For
reference

W9-CCR-936

Encyclopedia of

WARS

VOLUME II

(G TO R)

Charles Phillips
and
Alan Axelrod

☑®

Facts On File, Inc.

Encyclopedia of Wars

Facts On File, Inc.
132 West 31st Street
New York NY 10001

Library of Congress Cataloging in Publication Data
Phillips, Charles, 1948–
Encyclopedia of wars / Charles Phillips and Alan Axelrod
p. cm.
Includes bibliographical references and index.
ISBN 0-8160-2851-6 (set: alk. paper)
ISBN 0-8160-2852-4 (vol. 1)—ISBN 0-8160-2853-2 (vol. 2)—
ISBN 0-8160-2854-0 (vol. 3)
1. Military history—Encyclopedias. I. Axelrod, Alan, 1952– II. Title.
D25.A2P49 2004
355'.003—dc22   2003028010

Facts On File books are available at special discounts when purchased in bulk quantities for businesses, associations, institutions or sales promotions. Please call our Special Sales Department in New York at (212) 967-8800 or (800) 322-8755.

You can find Facts On File on the World Wide Web at http://www.factsonfile.com

Text adaptation by Erika K. Arroyo and David C. Strelecky
Cover design by Cathy Rincon
Maps by Sholto Ainslie

Printed in the United States of America

VB FOF 10 9 8 7 6 5 4 3 2 1

This book is printed on acid-free paper.

Contents

VOLUME I

List of Entries
iv

List of Maps
xvi

Contributors and Reviewers
xviii

Acknowledgments
xxi

Introduction
xxii

Entries A to F
1

VOLUME II

Entries G to R
505

VOLUME III

Entries S to Z
995

Chronology
1410

Selected Bibliography
1430

Index
1433

ENTRIES G TO R

G

Gabriel's Rebellion (1800)

PRINCIPAL COMBATANTS: African-American slaves of Virginia under Gabriel Prosser vs. the state's white citizens

PRINCIPAL THEATER(S): Richmond, Virginia, and environs

DECLARATION: No formal declaration.

MAJOR ISSUES AND OBJECTIVES: An attempt on the part of African-American slaves to win their freedom and to establish a black nation within the state of Virginia.

OUTCOME: The impending revolt was betrayed before it occurred, it was suppressed by Virginia officials, and the leaders of the movement were hanged.

APPROXIMATE MAXIMUM NUMBER OF MEN UNDER ARMS: Estimates of slave enlistments vary widely from 2,000 to 50,000. About 1,000 slaves gathered on the night of the planned assault. Contemporary papers report that the Virginia militia could have mustered no more than 500 soldiers.

CASUALTIES: Thirty-five leaders, including Prosser, were hanged.

TREATIES: No formal treaties

In 1800, Gabriel Prosser (d. 1800), a 24-year-old slave, planned a rebellion against the white slaveholders of Virginia. Prosser was a deeply religious man, as were most leaders of slave revolts, and he was inspired to act by the fight for freedom and the stirring words of equality he heard from his fellow Virginians, Thomas Jefferson (1743–1826) and George Washington (1732–99).

Prosser organized a three-pronged attack on Richmond. Assembling some six miles outside the city, one column planned to approach from the right to secure the arsenal and seize guns; the left column aimed for the powder house; the central column, attacking Richmond from both ends, was to kill every white person, except Frenchmen, Methodists, and Quakers. With Richmond secured, Prosser planned rapid assaults on other Virginia cities. If the scheme succeeded, Prosser would proclaim himself king of Virginia. If it failed, his army was to take to the woods and instigate a guerrilla war.

As Prosser's followers—estimated at about 1,000—gathered on the night of August 30, they did not know that their plans had been revealed to white officials. In truth, it hardly mattered because a thunderstorm washed out roads and bridges, making it impossible for Prosser to reach Richmond. Before he could regroup, he and 34 others were arrested, convicted, and hanged.

See also TURNER'S REBELLION; VESEY'S REBELLION.

Further reading: Douglas E. Egerton, *Gabriel's Rebellion: The Virginia Slave Conspiracies of 1800 and 1802* (Chapel Hill: University of North Carolina Press, 1993); Thomas Wentworth Higgenson, *Black Rebellion: Five Slave Revolts* (New York: Da Capo Press, 1998).

Galeruis's Invasion of Italy *See* ROMAN CIVIL WAR (306–307).

Gallic Wars: Ariovistusian Campaign (58 B.C.E.)

PRINCIPAL COMBATANTS: Rome vs. Germanic tribes under Ariovistus

PRINCIPAL THEATER(S): Central Gaul (eastern France)

DECLARATION: None

MAJOR ISSUES AND OBJECTIVES: Julius Caesar sought to drive out of Gaul a raiding tribe under Ariovistus.

OUTCOME: After a brief campaign of maneuver, Caesar fought a decisive battle that routed and purged the tribe.

APPROXIMATE MAXIMUM NUMBER OF MEN UNDER ARMS: Romans, 50,000; Ariovistus, 75,000

CASUALTIES: Numbers unknown, but very heavy among the followers of Ariovistus.

TREATIES: None

Following the GALLIC WARS: HELVETIAN CAMPAIGN in 58 B.C.E., Gaius Julius Caesar (100–44 B.C.E.) next faced a threat from Ariovistus (fl. 58 B.C.E.) leader of a Germanic tribe that had been raiding the Gauls of Aedui, Sequani, and Arverni (modern Alsace and Franche-Comté, France).

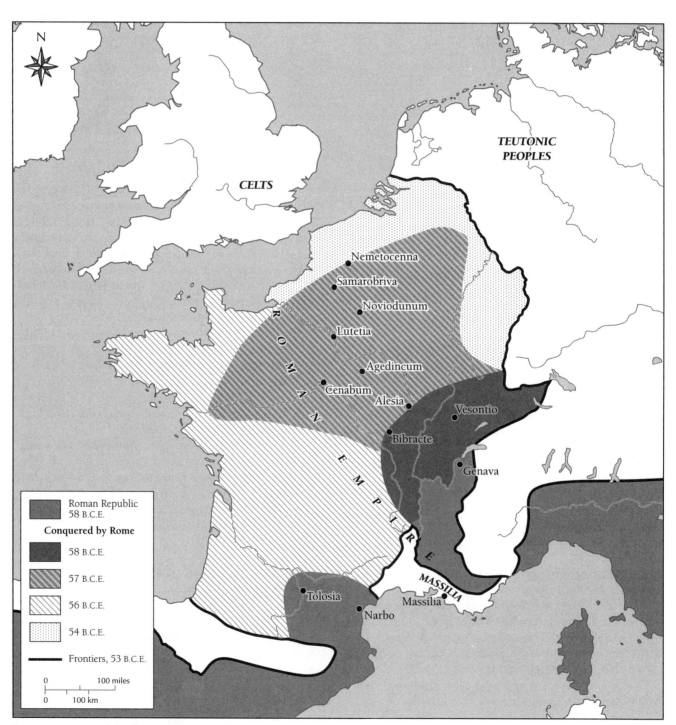

Roman conquest of Gaul, 58–52 B.C.E.

Caesar's force of 50,000 cautiously sparred with Ariovistus's 75,000 warriors in the country east of Vesontio (Besançon) until, on September 10, Caesar determined that the time and place were right for an attack. The battle came in the vicinity of modern Belfort, Mulhouse, or Cernay. Caesar moved swiftly and achieved total surprise. Seizing the initiative, he never relinquished it, and the Germans, despite their superior numbers, were routed. They retreated in disarray across the Rhine, with Caesar in pursuit.

This victory elicited from central Gaul general acknowledgment of Roman suzerainty. Caesar took his forces into winter quarters at Vesontio.

See also GALLIC WARS: BELGIAN CAMPAIGN; GALLIC WARS: MORINIAN AND MENAPIIAN CAMPAIGN; GALLIC WARS: VENETI CAMPAIGN; GALLIC WARS: FIRST INVASION OF BRITAIN; GALLIC WARS: GERMANIC CAMPAIGN; GALLIC WARS: REVOLT OF THE GAULS; GALLIC WARS: SECOND INVASION OF BRITAIN; GALLIC WARS: REVOLT OF THE BELGAE; GALLIC WARS: REVOLT IN CENTRAL GAUL; GALLIC WARS: FINAL PACIFICATION OF GAUL.

Further reading: Julius Caesar, *The Gallic War,* trans. Carolyn Hammond (New York: Oxford University Press, 1996).

Gallic Wars: Helvetian Campaign (58 B.C.E.)

PRINCIPAL COMBATANTS: Rome (with Gallic auxiliaries) and Helvetian migrants
PRINCIPAL THEATER(S): Gaul, principally the Jura Mountain region
DECLARATION: None
MAJOR ISSUES AND OBJECTIVES: Julius Caesar sought to repel a Helvetian invasion of Gaul.
OUTCOME: The Helvetians were defeated and suffered great losses; they withdrew to their original homeland in the region of modern Switzerland.
APPROXIMATE MAXIMUM NUMBER OF MEN UNDER ARMS: Helvetians, 100,000; Caesar, 30,000 legionnaires, plus about 25,000 Gallic warriors
CASUALTIES: Including many noncombatant civilians, 130,000 Helvetians died as a result of the Battle of Bibracte; Roman losses were heavy (though much smaller), but not precisely known.
TREATIES: None

In 58 B.C.E., Gaius Julius Caesar (100–44 B.C.E.), Roman triumvir and consul, became proconsul and governor of Gaul, taking in Istria, Illyricum, Cisalpine Gaul (the Po Valley), and Transalpine Gaul (southern France). He was immediately confronted by a migration—or invasion—of Helvetians, the Gallic tribe centered in modern Switzerland. Out of a population of nearly 400,000, 100,000 Helvetians were warriors.

Caesar gathered and concentrated his regular forces and also recruited various Gallic tribes who feared invasion by the Helvetians. By early spring, Caesar had mounted an effective blocking force, which sent the Helvetians into the Jura Mountains, north of the Rhône River. In June of 58, Caesar, leading a force of 34,000, intercepted the Helvetians as they crossed the Arar River. Caesar led his men on a forced night march, then immediately into a surprise attack. This daring move decimated the Helvetian force of 30,000 men who were still on the east bank of the Arar. Those who made it across, however, continued their march west toward the Liger (Loire) River. Caesar did not pursue, but warily followed them.

At Bibracte (Mount Beuvray), in July, the Helvetians, now about 70,000 strong, wheeled about and attacked Caesar's contingent of 30,000 legionnaires and 24,000 Gauls (this included 4,000 Gallic cavalrymen). Caesar's outnumbered forces quickly seized the initiative from the Helvetians, who were driven back to their camp. There tens of thousands of Helvetian migrants, men, women, and children, lived, and by the time the attack was over, 130,000 had perished. Those Helvetians who survived the battle surrendered and, at Caesar's demand, returned to their original homes east of the Jura Mountains.

See also GALLIC WARS: ARIOVISTUSIAN CAMPAIGN; GALLIC WARS: BELGIAN CAMPAIGN; GALLIC WARS: MORINIAN AND MENAPIIAN CAMPAIGN; GALLIC WARS: VENETI CAMPAIGN; GALLIC WARS: FIRST INVASION OF BRITAIN; GALLIC WARS: GERMANIC CAMPAIGN; GALLIC WARS: REVOLT OF THE GAULS; GALLIC WARS: SECOND INVASION OF BRITAIN; GALLIC WARS: REVOLT OF THE BELGAE; GALLIC WARS: REVOLT IN CENTRAL GAUL; GALLIC WARS: FINAL PACIFICATION OF GAUL.

Further reading: Julius Caesar, *The Gallic War,* trans. Carolyn Hammond (New York: Oxford University Press, 1996).

Gallic Wars: Belgian Campaign (57 B.C.E.)

PRINCIPAL COMBATANTS: Romans (with Gallic auxiliaries) vs. the Belgae, Nervii, and Aduatuci
PRINCIPAL THEATER(S): Belgica (modern Belgium and surrounding region)
DECLARATION: None
MAJOR ISSUES AND OBJECTIVES: Julius Caesar sought to preempt a massive Belgian invasion.
OUTCOME: The Romans prevailed, bringing all central Gaul under their control.
APPROXIMATE MAXIMUM NUMBER OF MEN UNDER ARMS: Belgae, 100,000; Romans, 40,000 legionnaires with 20,000 Gallic auxiliaries; Nervii, 75,000
CASUALTIES: At the Battle of the Sabis, Nervii losses were 60,000 (of 75,000 engaged); Roman losses are unknown, but were substantial
TREATIES: None

The Belgae were a Gallic-Germanic people living in northeastern Gaul (region of modern Belgium). Distressed by Gaius Julius Caesar's earlier triumphs in the area (*see* GALLIC WARS: ARIOVISTUSIAN CAMPAIGN and GALLIC WARS: HELVETIAN CAMPAIGN), they organized a vast coalition against the Roman legions, mustering some 300,000 warriors to overwhelm them. Timely intelligence alerted Caesar (100–44 B.C.E.) to the activities of the Belgae, and prompted him to act preemptively. In April 57 B.C.E., he led a force of 40,000 Roman legionnaires supplemented by 20,000 Gallic auxiliaries in an invasion of Belgica (Belgium). Taken by surprise, Galba (fl. 57–58 B.C.E.), king of Suessiones (Soissons), mustered some 75,000 to 100,000 warriors and met Caesar's advance at the Battle of the Axona (Aisne) River. Caesar defeated Galba, then continued his invasion. His victory prompted some of the tribes to submit to the Romans, but others, led by the Nervii, remained resistant.

In July 57, Caesar's invasion force reached the Sabis (Sambre) River. Uncharacteristically having failed to make proper reconnaissance, Caesar's forces were ambushed as they made camp on the Sabis. Some 75,000 Nervii attacked. So well-disciplined were the legionnaires, however, that, despite their surprise, they refused to panic and instead mounted an effective defense. After beating off successive attacks, the Romans assumed the offensive and inflicted some 60,000 casualties.

Caesar pressed on with the invasion and by the autumn of 57 had penetrated the country of the Aduatuci. In September he laid siege to Aduatuca, the tribal capital (Tongres). The Aduatuci surrendered, only to fall upon the Romans as they entered the town. Caesar successfully repelled these attacks, seized the initiative, and slaughtered the attackers. This demonstration brought most of Belgica to its knees in submission to Rome.

See also GALLIC WARS: MORINIAN AND MENAPIIAN CAMPAIGN; GALLIC WARS: VENETI CAMPAIGN; GALLIC WARS: FIRST INVASION OF BRITAIN; GALLIC WARS: GERMANIC CAMPAIGN; GALLIC WARS: REVOLT OF THE GAULS; GALLIC WARS: SECOND INVASION OF BRITAIN; GALLIC WARS: REVOLT OF THE BELGAE; GALLIC WARS: REVOLT IN CENTRAL GAUL; GALLIC WARS: FINAL PACIFICATION OF GAUL.

Further reading: Julius Caesar, *The Gallic War*, trans. Carolyn Hammond (New York: Oxford University Press, 1996).

Gallic Wars: Morinian and Menapiian Campaign (56 B.C.E.)

PRINCIPAL COMBATANTS: Romans vs. Morini and Menapii tribes

PRINCIPAL THEATER(S): Belgica (modern Belgium and the Netherlands)

DECLARATION: None

MAJOR ISSUES AND OBJECTIVES: Julius Caesar sought to suppress these rebellious tribes.

OUTCOME: Generally very successful in bringing Belgica under Roman control, Caesar nevertheless failed to run the Morini and Menapii to ground.

APPROXIMATE MAXIMUM NUMBER OF MEN UNDER ARMS: Unknown

CASUALTIES: Unknown

TREATIES: None

After successfully completing a campaign against the Veneti in 56 B.C.E. (*see* GALLIC WARS: VENETI CAMPAIGN), Gaius Julius Caesar (100–44 B.C.E.) turned to the suppression of rebellious tribes in the northwestern region of Belgica. All yielded rapidly except for the Morini and Menapii tribes, which successfully evaded the onslaught of the Roman legions by hiding in the marsh regions of the seacoast of the Low Countries or by making a break for the dense wilderness of the Ardennes. Caesar was never able to suppress these tribes, which were the sole holdouts against the Roman domination of all Gaul.

See also GALLIC WARS: HELVETIAN CAMPAIGN; GALLIC WARS: BELGIAN CAMPAIGN; GALLIC WARS: FIRST INVASION OF BRITAIN; GALLIC WARS: GERMANIC CAMPAIGN; GALLIC WARS: REVOLT OF THE GAULS; GALLIC WARS: SECOND INVASION OF BRITAIN; GALLIC WARS: REVOLT OF THE BELGAE; GALLIC WARS: REVOLT IN CENTRAL GAUL; GALLIC WARS: FINAL PACIFICATION OF GAUL.

Further reading: Julius Caesar, *The Gallic War*, trans. Carolyn Hammond (New York: Oxford University Press, 1996).

Gallic Wars: Veneti Campaign (56 B.C.E.)

PRINCIPAL COMBATANTS: Rome vs. the Veneti

PRINCIPAL THEATER(S): Armorica (Brittany), Aquitania, Normandy, and the Rhineland

DECLARATION: None

MAJOR ISSUES AND OBJECTIVES: Julius Caesar sought to suppress rebellion by the Veneti of Armorica.

OUTCOME: The rebellion was suppressed.

APPROXIMATE MAXIMUM NUMBER OF MEN UNDER ARMS: Unknown

CASUALTIES: Unknown

TREATIES: None

The Veneti were the tribal people of Armorica (Brittany). During the winter of 56 B.C.E., they took several Roman ambassadors captive, and they committed numerous acts of rebellion against Roman authority in the region. Come spring, Gaius Julius Caesar (100–44 B.C.E.) decided to act to suppress the Veneti. At the head of three legions, he marched into Armorica, north of the Loire River. He coordinated this advance with the operation of another legion, under General Decimus Brutus (85–43 B.C.E.), which manned a fleet stationed near the mouth of the Loire. Simultaneously, Marcus Licinius Crassus (d. 53 B.C.E.) led troops numbering somewhat more than legion strength in an invasion of Aquitania in northwestern Gaul. A smaller force, under Titus Labienus (100–45 B.C.E.), campaigned near the Rhine, while another force, led by Q. Titurius Sabinus (d. 54 B.C.E.), occupied the region of modern Normandy.

All of these forces worked to suppress the Veneti, systematically closing in on and laying siege to fortified towns. However, the major action took place at sea, in Quiberon Bay (the Gulf of Morbihan), where Roman galleys, though inferior to the ships of the Veneti, nevertheless outmaneuvered the larger vessels, enabling Roman legionnaires to slash the rigging of the Veneti ships by means of sickles lashed to long poles. This extraordinary tactic effectively disabled the Veneti fleet. Once the fleet was thus neutralized, the land campaign against the Veneti proceeded apace. Caesar was ruthless in visiting reprisals for the abuse inflicted on Roman ambassadors, and the Veneti, much abashed, acknowledged Roman suzerainty.

See also GALLIC WARS: HELVETIAN CAMPAIGN; GALLIC WARS: BELGIAN CAMPAIGN; GALLIC WARS: FIRST INVASION OF BRITAIN; GALLIC WARS: GERMANIC CAMPAIGN; GALLIC WARS: REVOLT OF THE GAULS; GALLIC WARS: SECOND INVASION OF BRITAIN; GALLIC WARS: REVOLT OF THE BELGAE; GALLIC WARS: REVOLT IN CENTRAL GAUL; GALLIC WARS: FINAL PACIFICATION OF GAUL.

Further reading: Julius Caesar, *The Gallic War,* trans. Carolyn Hammond (New York: Oxford University Press, 1996).

Gallic Wars: First Invasion of Britain
(55 B.C.E.)

PRINCIPAL COMBATANTS: Rome vs. the Britons
PRINCIPAL THEATER(S): Britain, on the Dover coast
DECLARATION: None
MAJOR ISSUES AND OBJECTIVES: This was a preliminary, exploratory invasion of Britain.
OUTCOME: Julius Caesar overcame local resistance, concluded a truce with the Britons, then withdrew to Gaul.
APPROXIMATE MAXIMUM NUMBER OF MEN UNDER ARMS: Rome, two legions; Britons, unknown
CASUALTIES: Unknown
TREATIES: Truce, 55 B.C.E.

Having secured Gaul by the summer of 55 B.C.E., Gaius Julius Caesar (100–44 B.C.E.) led two legions in an invasion of Britain, landing near Dubra (Dover) during August 55 B.C.E. The Britons resisted on the beaches, but Caesar bombarded the defenders with ship-mounted catapults. Softened up by this preinvasion bombardment, the Britons still fought hard, but were overcome quickly. A truce was concluded, and Caesar, having made his initial impression, withdrew to Gaul after occupying Britain for a mere three weeks.

See also GALLIC WARS: HELVETIAN CAMPAIGN; GALLIC WARS: BELGIAN CAMPAIGN; GALLIC WARS: VENETI CAMPAIGN; GALLIC WARS: GERMANIC CAMPAIGN; GALLIC WARS: REVOLT OF THE GAULS; GALLIC WARS: SECOND INVASION OF BRITAIN; GALLIC WARS: REVOLT OF THE BELGAE; GALLIC WARS: REVOLT IN CENTRAL GAUL; GALLIC WARS: FINAL PACIFICATION OF GAUL.

Further reading: Julius Caesar, *The Gallic War,* trans. Carolyn Hammond (New York: Oxford University Press, 1996).

Gallic Wars: Germanic Campaign (55 B.C.E.)

PRINCIPAL COMBATANTS: Rome vs. the Usipetes and Tencteri tribes
PRINCIPAL THEATER(S): Gaul, between the Meuse and Rhine Rivers
DECLARATION: None
MAJOR ISSUES AND OBJECTIVES: Julius Caesar sought to drive out Germanic invaders from Gaul—and to set a brutal example that would discourage future invasions.
OUTCOME: Caesar succeeded both in evicting (or killing) the Usipetes and Tencteri and in intimidating other tribes.
APPROXIMATE MAXIMUM NUMBER OF MEN UNDER ARMS: Roman strength was several legions; Usipetes and Tencteri fielded about 100,000 warriors.
CASUALTIES: Many of the 430,000 Usipetes and Tencteri in Gaul, men, women, and children, were slaughtered.
TREATIES: None

In 55 B.C.E., the Usipetes and Tencteri, Germanic tribes, invaded Gaul by crossing the Rhine River. Numbering some 430,000 and able to field at least 100,000 warriors, these people set up villages on the Meuse River near the modern city of Maastricht. Gaius Julius Caesar (100–44 B.C.E.) attempted to negotiate with the tribal leaders in May, hoping to persuade them to return to Germany. When Caesar discovered that they planned to attack during the negotiations, he resolved to act so vigorously against the invaders that no other German tribe would ever dare invade again.

Caesar embarked on the negotiations, but bested the Usipetes and Tencteri at their own game by making a surprise attack during the talks, hitting the invaders between the Meuse and the Rhine. Not only did his legions destroy the invading army, they were turned loose against the women and children as well.

The massacre was condemned in Rome, but Caesar argued that it had been necessary, and he took his campaign of terror into Germany itself. In June 55 B.C.E., he crossed the Rhine near the site of present-day Bonn and built a spectacular bridge across the river. He marched his legions en masse across the span, a feat that, as he had planned, thoroughly intimidated the local tribes. After securing their allegiance and submission, Caesar returned to Gaul—and destroyed the bridge, lest it be used at some future time by Germanic invaders.

See also GALLIC WARS: HELVETIAN CAMPAIGN; GALLIC WARS: BELGIAN CAMPAIGN; GALLIC WARS: VENETI CAMPAIGN; GALLIC WARS: FIRST INVASION OF BRITAIN; GALLIC WARS: REVOLT OF THE GAULS; GALLIC WARS: SECOND INVASION OF BRITAIN; GALLIC WARS: REVOLT OF THE BELGAE; GALLIC WARS: REVOLT IN CENTRAL GAUL; GALLIC WARS: FINAL PACIFICATION OF GAUL.

Further reading: Julius Caesar, *The Gallic War,* trans. Carolyn Hammond (New York: Oxford University Press, 1996).

Gallic Wars: Revolt of the Gauls
(54–53 B.C.E.)

PRINCIPAL COMBATANTS: Rome vs. the Gauls (especially Nervii)
PRINCIPAL THEATER(S): Northeastern Gaul
DECLARATION: None
MAJOR ISSUES AND OBJECTIVES: The Gauls attempted an uprising against Roman domination.
OUTCOME: Led by Julius Caesar, the Romans defeated the Nervii and suppressed the Gallic uprisings.
APPROXIMATE MAXIMUM NUMBER OF MEN UNDER ARMS: Gauls, potentially 1,000,000; actually fielded, more than 60,000 Nervii; total Roman strength was no more than 50,000 men.
CASUALTIES: Unknown
TREATIES: None

By 54 B.C.E., all Gaul was ready to erupt into rebellion. Potentially, the Gauls could muster 1,000,000 (a contemporary claim, probably grossly inflated) warriors, whereas the Roman army of occupation amounted to no more than 50,000 men. However, the Gallic tribes never fully united.

The principal uprising against Rome was led by the Nervii chief Ambiorix (fl. 54–52 B.C.E.), who attacked Q. Titurius Sabinus (fl. 54 B.C.E.) near Aduatuca. Ambiorix offered Sabinus a safe conduct to rejoin the other legions,

but as soon as the legions were on the march, Ambiorix attacked and destroyed them. He moved next against the major camp of Quintus Cicero (c. 102–43 B.C.E.), near the modern town of Binche. Cicero's forces repulsed the attack, whereupon Ambiorix tried to entice him into open battle. Cicero steeled his nerves and continued to defend the camp. He managed to dispatch a messenger to Gaius Julius Caesar (100–44 B.C.E.), who marched to Cicero's relief with a small force of 7,000 men—all he could muster on short notice.

Ambiorix marched to meet Caesar with 60,000 men, while keeping Cicero under siege with a substantial force. Vastly outnumbered, Caesar lured Ambiorix into a careless attack. Caesar was then able to mount a swift counterattack and drive Ambiorix from the field. Caesar went on to relieve Cicero and was soon joined by Titus Labienus (100–45 B.C.E.) and his forces. Thus united, the Romans established secure winter quarters.

See also GALLIC WARS: HELVETIAN CAMPAIGN; GALLIC WARS: BELGIAN CAMPAIGN; GALLIC WARS: VENETI CAMPAIGN; GALLIC WARS: FIRST INVASION OF BRITAIN; GALLIC WARS: GERMANIC CAMPAIGN; GALLIC WARS: SECOND INVASION OF BRITAIN; GALLIC WARS: REVOLT OF THE BELGAE; GALLIC WARS: REVOLT IN CENTRAL GAUL; GALLIC WARS: FINAL PACIFICATION OF GAUL.

Further reading: Julius Caesar, *The Gallic War,* trans. Carolyn Hammond (New York: Oxford University Press, 1996).

Gallic Wars: Second Invasion of Britain
(54 B.C.E.)

PRINCIPAL COMBATANTS: Rome vs. Britons under Chief Cassivellaunus
PRINCIPAL THEATER(S): Southeastern Britain (region of London)
DECLARATION: None
MAJOR ISSUES AND OBJECTIVES: Julius Caesar sought the submission of the Britons.
OUTCOME: Caesar received the submission of the Britons, but he did not occupy the country at this time.
APPROXIMATE MAXIMUM NUMBER OF MEN UNDER ARMS: Romans, 22,000; Britons, unknown
CASUALTIES: Unknown
TREATIES: None

After making a preliminary invasion the year before (*see* GALLIC WARS: FIRST INVASION OF BRITAIN), Gaius Julius Caesar (100–44 B.C.E.) returned to Britain in strength—five legions (20,000 men) with 2,000 cavalry troopers. As before, he landed at Dubra (Dover), and this time was unopposed—although a severe Channel storm posed a serious threat to his force.

Chief Cassivellaunus (fl. 54 B.C.E.) mustered a defensive force to counter the invasion, but it was no match for the advancing legions. The legions crossed the Thames west of the site of modern London and were frequently harassed by Cassivellaunus, who wisely avoided a head-on attack. When it was clear to the British chief that the Romans were not about to be intimidated into leaving the island, he sued for peace in a conference near Verulamium (St. Albans). Caesar contented himself with Cassivellaunus's professions of submission and made no attempt to occupy the country he had at least nominally conquered.

See also GALLIC WARS: HELVETIAN CAMPAIGN; GALLIC WARS: BELGIAN CAMPAIGN; GALLIC WARS: VENETI CAMPAIGN; GALLIC WARS: GERMANIC CAMPAIGN; GALLIC WARS: REVOLT OF THE GAULS; GALLIC WARS: REVOLT OF THE BELGAE; GALLIC WARS: REVOLT IN CENTRAL GAUL; GALLIC WARS: FINAL PACIFICATION OF GAUL.

Further reading: Julius Caesar, *The Gallic War,* trans. Carolyn Hammond (New York: Oxford University Press, 1996).

Gallic Wars: Revolt of the Belgae (53 B.C.E.)

PRINCIPAL COMBATANTS: Rome vs. the Belgae
PRINCIPAL THEATER(S): Belgica (around Belgium)
DECLARATION: None
MAJOR ISSUES AND OBJECTIVES: Julius Caesar wanted to suppress rebellion in Belgica.
OUTCOME: A strong show of force succeeded in suppressing rebellion throughout the region.
APPROXIMATE MAXIMUM NUMBER OF MEN UNDER ARMS: Rome, 10 legions
CASUALTIES: Unknown
TREATIES: None

Gaius Julius Caesar (100–44 B.C.E.) had only narrowly suppressed a Gallic rebellion led by Ambiorix (fl. 54–52 B.C.E.) of the Nervii (*see* GALLIC WARS: REVOLT OF THE GAULS) from 54 to 52 B.C.E. but by 53 he had mustered 10 full legions and was prepared to seize the initiative. He marched into Belgica, and although he did not force the rebellious Belgae into a major open battle, his ceaseless pursuit of rebel groups effectively wore them down. Understanding that some German tribes had assisted Ambiorix, Caesar built a new bridge across the Rhine as a demonstration of the ease with which he could invade and devastate the region. The pursuit and this demonstration brought Belgica under control.

See also GALLIC WARS: HELVETIAN CAMPAIGN; GALLIC WARS: BELGIAN CAMPAIGN; GALLIC WARS: VENETI CAMPAIGN; GALLIC WARS: FIRST INVASION OF BRITAIN; GALLIC WARS: GERMANIC CAMPAIGN; GALLIC WARS: REVOLT IN CENTRAL GAUL; GALLIC WARS: FINAL PACIFICATION OF GAUL.

Further reading: Julius Caesar, *The Gallic War,* trans. Carolyn Hammond (New York: Oxford University Press, 1996).

Gallic Wars: Revolt in Central Gaul (53–52 B.C.E.)

PRINCIPAL COMBATANTS: Rome vs. the Gauls under Vercingetorix
PRINCIPAL THEATER(S): Central Gaul
DECLARATION: None
MAJOR ISSUES AND OBJECTIVES: Vercingetorix led the biggest rebellion against Roman rule in Gaul.
OUTCOME: Although dramatically outnumbered, Julius Caesar defeated Vercingetorix and thereby broke the back of rebellion in central Gaul.
APPROXIMATE MAXIMUM NUMBER OF MEN UNDER ARMS: Vercingetorix's forces, 95,000; Gallic relief force, 240,000; Roman legions, 55,000
CASUALTIES: Unknown
TREATIES: None

The remarkable Arverni chieftain Vercingetorix (d. 46 B.C.E.) led a sudden rebellion among the tribes of central Gaul, which Gaius Julius Caesar (100–44 B.C.E.) had considered fully secure. For the first time, the disparate Gallic tribes united, and, under Vercingetorix, warriors became a disciplined and effective army. As the uprising began, most of the Roman legions were in northern Gaul, and Caesar himself was in Italy. Caesar was back in Gaul by January. In February 52, he led a small force from southern Gaul, through the Cevennes Mountains, and around Vercingetorix. He was able to join the legions in the Loire region, then launched an attack against Cenabum (Orléans), where the rebellion had begun. Caesar recaptured the town.

Dispatching legions under Titus Labienus (100–45 B.C.E.) to hold northern Gaul, Caesar led an expedition into southern Gaul, the heart of Vercingetorix's power. Caesar recaptured town after town as Vercingetorix made a highly destructive fighting retreat, in which he enforced a scorched-earth policy that inflicted great hardship on the legions.

In March 52, the Roman legions, hungry and short of supplies, were outside of Vercingetorix's stronghold at Avaricum (Bourges). They laid siege to the town, which fell but Vercingetorix eluded captured. Caesar pressed his weary troops southward and laid siege to Gergovia (modern Gergovie), the capital of the Arverni. Vercingetorix fortified the capital extensively and, during April and May 52, withstood Caesar's siege. Impatient and critically short of supplies, Caesar prematurely ordered an attack, which was repulsed with great loss of life. Caesar withdrew from Gergovia and joined Labienus in the north.

At this point, Caesar was forced to acknowledge that he had lost control of Gaul. He retreated to Province, his main base, to regroup with supplies and reinforcements. However, Vercingetorix, leading an army of 80,000 infantry and 15,000 cavalry, deployed his forces in the hill country along the Vingeanne, a tributary of the upper Saône. His object was to block Caesar and force him into battle.

In July, the Battle of the Vingeanne commenced. Vercingetorix hesitated, however, and thereby lost the initiative—which Caesar, as always, was quick to seize. Vercingetorix retreated, and Caesar pursued. The Arverni leader ensconced his forces in the fortified mountaintop town of Alesia (Alise-Ste-Reine), located on Mount Auxois. At this point, he had 90,000 men with which to oppose Caesar's 55,000, and he also enjoyed a superior position. As usual, Caesar did not let inferiority of numbers or position inhibit him. He attacked with great vigor, forcing the Gauls to hole up within the walls of Alesia. Then Caesar put his engineers to work building a giant siege-work wall, some 14 miles in circumference, around the town. After this great project had been completed, a tremendous Gallic force of 240,000 marched to the aid of Vercingetorix. This force laid siege to Caesar, even as he continued to hold Alesia under siege. Caesar, however, was fully prepared to withstand a long siege and had plenty of supplies. He allowed the relief force to make three attacks, all three times repulsing them and inflicting great losses. In the meantime, Vercingetorix and his followers were starving. When he tried to send women and children through the Roman lines, Caesar turned them back. At last Vercingetorix surrendered. This broke the back of the rebellion in central Gaul. The relief army dispersed. Vercingetorix was marched back to Rome, where he was there executed six years later.

See also GALLIC WARS: HELVETIAN CAMPAIGN; GALLIC WARS: BELGIAN CAMPAIGN; GALLIC WARS: VENETI CAMPAIGN; GALLIC WARS: FIRST INVASION OF BRITAIN; GALLIC WARS: GERMANIC CAMPAIGN; GALLIC WARS: REVOLT OF THE BELGAE; GALLIC WARS: REVOLT OF THE GAULS; GALLIC WARS: FINAL PACIFICATION OF GAUL.

Further reading: Julius Caesar, *The Gallic War,* trans. Carolyn Hammond (New York: Oxford University Press, 1996).

Gallic Wars: Final Pacification of Gaul
(51 B.C.E.)

PRINCIPAL COMBATANTS: Rome vs. Gallic rebels
PRINCIPAL THEATER(S): Gaul
DECLARATION: None

MAJOR ISSUES AND OBJECTIVES: A "mop-up" operation to ensure all pockets of rebellion had been crushed.
OUTCOME: The pacification was successful, and Gaul became a secure part of the Roman Empire.
APPROXIMATE MAXIMUM NUMBER OF MEN UNDER ARMS: Rome, about 55,000 men; no other figures known.
CASUALTIES: Few casualties in this campaign.
TREATIES: None

The defeat and execution of Vercingetorix (d. 46 B.C.E.), greatest of the Gallic chieftains (*see* GALLIC WARS: REVOLT IN CENTRAL GAUL), broke the back of rebellion in Gaul. However, Gaius Julius Caesar (100–44 B.C.E.) conducted an extensive "mop-up" operation, ensuring that he had thoroughly extinguished all pockets of persistent rebellion. This grand tour through Gaul was also intended to impress the people of that country with the might and majesty of the Roman legions, and in this Caesar was highly successful. Gaul was now securely in Roman hands and a key addition to the empire.

See also GALLIC WARS: HELVETIAN CAMPAIGN; GALLIC WARS: BELGIAN CAMPAIGN; GALLIC WARS: VENETI CAMPAIGN; GALLIC WARS: FIRST INVASION OF BRITAIN; GALLIC WARS: GERMANIC CAMPAIGN; GALLIC WARS: REVOLT OF THE BELGAE; GALLIC WARS: REVOLT OF THE GAULS; GALLIC WARS: REVOLT IN CENTRAL GAUL.

Further reading: Julius Caesar, *The Gallic War,* trans. Carolyn Hammond (New York: Oxford University Press, 1996).

Garibaldi's Invasion of Sicily (1860)

PRINCIPAL COMBATANTS: Giuseppe Garibaldi's "Thousand Redshirts" vs. forces of Naples
PRINCIPAL THEATER(S): Sicily
DECLARATION: None
MAJOR ISSUES AND OBJECTIVES: The nationalist Garibaldi sought to wrest Sicily from Neapolitan control preparatory to the conquest of Naples and, ultimately, the unification of Italy as a single kingdom.
OUTCOME: Sicily fell to Garibaldi.
APPROXIMATE MAXIMUM NUMBER OF MEN UNDER ARMS: The core of Garibaldi's force consisted of about 1,000 men, and 2,000 Sicilian guerrillas (the *Picciotti*) joined later; Neapolitan forces, 22,000.
CASUALTIES: Garibaldi lost 800 killed or wounded; the Neapolitans suffered 1,300 or more killed or wounded.
TREATIES: None

The Risorgimento, or reunification, of Italy spanned 1850 to 1870, and one of its military highlights was the liberation of Sicily from the Kingdom of Naples in 1860. This was led by Giuseppe Garibaldi (1807–82) and covertly supported by Victor Emmanuel II (1820–78), king of Piedmont, and his brilliant prime minister, Count Camillo Cavour (1810–61).

Although a revolt broke out in Naples in April 1860, only to be suppressed in May, Garibaldi sailed for Sicily—at the time part of the kingdom of Naples—with "The Thousand," a brigade of 1,000 Redshirt legionnaires loyal to him. The Thousand landed on May 11 and fought its first battle against Neapolitan forces on May 15 at Calatafami. For this encounter against 4,000 Neapolitan troops, Garibaldi's 1,000 Redshirts were augmented by 2,000 Sicilian guerrillas, known as the *Picciotti*. Although still outnumbered, Garibaldi and the Sicilians defeated the Neapolitan forces, opening the way, during May 26–27, for an assault on Palermo, chief city of Sicily. Garibaldi led 750 Redshirts and 3,000 Picciotti against a garrison of 18,000. Despite the disparity in numbers, the city fell to Garibaldi, and he advanced to Milazzo. There, on June 20, he was victorious, although his forces suffered severe losses—755 killed or wounded—compared to 162 casualties among the Neapolitans. Nevertheless, it was the Neapolitans who surrendered and gave up the city to Garibaldi.

The fall of Palermo and Milazzo signaled the liberation of Sicily, and from this conquest, Garibaldi led forces across the Strait of Messina to Naples, which fell to him on September 7.

See also ITALIAN WAR OF INDEPENDENCE (1859–1861).

Further reading: Denis Mack Smith, *Cavour and Garibaldi, 1860: A Study in Political Conflict* (New York: Cambridge University Press, 1985); George MacAway Trevelyan, *Garibaldi and the Making of Italy* (London: Phoenix Press, 2002).

Gascon Nobles' Revolt (1368)

PRINCIPAL COMBATANTS: Gascon nobles vs. Edward III
PRINCIPAL THEATER(S): Aquitaine
DECLARATION: None
MAJOR ISSUES AND OBJECTIVES: The nobles sought relief from Edward's irresponsible, oppressive, and economically burdensome government.
OUTCOME: Charles V (Charles the Wise) of France intervened, renewing the Hundred Years' War, to the disadvantage of Edward.
APPROXIMATE MAXIMUM NUMBER OF MEN UNDER ARMS: Not applicable
CASUALTIES: Not applicable
TREATIES: The document in question was the Treaty of Brétigny, May 8, 1360; Charles V now deemed invalid clauses relating to Edward's sovereignty over Aquitaine, thereby reigniting the Hundred Years' War.

This action was an episode of the HUNDRED YEARS' WAR and less a war in itself than an adroit diplomatic and strategic maneuver on the part of Charles V (Charles the Wise; 1338–80) of France.

Charles's nominal vassal, Edward III (r. 1327–77), ruler of Aquitaine, was an irresponsible monarch who did not hesitate to live extravagantly at the expense of the Gascons while ruling the realm through oppressive policies and burdensome taxes. At length, the Gascon nobles rebelled by appealing to Charles to intercede in 1368. In response, Charles turned to the Treaty of Brétigny, which had been concluded on May 8, 1360, between France and England. Among other things, the treaty gave Edward III full sovereignty over Aquitaine in exchange for his renunciation of his claim to the French throne and a further renunciation of any claim to sovereignty over territories outside of those specified in the treaty. Charles now recognized that although the treaty had been in force for eight years, certain key clauses regarding each king's renunciation of the other's newly agreed-to territories had been relegated to a separate document, which never had been officially ratified. Charles now summoned the eldest son of his vassal, Edward the Black Prince (1330–76), to Paris, presumably to inform him that his father's sovereignty over Aquitaine was invalid. As Charles had assumed, Edward refused to come. Charles then had a cause for resumption of the Hundred Years' War—this time in a context disadvantageous to Edward, whose territories rose up in rebellion, giving the French, under Charles, a series of advances.

Further reading: Richard Baker, *The Life and Campaigns of the Black Prince* (Rochester, N.Y.: Boydell & Brewer, 1997).

Gaston of Foix, Campaigns of (1511–1512)

PRINCIPAL COMBATANTS: France vs. papal-Spanish forces
PRINCIPAL THEATER(S): Northern Italy
DECLARATION: None
MAJOR ISSUES AND OBJECTIVES: Control of northern Italy
OUTCOME: The French achieved control of northern Italy, but the loss of the great French commander Gaston of Foix exposed France to later invasion.
APPROXIMATE MAXIMUM NUMBER OF MEN UNDER ARMS: Gaston's French forces, 23,000; papal-Spanish forces, 16,000 plus 5,000 garrison troops
CASUALTIES: France, 4,500 killed, 4,500 wounded; papal-Spanish forces, 9,000 killed, an unknown number wounded, many captured
TREATIES: None

Gaston of Foix (1489–1512), the duke of Nemours, joined in the Italian wars of Louis XII (1462–1515) with a brilliant series of campaigns against Bologna, Brescia, and Ravenna.

Although France had taken Bologna on May 13, 1511, a combined papal-Spanish force under Raymond of Cardona (fl. 1512), the Neapolitan viceroy, laid siege to the city in an effort to retake it. Gaston led an army to the relief of the city, driving off Raymond's forces. This accomplished, he turned to the north and advanced against Brescia, which was in the hands of the Venetians. Outside the city, Gaston defeated the Venetian forces, then laid siege to Brescia itself, which he captured in February 1512.

The capture of Brescia put most of northern Italy under Gaston's control. He therefore marched south, to lay siege against the Spanish in Ravenna. Wary of the remarkable Gaston of Foix, however, the combined papal-Spanish army moved with great caution toward Ravenna, seeking to establish an impregnable defensive position. Raymond of Cardona's force consisted of some 16,000 men, and the Ravenna garrison numbered 5,000. Against these, Gaston fielded 23,000, including some 8,500 German mercenaries, the *landsknechts*.

The Battle of Ravenna was fought on April 11, 1512. It was fierce and bloody, and one of its early casualties included Gaston of Foix, killed in an otherwise unremarkable skirmish. Beyond this, French losses were heavy, with some 4,500 killed and an equal number wounded. But papal-Spanish losses were heavier still: 9,000 killed and an unknown number wounded. Pedro Navarro (c. 1460–1528), the brilliant Spanish military engineer and commander of Spanish infantry, was captured, and when Spain declined to ransom him, he switched his allegiance to France. Although this acquisition was highly valuable, the French forces never overcame the loss of Gaston of Foix, and France was subsequently invaded by the English and, separately, by the Swiss.

See also ITALIAN WAR OF LOUIS XII.

Further reading: Frederic J. Baumgarther, *Louis XII* (London: Palgrave Macmillan, 1996).

Gaucho Revolution   *See* BRAZILIAN REVOLUTION.

Gempei War (Taira-Minamoto War) (1180–1185)

PRINCIPAL COMBATANTS: Minamoto clan vs. Taira clan
PRINCIPAL THEATER(S): Japan
DECLARATION: Call to war, 1180
MAJOR ISSUES AND OBJECTIVES: Minamoto Yoritomo sought to establish the dominance of his clan over that of the ruling Tairas.
OUTCOME: Yoritomo succeeded in bringing Japan under the control of the Minamotos and, in the process, established the shoguns as great powers in Japanese government.

APPROXIMATE MAXIMUM NUMBER OF MEN UNDER ARMS: Variable, but unknown; some battles fielded as many as 30,000 men on a side.
CASUALTIES: Unknown
TREATIES: No treaty, but an imperial proclamation named Minamoto Yoritomo sei-i-tai-shogun for life in 1191.

Also called the Taira-Minamoto War, this was the concluding contest between the Taira and Minamoto clans, which resulted in the Minamoto clan's establishment of the Kamakura shogunate, the military dictatorship that dominated Japan from 1192 to 1333.

In May 1180, Prince Mochihito, son of retired Emperor Go-Shirakawa (1127–92), issued a proclamation urging the Minamoto clan to rise against the Taira. In September, Minamoto Yoritomo (1147–99) responded to the call by raising an army in the eastern Japanese province of Kwanto, to which he had been exiled after his father, leader of the Minamoto clan, had been killed. Yoritomo's forces killed the local Taira governor, but they were defeated at the Battle of Ishibashiyama by a Taira force under Oba Kagechika (fl. 1180). Despite this defeat, Yoritomo's army continued to grow, and various local Taira officials were killed throughout Japan. By the spring of 1181, Yoritomo had the support of most of the prominent families in the Kanto domain. For a time, Yoritomo contented himself with consolidating his hold on this domain rather than attempting to spread the rebellion beyond it, but within two years, his forces were powerful enough to drive the Taira entirely out of Kwanto. Then, in 1183, Yoritomo led an advance on the Taira capital of Kyoto. After taking the capital, Yoritomo advanced into the western domains, where the Taira were still firmly established. In a series of battles, Yoritomo wore the Taira down. The culminating battle, Dan-no-ura, took place at sea in April 1185, when Yoritomo's fleet virtually destroyed that of the Taira at the western end of the Inland Sea. In this battle, the infant Emperor Antoku (d. 1185), a grandson of Taira no Kiyomori (1118–81), was drowned, as were many of the leaders of the Taira clan. Those who survived were, for the most part, executed. The battle itself became the stuff of Japanese legend through such classic literary accounts as the *Gempei seisui-ki* (Record of the rise and fall of the Minamoto and Taira), largely because of the loss of Antoku, along with a great sword, one of the Imperial Treasures of Japan brought from heaven by the first Japanese emperor. The loss of this sword betokened the revolutionary change created by Yoritomo's victory.

The victory at Dan-no-ura put Yoritomo on the path to assume control of the entire empire. Yoritomo had not merely suppressed a rival warrior clan, but had, for the first time in Japanese history, created an effective alliance among regional powers. In the process, he also built a government, establishing policies and institutions that supplanted aristocratic rule. The Minamoto created new government offices and appointed to them warriors whose loyalty to the Minamoto clan came before all else. In 1191, Yoritomo visited the new emperor in Kyoto, who certified Yoritomo's dominance of the empire by appointing him sei-i-tai-shogun ("barbarian-defeating generalissimo") for life. He thus became the first of the great shoguns, and this appointment marked the beginning of the great medieval courts of Japan and the power of the shoguns.

Further reading: John W. Hall, *Japan; From Prehistory to Modern Times* (Tokyo: C. E. Tuttle Co., 1971); Helen Craig McCullough, trans., *The Tale of the Heike* (Stanford, Calif.: Stanford University Press 1990); James Murdoch, *A History of Japan,* 3 vols. (New York: Routledge, 1996); George B. Samson, *A History of Japan,* 3 vols. (Palo Alto, Calif.: Stanford University Press, 1958–63); Pierre François Souyri, *The World Turned Upside Down* (New York: Columbia University Press, 2001).

Genghis Khan's Campaigns against the Khwarezmian Empire   *See* MONGOL-PERSIAN WAR, FIRST.

Genghis Khan's Chepe and Sübedei Expeditions   *See* MONGOL INVASION OF RUSSIA, FIRST.

Genghis Khan's Conquest of Kara-Khitai (1217)

PRINCIPAL COMBATANTS: Genghis (Chinggis) Khan vs. the Kara-Khitai
PRINCIPAL THEATER(S): Kara-Khitai (in modern Kyrgyzstan, Central Asia)
DECLARATION: None
MAJOR ISSUES AND OBJECTIVES: Conquest
OUTCOME: The Mongols defeated the Kara-Khitai forces of the usurper Kushluk, and Genghis Khan annexed the country.
APPROXIMATE MAXIMUM NUMBER OF MEN UNDER ARMS: Mongols, 20,000 men; Kara-Khitai, numbers unknown, but far superior
CASUALTIES: Unknown
TREATIES: None

Kushluk (fl. early 13th century), leader of the Naiman tribe, was defeated by Genghis Khan (c. 1162–1227) in the 1208 Battle of Irtysh. He fled the field and found refuge among the Kara-Khitai Tatars. During 1209–16, however, Kushluk, in concert with Mohammad Shah (r. 1098–1128) of Khwarazm, turned on his host and protector, the khan of Kara-Khitai, and carried out a coup d'état, which culminated in his usurpation of the Kara-Khitai

throne. From this position, Kushluk swore vengeance on Genghis Khan.

Genghis Khan knew that he had to check the threat posed by Kushluk, but he was also aware that his vast army was worn out by a decade of continual campaigning. Therefore, he detached the freshest troops, some 20,000 men, put them under the command of one of his ablest commanders, General Chepe (fl. early 13th century), then dispatched these forces to Kara-Khitai.

Outnumbered, Chepe understood that he had to employ what military tacticians call a "force multiplier," a means to compensate for his relatively small numbers. He therefore incited a rebellion among the Tatars. Once this was under way and the country thrown into chaos, Chepe attacked and defeated Kushluk's forces west of Kashgar. The treacherous usurper was captured and summarily executed, whereupon Genghis Khan annexed Kara-Khitai.

See also GENGHIS KHAN'S FIRST WAR WITH THE XI XIA EMPIRE; GENGHIS KHAN'S SECOND WAR WITH THE XI XIA EMPIRE; GENGHIS KHAN'S WAR WITH THE JIN EMPIRE; MONGOL INVASION OF RUSSIA, FIRST; MONGOL-PERSIAN WAR, FIRST.

Further reading: Paul Ratchnevsky, *Genghis Khan: His Life and Legacy* (London: Blackwell Publishers, 1991); J. J. Saunders, *The History of the Mongol Conquests* (Philadelphia: University of Pennsylvania Press, 2001).

Genghis Khan's First War with the Xi Xia Empire (1205–1209)

PRINCIPAL COMBATANTS: Mongols vs. Xia Tanguts
PRINCIPAL THEATER(S): Western Xia empire
DECLARATION: None
MAJOR ISSUES AND OBJECTIVES: Genghis (Chinggis) Khan sought suzerainty over the Xi Xia (Hsi Hsia) Empire, in part to control Chinese-Western trade routes and in part as a base from which to continue westward conquest.
OUTCOME: The Mongols waged a successful war of attrition against the Xi Xia, compelling them to accept Mongol suzerainty.
APPROXIMATE MAXIMUM NUMBER OF MEN UNDER ARMS: Unknown
CASUALTIES: Unknown
TREATIES: No surviving documents

Genghis Khan (c. 1162–1227) saw conquest of the Xi Xia, or Western Xia—a Chinese empire south of the Gobi Desert and west of Cathay, the empire of the Jin—as a means of controlling and profiting from the great caravan routes between China and the West. Although the Xi Xia were ruled by the Tanguts, a warrior people, the empire was poorly organized, weak, and ripe for conquest. Genghis Khan conducted the war as a series of massed, highly disciplined raids throughout the countryside during 1205, 1207, and 1209. No great cities were attacked, but the Xi Xia were so thoroughly worn down by three terrible raids that they sued for peace after the third, in 1209, and accepted Mongol dominion over them.

Far from being the brutal and rapacious conqueror popular history frequently portrays, Genghis Khan combined diplomacy and what today would be termed "nation building" with military conquest. He was eager to come to terms with the Xi Xia, to acquire control of the empire, but to allow the people to live their lives and, indeed, to live them better than they had under the Jin. From this conquest, Genghis Khan was in an excellent position to press Mongol expansion westward.

See also GENGHIS KHAN'S CONQUEST OF KARA-KHITAI; GENGHIS KHAN'S SECOND WAR WITH THE XI XIA EMPIRE; GENGHIS KHAN'S WAR WITH THE JIN EMPIRE; MONGOL INVASION OF RUSSIA, FIRST; MONGOL-PERSIAN WAR, FIRST.

Further reading: Paul Ratchnevsky, *Genghis Khan: His Life and Legacy* (London: Blackwell Publishers, 1991); J. J. Saunders, *The History of the Mongol Conquests* (Philadelphia: University of Pennsylvania Press, 2001).

Genghis Khan's Second War with the Xi Xia Empire (1226–1227)

PRINCIPAL COMBATANTS: Mongols vs. Tanguts of Xi Xia (Hsi Hsia)

PRINCIPAL THEATER(S): Xi Xia and Ning-Xia, imperial capital

DECLARATION: None

MAJOR ISSUES AND OBJECTIVES: Genghis Khan sought vengeance against his rebellious vassal.

OUTCOME: Ning-Xia was destroyed and Tangut hegemony in Xi Xia ended.

APPROXIMATE MAXIMUM NUMBER OF MEN UNDER ARMS: Mongols 180,000; Xia Tanguts, 300,000+

CASUALTIES: Xia Tanguts, 300,000 killed; Mongol casualties unknown

TREATIES: None

The Mongols' second war against the Xi Xia, or Western Xia Empire, came about when the Tangut vassal ruling that realm decided to assert autonomy by refusing to render to Genghis Khan (c. 1162–1227) the service appropriate from a vassal (*see* GENGHIS KAN'S FIRST WAR WITH THE XI XIA EMPIRE). Preparatory to launching his war against Persia (*see* MONGOL-PERSIAN WAR, FIRST), Genghis Khan called upon the Xi Xia for troops. Not only did the Tangut ruler of Xi Xia refuse to deliver the troops, he replied contemptuously that if Genghis Khan lacked sufficient numbers for conquest, he no longer had the right to rule.

In response to this act of rebellion, Genghis Khan invaded the Xia late in 1226, when the rivers were frozen, allowing for rapid passage of the Mongol army. Some 180,000 Mongols met 300,000 Xi Xias on a frozen battlefield: the Yellow River. From the beginning, Genghis Khan was in control of the battle. He enticed the Xia Tangut to advance onto the river, then attacked the Xia Tangut cavalry with dismounted archers. This threw the Xia Tangut into a confused panic, which the Mongols exploited in a series of charges. Simultaneously, Genghis Khan's infantry seized the initiative by attacking the Xia Tangut infantry still waiting on the far bank of the Yellow River. The Mongol victors reported virtually 100 percent casualties among the Tangut Xias, perhaps 300,000 killed.

Following the victory at Yellow River, the Mongols attacked Ning-Xia, capital of the Xi Xia empire. During the siege, Genghis Khan dispatched raiding units to lay waste to the surrounding countryside, However, Genghis Khan died before Ning-Xia fell. His commanders continued the war and took the capital. They put the entire population of the city to death and killed the rebellious Tangut emperor. With the destruction of Ning-Xia, Tangut rule over the empire ended forever.

See also GENGHIS KHAN'S CONQUEST OF KARA-KHITAI; GENGHIS KHAN'S WAR WITH THE JIN EMPIRE; MONGOL INVASION OF RUSSIA, FIRST.

Further reading: Paul Ratchnevsky, *Genghis Khan: His Life and Legacy* (London: Blackwell Publishers, 1991); J. J. Saunders, *The History of the Mongol Conquests* (Philadelphia: University of Pennsylvania Press, 2001).

Genghis Khan's Unification of Mongolia (1190–1206)

PRINCIPAL COMBATANTS: Genghis Khan vs. rival warlords of Mongolia

PRINCIPAL THEATER(S): Mongolia

DECLARATION: None

MAJOR ISSUES AND OBJECTIVES: Consolidation of empire

OUTCOME: Genghis Khan consolidated fractious Mongol tribes into a large and remarkably homogeneous empire, which, in turn, served as the core of a much larger empire of conquest and diplomacy.

APPROXIMATE MAXIMUM NUMBER OF MEN UNDER ARMS: Unknown

CASUALTIES: Unknown

TREATIES: Presumably no formal treaties

Temujin (c. 1162–1227), who would become known to history as Genghis Khan—Supreme Emperor—combined military conquest with brilliant diplomacy to bring together the disparate tribes of Mongolia into a large east-central Asian empire. By 1206, he had established the core of an empire that would become far vaster, all centered on the capital he created at Karakorum. From this nucleus, he would expand into China, India, Russia, and Europe.

See also GENGHIS KHAN'S FIRST WAR WITH THE HSIA EMPIRE; GENGHIS KHAN'S CONQUEST OF KARA-KHITAI; GENGHIS KHAN'S SECOND WAR WITH THE XI XIA EMPIRE; GENGHIS KHAN'S WAR WITH THE JIN EMPIRE; MONGOL INVASION OF RUSSIA, FIRST; MONGOL-PERSIAN WAR, FIRST.

Further reading: Paul Ratchnevsky, *Genghis Khan: His Life and Legacy* (London: Blackwell Publishers, 1991); J. J. Saunders, *The History of the Mongol Conquests* (Philadelphia: University of Pennsylvania Press, 2001).

Genghis Khan's War with the Jin Empire (1211–1215)

PRINCIPAL COMBATANTS: Genghis Khan vs. the Jin (Chin) Empire
PRINCIPAL THEATER(S): Northern China
DECLARATION: None
MAJOR ISSUES AND OBJECTIVES: Conquest
OUTCOME: Genghis Khan compelled the Jin emperor to yield to the suzerainty of the Mongols.
APPROXIMATE MAXIMUM NUMBER OF MEN UNDER ARMS: Unknown
CASUALTIES: Unknown
TREATIES: Concession of the Jin emperor, 1215

For two years, during 1211 and 1212, Genghis Khan (c. 1162–1227) attacked the cities of northern China in vain. His forces were repeatedly frustrated by the well-developed fortifications of the Chinese cities, and the Mongols, accustomed to conducting warfare on the run, using lightning raids, had never developed siegecraft. Genghis Khan recognized the need to develop a siege train, and he did so, returning in 1213. His forces penetrated as far as the Great Wall by the end of the year.

From 1213 on, Genghis Khan led his armies deeper into Jin lands, defeating the Jin in the central region of their own territory, between the Great Wall and the Yellow River. Taking one city after the other, Genghis Khan laid siege to Beijing, which fell to him in 1215. He sacked the Jin capital, forcing the Jin emperor to acknowledge Mongol suzerainty over his realm.

In a procedure typical of Genghis Khan, the conqueror co-opted local authority by offering key leaders positions of power rather than simply eliminating them. In this case, Yeh-lu Chu'u-ta'ai (fl. 1215), a Khitan in the service of the Jin, became one of the Khan's most important administrators. As Genghis Khan had recognized the need to adapt by developing siegecraft, so now he saw that the Khitan official had expertise in administering sedentary populations, a skill the Mongols lacked.

See also GENGHIS KHAN'S CONQUEST OF KARA-KHITAI; GENGHIS KHAN'S FIRST WAR WITH THE XI XIA EMPIRE; GENGHIS KHAN'S SECOND WAR WITH THE XI XIA EMPIRE; MONGOL INVASION OF RUSSIA, FIRST; MONGOL-PERSIAN WAR, FIRST.

Further reading: Paul Ratchnevsky, *Genghis Khan: His Life and Legacy* (London: Blackwell Publishers, 1991); J. J. Saunders, *The History of the Mongol Conquests* (Philadelphia: University of Pennsylvania Press, 2001).

German Civil Wars (938–941)

PRINCIPAL COMBATANTS: Otto I vs. his half brother Thankmur; Otto I vs. French-backed German nobles
PRINCIPAL THEATER(S): Germany
DECLARATION: None
MAJOR ISSUES AND OBJECTIVES: Control of Germany
OUTCOME: Otto increased his central authority over Germany.
APPROXIMATE MAXIMUM NUMBER OF MEN UNDER ARMS: Unknown
CASUALTIES: Unknown
TREATIES: None

The Carolingian Empire fell into decline immediately following the death of Charlemagne (742–814) and the ascension to power of his son, Louis I the Pious (768–840). A bad ruler and an even worse soldier, Louis faced increasingly bold Viking raiders just as his sons, squabbling over their inheritances, launched a civil war. For almost 50 years something approaching anarchy ruled Carolingian Europe as a result of this combination—continuous dynastic civil wars laced with frequent Viking raids. As the central authority of the Carolingian Empire fell into decline, the power of the nobility increased. In Germany more so than in France (where rulers would remain nominally Carolingian for another century), the nobles' growing power meant that old tribal organizations suddenly became independent duchies. And it opened the door to Europe for Muslim raiders from North Africa (*see* MAGYAR RAIDS IN FRANCE; MAGYAR RAIDS IN THE HOLY ROMAN EMPIRE; MAGYAR RAID INTO EUROPE, FIRST).

Central authority continued to decline in Germany until it was revived by the coming to power of a talented soldier, diplomat, and administrator named Henry the Fowler (r. 919–936) (Henry I). It was his son, Otto I the Great (912–973) who would decisively defeat the Muslims at the battle of Lechfield (*see* MAGYAR RAID, GREAT) and, in effect, create a new Holy Roman Empire. But before he faced the Magyars, Otto was forced to put down two rebellions in the early years of his reign.

The first was led by his half brother, Thankmur (fl. 10th century), and lasted less than a year during 938–939.

The second was more serious and lasted longer, from 939 to 941. A group of German nobles, led by Otto's younger brother Henry (fl. 10th century), launched a civil war once they had secured the backing of France's Louis IV (920–954). Otto won major victories in the 940 battle of Xanten and at the battle of Andernach in 941. These triumphs brought Lorraine under German control and enhanced Otto's power. Despite Henry's thwarted plot to murder his brother, Otto forgave him, although he severely punished his rebellious coconspirators. Henry remained loyal ever afterward and, in 947, Otto made him duke of Bavaria. Otto likewise bestowed the other German dukedoms on his relatives.

Secure at home, Otto invaded France the next year seeking revenge against Louis for supporting the German rebels. Louis quickly made peace and Otto withdrew.

Further reading: Geoffrey Barraclough, *The Origins of Modern Germany,* 3rd ed. (Oxford, England: B. Blackwell, 1988); Patrick J. Geary, *Before France and Germany; The Creation and Transformation of the Merovingian World* (New York: Oxford University Press, 1988).

German Civil War (1077–1106)

PRINCIPAL COMBATANTS: Henry IV of Germany vs. Pope Gregory VII; the Welf (Guelf) party vs. the Waiblingen; Henry IV vs. his son, Henry V

PRINCIPAL THEATER(S): Germany and Italy (primarily Rome)

DECLARATION: None

MAJOR ISSUES AND OBJECTIVES: Henry IV wanted absolute rule of Germany and desired to become Holy Roman Emperor; the papacy resisted his acquiring so much power.

OUTCOME: Although Henry IV ultimately prevailed, his death in 1106 put his rebellious son, Henry V, on the German throne; in contrast to his father, Henry V sought reconciliation with the papacy.

APPROXIMATE MAXIMUM NUMBER OF MEN UNDER ARMS: Unknown

CASUALTIES: Unknown

TREATIES: No controlling treaties were concluded

The always fractious German states erupted into civil war in 1077. Henry IV (1050–1106) became German king in 1056, when he was only six years old. During his minority, Germany was ruled by regents, who elevated the episcopacy to great power. After attaining his majority, Henry, in 1065, attempted to regain control of the government by choosing bishops who would answer directly to him. In response to Henry's bid for power, Pope Gregory VII (c. 1020–1085) objected to Henry's advocacy of lay investiture of bishops and also to Henry's demand that he be made the Holy Roman Emperor. For years, hostility increased between Henry and the papacy, until, in 1076, Henry convened a synod, which, at his bidding, proclaimed the deposition of Pope Gregory VII. Predictably, the pope responded by deposing the clergy of the synod and by excommunicating Henry IV. As part of the excommunication, the pope forbade Henry from exercising rule over his government.

The papal action moved Henry's nobles to the verge of rebellion against their king. In an ultimatum issued on February 22, 1077, they demanded that Henry secure papal absolution or they would abandon him. Immediately, Henry set out for the Diet at Augsburg. En route, he humbled himself before Gregory's representatives and thereby gained absolution. This, however, proved insufficient to move the Diet to reconsider its intention to reverse Henry's election. The Augsburg Diet deposed Henry IV and elected an antiking, their rival nominee for the throne.

The action of the Diet touched off a long civil war. The Welf party (known in Italy as the Guelfs) obtained papal support against Henry, whereas a majority of the German nobility honored their pledge to support Henry. These supporters formed a rival to the Welfs, the Waiblingen, named for a castle owned by Henry's family, the Hohenstaufens. (In Italy, the Waiblingen were known as the Ghibellines.)

In 1080, a council of the Waiblingen held at Brixton reaffirmed the original action of the synod that had deposed Pope Gregory VII and deposed him yet again. The council proclaimed an antipope, Guibert of Ravenna (1025–1100), who was called Clement III. Later that year, Henry IV led an army against the Welfs, but was defeated in his first engagement at the Battle of Thuringia. Strangely enough, this military defeat was negated by the death of the antiking and his replacement by a political unknown, whose presence actually diminished Welf power. Despite the military defeat, most Germans now believed that the death of the antiking was a sign of God's having elected Henry. Thus fortified by increased popular support, Henry was emboldened to expand the German civil war into an assault on Rome after Gregory defiantly demanded the new antiking's fealty.

After a long and costly struggle, Henry's army marched into Rome and occupied the city in 1084. Henry forcibly replaced Gregory with the antipope, Clement III, who, in turn, crowned Henry Holy Roman Emperor. No sooner was this done, however, than Pope Gregory's Norman adherents, under the leadership of Robert Guiscard (c. 1015–85), attacked the occupiers of Rome and drove them out. Rome, however, was then subject to the ravages of Robert's army, which sacked the city for three days after ejecting the forces of Henry. The sack of Rome turned Romans against Pope Gregory, who was forced into exile in Salerno. He died in 1085.

Thus, although he had again suffered a military defeat, Henry IV emerged triumphant. He returned to Germany, subdued another rival for the throne during 1086–87, returned to attack Rome in 1090–92, then found himself beset by his own sons. Backed by the successors of Pope Gregory, Henry's sons fought their father from 1092 to 1106. Henry IV was imprisoned by his son Henry (later Henry V, 1080–1125), who forced him to abdicate in 1105. The son now set about reconciling with the papacy, but Henry IV escaped from captivity, recruited a strong army, and defeated the forces of Henry V just outside of Visé, in modern Belgium. Having achieved military victory against a rival, Henry IV succumbed to illness and died, at Liège, in 1106. Thus Henry V assumed the German throne, and the civil war ended.

See also GERMAN CIVIL WARS (938–941); GERMAN CIVIL WAR (1197–1214); GERMAN CIVIL WAR (1314–1325); and GERMAN CIVIL WAR (1400–1411).

Further reading: Geoffrey Barraclough, *The Crucible of Europe: The Ninth and Tenth Centuries in European History* (Berkeley: University of California Press, 1976) and *The Origins of Modern Germany*, 3rd ed. (Oxford, England: Blackwell, 1988); R. I. Moore, *The First European Revolution, c. 970–1215* (London: Blackwell, 2000).

German Civil War (1197–1214)

PRINCIPAL COMBATANTS: Philip of Swabia (with aid from France) vs. Otto of Brunswick (with aid from England; later, Frederick (with papal support) vs. Otto of Brunswick; France vs. England (with aid from the Low Countries)

PRINCIPAL THEATER(S): Germany

DECLARATION: None

MAJOR ISSUES AND OBJECTIVES: Succession to the German throne and the imperial throne

OUTCOME: Frederick II was ultimately crowned, and Germany was more or less aligned with the pope; however, the long civil war had devastated the land.

APPROXIMATE MAXIMUM NUMBER OF MEN UNDER ARMS: At Bouvines, Philip II Augustus fielded 36,000 troops; Otto fielded 71,000.

CASUALTIES: Unknown

TREATIES: None

A conflict over the succession to the German and imperial throne following the death of Holy Roman Emperor Henry VI (1165–97) touched off a full-scale civil war with much outside involvement. The emperor-elect, Frederick II (1194–1250), was an infant. An additional contender, Philip of Swabia (c. 1176–1208), Henry's brother, was a member of the Waiblingen party (in Italy, known as the Ghibellines), whereas a third, Otto of Brunswick (c. 1175–1218), was a member of the rival Welfs (Italian, Guelfs). The Waiblingen was the nationalist party, and the Welfs constituted the papal party; their cause was sponsored behind the scenes by the new pope, Innocent III (1160 or 1161–1216).

Young Frederick was crowned nothing more than king of Sicily while the forces of Philip and Otto battled it out in a war that ravaged Germany. In 1198, Philip managed to be crowned with the support of the southern Germans and the French. However, Otto contested the coronation and found allies among the archbishop of Cologne, the northern Germans, and the English.

To obtain the support of Pope Innocent III, in 1201 Otto pledged to the papacy Italian lands under his control. This prompted the archbishop of Cologne to crown Philip at Aachen in 1205. Thus legitimated, Philip mounted a major offensive against Otto in 1206 and defeated him, thereby gaining Innocent's recognition—in exchange for certain concessions. Three years later, however, Philip was assassinated, and Otto regained ascendancy. After buying off the German church by relinquishing royal control over it, Otto invaded Italy and forced the pope to crown him Holy Roman Emperor Otto IV in 1209. This accomplished, Otto instantly reneged on his agreement with the German church and invaded Sicily. The pope responded by stirring up a new rebellion against Otto and crowning King Frederick II of Germany.

On July 27, 1214, King Philip II (1165–1223) (Philip Augustus) of France led his forces against those of Otto, his Flemish allies, and an army led by King John I ("Lackland"; 1199–1216) of England at the Battle of Bouvines. The main forces were those of Philip II Augustus—some 36,000 troops—and Otto of Brunswick, who fielded 71,000. Despite this disparity in numbers, Philip brilliantly outgeneraled Otto. Otto attempted to cut Philip's lines of communication and supply. Philip responded by feigning panic, which enticed Otto to make a premature attack on ground favorable to the French cavalry. Although the first French assault was repulsed by Flemish and German pikemen, Philip directed his knights against the very center of Otto's army. While Philip smashed through here, his right flank drove off repeated German attacks. Now it was Otto's turn to panic—in earnest. He fled the field, whereupon Philip turned his attention to the right flank of Otto's remaining forces, which included a small English contingent under John I. These warriors performed heroically, but were overwhelmed.

The French victory broke up the coalition among Otto, the Low Countries, and, most important, England. For King John, one consequence of this defeat was discredit among the English barons, who forced him as a result to sign the Magna Carta in 1215 (*see* ENGLISH CIVIL WAR [1215–1217]). As for Frederick II, he was crowned anew in Aachen in 1215, then reinstated the

Speyer concessions—the commitments to the church that Otto had reneged on—and embraced the papacy.

Frederick's ascension hardly brought peace and stability to Germany. The war fragmented an already fractious land, and a more or less permanent state of civil insurrection followed.

See also ANGLO-FRENCH WAR (1213–1214); GERMAN CIVIL WARS (938–941); GERMAN CIVIL WAR (1077–1106); GERMAN CIVIL WAR (1314–1325); GERMAN CIVIL WAR (1400–1411).

Further reading: Geoffrey Barraclough, *The Origins of Modern Germany,* 3rd ed. (Oxford, England: Blackwell, 1988); R. I. Moore, *The First European Revolution, c. 970–1215* (London: Blackwell, 2000).

German Civil War   (1314–1325)

PRINCIPAL COMBATANTS: Duke Frederick III of Austria vs. Duke Louis IV of Bavaria

PRINCIPAL THEATER(S): Germany and Italy

DECLARATION: None

MAJOR ISSUES AND OBJECTIVES: Succession to the German and imperial thrones

OUTCOME: Louis IV was crowned (though he shared the throne with Frederick III), but at the expense of alienating the papacy.

APPROXIMATE MAXIMUM NUMBER OF MEN UNDER ARMS: Unknown

CASUALTIES: Unknown

TREATIES: None

Under Holy Roman Emperor Henry VII (c. 1275–1313), the various princes of Germany, along with local church authorities, gained much power at the expense of the Holy Roman Empire and the papacy. Thus, many German princes felt entitled to even more when Henry died in 1313, and conflict developed over Henry's successor. Most of the princes supported the Hapsburg candidate, Duke Frederick III ("the Handsome") (1286–1330) of Austria. A significant minority favored the Wittelsbach candidate, Duke Louis IV of Bavaria (c. 1287–1347). In 1314, their respective supporters elected both men king of Germany, a fact that triggered a new civil war as both assumed the title of Holy Roman Emperor. Complicating matters was the fact that the papacy was vacant at the time, so that no supreme authority was available to adjudicate the election. Thus war seemed the only alternative.

After years of indecisive combat, in 1322 Louis IV achieved a decisive victory at the Battle of Mühldorf on the Inn River, some 45 miles east of Munich. Frederick was captured in the battle and imprisoned. Under duress, he acknowledged Louis as the rightful Holy Roman Emperor. The war quickly wound down, and by 1325 it was over—yet the underlying issues were not fully resolved. Pope John XXII (d. 1334) vehemently opposed Louis and refused to acknowledge his right to rule. In response, Louis denied a need for papal sanction and relied instead on the approval of the electors and the people. In 1327–28, he led an invasion of Rome. He captured the city and installed Nicholas V (d. 1333) as antipope. John XXII fled to Avignon, which became the new seat of the papacy. Louis had to content himself with a lay coronation as Holy Roman Emperor and joint rule with Frederick, who became Frederick III. As for the antipope, his reign was brief. Excommunicated by John in 1329, he renounced his claim to the papacy the following year.

See also GERMAN CIVIL WARS (938–941); GERMAN CIVIL WAR (1077–1106); GERMAN CIVIL WAR (1197–1214); GERMAN CIVIL WAR (1400–1411).

Further reading: F. R. H. Du Boulay, *Germany in the Later Middle Ages* (New York: St. Martin's Press, 1983); Friedrich Heer, *Holy Roman Empire,* trans. Janet Sondheimer (New York: Sterling, 2002); Joachim Leuschner, *Germany in the Late Middle Ages,* trans. Sabine MacCormack (New York: North-Holland Publishing, 1980).

German Civil War   (1400–1411)

PRINCIPAL COMBATANTS: King Wenceslaus IV vs. the German electors Rupert III, Sigismund, and Jobst

PRINCIPAL THEATER(S): Germany

DECLARATION: None

MAJOR ISSUES AND OBJECTIVES: Retention of the German throne and the imperial throne

OUTCOME: The conflict was a low-level civil war; an all-out war was averted by a scheme to mollify Wenceslaus and his supporters while allowing the electors their choice as German king and Holy Roman Emperor.

APPROXIMATE MAXIMUM NUMBER OF MEN UNDER ARMS: Unknown; no formal armies involved

CASUALTIES: Unknown

TREATIES: None

Wenceslaus (1361–1419), son of the Holy Roman Emperor Charles IV (1316–78), was king of Bohemia and Germany as well as Holy Roman Emperor. Although he was an earnest lover of peace, who willingly convened frequent diets in Germany from 1378 to 1389 to please and placate the always fractious German nobles, he was a weak and generally incompetent ruler, given to bouts of drunkenness. Worse, he spent most of his time in Prague, neglecting his German realm, and his absence prompted the nobles to demand that Wenceslaus appoint a *Reichsverweser* (imperial governor) for Germany. This the king stubbornly refused to do.

In the absence of effective rule, wars between town leagues and princes brought anarchy over Germany, and in August 1400, after Wenceslaus declined to attend one of many meetings demanded by the nobles, the princes deposed him and elected Rupert III (1352–1410), the elector of the Palatine, as the new Holy Roman Emperor. On the face of it, this was a wise and necessary step, but Wenceslaus, for all his incompetence, was popular with the German people. Nor did Wenceslaus leave quietly, but insisted on his right to retain the throne.

For the next decade, a low-level civil conflict simmered, continually threatening to erupt into a full-scale civil war. Only the death of Rupert in 1410 averted a major conflict, and Wenceslaus offered himself as candidate for emperor. The electors, however, refused to elect him and instead elevated Jobst (1351–1411), margrave of Moravia. But Jobst died in 1411, again clearing the way for Wenceslaus to stand for election. This time, Wenceslaus's brother, Sigismund (1368–1437), king of Hungary, maneuvered to allow Wenceslaus to retain the title of king of Germany and to receive a royal pension while he, Sigismund, became the actual German ruler and Holy Roman Emperor. Thus Wenceslaus and the people were placated, and a major civil war was avoided. Nevertheless, the low-level conflict that had ensued drained the German treasury and created a troubled reign for Sigismund.

See also GERMAN CIVIL WARS (938–941); GERMAN CIVIL WAR (1077–1106); German CIVIL WAR (1197–1214); GERMAN CIVIL WAR (1314–1325).

Further reading: Henry J. Cohn, *The Government of the Rhine Palatine in the Fifteenth Century* (London: Oxford University Press, 1978); Friedrich Heer, *Holy Roman Empire,* trans. Janet Sondheimer (New York: Sterling, 2002).

German East Africa Insurrection   *See* MAJI MAJI UPRISING.

Germanic Revolts of 1–5 C.E.   *See* ROMAN NORTHERN FRONTIER WARS.

German Peasants' War   *See* PEASANTS' WAR.

German Revolution   (1848)

PRINCIPAL COMBATANTS: German nationalists vs. Prussia's King Frederick William IV
PRINCIPAL THEATER(S): Berlin and southwest Germany
DECLARATION: None
MAJOR ISSUES AND OBJECTIVES: German liberals agitated for a constitutional monarchy ruling over a united Germany.

OUTCOME: Liberal reforms were short-lived, and the German nationalist movement collapsed.
APPROXIMATE MAXIMUM NUMBER OF MEN UNDER ARMS: Citizen movement, numbers unknown
CASUALTIES: Unknown, but mostly light; the only serious casualties were in Berlin, during April 1848.
TREATIES: None

The year 1848 saw revolutions—most short-lived—in France, Italy, Hungary, and Bohemia, as well as Germany. All shared a common theme—a desire for liberal reform— except for the German revolution, which had more to do with creating a unified nation than with liberalizing existing government.

Like the other European revolutions, that in Germany was inspired by the FRENCH REVOLUTION (1848). It began as public demonstrations in favor of the establishment of a German national parliament. The demonstrations had an effect. In Baden, for example, liberal reform was introduced into government. The Hanseatic states transformed themselves into democratic republics during March 1848. Up to this point, the "revolution" was bloodless, but after the repressive Klemens von Metternich (1753–1859) was driven out of Austria during the AUSTRIAN REVOLUTION in March 1848, Berlin suddenly exploded into armed revolt. On March 13, garrison troops, including dragoons and the garde du corps, confronted a street mob, which they dispersed at rifle point. Three days later, as demonstrations continued and intensified, cavalry as well as infantry were called out. Demonstrators hurled stones, and the troops replied with shots, which dispersed the crowd. Still, the demonstrations continued throughout the rest of the week, the crowd hurling stones, the troops replying with gunfire.

At last, on March 18, King Frederick William IV (1795–1861), who had assumed the Prussian throne in 1840, made a series of sweeping concessions, yielding to a call for a German confederation and even agreeing to some constitutional reforms. He stopped just short of accepting rule over a unified Germany as a constitutional monarch.

On May 18, 1848, a National Assembly convened at Frankfurt, but was soon deeply divided over whether Austria was to be part of the newly contemplated German confederation. While the assembly debated, troops forcibly put down the radical agitation of German laborers, and the revolution began to lose steam. By the end of the year, the radicalism that had triggered the revolution had petered out, and the National Assembly drifted steadily to the right. When the assembly offered Frederick William rule over a unified Germany within the confines of a liberal—but hardly democratic—constitution, he rejected the offer as too great an incursion on his royal prerogatives. His counterproposal was a somewhat liberalized, but still conservative plan for continued monarchy. This gave rise to abortive uprisings in the German southwest, which royal troops quickly put down.

By the beginning of 1849, a number of the king's liberal decrees of the previous year had been canceled. Austria once again emerged as a powerful rival to Prussian power and assumed leadership of the old German Confederacy Assembly. In effect, the pre-1848 status quo had been reasserted, and the drive for a democratic and united Germany would have to await the ascendancy of Otto von Bismarck (1815–98) and the FRANCO-PRUSSIAN WAR two decades later.

Germany's harsh suppression of its 1848 liberal revolutions led millions of Germans to emigrate during the next decade. When Bismarck came to power and introduced universal conscription into his brutal Prussian army, they were joined by young German draft dodgers and those from a number of religious sects whose beliefs forbade military service. For almost 40 years these millions of Germans scattered over Europe, nations adjacent to Europe, and North, Central, and South America. Wherever they went, these German intellectuals, revolutionaries, and true believers brought deeply held new doctrines and often startling new ideas whose unsettling impact was soon felt not merely in their adopted homelands but ultimately around the world.

Further reading: Werner E. Mosse, *The European Powers and the German Question, 1848–71* (New York: Cambridge University Press, 1981); Wolfram Siemann, *The German Revolution of 1848–49* (New York: St. Martin's Press, 1999); Veit Valentin, *1848: Chapters of Germany History* (Hamden, Conn.: Archon Books, 1965).

German Town War *See* "TOWN WAR."

Geronimo Campaign, The *See* UNITED STATES–APACHE WAR (1876–1886).

Ghassanid-Lakhmid Wars (c. 500–583)

PRINCIPAL COMBATANTS: Ghassanids (allied with Byzantium) vs. Lakhmids (allied with Persia)
PRINCIPAL THEATER(S): Arabia (modern region of Syria, Jordan, and Israel)
DECLARATION: None
MAJOR ISSUES AND OBJECTIVES: Ghassan and the Lakhmids were essentially client states of Byzantium and Persia, respectively, which promoted war between them as a means of gaining power and influence over Arabia.
OUTCOME: Neither dynasty proved enduringly dominant, and both ultimately succumbed to the Muslim conquest of Arabia.

APPROXIMATE MAXIMUM NUMBER OF MEN UNDER ARMS: Unknown
CASUALTIES: Unknown
TREATIES: None

Byzantium (the Eastern Empire of Rome) vied with Sassanid Persia for influence and hegemony in Arabia and backed rival dynasties in Arabia. The Byzantines supported the Ghassanids, whereas the Persians backed the Lakhmids, encouraging and perpetuating years of continual warfare between the dynasties.

Concentrated around Al-Syrah in southern Iraq, the Lakhmid kingdom emerged late in the third century and became an increasingly influential Iranian vassal state, approaching the height of its power by the end of the fifth century under King al-Mundhir I (c. 418–462). At the start of the sixth century, King al-Mundhir III (503–554) began raiding Byzantine Syria, particularly the pro-Byzantine Ghassanid Arab kingdom.

The Ghassanids endured much loss at the hands of the Lakhmid raiders until a battle in 528, in which the Ghassanid leader al-Harith ibn Jabalah (r. 529–569) defeated the Lakhmid forces and soon afterward became Ghassanid king. About 550, the Lakhmids returned to the offensive with strong attacks against Ghassan as well as Byzantine Syria, but these ultimately failed.

Byzantium turned against its ally in 583 when orthodox Byzantine leaders responded to the Monophysitic heresy rampant in Ghassan (the belief that Christ's human and divine natures are one rather than two). To suppress the heresy, Byzantium sent troops to seal Ghassan's borders and made Ghassan a vassal. Two decades later, the Lakhmid dynasty effectively came to an end with the death of its last ruler. Persian Christians had opposed his adherence to the Nestorian heresy (the belief that Mary was not the mother of God). What was left of both Ghassan and the Lakhmid dynasties was swept away during the balance of the seventh century by the great Muslim conquest.

Further reading: Cyril A. Mango, ed., *Oxford History of Byzantium* (New York: Oxford University Press, 2002); John Julius Norwich, *Byzantium: The Early Centuries.* (New York: Alfred A. Knopf, 2003); Mark Whittow, *The Making of Byzantium, 600–1025* (Berkeley: University of California Press, 1996).

Ghost Dance Uprising (1890–1891)

PRINCIPAL COMBATANTS: Various Sioux factions vs. United States
PRINCIPAL THEATER(S): South Dakota
DECLARATION: No formal declaration
MAJOR ISSUES AND OBJECTIVES: A religiously inspired Indian uprising against white domination

OUTCOME: Rebellion was suppressed, ending four centuries of warfare between whites and Indians in North America.

APPROXIMATE MAXIMUM NUMBER OF MEN UNDER ARMS: For the United States, 5,000 at Pine Ridge Reservation; for the Sioux, 150 warriors, supporters of Sitting Bull, otherwise, totals unknown

CASUALTIES: At Wounded Knee, possibly 300–350 Indians; United States, 25 killed, 39 wounded, most a result of friendly fire

TREATIES: No formal treaty

By the opening of the last decade of the 19th century, the so-called Indian Wars of the American West were by and large concluded. The tribes, hostile, friendly, and indifferent, were confined on nearly 200 reservations, encompassing some 181,000 square miles of land. For the most part, life on these reservations was at best harsh and at worst debilitating and demoralizing. The great Hunkpapa Sioux chief Sitting Bull (1831–90), domiciled with his followers at the Standing Rock Reservation, South Dakota, persistently refused to cooperate with the agent in charge and struggled to maintain the identity of his people.

In the meantime, among the reservation Sioux, a prophet arose. Wovoka (c. 1856–1932) was the son of a Paiute shaman and had spent part of his youth with a white rancher's family, from whom he learned Christian teachings and traditions, which he combined with Native religion. Wovoka began to preach of the coming of a new world in which only Indians dwelled and in which buffalo—virtually exterminated by white hunters and the encroachment of white civilization—were again plentiful. Generations of slain Indians would come back to life in the new world. Wovoka enjoined all Indians to dance the Ghost Dance in order to propitiate the millennium. His was a message born of discontent and desperation, to be sure, but Wovoka did not counsel violence. Quite the opposite, he preached a Christian ethic of peace.

Wovoka's message spread through the western reservations like wildfire, and among the Teton Sioux, his call for nonviolence was suppressed. Wovoka's message became a call to rebellion. Short Bull (c. 1845–1904) and Kicking Bear (c. 1847–1923)—Teton apostles of the Ghost Dance religion—urged a campaign to obliterate the white man, and they even fashioned a "ghost shirt," which, they said, afforded absolute protection against the whites' bullets.

But even in the absence of such bellicose posturings, the Ghost Dance itself was sufficient to alarm white authorities. The agent in charge of the Pine Ridge Reservation frantically telegraphed Washington, D.C., in November 1890: "Indians are dancing in the snow and are wild and crazy. We need protection and we need it now." Accordingly, on November 20, 1890, cavalry and infantry reinforcements arrived at Pine Ridge and at the Rosebud Reservation. This action served only to provoke the Sioux under Short Bull and Kicking Bear, and some 3,000 Indians gathered on a plateau at the northwest corner of Pine Ridge called the Stronghold. Sitting Bull, most venerated of all Sioux leaders, actively embraced the Ghost Dance doctrine at Standing Rock Reservation. James McLaughlin (1842–1923), the agent in charge there, decided to have Sitting Bull quietly arrested and removed from the reservation. To accomplish the arrest, McLaughlin wanted to use the reservation's own Indian policemen.

The skillful but vainglorious army commander in charge of western operations, Nelson A. Miles (1835–1925), thought that the arrest of Sitting Bull, which would signify the end of the Indian Wars once and for all, should not be quiet. Accordingly, Miles contacted the greatest showman the West has ever known: William F. Buffalo "Bill" Cody (1846–1917). Cody and Sitting Bull were, after all, friends, the Indian having formerly starred in Cody's Wild West Show. Cody would persuade Sitting Bull to step down—and, what is more, he would persuade him with a flourish.

McLaughlin, convinced that the publicity that would attend Miles's plan would provoke widespread rebellion, arranged for the commanding officer of nearby Fort Yates to detain Buffalo Bill at a local saloon when the showman arrived at Standing Rock on November 27, 1890, until he could secure orders cancelling Cody's mission. This he narrowly succeeded in doing just as Short Bull and Kicking Bear openly invited Sitting Bull to join them and their people at the Stronghold on the Pine Ridge Reservation.

McLaughlin dispatched 43 reservation policemen on December 15 to arrest Sitting Bull. A scuffle developed, and Sitting Bull was killed.

With many of the reservation Sioux clearly on the verge of violent resistance, General Miles ordered the arrest of another prominent chief, Big Foot (d. 1890) of the Miniconjou Sioux, who were living on the Cheyenne River. The tragic irony is that Big Foot had not only personally renounced the Ghost Dance religion, he was marching to Pine Ridge at the behest of Chief Red Cloud (c. 1822–1909), a Pine Ridge leader friendly to the whites, who had asked him to persuade the Stronghold party to surrender. Miles understood only that Big Foot was headed for the Stronghold, and that, he assumed, could mean only trouble.

Miles sent troops in a wide net across the prairies and badlands to intercept all Miniconjous. On December 28, 1890, a squadron of the Seventh Cavalry located the chief and about 350 Miniconjous near a stream called Wounded Knee Creek. During the night of the 28th, more troops moved into the area, so that by morning 500 soldiers, under Colonel James W. Forsyth, surrounded Big Foot's camp. Four Hotchkiss guns—small pieces of repeating artillery—were trained on the camp from the surrounding hills.

Forsyth's mission was to disarm the Indians and remove them from the "zone of military operations." His soldiers entered the camp and began a rough and provocative search for guns. Soon shots rang out—whether from the Indians or the soldiers is not known—and a full-scale massacre (the army persisted in calling it a battle) ensued. In less than an hour, Big Foot and 153 other Miniconjous are known to have been killed—most of them cut down by deadly fire from the Hotchkiss guns—but so many others staggered, limped, or crawled away that the exact death toll remains unknown. Probably 300 of the 350 who had been camped at Wounded Knee Creek ultimately perished. Most of the Seventh Cavalry's casualties—25 killed and 39 wounded—were the result of "friendly fire."

The Wounded Knee Massacre immediately provoked "hostile" and "friendly" Sioux factions to unite—though Chief Red Cloud continued to protest his people's participation—in a December 30 ambush of the Seventh Cavalry near the Pine Ridge Agency. The unit was rescued by the timely arrival of additional cavalry, and General Miles marshaled 3,500 troops (out of a total force of 5,000) around the outraged Sioux who had assembled 15 miles north of the Pine Ridge Agency along White Clay Creek. Despite the numerical superiority he enjoyed, Miles was wary of provoking further bloodshed. With great forbearance, he slowly closed in around the Indians, urging surrender and promising good treatment. On January 15, 1891, the Sioux at last surrendered, effectively bringing to a conclusion some four centuries of warfare between whites and Indians in North America.

See also UNITED STATES–SIOUX WAR (GREAT SIOUX UPRISING).

Further reading: Alan Axelrod, *Chronicle of the Indian Wars: From Colonial Times to Wounded Knee* (New York: Prentice Hall General Reference, 1993); Dee Brown, *Bury My Heart at Wounded Knee* (Reprint ed., New York: Henry Holt, 2000); Stephan J. Crum, "Ghost Dance," in *Encyclopedia of American West* vol. 2, edited by Charles Phillips and Alan Axelrod (Macmillan Reference USA, 1996); Robert M. Utley, *The Lance and the Shield: The Life and Times of Sitting Bull* (New York: Ballantine, 1994).

Gladiator's Revolt   *See* SERVILE WAR, THIRD.

Glencoe Massacre   (1692)

PRINCIPAL COMBATANTS: MacDonald clan vs. English troops and the Campbell clan
PRINCIPAL THEATER(S): Glencoe Valley, Scotland
DECLARATION: None
MAJOR ISSUES AND OBJECTIVES: King William III of England moved to exterminate the rebellious MacDonald clan of Scotland.

OUTCOME: Most of the clan was slaughtered; news of the atrocity, however, destroyed the reputation of William III in Scotland.
APPROXIMATE MAXIMUM NUMBER OF MEN UNDER ARMS: MacDonalds, number unknown; English, 80 troops
CASUALTIES: 38 MacDonalds were killed; probably an equal number later died of exposure.
TREATIES: None

Like many other English monarchs before him, King William III (1650–1702) was hard pressed to control Scotland. During 1689–90 he faced rebellion among the Highland Jacobites (*see* JACOBITE REBELLION [1689–1690]) and imposed upon the Scottish clan chiefs oaths of allegiance.

One clan leader, Maclain MacDonald (d. 1692) of Glencoe, refused to swear the oath. In response, William ordered the extirpation of the clan and dispatched troops commanded by Captain Robert Campbell (fl. 1692), a relative of Maclain MacDonald. Maclain MacDonald did not resist the troops, but received them hospitably. In the meantime, other royal soldiers sealed all approaches to the valley of Glencoe, and the visiting soldiers, aided by members of the Campbell clan, rivals to the MacDonalds, slaughtered the MacDonalds as they slept. They also burned their houses.

Unfortunately for King William, the slaughter was not total. Thirty-eight MacDonalds were slain, but others escaped, many succumbing to exposure, but some survived to broadcast news of the atrocity throughout Scotland, further hardening much of the country against William and English domination.

See also JACOBITE REBELLION (1715–1716); JACOBITE REBELLION (1745–1746).

Further reading: Bruce Lenman, *The Jacobite Risings in Britain 1689–1746* (Aberdeen: Scottish Cultural Press, 1995); John L. Roberts, *Clan, King, and Covenant: The History of the Highland Clans from the Civil War to the Glencoe Massacre* (Edinburgh: Edinburgh University Press, 2000).

Glendower's Revolt   (1402–1409)

PRINCIPAL COMBATANTS: Welsh rebels under Owen Glendower vs. England's King Henry IV
PRINCIPAL THEATER(S): Wales
DECLARATION: None
MAJOR ISSUES AND OBJECTIVES: Glendower wanted to evict the English from Wales.
OUTCOME: Despite many early victories and potentially powerful allies, Glendower was ultimately defeated, and the rebellion collapsed.
APPROXIMATE MAXIMUM NUMBER OF MEN UNDER ARMS: Unknown

CASUALTIES: Unknown
TREATIES: None

The Welsh had long protested and rebelled against onerous English taxation and inept administration. The situation came to a crisis during the tumultuous reign of King Henry IV (1367–1413) when a wealthy and powerful Welsh lord, Owen Glendower (c. 1354–1416), led a successful campaign against Henry's garrisons throughout Wales, driving them out of the country.

Glendower was descended from the princes of Powys and had inherited a number of manor properties in northern Wales. As a youth, he was sent to London to study law, then served in the army of Henry Bolingbroke (1366–1413), who opposed King Richard II (1367–1400). After this adventure, Glendower returned to Wales to discover that oppressive English rule had badly hobbled the Welsh economy and stirred popular resentment.

In September 1400, a year after Bolingbroke usurped the English throne, Glendower engaged in a feud with his neighbor, Reynold, Lord Grey of Ruthin (1362–1440), which rapidly expanded. Proclaimed prince of Wales, Glendower found allies in the English Edmund de Mortimer (1367–1409) in 1402 and the rebellious Percys in 1403. After Glendower captured the castles of Aberystwyth and Harlech in 1404, he won recognition from France's King Charles VI (1368–1422), who, eager for any opportunity to oppose the English, struck an alliance with the Welshman. Charles proved an unreliable ally. The troops he repeatedly promised Glendower never materialized, and, as a result, Glendower's forces suffered defeat after defeat between 1405 through 1409. Aberystwyth and Harlech were soon retaken, and Glendower fled into the remote Welsh mountains, where he died some seven years after the end of the war.

See also NORTHUMBERLAND'S REBELLION; PERCY'S REBELLION.

Further reading: John Davies, *A History of Wales* (New York: Viking Penguin, 1995); R. R. Davies, *Age of Conquest: Wales 1063–1415* (New York: Oxford University Press, 2000).

Glorious Revolution (1688)

PRINCIPAL COMBATANTS: Supporters of William and Mary vs. James II
PRINCIPAL THEATER(S): Devonshire
DECLARATION: None
MAJOR ISSUES AND OBJECTIVES: At the invitation of a delegation of Parliament, William and Mary came to England to replace James II.
OUTCOME: The revolution—the installation of new monarchs and a profound revision of the role of the English Crown—was wholly successful and entirely peaceful.
APPROXIMATE MAXIMUM NUMBER OF MEN UNDER ARMS: William and Mary were accompanied by a small Dutch force and gathered many more supporters; James II's army deserted him.
CASUALTIES: None
TREATIES: None

The catalogue of the offenses of England's King James II (1633–1701) is long: his reprisal against MONMOUTH'S REBELLION was disproportionately brutal, as was his attempt to force Catholicism upon the English; his general abridgment of rights, culminating in his proroguing (suspending) Parliament, brought the nation to the verge of civil war. Perhaps most outrageous of all was James's total lack of political consciousness, an understanding that his rash tyrannies would produce a conspiracy to remove him from the throne. But this is precisely what happened. In 1688, seven prominent Whig and Tory leaders invited Mary (1662–94) and her husband, William of Orange (1650–1702), to come from Holland to replace James II on the English throne. The two monarchs landed at Torbay, Devonshire, with a small Dutch army and acquired many additional supporters as they marched to meet the forces of James II at Salisbury. The English king's forces, under John Churchill (later, duke of Marlborough) deserted James, who fled, was intercepted at Kent, but then released and permitted to sail for France—ignominiously making his way across the Channel on a decrepit fishing smack, the only vessel immediately available.

William and Mary immediately assumed leadership of a provisional government while the Convention Parliament debated how power might be legally and permanently transferred to them. In 1689, the Convention Parliament finally ruled that the throne was indeed vacant, that James's flight constituted abdication, and the Parliament further asserted its authority to appoint William and Mary legal sovereigns. It was the first time in English history that the Parliament had appointed a monarch.

The Glorious Revolution had done much more than replace an abusive king with more palatable rulers. The Convention Parliament enacted a "Declaration of Rights" and a "Bill of Rights," which defined anew the relationship between monarch and subjects, and it explicitly barred future Catholic succession to the throne. The parliamentary acts ended the royal prerogative to suspend or abridge the law in any way, thereby subordinating the monarch to the law. The Crown was also explicitly forbidden to levy taxes or maintain a standing army in peacetime without parliamentary consent. Thus William and Mary came to power as England's first monarchs fully answerable to a Parliament and a constitution. Parliament, in effect, became the supreme governing body of England.

See also DUTCH WAR, THIRD.

Further reading: John Childs, *The Army, James II and the Glorious Revolution* (Manchester, England: Manchester University Press, 1980); Eveline Cruickshanks, *The Glorious Revolution* (New York: St. Martin's Press, 2000); John Miller, *The Glorious Revolution*, 2nd ed. (New York: Addison-Wesley, 1997).

Gold Coast Uprising   *See* ASHANTI UPRISING.

Golden Horde Dynastic War   (1359–1381)

PRINCIPAL COMBATANTS: Mamak and Urus, successors to Jöchi vs. Tamerlane (Timur) and Toktamish; Mamak vs. Dmitri Donskoi of Muscovy (Russia)

PRINCIPAL THEATER(S): Golden Horde (Kipchak Khanate, Mongol territory north and west of the Caspian Sea)

DECLARATION: None

MAJOR ISSUES AND OBJECTIVES: Control of the Golden Horde

OUTCOME: Thanks to his alliance with Tamerlane, Toktamish assumed rule over the Golden Horde.

APPROXIMATE MAXIMUM NUMBER OF MEN UNDER ARMS: Unknown

CASUALTIES: Unknown

TREATIES: None

Jöchi (d. 1227), son of the great Mongol ruler Genghis Khan (c. 1162–1227), was given the Mongol territory north and west of the Caspian Sea to rule. This territory and its subjects became the Kipchak Khanate, better known to history as the Golden Horde, because of its celebrated abundance and wealth.

In 1359, the last successor of Jöchi died, and with his death, the Golden Horde became the subject of violent dispute. Mamak and Urus (both fl. 14th century), two non-Mongols, ruled the Golden Horde (the Russian designation for the Ulus Juchi, the western part of the Mongol Empire) jointly for a time, but the conqueror Tamerlane (Timur) (1336–1405) pushed to obtain the throne for his ally and protégé Toktamish (d. 1398). Tamerlane high-handedly proclaimed Toktamish the khan of the Golden Horde in 1377. The proclamation notwithstanding, Mamak retained power, until he was defeated by Dmitri Donskoi (1363–89), prince of Muscovy (modern Russia). Donskoi led his Russian forces in a rebellion against the Mongols, who demanded tribute.

Hoping to exploit Mamak's defeat at the hands of the Russian, Toktamish attacked Mamak twice, but was twice defeated. Mamak died of natural causes, however, in 1380 and was followed, later that same year, by Urus. In this way, despite his military defeats, Toktamish came

to rule the Golden Horde. His first act was to return the Golden Horde to the Mongol fold and to launch attacks against Russia. Toktamish triumphed over the Russians and, flushed with victory, turned his back on his benefactor, Tamerlane. This triggered TAMERLANE'S FIRST WAR AGAINST TOKTAMISH, from 1385 to 1386 and TAMERLANE'S SECOND WAR AGAINST TOKTAMISH, from 1391 to 1395.

Further reading: Charles J. Halperin, *Russia and the Golden Horde: The Mongol Impact on Medieval Russian History* (Bloomington: Indiana University Press, 1987); David Morgan, *The Mongols* (New York: Oxford University Press, 1986).

Golden Horde–Il-Khan Civil War (1261–1262)

PRINCIPAL COMBATANTS: Hülegü, il-Khan (Mongol) ruler of Persia vs. Berke, khan of the Golden Horde (Kipchak Khanate)

PRINCIPAL THEATER(S): Western region of the Mongol Empire

DECLARATION: None

MAJOR ISSUES AND OBJECTIVES: Dominance over the two khanates

OUTCOME: The war was inconclusive, and the rival khanates remained bitter foes.

APPROXIMATE MAXIMUM NUMBER OF MEN UNDER ARMS: Unknown

CASUALTIES: Unknown

TREATIES: Alliance treaty between Golden Horde and Mamluk Turks, 1262

When Arik-Böke (fl. 1261–62) convened a *kuriltai*, a Great Assembly, in 1260, he provoked the MONGOL CIVIL WAR as well as the Golden Horde–Il-Khan Civil War. This second conflict broke out between Arik-Böke's brother Hülegü (r. 1256–65), who was the il-Khan (Mongol) ruler of Persia, and Berke, the khan of the Golden Horde, or Kipchak Khanate, the Mongol territory lying north and west of the Caspian Sea.

Hülegü attacked a protégé of Arik-Böke, which provoked Berke (fl. 1261–62), a Muslim enemy of Hülegü, to conclude a treaty with the Mamluk Turks, who were also enemies of the Il-Khan.

In 1262, Hülegü advanced northward and ambushed Berke's army in a devastating surprise attack. However, the tables suddenly turned when, while the troops crossed the frozen Terek River, the ice gave way beneath their feet, drowning much of Hülegü's army. Hülegü retreated with the survivors and quickly looked for a way to stop the war. He did so by marrying a Byzantine princess, thereby forming a powerful alliance with a traditional foe of the Muslims. Although this alliance created a stand-off that stopped the fighting, the khanates of Hülegü and Berke remained bitter, simmering foes.

See also GOLDEN HORDE DYNASTIC WAR.

Further reading: David Morgan, *The Mongols* (New York: Oxford University Press, 1986); Paul Ratchnevsky, *Genghis Khan: His Life and Legacy,* trans. and ed. Thomas N. Haining (New York: Oxford University Press, 1991).

Gordon's Khartoum Campaign, Charles "Chinese" *See* SUDANESE WAR (1881–1885).

Gothic (Italian) War (534–554)

PRINCIPAL COMBATANTS: Byzantine Empire vs. Goths
PRINCIPAL THEATER(S): Italy
DECLARATION: None
MAJOR ISSUES AND OBJECTIVES: Justinian I, emperor of the Eastern Roman (Byzantine) Empire, sought to wrest Italy from the Goths and thereby reunite the Eastern and Western Roman empires.
OUTCOME: Italy briefly came under Justinian's control, but at great cost to the Eastern Empire.
APPROXIMATE MAXIMUM NUMBER OF MEN UNDER ARMS: At war's end: Byzantine Empire, 20,000; Goths, 15,000
CASUALTIES: Byzantine numbers unknown; Goth losses at the culminating Battle of Taginae were 6,000 killed out of a force of 15,000.
TREATIES: No document survives

The Ostrogoth king, Theodoric the Great (c. 454–526), conquered Italy by 493, but he failed to establish a strong dynasty. The Gothic rulers who followed him were inept leaders, and, as the Byzantine emperor Justinian I (483–565) saw it, Italy was ripe for conquest. With the taking of Italy, Justinian hoped to reunite the Western Roman and Eastern Roman (Byzantine) empires.

Justinian dispatched an army under his leading general, Belisarius (c. 505–565), to command an expedition to retake Italy from the Goths. From Constantinople, Belisarius's forces landed at Sicily, invaded it, then used it as a jumping-off point to the southern Italian mainland. By 536, Belisarius had taken Naples as well as Rome. At Rome, the Goths counterattacked with a year-long siege during 537–538, but the disciplined and resourceful Byzantine invaders withstood it until the Goths were force to lift the siege and depart.

Belisarius continued his northward march up the Italian Peninsula, but he soon faced the chief problems of even highly successful invaders: supply and reinforcement. His often hungry troops were vulnerable to repeated hit-and-run attacks by the Goths. Nevertheless, Belisarius

scored a major victory at Ravenna in 539, capturing the Gothic king Vitiges, who was sent to Constantinople as a prisoner. Leaderless, the Gothic resistance collapsed, and, in 541, Belisarius heeded Justinian's order to return to Constantinople. For his part, Justinian was persuaded that Italy had been safely secured for the Byzantine Empire, and he did not want Belisarius and an army to remain in the region for fear that Belisarius would proclaim himself emperor of the West.

Yet no sooner had Belisarius withdrawn from Italy than the Goths mobilized under a new ruler, Totila (Baduila) (d. 552). Totila led Gothic forces in the reconquest of the cities and strongholds yielded to the Byzantines. Belisarius was dispatched to Italy again and led a series of five campaigns against the Goths, but without the success he had earlier enjoyed. Although he briefly retook Rome, it quickly fell again to the Goths. Justinian recalled Belisarius, and all of Italy, including even Sicily, was again in Goth hands.

In 552, Justinian sent Narses (c. 478–c. 573), an aged eunuch general, to lead a combined sea and land assault on Italy from the north via the Adriatic. The expedition marched across the Apennine range and, in July, engaged the Goths at the Battle of Taginae, an Apennine mountain village. Narses's archers proved his most destructive arm, and the general used them in superb coordination with his pikemen—the first time the bow and pike had been used effectively together.

From Taginae, Narses marched down the Italian Peninsula, methodically retaking the Goth strongholds. By the end of 552, Rome was again liberated from the Goths, and during 553, Justinian could again claim control of Italy. Constantinople did not retain that control for long.

See also JUSTINIAN'S SECOND PERSIAN WAR.

Further reading: Edward Gibbon, *Decline and Fall of the Roman Empire,* 7 vols., ed. by J. B. Bury (New York: Modern Library, 1995); Peter Heather, *The Goths* (London: Blackwell, 1996); John Julius Norwich, *Byzantium: The Early Centuries* (New York: Alfred A. Knopf, 2003).

Gothic-Roman Wars *See* ROMAN-GOTHIC WAR, FIRST; ROMAN-GOTHIC WAR, SECOND; ROMAN-GOTHIC WAR, THIRD; ROMAN-GOTHIC WAR, FOURTH; ROMAN-GOTHIC WAR, FIFTH.

Gothic-Sarmatian War (332–334)

PRINCIPAL COMBATANTS: Sarmatians and Byzantine Empire vs. Goths and allied Germanic tribes; subsequently, Sarmatians vs. Byzantine Empire
PRINCIPAL THEATER(S): Dacia (approximately modern Romania)
DECLARATION: None

MAJOR ISSUES AND OBJECTIVES: The Sarmatians secured the aid of the Byzantine Empire in resisting invasion by the Goths and their allies; when the Sarmatians betrayed the Byzantine alliance, the Byzantines withdrew aid and encouraged the Goths' conquest.
OUTCOME: The Sarmatians were destroyed as a people; some 300,000 were permitted to resettle within the Eastern Roman Empire; the Goths became *foederati* of the Byzantine Empire.
APPROXIMATE MAXIMUM NUMBER OF MEN UNDER ARMS: Unknown
CASUALTIES: Unknown
TREATIES: No documents survive

Goths and other Germanic "barbarian" tribes made frequent incursions into the territory of the Sarmatians, a people living in Dacia (approximately the region of modern Romania). The Sarmatians shared with the Scythians, a closely related people, a heritage of horsemanship and skill at arms. By the fifth century B.C.E., they had also proved themselves superb administrators, coming to control—and to govern well—all the lands between the Ural Mountains and the Don River. By the fourth century B.C.E., they crossed the Don and conquered the Scythians, and during the first century C.E., the Sarmatians became a powerful threat to the Roman Empire.

Although closely allied with several Germanic tribes, the Sarmatians were themselves overwhelmed by the Goths during the third century C.E., and their territory was reduced to Dacia (Romania) and the lower Danube region. Even so contracted, the Sarmatians were continually harassed and menaced by the Goths and therefore reluctantly requested military aid from Constantine I the Great (c. 285–337), emperor of the Eastern Roman Empire (Byzantium). Constantine dispatched an army under the command of his son. Operating in concert with the Sarmatians, the force attacked the Goths and Gothic allies during 332–33. In the midst of this action, however, the Sarmatians turned against their Byzantine allies by making forays against the Roman Empire. Outraged by the betrayal, Constantine threw his support behind the Goths. He urged them to act even more aggressively against the Sarmatians, as he withdrew Roman aid. Without this aid, the Sarmatians were instantly overwhelmed by the Gothic hordes.

In a curious act of magnanimity, Constantine permitted some 300,000 Sarmatian refugees to resettle within the Eastern Roman Empire. As for the Goths, they responded to the Christianizing efforts of the Byzantine bishop Ulfilas, and embraced membership in the Byzantine federation. In exchange for their good behavior, the Goths received Byzantine subsidies.

Further reading: Edward Gibbon, *Decline and Fall of the Roman Empire,* 7 vols., ed. by J. B. Bury (New York: Modern Library, 1995); Peter Heather, *The Goths* (London:

Blackwell, 1996); John Julius Norwich, *Byzantium: The Early Centuries* (New York: Alfred A. Knopf, 2003).

Granada, Siege of (1491–1492)

PRINCIPAL COMBATANTS: Christian Castile vs. Muslim Granada
PRINCIPAL THEATER(S): Granada (the capital city of the Muslim kingdom of Granada)
DECLARATION: None
MAJOR ISSUES AND OBJECTIVES: Christian Castile sought to complete its conquest of Muslim Granada.
OUTCOME: Granada, the last stronghold of Muslim Spain, fell.
APPROXIMATE MAXIMUM NUMBER OF MEN UNDER ARMS: Unknown
CASUALTIES: Unknown
TREATIES: None

The siege of Granada may be seen as a phase of the SPANISH CHRISTIAN-MUSLIM WAR (1481–1492). As a result of that conflict, most of Moorish Granada, in southern Spain, had by 1491 fallen to an invasion of Christian Castilians. The capital city of Granada, however, held out against the invaders, refusing to yield to the suzerainty of King Ferdinand V (1452–1516) and Queen Isabella I (1451–1504) of Castile and Aragon. About to fall under siege, the Muslims of Granada appealed to Sultan Muhammad XI (d. 1538), known as Boabdil, to come to their aid.

In 1483, Boabdil had marched against the Castilians, but was captured in battle. To ransom himself, he signed the Pact of Córdoba, by which he pledged to deliver into Castilian hands the portion of his holdings that were under the control of Abd al-Zaghall (fl. late 15th century) in return for Castilian aid in recovering a part of his territory that had been lost by his father. Thus Boabdil was able to reoccupy the Alhambra.

Boabdil's concession did not satisfy the Castilian appetite for conquest, and when, early in 1491, the Spanish invaded al-Zaghall's remaining holdings in eastern Granada and the district of Almería, Boabdil abrogated the Pact of Córdoba and came to al-Zaghall's aid. However, al-Zaghall soon surrendered to the Castilians and accepted a kind of voluntary exile, leaving Boabdil holding only the town of Granada.

In April 1491, Castilian forces laid siege to Granada, which now contained not only the original defenders, but Boabdil's army as well. In the process of investing Granada, the Castilians established Santa Fe, a western outpost that severed Granada's communication with the outside world. From within the besieged city, numerous sorties were launched, each repulsed by Christian forces. With the situation clearly hopeless, Boabdil sued for peace. After brief negotiations, he surrendered on January 2, 1492. The day before, the magnificent Alhambra, palace of the Moorish rulers of Granada, had fallen to Castile.

Ferdinand and Isabella rode into Granada on January 6, 1492. They administered their conquest with great liberality, granting the Granadans freedom of worship and a significant measure of self-government. They also allowed Moors who wished to migrate to North Africa to do so freely and in safety. However, the significance of the conquest of Granada was great. Muslim rule had ended in Spain, and a triumphant Spain was ready to explore and conquer a new world.

Further reading: David Coleman, *Creating Christian Granada: Society and Religious Culture in an Old-World Frontier City, 1492–1600* (Ithaca, N.Y.: Cornell University Press, 2003); John Edwards, *Spain of the Catholic Monarchs, 1474–1520* (London: Blackwell, 2001).

Grand Alliance, War of the (Nine Years' War, War of the League of Augsburg) (1688–1697)

PRINCIPAL COMBATANTS: France vs. England, the Dutch Republic (United Provinces), Spain, the Spanish Netherlands, Austria, the Holy Roman Empire, the Bishopric of Liège, Brandenburg-Prussia, Württemberg, Savoy-Piedmont, Bavaria, the Palatinate, Electorate of Cologne, Denmark; England vs. Ireland and Scotland
PRINCIPAL THEATER(S): The Spanish Netherlands, northeastern France, Duchy of Luxembourg, Bishopric of Liège, the Moselle valley, the Rhineland, Savoy-Piedmont, Dauphiné, Catalonia, Ireland
DECLARATION: Alliance declares war on France, 1689
MAJOR ISSUES AND OBJECTIVES: (1) The formation of an anti-French coalition aimed at restoring Europe to the frontiers agreed at the Peace of Westphalia in 1648 and the Peace of Nijmegen in 1678. (2) Savoy-Piedmont's need to free herself from French and Hapsburg/Spanish domination by regaining Pinerolo and Casale. (3) William of Orange's quest for international, particularly French, recognition of his entitlement to the throne of England.
OUTCOME: (1) France retained Strasbourg and Alsace but surrendered other territories gained since 1678. The Dutch were allowed to garrison selected fortresses in the Spanish Netherlands as a "barrier" against French aggression. (2) Savoy-Piedmont secured Pinerolo and neutralized Casale. (3) Louis XIV recognized William III as king of England.
APPROXIMATE MAXIMUM NUMBER OF MEN UNDER ARMS: The military establishments of most participants reached their peak between 1693 and 1695. France: 300,000; England: 100,000; Dutch Republic: 130,000; Savoy-Piedmont: 20,000; Austria and Holy Roman Empire: 100,000; Spain: 40,000; Brandenburg-Prussia: 40,000; Denmark: 32,000

CASUALTIES: France: c. 200,000; Austria/Imperial forces: c. 120,000; Spain, Savoy, England, and the Dutch Republic: c. 250,000. The principal killer of both civilians and soldiers was disease, usually spread by the presence and movement of armies.
TREATIES: Treaty of Limerick (October 13, 1691); Treaty of Turin (June 29–July 5, 1696); Truce of Vigevano (October 7, 1696); Peace of Rijswijk (Ryswick) (September 20–October 30, 1696)

This conflict enjoys seven names, each indicative of a particular historical perspective: the War of the GRAND ALLIANCE, the War of the League of Augsburg, KING WILLIAM'S WAR, the War of the English Succession, the First World War, the Palatine War, and the Nine Years' War. The latter nomenclature is neutral and thus the most satisfactory.

It was contemporary with the AUSTRO-TURKISH WAR (1683–1699). Only the Holy Roman Emperor and some German states—Austria, Bavaria, Saxony—were actively involved in both.

CAUSES

Louis XIV (1638–1715) of France emerged from the Third DUTCH WAR (1672–78) as the most powerful monarch in western Europe. He immediately consolidated and extended his gains seeking defensible frontiers in the Spanish Netherlands, Alsace, and the Rhineland. Between 1678 and 1688, a decade of "peace," the French army numbered 140,000 men, allowing Louis to support aggressive diplomacy with armed force. By 1680 Louis's diplomats had reclaimed Franche-Comté, Alsace, Lorraine, Orange, Toul, Metz, and Verdun, while his troops occupied most of the duchy of Luxembourg and were blockading Luxembourg City. When, in 1682, the governor of Luxembourg tried to break the blockade, French units invaded Flanders, ruined the countryside, and occupied the territory around Courtrai. On September 30, 1681, the French army simultaneously seized Strasbourg and took possession of Casale in Montferrat. Spain declared war on France in 1683 but this only resulted in the loss of Courtrai in November and Luxembourg City on June 3, 1684, following a formal siege. Under cover of the siege of Luxembourg, Louis's Mediterranean fleet bombarded Genoa whose politics were pro-Hapsburg and anti-French (May 1684). No power could stand alone against France.

Western Europe was alarmed but concerted action was slow to develop. Leopold I (1640–1705), the Holy Roman Emperor, was distracted, first by a revolt in Hungary (see HAPSBURG CONQUEST OF HUNGARY; HAPSBURG-OTTOMAN WAR FOR HUNGARY), and then, in 1683, by the Turkish invasion of Austria and the subsequent siege of Vienna (see AUSTRO-TURKISH WAR [1683–1699]; VIENNA, SIEGE OF). At Regensburg, or Ratisbon, on August 15, 1684, a truce was concluded between Austria, Spain, and

France, which guaranteed the expanded borders of France for 20 years. Having largely secured his frontiers, Louis commenced the climacteric of his campaign against the Huguenots by revoking the Edict of Nantes in 1685. Protestant refugees, living evidence of Louis's violence and intolerance, were welcomed into England, the Dutch Republic, Switzerland, and Brandenburg-Prussia.

During the four years following the Truce of Regensburg an anti-French confederation developed, largely through the initiative and leadership of the stadtholder of the United Provinces, William III of Orange (1650–1702). In 1685, a number of German states, of which the largest was Bavaria, formed the League of Augsburg to defend German soil. The persecution of the Huguenots and the Vaudois finally convinced the Republican Party in the United Provinces that Louis could not be trusted, particularly as the accession of the Catholic James II (1633–1701) of England in 1685 presaged an alliance between England and France that would endanger Dutch maritime commerce. Although the Dutch and Frederick William (1620–88), the Great Elector of Brandenburg-Prussia, did not join the league, they were supportive.

The balance of power was also shifting in central Europe. The Turks were beaten at Buda in 1686 and Mohács in 1687, and lost Belgrade in September 1688. Emperor Leopold could now reduce his military effort against the Turks and direct some of his forces, especially the German army of the Circles, toward the Rhine to protect the empire. Whereas Louis had accepted the Truce of Regensburg on the supposition that 20 years would provide ample opportunity to translate his seizures into permanent accretions through formal treaties, the retreat of the Turkish army undermined his assumptions. Instead of being coerced into confirming the truce, Leopold was about to lead a coalition of German princes dedicated to recapturing lands forfeited to France.

OUTBREAK

Affairs came to a head in the electorate of Cologne. Maximilian Heinrich (1621–88), the archbishop-elector, had been a French client since 1671. There were two contenders for his throne. The favorite was Cardinal Wilhelm Egon von Fürstenberg (1624–1704), one of Louis's advisers on German politics. When Maximilian Heinrich died on June 3, 1688, the succession of Fürstenberg, who had been accepted by the cathedral chapter as coadjutor in January 1688, seemed assured. The second candidate was Prince Joseph Clement (1671–1723) of Bavaria, a nephew of Maximilian II Emmanuel (1662–1726), elector of Bavaria, and a younger brother of Maximilian Heinrich. At the election, neither received the necessary two-thirds majority and the impasse was referred to Pope Innocent XI (1611–89). There was no prospect of Innocent, who had been insulted and ill-treated by Louis, finding in favor of Fürstenberg, and Joseph Clement was duly installed as archbishop-elector on August 26, 1688.

Rather than waiting to assess the impact of his defeat at Cologne, Louis, encouraged by his war minister, the marquis de Louvois, and aware of the mounting strength of his opponents beyond the Rhine, determined upon a preemptive strike against the Holy Roman Empire. When Brandenburg troops entered the city of Cologne in support of Joseph Clement, 16,000 French soldiers occupied the remainder of the electorate, including Bonn and Kaiserswerth. In return for a Dutch commitment to support Austrian claims to the Spanish succession, Emperor Leopold promptly joined the League of Augsburg.

On September 24, 1688, a French army under the dauphin and the duc de Duras, attended by the engineer, Sébastien Le Prestre de Vauban, invaded the Rhineland and besieged the imperial fortress of Philippsburg. Louis hoped for a short, sharp siege. Before they could mobilize, Leopold and the German princes would thus be presented with a fait accompli sufficient to persuade them to translate the Truce of Regensburg into a permanent settlement. If the worst occurred, and Louis was not pessimistic, the annexation of Philippsburg would at least complete the defense of France's eastern frontier.

THE RAVAGING OF THE PALATINATE

Aided by heavy rains, Philippsburg held out for two months. To make the Germans pay for the campaign, French detachments roamed the Rhineland extracting contributions and seizing supplies. The marquis de Boufflers surprised Kaiserslautern on October 2 and then attempted Coblenz. German reaction was swift. Frederick William of Brandenburg-Prussia, John George III of Saxony, Ernst Augustus of Hanover, and Karl of Hesse-Kassel agreed to mobilize their forces (the Concert of Magdeburg, October 15, 1688). From Hungary, the emperor recalled the Bavarian, Swabian, and Franconian troops and sent them, under the elector of Bavaria, to defend southern Germany. By the end of October, a German army of 20,000 men had concentrated at Frankfurt-am-Main and Boufflers had to withdraw before Coblenz. Louis's invasion of Germany also created an opportunity for William of Orange to invade England.

In attacking Philippsburg, Louis calculated that William of Orange would invade England only to become enmeshed in a civil war: simultaneously, the Turks would be encouraged to greater endeavors on the Danube. Instead, by the spring of 1689, France faced war with Spain and the Anglo-Dutch along her entire frontier from Dunkirk to Basel. The Rhineland would now become subsidiary to the main theater of war in the Spanish Netherlands. Louvois and Louis decided further to erode the military capability of the Rhineland through a campaign of devastation and destruction, the "ravaging of the Palatinate."

The resultant systematic destruction of towns, villages, fortresses, and supplies in the Palatinate, Trier, and

Württemberg was designed to create a cordon sanitaire through which the German armies could not operate toward the French border. Tübingen, Heilbronn, Heidelberg, Worms, Mainz, Mannheim, Eslingen, Oppenheim, Pforzheim, Kaiserslautern, Spiers, Coblenz, and Cochem were all partially or totally destroyed. French raiding parties reached as far into Germany as Nuremberg and Würzburg. This mixture of terror and crude economic warfare characterized the French conduct of the Nine Years' War. Catinat in Piedmont and the duc de Noailles and Marshal Vendôme in Catalonia used identical methods. In the case of the Palatinate, it was successful. Although the German princes did not come to the peace table, the Rhineland remained a secondary theater, and armies could undertake only limited operations.

ENGLAND

By the spring of 1688, the Catholic and francophile James II appeared to be sliding into a commitment to France. The Dutch calculated that it was imperative to secure England and her considerable resources. Exploiting internal disquiet, William of Orange, on behalf of the States-General, invaded England on November 15, 1688, during the opportunity created by the French siege of Philippsburg (see GLORIOUS REVOLUTION). King James fled to France, and William and his wife, Mary, were created joint sovereigns by the Convention Parliament. Louis quickly played James against the new regime in England. He was dispatched to Ireland, where the Catholics were already in revolt, entering Dublin on April 3, 1689 (see IRISH WAR). If William's energies could not be consumed by civil war in England, Louis was able to substitute Ireland.

THE GRAND ALLIANCE

The Dutch Republic declared war on France on March 9, 1689. This was followed by an offensive compact between the Dutch and the Holy Roman Emperor, the Grand Alliance, on May 12, which aimed to restore Europe to the boundaries that had been settled at the Peace of Westphalia in 1648 and the Peace of Nijmegen in 1678. Additionally, the Dutch agreed to support the imperial candidate to the Spanish succession (see SPANISH SUCCESSION, WAR OF THE). Spain and the Spanish Netherlands declared war on France on May 3, 1689. William, as king of England, declared war on May 17, 1689. England and Duke Charles V of Lorraine joined the Grand Alliance on December 19, 1689. The elector of Bavaria added his name to the Grand Alliance on May 4, 1690, and the duke of Savoy and the king of Spain declared war in June. The elector of Brandenburg was already allied with both the Dutch Republic and the emperor. Several states, including Denmark, Sweden, Hesse-Kassel, Württemberg, and Hanover, were prepared to rent troops to the Grand Alliance. Instead of a short war, France was faced by a coalition of the League of Augsburg, Spain, England, and the United Provinces.

THE NATURE OF THE WAR

All participants perceived that they were fighting defensively. However, the huge costs of waging war demanded the offensive so that armies could be maintained through contributions extracted from enemy lands. The imperative of making "war pay for war" involved the capture of territory resulting in positional campaigns, the extensive use of field fortifications or "lines," and the predominance of the siege. Constricting an opponent's freedom of maneuver through the consumption or destruction of material resources was a central strategic ploy.

Weaponry, tactical organization, the limitations imposed by logistics, and the rough equivalence of numbers between the allies and France rendered armies almost incapable of decisive action in battle. Destruction of an enemy's armed forces was not an objective because it was rarely possible. Politicians sought what their soldiers could deliver: the capture and retention of territory via the siege and fortification.

1689: THE SPREAD OF WAR

During a winter of raiding, all participants augmented their forces. The French withdrew from Germany and the bishopric of Liège having forced the prince-bishop, Jean-Louis d'Elderen (r. 1688–94), to declare his state neutral. Liège was obliged to abandon neutrality and join the Grand Alliance later in the year. The French formed two main armies: one to operate along the line of the Sambre River under the command of Marshal d'Humières and a second at Mainz directed by the duke de Duras. Although the allies were numerically superior, the French held the advantage of a central position, while the allies experienced difficulty in coordinating their campaigns. Not until 1691, when William III was able to leave England and Ireland, did the allied war effort benefit from some degree of synchronization.

The campaign opened in the Rhineland. The smaller of three German armies, commanded by the elector of Bavaria, held the "lines of Stollhofen" between the Black Forest and the Rhine, guarding central Germany against a French attack from Strasbourg and Kehl. The Army of the Middle Rhine consisted of 50,000 Austrians, Bavarians, Saxons, and Hessians around Frankfurt-am-Main, directed by Duke Charles V of Lorraine. Lorraine besieged Mainz on June 5: Marshal d'Huxelles resisted for 52 days. This was the major success in Germany in 1689. A victory at Herderbosch on March 11 by 40,000 Brandenburg and Hanoverian forces commanded by General Hans Adam von Schöning over the French under the marquis de Sourdis and the comte de Vertillac forced the French to evacuate most of the electorate of Cologne: Neuss fell on March 14, Siburg and Kempen on March 16, quickly followed by Zons and Soest on the Ruhr. The French hold on Cologne was reduced to Bonn, Rheinberg, and Kaiserswerth. This cleared the eastern flank of the Anglo-Dutch-Spanish army in the Spanish Netherlands, commanded by George

Friedrich von Waldeck, and reduced the danger of a French invasion of the United Provinces along the line of the Rhine River (see LOUIS XIV'S RHENISH INVASION). Kaiserswerth was bombarded on May 23 and then besieged (June 21–26), followed by the bombardment and siege of Bonn, which fell on October 10. The French, although they still held Philippsburg, had been pressed back to the Rhine, which they were to hold for the next seven years.

In Flanders, Waldeck resolved to cross the Sambre and invade France. Although Waldeck won the action at Walcourt on August 25, his invasion of France was effectively countered by d'Humières. Waldeck withdrew across the Sambre.

After James II's return to Ireland, his Catholic forces occupied most of the country, except Londonderry and Enniskillen in Ulster. Although he knew that the war would be decided in the Low Countries, William had to divert resources to the conflict in Ireland because the future of his throne depended upon its outcome. A French squadron under the comte de Château-Renault was surprised on May 11 by an allied squadron under Admiral Edward Herbert while landing supplies and reinforcements in Bantry Bay. Both sides claimed victory, but the allied ships withdrew. Londonderry withstood a low-intensity siege of 105 days (April 28–August 10) and, on August 23, Marshal Herman von Schomberg landed near Bangor with 14,000 allied troops but was unable to make strategic progress.

Scotland also rose in support of James II (see JACOBITE REBELLION [1689–1690]). A rebellion, led by John Claverhouse, viscount Dundee, beat a small Williamite army under General Hugh Mackay at Killiecrankie on July 27. Defeat at Dunkeld on August 21 marked the effective end of the Jacobite cause in Scotland.

In Catalonia, a peasant rising against Castilian rule, which had initially broken out in 1687, burst into life in the spring of 1689. In May, Marshal Noailles invaded Catalonia with 9,000 men and took the fortress of Camprodon in the face of extremely weak resistance. France could not spare enough troops to exploit this success, even though Barcelona was open to attack. At the end of June, Noailles withdrew into Roussillon, and the Spaniards advanced, then besieged and razed Camprodon before turning to suppress the peasant rising in their rear.

1690: SAVOY-PIEDMONT, BEACHY HEAD, THE BOYNE, AND FLEURUS

In 1690, a fifth theater of war opened. Savoy-Piedmont was sandwiched between France and Spanish Milan and dominated by the French fortresses of Pinerolo in the west and Casale in the east: Duke Victor Amadeus II (1666–1732), "could not afford to be honorable." France had treated him like a vassal since 1685. Forced by Louis to persecute his Protestant Vaudois subjects, from the spring of 1687 Victor Amadeus tried to move closer to Spain and the emperor. The outbreak of war along the Rhine allowed him greater freedom of action. On June 3 he signed a treaty with Spain for military assistance from Milan and concluded a similar deal with the emperor on June 4. He then declared war on Louis XIV. In return for promising to restore to the Vaudois all the rights they had enjoyed before 1686, Victor Amadeus formally allied with England and the United Provinces on October 20, 1690.

Initially, France regarded northern Italy as a subsidiary theater. William, though, saw Piedmont as the one region where the allies could act effectively, invading southern France to capture Toulon and foment rebellion among the Huguenots of Dauphiné, the Cevennes, and Languedoc. Victor Amadeus was less ambitious; his objective was to rid himself of French influence, avoid domination by Spain and Austria, and regain the fortresses of Pinerolo and Casale.

During the first weeks of the war, French troops overran Savoy with the exception of the fortress of Montmélian. Savoyard hatred of the French and religious discord resulted in a brutal war: massacres, atrocities, and the burning of towns and villages were frequent. Throughout, the French suffered guerrilla attacks by an armed populace, both Catholic and Vaudois. In return, they took draconian reprisals. By 1696, Savoy and much of southern and western Piedmont had been devastated and ruined.

In June, Catinat's army was in Pinerolo and Victor Amadeus's forces were at Turin. By ravaging the countryside and threatening Saluzzo, Catinat sought to bring Victor Amadeus to battle. Faced with a threat to this important town, Victor Amadeus accepted battle on August 18 at the Abbey of Staffarda. Surprised and defeated, the allied army lost 5,000 men and had to withdraw to Carmagnola to await reinforcements. Catinat exploited his victory by levying contributions from much of southern Piedmont. Early in November, Catinat hurried northward to besiege and capture Susa on the River Dora Riparia, a vital fortress on his communications with Briançon in Dauphiné.

In the more northerly theaters, the prospects for France were promising. William and most of the British troops were tied down in Ireland while the emperor was making his major effort in Hungary. There was also an unexpected naval success for France. So many English and Dutch ships had already been lost to French privateers that merchants demanded greater protection. This could only be provided by denuding the Channel fleet. While Vice-Admiral Henry Killigrew's 24 warships were escorting merchantmen toward Cadiz, a French fleet under the comte de Tourville entered the English Channel, greatly outnumbering the combined Anglo-Dutch Fleet of Arthur Herbert, now earl of Torrington. Torrington, who wanted to evade battle until Killigrew could rejoin, was instructed to fight. On July 10, off Beachy Head, Torrington's English vessels failed to support the Dutch, and the allied fleet was defeated losing five ships.

As they withdrew to the Nore River in Ireland, Tourville ruled the Channel, but an outbreak of sickness restricted exploitation to burning the fishing village of Teignmouth.

Although Tourville stood across his communications with England, William III campaigned actively in Ireland. Landing at Carrickfergus on June 24 with enough reinforcements to augment the allied army to 40,000 men, William assumed command from Schomberg and advanced south toward Dublin. James II marched north with a smaller army, approximately c. 25,000, including 6,600 French infantry, and took position along the River Boyne, but was defeated on July 11. While the Jacobite army withdrew to Limerick, James left Ireland for France, command passing to the duke of Tyrconnel. Bad weather saved Limerick from capture. To improve communications with England and boost his own prestige, the earl of Marlborough launched an amphibious operation that captured Cork (August 29) and Kinsale (October 15).

Waldeck was again given command of the allied army in the Spanish Netherlands. D'Humières had been relegated to command of the French troops in the lines of the Lys and the Scheldt, and the chief French command in Flanders went to their most capable general, the duke of Luxembourg. Taking a central position, he rapidly combined with the corps of Boufflers to the east of the Meuse and advanced with 40,000 men against Waldeck's 30,000. At Fleurus, on July 1, in a battle that lasted all day, Waldeck was beaten, although both sides lost approximately 7,000 men. Intelligence that a German attack might materialize from Coblenz along the line of the Moselle River prevented Luxembourg from exploiting his victory.

The Turkish recapture of Belgrade in October forced the emperor to recall imperial troops from the Rhineland, while a further 6,000 left Germany for northern Italy. Another setback was the death of the duke of Lorraine: The less able elector of Bavaria was appointed in his stead. Fleurus allowed the French to reinforce their corps in the Rhineland to 40,000, against which the German armies were unable to take significant action.

1691: MONS AND LEUSE

William III provided reinforcements sufficient to increase the Piedmontese army to 20,000 men, but plans to invade France through Savoy had to be abandoned after Catinat's preemptive capture of Nice early in March. He then prepared to attack Turin, taking Avigliana as a preliminary, but his forces were inadequate and he turned southward. Carmagnola fell on June 9 and Catinat then besieged Cuneo, the key post in southern Piedmont. The arrival of imperial reinforcements under Prince Eugene of Savoy enabled Victor Amadeus to force Catinat to abandon the siege. Catinat assumed the defensive, although Victor Amadeus's plans for an invasion of France were obstructed by the Austrians. Sensing that he might not achieve his political objectives by military means, in October Victor Amadeus sought a diplomatic contact with France. Giovanni Gropello (fl. late 11th century) was sent, during December, to open negotiations with the comte de Tessé, the commandant of Pinerolo. Nothing resulted from these overtures because Louis would offer nothing except recognition of the duke's neutrality.

In Catalonia, the French land forces were inactive as Noailles attempted to establish a supply base around Cardona. Instead, campaigning was pursued by the navy. Employing the bomb ketches that had proved so effective against Genoa, 36 French ships anchored off Barcelona on July 7 and bombarded the city on July 10, destroying over 300 houses. The fleet proceeded to Alicante on July 25 and fired 3,500 bombs into the town over a period of four days; 90 percent of the buildings were damaged. These terror attacks helped to unite Spain, including the Catalans, behind the leadership in Madrid, resulting in improved prospects for fighting effectively against France.

The Irish theater was brought to a conclusion during 1691. William III handed command to Godard van Reede, baron van Ginkel, later earl of Athlone. He emerged from winter quarters to secure a crossing of the Shannon River at Athlone (June 29–July 10) before defeating the Jacobite army under its French commander, the marquis de St. Ruth, at Aughrim on July 22. The Jacobite army withdrew into Limerick. With no prospects of further French assistance, the Jacobites signed the Treaty of Limerick (October 13), which ended the war on surprisingly generous terms.

On the Rhine, the German armies achieved little, epidemics of sickness affecting both the French and the imperial forces. Again, the main theater was the Spanish Netherlands. In an operation carefully planned by Louvois, the last before his death on August 16, the French surprised the Allies by besieging the fortress of Mons (March 15). William hurriedly concentrated an army at Halle, south of Brussels, but was unable to prevent the fall of the fortress on April 8. Having been outmaneuvered, William sought redemption through battle. Boufflers raided Liège in June, bombarding sections of the city and burning some of the suburbs, but he was unable to effect a siege. William left the field before the campaign was concluded, and Luxembourg took advantage by embarrassing the rear guard of the army, now under Waldeck, as it decamped from a position at Leuse on September 19.

1692: LA HOGUE, NAMUR, AND STEENKIRK

All participants were now feeling the economic strains of war Antigovernment factions in England were disillusioned with both the cost and the unimpressive results of fighting the French in Flanders: An alternative was discovered by resurrecting the Elizabethan strategy of mounting amphibious "descents" upon the enemy coast. Employing infantry returned from Ireland, the initial target (January 1692) was Dunkirk, but secrecy was compromised and the operation canceled.

The major French objective for 1692 was the capture of the vital Sambre-Meuse fortress of Namur (May 29–July 1). To delay William from marching to its relief, Louis arranged a simultaneous invasion attempt upon the south coast of England using 12,000 Irish troops, released under the terms of the Treaty of Limerick, supported by an equal number of Frenchmen. An essential preliminary was the acquisition of naval supremacy in the English Channel. During a five-day battle between Capes La Hogue and Barfleur on the northern coast of the Cotentin Peninsula (May 29–June 3), Edward Russell's Anglo-Dutch warships shattered Tourville's fleet. The invasion was canceled.

The fall of Namur opened the line of the Sambre-Meuse to Luxembourg and threatened Liège. William sought to restore the situation through battle. By a night march from his position at Halle, William surprised Luxembourg in his camp at Enghien, but inadequate reconnaissance reduced the allied assault to a partial blow against the French right wing around the village of Steenkirk (August 3). Although only half the armies were engaged, the battle cost each side 8,000 casualties.

The imperial forces in the Rhineland numbered 47,000 but were slow to enter the field. Two limited offensives across the Rhine brought no enduring success, failing to capture Eberenburg, while a counterattack by Marshal de Lorge seized Pforzheim. Lorge then brushed aside a small corps on the borders of Württemberg and proceeded to levy contributions throughout the duchy.

Although his preference was either to recapture Pinerolo and Susa or to invade Savoy and relieve Montmélian, Victor Amadeus was persuaded by William III to mount an invasion of France: Catinat's army had been drained to provide troops for other theaters and was incapable of an offensive. In the spring, a small force was sent to blockade Casale, while the main allied army invaded Dauphiné. In July, they besieged and took Guillestre, Embrun, and Gap, ruining the countryside as they progressed. This, however, was the limit of the advance and all attempts to foment a rising among the Huguenots failed. The campaign was already languishing when Victor Amadeus contracted smallpox. The allied army recrossed the Alps in the autumn. During the winter, as Victor Amadeus slowly recovered, further diplomatic approaches were made to Tessé.

1693: LANDEN, LA MARSAGLIA, AND CHARLEROI

The year 1693 was decisive. French harvests between 1689 and 1691 had been indifferent; that of 1692 was poor; the harvest of 1693 failed completely throughout France and northern Italy. Faced with a dwindling tax base, Louis had to prioritize expenditure. Money was accordingly diverted from the navy to the army. The former switched from fleet actions to commerce raiding in conjunction with privateers. The resultant "guerre de course" was to have a major impact on Anglo-Dutch commerce, more than 1,200 merchant ships being captured by the French between 1688 and 1695. The final, successful, French fleet action was the seizure, off Lagos, of 80 of the 400 merchantmen from the insufficiently escorted Smyrna fleet (June 27). Louis also decided to launch land offensives in Catalonia, Germany, and the Netherlands, as a prelude to dictating generous peace terms to the Grand Alliance. A concomitant diplomatic initiative arrested Swedish dalliance with the Grand Alliance before applying her good offices to open fissures among the German princes. Only the offer of an electoral title by Leopold persuaded Ernst August of Hanover not to desert the Grand Alliance, and concessions were also required to retain the wavering John George IV of Saxony. The major French diplomatic effort was directed toward Piedmont.

Victor Amadeus determined upon an offensive to capture Pinerolo. After sending minor forces under the Spanish general, the marquis de Leganez, to mask Casale, he advanced westward. Catinat left Tessé in command of the fortress and withdrew his field army to Fenstrelle to protect Tessé's communications with Susa. The attack on Pinerolo was halfhearted, more bombardment than siege, and ended with Victor Amadeus renewing his diplomatic overtures to Tessé through Gropello on September 22. As Victor Amadeus dithered, Louis prepared a counterattack. Reinforced with troops from Catalonia and the Rhine, Catinat advanced from the mountains above Pinerolo and was across Victor Amadeus's communications with Turin by September 29. Abandoning the bombardment, the allied army hastened eastward, encumbered by their siege train. At La Marsaglia on October 4, the outnumbered, fatigued, and out-generaled allied army lost 6,000 men. Although Cuneo and Turin lay open to attack, supply difficulties prevented Catinat from exploiting his victory. After levying contributions from as far south as Saluzzo, he retired into winter quarters.

His country exhausted and facing famine, Louis needed peace in Italy. With Savoy and Nice occupied, much of Piedmont devastated, and his army beaten at La Marsaglia, Victor Amadeus was receptive and talks reopened in October. Tessé was empowered to negotiate on the conclusion of a truce, followed by a junction of Franco-Savoyard forces to drive the imperial armies from Italy before declaring it a neutral zone. As a gesture of goodwill, Victor Amadeus promised to remain inactive for the campaign of 1694. By attempting to detach one member, Louis hoped to induce the collapse of the Grand Alliance and thus bring about a general settlement. Accordingly, he also made indirect contact with William III. Victor Amadeus maneuvered between both sides, pressing Louis to make peace on favorable terms but advertising the fact of these negotiations to persuade his allies to redouble their military efforts on his behalf.

Noailles besieged Rosas, the chief Catalan naval base, on May 28, using both his army and a fleet of 50 warships. It surrendered on June 9.

The comte de Lorge crossed the Rhine in May with 50,000 men and attacked Heidelberg, which was sacked for the second time in four years. He then advanced slowly into Franconia, but Ludwig of Baden occupied a strongly fortified blocking position at Ilzfeldt (July 26–August 28) through which Lorge and the dauphin could not penetrate.

Luxembourg commanded 68,000 men in the Netherlands supported by Boufflers with 48,000. William had 120,000. Luxembourg made light of this numerical inferiority by maneuvering so that William had to split his army into three corps to protect Flanders, Brussels, and Liège. Having achieved a local superiority of 66,000 to 50,000, Luxembourg trapped William in a confined and awkward position around the villages of Landen and Neerwinden, west of Maastricht, on July 29. Although the allied army lost only 12,000 compared to French casualties numbering 15,000, William withdrew from the field in some disorder and Luxembourg was able to exploit his victory by besieging and taking the Meuse fortress of Charleroi (October 11).

1694: HUY

The French victories of 1693 were insufficient to bring the Grand Alliance to negotiation. France was now so reduced in resources that she could not resume the offensive and depended upon diplomacy to disunite her opponents.

Following an ill-conceived and worse executed "descent" on Brest, which was repulsed on the beach of Camaret Bay (June 8), followed by the bombardment of Dieppe, St. Malo, and Le Havre, the powerful Anglo-Dutch navy was employed in a strategic role. On May 17, Noailles's 26,000 men beat a Spanish army of 16,000 on the banks of the River Ter, French warships providing flanking fire and logistic support. Palamós was stormed on June 7 and Gerona on June 19, opening the route to Barcelona. The Anglo-Dutch fleet was ordered to the Mediterranean: 75 ships under Edward Russell anchored off Barcelona on August 8. The French ships immediately departed for the safety of Toulon, obliging Noailles to withdraw to the line of the Ter, harassed by the Catalan guerrillas, the *miquelets,* under their general, Blas Trinxería. Seapower had proved decisive. Instead of returning to home waters, Russell was instructed to winter at Cadiz in readiness for operations off Catalonia in the spring. There was also the possibility that the allied fleet could assist the duke of Savoy in recapturing Nice, especially because Catinat's army had been depleted to reinforce Noailles. The duke demurred, explaining that the season was too far advanced for such complex maneuvers. Either Victor Amadeus was abiding by his pledge to remain inac-

tive or, more probably, the devastated Piedmontese countryside could no longer support sustained operations, a situation exacerbated by an acute shortage of grain throughout northern Italy in the winter of 1694, occasioned by the failure of the harvest. Late in the year, imperial envoys proposed Casale as the target for the next year. This did not accord with Victor Amadeus's aim of regaining Savoyard control over Casale, and he promptly renewed his negotiations with Tessé: Peace had to be secured.

In both Germany and the Netherlands, the French remained on the defensive. Lorge sallied across the Rhine early in June but an advance by Ludwig of Baden forced him to recross at Philippsburg on June 28 following a sharp engagement. Baden then occupied a series of fortified camps to deter the French from reentering Germany. Although he was able to protect Flanders, Luxembourg could not prevent William from seizing the small Meuse fortress of Huy (September 27), an essential preliminary to future operations against Namur.

1695: THE GREAT SIEGE OF NAMUR

Despite winter negotiations, William concluded that he had more to gain from weakening France through military action, while Louis trusted that Savoy-Piedmont could be detached from the Grand Alliance.

Taking advantage of the Anglo-Dutch fleet, the marquis de Castañaga unsuccessfully attacked Palamós (August 15–25). When the fleet departed from the Mediterranean in the autumn, the French were free to resume their advance toward Barcelona. Neither could the allied fleet affect events in Savoy-Piedmont. Victor Amadeus knew that the imperial forces intended to attack Casale. Concerned to restrict the extension of Austrian Hapsburg power in Milan, on March 15 the duke instructed Gropello to warn Tessé. Instead of letting the emperor conquer Casale, Gropello proposed that the garrison should surrender after a brief siege by the Piedmontese on condition that the fortifications were then dismantled and the fortress returned to its rightful owner, the duke of Mantua. On April 29, 1695, Louis consented and Victor Amadeus undertook to prevent his allies from attacking any other French possession during 1695.

The siege of Casale began on June 25 and, after token resistance, the French garrison surrendered on July 9. Despite the suspicions of his allies, Victor Amadeus avoided any further action and the rest of the summer was spent demolishing the fortifications, a task not completed until mid-September, by which time it was too late to begin further operations. On November 23, Gropello proposed to Tessé that Victor Amadeus would abandon his allies if France would cede Pinerolo. Although Louis was reluctant to give up territory, he grew more amenable to the proposal as he realized that the defection of Savoy-Piedmont might well shatter the Grand Alliance. In

February 1696 he instructed Tessé to draw up a settlement on these lines.

Luxembourg died in January 1695, to be succeeded by the less able duc de Villeroi. Villeroi has 115,000 men in the Spanish Netherlands but was outnumbered by William. The allies feinted toward Flanders, and attacked Fort Knokke (June 17–24) to commit Villeroi, before hurrying eastward to besiege Namur (July 8), which was defended by Boufflers with a garrison of 15,000 men. Villeroi was slow to march to relieve Namur, thinking that the fortress could endure almost indefinitely. He was shadowed by the prince de Vaudémont with a corps of 37,000 men whose rearguard action at Aarsele (July 14–15) was one of the tactical masterpieces of the war. Slowly, Villeroi edged toward Namur, bombarding Brussels en route (August 13–15) to draw William away from the Meuse River. Some 4,000 shells and red-hot shot were fired, destroying more than 2,000 buildings. Finally, Villeroi approached Namur but was held off by William's covering army. Boufflers surrendered on September 22. For William, this achievement greatly enhanced his own prestige and that of the Grand Alliance. Strategically, the recapture of Huy in 1694 and Namur in 1695 restored the allied position on the Meuse and secured communications between their armies in the Low Countries and those on the Rhine and the Moselle.

1696: EXHAUSTION AND STALEMATE

The campaign of 1696 was dominated by a monetary crisis in England and the defection of Savoy-Piedmont from the Grand Alliance. Without money to pay his troops in the Netherlands, William was unable to undertake significant operations. Without operations in the Netherlands to distract the French, there was no prospect of the imperial armies in the Rhineland functioning effectively. The sole operation of note was the raid on the French magazine at Givet (March 15–17) by Menno van Coehoorn. The destruction of 4 million rations may have forced the French to abandon an attempt to retake Namur. The raid on Givet possibly persuaded Louis that economic salvation might be found in the New World; as a result, in 1697, the baron de Pointis led a naval expedition that captured and looted Cartagena, Colombia.

Louis also attempted an invasion of England. The murder of William III by Jacobite assassins as he traveled to Windsor was to be the signal for a landing in Kent by 14,000 French soldiers under Boufflers and d'Harcourt. The discovery of the assassination plot on March 2 ended this scheme, which could not have succeeded because the Anglo-Dutch fleet retained command of the English Channel.

Determined to capture Pinerolo either through diplomacy or war, Victor Amadeus prepared to attack. He was preempted by Louis's offer of peace and on May 30 Tessé and Gropello signed a draft treaty. The final version of the Treaty of Turin was signed on June 29 and ratified by

Louis on July 6. France ceded Pinerolo, its fortifications demolished, plus its land corridor into Dauphiné, and would restore Savoyard territory seized during the war as soon as all allied forces had evacuated Italy. An immediate truce was to be declared, before the French and Savoyard armies combined to force Savoy's ex-allies to accept the neutralization of northern Italy. Victor Amadeus's daughter, Marie Adelaide, was to marry the duke of Burgundy.

On July 12, Catinat's army, suitably reinforced, advanced on Turin as if to attack, offering Victor Amadeus the pretext to sue for peace. He did so and dropped from the Grand Alliance. Early in August, the remaining allied forces left Turin and withdrew toward Lombardy. When the truce expired, the French and Savoyard armies marched into the Milanese and besieged Valenza. The Allies were forced to sue for peace. A truce was proclaimed at Vigevano on October 7, declaring Italy to be a neutral zone. During the next two months, the allied armies departed. Although Victor Amadeus had secured his war aims of capturing Pinerolo and neutralizing Casale, the price, both to his reputation and the economy of the duchy, was high.

1697: ATH, BRUSSELS, AND BARCELONA

Financially exhausted, England, the United Provinces, and Spain did not want another campaign. Peace had seemed within reach in 1696 when the defection of Savoy wrecked their expectations and encouraged France to further military effort. Catinat's 40,000 men were redeployed to reinforce the French armies in Catalonia and the Netherlands; success in either or both theaters would force the Grand Alliance to make peace on French terms. The allies did not enjoy such riches. The Savoyard army was forfeit while the Spanish troops that had fought for Savoy-Piedmont had to remain in northern Italy to police the truce and cover Milan.

The campaign in the Netherlands had not properly opened when the peace plenipotentiaries met in the Palace of Rijswijk on the outskirts of The Hague on May 6. Nevertheless, the French assumed the offensive, besieging Ath (May 7–June 5) "to make a noise" during the peace negotiations. Three French armies, under Villeroi, Boufflers, and Catinat, then threatened Brussels, but the allies retreated through the night of June 22–23 to take up a blocking position around Koekelberg near Anderlecht. Here the armies remained until the signature of peace.

In Catalonia, where the duke de Vendôme had succeeded Noailles, the French advanced during June and besieged Barcelona on June 12 with 25,000 troops and a sizable fleet. Barcelona fell on August 10. This convinced the king of Spain to make peace.

THE COLONIES

Although not affecting the campaigns in Europe, there was some fighting in the Americas and India. Protection of trade—sugar, tobacco, fishing, and precious metals—was the major concern. The petty operations, which usually consisted of raids conducted by local militias, occasionally supported by troops from Europe, were not strategically significant.

The French seized St. Kitts on August 15, 1689, but it was recaptured on July 22, 1690. A British attempt to take Guadeloupe in April 1691 was unsuccessful. During 1695, the British attacked French bases on Hispaniola following raids on Jamaica. In 1697, the baron de Pointis and the marquis de Château-Renault brought a squadron into the Caribbean in search of the Spanish treasure fleet. Unable to locate the *flota,* they looted Cartagena, the entrepôt for the South American silver traffic. Also in 1697, a British squadron tried to regain control of Newfoundland but achieved little.

Whereas the war in the Caribbean was mostly conducted by Europeans and white settlers, in North America the Nine Years' War relied upon the native Indians: the Five Nations of the Iroquois were allied to the British and the Algonquian tribes to the French. Vicious frontier raiding was the characteristic military operation, except for the capture of Port Royal by Sir William Phips, the governor of New York, on May 21, 1690, and an unsuccessful attack on Quebec later in the same year.

In India, Admiral Duquesne-Guiton sailed in October 1690 into Madras harbor and bombarded the Anglo-Dutch fleet. Three years later, in September 1693, the Dutch besieged and captured the tiny French garrison at Pondicherry.

THE PEACE OF RIJSWIJK, 1697

Negotiations were formally conducted at Rijswijk, but proceedings were hastened by nine private conversations between the earl of Portland and Marshal Boufflers, beginning at Brucom, near Halle, on July 8. Peace was signed at Rijswijk on September 20, the emperor adding his signature on October 30 when he finally accepted that his allies would not support his request for the return of Strasbourg.

The peace settlement represented a substantial victory for the Grand Alliance. William III was recognized as king of England and Louis XIV undertook not to support actively the candidacy of James II's son. The forward defense of the United Provinces was formalized by permitting the Dutch to garrison a line of Spanish fortresses from Nieuport to Namur, including Charleroi, in the south of the Spanish Netherlands, the "Dutch Barrier." The territorial settlement largely obeyed the rule of status quo ante bellum. The French surrendered Philippsburg, Breisach, Freiburg-im-Breisgau, and Kehl, while their new fortresses at La Pile, Mont Royal, and Fort Louis were to be demolished. They retained, however, Alsace and Strasbourg. The duke of Lorraine was restored to his duchy. With an eye on the Spanish succession, Louis allowed Spain to regain Luxembourg, Chimay, Mons, Courtrai, Charleroi, Ath, and evacuated Barcelona and Catalonia. Dinant was

returned to the bishop of Liège. With the question of the Spanish succession unresolved, the Peace of Rijswijk was simply a truce in the long struggle between France and the Hapsburg-Dutch coalition.

Further reading: John Childs, *The Nine Years' War and the British Army, 1688–97: The Campaigns in the Low Countries* (Manchester, England: Manchester University Press, 1991) and "Secondary Operations of the British Army during the Nine Years' War, 1688–1697," *Journal for the Society for Army Research* 73 (1995): 73–98; G. N. Clark, *The Dutch Alliance and the War against the French Trade, 1688–1697* (Manchester, England: Manchester University Press, 1993); N. M. Crouse, *The French Struggle for the West Indies, 1665–1713* (New York: Octagon Books, 1966); John Erman, *The Navy in the War of William III, 1689–1697* (New York: Cambridge University Press, 1953); Douglas E. Leach, *Arms for Empire: a Military History of the British Colonies in North America, 1607–1763* (New York: Macmillan, 1973); E. N. Lloyd, "Catinat," *English Historical Review* 9 (1984): 493–530; W. T. Morgan, "The British West Indies during King William's War, 1689–97," *Journal of Modern History* 2 (1930): 378–409; J. G. Simms, *Jacobite Ireland, 1685–1691* (London: Routledge and Kegan Paul, 1969); Paul Sonnio, "The Origins of Louis XIV's Wars," in *The Origins of War in Early Modern Europe,* ed. Jeremy Black (Highlands, N.J.: Humanities Press, 1987); Claude Sturgill, *Marshall Villars and the Spanish Succession* (Lexington: University of Kentucky Press, 1965); Geoffrey Symcox, *Victor Amadeus II: Absolutism in the Savoyard State, 1675–1730* (Berkeley: University of California Press, 1983) and *The Crisis of French Sea Power, 1688–1697* (The Hague: M. Nijhoff, 1974); John B. Wolf, *The Emergence of the Great Powers, 1685–1715* (New York: Harper, 1951).

Grattan Massacre   (1854)

PRINCIPAL COMBATANTS: The United States vs. the Lakota People (also called the Teton Sioux, and consisting of the Brulé, Hunkpapa, Minneconjou, and Oglala tribes, among others)

PRINCIPAL THEATER(S): North Platte River, seven miles east of Fort Laramie, Wyoming

DECLARATION: None

MAJOR ISSUES AND OBJECTIVES: On August 18, 1854, High Forehead, member of a hunting party of various Lakota tribes, killed a cow belonging to a passing Mormon emigrant; when the Mormon complained to Fort Laramie, a sortie was dispatched to arrest the Sioux hunter.

OUTCOME: Brevet Second Lieutenant John L. Grattan and a small troop from the Sixth U.S. Infantry, plus their interpreter, were killed by Brulé Sioux soldiers after Grattan attacked when they refused to give up High Forehead. Subsequently labeled the "Grattan Massacre," the episode foreshadowed a generation of bloodletting on the northern plains.

APPROXIMATE MAXIMUM NUMBER OF MEN UNDER ARMS:
U.S. Army: 30; Sioux: unknown
CASUALTIES: United States, 31; Sioux, 1
TREATIES: None

For more than half a century before the Grattan Massacre, a mutually suspicious, but carefully guarded relationship existed between the expansionist United States and the Indian tribes of the northern Great Plains. Federal employees and soldiers, explorers, missionaries, and traders were welcomed across the region as long as they behaved decently. Tribal members and non-Indian hunters, sometimes together, harvested beaver pelts, buffalo hides, and other animal resources to the commercial advantages of white investors in the fur trade. The Indians exchanged some of the natural bounty of their hunting grounds and their labor for American- and European-manufactured goods that improved their military capabilities, made their lives more convenient or luxurious, and embellished their culture, its ceremonies and art.

But many on both sides grew increasingly fearful over the years that such occasional clashes as the ARIKARA WAR of 1823 might someday escalate into a more generalized war. In many ways, the clashes had structural roots in the changing economy and society of the Great Plains: Fur traders and professional hunters were so depleting the wildlife that they posed an essential threat to the traditions of tribal life; during the 1840s, overland travelers to the Pacific coast violated the boundaries of tribal lands without permission; and by mid-century, a significant number of emigrants were settling close enough to Indian communities to create many cross-cultural conflicts.

It was just about that time that strategists in the U.S. Army, increasingly worried about the potential for violence, changed the military's policies toward the northern plains. Since 1819, when the United States had established Forts Snelling and Atkinson, and 1825, when the Atkinson-O'Fallon Commission had made treaties with the Plains tribes during the Yellowstone Expedition, the army high command had reduced its forces north of Kansas to meet the military exigencies of the southern Great Plains. In 1848, however, federal troops had built Fort Kearney and, in 1849, the government had purchased Fort Laramie from traders. These moves were aimed at protecting the new migration of Mormons, California gold rush emigrants, and others traveling west from Omaha along the sides of the Platte River basin.

The Treaty of Fort Laramie in 1851 arranged safe passage for these overlanders. Its diplomatic mechanism was familiar to the region's tribal leaders. Treaties, like those produced by the Atkinson-O'Fallon Commission, traditionally recognized the territorial claims negotiated among the tribes themselves for the privilege of passage or for hunting rights. The Fort Laramie treaty extended this intertribal diplomacy to cover non-Indians by offering annuities as tolls for travel across Sioux, Cheyenne, and Arapaho lands. For three years after the treaty was signed, tribal soldiers allowed non-Indians to migrate unmolested until a trivial misunderstanding provoked a bloody confrontation.

The 1851 Fort Laramie Treaty obliged the Plains Indian tribes to assemble each autumn to receive the food and trade goods they were paid for allowing travelers to pass through their territory. As Indians collected near Fort Laramie in August 1854, a member of a hunting party made up of Brulé Sioux and other Lakota soldiers killed a lame cow that belonged to a Mormon family traveling overland with a nearby wagon train. The cow's Mormon owner reported the "theft" to Fort Laramie and demanded restitution. Such incidents were not uncommon at these meetings of cultures, perhaps inherently volatile, among Indian hunters, the U.S. military, and American emigrants. They awaited only the right spark to make of them a crossroads to conflict, and, in this case, the spark proved to be Lieutenant John L. Grattan (1830–54).

A recent graduate of West Point, eager to prove his own mettle, Grattan asked for command of a sortie to the camp of Brulé chief Conquering Bear (sometimes translated as Brave Bear) to arrest the Sioux "thief." Post commander Captain Hugh B. Fleming reluctantly agreed to the expedition, but he warned the young West Pointer to exercise discretion and to avoid any violent engagement. Giving little heed to the warning, Grattan sallied forth on the day following the incident, August 19, with 27 privates and two NCOs, armed with a 12-pounder howitzer and a 12-pounder mountain gun.

On the march toward the Indian village, Grattan's interpreter, Auguste Lucien (d. 1854), got drunk, and upon the army's arrival at the camp, the interpreter began hurling insults at the Sioux as the parley got under way. Conquering Bear (d. 1854) calmly pointed out that the hunting party, in need of food, assumed the lame cow, of no use to others, was fair game. In addition, the party consisted of other tribal members, some Oglala and some Minneconjou Sioux, over which he had no direct authority. In fact, it had been one of them who put the ox out of its misery. Trying to forestall a confrontation, Conquering Bear offered amends to the Mormon family, but his offer was refused. When High Forehead (fl. 1854), the Minneconjou who had killed the cow, refused to surrender, the tension, never far from the surface, increased. Forty-five-minutes after the parley had opened, the overconfident Grattan rashly ordered his troops to open fire on the village, fatally wounding Conquering Bear—as it turns out, the only Sioux to die that day.

Unfortunately for the thoughtless lieutenant and his command, Grattan had set his two artillery pieces too high to be effective. The next shots caused no injury and little damage, but did incite the fury of the Brulé soldiers, who—joined by some of the Oglala—responded quickly and forcefully. Lucien was among the first to fall; so was Grattan. By nightfall, all the troops except Private John Cuddy (d. 1854) lay dead. Cuddy survived long enough to return to Fort Laramie, but he lapsed into a coma and died on August 21.

The news shocked and alarmed citizens throughout the United States, but despite their outrage, not all officials joined in the growing cry for revenge. To the contrary, the Bureau of Indians Affairs, after hearing reports from Fort Laramie, quickly concluded that the army had blundered. The War Department, on the other hand, demanded a response. When young Sioux warriors, buoyed by the victory over Grattan, began raiding along the major emigrant routes, Secretary of War Jefferson Davis (1808–89) decided that the "massacre"—the word was often used to describe Indian victories—had been deliberate. Action, Davis declared, had to be taken to "punish" the Sioux if future raids were to be avoided. He recalled the fiery-tempered but experienced Indian-fighter, Colonel William S. Harney (1800–89) home from leave in Paris to direct operations against the Sioux, which in turn led to the first serious confrontation between the Lakota and the U.S. Army at Blue Water Creek in early September 1855 (see UNITED STATES–SIOUX WAR [1854–1857]).

The Grattan Massacre initiated half a century of military conflict on the northern Great Plains.

Further reading: George Rollie Adams, *General William S. Harney: Prince of Dragoons* (Lincoln: University of Nebraska Press, 2001); Alan Axelrod, *Chronicle of the Indian Wars: From Colonial Times to Wounded Knee* (New York: Prentice Hall General Reference, 1993); Edward Lazarus, *Black Hills, White Justice: The Sioux Nation versus the United States* (New York: HarperCollins, 1991); Lloyd E. McCann, "The Grattan Massacre," *Nebraska History* 37 (1956): 1–26; Charles Phillips and Alan Axelrod, *Encyclopedia of the American West* (New York: Macmillan Reference USA, 1996); Robert M. Utley, *Frontiersman in Blue: The United States Army and the Indian, 1848–1865* (Lincoln: University of Nebraska Press, 1981).

Great Indian Mutiny   *See* INDIAN MUTINY (1857–1858).

Great Java War   *See* JAVA WAR, GREAT (1815–1830).

Great Kaffir War   *See* KAFFIR WAR, EIGHTH (1850–1853).

Great Northern War   *See* NORTHERN WAR, SECOND (1700–1711).

Great Peloponnese War   *See* PELOPONNESE WAR, SECOND.

Greco-Persian Wars   (500–448 B.C.E.)

PRINCIPAL COMBATANTS: Persia vs. Greek city-states (mostly Athens, Sparta, and the Delian League)
PRINCIPAL THEATER(S): Greece and Asia Minor
DECLARATION: None
MAJOR ISSUES AND OBJECTIVES: Persia began the war with the intention of punishing Athens; ultimately, its goal was to occupy European Greece.
OUTCOME: The Persian invasion was ultimately repulsed, and the Persians driven out of Europe and Asia Minor.
APPROXIMATE MAXIMUM NUMBER OF MEN UNDER ARMS: At Marathon: Persian, 15,000; Greek, 10,000; at Thermopylae: Persian, 100,000; Greek, 5,300
CASUALTIES: Totals unknown; naval losses among the Persians were particularly devastating.
TREATIES: Peace of Callias, 448

From about 500 to 493 B.C.E. Athens (with Eretria) helped Miletus and other Ioanian city-states in their revolt against the Persian Empire (see IONIAN REVOLT). This incited Darius I (550–486 B.C.E.), king of Persia, to seek vengeance on the Athenians. In 492 B.C.E. he sent his son-in-law Mardonius with an army to invade European Greece. Mardonius enjoyed great success against Thrace and Macedonia, quickly subduing them, but then was forced to return to Asia when a massive storm wrecked most of his fleet. In 490, a second Persian expedition made the Aegean crossing under the leadership of Artaphrenes the Younger (fl. 490 B.C.E.) and Datis (fl. 490 B.C.E.), Darius's nephew, who, together, conquered Eretria in a week's time. Datis then led a 15,000-man force in a landing at Marathon, 24 miles northeast of Athens. Miltiades (d. 489 B.C.E.), the Greek general, mustered all the men he could—about 10,000 Athenian citizen-soldiers and another 1,000 Plataean troops. He decided to take the offensive—a bold move against a superior, and hitherto undefeated, force. On September 12, 490, Miltiades arranged his infantry (hoplites) in a long, thin line across the two-mile-wide Marathon plain. The line charged the Persian invaders, who readily beat back the Greek center. Miltiades, however, had augmented his flanks, and these now wheeled inward to envelop the Persian center. Datis was thereby routed and forced to retreat to his ships. Unable to attack strongly defended Athens, Datis returned to Asia in defeat.

Greek losses were a mere 192 men, whereas the Persians had lost 6,400.

It was 480 before Darius mounted another invasion. This time he sent a massive force of 100,000 men, led by his son Xerxes I (d. 465 B.C.E.), across the Hellespont (Dardanelles) on a boat bridge. The army marched through Thrace and Macedonia, then turned into Thessaly. There, at Thermopylae Pass, the narrow gateway into Boeotia—and Attica, the Athenian homeland—the vastly outnumbered Greeks established a strong defensive position, but with a mere 5,300 men. In one of the great heroic stands of all history, 300 Spartans, under Leonidas I (d. 480 B.C.E.), held off 100,000 Persians at the pass. They fought to the last man, but bought sufficient time in the three-day battle for the main body of 5,000 hoplites to escape.

Following Thermopylae, the Greeks yielded Attica to Xerxes, who sacked Athens. The Greek forces took up positions behind a great wall they built across the Isthmus of Corinth, and the Persians followed. The plan now was for the vast Persian fleet of some 600 galleys to attack the Greek position. In September 480, the Persian land forces watched as Xerxes' 600 vessels seemingly entrapped the 366 triremes (superior war galleys with three rows of oars) of the Greek fleet in the Saronic Gulf. Themistocles (c. 525–462 B.C.E.), the Greek commander, lured Xerxes' fleet into the dangerously narrow waters off Salamis, thereby depriving the unwieldy craft of maneuverability. With the enemy thus rendered vulnerable, the Spartan admiral Eurybiades (fl. 480 B.C.E.) led the Athenian triremes in a furious attack. Two hundred to three hundred Persian vessels were destroyed, whereas the Greeks lost perhaps 40 of their own. Xerxes was thus forced to break off the ground campaign, postponing further attacks until the next year—by which time the Greek city-states had been able to unite and pool their military resources. At the Battle of Cape Mycale, in 479, the already diminished Persian fleet was destroyed.

While the Persians suffered defeat at sea, the Greek land forces also managed to take the main Persian base at Plataea, southern Boeotia. This put an end to the immediate threat of a Persian invasion and prompted the Ionian states, with the aid and urging of Athens, to form the Delian League in 478. The Athenian general Cimon (c. 510–450 B.C.E.), son of Miltiades, led the forces of the Delian League in a counteroffensive that retook the cities of Thrace as well as those along the Aegean.

In 466, at the mouth of the Eurymedon River, in southern Asia Minor, Cimon's forces routed the reconstituted Persian fleet and scattered its land forces. This brought southern Asia Minor into the Delian League and ended the Persian threat of further invasion. Athens, however, continued to act against the Persians elsewhere, sending Pericles (c. 495–29 B.C.E.) to lead forces in aid of rebellions in Egypt. Pericles blockaded Memphis in 459, but was badly defeated by the Persians in 456 and besieged on an island in the Nile. In one of the greatest feats of military engineering in all history, the Persian forces diverted the Nile's flow and were thereby able to attack and destroy the Greeks in 454. At this point, Cimon, who had fallen from power with the ascension of his rival Pericles, was recalled. In 450, he won a victory over the Persians at Salamis in Cyprus, thereby recovering most of Cyprus. In 449, however, Cimon died (either of illness or of battle wounds) during the siege of Citium, bringing the war to a close the following year. By the Peace of Callias, Persia pledged to stay out of the Aegean forever. The peace endured for 40 years.

See also PERSIAN INVASION OF GREECE.

Further reading: A. R. Burn, *Persia and the Greeks: The Defence of the West, c. 546–478 B.C.* (Palo Alto, Calif.: Stanford University Press, 1984); David Califf, *Marathon* (Philadelphia: Chelsea House, 2002); Peter Green, *The Greco-Persian Wars* (Berkeley: University of California Press, 1996); J. F. Lazenby, *The Defence of Greece, 490–479 B.C.* (Warminster, England: Aris and Phillips, 1993).

Greco-Turkish War (Thirty Day's War) (1897)

PRINCIPAL COMBATANTS: Greece vs. the Ottoman Empire
PRINCIPAL THEATER(S): Crete and Thessaly
DECLARATION: Greece against Ottoman Empire
MAJOR ISSUES AND OBJECTIVES: Greece attempted to annex Crete.
OUTCOME: Greek forces were decisively defeated, but Crete was put under an international protectorate governed by Prince George of Greece.
APPROXIMATE MAXIMUM NUMBER OF MEN UNDER ARMS: Unknown
CASUALTIES: Greece, 600 killed; Turkey, 1,300 killed
TREATIES: Armistice and treaty, 1897

The CRETAN UPRISING (1896) had pitted Islamic Ottomans against Orthodox Greeks on the Ottoman-ruled island of Crete. In response to Ottoman persecution of Orthodox Cretans, Greece commenced a war on April 17, 1897, to annex Crete. The Greeks launched two campaigns, one on Crete itself, the other in Thessaly. The Ottoman forces defended their positions vigorously, defeating the Greeks on Crete at the Battle of Vestinos on May 5 and at Pharsalus on May 6. The Turks forced the withdrawal of 9,000 Greek troops from the island. In Thessaly, the Greeks were fought to a standstill which persuaded them to sign an armistice on May 19, 1897. The war had lasted a month and is sometimes called the Thirty Days' War. Four months later, a final peace treaty was concluded.

Greece suffered a serious defeat and was compelled to pay an indemnity and to cede part of Thessaly to the Ottoman Empire. The Greek government also yielded a degree of its sovereignty to an international commission, appointed to supervise its economic affairs. Nevertheless, the Ottomans were also compelled to withdraw militarily from Crete and to cede it to an internationally supervised protectorate under Prince George of Greece. The protectorate endured until the end of the First BALKAN WAR in 1913, when, by the Treaty of London, Crete was formally annexed to Greece.

See also GREEK WAR OF INDEPENDENCE.

Further reading: Alan Warwick, *The Decline and Fall of the Ottoman Empire* (New York: Barnes and Noble Books, 1995).

Greco-Turkish War (1920–1922)

PRINCIPAL COMBATANTS: Greece vs. Turkey
PRINCIPAL THEATER(S): Smyrna, Thrace, and Anatolia
DECLARATION: None
MAJOR ISSUES AND OBJECTIVES: Greece wanted to expand its World War I acquisition, Smyrna, to include Turkish territory in Thrace and Anatolia.
OUTCOME: Greece was decisively defeated and compelled to renounce all Anatolian claims and to return Thrace to Turkey.
APPROXIMATE MAXIMUM NUMBER OF MEN UNDER ARMS: About 50,000 on each side at any given time
CASUALTIES: Greece, 105,000 killed, wounded, or taken prisoner; Turkey, 13,000 killed, 35,000 wounded. Many noncombatant deaths on both sides
TREATIES: Treaty of Lausanne, July 24, 1923

After WORLD WAR I, the Allied Powers supported Greek occupation of Smyrna, which had been part of the German-allied Ottoman Empire. In the meantime, Mustafa Kemal (1881–1938) (later renowned as Kemal Atatûrk) successfully led a revolution against the government of Sultan Muhammad VI (r. 1918–22) and set up a new provisional republican Turkish government at Ankara in 1920. For their part, the Greeks wanted to expand what the post–World War I Treaty of Sèvres had given them, Smyrna, to include Thrace and as much of Anatolia as they could manage to acquire. On June 22, 1920, the Greek army under Alexander I (1893–1920) began its advance inland, taking Alasehir on June 24. The advance paused here while Greeks and Turks negotiated at Constantinople (later Istanbul). Muhammad VI had agreed to certain concessions, which Kemal now refused to honor. The negotiations broke down, and the Greek offensive resumed on March 23, 1921.

At Inönü 150 miles west of Ankara, a Turkish force under Ismet Pasha (1884–1973) retarded the advance of 37,000 Greek troops. By August 24, 1921, however the Greeks had reached the Sakarya River, 70 miles outside Ankara, where they would fight the decisive battle of the war. The battle commenced on August 24, 1921, and pitted 50,000 Greeks against 44,000 Turks, who were subse-

quently reinforced by an additional 8,000. Although the Greeks initially succeeded in driving back the Turkish center, on September 10, Kemal led a small reserve force in an attack on the Greek left flank. Fearing envelopment, the Greeks disengaged and withdrew to Smyrna, having lost 3,897 killed and 19,000 wounded. An additional 15,000 had been captured or were missing in action. Turkish losses were 3,700 killed, 18,000 wounded, and 1,000 missing or taken prisoner.

Following their victory at the Sakarya, the Turks intensified their counteroffensive, beginning on August 18, 1922, laying siege to Smyrna. It fell to the Turks on September 9, and the Greek forces were expelled from the island.

The Treaty of Lausanne was concluded on July 24, 1923, by which Greek claims to Anatolia were vacated, and the Greeks were compelled to return Thrace to the Turks. The Turkish border in Europe was fixed at the Maritsa River. The Turkish triumph also propelled Mustafa Kemal to the presidency of the newly proclaimed Turkish republic.

See also BALKAN WAR, FIRST; BALKAN WAR, SECOND; GRECO-TURKISH WAR (1897); GREEK WAR OF INDEPENDENCE.

Further reading: Marjorie Housepian Dobkin, *Smyrna 1922: The Destruction of a City* (New York: New Mark Press, 1999).

Greek Civil War (1944–1949)

PRINCIPAL COMBATANTS: Greek Communists vs. Greek government forces
PRINCIPAL THEATER(S): Greece
DECLARATION: None
MAJOR ISSUES AND OBJECTIVES: The Greek communists wanted to overthrow the British- and American-supported democratic government.
OUTCOME: With British and then U.S. support, the government ultimately crushed the communist insurgency.
APPROXIMATE MAXIMUM NUMBER OF MEN UNDER ARMS: Greek government forces, 205,000,—with 40,000 British troops; Greek Communists, about 28,000 guerrillas, maximum
CASUALTIES: Government forces, 15,969 killed, 38,557 wounded, 2,001 missing; communist forces, 50,000 killed; total fatalities, including noncombatants, 158,000
TREATIES: None; cease-fire signed October 16, 1949

Early in WORLD WAR II, Greece was invaded and occupied by Nazi forces. During the occupation, an active partisan resistance was conducted, chiefly by the Communist National Liberation Front (EAM) and its military arm, the People's National Army of Liberation (ELAS). The British drove the Germans out in September 1944, and liberated Greece was occupied by the British, who brought the former government of Greece, which now included the EAM, back into power. Certain elements of the ELAS resisted cooperation with the British-supported government and threatened armed insurrection. The British response was a proposal to disarm the ELAS, which elicited a Communist protest in the form of a general strike in Athens declared on December 2, 1944. The next day, police and the ELAS clashed in the streets, but after British prime minister Winston Churchill (1874–1965) visited, a truce was signed, and ELAS guerrillas withdrew from Athens. A further agreement was concluded on February 12, 1945, calling for the ELAS to surrender its weapons within two weeks. Despite the agreement, however, fighting continued. The Greek government was unstable, and Greece was embroiled in territorial disputes with Yugoslavia and Albania.

Marshal Tito (Josip Broz) (1892–1980), head of Communist Yugoslavia, supported the EAM-ELAS, as did Albania and Bulgaria. With this support, the Communist forces were able to retreat intact north into the mountains. There they received supplies directly from Yugoslavia and Albania. To counter this, Britain sent 40,000 troops to Greece and gave financial aid to the government, which soon became entirely dependent on the troops and the cash to maintain power. Devastated itself by the just-concluded war, however, Great Britain announced that it could not continue its support beyond March 31, 1947, the day of Greek elections. On February 21, 1947, Britain turned to the United States. It requested aid for Greece as well as Turkey. President Harry S. Truman (1884–1972) secured an appropriation from Congress of $400 million for this purpose as part of the so-called Truman Doctrine—a policy of aiding the "free" nations of Europe to resist the incursion of Soviet-sponsored communism (see COLD WAR). The ELAS responded to the Truman Doctrine by announcing the formation of a Communist government, the "Free Greek Government," and, with 20,000–30,000 guerrillas, it fought its way south, penetrating nearly to Athens.

As U.S. military and financial aid began to reach government forces, 40,000 loyalist troops were able to mount a major attack on the main Communist base in the Grammos Mountains during June 19–August 20, 1948. It was the biggest battle of the war, and it proved decisive. The rebels, under General "Markos" Vaphiades (1906–92), broke out of an encirclement by three columns of government troops, but, in doing so, they suffered catastrophic losses: 3,128 killed, 6,000 wounded, and 598 taken prisoner. (Government forces lost 801 killed, 5,000 wounded, and 31 missing.)

With the Communist rebels reeling, the government launched 50,000 troops against a force of 12,500 Communists in the Vitsi Mountains. In heavy fighting, the government did not succeed in dislodging the Communists, but did inflict heavy casualties.

With the onset of winter 1948–49, government troops concentrated on the Peloponnese, clearing it of some 4,000 rebels by the middle of March 1949. However, in Macedonia, it was the rebels who took the offensive. The town of Carpenisi was occupied on January 12, 1949, and it took government forces 16 days to recapture it. The government garrison at Florina came under attack from 4,000 communist troops on February 12, 1949. The siege was broken after four days of bitter combat.

The Communist offensive created heavy casualties on both sides, but Communist losses were heavier—and, in proportion to the numbers of men fielded, much more devastating. The rebel forces kept fighting, but had been greatly reduced, and in July 1949, Tito, responding to divisions within the Soviet sphere of influence, withdrew support for the Greek Communists after they announced their allegiance to Tito's nemesis, Joseph Stalin (1879–1953). By August, the last of the Communist guerrillas had been captured, and the country was declared secure on August 28, 1949. The People's National Army of Liberation (ELAS), principal Greek communist military force, formally surrendered on October 16, 1949.

Further reading: John O. Iatrides and Linda Wrigley, eds., *Greece at the Crossroads: The Civil War and Its Legacy* (State College: Pennsylvania State University Press, 1995); Amikam Nachmani, *International Intervention in the Greek Civil War: The United Nations Special Committee on the Balkans, 1947–1952* (Westport, Conn.: Greenwood Publishing Group, 1990); Peter J. Stavrakis, *Moscow and Greek Communism, 1944–1949* (Ithaca, N.Y.: Cornell University Press, 1989).

Greek War *See* LAMIAN WAR.

Greek War of Independence (1821–1832)

PRINCIPAL COMBATANTS: Greek nationalists (later with British, Russian, and French allies) vs. Ottoman and Egyptian forces
PRINCIPAL THEATER(S): Greece and Balkans
DECLARATION: Declaration of independence, January 13, 1822
MAJOR ISSUES AND OBJECTIVES: Greek nationalists sought independence from the Ottoman Empire.
OUTCOME: With Anglo-Franco-Russo aid, the nationalists achieved autonomy, then independence.
APPROXIMATE MAXIMUM NUMBER OF MEN UNDER ARMS: Ottoman and Egyptian forces, 24,000; Greek and allied forces, 25,000
CASUALTIES: Greece, 15,000 killed; Ottoman and Egyptian forces, about 6,000 killed
TREATIES: Treaty of Adrianople, September 14, 1829; Treaty of London, August 30, 1832

Greece had long been under Ottoman rule when the "Hellenic movement"—in part driven by early 19th-century archaeological discoveries that reawakened a passion for classical Greek culture—nurtured a nationalist movement. Educated Greeks were attracted to cultural-political societies, the most prominent of which was the Philike Hetairia (Society of Friends), whereas the lower classes gravitated toward quasi-guerrilla bandit bands, known as the *klephts*.

The beginning of a war for independence was signaled by the so-called YPSILANTI REBELLIONS. The Ypsilantis were a prominent Greek family in Constantinople (and therefore known as Phanariots, Greeks of Constantinople) that had been exiled to Russia because of a dispute with the Sublime Porte, the Ottoman government. In Russia, Alexander Ypsilanti (1792–1832) became a general in the czar's army, and in 1820, military leader of the Philike Hetairia. His ambition was to incorporate Greece in a pan-Balkan rebellion against Ottoman domination, and in March 1821 he led a "Sacred Battalion" in an invasion of Moldavia. He took its capital, Jassy (modern Iasi, Romania), then entered Bucharest. Ypsilanti received acclaim and support from the Phanariot governor of Moldavia and Greeks living in Wallachia, but the czar, responding to pressure from the Austrian minister Metternich, repudiated the action. Presumably acting at the czar's urging, the Greek ecumenical patriarch excommunicated Ypsilanti. Worse, Romania failed to support Ypsilanti. Romania had its own agenda of independence, which included not only freedom from Ottoman oppression but from the oppression of Phanariot officials as well.

Lacking sufficient backing, Ypsilanti suffered a decisive defeat at the Battle of Dragasani, 90 miles west of Bucharest, on June 9, 1821. The general fled to Austria, only to be arrested by imperial order and imprisoned for the next six years. Alexander Ypsilanti's brother, Demetrios (1793–1832), also fled, from Moldavia to Morea (Peloponnese). Here he assembled Greek rebels to begin the war of independence in earnest and on Hellenic territory.

On January 13, 1822, Demetrios Ypsilanti was instrumental in a declaration of independence at Epidaurus, Greece. He led rebel bands by land and sea against the Ottoman garrisons and ports of Morea. His men seized supplies from Ottoman ships there. The rebels took the major Ottoman fortress of Tripolitza and then Athens itself. The Turks responded, during 1822–23, by invading Greece, but their assault on the Greek fortress of Missolonghi (at the mouth of the Gulf of Corinth) failed, and the troops withdrew.

On Crete, however, the Turks made horrific inroads, killing the Orthodox residents there and then going on to devastate the island of Chios, actually enslaving some 100,000 Greeks. Yet Morea held out—until internecine quarreling among the Greeks sparked a civil war in the midst of the rebellion. In 1825, Ottoman sultan Mahmud II (1784–1839) secured military aid from Egypt, which

put under the leadership of Ibrahim Ali (1789–1848), son of the Egyptian pasha, an amphibious force aimed at Morea. The Greeks, debilitated by internal strife, were easily defeated, and the Turks soon retook Morea on February 24, 1825, then took Krommydi on April 19. Missolonghi, a key Greek stronghold, was besieged from May 7, 1825, to April 23, 1826. The Egyptians stormed the fortress, killing 500; in the course of the entire siege, 3,000 Greeks died. After the fall of Missolonghi, Athens was retaken on June 5, 1827.

Throughout western Europe, governments and individuals (including, most famously, the British poet George Gordon, Lord Byron [1788–1824]) rallied to the cause of Greek independence. For one thing, western Europe favored a weak Ottoman Empire, and, for another, people felt genuine outrage at the oppression of the "noble" Greeks by the "barbaric" Turks. Britain, Russia, and France agreed to mediate between the Turks and the Greeks, with the ultimate object of obtaining Greek autonomy, if not outright independence. The three nations also demanded the immediate withdrawal of Egyptian forces from Greece. The response of the Ottomans as well as the Egyptians was defiant. The Ottoman Porte rejected any armistice, and the Egyptians refused to evacuate Greek territory. Britain, Russia, and France then launched a naval expedition against the Turkish-Egyptian fleet at Navarino, destroying most of it on October 20, 1827. Navarino was the decisive battle of the war, and it was entirely the work of British, French, and Russian naval commanders and some 17,500 naval personnel from those nations. Not a single Greek was involved. The Turks lost three ships-of-the-line, 12 frigates, two fireships, and 45 smaller craft—a disaster for the Ottoman navy. Four thousand Turks, Egyptians, and Algerians died in the battle, whereas the allies lost 177 men killed in action. Navarino is especially significant in military history in that it was the last great sea battle between wooden ships.

After Navarino, French land forces aided the Greeks in expelling Ibrahim's army.

At this point, Turkey and Russia came to blows in the RUSSO-TURKISH WAR (1828–29), which resulted in a series of Turkish defeats and ended with the Treaty of Adrianople, whereby the Ottoman Porte ceded sovereignty of Moldavia and Wallachia (the so-called Danubian Principalities) and granted Greece autonomous status. Full independence was recognized by the Porte in 1832 when the Treaty of London was signed.

Further reading: David Brewer, *The Greek War of Independence* (New York: Penguin Putnam, 2003).

Grenada, Invasion of (1983)

PRINCIPAL COMBATANTS: United States forces vs. Cuban and Grenadan forces

PRINCIPAL THEATER(S): Grenada, West Indies

DECLARATION: None

MAJOR ISSUES AND OBJECTIVES: The United States wanted to remove the Cuban military presence in Grenada and to protect approximately 1,000 U.S. nationals resident in the country.

OUTCOME: U.S. objectives were achieved.

APPROXIMATE MAXIMUM NUMBER OF MEN UNDER ARMS: Two U.S. Marine amphibious units, two Army Ranger battalions, a brigade of the 82nd Airborne Division, special operations units, and major naval vessels vs. 500–600 Grenadian regulars, 2,000–2,500 organized militiamen, and about 800 Cuban military construction personnel

CASUALTIES: United States, 18 killed, 116 wounded; Grenada, 25 dead, 59 wounded; Cuba, 45 dead, 350 wounded

TREATIES: None

On October 25, 1983, President Ronald Reagan (b. 1911) authorized U.S. forces to invade the island nation of Grenada in the West Indies. Intelligence reports revealed that Cuban troops had been sent to the tiny country (population 110,100) at the request of its anti-American dictatorship. In keeping with the COLD WAR policy of containment of communism, President Reagan was determined to prevent a Cuban presence from being established in Grenada. More immediately, the military was assigned the task of protecting the approximately 1,000 American citizens there, most of whom were students at a local medical college.

The background of the invasion is this: In 1979, a Marxist-Leninist coup led by Maurice Bishop (1944–83) and his New Jewel movement overthrew the government of Grenada. The United States became alarmed when the new communist regime devoted inordinate resources to the construction of a 9,800-foot airstrip, a facility clearly intended for military purposes. The Bishop administration proved to be short-lived. He, together with others in his government, were killed in a 1983 coup that put Deputy Prime Minister Bernard Coard (b. 1944) and General Hudson Austin (b. 1939) in charge of the government. At this point, Sir Paul Scoon (b. 1935), Grenada's governor general, secretly communicated with the Organization of Eastern Caribbean States (OECS) for aid in restoring order. It was the OECS that, in turn, asked for U.S. military intervention.

The United States launched Operation Urgent Fury, which included a naval battle group centered on the aircraft carrier *Independence*, as well as the helicopter carrier *Guam*, two U.S. Marine amphibious units, two Army Ranger battalions, a brigade of the 82nd Airborne Division, and special operations units. These massive forces landed on Grenada on October 25, 1983, and found themselves facing no more than 500–600 Grenadan regulars, 2,000 to 2,500 poorly equipped and poorly organized militiamen, and about 800 Cuban military construction

personnel. The invaders quickly seized the airport and destroyed Radio Free Grenada, a key source of government communications. The U.S. nationals were safely evacuated, and Grenada was under complete U.S. military control by October 28.

The operation was highly successful in that it achieved its objectives, rescuing the U.S. nationals and evicting the Cubans. It was plagued, however, by poor intelligence and inadequate communication and coordination among the army, navy, and marines.

Further reading: William C. Gilmore, *Grenada Intervention: Analysis and Documentation* (New York: Facts On File, 1985); Peter A. Hutchausen, *America's Splendid Little Wars: A Short History of U.S. Military Engagements: 1975–2000* (New York: Viking, 2003); Anthony J. Payne, Paul Sutton, and Tony Thorndike, *Grenada: Revolution and Invasion* (New York: St. Martin's Press, 1986).

Guatemalan Revolution (1954)

PRINCIPAL COMBATANTS: U.S.-backed anticommunist rebels vs. Republic of Guatemala

PRINCIPAL THEATER(S): Guatemala

DECLARATION: None

MAJOR ISSUES AND OBJECTIVES: When a newly elected Guatemalan president began nationalizing fallow land leased to the United Fruit Company, the United States mounted a military coup.

OUTCOME: The president was ousted and replaced by a military junta that brutally repressed suspected communists and left-wing sympathizers.

APPROXIMATE MAXIMUM NUMBER OF MEN UNDER ARMS: 500 rebels; government troop strength unknown

CASUALTIES: About 100 killed on each side

TREATIES: None

Guatemala had been a "banana republic" since 1913, when the Boston-based United Fruit Company established the Tropical Radio and Telegraph Company in the impoverished Central American country, creating a monopoly of the little nation's communications system and placing a stranglehold on its infrastructure—a shining example of America's "dollar diplomacy." Imperialism disguised as economic development, dollar diplomacy allowed the United States in the name of free trade and capital investment to promote its interests—and be spared the inconvenience, not to mention the political headaches, of setting up a colonial government—through the auspices of huge export firms doing business in Central America and the Caribbean.

In Guatemala dollar diplomacy worked like this: Guatemala's ruling elite were persuaded to grant United Fruit tax exemptions, vast acreages for its plantations, and the ownership of Guatemala's main port exchange in return for help in building a railroad, since Queen Victoria's (1819–1901) heyday the sine qua non for any nation that wanted to count for something. Seduced by promises of further American investment, Guatemalan leaders turned over control of all the nation's railways to the company, whose merchant navy already dominated local shipping. Here also—and in other Latin American countries—United Fruit functioned as a shadow government.

Like the other big fruit companies—Standard Fruit and Steamship in Honduras, for example—United Fruit ruled its vast plantations with an iron fist. Company commissaries drove peasants into unredeemable debt, and thus peonage. When malaria weakened its much exploited workers, the company imported black workers from Jamaica and the West Indies—whose immune systems were supposedly resistant to the disease—to get the crop picked, imposing a U.S.-style racial segregation on those it forced to work together. True, the company built a number of hospitals, but that made sense if it wanted to keep its workers healthy enough to harvest its products. On the other hand, the company did not bother much with schools, building only a few and those mostly for show; it did not need many workers who could read, and consequently Guatemalan literacy rates remained shamefully low. Peasants owned tiny plots, whereas United Fruit kept hundreds of thousands of acres in reserve and uncultivated. By 1930, the company had made so much money that it easily absorbed 20 of its closest rivals, becoming Central America's biggest employer. In the absence of major investments of capital and because so much land was dedicated to agriculture, Guatemala could hardly industrialize, and it thus remained hostage to the constantly shifting world demand for its two cash crops, coffee and bananas—a predicament that continues to plague both Central and much of South America today.

When America began to develop its secret intelligence organizations after WORLD WAR I, their personnel—like many in the country's foreign service—tended to be agents of the dollar diplomats as well. It was the managing partner of the Wall Street law firm, Sullivan and Cromwell, who in 1936 put together the deal that gave its client, United Fruit, control of the International Railways of Central America (IRCA) and drew up the papers for a new 99-year lease in Guatemala signed by the Guatemalan caudillo (military leader) Jorge Ubico y Castañeda (1878–1946). Ubico was a man who so despised the Mayan rabble that constituted a majority of his subjects (and United Fruit's workers) that he had his initials stamped in every bullet fired by his soldiers to ensure that malcontents "would carry his personal emblem into eternity." A 1944 revolution led by reform-minded army officers ousted Ubico and set up national elections, the second of which six years later brought to power Jacobo Arbenz Guzmán (1913–71).

Pledging "to convert Guatemala from a backwater country with a predominantly feudal economy into a modern capitalist state," President Arbenz planned to open a second port on the Gulf of Mexico, build a national highway to break IRCA's monopoly on transport, and generally compete with United Fruit. In 1952, he squeezed through a legislature corrupted by foreign bribes an agricultural reform bill and began expropriating uncultivated land leased by United Fruit. By 1954, he had nationalized some 400,000 acres—a seventh of the arable acreage in Guatemala—when United Fruit struck back with a vengeance.

In the U.S. Senate, Boston's Henry Cabot Lodge (1902–85) (dubbed "the senator from United Fruit") and House Speaker John McCormack (1891–1980), also from Massachusetts, set off a drum roll in Congress demanding action to clean up the mess in Guatemala. Back in 1952 John Foster Dulles (1888–1959)—from the Wall Street firm of Sullivan and Cromwell—became the U.S. secretary of state, and his brother, Allen (1893–1969), head of the CIA, and now they arranged for the United States to meet with several Latin American nations in a Pan-America conference that condemned the growing influence of the communist movement in the Western Hemisphere.

Suddenly Arbenz found himself accused of consorting with communists and subverting the free world, and a CIA-backed coup was underway. Kermit Roosevelt, the United States's man in Teheran, who had helped engineer the fall from power of Iran's prime minister and the return of the shah earlier in the year, declined the Dulles brothers' invitation to participate, stating that the plan reeked of Nazi methodology. At any rate, the U.S. government claimed a Polish ship carrying communist-made arms had docked in Guatemala and then sent U.S. arms to Honduras and Nicaragua for "defensive" purposes. One of those purposes at least was the invasion launched from Honduras on June 18, 1954, of a 2,000-man anticommunist army under Lieutenant Colonel Carlos Castillo Armas (1914–57). Castillo Armas, encountering almost no resistance from Arbenz's army, quickly penetrated deep into Guatemala. Arbenz turned to the United Nations for help, and the Organization of American States began an investigation into the one-sided conflict, but before either could reach any conclusions Arbenz was ousted on June 28, 1954, and fled to Mexico City.

Castillo Armas occupied Guatemala City as head of a military junta that would now run the country. He brought back Ubico's head of security, a man adept at terror and torture. Suspected communists were treated as common criminals, which meant none too gently, and the hunt was on. Castillo Armas just missed capturing a young, contemplative left-winger named Che Guevara (1928–67), who left the country for glory elsewhere (see the CUBAN REVOLUTION). If the Dulles brothers took pause at overthrowing the democratically elected president of a sovereign power and replacing him with a brutal dictator, they never mentioned it. Their clients—the government they served, the old Wall Street law firm at which they once had worked, the United Fruit board of directors for whom they reclaimed Guatemala—were pleased, and they felt covert action had been vindicated. They would use it again.

See also GUATEMALAN WAR.

Further reading: Piero Gleijeses, *Shattered Hope: The Guatemalan Revolution and the United States, 1944–1954* (Princeton, N.J.: Princeton University Press, 1992); Burton Hersh, *The Old Boys: The American Elite and the Origins of the CIA* (New York: Scribner's, 1992); Richard H. Immerman, *The CIA in Guatemala: The Foreign Policy of Intervention* (Austin: University of Texas Press, 1982).

Guatemalan War (1885)

PRINCIPAL COMBATANTS: Guatemala vs. El Salvador (with Nicaraguan, Costa Rican, and Mexican support)
PRINCIPAL THEATER(S): El Salvador border region
DECLARATION: None
MAJOR ISSUES AND OBJECTIVES: Justo Rufino Barrios, dictator of Guatemala, sought to forge a single, unified Central American state, with himself as its president.
OUTCOME: In a single major battle, Barrios was killed and his army defeated.
APPROXIMATE MAXIMUM NUMBER OF MEN UNDER ARMS: Guatemala, 7,000; Salvadoran and allied strength unknown
CASUALTIES: Guatemala, 800 killed; El Salvador, 200 killed
TREATIES: None

A liberal coup in 1871 ended the string of conservative regimes that had ruled Guatemala for years. Miguel García Granados (served 1871–73) assumed the presidency and was succeeded upon his retirement in 1873 by fellow revolutionary Justo Rufino Barrios (1835–85), who had been commander of the army during the Granados presidency. The military man approached the task of government as a dictator, diminishing the power of the church, but improving the Guatemalan economy by developing its coffee industry. Barrios favored a union of Central American states, which he effected in 1876. From a union of states, his ambitions escalated to the creation of a single united Central American republic—with himself as president and commander of the army. Honduras eagerly joined Guatemala in this enterprise, but El Salvador, Nicaragua, and Costa Rica rejected the proposal. Although Mexico was not encompassed by the proposal, its president, Porfirio Díaz (1830–1915), also objected to it, fearing the presence of a large republic on its border. Díaz dispatched troops along the border with Guatemala. Violence broke out when Barrios invaded El Salvador with 7,000 men. The invasion was quickly checked at the Battle of Chalchuapa, April 2, 1885, the only major armed exchange of the Guatemalan War. Eight hundred Guatemalans, including Barrios, fell in this battle, and the Guatemalan plan to create a single Central American republic instantly collapsed.

Further reading: Greg Grandi, *The Blood of Guatemala: A History of Race and Nation* (Durham, N.C.: Duke University Press, 2000); Jim Handy, *Gift of the Devil: A History of Guatemala* (Boston: South End Press, 1990).

Guerre Folle ("Mad War") (1488–1491)

PRINCIPAL COMBATANTS: The first phase of the war was fought by rivals for the regency of French king Charles VIII; the second phase was fought between France and Brittany (with allies Austria, Aragon, and England).
PRINCIPAL THEATER(S): Brittany
DECLARATION: None
MAJOR ISSUES AND OBJECTIVES: The first phase of the war was a dispute over the regency of King Charles VIII of France; the second phase was a dispute over Anne of Brittany's marriage to King Maximilian of Austria.
OUTCOME: Anne of Brittany agreed to marry Charles VIII of France; France guaranteed Breton autonomy.
APPROXIMATE MAXIMUM NUMBER OF MEN UNDER ARMS: Unknown
CASUALTIES: Unknown
TREATIES: The Treaty of Sablé (1488) ended the first phase of the war; the Treaty of Laval (1491) ended the second.

During the minority of King Charles VIII (1470–98) of France, a dispute broke out among rival claimants to the regency. The young king's sister Anne of France (1460–1522) was opposed to the insurgent claims of Duke Louis (1462–1515) of Orléans, who had gained the support of Brittany's duke Francis II (1435–88). Anne of France dispatched troops, who defeated the forces of Louis and Francis II at the Battle of Saint-Aubin-du-Cormier in 1488. A settlement, the Treaty of Sablé, was drawn up, stipulating the evacuation of all foreign troops from Brittany and obliging Anne of Brittany (1477–1514), Duke Francis's heir, to secure royal permission before marrying.

After Francis died later in 1488, Anne—without the required permission—married Austria's King Maximilian (1459–1519) by proxy, thereby menacing Charles with Austrian encirclement. Accordingly, Charles petitioned Anne of Brittany to renounce the marriage in favor of marriage to himself. The petition touched off a conflict in which King Ferdinand II (1452–1516) of Aragon and King Henry VII (1457–1509) of England backed the Austrian monarch. France sent a large force to Rennes, prompting Maximilian and his allies to back down and agree to the Treaty of Laval, whereby Anne of Brittany agreed to marry Charles in exchange for a pledge of Breton autonomy.

Further reading: David Potter, *History of France, 1460–1560* (New York: St. Martin's Press, 1995).

"Güglers" War (1375–1376)

PRINCIPAL COMBATANTS: French-sponsored English and French mercenaries (*Güglers*) vs. Swiss citizens
PRINCIPAL THEATER(S): Aargau, Switzerland
DECLARATION: None
MAJOR ISSUES AND OBJECTIVES: Lord Enguerrand VII de Coucy claimed the Aargau by right of inheritance and therefore waged war against Leopold of Austria for possession of the territory.
OUTCOME: A combination of a scorched-earth policy and the skill and determination of Swiss citizen-soldiers defeated the Güglers.
APPROXIMATE MAXIMUM NUMBER OF MEN UNDER ARMS: 10,000 Güglers against an unknown number of Swiss citizen-soldiers
CASUALTIES: Unknown, but starvation was high among the Güglers.
TREATIES: None

This ugly conflict associated with the HUNDRED YEARS' WAR was named for the dress of the 10,000-man French and English mercenary army hired to prosecute the war. The troops wore cloaks with pointed hoods, called in Swiss-German *Güglers*.

By right of inheritance from his mother, Lord Enguerrand VII de Coucy (1340–97) (later count of Soissons) claimed the Swiss territory of Aargau, which was held by Duke Leopold III (1351–86) of Austria, Enguerrand's cousin. The French-financed Enguerrand's hiring of the Gügler mercenaries, who were augmented by French knights. This force swept through France and Alsace en route to Basel. By November 1375, they had crossed the Jura mountains and were in lower Aargau. At this point, the Güglers had laid waste to a swath of countryside, and they entered Aargau unopposed by Leopold, who refused to fight. Instead, he ordered a scorched-earth policy, pillaging and essentially destroying the region to ensure that the Güglers would have nothing—no booty and no food.

The hungry and enraged Güglers divided their force into three units, believing this to be the most effective way to fight the citizen armies that, in the absence of official aid from Leopold, had formed to oppose them. In fact, the citizen armies proved devastatingly effective against the starving Güglers. At the culminating Battle of Fraubrunnen on December 26, 1376, Bernese troops decisively defeated the Güglers, who began a long, costly retreat back through the Jura Mountains and into France—all the way pursued and harried by Swiss citizen forces.

Further reading: Christopher Allmand, *The Hundred Years' War: England and France at War, c. 1300–1450* (New York: Cambridge University Press, 1988); Anne Curry, *The Hundred Years War*, 2nd ed. (New York: Palgrave Macmillan, 2003); Robin Neillands, *The Hundred Years' War* (New York: Routledge, 2001); Jonathan Sumption, *The Hundred Years' War* (Boston: Faber and Faber, 1999).

Guinea-Bissauan War of Independence (1962–1974)

PRINCIPAL COMBATANTS: Guinean revolutionaries vs. Portugal
PRINCIPAL THEATER(S): Guinea-Bissau
DECLARATION: None; independence proclaimed, 1973
MAJOR ISSUES AND OBJECTIVES: The PAIGC party wanted to lead Guinea-Bissau to independence from Portugal.
OUTCOME: After a prolonged struggle, independence was achieved.
APPROXIMATE MAXIMUM NUMBER OF MEN UNDER ARMS: Revolutionaries, 6,200; Portuguese forces, 55,000
CASUALTIES: Revolutionaries, 2,000 military and 5,000 civilians killed; Portuguese forces, 1,000
TREATIES: Portuguese recognition of the Republic of Guinea-Bissau, 1974

Guinea-Bissau was an overseas province of Portugal and known as Portuguese Guinea. In 1956, the African Party for the Independence of Guinea and Cape Verde (PAIGC), founded by Amilcar Cabral (1924–73), attempted to negotiate independence for Guinea-Bissau and the Cape Verde Islands, which were also Portuguese possessions. When talks failed, the PAIGC worked vigorously at the grass roots to acquire support for a war of independence throughout the Guinean villages on the mainland of West Africa. By the end of 1962, guerrilla units had formed and were increasingly effective in their raids on Portuguese army outposts and police stations. Within months, many areas had been taken over by the guerrillas and completely cleared of Portuguese. The Portuguese garrisons were confined to the cities and their own bases. They dared not venture into the countryside. The Portuguese government sought to reclaim the country by attacking, mainly from the air, guerrilla forest bases. The 27,000 Portuguese garrison troops were substantially reinforced, more than doubled to 55,000.

During the Portuguese offensive, the guerrilla units also suffered from internal dissension, as tribal affiliations conflicted with political organization. A pervasive belief in witchcraft also undermined unified effort. At this point, Cabral realized that the war for independence in Guinea-Bissau had to be prosecuted in a twofold manner. It was a struggle against Portuguese imperialism but also against outmoded tribalism and superstition, which were incompatible with united resistance to colonial rule. Cabral worked vigorously through his commanders to gain control of the situation, and, by the early 1970s, he had made significant progress. He did not aim to defeat the Portuguese militarily, but to wear down the will of the Portuguese government to continue the struggle. By 1973, most of Portuguese Guinea was solidly under Cabral's control and the PAIGC formally proclaimed the independence of the Republic of Guinea-Bissau.

Portugal refused to recognize the independence of its colony, and Amilcar Cabral was assassinated, apparently by PAIGC members who had been compromised by Portuguese agents. But the assassination did nothing to halt the independence movement, and a 1974 military coup in Portugal installed a new government willing to recognize the republic. Luis de Almeida Cabral (b. 1931), brother of the slain Amilcar Cabral, was elected president. The following year, Cape Verde Islands also achieved independence.

Further reading: Carlos Lopes, *Guinea-Bissau: From Liberation Struggle to Independent Statehood* (Denver: Westview, 1987).

Gulf War *See* PERSIAN GULF WAR (1990–1991).

Gupta Dynasty, Conquests of the (320–467)

PRINCIPAL COMBATANTS: The Guptas and the Kushans (and others); the Guptas and the White Huns
PRINCIPAL THEATER(S): Northern India
DECLARATION: None
MAJOR ISSUES AND OBJECTIVES: The Guptas sought expansion and unification.
OUTCOME: The Gupta kingdom reached its height and greatest extent under Chandragupta II in the early 400s. With his death, repeated invasion rapidly reduced the kingdom, which effectively ceased to exist about 467.
APPROXIMATE MAXIMUM NUMBER OF MEN UNDER ARMS: Extremely variable
CASUALTIES: Unknown
TREATIES: No surviving documents

Chandragupta I (r. c. 320–c. 330) came to the throne of the Magadha kingdom through marriage. Once established, he took advantage of the weakness of the Kushan-held west by expanding his kingdom as far as Allahabad. When he assumed the throne on the death of his father, Samudragupta (335–80) pushed the boundaries of the kingdom eastward, to Assam, then extended it west, beyond Allahabad, to the Punjab borderlands. The entire Deccan paid him homage.

Samudragupta began a war with the Shakas in their capital at Ujjain, and his son, Chandragupta II (380–413), prosecuted the war to its conclusion, conquering all of the

Shaka kingdom, which covered the territory of modern Bombay state. At this point, the Gupta dominated all of northern India, save for the extreme northwestern corner. This proved to be the dynasty's Achilles' heel, for it admitted passage to invaders. By the fifth century, White Hun invasions had ravaged and sapped the Gupta kingdom, so that by about 467 it had been reduced to no more than a portion of Bengal. The dynasty ended completely by 499.

The Guptas had brought India to its classical height. Following the barbarian invasions, the former Gupta realm fragmented into a mass of small states, which devoted themselves to warring against one another.

Further reading: Ashvini Agrawal, *Rise and Fall of the Imperial Guptas* (Delhi: Motilal Banarsidass, 1989); Sachindra Kumar Maity, *The Imperial Guptas and Their Times* (New Delhi: Munshiram Manoharlal Publishers Pvt. Ltd., 1963); R. C. Majumdar, *Ancient India* (Delhi: Motilal Banasidass, 1982); Francis Watson, *A Concise History of India* (London: Thames and Hudson, 1981).

Gurkha War (1814–1816)

PRINCIPAL COMBATANTS: Britain (British East India Company) vs. the Gurkhas
PRINCIPAL THEATER(S): Nepal (near the Indian border)
DECLARATION: None
MAJOR ISSUES AND OBJECTIVES: The East India Company and the Gurkhas disputed possession of a region bordering Nepal and India.
OUTCOME: The disputed territory came under East India Company control, and Nepal and the Gurkhas became British allies.
APPROXIMATE MAXIMUM NUMBER OF MEN UNDER ARMS: British East India Company, 40,000; Gurkhas, 12,000
CASUALTIES: British forces, 3,000 killed or wounded; Gurkhas, 1,500 killed or wounded
TREATIES: Treaty of Sagauli, November 28, 1815

The Gurkhas, a tribe of the western Himalayas, conquered the Nepal valley by 1768. From this territory, they gradually built up a powerful realm with formidable military strength. Conflict between the Gurkhas and the English began in 1801, when the East India Company occupied the Gorakpur district, which bordered Gurkha country. The Gurkhas took Bhutwal, which was subsequently retaken by the East India Company. The dispute over Bhutwal simmered until 1814, when the British government warned the Raja of Nepal that troops would be dispatched to take possession of Bhutwal once and for all. In response, the Gurkhas evacuated—only to return once the British troops had been withdrawn during the rainy season. The territory was patrolled by a small police force, some of whom the Gurkhas killed. In response, the governor-general of British India, Warren, Lord Hastings (1732–1818), sent a letter to the raja of Nepal, accusing him of deliberately making war on the British government and warning him that troops would be sent into Nepal as soon as the cold weather set in.

When it began, the war went badly for the British. Three of the first four expeditions sent were defeated. The worst disaster came when 3,500 troops attempted to storm the small fort of Kalanga, a few miles north of Debra Dun. The first British attack was beaten back, and then the commanding general of the force was killed while rallying his men for a second attack. The British kept up the pressure for weeks, finally making a breach in the Gurkha line. However, the British were so thoroughly intimidated that, on November 27, 1814, they refused to advance on the fort, even though it was held by only 600 men. Instead of charging the fort, the British bombarded it, finally forcing the Gurkhas to abandon it three days later. Even after achieving this small victory, the intimidated British broke and ran under Gurkha attack at the end of the year.

Two additional expeditions against the eastern end of the Gurkha territory bogged down, and a major British baggage train was attacked and pillaged. Reinforcements were called for, bringing the number of troops massed against the Gurkhas to about 13,000. Even with these numbers, reports of the Gurkhas' fierce fighting capabilities discouraged any offensive action. Yet the fact was that the Gurkhas had neither the manpower nor the resources to withstand the full military might of the British East India Company for any length of time. All that was required was an injection of nerve and the will to mount a concerted campaign.

By early 1815, the East India Company had mustered almost 40,000 troops against perhaps 12,000 Gurkhas, and in the spring the now overwhelmingly superior British forces made headway. By April 1815, the main Gurkha military leader, Amar Singh (fl. 1815), was blockaded on a single mountain ridge. His troops were beginning to talk of surrender. While this was going on, an irregular force of British and Indian troops penetrated deep into Gurkha territory. On April 28, 1815, the Gurkhas hoisted a flag of truce and surrendered, agreeing to evacuate Almora and the whole province of Jumaon and to withdraw all their troops to the east of the Kali River. With this capitulation, Amar Singh's troops began to desert and go over to the British. On May 10, Amar Singh surrendered. All of the disputed territory was now under British hands. Negotiations between the East India Company and the Gurkhas dragged on until November 1815, when the Treaty of Sagauli was signed—however, the major Nepalese leader Nepal Durbar (fl. 1815) refused to ratify it.

Fighting was resumed early in 1816. A British force of 20,000 advanced on Khatmandu and, by strenuous and stealthy maneuvering, surprised the Gurkhas with an attack from behind. The Gurkhas, panic stricken, withdrew without giving battle. A few days later, in March, a representative of Nepal Durbar offered to ratify the 1815 treaty. A lasting peace was made. Nepal remained an independent kingdom, allied to the British, but never a vassal to them, and many Gurkhas voluntarily joined the British colonial military service, in which they became elite troops of great renown and tradition.

Further reading: David Bolt, *Gurkhas* (New York: White Lion Publishers, 1975); Byron Farwell, *The Gurkhas* (New York: Norton, 1990); Harold James and Denis Sheil-Small, *The Gurkhas* (Harrisburg, Pa.: Stackpole Books, 1966).

Guyanan Rebellion (1969)

PRINCIPAL COMBATANTS: Rebel guerrillas vs. Guyanan police and military forces
PRINCIPAL THEATER(S): Southwestern Guyana, on the Brazilian border
DECLARATION: None
MAJOR ISSUES AND OBJECTIVES: The rebels were apparently sponsored by American owners of ranches in southwestern Guyana who wanted to establish an independent state in which they could operate without restrictions of any kind.
OUTCOME: The rebellion was quickly crushed.
APPROXIMATE MAXIMUM NUMBER OF MEN UNDER ARMS: Unknown
CASUALTIES: A few fatalities
TREATIES: None

This brief conflict began on January 2, 1969, when guerrillas from Brazil invaded Guyana and took the border towns of Lethem and Annai. The Guyanan army and government police officers were quickly deployed to the region and drove the guerrillas back across the border. Casualties on both sides were light in this ultimately abortive rebellion, which was apparently backed by American nationals who owned extensive cattle ranches in the border region and wanted to create a separate state to allow them to operate without restriction or taxation.

Further reading: Chaitram Singh, *Guyana: Politics in a Plantation Society* (Westport, Conn.: Greenwood Publishing Group, 1988).

H

Haitian Civil War (1805–1820)

PRINCIPAL COMBATANTS: Southern Haiti ("jaunes") vs. northern Haiti ("noirs") (with involvement of French and Spanish colonists in Santo Domingo)
PRINCIPAL THEATER(S): Haiti and Santo Domingo (modern Dominican Republic)
DECLARATION: None
MAJOR ISSUES AND OBJECTIVES: Henry Christophe (northern leader) vied with Alexandre Pétion (leader in the south) for control of Haiti.
OUTCOME: Jean-Pierre Boyer, successor to Pétion, prevailed, unifying all Haiti under his presidency after the suicide of Christophe.
APPROXIMATE MAXIMUM NUMBER OF MEN UNDER ARMS: Northerners (noirs), 30,000; Southerners (jaunes), 20,000
CASUALTIES: Unknown, but widespread among combatants and noncombatants alike.
TREATIES: None

Jean-Jacques Dessalines (1758–1806), who had crowned himself Emperor Jacques I of Haiti after the HAITIAN-FRENCH WAR of 1801–04, was a brutal and aggressive dictator. During February–March 1805, he led 30,000 Haitians in an invasion of neighboring Santo Domingo. When a French fleet showed itself off Santo Domingo, Dessalines retreated, ravaging the countryside along the way back to the Haitian frontier.

Dessalines's depredations incited the mulattoes (jaunes) of the south to rebellion, and when Dessalines led an expedition to crush the uprising, he was killed on October 17, 1806. Henry Christophe (1767–1820) succeeded him, but by this time Haiti had fractured into a mostly black (noir) north (soon to become the Kingdom of Haiti) and predominantly jaune south. In 1807, when Henry Christophe declared himself king, the forces loyal to him fought those of the Republic of Haiti under President Alexandre Pétion (1770–1818) sporadically over the next 13 years.

Christophe launched a major offensive in mid-1812, but it petered out indecisively. His forces continually harassed the republic from February 1807 to May 1819, successfully defeating a series of punitive expeditions. However, in 1819, Jean-Pierre Boyer (1776–1850) dispatched six regiments into the mountainous region of the Grand' Anse (southern panhandle) to find the noir rebel leader known only as Goman (d. 1819). When Goman was cornered, he committed suicide by leaping off a cliff.

With the death of Goman, the last of the major organized noir resistance crumbled. In 1820, Henry Christophe, ill and despondent, killed himself, leaving Boyer to unify the nation.

See also HAITIAN RECONQUEST OF SANTO DOMINGO; HAITIAN REVOLT (1858–1859); HAITIAN REVOLT (1915); HAITIAN REVOLT (1918–1920); TOUSSAINT LOUVERTURE, REVOLT OF.

Further reading: Alex Dupuy, *Haiti in the World Economy: Class, Race, and Underdevelopment since 1700* (Boulder, Colo.: Westview Press, 1997); Rayford W. Logan, *Haiti and the Dominican Republic* (New York: Oxford University Press, 1968); David Nicholls, *From Dessalines to Duvalier: Race, Color, and National Independence in Haiti,* rev. ed. (New Brunswick, N.J.: Rutgers University Press, 1995); Médéric-Louis-Elie Moreau de Saint-Méry, *A Civilization That Perished: The Last Years of White Colonial Rule in Haiti,* ed. Ivor D. Spencer, 2 vols. (Lanham, Md.: University Press of America, 1985).

Haitian-French War (1801–1804)

PRINCIPAL COMBATANTS: French vs. Haitian independence fighters
PRINCIPAL THEATER(S): Hispaniola, especially modern Haiti
DECLARATION: None
MAJOR ISSUES AND OBJECTIVES: The French sought to wrest Hispaniola from the island's governor-general, François-Dominique-Toussaint Louverture.
OUTCOME: French forces withdrew, mainly because of casualties caused by tropical disease.
APPROXIMATE MAXIMUM NUMBER OF MEN UNDER ARMS: French, 25,000; Haitian, variable—but always fewer than the French
CASUALTIES: Battle deaths unknown; the French succumbed to disease at a high rate. At least 5,000 French settlers were massacred during 1805.
TREATIES: None

As a result of the REVOLT OF TOUSSAINT LOUVERTURE, Toussaint Louverture (c. 1743–1803) became governor-general of Hispaniola and put the island's government under a new constitution. At this time, Napoleon Bonaparte (1769–1821) dispatched his brother-in-law, Charles Victor Leclerc (1772–1802), at the head of 25,000 French troops to wrest control of Hispaniola from Toussaint Louverture and reestablish slavery. The French force landed at Cap-Français (Cap-Haïtien, Haiti) on February 5, 1802, only to find that retreating black forces under Henry Christophe (1767–1820) (*see* HAITIAN CIVIL WAR) had put the port city to the torch. This was a prelude to worse. As they advanced inland, the French troops were attacked by guerrillas, who avoided open battle, but nevertheless took a heavy toll on the French. An even more destructive enemy proved to be yellow fever, which was endemic to the island. The French forces dwindled rapidly.

Despite all they suffered, the French scored a victory against a force of some 1,200 troops led by Jean-Jacques Dessalines (1758–1806) at the Battle of Crête-à-Pierrot. This apparently persuaded both Dessalines and Christophe to turn coat and defect to the French. With his leading commanders having gone to the other side, Toussaint Louverture accepted a French offer of amnesty and laid down his arms. He was summarily taken prisoner and sent back, in chains, to France. He died in a French prison about a year later. In the meantime Dessalines and Christophe cooperated with the French to put down those black and mulatto guerrillas who persisted in fighting, but, when they discovered Napoleon's intention to return slavery to the island, they deserted the French fold and joined the guerrillas. In March 1805, Dessalines ordered the massacre of every *blanc*—white person—remaining in Haiti. Beginning in the town of Jérémie, in southwest Haiti, Dessalines slaughtered some 1,400 white French men, women, and children. He progressed east and executed 800 French whites in Port-au-Prince, then marched north to Le Cap, where, during late April, 2,000 whites were killed. Historians estimate that no fewer than 5,000 whites were massacred on Haiti at the behest of Dessalines, who wanted to ensure that no European army would ever dare invade again.

In the end, it was not only the desertion of Dessalines and Christophe, the ongoing resistance of guerrillas, and the massacre of 1805 that defeated the French army on Hispaniola. Another vanquisher was tropical disease, primarily yellow fever. Napoleon decided to cut his losses and withdraw forces from the Caribbean. Indeed, he decided to abandon the New World altogether and, in 1804, through his minister, Charles Maurice de Talleyrand-Périgord (1754–1838), negotiated the sale to the fledgling United States of its only other major piece of American real estate: the Louisiana territory.

See also HAITIAN RECONQUEST OF SANTO DOMINGO; HAITIAN REVOLT (1858–1859); HAITIAN REVOLT (1915); HAITIAN REVOLT (1918–1920).

Further reading: Alex Dupuy, *Haiti in the World Economy: Class, Race, and Underdevelopment since 1700* (Boulder, Colo.: Westview Press, 1997); Rayford W. Logan, *Haiti and the Dominican Republic* (New York: Oxford University Press, 1968); David Nicholls, *From Dessalines to Duvalier: Race, Color, and National Independence in Haiti*, rev. ed. (New Brunswick, N.J.: Rutgers University Press, 1995); Médéric-Louis-Elie Moreau de Saint-Méry, *A Civilization That Perished: The Last Years of White Colonial Rule in Haiti*, ed. Ivor D. Spencer, 2 vols. (Lanham, Md.: University Press of America, 1985).

Haitian Reconquest of Santo Domingo (1822)

PRINCIPAL COMBATANTS: Haiti vs. Spain
PRINCIPAL THEATER(S): Santo Domingo (Dominican Republic)
DECLARATION: Santo Domingan declaration of independence, November 30, 1821
MAJOR ISSUES AND OBJECTIVES: Haiti chose to interpret Santo Domingo's declaration of independence from Spain as submission to the government of Haiti and responded by driving the Spanish out of Santo Domingo and annexing the country.
OUTCOME: Haiti and Santo Domingo were united under the presidency of Jean-Pierre Boyer.
APPROXIMATE MAXIMUM NUMBER OF MEN UNDER ARMS: Unknown
CASUALTIES: Unknown
TREATIES: None

Santo Domingo (Dominican Republic) had been a Spanish colony when it was ceded to France and then conquered by the Haitians in 1820 (*see* HAITIAN CIVIL WAR [1805–1820]). Through this, many Santo Domingans remained loyal to Spain until they began to suffer under the repressive rule of the ultraconservative Spanish monarch Ferdinand VII (1784–1833). On November 30, 1821, Santo Domingo declared itself independent from Spain and called itself the Dominican Republic. The people sent a representative to Simon Bolívar (1783–1830), the "Great Liberator" of South America, and asked for union with Great Colombia. Before this envoy reached Bolívar, however, Jean-Pierre Boyer (1776–1850) Haiti's president, declared that Santo Domingo had not declared independence but, in breaking with Spain, had submitted to the government of Haiti. He dispatched an army into Santo Domingo, drove out the Spanish, and asserted his control of the entire island of Hispaniola—Haiti and Santo Domingo. Hait occupied so-called Spanish Haiti until 1844, when the Dominicans rejected Haitian hegemony and again declared their own sovereignty.

See also HAITIAN REVOLT (1915); HAITIAN REVOLT (1918–1920).

Further reading: Alex Dupuy, *Haiti in the World Economy: Class, Race, and Underdevelopment since 1700* (Boulder, Colo.: Westview Press, 1997); Rayford W. Logan, *Haiti and the Dominican Republic* (New York: Oxford University Press, 1968); David Nicholls, *From Dessalines to Duvalier: Race, Color, and National Independence in Haiti*, rev. ed. (New Brunswick, N.J.: Rutgers University Press, 1995).

Haitian Revolt (1858–1859)

PRINCIPAL COMBATANTS: Forces of self-proclaimed Haitian emperor Faustin I vs. mulatto rebels
PRINCIPAL THEATER(S): Haiti
DECLARATION: None
MAJOR ISSUES AND OBJECTIVES: The mulattoes, having been betrayed by Faustin I, wanted to overthrow his repressive and corrupt regime.
OUTCOME: Faustin was overthrown in a brief but bloody revolt, his repressive regime replaced by anarchy.
APPROXIMATE MAXIMUM NUMBER OF MEN UNDER ARMS: Unknown
CASUALTIES: Unknown
TREATIES: None

Jean-Pierre Boyer (1776–1850), who became president of Haiti as a result of the HAITIAN CIVIL WAR, ruled the nation as a fiefdom, his long administration steeped in corruption and maintained by terror and coercion. In 1843, his regime was overthrown by a coup, and in 1847, after a period of great instability, Faustin Élie Soulouque (c. 1785–1867), a former slave, assumed the presidency,

with the backing of mulatto leaders, who believed he would make a compliant puppet. In 1849, Soulouque turned on his backers and created around himself a cult of personality. Emboldened, he crowned himself Emperor Faustin I, instituting a regime even more brutally oppressive and corrupt than that of Boyer. While his people languished in poverty, Faustin assembled a court as lavish as many in Europe. He sought to extend his rule into the Dominican Republic, but was repeatedly defeated. In the meantime, opposition to him grew within Haiti, even as the United States, France, and Great Britain applied diplomatic and economic pressure to force his resignation. At last, Faustin I was overthrown in a revolt led by the mulattoes originally allied with him.

Although the revolt was violent, Faustin himself escaped into exile. One of the emperor's former generals, Nicholas Fabre Geffrard (1806–79), took up the reins of government, declaring a republic and immediately achieving election as president. He made valiant attempts to institute badly needed reforms, but was repeatedly foiled by reactionaries, who finally succeeded in toppling his government in 1867, sending him into exile and returning the nation to violent chaos.

See also HAITIAN-FRENCH WAR (1801–1804); HAITIAN REVOLT (1915); HAITIAN REVOLT (1918–1920).

Further reading: Alex Dupuy, *Haiti in the World Economy: Class, Race, and Underdevelopment since 1700* (Boulder, Colo.: Westview Press, 1997); Rayford W. Logan, *Haiti and the Dominican Republic* (New York: Oxford University Press, 1968); David Nicholls, *From Dessalines to Duvalier: Race, Color, and National Independence in Haiti*, rev. ed. (New Brunswick, N.J.: Rutgers University Press, 1995).

Haitian Revolt (1915)

PRINCIPAL COMBATANTS: U.S. Marines vs. Haitian antigovernment mobs ("Cacos")
PRINCIPAL THEATER(S): Haiti
DECLARATION: None
MAJOR ISSUES AND OBJECTIVES: The United States sought to protect U.S. interests in Haiti by establishing a protectorate over it.
OUTCOME: A U.S. protectorate was established.
APPROXIMATE MAXIMUM NUMBER OF MEN UNDER ARMS: 2,000 U.S. Marines; Caco numbers unknown
CASUALTIES: Relatively light
TREATIES: Treaty of September 16, 1915, establishing a U.S. protectorate

Throughout the 19th century, Haiti had suffered great instability under a series of corrupt and repressive regimes. Vilbrun Guillaume Sam (d. 1915) led a revolt against the weak, chronically unstable government in 1915, assuming the title of president, briefly, until his assassination at the hands of a mob on July 28, 1915. In the wake of Sam's death, Haiti effectively lacked all government and was in a state of violent anarchy. President Woodrow Wilson (1856–1924), seeking to protect U.S. interests in the island nation, dispatched two companies of U.S. Marines in March 1915 to restore order and supervise election of a new president.

The first marine contingent advanced on Port-au-Prince, the Haitian capital, and restored order there. Reinforcements were called, and by late August 1915, approximately 2,000 marines were in country. The marines engaged in a number of small but intense battles, including fierce hand-to-hand combat in an abandoned French fort atop a 4,000-foot mountain, against insurgents known as the Cacos.

Once the Cacos had been suppressed, the Wilson administration backed the new government of President Philippe Sudre Dartiguenave (1863–1926), who signed a treaty agreeing to place Haiti under a U.S. protectorate. The marines remained in the country through 1934, supervising a U.S.-sponsored Haitian police corps. Although the marine presence and the protectorate status were blatant acts of American imperialism, they provided undeniable benefits to the war-weary and poverty-plagued nation. Throughout Haiti, a small contingent of marines supervised the building of an infrastructure of public works, roads, and utilities, and were reasonably effective at providing the people with physical protection—albeit at the expense of their sovereignty.

See also HAITIAN CIVIL WAR; HAITIAN RECONQUEST OF SANTO DOMINGO; HAITIAN REVOLT (1858–1859); HAITIAN REVOLT (1918–1920).

Further reading: Alex Dupuy, *Haiti in the World Economy: Class, Race, and Underdevelopment since 1700* (Boulder, Colo.: Westview Press, 1997); Rayford W. Logan, *Haiti and the Dominican Republic* (New York: Oxford University Press, 1968); David Nicholls, *From Dessalines to Duvalier: Race, Color, and National Independence in Haiti*, rev. ed. (New Brunswick, N.J.: Rutgers University Press, 1995).

Haitian Revolt (1918–1920)

PRINCIPAL COMBATANTS: Haitian anti-U.S. rebels (including "Cacos") vs. U.S. Marines and Haitian gendarmerie
PRINCIPAL THEATER(S): Haiti, principally Port-au-Prince
DECLARATION: None
MAJOR ISSUES AND OBJECTIVES: The rebels wanted to end the U.S. protectorate of Haiti.
OUTCOME: The rebellion, though briefly fierce, was quickly crushed.

APPROXIMATE MAXIMUM NUMBER OF MEN UNDER ARMS: Rebels, 20,000–40,000; U.S. Marines, 1,500+; Haitian gendarmerie, 2,700
CASUALTIES: Cacos, 2,004 killed; Marines, 28 killed; gendarmerie, 70 killed
TREATIES: None

Since 1915, Haiti had been a protectorate of the United States, was occupied by a small force of U.S. Marines, and was policed by a U.S.-backed Haitian gendarmerie. In 1918, the marines supervised a plebiscite by which a new constitution was overwhelmingly adopted (the vote was suspect), even while the U.S. protectorate remained in effect. No new elections followed the adoption of the constitution, and the country continued to be governed by the president the United States had supported, Philippe Sudre Dartiguenave (1863–1926), and the government itself staffed by American bureaucrats. This situation created a considerable degree of resentment among many Haitians. Worse, the Haitian police began enforcing a *corvée,* or labor draft, inducting rural Haitians into a labor force for public works. The enforcement of the *corvée* triggered a revolt against the U.S. presence.

Rebel forces were large, numbering between 20,000 and 40,000, but were poorly organized and even more poorly equipped. They were driven, however, by an intense belief in the native religion of Haiti, Vodun (Voodoo), and their leaders supplied them with various powders and potions said to confer invulnerability upon them. Thus they attacked boldly and fiercely throughout the countryside, finally focusing on the capital city of Port-au-Prince. Marines and the Haitian gendarmerie, although outnumbered, readily defeated the poorly armed rebels.

The most serious threat came from about 5,000 rugged northern mountaineers known as the Cacos. They became very active in March 1919, and during the summer of that year two marines and a Haitian constable penetrated the camp of Caco leader Charlemagne Péralte (1886–1919), whom they assassinated. When a new Caco leader, Benoît Batraville (d. 1920), emerged, the First Marine Brigade, reinforced by the Eighth Marines, conducted a systematic campaign against the Cacos. By May 19, 1920, when a marine patrol killed Batraville, completely suppressing the rebellion, 2,004 Cacos had died, the marines had sustained 28 battle deaths, and 70 Haitian gendarmes were also killed.

The uprising caused the American protectorate, slated to last 10 years, from 1915 to 1925, to be extended to 1934.

See also HAITIAN CIVIL WAR; HAITIAN RECONQUEST OF SANTO DOMINGO; HAITIAN REVOLT (1858–1859); HAITIAN REVOLT (1915).

Further reading: Alex Dupuy, *Haiti in the World Economy: Class, Race, and Underdevelopment since 1700* (Boulder, Colo.: Westview Press, 1997); Rayford W. Logan, *Haiti and the Dominican Republic* (New York: Oxford University Press, 1968); David Nicholls, *From Dessalines to Duvalier: Race, Color, and National Independence in Haiti,* rev. ed. (New Brunswick, N.J.: Rutgers University Press, 1995).

Hamdanid Invasion of Anatolia

See BYZANTINE-MUSLIM WAR (960–976).

Hammurabi's Unification of Mesopotamia

(1787–1750 B.C.E.)

PRINCIPAL COMBATANTS: Babylon vs. surrounding kingdoms
PRINCIPAL THEATER(S): Mesopotamia
DECLARATION: None
MAJOR ISSUES AND OBJECTIVES: Imperial expansion and conquest
OUTCOME: Babylon expanded, Hammurabi consolidated his hold on a unified Mesopotamian empire, but also stretched his borders thin and rendered them vulnerable.
APPROXIMATE MAXIMUM NUMBER OF MEN UNDER ARMS: Unknown
CASUALTIES: Unknown
TREATIES: No documents survive

In Babylon, Hammurabi (d. 1750 B.C.E.) inherited a powerful kingdom with a formidable military. He resolved to use his armies to gain control of the Euphrates River, which would give him control of vast tracts of arable lands, since agriculture in the region was wholly dependent on irrigation. Of course, his strategy brought Babylon into conflict with Larsa, a kingdom downstream. In 1787 B.C.E., Hammurabi conquered the Larsan cities of Uruk (Erech) and Isin, reengaged Larsan forces again the following year, then, in 1784, abruptly shifted the direction of operations to the north and east. This was followed by nearly two decades of peace—but not the cessation of military activity. Hammurabi devoted these years to thoroughly fortifying key cities on his northern borders, especially during 1776–68.

Poised for war, Hammurabi spent the last 14 years of his reign fighting continual battles. In 1764, he broke up a coalition among Ashur, Eshnunna, and Elam, the chief powers east of the Tigris River. The coalition threatened to bar Babylon's access to the metal-producing areas of Iran. The next year, Hammurabi attacked Rim-Sin of Larsa, apparently using a spectacular military engineering tactic. Hammurabi seems to have dammed a main watercourse, then he either, at a critical moment, caused the waters to be suddenly released, creating a catastrophic flood, or simply withheld the water from Larsa, forcing the people into submission when Hammurabi laid siege to the state.

In 1762, Hammurabi turned to the east and expanded his borders, then, the following year, he attacked his ally, Zimrilim (c. 1800–1750 B.C.E.), king of Mari. Likely, this treachery against an ally of long standing was motivated by a claim on precious water, although it is also possible that Hammurabi simply wanted to gain the advantage of acquiring Mari's strategically superb location at what was the crossroads of the Middle East's overland trade.

In 1759 B.C.E., Hammurabi led his armies east once again, where he fought against Eshnunna, destroying that kingdom by means of another damming operation. Although victory was achieved, the expansion of the Babylonian kingdom through Eshunna removed a valuable buffer zone between Hammurabi's realm and the more aggressive people of the East. This necessitated a new program of fortification building to strengthen the kingdom's defenses. Hammurabi undertook this great work during his own physical decline. He died about 1750 B.C.E. having effectively expanded Babylon while simultaneously consolidating his power over it, yet, in extending his borders, he rendered the kingdom vulnerable to frontier incursions and, ultimately, full-scale invasion.

Further reading: A. Leo Oppenheim, *Ancient Mesopotamia: Portrait of a Dead Civilization* (Chicago: University of Chicago Press, 1986).

Hancock's Campaign   (1867)

PRINCIPAL COMBATANTS: United States vs. Plains Indians
PRINCIPAL THEATER(S): Kansas and Nebraska
DECLARATION: None
MAJOR ISSUES AND OBJECTIVES: Even as a government peace commission worked to end hostilities with Red Cloud's Sioux and their Cheyenne allies in the Dakotas, a frustrated U.S. Army set out to "punish" the bellicose tribes of the central and southern Great Plains.
OUTCOME: General Hancock's troops chased Indians throughout the area without ever engaging them in decisive battle, while the Indians used the pursuit as an excuse to terrorize Kansas; the army—forced on the defensive—withdrew in utter failure.
APPROXIMATE MAXIMUM NUMBER OF MEN UNDER ARMS: United States—4,000 troops; Plains Indians—unknown
CASUALTIES: U.S. troops, under 100 killed and wounded; Indians, 100+ killed or wounded
TREATIES: Treaty of Medicine Lodge Creek, Kansas, 1867

In the wake of the FETTERMAN MASSACRE on December 21, 1866 (*see* BOZEMAN TRAIL, WAR FOR THE), General William Tecumseh Sherman (1820–91), newly in command of the Division of the Missouri (which encompassed the Great Plains and included the U.S. Army's departments of the Missouri, Platte, Dakota, and Arkansas) telegraphed his commander Ulysses S. Grant (1822–85), who had just been promoted to the recently established rank of general of the armies of the United States: "We must act with vindictive earnestness against the Sioux, even to their extermination, men, women, and children."

Much of nonmilitary Washington, however, continued to favor conciliation. The government was then in the middle of a bureaucratic struggle over who would handle Indian affairs, the civil servants of the Indian Bureau or the officers of the U.S. military, a tussle that ultimately would result in Grant's "Peace Policy," when the Civil War hero became president two years later. President Grant would surprise and dismay many in the army by entering the lists on the side of the civilian "liberals," announcing a policy of what he called "conquest by kindness," under which Native American tribes were no longer to be considered sovereign nations, but wards of the state under civilian—not military—supervision; the Indians would be concentrated on reservations where they would be "civilized," that is, educated, Christianized, and taught to become self-supporting farmers.

Meanwhile, however, the army loudly wrangled with the Indian Bureau, which answered not to the War Department but to the Department of the Interior, over policy throughout 1866–67, particularly over the issue of arms sales. The army, understandably, protested against arming hostile Indians. The Indian Bureau argued that the Indians needed weapons in order to hunt; if they could not hunt, they could not feed themselves, and if they could not feed themselves, they would make war. The War Department sponsored a bill, introduced before the Senate on February 9, 1867, to transfer full authority over the Indians from the Department of the Interior to the Department of War. The bill came up against the report of a Senate investigative committee chaired by Wisconsin senator James R. Doolittle (1815–97), which frankly assessed the root causes of Indian-white warfare and recommended against the transfer of the Indian Bureau to the War Department, detailing military blunders and outrages (with a stress on the SAND CREEK MASSACRE) in the West. In light of the report, the War Department's bid for transfer of the Indian Bureau carried the House of Representatives but failed in the Senate, and another peace commission was sent into the field. Sherman had planned to send Colonel John Gibbon (1827–96) with a force of 2,000 cavalry and infantry to "punish" the Sioux and Cheyenne of the Powder River country; this campaign would have to be tabled until the peace commission had failed—as Sherman was certain it would.

The peace commission was not, however, calling on the tribes of the central and southern Plains—the Southern Cheyenne, the Southern Arapaho, Kiowa, and Oglala and Southern Brulé Sioux—and Sherman did not have to wait to campaign against these groups. He dispatched General Winfield Scott Hancock (1824–86)—an impressive Civil War commander, though new to Indian fighting—to do the job.

The Indians of this region at this time were neither unambiguously hostile nor friendly. They tended to be fragmented, the older leaders favoring peace and accommodation, the younger warriors restless and spoiling for a fight. Menacing words and minor raiding activity were common, and Sherman ordered the hostility checked. On April 7, 1867, Hancock turned out 1,400 troopers of the Seventh Cavalry, the 37th Infantry, and the Fourth Artillery at Fort Larned, Kansas. He summoned a body of Cheyenne chiefs to the fort for a conference and to see for themselves the might of the U.S. Army. Bad weather delayed the meeting and resulted in a small turnout—two chiefs and 12 warriors—so Hancock decided to march a column of soldiers the next day to a combined Cheyenne and Sioux village on the Pawnee fork of the Arkansas River in order to deliver his stern message to more chiefs. Doubtless recalling the treachery of Sand Creek, the women and children of the village scattered for the hills as they saw the soldiers approaching. Although Hancock instructed his principal field officer, Lieutenant Colonel George Armstrong Custer (1839–76), commanding the Seventh Cavalry, to surround the village to prevent the men from escaping as well, by morning the lodges were all deserted. Hancock concluded that war had commenced. Responding to Custer's report that the Indians had given him the slip and burned a station on the Smoky Hill route, Hancock torched the Indian village, then marched to Fort Larned, where his campaign would come to an end in May.

In the meantime, he had sent Custer's cavalry out to chase Indians. At 25, Custer had attained the brevet rank of major general in the Civil War, earning a reputation as a brilliant, if erratic and egotistical, cavalry commander. The flamboyant, yellow-haired "boy general" was, like many other officers, reduced in rank at the conclusion of the war. He was determined to recover his former glory by fighting Indians and fighting them unrelentingly. Acting on Hancock's orders, he led his Seventh Cavalry in hot pursuit of the fleeing Cheyenne and Sioux. When Custer arrived at Fort Hays, Kansas, however, his cavalry was immobilized because forage—which was to have been stored there for him—had not arrived. While Custer waited, the Indians attacked, wreaking havoc on the local Kansas countryside. Ultimately Custer took to the field under orders from General Sherman.

From April through July, he and his men followed the chase through Kansas and Nebraska, always in vain, as the Indians terrorized the region. Though he engaged Indians several times, he was never able to fight a decisive battle, and Custer and the Seventh Cavalry, exhausted, had at last to withdraw. What had begun as an offensive campaign became a series of desperate and futile attempts at defense—desperate and futile because 4,000 officers and men broadcast over 1,500 miles of major trails could hardly be expected to patrol the region effectively.

In July, Custer went to Fort Riley to see his wife and obtain supplies and was subsequently court-martialed for absenting himself from his command without leave and for abusing men and animals. He was sentenced to suspension from rank and pay for one year. Hancock's campaign and Custer's court-martial played right into the hands of the Indian Bureau. An Indian agent with Hancock, E. W. Wyncoop (1836–91), severely criticized Hancock's management of the campaign, and others blamed both Hancock and Custer for the Indian depredations that spread along the Kansas frontier that summer.

Hancock's campaign was yet another costly army failure and prompted a peace offensive on the southern and central Plains to complement the peace activities in the north. Commissioners negotiated two sets of treaties, at Medicine Lodge Creek, Kansas, in 1867, and at Fort Laramie the next year. The Medicine Lodge treaties established Cheyenne, Arapaho, Kiowa, Comanche, and Kiowa-Apache reservations in Indian Territory (present-day Oklahoma), and the Fort Laramie treaties gave to Red Cloud most of what he had fought for in the War for the Bozeman Trail, including the designation of the Powder River country as "unceded Indian territory."

Further reading: Alan Axelrod, *Chronicle of the Indian Wars: From Colonial Times to Wounded Knee* (New York: Prentice-Hall General Reference, 1993); Donald J. Berthrong, *The Southern Cheyenne* (Norman: University of Oklahoma Press, 1963); William H. Lecke, *The Military Conquest of the Southern Plains* (Norman: University of Oklahoma Press, 1963); Robert Utley, *Cavalier in Buckskin: George Armstrong Custer and the Western Military Frontier* (Norman: University of Oklahoma Press, 1988) and *Frontier Regulars: The United States Army and the Indians, 1866–1890* (Lincoln: University of Nebraska Press, 1984).

Hannibal's Destruction of Himera
(409 B.C.E.)

PRINCIPAL COMBATANTS: Carthage vs. Syracuse
PRINCIPAL THEATER(S): Himera, on the north coast of Sicily
DECLARATION: None
MAJOR ISSUES AND OBJECTIVES: Seeking revenge for the humiliating defeat in the Carthaginian-Syracusan War, a general named Hannibal besieged and captured the city-state of Himera.
OUTCOME: Carthage defeated Syracuse's opposition, looted Himera, and burned the city to the ground.

APPROXIMATE MAXIMUM NUMBER OF MEN UNDER ARMS: Unknown
CASUALTIES: Unknown
TREATIES: None

The Carthaginian general, Hamilcar Barcas (c. 270–28 B.C.E.) and his famous son Hannibal (247–183 B.C.E.), who won their glory during the PUNIC WARS, descended from a powerful family with a long history of military service to their North African homeland. Not only their family name, Barcas, but their first names as well, frequently appeared in the annals of Carthage's storied past. An earlier Hamilcar (fl. 480 B.C.E) attempted to conquer Sicily but was repulsed by Syracuse at the battle of Himera in 480 B.C.E, preserving the island's Greek city-states from Carthagian domination for the better part of another century (see CARTHAGINIAN-SYRACUSAN WAR [481–480 B.C.E]). Hamilcar died during the war, which so soundly shook Carthage that it adopted an isolationist policy until Hamlicar's grandson Hannibal (d. 406 B.C.E.) rose to military prominence two generations later. Seeking revenge for his grandfather's death and renewed glory for the Barcas and for Carthage, this ancestor and namesake of the Hannibal who would one day challenge Rome raised a large invasion force and in 409 laid siege to Himera, again facing the Syracusans. Only this time, the opposition of Syracuse proved futile. Hannibal and his troops entered the city-state, looted the denizens, and departed—after first reducing Himera to ruins.

See also HANNIBAL'S SACK OF ACRAGAS.

Further reading: Serge Lancel, *Carthage: A History* (London: Blackwell, 1994).

Hannibal's Sack of Acragas   (406 B.C.E.)

PRINCIPAL COMBATANTS: Carthage vs. Syracuse
PRINCIPAL THEATER(S): The south coast of Sicily
DECLARATION: None
MAJOR ISSUES AND OBJECTIVES: Three years after destroying Himera, the first Hannibal returned with his soon-to-be-renowned nephew, Himilco, in the first salvo of a longer campaign called Himilco's War.
OUTCOME: The settlement of Acragas was severely defeated, but the first Hannibal was killed in the fighting.
APPROXIMATE MAXIMUM NUMBER OF MEN UNDER ARMS: Syracuse sent 35,000 men to relieve the besieged garrison.
CASUALTIES: Unknown
TREATIES: None

Three years after HANNIBAL'S DESTRUCTION OF HIMERA, the Carthaginian general (not the Hannibal [247–183 B.C.E.]

famous for his exploits in the Second PUNIC WAR) returned to Sicily to seek victories against the Syracusans. This early Hannibal (d. 406 B.C.E.) took with him on the expedition his soon-to-be-illustrious nephew, Himilco (d. 397 B.C.E.), and together they besieged Acragas, a settlement on the island's south coast. He defeated the city's garrison, which was commanded by the able Spartan Dexippus (d. 406 B.C.E.), who died in the battle. However, Hannibal himself succumbed to an epidemic that swept the Carthaginian camp before the siege was completed. It fell to Himilco to finish the triumph and to resist the onslaught of a 35,000-man Syracusan relief column, fighting a fierce battle outside the city's walls. The Syracusans nearly prevailed, but, on the verge of victory, fell to disputing among themselves, thus giving the advantage to Carthage.

The relief column defeated, Himilco turned his men loose on Acragas. Its brutal sacking was the first assault of many along Sicily's coast in what is now called HIMILCO'S WAR.

Further reading: Serge Lancel, *Carthage: A History* (London: Blackwell, 1994).

Hanoi Incident   *See* FRENCH INDOCHINA WAR (1873–1874).

Hapsburg-Bohemian War (1274–1278)

PRINCIPAL COMBATANTS: Hapsburg emperor Rudolf I (and allies) vs. Bohemian king Ottokar II
PRINCIPAL THEATER(S): Austria
DECLARATION: None
MAJOR ISSUES AND OBJECTIVES: Rudolf fought to make good his claim on Austria.
OUTCOME: Rudolf prevailed, establishing Hapsburg rule over Austria and the entire Danube valley.
APPROXIMATE MAXIMUM NUMBER OF MEN UNDER ARMS: Unknown
CASUALTIES: Unknown
TREATIES: None

The war was fought over a disputed claim to Austria. Both the Holy Roman Emperor Rudolf I (1218–91) of Hapsburg and Bohemia's King Ottokar II ("Ottokar the Great") (c. 1230–78) laid claim to it. In 1274, the Diet of Regensburg vacated Ottokar's claim to Austria, as well as his claims to Styria and Carniola. Thus sanctioned, Rudolf forged an alliance with a group of disaffected Bohemian nobles, then attacked Ottokar in Austria. After making additional agreements with Bavarian knights, Rudolf besieged Vienna, Ottokar's well-fortified stronghold. Unfortunately for Ottokar, his troops proved as disloyal as some of his

nobles, and they deserted Vienna. The Bavarian knights overran and captured a supply center at Klosternberg, which provisioned the siege forces for the long haul. Vienna, starving, had no choice but to surrender and to recognize Rudolf as king. Ottokar personally capitulated soon afterward, in 1275, and, in accordance with the Diet's ruling, renounced his claims to Austria, Styria, and Carniola, retaining only Bohemia and Moravia for his kingdom.

Humiliated, the Bohemian king was never reconciled to his defeat. He soon raised a new army, which led back to Vienna in 1278. There Rudolf, his force now augmented by Alsatians and Swabians, as well as Hungarian units under Ladislas IV (1262–90), engaged him on August 26, 1278, at the Battle of Marchfield (Durnkrut), a plain north of the Danube from Vienna. Ottokar was not only defeated but killed. His son, Wenceslas II (1271–1305), aged seven, assumed the throne under a Hapsburg regency directed by Rudolf, and the Hapsburgs would rule Austria and the Danube valley through the end of WORLD WAR I in 1918.

Further reading: Jean Berenger, *History of the Hapsburg Empire, 1273–1700* (London: Longman Publishing Group, 1995); Archdeacon William Coxe, *History of the House of Austria*, 3rd ed., 4 vols. (reprint, New York: Arno Press, 1971); Adam Wandruska, *The House of Hapsburg: Six Hundred Years of European Dynasty*, trans. Cathleen and Hans Epstein (Westport, Conn.: Greenwood Press, 1975).

Hapsburg Brothers' War (1601–1612)

PRINCIPAL COMBATANTS: Rudolf II, Holy Roman Emperor, vs. Matthias, governor of Austria
PRINCIPAL THEATER(S): Austria and Bohemia
DECLARATION: None
MAJOR ISSUES AND OBJECTIVES: The mentally unbalanced Rudolf invited forces under his cousin to raid and pillage Austria and Bohemia in a misguided effort to wrest them from his brother Matthias.
OUTCOME: Rudolf was ultimately forced to abdicate.
APPROXIMATE MAXIMUM NUMBER OF MEN UNDER ARMS: Unknown
CASUALTIES: Unknown
TREATIES: None

The war was the result of an internecine dispute within the Hapsburg family. The apparent insanity of the Holy Roman Emperor, Rudolf II (1552–1612), touched off a contest for control of various parts of the Hapsburg realm. In 1605, in an attempt to resolve the already violent dispute, a Hapsburg conference decided that Matthias (1557–1619), governor of Austria, would also assume governance of Hungary, taking the reins from his brother Rudolf. Matthias understood that many in Hungary looked to Turkey for relief from Hapsburg religious persecution: the Catholic Hapsburgs promoted the Counter Reformation in Protestant Hungary. Matthias wanted to avert war with the Turks. He therefore ended the Hapsburg policy of support for the Counter Reformation. This, however, triggered a violent response from Rudolf, who was a zealous Catholic. To checkmate his brother, Matthias summarily proclaimed himself head of the Hapsburg family. Although Rudolf remained Holy Roman Emperor, Matthias now took control of Bohemia and Austria, in addition to Hungary. Rudolf resisted this, and the nobles of Bohemia sided with him.

An all-out war within the Hapsburg family seemed inevitable, but timely compromise staved it off—until Rudolf, increasingly unstable, called on his cousin, Leopold V (1586–1632) archduke of Austria and a Catholic archbishop, to lead an army through Austria and Bohemia, plundering as he marched. This expedition, which took place in 1611, prompted the Bohemian nobles to transfer their allegiance from Rudolf to Matthias. With the aid of the Bohemian nobles, Matthias forced Rudolf to abdicate the Bohemian throne. Rudolf was permitted to continue styling himself Holy Roman Emperor, but he had no real power, and, on his death in 1612, Matthias succeeded him in fact as Holy Roman Emperor.

See also HAPSBURG DYNASTIC WARS.

Further reading: Jean Berenger, *History of the Hapsburg Empire, 1273–1700* (London: Longman Publishing Group, 1995); Archdeacon William Coxe, *History of the House of Austria*, 3rd ed., 4 vols. (reprint, New York: Arno Press, 1971); Adam Wandruska, *The House of Hapsburg: Six Hundred Years of European Dynasty*, trans. Cathleen and Hans Epstein (Westport, Conn.: Greenwood Press, 1975).

Hapsburg Dynastic Wars (1439–1457)

PRINCIPAL COMBATANTS: Frederick V, duke of Inner Austria (later Holy Roman Emperor Frederick III) vs. Hungary's John Hunyadi and, separately, Ulrich of Cilli.

PRINCIPAL THEATER(S): Austria

DECLARATION: None

MAJOR ISSUES AND OBJECTIVES: Frederick, Hunyadi, and Ulrich each sought control of Ladislas, infant king of Bohemia and Hungary.

OUTCOME: After prolonged war alternating with compromise, Ladislas asserted his majority and ruled Hungary and Bohemia until his death, apparently by assassination.

APPROXIMATE MAXIMUM NUMBER OF MEN UNDER ARMS: Totals unknown. The biggest military operation, the siege of Wiener Neustadt, was carried out by 16,000 soldiers loyal to Ulrich of Cilli.

CASUALTIES: Unknown
TREATIES: None

Albert II (1397–1439), the first of the Hapsburg Holy Roman Emperors, also ruled Austria, Bohemia, and Hungary. A peacemaker and brilliant administrator, he convened the Diet of Nürnberg in 1438 at which he settled all feuds based on the right of private warfare and set up a system of arbitration. He also organized Germany into efficient "administrative circles." Despite all of this, his death in 1439 following a long campaign against the Turks precipitated a crisis of succession. A son, Ladislas (1440–57), was born to him posthumously, but it was Albert's cousin, Frederick V, duke of Inner Austria, who became effective head of the Hapsburg family upon Albert's death. Frederick was guardian of the infant Ladislas, but he had not been designated regent. Nevertheless, he freely exploited his ward's claims to both the Hungarian and Bohemian thrones. Opposing Frederick was John Hunyadi (1387–1456), a Hungarian general who, for all intents and purposes, was the real ruler of Hungary. Hunyadi wanted to control Ladislas as a means of preserving his own power in Hungary. To this end, Hunyadi invaded Styria (part of Inner Austria) in 1446. Backed by his men, Hunyadi demanded that Ladislas be surrendered to him. Instead of relinquishing the boy to Hunyadi, Frederick put him in the care of an arbitrator, a Roman Catholic cardinal. Hunyadi was immediately distracted by an invitation to crusade against the Turks, which he did.

This did not end Frederick's troubles, however. No sooner had he dodged John Hunyadi than, in 1451, he faced an insurrection among many Austrian nobles, who demanded Ladislas. The insurrection was put down with little bloodshed by legal maneuvering that conferred on Frederick full regent powers in Austria. Almost simultaneously, Frederick resolved the dispute with Bohemia by naming George of Podebrad (1420–71) the boy's regent for Bohemia.

Physical possession of Ladislas still remained an issue, however, with dissident Austrians. In 1452, Ulrich of Cilli (d. 1456), the boy's cousin and the single most powerful man in Austria, led 16,000 troops in a siege against Frederick—now Holy Roman Emperor Frederick III—in his capital, Wiener Neustadt, Austria. Frederick had no choice but to surrender Ladislas to him, and the boy was taken to Vienna. The following year, 1453, Ulrich was deposed by a coup—yet Ladislas remained the presumptive monarch. The boy was crowned Ladislas V in 1453, then, two years later, claimed his majority in opposition to John Hunyadi and George of Podebrad. Ladislas assumed active rule of Bohemia and Hungary, only to die in 1457, probably the victim of murder by poisoning.

Following the death of Ladislas, Bohemia elected George of Podebrad as its king, and Hungary elected Matthias I Corvinus (1443–95).

See also HAPSBURG BROTHERS' WAR.

Further reading: Jean Berenger, *History of the Hapsburg Empire, 1273–1700* (London: Longman Publishing Group, 1995); Archdeacon William Coxe, *History of the House of Austria*, 3rd ed., 4 vols. (reprint, New York: Arno Press, 1971); Adam Wandruska, *The House of Hapsburg: Six Hundred Years of European Dynasty*, trans. Cathleen and Hans Epstein (Westport, Conn.: Greenwood Press, 1975).

Hapsburg-Ottoman War for Hungary
(1662–1683)

PRINCIPAL COMBATANTS: Hapsburgs with Polish alliance vs. the Ottoman Turks
PRINCIPAL THEATER(S): Hungary
DECLARATION: None
MAJOR ISSUES AND OBJECTIVES: The Turks sought conquest of Hungary and the capture of Vienna.
OUTCOME: Hungary fell to the Turks; however, with Polish aid, the Hapsburgs lifted the siege of Vienna, and a new alliance was concluded against the Turks with the object of ejecting them once and for all from Hungary.
APPROXIMATE MAXIMUM NUMBER OF MEN UNDER ARMS: Hapsburgs, 45,000; Polish forces, 30,000; Turks, 200,000 men
CASUALTIES: Heavy among Turkish forces at the Battle of Vienna (1683); as many as 17,000 may have died on both sides during the war.
TREATIES: Peace of Vasavar, August 11, 1664; Peace of 1682

At the Battle of Nagyszollos, January 22, 1662, Janos Kemeny (d. 1662), prince of Transylvania, was defeated and killed by Turkish forces under Mehmed Kucuk (fl. 1662). This restored control of Transylvania to the Ottomans.

Following the victory in Transylvania, Turkish forces under the Grand Vizier Fazil Ahmed Koprulu Pasha (1635–76) invaded Hapsburg Hungary with 80,000 men. His object was to capture Vienna, but he failed to seize the initiative and, once delayed, found himself confronting stiff resistance from Hapsburg fortresses. Koprulu Pasha initiated peace negotiations with the Hapsburgs, but, in the meantime, attacked at the Raab River on August 1, 1664. Repulsed, the Turks retreated to Buda. For their part, the Hapsburgs declined to exploit the victory. They did not pursue, and, on August 11, 1664, the Peace of Vasavar was concluded.

The Peace of Vasavar did not please the Magyar nobility in Hungary, and during 1664–73, small-scale rebellions sporadically broke out against the Hapsburgs. The Magyars staged a full-scale revolt in 1678, calling on the Turks for aid. Pressure on the Hapsburgs was so great that, in 1682, they concluded a peace with Count Imre Thokoly (1656–1705), the leader of the Magyar revolt. Thokoly assumed de facto control of all Hungary, except for Transylvania. In the meantime, the Hapsburgs concluded an alliance with the Poles on March 31, 1683. This came just in time to resist a Turkish invasion of Austria by an army of some 200,000 men. Before this onslaught, the badly outnumbered Hapsburg forces—about 45,000 men —retreated, and on July 14, 1683, the Turks laid siege to Vienna.

The Vienna siege lasted into September, when Polish forces under John Sobieski arrived with an army of 30,000. Surprised, the Turks now faced a combined force of about 76,000 in the Battle of Vienna on September 12, 1683. The result was the defeat of the numerically superior Turks, who suffered heavy losses. However, once the siege was broken, Sobieski declined immediate pursuit. The delay extended into December, allowing the surviving portion of the Turkish army to escape intact.

The next year, the Treaty of Linz was concluded (March 31, 1684), creating a Holy League to continue to oppose the Turks and reclaim all Hungary (see AUSTRO-TURKISH WAR [1683–1699]; VIENNA, SIEGE OF [1683]).

See also HAPSBURG BROTHERS' WAR.

Further reading: Jean Berenger, *History of the Hapsburg Empire, 1273–1700* (London: Longman Publishing Group, 1995); Archdeacon William Coxe, *History of the House of Austria*, 3rd ed., 4 vols. (reprint, New York: Arno Press, 1971); Adam Wandruska, *The House of Hapsburg: Six Hundred Years of European Dynasty*, trans. Cathleen and Hans Epstein (Westport, Conn.: Greenwood Press, 1975).

Hapsburg-Valois War (1547–1559)

PRINCIPAL COMBATANTS: Hapsburg-ruled Spain (allied with Florence) vs. France
PRINCIPAL THEATER(S): Italy
DECLARATION: None
MAJOR ISSUES AND OBJECTIVES: France wanted to achieve control of as much of Italy as possible, but was resisted by Hapsburg-ruled Spain.
OUTCOME: France was defeated in this and related wars and therefore relinquished most of its claims to Italian territory.
APPROXIMATE MAXIMUM NUMBER OF MEN UNDER ARMS: Hapsburgs and France each fielded no more than 50,000 men at any given time.

CASUALTIES: Hapsburgs, 28,050 killed or wounded; France, 42,400 killed or wounded

TREATIES: Treaty of Câteau-Cambrésis, April 3, 1559

Determined to assert French hegemony over the bulk of Europe, Henry II (1519–59) of France embarked on war against Holy Roman Emperor Charles V (1500–58), beginning in 1547. By April 1552, Henry had taken Lorraine, and when Charles attempted to take the fortress city of Metz during October–December 1552, he was repulsed. That same year, a French force invaded Tuscany, but imperial troops defeated the invaders at the Battle of Marciano on August 2, 1553. Survivors of the battle withdrew to Siena, where they were laid under siege until 1554, when they capitulated.

By 1556, Charles V, exhausted by war, abdicated the throne. His son, Philip II (1527–98), assumed the crown of Spain, and Charles's brother, Ferdinand, became Holy Roman Emperor. The war with France continued, but shifted from Italy to northern France and into Flanders.

Philip, with Duke Emmanuel Philibert of Savoy (1528–80), led an army of 50,000 into Picardy while most of the French army was still in Italy. A French force of some 26,000 troops was hastily raised, and an attempt was made to check the invasion at St. Quentin on August 10, 1557. However, as the French army crossed the Somme River, imperial forces attacked, and some 6,000 Frenchmen were killed. The imperial forces sustained no more than 500 casualties. Incredibly, however, the imperial commanders failed to exploit this tremendous triumph and withdrew into the Netherlands. This gave Henry II sufficient time to summon reinforcements from Italy.

On January 1, 1558, the duke of Guise (1519–63) led 25,000 men from Italy against an imperial-allied English force at Calais. The defeat of this English garrison forever ended Britain's occupation of this piece of the Continent. Then, on June 30, 1558, another French force—about 10,500 strong—invaded Spanish Flanders and pillaged Dunkirk before falling back on Calais. A Spanish force of 13,000 men routed the French invaders on July 13, virtually wiping out the entire French force. This catastrophe prompted France to sue for peace, which came in the form of the Treaty of Câteau-Cambrésis (April 3, 1559), by which France relinquished almost all of its Italian possessions.

Further reading: Jean Berenger, *History of the Hapsburg Empire, 1273–1700* (London: Longman Publishing Group, 1995); Archdeacon William Coxe, *History of the House of Austria*, 3rd ed., 4 vols. (reprint, New York: Arno Press, 1971); Adam Wandruska, *The House of Hapsburg: Six Hundred Years of European Dynasty,* trans. Cathleen and Hans Epstein (Westport, Conn.: Greenwood Press, 1975).

Harsha's Conquests *See* CHALUKYAN WAR AGAINST HARSHA.

Hawaiian Wars (Unification of Hawaii) (1782–1810)

PRINCIPAL COMBATANTS: Forces of Kamehameha I vs. rival chieftains and the chiefs of Molokai, Lanai, Oahu, and Kauai

PRINCIPAL THEATER(S): Hawaiian Islands

DECLARATION: None

MAJOR ISSUES AND OBJECTIVES: Kamehameha I sought to unite all of the Hawaiian Islands under his rule.

OUTCOME: Through a combination of war and negotiation, Kamehameha I created the kingdom of Hawaii.

APPROXIMATE MAXIMUM NUMBER OF MEN UNDER ARMS: The largest force consisted of 12,000 warriors led by Kamehameha.

CASUALTIES: Unknown, but particularly devastating among the defenders of Oahu.

TREATIES: None

Kamehameha I (c. 1758–1819) the Great inherited, with his cousin, Kiwalao (d. 1782), rule over the big island of Hawaii in 1782. Almost immediately, Kamehameha fell to disputing with Kiwalao and waged a war against him, killing him at the Battle of Mokuohai, fought later in 1782. Other rivals also emerged, all of whom Kamehameha subdued, even as he struck out from the island of Hawaii to gain control over the other islands in the Hawaiian chain, each of which was governed by other chieftains.

Maui fell to him in 1790, after a bloody invasion. By 1791, Kamehameha had acquired firearms from American and European traders and used these to attack chieftains from Oahu and Kauai after they had retaken Maui and attacked Hawaii. Using the bought weapons, Kamehameha defeated the armies from Oahu and Kauai to emerge as sole ruler of the big island. When a new rival, Keovu (d. 1791), emerged at this time, Kamehameha invited him to a parley—then assassinated him upon his arrival.

Having taken the big island, Kamehameha invaded the other islands beginning in 1795. With 12,000 warriors in 1,200 large war canoes, he invaded Molokai, Lanai, and Oahu. On Oahu, the invaders drove the defenders to a desperate stand at Nuuanu Pali, a 1,200-foot cliff near modern Honolulu. The defenders, to a man, fell to their deaths from this height—either pushed or having committed suicide. Their leader, Kalunikupule (d. 1795) was summarily executed.

After his victory at Oahu, only the islands of Kauai and Niihau remained to be taken. Kamehameha mounted a major expedition against them in 1800, but was caught in a destructive storm. He and his surviving crews turned back. Four years passed before he made another attempt, but an epidemic swept his army, killing many warriors before the invasion could be launched, This mishap prompted Kamehameha to turn to negotiations with the leaders, who, in 1809, acknowledged Kamehameha as their king. By 1810, all of the Hawaiian chain was consolidated under Kamehameha's control.

Further reading: Gavan Daws, *Shoal of Time: A History of the Hawaiian Islands* (New York: Macmillan, 1968); Ruth M. Tabrah, *Hawaii. States and the Nation.* (New York: W. W. Norton, 1984); Richard William Tregaskis, *The Warrior King: Kamehameha the Great* (New York: Simon and Schuster, 1973).

Heiji War (1159–1185)

PRINCIPAL COMBATANTS: Taira vs. Minamoto warrior clans

PRINCIPAL THEATER(S): Japan

DECLARATION: None

MAJOR ISSUES AND OBJECTIVES: The rival clans sought control of the Japanese government.

OUTCOME: The Minamoto clan emerged as dominant, and the war heralded the emergence of feudal Japan.

APPROXIMATE MAXIMUM NUMBER OF MEN UNDER ARMS: Unknown

CASUALTIES: Unknown

TREATIES: None

The Heian period, 792–1192, brought a great measure of peace and stability to early Japan; however, during the later Heian period, certain leading families acquired large territories and hired private standing armies to defend their property. Soon, these armies displaced the standing forces of the Heian government. This situation produced a number of warrior clans, the two most important of which were the Taira, also called the Heike, and the Minamoto, also known as the Genji (*see* GEMPEI WAR). By the 1150s, the Minamoto controlled most of eastern Japan, whereas the Taira dominated the west.

As the power of the two great warrior clans grew, another clan, the Fujiwara, gained control of the emperor and, from 856 to 1086 the Fujiwara were effectively the principal executive authority in the government of Japan. In 1155, the succession to the throne fell vacant, and Go-Shirakawa (1127–92) was named emperor, an action that touched off a minor revolt known as the HOGEN WAR, which the Taira and Minamoto clans quarreled. Although the Hogen War itself was not of great military scope, it signaled a turning point in Japanese affairs, for power had clearly passed to the warrior clans. Go-Shirakawa (Shirakawa II) was succeeded by Nijo (1143–65), and, during his reign, the ambitious and shrewd yet morally bankrupt

Taira lord, Kiyomori (1118–81), insinuated himself at court and acquired great influence with the emperor. Seeking to control Kiyomori, the retired emperor Go-Shirakawa, with the help of a minor Minamoto lord, laid a military trap for him. The plot collapsed and created a great rift between the Taira and the retired emperor on the one hand and the Taira and Minmoto clans on the other.

In 1179, the head of the Taira, Shigemori (d. 1179), died and was succeeded by his brother Muenemori (1147–85). In contrast to Shigemori, who had been a forceful and successful leader, Muenemori was cowardly and inept in military and political matters. Go-Shirakawa recognized Muenemori's weakness and decided to take steps to reduce Taira power. He dismissed many influential Taira in the capital. Kiyomori stepped in, however, dismissed even more court officials, then marched on the capital and forced the new emperor, Takakura (1161–81), off the throne, installing in his place his own year-old grandson, Antoku (1178–85). The deposed emperor recruited the Minamoto—the Genji—to come to his aid, and the Heiji War became a full-scale civil war.

Kiyomori's seizure of the capital was virtually a military coup. It was opposed by Minamoto Yoritomo (1147–99), who, after coming to control all of eastern Japan, overran the capital in 1185, forced the Taira out of the city, and ended the Heiji War. In its aftermath, Minamoto Yoritomo set up an alternative military government in Kamakura, 30 miles south of Tokyo. The Kamakura military leaders ruled as shoguns—hereditary military governors—and their government eventually came to dominate the country. The Heiji War, therefore, inaugurated the long period of feudal Japan, run by a network of provincial generals and lords who served the shogun as his vassals.

See also JAPANESE CIVIL WAR (936–941); JAPANESE CIVIL WAR (1331–1333).

Further reading: William Wayne Ferris, *Heavenly Warriors: The Evolution of Japan's Military, 500–1300* (Cambridge, Mass.: Harvard University Press, 1996); John W. Hall, *Japan; From Prehistory to Modern Times* (Tokyo: C. E. Tuttle, 1971); Jeffrey P. Mass, *Warrior Government in Early Medieval Japan* (New Haven, Conn.: Yale University Press, 1974); James Murdoch, *A History of Japan*, 3 vols. (New York: Routledge, 1996); George B. Samson, *A History of Japan*, 3 vols. (Palo Alto, Calif., Stanford University Press, 1958–63).

Henry II's Campaigns in Wales (1157, 1165)

PRINCIPAL COMBATANTS: Norman England vs. Wales

PRINCIPAL THEATER(S): Wales

DECLARATION: None

MAJOR ISSUES AND OBJECTIVES: Taking advantage of a chaotic period in English rule, the Welsh rebelled against the Norman barons sent to control them; Henry II invaded to put down the rebellion.

OUTCOME: Henry received the homage of Wales despite failing to conquer the Welsh.

APPROXIMATE MAXIMUM NUMBER OF MEN UNDER ARMS: Unknown

CASUALTIES: Unknown

TREATIES: None

Following the NORMAN CONQUEST of 1066, Wales came under control of feudal barons and their retinues who owed fealty to the French-speaking English kings. Then, in 1157, the chaotic reign of England's King Stephen (c. 1097–1154) gave the Welsh the opportunity to rise against the "foreign" barons. The revolt was led by two Welsh nobles, Owain of Gwynnedd (d. 1170), prince of the north, and Rhys ap Gruffydd (c. 1132–97), lord of the south.

England was hardly in shape to resist. The ambitious Henry Plantagenet (1133–89) had fast been adding titles to his name. Already duke of Normandy in 1150, he became count of Anjou upon the death of his father, Geoffrey (1113–51). The next year, he acquired lordship of aquitaine by marrying the beautiful and talented Eleanor (1122–1204). Now he laid claim to the English throne as the grandson (through his mother) of Henry I (1069–1135). Faced by invasion, Stephen agreed in 1153 to accept Plantagenet as coadjutor and heir. When Stephen died the following year, Henry II became king over territories stretching from Scotland to the Pyrenees. His succession came virtually without opposition, except from those already fighting in Wales.

Now, in fact, Wales won back lands taken as a result of the Norman Conquest, defeating the invasion force mounted by the new king. Even though he failed to prevail on the battlefield, Henry persuaded Owain to give him his allegiance and began rebuilding the English fortresses in Wales. By 1165, Owain had again had enough of the overbearing English barons, and he incited a new rebellion, which led to yet another invasion. This time Henry and Owain fought to a draw in a campaign plagued by bad weather and short supplies on both sides. Henry had managed in general to drive the Welsh back from the English border, but the individual lords kept control of their own districts. As the Welsh looked on, once again the English began building new fortresses for their borderland barons.

See also ANGLO-FRENCH WAR (1159–1189).

Further reading: Richard W. Barker, *Henry Plantagenet, A Biography* (London: Barrie and Rockcliff, 1964); Paul Barbier, *The Age of Owain Gwynedd; An Attempt at a Connected Account of the History of Wales from December, 1135 to November, 1170* (Felinfach, Wales: Llanerch, 1990).

Henry VII's First Invasion of Brittany
(1488)

PRINCIPAL COMBATANTS: England vs. Brittany

PRINCIPAL THEATER(S): Brittany

DECLARATION: None

MAJOR ISSUES AND OBJECTIVES: Henry VII sought to assert English control of Brittany in order to secure his precarious hold on the English throne.

OUTCOME: An English invasion failed, and Brittany declared its allegiance to France.

APPROXIMATE MAXIMUM NUMBER OF MEN UNDER ARMS: Unknown

CASUALTIES: Unknown

TREATIES: Treaty of Sablé, 1488

The Wars of the ROSES, from 1455 to 1485, made Henry VII (1457–1509) king of England. He was, however, keenly aware that his reign was vulnerable, and in an effort to protect his hold on the throne, he decided to invade Brittany. Although Brittany was, at the time, a duchy nominally controlled by England, it was weakly held and therefore in danger of falling to Charles VIII (1470–98) of France. To avert this, Henry VII appealed to English patriots to finance an invasion. The king loaded three warships with volunteers and invaded—only to be rapidly and readily repulsed.

In the wake of victory over the English, Francis II (1435–88), the duke of Brittany, shifted his allegiance from Henry to Charles. For his part, Charles, who wanted to marry the duke's daughter, Anne of Brittany (1477–1514), was eager to accept Francis's fealty. Defeated, Henry cut his losses by renewing a truce under the Treaty of Sablé.

See also HENRY VII'S SECOND INVASION OF BRITTANY.

Further reading: J. D. Mackie, *The Earlier Tudors, 1485–1558* (New York: Oxford University Press, 1994); Anthony Pickering, *Lancastrians to Tudors: England 1450–1509* (New York: Cambridge University Press, 2000).

Henry VII's Second Invasion of Brittany
(1489–1492)

PRINCIPAL COMBATANTS: England vs. France

PRINCIPAL THEATER(S): Brittany

DECLARATION: None

MAJOR ISSUES AND OBJECTIVES: Henry VII of England sought to block the absorption of Brittany by France.

OUTCOME: King Charles VIII settled with Henry VII for a sum of money and a pension, in exchange for Henry's relinquishing all claims on Brittany.

APPROXIMATE MAXIMUM NUMBER OF MEN UNDER ARMS:
Unknown
CASUALTIES: Unknown
TREATIES: Treaty of Etaples, 1492

Almost immediately after Henry VII (1457–1509) of England signed the Treaty of Sablé with France and Brittany, ending HENRY VII's FIRST INVASION OF BRITTANY in 1488, Francis II (1435–88), duke of Brittany, died. Charles VIII (1470–98) of France immediately laid claim to Brittany and to Anne of Brittany (1477–1514), Francis's daughter, whom he had wanted to marry. Henry responded by calling for a Breton regency. To Brittany, he offered his services as mediator. He also offered military aid to resist French conquest, and he strengthened his own position by an alliance with Spain, by which Catherine of Aragon (1485–1536) would marry his son, Arthur (d. 1502). But, even as Henry's troops were en route to Brittany, Anne of Brittany agreed to the marriage and agreed to yield Brittany to Charles, and Spain made a secret alliance with France.

Henry, seeking to salvage something from the situation, invaded France in 1490 and laid siege against Boulogne the following year. Charles VIII bought him off with 745,000 gold crowns and a pension, terms agreed to in the 1492 Treaty of Etaples, which ended the war. In exchange, Henry VII renounced all claims to Brittany, which became a French province.

See also "GUERRE FOLLE."

Further reading: J. D. Mackie, *The Earlier Tudors, 1485–1558* (New York: Oxford University Press, 1994); Anthony Pickering, *Lancastrians to Tudors: England 1450–1509* (New York: Cambridge University Press, 2000).

Henry of Bolingbroke's Revolt   (1399)

PRINCIPAL COMBATANTS: Followers of Henry of Bolingbroke vs. King Richard II of England
PRINCIPAL THEATER(S): Yorkshire and London
DECLARATION: None
MAJOR ISSUES AND OBJECTIVES: Bolingbroke revolted when Richard withheld his inheritance from him; he then sought the throne.
OUTCOME: Bolingbroke prevailed, captured, and disposed of Richard II, and assumed the throne as Henry IV, first of the house of Lancaster to become king of England.
APPROXIMATE MAXIMUM NUMBER OF MEN UNDER ARMS:
Unknown
CASUALTIES: Few, if any—excluding Richard II himself
TREATIES: None

As a young king, England's Richard II (1367–1400) was controlled by his uncle, John of Gaunt (1340–99)—head of the house of Lancaster and the country's regent. During the early years of Richard's reign, John of Gaunt's ambitious son, Henry of Bolingbroke (1367–1413), appeared content to remain in the background while his father ran the government. But when Gaunt led an expedition against Spain in 1386, Bolingbroke joined a group a young nobles opposed to the king called "the lords appellants," who from 1387 until 1389 forcibly isolated Richard from his closest associates and thereby dominated the kingdom. Richard had just taken back control of his government when Gaunt returned home.

The former regent managed—at least publicly—to effect reconciliation between the king and the lords appellants before charging off once more, this time on crusades into Lithuania in 1390 and Prussia in 1392. While he was gone, the still bitter King Richard used a dispute between Bolingbroke and another of the former lords appellants, Thomas Mowbray (1366–99), duke of Norfolk, to banish both men from his kingdom. Upon John of Gaunt's death in January 1399, the vindictive Richard seized all the Lancastrian estates, depriving the exiled Bolingbroke of his inheritance and giving him clear excuse to attack England. Bolingbroke invaded Yorkshire, sailing across the English Channel from France while Richard was absent on his second expedition against Ireland. Henry landed at Ravenspur at the mouth of the Humber River on July 4, 1399, and encountered no organized resistance. The northern barons flocked to his side, and, with them, Bolingbroke marched on London. By the time Richard returned to London, the revolt was too advanced to counter. The king felt he had no choice but to surrender. Bolingbroke imprisoned him in Pontefract Castle, where he died in 1400. It is believed that he was murdered outright or deliberately starved to death. Henry of Bolingbroke then usurped the throne using his descent from King Henry III (1207–72) to justify his rule as Henry IV, first of the Lancastrian monarchs.

See also ENGLISH INVASIONS OF IRELAND; HUNDRED YEARS' WAR.

Further reading: Mary Louise Bruce, *The Usurper King: Henry of Bolingbroke, 1355–99* (London: Rubicon Press, 1985); Anthony Tuck, *Crown and Nobility, 1272–1461: Political Conflict in Late Medieval England* (New York: Barnes and Noble Books, 1986).

Henry the Wrangler's Revolts   (973–1002)

PRINCIPAL COMBATANTS: Bavaria and Bohemia vs. Germany
PRINCIPAL THEATER(S): Bavaria and Bohemia
DECLARATION: None
MAJOR ISSUES AND OBJECTIVES: Henry II, duke of Bavaria, and other German-speaking princes rebelled against the hegemony of Germany's Otto II.

OUTCOME: Henry's revolts were crushed, and he was forced into exile.

APPROXIMATE MAXIMUM NUMBER OF MEN UNDER ARMS: Unknown

CASUALTIES: Unknown

TREATIES: None

After the death of Otto I the Great (912–973), his son Otto II (955–983) ascended to the German throne in 973, and the German states of the Holy Roman Empire descended into five years of civil war. These were led by the duke of Bavaria, Henry II (973–1024), known as "Henry the Wrangler" (or "Henry the Quarrelsome") and Boleslav of Bohemia. By 983, the rebellions had been suppressed by Otto, despite the distraction of the FRANCO-GERMAN WAR, fought from 978 to 980. Forced into exile, Henry left his son, also called Henry (973–1024), with Abraham, bishop of Friesling. When Otto II died, Otto III (980–1002) was a mere three years old, and during his minority Germany was ruled by his formidable mother, Theophano, who had to face a number of revolts led by Henry the Wrangler until 1002. Otto III would travel to Italy at age 13 and, in 996, he appointed a new pope, Gregory V (972–999), and had himself crowned emperor. When Otto died while suppressing another revolt in Rome in 1002 (*see* ARDOIN'S REVOLT), Henry the Wrangler's son ascended to the German throne as Henry II, Holy Roman Emperor.

See also ARDOIN'S WARS; BALDWIN OF FLANDERS, REVOLT OF.

Further reading: K. J. Leyser, *Medieval Germany and Its Neighbors, 900–1250* (London: Hambledon, 1982).

Herero Uprising (1904–1908)

PRINCIPAL COMBATANTS: Herero (and allied tribes, especially the Hottentots) vs. Germany

PRINCIPAL THEATER(S): German Southwest Africa

DECLARATION: None

MAJOR ISSUES AND OBJECTIVES: The Herero sought to eject German invaders.

OUTCOME: After a long and bitter struggle, three-quarters of the Herero were wiped out, and the remainder removed to other lands.

APPROXIMATE MAXIMUM NUMBER OF MEN UNDER ARMS: Unknown

CASUALTIES: Disastrous among the Herero, who lost about 80 percent of their number, combatants and noncombatants alike.

TREATIES: None

The Herero are Bantu-speaking people of southwestern Africa, who currently inhabit parts of central Namibia and Botswana. They were never a large tribal group, but they had long been powerful in disproportion to their numbers. From the 17th through the later 19th century, they held sway over the Central Highland north of Windhoek. Thus when the German colonial interests encroached on them during 1904–07, the Herero were quick to resist, and because their influence was so great in the region, the Herero uprising attracted other tribes as well, most notably the Hottentots.

German forces had a great deal of trouble suppressing the uprising, and the German government was forced to send significant numbers of troops to fight a guerrilla war of attrition. The Herero uprising inspired a similar uprising against the Portuguese in Angola.

The final suppression of the Herero, when it came, was brutal in the extreme. The Germans subjugated the tribe only by killing 80 percent of the members and compelling survivors to move to the arid sand veldt that is today called Hereroland.

See also HOTTENTOT UPRISING.

Further reading: Helmut Bley, *Namibia under German Rule* (Hamburg and Windhoek, Namibia: Namibia Scientific Society, 1996); Jon Bridgman, *The Revolt of the Hereros* (Berkeley: University of California Press, 1981); San-Bart Gewald, *Herero Heroes: A Socio-Political History of the Herero of Namibia, 1890–1923* (Athens: Ohio University Press, 1999).

Himilco's War (405 B.C.E.)

PRINCIPAL COMBATANTS: Carthage vs. Syracuse

PRINCIPAL THEATER(S): Sicily

DECLARATION: None

MAJOR ISSUES AND OBJECTIVES: Carthage sought control of parts of Sicily.

OUTCOME: Syracuse, defeated, made major cessions to Carthage.

APPROXIMATE MAXIMUM NUMBER OF MEN UNDER ARMS: Unknown

CASUALTIES: Unknown

TREATIES: Treaty of 405 B.C.E., by which Syracuse relinquished about half of Sicily to Carthage

The Carthaginian general Himilco (d. 396 B.C.E.) invaded southern Sicily, where he fought an army led by Dionysius I (c. 430–367 B.C.E.), tyrant of Syracuse. Himilco defeated Dionysius at Gela and at Camarina (Santa Croceo). Dionysius not only ceded these cities to Himilco, but concluded a treaty by which Syracuse relinquished to Carthage half of Sicily. It was the first time Syracuse had found it necessary to enter into a treaty with Carthage, against which it had long struggled.

In the First DIONYSIUS WAR, from 398 to 397 B.C.E., Dionysius reclaimed what he had lost, driving the Carthaginians out of Sicily and Himilco to suicide.

See also Dionysius War, Second; Dionysius War, Third; Dionysius War, Fourth; Hannibal's Destruction of Himera; Hannibal's Sack of Acragas.

Further reading: Brian Caven, *Dionysius I: War-Lord of Sicily* (New Haven, Conn.: Yale University Press, 1990).

Hittite Conquest of Anatolia
(c. 1700–c. 1325 B.C.E.)

PRINCIPAL COMBATANTS: Hittites vs. Mitanni and, subsequently, Egypt
PRINCIPAL THEATER(S): Anatolia (modern Turkey), Syria, and Cilicia
DECLARATION: None
MAJOR ISSUES AND OBJECTIVES: The Hittites craved expansion of their empire.
OUTCOME: Twice, during this long period, the Hittites succeeded in dominating Anatolia.
APPROXIMATE MAXIMUM NUMBER OF MEN UNDER ARMS: Unknown
CASUALTIES: Unknown
TREATIES: Unknown

The earliest records of Hittite presence in Anatolia (Turkey) date from about 2000 B.C.E. Twice, during the period 1700 to 1325 B.C.E., they came to dominate the region. Under King Hattusilis, who ruled from about 1650 to 1620 B.C.E., and his successors, the Hittites created what is known as the Old Kingdom, extending their holdings throughout Anatolia and into Syria and Cilicia. In fighting to acquire Cilicia, which was taken, lost to the Mitanni, then retaken, Hattusilis was severely wounded and had to be taken home, where he eventually died of his wounds. Three sons ruled briefly in succession—all poorly—but his adoptive grandson, Mursilis (Murshilish) (c. 1620–1590 B.C.E.), resumed aggressive campaigning in northern Syria. During one of these campaigns, he subdued and destroyed the city of Aleppo. After this, he turned his attention to Babylon, where he defeated and deposed the powerful Amorite dynasty. Later, after defeating the Hurrians along the Euphrates River, Mursilis returned to the Hittite capital, Huttusas, where he was subsequently assassinated by conspirators in service to his brother-in-law, Hantilis.

Following the death of Mursilis, the Mitanni regained much of what they had lost to the Hittites. As a result of the Hittite-Hurrian Wars, from around 1620 to about 1325 B.C.E., the Mitanni established in northern Syria the Hanigabat kingdom. However, about 1400 B.C.E., a new Hittite king, Suppiluliumas (c. 1375–c. 1335 B.C.E.), founded the Hittite New Kingdom and reigned as most powerful of the Hittite rulers, called by some scholars the "Charlemagne of the Near East." Continually fighting the Mitanni in the east, Suppiluliumas spread Hittite influence over much of Syria and throughout the Euphrates River valley. He rebuilt the Hittite capital at Hattusas and extended his kingdom to the proportions of a truly great empire.

Feared by his neighbors, Suppiluliumas commanded the wary respect of even the powerful Egyptians, who cultivated an alliance. The widow of the pharaoh Tutankhamen (fl. 1333–1323 B.C.E.) invited Suppiluliumas to send one of his sons to be her new husband. By the time the young man arrived in Egypt, however, an anti-Hittite movement had been organized, and the unfortunate son was assassinated. Suppiluliumas launched a campaign against the Egyptians, but was soon dead himself, apparently having succumbed to plague, introduced into his homeland by Egyptian prisoners of war.

See also Assyrian-Hurrian Wars; Hurrian Conquests.

Further reading: Trevor Bryce, *The Kingdom of the Hittites* (New York: Oxford University Press, 1998); O. R. Gurney, *The Hittites* (New York: Penguin Books, 1990); J. G. Macqueen, *The Hittites and Their Contemporaries in Asia Minor* (London: Thames and Hudson, 1986).

Hittite-Hurrian Wars (c. 1620–c. 1325 B.C.E.)

PRINCIPAL COMBATANTS: Hittites vs. Hurrian Mitanni (later with Assyrian allies); separately, Egypt vs. Hurrian Mitanni
PRINCIPAL THEATER(S): Anatolia (Turkey) and the region of modern Palestine and modern Syria
DECLARATION: None
MAJOR ISSUES AND OBJECTIVES: The Hittites and Hurrians struggled to dominate Anatolia.
OUTCOME: Dominance seesawed between the Hittites and Hurrian Mitanni but ultimately fell to Assyria, which became the dominant force in the region by the end of these wars.
APPROXIMATE MAXIMUM NUMBER OF MEN UNDER ARMS: Unknown
CASUALTIES: Unknown
TREATIES: No documents survive

The Hittite-Hurrian Wars are especially significant for having included the earliest battle of which a record—however incomplete—exists: the Battle of Megiddo, 1469 or 1479 B.C.E.

The Hurrians and Hittites vied for centuries to control Anatolia, the territory of modern Turkey (*see* Hittite Conquest of Anatolia). The long series of wars between them began about 1620 B.C.E. when the Hittites fought the Arzawa, a kingdom on their southwest border. Because the Hittites devoted most of their military resources to this struggle, they left south and southeast Anatolia undefended, and the Hurrian kingdom of Mitanni invaded and seized this region. In response, Hittite forces were rushed to the area and succeeded in ejecting the Hurrian Mitanni but, about 1600 B.C.E., were again involved in a pitched struggle for the city of Aleppo. After approximately five years of fighting, the Mitanni finally withdrew.

Some time after this victory, internal struggles within the Hittite kingdom weakened its military position, and the Hurrian Mitanni wrested Cilicia from the Hittites, establishing a kingdom called Kizzuwada about 1590 B.C.E. In a bold strategic move, the Mitanni also created the Hanigabat kingdom in the southeast, which effectively cut the Hittites off from northern Syria. This led to the Battle of Megiddo in 1469 or 1479 B.C.E., not between the Hurrian Mitanni and the Hittites, but between the forces of Egypt, under Pharaoh Thutmose III (fl. c. 1500–1447 B.C.E.), and Saustater (fl. 1500–1450 B.C.E.), the Mitanni king of the Syrian city of Kadesh. With the failure of the Hittites to contain Mitanni expansion, Thutmose feared losing influence in Syria and Palestine. He therefore led an army around the eastern end of the Mediterranean Sea to extinguish what he interpreted as a revolt in northern Palestine led by the king of Kadesh. The king's rebel army marched south to Megiddo, which overlooked the pass leading to the Plain of Esdraelon and was thus a strategically placed high-ground position, the gateway to all Mesopotamia. Deploying his army in three groups, Thutmose made a surprise attack on the Mitanni position at dawn and routed the opposing force, which withdrew behind Megiddo's walls. Had Thutmose proceeded against Megiddo immediately, the city would have quickly fallen. But his troops paused to loot the abandoned Mitanni camp, giving the defenders time to prepare strong defenses. As a result, Megiddo fell only after a seven-month siege. The Battle of Megiddo must have involved very large forces, for it was probably the site of the Armageddon battle described in the New Testament.

The Egyptian victory at Megiddo stopped the Mitanni expansion. The Hittite "Old Kingdom" still languished in decline, however, until the advent of a new leader, Suppiluliumas (c. 1375–c. 1335 B.C.E.), who founded the "New Kingdom" and brought the Hittites to renewed power and influence. He resolved to end the Hurrian presence in Syria altogether by mounting a massive invasion into Syria. With strategic aplomb, he invaded via an unexpected route, through the eastern valley of the Euphrates, which caught the Mitanni entirely unawares. They offered only feeble resistance and, by about 1370, yielded all territory north of Damascus and all of present-day Lebanon.

Seeking to halt the Hittite advance, the Mitanni struck an alliance with Assyria, a rival of the Hittites, but the Hittites checked this move by conquering the Mitanni city of Carchemish on the Euphrates in about 1340. This gave the Hittites a buffer state between them and Assyria. It would be years before the Mitanni-Assyrian alliance retook the region in 1325. After the area around Carchemish had been retaken, the Hurrian Mitanni also reestablished Hanigabat as a subkingdom. By this time, however, both the Hurrians and the Hittites had greatly receded in importance relative to the Assyrians, who were rapidly becoming the dominant people in the region and were destined to possess all of Anatolia.

See also ASSYRIAN-HURRIAN WARS; HURRIAN Conquests.

Further reading: Trevor Bryce, *The Kingdom of the Hittites* (New York: Oxford University Press, 1998); O. R. Gurney, *The Hittites* (New York: Penguin Books, 1990); J. G. Macqueen, *The Hittites and Their Contemporaries in Asia Minor* (London: Thames and Hudson, 1986).

Hogen War (1156)

PRINCIPAL COMBATANTS: Go-Shirakawa vs. Sutoku
PRINCIPAL THEATER(S): Japan
DECLARATION: None
MAJOR ISSUES AND OBJECTIVES: The dispute was over succession to the imperial throne.
OUTCOME: The supporters of Go-Shirakawa prevailed, and he assumed the Japanese throne; but the Fujiwara family was finished as effective rulers of Japan.
APPROXIMATE MAXIMUM NUMBER OF MEN UNDER ARMS: Unknown
CASUALTIES: Unknown
TREATIES: None

As the prelude to the larger HEIJI WAR, from 1159 to 1185, the Hogen War marked the end of the Fujiwara family's feudal control over the Japanese monarchy and sparked a period of prolonged fighting. The conflict centered around who in fact ran the imperial court, the retired emperor Sutoku (1119–64) or the reigning emperor Go-Shirakawa (Shirakawa II) (1127–92). In Japan of the Heian period (792–1192), it was customary for emperors to step down later in life, abdicating in favor of a son, then enter a monastery. There, they would live out the remainder of their lives in semiretirement, intervening in affairs of state only as necessary. Toba was one such retired emperor, who, displeased with the rule of his first son, Sutoku, compelled him to abdicate. Sutoku himself retired to a monastery.

After Toba died in 1156, trouble between the new emperor, his third son, Go-Shirakawa, and his first, Sutoku, was perhaps inevitable. Sutoku resolved to come out of retirement and resume what he considered his rightful place on the throne. This action sharply divided the imperial Fujiwara family between those who favored Go-Shirakawa and those who favored Sutoku. When the kampu (or chief counselor, a position controlled since 857 by the head of the Fujiwara family), backed Go-Shirakawa, Sutoku quickly called on the support of the warrior clan led by the shogun (military governor or, perhaps, supreme general) Minamoto Tameyoshi (d. 1156). In response, those warriors led by rival shogun Taira Kiyomori, came to the aid of Go-Shirakawa's faction.

Go-Shirakawa and his partisans won the brief and violent struggle, forcing Sutoku back into exile and killing his chief supporters. Tameyoshi was executed, and the Minamoto clan declined in power as the Taira family took effective control of the government.

By the time Go-Shirakawa himself decided to respect the custom of retiring to a monastery after abdicating to a son, real power was no longer in the hands of the emperors, but in those of the shoguns.

See also GEMPEI WAR.

Further reading: William Wayne Ferris, *Heavenly Warriors: The Evolution of Japan's Military, 500–1300* (Cambridge, Mass.: Harvard University Press, 1996); Jeffrey P. Mass, *Warrior Government in Early Medieval Japan* (New Haven, Conn.: Yale University Press, 1974).

Holy League, War of the (1510–1514)

PRINCIPAL COMBATANTS: Holy League (Italian states, Swiss cantons, Spain, and England) vs. France
PRINCIPAL THEATER(S): Italy
DECLARATION: None
MAJOR ISSUES AND OBJECTIVES: With papal support, the Holy League sought to oust the French from Italy.
OUTCOME: The French were forced out of Italy, but the Holy League did not long survive the death of the pope who had created it, and the French, now allied with the Swiss, returned to Italy after the war.
APPROXIMATE MAXIMUM NUMBER OF MEN UNDER ARMS: At the most important battle, Novara, the French fielded 10,000 men vs. an Italian-Swiss force of 13,000.
CASUALTIES: At Novara, at least 5,000 French troops and French-employed German mercenaries were killed or wounded; Holy League forces, 1,300 killed or wounded.
TREATIES: All the allies, unable to agree, made separate peace agreements with France.

When France threw its support behind Alfonso I (1486–1534) of Este against Pope Julius II (1443–1513), the pope organized a "Holy League" of Italian states, Swiss cantons, Spain, and England to field an army with the mission of pushing France out of Italy. In a vigorous campaign, the Holy League drove the French out of a number of Italian cities, including, most significantly, Milan, by the spring of 1512. Then, on June 6, 1513, a Swiss-Italian force engaged the French at Novara, 28 miles west of Milan. The French army, 10,000 men under Louis de La Trémoille (1460–1525), was surprised by an attack of the 13,000-man Swiss-Italian army, which included deadly pikemen. Although the attackers suffered heavy losses including 700 pikemen killed or wounded, they inflicted

at least 5,000 casualties on the French—a stunning casualty rate of 50 percent—which caused the desertion of German mercenaries fighting in the French ranks (those who surrendered to the Swiss were summarily executed) and forced the French to withdraw from Italy entirely. Yet the French surrendered to the Swiss, and not the Holy League, which, in fact, did not prove durable. With the death of Pope Julius II later in 1513, the league began to dissolve. The French and the Swiss would subsequently fight and then conclude an alliance that would give them control over much of Italy.

See also LEAGUE OF CAMBRAI, WAR OF THE.

Further reading: Christine Shaw, *Julius II, The Warrior Pope* (Cambridge, England: Blackwell, 1993).

Holy Roman Empire–Papacy War (1081–1084)

PRINCIPAL COMBATANTS: Holy Roman Emperor Henry IV vs. Pope Gregory VII (with his ally, Robert Guiscard)
PRINCIPAL THEATER(S): Italy, especially Rome
DECLARATION: None
MAJOR ISSUES AND OBJECTIVES: Henry IV wanted to depose Gregory VII and replace him with a pliant antipope, who would crown him Holy Roman Emperor.
OUTCOME: Henry IV deposed Gregory VII and did become Holy Roman Emperor, but he was forced out of Italy, and the supremacy of papal authority over the Holy Roman Empire in ecclesiastical matters was vindicated.
APPROXIMATE MAXIMUM NUMBER OF MEN UNDER ARMS: Unknown
CASUALTIES: Unknown
TREATIES: None

As a result of the ongoing GERMAN CIVIL WAR (1077–1106), the German king Henry IV (1050–1106) had been excommunicated by Pope Gregory VII (c. 1020–85). Despite having been defeated by forces of the Welfs (the papal party, known in Italy as Guelfs) in 1080, Henry invaded Italy the following year and laid siege against Rome. The city held out heroically, even after the fall of the Vatican and St. Peter's in 1083. Once established in the Vatican—Gregory VII fled to the castle of St. Angelo—Henry bribed key officials and thereby secured the surrender of Rome in 1084. Henry entered the city and installed the antipope Clement III (c. 1030–1100), who promptly named Henry IV Holy Roman Emperor.

At this point, Robert Guiscard (c. 1015–85), ruler of Apulia and Calabria, answered the pope's call for aid by leading a large army—mostly Norman, but including a motley assortment of men, even Muslim soldiers of fortune—against Rome. Overwhelmed, Henry's troops offered no resistance and returned to Germany. Unfortunately, Robert Guiscard's army did not merely liberate

Rome, but sacked it, causing much destruction. Pope Gregory VII was liberated, only to find himself effectively a prisoner of Robert Guiscard's men, who escorted him to exile in Salerno. There he was presumably to wait out the storm sweeping Rome in the aftermath of its sacking, but Gregory's health rapidly deteriorated, and he died in Salerno in 1085.

Although Gregory personally was a victim of the war, it ended as a victory for the power of the papacy over that of the Holy Roman Empire. In 1073, Gregory had issued a decree banning lay investiture—that is, the practice whereby lay rulers awarded churches to prelates. The 1081–84 war enforced this decree, thereby depriving the kings and princes of the Holy Roman Empire of important power over ecclesiastics, reserving that to the pope.

See also HOLY ROMAN EMPIRE–PAPACY WAR (1228–1241).

Further reading: H. E. J. Cowdrey, *Pope Gregory VII, 1073–1085* (New York: Oxford University Press, 1998).

Holy Roman Empire–Papacy War
(1228–1241)

PRINCIPAL COMBATANTS: Holy Roman Emperor Frederick II vs. Pope Gregory IX (with the Lombard League)

PRINCIPAL THEATER(S): Italy

DECLARATION: None

MAJOR ISSUES AND OBJECTIVES: The Holy Roman Empire and the papacy struggled for political supremacy.

OUTCOME: Largely undecided, although Frederick II made significant inroads into Italy

APPROXIMATE MAXIMUM NUMBER OF MEN UNDER ARMS: Variable

CASUALTIES: Unknown

TREATIES: The Peace of San Germano, 1230, brought an uneasy truce, which was soon broken.

The GERMAN CIVIL WAR (1077–1106) and the HOLY ROMAN EMPIRE–PAPACY WAR (1081–1084) were part of an ongoing dispute between the papacy and the Holy Roman Empire, both of which struggled to consolidate dominance over European affairs. The Holy Roman Emperor Frederick II (1194–1250) had been raised under papal care and was crowned in 1220. The assumption of Pope Honorius III (d. 1227) was that here, at long last, was an emperor who would be compliant and submissive to the papal will. On the contrary, Frederick II vigorously asserted the rights and authority of lay rulers. In an effort to control Frederick II, Honorius III ordered him to lead a crusade to Jerusalem; instead, the emperor sent troops under the command of others. The pope then arranged a marriage between Frederick and Isabella (Yolande) of Brienne (1212–28), the heiress to the kingdom of Jerusalem in 1225, and then, two years later, compelled him to undertake the Sixth CRUSADE.

This time, Frederick went, but, falling ill, returned early—and was promptly excommunicated by Honorius's successor, Gregory IX (c. 1143–1241).

In 1228, Gregory offered Frederick restoration to grace if he would sail to the Holy Land again. Although Frederick fought valiantly and successfully, recovering Jerusalem and becoming its king, Gregory incited rebellion in his territories. When, on his return to Europe, Frederick warred against papal forces in order to regain Sicily, Gregory once again excommunicated him—only to come to a grudging accommodation in the Peace of San Germano in 1230.

The peace was an uneasy one. Although Sicily remained quiet, Frederick fought throughout Italy in an effort to unite it under his rule. He was victorious against papal-sponsored Lombard resistance in 1231, then boldly summoned the Diet of the Empire at Piacenza in 1236 to compel Italian cooperation with him. Following this, he annexed church lands, thereby bringing upon himself yet another excommunication decree.

During 1236–37, Frederick conquered the Veronese March (borderlands) and routed the Welf (called Guelf in Italy) forces of the Lombard League at the Battle of Cortenuova on November 27, 1237. From this triumph, he went on to smash Milan. The following year, however, Frederick failed to take Brescia after a long siege. The pope, in the meantime, issued yet another excommunication and allied himself, secretly, with Genoa and Venice. Frederick laid siege to Milan, which also failed, and then, in 1240, he opened an assault on Rome. This served to initiate peace negotiations, which Gregory cut short in 1241, summarily summoning a General Council. Frederick asserted himself by forcibly preventing the council delegates from assembling. The war ended, suddenly, without further resolution when Pope Gregory IX died later in 1241. The struggle would resume just three years later.

See also HOLY ROMAN EMPIRE–PAPACY WAR (1243–1250), LOMBARD LEAGUE, WARS OF THE.

Further reading: David Abulafia, *Frederick II: A Medieval Emperor* (New York: Oxford University Press, 1992); Paul Wiegler, *The Infidel Emperor and His Struggles against the Pope: A Chronicle of the Thirteenth Century* (New York: E. P. Dutton, 1930).

Holy Roman Empire–Papacy War
(1243–1250)

PRINCIPAL COMBATANTS: Holy Roman Emperor Frederick II vs. papal-sponsored rebels, and Pope Innocent IV

PRINCIPAL THEATER(S): Italy

DECLARATION: None

MAJOR ISSUES AND OBJECTIVES: This war was a continuation of the seemingly endless struggle between the papacy and the Holy Roman Empire for control of the European (especially Italian) political sphere.

OUTCOME: The balance of victory seesawed between the belligerents, but, on balance, favored the Holy Roman Empire, pointing to a future in which the power of the papacy would be confined to matters of religion.
APPROXIMATE MAXIMUM NUMBER OF MEN UNDER ARMS: Unknown
CASUALTIES: Unknown
TREATIES: None

The death of Pope Gregory IX (c. 1143–1241) brought an abrupt end to the HOLY ROMAN EMPIRE–PAPACY WAR 1228–41, which proved nothing more than an intermission in the ongoing conflict between the lay rulers of the Holy Roman Empire and the ecclesiastical authorities of the papacy. In 1241, a new pope, Celestine IV (d. 1241), was elected to replace Gregory, only to die himself just 17 days later. Frederick II (1194–1250), the Holy Roman Emperor, took advantage of the chaos within the papacy to subdue the Papal States that had not been subdued during the war just concluded, and he planned a major naval assault on the papal strongholds of Genoa and Venice. In the meantime, he also lobbied for election of a compliant pope. But Innocent IV (d. 1254), sophisticated, smooth, and ruthless, was anything but compliant.

While Frederick negotiated with Innocent, seeking to lift his excommunication, the pope laid siege to Viterbo, hitherto an independent Italian city, in 1243. At the same time, Innocent stirred up a rebellion against Frederick in Lombardy, and then, in 1244, marched his forces into Rome in an effort to awe the emperor. Frederick responded by essentially renouncing the agreement he and the pope had negotiated beginning in 1239. This escalated to a military threat that called Innocent's bluff in Rome, and the pope retreated first to Genoa and then to Lyon. Innocent convened an ecumenical council in Lyon in 1245. The delegates managed to evade all of Frederick's attempts to prevent their reaching Lyon, including his blockade of all Alpine passes. They endorsed Innocent's new excommunication of Frederick and his order that the emperor be deposed on charges of violating the peace, sacrilege, and heresy. In 1246, the pope called on the German princes to elect a new emperor, and they selected Henry Raspe (c. 1202–47), landgrave of Thuringia. Upon his death, the princes selected William (1228–56) of Holland. Meanwhile, the pope engineered a rebellion against the Holy Roman Empire in Sicily. For their part, the Germans continued to support Frederick and rebelled against his replacement.

Frederick, in the meantime, concentrated on defeating the pope in Italy. In 1245, he invaded and sacked Viterbo, attacked Piacenza, and, the following year, decisively defeated the Welfs (papal forces known in Italy as Guelfs) at Parma. His attempt to take that city by storm, however, resulted in a prolonged siege, which was lifted under counterattack in 1248. After this, the situation in Italy worsened for Frederick. He suffered massive defeat in Tuscany, which he relinquished in 1249, then suffered the capture of his son in Sardinia. Yet the emperor refused to yield. Later in the year, he crushed a new rebellion in Sicily and retook Parma. The following year, 1250, the war suddenly ended with Frederick's death, much as the 1228–41 war had ended with the death of Gregory IX.

Although the war ended without full resolution of the struggle between the papacy and the Holy Roman Empire, Frederick's example pointed toward a future in which the role of the papacy would become increasingly limited to the ecclesiastical or spiritual realm, whereas the affairs of temporal politics would rest with lay rulers.

See also CRUSADE, SEVENTH; MONGOL INVASION OF EUROPE.

Further reading: David Abulafia, *Frederick II: A Medieval Emperor* (New York: Oxford University Press, 1992); Paul Wiegler, *The Infidel Emperor and His Struggles against the Pope: A Chronicle of the Thirteenth Century* (New York: E. P. Dutton, 1930).

Honduran Civil War (1909–1911)

PRINCIPAL COMBATANTS: Conservatives led by Manuel Bonilla vs. liberals led by incumbent president Miguel R. Dávila
PRINCIPAL THEATER(S): Nicaragua
DECLARATION: None
MAJOR ISSUES AND OBJECTIVES: Bonilla and the conservatives wanted to overthrow and replace the liberal Dávila, who had been placed in office by the dictator of Nicaragua.
OUTCOME: The war itself was inconclusive, but, following the armistice, Bonilla defeated Dávila in a peaceful election.
APPROXIMATE MAXIMUM NUMBER OF MEN UNDER ARMS: Unknown
CASUALTIES: Unknown
TREATIES: Armistice of February 8, 1911

This low-level conflict ensued after Nicaraguan dictator José Santos Zelaya (1853–1919) virtually installed Miguel R. Dávila (d. 1927) in the presidency of Honduras following Honduran defeat in the HONDURAN-NICARAGUAN WAR. The former Honduran president, Manuel Bonilla (1849–1913), led conservative supporters in a rebellion against the liberal Dávila, touching off an inconclusive civil war that was ended by mutual agreement to an armistice on February 8, 1911. New elections were called, and Bonilla was elected to replace Dávila.

See also NICARAGUAN CIVIL WAR (1909–1912).

Further reading: Dario Euraque, *Region and State in Honduras, 1870–1972: Reinterpreting the Banana Republic* (Chapel Hill: University of North Carolina Press, 1997); Harvey Kessler Meyer and Jessie H. Meyer, *Historical*

Dictionary of Honduras, 2nd ed. (Lanham, Md.: Rowman and Littlefield, 1994); Nancy Peckenham and Anne Streets, eds. *Honduras: Portrait of a Captive Nation* (New York: Praeger, 1985).

Honduran Guerrilla War (1981–1990)

PRINCIPAL COMBATANTS: Communist guerrillas (supported by Nicaragua's Sandinistas) vs. Honduran government forces (aided by the United States)
PRINCIPAL THEATER(S): Honduras
DECLARATION: None
MAJOR ISSUES AND OBJECTIVES: Leftist guerrillas sought to topple the right-wing Honduran government, which supported anti-Sandinista forces (or "contras") in El Salvador and Nicaragua.
OUTCOME: The war ended after Sandinista power diminished following the Nicaraguan elections of 1990.
APPROXIMATE MAXIMUM NUMBER OF MEN UNDER ARMS: Variable
CASUALTIES: In the thousands, principally civilian
TREATIES: None

The NICARAGUAN CIVIL WAR (1982–90) and the SALVADORAN CIVIL WAR produced large numbers of refugees, many of whom fled to Honduras. As a consequence of this influx, the Honduran government feared that Honduras would be exposed to attack by guerrillas from El Salvador and Nicaragua. The fears rapidly proved well founded as Cuban-trained guerrillas hit Honduran military and police installations and terrorized the Honduran capital of Tegucigalpa, even attacking the U.S. embassy there. The United States supplied large amounts of military hardware to Honduran government forces in an effort to combat the rebels.

In the meantime, the anti-Sandinista (the Sandinistas were the revolutionaries who had seized power in Nicaragua) Nicaraguan Democratic Force (FDN) formed within Honduras and, from bases there, launched raids into Nicaragua. This provoked the Sandinistas to invade Honduras to raid the FDN bases. In response, the United States provided helicopters and pilots to carry Honduran troops to the border regions to repel the invasion. The United States then sent 3,200 combat troops to assist the anti-Sandinista forces, which were collectively called *contras*. This, however, provoked left-wing violence within Honduras, as many objected to the American military presence in the country.

In actuality, the United States had a deeper and more extensive involvement in the Honduran war than was generally known at the time. The administration of Ronald Reagan (1911–2004) came into office in 1981, with two of its top priorities being an end to the war in El Salvador and aiding the contra guerrilla war against the Sandinistas in Nicaragua. Honduras, located between El Salvador and Nicaragua and embroiled in a guerrilla warfare spawned by the conflicts of its neighbors, effectively became the base for all U.S. operations in Central America. The U.S. Central Intelligence Agency (CIA) supported covert operations, including the U.S.-trained Battalion 316, a secret Honduran army intelligence unit formed in 1982. Battalion 316 soon became notorious for committing human rights abuses. With U.S. support, the Honduran army suppressed the small Honduran guerrilla movement between 1980 and 1984, typically by the most brutal means available, including imprisonment and torture, in addition to outright murder.

By 1990, the Honduran war quickly wound down after the Sandinistas were defeated in the Nicaraguan elections. Revelations concerning the Reagan administration's illegal covert support of the contras prompted the U.S. Congress to eliminate much of the U.S. military presence in Central America at this time as well. Nevertheless, the end of the war did not bring an immediate end to the killing. Peasants seeking land reforms and threatening to seize land in default of government action were attacked and killed in 1991 after they began farming idle land. When this outrage was exposed, publicly contrite government officials pledged to bring an end to human rights abuses in Honduras and to introduce land reform.

Further reading: Thomas P. Anderson, *Politics in Central America: Guatemala, El Salvador, Honduras, and Nicaragua* (New York: Praeger, 1988); Jonathan R. Barton, *Political Geography of Latin America* (New York: Routledge, 1997); Harvey Kessler Meyer and Jessie H. Meyer, *Historical Dictionary of Honduras,* 2nd ed. (Lanham, Md.: Rowman and Littlefield, 1994); Nancy Peckenham and Anne Streets, eds. *Honduras: Portrait of a Captive Nation* (New York: Praeger, 1985); Donald E. Schulz and Deborah Sundloff Schulz, *The United States, Honduras, and the Crisis in Central America* (Boulder, Colo.: Westview Press, 1994).

Honduran-Nicaraguan War (1907)

PRINCIPAL COMBATANTS: Honduras vs. Nicaragua
PRINCIPAL THEATER(S): Honduras
DECLARATION: None
MAJOR ISSUES AND OBJECTIVES: Ostensibly, Nicaragua was responding to a Honduran violation of its sovereignty; however, the war was a product of Nicaragua president Zelaya's desire to gain control of his Central American neighbors toward the eventual end of uniting Central America under his rule.
OUTCOME: Honduras accepted the installation of Zelaya's handpicked candidate for Honduran president.
APPROXIMATE MAXIMUM NUMBER OF MEN UNDER ARMS: Unknown
CASUALTIES: Unknown
TREATIES: None

After José Santos Zelaya (1853–1919) became president of Nicaragua as a result of a liberal revolt in 1893, he not only assumed dictatorial authority within his own borders, but sought to unite other Central American countries under his leadership. Toward this end, he often interfered in the internal affairs of his neighbors. When, in 1903, the conservative Honduran politician Manuel Bonilla (1849–1913) led a successful coup against the liberal government Zelaya had supported in Honduras, Zelaya enthusiastically supported Honduran rebels who sought to topple Bonilla. When a 1906 revolt failed, Honduran troops pursued fleeing rebels across the border with Nicaragua. An indignant Zelaya demanded reparations from Honduras for having violated Nicaraguan sovereignty. Honduras refused, and, in response, Nicaraguan forces invaded. The resulting war is notable for the Battle of Namasigue, fought on Honduran territory on March 18, 1907, using (among other weapons) machine guns. It was the first use of this weapon in Central America.

The Nicaraguans prevailed at Namasigue and went on to overrun Tegucigalpa, the Honduran capital. Bonilla sought refuge in the United States, and Zelaya installed Miguel R. Dávila (d. 1927) as his handpicked president of a new liberal Honduran regime. This led to the HONDURAN CIVIL WAR.

Further reading: Dario Euraque, *Region and State in Honduras, 1870–1972: Reinterpreting the Banana Republic* (Chapel Hill: University of North Carolina Press, 1997); Harvey Kessler Meyer and Jessie H. Meyer, *Historical Dictionary of Honduras,* 2nd ed. (Lanham, Md.: Rowman and Littlefield, 1994); Thomas W. Walker, *Nicaragua,* 4th ed. (Boulder, Colo.: Westview Press, 2003).

Honduran-Salvadoran War *See* SOCCER WAR (FOOTBALL WAR).

Hono Heke's War *See* BAY OF ISLANDS WAR (1844–1847).

Hottentot Uprising (1904–1907)

PRINCIPAL COMBATANTS: Germany vs. the "Hottentots" (including Herero, Ovambo, Nama, and Oorlam tribes)
PRINCIPAL THEATER(S): German Southwest Africa (Namibia)
DECLARATION: None
MAJOR ISSUES AND OBJECTIVES: Tribal resistance to German colonial incursions and outrages
OUTCOME: Resistance was ultimately crushed.
APPROXIMATE MAXIMUM NUMBER OF MEN UNDER ARMS: Germany, 80,000; tribes, 100,000
CASUALTIES: Germany, 6,000; tribes, 30,000
TREATIES: None

Early in the 20th century, German settlers arrived in great numbers in southwest Africa, mainly to exploit copper and diamond mining. Beginning in 1904, a group of tribes, generally called Hottentots by the Germans, rose up in rebellion.

The first tribe to rebel was the Herero—and, in a single encounter, the Ovambo, who attacked Fort Namutoni near the Etosha Pan. The first phase of the war ended when General Lother van Trotha (1848–1920) defeated the main force of Herero warriors at the Battle of Waterburg. The German victors took no prisoners, but instead drove the survivors of the battle into the Kalahari Desert, where most died. These in effect mass execution tactics were typical of the German approach to warfare in the region. Although the tribes came close to expelling the Germans from the region, the German response was vigorous and ruthless. Mass execution and confinement in squalid concentration camps were common. By the end of the war, the population of the Herero tribe was reduced by some 80 percent.

The later phases of the uprising were dominated by resistance from the Nama tribe. This uprising was crushed by 1907, and Nama survivors were confined to concentration camps, which were, in fact, death camps. Starvation, disease, and general privation killed two-thirds of the Nama confined.

See also HERERO UPRISING.

Further reading: Helmut Bley, *Namibia under German Rule* (Hamburg and Windhoek, Namibia: Namibia Scientific Society, 1996); Jon Bridgman, *The Revolt of the Hereros* (Berkeley: University of California Press, 1981); San-Bart Gewald, *Herero Heroes: A Socio-Political History of the Herero of Namibia, 1890–1923* (Athens: Ohio University Press, 1999).

Hot Water War *See* FRIES'S REBELLION (HOT WATER WAR).

Huguenot Revolt *See* BÉARNESE REVOLT, SECOND (1625–1626).

Huguenot Wars *See* RELIGION, FIRST WAR OF; RELIGION, SECOND WAR OF; RELIGION, THIRD WAR OF; RELIGION, FOURTH WAR OF; RELIGION, FIFTH WAR OF; RELIGION, SIXTH AND SEVENTH WARS OF; RELIGION, EIGHTH WAR OF; RELIGION, NINTH WAR OF.

Hukbalahap Rebellion (1946–1954)

PRINCIPAL COMBATANTS: "Huk" guerrillas vs. Japan (during its World War II occupation of the Philippines) and, after the war, the newly independent Filipino government

PRINCIPAL THEATER(S): Philippines

DECLARATION: None

MAJOR ISSUES AND OBJECTIVES: During World War II, the Huks resisted the Japanese occupiers of the islands; after the war, they sought to introduce a communist presence in the newly independent Philippine government.

OUTCOME: Although the Huks were highly effective against the Japanese and, initially, against the postwar government, they were no match for U.S.-supplied weaponry and the reform government of Ramón Magsaysay.

APPROXIMATE MAXIMUM NUMBER OF MEN UNDER ARMS: Unknown

CASUALTIES: Unknown

TREATIES: None

Much of the resistance to the Japanese occupation of the Philippines during WORLD WAR II came from "Huks," members of the Hukbalahap, translated as "People's Anti-Japanese Army." The origin of the Hukbalahap may be found in various communist and socialist grassroots political groups that flourished in the Philippines beginning in the 1930s. The Huks became a highly effective guerrilla force, responsible for the deaths of thousands of Japanese soldiers, as well as Filipinos who collaborated with the invaders.

The Huks came to control most of central Luzon by 1945 and created a functioning government that collected taxes and administered laws. Although some of those who collaborated with the Japanese had also secretly helped the guerrillas, many Huks—especially the rank-and-file who had remained in the hills—came out of the war bitterly against those who appeared to have benefited from the occupation. The differences between these two extreme groups would mark the politics of the postwar Philippines.

After the war, the Huks took part in the elections that followed Philippine independence on July 4, 1946, but managed to gain only a single seat in Congress. The newly constituted government refused to seat the Huk representative, however, and the Huks reactivated their guerrilla organization, this time in opposition to the new government. The guerrilla movement fed off a growing sense of social injustice among tenant farmers, especially in central Luzon. Soon, government forces proved virtually powerless against the sophisticated guerrilla organization, and in 1950 the Huks ventured out of their jungle encampments to make an assault on Manila. This time, however, government forces were ready, having identified the location of the Huk headquarters within the city. On the eve of the attack, government troops raided the headquarters and arrested all the principal Huk leaders. The attack was called off.

To forestall further Huk activity, the United States sent weapons and other military equipment to the government forces, which made them far more effective in combating the guerrillas—although a low-level state of civil insurrection persisted through 1954. Even more effective against the Huks than U.S. weapons was the presidency of Ramón Magsaysay (1907–57), whose bold political and economic reforms, beginning in 1953, quickly eroded popular support for the communist movement. The last leader of the Huks surrendered in 1954.

See also WORLD WAR II: PACIFIC.

Further reading: Lawrence M. Greenberg, *The Hukbalahap Insurrection: A Case Study of a Successful Anti-Insurgency Operation in the Philippines, 1946–1955* (Washington: D.C.: Analysis Branch, U.S. Army Center of Military History, 1987); Edward Geary Lansdale, *In the Midst of Wars: An American's Mission to Southeast Asia* (New York: Fordham University Press, 1991).

Hundred Days' War (1815)

PRINCIPAL COMBATANTS: France vs. the allied countries of Great Britain, Austria, Russia, and Prussia

PRINCIPAL THEATER(S): France

DECLARATION: The allies declared Napoleon an international outlaw after he returned to France and reclaimed the throne.

MAJOR ISSUES AND OBJECTIVES: Napoleon sought to regain rule of France.

OUTCOME: Napoleon's forces were defeated, and he died in exile.

APPROXIMATE MAXIMUM NUMBER OF MEN UNDER ARMS: France, 188,000 troops in the field, 100,000 in garrisons; allies, 721,000

CASUALTIES: France, 43,000 killed or wounded; Allies, 11,400 killed or wounded

TREATIES: Second Peace of Paris, November 20, 1815

While in exile on Elba, Napoleon (1769–1821)—brooding over his fate and unhappy with his treatment—became aware of France's dissatisfaction over the restoration of the Bourbon dynasty, and he returned to France in 1815. Landing at Cannes on March 1, with a detachment of his guard, he was greeted by many not as a fallen emperor but as the embodiment of the spirit of the Revolution and the returning savior of the nation's glory. As he crossed the Alps, the republican peasantry rallied round him, and near Grenoble, he won over the soldiers sent to arrest him. King Louis XVIII (1755–1824) fled in terror, and Napoleon marched into Paris on March 20, commencing the period known as the "Hundred Days." Napoleon knew that his exhausted nation and greatly reduced army were in no condition to take on all of Europe. Accordingly, he proclaimed peaceful intentions. But the allies—Austria, Great Britain, Russia, and Prussia—meeting at the Congress of Vienna, declared him an outlaw, summarily prepared for renewed war, and made plans to invade France.

To rally the French masses to his cause, he probably should have allied himself once more with the Jacobins, but he was afraid to do so and alienate the bourgeoisie whose support was critical and whose predominance he himself had always assured. The bourgeoisie feared above everything a revival of the socialist experiments France had suffered at the hands of Jacobin radicals in 1793 and 1794. Thus, all Napoleon had to offer was a political regime not unlike that of Louis XVIII, except with himself at the top. Enthusiasm ebbed, and his latest adventure seemed a dead end. In these circumstances, Napoleon, as always, chose action. Rather than adopt a defensive posture, Napoleon determined that his only chance was to separate the Prussian and Anglo-Dutch armies in order to defeat them in detail in what is now Belgium.

He took the field at the head of a 125,000-man army and marched north. He captured Charleroi and, on June 16, 1815, defeated the Prussians, led by Field Marshall Gebhard von Blücher (1749–1819), at Ligny. That same day, the British under Sir Arthur Wellesley, Lord Wellington (1769–1852), defeated another French force at Quartre-Bras but in so doing was prevented from rushing to von Blücher's defense. Buoyed by his victory Napoleon attacked the combined forces of the Lord Wellington and von Blücher at Waterloo on June 18, 1815, and was utterly defeated in one of the most famous battles in history. The routed French fled, and the allies marched on to Paris unopposed.

Returning to Paris ahead of the enemy, Napoleon abdicated for the second time on June 23. He took flight to Aix, where he surrendered to the captain of the British warship *Bellerophon* and was exiled, as a prisoner of war, to the island of St. Helena, where he died on May 5, 1821.

See also COALITION, WAR OF THE FIRST; COALITION, WAR OF THE SECOND; COALITION, WAR OF THE THIRD; FRENCH REVOLUTION (1789–1799); FRENCH REVOLUTIONARY WARS; NAPOLEONIC WARS; NAPOLEON'S INVASION OF RUSSIA; NAPOLEON'S WAR WITH AUSTRIA; PENINSULAR WAR.

Further reading: Donald Frederick, *Imperial Sunset: The Fall of Napoleon, 1813–1814* (New York: Cooper Square Press, 2001); Peter Hofschoröer, *1815, The Waterloo Campaign: Wellington and His German Allies and the Battles of Ligny and Quatre Bras* (Mechanicsburg, Pa.: Stackpole Books, 1998) and *1815, the Waterloo Campaign: The German Victory: From Waterloo to the Fall of Napoleon* (Mechanicsburg, Pa.: Stackpole Books, 1999).

Hundred Years' War (1337–1453)

PRINCIPAL COMBATANTS: England vs. France
PRINCIPAL THEATER(S): France
DECLARATION: None
MAJOR ISSUES AND OBJECTIVES: King Edward III of England sought to press his claim to the throne of France; his successors, though they relinquished the claim, wanted to preserve England's holdings in Guyenne (Guienne) and Calais.
OUTCOME: England was crippled by the cost of war that lasted for more than 100 years, while France became more unified and less feudal in nature.
APPROXIMATE MAXIMUM NUMBER OF MEN UNDER ARMS: Size of the armie varied over time, Edward probably had 10,000 men on his 1359 campaign; Henry V 15,000.
CASUALTIES: Unknown but they were enormous. Some estimate that the war and the plague reduced Europe's population by half.
TREATIES: Treaty of Brétigny (1360), Peace of Paris (1396), Treaty of Troyes (1420)

When Charles IV (1249–1328) died in 1328 with no male children, a crisis of succession was sparked in France. Before his death, Charles had made plans to forestall such a crisis by stipulating that Philip of Valois (1293–1350), his cousin, would be named king in the event that his wife, pregnant at the time of his death, gave birth to a girl. Philip indeed claimed the throne as Philip VI upon the death of Charles, but also entering the fray was Isabella (1292–1358), Charles's sister and the mother of Edward III (1312–77) of England. The French assembly, despite the closer line of descent of Isabella, recognized Philip's claim, sparking a period of war between France and England that lasted until 1453.

When Edward III succeeded to the English throne, he lacked the power to press his claim to France, but he did have control of Guienne, a long strip of coastline from La Rochelle to Bayonne and the Pyrenees. Vital to England for trade, this region had been held by England as feudatory to the king of France since 1259. England also held Ponthieu, whose major towns were Abbeville and Crécy. Not only was Edward III determined to hold Guienne and Ponthieu, he was also intent on punishing Philip VI for giving refuge to David II (1324–71), king of Scotland, England's enemy to the north.

In 1337, Edward claimed the French throne, while Philip negated England's right to Guienne. The ensuing war occurred in four phases.

Between 1337 and 1360, Edward was victorious at several battles but at last had to renounce his claim to the French throne. At the Battle of Sluys, Edward won a major victory at sea. In the daylong fight, the English fleet of 150 ships gained command of the English Channel and sank or captured 166 out of the total 190 French ships. A truce between the warring nations lasted for about two years. At the Battle of Crécy, the English army defeated a French force nearly three times its size. The French made 15 or 16 separate attacks in their attempt to push Edward from the field, but by the end of the fighting on the night of August 26, 1346, France had lost 1,542 lords and knights and 10,000 to 20,000 men-at-arms, crossbowmen, and infantry. England lost two knights, and 40 men-at-arms and archers, and an unknown but small number of Welsh infantrymen. Edward reached Calais on September 4, 1346, and laid siege on the city. After a year, the city was England's.

Over the next several years, England and France were unable to mount significant campaigns due to the ravages of the Black Death. But in 1355, Edward was once again ready to cross the Channel and lead his army in devastating raids across northern France. In the meantime, Edward's sons, John of Gaunt (1340–99) and Edward (1330–76), prince of Wales (known as the Black Prince) raided Brittany and Languedoc, respectively.

The war took a new turn with the capture of French king John II (1319–64) (who had been crowned at the death of Philip VI in 1350) at the Battle of Poitiers on September 19, 1356. In this battle, the Black Prince sent a small party to attack the French rear lines, and this proved too much for the French soldiers, whose ranks had been riddled by arrows from English longbows. Both John II and his son, the dauphin, later to be crowned as Charles V (1337–80), were captured and taken to England under a ransom of 3 million crowns.

Among those most affected by the uncontrolled sweep of the English army were French peasants, who could not work in the fields without posting a watchman and who had given up their homes for the relative safety of caves and forests. In 1358, the French peasants rose in rebellion, protesting the inability of the nobility to protect them against English depredations and the costly demands of the army for food and money. Known as the revolt of the JACQUERIE after the scornful nickname "Jacques" for French peasants, the revolt ended when Charles II (1332–87) of Navarre and other French nobles massacred the peasant mob near Meaux.

Meanwhile, Edward's raids continued right up to the gates of Paris. Edward rarely had trouble filling the ranks of his invading army because of the success of the raids. In fact, many Englishmen of less than noble status made fortunes from looting and pillaging northern France. On October 24, 1360, Edward negotiated the Treaty of Brétigny, by which English holdings in southwestern France, known as Aquitaine, were increased significantly and were to be held in full sovereignty, and France recognized English control of Calais and Ponthieu. Edward renounced his claim to the throne, and John II was ransomed.

The second phase of the war began with the death of John II. He was succeeded by Charles V (1337–80), and over the span of his reign (from 1360 to 1380) he defeated England and regained control of Aquitaine. John of Gaunt set out to reverse the tide of English losses, but defeats continued to mount up—at Poitiers, Poitou, and La Rochelle. By 1373, Aquitaine no longer existed. The French under Charles V made raids on English soil, penetrating as far as Rye, Lewes, Plymouth, Hastings, Winchelsea, and Gravesend. At the deaths of the Black Prince in 1376, Edward III of England in 1377, and

Charles V of France in 1380, the tide had turned in the war, which by 1380 had been raging for 43 years.

The following year, England was plagued with a peasant revolt similar to the Jacquerie in France. (See ENGLISH PEASANT REVOLT.) Spreading from Essex to Kent and then to all of England, the peasant rebels marched to London and beheaded Simon of Sudburg (d. 1381), archbishop of Canterbury and chancellor, and Sir Robert Hales, the treasurer. Eventually the rabble was dispersed, and King Richard II (1367–1400), in retaliation, reneged on his promises of relief to them.

Between 1386 and 1396, periods of truce were interspersed with periods of fighting. Then in 1396, the Peace of Paris was negotiated. Richard II of England and Charles VI (1380–1422) of France agreed to abide by a truce for the next 30 years. By the terms of the treaty, England retained control of Calais and part of Gascony between Bordeaux and Bayonne.

However, peace lasted only a short time. The French continued raiding the southern coast of England and providing aid to Scotland and Wales in their struggles with England. In the meantime, John the Fearless (1371–1419), duke of Burgundy, and Louis I (1372–1407), duke of Orléans, engaged in a power struggle that ultimately grew to a full-scale civil war in France. Then in April 1415, Henry V (1387–1422) of England declared war on Charles VI of France and set sail with an army of 12,000 men to Normandy in phase three of the war. After capturing Harfleur and winning a battle at Agincourt, Henry captured Rouen in 1419. The French government then signed the Treaty of Troyes in 1420. Control of northern France went to Henry V and the duke of Burgundy, and Henry became the heir of Charles VI. Married to Charles VI's daughter Catherine, Henry V spent much of his time consolidating his holdings in northern France. In 1422, he died, leaving nine-month-old Henry VI (1421–71) king of England and France. South of the Loire, however, the French recognized the dauphin, Charles VII (1403–61), as king, and a rival government was created in Bourges. Between 1423 and 1426, the English won battles at Cravant, Verneuil, and St. James, and by 1428, they had consolidated their control of northern France. In 1428, the English set out from Paris toward Orléans, where they laid siege against the town (see ORLÉANS, SIEGE OF). Jeanne d'Arc (1412–31) (Joan of Arc) as 17-year-old peasant girl from Champagne, came to the aid of the dauphin and convinced many in the French army that her divine mission was to expel the English from French soil. Jeanne was ultimately victorious at Orléans, and the dauphin was crowned Charles VII at Rheims on July 16, 1429. Captured by the Burgundians and turned over to the English, Jeanne was convicted of heresy and was burned at the stake on May 30, 1431. Though she had helped him become king, Charles VII did nothing to aid her.

The final phase of the war began when the English lost control of Paris in 1436, Normandy in 1449 and 1450, and Guienne in 1451. Recovering to a degree, the English captured Bordeaux in 1452, but on October 19, 1453, Bordeaux fell to the French, and the Hundred Years' War came to a close.

By the end of the war, the government of England was bankrupt, and the Lancastrian dynasty was discredited. Civil war in the form of the Wars of the ROSES would soon follow in 1455. For the French, the Hundred Years' War brought national unity and the beginnings of a dismantling of feudalism.

See also BRETON SUCCESSION, WAR OF THE; BLACK PRINCE'S NAVARETTE CAMPAIGN; GASCON NOBLES' REVOLT; "GÜGLERS" WAR; HENRY OF BOLINGBROKE'S REVOLT; NORMAN CONQUEST; EDWARD, THE BLACK PRINCE, RAIDS OF.

Further reading: Christopher Allmand, *The Hundred Years War: England and France at War, c. 1300–1450* (New York: Cambridge University Press, 1988); Anne Curry, *The Hundred Years War* (New York: Palgrave Macmillan, 2003); Robin Neillands, *The Hundred Years War* (New York: Routledge, 2001); Jonathan Sumption, *The Hundred Years War* (Boston: Faber and Faber, 1999).

Hungarian-Bohemian Wars   *See* BOHEMIAN-HUNGARIAN WAR (1260–1270); BOHEMIAN-HUNGARIAN WAR (1468–1478).

Hungarian Civil War   (1301–1308)

PRINCIPAL COMBATANTS: Aspirants to the Hungarian crown following the death of King Andrew III vs. last of the Árpád dynasty
PRINCIPAL THEATER(S): Hungary
DECLARATION: None
MAJOR ISSUES AND OBJECTIVES: Succession to the Hungarian throne
OUTCOME: After much strife, Charles Robert of Naples was elected by the Hungarian diet as king.
APPROXIMATE MAXIMUM NUMBER OF MEN UNDER ARMS: Unknown
CASUALTIES: Unknown
TREATIES: None

Hungary's Árpád dynasty had come dangerously close to extinction when the death of Stephan V (1239–72) left the country in the hands of his Cuman widow Elizabeth, whose regency (1272–77) was bedeviled by a wild and unruly son and much civil unrest. Ladislav IV (1262–90), kidnapped by rebels as a child, grew up so nearly pagan that Pope Nicholas IV (d. 1292) called for a crusade against him when he reached his majority. When he was assassinated by Cuman tribesmen following years of upheaval and uncertainty, the Hungarian throne was left without a legitimate heir. Those in the female line—

including some of Europe's important houses in Bohemia, Bavaria, and Naples—quickly prepared to stake their claim.

Then one male of Árpád descent was discovered in Italy. Although some impugned his legitimacy, his supporters smuggled him into the country, where he assumed the throne as the surprisingly adept and wise Andrew III. However, when he died without male issue in 1301, the national dynasty did indeed become extinct. Though Hungary was now entitled to choose a successor, bloodlines remained a major concern. The maneuverings of those basing their hopes yet again on claims of descent from an Árpád in the female line touched off a war of succession.

Those fighting to seize the Hungarian throne were Bohemia's Wenceslaus III (1289–1306), Bavaria's Duke Otto III (d. 1312), and Naples's Charles Robert of Anjou (1288–1342), who was aided by his uncle, King Albert I (c. 1250–1308) of Germany, as well as Pope Boniface VIII (c. 1235–1303). Albert called upon Bohemia's King Wenceslaus II (1271–1305), father of Wenceslaus III, to renounce all claim to Hungary's crown of St. Stephen and to remove his son from the Hungarian throne—despite the fact that the Hungarian diet had elected Wenceslaus III in 1301. Wenceslaus II refused Albert's demand, whereupon Albert invaded Bohemia in 1304. However, he met stiff resistance from the armies of Wenceslaus II, which not only pushed Albert's forces back but were about to take the offensive and invade Austria when Wenceslaus II died. At this point, in 1305, Wenceslaus III, now king of Bohemia, relinquished the Hungarian throne to Duke Otto. Far from resolving the civil strife, this led to a period of intense disorder until the Hungarian diet elected Charles Robert as King Charles I in 1308; he was crowned in 1310. During the first 15 years of his reign, Charles I was engaged in continuous struggles to subdue the Hungarian nobles.

Further reading: Pál Engel, *The Realm of St. Stephen: A History of Medieval Hungary, 895–1526,* trans. Tamás Pálosfalvi (New York: I. B. Tauris, 2001); Paul Ignotus, *Hungary* (New York: Praeger, 1972); Dominic G. Kosáry, *A History of Hungary* (New York: Arno Press, 1971); C. A. Macartney, *Hungary, a Short History* (Edinburgh, Scotland: Edinburgh University Press, 1962); Denis Sinor, *History of Hungary* (Westport, Conn.: Greenwood Press, 1976); Domokos Varga, *Hungary in Greatness and Decline: The 14th and 15th Centuries,* trans. Martha Szacsvay Lipták (Corvino Kiadó and Stone Mountain, Ga.: Hungarian Cultural Foundation, 1982).

Hungarian Civil War   (1439–1440)

PRINCIPAL COMBATANTS: Contenders for the Hungarian throne following the death of King Albert II
PRINCIPAL THEATER(S): Hungary
DECLARATION: None

MAJOR ISSUES AND OBJECTIVES: Succession to the throne
OUTCOME: Backed by a powerful general, Ladislas III, whom the majority of nobles supported, became king.
APPROXIMATE MAXIMUM NUMBER OF MEN UNDER ARMS: Unknown
CASUALTIES: Unknown
TREATIES: None

When King Albert II (1397–1439), monarch of Hungary and Bohemia, died, he left a pregnant widow whose unborn son had a claim to the Hungarian throne. But his death sparked a war of succession, in part because the fatherless newborn came under the guardianship of Frederick III (1415–93), king of Germany and subsequently the Holy Roman Emperor. Frederick was despised by the Hungarian nobility, led by General John Hunyadi, hero of the HUNGARIAN-TURKISH WAR (1437–1438), and they turned instead to Poland's King Ladislav III (1387–1456). Civil war erupted, but Hunyadi's faction succeeded in placing the Polish pretender on the throne as Uladislas I in 1440. His reign would last for only a few years, and after his death at the battle of Varna in 1444 during the HUNGARIAN-TURKISH WAR (1444–1456), the now four-year-old son of Albert II, also known as Ladislav, was proclaimed Hungary's King Ladislav V (sometimes called Ladislav V Posthumous) (1440–57) with Hunyadi serving as regent.

Further reading: Pál Engel, *The Realm of St. Stephen: A History of Medieval Hungary, 895–1526,* trans. Tamás Pálosfalvi (New York: I. B. Tauris, 2001); Joseph Held, *Hunyadi: Legend and Reality* (Boulder, Colo., and New York: East European Monographs, distributed by Columbia University Press, 1985); Paul Ignotus, *Hungary* (New York: Praeger, 1972); Dominic G. Kosáry, *A History of Hungary* (New York: Arno Press, 1971); C. A. Macartney, *Hungary, a Short History* (Edinburgh, Scotland: Edinburgh University Press, 1962); Denis Sinor, *History of Hungary* (Westport, Conn.: Greenwood Press, 1976); Domokos Varga, *Hungary in Greatness and Decline: The 14th and 15th Centuries,* trans. Martha Szacsvay Lipták (Corvino Kiadó and Stone Mountain, Ga.: Hungarian Cultural Foundation, 1982).

Hungarian Civil War (1526–1529)

PRINCIPAL COMBATANTS: Forces of John Zápolya (with Ottoman aid) vs. forces of Frederick III of Germany
PRINCIPAL THEATER(S): Hungary
DECLARATION: None
MAJOR ISSUES AND OBJECTIVES: Ascension to the Hungarian throne
OUTCOME: With Ottoman aid, John Zápolya regained the throne.
APPROXIMATE MAXIMUM NUMBER OF MEN UNDER ARMS: Unknown
CASUALTIES: Unknown
TREATIES: None

In the wake of the HUNGARIAN-TURKISH WAR (1521–1526), John Zápolya (1487–1540) of Transylvania was elected king of Ottoman Hungary. However, Austria's Archduke Ferdinand (1503–64)—subsequently Holy Roman Emperor—asserted his claim to the throne as the brother-in-law of the preceding Hungarian king, Louis II (1506–26). He persuaded the Hungarian diet, which approved him king in 1527. Thus authorized, Ferdinand invaded Hungary, capturing Raab, Gran (Esztergom), and Buda. The decisive battle was fought at Tokay in 1527 and resulted in the defeat of Zápolya and his army.

At this juncture, John Zápolya appealed to the Ottoman sultan Süleyman I the Magnificent (1496–1566), who responded by invading Hungary. After recapturing Buda, Süleyman returned Zápolya to the throne in 1529, and the restored monarch accompanied the sultan on his campaign against Vienna in the AUSTRO-TURKISH WAR (1529–1533).

Further reading: Pál Fódor and Géza Dávid, eds., *Ottomans, Hungarians, and Hapsburgs in Central Europe* (Boston: Brill, 2000); Paul Ignotus, *Hungary* (New York: Praeger, 1972; Dominic G. Kosáry, *A History of Hungary* (New York: Arno Press, 1971); C. A. Macartney, *Hungary, a Short History* (Edinburgh, Scotland: Edinburgh University Press, 1962); Denis Sinor, *History of Hungary* (Westport, Conn.: Greenwood Press, 1976).

Hungarian Civil War (1540–1547)

PRINCIPAL COMBATANTS: Archduke Ferdinand of Austria vs. John II Sigismund (with Ottoman aid)
PRINCIPAL THEATER(S): Hungary
DECLARATION: None
MAJOR ISSUES AND OBJECTIVES: Succession to the Hungarian throne
OUTCOME: Hungary was partitioned among Austria's Ferdinand, Hungary's John II Sigismund, and the Ottoman Empire's Sultan Süleyman I the Magnificent.
APPROXIMATE MAXIMUM NUMBER OF MEN UNDER ARMS: Unknown
CASUALTIES: Unknown
TREATIES: Truce of 1547

The AUSTRO-TURKISH WAR (1537–1547) produced the secret Treaty of Nagyvárad, by which Hungary was partitioned: Austria's Archduke Ferdinand (1503–64) received Croatia, Slavonia, and western Hungary, whereas John Zápolya (1487–1540) retained the title of king of Hungary and the remainder of the country, including the capital, Buda. The secret treaty further stipulated that the title, throne, and Zápolya's lands would go to Ferdinand on

Zápolya's death. When John Zápolya died, however, it was his infant son who was named king as John II Sigismund (1540–71). Ferdinand invoked the secret treaty, claimed the kingdom, and laid siege to Buda, whereupon Zápolya's widow appealed to the Ottoman sultan Süleyman I (the Magnificent; 1496–1566) for help.

Süleyman did not want Austria to make any gains in Hungary and eagerly dispatched an army to seize Buda, as well as other cities. He set up a Turkish administration throughout the country while fighting raged through 1547. At that point, the demands of the TURKO-PERSIAN WAR (1526–1555) forced Süleyman to conclude a five-year truce, which gave Ferdinand control of Austrian Hungary in return for tribute paid to the Ottomans. John II Sigismund received Transylvania and neighboring areas, along with the title "prince." The Ottomans held southern and central Hungary.

See also AUSTRO-TURKISH WAR (1551–1553).

Further reading: Pál Fódor and Géza Dávid, eds., *Ottomans, Hungarians, and Hapsburgs in Central Europe* (Boston: Brill, 2000); Paul Ignotus, *Hungary* (New York: Praeger, 1972); Dominic G. Kosáry, *A History of Hungary* (New York: Arno Press, 1971); C. A. Macartney, *Hungary, a Short History* (Edinburgh, Scotland: Edinburgh University Press, 1962); Denis Sinor, *History of Hungary* (Westport, Conn.: Greenwood Press, 1976).

Hungarian Civil War (1921)

PRINCIPAL COMBATANTS: Former Austro-Hungarian emperor Charles I vs. the government forces of Admiral Horthy
PRINCIPAL THEATER(S): Hungary
DECLARATION: None
MAJOR ISSUES AND OBJECTIVES: Charles I wanted to regain the Hungarian throne.
OUTCOME: Charles was defeated and exiled; Austrian claims on the Hungarian throne were nullified.
APPROXIMATE MAXIMUM NUMBER OF MEN UNDER ARMS: Unknown
CASUALTIES: Unknown
TREATIES: None

The former Austro-Hungarian emperor Charles I (1887–1922) had fled to Switzerland in 1919 during KUN'S RED TERROR. In March 1921, he returned to Hungary in a bid to recover his throne and called on the current regent and de facto head of state, the aristocratic, anticommunist Admiral Nicholas Horthy de Nagybánya (1868–1957), to step down.

Popular opposition to Charles was intense, and even the monarchists challenged the legitimacy of his title to the throne. His attempts to return to power set the stage for the rise of Count István Bethlen (1874–1946), who

dominated Hungarian politics for the next 10 years. In effect, Charles's return split Hungary's main tradition-minded political parties between conservatives who favored a return to Hapsburg rule and radical right-wing nationalists who supported the election of a Hungarian king. Bethlen was a right-wing member of the parliament, but he was unaffiliated with a major party, and he took advantage of this rift. He persuaded the Christian National Union, a party opposed to Charles's restoration, to merge with the Smallholders' Party and form a new Party of Unity. When Bethlen emerged as the leader of this new party, Horthy was forced to appoint him prime minister.

In October 1921, frustrated by the resistance to his return, Charles led troops from Odenburg (Sopron), Hungary, and marched on Budapest. He was met by government forces, which pushed his army back and placed Charles under arrest. The former monarch was exiled to Madeira, and the Hungarian diet summarily and officially nullified all Austrian (Hapsburg) claims to the throne. In May 1922, the Party of Unity captured a large parliamentary majority. Later that year, Charles died in exile.

See also HUNGARIAN REVOLUTION (1918); WORLD WAR I: EASTERN FRONT.

Further reading: Jörg K. Hoensch, *A History of Modern Hungary, 1867–1994,* trans. Kim Traynor, 2nd ed. (New York: Longman, 1996); Paul Ignotus, *Hungary* (New York: Praeger, 1972); Dominic G. Kosáry, *A History of Hungary* (New York: Arno Press, 1971); C. A. Macartney, *Hungary, a Short History* (Edinburgh, Scotland: Edinburgh University Press, 1962); Denis Sinor, *History of Hungary* (Westport, Conn.: Greenwood Press, 1976); John C. Swanson, *The Remnants of the Hapsburg Monarchy: The Shaping of Modern Austria and Hungary, 1918–1922* (Boulder, Colo., and New York: East European Monographs, distributed by Columbia University Press, 2001).

Hungarian-Czechoslovakian War   *See* KUN'S RED TERROR.

Hungarian Pagan Uprising (1046)

PRINCIPAL COMBATANTS: Hungarian pagans and others vs. Peter Orseolo, unpopular successor to the Hungarian throne
PRINCIPAL THEATER(S): Hungary
DECLARATION: None
MAJOR ISSUES AND OBJECTIVES: Succession to the Hungarian throne
OUTCOME: Peter Orseolo was overthrown, and a quasi-pagan king was installed on the Hungarian throne.
APPROXIMATE MAXIMUM NUMBER OF MEN UNDER ARMS: Unknown

CASUALTIES: Unknown
TREATIES: None

The death of Hungary's King Stephen I (Saint Stephen) (c. 975–1038) left much of the work he began—Christianizing Hungary—unfinished. Even his own Árpád dynasty was not fully converted, and Stephen had exiled recalcitrant family members. Since his only son, Emeric, died before he did, Stephen had chosen Peter Orseolo (1011–46), son of the doge of Venice and a distant relative, as a safe Christian successor. Peter arrived in Hungary only to fall victim to various court plots against him. The nation rebelled against this designated but foreign successor, and he fled for his life in 1041 to the Holy Roman Emperor Henry III (1017–56).

Peter assembled an army of Henry's troops and returned to Hungary to reclaim his throne in 1044 from the "national" king, Samuel Aba, who had taken his place. However, many Hungarians regarded him as an interloper and Henry's vassal, who would bring about Hungary's domination by foreign powers. The church likewise disapproved of him. It was not difficult for two of the exiled Árpáds to find support for an invasion in 1046. Supported by Russian troops from Kiev, they also garnered pagan backing in the country and marched on Peter's palace. The mob massacred a delegation of bishops and Hungarian nobles, who supported their proposed overthrow of the hated king, then stormed the palace, captured Peter, blinded him, and cast him into prison, where he died of his wounds.

Andrew I (d. 1060), an Árpád, converted to Orthodox Christianity while he was in Russia. It was he who became the Hungarian king (1047), but he exploited the country's paganism to keep himself in power, maintaining only the merest show of Christianity in order to appease the converted nobility. During this period, he resisted domination by the Holy Roman Empire.

Further reading: Pál Engel, *The Realm of St. Stephen: A History of Medieval Hungary, 895–1526,* trans. Tamás Pálosfalvi (New York: I. B. Tauris, 2001); Paul Ignotus, *Hungary* (New York: Praeger, 1972); Dominic G. Kosáry, *A History of Hungary* (New York: Arno Press, 1971); C. A. Macartney, *The Magyars in the Ninth Century* (reprint, New York: Cambridge University Press, 1968); Denis Sinor, *History of Hungary* (Westport, Conn.: Greenwood Press, 1976).

Hungarian Peasants' Revolt   *See* DÓZSA'S REBELLION.

Hungarian Revolt (1956)

PRINCIPAL COMBATANTS: Hungarian freedom fighters and police vs. Soviet troops

PRINCIPAL THEATER(S): Hungary
DECLARATION: None
MAJOR ISSUES AND OBJECTIVES: On October 24, 1956, Hungary's prime minister Imre Nagy defied the USSR by announcing an end to one-party rule, thereby igniting the movement to remove Hungary from the Soviet sphere of influence established in Eastern Europe at the end of World War II, a movement the West came to call the Hungarian Revolution.
OUTCOME: Soviet troops and tanks invaded Hungary and crushed the revolution.
APPROXIMATE MAXIMUM NUMBER OF MEN UNDER ARMS: Unknown number of Hungarian students, workers, and freedom fighters; 200,000 Soviet troops
CASUALTIES: Unknown but in the tens of thousands; nearly 250,000 fled the country; Soviet losses, 669 killed, 1,540 wounded, 51 missing
TREATIES: Agreement for continued Soviet control signed in 1957

The Treaty of Versailles that ended WORLD WAR I not only penalized Germany but dismembered the tottering Austro-Hungarian Empire, leaving Hungary a nation greatly shrunken. The Treaty of Trianon, which followed the Versailles document in 1920, stripped the empire of nearly three-quarters of its territory. Between 1920 and 1944, Admiral Nicholas Horthy de Nagybánya (1868–1957), the Magyar regent of Hungary, worked to regain the nation's former lands, securing from Germany some revision of its frontiers in exchange for an alliance in WORLD WAR II. The territorial gains were short-lived, and the alliance meant that Hungary was defeated with Germany and, like other eastern European nations, was overrun by a Soviet occupation force.

Following the war, an uneasy coalition government was formed for three years, after which, the communists established a one-party dictatorship under Mátyás Rákosi (1892–1971)—which they, of course, called the Hungarian Revolution. In Stalinist fashion, the party imposed forced collectivization of farms and a program of industrialization, both enforced by terror tactics and the secret police. Rákosi, however, was forced out after the death of Soviet premier Joseph Stalin (1879–1953) and replaced by Imre Nagy (1896–1958), who introduced more liberal policies. The "thaw" was short-lived: in 1955, Rákosi returned to oust Nagy and reintroduced unalloyed Stalinism. Because of his open criticism of Soviet influence in Hungary, Nagy was expelled from the Communist Party in early 1956.

But the brief breath of democracy had emboldened the Hungarian resistance to communism, and opposition to Rákosi mounted. On October 23, students, workers, and others began a march in Budapest. They protested the Hungarian government's draconian tactics, demanding free elections, economic reforms, the withdrawal of Soviet troops stationed in Hungary since the war, and the reinstatement of Nagy. The police fired on a peaceful student demonstration; street fighting broke out and soon spread across the country. Most Hungarian soldiers joined the demonstrators, which left the government virtually helpless. Within a very few days, revolutionary elements had seized control of many important institutions and facilities, including the radio stations, and freed the imprisoned anticommunist leader Cardinal Josef Mindszenty (1892–1975). Soviet troops pulled back, withdrawing from Hungary, and Nagy (who had been reinstated as prime minister on October 24) announced an end to one-party rule—a second Hungarian "Revolution" in little more than a decade.

The pro-Western new democratic regime renounced the Warsaw Pact, a COLD WAR Soviet defense alliance with Hungary and other Eastern bloc countries, and asked the United Nations to grant it status as an internationally neutral country. Despite the United States's stance on the "containment" of communism as expressed in the Truman Doctrine, the Eisenhower government declined to intervene in the anti-Soviet revolution, and—much to the shock of the Hungarians—announced that it would offer no aid to the new government. Accordingly, the Soviets, who had been quietly building up their forces on the border, attacked on November 4 with 200,000 troops and 2,800 tanks. Despite impassioned radio pleas to the United States and Nagy's personal plea to the UN for aid, no help was forthcoming. Hungarian freedom fighters put up a valiant resistance, but within weeks, the revolution was destroyed, and Hungary, barely recovered from the devastation of the world war, was in shambles. Nagy fled, only to be seized later by the Soviet secret police, and the Soviets replaced him with János Kádár (1912–89) as premier. The Soviets killed tens of thousands of people and imprisoned more. Almost a quarter-million Hungarians fled the country. The Soviets legitimized their military occupation through signed agreements with Kádár, which they then used to justify communist control for decades.

The 1956 Hungarian Revolt was one of the earliest indications that the Soviet juggernaut was not unstoppable, but it also tested—and found wanting—the West's resolve to act against a Soviet superpower armed with nuclear weapons. To many in the West, after 1956, the Iron Curtain seemed more impenetrable than ever. Indeed, a period of extreme repression followed the revolt. Yet Hungary's willingness to stand up to the Soviets led the USSR to treat the country more cautiously than it did many of its other Eastern-bloc puppets and, by the late 1960s, the Hungarians had succeeded in establishing a more liberal regime under János Kádár, who over time transformed Hungary into the most economically and politically successful nation of the Soviet bloc. When the East European bloc began to crumble in the late 1980s, the Kádár regime was supplanted by the Reform Communists, who reintroduced multiparty government, which, in turn, ousted the Communist Party and replaced it with the Hungarian Democratic Forum in 1990.

See also CZECHOSLOVAKIA, SOVIET INVASION OF.

Further reading: Sander Balogh, *The History of Hungary after the Second World War, 1944–1980* (Corvina, Hungary: Utura, 1986); Ray Gading, *Cry Hungary: Uprising 1956* (New York: Macmillan, 1986); Charles Gati, *Hungary and the Soviet Bloc* (Durham, N.C.: Duke University Press, 1986); Jörg K. Hoensch, *A History of Modern Hungary, 1867–1994,* trans. Kim Traynor, 2nd ed. (New York: Longman, 1996); Paul E. Zinner, *Revolution in Hungary* (Freeport, N.Y.: Books for Libraries Press, 1972).

Hungarian Revolution (1848–1849)

PRINCIPAL COMBATANTS: Hungarian nationalists vs. Russian-allied Austria

PRINCIPAL THEATER(S): Hungary

DECLARATION: None

MAJOR ISSUES AND OBJECTIVES: Hungary wanted to achieve autonomy and, ultimately, full independence from Austrian rule.

OUTCOME: Initially, the revolution was successful, but counterattacks from Austrian and Russian forces crushed it, and a new, even more repressive regime was installed.

APPROXIMATE MAXIMUM NUMBER OF MEN UNDER ARMS: Hapsburg forces, 370,000; Hungarian forces, 152,000; Russian forces, 360,000

CASUALTIES: Hapsburg forces, 16,600 killed or wounded, 14,200 prisoners, 41,000 dead of disease; Russian forces, 903 killed, 1,585 wounded, 13,554 dead of disease; Hungarian forces, an estimated 45,000 dead from all causes.

TREATIES: None

The tumultuous year 1848 saw revolution sweep through Europe. In Hungary, the great nationalist leader Louis (Lajos) Kossuth (1802–94) brought simmering Hungarian nationalism to a boil with his March 3, 1848, speech before the Hungarian Diet, denouncing life under the Austrian monarchy. He did not call for independence, but for a democratic constitution, under which Hungary would enjoy a significant degree of autonomy. In this, Kossuth was in sync with the AUSTRIAN REVOLUTION, which likewise demanded constitutional monarchy.

Kossuth rallied behind him a broad cross-section of the Hungarian people, including peasants, workers, students, and the Magyars, the Hungarian upper class. The Diet enacted the March Laws, which effectively set up an autonomous government for Hungary, still under Austrian auspices. The beleaguered Emperor Ferdinand (1793–1875) reluctantly accepted the March Laws.

The new imperial government, however, was beset by enemies—conservatives resented its land reforms and centrists in Vienna its threat to the integrity of the Hapsburg monarchy. They found common cause with many among the empire's disaffected nationalities, notably the Serbs and Romanians, but especially with the Croats, whose leader was a Croatian noble and a general in the Austrian army named Joseph Jellačić (1801–59). Jellačić rejected the Diet's authority and started a movement for Croatian independence. This, in turn, prompted independence movements in Serbia, Slovakia, Bohemia, and Romania. Alarmed by the imminent disintegration of the empire, Ferdinand withdrew his support for Hungarian premier Louis Batthyány (c. 1806–49), head of Hungary's independent government, and turned to Jellačić instead. He co-opted the rebel leader by naming him to command imperial forces set to invade Hungary. Batthyány and others immediately resigned in protest, leaving Kossuth in charge, and he rallied Hungarians to resist the invasion, which they did, improvising a national army. However, the Austrian forces continued their relentless advance through Hungary, prompting the Diet to remove Debrecen as city after city fell and Budapest was threatened. In January, Budapest did fall to the Austrian invaders, and Batthyány and others were arrested.

In the face of the Austrian advance, the outnumbered Hungarian force, commanded by a young soldier of genius named Arthur von Görgey (1818–1916), withdrew to positions in the mountains north of Budapest. In the meantime, Henry Dembinski (1791–1864), a Pole, led another Hungarian force in an attempt to liberate Budapest but met defeat at the Battle of Kápolna during February 26–27, 1849. The rebels had held firm through the 26th, but when the Austrians, under Prince Alfred Windischgrätz (1787–1862), counterattacked, the Hungarians fell back in disorder.

Next, Austria called on Russia for aid in suppressing the rebellion. A small Transylvanian force under Joseph Bem (1794–1850) held off the Austrians until the onslaught of the Russians in July 1849. By that time, however, General Görgey had reorganized his forces and, fighting a series of small actions, managed to push Windischgrätz out of Austria by April. This led to the proclamation of the independent republic of Hungary on April 13, 1849, with Kossuth as governor-president. However, a new Austrian invasion, this time bolstered by the Russians, swept through Hungary during June and July 1849, driving Görgey's forces into southeastern Hungary. The new government followed him there. But the Austro-Russian army kept the pressure on, and, on August 9, 1849, General Julius von Haynau (1786–1853) led an Austrian force that completed the defeat of Görgey at the Battle of Temesvár. Kossuth relinquished the reins of government to Görgey, then fled to the Ottoman Empire. Görgey surrendered to Russian forces two days afterward.

The repercussions against Hungary were vicious and iron-handed. At the direction of the emperor, Haynau ordered the execution of Batthyány and hundreds of others. Still more Hungarian leaders were imprisoned. All pretense of Hungarian nationalism was stripped away, as Austria installed a German-speaking bureaucracy to govern the recalcitrant province, the so-called Bach regime after Alexander Bach (1813–93), Austria's draconian minister of the interior.

See also Hungarian Revolution (1918).

Further reading: István Deák, *The Lawful Revolution: Louis Kossuth and the Hungarians, 1848–1849* (London: Phoenix, 2001); Ian W. Roberts, *Nicholas I and the Russian Intervention in Hungary* (Houndsville, Basingstoke, Hampshire: Macmillan, in association with the School of Slavic and Eastern European Studies, University of London, 1991); György Spira, *The Nationality Issue in the Hungary of 1848–49* (Budapest: Akadémiai Kiadó, 1992); Adam Wandruska, *The House of Hapsburg: Six Hundred Years of European Dynasty* trans. Cathleen and Hans Epstein (Westport, Conn.: Greenwood Press, 1975).

Hungarian Revolution (1918)

PRINCIPAL COMBATANTS: Hungarian nationalists vs. Austro-Hungarian Empire

PRINCIPAL THEATER(S): Hungary

DECLARATION: No official declaration, but the rebellion was triggered by the establishment of a Hungarian national council on October 25, 1918

MAJOR ISSUES AND OBJECTIVES: Hungary sought to achieve its long-held goal of independence from the Austro-Hungarian Empire.

OUTCOME: With the collapse of the Austro-Hungarian Empire immediately following the end of World War I, Hungary successfully declared its independence.

APPROXIMATE MAXIMUM NUMBER OF MEN UNDER ARMS: Unknown

CASUALTIES: Unknown

TREATIES: None—although the Treaty of Versailles and other treaties relating to the end of World War I affirmed the dismantlement of the Austro-Hungarian Empire and the independence of Hungary

As World War I ground to its end, Hungarian nationalists saw an opportunity to make a break for independence from the Austro-Hungarian Empire. In the early autumn of 1918, the Hungarian Diet defiantly recalled its troops from the front, and Count Michael Károlyi (1875–1955) created a national council, to replace the Diet altogether, on October 25, 1918. The public rallied to Károlyi in open demonstrations of rebellion, calling for an immediate end to Hungarian participation in the war, the dismissal of the

Austrian-sanctioned Diet, universal suffrage, and an end to the dual monarchy of Austria-Hungary. On October 31, Austrian emperor Charles I (1887–1922) named Károlyi Hungarian premier in an effort to appease the revolutionaries and restore order, and a genuine radical-socialist coalition came into power. However, as had occurred during the HUNGARIAN REVOLUTION (1848–1849), ethnic nationalism undermined the unity of the Hungarian revolution. Slovaks, Serbs, and Romanians threatened to withdraw from the Hungarian coalition. Károlyi acted quickly to restore unity by concluding a separate peace between Hungary and France. As part of the agreement, he withdrew Hungarian troops from the southeastern portion of the nation, allowing Serbs to occupy the south, Romanians to occupy Transylvania, and Bohemian troops to hold Slovakia. At this point, World War I ended, and, with its end, the Austro-Hungarian Empire collapsed, the emperor withdrawing from all state affairs. This left the way open for Hungary to declare its independence as a republic on November 16, 1918, just five days after the World War I armistice.

While the separation from Austria was popular, it proved disastrous for Károlyi and his government. Serb, Czech, and Romanian troops took control of various sections in two-thirds of the prostrate country, destroying any possibility of orderly political development or social reform. The government itself moved steadily to the left until, on March 21, 1919, it was replaced by a soviet republic controlled by the revolution-minded Béla Kun (1885–c. 1939).

See also HUNGARIAN CIVIL WAR (1921); KUN'S RED TERROR.

Further reading: Jörg K. Hoensch, *A History of Modern Hungary, 1867–1994*, trans. Kim Traynor, 2nd ed. (New York: Longman, 1996); Paul Ignotus, *Hungary* (New York: Praeger, 1972); Dominic G. Kosáry, *A History of Hungary* (New York: Arno Press, 1971); C. A. Macartney, *Hungary, a Short History* (Edinburgh, Scotland: Edinburgh University Press, 1962); Denis Sinor, *History of Hungary* (Westport, Conn.: Greenwood Press, 1976); John C. Swanson, *The Remnants of the Hapsburg Monarchy: The Shaping of Modern Austria and Hungary, 1918–1922* (Boulder, Colo., and New York: East European Monographs, distributed by Columbia University Press, 2001); Rudolf L. Tökés, *Béla Kun and the Hungarian Soviet Republic: The Origins and Role of the Communist Party in the Revolutions of 1918–1919* (New York: Praeger, 1967).

Hungarian-Turkish War (1437–1438)

PRINCIPAL COMBATANTS: Hungary vs. the Ottoman Turks
PRINCIPAL THEATER(S): Belgrade area and Romania
DECLARATION: None
MAJOR ISSUES AND OBJECTIVES: Hungary resisted an Ottoman invasion.

OUTCOME: The Ottomans were cleared from Hungary and Romania.
APPROXIMATE MAXIMUM NUMBER OF MEN UNDER ARMS: Unknown
CASUALTIES: Unknown
TREATIES: None

The Ottoman invasion of Hungary was blocked by the Transylvanian leader John Hunyadi (1387–1456), who had overseen the highly effective fortification of Belgrade and then the relief of the siege of the Sememdria (Smederevo) fortress on the Danube. After breaking the siege here, Hunyadi went on the offensive and achieved great success in pushing the Turks out of Hungary. In recognition of his victories, he was named *bán*, military governor, of Severin, Wallachia (now part of Romania) and, from this post, continued to fight the Turks in the HUNGARIAN-TURKISH WAR (1441–1444).

See also HUNGARIAN CIVIL WAR (1439–1440); HUNGARIAN-TURKISH WAR (1444–1456); HUNGARIAN-TURKISH WAR (1463–1483); HUNGARIAN-VENETIAN WAR (1378–1381).

Further reading: Pál Engel, *The Realm of St. Stephen: A History of Medieval Hungary, 895–1526*, trans. Tamás Pálosfalvi (New York: I. B. Tauris, 2001); Pál Fódor and Géza Dávid, eds., *Ottomans, Hungarians, and Hapsburgs in Central Europe* (Boston: Brill, 2000); Joseph Held, *Hunyadi: Legend and Reality* (Boulder, Colo., and New York: East European Monographs, distributed by Columbia University Press, 1985); Colin Imber, *The Ottoman Empire, 1300–1650: The Structure of Power* (New York: Palgrave, 2002); Domokos Varga, *Hungary in Greatness and Decline: The 14th and 15th Centuries*, trans. Martha Szacsvay Lipták (Corvino Kiadó and Stone Mountain, Ga.: Hungarian Cultural Foundation, 1982).

Hungarian-Turkish War (1441–1444)

PRINCIPAL COMBATANTS: Hungarians vs. Ottoman Turks
PRINCIPAL THEATER(S): Balkan region
DECLARATION: None
MAJOR ISSUES AND OBJECTIVES: The Hungarian forces sought to repel an Ottoman invasion.
OUTCOME: Hungarian forces were consistently and overwhelmingly successful against the invaders.
APPROXIMATE MAXIMUM NUMBER OF MEN UNDER ARMS: Unknown
CASUALTIES: Unknown
TREATIES: Peace of Szeged (Hungary), July 12, 1444

After having been ejected from Hungary in the HUNGARIAN-TURKISH WAR (1437–1438), the Ottomans invaded Hungary again in 1441. John Hunyadi (1387–1456), who had successfully repelled the Ottomans during the last war, led an army of Slavs and Magyars (Hungarian gentry) against the new invasion, which had been mounted ostensibly to punish Hungary for having supported the claim of the "false Mustafa" to the Ottoman throne held by Murad II (c. 1403–51).

Hunyadi prevailed at the Battle of Semendria (Smederevo), site of an important Hungarian fortress, in 1441 and at the Battle of Herrmannstadt the following year. After the Ottomans were also defeated at Vassag and Nagyszeben, Pope Eugenius IV (1383–1447) persuaded King Ladislas III (1424–44) of Hungary and Poland that the time was ripe for a full-scale crusade against the Muslim Turks. Ladislas's army drove the Ottomans from Semendria in 1442, and, the next year, Hunyadi defeated Turkish forces at Nish, Serbia, then captured Sofia. After this victory, Hunyadi united his army with that of King Ladislas and, together, they engaged the Ottomans at Snaim (Kustinitza), scoring a spectacular victory in 1443 that broke the Ottoman hold on the Balkans. Murad sued for peace and, at Szeged, Hungary, concluded a 10-year truce on July 12, 1444. By the terms of this treaty, Hungary acquired control over Serbia and Wallachia.

Almost immediately after signing the treaty, Murad II abdicated, and, within a few days, Hungary violated the "10-year" truce by starting the HUNGARIAN-TURKISH WAR (1444–1456).

See also HUNGARIAN-TURKISH WAR (1463–1483); HUNGARIAN-TURKISH WAR (1492–1494).

Further reading: Pál Engel, *The Realm of St. Stephen: A History of Medieval Hungary, 895–1526,* trans. Tamás Pálosfalvi (New York: I. B. Tauris, 2001); Pál Fódor and Géza Dávid, eds., *Ottomans, Hungarians, and Hapsburgs in Central Europe* (Boston: Brill, 2000); Joseph Held, *Hunyadi: Legend and Reality* (Boulder, Colo., and New York: East European Monographs, distributed by Columbia University Press, 1985); Colin Imber, *The Ottoman Empire, 1300–1650: The Structure of Power* (New York: Palgrave, 2002); Domokos Varga, *Hungary in Greatness and Decline: The 14th and 15th Centuries,* trans. Martha Szacsvay Lipták (Corvino Kiadó and Stone Mountain, Ga.: Hungarian Cultural Foundation, 1982).

Hungarian-Turkish War (1444–1456)

PRINCIPAL COMBATANTS: Hungary vs. the Ottoman Empire
PRINCIPAL THEATER(S): Balkans, especially Serbia
DECLARATION: None
MAJOR ISSUES AND OBJECTIVES: Encouraged by the pope, Hungary mounted a "crusade" against the Ottomans with the object of driving them out of the Balkans.
OUTCOME: For the present, the Ottoman forces withdrew to Constantinople, but the death of the Hungarians' principal commander, John Hunyadi, prevented the Hungarian forces from further capitalizing on their victory.
APPROXIMATE MAXIMUM NUMBER OF MEN UNDER ARMS: At the Battle of Kosovo: Hungary, 24,000; Ottoman Empire, about 30,000
CASUALTIES: At Kosovo: Hungary, about 12,000 killed and wounded; Ottoman Empire, about 10,000 killed and wounded
TREATIES: None

Just 19 days after signing a treaty ending the HUNGARIAN-TURKISH WAR (1441–1444), Hungary exploited the disarray in Ottoman leadership caused by the sudden abdication of Sultan Murad II (c. 1403–51) by mounting an all-out attack against Turkey—in violation of the truce just concluded and slated to last 10 years. Encouraged by Pope Eugenius IV (1383–1447) (who wanted a new Crusade against Islam) King Ladislas III (1424–44) of Hungary and Poland formed an alliance with Venice and, with John Hunyadi (1387–1456) and Cardinal Julian Cesarini (1398–1444), led an army through Bulgaria to the Black Sea, where they destroyed most of the Turkish fleet, and then went on to capture Sunium, Pezech, and Kavanna. After this, the Hungarian-Venetian force laid siege to Varna, the Turks' key Black Sea port. The plan was to meet here the ships of Venice, but they remained at Gallipoli and did not even attempt to prevent Murad, recalled to the throne in this crisis, from rushing back to Europe from Asia Minor. The sultan and his army arrived at Varna on November 10, 1444. Hunyadi engaged the force in a bold but desperate frontal assault, which Murad beat back. Then the sultan counterattacked, rapidly routing the Europeans and killing both Ladislas and Cesarini. Hunyadi managed to escape what became a general slaughter.

As a result of Varna, Murad reclaimed control of Serbia and Bosnia, and when Hunyadi led a new army of 24,000 men against him in 1448, the Hungarian commander was defeated in the two-day Battle of Kosovo, during October 16–17. Murad's forces were considerably larger and well organized. On the first day, Murad used his Janissary infantry and spahi cavalry against Hunyadi's center-positioned German mercenary infantry, armed with guns and pikes, and flank-positioned hussars (cavalry). (A unit of Wallachian troops had deserted him). Neither side carried the day, and both suffered heavy losses. On the second day, however, Murad's heavily armored spahis broke through Hunyadi's hussars, and the Hungarian-German force turned in retreat and withdrew from the field. Hunyadi had lost about half of his force, whereas Murad lost perhaps a third.

Hunyadi returned to raid the Turks in Serbia in 1449, causing considerable damage. Muhammad II (1430–81), Murad's son and successor, terrorized Serbia in 1453, abducting 50,000 Serb Christians. The following year, Hunyadi invaded the region again and ultimately pushed the Ottomans out of Semendria (Smederevo) and back to

Kruševac. There Hunyadi met with Muhammad II to negotiate peace terms. None were forthcoming, and, in July 1456, Muhammad laid siege to Belgrade. After three weeks, however, the siege was lifted when Hunyadi broke through a naval blockade on the Danube, defeated the Ottoman forces, and secured the city.

Muhammad withdrew to Constantinople. On August 11, 1456, Hunyadi succumbed to an illness, probably cholera, which was epidemic in his camp. Without their commander, the Hungarian forces failed to pursue the Turks or otherwise exploit their hard-won victory.

See also HAPSBURG DYNASTIC WARS; VENETIAN-TURKISH WAR (1443–1453).

Further reading: Pál Engel, *The Realm of St. Stephen: A History of Medieval Hungary, 895–1526,* trans. Tamás Pálosfalvi (New York: I. B. Tauris, 2001); Pál Fódor and Géza Dávid, eds., *Ottomans, Hungarians, and Hapsburgs in Central Europe* (Boston: Brill, 2000); Joseph Held, *Hunyadi: Legend and Reality* (Boulder, Colo., and New York: East European Monographs, distributed by Columbia University Press, 1985); Colin Imber, *The Ottoman Empire, 1300–1650: The Structure of Power* (New York: Palgrave, 2002); Domokos Varga, *Hungary in Greatness and Decline: The 14th and 15th Centuries,* trans. Martha Szacsvay Lipták (Corvino Kiadó and Stone Mountain, Ga.: Hungarian Cultural Foundation, 1982).

Hungarian-Turkish War (1463–1483)

PRINCIPAL COMBATANTS: Hungary vs. the Ottoman Empire
PRINCIPAL THEATER(S): Bosnia and Herzegovina
DECLARATION: None
MAJOR ISSUES AND OBJECTIVES: The Hungarians (with some Venetian and papal support) sought to check Ottoman advances in Bosnia.
OUTCOME: The Hungarians reclaimed northern Bosnia, but the remainder of the country fell to the Ottomans, as did Herzegovina.
APPROXIMATE MAXIMUM NUMBER OF MEN UNDER ARMS: Unknown
CASUALTIES: Unknown
TREATIES: None

Under papal auspices, Hungary and Venice allied against the Ottoman Empire to counter Turkish conquests in Serbia after the Turks took Bosnia in the BOSNIAN-TURKISH WAR. Under King Matthias Corvinus (1440–90), Hungarian forces poured into Bosnia and scored several victories against the Ottomans, unseating them from a number of fortresses. An Ottoman army under Muhammad II (1429–81) besieged the town of Jajce, but Hungarian forces held the town and reclaimed much of northern Bosnia. The rest of the country remained firmly in Ottoman hands, although the Hungarians did score a signifi-

cant victory in taking the large Turkish fortress at Sazbács, on the Sava River. With Muhammad's death in 1481, the war assumed the character of a low-level conflict, although the Ottomans made one more significant inroad in 1483, conquering Herzegovina, south of Bosnia.

See also HUNGARIAN-TURKISH WAR (1444–1456); VENETIAN-TURKISH WAR (1463–1479).

Further reading: Pál Engel, *The Realm of St. Stephen: A History of Medieval Hungary, 895–1526,* trans. Tamás Pálosfalvi (New York: I. B. Tauris, 2001); Pál Fódor and Géza Dávid, eds., *Ottomans, Hungarians, and Hapsburgs in Central Europe* (Boston: Brill, 2000); Colin Imber, *The Ottoman Empire, 1300–1650: The Structure of Power* (New York: Palgrave, 2002); Domokos Varga, *Hungary in Greatness and Decline: The 14th and 15th Centuries,* trans. Martha Szacsvay Lipták (Corvino Kiadó and Stone Mountain, Ga.: Hungarian Cultural Foundation, 1982).

Hungarian-Turkish War (1492–1494)

PRINCIPAL COMBATANTS: Hungary vs. the Ottoman Empire
PRINCIPAL THEATER(S): Region of Belgrade, Transylvania, Croatia, and southern Austria
DECLARATION: None
MAJOR ISSUES AND OBJECTIVES: The Ottomans wanted to extend their dominion in Europe and were opposed by Holy Roman Emperor Maximilian I.
OUTCOME: Maximilian was unable to muster sufficient support from other European rulers to drive the Turks from the Balkans.
APPROXIMATE MAXIMUM NUMBER OF MEN UNDER ARMS: Unknown
CASUALTIES: Unknown
TREATIES: None

Bayazid II (1447–1513), the Ottoman sultan, made a surprise assault on Belgrade in 1492, but the Hungarian forces holding the city stood firm, and an army under Holy Roman Emperor Maximilian I (1459–1519) defeated the Ottoman invaders at the Battle of Villach, in Carinthia (the southern region of Austria). Bayazid did not withdraw from the region following his defeat, however, and instead invaded Transylvania, Croatia, Styria, and Carniola (the latter two in Austria). Overwhelmed, Maximilian appealed to the Christian rulers of other European states but was unable to raise a force sufficient to dislodge the Turks. Despite this, Bayazid did not mount a full-scale war in the Balkans and Austria, but contented himself with skirmishing against whatever low-level resistance he encountered.

Further reading: Pál Engel, *The Realm of St. Stephen: A History of Medieval Hungary, 895–1526,* trans. Tamás Pálosfalvi (New York: I. B. Tauris, 2001); Pál Fódor and Géza Dávid, eds., *Ottomans, Hungarians, and Hapsburgs in Central Europe* (Boston: Brill, 2000); Colin Imber, *The*

Ottoman Empire, 1300–1650: The Structure of Power (New York: Palgrave, 2002); Domokos Varga, *Hungary in Greatness and Decline: The 14th and 15th Centuries,* trans. Martha Szacsvay Lipták (Corvino Kiadó and Stone Mountain, Ga.: Hungarian Cultural Foundation, 1982).

Hungarian-Turkish War (1521–1526)

PRINCIPAL COMBATANTS: Hungary vs. the Ottoman Empire
PRINCIPAL THEATER(S): Hungary
DECLARATION: None
MAJOR ISSUES AND OBJECTIVES: Süleyman I sought tribute from Hungary.
OUTCOME: Hungarian forces were disastrously defeated; Süleyman left a Transylvanian puppet to rule over Magyar Hungary.
APPROXIMATE MAXIMUM NUMBER OF MEN UNDER ARMS: Hungary, 20,000–30,000; Ottomans, 100,000–200,000
CASUALTIES: At Mohacs: Hungary, 10,000–15,000 killed; Ottoman losses were described as "heavy." The Ottomans took 105,000 Hungarians captive.
TREATIES: None

When Vladislav II (1456–1516), king of Bohemia and—as Ladislas II—of Hungary, died, his nine-year-old son, Louis II (1506–26), was proclaimed king. The defenses of the kingdom grew weaker under Louis's minority rule as the Hungarian magnates took advantage of his youth to disband the king's standing army—known since the days of Matthias Corvinus (1440–90) as the dreaded Black Army (after its original commander "Black John" Haugwitz).

In 1521, the new Ottoman sultan, Süleyman I the Magnificent (c. 1496–1566) recognized the realm's subsequent vulnerability and demanded tribute from the teenaged ruler of Bohemia and Hungary. Louis petulantly refused and deliberately insulted the Turkish ambassador. To these affronts, Süleyman responded with an invasion, thus renewing the chronic warfare between Hungary and the Ottoman Empire.

Hungary's powerful magnates, suddenly aware of the renewed threat, voted to reestablish a standing army. None of the various factions, however, wanted to pay for its upkeep and kept trying to slough the burden onto the shoulders of their rivals. Thus nothing was done to raise the army, and most Hungarian forces were quickly demolished or captured, when the sultan advanced into Hungary in 1526. Belgrade fell to the Turks, who used it as an advanced base of operations into the north. In the meantime, Hungary called on an alliance with Persia and the Holy Roman Empire for help, but France threw its support behind the Ottomans—despite their being Muslims. Süleyman's forces were huge. He fielded 100,000 to 200,000 men against 20,000 to 30,000 Hungarians (with

some assistance from Sigismund I [1467–1548] of Poland) on the plain of Mohacs, along the Danube, on August 29, 1526. Louis foolishly unleashed a frontal assault against these massively superior forces, using a mixed force of knights and peasants, neither of which was well disciplined. The Turks, in contrast, were a highly trained force commanded with intelligence. They beat the Christians thoroughly on August 29, then swept them from the field on August 30. European losses numbered at 10,000 to 15,000 dead, including King Louis II (who drowned while fleeing), seven bishops, and many high nobles. Losses among the Ottomans were also heavy.

From Mohacs, Süleyman advanced to Buda, which he occupied unopposed, but, despite his stunning victory, the sultan soon withdrew to Turkey to attend to the TURKO-PERSIAN WAR (1526–1555). He took with him 105,000 Hungarian captives and appointed a Transylvanian, John Zápolya (1487–1540), to rule over the Magyars. This led to the HUNGARIAN CIVIL WAR (1526–1529).

See also AUSTRO-TURKISH WAR (1529–1533).

Further reading: Pál Engel, *The Realm of St. Stephen: A History of Medieval Hungary, 895–1526,* trans. Tamás Pálosfalvi (New York: I. B. Tauris, 2001); Pál Fódor and Géza Dávid, eds., *Ottomans, Hungarians, and Hapsburgs in Central Europe* (Boston: Brill, 2000); Colin Imber, *The Ottoman Empire, 1300–1650: The Structure of Power* (New York: Palgrave, 2002); Metin Kunt and Christine Woodhead eds., *Suleyman The Magnificent and His Age: The Ottoman Empire in the Early Modern World* (New York: Longman, 1995).

Hungarian-Venetian War (1171)

PRINCIPAL COMBATANTS: Hungary vs. Venice
PRINCIPAL THEATER(S): Dalmatian coast
DECLARATION: None
MAJOR ISSUES AND OBJECTIVES: Hungary attempted to take and hold various Venetian-held Dalmatian-coast seaports.
OUTCOME: The Hungarians were initially successful in taking the Dalmatian-coast seaports, but they were quickly recaptured by Venice.
APPROXIMATE MAXIMUM NUMBER OF MEN UNDER ARMS: Unknown
CASUALTIES: Unknown
TREATIES: None

Hungary's aggressive King Stephen III (d. 1172) exploited the VENETIAN-BYZANTINE WAR to grab up Venetian-held towns along the Dalmatian coast during 1171. With Norman allies, Venice recaptured the seaports of Zara (Zadar) and Ragusa (Dubrovnik), ending the war. Later, in 1173, Hungarians under King Béla III (r. 1173–96) twice attempted to recover the lost Dalmatian territory and met with limited success, retaking Zara and a few lesser objectives.

Further reading: Pál Engel, *The Realm of St. Stephen: A History of Medieval Hungary, 895–1526,* trans. Tamás Pálosfalvi (New York: I. B. Tauris, 2001); Paul Ignotus, *Hungary* (New York: Praeger, 1972); Dominic G. Kosáry, *A History of Hungary* (New York: Arno Press, 1971); C. A. Macartney, *Hungary, a Short History* (Edinburgh, Scotland: Edinburgh University Press, 1962); Denis Sinor, *History of Hungary* (Westport, Conn.: Greenwood Press, 1976).

Hungarian-Venetian War (1342–1346)

PRINCIPAL COMBATANTS: Hungary vs. Venice
PRINCIPAL THEATER(S): Dalmatia
DECLARATION: None
MAJOR ISSUES AND OBJECTIVES: Hungary wanted to recover Dalmatian territories lost to Venice.
OUTCOME: The Venetians repelled the Hungarian invasion and defeated the Hungarians decisively at the Battle of Zara.
APPROXIMATE MAXIMUM NUMBER OF MEN UNDER ARMS: Unknown
CASUALTIES: Unknown
TREATIES: None

Hungary yielded most of Dalmatia to Venice during the reign of Hungary's Charles I (1288–1342). His successor, Louis I (1326–82) (known as Louis the Great) immediately invaded Dalmatia in an effort to regain the territory, but was defeated in the Battle of Zara (Zadar) in 1346.

See also HUNGARIAN-VENETIAN WAR (1357–1358); HUNGARIAN-VENETIAN WAR (1378–1381).

Further reading: Pál Engel, *The Realm of St. Stephen: A History of Medieval Hungary, 895–1526,* trans. Tamás Pálosfalvi (New York: I. B. Tauris, 2001); Paul Ignotus, *Hungary* (New York: Praeger, 1972); Dominic G. Kosáry, *A History of Hungary* (New York: Arno Press, 1971); C. A. Macartney, *Hungary, a Short History* (Edinburgh, Scotland: Edinburgh University Press, 1962); Denis Sinor, *History of Hungary* (Westport, Conn.: Greenwood Press, 1976); Domokos Varga, *Hungary in Greatness and Decline: The 14th and 15th Centuries,* trans. Martha Szacsvay Lipták (Corvino Kiadó and Stone Mountain, Ga.: Hungarian Cultural Foundation, 1982).

Hungarian-Venetian War (1357–1358)

PRINCIPAL COMBATANTS: Hungary vs. Venice
PRINCIPAL THEATER(S): Dalmatia
DECLARATION: None

MAJOR ISSUES AND OBJECTIVES: Hungary wanted to recover Dalmatian territories lost earlier to Venice.
OUTCOME: Hungary obtained the cession of most of Dalmatia.
APPROXIMATE MAXIMUM NUMBER OF MEN UNDER ARMS: Unknown
CASUALTIES: Unknown
TREATIES: Treaty of Zara, February 1358

Thanks to the efforts of King Louis I (1326–1382)—known as "Louis the Great" or Lajos Nagy—Hungary recovered some of its former power and prestige during 1357–58. Louis invaded Venetian-held Dalmatia and rapidly seized many towns, which he himself had lost to Venice in the HUNGARIAN-VENETIAN WAR (1342–1346). Venice, unable to mount a credible defense, ceded most of Dalmatia to Hungary in February 1358 by the Treaty of Zara (Zadar). This bolstered Hungary's prestige and put it in position to expand at the expense of the Turks in northern Bulgaria. Moreover, Casimir III (1310–70) named Louis as his successor to the Polish throne.

See also HUNGARIAN-VENETIAN WAR (1378–1381).

Further reading: Pál Engel, *The Realm of St. Stephen: A History of Medieval Hungary, 895–1526,* trans. Tamás Pálosfalvi (New York: I. B. Tauris, 2001); Paul Ignotus, *Hungary* (New York: Praeger, 1972); Dominic G. Kosáry, *A History of Hungary* (New York: Arno Press), 1971); C. A. Macartney, *Hungary, a Short History* (Edinburgh, Scotland: Edinburgh University Press, 1962); Denis Sinor, *History of Hungary* (Westport, Conn.: Greenwood Press, 1976); Domokos Varga, *Hungary in Greatness and Decline: The 14th and 15th Centuries,* trans. Martha Szacsvay Lipták (Corvino Kiadó and Stone Mountain, Ga.: Hungarian Cultural Foundation, 1982).

Hungarian-Venetian War (1378–1381)

PRINCIPAL COMBATANTS: Hungary (with Genoese allies) vs. Venice
PRINCIPAL THEATER(S): Dalmatian coast
DECLARATION: None
MAJOR ISSUES AND OBJECTIVES: Having taken inland Dalmatia in the War of Chioggia, Hungary aimed at acquiring control of the coast as well.
OUTCOME: Venice ceded the Dalmatian coast to Hungary.
APPROXIMATE MAXIMUM NUMBER OF MEN UNDER ARMS: Unknown
CASUALTIES: Unknown
TREATIES: Peace of Turin, August 8, 1377

Hungary's King Louis I (1326–82) suffered defeat at the hands of Venice in the HUNGARIAN-VENETIAN WAR

(1342–1346) and was forced to yield some territory and cities. He fared much better in his second war against Venice, the HUNGARIAN-VENETIAN WAR (1357–1358), and managed to recover some Dalmatian coastal towns. Next, in the War of CHIOGGIA (1378–81), he succeeded in recovering inland Dalmatia. But this time, Louis also allied Hungary with Genoa (longtime rival of Venice) to capture those parts of the Dalmatian coast he had not taken in the 1357–58 war. The Genoese did not fare well in this war, but Hungary wrested control of the Balkans from the Ottoman Empire, which thereby put Louis I in a position of sufficient strength to force Venice to yield the Dalmatian seacoast by the 1381 Peace of Turin.

The final conquest of all Dalmatia, coupled with Hungary's hard-won dominion over the Balkans, made the Hungarian kingdom the most powerful in eastern Europe. Louis, king of Poland as well as Hungary since 1370, emerged as the most significant ruler of the region.

Further reading: Pál Engel, *The Realm of St. Stephen: A History of Medieval Hungary, 895–1526*, trans. Tamás Pálosfalvi (New York: I. B. Tauris, 2001); Paul Ignotus, *Hungary* (New York: Praeger, 1972); Dominic G. Kosáry, *A History of Hungary* (New York: Arno Press, 1971); C. A. Macartney, *Hungary, a Short History* (Edinburgh, Scotland: Edinburgh University Press, 1962); Denis Sinor, *History of Hungary* (Westport, Conn.: Greenwood Press, 1976); Domokos Varga, *Hungary in Greatness and Decline: The 14th and 15th Centuries,* trans. Martha Szacsvay Lipták (Corvino Kiadó and Stone Mountain, Ga.: Hungarian Cultural Foundation, 1982).

Hungarian War with the Holy Roman Empire (1477–1485)

PRINCIPAL COMBATANTS: Hungary vs. the Holy Roman Empire (chiefly Austria)
PRINCIPAL THEATER(S): Austria
DECLARATION: None
MAJOR ISSUES AND OBJECTIVES: The Holy Roman Emperor Frederick III wanted to assume the throne of Hungary; Matthias Corvinus, elected to that throne, resisted.
OUTCOME: Matthias Corvinus's resistance to the Holy Roman Empire was highly successful, and Hungary dominated much of central and southeastern Europe from 1485 until the death of Matthias in 1490.
APPROXIMATE MAXIMUM NUMBER OF MEN UNDER ARMS: Unknown
CASUALTIES: Unknown
TREATIES: None

When, as a child, Ladislav V (Posthumous; 1440–570) was proclaimed king of Hungary by its ruling magnates, the great Hungarian general and hero John Hunyadi (1387–1456) was appointed his guardian and became, for

a while, the country's governor. Upon Hunyadi's death, however, Ladislav's powerful uncle, Ulrich of Cilli (d. 1456), well aware of the country's devotion to the general, had his eldest son assassinated and his younger son, Matthias Corvinus (1440–90), imprisoned in Prague. Ladislav died suddenly, unmarried and childless, the following year, and the Hungarian nobility proclaimed Matthias king at a Diet convened in 1458 in Buda and Pest. Matthias proved a most able monarch, not only quelling dissension within Hungary, but successfully defending against Ottoman incursions with the help of a 30,000-strong standing army, made up of mercenaries (most of them defeated Hussites) and known, after its commander "Black John" Haugwitz, as the Black Army.

The Hapsburgs, however, under Holy Roman Emperor Frederick III (1415–93) repeatedly contested Matthias's right to rule. At last, in 1477, when the marriage of Frederick's son Maximilian (1459–1519) to Mary of Burgundy (1457–82) dramatically enhanced the power of the House of Hapsburg, Frederick pushed harder for control of Hungary. In response, Matthias secured allies from among Frederick's enemies in Austria and Germany, and launched a series of highly destructive raids into Austria during 1477, 1479, and 1482. In 1485, Matthias laid siege to Vienna, which soon fell to him. Matthias occupied Vienna for the next five years—until his death in 1490. Only after the dynamic Hungarian king had died was Maximilian able to retake Vienna and, subsequently, other Austrian territory taken by Matthias. Maximilian became Holy Roman Emperor in 1490.

Further reading: Jean Berenger, *History of the Hapsburg Empire, 1273–1700* (London: Longman Publishing Group, 1995); Pál Engel, *The Realm of St. Stephen: A History of Medieval Hungary, 895–1526,* trans. Tamás Pálosfalvi (New York: I. B. Tauris, 2001); Domokos Varga, *Hungary in Greatness and Decline: The 14th and 15th Centuries,* trans. Martha Szacsvay Lipták (Corvino Kiadó and Stone Mountain, Ga.: Hungarian Cultural Foundation, 1982); Adam Wandruska, *The House of Hapsburg: Six Hundred Years of European Dynasty,* trans. Cathleen and Hans Epstein (Westport, Conn.: Greenwood Press, 1975).

Hun Invasion of Gothic Empire (376)

PRINCIPAL COMBATANTS: The Huns vs. the Ostrogoths and Visigoths
PRINCIPAL THEATER(S): Gothic Empire (southeastern Europe)
DECLARATION: None
MAJOR ISSUES AND OBJECTIVES: Conquest
OUTCOME: The Huns overran the Gothic realm, as the Goths sought refuge within the Roman Empire.
APPROXIMATE MAXIMUM NUMBER OF MEN UNDER ARMS: In the hundreds of thousands on both sides; the Gothic warrior class numbered more than 200,000.

CASUALTIES: As many as 1 million Gothic refugees were created by the invasion.

TREATIES: None, save a disarmament agreement between Rome and the Visigoths.

Ermanaric (d. c. 370–376), leader of the Ostrogoths, was killed (or committed suicide) during the onslaught of the Huns, who invaded the Gothic Empire by way of the Dnieper River. Withimer assumed leadership of the embattled Ostrogoths but soon fell in battle and was replaced by Alatheus and Saphrax, who could offer nothing more than leadership in an Ostrogoth flight across the Dniester.

In contrast to the Ostrogoth leaders, Athanaric (d. 381), leader of the Visigoths, was determined to take a stand against the Hun invasion. Unfortunately, the majority of his people emulated the Ostrogoths and fled toward the Danube, led by Fritgern and Alavius. Perhaps as many as 1 million Ostrogoths and Visigoths were displaced as refugees, including 200,000 warriors. With a minority following, Athanaric sought refuge in the forests of Carpathia and Transylvania.

The Visigoths appealed to Valens (c. 328–378), Roman emperor of the East, for refuge. The Roman agreed, on condition that the Visigoths disarm and further surrender their male children under military age as hostages. By the time the Ostrogoths arrived at the frontier of the Roman Empire and likewise appealed for refuge, the Romans refused. However, preoccupied with the influx of Visigoths, the Romans could not prevent the Ostrogoths from crossing the Danube.

See also HUN RAIDS.

Further reading: Thomas S. Burns, *A History of the Ostro-Goths* (Bloomington: Indiana University Press, 1984); Arther Ferrill, *The Fall of the Roman Empire: The Military Explanation* (New York: Thames and Hudson, 1986); Peter Heather, ed., *The Visigoths from the Migration Period to the Seventh Century* (Rochester, N.Y.: Boydell Press, 1999); Otto J. Maenchen-Helfen, *The World of the Huns* (Berkeley: University of California Press, 1973); E. A. Thompson, *The Huns* (Cambridge, England: Blackwell, 1996).

Hun Raids: Hun Invasion of Thrace (409)

PRINCIPAL COMBATANTS: Huns vs. Eastern Roman Empire
PRINCIPAL THEATER(S): Thrace
DECLARATION: None
MAJOR ISSUES AND OBJECTIVES: Conquest
OUTCOME: The Eastern Roman forces repulsed the Hun invasion.
APPROXIMATE MAXIMUM NUMBER OF MEN UNDER ARMS: Unknown
CASUALTIES: Unknown
TREATIES: None

From 408 to 450, the Eastern Roman Empire (Byzantine Empire) was menaced by Hun incursions, invasions, and raids. One of the biggest was led by the Hun king Uldin against Thrace in 409. Anthemius (d. 472), the Praetorian prefect who, with his sister Pulcheria (399–453), had taken over the imperial government as regents for the infant Theodosius II (401–450) on the death of Arcadius (c. 377–408), led a defensive force against the Hun onslaught. Anthemius was able to repulse the Huns, who were driven back across the Danube.

See also HUN INVASION OF GOTHIC EMPIRE; HUN RAIDS: ATTILA'S EASTERN CONQUESTS; HUN RAIDS: ATTILA'S FIRST INVASION OF EASTERN EMPIRE; HUN RAIDS: ATTILA'S SECOND INVASION OF EASTERN EMPIRE; HUN RAIDS: ATTILA'S INVASION OF WESTERN EMPIRE; HUN RAIDS: EASTERN EMPIRE'S ITALIAN EXPEDITION; HUN RAIDS: EASTERN EMPIRE'S AFRICAN EXPEDITION.

Further reading: Arther Ferrill, *The Fall of the Roman Empire: The Military Explanation* (New York: Thames and Hudson, 1986); Otto J. Maenchen-Helfen, *The World of the Huns* (Berkeley: University of California Press, 1973); E. A. Thompson, *The Huns* (Cambridge, England: Blackwell, 1996).

Hun Raids: Eastern Empire's Italian Expedition (against John) (424–425)

PRINCIPAL COMBATANTS: Eastern Roman Empire vs. John, Hunnish usurper of the Western Roman throne
PRINCIPAL THEATER(S): Italy, principally Ravenna
DECLARATION: None
MAJOR ISSUES AND OBJECTIVES: Overthrow of the usurper, and elevation of a Roman to the throne
OUTCOME: The usurper was deposed, and Valentinian enthroned as a puppet of his mother, Placidia.
APPROXIMATE MAXIMUM NUMBER OF MEN UNDER ARMS: Unknown
CASUALTIES: Unknown
TREATIES: None

Constantius (d. 421), leading general of the Eastern Empire, died in 421, whereupon his widow, Placidia (c. 390–450), having become estranged from her brother Honorius (384–423), emperor of the West, fled to Constantinople and, with her son Valentinian III (419–455), found refuge in the court of Theodosius II (401–450), emperor of the East. Soon after this, Honorius died, and his vacant throne was usurped by his prime minister, John. Theodosius resolved to unseat the usurper and sent Ardaburius and Aspar (d. 471), father and son generals, at the head of an army to depose John at his court in Ravenna.

The fleet of Ardaburius was dispersed by a storm en route, and although the general survived, he was taken prisoner. Aspar, having taken the overland route, approached Ravenna and, with the help of agents and allies within the city, captured it in 425. Moving swiftly, Aspar's forces captured and killed John. Valentinian was enthroned in his place, and, through him, his mother Placidia ruled the Western Empire. Theodosius picked up Illyricum as a reward for his aid in overthrowing the usurper.

See also HUN INVASION OF GOTHIC EMPIRE; HUN RAIDS: ATTILA'S EASTERN CONQUESTS; HUN RAIDS: ATTILA'S FIRST INVASION OF EASTERN EMPIRE; HUN RAIDS: ATTILA'S SECOND INVASION OF EASTERN EMPIRE; HUN RAIDS: ATTILA'S INVASION OF WESTERN EMPIRE; HUN RAIDS: EASTERN EMPIRE'S AFRICA EXPEDITION; HUN RAIDS: HUN INVASION OF THRACE.

Further reading: Arther Ferrill, *The Fall of the Roman Empire: The Military Explanation* (New York: Thames and Hudson, 1986); Thomas Hodkins, *Huns, Vandals, and the Fate of the Roman Empire* (Mechanicsburg, Pa.: Stackpole Books, 1996); Otto J. Maenchen-Helfen, *The World of the Huns* (Berkeley: University of California Press, 1973); E. A. Thompson, *The Huns* (Cambridge, England: Blackwell, 1996).

Hun Raids: Eastern Empire's African Expedition (431)

PRINCIPAL COMBATANTS: Rome and the Eastern Empire vs. the Vandals and Alans

PRINCIPAL THEATER(S): Northwestern Africa

DECLARATION: None

MAJOR ISSUES AND OBJECTIVES: The barbarians sought to conquer northwestern Africa.

OUTCOME: Under Gaiseric, the barbarians came to control most of northwestern Africa.

APPROXIMATE MAXIMUM NUMBER OF MEN UNDER ARMS: Vandals and Alans (barbarians), 50,000; Roman and East Roman forces were similar in number.

CASUALTIES: Unknown

TREATIES: None

During the Huns' attacks on Rome's eastern lands from 424 to 425 (*see* HUN RAIDS: EASTERN EMPIRE'S ITALIAN EXPEDITION [AGAINST JOHN]), Bonifacius, a Roman-barbarian general in service to the Eastern Empire, remained loyal to Valentinian III (419–455) and Placidia (c. 390–450) and opposed the uprising of John. For this, Placidia rewarded Bonifacius with the governorship of Africa. Bonifacius subsequently rebelled against the Eastern Empire and invited Gaiseric (Genseric, 390–477) and some 50,000 Vandals and Alans to invade Africa in 429. Within a short time, however, Bonifacius reconciled with Placidia and the Eastern Empire but now found that he

could not eject the barbarians in his midst. He requested military aid from Placidia, who, in turn, appealed to Theodosius II (401–450) and Pulcheria (399–453) to send a force to Africa.

In 431, a land and naval force was sent under the Roman general Aspar (d. 471) to reinforce the army of Bonifacius. Bonifacius assumed overall command of the combined Roman–East Roman force, which was quickly defeated by Gaiseric's barbarians. They resumed the siege of Hippo, which the African expedition had interrupted, and Aspar, apparently after a dispute with Bonifacius over command, withdrew his forces back to Constantinople. By 435, the Vandals were in control of all northwestern Africa, except for eastern Numidia (Tunisia).

See also HUN INVASION OF GOTHIC EMPIRE; HUN RAIDS: ATTILA'S EASTERN CONQUESTS; HUN RAIDS: ATTILA'S FIRST INVASION OF EASTERN EMPIRE; HUN RAIDS: ATTILA'S SECOND INVASION OF EASTERN EMPIRE; HUN RAIDS: ATTILA'S INVASION OF WESTERN EMPIRE; HUN RAIDS: EASTERN EMPIRE'S ITALIAN EXPEDITION; HUN RAIDS: HUN INVASION OF THRACE.

Further reading: Arther Ferrill, *The Fall of the Roman Empire: The Military Explanation* (New York: Thames and Hudson, 1986); Thomas Hodkins, *Huns, Vandals, and the Fate of the Roman Empire* (Mechanicsburg, Pa.: Stackpole Books, 1996); Otto J. Maenchen-Helfen, *The World of the Huns* (Berkeley: University of California Press, 1973); E. A. Thompson, *The Huns* (Cambridge, England: Blackwell, 1996).

Hun Raids: Attila's Eastern Conquests (433–441)

PRINCIPAL COMBATANTS: The Huns vs. Scythia, Media, and Persia

PRINCIPAL THEATER(S): Scythia, Media, and Persia

DECLARATION: None

MAJOR ISSUES AND OBJECTIVES: Conquest

OUTCOME: The Huns came to control Scythia, Media, and Persia

APPROXIMATE MAXIMUM NUMBER OF MEN UNDER ARMS: Unknown

CASUALTIES: Unknown

TREATIES: Between the Eastern Empire and the Huns, renewed 433

In 432, Theodosius II (401–450), emperor of the East, concluded a treaty with Ruas, king of the Huns, intended to prevent conflict between the Huns and the Byzantines. With the death of Ruas in 433, Attila (c. 406–453) and Bleda (d. 445), his nephew, jointly assumed the Hun throne. The pair renewed the treaty, and Attila and Bleda turned their attention to making conquests in Scythia, Media, and Persia, all beyond the bounds of the Eastern Empire.

See also HUN INVASION OF GOTHIC EMPIRE; HUN RAIDS: HUN INVASION OF THRACE; HUN RAIDS: EASTERN EMPIRE'S AFRICA EXPEDITION; HUN RAIDS: EASTERN EMPIRE'S ITALIAN EXPEDITION; HUN RAIDS: ATTILA'S FIRST INVASION OF EASTERN EMPIRE; HUN RAIDS: ATTILA'S SECOND INVASION OF EASTERN EMPIRE; HUN RAIDS: ATTILA'S INVASION OF WESTERN EMPIRE.

Further reading: Roger Carintini, *Attila* (Paris: Hachette, 2000); Arther Ferrill, *The Fall of the Roman Empire: The Military Explanation* (New York: Thames and Hudson, 1986); Otto J. Maenchen-Helfen, *The World of the Huns* (Berkeley: University of California Press, 1973); E. A. Thompson, *The Huns* (Cambridge, England: Blackwell, 1996); Robert N. Webb, *Attila, King of the Huns* (New York: F. Watts, 1965).

Hun Raids: Attila's First Invasion of Eastern Empire (441–443)

PRINCIPAL COMBATANTS: The Huns vs. the Eastern Roman Empire
PRINCIPAL THEATER(S): The Balkans
DECLARATION: None
MAJOR ISSUES AND OBJECTIVES: The Hun raids were aimed chiefly at extracting massive tribute from the Eastern Empire.
OUTCOME: After defeating and nearly destroying the imperial army under General Aspar, Attila prevailed, extensively raiding the Balkan Peninsula and forcing a new and exorbitant tribute from Emperor Theodosius.
APPROXIMATE MAXIMUM NUMBER OF MEN UNDER ARMS: Unknown
CASUALTIES: Unknown, but catastrophic for imperial forces
TREATIES: Peace and tribute agreement, August 443

Attila (c. 406–453) violated the Hun treaty with the Eastern Empire (*see* HUN RAIDS: ATTILA'S EASTERN CONQUESTS) after the Vandal leader Gaiseric (Genseric, 390–477) bribed and cajoled him. Attila launched an invasion into Illyricum in 441. The Eastern Empire responded by suing for a truce, which was quickly concluded and endured for less than a year before Attila invaded Moesia and Thrace, then advanced to the walls of Constantinople itself.

Attila's forces pushed the imperial army, led by the Roman general Aspar (d. 471), into retreat to the Chersonese Peninsula. There, without room for maneuver, the Eastern army was all but completely destroyed. Aspar and a small number of others made their escape by sea.

In the absence of an opposing army, Attila raided the Balkan Peninsula fiercely. Only at Asemus (Osma, near Sistova) did the Huns encounter serious resistance. A local force repulsed them, forcing Attila to fall back with significant losses. This was hardly sufficient to counterbalance the losses suffered by the Eastern Empire. In August 443, Theodosius II (401–450), the Eastern emperor, sued for peace, agreeing to a massive increase in tribute money paid to Attila.

Further reading: Roger Carintini, *Attila* (Paris: Hachette, 2000); Arther Ferrill, *The Fall of the Roman Empire: The Military Explanation* (New York: Thames and Hudson, 1986); Otto J. Maenchen-Helfen, *The World of the Huns* (Berkeley: University of California Press, 1973); E. A. Thompson, *The Huns* (Cambridge, England: Blackwell, 1996); Robert N. Webb, *Attila, King of the Huns* (New York: F. Watts, 1965).

Hun Raids: Attila's Second Invasion of Eastern Empire (447)

PRINCIPAL COMBATANTS: The Huns vs. the Eastern Roman Empire
PRINCIPAL THEATER(S): Thrace and Greece
DECLARATION: None
MAJOR ISSUES AND OBJECTIVES: Conquest
OUTCOME: Attila extracted from the Eastern Empire three times the earlier tribute, together with an extensive cession of territory along the Danube.
APPROXIMATE MAXIMUM NUMBER OF MEN UNDER ARMS: Unknown
CASUALTIES: Unknown
TREATIES: Peace of 447

In 445, Attila (c. 406–453) murdered Bleda (d. 445) to become the sole ruler of the Huns, who now commanded an empire of vast extent. Two years later, Attila led a new invasion of the Eastern Empire, despite the highly favorable peace terms that had been reached with Emperor Theodosius II (401–450) after his first invasion of the Eastern Empire (HUN RAIDS: ATTILA'S FIRST INVASION OF EASTERN EMPIRE, 441–443).

So feared were the Huns that, even as they advanced toward Thrace, there was panic in Constantinople. This was not without good reason: a recent earthquake had damaged the city's walls, making it that much more vulnerable to assault.

Theodosius dispatched an army to intercept the advance of the Huns. The Battle of the Utus was ultimately indecisive, but it did temporarily halt the Hun advance. Although the Eastern Roman army withdrew, the action put the Huns off their Constantinople-bound course and sent them toward Greece. Encountering the formidable fortifications of Thermopylae, a narrow pass, the Huns were halted.

At this juncture, Theodosius sued to renew the peace. The price he paid was catastrophically high: a tribute assessed at three times the earlier exorbitant amount, together with the cession of a 50-mile-wide swath of the right bank of the Danube, from Singidunum (Belgrade) to Novae (Svistov, Bulgaria).

Further reading: Roger Carintini, *Attila* (Paris: Hachette, 2000); Arther Ferrill, *The Fall of the Roman Empire: The Military Explanation* (New York: Thames and Hudson, 1986); Otto J. Maenchen-Helfen, *The World of the Huns* (Berkeley: University of California Press, 1973); E. A. Thompson, *The Huns* (Cambridge: Blackwell, 1996); Robert N. Webb, *Attila, King of the Huns* (New York: F. Watts, 1965).

Hun Raids: Attila's Invasion of Western Empire (450–452)

PRINCIPAL COMBATANTS: The Huns vs. the Western Roman Empire

PRINCIPAL THEATER(S): France and Italy

DECLARATION: None

MAJOR ISSUES AND OBJECTIVES: Conquest

OUTCOME: Attila's failure to prevail at the Battle of Châlons forfeited his main opportunity to seize control of the Western Empire and thereby introduce Asian rule into Europe; his later withdrawal from Italy ended his western European invasion.

APPROXIMATE MAXIMUM NUMBER OF MEN UNDER ARMS: Huns, perhaps as many as 500,000 or as few as 100,000 men; the armies of the Eastern Empire and its allies never numbered more than about half the troops the Huns fielded.

CASUALTIES: Unknown, but certainly heavy among the Huns as a result of the Battle of Châlons and, later, in Italy, as a result of epidemic disease.

TREATIES: None

It was at the behest of his ally, the Vandal leader Gaiseric (Genseric, 390–477), that Attila (c. 406–453) ventured into the Western Empire. Gaiseric needed a diversion against Theodoric (d. 534) of Toulouse, who was about to invade North Africa. Moreover, Attila wanted to avenge himself against the Western emperor, Valentinian III (419–455), who had rebuffed a suit for the hand of his sister, Honoria—and for half of the Western Empire.

Thus motivated, Attila was on the march in 450 and crossed the Rhine in 451 with the greatest army he had ever led—reportedly 500,000 warriors (modern historians believe the actual figure was no more than 100,000).

The Rhine crossing came just north of Moguntiacum (Mainz), which was in the territory of his allies, the Franks, and thus there was no resistance to his crossing. The front of the advance was vast, nearly 100 miles across. With this great scythe, Attila swept through the cities and towns of northern Gaul, sacking all save Paris (spared, it was said, through the intercession of St. Geneviève).

While ravaging the countryside, Attila repeatedly invited Theodoric to join him in a united campaign against Roman rule in Gaul.

The Roman general Aetius (d. 454) mustered a large army consisting of Gauls and Romans, with Franks, Burgundians, Germans, and Alans. Despite the diversity of those recruited, Aetius commanded no more than half the strength of Attila. Theodoric considered whether to join Attila, but, persuaded by the charisma and conviction of Aetius, he sided with Rome against the Huns.

Attila marched through Metz on April 7, 451, and swept through the valley of the Loire, then set up a siege of Orléans using about half of his army. The other half Attila deployed in a massive raid of northern France. Just as Orléans was about to surrender to the besiegers, Aetius and Theodoric attacked. However, after brief skirmishing, Attila suddenly broke off the siege, retreated, and called for the rest of his army. In the meantime, Aetius gave chase. Attila reunited his forces between Troyes and Châlons. He quickly set up a great redoubt near Méry-sur Seine, digging into massive entrenchments. It was in this fortified position that Aetius found the Huns in June. A titanic battle—the Battle of Châlons—ensued. Aetius and Theodoric held out against Attila's massive assaults on the center and right. The allies mounted an offensive with their left against Attila's right. Theodoric fell, but Attila was forced to withdraw.

Attila assumed that Aetius would give chase, but his troops had taken heavy losses, and he did not attack. This is understandable, but it is unclear why Aetius also failed to blockade the Huns to cut them off and starve them into submission. The Roman general was not usually prone to such strategic lapses. Attila withdrew from Gaul, quietly and without further destruction to the countryside. Had he prevailed at the Battle of Châlons, Attila would have conquered the Western Empire, and it is quite possible that the subsequent course of European history would have been dominated by Asian peoples.

As it was, Attila returned to his home base in Pannonia (Hungary). He once again asked Valentinian for the hand of Honoria and was again refused. He launched a new foray into western Europe, this time by way of the Julian Alps into northeastern Italy. Attila laid waste to Aquileia and cleaned out Venetia, whose inhabitants (it is said) withdrew to the coastal islands and founded Venice. Padua was sacked, and the Mincio was devastated.

Aetius, rushing back from Gaul, reached Italy in time to take up positions at the Po River. Although Aetius's force was much smaller than Attila's, he managed to hold the Po crossings, probably because Attila had by this time decided to withdraw from Italy. He faced a rebellion in northeastern Illyricum, which needed attending to, and his army was swept by pestilential disease in Italy. The Catholic Church holds that a visit by Pope Leo I (c. 400–474) persuaded Attila—awed by his presence—to quit Italy. This tradition is almost certainly apocryphal. Faced with a pressing emergency elsewhere and fearing destruction by disease, he withdrew—and died the following year.

Further reading: Roger Carintini, *Attila* (Paris: Hachette, 2000); Arthur Ferrill, *The Fall of the Roman Empire: The Military Explanation* (New York: Thames and Hudson, 1986); Otto J. Maenchen-Helfen, *The World of the Huns* (Berkeley: University of California Press, 1973); E. A. Thompson, *The Huns* (Cambridge, England: Blackwell, 1996): Robert N. Webb, *Attila, King of the Huns* (New York: F. Watts, 1965).

Hurrian Conquests (c. 1700–c. 1500 B.C.E.)

PRINCIPAL COMBATANTS: Hurrians vs. Hittites and Egyptians
PRINCIPAL THEATER(S): Mesopotamia, Anatolia, Syria
DECLARATION: None
MAJOR ISSUES AND OBJECTIVES: The Hurrians expanded from their original migratory settlements between Lake Van and the Zagros Mountains in western Iran.
OUTCOME: By 1500 B.C.E., Hurrians had settled as far west as Anatolia and as far north as Syria.
APPROXIMATE MAXIMUM NUMBER OF MEN UNDER ARMS: Extremely variable
CASUALTIES: Unknown
TREATIES: No surviving documents

By about 1700 B.C.E., the Hurrians, whose origin lay in the Caucasus, had migrated into northern Mesopotamia and had become sufficiently well established to overthrow their Semitic overlords. They took over the region between Lake Van and the Zagros Mountains, then expanded west and south into eastern Anatolia (Turkey) and northern Syria. This expansion was complete by about 1500 B.C.E. Very little is known about the course of the wars that must have accompanied this expansion.

In Anatolia and Syria, the Hurrians established the kingdom of Mitanni, which frequently warred with Egypt and with the Hittites (*see* HITTITE CONQUEST OF ANATOLIA and HITTITE-HURRIAN WARS).

The greatest of the Hurrian kingdoms, Mitanni, declined during the two centuries following the period of these conquests. After 1350 B.C.E., Mitanni encompassed no more than Hanigabat, which was overrun by Assyria around 1245 B.C.E. The Mitanni and the Hurrians generally ceased to exist as an ethnically recognizable people by 1000 B.C.E.

See also ASSYRIAN-HURRIAN WARS.

Further reading: Trevor Bryce, *The Kingdom of the Hittites* (New York: Oxford University Press, 1998); Ignace Gelb, *Hurrians and Subarians* (Chicago: University of Chicago Press, 1944); O. R. Gurney, *The Hittites* (New York: Penguin Books, 1990); J. G. Macqueen, *The Hittites and Their Contemporaries in Asia Minor* (London: Thames and Hudson, 1986).

Hussite Civil War (1423–1434)

PRINCIPAL COMBATANTS: Utraquist Hussites vs. Taborite Hussites
PRINCIPAL THEATER(S): Bohemia
DECLARATION: None
MAJOR ISSUES AND OBJECTIVES: The radical Taborites wanted to suppress the moderate Utraquists to make a break with the Catholic Church and the ruling government of Bohemia.
OUTCOME: For most of the war, the Taborites prevailed until the Utraquists reached an accommodation with the church and thereby acquired allies among the Bohemian nobility.
APPROXIMATE MAXIMUM NUMBER OF MEN UNDER ARMS: Unknown
CASUALTIES: Unknown
TREATIES: The Compactata of 1433 created the alliance that enabled the Utraquists to defeat the Taborites.

The Hussite Civil War was partly contemporaneous with the HUSSITE WARS from 1419 to 1436) that followed the martyrdom of the Bohemian religious reformer John Huss (1369–1415). Huss sought to reform the Catholic Church and, in particular, held that the pope was not divinely placed in authority, but was elected by the rule of men. Huss was burned as a heretic, but his followers were legion among the Bohemian knights and nobility, who not only published a protest against Huss's martyrdom but also offered protection to those persecuted for their faith. However, his followers became factionalized within a few years of death. The radical Taborites (named after their stronghold, Tabor, located south of Praque) were uncompromising in their demands for reforms, whereas the moderate Utraquists saw the possibility of coming to an accommodation with church and government in Bohemia. The Taborite leader John Ziska (c. 1360–1424) sought to suppress the Utraquists and defeated them at the battles of Horid and Strachov in 1423. In 1424, Taborite forces under Ziska were victorious at the Battle of Skalic and then the Battle of Malesov. Despite what amounted to a long truce, from 1424 to 1433, the Utraquists remained stubbornly active, and when Ziska died in 1424, his successor, Andrew Prokop (c. 1380–1434, also known as Prokop the Great), was unable to prevent their reemergence. In 1433, the civil war heated up again. The Utraquists agreed to the Compactata, a 1433 compromise with the Catholic Church that not only readmitted them into the church but created a military alliance with the Bohemian nobility. Thus allied, the Utraquists defeated the

Taborites at the Battle of Lipany on May 20, 1434, combat in which Prokop the Great was killed.

See also BOHEMIAN CIVIL WAR (1390–1419; GERMAN CIVIL WAR (1400–1411).

Further reading: Frabtisk Michalek Bartos, *The Hussite Revolution, 1424–1437* (Boulder, Colo., and New York: East European Monographs, distributed by Columbia University Press, 1986); Josef Kalvoda, *The Genesis of Czechoslovakia* (Boulder, Colo., and New York: East European Monographs, distributed by Columbia University Press, 1986).

Hussite Wars (1419–1436)

PRINCIPAL COMBATANTS: Hussite rebels vs. German (Holy Roman Empire) forces of King Sigismund
PRINCIPAL THEATER(S): Bohemia, Hungary, Austria, and Germany
DECLARATION: None
MAJOR ISSUES AND OBJECTIVES: The Hussites wanted independence from the Holy Roman Empire and the Roman Catholic Church.
OUTCOME: Despite overwhelming military victories against Sigismund, the Hussites were ultimately undermined by the Hussite Civil War (1423–34) between the Taborite and Utraquist Hussite factions; this led to the destruction of the Bohemian military, and capitulation to Sigismund.
APPROXIMATE MAXIMUM NUMBER OF MEN UNDER ARMS: Hussites, 25,000; Sigismund's forces, 50,000
CASUALTIES: Hussite losses at Český-Brod, 18,000 killed; Sigismund's losses often ran between 30 and 50 percent of his forces, well into the tens of thousands.
TREATIES: The Compactata of 1433

John Huss (1369–1415), a Bohemian priest and religious reformer, sought to reform the Catholic Church, in the process attacking the doctrine that the papacy is divinely decreed. Huss argued that popes are elected by men, not placed in office by God. This, among other doctrines he proposed, earned Huss a trial for heresy and, ultimately, execution at the stake in 1415. By the time of his death, Huss had attracted many followers, the Hussites, who endured persecution that seemed only to strengthen their resolve to resist state-sponsored religious tyranny. In 1419, the Hussites rebelled against Catholics and German king Sigismund (1368–1437), who had inherited the Bohemian throne and who was believed to have condoned the execution of Huss.

Pope Martin V (1368–1431) proclaimed a crusade against the Hussite rebels, sanctioning Sigismund to send troops of the Holy Roman Empire to Prague. The Hussites rallied behind the dynamic leader John Ziska (c. 1360–1424), head of the radical Taborite Hussite faction.

Ziska closed the gates of the city and deployed his forces in trenches outside the walls of Prague on the commanding Hill of Witkov. Sigismund's forces attacked on July 14, 1420. With only 9,000 men under his command, Ziska repelled the invaders.

Following this repulse, Sigismund took personal command of the imperial troops, arriving in Bohemia late in 1421 leading a massive German army—estimated at tens of thousands of men—against a significantly smaller Hussite force of no more than 25,000 led by John Ziska. Ziska was, however, a natural military genius, who knew how to make the most of the resources he had. Not only were his men well trained, they were incredibly mobile. Ziska made use of mobile artillery—unheard of at the time—and he used his baggage wagons as mobile forts. When Sigismund confronted the Hussite army at Kutná Hora, 45 miles southeast of Prague, on January 6, 1422, he was stopped by a ring of wagon-forts. After pounding against these to no avail—and suffering heavy losses in the process—Sigismund suddenly found himself under heavy attack by a Hussite charge. Sigismund had no choice but to fall back. He withdrew 15 miles to the southeast, taking a stand at Nemecky-Brod. There, on January 10, 1422, Ziska attacked with about 11,000 troops against Sigismund's 23,000. When it was over, Sigismund had lost more than half of his army and was forced to flee to avoid capture.

While fighting Sigismund, Ziska was also embroiled in the HUSSITE CIVIL WAR (1423–34), and died in 1424. Andrew Prokop (c. 1380–1434) or Prokop the Great, replaced Ziska as leader of the Taborite Hussites, who, despite the death of Ziska, still wholly intimidated Sigismund's Germans. For two years, neither Sigismund nor the pope was able to form an army willing to confront the Hussites. Finally, in 1426, a large force of 50,000 Germans made a stand at Ústí nad Labem, only to be defeated by the smaller Hussite force, which inflicted some 15,000 casualties on the enemy, forcing the Germans to flee in panic. After this, the Hussites took the offensive, invading Hungary, Austria, and Germany, burning a swath of destruction along the way.

But the Hussite Civil War continued to take its toll. The moderate Utraquists, opposed to the radical Taborites, made an accommodation with the Catholic Church and struck up an alliance with conservative Bohemian nobles. The combined Utraquist-Bohemian army met Prokop the Great's Taborite force at Český-Brod on May 30, 1434, 19 miles east of Prague. Casualties on both sides included some 18,000 dead, including Prokop. With the Bohemian army thus shattered, the path was clear to ultimate surrender to Sigismund, which occurred two years later. In 1436, Bohemia recognized Sigismund as its king.

See also BOHEMIAN CIVIL WAR (1390–1419); GERMAN CIVIL WAR (1400–1411).

Further reading: Frabtisk Michalek Bartos, *The Hussite Revolution, 1424–1437* (Boulder, Colo., and New York:

East European Monographs, distributed by Columbia University Press, 1986); Josef Kalvoda, *The Genesis of Czechoslovakia* (Boulder, Colo., and New York: East European Monographs, distributed by Columbia University Press, 1986).

Hyksos Invasion of Egypt (c. 1674–1567 B.C.E.)

PRINCIPAL COMBATANTS: Hyksos vs. Egyptians
PRINCIPAL THEATER(S): Lower Egypt
DECLARATION: None
MAJOR ISSUES AND OBJECTIVES: The Hyksos invaded or infiltrated Egypt for the purpose of taking over leadership of its government.
OUTCOME: The Hyksos assumed power in Egypt as the concurrent 15th and 16th dynasties.
APPROXIMATE MAXIMUM NUMBER OF MEN UNDER ARMS: Unknown
CASUALTIES: Unknown
TREATIES: No surviving documents

The Hyksos were a Semitic people who invaded Egypt about 1700 B.C.E. and founded the 15th and 16th Egyptian dynasties. They laid siege to Memphis around 1674 B.C.E., while ruling Egypt from a Nile delta capital they called Avaris.

Was the Hyksos invasion a full-scale war? Manetho (fl. c. 300 B.C.E.), an Egyptian historian, portrays the Hyksos progress into Egypt as nothing less. Using archaeological evidence, modern scholars have suggested that the "invasion" was more in the nature of a gradual infiltration, which led to a coup d'état in lower Egypt. After the coup—which may or may not have been particularly violent—the Hyksos apparently ruled Egypt peacefully. The lower kingdom they ruled directly, governing the upper kingdom through a series of vassals.

However the Hyksos came to power, their reign seems to have ended rather abruptly in 1567, when native Egyptian forces retook Memphis and expelled the Hyksos from it. Egyptian records make no mention of the Hyksos after 1567, and archaeologists have found no traces of this ethnic group after this year.

Further reading: William C. Hayes, *Hyksos Period and the New Kingdom, 1675–1080 B.C.* (New York: Metropolitan Museum of Art, 1959); Sabatino Moscati, *Ancient Semitic Civilizations* (New York: G. P. Putnam's Sons, Capricorn Books, 1960).

I

Iconoclastic War, First (726–731)

PRINCIPAL COMBATANTS: Forces of Leo III, Byzantine emperor opposed to holy icons, vs. Byzantine rebels who supported icon worship
PRINCIPAL THEATER(S): Greece and Ravenna, Italy
DECLARATION: No declaration, but the war was begun by Leo's proclamation of his opposition to the worship of holy icons.
MAJOR ISSUES AND OBJECTIVES: Leo III wanted to end icon worship in the Byzantine Empire.
OUTCOME: Inconclusive, except that parts of the Byzantine Empire slipped further from imperial control
APPROXIMATE MAXIMUM NUMBER OF MEN UNDER ARMS: Unknown
CASUALTIES: Unknown
TREATIES: None

Byzantine emperor Leo III (c. 680–741) came to power by overthrowing, in March 717, Emperor Theodosius III (d. after 717). Leo's early reign was marked by continual resistance to Arab invasion, alternating with Byzantine counterinvasion into Arab territory. By the mid-720s, however, the Arab threat had been reduced, and Leo turned his attention to the realization of his own religious campaign. In the Eastern Roman Empire, the veneration of holy icons had become an overwhelmingly important part of religious ritual, growing into what Leo deemed spiritually and politically dangerous cult status. Supported by like-minded "Iconoclastic"—literally, "icon-destroying"—clergymen, Leo made public his opposition to the veneration of icons in 726. At first, he confined his

opposition to making speeches, but these speeches incited troops to destroy, in Constantinople, a particularly important icon depicting Christ. The act nearly provoked a popular revolt, when a mob killed the officer who had brought down the icon. Amid papal denunciation of the Iconoclasts, this incident triggered a revolt of the troops of the Theme of Hellas (Greece) in 727. The Greek sent a rebel fleet to Constantinople, one of the ship bearing a proposed anti-emperor. Leo's navy intercepted the fleet and destroyed it.

In 730, Leo ordered the destruction of all holy icons in the empire. When the head of the Eastern Orthodox Church, the patriarch of Constantinople, refused to comply, Leo deposed and replaced him. These actions created stiffening resistance throughout the Byzantine Empire, and, in 731, the populace of Ravenna, Italy, a Byzantine exarchate (or province), revolted, prompting Leo to dispatch a fleet to capture the rebellious city. A storm ravaged the fleet, however, and the defenders of Ravenna turned it back. Having failed to restore order by military means, Leo declared Calabria, Sicily, and Illyria to be under the control of the new Eastern Orthodox patriarch of Constantinople, thereby denying the Roman Catholic pope's authority in these places. With this, the First Iconoclastic War came to an uneasy end.

See also BYZANTINE-MUSLIM WAR (741–752); ICONO-CLASTIC WAR, SECOND.

Further reading: Stephen Gero, *Byzantine Iconoclasm during the Reign of Leo III* (Louvain, Belgium: Secretariat du Corpus SCO, 1973); John Julius Norwich, *Byzantium: The Early Centuries* (New York: Alfred A. Knopf, 2003); Cyril A. Mango, ed., *Oxford History of Byzantium* (New York: Oxford University Press, 2002); Mark Whittow, *The*

Making of Byzantium, 600–1025 (Berkeley: University of California Press, 1996).

Iconoclastic War, Second   (741–743)

PRINCIPAL COMBATANTS: Icon-worshiping rebels led by Artavasdos vs. Constantine V, Iconoclast Byzantine emperor
PRINCIPAL THEATER(S): Byzantium
DECLARATION: None
MAJOR ISSUES AND OBJECTIVES: Artavasdos led a rebellion against the Iconoclast emperor Constantine V with the aim of installing himself on the Byzantine throne and restoring icon worship throughout the realm.
OUTCOME: Constantine V put down the rebellion and recovered the throne.
APPROXIMATE MAXIMUM NUMBER OF MEN UNDER ARMS: Unknown
CASUALTIES: Unknown
TREATIES: None

Constantine V (718–775), the successor of Byzantine emperor Leo III (c. 680–741), who had started the First ICONOCLASTIC WAR in 726, intensified the persecution of icon worshipers, thereby stirring elements of the empire to rebellion. When Constantine was off fighting the BYZANTINE-MUSLIM WAR (741–752), Artavasdos (fl. 740s), his brother-in-law, incited and led a military and religious revolt in favor of the icon worshipers. Against reduced imperial forces, the rebels scored a victory that emboldened Artavasdos to proclaim himself emperor. He immediately restored icon worship throughout the realm. His reign, however, was brief. At the battles of Sardes and Modrina, both fought in 743, imperial forces, personally led by Constantine, easily defeated the rebels. Constantine reclaimed the throne and, by way of punishment, blinded his brother-in-law. The iconoclastic movement resumed.

Further reading: Stephen Gero, *Byzantine Iconoclasm during the Reign of Constantine V* (Louvain, Belgium: Corpussco, 1977); John Julius Norwich, *Byzantium: The Early Centuries* (New York: Alfred A. Knopf, 2003); Cyril A. Mango, ed., *Oxford History of Byzantium* (New York: Oxford University Press, 2002); Mark Whittow, *The Making of Byzantium, 600–1025* (Berkeley: University of California Press, 1996).

Illyrian War, First   (229–228 B.C.E.)

PRINCIPAL COMBATANTS: Rome vs. Illyria
PRINCIPAL THEATER(S): Greece, mainly Corfu
DECLARATION: Roman Senate against Illyria, 229 B.C.E.
MAJOR ISSUES AND OBJECTIVES: Rome wanted to put an end to Illyrian piracy, which menaced Roman trade with Greece.
OUTCOME: The Illyrians were quickly—and almost bloodlessly—defeated at Corcyra (Corfu); they renounced territorial claims, and piracy was suppressed.
APPROXIMATE MAXIMUM NUMBER OF MEN UNDER ARMS: Unknown
CASUALTIES: Unknown
TREATIES: No documents survive

The Illyrians, who lived on the eastern shore of the Adriatic on the Balkan Peninsula, were a warlike people, who regularly sent pirate fleets to prey on Roman and Greek shipping. The Greeks generally ignored the Illyrians and did their best to avoid them. The Romans, however, sought to establish a trading relationship. In 230 B.C.E., a Roman trading fleet fell victim to Illyrian pirates, and when the Romans sent a delegation to negotiate with the queen of Illyria, Teuta (fl. 230s–220s B.C.E.), the ambassadors were not only treated with contempt at court, but were set upon and assassinated on their return trip. This provoked the Roman Senate to declare war.

Roman legions attacked the Illyrians while they were in the process of laying siege to a number of Greek city-states. At Corcyra (Corfu), Greece, the Romans attacked the Illyrians in 229 B.C.E. Awed by the Roman legion and fleet, the Illyrian besieging force surrendered with hardly a fight, and the haughty Queen Teuta capitulated the following year. She renounced territorial claims and agreed to pay a war indemnity to Rome. To ensure the longevity of its victory, Rome struck an alliance with Macedonia, which would serve as a buffer on Illyria's flank.

See also ILLYRIAN WAR, SECOND; MACEDONIAN WAR, FIRST.

Further reading: M. Cary, *A History of the Greek World from 323 to 146 B.C.* (New York: Barnes and Noble, 1963); F. W. Walbank, *The Hellenistic World* (Cambridge, Mass.: Harvard University Press, 1993).

Illyrian War, Second   (219 B.C.E.)

PRINCIPAL COMBATANTS: Rome vs. Illyria
PRINCIPAL THEATER(S): Dinale and Pharos, Illyria (on the Balkan Peninsula)
DECLARATION: None
MAJOR ISSUES AND OBJECTIVES: When Illyria violated the peace imposed by Rome after the First Illyrian War, Roman legions swiftly attacked.
OUTCOME: The war ended in one week, and the Roman-imposed peace was reestablished.
APPROXIMATE MAXIMUM NUMBER OF MEN UNDER ARMS: Unknown

CASUALTIES: Unknown
TREATIES: No documents survive

Roman victory in the First ILLYRIAN WAR, from 229 to 228 B.C.E. resulted in a firm peace with the warlike Illyrians; however, Demetrius of Pharos (d. 214 B.C.E.), the new ruler of Illyria, violated the peace in 220 B.C.E. by invading various Roman-protected territories and by resuming the piracy that had long preyed upon Roman and Greek shipping. In 219, Roman legions laid siege to two major Illyrian fortress cities, Dinale and Pharos. Dinale was besieged for a week before it surrendered. Pharos, which was attacked by legions from two sides, held out for less than a day. Demetrius of Pharos fled the city before it fell; however, the Romans successfully reestablished the peace that had been won in the First Illyrian War.

See also PUNIC WAR, SECOND.

Further reading: M. Cary, *A History of the World from 323 to 146 B.C.* (New York: Barnes and Noble, 1963); F. W. Walbank, *The Hellenistic World* (Cambridge, Mass.: Harvard University Press, 1993).

Inca Revolt (1535–1536)

PRINCIPAL COMBATANTS: The Incas vs. the Spanish conquistadores
PRINCIPAL THEATER(S): Peru, especially Cuzco and vicinity
DECLARATION: None
MAJOR ISSUES AND OBJECTIVES: The Incas wanted to oust the Spanish invaders from their country.
OUTCOME: Ultimately, the rebellion was put down after the failure of the Inca siege of Spanish-held Cuzco.
APPROXIMATE MAXIMUM NUMBER OF MEN UNDER ARMS: Unknown
CASUALTIES: Unknown
TREATIES: None

Desiring, as many Spanish did, to emulate the success of Hernán Cortés (1485–1547) enjoyed in the SPANISH CONQUEST OF MEXICO (1519–21), the Spanish conquistador Francisco Pizarro (c. 1475–1541) successfully invaded the realm of the Peruvian Incas in 1531, having twice failed in the 1520s. He landed at Tumbez on the Pacific coast, just south of the equator, and from there marched to Cuzco, the Inca capital. Along the way, he avoided most armed clashes by exploiting an ongoing civil war among tribal factions allied to rival heirs to the chieftainship. Pizarro explained to each group he encountered that he was the enemy of the other. At Cajamarca, en route to Cuzco, Pizarro captured Atahualpa (c. 1500–33), one of the candidates for chief. While Pizarro's soldiers busied themselves plundering Inca treasure, Pizarro negotiated with Atahualpa's rival, Manco Capac II (c. 1500–44), even as Atahualpa managed secretly to assemble a force to expel the Spanish. But before Atahualpa could muster his forces, Pizarro had him tried for usurpation, idolatry, and polygamy, found him guilty, and had him executed. With Atahualpa disposed of, the Spanish crowned Manco, as the more pliable puppet chief.

Yet Manco had an agenda of his own. When Pizarro and his lieutenant, Diego de Almagro (c. 1475–1538), were absent, Manco organized an Inca revolt. The resulting uprising resulted in the slaughter of a number of conquistadores, and the Incas laid siege to Spanish-held Cuzco, holding that city in thrall for 10 months. At length, however, the Spanish prevailed, breaking the siege. Once this happened, the Inca revolt abruptly folded, as the Indians went home to tend to their crops. The revolt collapsing around him, Manco Capac II fled to the hills with a band of loyal followers. There he decreed what was in effect an Incan government in exile and directed an ongoing campaign of raids against the Spanish. In 1544, some of his followers turned on him and assassinated him.

See also SPANISH CONQUEST OF PERU.

Further reading: John Hemming, *The Conquest of the Incas,* rev. ed. (New York: Penguin Books, 1983); Alfred Métraux, *The History of the Incas,* trans. George Ordish (New York: Pantheon Books, 1969); Fred Ramon, *Francisco Pizarro: The Exploration of Peru and the Conquest of the Inca* (New York: Rosen Publishing Group, 2003).

India, Mongol Invasion of   *See* MONGOL INVASIONS OF INDIA.

Indian Civil War (1947–1948)

PRINCIPAL COMBATANTS: Hindus vs. Muslims
PRINCIPAL THEATER(S): India
DECLARATION: None
MAJOR ISSUES AND OBJECTIVES: The two religious groups each wanted to dominate newly independent India.
OUTCOME: The civil war was largely a fight between civilians and led to no definite conclusion but ended, uneasily, after the assassination of Gandhi.
APPROXIMATE MAXIMUM NUMBER OF MEN UNDER ARMS: Millions of civilians were involved in the rioting.
CASUALTIES: The "war" created some 7 million refugees, at least 1 million of whom perished in rioting.
TREATIES: None

Born in India, Mohandas Gandhi (1869–1948) studied law at Oxford and practiced at the bar in Bombay before taking a job with an Indian firm in South Africa. Appalled by the politics of apartheid, he perfected the techniques of his "progressive nonviolent noncooperation" in demonstrations against the racist white government of South Africa. Returning to India in 1915, he became a labor organizer and a thorn in the side of the British colonial government as he used his peculiar style of political protest in a series of strikes, boycotts, and dramatic demonstrations to agitate constantly for India's independence.

Frequently imprisoned, Gandhi turned even that into an instrument of protest, resorting to widely publicized hunger strikes as part of his program of civil disobedience. Although Great Britain had begun to make some concessions by the 1930s, the British threw the troublesome leader back in jail during WORLD WAR II, and from 1942 to 1944 the world-famous prisoner demanded complete withdrawal of the British colonial forces from India, directing this "Quit India" movement from his cell.

The movement he fostered ultimately prevailed, because Great Britain, subtly but persistently pressed by the United States after the war to give up much of its empire, granted India's independence in 1947. Yet for Gandhi, this victory was tempered by what he took as his personal failure to unite India's Hindu majority with the new nation's many minorities, especially its large Muslim population.

Led by Muhammad Ali Jinnah (1876–1949) the Muslim League and the Hindu-dominated Congress went their separate ways over the issue of religion in the new state. Riots between Hindus and Muslims broke out, the worst of which was the "Great Calcutta Killing" of August 16–20, 1946, which spread throughout much of the subcontinent. To many, and especially the British, the only resolution seemed to be partition of the new nation into a predominantly Hindu India and a predominantly Muslim Pakistan.

The British sanctioned the partition which was set for August 14, 1947. Two days after it was effected, civil war broke out between the Hindus and Muslims in the Punjab. From there, fighting spread throughout the country. The nation suddenly experienced a mass movement of refugees unprecedented in history. Some 5.5 million people moved between Pakistan and India, Muslims one way, Hindus another. Another 1.25 million moved from eastern Pakistan into western Bengal, while 400,000 Hindus left Sind (in western Pakistan) and settled in India. The movement of refugees was accompanied by continual rioting, and deaths among the refugees amounted to perhaps 1 million persons. Britain offered to intervene militarily, but Indian prime minister Jawaharlal Nehru (1889–1964), whose country had so recently won its independence, refused to accept help from the former oppressor.

The civil war was made worse by the outbreak of the INDO-PAKISTANI WAR (1947–1948), which erupted over a dispute concerning the partition of Kashmir. Throughout the firestorm, Gandhi, father of Indian independence, who had accepted no office in new India, pleaded for order. He walked barefoot through riot-torn Bengal and Bihar, trying by his simple presence to stop the slaughter. Then he returned to New Delhi, where he preached nonviolence daily until he was assassinated on January 30, 1948 by an orthodox Hindu Brahmin fanatic, who felt that Gandhi had betrayed his allegiance to India. So venerated was Gandhi, that his murder—a martyr's death—did much to bring an end to the rioting and to unify the government of India, albeit as a nation separate from Pakistan.

See also INDO-PAKISTANI WAR (1965); INDO-PAKISTANI WAR (1971).

Further reading: Allen Hayes Merriam, *Gandhi vs. Jinnah: The Debate over the Partition of India* (Calcutta: Minerva, 1980); C. H. Phillips and Mary Doreen Wainwright, eds., *The Partition of India: Policies and Perspectives, 1935–1947* (Cambridge, Mass.: M.I.T. Press, 1970); Rajan Mahan Ramakant, ed., *India's Partition: Preludes and Legacies* (Jaipur, India: Rawat Publications, 1998).

Indian Mutiny (1857–1859)

PRINCIPAL COMBATANTS: Indian rebel groups (initially led by the sepoys) vs. Great Britain (the East India Company government)
PRINCIPAL THEATER(S): India
DECLARATION: None
MAJOR ISSUES AND OBJECTIVES: The Indian rebels sought to overthrow British colonial rule.
OUTCOME: The extremely brutal uprising was largely suppressed in 1858 and definitively ended in 1859.
APPROXIMATE MAXIMUM NUMBER OF MEN UNDER ARMS: 160,000 total, many of whom rebelled against the British; loyal British forces at any one place and time numbered about 30,000; rebel forces typically outnumbered the British but were less well equipped
CASUALTIES: Britain, 2,034 killed in battle, 8,987 died of disease and other causes; Indian, unknown
TREATIES: None

Also called the Sepoy Rebellion, the Great Mutiny, and the First Indian War of Independence, this was an uprising against the British colonial regime in India begun by Indian troops—called *sipahi,* anglicized to *sepoys*—in service to the British East India Company.

By the middle of the 19th century, the East India Company controlled the region of modern India, Pakistan, Bangladesh, Burma (Myanmar), and Ceylon (Sri Lanka). The Great Mogul emperor of India was now no more than a figurehead; the real government was contained within a British civil and military administration and the British-controlled army numbering 160,000 men, of whom only 24,000 were British. The rest were native troops in the British service. Over the years, friction developed between the native troops and their East India Company employers. The British refused to respect Indian religious and cultural traditions. In an atmosphere of growing discontent there arose a rumor among the sepoys late in 1856 that the cartridges for the newly issued Lee-Enfield rifles were greased with the fat of cows and pigs. Cows are sacred to Hindus and must not be eaten, whereas pigs are regarded by Muslims as unclean—and must not be eaten. Prior to loading a rifle of the period, it was necessary to bite off the end of the paper cartridge; for the Hindu or Muslim soldier, doing so meant coming into contact with cow or pig and was, therefore, a grave pollution. In the Bengal army, some soldiers refused to use the new cartridges, but a full-scale mutiny broke out in Meerut, northeast of Delhi, where 85 men of the third light cavalry refused to use the cartridges on April 23, 1857. Convicted of mutiny, they were sentenced to imprisonment, publicly fettered, and ceremonially stripped of their military insignia. This served only to incite further rebellion. Members of the 11th and 20th infantry regiments revolted on May 10, freeing their imprisoned comrades—and many civilian prisoners as well. Following this, they rioted, killing 40 British officers and civilians in Meerut. From here, they marched to Delhi, where other Indian regiments joined the mutiny. In the city, the sepoys slaughtered many more British soldiers and civilians and restored to power the aged Mogul emperor, Muhammad Bahadur Shah (1775–1862).

News of the rebellion exploded throughout the subcontinent. Regiments throughout the Bengal army mutinied, and north and central India generally rose up against British rule. At first, the British were overwhelmed and at a loss for a response. In the Punjab, British commanders disarmed the sepoys and assembled a small army to advance on Delhi. The force took up a position outside the city. In Kolkata, the British contained the rebellion and managed to retain control of the Ganges River and communications lines as far upriver as Allahabad. In central India, several thousand British troops fought many pitched battles against the forces of local princes and Rani (Queen) Lakshmibai (c. 1830–58) of Jhansi, all of whom had joined the uprising.

In the central Ganges River valley, Oudh, recently annexed by the British, became an area of intense rebellion. On May 30, 1857, rebels besieged Europeans along with loyal Indians at the British Residency in Oudh's capital, Lucknow. Shortly after this, the British garrison at Cawnpore (Kanpur) came under siege through June 27, when the survivors negotiated with the rebel leader, Nana Sahib (c. 1821–c. 1858), for safe passage. Despite this, they were attacked while evacuating to boats on the Ganges River. Most of the British soldiers were killed. Some 200 British women and children, captured, were subsequently slain in prison. In retaliation, the British forces authorized a brutal pogrom of similar atrocities directed against Indian combatants and noncombatants alike.

In the meantime, outside the walls of Delhi, inconclusive battles were fought until the British army was sufficiently reinforced to attack the city on September 15. After five days of bitter fighting, the British retook Delhi. On September 25, a relief column reached the Lucknow residency, but it was pinned down there through late November, when a second relief force arrived, broke the siege, and evacuated the survivors. When the British returned to Oudh in February 1858, it was with an army of more than 30,000 men, including Nepalese troops. Lucknow fell to the British on March 23, 1858, and the rebel forces in north India dispersed. The rebel fort at Jhansi capitulated in April, and the rani was subsequently killed in battle. With this, the mutiny, for all practical purposes, ended; however, sporadic fighting continued into the next year, as British forces engaged small rebel forces. Early in the year, rebel leader Nana Sahib's leading general, Tantia Topi (1819–59), was captured, and, with his execution in April 1859, the revolt was completely ended.

The consequences of the Indian Mutiny were profound. The British government officially abolished the Mogul Empire once and for all, exiling the aged emperor Muhammad Bahadur Shah to Burma. Equally significant was the assumption of British direct rule of India, ending the administration of the East India Company. British military recruiters now looked to the Punjab and Nepal for new native troops, for these regions had remained steadfastly loyal during the rebellion. Perhaps most far reaching was the general change in attitude of the British administration toward Indians. The relationship was now pervaded by distrust, and the policy of the British turned from exploitive paternalism to frank repression.

Further reading: Agha Humayun Amin, *The Sepoy Rebellion of 1857–59, Reinterpreted* (Lahore, Pakistan: Strategies and Tactics, 1998); C. Hibbert, *The Great Mutiny: India 1857* (London: Allen Lane, 1978).

Indian-Nepalese War   *See* GURKHA WAR.

Indian War   *See* MARYLAND AND VIRGINIA'S WAR WITH THE SUSQUEHANNOCKS.

Indonesian-Malaysian War   (1963–1966)

PRINCIPAL COMBATANTS: Indonesia vs. Malaysia
PRINCIPAL THEATER(S): Malaysia, especially Sabah and Sarawak (both in Borneo), and Singapore Harbor
DECLARATION: Indonesia against Malaysia, 1963
MAJOR ISSUES AND OBJECTIVES: Indonesia refused to recognize the Republic of Malaysia.

OUTCOME: Drained by internal dissension, Indonesia agreed to peace in 1966; Malaysia endured as an independent republic.
APPROXIMATE MAXIMUM NUMBER OF MEN UNDER ARMS: Unknown
CASUALTIES: During the period, 150,000–500,000 Indonesian communists were killed.
TREATIES: Treaty of Jakarta, August 11, 1966

Achmed Sukarno (1901–70), president (and dictator) of Indonesia, refused to recognize the newly proclaimed Federation of Malaysia (the union of Malaya, Sabah, Sarawak, and—until 1965—Singapore). Sukarno stirred his nation to war against Malaysia, which sought and received military aid from Great Britain when Indonesian guerrillas penetrated Sabah and Sarawak. Sukarno fought no set battles but waged a low-level guerrilla war, using paratroopers behind Malaysian lines and underwater demolition teams to mine the harbor of Singapore. During the war, dissension broke out at home, as communists staged a coup d'état (which failed) on September 30, 1965. General Suharto (b. 1921), Sukarno's general in chief, led Indonesian forces against the communist insurgents, then launched a nationwide purge of communists and leftists.

The purge, ostensibly in retaliation for the communist abduction and killing of six top Indonesian generals, was carried out by a combination of the Indonesian army and right-wing Muslim political groups. It was a slaughter, in which an estimated 150,000 to as many as 500,000 communists were killed (the most widely accepted figure puts the toll at between 200,000 and 250,000). Most of the deaths occurred within eight weeks after the September 30, 1965, coup attempt, but the killings continued well into 1966. The death toll on Indonesian-held Bali was at least 50,000 and, on east Java, 100,000. The leftist leader Dipoa Nusuntara Aidit (d. 1966) was killed, and those communists who were not executed or murdered were imprisoned in untold numbers. By 1976, there were still 70,000 political prisoners from this period being held.

Although the communist takeover was crushed, the effort monopolized Indonesian military resources, and Sukarno agreed to open peace negotiations with Malaysia at Bangkok. An armistice was concluded on June 1, 1966, followed by a formal treaty, signed at Djakarta, on August 11, 1966. Nor did Sukarno retain true power in Indonesia. On March 11, 1966, the army compelled him to relinquish much authority on army chief of staff Suharto.

See also INDONESIAN WARS.

Further reading: Benedict R.O.G. Anderson, ed., *Violence and State in Suharto's Indonesia* (Ithaca, N.Y.: Southeast Asia Program Publishing, Cornell University Press, 2001); J. A. C. Mackie, *Konfrontasi: The Indonesia-Malaysia Dispute, 1963–1966* (Kuala Lumpur and New York: Published for the Australian Institute of International Affairs by Oxford University Press, 1974).

Indonesian War in East Timor (1975–1999)

PRINCIPAL COMBATANTS: East Timorese rebels vs. Portugal, then various factions in East Timor and Indonesia
PRINCIPAL THEATER(S): East Timor
DECLARATION: None
MAJOR ISSUES AND OBJECTIVES: Independence of East Timor, first from Portugal, then from Indonesia
OUTCOME: With United Nations intervention, independence was achieved (2002), but East Timor was left in ruins.
APPROXIMATE MAXIMUM NUMBER OF MEN UNDER ARMS: Unknown
CASUALTIES: More than 200,000 East Timorese died during the long struggle for independence from Indonesia. Almost 1 million became refugees in 1999.
TREATIES: Various UN agreements, the most important of which was concluded in 1999 among Portugal, Indonesia, and East Timor

East Timor, the eastern portion of Timor Island, in the Malay Archipelago, was settled by the Portuguese in 1520 and became a Portuguese colony in 1859. Through the 20th century, Portuguese rule on East Timor became a dictatorship, which was overthrown in 1974 in a bloodless military coup. In the absence of the Portuguese, rival political parties quickly formed, and, in 1975, a civil war broke out, triggered by military intelligence operations and a declaration of independence of FRETILIN (Revolutionary Front for the Independence of East Timor). Exploiting the disarray in East Timor, Indonesian forces invaded in 1975. The following year, East Timor was incorporated as Indonesia's 27th province. However, the United Nations refused to recognize Indonesia's claim on what it considered an independent nation. Through 1999, East Timor would be torn by violence between the independence-seeking factions and the Indonesian military presence in the region. Between 1975 and 1999, it is estimated that more than 200,000 East Timorese were killed.

During 1977–78, the Indonesian air force conducted heavy bombardment of East Timor. This was followed by years of essentially guerrilla warfare. In 1988, the European Union (EU) voted its support of East Timor's right to self-determination, and the United Nations followed suit in 1989. Nevertheless, Indonesia continued to assert its claim, and in 1991 more than 250 mourners and demonstrators were cut down by Indonesian army forces at the Santa Cruz Cemetery in East Timor's capital city of Dili.

Although the Indonesian government launched a formal inquiry into the massacre, issuing a 1992 report condemning the military. The troops and officers involved were given light sentences whereas East Timorese protesters were sentenced to as much as 10 years imprisonment. The following year, 1993, FRETILIN leader Xanana Gusmão (b. 1946) was captured and sentenced to a 20-year term. His leadership role in the Revolutionary Front was assumed by Konis Santana.

Throughout the 1990s, the Indonesian military presence was increased in East Timor, and in 1997, the Indonesian army clamped down on pro-independence demonstrations that came in the wake of the announcements that internationally recognized independence leaders Bishop Carlos Belo (b. 1948) and José Ramos-Horta (b. 1949) were to be awarded jointly the Nobel Peace Prize. At this point, in 1998, the Catholic Church convened a conference of Timorese leaders in the town of Dare to avert clashes among factions fighting for independence and to map out a road to reconciliation with Portugal and Indonesia. At last, on May 5, 1999, an agreement was signed at the United Nations, among Portugal, Indonesia, and the Timorese leadership regarding a resolution to the East Timor crisis. On June 11, 1999, UNAMET (United Nations Mission in East Timor) was established to assist in the holding of a plebiscite on the question of East Timorese independence. On August 30, 1999, East Timor voted for independence. The results were announced on September 4, 1999: 78.5 percent of East Timorese favored complete independence from Indonesia.

Despite the UN-brokered agreements, Indonesia armed pro-Indonesian East Timorese militia forces, which brought a reign of terror on pro-independence supporters. The result was a chaotic, anarchic renewal of civil war, which killed thousands and left the capital city of Dili in ruins. It is estimated that 85 percent of the buildings in the country, including virtually all schools and nearly all businesses, were destroyed in the 1999 violence. Approximately 1 million East Timorese became refugees, fleeing to West Timor, other Indonesian islands, and Australia.

On September 20, 1999, a UN-sanctioned International Force for East Timor (INTERFET) entered East Timor to restore peace and order and to protect UNAMET, so that it could carry out its mandate to assist in enforcing East Timorese independence.

On October 25, 1999, a United Nations Transitional Administration in East Timor (UNTAET) was created to act as an interim government until an election could be held. At the start of 2002, East Timor was declared an independent nonself-governing territory under United Nations supervision, and in February the provisional government drafted a constitution, which was subsequently approved. In April, under the new constitution, Xanana Gusmão, who had been imprisoned in 1993, was elected East Timor's first president, and on May 20 the nation became fully independent.

Further reading: Geoffrey C. Gunn, *East Timor and the U.N.: The Case for Intervention* (Trenton, N.J.: Red Sea Press, 1997); Matthew Jardine, *East Timor: Genocide in Paradise* (Tucson, Ariz.: Odonian Press, 1999); Michael G. Smith, *Peacekeeping in East Timor: The Path to Independence* (Boulder, Colo.: Lynne Rienner Publishers, 2003).

Indonesian War of Independence
(1945–1949)

PRINCIPAL COMBATANTS: The Indonesian republicans vs. the Netherlands; also Indonesian Muslim fundamentalists and (separately) the People's Democratic Front (Indonesian communists) vs. Indonesian republicans
PRINCIPAL THEATER(S): Indonesia, especially Java
DECLARATION: Independence proclaimed, August 17, 1945
MAJOR ISSUES AND OBJECTIVES: Indonesian republicans wanted independence from Dutch colonial rule (and to suppress rival agitators for Muslim and for communist government).
OUTCOME: Independence was fully recognized in 1949.
APPROXIMATE MAXIMUM NUMBER OF MEN UNDER ARMS: The Netherlands, 175,000; Indonesia, 160,000 plus 175,000 irregulars
CASUALTIES: The Netherlands, 2,526 military casualties, 22,000 civilian casualties; Indonesia, 80,000
TREATIES: Cheribon Agreement of 1946, followed by The Hague Accord, November 2, 1949

In the years between the two world wars, the Dutch East Indies witnessed the rise and rebuff of two challenges to colonial rule, a communist revolt and an Islamic nationalist movement. In 1927 a new challenge was mounted by a young engineer, fresh out of school, named Achmed Sukarno (1901–70), who founded a "general study club" in Bandung, which became the nucleus of the independence-minded Indonesian Nationalist Party (Partai Nasional Indonesia, or PNI). Arrested, tried, and imprisoned by the Dutch in 1929, Sukarno was ultimately exiled to southern Sumatra in 1933, but a reconstituted PNI under the leadership of Mohammad Hatta (1902–80) and Sutan Sjahrir (1909–66) continued to agitate for independence until the Japanese invaded and occupied the country in 1942.

Initially hailed by many Indonesian nationalists as liberators, the Japanese established themselves as vicious overlords, and the East Indies' dreams of independence vanished into the fog of WORLD WAR II. Then, in late 1944, as the war was clearly turning against it, Japan announced its intention to prepare the Indies for self-government. On the eve of the Japanese surrender, Terauchi Hisaichi (1879–1945), commander of Southeast Asia, summoned Sukarno and Hatta to Saigon, where he promised them an immediate transfer of independence. Pressured by their own followers to act, Sukarno proclaimed independence—after confirming the news of the Japanese surrender—early on the morning of August 17, 1945. The proclamation sparked a series of uprisings that worried the British who arrived to accept the Japanese surrender. As the self-proclaimed government began to draft a constitution and install an ad hoc parliament called the Central Indonesian National Committee under President Sukarno, the Netherlands refused to recognize the independence of the East Indies. In conjunction with the British, Dutch troops landed at Batavia (Jakarta, Java) with the dual mission of disarming and repatriating Japanese soldiers still in the islands and restoring the status quo ante bellum (the way things were before the war), that is, a Dutch government in the East Indies.

The Dutch-British force soon found itself under attack by the Indonesian People's Army, which was concentrated in Bandung and Surabaya, Java. The violence was sufficient to prompt the Netherlands to enter into negotiations with the Indonesians, producing the Cheribon Agreement of 1946, whereby the Netherlands allowed the creation of a United States of Indonesia as a dominion under the Netherlands Crown. The agreement was signed, but soon sharp differences of interpretation broke out and were expressed in violence in Java and elsewhere. On July 20, 1947, Dutch troops (the British left in November 1946) cracked down with a "police action" of considerable brutality—and effectiveness.

The republicans—those who favored an independent Indonesian democracy—were forced to fight not only the Dutch but also Muslim extremists, who wanted to create a fundamentalist Islamic state. Into this melee was added the communist People's Democratic Front. The republican government was able to crush the communists at Madioen, Java, in September 1948, but failed in its resistance against the Dutch, who captured the rebel capital, Jogjakarta, during the same year and placed key republican leaders under arrest. In the villages, however, at the grassroots, guerrilla resistance to Dutch occupation continued.

The Dutch eventually realized the impracticability of suppressing the republican movement. From August 23 to November 2, 1949, Dutch representatives met with Indonesians at The Hague and negotiated the transfer of full sovereignty to Sukarno's United States of Indonesia. Guerrilla warfare between Indonesian republicans and the Islamic fundamentalists continued, especially after 1950, when the nation officially became the Republic of Indonesia.

See also INDONESIAN-MALAYSIAN WAR; INDONESIAN WARS.

Further reading: William H. Frederick, *Visions and Heat: The Making of the Indonesian Revolution* (Athens: Ohio University Press, 1989); George McTurnan Kahin, *Nationalism and Revolution in Indonesia* (Ithaca, N.Y.: Southeast Asia Program Publications, Cornell University, 2003); Anthony Reid, *The Indonesian National Revolution, 1945–1950* (Westport, Conn.: Greenwood Press, 1986).

Indonesian Wars (1957–1962)

PRINCIPAL COMBATANTS: Indonesia vs. the Netherlands
PRINCIPAL THEATER(S): West New Guinea
DECLARATION: None
MAJOR ISSUES AND OBJECTIVES: Indonesia wanted possession of Dutch-held West New Guinea (Irian Jaya)
OUTCOME: Negotiated peace included an orderly transfer of West New Guinea from Dutch authority, through the agency of the United Nations, and ultimately into Indonesian authority.
APPROXIMATE MAXIMUM NUMBER OF MEN UNDER ARMS: Unknown
CASUALTIES: Unknown
TREATIES: Indonesian-Dutch Agreement of August 15, 1962

In 1949, when Indonesia achieved full independence from the Netherlands (*see* INDONESIAN WAR OF INDEPENDENCE), Achmed Sukarno (1901–70) was named president for life. His rule was dictatorial and gave rise to a number of military revolts in 1957. Sukarno's response was swift and decisive. He used the army to crush these rebellions; in 1959, he dropped all pretense of democratic rule by dissolving the assembly and giving himself full dictatorial powers. He also aligned the government increasingly with the communists.

In the meantime, while bringing iron-fisted order to the new republic, Sukarno called on the United Nations to intervene in resolving the republic's dispute with the Netherlands over possession of West New Guinea, which was still under Dutch rule, but which Indonesia claimed as the state of Irian Jaya. When the UN failed to reach a solution to the crisis, Sukarno called a general strike against all Dutch-owned businesses in Indonesia, expelled Dutch nationals, and seized and nationalized many Dutch holdings. Immediately, some 40,000 Netherlanders fled the country, and the army was drawn into the management of their abandoned enterprises. As a result, military entrepreneurs would come to play an ever-increasing role in the economic affairs of Sukarno's Indonesia.

Meanwhile, under the pressure applied by Sukarno, the Netherlands opened talks with Indonesia concerning West New Guinea. When the negotiations broke down, the Dutch prepared defenses in West New Guinea. Indonesian paratroopers landed in 1962 and coordinated with indigenous guerrillas an offensive against the Dutch. The Dutch responded with stiff and effective resistance. The violence rapidly escalated, and, in a bid to forestall all-out war, both the United States and the United Nations sponsored new peace talks. Negotiations led to the

Indonesian-Dutch Agreement of August 15, 1962, by which the Netherlands agreed to transfer administration of West New Guinea to the United Nations, which would later transfer it to Indonesia. The final transfer occurred in 1963.

See also INDONESIAN-MALAYSIAN WAR; INDONESIAN WAR IN EAST TIMOR.

Further reading: Herbert Feith, *The Decline of Constitutional Democracy in Indonesia* (Ithaca N.Y.: Cornell University Press, 1962); Audrey R. Kahin and George McTurnan Kahin, *Subversion as Foreign Policy: The Secret Eisenhower and Dulles Debacle in Indonesia* (New York: New Press, 1995); J. D. Legge, *Sukarno: A Political Biography* (New York, Praeger, 1972); Daniel S. Lev and Ruth McVey, eds., *Making Indonesia* (Ithaca, N.Y.: Southeast Asia Program, Cornell University, 1996); Rex Mortimer, *Indonesian Communism under Sukarno: Ideology and Politics, 1959–1965* (Ithaca, N.Y.: Cornell University Press, 1974).

Indo-Pakistani War (1947–1948)

PRINCIPAL COMBATANTS: India vs. Pakistan
PRINCIPAL THEATER(S): Jammu and Kashmir
DECLARATION: None
MAJOR ISSUES AND OBJECTIVES: India and Pakistan disputed governance of Jammu and Kashmir.
OUTCOME: A 1948 cease-fire created a de facto partition of the region at the current battle line.
APPROXIMATE MAXIMUM NUMBER OF MEN UNDER ARMS: Unknown
CASUALTIES: India, 1,500 killed, 3,500 wounded, 1,000 missing; Azad Kashmir and Pakistan, 1,000 killed; Pathan tribesmen and Kashmir; civilians, 5,000 killed
TREATIES: United Nations cease-fire, April 1948

The INDIAN CIVIL WAR resulted, in part, in the partition of the Indian subcontinent into Hindu-dominated India and Muslim-dominated Pakistan; however, Jammu and Kashmir (commonly known as Kashmir) remained an independent kingdom bordering West Pakistan. Its situation was complicated by the fact that, while its population was chiefly Muslim, its maharaja was a Sikh named Hari Singh (r. 1925–48). He wished the nation to remain both independent and neutral, and while this was in essence acceptable to Kashmir's Hindu-Muslim national conference, the members wanted to bring democracy to the country first. Tensions exploded in October 1947 when the Pathan Muslims of Poonch rebelled against the Hindu landowners of Kashmir. On October 22, Pakistan sent troops into the region, brutally taking Muzaffarabad and Uri, burning a swath of destruction wherever they marched, and killing Hindu civilians. As the troops closed in on the Kashmiri capital of Srinagar, the Kashmiri ruler summarily ceded

Jammu and Kashmir to India on October 27, 1947, simultaneously pleading for Indian military aid. In response, Sikh troops entered the region and pushed the invaders back toward the Pakistani border. Pakistan prepared to send more troops to fight it out in Pakistan, but the British officers who commanded the Pakistani army in the field threatened to resign. Pakistan then withdrew its regular army and sent instead "volunteers" to defend what they now called *Azad Kashmir*—Free Kashmir. This incursion created a flood of Hindu refugees pouring out of Kashmir and greatly exacerbating the ongoing civil war in India.

As the war between Pakistan and India and the civil war in India both escalated out of control, the father of Indian independence, Mohandas Gandhi (1869–1948) embarked on a campaign to bring about Muslim-Hindu conciliation and harmony. In the midst of this, a Hindu extremist assassinated the great leader, on January 30, 1948, an action that suddenly brought a degree of unity to the warring factions. More fighting broke out in April 1948, but United Nations intervention brought a cease-fire after three weeks. The battle line as of April 1948 became a de facto border in the region between Pakistan and India as the two sides held to an uneasy armistice.

See also INDO-PAKISTANI WAR (1965); INDO-PAKISTANI WAR (1971).

Further reading: M. J. Akbar, *India: The Siege Within: Challenges to a Nation's Unity* (New Delhi: UBSPD, 1996); Balraj Puri, *Jammu and Kashmir: Triumph and Tragedy of Indian Federalism* (New Delhi: Sterling Publishers, c. 1981); Robert Wirsing, *India, Pakistan, and the Kashmir Dispute: On Regional Conflict and Its Resolution* (New York: St. Martin's Press, 1994).

Indo-Pakistani War (1965)

PRINCIPAL COMBATANTS: India vs. Pakistan
PRINCIPAL THEATER(S): Rann of Kutch and Pakistan-India border region
DECLARATION: None
MAJOR ISSUES AND OBJECTIVES: India feared that Pakistan's friendship with China would compromise the integrity of Kashmir's border with China.
OUTCOME: A cease-fire reestablished earlier battle lines, and India renewed its promise of a Kashmiri plebiscite.
APPROXIMATE MAXIMUM NUMBER OF MEN UNDER ARMS: India, 900,000; Pakistan, 233,000
CASUALTIES: India, 3,712 killed, 7,638 wounded; Pakistan, 1,500 killed, 4,300 wounded
TREATIES: Conference at Tashkent, 1966

In 1958, General Muhammad Ayub Khan (1907–74), with substantial military backing from the United States, seized power in Pakistan. By the time India's powerful first prime minister, Jawaharlal Nehru (1889–1964), died and was succeeded by the lackluster Lal Bahadur Shastri (1904–66), Ayub was ready to test India's frontier outposts in Kashmir. Since the IINDO-PAKISTANI WAR (1947–1948), the Kashmir region had existed as a state divided between Pakistan and India. About a third of it was under Pakistani administration as *Azad Kashmir*—Free Kashmir—and about two-thirds was occupied by Indian forces—despite an Indian promise, never fulfilled, of a Kashmiri plebiscite. Always a flashpoint, Kashmir became a renewed cause of conflict when Ayub signed a treaty of friendship with China. As India saw it, this put in jeopardy the boundary between Kashmir and China. Fevered talks began between India and Pakistan, but predictably broke down, and a border war flared in the Rann of Kutch during April 9–30, 1965. Pakistan's American-supplied Patton tanks rolled to an easy victory over India's British Centurions, and the country's new prime minister quickly turned to the United Nations for succor. The United Nations engineered a cease-fire and both sides withdrew their troops.

Despite this mutual acceptance of the borders established in 1948, Pakistan believed that it had actually won the war and that India's army was weak. At least, those were the reasons Ayub's foreign minister, Zulfikar Ali Bhutto (1928–79), gave when he argued for another campaign in Kashmir during the summer of 1965. Pakistan launched "Operation Grandslam"—aimed at cutting off Kashmir along its narrow south neck before India could respond with its ragtag tanks—in mid-August.

Now, the long-simmering dispute rapidly escalated into a major war on September 6, 1965, when India sent 900,000 troops across the border toward Lahore, Pakistan. The city was in range of the Indian tanks when the United Nations was able to broker a new cease-fire on September 27—but not before a large number of Pakistani tanks had been destroyed and a number of troops killed.

During the cease-fire, both sides withdrew to the battle lines established before August. The cease-fire also kept China out of the war, and it gave sufficient breathing space for mediation. The United States, Britain, and the Soviet Union met at a Tashkent conference sponsored by the Russians, which resulted in a pledge of cooperation and a new Indian promise of a Kashmiri plebiscite. Unfortunately, Indian prime minister Lal Bahadur Shastri died just after the conference. His successor, Indira Gandhi (1917–84), followed through on most of Shastri's promises, but not all of them. Most significantly, the plebiscite remained unimplemented. War would be renewed in 1971 (*see* INDO-PAKISTANI WAR, 1971).

Further reading: M. J. Akbar, *India: The Siege Within: Challenges to a Nation's Unity* (New Delhi: UBSPD, 1996,); Balraj Puri, *Jammu and Kashmir: Triumph and Tragedy of Indian Federalism* (New Delhi: Sterling Publishers, c. 1981); Robert Wirsing, *India, Pakistan, and the Kashmir Dispute: On Regional Conflict and Its Resolution* (New York: St. Martin's Press, 1994).

Indo-Pakistani War (1971)

PRINCIPAL COMBATANTS: India vs. Pakistan
PRINCIPAL THEATER(S): West Pakistan and East Pakistan (Bangladesh)
DECLARATION: India on Pakistan, December 3, 1971
MAJOR ISSUES AND OBJECTIVES: India sought to establish the independence of Bangladesh from Pakistan.
OUTCOME: Bangladesh gained its independence, at great cost to Pakistan.
APPROXIMATE MAXIMUM NUMBER OF MEN UNDER ARMS: Unknown
CASUALTIES: India, unknown; Pakistan, 90,000 POWs
TREATIES: Cease-fire of December 17, 1971

In December 1970 Pakistan held its first general elections since independence in 1947. President Muhammad Ayub Khan (1907–74), who seized power in a military coup in 1958, had resigned in 1968 and passed the reins of power on to General Agha Yahya Muhammad Khan (1917–77). When the Awami League, headed by East Pakistan's popular Bengali leader, Sheikh Mujib (Mujibur Rahman) (1920–75), won a majority of seats in the new assembly two years later, the West Pakistan general simply turned his back on his nation's first-time voters. He refused to honor the election or even to lift the martial law imposed back when Ayub initially seized power.

Negotiations between General Yahya and the duly elected Mujib failed to lead anywhere when the latter demanded virtual independence for East Pakistan. By March 1971, the talks had collapsed, and at the end of the month Yahya directed a massacre in Dhaka, in East Pakistan. During the slaughter, his military arrested Mujib and spirited him by air to West Pakistan. But the Pakistanis failed to silence Mujib before he called upon his followers in the east to rise up, seize power, and declare their independence as Bangladesh, which means "Land of the Bengalis."

These events sparked a massive surge of some 10 million refugees from East Pakistan—Bangladesh—into West Bengal, India, one of the most impoverished districts of one of the world's poorest nations. Over the next eight months the Indian government appealed to the world for assistance in coping with the refugee crisis but received little help. Worse, U.S. president Richard M. Nixon (1913–94) took a hard line against India and in favor of the U.S. client state, Pakistan. Nixon declared that the Pakistani civil war had resulted from Indian efforts to undermine and destabilize its neighbor. Accordingly, in the midst of the refugee crisis, Nixon cut off India's American credit.

Thus encouraged, Pakistan sent air force planes after the monsoon season to attack Indian airfields in Kashmir on December 3, 1971. This triggered a 12-day war in which India seized and held the initiative. Indian troops invaded both West Pakistan and East Pakistan and marched virtually unopposed to the gates of Dhaka. On December 6, 1971, India recognized Bangladesh as a newly independent nation, then, on December 16, launched a combined ground and air assault on Dhaka. The city fell to Indian forces, and Pakistani troops surrendered in Bangladesh. Some 90,000 Pakistani soldiers became Indian prisoners of war, prompting Pakistan to agree to a general cease-fire on December 17, 1971. Mujib, released by the Pakistanis, flew home a hero to become the first prime minister of the People's Republic of Bangladesh in January 1972.

India was able to achieve a triumph so swift and stunning because of military and diplomatic backing from the Soviet Union, to which India had naturally turned, given the American infatuation with Pakistan. Under the 1971 Treaty of Peace, Friendship, and Cooperation, the USSR provided India with the firepower it deployed to win the war. Thus, not only did the victory give birth to Bangladesh, it made India the dominant power in South Asia, and caused its foreign policy—still officially nonaligned—to tilt more dramatically toward the Soviet Union.

Richard Nixon was not ready to give up so easily. He dispatched a nuclear-armed aircraft carrier from the Pacific Fleet, purportedly to help evacuate refugees from Dhaka, but in truth to stiffen the backs of the Pakistani military leaders. The war ended before the U.S. Navy could do much of anything, but India took notice. By 1972, India had launched its own nuclear program in response to this American nuclear saber rattling, making the entire world a much more dangerous place.

Although the United States extended aid to Pakistan, the nation was devastated by the brief war. With the loss of Bangladesh, Pakistan's population was halved, and its economy, never strong, was on the verge of total collapse. The United States held off recognizing Bangladesh until April 4, 1972, and Pakistan recognized its independence, grudgingly, two years later.

See also INDO-PAKISTANI WAR (1947–1948); INDO-PAKISTANI WAR (1965).

Further reading: G. W. Choudhury, *The Last Days of United Pakistan* (Bloomington: Indiana University Press, 1974); Kathryn Jacques, *Bangladesh, India and Pakistan: International Relations and Regional Tensions in South Asia* (New York: St. Martin's Press, 1999); Lawrence Lifschultz, *Bangladesh, The Unfinished Revolution* (London: Zed Press, 1979); Taluder Maniruzzaman, *The Bangladesh Revolution and Its Aftermath* (Dacca: Bangladesh Books International, 1980).

Indochina War

See FRENCH INDOCHINA WAR (1858–1863); FRENCH INDOCHINA WAR (1873–1874); FRENCH INDOCHINA WAR (1882–1885); FRENCH INDOCHINA WAR (1946–1954).

Ionian Revolt (c. 500–493 B.C.E.)

PRINCIPAL COMBATANTS: Persia vs, the Ionian city-states (with Athenian and Eretrian aid)
PRINCIPAL THEATER(S): Ionia (Asia Minor)
DECLARATION: None
MAJOR ISSUES AND OBJECTIVES: The Ionians sought independence from oppressive rule by Persian-sponsored tyrants.
OUTCOME: After initial triumph, the rebellion was crushed and Ionia retaken by the Persians.
APPROXIMATE MAXIMUM NUMBER OF MEN UNDER ARMS: Unknown
CASUALTIES: Unknown
TREATIES: None

The Greek city-states of Ionia (the region along the coast of Asia Minor in present-day Turkey) were, during the sixth century B.C.E., under the ruthless domination of Persia and under the immediate government of Persian puppet tyrants. About 500 B.C.E., the Ionian port city of Miletus rose up against the tyranny and was eagerly assisted by Athens and Eretria, Sparta demurring. The revolt in Miletus soon spread to other city-states in Ionia, which not only removed the Persian tyrants, but, in 498, drove Artaphernes (r. 513–493), the Persian satrap (governor of the region), out of his capital, Sardis. The rebels then sacked and destroyed the city.

The rebels, poorly organized, failed to capitalize on their victories. After ousting the satrap and destroying the capital, they dispersed, making it easy for fresh Persian forces to retake all of the Ionian city-states. The land battles ended by 499. At sea, the culminating battle took place in 494, when the Persians blockaded Miletus. Hoping to raise the blockade, a Greek fleet of 353 Lesbian, Samian, and Chian vessels attacked the Persian fleet off the island of Lade. From the beginning, it was a desperate effort, as the allied Greek fleet was significantly outnumbered. Worse, panic-stricken Samians and Lesbians deserted the attack at the last minute, leaving the remaining Greek ships vulnerable. The Greek fleet was destroyed, and the Persians landed at Miletus, sacking and destroying the city. With this, the Ionian revolt was crushed, leaving Artapheres' brother and Persian king Darius (c. 558–486) free to punish Athens and Eretria for their complicity in the revolt (*see* GRECO-PERSIAN WARS.

Further reading: J. M. Cook, *The Greeks in Ionia and the East* (New York: Praeger, 1963).

Iranian Revolution (1979)

PRINCIPAL COMBATANTS: Iranian revolutionaries vs. the shah of Iran

PRINCIPAL THEATER(S): Iran
DECLARATION: None
MAJOR ISSUES AND OBJECTIVES: A coalition of liberals and conservatives united under the Ayatollah Ruhollah Khomeini to overthrow the government of the shah of Iran.
OUTCOME: With the shah in self-imposed exile, the government fell and Khomeini established an Islamic republic in its place.
APPROXIMATE MAXIMUM NUMBER OF MEN UNDER ARMS: Millions of Iranian demonstrators; the shah's army declared neutrality and refused to fight
CASUALTIES: At least 10,000 opponents of the Khomeini regime were killed in rioting or executed by 1983.
TREATIES: None

Shah Muhammad Reza Pahlavi (1919–80) governed Iran as an autocrat and even a dictator, aligning himself with the Western democracies, but keeping order through a loyal corps of secret police. Liberal and intellectual elements in Iran bridled under his repressive rule; the most conservative, fundamentalist Islamic elements also objected to the shah, not necessarily because of his repressiveness, but for his pro-Western stance. In mutual opposition to the shah, the liberals and conservatives found common ground and rallied behind an elderly religious leader living in Parisian exile, Ayatollah Ruhollah Khomeini (1902–89). By the end of the 1970s, rioting had compelled the shah to seek refuge in Egypt in January 1979. He named a regency council to rule during his absence, a sign of weakness that the exiled Khomeini was quick to exploit. From Paris, Khomeini urged the overthrow of the government. Demonstrations assumed spectacular proportions, often massing more than 1 million marchers. When the army refused to fight the protesters, Khomeini returned to Iran, and by February 1979, the government had collapsed. In its place, Khomeini declared Iran to be an Islamic republic and ruled through a revolutionary council. A reign of terror ensued, in which thousands of "subversives" and "counterrevolutionaries" were paraded through show trials and led to imprisonment or execution.

As the ayatollah's regime grew increasingly repressive, dissidents risked their lives to protest. Women, who objected to being repressed by a return to Muslim fundamentalism, were in the forefront of the protests, as were ethnic groups such as the Kurds. Yet Khomeini pointed to the results of a popular referendum, which, he said, revealed that 99 percent of the people of Iran supported his revolution and reforms. Nevertheless, disorder and rebellion increased, prompting the revolutionary council to create the Army of the Guardians of the Islamic Revolution on May 6, 1979. This new force moved even more vigorously against dissidents, and the number of trials and executions increased. Iran became increasingly cut off from the West—and also from the rest of the Islamic world in the Middle East.

Americans became instantly aware of the magnitude of the Iranian revolution on November 4, 1979, when Iranian "students" stormed the U.S. embassy at Tehran and took hostage the embassy staff, 66 people. The mass abduction had been triggered when President Jimmy Carter (b. 1924) allowed the shah, who had been diagnosed with cancer, to enter the United States for treatment. The president refused to yield to the terrorists' demands to surrender the shah to them; however, the shah left the United States voluntarily early in December. Fifty-three hostages remained in captivity; 13 African Americans and women had been released on November 19 and 20. President Carter authorized a U.S. Army Special Forces unit to attempt a rescue on April 24, 1980, but a combination of mechanical problems with helicopters and other equipment and human blunders caused the mission to be aborted. The failed mission did not result in harm to the hostages, but it was a great embarrassment to the United States, and it served to embolden the Iranians.

It was not until November 1980 that the Iranian parliament proposed conditions to secure the release of the hostages. Among these was a U.S. pledge not to interfere in Iranian affairs, an agreement to release Iranian assets frozen by presidential order in the United States, the lifting of all U.S. sanctions on Iran, and the return of the shah's property to the people of Iran. An agreement was signed in January 1981, but Khomeini, as a gesture of insult to President Carter, delayed the release of the hostages until January 20, the day Carter left office and Ronald Reagan (1911–2004) was inaugurated. President Reagan asked Carter to serve as a special envoy to greet the returning hostages at a U.S. air base in West Germany. They had been held captive for 444 days.

See also IRAN-IRAQ WAR; PERSIAN REVOLUTION (1921).

Further reading: Haleh Afshar, ed., *Iran: A Revolution in Turmoil* (Albany: State University of New York Press, c. 1985); Mohammed Amjab, *Iran: From Royal Dictatorship to Theocracy* (New York: Greenwood Press, 1989); David Lesch, *1979: The Year That Shaped the Modern Middle East* (Boulder, Colo.: Westview Press, 2001); Mohsen M. Milani, *The Making of Iran's Islamic Revolution: From Monarchy to Islamic Republic,* 2nd ed. (Boulder, Colo.: Westview Press, 1994).

Iran-Iraq War (1980–1988)

PRINCIPAL COMBATANTS: Iraq vs. Iran
PRINCIPAL THEATER(S): Iraq and Iran
DECLARATION: None
MAJOR ISSUES AND OBJECTIVES: On September 21–22, 1980, Saddam Hussein launched Iraqi warplanes and troops on an invasion of Iran in an attempt to topple the regime of the Ayatollah Khomeini.

OUTCOME: Both sides claimed victory, but with the United States helping to tip the balance in Iraq's favor, Khomeini's forces suffered more damage, whereas Hussein came out of the war somewhat poorer but more inclined to exercise his muscle in the region.

APPROXIMATE MAXIMUM NUMBER OF MEN UNDER ARMS: Iraq: 500,000 men; Iran: 2 million

CASUALTIES: Iran, 262,000 killed, 600,000 wounded, 45,000 captured; Iraq, 105,000 killed, 400,000 wounded, 70,000 captured

TREATIES: None

Iraq and Iran had long disputed control of a 120-mile-long tidal river, the Shatt al-Arab, which flows past the important Iraqi port of Basra and Iran's Persian Gulf port of Abadan. Following the IRANIAN REVOLUTION, which overthrew Shah Muhammad Reza Pahlavi (1919–80) and elevated the fundamentalist Shi'ite Ayatollah Ruhollah Khomeini (1902–89) to power, the dispute grew into a holy war of terror aimed against Iraq's president, Saddam Hussein (b. 1935). Members of the Iranian terrorist group Al Dawa ("the Call") targeted Hussein and also made an attempt on the life of Iraq's deputy premier. Iran backed civil disturbances in Baghdad, attacked Iraq's embassy in Rome, attempted to incite Iraq's Shi'ite minority to rebellion, and shelled Iraqi border towns, killing civilians. At last, during September 21–22, 1980, Saddam Hussein launched fighter planes and ground troops against Iran, hoping for a quick victory, which would bring an end to the Khomeini regime.

Initially, Iraq did deal Iran severe blows, sinking gunboats in the Shatt al-Arab and destroying airfields and oil refineries. But Khomeini, whose revolutionary nation was by no means unified behind him, saw the attacks as an opportunity to bring his people together against a common threat. Accordingly, Khomeini called for an all-out military response, including suicidal attacks on the more technologically advanced Iraqi forces, which were equipped with the latest Soviet-built tanks, missiles, and artillery as well as French-made fighter planes. The Iraqi military, however, with some 500,000 men under arms was vastly outnumbered by the Iranians, who mustered an ill-equipped army of 2 million.

The result was neither the quick victory Hussein had hoped for nor the overwhelming victory Khomeini had urged, but a long stalemate that evolved into one of the bloodiest, most extended, and most futile wars ever fought in this volatile region. Iraq threatened to disrupt oil shipments through the Strait of Hormuz in the Persian Gulf, and both the United Nations and an Islamic conference, including most of the important powers in the Middle East, tried but failed to put a stop to the war.

The Iraqis soon found themselves on the defensive, hunkered down behind fortifications of earthworks and sandbagged bunkers stretching across a 300-mile front as Iran threw wave after wave against them, using everything from regular army troops to teen-aged Revolutionary Guards, inflicting heavy losses while incurring even heavier losses. A measure of Iran's fanaticism came in March 1984, when 10,000 children were roped together and sent into an Iraqi minefield ahead of assault troops. Iraq responded with chemical warfare, launching mustard gas shells against the children—something that had not been used (except by Iraq against rebellious Kurdish tribesmen) since WORLD WAR I. Two years later, Iraq used nerve gas as well as mustard gas against the Iranians.

Because neither side proved capable of mounting a decisive offensive, the war settled into a contest of attrition and great suffering. But it was precisely in the attrition that Saddam Hussein found his secret weapon: the willingness to endure substantial losses and take great punishment while exhausting the enemy. Both powers at length tried to cut the other's economic lifeline, which in the Middle East meant bombing oil shipments. Their attacks against various tankers plying the Gulf dangerously escalated the war of attrition, and the United States—already inclined to hold Iran responsible for much of the terrorism against Americans in the region—eventually tilted the political balance intentionally toward Iraq. Promising to keep the Persian Gulf open to international trade, the Americans made clear they intended to safeguard the main source of oil for Western Europe and Japan.

For now, Hussein's military was like some third-rate boxer, outclassed but able to take punishment until his opponent fell from sheer exhaustion. With some trepidation, the United States began selling military equipment to Iraq, hoping, like Hussein, that the Khomeini regime would fall. The quasi-alliance between the two countries was tested in May 1987 when an Iraqi fighter struck an American destroyer, the USS *Stark* with a French-made Exocet anti-ship missile. Although the United States officially accepted Iraq's explanation that the attack had been an accident, President Ronald Reagan (1911–2004) soon acted to "reflag" Kuwaiti oil tankers leaving the Gulf—temporarily giving them U.S. registry—to legitimate armed escorts.

In general, the result was a buildup of U.S. warships in the region. On April 14, 1988, one of the vessels, the USS *Samuel B. Roberts,* escorting a reflagged Kuwaiti tanker, struck an Iranian mine. In response, President Reagan authorized Operation Praying Mantis, a combined raid by army helicopters and marine commandos, supported by naval gunfire and air strikes, against Iranian oil facilities and military installations. The Iranians threw their small naval forces—four combat ships and a few patrol boats—against the U.S. fleet in the Gulf. Following a 10-hour battle, Iran lost three of its principal ships and suffered severe damage to the fourth.

Defeated at sea, Iran launched a missile attack against Baghdad, using 60 Soviet-made "Scud" medium-range ballistic missiles. Iraq retaliated by launching more than 200 Scuds in what came to be called the Battle of the Cities. The missile battles and the earlier naval losses were the prelude to a campaign the Iraqis called "Tawakalna Ala Allah," a final offensive in which Hussein laced his regular troops with 100,000 crack Republican Guards in an invasion of Iran. The invasion began on April 17, 1988, and the long and costly war was over within four months.

Officially, both sides claimed victory, but, in fact, Iran emerged from the conflict with its armed forces shattered and its people exhausted, whereas Iraq, despite the heavy losses it had incurred, was strengthened in its resolve to prevail at any cost. Tactically, Saddam Hussein had lost the war, yet, for all practical purposes, he had prevailed, and that taught him a style of international thuggery that would prompt him to invade Kuwait and touch off the PERSIAN GULF WAR, where the United States, determined to protect the region's oil, would itself fight Iraq.

Further reading: Shahram Chubin and Charles Tripp, *Iran and Iraq at War* (New York: I. B. Tauris, 1988); Dilip Hino, *The Longest War: The Iran-Iraq Military Conflict* (New York: Routledge, 1991); Majid Khadduri, *The Gulf War: The Origins and Implications of the Iraq-Iran Conflict* (New York: Oxford University Press, 1988); Edgar O'Ballance, *The Gulf War* (London and Washington, D.C.: Brassey's Defence Publishers, 1988).

Irish Convict Revolt   See AUSTRALIAN IRISH CONVICT REVOLT (1804).

Irish Raids in Britain   (395–405)

PRINCIPAL COMBATANTS: Irish raiders vs. Britain and Wales
PRINCIPAL THEATER(S): Roman Britain and Wales
DECLARATION: None
MAJOR ISSUES AND OBJECTIVES: The raiders wanted goods and slaves.
OUTCOME: When northern Wales mounted an effective defense, the raiding ended.
APPROXIMATE MAXIMUM NUMBER OF MEN UNDER ARMS: Unknown
CASUALTIES: Unknown
TREATIES: None

Roman Britain was the target of raids by Saxons and Picts as well as from Ireland, under the leadership of Niall (d. 405) of the Nine Hostages. His bands attacked from Strathclyde into Wales, concentrating on the coast and abducting thousands of prisoners as slaves. Among the captives was one Patricius, who was abducted about 400, pressed into service as a swineherd, subsequently escaped, then returned to Ireland as the missionary Saint Patrick (c. 389–c. 461).

Around 400, Gwynedd, the northernmost Welsh kingdom, mounted an effective defense against the Irish raiders and expelled them. This brought raiding to an end by 405.

See also SAXON RAIDS.

Further reading: Jacqueline O'Brien and Peter Harbison, *Ancient Ireland: From Prehistory to the Middle Ages* (New York: Oxford University Press, 2001).

Irish Rebellion, Great   (1641–1649)

PRINCIPAL COMBATANTS: Irish rebels vs. England
PRINCIPAL THEATER(S): Ireland
DECLARATION: None
MAJOR ISSUES AND OBJECTIVES: The Irish rebelled against English despotism.
OUTCOME: The war ended with an Irish victory over English forces, but, subsequently, Oliver Cromwell brutally suppressed the rebellion.
APPROXIMATE MAXIMUM NUMBER OF MEN UNDER ARMS: At Rathmines, Irish rebels, 5,000; English and royalists, 19,000
CASUALTIES: At Rathmines, English and royalists, 4,000 killed or wounded, 2,000 captured; Irish casualties unknown
TREATIES: None

In 1641, 40 years after TYRONE'S REBELLION, the Irish rose once again in revolt, first in Ulster, then throughout the entire island. Some 3,000 English and Scottish settlers were killed in the initial uprising on the Plantation lands, though the Puritan-dominated English Parliament wildly inflated the figure in its propaganda to hundreds of thousands massacred by Catholic savages and refused to entrust King Charles I (1600–49) with an army to put down the rebellion. Fearing that Charles would not only make peace with the Irish, but use them against the Puritans in the First (Great) ENGLISH CIVIL WAR that broke out in 1642, Parliament recruited volunteers at large to quell the revolt, promising them Irish lands in return for their service. Parliament also sent Scottish troops into the country, which, by this time, had fallen almost entirely under the control of the rebels, who established a provisional government in Kilkenny. The English forces were at first commanded by James Butler (1610–88), duke of Ormonde and lord lieutenant of Ireland, whom King Charles ordered to negotiate an end to the rebellion. Both the Parliament in London and a newly constituted parliament in Dublin rejected the terms produced by the negotiations. In 1645, with Charles in the clutches of an Oliver Cromwell (1599–1658)–dominated Parliament, Ormonde himself now was leading the rebellion as the head of the Confederacy, an alliance of all Royalists in Ireland. Some among the Irish chose not so to be led, such as Murrough O'Brien, baron of Inchiquin (d. 1551), who was an Irish Protestant stationed in Munster. He not only rejected the leadership of the Confederacy, but also laid waste to Munster for Parliament, which earned him the everlasting spite of his fellow Irishmen and the memorable if somber sobriquet "Murrough of the Burnings." Some, however, such as Owen Roe O'Neill (1582–1649), were simply pure Irish Catholic rebels and disliked riding with their former enemies, the English overlords. O'Neill, the nephew of Hugh O'Neill, earl of Tyrone (1540–1616), and a veteran of the Spanish army, kept his Ulster followers from joining Ormonde. Then, in 1647, for no discernible reason, Baron Inchiquin switched sides and joined the duke of Ormonde.

A turning point came in 1649, when Colonel Michael Jones landed with 2,000 troops, expelled Ormonde from Dublin and defeated him and his Royalist-Catholic forces at the Battle of Rathmines on August 2. Ormonde's power was broken, but there remained a number of rebel strongholds either in Confederate or Irish hands. It was to capture these and completely crush the rebellion that Oliver Cromwell set sail for Ireland on August 13, 1649 (*see* CROMWELL'S IRISH CAMPAIGN).

See also ENGLISH CIVIL WAR, SECOND.

Further reading: Padraig Lenihan, *Confederate Catholics at War, 1641–49* (Cork, Ireland: Cork University Press, 2001); John O'Beirn Ranelagh, *A Short History of Ireland* (New York: Cambridge University Press, 2000).

Irish Tithe War (1831)

PRINCIPAL COMBATANTS: The Irish "Catholic Association" vs. the British government in Ireland
PRINCIPAL THEATER(S): Ireland
DECLARATION: None
MAJOR ISSUES AND OBJECTIVES: The Catholic Association sought relief from an Anglican tithe imposed on them.
OUTCOME: The tithe was partially rescinded.
APPROXIMATE MAXIMUM NUMBER OF MEN UNDER ARMS: Unknown
CASUALTIES: At least 22 protesters and 26 police officials were killed.
TREATIES: None

Irish Catholics bridled under the law that forced them to pay tithes to the Church of England. A group of them banded together in the Catholic Association, founded in 1823 by Daniel O'Connell (1775–1847), and began a campaign of resistance to the tax.

Using techniques of passive resistance, the Catholic Association succeeded in crippling the Anglican Church in Ireland. But the group's protests turned violent in 1831. At Newtownforbes, Ireland, a dozen men protesting the impoundment of cattle were killed by British soldiers. At Carrickshook, Irish farmers used their farm implements to kill 18 police officers. At Castlepollard, police officers shot 10, and at Gortroche, a Catholic priest ordered his parishioners to fire on officials: eight died, and another 13 were wounded. The British army briefly redoubled its collection efforts but soon withdrew. At this, the Catholic Association returned to predominantly peaceful methods of resistance, and the so-called Tithe War came to an end following new legislation partially abolishing the tax in 1836.

See also IRISH REBELLION, GREAT.

Further reading: Christopher Haigh, ed., *The Cambridge Historical Encyclopedia of Great Britain and Ireland* (New York: Cambridge University Press, 1985); Alvin Jackson, *Ireland, 1798–1998: Politics and War* (London: Blackwell, 1999); R. B. McDowell, *Public Opinion and Government Policy in Ireland, 1801–1846* (Westport, Conn.: Greenwood Press, 1975).

Irish War (1689–1691)

PRINCIPAL COMBATANTS: Irish Jacobites (with French allies) vs. an Anglo-Dutch force in support of William and Mary
PRINCIPAL THEATER(S): Ireland
DECLARATION: None
MAJOR ISSUES AND OBJECTIVES: The Irish Catholics aided James II in his bid to regain the English throne.
OUTCOME: The Jacobites were suppressed but granted amnesty.
APPROXIMATE MAXIMUM NUMBER OF MEN UNDER ARMS: Anglo-Dutch army, 36,000; Irish-French army, 28,600
CASUALTIES: At Londonderry, Anglo-Dutch: 3,000 killed or wounded; Irish-French, 5,000 killed or wounded. At Newtown Butler, Irish-French, 2,000. At Boyne River, Anglo-Dutch, 500; Irish-French, 1,500. At Limerick, Anglo-Dutch, 2,000. At Aughrim, Anglo-Dutch, 1,600; Irish-French, 7,000.
TREATIES: Treaty of Limerick, October 3, 1691

When King James II (1633–1701) of England was forced off the throne in 1688 by the GLORIOUS REVOLUTION, he turned to the Irish for aid in regaining power. The Irish, having suffered at the hands of Oliver Cromwell (1599–1658) (*see* CROMWELL'S IRISH CAMPAIGN) from 1649 to 1650, were willing to help. In 1689, therefore, when James landed in Ireland with soldiers and cash supplied by France's Louis XIV (1638–1715), he was acknowledged king by an Irish parliament convened in Dublin. The parliament confiscated

Protestant lands in Ireland, assembled an Irish-French army, and advanced on Londonderry, a predominantly Protestant town that had affirmed loyalty to King William III (1650–1702) and Queen Mary II (1662–94). The Irish-French army laid siege against Londonderry for 15 weeks, but the town held firm. Then, in 1690, William led an Anglo-Dutch army against James, landing at Carrickfergus and marching south with 35,000 troops to the Boyne River, which marked the battle line held by James's army. The Irish-French army was supported by the Irish Jacobite Patrick Sarsfield, Earl of Lucan (d. 1693).

On July 11, 1690, William sent a detachment under Duke Friedrich Herman von Schomberg (1615–90) to cross the Boyne three miles west of Drogheda. Simultaneously, he dispatched another detachment to cross the river upstream. James's army was flanked, and he was routed, losing more than 1,000 men. James fled the field to France, and William returned to England, leaving his army under the command of the Dutch-born general Godard van Reede, Heer van Ginkel (1644–1702/1703). After completing the conquest of Athlone, along the upper Shannon River, Ginkel marched west and, on July 12, 1691, engaged the rebel forces at Aughrim, about 30 miles east of Galway. The Irish-French forces were led by the Earl of Lucan and French general Charles Chalmont, marquis de Saint-Ruth. Although they fought valiantly, Ginkel out-generaled his rivals and managed to turn the rebel flank. After Saint-Ruth fell when Ginkel's forces stormed the defensive entrenchments, the rebels fled the field, making no attempt to fight a rearguard action and thereby incurring heavy losses numbering in the thousands. In fact, Aughrim was the bloodiest battle ever fought on Irish soil. One general, three major-generals, seven brigadiers, 22 colonels, 17 lieutenant-colonels, and over 7,000 others were killed, and so devastating were the losses that the Jacobite rebellion in Ireland was effectively finished (*see* JACOBITE REBELLION [1689–1690]).

Nevertheless, after the battle, Lucan kept some hope alive when he holed up in Limerick, headquarters of the Jacobite rebellion. Ginkel laid siege against Limerick, and, on October 3, 1691, the garrison there surrendered. In the so-called pacification of Limerick, King William, always a practitioner of toleration, allowed the Irish Jacobites to take an oath of allegiance to William and Mary or to leave the country—transportation to France was provided. On their own, however, the Protestant Irish parliament passed a series of anti-Catholic laws, which amounted to state-sanctioned persecution. Still, following the treaty of Limerick, which Lucan signed on October 3, 1691, a century of peace ensued in Ireland.

See also GRAND ALLIANCE, WAR OF THE; IRISH REBELLION, GREAT.

Further reading: R. F. Foster, *Modern Ireland, 1690–1792* (New York: Penguin USA, 1989); Christopher Haigh, ed., *The Cambridge Historical Encyclopedia of Great Britain and Ireland* (New York: Cambridge University Press, 1985).

Iroquoian Beaver Wars *See* BEAVER WARS.

Iroquois-French Wars (1642–1696)

PRINCIPAL COMBATANTS: The Iroquois tribes vs. French settlers and traders
PRINCIPAL THEATER(S): Region of St. Lawrence and Ottawa rivers; Montreal area
DECLARATION: None
MAJOR ISSUES AND OBJECTIVES: In part, Iroquois desire for vengeance against the French; in part, Iroquois strategy to eliminate trading competition
OUTCOME: Despite a 1701 treaty, fighting remained chronic.
APPROXIMATE MAXIMUM NUMBER OF MEN UNDER ARMS: Variable
CASUALTIES: Unknown
TREATIES: 1701 treaty with France, pledging Iroquois neutrality in French and English disputes

In 1609, the French explorer Samuel de Champlain (c. 1567–1635), in company with a Huron Indian war party, encountered, engaged, and killed some Iroquois Indians. This incident created bad blood between the Iroquois and the French, and after Champlain died in 1635, Iroquois raiders set about terrorizing French settlements along the St. Lawrence and Ottawa Rivers, including the Jesuit missions. The Hurons, allies of the French, were also targets of Iroquois aggression and were all but wiped out in the IROQUOIS-HURON WAR from 1648 to 1650.

After the Iroquois defeated the Hurons, they established bases of operation at various strategic points along the St. Lawrence and Ottawa Rivers. From these centers, they attacked the French by water as well as by land. Traditionally, most Indian tribes fought only in the warmer seasons and then only during the day. Remarkably, the Iroquois fought relentlessly and continuously, in all seasons, sometimes attacking by day, and sometimes by night. Reeling from ceaseless attack, the French repeatedly attempted to come to peace terms with the Iroquois. Brief truces were concluded but quickly broken. Moreover, Dutch traders at Fort Orange (Albany, New York), rivals of the French for the Indian trade, ensured that the Iroquois were well supplied with weapons and ammunition. The Dutch actively worked to perpetuate the war.

By the mid-17th century, the issue had gone far beyond mere vengeance for the deeds of Samuel de Champlain. The war between the Iroquois and the French was a struggle for control of the profitable beaver fur trade. The

Iroquois objective was to monopolize the trade, diverting it from French outposts exclusively to the Dutch at Fort Orange (*see* BEAVER WARS, of which the Iroquois-French Wars may be seen as an aspect). At this point, the Iroquois had carried the war almost to Montreal, and it was not until 1666 that soldiers were sent from France to take the offensive.

The arrival of French regulars turned the tide of the war, pushing the Iroquois not only out of Canada but into their homelands, where they were repeatedly defeated. Within months, it was the Iroquois who sued for peace. The truce hammered out lasted nearly two decades, until French settlement began to expand westward. This aggravated chronic, violent rivalry with the English, who were allied with the Iroquois. A new French governor, the marquis de Denonville (d. 1710), arrived in 1685 and decided that the time was ripe for an offensive move against the Senecas, westernmost of the Iroquois tribes. The governor led a large force into western New York and destroyed four Seneca villages in 1687. Far from subduing the Senecas, however, this action moved them to vengeance. In 1689, Seneca warriors advanced down the St. Lawrence River in large numbers to attack the French-Canadian settlement of Lachine, which was all but destroyed, many of its inhabitants brutally massacred. From the site of this victory, Seneca war parties fanned out to terrorize the countryside as far as Montreal.

The Senecas returned repeatedly to attack Lachine. They also targeted other French forts, towns, and small settlements. When the comte de Frontenac (1620–1698) returned as governor of New France in 1689, he devoted himself to an organized campaign against the Iroquois generally and the Seneca in particular. Peace was restored in 1696, and, in 1701, the Iroquois signed a treaty with France, by which they pledged neutrality in the various colonial wars between the French and English, which culminated in the FRENCH AND INDIAN WAR. No treaty, however, could repair the damage the Iroquois-French Wars had done to Iroquois unity. Despite the Iroquois pledge to maintain a policy of neutrality, individual Iroquois tribes often violated these terms, siding with the English, in the empty hope of regaining the military and economic dominance they had formerly enjoyed in western New York and the Ohio country.

Further reading: Alan Axelrod, *Chronicle of the Indian Wars: From Colonial Times to Wounded Knee* (New York: Prentice Hall General Reference, 1993); José Antonio Brandas, *Your Fyre Shall Burn No More: Iroquois Policy toward New France and Its Native Allies to 1701* (Lincoln: University of Nebraska Press, 1997).

Iroquois-Huron War   (1648–1650)

PRINCIPAL COMBATANTS: The English-allied Iroquois vs. the French-allied Huron

PRINCIPAL THEATER(S): Ontario, Canada
DECLARATION: None
MAJOR ISSUES AND OBJECTIVES: Traditional enmity and competition for trade
OUTCOME: Great reduction of the Huron tribe
APPROXIMATE MAXIMUM NUMBER OF MEN UNDER ARMS: Unknown
CASUALTIES: Unknown
TREATIES: None

The Huron Indians, who, in the 17th century, inhabited present-day Ontario, Canada, were longtime trading partners with the French and traditional enemies of the Iroquois. In 1648, the Dutch traders at Fort Orange (Albany, New York), desiring to preempt French trade, began supplying the Iroquois—their chief trading partners—with guns and ammunition to enable them to mount a major invasion of Huron territory. The invasion was swift and destructive. Two French Jesuit missionaries, Jean de Brébeuf (1593–1649) and Gabriel Lalemant (1610–49), were tortured to death, and the Huron tribe was decimated, the survivors sent fleeing to various neighboring tribes in search of refuge.

The traditional battle tactics of the East Coast Indians employed short, violent attacks, followed by withdrawal. In this war, however, the Iroquois relentlessly pursued the Huron refugees, in the process also attacking and virtually wiping out the Tobaccos, who had given shelter to many Hurons. The Iroquois went on to destroy much of the so-called Neutral Nation in 1650.

Historians sometimes treat the Iroquois-Huron War as a phase of the BEAVER WARS.

See also FRENCH AND INDIAN WAR; IROQUOIS-FRENCH WARS.

Further reading: Alan Axelrod, *Chronicle of the Indian Wars: From Colonial Times to Wounded Knee* (New York: Prentice Hall General Reference, 1993); José Antonio Brandas, *Your Fyre Shall Burn No More: Iroquois Policy toward New France and Its Native Allies to 1701* (Lincoln: University of Nebraska Press, 1997).

Isaurian War   (492–498)

PRINCIPAL COMBATANTS: Isauria vs. the Byzantine Empire
PRINCIPAL THEATER(S): Western Anatolia and Isauria (Turkey)
DECLARATION: Byzantine Empire on Isauria, 492
MAJOR ISSUES AND OBJECTIVES: Isauria rebelled against the removal of Isaurians from powerful imperial office.
OUTCOME: The Byzantine forces consistently proved victorious, but the Isaurians continued stubbornly to resist until virtually all of their strongholds had been captured or destroyed and the survivors forcibly relocated.

APPROXIMATE MAXIMUM NUMBER OF MEN UNDER ARMS:
Unknown
CASUALTIES: Unknown
TREATIES: None

The Eastern Roman (Byzantine) emperor Zeno (426–491), a native of Isauria (south-central Turkey), appointed many kinsmen and other Isaurians to key positions in the empire. When Zeno died, Anastasius (c. 430–518), a powerful financial administrator (who would later perfect the Byzantine monetary system), was chosen by Zeno's widow, Aviadne (fl. fifth century), to succeed him. As Emperor Anastasius I, he summarily removed all of the Isaurian officials and expelled all Isaurian troops from the Byzantine capital city of Constantinople. In response to these actions, the Isaurians revolted, invading western Anatolia (encompassing much of modern Turkey). The emperor responded by declaring war on Isauria and sent his army, recruited mostly from among the Goths, to engage the Isaurians at the Battle of Cotyaeum in 493. The Isaurians were badly defeated in this battle and withdrew into the mountains of Isauria.

Although beaten and consistently outnumbered, the Isaurians refused to break off the war and continued to battle imperial forces. When, at last, all of the Isaurian strongholds had been captured or destroyed, Anastasius I resettled the survivors in Thrace, where they could be controlled and where they presented little threat to Anatolia.

Further reading: Cyril A. Mango, ed., *Oxford History of Byzantium* (New York: Oxford University Press, 2002); John Julius Norwich, *Byzantium: The Early Centuries* (New York: Alfred A. Knopf, 2003).

Israeli-Arab Wars *See* ARAB-ISRAELI WAR (1948–1949); ARAB-ISRAELI WAR (1956); ARAB-ISRAELI WAR (1967); ARAB-ISRAELI WAR (1973).

Israeli Invasion of Lebanon *See* LEBANESE CIVIL WAR (1975–1992).

Italian Revolts (1831–1834)

PRINCIPAL COMBATANTS: Italian republicans vs. papal and Austrian forces
PRINCIPAL THEATER(S): Modena, Parma, Romagna, the Marches, Umbria
DECLARATION: The declaration of Modena, 1831, triggered the series of revolts.
MAJOR ISSUES AND OBJECTIVES: A group of Italian states wanted to unite under a single republican government, independent from Austrian autocracy.

OUTCOME: The rebellion was crushed by Austrian intervention.
APPROXIMATE MAXIMUM NUMBER OF MEN UNDER ARMS:
Unknown
CASUALTIES: Unknown
TREATIES: None

Prior to the arrival of Giuseppe Mazzini (1805–72) on the stage of Italian politics, liberal uprisings in the 19th century had been mostly the purview of the Carbonari, members of a secret political association first organized about 1811 with the goal of establishing a republic. By 1831, the hopes raised by the July 1830 revolution in Paris (*see* FRENCH REVOLUTION [1830]), had set afoot in Italy a conspiracy led by two Carbonari—Enrico Misley (1801–63) and Ciro Menotti (1758–1831). As a result, Mazzini advocated the union of the disparate Italian states under a republican government. In Modena, in 1831, an assembly declared the overthrow of the Austrian puppet government of Duke Francesco IV (1779–1846). This triggered similar declarations in Parma, Romagna, the Marches, and Umbria, all of which set up new provisional republican governments, then united to create a provincial government headquartered at Bologna. Bologna had been governed by a papal legate, who was forced to step down. The Vatican responded by asking for Austrian intervention. Austrian forces quickly put down the revolt, restoring all the autocrats to power.

The abject failure of the latest attempts to foment change left Italy's moderate liberal leaders, most of them Carbonari, disheartened and leery of Jacobin-style revolution. Not only were they ready to work with an absolute monarchy, they had come to deeply abhor those republicans and democrats who sought to achieve unification and social reform through force of arms.

Thus it fell to the young Genoese Mazzini, who had been exiled to France at the age of 25, to pick up the mantle of French liberalism. In distinction to the Carbonaria, Mazzini's organization—Giovane Italia (Young Italy)—advocated the union of disparate Italian states under a republican government.

Young Italy and Mazzini put their trust in the education and participation of the people, but the group had no radically egalitarian leanings. This new faction spread like wildfire, especially in upper Italy, absorbing Carbonari and old Jacobin alike.

In 1833 and 1834 came the earliest, quickly quelled, Mazzinian uprisings in Savoy and at Genoa, the latter organized by Giuseppe Garibaldi (1807–82), who afterward fled to France. By the end of 1834, the Austrian police had a list of some 2,000 members of Young Italy in Lombardy alone. Although the revolts failed, Mazzini, who had been living in exile in Switzerland, became as a result enough of a revolutionary celebrity to establish firm relationships with radicals in other countries. In 1836, many of them joined him in founding Giovane Europa (Young Europe), after which he resettled in London.

See also ITALIAN REVOLUTION (1848–1849).

Further reading: Christopher Duggan, *A Concise History of Italy* (New York: Cambridge University Press, 1994); Raymond Grew, *A Sterner Plan for Italian Unity* (Princeton, N.J.: Princeton University Press, 1963).

Italian Revolution (1848–1849)

PRINCIPAL COMBATANTS: Italian nationalists vs. Austria and Austrian-dominated Italian rulers (with French and Spanish allies)

PRINCIPAL THEATER(S): Italy

DECLARATION: Sardinia against Austria, 1848

MAJOR ISSUES AND OBJECTIVES: Italian nationalists wanted to unify the states of Italy in independence from Austrian domination.

OUTCOME: Despite successes, the revolution was crushed by Austrian forces allied with those of France and Spain.

APPROXIMATE MAXIMUM NUMBER OF MEN UNDER ARMS: Republican fighters across Italy numbered in the 100,000s if rebellious city mobs are included, but well-armed patriots numbered in the 10,000s. The total for the Austrian army reached 70,000. In Rome, forces backing the Vatican totaled between in excess of 35,000 (15,000 Austrian, 7,000 French, 12,000 Neapolitan, 6,000 Spaniard, and 2,000 Tuscan soldiers fought there at some point) against 18,600 Republicans, including 5,000 of Garibaldi's Red Shirts. In Venice, 30,000 Austrians besieged 17,000 Civic Guards supported by a 4,000-man navy.

CASUALTIES: Varied across Italy. In the siege of Rome, Republicans lost 4,300-plus, the French around 2,000. In Venice, 900 defenders died in battle, but 8,000 fell sick, while the Austrians lost 1,200 in battle and 8,000 wounded, with like numbers (8,000) contracting cholera.

TREATIES: Austria and Piedmont, August 9, 1849

In a year of revolution throughout Europe (in France, Germany, and Hungary), Italians rose up under the leadership of King Charles Albert (1798–1849) of Sardinia, who proposed a *Risorgimento,* a movement that would not only liberate Italy from Austrian domination but unify the Italian states under a single government. Milan rebelled against Austrian government in the "FIVE DAYS" REVOLT of 1848, which inspired Charles Albert to declare war on Austria. This, in turn, triggered a revolt in Venice, with the proclamation of an independent republic under the leadership of Daniele Manin. In Piedmont, Count Camillo Cavour (1810–61) supported Sardinia's declaration of war, as did Pope Pius IX (1792–1878), and political leaders in Modena, Parma, Tuscany, and Naples. Charles Albert was thus able to assemble a large allied Italian army, which he fielded against

the smaller, 70,000-man Austrian army under Field Marshal Joseph Radetzky (1766–1858). Radetzky, however, was a brilliant commander, who deployed his forces in very strong defensive positions in a region bounded by Mantua, Verona, Peschiera, and Legnago. Frequently, he would take the offensive against Charles Albert, who proved to be an indecisive military commander. The Tuscans were quickly routed, and Radetzky seized the entire papal force, holding it hostage. These two defeats unnerved the united armies of Italy. Naples recalled its forces, leaving Piedmont to fend for itself. On July 24, 1848, Radetzky's force met the Piedmontese army at the Battle of Custoza, 11 miles southwest of Verona. The result was an overwhelming defeat for the outnumbered Italians, who were driven out of Lombardy altogether. This led to an armistice on August 9 and Austria's resumption of control over all of its lost territory, save Venice. Radetzky occupied Milan.

The armistice was displeasing to both sides, and the war resumed after a seven-month intermission after Charles Albert denounced the truce on March 12, 1849. In response, Radetzky seized the fortress of Mortara, which precipitated a battle at nearby Novara, 28 miles west of Milan, on March 23. Radetzky and his superbly trained Austrian regulars took and never relinquished the initiative, decisively defeating the ragtag Piedmontese force. A week after Novara, Radetzky's subordinate, Baron Julius von Haynau (1786–1853), defeated the Italians at Brescia, 54 miles northeast of Milan. This prompted Charles Albert to abdicate in favor of his son Victor Emmanuel II (1820–78) (who was destined later to become the first king of unified Italy). On August 9, 1849, Victor Emmanuel II concluded a treaty with Austria, agreeing to harsh terms imposed by the Austrians, including a punishing financial indemnity.

Elsewhere in Italy, disorder continued to reign—although the revolution as such had died. In the Kingdom of the Two Sicilies, King Ferdinand II (1810–59) ordered artillery fire against Messina and Palermo to suppress civil disorder there. In Rome, governed by a revolutionary tribunal, Pius IX asked to be reinstated, and Louis Napoleon (1808–73) dispatched a French army to restore order. Giuseppe Garibaldi (1807–82) led 5,000 Italian legionnaires—the celebrated Red Shirts—and forced the French to withdraw from Rome in April 1849, whereupon the Austrians, Neapolitans, and Spanish converged on Rome to aid the French. Garibaldi led the Roman resistance against the Neapolitans, driving them back and prompting the Spanish likewise to withdraw. But the continual reinforcement of the French finally compelled Garibaldi to withdraw. Rome fell in June, and the papal government was restored.

In the meantime, Manin held out against the siege in Venice from May to August 1849, but Radetzky's bombardment was relentless and his blockade impregnable. The people of Venice languished under starvation and disease (epidemic cholera). Two weeks after Victor Emmanuel II signed his treaty with Austria, Manin surrendered

Venice, and Italy's great war for independence came to an end, crushed not just by Austria but the combined forces of European aristocratic conservatism.

See also ITALIAN REVOLTS (1831–1834).

Further reading: Christopher Duggan, A Concise History of Italy (New York: Cambridge University Press, 1994); Raymond Grew, A Sterner Plan for Italian Unity (Princeton, N.J.: Princeton University Press, 1963); Denis Mack Smith, Cavour and Garibaldi, 1860: A Study in Political Conflict (New York: Cambridge University Press, 1985).

Italian Uprisings (1914)

PRINCIPAL COMBATANTS: Italian socialists vs. government troops
PRINCIPAL THEATER(S): Romagna and the Marches, Italy
DECLARATION: Romagna declared itself a republic in June 1914.
MAJOR ISSUES AND OBJECTIVES: Laborers and socialists agitated for a government more responsive to their needs.
OUTCOME: The rebellion was put down by a major show of force.
APPROXIMATE MAXIMUM NUMBER OF MEN UNDER ARMS: 100,000 Italian regulars were dispatched to restore order in the region.
CASUALTIES: Unknown
TREATIES: None

"Red Week" was a series of popular socialist uprisings beginning on June 7, 1914, in the Marches and Romagna (often referred to as "Red Romagna") in response to the formation of a new, fairly conservative government by Premier Antonio Salandra (1853–1931). The demonstrators demanded higher wages, lower taxes, and an abandonment of militarism (as Europe drifted toward WORLD WAR I). Red Week saw the rise of such popular leaders as Benito Mussolini (1883–1945), who began his political career not as an anticommunist but as a radical socialist. Rioting was general, with a massive workers' strike, destruction of private property, and vandalism of telegraph lines and railroad tracks. Romagna declared itself an independent republic, and the governments of Ferrara and Ravenna surrendered to the rebels. Order was restored by some 100,000 troops transported into the region. Italy's determination to remain neutral after World War I began at the end of July (this despite Italian membership in the Triple Alliance with Germany and Austria) pacified some of the workers' concerns.

See also FASCIST MARCH ON ROME.

Further reading: Alan Axelrod, Life and Work of Benito Mussolini (New York: Alpha, 2002); R. J. B. Bosworth, Mussolini (London: Edward Arnold, 2002); Christopher Duggan, A Concise History of Italy (New York: Cambridge University Press, 1994).

Italian War   See GOTHIC (ITALIAN) WAR.

Italian War between Charles V and Francis I, First (1521–1525)

PRINCIPAL COMBATANTS: French king Francis I and his Swiss and Venetian allies vs. the Holy Roman Emperor Charles V with his Spanish, English, Italian, and Papal allies
PRINCIPAL THEATER(S): Mostly Lombardy and northern Italy
DECLARATION: Francis I invaded Luxembourg and Navarre in May and June 1521.
MAJOR ISSUES AND OBJECTIVES: France tried to establish hegemony in Italy but found herself opposed by the Holy Roman Empire and the pope.
OUTCOME: French ambitions were stymied, and Charles V took Francis I prisoner, forcing him to renounce all claims to Italy and to surrender French territory to the Hapsburgs.
APPROXIMATE MAXIMUM NUMBER OF MEN UNDER ARMS: France and allies, 41,000; Holy Roman Empire and allies, 20,000
CASUALTIES: At Bicocca, 3,000 Swiss killed; 200 Imperial forces killed
TREATIES: Treaty of Madrid, January 14, 1525

For the first half of the 16th century, the French tried repeatedly to gain ascendancy in Italy. For four decades, beginning with the accession of Charles V (1500–58) to the Hapsburg throne, the struggle for supremacy was not merely between the states of the Holy Roman Empire and France but also a personal feud between the emperor and Francis I (1494–1547). Usually, not only were the Hapsburgs—that is the Empire and Spain—allied against the French, but so too were the English and most of the Italian city-states. The Swiss, and an Italian city-state, seeing here or there an advantage, would occasionally line up behind the French. By 1521, Charles had managed to enlist the Vatican to his cause as well, and that year it moved to replace French rule in Milan with the pope's ally and client, Francesco Maria Sforza (1491–1530).

On April 22, 1522, the 15,000-strong French army, led by Marshal Odet de Lautrec (d. 1528) and backed by some 8,000 Swiss and 10,000 Venetians, met the imperial forces—20,000 men (German, Spanish, and papal) led by a condottiere general named Prosper Colonna—at the decisive battle of Bicocca near Milan. Colonna had set up in a strong defensive position, and the Swiss troops, their pay in arrears and seeing the lay of the land, threatened to depart unless they got their back wages immediately. Instead, Lautrec wheeled them into one battle before they withdrew, thus giving himself little choice but to attack. Prudently planning to maximize the use of his artillery, Lautrec could not control the impatient Swiss, who attacked without orders before he could get his guns into position. They were caught short at the Hapsburg entrenchments and cut to shreds by the Spanish harquebusiers: in half an hour, 3,000 Swiss lay dead and the charge had been repulsed. French heavy cavalry tried a diversionary strike, but the horsemen too were driven off. Lautrec retreated into Venetian territory, while the Allies celebrated a victory that cost them only a few hundred men.

The battle struck a massive blow at Swiss morale and was one of the earliest demonstrations of the effectiveness of gunpowder small arms. Although Italy was the main battleground for the war, some of the combat occurred in Navarre, in northern Spain, where back in 1521 an invading French army had lost to the Spaniards near Pamplona and was driven out. Also, in 1522 and 1523, the English, based in Calais, first under the earl of Surrey and then the duke of Suffolk, launched raids into Picardy. By 1523, the Venetians had had enough, and sued for peace, forcing the remnants of the French army to withdraw from Italy entirely back into France. There, they planned to invade Italy again, but were stymied when the treasonous Prince Charles of Bourbon (1490–1527), constable of France, fled to Germany to join Charles V.

In 1524, Francis did indeed launch another invasion of Italy to regain lost territory. At the Battle of Pavia on February 24, 1525, an Italian-Spanish-German army defeated the French in a two-hour pitched battle that could easily have gone the other way. Instead, Francis was captured and imprisoned in Madrid, where he signed a treaty giving up all his claims in Italy and surrendering Burgundy, Artois, and Flanders to Charles V. Despite the defeats here and in most of the future Hapsburg-Valois wars (*see* ITALIAN WAR BETWEEN CARLES V AND FRANCIS I, SECOND; ITALIAN WAR BETWEEN CHARLES V AND FRANCIS I, THIRD; ITALIAN WAR BETWEEN CHARLES V AND FRANCIS I, FOURTH), the constant adversity France faced in these struggles helped to temper and hone the French national spirit, which had in effect been created by Joan of Arc (1421–31) during the HUNDRED YEARS' WAR. The surprise was not that the French lost, but that they came so close to winning so often.

Further reading: Jean Berenger, *History of the Hapsburg Empire, 1273–1700* (London: Longman Publishing Group, 1995); William Peter Blockmans, *Emperor Charles V, 1500–1558,* trans. Isola van den Hoven-Varden (London: Arnold, 2002); Francis Hackett, *Francis the First* (New York: Greenwood Press, 1968); Julius Kirshner, ed., *The Origins of State in Italy, 1300–1600* (Chicago: University of Chicago Press, 1996); Robert Jean Knecht, *Francis I* (New York: Cambridge University Press, 1982); Adam Wandruska, *The House of Hapsburg: Six Hundred Years of European Dynasty,* trans. Cathleen and Hans Epstein (Westport, Conn.: Greenwood Press, 1975).

Italian War between Charles V and Francis I, Second (1526–1530)

PRINCIPAL COMBATANTS: The League of Cognac (France, Milan, Venice, Florence, and the papacy) led by Francis I vs. Spanish and German mercenaries in the hire of Charles V.

PRINCIPAL THEATER(S): Italy

DECLARATION: Francis I repudiated the Treaty of Madrid on May 22, 1526.

MAJOR ISSUES AND OBJECTIVES: When the pope, alarmed by the Hapsburgs' growing power, joined Francis I in the League of Cognac, Holy Roman Emperor Charles V sent troops into Italy to destroy the new alliance.

OUTCOME: A draw in which Francis I and Charles V returned to the status quo, while most of the Italian city-states fell under the control of the Spanish Hapsburgs.

APPROXIMATE MAXIMUM NUMBER OF MEN UNDER ARMS: In the sack of Rome, German and Spanish mercenaries, 22,000. At Naples, League of Cognac forces, 25,000

CASUALTIES: In the sack of Rome, 4,000 civilians killed. During the League's retreat from Naples, 18,000 killed.

TREATIES: Treaty of Cambrai and Treaty of Barcelona, both in 1529

On May 22, 1526, France repudiated the Treaty of Madrid, which had ended the First ITALIAN WAR BETWEEN CHARLES V AND FRANCIS I, because the French king Francis I (1494–1547) claimed he had been forced to sign it under duress (he was a captive of the Holy Roman Empire at the time). That same year, Pope Clement VII (1478–1534), alarmed by the increasing power of the Hapsburgs as a result of the recent war, withdrew papal support from Emperor Charles V (1500–58) and formed the League of Cognac with Francis. Also joining the league were Francesco Maria Sforza (1495–1535), an erstwhile ally whom Charles V had made ruler of Milan after ousting the French, and the rulers of Venice and Florence. Spanish and German mercenaries, led by the French turncoat Charles of Bourbon (1490–1527), then invaded Italy in 1526 to oppose the league.

The defending French forces and their allies had the worst of a war of attrition, and the Hapsburg mercenaries sacked Rome in early May 1527. When their leader, Charles of Bourbon, constable of France, was killed, the hired soldiers, starving and unpaid, committed horrible atrocities in the city, briefly imprisoning the pope himself. In 1528, a revolt in Genoa, led by Andrea Doria (1466–1560), cost the French their most important base in Italy, and a French army was decisively defeated at the Battle of Landriano. Despite a late rally led by the Vicomte Odet de Foix Lautrec (d. 1528), the disastrous defeats and Genoa's alliance with Charles V made the French anxious for peace. In 1529, Francis I and Charles V signed the

Treaty of Cambrai, known as the "Ladies' Peace" because it was reached through the efforts of Charles's aunt, Margaret of Austria (1480–1530), and Francis's mother, Louise of Saray (1476–1531). Charles, as it turned out, was as anxious to sign as Francis, due to a growing threat from the Turks at his rear. The treaty restored the status quo, with Francis agreeing to pay a nominal indemnity and again renouncing his claims in Italy, whereas Charles withdrew his claim to Burgundy under the Treaty of Madrid.

As for the pope, Clement realized his long-term interest lay with Hapsburg Spain, and he signed the Treaty of Barcelona in 1529 in return for imperial help from Charles in fighting the still rebellious Florentine republic. Though suddenly abandoned by France in the unexpected "Ladies' Peace," Florence was led by an able soldier, Francesco Ferruccio (1489–1530), who continued to fight the empire's forces under Philibert de Chalon, prince of Orange (d. 1530). Both leaders were killed at the Battle of Gavinana on August 2, 1530, and on August 12, Florence surrendered. As a result Alessandro de' Medici (1510–37) became duke, and the independent Italian states—except for Milan and Genoa—came under Spanish control. Pope Clement crowned Charles king of Lombardy in 1530. Meanwhile, Francis was reorganizing his army. He established infantry legions, standing units of 6,000 mixed pikemen and harquebusiers, of Picardy, Languedoc, Normandy, and Champagne—clearly preparing for the next war.

See also ITALIAN WAR BETWEEN CHARLES V AND FRANCIS I, THIRD; ITALIAN WAR BETWEEN CHARLES V AND FRANCIS I, FOURTH.

Further reading: Jean Berenger, *History of the Hapsburg Empire, 1273–1700* (London: Longman Publishing Group, 1995); William Peter Blockmans, *Emperor Charles V, 1500–1558,* trans. Isola van de Hoven-Varden (London: Arnold, 2002); Francis Hackett, *Francis the First* (New York: Greenwood Press, 1968); Julius Kirshner, ed., *The Origins of State in Italy, 1300–1600* (Chicago: University of Chicago Press, 1996); Robert Jean Knecht, *Francis I* (New York: Cambridge University Press, 1982); Adam Wandruska, *The House of Hapsburg: Six Hundred Years of European Dynasty,* trans. Cathleen and Hans Epstein (Westport, Conn.: Greenwood Press, 1975).

Italian War between Charles V and Francis I, Third (1535–1538)

PRINCIPAL COMBATANTS: Charles V vs. Francis I
PRINCIPAL THEATER(S): Northwestern Italy and southeastern France
DECLARATION: None
MAJOR ISSUES AND OBJECTIVES: When Charles V made his son Philip duke of Milan, Francis I invaded Italy to retake the city-state but fell short of his goal, seizing only Turin; Charles responded by invading France.

OUTCOME: A truce was declared before any major engagements, reestablishing the status quo, except that France remained in control of Turin.
APPROXIMATE MAXIMUM NUMBER OF MEN UNDER ARMS: Unknown
CASUALTIES: Unknown
TREATIES: Truce of Nice, 1538

Under the Treaty of Cambrai, which ended the Second ITALIAN WAR BETWEEN CHARLES V AND FRANCIS I, the Holy Roman Emperor Charles V (1500–58) was to take possession of Milan upon the death without issue of its ruler, Duke Francesco Maria Sforza (1495–1535). When the duke died in 1535, Charles made his son Philip (1527–98)—later King Philip II of Spain—the duke. Seeking to regain at least some control of Italy, a large French army unexpectedly invaded and captured Turin but was unable to reach Milan. In response, Charles V attempted two counterattacks against Francis I (1494–1547), personally leading one through Provence and sending the other through Picardy. The northern invasion bogged down, but Charles continued his march through southeastern France, advancing as far as Aix. But when he discovered that Francis was ensconced at Avignon and ready to fight, the emperor suddenly declined the challenge and withdrew. A temporary peace was patched up under the Truce of Nice, intended to restore the status quo for 10 years, although the status quo now meant that Francis retained his toehold in northwest Italy.

See also ITALIAN WAR BETWEEN CHARLES V AND FRANCIS I, FIRST; ITALIAN WAR BETWEEN CHARLES V AND FRANCIS I, FOURTH.

Further reading: Jean Berenger, *History of the Hapsburg Empire, 1273–1700* (London: Longman Publishing Group, 1995); Archdeacon William Coxe, *History of the House of Austria,* 3rd ed. 4 vols. (reprint, New York: Arno Press, 1971); Francis Hackett, *Francis the First* (New York: Greenwood Press, 1968); Robert Jean Knecht, *Francis I* (New York: Cambridge University Press, 1982); Adam Wandruska, *The House of Hapsburg: Six Hundred Years of European Dynasty,* trans. Cathleen and Hans Epstein (Westport, Conn.: Greenwood Press, 1975).

Italian War between Charles V and Francis I, Fourth (1542–1544)

PRINCIPAL COMBATANTS: Charles V, emperor of the Holy Roman Empire, Henry VIII, king of England vs. Francis I, king of France, Süleyman the Magnificent, sultan of the Ottoman Turks
PRINCIPAL THEATER(S): Northern Italy and much of France
DECLARATION: None

MAJOR ISSUES AND OBJECTIVES: After Francis I, seeking to take advantage of Charles V's troubles with the Turks, allied with Ottoman Sultan Süleyman and attacked Nice, Charles joined Henry VII to invade France.

OUTCOME: After an inconclusive French victory at Ceresole and a poorly coordinated dual invasion by the Germans and the English, Charles and Francis signed a peace returning to the status quo ante bellum.

APPROXIMATE MAXIMUM NUMBER OF MEN UNDER ARMS: imperial forces, 59,000; France, 45,000

CASUALTIES: At Ceresole, imperial forces, 6,000 killed, 3,200 wounded; France, 2,000 killed or wounded

TREATIES: Peace of Crépy, September 18, 1544

To the horror of many French and the astonishment of others throughout Europe, Francis I (1494–1547) took advantage of a number of setbacks for the Holy Roman Empire to ally himself with Charles V's (1500–58) enemy, Süleyman I the Magnificent (c. 1496–1566), sultan of the Ottoman Turks. For the first two years, the fighting—centered mostly in northern Italy and Roussillon—was inconclusive. A joint Franco-Turkish fleet under Ottoman admiral Khair el-Din sailed on Nice, bombarding, besieging, and sacking the imperial port in 1543. In September Charles invaded Picardy and besieged Landrecies in northern France. Francis approached with a large army the following month, and—after some futile maneuvering—both sides retired to winter quarters. Meanwhile, Charles had colluded with Henry VIII (1491–1547) of England to advance from Calais while Imperial forces invaded through Lorraine and Champagne (see ANGLO-FRENCH WAR [1542–1546]).

At Ceresole, south of Turin, the 20,000-strong imperial forces under the Spanish Marqués del Vasto met 15,000 French, Swiss, and Italian troops under Francis of Bourbon on April 14, 1544. After a prolonged harquebus skirmish and a long-range artillery duel, both infantries became locked in a sanguinary battle. The 7,000 imperial *landsknechts* (German mercenary soldiers) were almost completely destroyed by the combined efforts of the Swiss infantry and the French cavalry. At the same time, the French infantry was being overwhelmed by hardened Spanish and German veterans before Bourbon saved the day with an enveloping cavalry charge. In the less-than-complete French victory at the Battle of Ceresole, del Vasto was forced to retreat after losing more than 6,000 dead and 3,200 wounded, compared to French losses of some 2,000. The battle reaffirmed the lessons being learned in the Hapsburg-Valois conflicts: the infantry of the time—whether harquebusiers, landsknechts, or pikemen—could repulse any cavalry attack. But if an army deployed its cavalry against the flank of an enemy infantry already doing battle with its own infantry, the maneuver was likely to be decisive.

In general, because the English and imperial advances were slow and not well coordinated, the French could mass their forces and stop them. In May and August of 1544, for example, Charles's invasion of eastern France was delayed by the gallant defense at St. Dizier, which gave Francis time to recall his troops from Italy and reinforce them at home in defense of Paris. Thus, the imperial army halted after seizing Épernay, Château-Thierry, Soissons, and Meaux. Meanwhile, Henry's 40,000-man English army, including many foreign mercenaries, made a leisurely crossing to Calais in July, giving Francis more than adequate warning. Though Henry managed to capture Boulogne, he made no attempt to coordinate with Charles's Germans.

A discouraged Charles was more than eager to accept Francis's offers of peace, which left the English suddenly without allies. Henry returned home, leaving a garrison in Boulogne. The Peace of Crépy on September 18 reaffirmed the status quo. The French retained northwest Italy, but for the third time, Francis gave up all claims to Naples.

See also HAPSBURG-VALOIS WAR; ITALIAN WAR BETWEEN CHARLES V AND FRANCIS I, FIRST; ITALIAN WAR BETWEEN CHARLES V AND FRANCIS I, SECOND; ITALIAN WAR BETWEEN CHARLES V AND FRANCIS I, THIRD.

Further reading: Jean Berenger, *History of the Hapsburg Empire, 1273–1700* (London: Longman Publishing Group, 1995); William Peter Blockmans, *Emperor Charles V, 1500–1558*, trans. Isola van den Hoven-Varden (London: Arnold, 2002); Francis Hackett, *Francis the First* (New York: Greenwood Press, 1968); Julius Kirshner, ed., *The Origins of State in Italy, 1300–1600* (Chicago: University of Chicago Press, 1996); Robert Jean Knecht, *Francis I* (New York: Cambridge University Press, 1982); Adam Wandruska, *The House of Hapsburg: Six Hundred Years of European Dynasty*, trans. Cathleen and Hans Epstein (Westport, Conn.: Greenwood Press, 1975).

Italian War of Charles VIII (1494–1495)

PRINCIPAL COMBATANTS: France vs. Naples and the papal League of Venice

PRINCIPAL THEATER(S): Northern Italy

DECLARATION: None

MAJOR ISSUES AND OBJECTIVES: Charles VIII wanted to annex Naples as an Angevin possession.

OUTCOME: Pope Alexander VI's League of Venice defeated Charles, foiling his plan for annexation.

APPROXIMATE MAXIMUM NUMBER OF MEN UNDER ARMS: France, 25,000

CASUALTIES: At Fornovo, France, 400 killed or wounded; League of Venice, 3,350 killed

TREATIES: None

In the last decade of the 15th century, Lodovico ("the Moor") Sforza (1451–1508) usurped the duchy of Milan from his nephew, Gian Galeazzo (1469–1494), whom Lodovico had served as regent, setting in motion events that would soon bring to an end the independence of the Italians until the 19th century.

Years before Lodovico laid claim to Milan, the legitimate heir had married the granddaughter of Ferrante of Naples (1458–94), Isabella of Aragon, who in 1490 gave birth to a son. Thus, the direct interest of Naples in the disposition of the Milanese duchy left the new duke feeling vulnerable. As a result Sforza—ignoring the larger interests of Italy—invited the French king, Charles VIII (1470–98), to press his Angevin claim to Naples.

Charles was interested in the offer for reasons beyond the outstanding claims he had against both Naples and Milan—the latter of which both rulers chose conveniently to ignore. He apparently accepted the medieval notion that it was France's mission to save Italy from its own corruption and purify Rome. From this renewed Italy, he dreamed of leading a crusade against the Turks. Accordingly, a French army augmented by Swiss mercenary troops and heavy artillery invaded Italy by way of the Alps in 1494.

The army toppled Pietro de' Medici (1471–1503) in Florence, replacing his autocratic rule with a constitutional republic sponsored by the popular leader Girolamo Savonarola (1452–98), a powerful demagogue who preached hellfire and damnation as a result of God's wrath against Italy, and thus the need for not only repentance but also democratic reforms. Savonarola had strongly denounced Pope Alexander VI (1492–1503) and called for the intervention of a foreign scourge of God to invade and chastise Italy and open a new age of righteousness.

Not surprisingly, the pope soon became one of Savonarola's direst enemies. Nor is it surprising that he formed the League of Venice to oppose Charles, who was also plagued by disease among his troops as well as military reversals. He broke off his conquest of Naples and returned to France in 1495, barely escaping annihilation at the Battle of Fornovo (Taro) on July 6. Following Charles's withdrawal, the pope awarded King Ferdinand II (1452–1516) of Aragon governance of Naples.

From Charles's point of view, the war was costly and utterly futile. To the rest of Europe, however, it revealed just how vulnerable Italy was. The fragmented states refused to unite, even to defend the common good. It was a lesson that later French rulers headed well, and the independence of the Italian states was doomed.

See also ITALIAN WAR BETWEEN CHARLES V AND FRANCIS I, FIRST; NEAPOLITAN REVOLT (1485–1486).

Further reading: David Abulafia, *The French Descent into Renaissance Italy, 1494–1495: Antecedents and Effects* (Brookfield, Vt.: Ashgate Publishing, 1995); Gene A.

Bruckner, *Florence, the Golden Age, 1138–1737* (Berkeley: University of California Press, c. 1998).

Italian War of Independence (1848–1849)

See ITALIAN REVOLUTION.

Italian War of Independence (1859–1861)

PRINCIPAL COMBATANTS: Italian nationalists (mainly Piedmontese) with French allies vs. Austria and the Austrian-controlled Kingdom of the Two Sicilies
PRINCIPAL THEATER(S): Italy
DECLARATION: Austria against Piedmont, April 1859
MAJOR ISSUES AND OBJECTIVES: Piedmont sought to unite Italy under a single ruler, independent of Austria.
OUTCOME: Union and independence were achieved, except for Rome and Venetia.
APPROXIMATE MAXIMUM NUMBER OF MEN UNDER ARMS: At the biggest battle, Solferino: Franco-Piedmontese, 100,000; Austrian, 100,000
CASUALTIES: At Solferino: Franco-Piedmontese, 20,000 killed, wounded, and missing; Austrian losses were comparable
TREATIES: Peace of Zurich (France and Austria), 1859

Camillo Cavour (1810–61) had been a young Piedmontese politician who supported the ITALIAN REVOLUTION (1848–49). After the revolution, he became known as a moderate. Seeking to solve the problems of the Piedmont (a part of the Kingdom of Sardinia) and of Italy as a whole not so much by revolution as through international politics, he had by 1857 established a new monarchist-unionist party, the Italian National Society (Società Nazionale Italiana). Boasting revolutionary firebrands Daniele Manin (1804–57) and Giuseppe Garibaldi (1807–82) as president and vice president, respectively, the party appealed to the radicals although it was controlled by the more cautious Count Cavour, who as Piedmont's prime minister struck an alliance on December 10, 1858, with Napoleon III (1808–73) of France specifically designed to expel Austria from the region. The arrangement with Napoleon called for the French to intervene should the Piedmont be invaded by Austria, which—as Cavour hoped—did indeed provoke just such an invasion. Austria declared war on the Piedmont in April 1859.

Austrian forces of some 50,000 men were met by a Franco-Piedmontese army and defeated at the Battle of Magenta on June 4. In chaotic combat, the losses to both sides were heavy, but the French-Piedmontese alliance pushed the Austrians back. For his victory, the French marshal Comte Marie-Edmé-Patrice de MacMahon (1808–93) was named duke of Magenta.

Following its defeat at Magenta, the Austrian army withdrew east across Lombardy, taking up a position at Solferino, five miles before the Mincio River. Here, the 100,000-man force was deployed in entrenchments on a series of hills, and Austrian emperor Franz Josef (1830–1916) arrived to assume personal command. The Franco-Piedmontese army, now also numbering about 100,000, had pursued the Austrians from Magenta. On June 24, 1859, these forces prepared to attack—led, like the Austrians, by the monarchs themselves, Napoleon III of France and Victor Emmanuel II (1820–78) of Piedmont, although field command was actually handled by the French generals.

The allies concentrated on the Austrian center, smashing through it after a full day of combat. Franz Josef ordered his troops to withdraw across the Mincio, having lost 20,000 killed, wounded, and missing. Losses among the Franco-Piedmontese forces were comparable, prompting Louis Napoleon to conclude a separate peace—the Treaty of Zurich—with Austria, which left the Piedmontese in the lurch. Austria ceded Lombardy to France, which, by way of compensating its ally, allowed Piedmont to annex it. France received Nice and Savoy. Austria retained Venetia, dominated by Venice.

Despite the loss of the French alliance, the Italians continued the fight. On April 15, 1860, Cavour held a plebiscite, by which Modena, Parma, Romagna, and Tuscany united with Piedmont. In this way, the Kingdom of Sardinia, of which Piedmont was a part, became the Kingdom of Italy—a union of most of northern and central Italy.

Italian democrats, however, refused to concede that the national revolution was complete—not with so many states in Italy still under the control of their old, traditional sovereigns. Sicily, where revolutionary opposition to the Bourbon government was endemic, ranked high on the radicals' list for democratic revival. Though a popular insurrection in Palermo in April 1860 had been quickly suppressed, revolutionaries had spread underground throughout the island's cities and countryside. In May 1860, Italian democrats from all over the peninsula—from Lombardy and Venetia, from all the old states—overcame the deep rifts that had divided them for a decade or more and, with the tacit approval of Cavour, lined up behind the great nationalist Giuseppe Garibaldi.

Garibaldi landed on May 11, 1861, with his "Thousand Red Shirts" at Marsala, Sicily, and led the Red Shirts and another 1,000 Sicilians against the Austrian puppet Francis II (1836–94), king of the Two Sicilies (Sicily and Naples), fighting the Neapolitan army at Calatafimi on May 15. After defeating Francis, the rebels took Palermo 12 days later. For his part, Cavour had not believed Garibaldi would succeed in the south. Now that he had, Cavour took steps to annex the Two Sicilies to the Kingdom of Italy. Garibaldi did not trust Cavour and quickly seized Naples, only to be checked by the Bourbon army at the Liri River.

Cavour now invaded the Papal States, taking Umbria and the Marches after defeating papal forces at Castelfidardo on September 18, 1860. From this victory, he advanced to Naples, hoping that Garibaldi would relinquish his territory to him. Garibaldi did so after plebiscites indicated a popular desire to join the Kingdom of Italy. He bowed out, retiring to Caprera.

In February 1861, a provisional government was formed, which declared Victor Emmanuel II king of Italy, under a constitution. Venetia (occupied by Austria) and Rome (occupied by France) remained outside the new Kingdom of Italy. Upon Cavour's death later in 1861, Garibaldi emerged from retirement to lead an assault on Rome, but was now checked by the new Italian government, which was loath to precipitate a crisis with France. The war of independence was over, but Garibaldi did battle with government forces and was wounded at the Battle of Aspromonte on August 29, 1862. His forces defeated, he was captured and imprisoned, but subsequently pardoned.

See also "FIVE DAYS" REVOLT; ITALIAN REVOLUTION.

Further reading: Arnold Blumberg, *A Carefully Planned Accident: The Italian War of 1859* (Cranbury, N.J.: Associated University Presses, 1990); Denis Mack Smith, *Cavour and Garibaldi, 1860: A Study in Political Conflict* (New York: Cambridge University Press, 1985).

Italian War of Louis XII (1499–1504)

PRINCIPAL COMBATANTS: France (with Venetian, Swiss, and Aragonese allies) vs. Lodovico Sforza, duke of Milan; subsequently, France vs. Aragon

PRINCIPAL THEATER(S): Milan and the Kingdom of the Two Sicilies

DECLARATION: None

MAJOR ISSUES AND OBJECTIVES: France wanted control of Milan and, subsequently, Sicily and Naples.

OUTCOME: Milan and Genoa fell to France, the Kingdom of the Two Sicilies to Aragon.

APPROXIMATE MAXIMUM NUMBER OF MEN UNDER ARMS: France and allies, 22,000; Milan and Aragon, 15,000

CASUALTIES: French losses, 3,000–4,000 killed; other losses unknown

TREATIES: Treaty of Granada, 1500; Treaty of Blois, 1504

When Louis XII (1462–1515) succeeded Charles VIII (1470–98) as king of France in 1498, he determined to conclude an alliance with Venice and the Swiss to help him press his claim to the throne of Milan, which he had inherited from his grandmother Valentina Visconti (1366–1408). The duke of Milan, Lodovico Sforza

(1451–1508), quickly fled Milan to assemble an army of Swiss mercenaries to resist the French and their allies. But when he returned to the city, he found it occupied by Gian Giacomo Trivulzio (c. 1441–1518), condottiere (mercenary) in service to France. When Sforza's mercenaries confronted the condottiere at Novara in 1500, the Swiss refused to fight the other mercenary force, and Louis XII won virtually by default, becoming duke of Milan. Sforza was made a prisoner and taken to France.

After this victory, Louis, allied with Ferdinand II Ferdinand II (Ferdinand the Catholic; 1452–1516), king of Aragon, conquered Naples in 1501. Following this victory, Louis and Ferdinand quarreled. In 1500, the two had agreed by the Treaty of Granada that the Kingdom of the Two Sicilies (that is, Sicily and Naples) would be divided, which canceled Aragon's claim on the kingdom. After the joint victory, however, Ferdinand insisted on French recognition of the Two Sicilies under the Spanish Crown. Now Louis fought his Aragonese ally at the Battle of Cerignola on April 28, 1503. The French (and their Swiss mercenaries) were defeated largely by Spanish harquebusiers—musketeers—who, under the leadership of Gonzalo de Cordoba (1453–1515), known as the "Great Captain," cut down the enemy's swordsmen. The rout was so swift and thorough that Louis's artillery was captured before it could even be put into action. As many as 4,000 French troops died. Naples was abandoned to Aragon on May 13 as the French retreated. Louis signed the Treaty of Blois on September 22, 1504, by which he acknowledged Spanish rule of the Two Sicilies. Genoa and Milan, however, came under French control.

See also ITALIAN WAR OF CHARLES VIII; ITALIAN WARS BETWEEN CHARLES V AND FRANCIS I.

Further reading: Christopher Duggan, *A Concise History of Italy* (New York: Cambridge University Press, 1994); Geoffrey Trease, *The Condottieri, Soldiers of Fortune* (New York: Holt, Rinehart and Winston, 1971).

Italo-Ethiopian War (1887–1889)

PRINCIPAL COMBATANTS: Italy vs. Eritrea and Ethiopia
PRINCIPAL THEATER(S): Eritrea
DECLARATION: Italy on Emperor Yohannes IV of Ethiopia, 1887
MAJOR ISSUES AND OBJECTIVES: Italy wanted to acquire control of Ethiopia and Eritrea.
OUTCOME: Italy believed it had acquired a protectorate over Ethiopia, a conclusion disputed by Emperor Menelik II, Yohannes's successor.
APPROXIMATE MAXIMUM NUMBER OF MEN UNDER ARMS: Italy, 20,000; Ethiopian and Eritrean forces, variable
CASUALTIES: At the Battle of Dogali, Italian losses were 500 killed; most other losses were the result of disease.
TREATIES: Treaty of Uccialli, May 2, 1889

Italy acquired a colonial foothold in Africa by establishing a colony at Assaf on the Eritrean coast in 1882. Massawa, also part of Eritrea, was added in 1885. Wanting to expand their African holdings, the Italians marched inland in 1887, seeking a foothold in Ethiopia. From their bases in Assaf and Massawa, Italy reached an agreement with the leader of the Shewa (who would go on to become the Ethiopian emperor Menelik II [1844–1913]) allowing penetration into the Eritrean interior. The advance, however, was opposed by Ethiopian forces under Emperor Yohannes IV (1831–89), who defeated the Italians at the brutal Battle of Dogali on January 26, 1887, killing 500 Italians. In response to this defeat, Italy invaded Eritrea with 20,000 men, who were established in garrisons. However, this proved an even greater disaster. Yohannes generally avoided battle with the Italians, instead allowing diseases endemic in the region to take their toll among the Italian troops. He understood that, confined to close quarters in garrisons, Europeans in Africa died like flies. The surviving Italian troops were recalled.

While the Italian garrison languished, Yohannes fought a Mahdist (messianic Muslim) invasion in the north and was killed at the Battle of Metemma on March 12, 1889. With the death of Yohannes, Menelik, the Shewa ally of the Italians, assumed the throne of Ethiopia and concluded the Treaty of Uccialli with Italy on May 2, 1889. The ambiguous wording of the document would give rise to the ITALO-ETHIOPIAN WAR (1895–1896): Italy interpreted the treaty as giving it a protectorate over Ethiopia, whereas Emperor Menelik II asserted Ethiopia's absolute sovereignty.

Further reading: Harold G. Marcus, *The Life and Times of Menelik II, Ethiopia, 1844–1913* (Lawrenceville, N.J.: Red Sea Press, 1995).

Italo-Ethiopian War (1895–1896)

PRINCIPAL COMBATANTS: Italy vs. Ethiopia
PRINCIPAL THEATER(S): Ethiopia
DECLARATION: None
MAJOR ISSUES AND OBJECTIVES: Italy wanted to enforce what it interpreted as its right to a protectorate over Ethiopia.
OUTCOME: Ethiopia decisively defeated Italy, which relinquished all claims except in Eritrea.
APPROXIMATE MAXIMUM NUMBER OF MEN UNDER ARMS: Italy, 20,000; Ethiopia, 80,000
CASUALTIES: Italian losses at the decisive Battle of Adwa were 6,500 killed and 2,500 taken prisoner
TREATIES: Treaty of Addis Ababa, October 26, 1896

This war flowed from a disputed reading of the Treaty of Uccialli, May 2, 1889, which was concluded at the end of the ITALO-ETHIOPIAN WAR of 1887–89. Italy interpreted the treaty as awarding it a protectorate over Ethiopia, an interpretation rejected by Ethiopia's Emperor Menelik II (1844–1913), who asserted the absolute sovereignty of his victorious kingdom. With positions irreconcilable and Italians wanting to avenge their defeat in the earlier war, a force of 2,400 was deployed to invade the Ethiopian district of Tigre in 1895. Menelik responded with an army that defeated the Italians at the Battle of Menkele. This prompted Italy to send 20,000 men, who were met at the Battle of Adwa on March 1, 1896, by an Ethiopian force of 80,000. Approximately 6,500 Italians were killed and another 2,500 made prisoner. Following this humiliating defeat, Italy concluded the Treaty of Addis Ababa on October 26, 1896, by which Italy recognized Ethiopian independence but held the coastal colony of Eritrea. Subsequently, in 1900, Italy agreed to further reductions in its Eritrean holdings. The humiliations of 1896 and 1900 simmered among Italian imperialists for decades, motivating Benito Mussolini (1883–1945) to embark on the ITALO-ETHIOPIAN WAR (1935–1936).

Further reading: Harold G. Marcus, *The Life and Times of Menelik II, Ethiopia, 1844–1913* (Lawrenceville, N.J.: Red Sea Press, 1995).

Italo-Ethiopian War (1935–1936)

PRINCIPAL COMBATANTS: Italy vs. Ethiopia
PRINCIPAL THEATER(S): Ethiopia
DECLARATION: Italy invaded without declaration
MAJOR ISSUES AND OBJECTIVES: Italy wanted to annex Ethiopia, partly to avenge its humiliation in the Italo-Ethiopian War of 1895–1896.
OUTCOME: Ethiopia was ravaged and annexed to Italy's other African holdings.
APPROXIMATE MAXIMUM NUMBER OF MEN UNDER ARMS: Italian, 500,000; Ethiopian, 350,000 (but only one-quarter of these with any military training)
CASUALTIES: Italy: 4,359 killed (2,323 italians, 1,086 Eritreans, 507 Somalis, 453 Italian workingmen); Ethiopia: estimates reach 275,000 military and civilian dead (many from mass bombings and mustard gas attacks)
TREATIES: Formal annexation, 1936

Benito Mussolini (1883–1945), made dictator of Italy in 1922, sought to restore Italy to its ancient glory as the Roman Empire. More specifically, he wanted to avenge the humiliating loss of Ethiopia in the ITALO-ETHIOPIAN WAR (1895–1896). Through the manipulation of previous treaty documents, most notoriously the Treaty of Addis Ababa (October 26, 1896), Mussolini persuaded the League of Nations to recommend partition of Ethiopia by the Hoare-Laval Plan, which would have delivered most of the country into Italian hands. The North African nation indignantly rejected this fraud, and, in December 1934, Italian and Ethiopian forces clashed at the Battle of Ualual in a disputed region of the border between Ethiopia and Italian Somaliland. Although Ethiopian emperor Haile Selassie I (1891–1975) wanted to avoid war with Italy and pulled his troops back 20 miles from the Eritrean border, Mussolini seized on the incident as a pretext for launching an invasion of Ethiopia on October 3, 1935. He did so without declaring war.

The invasion was led by Generals Rodolfo Graziani (1882–1955) and Pietro Badoglio (1871–1956), and brought to bear large forces with modern weapons, including intensive use of assault aircraft. The Ethiopians were poorly equipped and essentially defenseless against a modern army. The major Italian breakthrough came at the Battle of Lake Ashanga on April 9, 1936, which was followed by the fall of Addis Ababa, the Ethiopian capital, on May 5. Emperor Haile Selassie had fled on May 2 and, with great and moving dignity, appealed to the League of Nations for intervention. Italian forces executed the archbishop of the Ethiopian Coptic Church, murdered Coptic monks, and sacked Addis Ababa. But the emperor's pleas were in vain. Mussolini arranged it so that Italy's King Victor Emmanuel III (1869–1947) was now designated "emperor of Ethiopia," which was formally united with Eritrea and Italian Somaliland to form Italian East Africa.

Italy was destined to lose its Italian empire early in WORLD WAR II, when Ethiopia was liberated by British, Free French, and Ethiopian troops, and Haile Selassie was restored to power on May 5, 1941.

See also ITALO-TURKISH WAR (1911–1912).

Further reading: S. K. B. Asante, *Pan-African Protest: West Africa and the Italo-Ethiopian Crisis, 1934–1941* (London: Longman, 1977); Thomas M. Coffey, *Lion by the Tail: The Story of the Italian-Ethiopian War* (New York: Viking Press, 1974).

Italo-Turkish War (1911–1912)

PRINCIPAL COMBATANTS: Italy vs. Turkey
PRINCIPAL THEATER(S): Libya, Rhodes, and the Dodecanese Islands
DECLARATION: Italy against Turkey, September 29, 1911
MAJOR ISSUES AND OBJECTIVES: Italy wanted to establish a North African empire.
OUTCOME: Turkey ceded Libya, Rhodes, and the Dodecanese to Italy.
APPROXIMATE MAXIMUM NUMBER OF MEN UNDER ARMS: Italy, 50,000; Turkey, far fewer, including native Arab troops
CASUALTIES: Italy, 4,000 killed, 6,000 wounded, 2,000 died from disease; Turkey, 14,000 killed or died from disease
TREATIES: Treaty of Ouchy, October 17, 1912

At the end of the 19th century, Italy felt itself woefully behind other nations in acquiring colonial holdings. With the Ottoman Empire crumbling, Italy targeted the Turkish provinces of Tripolitania and Cyrenaica (eastern Libya) in North Africa as prizes ripe for the picking. Italy began by sending merchants and immigrants into the region during the 1880s. By 1911, these areas had accumulated a substantial population of Italian nationals, and on September 28, 1911, the Italian government, claiming that its nationals were being abused, presented the Sublime Porte (the Ottoman government) with a 24-hour ultimatum, threatening immediate invasion. Receiving no satisfactory reply, Italy declared war and invaded North Africa the next day with 50,000 troops. Caught by surprise, the Turks could do little as Italian forces bombarded Tripoli with 10 battleships and cruisers for two days. A landing force occupied Tripoli on October 5, encountering little resistance.

Having declared itself neutral, Egypt refused passage to Ottoman troops, so that Turkey had to enlist the aid of Arabs, who occupied coastal regions and brought the war to a standstill in November 1911. Italy sought to break the stalemate with the naval bombardment of Beirut and Smyrna, then followed this by occupying Rhodes, Jos, and other islands of the Dodecanese. Italian vessels bombarded Turkish fortifications protecting the Dardanelles, which forced the closure of the straits. The toughest battle the Italians faced in Libya was not against the Turks, however, but against pro-Turkish Senussi tribal warriors, who made a fierce attack on Tripoli during October 23–26, 1911, in an attempt to retake the Libyan capital. The Italian defenders lost 382 killed and 1,158 wounded in repulsing the attack. The tribesmen lost about 1,000 killed and wounded, but were forced to withdraw.

If the Italians faced fierce "primitive" opposition, they themselves employed some very modern weapons. In addition to naval bombardment, the Italians introduced into the land war the first armored fighting vehicle. The Bianchi, a wheeled armored car, fought in Libya in 1912 with good results. The Bianchi heralded the use of armored cars and tracked vehicles—tanks—in WORLD WAR I.

Despite the Senussi resistance, the Ottoman forces were simply overwhelmed. Moreover, the Sublime Porte was reeling in the aftershock of the recently concluded YOUNG TURKS' REVOLT from 1908 to 1909. Therefore, the Ottoman government concluded the Treaty of Ouchy on October 17, 1912, by which the Turks ceded Libya, Rhodes, and the Dodecanese to Italy.

See also ITALO-ETHIOPIAN WAR (1895–1896); ITALO-ETHIOPIAN WAR (1935–1936).

Further reading: Denis Mack Smith, *Italy, a Modern History* (Ann Arbor: University of Michigan Press, 1969); Rachel Simon, *Libya between Ottomanism and Nationalism: The Ottoman Involvement in Libya during the War with Italy 1911–1919* (Berlin: K. Schwarz, 1987).

J

Jacobite Rebellion (1689–1690)

PRINCIPAL COMBATANTS: Scottish government forces (favoring William and Mary) vs. Jacobite rebels (favoring the restoration of James II)
PRINCIPAL THEATER(S): Scottish Highlands
DECLARATION: None
MAJOR ISSUES AND OBJECTIVES: The Jacobites sought to restore James II to the English throne, which was occupied by William and Mary.
OUTCOME: The rebellion was crushed.
APPROXIMATE MAXIMUM NUMBER OF MEN UNDER ARMS: Scottish government, 4,000; Jacobites, a lesser number
CASUALTIES: At Killiecrankie Pass, 2,000 government troops died in the single greatest loss of the war; throughout the rest of the war, losses among the Jacobites were heavy.
TREATIES: None

In 1688, the British Parliament invited William of Orange (1650–1702) to come from Holland and replace James II (1633–1701) as king of England. He did so in the GLORIOUS REVOLUTION of 1688, but a body of Tories and Stuarts rejected William and Mary II (1662–94) and were determined to restore James II to the throne. These Jacobites staged a rebellion in the Scottish Highlands, although James himself was off elsewhere, leading an army in the IRISH WAR (1689–91). Throughout most of Scotland, William and Mary had been accepted as Britain's new monarchs, and Scots authorities sent troops to suppress the Jacobites. At Killiecrankie Pass, in the Grampian Mountains, on July 27,

1689, 4,000 government troops under General Hugh Mackay (c. 1640–92) were ambushed by a smaller Jacobite force led by John Graham (c. 1649–89), viscount Dundee. Dundee's swift surprise attack killed half of Mackay's men, but the brilliant Dundee fell in the attack, rendering this a Pyrrhic victory because, leaderless, the Jacobites dispersed.

The Jacobites reformed and attacked at Dunkeld but were this time severely beaten and retreated into the hills. In 1690, the Battle of Cromdale also proved disastrous to the Jacobites. In the meantime, on July 1, James's forces were decisively defeated in Ireland at the Battle of the Boyne, and James fled to France, where he died in 1701 without again attempting to retake the English throne. Although William's forces had prevailed in Scotland, the new monarchs were never able to win the full loyalty of the Highlanders.

See also GRAND ALLIANCE, WAR OF THE; JACOBITE REBELLION (1715–1716).

Further reading: Leo Gooch, *The Desperate Faction?: The Jacobites of North-East England, 1688–1745* (Hull, England: University of Hull Press, 1995); Bruce Lenman, *The Jacobite Risings in Britain, 1689–1746* (London: Scottish Cultural Press, 1995.

Jacobite Rebellion (1715–1716)

PRINCIPAL COMBATANTS: Jacobites (supporters of James Edward, the Old Pretender) vs. British supporters of King George I
PRINCIPAL THEATER(S): Scotland and northern England
DECLARATION: None

MAJOR ISSUES AND OBJECTIVES: Dissatisfied with Hanoverian rule in Britain and the Union of England and Scotland, the Jacobites rallied to the cause of James Edward, the Old Pretender, seeking his elevation to the English throne as James III.

OUTCOME: The rebellion was crushed, its leaders executed or exiled.

APPROXIMATE MAXIMUM NUMBER OF MEN UNDER ARMS: Combined Scots and English Jacobite force, 12,000; government forces were larger

CASUALTIES: At Preston, rebels, 42; loyalists, 276. At Sheriffmuir, rebels, 150; loyalists 490. Overall estimate of fatalities, 3,000.

TREATIES: None

Popularly called "The Fifteen," this revival of the effort to restore the Stuarts to the throne of England (see JACOBITE REBELLION [1689–1690]) began in response to the plea of James II's (1633–1701) son James Edward (known as the "Old Pretender"; 1688–1766) for a clan uprising in Scotland a year after George I (1660–1727), the first of the House of Hanover to rule Great Britain, arrived in London. The Jacobites, who had unsuccessfully opposed the Union of Scotland and England in 1707 and then lost a vote to repeal the union in 1713, answered James Edward's call. John Erskine (1675–1732), the earl of Mar, proclaimed James Edward James III of England and James VIII of Scotland, and denounced the union. Some 18 Scottish lords rallied behind the Pretender's banner when it was raised by Mar, bringing with them 5,000 men. At that point government troops in Scotland numbered only about 1,500, so had Mar acted forcefully at the start of the rebellion it might have turned out differently. Instead, he marched on Perth, which his forces seized, but he did not continue on to Sterling, the next logical target. Instead he delayed as he waited for reinforcements. It was a blunder that gave the English time to rally and march north.

King George's government was also afforded the time to concentrate on the Jacobite threat in England proper. Parliament granted the new king the right to imprison anyone he suspected of conspiring against him, and beginning in September 1715, he did so with alacrity. The first arrest was an officer in the Guards, accused of enlisting men for the Stuart cause, but soon six members of Parliament were also rounded up, including Sir William Wyndham (1687–1740), suspected of plotting a revolt in the West Country.

Another MP, Thomas Forster (c. 1675–1738), did indeed lead a rising in the north along with James Radcliffe (1689–1716), third earl of Derwentwater. Together they marched about 2,000 men south hoping to hook up with Mar but were intercepted on November 14 and defeated by the government on November 15, 1715, at the battle of Preston. Meanwhile, Mar—with some 10,000 troops—had engaged 3,500 soldiers under General John Campbell (1678–1743), second duke of Argyll, at Sheriffmuir on November 13 in an indecisive battle whose outcome was nevertheless enough, along with the defeat at Preston, to herald the collapse of the Jacobite challenge.

By the time James himself reached Scotland in December, Mar's army had withered away even as Argyll's was reinforced, including the arrival of a Dutch contingent. James abandoned his lost cause, leaving England never to return, and taking with him back to France the earl of Mar. "The Fifteen" collapsed, and Derwentwater, along with 29 others, was executed in 1716. Other Jacobite leaders were deported, peerages were forfeited, and clans were disarmed.

See also JACOBITE REBELLION (1745–1746).

Further reading: Leo Gooch, *The Desperate Faction?: The Jacobites of North-East England, 1688–1745* (Hull, England: University of Hull Press, 1995); Bruce Lenman, *The Jacobite Risings in Britain, 1689–1746* (London: Scottish Cultural Press, 1995).

Jacobite Rebellion (1745–1746)

PRINCIPAL COMBATANTS: Jacobites (supporters of the Young Pretender, Charles Edward Stuart, "Bonnie Prince Charlie") vs. English government forces

PRINCIPAL THEATER(S): Scottish Highlands and northern England

DECLARATION: None

MAJOR ISSUES AND OBJECTIVES: The Jacobites wanted to bring Charles Edward Stuart to the English throne.

OUTCOME: After scoring many victories against the English, the Jacobites were definitively crushed at the Battle of Culloden Moor, and the last Jacobite rebellion ended.

APPROXIMATE MAXIMUM NUMBER OF MEN UNDER ARMS: English, 10,000; Jacobite, 8,000

CASUALTIES: At Culloden: English, 300 killed; Jacobite losses approached 8,000 at this battle

TREATIES: None

This renewal of Jacobite support for the restoration to the British throne of descendants of James II (1633–1701) (see JACOBITE REBELLION (1689–1690]) and JACOBITE REBELLION (1715–1716]) was popularly called "The Forty-Five." In 1745, Charles Edward Stuart (1720–88), son of the "Old Pretender," James Edward Stuart (1688–1766), and grandson of King James II, came to Scotland with just seven followers, but, when his father was again proclaimed by the Jacobites King James III, "Bonnie Prince Charlie" or the "Young Pretender" (as Charles Edward was dubbed) drew to him a large following from among the Scottish clans, about 2,000 men. He led them skillfully, this last feudal army to be raised in Europe, capturing Perth, then defeating two regiments of the Hanoverian king's troops at Coltbridge. General Sir John Cope (d. 1760) marched north from Stirling with a 4,000-troop-strong British army to intercept the Scottish forces. When he found them entrenched and apparently impregnable along the Corrieyairack Pass, he turned for Inverness, giving Charles leave to proceed on to Edinburgh, where he took the town but not the castle. Meanwhile, Cope sailed from Inverness to the Firth of Forth, landing his army to engage the Jacobites at Prestonpans on September 21, 1745. Although outnumbered, the Highlanders charged into Cope's command and routed the government forces. The royalists lost 1,000 as prisoners, and hundreds were killed or wounded.

After the victory at Prestonpans, Bonnie Prince Charlie invaded Lancashire, England, with an army now some 5,500 strong, including elements of Scots and Irish regiments under French command. To avoid a superior force at Newcastle, which included some 6,000 Dutch soldiers, Charles turned south, capturing Carlisle and Manchester. From there he raided Derby on December 4.

With British forces confused and ill-deployed, nothing—no army, at least—now stood between the Pretender to the throne and the throne itself in London. The 4,000 regulars deployed in the city were quickly mobilized to protect its northern approach at Finchley, but on December 6 Charles and his advisers—having recruited fewer to their cause than they'd hoped and cognizant that hostile and superior forces were perhaps a day's march away—decided to retreat to Scotland, a decision whose soundness would be debated down through the ages.

In any case, Charles returned to Scotland, with English forces in pursuit. On January 17, 1746, at Falkirk, the Jacobite army, now numbering about 8,000 men, suddenly turned on its pursuers, whose numbers were approximately equal. The Jacobites charged, breaking the English line and inflicting heavy casualties: 600 killed, 700 captured. The English also lost their baggage and artillery. Losses to the Jacobites were about 150 killed and wounded.

From Falkirk, the Jacobites marched north to occupy Inverness. The English army was reorganized under King George II's (1683–1760) son the duke of Cumberland (1721–65) (William Augustus), who skillfully deployed his 10,000 men, with artillery, at Culloden Moor on April 16, 1746. Thus positioned, he allowed the Highlanders to do what had served them so well in the past—charge—only, this time, the English defenses were so well prepared that each charge proved costly to the Jacobites, reducing their already outnumbered forces. Finally, Cumberland's cavalry charged and swept all before them. The Scots ran, only to be cut down. Cumberland, determined to put an end to the rebellion, had ordered that no quarter be given, and thus even the wounded were slain. Most of the Jaco-

bite force at Culloden was killed, whereas Cumberland—dubbed "the Butcher"—lost no more than 300 men. With this battle, "the Forty-Five" ended, but Bonnie Prince Charlie escaped. He hid in the Highlands until he eventually returned to France, where he died, a permanent exile.

Further reading: Jeremy Black, *Culloden and the '45* (Gloucester, England: Palgrave Macmillan, 1991); Leo Gooch, *The Desperate Faction?: The Jacobites of North-East England, 1688–1745* (Hull, England: University of Hull Press, 1995); Bruce Lenman, *The Jacobite Risings in Britain, 1689–1746* (London: Scottish Cultural Press, 1995); F. J. McLynn, *The Jacobite Army in England, 1745: The Final Campaign* (Atlantic Highlands, N.J.: Humanities Press, 1983); Stuart Reid, *1745: A Military History of the Last Jacobite Rising* (Staplehurst, Kent: Spellmount, 1996).

Jacquerie (1358)

PRINCIPAL COMBATANTS: French peasant groups vs. French nobility
PRINCIPAL THEATER(S): Countryside near Paris
DECLARATION: None
MAJOR ISSUES AND OBJECTIVES: Oppressed during the Hundred Years' War, a large group of French peasants sought vengeance on their overlords.
OUTCOME: The rebellion was quickly and cruelly crushed.
APPROXIMATE MAXIMUM NUMBER OF MEN UNDER ARMS: Unknown
CASUALTIES: Unknown
TREATIES: None

The Jacquerie was the name given to a French peasants' revolt, which took place during the HUNDRED YEARS' WAR. The name derives from the mocking sobriquet the French nobility bestowed upon the peasants, whom they sneeringly referred to as Jacques or Jacques Bonhommes, a common term of contempt during this period.

The Hundred Years' War was ruinous to many in Europe. But none suffered more than the French peasantry. They were beset by both the invading English soldiers and their own lords. Many lost their homes. Few could work their land, unless sentinels were present. Many retreated to caves and forests for shelter. The invaders robbed and raped or simply extorted money and food on pain of death. Turning to their own lords, the people were met with demands for crops and animals to pay ransoms, finance military actions, or recover losses incurred during the Black Death, which had become epidemic in the course of the war.

At last, on May 21, 1358, near Compiègne, north of Paris, peasants led by Guillaume Calé (d. 1358) rampaged throughout the countryside, putting castles to the torch and murdering whatever nobles they encountered. The rebellion spread to Paris itself, then farmers joined urban rebels, who were led by Étienne Marcel (d. 1358). Whereas the peasants wanted revenge and justice, Marcel had a more focused political objective: the overthrow of King Charles V (1338–80).

Even with their forces combined, the revolt was short-lived. Charles II (1332–87) of Navarre, with others, organized an army against the peasants and the forces of Marcel. The Parisian rebels were defeated at Meaux by Gaston Phoebus of Foix (1331–91) and Jean III de Grailly (d. 1376–77) on June 9. Charles II himself defeated Calé at Clermont-en-Beavais the following day. Following these battles, Marcel was murdered, and Charles led a punitive expedition throughout the countryside, rounding up those identified as leaders, who were summarily executed or, indeed, slaughtered.

See also ENGLISH PEASANTS' REVOLT.

Further reading: Christopher Allmand, *The Hundred Years' War: England and France at War, c. 1300–1450* (New York: Cambridge University Press, 1988); Anne Curry, *The Hundred Years' War,* 2nd ed. (New York: Palgrave Macmillan, 2003); Robin Neillands, *The Hundred Years' War* (New York: Routledge, 2001); Jonathan Sumption, *The Hundred Years' War* (Boston: Faber and Faber, 1999); Nicholas Wright, *Knights and Peasants: The Hundred Years' War in the French Countryside* (Rochester, N.Y.: Boydell and Brewer, 2001).

Jamaica, Seizure of   *See* ANGLO-SPANISH WAR (1655–1659).

Jameson Raid   (1895–1896)

PRINCIPAL COMBATANTS: "Renegade" Englishman L. Starr Jameson and 500 adventurers vs. the Boer commandos from the Republic of South Africa (Transvaal).

PRINCIPAL THEATER(S): The Transvaal south of Johannesburg.

DECLARATION: No formal declaration.

MAJOR ISSUES AND OBJECTIVES: Jameson, under instructions from Cecil Rhodes, planned to spark an uprising among those the Boers considered outsiders in Johannesburg. The idea was "unofficially" to destabilize the Boer republic, thus requiring Great Britain to intervene, reestablish order, and add the Boer lands once again to the British Empire. The Boers sought not only to defeat Jameson and prevent the uprising, but to receive assurances from the British government that it respected their autonomy.

OUTCOME: Jameson was captured, turned over to Britain, tried, convicted, and given a slap on the wrist. Rhodes was removed as prime minister of the Cape Colony. Suspicion of British intentions grew among the Boers, paving the way for the Boer War three years later.

APPROXIMATE MAXIMUM NUMBER OF MEN UNDER ARMS: Jameson's force, 494; Boers, 2,000–3,000.

CASUALTIES: Jameson's forces, 17 dead, 55 wounded, 35 missing; Boers, negligible.

TREATIES: None

In 1886, five years after the Boers—descendants of early Dutch settlers in South Africa—had won autonomy from the British in the First BOER WAR, a huge gold deposit was discovered a few miles south of Johannesburg. Overnight, a city of tents sprang up, housing the largest concentration of white men in Africa—several thousand Britons, Americans, Germans, and Scandinavians, whom the Boers dubbed derisively *Uitlanders*—"outsiders" in Afrikaans, the dialect of Dutch spoken in South Africa. The area was called the Witwatersrand, the Rand for short, and it was fast becoming the greatest source of gold in the world, exceeding the combined production of the United States, Russia, and Australia. The Transvaal Republic's president, S. J. Paul Kruger (1825–1904) viewed the Uitlanders askance from his clean and manicured capital in Pretoria. They seemed to him a godless lot—lawless, violent, and dirty. To make sure the Boers remained in control of these men, whom Kruger publicly referred to as "thieves and murderers," he set up a five-year residency requirement for citizenship, then increased it to 14 years. The Boers discriminated against the miners, taxing them liberally, insisting their children attend Boer schools and learn to speak Afrikaans.

Talk of an armed uprising against the Boers began to spread, and in such talk, Cecil Rhodes's name always seemed to crop up.

Cecil John Rhodes (1853–1902) was the son of a stern vicar and a doting mother, the sixth of nine children, and he had come to Africa at age 20 in 1873 to help his brother grow cotton. He fell in love with the country when diamonds were discovered in the northern reaches of the Cape Colony, and he was lucky enough to stake a claim that made him rich. After buying himself an Oxford education, he had returned in 1881 to consolidate his mining interests and to fulfill his dream of establishing a federation of South African states within the British Empire. By 1890, his company, De Beers Consolidated Mines, Ltd., owned 90 percent of the world's production of diamonds, and he was prime minister of the Cape Colony. He was reported to have exclaimed one night, as he stared up at the African heavens, that he would annex the planets if he could. Now he was willing to settle for the Transvaal and the Orange Free State, the major obstacles to his plans for expanding the Cape Colony northward, creating a British federation of South African states, building a Cape Town-to-Cairo railway, and opening eastern Africa to Rhodesian colonizing.

The trouble was that one British prime minister, Benjamin Disraeli (1804–81), listening to the siren calls of imperialists like Rhodes, had already tried back in 1877 to annex the Boer lands and failed. Since the Treaty of Pretoria in 1881, the official position of the British government in London was that the Boer republic was independent in its internal affairs, though in matters of foreign policy it was supposed to seek approval of the Crown. Armed rebellion thus seemed the only decent alternative, and by 1895 Rhodes had launched a plot against the Transvaal government. He had seen to it that 4,000 rifles, three machine guns, and more than 200,000 rounds of ammunition had been smuggled into Johannesburg under loads of coal and in false-bottom oil tanks. In the spring, he entertained three Uitlander leaders on his wicker-bedecked veranda in Cape Town, conspiring against Kruger. British troops, of course, could not be used, at least officially, he told them, but he had recruited a private army to help out. It consisted of mercenaries who worked for the South Africa Company, of which he was chair, and he had already used them to good effect in Matabeleland. At their head would be a man he trusted, his best friend and factotum, Leander Starr Jameson (1853–1917)—known thereabouts as "Doctor Jim."

Later Jameson would claim that all the thinking and planning about Africa came from Rhodes. At Rhodes's request, he had taken on and defeated the Matabele, capturing their king, then treating him for gout. Now, in October 1895, he was gathering men at Mafeking on the western border of Transvaal, about 140 miles from Johannesburg, declaring that anyone could take the Transvaal from the arrogant and stuffy Boers with half a dozen revolvers. And *he* had 494 men—including a number of British officers "on leave" from the regular army—as well as six machine guns, and the three pieces of artillery. Two months Jameson waited for word from the Uitlanders to launch his raid, but they procrastinated and fretted over such questions as whether the uprising could succeed, what would be their future relationship to the Cape Colony, how London might respond to such an undertaking. At length, they fixed December 28, 1895, as the date, then postponed it at the last moment indefinitely. Jameson, always impatient, announced he was through waiting. The next night he led his little band on its fantastical dash into the Transvaal.

It was military madness, a four-day opéra-bouffe performance in which Jameson's raiders slowly fought their way against the Boers—who dropped their plows and picked up their rifles—to within 14 miles of Johannesburg. There, at Krugersberg, exhausted from four nights without sleep, his ranks thinned—17 dead, 55 wounded, 35 missing—by hard-bitten, straight-shooting Boer commandos, surrounded, outnumbered nearly six to one, Jameson raised a white flag and let his men be rounded up like cattle. The Uitlander leaders in Johannesburg never showed their faces, and the half-baked uprising failed without ever starting. The Boers turned Jameson and those left of his men over to the Cape government on the Natal border. From there, the whole bunch was shipped off to England for trial.

The British government immediately repudiated the raid and the colonial secretary promised to bring Jameson and five of his officers into the dock of the Old Bailey to answer charges they had infringed on the Foreign Enlistment Act. In the months before the trial, the defendants remained free, however, and Jameson became a celebrity. Margot Tennant, who would one day marry future Liberal prime minister H. H. Asquith, confessed that "Doctor Jim had personal magnetism and could do what he liked with my sex." Even during the nine-day trial in July 1896, Jameson remained the toast of the town. The lord chief justice had to suppress pro-Jameson demonstrations in the courtroom, and the *Times* of London mused that Doctor Jim's only real crime was an "excess of zeal." Nevertheless, he was convicted and sentenced to 15 months in a comfortable jail. His officers served less time and were stripped of their regular army commissions. Cecil Rhodes was forced to step down as the Cape Colony's prime minister because of the controversy. Jameson grew despondent and fell ill, whereupon Queen Victoria (1819–1901) pardoned him and sent him home. He had served four months of his sentence. Within a decade, the good doctor was himself prime minister of the Cape Colony. In 1911, King George V (1865–1936) made him a baronet. In 1912, Sir Leander Starr Jameson left Africa for good and settled in England.

Meanwhile, the Boers recognized a mere slap on the wrist when they saw one. Kruger and his minions, never the most trusting of men, felt utterly betrayed by the British. The ill will from Jameson's raid paved the way to open warfare between England and the Boers of the Transvaal and the Orange Free State.

See also BOER WAR, SECOND.

Further reading: T. R. H. Davenport, *The Afrikaner Bond: The History of a South African Political Party, 1880–1911* (New York: Oxford University Press, 1966); Frederick A. Johnstone, *Class, Race, Gold* (Boston: Routledge and Kegan Paul, 1987); Charles van Onselen, *Studies in the Social and Economic History of the Witwatersrand, 1886–1914*, 2 vols. (New York: Longman, 1982); Thomas Pakenham, *The Boer War* (New York: Random House, 1979); Peter Warwick, ed., *The South African War* (Harlow, Essex: Longman, 1980); William H. Worger, *South Africa's City of Diamonds: Mine Workers and Monopoly Capitalism in Kimberly, 1867–1895* (New Haven, Conn.: Yale University Press, 1987).

Janissaries' Revolt (1621–1622)

PRINCIPAL COMBATANTS: Janissaries vs. Sultan Osman II
PRINCIPAL THEATER(S): Royal court, Constantinople

DECLARATION: None

MAJOR ISSUES AND OBJECTIVES: The Janissaries overthrew a sultan they no longer considered competent.

OUTCOME: Osman II was assassinated, and the queen mother was installed to rule through her imbecile son, Mustafa I.

APPROXIMATE MAXIMUM NUMBER OF MEN UNDER ARMS: Unknown

CASUALTIES: Osman II, the chief eunuch of the seraglio, and the grand vizier were assassinated.

TREATIES: None

The Janissary corps was formed by Ottoman sultan Murad I (1319–89) in the 14th century as a non-Turkish elite mercenary force, originally staffed by young Christian converts to Islam, drawn from the Ottoman Empire's Balkan provinces. Murad II (1403–51) restyled the Janissaries as a palace guard under his direct control in the 15th century. The idea was to create a militarily effective force that would be absolutely loyal to the sultan because it owed family or clan allegiance to no one else. By the end of the 16th century, however, the Janissaries became a major political force in Turkish court life and politics, with a deep allegiance only to themselves. The Ottoman rulers lived under continual threat of a Janissaries' revolt, especially in times of external peace, because these mercenaries were paid only during war. At the very heart of Ottoman government was a nest of vipers.

In 1618, it was the Janissary corps that deposed Sultan Mustafa I (1591–1639), who was mentally retarded, and replaced him with Osman II (1604–22), a teenager animated by dreams of conquest. His campaign against the Poles in 1621 produced Turkish losses so substantial that the troops eventually mutinied. At this, Osman simply returned to Constantinople and boasted of his "victory." The Janissaries—as yet unpaid—were outraged by the young sultan's false claim and threatened revolt. In response, Osman decided to eliminate the Janissaries once and for all. He set about creating a militia with the stated purpose of campaigning in Asia; secretly, however, Osman instructed them to march off, double back, then make a surprise attack on the Janissaries, killing all of them. In the climate of intrigue that was the Ottoman court, secrecy was nearly impossible, and word of the sultan's plot leaked out. The Janissaries made good on their threats and staged a revolt. In a panic, Osman promised to call off the militia, but this was to no avail. Unforgiving, the Janissaries seized the deposed sultan Mustafa I, killed the grand vizier and the chief eunuch of the seraglio, crowned the retarded Mustafa, and brought Osman back to their barracks. Here, they strangled the hapless monarch to death—the traditional mode of execution in Ottoman official circles. It was the first regicide in the history of the Ottoman Empire.

The revolt was not merely a spontaneous expression of anger, but had been planned in consultation with Valide (fl. 17th century), the queen mother. She approved of Osman's assassination and planned to rule, through Mustafa, as the power behind the throne. The Janissaries sent Valide Osman's ear as proof that the deed had been done.

However, as for Valide and Mustafa, the Janissaries did not long approve of their reign and backed instead the ascension of Murad IV (1609–40) in 1623. With that support, he did ascend the troubled Ottoman throne.

See also JANISSARIES' REVOLT (1703); JANISSARIES' REVOLT (1730); JANISSARIES' REVOLT (1807–1808); JANISSARIES' REVOLT (1826).

Further reading: Godfrey Goodwin, *The Janissaries* (London: I. B. Tauris, 1997); Lord Kinross, *The Ottoman Centuries: The Rise and Fall of the Turkish Empire* (New York: Morrow, 1977); Kemal H. Karpat, ed., *The Ottoman State and Its Place in World History* (Leiden, Netherlands: Brill, 1974); Stanford J. Shaw and E. K. Shaw, *History of the Ottoman Empire and Modern Turkey*, 2 vols. (New York: Cambridge University Press, 1976–1977).

Janissaries' Revolt (1703)

PRINCIPAL COMBATANTS: Janissaries vs. Sultan Mustafa II

PRINCIPAL THEATER(S): Constantinople and Adrianople

DECLARATION: None

MAJOR ISSUES AND OBJECTIVES: Unpaid, the Janissaries rebelled against Mustafa II.

OUTCOME: Mustafa II was forced to abdicate in favor of Ahmed III.

APPROXIMATE MAXIMUM NUMBER OF MEN UNDER ARMS: Unknown

CASUALTIES: Unknown

TREATIES: None

The Janissaries were an important military asset to the Ottoman sultans, but also a continual threat to them. The Janissary corps was paid only in time of war, and often Sultans reneged on that payment. When the Sublime Porte (Ottoman government) failed to pay in 1703, the Janissaries revolted for six weeks in an action that nearly escalated to full-scale civil war. The response of Sultan Mustafa II (1664–1704) was to go into hiding in Adrianople, where he assembled an army to confront the Janissaries. In the meantime, he refused all demands that he return to Constantinople, whereupon the Janissaries took possession of the Prophet's sacred standard, the chief symbol of authority, assumed the offensive, and sought Mustafa II out in his hiding place. Finding him, they compelled his abdication in favor of Ahmed III (1673–1736).

Raised to power by the Janissaries, Ahmed III was destined also to fall from power, likewise through their agency, in the JANISSARIES' REVOLT (1730).

See also JANISSARIES' REVOLT (1807–1808); JANISSARIES' REVOLT (1826). For an explanation of the Janissaries' role in the Ottoman military and politics, *see* JANISSARIES' REVOLT (1621–1622).

Further reading: Godfrey Goodwin, *The Janissaries* (London: I. B. Tauris, 1997); Lord Kinross, *The Ottoman Centuries: The Rise and Fall of the Turkish Empire* (New York: Morrow, 1977); Kemal H. Karpat, ed., *The Ottoman State and Its Place in World History* (Leiden, Netherlands: Brill, 1974); Stanford J. Shaw and E. K. Shaw, *History of the Ottoman Empire and Modern Turkey,* 2 vols. (New York: Cambridge University Press, 1976–1977).

Janissaries' Revolt (1730)

PRINCIPAL COMBATANTS: Janissaries and Albanian rebels vs. Sultan Ahmed III and, subsequently, Sultan Mahmud I
PRINCIPAL THEATER(S): Constantinople
DECLARATION: None
MAJOR ISSUES AND OBJECTIVES: The Janissaries wanted to unseat Sultan Ahmed III and then decided to support a general revolt against the Sublime Porte (Ottoman government).
OUTCOME: Ahmed was deposed and replaced by Mahmud I, who put down the rebellion by killing or exiling many of the rebels, thereby persuading the Janissaries to return to his service.
APPROXIMATE MAXIMUM NUMBER OF MEN UNDER ARMS: Albanian rebels, 12,000
CASUALTIES: In a single campaign, Mahmud I killed 7,000 rebels.
TREATIES: None

Sultan Ahmed III (1673–1736), who had been placed on the throne as a result of the JANISSARIES' REVOLT (1703), failed to call the Janissaries into action during the PERSIAN CIVIL WAR (1725–1730). Not committed to the war, the Janissaries were not paid—a situation that always produced great discontent, and that, inexplicably, the sultans never addressed. When the Persian Civil War prompted incursions into Ottoman territory, the TURKO-PERSIAN WAR of 1730–36 broke out. This time, Ahmed called on the Janissaries, who rebelled by delaying their deployment for two months while they supported a rebellion against the sultan by 12,000 Albanian troops. During this time, the Janissaries assassinated (by strangulation—traditional Ottoman mode of execution) the grand vizier, the admiral in chief, and other government and military officials. The life of the sultan they spared, but forced him to abdicate in favor of his nephew, Mahmud I (1696–1754).

Yet the installation of the new sultan did not quell the revolt. Mahmud did not act directly against the Janissaries, but instead moved against the rebels they supported. Ahmed invited the rebel leader, under a promise of safe conduct, to meet with him and the Divan (his privy council). Treacherously, Mahmud took the leader prisoner, then had him strangled as he looked on. This accomplished, the sultan oversaw the systematic slaughter of the rebels, some 7,000 of them over the course of three bloody weeks, in a display of brutality that rapidly diminished the passion for rebellion among the Albanians and prompted the Janissaries to withdraw their support. By the time the sultan had finished disposing of rebels—through either execution or banishment—his empire's military assets had been reduced by 50,000 men; nevertheless, the remaining Janissaries were now prepared for service against the Persians.

See also JANISSARIES' REVOLT (1807–1808); JANISSARIES' REVOLT (1826). For an explanation of the Janissaries' role in the Ottoman military and politics, *see* JANISSARIES' REVOLT (1621–1622).

Further reading: Godfrey Goodwin, *The Janissaries* (London: I. B. Tauris, 1997); Lord Kinross, *The Ottoman Centuries: The Rise and Fall of the Turkish Empire* (New York: Morrow, 1977); Kemal H. Karpat, ed., *The Ottoman State and Its Place in World History* (Leiden, Netherlands: Brill, 1974); Stanford J. Shaw and E. K. Shaw, *History of the Ottoman Empire and Modern Turkey,* 2 vols. (New York: Cambridge University Press, 1976–1977).

Janissaries' Revolt (1807–1808)

PRINCIPAL COMBATANTS: Janissaries vs. Sultan Selim III and Mustafa IV
PRINCIPAL THEATER(S): Constantinople
DECLARATION: None
MAJOR ISSUES AND OBJECTIVES: The Janissaries fought to preserve their position and livelihood.
OUTCOME: The Janissaries remained a terror to the sultans.
APPROXIMATE MAXIMUM NUMBER OF MEN UNDER ARMS: Unknown
CASUALTIES: Unknown
TREATIES: None

In 1805, Sultan Selim III (1761–1808) decided to neutralize the always troublesome Janissaries once and for all by forming an army according to a "New Order," based on Western-style (i.e., Napoleonic) regimental organization, discipline, weaponry, and uniforms. The Janissaries threatened revolt, however, and Selim withdrew the New Order decree, although reform of uniforms was still advanced. This alone was sufficient to prompt a rebellion, in 1807, among the Yamaks, the sultan's second-line or auxiliary troops. The Janissaries decided to join them, as did the grand mufti, who ruled that the Western-style uniforms were contrary to Muslim law because they were Christian garb. This ruling gave the rebels the moral basis from which they promoted legal prosecution of the reformers in the sultan's government. Tried, they were all executed, and Selim III himself deposed.

Mustafa IV (1779–1808), a relative of Selim, agreed to ascend the throne, but soon found himself under attack by Selim's supporters. When they discovered that Mustafa had ordered Selim strangled, the Janissaries turned on Mustafa, dragged him from the throne, and strangled him. They now saw to the elevation of Mahmud II (1784–1839) to the throne. The new sultan judiciously appointed the leader of the Janissaries to the post of grand vizier. He now reintroduced Selim's New Order. This time, the Janissaries held off open revolt and made a show of acceptance. Once the grand vizier had been lulled into confidence that the reform had been accomplished, the Janissaries effected his arrest and execution. In this way, through intrigue and ruthless terror, the Janissaries staved off their demise.

See also JANISSARIES' REVOLT (1703); JANISSARIES' REVOLT (1730); JANISSARIES' REVOLT (1826). For an explanation of the Janissaries' role in the Ottoman military and politics, *see* JANISSARIES' REVOLT (1621–1622).

Further reading: Godfrey Goodwin, *The Janissaries* (London: I. B. Tauris, 1997); Lord Kinross, *The Ottoman Centuries: The Rise and Fall of the Turkish Empire* (New York: Morrow, 1977); Kemal H. Karpat, ed., *The Ottoman State and Its Place in World History* (Leiden, Netherlands: Brill, 1974); Stanford J. Shaw and E. K. Shaw, *History of the Ottoman Empire and Modern Turkey,* 2 vols. (New York: Cambridge University Press, 1976–1977).

Janissaries' Revolt (1826)

PRINCIPAL COMBATANTS: Janissaries vs. Sultan Mahmud II
PRINCIPAL THEATER(S): Constantinople and the Turkish provinces
DECLARATION: None
MAJOR ISSUES AND OBJECTIVES: Mahmud II wanted to rid the government of the Janissary menace once and for all.
OUTCOME: The Janissaries were slain, virtually to a man.
APPROXIMATE MAXIMUM NUMBER OF MEN UNDER ARMS: Mahmud's forces, 14,000
CASUALTIES: Janissary losses, 4,000 killed in barracks; many more slain throughout the provinces
TREATIES: None

Like Sultan Selim III (1761–1808) before him [see JANISSARIES' REVOLT (1807–1808)], Mahmud II (1784–1839)—Mahmud the Reformer—wanted to neutralize the dangerous Janissary corps, which had repeatedly shown itself to be the greatest threat to the sultan within the empire. Moreover, in the GREEK WAR OF INDEPENDENCE from 1821 to 1832, the Janissaries had performed so poorly that Mahmud had had to call in Egyptian mercenaries. Nevertheless, Mahmud was all too aware that

"reforming" the Janissaries out of existence was a dangerous proposition, bound to incite them to rebellion. Accordingly, he proceeded carefully, ensuring himself of the support of the grand mufti, then improving his own personal army by building up a 14,000-man force equipped with the latest Western artillery, and finally decreeing a highly modified version of Selim's "New Order" military. The Janissaries would not be dismissed, but they would be separated and dispersed. Mahmud decreed that 150 from each Janissary battalion would be integrated into each division of the new corps he was creating under the New Order. This, Mahmud explained, was actually a revival of an *old* Ottoman military order, not a reformist innovation.

Despite Mahmud's assurances and deceptions, the Janissaries revolted. On June 14, 1826, they assembled in the Constantinople Hippodrome and demanded an audience. By way of response, Mahmud used his new artillery, firing against Janissaries with grapeshot, forcing them to retreat to their barracks. Once they were concentrated there, Mahmud opened up on them in earnest, subjecting the barracks to an intensive artillery bombardment. This action incited Turkish mobs to attack the hated Janissaries as well, and Mahmud did not interfere with them. Indeed, he allowed the rioters free rein. In the end, 4,000 Janissaries died in and around their barracks, and many more thousands who fled to the provinces fell victim to mob violence.

Having eliminated the Janissaries, Mahmud II decided to obliterate their legacy as well, outlawing even the use of the word *Janissary* and banning the Bektashi dervishes, the Janissaries' allies and abettors from the empire.

See also JANISSARIES REVOLT (1703); JANISSARIES REVOLT (1730). For an explanation of the Janissaries' role in the Ottoman military and politics, *see* JANISSARIES' REVOLT (1621–1622).

Further reading: Godfrey Goodwin, *The Janissaries* (London: I. B. Tauris, 1997); Lord Kinross, *The Ottoman Centuries: The Rise and Fall of the Turkish Empire* (New York: Morrow, 1977); Kemal H. Karpat, ed., *The Ottoman State and Its Place in World History* (Leiden, Netherlands: Brill, 1974); Stanford J. Shaw and E. K. Shaw, *History of the Ottoman Empire and Modern Turkey,* 2 vols. (New York: Cambridge University Press, 1976–1977).

January Insurrection *See* POLISH REBELLION (1863–1864).

Japanese Civil War (672)

PRINCIPAL COMBATANTS: Prince Otomo vs. Prince Oama
PRINCIPAL THEATER(S): Omi province, Shiga prefecture, Japan
DECLARATION: None

MAJOR ISSUES AND OBJECTIVES: This was a contest for succession to the Japanese throne.
OUTCOME: Oama's forces defeated those of Otomo, and Oama ascended the throne as Emperor Temmu Tenno.
APPROXIMATE MAXIMUM NUMBER OF MEN UNDER ARMS: Unknown
CASUALTIES: Unknown
TREATIES: None

In Japan, the war is called *Jinshinno-ran*. It broke out over the issue of imperial succession following the death of Emperor Tenchi (626–671). Tenchi had struggled valiantly to centralize Japanese government, enhancing the authority of the emperor over that of the noble families. Throughout his reign, the Nakatomi and Soga families had done their utmost to block the aggrandizement of imperial authority. Tenchi had designated Prince Otomo as his successor. Obediently, Tenchi's other son, Oama (673–686), retired to a secluded life in a Buddhist monastery. Doubtless, he realized that he might be killed if he remained in court.

Upon Tenchi's death, the Nakatomi and Soga put Prince Otomo (fl. 672) on the throne. Oama returned from the monastery and raised an army to fight the supporters of Otomo in a single battle that took place just outside of Otomo's capital in Omi province, Shiga prefecture. Otomo was defeated in their Battle of Jinshin, and Oama's way to the throne was thereby cleared. He ruled as Temmu Tenno, establishing his capital at Asuka, Yamato Province, Nara prefecture, a location remote from the seats of the Nakatomis and Sogas.

Further reading: John W. Hall, *Japan: From Prehistory to Modern Times* (Tokyo: C. E. Tuttle Co., 1971); James Murdoch, *A History of Japan,* 3 vols. (New York: Routledge, 1996); George B. Samson, *A History of Japan,* 3 vols. (Palo Alto, Calif.: Stanford University Press, 1958–63).

Japanese Civil War (764–765)

PRINCIPAL COMBATANTS: Oshikatsu (Nakamato), minister under Emperor Junnin, vs. Dokyo, favorite of the "retired" but still powerful empress, Koken (Shotoku)
PRINCIPAL THEATER(S): Japan
DECLARATION: None
MAJOR ISSUES AND OBJECTIVES: Control of the Japanese throne and government
OUTCOME: Oshikatsu and his adherents were defeated and killed; Koken reascended the Japanese throne (as Empress Shotoku), deposed Emperor Junnin, and made Dokyo prime minister.
APPROXIMATE MAXIMUM NUMBER OF MEN UNDER ARMS: Unknown
CASUALTIES: Unknown
TREATIES: None

In 758, Empress Koken (718–770) retired to life as a nun, abdicating the Japanese throne in favor of Emperor Junnin (d. c. 766). However, as was often true in the case of "retired" Japanese monarchs, Koken retained considerable actual power. Moreover, she exercised this power not simply in her own right, but with the advice and under the influence of a Buddhist priest, Dokyo (d. 772), who was almost certainly her lover. Although the Japanese court was willing to accept the power arrangement between Koken and Junnin, the emperor's principal minister, Oshikatsu (Nakamaro) (d. 765), soon became jealous of the degree of power Dokyo was attaining. The conflict grew and developed into a civil war by 764.

After brief but intense fighting, Oshikatsu and most of his adherents were killed. Seeking to avert further warfare, Koken reascended the throne, now as Empress Shotoku, and moved quickly against Junnin, who was placed under arrest, then exiled to the island of Awaji. With the hapless emperor thus disposed of, Koken/Shotoku called Dokyo to court and appointed him prime minister. He was also anointed with a special title, *Ho-o,* a religious distinction roughly translated as "pope." This theoretically put him into position to assume the throne on the death of Koken in 770, but opposition was too strong, and Dokyo was banished.

Further reading: John W. Hall, *Japan: From Prehistory to Modern Times* (Tokyo: C. E. Tuttle Co., 1971); Richard J. Miller, *Japan's First Bureaucracy: A Study of Eighth-Century Government* (Ithaca, N.Y.: China-Japan Program, Cornell University, 1978); James Murdoch, *A History of Japan,* 3 vols. (New York: Routledge, 1996); George B. Samson, *A History of Japan,* 3 vols. (Palo Alto, Calif.: Stanford University Press, 1958–63).

Japanese Civil War (936–941)

PRINCIPAL COMBATANTS: In the west, Fujiwara Sumitomo vs. Kyoto government; separately, in the east, Masakado vs. a rival Taira chieftain
PRINCIPAL THEATER(S): Japan's western and eastern provinces
DECLARATION: None
MAJOR ISSUES AND OBJECTIVES: Control of portions of Japan
OUTCOME: Sumitomo's rebellion was crushed by imperial forces; Masakado's rebellion was neutralized by other members of the Taira family.
APPROXIMATE MAXIMUM NUMBER OF MEN UNDER ARMS: Unknown
CASUALTIES: Unknown
TREATIES: None

The 903 revolt of Taira-no-Masakado (d. 903), a leader of the Kanto district, destabilized the Kyoto government and encouraged various acts of disobedience, including piracy off the coast in the Inland Sea. In 936, the pirate attacks grew to unprecedented intensity, and the Kyoto court dispatched Sumitomo (d. 941), of the powerful Fujiwara family, to combat the pirates. He did this with great success but then led his followers in raids throughout the western provinces. When Sumitomo failed to obey the emperor's command to cease and desist, imperial troops were sent against him. Joining the imperial forces was the chief of a western military family, the Minamoto, and, together, the combined imperial and Minamoto forces crushed Sumitomo's rebellion and killed Sumitomo himself.

Although the defeat and death of Sumitomo brought peace in the western provinces, the eastern region of Kanto erupted into rebellion. There Masakado (d. 940), of the Taira family, having steadily expanded his territorial holdings, declared himself emperor of Kanto in 939. The following year, however, another Taira chieftain vied for the new Kanto throne and deposed Masakado. With this, the eastern region also returned to peace.

Further reading: Karl Friday, *Hired Swords: The Rise of Private Warrior Power in Early Japan* (Palo Alto, Calif.: Stanford University Press, 1992); John W. Hall, *Japan: From Prehistory to Modern Times* (Tokyo: C. E. Tuttle Co., 1971); James Murdoch, *A History of Japan,* 3 vols. (New York: Routledge, 1996); George B. Samson, *A History of Japan,* 3 vols. (Palo Alto, Calif.: Stanford University Press, 1958–63).

Japanese Civil War (1156)   *See* HOGEN WAR.

Japanese Civil War (1159–1160)   *See* HEIJI WAR.

Japanese Civil War (1180–1185)   *See* GEMPEI WAR.

Japanese Civil War (1221)   *See* JOKYU WAR.

Japanese Civil War   (1331–1333)

PRINCIPAL COMBATANTS: Hojo shogunate vs. Emperor Daigo II (subsequently aided by Hojo defectors)
PRINCIPAL THEATER(S): Japan, especially Kamakura
DECLARATION: None
MAJOR ISSUES AND OBJECTIVES: Control of Japanese government
OUTCOME: The shogunate forced the exile of the emperor; he returned, raised an army, and ended the power of the Hojo shogunate.

APPROXIMATE MAXIMUM NUMBER OF MEN UNDER ARMS: Unknown
CASUALTIES: Unknown
TREATIES: None

By the 14th century, Japanese government was sharply divided between the imperial court at Kyoto and the military, headquartered at the Bakufu in the Kamakura district. Although the emperor enjoyed high status, it was the Hojo shogunate—the military authority—that wielded the greater power. This situation—the emperor divine, yet with little secular power, the military all powerful—endured for a long while, but by the 14th century it began to show signs of eroding. In 1331, a crisis came when shogunate agents discovered that Emperor Daigo II (Go-Daigo; 1288–1339) was plotting to attack and destroy Kamakura. Once apprised of this, the shogunate acted quickly and dispatched an army to Kyoto, Daigo II offered resistance, but his forces were no match for those of the shogun. Quickly overwhelmed, he was taken prisoner, and he was exiled to the island of Oki the next year.

Doubtless because of his divine status, Daigo II escaped death, which was unfortunate for the shogunate, because, in 1333, he escaped from exile and rallied an army to the cause of his restoration. Warriors poured in, and at the Bakufu, many troops defected to the emperor. Ashikaga Takauji (1305–58), a general of the Minamoto family, long the chief supporters of the shogunate, turned his Bakufu army against the military and placed himself and his forces in the emperor's service. With another Bakufu defector, he launched an incendiary attack against Kamakura, burning the city down. This brought a sudden end to the rule of the Hojo shogunate—but it proved only a prelude to the JAPANESE CIVIL WARS (1336–1392).

Further reading: John W. Hall, *Japan: From Prehistory to Modern Times* (Tokyo: C. E. Tuttle Co., 1971); Jeffrey Mass, *Warrior Government in Early Medieval Japan* (New Haven, Conn.: Yale University Press, 1974); James Murdoch, *A History of Japan,* 3 vols. (New York: Routledge, 1996); George B. Samson, *A History of Japan,* 3 vols. (Palo Alto, Calif.: Stanford University Press, 1958–63).

Japanese Civil Wars   (1336–1392)

PRINCIPAL COMBATANTS: Yoshino-based government vs. Kyoto-based government (south versus north)
PRINCIPAL THEATER(S): All Japan
DECLARATION: None
MAJOR ISSUES AND OBJECTIVES: Control of Japan
OUTCOME: The struggle between northern and southern rivals brought utter chaos to Japan, nearly destroying the country's economy; with great patience, order was

restored by the ascendancy of the Ashikaga shogun Yoshimitsu.

APPROXIMATE MAXIMUM NUMBER OF MEN UNDER ARMS:
Unknown
CASUALTIES: Unknown
TREATIES: New treaties concluded with China and Korea by the 1390s

The Minamoto general Ashikaga Takauji (1305–58) had defected from the *bakufu,* or shogunate (military dictatorship), to aid Emperor Daigo II (Go-Daigo; 1288–1339) in overthrowing the Hojo-controlled regime and reestablishing Daigo on the imperial throne in the JAPANESE CIVIL WAR (1331–1333). In 1335, however, he changed sides again, their time against Daigo II, joining a new rebel movement in Kanto. These forces were opposed to both the Hojo shogunate and to the emperor. As commander of the rebel army, Ashikaga captured the Kyoto capital and took Daigo II prisoner. Although the ever-resourceful emperor subsequently escaped and took refuge in the mountains, Ashikaga Takauji set up a puppet on the throne, who compliantly named him shogun.

From exile, Daigo denounced Ashikaga Takauji and his puppet, and he rallied to himself the constituents of a rival court he set up in the south of Japan, at Yoshino. Now Kyoto and Yoshino became the poles around which a series of civil wars was generated. All of Japan erupted into combat, and the government was reduced to anarchy. The allegiances of the feudal lords shifted with the wind in a period dubbed the "Age of the Turncoats." In the absence of strong central authority, the countryside was torn by general lawlessness and rapine. It was the nadir of medieval Japanese life.

At last, in 1367, Yoshimitsu (1358–95), the most charismatic and able of the Ashikaga shoguns, emerged as dominant among the warlords. Gradually, he was able to reestablish a central government. He resumed trading relations with Korea and China in an effort to restore Japan's battered economy, and he launched numerous campaigns against pirates and other brigands. Having brought a significant measure of order back to the country, in 1392 he possessed sufficient credibility to persuade the ruler at Yoshino to abdicate in favor of the ruler at Kyoto. In return, the southern ruler was granted a large pension and official state status. Although low-level warfare and interclan feuding persisted, Japan generally began to recover.

Further reading: John W. Hall, *Japan; From Prehistory to Modern Times* (Tokyo: C. E. Tuttle Co., 1971); James Murdoch, *A History of Japan,* 3 vols. (New York: Routledge, 1996); George B. Samson, *A History of Japan,* 3 vols. (Palo Alto, Calif.: Stanford University Press, 1958–63); H. P. Varley, *Imperial Restoration in Medieval Japan* (New York: Columbia University Press, 1971).

Japanese Civil Wars (1450–1550)

PRINCIPAL COMBATANTS: Rival warlords (daimyo) of Japan
PRINCIPAL THEATER(S): All Japan
DECLARATION: None
MAJOR ISSUES AND OBJECTIVES: In a time of anarchy, rival warlords continually fought with one another to claim more territory and power.
OUTCOME: The war resolved no issue; it ended with the rise of the powerful daimyo Oda Nobunaga.
APPROXIMATE MAXIMUM NUMBER OF MEN UNDER ARMS:
Unknown
CASUALTIES: Unknown
TREATIES: None

The century between 1450 and 1550 is called in Japanese history the Warring States Period. During this time, civil war was continual, creating anarchy that spawned piracy and brigandage, as well as interclan feuding. Both of the traditional rivals for power, the imperial government and the shogunate (military dictatorship), lost control of the country. Rebels and warlords vied for pieces of territory, and the only semblance of stable government was to be found in and around the ancient imperial capital of Kyoto. Beyond this region, the force of government, whether imperial or shogunate, was hardly felt.

Amid the chaos, a new warrior class grew to prominence, the samurai. Instead of aligning themselves with either the shogunate or the emperor, the samurai gave their allegiance variously to local warlords, some of whom amassed sufficient power to become territorial rulers, or daimyo. Each daimyo created a private empire, wholly independent of central authority and maintained by means of a private army. Although chronic instability generally weakened the national economy, the existence of the private armies afforded the peasantry unprecedented opportunity for rising to power. Moreover, the samurai introduced their own rigid moral code, which probably represented what little order existed across the country during this long period. Nevertheless, with so many daimyo controlling so many private armies, strife was frequent. The daimyo continually warred against one another. These disputes often developed into interclan feuds. The spirit of war was so powerful in Japan during this period that rival Buddhist monasteries began feuding and warring with one another.

The Warring States Period came to an end with the rise of the powerful daimyo Oda Nobunaga (1534–82).

See also JAPANESE CIVIL WARS (1560–1584); MONKS, WAR OF THE; ONIN WAR.

Further reading: John W. Hall, *Japan: From Prehistory to Modern Times* (Tokyo: C. E. Tuttle Co., 1971); Thomas Keirstead, *The Geography of Power in Medieval Japan* (Princeton, N.J.: Princeton University Press,

1992); James Murdoch, *A History of Japan*, 3 vols. (New York: Routledge, 1996); George B. Samson, *A History of Japan*, 3 vols. (Palo Alto, Calif.: Stanford University Press, 1958–63).

Japanese Civil War (1467–1477) *See* ONIN WAR.

Japanese Civil Wars (1560–1584)

PRINCIPAL COMBATANTS: Oda Nobunaga vs. rival daimyo; after Nobunaga's death, the fight was taken over by his able general Toyotomi Hideyoshi
PRINCIPAL THEATER(S): Japan
DECLARATION: None
MAJOR ISSUES AND OBJECTIVES: The unification of Japan under a single ruler
OUTCOME: After a long war, most of Japan was effectively unified under Hideyoshi.
APPROXIMATE MAXIMUM NUMBER OF MEN UNDER ARMS: Probably the largest army fielded at any one time was the 30,000 men Hideyoshi led against Kyoto.
CASUALTIES: Unknown
TREATIES: Treaty between Hideyoshi and his potential chief rival, Tokugawa Iyeyasu, 1584

Out of the chaos of the JAPANESE CIVIL WARS (1450–1550), 16-year-old Oda Nobunaga (1534–82) emerged as daimyo (warlord) of Owari, eastern Japan. The head of the Imagawa family Imagawa Yoshimoto (1519–60), daimyo to the north of Owari, decided to exploit Oda Nobunaga's inexperience by attempting what he believed would be an easy conquest. Nobunaga led a defense with extraordinary skill and defeated Imagawa, who was slain in battle.

The attack moved Nobunaga to further action. He concluded an alliance with Tokugawa (1542–1616) the daimyo of Mikawa, and another alliance with the daimyo of Kari. These alliances secured his position in the east. Thus emboldened, Nobunaga decided to move aggressively and, in 1562, advanced against the province of Mino to the west. After a two-year campaign, the province fell to him. He moved next to the south and invaded Ise. Here he met powerful resistance and was never able to conquer the territory completely. But the performance of his leading general, Toyotomi Hideyoshi (1536–98), was so brilliant that most of the provincial daimyos flocked to Nobunaga's side.

Ogimachi (1517–93), the emperor himself, recognized Oda Nobunaga's great power and influence when, in 1567, he asked him to come to the imperial capital, Kyoto, to quell the violence of an uprising triggered by a dispute over the succession of the shogun (military

overlord). Within a year Nobunaga had brought order to Kyoto and was named vice shogun. He used this position as a springboard to what amounted to control of all Japan. However, his rapid rise met with resistance. Those who had formerly allied with him feared that he would become a tyrant, and they rebelled against him. Of all the daimyos, only Iyeyasu and a few minor daimyos remained loyal.

Nobunaga and his small coterie of allies fought the other daimyos between 1570 and 1573. Although he faced superior numbers, Nobunaga emerged victorious and, flushed with victory, advanced against Kwanto in the northeast. He conquered this province, then also took the territory between Kwanto and the outlying vicinity to Kyoto. With this region secured, Nobunaga turned next against the Buddhist monasteries in the hills of Hiyesia above Kyoto, for these had been centers of resistance against him. Toward the militant monks Nobunaga was ruthless, massacring them and destroying their settlements.

Nobunaga himself fell to an assassin in 1582, while he was marching to fight alongside Hideyoshi on the island of Shikoku. A vassal, Akechi (fl. 16th century), wounded Nobunaga, who subsequently committed suicide. Akechi then proclaimed himself shogun. In the meantime, Hideyoshi made peace with his rivals on Shikoku and returned quickly to Kyoto at the head of 30,000 men. He swiftly avenged the death of his great ally, then assumed the office of *kwampaku*, effectively regent. This incited jealousy among the heirs of the slain Oda Nobunaga, who now rebelled against Hideyoshi. The alliance fragmented, but Hideyoshi combined adroit diplomacy with brilliance at arms to put down the rebellion and reunite the daimyo. By 1584, he had become the chief ruler of Japan. To secure this position, Hideyoshi concluded a treaty with a potential rival, Iyeyasu, and, thanks to a generous and conciliatory policy toward his many former enemies, Hideyoshi succeeded in forging a genuine unified nation out of what had been a collection of feuding warlord territories.

See also MONKS, WAR OF THE.

Further reading: John W. Hall, *Japan: From Prehistory to Modern Times* (Tokyo: C. E. Tuttle Co., 1971); John W. Hall, Bagahari Keiji, and Kozo Yamamura, eds., *Japan Before Tokugawa: Political Consolidation and Economic Growth, 1500–1650* (Princeton, N.J.: Princeton University Press, 1981); James Murdoch, *A History of Japan*, 3 vols. (New York: Routledge, 1996); George B. Samson, *A History of Japan*, 3 vols. (Palo Alto, Calif.: Stanford University Press, 1958–63).

Japanese Civil War (1863–1868) *See* MEIJI RESTORATION.

Japanese Earlier Nine Years' War
(1051–1062)

PRINCIPAL COMBATANTS: Abe family vs. the governors of Mutsu and Dewa provinces as well as imperial-sanctioned troops led by Minamoto Yoriyoshi

PRINCIPAL THEATER(S): Northeastern Japan

DECLARATION: None

MAJOR ISSUES AND OBJECTIVES: Control of northeastern Japan and assertion of imperial control over the rebellious Abe clan

OUTCOME: After over a decade of struggle (of which only nine years was spent actually fighting), the Abe rebellion was suppressed.

APPROXIMATE MAXIMUM NUMBER OF MEN UNDER ARMS: Unknown

CASUALTIES: Unknown

TREATIES: None

The refusal of the Abe family, ruling clan of the portion of Mutsu Province bordering the Kitakami River in northeastern Japan, to pay taxes owed to the province created enmity with other clans and warlords. When the Abe then began to expand their holdings, the governors of Mutsu Province and Dewa, the neighboring province, pooled their resources and marched against the Abe's army. The Abe forces were victorious, however, and pushed the governors' armies into retreat.

News of the warfare in the provinces reached the emperor, Go-Reizei (1045–68), who dispatched an army under Minamoto Yoriyoshi (988–1075) and his son Yoshiie (1039–1106) to Mutsu to deal once and for all with the upstart Abes. At the first battle, in 1056, Abe Yoritoki (d. 1056), the patriarch of the clan, was fatally wounded by an arrow, but his son Sadato (1019–62) immediately assumed command of the army, which was able to continue the fight. Under Sadato, the Abe forces defeated Minamoto at Kawasaki in 1058. The timely commencement of a snowstorm provided concealment for a small fraction of the defeated army to escape. Only after a hiatus of four years was Minamoto able to recruit a new army, augmented by a contingent from the Kiyohara family (based in Dewa), to mount a fresh attack on the Abes.

One Abe army, under Yoritoki's second son, Abe Muneto, quickly folded, but Abe Sadato continued to resist. He was twice defeated, yet refused to capitulate. At last, the Minamoto forces overran his base in Kuriyagawa, his fort was set ablaze, and Sadato was killed. A triumphant Minamoto delivered his severed head to the emperor. More than a decade after it began, after nine years of actual fighting, the war was over.

See also JAPANESE LATER THREE YEARS' WAR.

Further reading: John W. Hall, *Japan: From Prehistory to Modern Times* (Tokyo: C. E. Tuttle Co., 1971); Jeffrey Mass, *Warrior Government in Early Medieval Japan* (New Haven, Conn.: Yale University Press, 1974); James Murdoch, *A History of Japan*, 3 vols. (New York: Routledge, 1996); George B. Samson, *A History of Japan*, 3 vols. (Palo Alto, Calif.: Stanford University Press, 1958–63).

Japanese Invasion of Korea (1592–1599)

PRINCIPAL COMBATANTS: Japan vs. Korea (with Chinese aid)

PRINCIPAL THEATER(S): Korea

DECLARATION: None

MAJOR ISSUES AND OBJECTIVES: Japan sought conquest of Korea.

OUTCOME: Korea was occupied for a time, but Japan's failure to gain control of the sea made its triumph only temporary; ultimately, the Japanese invaders withdrew from the country they had devastated.

APPROXIMATE MAXIMUM NUMBER OF MEN UNDER ARMS: Japan, 138,900 (plus 51,950 reserves); Korea, 70,000; China, 80,000

CASUALTIES: Unknown, but in the thousands

TREATIES: Truce of 1592; armistice of 1599

Toyotomi Hideyoshi (1536–98) emerged from the JAPANESE CIVIL WARS (1560–1584) as the leader of a unified Japan. Having achieved this titanic and seemingly impossible feat, he decided to move next on a great campaign of conquest to include Korea and China.

Hideyoshi assembled a vast army of 138,900 men, plus a reserve force of 51,950 more, to advance across the Straits of Tshushima and attack Pusan, principal port of southeast Korea. He would have to overcome the superb Korean navy, especially the fleet of Cholla Province, which included history's very first ironclad vessels, called "turtles." Driven by galley oars, they carried mounted iron rams as well as at least two cannon each. Archers on board were armed with incendiary arrows. Although the Japanese would later be known as a seafaring people, this was not the case in the late 16th century. Thus Korean admiral Yi Sun Sin (fl. late 16th century), with 45 formidable ships, won the first battle of the invasion, destroying 26 of 50 Japanese ships on May 7, 1592. Eighteen more Japanese vessels were sunk the next day.

Despite Yi's magnificent victories, a Japanese force was able to land at Pusan on May 24. A 5,000-man vanguard assaulted Pusan Castle, which was defended by about 10,000 Koreans; however, whereas the Japanese were armed with modern muskets, the Koreans had nothing but lances and bows. The castle fell, and the Japanese invaders reportedly collected the heads of 8,000 garrison members.

On May 25, 10,000 Japanese defeated 20,000 Koreans at Tong-Nae Castle, with the loss of 5,000 of the defenders and only 100 Japanese (plus 400 wounded). Following this, the Japanese began deploying their main forces; 39,500 men were sent in two columns to attack Seoul. They were met by a 70,000-man Korean army at Chung-Ju on June 7, but the outnumbered Japanese managed a flank attack, which killed some 3,000 Koreans and forced the surrender of the rest. Some 11,000 Japanese advanced northward to the city of Pyongyang. Here they encountered 5,000 Chinese, whom they swept aside on October 3, killing at least 3,000.

The Chinese disaster at Pyongyang prompted the Ming government to order full-scale intervention in Korea. Li Ju-Sung (fl. 16th century) led 51,000 Chinese against the Japanese. However, on February 25, 1593, the Chinese cavalry became mired in the mud at Pyokcheg-wan and were exposed to furious Japanese swordsmen. At this place, perhaps 70,000 Chinese and Korean troops faced 40,000 Japanese. At least 10,000 Chinese and Koreans fell before withdrawing.

Despite the overwhelming success of the Japanese on land, Admiral Yi gained mastery of the sea, virtually destroying the Japanese navy in the course of several battles. Hideyoshi, realizing that his army, however victorious, was now cut off for lack of ships, agreed to a cease-fire. During this period, from 1593 to 1596, negotiations ground on without result. At last, in March 1597, Hideyoshi resumed the war, deploying a new invasion of some 149,000 men in 500 ships. Admiral Yi was not present when the Japanese vessels surprised the Korean fleet in a night attack on July 16, 1597. Of 180 Korean ships, only 12 escaped destruction. The Japanese not only failed to rescue drowning crews, they beheaded the survivors they encountered.

A landing force swept ashore, took the fortress of Nam-won, and collected 3,726 Chinese heads. At this juncture, Admiral Yi returned to command, and with 12 capital ships he managed to force the Japanese fleet into the narrow waters of the Myongyang Strait. On September 16, 1597, he attacked and destroyed the Japanese flagship, then displayed the severed head of Admiral Kurushima Michifusa (d. 1597) on a Korean mast. The sight so demoralized the rest of the Japanese fleet that they fled in panic, crashing into a chain the Koreans had laid across the strait. More than 100 Japanese vessels foundered and were lost.

Yi's victory at sea halted the Japanese land advance 17 miles outside of Seoul. A Chinese army of 80,000 attacked the Japanese camp at Uru-san in January 1598. The Japanese held out until the arrival of Chinese reinforcements persuaded Hideyoshi to evacuate the Korean Peninsula.

Further reading: John W. Hall, *Japan: From Prehistory to Modern Times* (Tokyo: C. E. Tuttle Co., 1971); Mikiso Hane, *Modern Japan: A Historical Survey,* 3rd ed. (Boulder, Colo.: Westview Press, 2001); James Murdoch, *A History of Japan,* 3 vols. (New York: Routledge, 1996); George B. Samson, *A History of Japan,* 3 vols. (Palo Alto, Calif.: Stanford University Press, 1958–63); Conrad Totman, *Early Modern Japan* (Berkeley: University of California Press, 1993).

Japanese Later Three Years' War
(1083–1087)

PRINCIPAL COMBATANTS: Kiyowara clan vs. Mutsu Province (with aid from Fujiwara clan)
PRINCIPAL THEATER(S): Northern Japan
DECLARATION: None
MAJOR ISSUES AND OBJECTIVES: The provincial governor of Mutsu sought to suppress the perpetually warring Kiyowara clan.
OUTCOME: The Kiyowara were defeated and stability restored to Mutsu.
APPROXIMATE MAXIMUM NUMBER OF MEN UNDER ARMS: Unknown
CASUALTIES: Unknown
TREATIES: None

The ruling clan of Mutsu Province in northern Japan, the Kiyowara, splintered into various branches and factions, which habitually quarreled. Often, the fighting was violent, causing great hardship in the province. Minamoto Yoshiie (1039–1106), the provincial governor, repeatedly tried to quell the violence but ultimately decided that his military intervention was called for. In 1086, he led an assault on a winter fort harboring Iyehira and his Kiyowara faction. Minamoto Yoshiie laid a siege, but it failed as many of his men succumbed to the hardships of a harsh northern winter. Calling his men into retreat, Yoshiie regrouped and reinforced his army with troops from his younger brother and from the Fujiwara family, rivals to Kiyowara. The united forces chose a new target, the great Kiyowara fortress at Kanazawa. The defenders capitulated after an arduous four-month siege. However, the Kiyowara leaders made a break for it and were promptly killed. The war is called the "Three Years' War" because, although the period of hostility spanned a full four years, the actual fighting occupied only in three.

See also JAPANESE EARLIER NINE YEARS' WAR.

Further reading: John W. Hall, *Japan: From Prehistory to Modern Times* (Tokyo: C. E. Tuttle Co., 1971); Jeffrey Mass, *Warrior Government in Early Medieval Japan* (New Haven, Conn.: Yale University Press, 1974); James Murdoch, *A History of Japan,* 3 vols. (New York: Routledge, 1996); George B. Samson, *A History of Japan,* 3 vols. (Palo Alto, Calif.: Stanford University Press, 1958–63).

Javanese-Chinese-Dutch War (1740–1743)

PRINCIPAL COMBATANTS: Dutch East India Company vs. Chinese on Java; some Javanese sided with the Chinese, some with the Dutch
PRINCIPAL THEATER(S): Java
DECLARATION: None
MAJOR ISSUES AND OBJECTIVES: Dutch East India Company deportations of Chinese on Java incited a rebellion against the Dutch.
OUTCOME: The rebellion was put down and peace was restored between the Dutch and Chinese on Java.
APPROXIMATE MAXIMUM NUMBER OF MEN UNDER ARMS: Totals unknown, but in 1741, the Dutch post at Semarang was besieged by 23,500 Chinese and Javanese rebels.
CASUALTIES: About 10,000, on all sides died.
TREATIES: None

Chinese trade with Java was a long-established fact centuries before the Dutch entered the Javanese trade under the auspices of the Dutch East India Company. Chinese traders became integrated into the Dutch-Javanese trade after the Dutch East India Company established its headquarters at Batavia (Djakarta). The Chinese population in Batavia and vicinity grew, so that, by the mid-18th century, it greatly outnumbered Dutch residents. Dutch colonial administrators feared that the Chinese, many of whom were impoverished and unemployed, would rise in rebellion. To forestall this, officials began deporting Chinese to Ceylon (Sri Lanka) and the Cape of Good Hope (Cape Town, South Africa). This action served only to incite an uprising. In 1740, the Chinese of Batavia rebelled and, initially, were mowed down by well-armed Dutch East India Company military forces. However, Javanese dissidents, who had long resented the Dutch imperial presence, joined the Chinese cause, and the rebellion soon spread beyond Batavia to engulf all of Java. In 1741, the Dutch post at Semarang withstood a siege by 23,500 Chinese and Javanese rebels.

The impact on the Dutch was both military and economic, as the sugar industry came to a standstill. There was a real question as to whether the Javanese royal government, in the person of King Pakubuwono II (d. 1743), ruler of Mataram, would back the Chinese or the Dutch. At first, he sided with the Chinese, participating in the slaughter of the Dutch garrison at Kartosuro, but, realizing that the Dutch had far more resources than the Chinese, he changed allegiance and allied himself with the Dutch. In 1743, Pakubuwono ceded to the Dutch the northern coastal region of Java, which effectively hemmed in the Chinese. With this, the rebellion ended—as did the deportations. The war had reduced the Chinese population, but those who remained functioned peacefully as participants in the Javanese-Dutch trade.

See also JAVANESE WAR OF SUCCESSION, FIRST; JAVANESE WAR OF SUCCESSION, SECOND; JAVANESE WAR OF SUCCESSION, THIRD.
Further reading: Lucas Wilhemus Nagtegaal, *Riding the Tiger: The Dutch East Indies Company and the Northeast Coast of Java, 1680–1743* (Leiden, Netherlands: KITLV Press, 1996); Y. Stamford Raffles, *The History of Java* (New York: Oxford University Press, 1985).

Javanese Invasion of Malacca (1574)

PRINCIPAL COMBATANTS: Javanese Muslims vs. Portuguese colonial forces
PRINCIPAL THEATER(S): Malacca
DECLARATION: None
MAJOR ISSUES AND OBJECTIVES: The Javanese Muslims sought to drive the Christian Portuguese from the region.
OUTCOME: The Portuguese drove off the attack.
APPROXIMATE MAXIMUM NUMBER OF MEN UNDER ARMS: Unknown
CASUALTIES: Unknown
TREATIES: None

In 1574, Muslim raiders from Java attacked Portuguese-held Malacca in an attempt to eject Christians from the region. Portuguese reinforcements were summoned from Goa in sufficient force to drive the raiders off.
Further reading: Y. Stamford Raffles, *The History of Java* (New York: Oxford University Press, 1985).

Javanese War of Succession, First (1704–1707)

PRINCIPAL COMBATANTS: Javanese rebels vs. Dutch East India Company
PRINCIPAL THEATER(S): Java
DECLARATION: None
MAJOR ISSUES AND OBJECTIVES: Javanese rebels sought independence from Dutch domination.
OUTCOME: The rebellion was crushed.
APPROXIMATE MAXIMUM NUMBER OF MEN UNDER ARMS: Unknown
CASUALTIES: Unknown
TREATIES: None

The Dutch East India Company was founded in 1602 and, in the course of the century, became a major economic and political power in Java, dominating the chief coastal city of Batavia (Djakarta) and often intruding itself into the affairs of local kings and sultans, as well as rulers throughout the East Indies (the Malay archipelago). This incited several uprisings against the Dutch presence in the region. In turn, that presence destabilized Javanese government and issues of succession. The Dutch frequently took advantage of this instability to gain a stronger hold on Java.

In 1704, Surapati (d. 1707), a fugitive Balinese slave, rallied a band of natives against Dutch traders. Dutch East India Company forces attempted to capture him, which drove Surapati to seek refuge from King Amangkurat III (fl. 1703–08) of Mataram, the key central Javanese kingdom. Amangkurat harbored Surapati for a time, and then the former slave moved to northeastern Java, where he declared himself a king. In the meantime, the Dutch sought vengeance against Amangkurat for having sheltered the fugitive troublemaker, and they sponsored a rival to the throne, Pakubuwono I (d. 1719), Amangkurat's uncle. His followers united with Dutch East India Company troops to defeat Amangkurat in battle. The deposed king fled to the northeast, where he now sought refuge with Surapati.

But the Dutch were not through. They relentlessly pursued Amangkurat and ran him to ground in the northeast, along with Surapati. The fugitive slave was executed in 1708, and Amangkurat was exiled to Ceylon (Sri Lanka).

See also JAVANESE WAR OF SUCCESSION, SECOND; JAVANESE WAR OF SUCCESSION, THIRD.

Further reading: Lucas Wilhemus Nagtegaal, *Riding the Tiger: The Dutch East Indies Company and the Northeast Coast of Java, 1680–1743* (Leiden, Netherlands: KITLV Press, 1996); Y. Stamford Raffles, *The History of Java* (New York: Oxford University Press, 1985).

Javanese War of Succession, Second
(1719–1723)

PRINCIPAL COMBATANTS: Dutch East India Company vs. Javanese leaders hostile to the company
PRINCIPAL THEATER(S): Java
DECLARATION: None
MAJOR ISSUES AND OBJECTIVES: The Dutch East India Company sought to ensure a friendly government in Java.
OUTCOME: Rivals were killed or exiled, and the company expanded its influence and control throughout most of Java.
APPROXIMATE MAXIMUM NUMBER OF MEN UNDER ARMS: The Dutch employed more than 1,000 men on Java; Javanese numbers unknown
CASUALTIES: Unknown, but described as massive by historians
TREATIES: None

In the First JAVANESE WAR OF SUCCESSION, from 1704 to 1707, the forces of the Dutch East India Company had

placed on the throne of Mataram, most important of the Javanese kingdoms, King Pakubuwono I (d. 1719), who was compliant with the company's wishes. His death in 1719 brought a number of claimants to succession. The Dutch allied themselves to whatever they perceived as the winning side, then were determined to eliminate all rivals hostile to their presence and commercial prosperity. Accordingly, they conducted a campaign to find and kill or exile all potential rivals for power. In the course of this campaign, the Dutch East India Company expanded its control of Java.

See also JAVANESE WAR OF SUCCESSION, THIRD.

Further reading: Lucas Wilhemus Nagtegaal, *Riding the Tiger: The Dutch East Indies Company and the Northeast Coast of Java, 1680–1743* (Leiden, Netherlands: KITLV Press, 1996); Y. Stamford Raffles, *The History of Java* (New York: Oxford University Press, 1985).

Javanese War of Succession, Third
(1746–1757)

PRINCIPAL COMBATANTS: Dutch East India Company vs. rivals to King Pakubuwono III
PRINCIPAL THEATER(S): Mataram, Java
DECLARATION: None
MAJOR ISSUES AND OBJECTIVES: The Dutch helped their puppet, Pakubuwono III, resist challenges by two rival claimants to the throne of Mataram.
OUTCOME: The kingdom was partitioned to satisfy all claimants to the throne.
APPROXIMATE MAXIMUM NUMBER OF MEN UNDER ARMS: Dutch numbers unknown; rebel forces, 13,000
CASUALTIES: Unknown
TREATIES: Gianti Agreement, 1755

Through the First JAVANESE WAR OF SUCCESSION, from 1704 to 1707, the Second JAVANESE WAR OF SUCCESSION, from 1719 to 1723, and the JAVANESE-CHINESE-DUTCH WAR, from 1740 to 1743, the central Javanese kingdom of Mataram had become a client or vassal realm of the Dutch East India Company, which supported rulers friendly to it and suppressed those who dared to oppose it. When King Pakubuwono III (fl. 1743–57) was assailed by rivals to the throne, mainly Mangkubumi (1717–92) in 1746, the company sided with the compliant king. War became chronic, and by 1747, the Dutch faced some 13,000 rebels. In 1751, the Dutch suffered a serious setback in a battle at the Bogowonto River. At last, in 1755, by the Gianti Agreement, the company agreed to allow the partition of Mataram. Pakubuwono continued to rule in the east, from his capital Surakarta, and Mangkubumi took over the western portion of the kingdom, ruling from Jogjakarta. This left sporadic guerrilla warfare raging against the Dutch through 1757 in the east. However, the Dutch bided their time, understanding that warfare among the Javanese ultimately strengthened their position as a colonial power.

Further reading: Lucas Wilhemus Nagtegaal, *Riding the Tiger: The Dutch East Indies Company and the Northeast Coast of Java, 1680–1743* (Leiden, Netherlands: KITLV Press, 1996); Y. Stamford Raffles, *The History of Java* (New York: Oxford University Press, 1985).

Java Revolt   (1849)

PRINCIPAL COMBATANTS: Javanese vs. Netherlands Indies forces
PRINCIPAL THEATER(S): Java
DECLARATION: None
MAJOR ISSUES AND OBJECTIVES: Suppression of anticolonial rebellion in Java
OUTCOME: Java came under the full control of the Dutch.
APPROXIMATE MAXIMUM NUMBER OF MEN UNDER ARMS: Unknown
CASUALTIES: Unknown
TREATIES: None

The Dutch East India Company was granted virtual sovereignty over Java by the government of the Netherlands during the 17th century. Relations between the Javanese natives and the Dutch were often strained and violent during the centuries of colonial occupation. In 1849, a major revolt developed, to which the colonial authorities responded by sending a major Netherlands Indies military force to Bali in April. The Javanese military leader Gusti Ketut Jilantik was killed in a clash with these forces, and the Netherlands colonial government assumed control of Buleleng and the north coast of Bali.

In May, the Netherlands Indies forces advanced into southern Bali for the first time. They marched through Karangasem and Klungkung and put down resistance in these places. Forces under the raja of Lombok, allied to the Dutch, attacked and took Karangasem while the Netherlands Indies forces assumed full control in Palembang. By 1850, Dutch missionaries were beginning their work among Bataks of north Sumatra, and a great famine in central Java ended all hope of renewed resistance. The Dutch further consolidated their hold on Java in 1850 by purchasing the remaining Portuguese posts on Flores.

Further reading: C. A. Bayly and D. H. A. Kolff, eds., *Two Colonial Empires: Comparative Essays on the History of India and Indonesia in the Nineteenth Century* (Norwell, Mass.: Kluwer Academic Pub., 1986); George Musselman, *The Cradle of Colonialism* (New Haven, Conn.: Yale University Press, 1963); Y. Stamford Raffles, *The History of Java* (New York: Oxford University Press, 1985).

Java War, Great   (1815–1830)

PRINCIPAL COMBATANTS: Dutch East India Company forces vs. Javanese guerrillas led by Dipo Negoro
PRINCIPAL THEATER(S): Java
DECLARATION: Jihad proclaimed, 1815
MAJOR ISSUES AND OBJECTIVES: Dipo Negoro's rebels wanted to suppress Dutch economic and political domination of Java.
OUTCOME: The rebels were ultimately defeated, at great cost, but the Dutch did liberalize administration of Java.
APPROXIMATE MAXIMUM NUMBER OF MEN UNDER ARMS: Dutch forces, 100,000
CASUALTIES: Dutch losses may have been as high as 15,000 killed; Javanese losses, 200,000, including 20,000 battlefield deaths
TREATIES: None

The war is sometimes referred to as Dipo Negoro's War, after Prince Dipo Negoro (c. 1785–1855), the disgruntled eldest son of the king of Jogjakarta, who was passed over for succession to the throne when the Dutch East India Company, under Governor Johannes Bosch (fl. early 19th century), supported a younger and more compliant rival. Dipo Negoro recruited support for his war against the Dutch by appealing to indigenous Muslim property owners, who had lost land to Dutch policies of land reform and redistribution. Dipo Negoro further bolstered his cause by transforming it into a jihad, a Muslim holy war against the infidel Dutch. This cause came to the fore after the Dutch built a road beside a sacred tomb, an act of sacrilege. It united Muslim aristocrats and common folk alike.

Dipo Negoro led a low-level guerrilla war against the Dutch from 1815 to 1828, when the Dutch at last managed to force a major battle in the open. Better equipped than the prince's forces, the Dutch scored a significant victory, which gained them the momentum needed to support a major effort. The Dutch government financed the building of stronghold forts throughout the region, linked by good roads. Now forces could be concentrated quickly anywhere resistance was met. Although costly to maintain, the fortress network ended Dipo Negoro's effectiveness. In 1829, two of his chief lieutenants surrendered, and on March 28, 1830, the prince himself offered to negotiate. When he drew the line at relinquishing his title of protector of Islam, Dutch authorities violated their pledge of safe conduct, arrested Dipo Negoro, and exiled him to the Celebes. From the Javanese point of view, the war had not been fought entirely in vain, however. Having experienced heavy losses and having been forced to invest expensively in defense, the Dutch now deemed it prudent to bend in their administration of Java, and fairer economic and political policies were instituted.

See also ANGLO-DUTCH WAR IN JAVA; JAVANESE WAR OF SUCCESSION, SECOND; PADRI WAR.

Further reading: C. A. Bayly and D. H. A. Kolff, eds., *Two Colonial Empires: Comparative Essays on the History of India and Indonesia in the Nineteenth Century* (Norwell, Mass.: Kluwer Academic Pub., 1986); George Musselman, *The Cradle of Colonialism* (New Haven, Conn.: Yale University Press, 1963); Y. Stamford Raffles, *The History of Java* (New York: Oxford University Press, 1985).

Jenkins' Ear, War of (1739–c. 1743)

PRINCIPAL COMBATANTS: England and the English colony of Georgia vs. Spain and the Spanish colony of Florida
PRINCIPAL THEATER(S): Georgia and Florida
DECLARATION: Great Britain declared war on Spain, October 19, 1739.
MAJOR ISSUES AND OBJECTIVES: British outrage over an assault on a merchant captain by Spanish authorities seeking to regulate trade with Spanish colonies, set against European conflicts and alliances
OUTCOME: Inconclusive, an event in the War of the Austrian Succession (1740–48)
APPROXIMATE MAXIMUM NUMBER OF MEN UNDER ARMS: In Florida, Oglethorpe commanded 1,300 regulars and militia plus 500 Indian allies; Spanish forces, 1,100
CASUALTIES: At St. Augustine, Oglethorpe lost 122 men killed, 50 wounded, 20 captured; Spanish losses, 200 killed, wounded or captured
TREATIES: No treaty, one of a series of actions of the War of the Austrian Succession

As with KING WILLIAM'S WAR and QUEEN ANNE'S WAR, the causes of KING GEORGE'S WAR were rooted in European alliances and conflicts that profoundly affected the farthest-flung colonies of empire. The War of Jenkins' Ear was a kind of overture to King George's War, as the American theater of the War of the AUSTRIAN SUCCESSION was called. At the conclusion of Queen Anne's War (the European phase of which was the War of the SPANISH SUCCESSION) in 1713, Great Britain concluded a treaty with France's ally Spain. It included a provision called the "Asiento," a contract that permitted and regulated English trade in slavery and goods with the Spanish colonies.

English traders were quick to violate the regulatory provisions of the Asiento, thereby provoking Spanish officials to deal harshly with British merchant sailors in the West Indies. Robert Jenkins (fl. 1730s), captain of the merchant ship *Rebecca,* claimed that Spanish coast guards had cut off his ear while interrogating him. When word of this—and other incidents—reached Great Britain, outrage ignited open hostilities.

On October 19, 1739, Great Britain declared war on Spain, and in January 1740, James Oglethorpe (1696–1785), the principal founder of the English colony of Georgia, invaded Spanish-held Florida. Spanish abuses of the Creek, Cherokee, and Chickasaw Indians in the region sent them into the English camp, and, with their aid, Oglethorpe captured Fort San Francisco de Pupo and Fort Picolata, both on the San Juan River. He next laid siege to Saint Augustine from May through July but was forced to break off at the approach of Spanish relief forces. Oglethorpe repelled a Spanish counterattack on Saint Simon's Island, Georgia, in the Battle of Bloody Marsh, June 9, 1742, but the Georgians' second attempt to capture Saint Augustine, in 1743, also failed. Oglethorpe then withdrew from Florida.

The War of Jenkins' Ear did not formally end but was swallowed up in the much larger conflict over the Austrian succession fought in Europe.

Further reading: Phinizy Spalding, *Oglethorpe in America* (Chicago: University of Chicago Press, 1977); Philip Woodfine, *Britannia's Glories: The Walpole Ministry and the 1739 War with Spain* (Rochester, N.Y.: Boydell and Brewer, 1998).

Jericho, Fall of (c. 8000 B.C.E.)

PRINCIPAL COMBATANTS: Israelites vs. Canaanites
PRINCIPAL THEATER(S): Canaan
DECLARATION: None
MAJOR ISSUES AND OBJECTIVES: Conquest of Canaan
OUTCOME: Jericho fell, thereby opening the way for the Israelite conquest of all Canaan.
APPROXIMATE MAXIMUM NUMBER OF MEN UNDER ARMS: Unknown
CASUALTIES: Unknown; according to the Old Testament, Jericho was virtually annihilated.
TREATIES: None

According to the Book of Joshua (Old Testament), Joshua became leader of the Israelite tribes after the death of Moses. Under Joshua, the Israelites conquered Canaan, and it was Joshua who distributed Canaan's lands to the 12 tribes of Israel.

Joshua was apparently a very able military leader, who sent spies into Canaan to assess the Canaanites' morale. Based on this intelligence, Joshua led the Israelites in an invasion across the Jordan River. The first obstacle to be overcome was the walled city of Jericho, which, even then, was one of the oldest known cities, having been established at least as early as 9000 B.C.E. Joshua's forces breached the walls of Jericho and took the city. This accomplished, the Israelites were able to capture other towns in the north and south until most of Palestine was brought under Israelite control.

As far as can be determined, following its destruction by the Israelites, Jericho was abandoned until Hiel the

Bethelite established himself there in the ninth century B.C.E. (as recorded in 1 Kings 16:34).

Further reading: David Neev, *The Destruction of Sodom, Gomorrah, and Jericho: Geological, Climatological, and Archaeological Background* (New York: Oxford University Press, 1995).

Jewish-Philistine Wars (1028–c. 1000 B.C.E.)

PRINCIPAL COMBATANTS: Israel vs. the Philistines
PRINCIPAL THEATER(S): Israel
DECLARATION: None
MAJOR ISSUES AND OBJECTIVES: Israel sought to drive out the Philistine oppressors and overlords.
OUTCOME: Under King Saul, Israel enjoyed limited but significant success against the Philistines; under King David, the Philistines were entirely neutralized.
APPROXIMATE MAXIMUM NUMBER OF MEN UNDER ARMS: Unknown
CASUALTIES: Unknown
TREATIES: Unknown

Between 1080 and 1028 B.C.E., the Philistines rose, invaded, and came to dominate the territories of Israel. Under the reign of King Saul (fl. c. 1021–1000 B.C.E.), the Jews rebelled against their Philistine overlords. Saul had significant success against the Philistines; however, internal struggles and factionalism within Israel ultimately impeded the struggle, and Saul was never able to drive the Philistines completely out of Israel. Saul was killed at the important Battle of Mount Gilboa.

David (d. c. 962 B.C.E.) succeeded to the throne vacated on the death of Saul, and from 1010 to about 1000 B.C.E., he succeeded in neutralizing the Philistine threat. He did this by three means: prowess at arms, an ability to unite the always fractious Israelites, and the diplomatic daring to recruit soldiers from among the very Philistines he had defeated. This last step co-opted Philistine resistance and also provided Israel with an army to combat other external threats and to expand the kingdom.

Further reading: Neal Bierling, *Philistines: Giving Goliath His Due* (Warren Center, Pa.: Shangri-La Publications, 2002); Trude Krakauer Dothan and M. Dothan, *People of the Sea: The Search for the Philistines* (New York: Macmillan, 1992); Carl S. Ehrlich, *The Philistia in Transition, A History from ca. 1000–730 BCE* (Boston: Brill Academic, 1996).

Jewish Revolt (168–143 B.C.E.) *See* MACCABEES, REVOLT OF THE.

Jewish Revolt (66–73)

PRINCIPAL COMBATANTS: Palestine vs. Rome
PRINCIPAL THEATER(S): Jerusalem and the deserts of Palestine
DECLARATION: None
MAJOR ISSUES AND OBJECTIVES: A band of Jewish rebels sought to expel the Romans from Palestine.
OUTCOME: After much effort, the rebellion was crushed.
APPROXIMATE MAXIMUM NUMBER OF MEN UNDER ARMS: Unknown
CASUALTIES: 3,600 Jerusalemites killed
TREATIES: None

Cestius Gallus (fl. first century), the governor of first-century Rome's Middle Eastern possessions, was a rash and inept administrator, easily antagonized by a band of Jewish zealots bent on expelling the Romans from Palestine. An explosive situation soon developed. It took only the additional ineptitude of Judea's Roman procurator, Gessius Florus (fl. first century), to light the fuse. As the result of a dispute in Caesarea, the capital of Judea, Florus imposed a heavy fine on the Temple at Jerusalem. When the Jews refused to pay the fine, Gessius Florus met with a Jewish delegation in Jerusalem. The Jews protested the procurator's looting of the land, whereupon Florus brought the meeting to an end by ordering the deaths of 3,600 Jerusalemites. Instead of cowering in fear, the Jews revolted against the Romans. The rebellion spread rapidly through Palestine as zealots took a series of Roman frontier fortresses, most notably Masada, in 66.

In response to the spreading conflict, Gallus led troops to Jerusalem, where he attacked the temple, but was beaten back. Retreating through the Jerusalem suburb of Bezetha, he lost 6,000 men, equipment, and a siege train to Jewish forces. News of the loss outraged the Roman emperor Nero (37–68), who dispatched an army under Titus Flavius Vespasian (9–79) to crush the revolt.

Vespasian was an able professional commander. He began his campaign systematically, in Galilee, where he laid siege to Jotapata, an important Jewish-held Galilean fortress. After a 47-day siege, Jotapata fell, and its commander, Joseph Ben Matthias (37–c. 95), became a Roman prisoner. Changing his name to Flavius Josephus, he wrote *The Jewish War,* an extraordinary eyewitness account of the rebellion.

After the fall of Jotapata, Vespasian sought an early end to the bloodshed through a peace conference but was rebuffed. His forces were met in battle at Tiberias, Gischala, and the fortress Gamala. Victorious in each, his troops laid waste to many rebel cities as they inexorably advanced on Jerusalem in 68. That city was already beset by civil strife; for the zealots had slaughtered not only Roman residents but many of the Jews who supported them. However, Jerusalem was given a reprieve when Vespasian, who would become emperor, was obliged to withdraw from the field of battle and return to Rome following the murder of Nero.

Vespasian turned over command of the army to his son Titus (c. 40–81), who arrived from Rome and immediately carried out the siege of Jerusalem in the spring of 70. The city presented a formidable objective because it was enclosed by great walls. Titus breached the outer wall in the north and the west, then, using assault towers, his troops went to work on the inner wall. The city's defenders sent Titus a surrender offer, and the general called a halt to the siege. But it was only a ruse to buy time for the Jewish troops to withdraw into the upper city and the temple areas. Titus resumed the siege, broke through the inner wall, and invaded the city, only to find the immediate area deserted. Deciding that it would be costly to fight it out, Titus instead erected a siege wall around Jerusalem to starve out its defenders. Although a few Jews surrendered, the majority fought on with a fierceness born of desperation. Relentlessly, Titus took increasing numbers of captives, whom he crucified, sometimes 500 at a time, all in full sight of the remaining defenders.

Titus next moved against the Antonia fortress, which defended the temple. Day and night he battered the fortress with rams until it crumbled. At this, the zealots hunkered down in the fortified temple itself. To breach it, the Romans set fire to the gates, unintentionally igniting the entire temple. Once it fell to the Romans, soldiers looted its treasure.

The Jews were still in possession of the Upper City. Titus opened negotiations, but these soon broke down, whereupon the general ordered the burning of the lower city. He next attacked and breached the walls of the upper city. There he found no one left to fight—only the bodies of those who had died in the siege. Putting the rest of Jerusalem to the torch, the Romans took additional prisoners, whom they crucified or enslaved.

In the meantime, Roman forces marched through the desert to root out the rebels hidden in far-flung fortresses. The fortress at Herodium fell quickly. The fortress at Machaerus surrendered after the capture of its leader in 71. But Masada, taken back in 66, resisted capture. Its position was virtually unassailable, perched on a mountaintop 1,400 feet above the level of the Dead Sea and fitted out with two palaces and formidable fortifications, which had been built by Judea's king, Herod the Great (73–4 B.C.E.).

Masada was besieged in 72 (see MASADA, SIEGE OF). Defended by fewer than 1,000 men, led by Eleazar ben Yahir, women, and children against a Roman legion consisting of some 15,000 men, the fortress held out for almost two years. The Romans dug a siege wall, set up eight camps, and erected a massive ramp for a siege tower and battering ram. Yet they managed to make only a single breach in Masada's stone wall, which was readily repaired with a wall of wood and earth. The Romans, however, set fire to the wooden wall and finally entered Masada, where they were stunned to find just two women and five children, holed up in a cave, still alive. When the situation was hopeless, the zealots had chosen mass suicide rather than capture and enslavement.

Further reading: Rupert Furneaux, *The Roman Siege of Jerusalem* (New York: D. McKay Co., 1972); Flavius Josephus, *The Jewish War,* in *Complete Works,* trans. William Whitson (Nashville: Nelson Reference and Electronic, 2003); Mikhah Livneh, *The Last Fortress: The Study of Masada and Its People* (Tel Aviv: Ministry of Defense, 1989); John W. Welch, *Masada and the World of the New Testament* (Provo, Utah: Brigham Young University Press, 1997); Yigael Yadin, *Masada: Herod's Fortress and the Zealots' Last Stand* (New York: Random House, 1966).

Jewish Revolt (115–117)

PRINCIPAL COMBATANTS: Jewish rebels vs. Roman imperial forces

PRINCIPAL THEATER(S): Primarily the Roman province of Cyrenaica; also Egypt, Cyprus, Asia Minor, Judea, and Mesopotamia

DECLARATION: None

MAJOR ISSUES AND OBJECTIVES: The Jews sought relief from Roman repression.

OUTCOME: Despite isolated Jewish victories, the rebellion was ruthlessly crushed.

APPROXIMATE MAXIMUM NUMBER OF MEN UNDER ARMS: Unknown

CASUALTIES: Unknown

TREATIES: None

The revolt began in the Roman province of Cyrenaica (eastern Libya), which was populated in large part by Greeks and Jews. The Jews, who had long felt themselves oppressed by the Greeks, now rebelled against the even more oppressive Romans. Zealots instigated a revolt in the city of Cyrene in 115 under the leadership of one Lukuas or Andreas (fl. second century). After Roman citizens were slain and buildings destroyed, the Roman emperor Trajan (53–117) dispatched forces to crush the rebellion and punish the Jews.

In the meantime, the revolt spread to Jews in Egypt, Cyprus, Asia Minor, Judea, and Mesopotamia. In each place, the Romans soon regained control. In Alexandria, the Jewish rebels enjoyed a measure of triumph, especially in the areas outside the city. In the Cypriot city of Salamis, Jewish rebels massacred all non-Jews and then sacked the city. Yet by 117, the rebellion was well under control—although sporadic outbreaks continued beyond the reign of Trajan, and the prevailing spirit of rebellion and defiance prompted subsequent Roman emperors to appoint repressive governors throughout the region.

See also JEWISH REVOLT (66–73).

Further reading: A. Hayim Ben-Sasson and Haum H. Ben-Sasson, *History of the Jewish People* (Cambridge, Mass.: Harvard University Press, 1985); Paul M. Johnson, *A History of the Jews* (New York: HarperCollins, 1988); Max L. Margolis and Alexander Marx, *A History of the Jewish People* (New York: Simon and Schuster, 1972).

Jewish Revolt (132–135) *See* BAR COCHEBA'S REVOLT.

Jin Invasion of South China *See* JUCHEN MONGOL INVASION OF THE SONG EMPIRE.

Johnson County War (1892)

PRINCIPAL COMBATANTS: Small ranchers and cowboys of Johnson County, Wyoming, vs. the cattle barons of the Wyoming Stock Growers' Association
PRINCIPAL THEATER(S): Johnson County, Wyoming
DECLARATION: None
MAJOR ISSUES AND OBJECTIVES: Cattle barons blamed an outbreak of rustling on their former cowhands and other small ranchers, and when the courts refused to act, they took matters into their own hands.
OUTCOME: Inconclusive; no one was convicted of rustling, but neither were others convicted of vigilantism and murder; the "war" polarized politics in the state for generations.
APPROXIMATE MAXIMUM NUMBER OF MEN UNDER ARMS: 50 cattle barons and their hired guns; 200 cowboys and small ranchers
CASUALTIES: Two small ranchers
TREATIES: None

The Johnson County War (or "Invasion") in 1892 was one of the more infamous and one of the last of the major vigilante conflicts in the American West of the 19th century. The perpetrators of the incident were the owners of large cattle ranches, many of whom lived in Cheyenne, Wyoming, and left the day-to-day operations of their Wyoming ranches to managers. Most of the big ranchers were members of the Wyoming Stock Growers' Association, a private organization that had received quasi-governmental status through control over roundups and disposition of "mavericks."

By the 1890s, the cattle barons had become accustomed to using state action for their purposes, and they were heard to complain constantly that the courts, particularly in Johnson County, were refusing to convict cattle thieves. They hired former Johnson County sheriff Frank M. Canton (1849–1927) to put a stop to the rustling by any means necessary. Canton—who was later implicated in the murders of two small ranchers who the cattlemen thought were rustlers—became a source of intimidation by the big ranchers against homesteaders in general. Still, the "problem" persisted, and the big operators planned a daring strike by a band of vigilantes they called "Regulators" and the people of Johnson County called "Invaders."

On April 5, 1892, a special train made up of six cars pulled out of the station at Cheyenne bound for Casper. Aboard were 19 cattlemen, 5 stock detectives, 22 Texas gunmen, 1 Idaho gunman, 2 newspaper reporters, and 4 observers. Leading the secret expedition were Frank Canton and cattleman Frank Wolcott. A good number of the Wyoming participants had been prominent in state affairs; five had been delegates to the state constitutional convention three years before. These invaders disembarked at Casper and set out on horses for Buffalo, county seat of Johnson County, some 100 miles to the north. They carried with them a "death list" of men they believed were rustlers or were sympathetic to rustling.

Forty-six miles short of their goal, the invaders came upon two of the men on their list. Nate Champion and Nick Ray were staying in a cabin on the KC ranch, near the present-day town of Kaycee. The invaders surrounded the cabin. Ray was shot and killed, but Champion was able to stand off the 50 gunmen for almost 12 hours. At 4 P.M., the invaders set fire to the cabin and shot Champion dead when he ran from the burning building. During the stand-off, Buffalo editor Jack Flagg and his son happened by in a buggy. They escaped capture and got word to the citizens of Buffalo. The invaders came within six miles of Buffalo but turned back when they were told the town had been warned. They took refuge in a barn at the TA Ranch, 13 miles south of Buffalo.

Led by Red Angus, county sheriff, about 200 Buffalo residents set out to intercept the invading force. On the morning of April 11, 1892, the invaders were surrounded. As they approached Buffalo, they had cut the telegraph lines and persuaded acting governor Amos Barber not to answer calls from Buffalo citizens for military intervention. Now, the invaders needed army protection. They managed to send word to Barber, who immediately sent messages to Washington, D.C., to Senators Francis E. Warren (1844–1924) and Joseph Maull Carey (1845–1924), both sympathetic to the invaders. Some claim that the senators roused President Benjamin Harrison (1833–1901) from bed to give an order to send troops. The cavalry, stationed at Fort McKinney near Buffalo, arrived in time to prevent further casualties.

Most of the invaders waited in the comfort of the officers' quarters at Fort D. A. Russell, where they were held pending trial. Following nine months of delays, the case was dismissed because Johnson County could no longer afford the high costs of prosecution.

The inept invasion split the state politically for several years, most people taking the side of Johnson County against the wealthy few who supported the big ranchers. It left two generations of hard feelings, and traces of bitterness were said to remain a century later. In the immediate aftermath of the invasion, Cheyenne newspaperman Asa Mercer wrote an exposé, "Banditti of the Plains: The Crowning Infamy of the Ages," condemning the invasion. Owen Wister (1860–1938), a friend of the invaders, canceled a vacation to the area in the summer of 1892, fearing involvement in the fallout, but the "war" became the inspiration for his novel *The Virginian,* as well as the novel and film *Shane* and the movie *Heaven's Gate.*

Further reading: John Clay, *My Life on the Range* (Norman: University of Oklahoma Press, 1962); Jack R. Gage, *The Johnson County War* (Cheyenne, Wyo.: Flintrock Pub. Co., 1967); Helena Huntington Smith, *The War on Powder River* (New York: McGraw Hill, 1966).

Jokyu War (1221)

PRINCIPAL COMBATANTS: The Hojo vs. former emperor Toba II
PRINCIPAL THEATER(S): Kyoto, Japan
DECLARATION: None
MAJOR ISSUES AND OBJECTIVES: Toba wanted to overthrow the Hojo-controlled Bakufu (military government).
OUTCOME: The Hojo quickly crushed Toba's rebellion.
APPROXIMATE MAXIMUM NUMBER OF MEN UNDER ARMS: Unknown
CASUALTIES: Unknown
TREATIES: None

During the Kamakura period, Japanese political life was a complicated and subtle web of officially constituted authority manipulated by unofficial powers. In 1192, the Bakufu, a military government, was established at Kamakura, ruled by a shogun, a military leader whose authority was hereditary. At this time, the role of emperor had degenerated to that of a mere puppet. Initially, the shoguns enjoyed the real power, but they, too, soon deliquesced to the level of mere instruments of the powerful Hojo family, led by a *shikken* (regent).

Early in the 12th century, Emperor Toba II (1180–1239) abdicated, realizing that, in the present state of Japanese government, he commanded more influence off the throne than on it. In 1221, Toba recruited the support of Japanese monasteries, which possessed great military strength. He led the monasteries against the Bakufu but soon found himself checked by the Hojo—supporters of the Bakufu—at a battle in Kyoto. This effectively crushed the rebellion, and Toba was banished.

To prevent further rebellion, the Hojo boldly installed two of their own military governors in Kyoto and simultaneously seized both the imperial court and the imperial succession. Those loyal to Toba forfeited their estates, which were redistributed to individuals and families friendly to the Hojo. Thus the brief Jokyu War firmly bolstered the feudal nature of Japanese society during this period and linked feudalism to a strong military establishment.

Further reading: John W. Hall, *Japan: From Prehistory to Modern Times* (Tokyo: C. E. Tuttle Co., 1971); Jeffrey Mass, *Warrior Government in Early Medieval Japan* (New Haven, Conn.: Yale University Press, 1974); Jeffrey Mass, ed., *Court and Bakufu in Japan: Essays in Kamakura History* (New Haven, Conn.: Yale University Press, 1982); James Murdoch, *A History of Japan,* 3 vols. (New York: Routledge, 1996); George B. Samson, *A History of Japan,* 3 vols. (Palo Alto, Calif.: Stanford University Press, 1958–63).

Jordanian Civil War (1970–1971)

PRINCIPAL COMBATANTS: Jordan vs. Palestinian guerrillas
PRINCIPAL THEATER(S): Jordan
DECLARATION: Martial law decree, September 16, 1970
MAJOR ISSUES AND OBJECTIVES: Jordan's King Hussein wanted to purge Jordan of Palestinian terrorists.
OUTCOME: The Palestinians were suppressed.
APPROXIMATE MAXIMUM NUMBER OF MEN UNDER ARMS: Jordanians, 54,000; Palestinians, 20,000
CASUALTIES: Jordan army, 750 killed, 1,250 wounded. Total casualties for both sides are estimated at 3,440 killed and 10,840 wounded.
TREATIES: None

The Six-Day War between Egypt and Israel produced some 400,000 Palestinian refugees, who fled the West Bank when it was forfeited to victorious Israel (*see* ARAB-ISRAELI WAR [1967]). This vast influx of dispossessed Palestinians joined the even larger Palestinian population already resident in Jordan, which immediately became a base from which Palestinians conducted terrorist attacks on Israel. The most visible and militant of the Palestinian terrorist groups was the Palestine Liberation Organization (PLO), led by Yasser Arafat (b. 1929). In defiance of Jordan's king Hussein (1935–99), Arafat asserted the PLO's right to conduct war from Jordanian territory with the objective of reclaiming the West Bank as a Palestinian state. Hussein could not long tolerate the threat to his own reign and to the sovereignty of his nation.

In February, 200 were killed and 500 wounded in four days of fighting. This was followed on September 1 by a Palestinian-backed assassination attempt against the Jordanian king. The final straw came with "Black September," a rash of PLO hijackings of commercial airliners during

September 6–9, 1970, which were flown to Amman, Jordan. Risking the alienation of other Arab states—who wanted to see the defeat of Israel and who therefore supported the PLO—Hussein declared martial law on September 16, 1970, and conducted a 10-day campaign against the Palestinians, containing the refugee camps, disarming guerrillas, and deporting key leaders. King Hussein deployed his Bedouin army of 52,000 and his 2,000-man, 40-plane air force against the outclassed forces—about 20,000 men—fielded by the Palestinians. Syria deployed two armored brigades on September 20, threatening out-and-out war, but Hussein did not back down. Some 300 Syrian tanks advanced across the border, only to be pushed back by September 23 with the loss of 60 vehicles. President Gamal Abdel Nasser (1918–70) of Egypt intervened and brokered a cease-fire on September 27.

Low-level guerrilla resistance continued throughout Jordan well into 1971; however, Amman was cleared of Palestinians by April, and, by July, PLO bases throughout Jordan had been destroyed. The PLO and other Palestinian guerrillas moved on to bases in Lebanon.

See also LEBANESE CIVIL WAR (1975–1992).

Further reading: Clinton Baily, *Jordan's Palestinian Challenge, 1948–1983: A Political History* (Boulder, Colo.: Westview Press, 1984).

Juchen Mongol Conquest of the Liao
(1114–1122)

PRINCIPAL COMBATANTS: Juchen Mongols vs. the Liao (Khitan) dynasty; China also attacked the Liao during this period
PRINCIPAL THEATER(S): Manchuria
DECLARATION: None
MAJOR ISSUES AND OBJECTIVES: Conquest of southern Manchuria
OUTCOME: The Juchen Mongols not only took southern Manchuria but penetrated deep into China to establish the Jin (Chin) dynasty at Beijing.
APPROXIMATE MAXIMUM NUMBER OF MEN UNDER ARMS: Unknown
CASUALTIES: Unknown
TREATIES: None

For many years, the Juchen Mongol tribes of northern Manchuria recognized the suzerainty of the Liao (Khitan) dynasty in southern Manchuria. Then, in 1114, the leader of the Juchen Mongols suddenly severed relations with the overlord of the Khitan tribe that had founded the Liao dynasty. This was the prelude to a Mongol attack on the Liao, which came swiftly and massively as thousands of Juchen tribesmen poured in from the north.

The Liao situation was made worse by an attack by the Chinese from the south; China sought to exploit an opportunity to avenge the disloyalty of people who had been its former vassal.

Squeezed between two great forces, the Liao evacuated Manchuria by 1116. The Juchen Mongols held that territory and continued to pursue the Liao into Shanxi (Shansi) and Zhili (Chihli) in present-day China. By the end of the war, 1122, the Juchen Mongols had taken Beijing and established the Jin dynasty. Liao survivors settled in the west, where they founded Kara-Khitai in the valley of the Ili River. Their once great dynasty, however, was totally obliterated by 1125.

See also CHINESE WAR WITH THE KHITANS; CHINESE WAR WITH THE TANGUTS, FIRST; CHINESE WAR WITH THE TANGUTS, SECOND.

Further reading: Hok-lam Chan, *Legitimation in Imperial China: Discussions under the Jurchen-Chin Dynasty, 1115–1234* (Seattle: University of Washington Press, 1984); Wolfram Eberhart, *A History of China*, 3d ed. (Berkeley: University of California Press, 1969); Charles O. Hucker, *China's Imperial Past: An Introduction to Chinese History and Culture* (Stanford, Calif.: Stanford University Press, 1975); Jing-shen Tao, *The Jurchen in Twelfth-Century China: A Study in Sinicization* (Seattle: University of Washington Press, 1976); Hogt Cleveland Tillman and Stephen H. West, eds., *China under Jurchen Rule* (Albany: State University of New York Press, 1995).

Juchen Mongol Invasion of the Song Empire (1125–1162)

PRINCIPAL COMBATANTS: Juchen Mongols (Jin [Chin] dynasty) vs. Song (Sung) dynasty and, subsequently, Southern Song
PRINCIPAL THEATER(S): China
DECLARATION: None
MAJOR ISSUES AND OBJECTIVES: Control of China
OUTCOME: In the early phases of the war, the Song were defeated and pushed to the south; subsequently, the Southern Song staged a successful counteroffensive campaign, which drove the Chin northward. A treaty was concluded, dividing rule of China between the two dynasties.
APPROXIMATE MAXIMUM NUMBER OF MEN UNDER ARMS: Unknown
CASUALTIES: Unknown
TREATIES: Treaties between Southern Song and Chin, dividing rule, 1141 and 1162

During the JUCHEN MONGOL CONQUEST OF THE LIAO, from 1114 to 1122, the Chinese Song dynasty had helped the Juchen Mongols take the territory of the Liao in southern Manchuria and Shanxi (Shansi). In 1125, however, the Juchen Mongols, who had established the Jin dynasty at Beijing, suddenly turned on the Song by invading Song holdings north of the Yellow River. In 1126, the Juchen Mongols went on to cross the Yellow River and surround the Song capital of Kaifeng (K'ai-feng). After a year-long siege, that city fell, and the Song emperor, Huizong (Hui Tsung; 1082–1135), was captured, along with his family. All were sent into exile; however, one son, Gaozong (Kao Tsung;1107–87), escaped and fled to Nanjing (Nanking). There he founded the Southern Song dynasty.

In 1129, the Juchen Mongols followed Gaozong. Crossing the Yangtze River, they attacked and captured Nanjing, Gaozong's capital city. The indefatigable Southern Song emperor fled again, this time to Hangzhou (Hangchow), and organized armies under General Yo Fei (Yue Fei; d. 1141). Coordinating a land assault with the Song Yangtze River fleet, Yo Fei scored a victory against the Juchen Mongols—the Jin—pushing them back north across the river. This marked a turning point in the war, as Southern Song forces pushed the Jin farther and farther north.

By the early 1140s, many within the Southern Song hierarchy, weary of war, called for a treaty with the Jin. Yo Fei was adamant that the war should continue, but in 1141, he was relieved of command, recalled, and then executed, whereupon the Song and Jin concluded a treaty dividing China along the watershed of the Yangtze valley and the Yellow River valley. For two decades, an uneasy peace, frequently punctuated by outbursts of violence, prevailed. At last, in 1161, Jin forces mounted an invasion of Southern Song territory, but were devastatingly rebuffed in a battle outside of Nanjing. Military historians believe that this battle was marked by the first use of explosives (gunpowder). Much abashed, the Jin concluded a new treaty with Gaozong and the Southern Song.

See also MONGOL CONQUEST OF THE CHIN EMPIRE; MONGOL CONQUEST OF THE SONG EMPIRE.

Further reading: Hok-lam Chan, *Legitimation in Imperial China: Discussions under the Jurchen-Chin Dynasty, 1115–1234* (Seattle: University of Washington Press, 1984); Wolfram Eberhart, *A History of China*, 3rd ed. (Berkeley: University of California Press, 1969); Charles O. Hucker, *China's Imperial Past: An Introduction to Chinese History and Culture* (Stanford, Calif.: Stanford University Press, 1975); Jing-shen Tao, *The Jurchen in Twelfth-Century China: A Study in Sinicization* (Seattle: University of Washington Press, 1976); Hogt Cleveland Tillman and Stephen H. West, eds., *China under Jurchen Rule* (Albany: State University of New York Press, 1995).

Jugurthine War (Numidian War) (112–106 B.C.E.)

PRINCIPAL COMBATANTS: Followers of Jugurtha vs. Roman and Roman-led African forces
PRINCIPAL THEATER(S): Numidia
DECLARATION: None

MAJOR ISSUES AND OBJECTIVES: The Romans wanted to depose Jugurtha in favor of the son of the previous king of Numidia.
OUTCOME: Jugurtha was captured and removed from the Numidian throne.
APPROXIMATE MAXIMUM NUMBER OF MEN UNDER ARMS: Unknown
CASUALTIES: Unknown
TREATIES: None

This conflict, sometimes called the Numidian War, is named for Jugurtha (c. 156–104), the king of Numidia from 118 to 105 B.C.E., who tried to free his North African kingdom from Rome. Jugurtha was an illegitimate grandson of Masinissa (d. 148 B.C.E.), the Numidian ruler who had first allied his country with the Romans, and the nephew of his successor, King Micipsa (d. 116 B.C.E.). As a young man, Jugurtha had become so popular among the Numidians that his uncle felt the need to send him away, and the king placed the youth in the service of Scipio Africanus the Younger (185/184–129 B.C.E.), when the Roman general led an expedition to besiege Spain. Once in Rome, Jugurtha managed to establish close relationships with several powerful Roman senators, who evidently persuaded Micipsa to adopt Jugurtha in 120.

Thus it was that, upon Micipsa's death, Jugurtha came to share rule over Numidia with Micipsa's two sons, Himpsal and Adherbal, the first of whom Jugurtha assassinated, prompting the second to flee to Rome in search of aid. Adherbal had reason to hope, since a change of government in his country required Roman approval, but Jugurtha knew Rome and the Romans better, bribing Roman officials through envoys and obtaining the Senate's authorization to divide Numidia east and west. Jugurtha took the vastly richer western half, saddling Adherbal with the east.

Hardly content to let matters rest there, in 112 Jugurtha attacked Adherbal's diminished kingdom, trusting his influence in Rome to smooth over any senatorial feathers he might ruffle in the process. But when he captured Adherbal's capital at Cirta, he overstepped the boundaries, killing not only his rival king but also a number of Roman businessmen.

Popular outrage at the death of Roman citizens swept the city, forcing the Senate to declare war on Numidia. Even then, however, Jugurtha's contacts helped. In 111, the Roman consul, Lucius Calpurnius Bestia, made a favorable settlement with Jugurtha, though the Senate summoned him to Rome to explain just how he had managed to obtain so generous a treaty. While in the capital, he had a potential rival for the throne assassinated, which led even the staunchest of his Roman friends to wash their hands of him.

In 109, the Roman general Quintus Caesilius Metellus (d. 99 B.C.E.) led a large African army in a sweep through Numidia, devastating much of the kingdom. Unable to defeat the invaders in open battle, Jugurtha resorted to guerrilla warfare. To combat this, Rome dispatched an army under Gaius Marius (c. 155–86 B.C.E.), who picked up where Caesilius had left off, ravaging the kingdom. This, however, failed to extinguish the flame of resistance. Ultimately, the Jugurthine War was ended not by military victory, but through the treachery of Jugurtha's father-in-law, who delivered the ruler into Roman hands. Marius was thus able to leave Numidia and return to Rome with Jugurtha his prisoner.

Further reading: J. R. Hawthorn, ed., *Sallust, Rome and Jugurtha: Being Selections from Saullust's Bellum Iugurthinum* (New York: St. Martin's Press, 1969); Paul MacKendrick, *The North African Stones Speak* (Chapel Hill: University of North Carolina Press, 1980); Colin Wells, *The Roman Empire,* 2nd ed. (Cambridge, Mass.: Harvard University Press, 1995).

Julian's First Campaign   *See* ROMAN-PERSIAN WAR (337–363).

Jülich Succession, War of the   (1609–1614)

PRINCIPAL COMBATANTS: Brandenburg and Palatinate-Neuberg (with Dutch and French support) vs. Austria (Holy Roman Empire); later, Brandenburg vs. Palatinate-Neuberg (with Catholic League support)
PRINCIPAL THEATER(S): Duchies of Jülich, Cleves, Mark, and Berg
DECLARATION: None
MAJOR ISSUES AND OBJECTIVES: The parties contested succession to the duchies of Jülich, Cleves, Mark, and Berg.
OUTCOME: Rule of the duchies was divided between Brandenburg (Cleves and Mark) and Palatinate-Neuberg (Jülich and Berg).
APPROXIMATE MAXIMUM NUMBER OF MEN UNDER ARMS: Unknown
CASUALTIES: Unknown
TREATIES: Treaty of Xanten, November 12, 1614

The death of Duke John William of Jülich (d. 1609) in 1609 precipitated a war for succession to his territories, the duchies of Jülich, Mark, Berg, and Cleves. Three rulers vied for succession: John Sigismund (1572–1619), the elector of Brandenburg (who claimed title by descent through the female line), Wolfgang William, the count of Palatinate-Neuberg (who made the same claim), and the elector of Saxony (who deemed the duchies his as an imperial fief). A fourth ruler, the Holy Roman Emperor, wanted to deliver the territories to Spain. A confusing conflict then began. The Brandenburg elector and the count of Palatinate-Neuberg agreed to rule the duchies jointly, but Austrian troops commanded by Leopold (1586–1633), the brother of the Holy Roman Emperor, invaded and held the duchies during 1609–10. Dutch and German Protestant troops, allied with the French, invaded in 1610, and pushed the Austrians out, capturing Jülich's fortress on September 1, 1610.

Yet the conflict was not over. In 1613, the elector of Brandenburg and the count of Palatinate-Neuberg fell out, dissolving their agreement for joint rule. The count now appealed to Catholic forces for aid in evicting the Brandenburg elector, and the war began to develop into a religious conflict between Protestants and Catholics. However, before a new outbreak of fighting occurred, Brandenburg and Palatinate-Neuberg concluded the Treaty of Xanten on November 12, 1614, whereby Brandenburg received Cleves and Mark (as well as, separately, Ravensberg) and Palatinate-Neuberg received Jülich and Berg (and Ravenstein). Concerned not to alienate the Catholic League, the count of Palatinate-Neuberg pledged to foster a conversion to Catholicism throughout his realm. Sigismund, the Brandenburg elector, remained faithful to his Calvinist Protestantism but instituted general religious toleration throughout his possessions.

See also THIRTY YEARS' WAR.

Further reading: Geoffrey Barraclough, *The Origins of Modern Germany,* 3rd ed. (Oxford, England: B. Blackwell, 1988); Frank Eyck, *Religion and Politics in German History* (New York: St. Martin's Press, 1998); Friedrich Heer, *Holy Roman Empire,* trans. Janet Sondheimer (New York: Sterling, 2002); James A. Vann and Steven Rowan, eds., *The Old Reich: Essays in German Political Institutions, 1495–1806* (Brussels: Editions de la librarie encyclopédique, 1974).

July Revolution (1830)   *See* FRENCH REVOLUTION (1830).

July Revolution (1854)   *See* SPANISH REVOLUTION (1854).

Justinian's Gothic War   *See* GOTHIC (ITALIAN) WAR.

Justinian's First Persian War   (524–532)

PRINCIPAL COMBATANTS: Byzantine Empire vs. Sassanid Persia
PRINCIPAL THEATER(S): Mesopotamia, at the Persian frontier
DECLARATION: None
MAJOR ISSUES AND OBJECTIVES: Byzantine emperor Justinian I wanted to end chronic Persian invasions of Byzantine territory.
OUTCOME: The invasions were halted when Persia concluded an "eternal" peace with the Byzantine Empire.

APPROXIMATE MAXIMUM NUMBER OF MEN UNDER ARMS: At most, both sides fielded about 40,000 men each.
CASUALTIES: At Dara, Persian losses were 8,000 dead; Byzantine losses are unknown.
TREATIES: "Eternal" peace between Chosroes of Persia and Justinian I of the Byzantine Empire, 532

In the sixth century, Persians continually made incursions into Byzantine territory, and, during 524, they invaded Mesopotamia. Emperor Justinian I (483–565) sent forces to repulse them and, over the next few years, engaged in frontier skirmishes. At last, in 527, Justinian ordered the leading Byzantine general, Belisarius (c. 505–565), to lead a major campaign against the Persians to end the threat to Mesopotamia once and for all. In 528, as part of this campaign, Belisarius built a large fort at Dara, in northern Mesopotamia, and garrisoned it. The construction of the fort provoked Kavadh I (d. 531), Sassanid king of Persia, to mount a major invasion with a combined Persian-Arab army of 40,000 men. Belisarius sallied out of Dara to intercept the invasion, attacking frontally with his own troops and conducting flanking attacks using Hun cavalry. The Persian-Arab force was routed and fled the field, leaving some 8,000 dead behind.

Some authorities date the Battle of Dara at 528, some at 530. What is certain is that, in 531, Kavadh I resumed the offensive, striking Belisarius at Callinicum on the east bank of the Euphrates. This time, the Persians seized the initiative, and it was Belisarius who suffered a severe defeat, saving his army only by taking refuge on islands in the river. Although Belisarius lost, the fact that he had saved most of his army meant that Callinicum was a draw, and it prompted Chosroes (d. 579), son of Kavadh I—who died shortly after the Callinicum battle—to conclude peace with Byzantium. It was not destined to last long (*see* JUSTINIAN'S SECOND PERSIAN WAR).

Further reading: John W. Barker, *Justinian and the Later Roman Empire* (Madison: University of Wisconsin Press, 1966); John Julius Norwich, *Byzantium: The Early Centuries* (New York: Alfred A. Knopf, 2003).

Justinian's Second Persian War (539–561)

PRINCIPAL COMBATANTS: Byzantine Empire vs. Persia
PRINCIPAL THEATER(S): Mesopotamia and Georgia
DECLARATION: None
MAJOR ISSUES AND OBJECTIVES: Justinian I defended the frontiers of his empire against renewed Persian invasion.
OUTCOME: Justinian paid Persia annual tribute money to maintain the peace.
APPROXIMATE MAXIMUM NUMBER OF MEN UNDER ARMS: Unknown
CASUALTIES: Unknown
TREATIES: Peace treaty and subsidy agreement, 561

Chosroes (d. 579), Sassanid king of Persia, concluded an "eternal" peace with Justinian I (483–565), Byzantine emperor, ending JUSTINIAN'S FIRST PERSIAN WAR (524–532), but renewed combat in 539 when he invaded Syria and sacked Antioch, a major city of the Eastern Empire. He held the city for a short time through 540. Chosroes resettled many Antiochan prisoners in a new town near his capital, Ctesiphon. In this way, he could ensure better control of the subject population. Chosroes went on to ravage Mesopotamia and Lazica (western Georgia), finally concluding an armistice with the hard-pressed Justinian I in 545. The Byzantine emperor judged it more expedient to pay Chosroes a hefty annual tribute than to fight him, but even this did not stop the combat, and the war continued at a low level of intensity through 561, when a major treaty was signed. In return for continuation of an annual subsidy, the Byzantines were permitted to maintain fortresses in the Caucasus.

See also NIKA REVOLT; ROMAN-PERSIAN WAR (502–506); VANDAL-ROMAN WARS IN NORTH AFRICA.

Further reading: John W. Barker, *Justinian and the Later Roman Empire* (Madison: University of Wisconsin Press, 1966); John Julius Norwich, *Byzantium: The Early Centuries* (New York: Alfred A. Knopf, 2003).

Kaffir War, First (1779)

PRINCIPAL COMBATANTS: The Boers vs. the Xhosa tribespeople (derisively called Kaffirs)
PRINCIPAL THEATER(S): South Africa
DECLARATION: None
MAJOR ISSUES AND OBJECTIVES: Control of farming and pasturage lands
OUTCOME: The Boers succeeded in pushing the Xhosa beyond the Great Fish River; however, no formal boundary resolution was reached.
APPROXIMATE MAXIMUM NUMBER OF MEN UNDER ARMS: Unknown
CASUALTIES: Unknown
TREATIES: None

Kaffir was the disparaging name the Boers—the Dutch farmers of South Africa—gave to native Africans. During the last quarter of the 18th century, Boers began migrating from the coastal regions of the South African colony to inland territory 400 miles northeast of Cape Town. This brought them into conflict with the Xhosa, a Bantu tribe that worked the pastureland along the Great Fish River. Both sides made efforts to demarcate boundaries of settlement, but individual Boers continually violated the boundaries, and in 1779, perhaps motivated by vengeance after Boers killed some tribesmen, the Xhosa raided Boer herders. Cattle were appropriated or slaughtered, and several herdsmen were killed. In response, the Boers organized guerrilla-style raids against the Xhosa. Not only were people targeted, but cattle was stolen in large numbers—reportedly in excess of 5,000 head.

The Boer raids succeeded in driving the Xhosa across the Great Fish River, which served as a natural boundary to settlement, but hardly resolved the underlying conflicts. Boer-Xhosa violence became endemic, and a Second KAFFIR WAR in 1793 ultimately erupted.

See also AXE, WAR OF THE; KAFFIR WAR, THIRD; KAFFIR WAR, FOURTH; KAFFIR WAR, FIFTH; KAFFIR WAR, SIXTH; KAFFIR WAR, EIGHTH; KAFFIR WAR, NINTH.

Further reading: Richard Elphick and Hermann Giliomee, eds., *The Shaping of South African Society, 1652–1820* (Cape Town: Longman, 1979); Noel Mostert, *Frontiers: The Epic of South Africa's Creation and the Tragedy of the Xhosa People* (New York: Alfred A. Knopf, 1993); J. B. Peires, *The House of Phalo: A History of the Xhosa People in the Days of Their Independence* (Berkeley: University of California Press, 1982); Leonard Thompson, *A History of South Africa,* 3rd ed. (New Haven, Conn.: Yale University Press, 2001).

Kaffir War, Second (1793)

PRINCIPAL COMBATANTS: The Boers vs. the Xhosa tribespeople (derisively called Kaffirs)
PRINCIPAL THEATER(S): South Africa
DECLARATION: None
MAJOR ISSUES AND OBJECTIVES: Dispute over boundary between Boer and Xhosa farming lands
OUTCOME: The war was abortive; after indecisive raids on both sides, the Boer force disbanded over a dispute with its Dutch East India Company leader.
APPROXIMATE MAXIMUM NUMBER OF MEN UNDER ARMS: Unknown

CASUALTIES: Unknown

TREATIES: A boundary treaty between the Boers and the Xhosa had been concluded before the war began but, unenforceable, was without practical effect.

After the First KAFFIR WAR in 1779, violence between the Xhosa tribe and the Boers (Dutch farmers in South Africa) continued. The Boers eventually solicited aid from the Dutch East India Company, the powerful colonizing force in the region. A company agent known to history only as Maynier (fl. 1793) was sent to the Xhosa to negotiate a resolution to the territorial dispute. Although an arrangement was agreed to, it had no practical effect, because the Dutch East India Company furnished no troops or police force to enforce the terms of the agreement. Both Xhosa tribespeople and Boers continued frequently to encroach on one another's territory.

In 1793, a severe drought swept South Africa. Desperate Boer farmers drove their herds into Kaffirland *Kaffir* was the term Boers applied to all African natives) in search of pasturage. A farmer named Lindeque (fl. 1793) organized a group that sought more than pasturage. These renegade Boers, violating the Dutch East India Company agreement, began raiding Xhosa cattle. In response, the Xhosa invaded the Boer territory. Agent Maynier recruited a guerrilla force from among the Boers, but the planned general assault against the Xhosa failed to materialize when the guerrilla force disbanded; Maynier refused to demand that the Xhosa surrender a large number of cattle as reparation for Boer losses.

See also AXE, WAR OF THE; KAFFIR WAR, THIRD; KAFFIR WAR, FOURTH; KAFFIR WAR, FIFTH; KAFFIR WAR, SIXTH; KAFFIR WAR, EIGHTH; KAFFIR WAR, NINTH.

Further reading: Richard Elphick and Hermann Giliomee, eds., *The Shaping of South African Society, 1652–1820* (Cape Town: Longman, 1979); Noel Mostert, *Frontiers: The Epic of South Africa's Creation and the Tragedy of the Xhosa People* (New York: Alfred A. Knopf, 1993); J. B. Peires, *The House of Phalo: a History of the Xhosa People in the Days of Their Independence* (Berkeley: University of California Press, 1982); Leonard Thompson, *A History of South Africa*, 3rd ed. (New Haven, Conn.: Yale University Press, 2001).

Kaffir War, Third (1799–1801)

PRINCIPAL COMBATANTS: The Boers (with British aid) vs. the Xhosa in alliance with the Khosians *Kaffir* was the Dutch generic term for native Africans.)

PRINCIPAL THEATER(S): South Africa

DECLARATION: None

MAJOR ISSUES AND OBJECTIVES: Dispute over boundary between Boer and Xhosa farming lands

OUTCOME: British diplomatic intervention broke up the alliance between the Xhosa and Khosians, but military campaigning failed to expel the Xhosa from the disputed region; the war petered out, ending indecisively.

APPROXIMATE MAXIMUM NUMBER OF MEN UNDER ARMS: Unknown

CASUALTIES: Unknown

TREATIES: Treaty of Amiens (between France and Britain), 1802, temporarily took Britain out of the chronic conflict between the Boers and the Xhosa.

In 1795, the Boers of Swellendam and Graaf-Reinet, both South African regions, declared independence, but it would not last long. The British, following the defeat of the Dutch by Napoleonic France (*see* COALITION, WAR OF THE FIRST), took over the Boer lands. They inherited not only the territory but also the chronic Boer territorial dispute with the Xhosa tribe. The Third Kaffir War would be the first involving the British and the British regular army. At issue, as always, was farmland and cattle pasturage.

In 1799, the Xhosa made common cause with the Khosian servants of the Boers, a people also known as the Hottentots and generally considered to be the first inhabitants of South Africa. These individuals deserted the Boers en masse, bringing with them guns and horses. Thus allied with the Khosians, the Xhosa raids against the Boers became both more destructive and more effective.

The British intervened with troops in May. They also acted diplomatically, by co-opting and undermining the alliance between the Xhosa and the Khosians. Territorial and other concessions to the Khosians succeeded in breaking the alliance, but the British goal of expelling the Xhosa from the disputed territories was not achieved. Nevertheless, by 1801, the war wound down on its own, and Britain temporarily washed its hands of the conflict by terms of the 1802 Treaty of Amiens (between France and Britain), which returned the Cape region to the Dutch.

See also AXE, WAR OF THE; HOTTENOTOT UPRISING; KAFFIR WAR, FIRST; KAFFIR WAR, SECOND; KAFFIR WAR, FOURTH; KAFFIR WAR, FIFTH; KAFFIR WAR, SIXTH; KAFFIR WAR, EIGHTH; KAFFIR WAR, NINTH.

Further reading: Richard Elphick and Hermann Giliomee, eds., *The Shaping of South African Society, 1652–1820* (Cape Town: Longman, 1979); Noel Mostert, *Frontiers: The Epic of South Africa's Creation and the Tragedy of the Xhosa People* (New York: Alfred A. Knopf, 1993); J. B. Peires, *The House of Phalo: A History of the Xhosa People in the Days of Their Independence* (Berkeley: University of California Press, 1982); Leonard Thompson, *A History of South Africa*, 3rd ed. (New Haven, Conn.: Yale University Press, 2001).

Kaffir War, Fourth (1811–1812)

PRINCIPAL COMBATANTS: The Boers vs. the Xhosa; British authorities attempted to police both Boers and Xhosa, to enforce a border between them.
PRINCIPAL THEATER(S): South Africa
DECLARATION: None
MAJOR ISSUES AND OBJECTIVES: Dispute over the boundary between Boer and Xhosa farming lands
OUTCOME: The underlying border issue remained unresolved; although the British built a string of forts to protect the border between the Boers and the Xhosa, they lacked sufficient troop strength to ensure an inviolate border.
APPROXIMATE MAXIMUM NUMBER OF MEN UNDER ARMS: Anglo-Boer-Khosian force, 2,000; Xhosa, 5,500
CASUALTIES: Boers, 15 killed; Xhosa, 500 killed
TREATIES: None

The peace brought by the Treaty of Amiens (*see* Third KAFFIR WAR) was short-lived, and alliances were realigned, such that Holland, formerly allied with Britain, now sided with France. In response, the British Royal Navy sailed into Cape Town harbor and retook control of the entire Cape region of South Africa. Against this background of European colonial conflict, the war between the Boers and Xhosa erupted anew, as "Kaffir" (the Boer term for any native African) refugees from colonial conflicts throughout the region poured into the Cape area in 1811. On December 27 of that year, Xhosa tribesmen massacred 15 Boers at a peace conference in the Zuurberg Mountains. A combined English, Boer, and Khosian (Hottentot) force of 2,000 was raised and pursued 5,500 Xhosa warriors across the Great Fish River by March 1812. Fought to a standstill, 500 Xhosa men were killed.

The British attempted to maintain strict borders between Xhosa and Boers, and they blamed the Boers unilaterally for violating the boundaries. The effort to enforce the borders was largely futile, however, since the British did not have the troop strength to police the region. After driving the Xhosa back across the Great Fish River, the British did establish a loose line of forts in an attempt to keep both sides separated.

See also AXE, WAR OF THE; HOTTENOTOT UPRISING; KAFFIR WAR, FIRST; KAFFIR WAR, SECOND; KAFFIR WAR, FOURTH; KAFFIR WAR, FIFTH; KAFFIR WAR, SIXTH; KAFFIR WAR, EIGHTH; KAFFIR WAR, NINTH.

Further reading: Richard Elphick and Hermann Giliomee, eds., *The Shaping of South African Society, 1652–1820* (Cape Town: Longman, 1979); Noel Mostert, *Frontiers: The Epic of South Africa's Creation and the Tragedy of the Xhosa People* (New York: Alfred A. Knopf, 1993); J. B. Peires, *The House of Phalo: A History of the Xhosa People in the Days of Their Independence* (Berkeley: University of California Press, 1982); Leonard Thompson,

A History of South Africa, 3rd ed. (New Haven, Conn.: Yale University Press, 2001).

Kaffir War, Fifth (1818–1820)

PRINCIPAL COMBATANTS: The Boers vs. the Xhosa; Great Britain vs. the Xhosa; Great Britain vs. the Boers
PRINCIPAL THEATER(S): South Africa
DECLARATION: None
MAJOR ISSUES AND OBJECTIVES: In an effort to settle the chronic land dispute between the Boers and the Xhosa tribe, the British colonial government created a wide neutral zone, on which it settled British farmers; this action only exacerbated, complicated, and enlarged the territorial dispute.
OUTCOME: The boundary remained unresolved, and hostilities in this region were compounded, involving Boers, Xhosa, and the British.
APPROXIMATE MAXIMUM NUMBER OF MEN UNDER ARMS: Xhosa, 10,000; Anglo-Boer force, 2,300
CASUALTIES: At Grahamstown, Britain, 3; Xhosa, 1,000
TREATIES: None

The stress of continual warfare (*see* KAFFIR WAR, FIRST, KAFFIR WAR, SECOND, KAFFIR WAR, THIRD, and KAFFIR WAR, FOURTH) eroded the internal unity of the Xhosa tribe. A power struggle developed between two rival chieftains, Ndlambi (fl. 1810s) and Gaika (fl. 1810s), resulting in a civil war beginning in October 1818. Ndlambi's partisans defeated those of Gaika, slaughtering thousands, but the British Cape government, deciding that Gaika was more compliant with colonial policy, continued to back him. On Christmas 1818, Xhosa warriors crossed the Great Fish River, the boundary between white settlement and Xhosa lands. This gave British authorities a pretext for dispatching troops to attack partisans of Ndlambi. In response, Ndlambi launched an attack on Grahamstown, a Boer settlement. This, in turn, touched off the Fifth Kaffir War.

Violence raged without resolution for about one year, reaching a climax at Grahamstown on April 22, 1819, when 10,000 Xhosa attacked an Anglo-Boer force of 450 men plus 150 friendly Khosians (Hottentots). Thanks largely to British howitzers, the attack was repulsed. About 1,000 Xhosa warriors fell, whereas losses among the defenders were 3 killed and 5 wounded. An Anglo-Boer offensive followed in August 1820, with an army of 2,300, but as usual, the fighting petered out when both sides tired of it. This time, Lord Charles Somerset (fl. early 19th century), the British governor of the Cape Colony, was determined to bring permanent resolution to the chronic and costly conflict between the Boers and Xhosa. He declared not a mere border, but a neutral strip, closed to both sides, between the Great Fish River and the Keiskama River. The idea was to establish a no-man's-land, a wide buffer. It was, however, a misguided policy: instead of alienating one side or the other, it alienated both. The valuable pasturage, watered by the rivers in an arid land, was badly needed. To make matters worse, Somerset settled *British* farmers in the neutral zone. Immediately, both Xhosa *and* Boers fell upon the settlers, who quickly fled. The war ended without resolution, but with great bitterness—now very much a three-way affair, with the Xhosa, the Boers, and the British locked in mutual hostility.

See also AXE, WAR OF THE; HOTTENOTOT UPRISING; KAFFIR WAR, SIXTH; KAFFIR WAR, EIGHTH; KAFFIR WAR, NINTH.

Further reading: Richard Elphick and Hermann Giliomee, eds., *The Shaping of South African Society, 1652–1820* (Cape Town: Longman, 1979); Noel Mostert, *Frontiers: The Epic of South Africa's Creation and the Tragedy of the Xhosa People* (New York: Alfred A. Knopf, 1993); J. B. Peires, *The House of Phalo: A History of the Xhosa People in the Days of Their Independence* (Berkeley: University of California Press, 1982); Leonard Thompson, *A History of South Africa*, 3rd ed. (New Haven, Conn.: Yale University Press, 2001).

Kaffir War, Sixth   (1834–1835)

PRINCIPAL COMBATANTS: The Boers vs. the Xhosa (derisively called Kaffirs); British intervened against the Xhosa
PRINCIPAL THEATER(S): South Africa
DECLARATION: None
MAJOR ISSUES AND OBJECTIVES: Dispute over the boundary between Boer and Xhosa farming lands
OUTCOME: In an effort to settle the border dispute, the British expelled the Xhosa, then opened their lands to Boer settlement; unable to defend the newly opened territory, the British abandoned the Boers, many of whom migrated northward in the Great Trek. Anglo-Boer relations worsened, as did British relations with the Xhosa.
APPROXIMATE MAXIMUM NUMBER OF MEN UNDER ARMS: British forces, 2,000; Xhosa, 15,000
CASUALTIES: Boers and British, 200 killed; Xhosa, 2,000 killed
TREATIES: None

By the 1830s, in the Cape Colony of South Africa, the Boers, whose farmlands baked under prolonged drought, continually moved farther into Kaffirland (as they called the territory of the Xhosa tribe), thus provoking more Boer-Xhosa violence. The British government of the colony, hoping to maintain profitable trade (centered at the British settlement of Port Elizabeth) with both the Boers and the Xhosa, succeeded only in antagonizing both sides and, if anything, intensifying the chronic conflict.

In 1834, Sir Benjamin D'Urban (1777–1849), British governor of the colony, decided to act against the Xhosa by expelling them from the disputed region. This accomplished, he curried favor with the Boers by declaring the Xhosa lands open to settlement. In response, on December 21, 1834, 15,000 Xhosa warriors invaded the Cape Colony along a front 100 miles wide, killing dozens of whites. About 1,200 British troops counterattacked in February 1835, pushing a few thousand Xhosa out of the Fish River bush and killing 100. In April, 2,000 British troops attacked again, forcing the Xhosa into the Amatola Mountains and capturing Chief Hintsa (d. 1835). When he was killed on May 12, 1835, in an escape attempt, the Xhosa resistance collapsed. However, D'Urban realized that he was powerless to defend in the future the lands he himself had opened. He therefore ordered the territory deannexed, leaving the Boer settlers isolated and abandoned, greatly exacerbating tensions with the British. Disgusted with British inconstancy, many Boers began the northern migration known as the Great Trek. As for British relations with the Xhosa, tribal resentment of the annexation would ultimately lead to the War of the AXE in 1846 (the Seventh Kaffir War) and the Eighth KAFFIR WAR in 1850.

See also KAFFIR WAR, FIRST; KAFFIR WAR, SECOND; THIRD; KAFFIR WAR, FOURTH; KAFFIR WAR, FIFTH; KAFFIR WAR, NINTH.

Further reading: Noel Mostert, *Frontiers: The Epic of South Africa's Creation and the Tragedy of the Xhosa People* (New York: Alfred A. Knopf, 1993); J. B. Peires, *The House of Phalo: A History of the Xhosa People in the Days of Their Independence* (Berkeley: University of California Press, 1982); Leonard Thompson, *A History of South Africa*, 3rd ed. (New Haven, Conn.: Yale University Press, 2001).

Kaffir War, Seventh   *See* AXE, WAR OF THE (1846–1847).

Kaffir War, Eighth   (1850–1853)

PRINCIPAL COMBATANTS: British colonial forces vs. the Xhosa tribe
PRINCIPAL THEATER(S): South Africa
DECLARATION: None
MAJOR ISSUES AND OBJECTIVES: The Xhosa resented British annexation of Xhosa territory.
OUTCOME: The Xhosa uprising was defeated.
APPROXIMATE MAXIMUM NUMBER OF MEN UNDER ARMS: Unknown
CASUALTIES: British colonials, 1,400 killed; Xhosa, 16,000 killed or captured
TREATIES: Peace of March 2, 1853

As a result of the Sixth KAFFIR WAR, from 1834 to 1835, and the War of the AXE (the Seventh Kaffir War), from 1846 to 1847, the British not only annexed all Xhosa tribal territory but sharply limited the power of the Xhosa chiefs.

British authorities dispatched a force of 650 men to arrest Sandile (fl. 1850s), a Xhosa chief. At Boma Pass, on December 24, 1850, the force was ambushed and 23 British soldiers killed. A second British patrol was ambushed on the same day, with the loss of 15 troops. Then, on Christmas day, Xhosa warriors raided a British settlement, killing 46 civilians.

On December 29, the Xhosa struck again, 1,000 warriors attacking a British patrol of 150 just outside of Fort Hare. The patrol retreated into the fort, but lost 24 killed and 18 wounded. Then some 5,000 warriors attacked the fort on January 21, 1851. The garrison of 1,000 (mostly militia) repulsed the attack, inflicting perhaps 100 casualties on the Xhosa. Simultaneously, rebels of the Khoikhoi tribe attacked other forts and settlements, taking Fort Armstrong and the Khoikhoi Kat River Settlement.

By early 1851, some 20,000 warriors of several Bantu tribes were in rebellion. The British were outnumbered about 2 to 1, but, reinforced by the end of the year, British forces assumed the offensive and penetrated deep into Xhosa country in the Waterkloof region. They destroyed vast herds, some 80,000 head of cattle, the principal source of tribal wealth as well as sustenance, and they captured or killed about 16,000 warriors.

British losses were 1,400 killed or dead from disease. In addition, on February 26, 1852, the steamer *Birkenhead* foundered on rocks off Cape Agulhus with the loss of 445 Royal Navy sailors and army reinforcements. A peace was concluded on March 2, 1853.

See also KAFFIR WAR, FIRST; KAFFIR WAR, SECOND; KAFFIR WAR, THIRD; KAFFIR WAR, FOURTH; KAFFIR WAR, FIFTH; KAFFIR WAR, SIXTH; KAFFIR WAR, SEVENTH; KAFFIR WAR, EIGHTH; KAFFIR WAR, NINTH.

Further reading: Noel Mostert, *Frontiers: The Epic of South Africa's Creation and the Tragedy of the Xhosa People* (New York: Alfred A. Knopf, 1993); Leonard Thompson, *A History of South Africa,* 3rd ed. (New Haven, Conn.: Yale University Press, 2001).

Kaffir War, Ninth (1877–1878)

PRINCIPAL COMBATANTS: Great Britain colonials vs. the Xhosa tribe
PRINCIPAL THEATER(S): South Africa
DECLARATION: None
MAJOR ISSUES AND OBJECTIVES: The Xhosa made a last-ditch effort to recover lands lost in previous wars.
OUTCOME: The British swiftly suppressed this latest rebellion, then cracked down harder than before, seizing and annexing all remaining Xhosa lands.

APPROXIMATE MAXIMUM NUMBER OF MEN UNDER ARMS: Unknown
CASUALTIES: British colonials, 193 killed; Xhosa, 3,680 killed
TREATIES: None

The Xhosa defeat in the Eighth KAFFIR WAR in 1853 had been total and terrible, driving the already desperate tribe to even greater desperation. At the behest of Chief Sarili (fl. 1870s) and as they had done in preparation for the 1850–53 war, the Xhosa destroyed their own crops and cattle in 1856, persuaded that such a sacrifice would propitiate the spirits of their ancestors and bring them aid in combating the British. The result of this destruction was increased starvation and the deaths of as many as 55,000 Xhosa.

By the 1870s, the self-destruction had ceased, and the Xhosa, though badly depleted, began gearing up again for war. An uprising exploded in August 1877 but was quickly suppressed by June 1878. Chief Sandile (d. 1878) was killed, as was Chief Siyolo (d. 1878), and the Xhosa's remaining lands were annexed by the British, who reduced the proud tribe to total economic dependency. The Xhosa became a conquered people.

See also AXE, WAR OF THE; KAFFIR WAR, FIRST; KAFFIR WAR, SECOND; KAFFIR WAR, THIRD; KAFFIR WAR, FOURTH; KAFFIR WAR, FIFTH; KAFFIR WAR, SIXTH.

Further reading: James Lawrence, *The Savage Wars: British Campaigns in Africa, 1870–1920* (New York: St. Martin's Press, 1985); Noel Mostert, *Frontiers: The Epic of South Africa's Creation and the Tragedy of the Xhosa People* (New York: Alfred A. Knopf, 1993); Leonard Thompson, *A History of South Africa,* 3rd ed. (New Haven, Conn.: Yale University Press, 2001).

Kalmar, War of (1611–1613)

PRINCIPAL COMBATANTS: Sweden vs. the Kingdom of Denmark and Norway
PRINCIPAL THEATER(S): Finnmark and southern Swedish coast
DECLARATION: Mutual, 1611
MAJOR ISSUES AND OBJECTIVES: The two sides fought for possession of the Finnmark region.
OUTCOME: Denmark and Norway gained control of Finnmark.
APPROXIMATE MAXIMUM NUMBER OF MEN UNDER ARMS: Unknown
CASUALTIES: Unknown
TREATIES: Peace of Knäred, 1613

Sweden's king Charles IX (1550–1611) attempted to wield absolute control over the Finnmark portion of the Scandinavian peninsula, the far northern region that offered a bounty in fisheries and fur trapping. Charles coupled this with various other attempts to curtail Danish trade in the Gulf of Riga and the eastern Baltic generally. In response, King Christian IV (1577–1648) of Denmark and Norway dispatched a fleet to defend trade in the Öresund (Danish Sound), then invited negotiation with Charles. The Swedish king refused to attempt peaceful resolution of Swedish-Danish border difficulties, and both nations declared war.

The Danes opened up with an offensive through Västergötland while the Norwegians laid siege against the Swedish port of Kalmar. Charles and his son Gustavus Adolphus (1594–1632) led a relief force to Kalmar, but the Danes then reinforced the assault, and the Swedes fell back to Visby, relinquishing Kalmar to the Danes by the summer of 1611. Incredibly, the frustrated Charles, defeated in battle, challenged Christian to a duel as a means of settling the fate of Kalmar. The king of Denmark and Norway wisely declined, then attacked the Swedes at Visby, but withdrew after a three-day drawn battle.

Charles IX died late in 1611, leaving the war to his son Gustavus II. He fared no better than his father, however, losing Finnmark and the port of Älvsborg in southeastern Sweden in May 1612. Exhausted, Gustavus II concluded the Peace of Knäred early in 1613, yielding to Danish-Norwegian control Finnmark but reclaiming Älvsborg in exchange for an annual tribute. Kalmar was also returned to Sweden.

See also KALMAR CIVIL WAR; THIRTY YEARS' WAR.

Further reading: Byron J. Nordstrom, *The History of Sweden* (Westport, Conn.: Greenwood Press, 2002); Michael Roberts, *Gustavus Adolphus: A History of Sweden, 1611–1632,* 2 vols. (London and New York: Longmans, Green, 1953–1958); Franklin D. Scott, *Sweden, the Nation's History* (Carbondale: Southern Illinois University Press, 1988).

Kalmar Civil War (1520–1523)

PRINCIPAL COMBATANTS: Swedish rebels vs. the Kalmar Union
PRINCIPAL THEATER(S): Sweden
DECLARATION: None
MAJOR ISSUES AND OBJECTIVES: Sweden wanted to end oppression by the Kalmar Union monarch Christian II.
OUTCOME: Led by Gustavus Eriksson Vasa, the rebellion deposed Christian II, drove the Danes out of Sweden, and put Gustavus on the throne of an independent Sweden.
APPROXIMATE MAXIMUM NUMBER OF MEN UNDER ARMS: Unknown
CASUALTIES: Christian II ordered the execution of nearly 100 Swedish nobles.
TREATIES: None

By virtue of the Kalmar Union (1397), King Christian II (1481–1559) was king of Denmark, Sweden, and Norway. A Swedish rival presented himself, however, in Sten Sture the Younger (c. 1493–1520), regent to the Swedish throne. Christian led a Danish army in an invasion of Sweden in 1520 and was met in battle at Bogesund by Sten Sture. The regent was fatally wounded in the battle, whereupon his widow encouraged the Stockholm garrison to resist a siege, which the garrison did for five months before surrendering on November 4, 1520. Christian II was crowned in Stockholm the next day, on November 5, 1520, and, three days later, convened a "spiritual court" to justify, on religious grounds, a general purge of all opponents. The purge was nothing less than a massacre (later dubbed the Stockholm Massacre or the Bath of Blood) of nearly 100 Swedish noblemen. This provoked a rebellion, beginning among the peasants of the central Swedish province of Dalecarlia, led by a fugitive noble, Gustavus Eriksson Vasa (1496–1560).

Beginning with his peasant army, Vasa gradually conquered Danish-held areas. With each triumph, he attracted more recruits. He progressed through Uppsala and enjoyed such success that the Swedish Diet officially proclaimed Vasa liberator and administrator in August 1521. Thus sanctioned, he laid siege against Stockholm, which fell to him on June 20, 1523, whereupon Christian left the throne and was driven out of Sweden as well as Denmark. Vasa assumed the Swedish throne as Gustavus I later in 1523, thereby dissolving the Kalmar Union and rendering Sweden independent. In 1524, Frederick I (c. 1471–1533), successor to Christian in Denmark, met with Gustavus peacefully to settle lingering boundary differences between Denmark and Sweden. (The Kalmar Civil War is also known as the Swedish Civil War of 1520–23.)

See also DANISH-SWEDISH WAR (1563–1570); KALMAR, WAR OF.

Further reading: Byron J. Nordstrom, *The History of Sweden* (Westport, Conn.: Greenwood Press, 2002); Franklin D. Scott, *Sweden, the Nation's History* (Carbondale: Southern Illinois University Press, 1988).

Kalmar War with Holstein (1409–1435)

PRINCIPAL COMBATANTS: Kalmar Union vs. Holstein (with the Hanseatic League)
PRINCIPAL THEATER(S): Holstein, Öresund, and Copenhagen and vicinity
DECLARATION: None
MAJOR ISSUES AND OBJECTIVES: Erik VII, king of the Kalmar Union, wanted possession of Schleswig; the count of Holstein resisted.
OUTCOME: After a very long war, Erik returned Schleswig to Holstein.
APPROXIMATE MAXIMUM NUMBER OF MEN UNDER ARMS: Unknown

CASUALTIES: Unknown
TREATIES: 1435 agreement returning Schleswig to the count of Holstein

The Kalmar Union was a combination of the three crowns of Denmark, Sweden, and Norway, which, in 1409 was ruled by Erik of Pomerania as Erik VII (1382–1459). In this year, challenging the count of Holstein's possession of the duchy of Schleswig, Erik seized it, prompting Holstein to the desperate stratagem of opening the ports of Schleswig to the Victualling Brothers, a notorious band of pirates. These men successfully pushed Erik's invading force out of Schleswig. Although Erik suffered further reverses during 1416–18, he regained Fehman Island, which emboldened him to oppose the powerful Hanseatic League. In 1422, he issued an edict permitting only Danes to practice trades and crafts, effectively shutting out Hanseatic League members, whereupon the league allied itself with Holstein in the KALMAR WAR WITH THE HANSEATIC LEAGUE from 1422 to 1435.

Erik now turned his attention to the defense of Pomerania, which he feared would be invaded by the Swedes of Kalmar. Leaving his army to hold Flensburg, he led his navy in the defeat of the Hanseatic League's fleet in the Öresund. He sought to capitalize on this victory by levying in 1428 a heavy toll on ships sailing through the Öresund. This served only to provoke new opposition from the Hanseatic League and Holstein, which besieged the Danish capital of Copenhagen. Copenhagen resisted and withstood the siege, but Flensburg finally fell to Holstein and the league in 1431. Desultory fighting continued for another four years before Erik finally concluded a treaty with Holstein and with the Hanseatic League, by which Schleswig was returned to Holstein. Thus a quarter century of warfare netted Erik nothing at all.

Further reading: Byron J. Nordstrom, *The History of Sweden* (Westport, Conn.: Greenwood Press, 2002); Franklin D. Scott, *Sweden, the Nation's History* (Carbondale: Southern Illinois University Press, 1988).

Kalmar War with the Hanseatic League (1422–1435)

PRINCIPAL COMBATANTS: Erik VII (Kalmar Union) vs. Hanseatic League (with Holstein)
PRINCIPAL THEATER(S): Baltic Sea and Flensburg
DECLARATION: Hanseatic League on King Erik VII of the Kalmar Union
MAJOR ISSUES AND OBJECTIVES: The Hanseatic League wanted to break Erik's attempts to monopolize trade with Norway and extort exorbitant taxes on league vessels.
OUTCOME: Erik was defeated.
APPROXIMATE MAXIMUM NUMBER OF MEN UNDER ARMS: Unknown

CASUALTIES: Unknown
TREATIES: 1435 agreement returning Schleswig to the count of Holstein

While Danish King Erik VII (1382–1459), ruler of the Kalmar Union (the three crowns of Denmark, Sweden, and Norway), warred—from 1409 to 1435—with Holstein over possession of Schleswig (*see* KALMAR WAR WITH HOLSTEIN), Holstein's ally, the Hanseatic League declared war on Erik. Erik had levied exorbitant tolls on ships navigating the Öresund (Danish Sound) and had blocked non-Danish trade to Norway. The mercantile Hanseatic League sought to wrest control of the Öresund from Erik by retaking Flensburg, the Baltic port Erik had seized in the war with Holstein. An amphibious assault by the Hanseatic League failed to capture Copenhagen in 1428, but the Battle of Stralsund, on the Baltic, nearly destroyed the Swedish fleet. With the fleet greatly diminished, Erik could no longer effectively defend Flensburg, which surrendered to the Hanseatic League in 1431. Both the war with Holstein and the war against the Hanseatic League dragged on after this in a desultory manner until 1435, when Erik, realizing the futility of the struggle, concluded peace with both Holstein and the league. Holstein regained Schleswig, and the vessels of the Hanseatic League freely traversed the Öresund and traded with Norway. As in the war with Holstein, Erik had gained absolutely nothing in what amounted to a quarter century of war.

See also SCANDINAVIAN REVOLT.

Further reading: Philippe Dollinger, *The German Hansa,* trans. D. S. Ault and S. H. Steinburg (Palo Alto, Calif.: Stanford University Press, 1970); Byron J. Nordstrom, *The History of Sweden* (Westport, Conn.: Greenwood Press, 2002); Franklin D. Scott, *Sweden, the Nation's History* (Carbondale: Southern Illinois University Press, 1988).

Kampuchean Civil War (1978–1998)

PRINCIPAL COMBATANTS: Khmer Rouge vs. Vietnam-supported anti–Khmer Rouge forces
PRINCIPAL THEATER(S): Kampuchea (Cambodia)
DECLARATION: None
MAJOR ISSUES AND OBJECTIVES: Pol Pot's Khmer Rouge sought to retain its rule over Kampuchea.
OUTCOME: The Khmer Rouge gradually disintegrated under the combined pressure of several anti–Khmer Rouge forces, which formed a coalition government.
APPROXIMATE MAXIMUM NUMBER OF MEN UNDER ARMS: Anti–Khmer Rouge forces (Vietnamese occupiers), 140,000; Khmer Rouge, 40,000
CASUALTIES: Combat casualties pale in comparison to the deaths related to Pol Pot's "cultural revolution": about 2 million.
TREATIES: Paris Peace Agreement, October 23, 1991

Born on May 19, 1928, in Cambodia, Pol Pot (1928–98) became a follower of Vietnam's Ho Chi Minh (c. 1890–1969) and joined Ho's Indochinese Communist Party during World War II. Pol Pot assumed leadership of the Khmer Rouge guerrilla movement, which overthrew the U.S.-backed Cambodian government of Lon Nol (1913–85) in 1975 (*see* CAMBODIAN CIVIL WAR). Pol Pot then became prime minister of Democratic Kampuchea, the new regime's name for Cambodia, in April 1976. Under Pol Pot, the Khmer Rouge sought to implement a radical form of Mao Zedong's (1893–1976) ideal of agrarian communism. Pol Pot's regime appropriated land and sought to refashion society, not only through education and indoctrination, but, more directly, by the mass murder of approximately 2 million Cambodians.

While his Khmer Rouge forces turned the nation into "killing fields," Kampuchea also fended off border attacks from Vietnam. The Vietnamese urged Kampuchean rebels to step up efforts to overthrow the Pol Pot regime. Finally, in 1978, an army of 200,000 Vietnamese troops invaded Kampuchea, taking the capital city of Phnom Penh on January 9, 1979. The Vietnamese installed Heng Samrin (b. 1931), a dissident member of the Khmer Rouge, as president of occupied Kampuchea, but Pol Pot continued to lead a Khmer Rouge guerrilla campaign against the new government and the Vietnamese invaders.

In 1982, three Khmer forces united to oust the Vietnamese invaders and overturn the Vietnamese-bolstered government. Prince Norodom Sihanouk (b. 1922), exiled former ruler of Cambodia, formed a coalition government-in-exile that included the Khmer Rouge and which received United Nations recognition. The government stood ready to replace the Vietnamese-supported regime whenever that proved militarily feasible. In 1984, however, Vietnamese forces campaigned vigorously against Khmer camps along the Thai-Kampuchean border but continued to encounter stiff resistance from the guerrillas. The Vietnamese secured Soviet aid in fighting the guerrillas, but by the late 1980s, the Soviets counseled the Vietnamese to begin withdrawing from Kampuchea. The Khmer Rouge, by the late 1980s about 40,000 strong, attempted to regain territory as the Vietnamese pulled out, but with no success. At last, in 1989, the regime in Phnom Penh restored the country's original name, Cambodia, and, on October 23, 1991, the four Khmer factions, those siding with Sihanouk, the Kampuchean People's National Liberation Front, the Khmer Rouge, and the Phnom Penh government, signed a peace accord in Paris. The United Nations supervised the disarming of at least some of the Khmer factions and repatriated approximately 375,000 refugees who had fled to Thailand. Later in 1991, Prince Sihanouk returned from exile to Phnom Penh as an elected president, replacing Heng Samrin.

All was far from well, however. Almost immediately, in 1992, Khmer Rouge rebels attacked the United Nations forces. Prince Sihanouk failed to introduce unity into the Phnom Penh government, which was torn by dissension. Nevertheless, Khmer Rouge forces suffered severe defeats in Pailin and Phnom Malai, relinquishing bases there in 1996. The Khmer Rouge was falling apart, its constituents fleeing into the jungle.

Yet while the threat from the Khmer Rouge decreased, internal strife in Phnom Penh rapidly escalated. Rival prime ministers, Prince Norodom Ranariddh—Sihanouk's son—and Hun Sen (b. 1951), each sought to recruit dispersed Khmer Rouge rebels to bolster their positions. In July 1997, fighting developed in the capital, and Hun Sen ousted Ranariddh, who barely escaped with his life. His father, President Sihanouk, was soon forced to leave the country as well—though not for political reasons so much as medical ones: he had cancer.

With Ranariddh out of the way, Hun Sen had little use now for the Khmer Rouge, whose disintegration became more rapid. Those who were left in the organization turned against Pol Pot, whom they replaced with Ta Mok (b. 1918). In 1997, the Khmer Rouge remnants tried Pol Pot in absentia and sentenced him to house arrest for life. As the Khmer Rouge continued to disintegrate, Pol Pot met his death on April 15, 1998, either at the hands of the Khmer Rouge or from illness. He had never been officially brought to trial for genocide. In December, the last of the Khmer Rouge surrendered to the government and voluntarily disarmed. Ta Mok was placed under arrest in 1999 and held in prison, where he remained for years awaiting trial by a United Nations tribunal on war crimes.

See also KAMPUCHEAN-THAI BORDER WAR.

Further reading: Ben Kiernan, *How Pol Pot Came to Power* (London: Verso, 1985); William Shawcross, *Cambodia's New Deal: A Report* (Washington, D.C.: Carnegie Endowment for International Peace, Brookings Institution, 1994) and *The Quality of Mercy: Cambodia, Holocaust, and Modern Conscience* (New York: Simon and Schuster, 1984).

Kampuchean-Thai Border War (1977–1995)

PRINCIPAL COMBATANTS: Kampuchea (including occupying Vietnamese forces) vs. Thailand
PRINCIPAL THEATER(S): Thai-Kampuchean borderlands
DECLARATION: None
MAJOR ISSUES AND OBJECTIVES: Thailand sought to defend its border against incursions by various Cambodian factions and Vietnamese occupying forces.
OUTCOME: Thanks in part to United Nations intervention, the border war wound down without ultimate resolution.
APPROXIMATE MAXIMUM NUMBER OF MEN UNDER ARMS: Variable on all sides; the United Nations effectively policed the borderlands with about 16,000 peacekeepers.
CASUALTIES: Unknown; approximately 375,000 Kampuchean refugees crossed the Thai border.
TREATIES: None

The reign of terror of Pol Pot (1928–98) and the KAMPUCHEAN CIVIL WAR from 1978 to 1998 created hundreds of thousands of Kampuchean (Cambodian) refugees beginning in 1975. Pol Pot's radical and fierce Khmer Rouge frequently attacked the Thai border near Aranyaprathet, and Thailand responded by closing its borders and using aircraft and artillery to repel the enemy attacks. During 1979–80, Vietnamese forces occupying Kampuchea also invaded Thai borderlands in an effort to find Khmer Rouge guerrillas, who reportedly infiltrated the refugee camps and hid in them. Thailand found itself fighting Khmer Rouge and Vietnamese forces in addition to rebel Thai communists, antigovernment Meo tribesmen, Thai Muslim separatists, opium dealers, and others who used the general conflict to achieve their ends. Ultimately, Thailand did provide support to the Khmer Rouge in the hope that it would bring a Kampuchean government friendlier to it than alternative regimes. Besides, by appeasing the Khmer Rouge, Thai officials sought to deprive their own communist rebels of an ally and reduce the number of enemy threats they had to face. Nevertheless, Thailand suffered the moral censure of the international community for supporting so vicious a regime. The United Nations intervened, and by 1992, the intervention was having a positive effect. Approximately 375,000 Cambodian refugees were being repatriated, and the situation along the Thai-Cambodian border steadily improved, so that, by 1995, the war gradually came to an end.

Further reading: Ben Kiernan, *How Pol Pot Came to Power* (London: Verso, 1985); Stephen Reynell, *Political Pawns: Refugees in the Thai-Kampuchean Border* (Oxford: Refugee Studies Program, 189); William Shawcross, *Cambodia's New Deal: A Report* (Washington, D.C.: Carnegie Endowment for International Peace, Brookings Institution, 1994) and *The Quality of Mercy: Cambodia, Holocaust, and Modern Conscience* (New York: Simon and Schuster, 1984).

Kansas-Missouri Border Wars (Wakarusa War; the Sack of Lawrence; "Bleeding Kansas"; Pottawatomie Massacre) (1855–1860)

PRINCIPAL COMBATANTS: Antislavery factions, mostly in Kansas, vs. proslavery factions, mostly in Missouri
PRINCIPAL THEATER(S): Kansas-Missouri border regions
DECLARATION: None
MAJOR ISSUES AND OBJECTIVES: The Kansas-Nebraska Act had made slavery a local option, and settlers on both sides of the issue fought to make sure that Kansas entered the union expressing their point of view.
OUTCOME: Kansas was not accepted into the Union until 1861, and the border wars continued to the eve of the American Civil War, fought over the same issues.

APPROXIMATE MAXIMUM NUMBER OF MEN UNDER ARMS: Unknown
CASUALTIES: In Kansas, 55 killed between 1855 and 1858; at the Sack of Lawrence, 183 killed
TREATIES: None

In 1854, the U.S. Congress passed the Kansas-Nebraska Act, throwing the decision of whether to allow slavery in the territories seeking statehood back to the respective territories. Leaving the question of slavery up to the "popular sovereignty" of the settlers ensured that violence would erupt in the territories sooner or later.

The act spawned the Republican Party and led U.S. senator David R. Atchison (1807–86) of Missouri, who had already broken with his hoary and respected former fellow senator Thomas Hart Benton (1782–1852) over slavery, to swear that he would let the territory "sink in hell" before allowing it to be organized as a Free-Soil state. Nebraskans, clearly, would opt for freedom, but Kansas was up for grabs. Abolitionists in the North organized the Emigrant Aid Society and financed free settlers in Kansas. New England authors like William Cullen Bryant (1794–1878) and John Greenleaf Whittier (1807–92) mounted one of history's great propaganda campaigns, quickly aided by newspaperman Horace Greeley (1811–72) and correspondents sent by eastern newspapers to report on the Kansas "situation."

In response, fearing and hating the "Yankee slavestealers" and egged on by Atchison, thousands of proslavery Missourians, mainly from the tobacco- and hemp-growing western counties, flooded into Kansas to vote illegally and then return home to their farms. Overwhelming the Kansas settlers, the majority of whom were probably Free-Soilers, the Missouri emigres elected a territorial legislature that immediately legalized slavery and won official recognition from the federal government. Free Soilers poured in from around the country to settle the land, formed their own legislature, set their capital up at Lawrence, and petitioned Congress for admission to the Union as a free state. When an antislavery man was murdered in November 1855, open warfare broke out along the Kansas-Missouri border.

At first it was called the Wakarusa War because a series of clashes between pro- and antislavery factions occurred along the Wakarusa River near Lawrence from November 26, 1855, to December 7, 1855, in which a few casualties occurred. Atchison resigned his seat in the Senate to lead the fight, organized a posse of Missourians, and—under the ruse of answering a U.S. marshal's summons—raided Lawrence. Popularly dubbed "border ruffians," the posse set fire to a hotel and a few houses, chopped up a printing press, arrested several free-state leaders, and killed three others in the process. A monomaniacal abolitionist named John Brown (1800–59) retaliated by murdering five pro-slavery settlers on the Pottawatomie Creek, none of whom had been involved in the violence against free-state settlers, then mutilating their bodies. Ideologically motivated assassination had begun. The Sack of Lawrence and the Pottawatomie Massacre threw Kansas into chaos.

John Brown became a hero in the North, which had grown to despise pro-slavery Missourians, like those Brown butchered, as subhumans. Missourians on the other hand considered Free Soilers foreign foes and hypocrites, who had come to Kansas for no other purpose than to steal and hide runaway slaves from Missouri.

By the time the federal government could join up with the governments of Missouri and Kansas to bring the guerrilla fighting (and the house and crop burnings, the cattle theft, the tarring and feathering, the torture, the murder, the continuing mutilation of the slain) in "Bleeding Kansas" more or less to an end, more than 200 people were dead and $2 million worth of property had been destroyed. In the fall of 1856, John Geary (1819–73), a former mayor of San Francisco, now governor of Kansas, nationalized both the pro-slavery and free-state militias, deploying them along with federal troops to stop the fighting.

But the ideological war continued in the pro-slavery-dominated legislature, which overrode Geary's veto and set up a constitutional convention. The convention phrased a referendum on the constitution so that a vote "yes" and a vote "no" *both* approved slavery. The Lecompton Constitution, as it was called, passed in 1857, not only making slavery legal but making it permanent: the constitution forbade future voters from outlawing human bondage. Free Soilers boycotted the vote; pro-slavers submitted the document to Congress in an application for statehood. President James Buchanan (1791–1868) accepted it, but Senator Stephan Douglas (1813–61), leading the opposition, denounced the document as a travesty, and Congress refused to allow Kansas into the Union as a slave state.

The fighting started all over again, erupting into civil war, which lasted until federal troops again intervened and restored order in 1860, on the eve of that larger UNITED STATES CIVIL WAR that the Kansas border wars had done so much to encourage.

Further reading: Eric Corder, *Prelude to Civil War: Kansas-Missouri* (New York: Crowell-Collier Press, 1990); Perry McCandless, *A History of Missouri: Volume II, 1820–1860* (Columbia: University of Missouri Press, 1972); Jay Monaghan, *Civil War on the Western Border, 1854–1864* (Lincoln: University of Nebraska Press, 1985); William E. Parish, *A History of Missouri, Volume 3: 1860–1875* (Columbia: University of Missouri Press, 1973); Charles Phillips, *Missouri: Crossroads of the Nation* (Sun Valley, Calif.: American Historical Press, 2003).

Kappel Wars (1529 and 1531)

PRINCIPAL COMBATANTS: Zurich Protestant reformers vs. Catholic cantons of the Christian Union
PRINCIPAL THEATER(S): Border between Zurich and Zug
DECLARATION: Christian Union on Zurich, 1529 and 1531
MAJOR ISSUES AND OBJECTIVES: Zurich Protestant reformers wanted to convert more Swiss cantons to Protestantism; five Catholic cantons, the Christian Union, resisted.
OUTCOME: Zurich was compelled to recognize Catholic rights in the Christian Union cantons.
APPROXIMATE MAXIMUM NUMBER OF MEN UNDER ARMS: Unknown
CASUALTIES: Unknown
TREATIES: First Peace of Kappel, June 26, 1529; Second Peace of Kappel, October 1531

In the 16th century, Zurich was a Protestant city driven by the religious reformer Huldreich Zwingli (1484–1531) to proselytize its neighboring Swiss cities and cantons. When it imposed a trade embargo on those cantons still loyal to the pope, five cantons—Uri, Schwyz, Lucerne, Unterwalden, and Zug—formed the Christian Union to oppose Zurich. This led to low-level battles during 1529, quickly quelled by an armistice (First Peace of Kappel) concluded at Kappel, a monastery on the border between Zurich and Zug. A key condition of the armistice was the severance of ties between Austria and the Christian Union.

Just three years after the armistice was agreed to, the Christian Union declared war on Zurich because it believed that a non-Union Catholic canton, Thurgau, was being forced into Protestantism. The declaration and offensive came so quickly that the war was concluded in a single battle, at Kappel. The hastily assembled and badly outnumbered Protestant army charged the Catholic forces on October 11, 1531, only to be crushed. Among the casualties was Huldreich Zwingli. By the Second Peace of Kappel, Zurich agreed to recognize and respect the rights of Catholics within the cantons of the Christian Union. The peace endured.

See also PEASANTS' WAR; SCHMALKALDIC WAR; VILLMERGEN WAR, FIRST; VILLMERGEN WAR, SECOND.

Further reading: Edgar Bonjour, H. S. Offler, and G. R. Potter, *A Short History of Switzerland* (Westport, Conn.: Greenwood Press, 1985); William Martin, *Switzerland: From Roman Times to the Present* (London: Elek, 1971).

Karmathian Revolt (899–906)

PRINCIPAL COMBATANTS: Karmathians vs. Caliph al-Mu'tadid
PRINCIPAL THEATER(S): Mesopotamia and Syria

DECLARATION: None
MAJOR ISSUES AND OBJECTIVES: The Shi'ite Karmathians rebelled against the orthodox Islam thrust upon them by the caliph.
OUTCOME: The Karmathians overran large areas but were eventually suppressed.
APPROXIMATE MAXIMUM NUMBER OF MEN UNDER ARMS: Unknown
CASUALTIES: Unknown
TREATIES: None

The Karmathians (Qarmatians) of lower Mesopotamia, members of the Ismailite Shi'ite sect, rebelled against the orthodox rule imposed on them by Caliph al-Mu'tadid (d. 902). In response to the rebellion, the caliph sent an army to suppress the rebels. Not only did this effort at suppression fail, but the Karmathians, under Abu Sa'id al-Djannabi (d. 913) invaded territory throughout Mesopotamia, penetrating as far as Syria. Many major cities fell to the Karmathians, including Basra, near the Persian Gulf (in modern Iraq). With great difficulty, the Karmathians were driven out of most of the areas they had overrun and, by 906, were totally cleared out of Syria, only to return to invade Iraq several times in 930.

See also MECCA, SACK OF.

Further reading: Hugh Kennedy, *The Prophet and the Age of the Caliphates: The Islamic Near East from the Sixth to the Eleventh Century* (New York: Longman, 1986); Michel C. Morony, *Iraq after the Muslim Conquest* (Princeton, N.J.: Princeton University Press, 1984).

Kett's Rebellion (1549)

PRINCIPAL COMBATANTS: England's landed nobles vs. English peasants
PRINCIPAL THEATER(S): Norfolk County
DECLARATION: No formal declaration
MAJOR ISSUES AND OBJECTIVES: England's peasants rebelled against the enclosure laws that drove them off their farms.
OUTCOME: The revolt was suppressed, and its leaders were executed.
APPROXIMATE MAXIMUM NUMBER OF MEN UNDER ARMS: Peasants, under Robert Kett, about 16,000; John Dudley, earl of Warwick, 1,400 German landsknechts
CASUALTIES: Peasants, 3,500; nobles, 40 killed
TREATIES: No formal treaty

When England's landed nobles passed the enclosure acts, families were thrown off their farms so the nobles could make more money grazing livestock. The peasants, having no place to go, staged a revolt in July 1549 during a routine feast in the town of Wymondham. Robert Kett (d. 1549), a tanner or a small landowner, led the peasant forces to Norwich, the town seat of Norfolk County. Kett formed a camp on nearby Mousehold Heath and took time to introduce a system of discipline and justice among his 16,000 followers. When he received a royal offer of amnesty, he refused it and, on August 1, led his forces in an attack on Norwich, which they captured. For most of a month, Kett and the rebels destroyed enclosing fences and hedges surrounding nobles' lands and plundered their property.

On August 27, Kett faced John Dudley (1502–53), earl of Warwick, and his forces of well-trained soldiers. Dudley's troops, better disciplined and skilled, quickly defeated the rebels. Kett was hanged, and the rebellion was over.

Further reading: S. T. Bindoff, *Kett's Rebellion, 1549* (London: The Historical Association, 1949); L. A. Clarkson, *The Pre-industrial Economy in England, 1500–1750* (New York: Schocken Books, 1972); G. R. Elton, *Reform and Reformation in England, 1509–1558* (London: Arnold, 1977).

Kharijite Rebellion (934–947)

PRINCIPAL COMBATANTS: Kharijites vs. Fatimids
PRINCIPAL THEATER(S): Central North Africa
DECLARATION: None
MAJOR ISSUES AND OBJECTIVES: Political and religious rebellion against the prevailing dynasty
OUTCOME: After a long guerrilla struggle, the Kharijite opposition was defeated by the Fatimids under Caliph al-Mansur.
APPROXIMATE MAXIMUM NUMBER OF MEN UNDER ARMS: Unknown
CASUALTIES: Unknown
TREATIES: None

The Kharijites, a heretical and politically rebellious Muslim sect, which had been instrumental in the overthrow of the Omayyad dynasty in Morocco (*see* KHARIJITE REVOLT) in 742, rose up in 934 against the Fatimid dynasty in central North Africa. Under the leadership of Abu Yazid Makhlad, the Kharijites conducted a war of raiding and guerrilla action, which spanned 13 years until, at last, a combination of persistence and attrition suppressed them. The Fatimid victors were led by Caliph al-Mansur (d. 953).

Further reading: P. M. Holt, Ann K. S. Lambton, and Bernard Lewis, *The Cambridge History of Islam,* 2 vols. (New York: Cambridge University Press, 1970).

Kharijite Revolt (741–742)

PRINCIPAL COMBATANTS: Kharijites and Berbers vs. Omayyads
PRINCIPAL THEATER(S): Morocco

DECLARATION: None

MAJOR ISSUES AND OBJECTIVES: Rebellion against Omayyad control of Morocco

OUTCOME: The Omayyads were ousted from Morocco and went into a general decline, heralding their overthrow by the Abbasids in 750.

APPROXIMATE MAXIMUM NUMBER OF MEN UNDER ARMS: Unknown

CASUALTIES: Unknown

TREATIES: None

The Kharijites, a heretical Muslim sect, united briefly with Berbers in armed rebellion against the Omayyad dynasty, which controlled Morocco. The Omayyad forces were driven out of the country, and, thanks to continual Kharijite pressure, the Omayyads nearly lost control of their other provinces in North Africa. The Omayyad caliphate entered a period of sharp decline, which culminated in 747 with the outbreak of the Abbasid rebellion and, by 750, the overthrow of the Omayyads by the Abbasids.

See also KHARIJITE REBELLION.

Further reading: P. M. Holt, Ann K. S. Lambton, and Bernard Lewis, *The Cambridge History of Islam,* 2 vols. (New York: Cambridge University Press, 1970).

Khazar-Muslim Caucasus War (727–733)

PRINCIPAL COMBATANTS: Khazars vs. Muslims (under Caliph Hisham)

PRINCIPAL THEATER(S): Caucasus region, especially Georgia

DECLARATION: None

MAJOR ISSUES AND OBJECTIVES: Muslim religious expansion and conquest

OUTCOME: At first driven from the region, the Muslims returned in greater force, overcame the Khazars, and reestablished control of Georgia.

APPROXIMATE MAXIMUM NUMBER OF MEN UNDER ARMS: Unknown

CASUALTIES: Unknown

TREATIES: Unknown

During the eighth century, Muslim forces swept into the Caucasus, where they enjoyed initial military success and were able to establish themselves north of the Daryal Pass. However, the Khazar warriors of this region counterattacked, driving the Muslim forces back into Mesopotamia. Recovering from their retreat, the Muslims regrouped and reinforced their numbers, then renewed the attack, this time overwhelming the Khazars. The Muslims retook Georgia and pushed the limit of their northern frontier to the Caucasus. Derbent became an advanced Muslim outpost, which kept the Khazars in check.

Further reading: Sir John Bagot Glubb, *The Great Arab Conquests* (London: Hodder and Stoughton, 1963); P. M. Holt, Ann K. S. Lambton, and Bernard Lewis, *The Cambridge History of Islam,* 2 vols. (New York: Cambridge University Press, 1970); Arthur Koestler, *The Thirteenth Tribe: The Khazar Empire and Its Heritage* (New York: Random House, 1976).

Khmer-Cham War (1050–1051)

PRINCIPAL COMBATANTS: Khmer vs. Cham forces (with Cham-allied Khmer rebels)

PRINCIPAL THEATER(S): Champa (central Vietnam) and the southern portions of the Khmer Empire (Cambodia)

DECLARATION: None

MAJOR ISSUES AND OBJECTIVES: Cham kings wanted to conquer the Khmer Empire.

OUTCOME: Cham military action incited a southern Khmer rebellion; however, the rebellion was crushed, and the Khmer Empire remained intact.

APPROXIMATE MAXIMUM NUMBER OF MEN UNDER ARMS: Unknown

CASUALTIES: Unknown

TREATIES: None

The kingdom of Champa (central Vietnam) and the southern portions of the Khmer Empire (Cambodia and portions of Laos) were torn by civil disorder during the 11th century. Then, in 1050, Jaya Paramesvarman (d. 1060), the Cham king, and his son Yuvaraja Mahasenapati (d. c. 1092) succeeded in putting down a revolt in Panduranga, a Champan province. After this, Yuvaraja's forces went on to triumph over the Khmers, taking the city of Sambhupura, demolishing the temples there, and donating loot and prisoners to the Mi-son temples. In the south, the Khmers rebelled in 1051, led by a Khmer vassal king or a Cham chieftain and supported by the Chams. The result of the rebellion was that the southern Khmer Empire fell into Cham hands.

A series of Khmer expeditions were sent against the rebel forces, which withstood all such assaults until late in 1051, when they were finally defeated and fled to Champa. The Khmers donated their booty to an Isvaran temple at Rajatirtha.

See also VIETNAMESE-CHAM WAR (1000–1044).

Further reading: Lawrence Palmer Briggs, *The Ancient Khmer Empire* (Philadelphia: American Philosophical Society, 1951); D. G. E. Hall, *A History of South-East Asia,* 4th ed. (New York: St. Martin's Press, 1981).

Khmer-Cham War (1144–1150)

PRINCIPAL COMBATANTS: Khmer Empire vs. Champa

PRINCIPAL THEATER(S): Champa (central Vietnam)

DECLARATION: None
MAJOR ISSUES AND OBJECTIVES: The Khmer emperor wanted to conquer Champa.
OUTCOME: Defiant leaders in southern Champa defeated Khmer forces.
APPROXIMATE MAXIMUM NUMBER OF MEN UNDER ARMS: Unknown
CASUALTIES: Unknown
TREATIES: None

When Dai Viet, also called Annam (northern Vietnam), concluded a peace with the kingdom of Champa (central Vietnam), Champa declined an alliance with the Khmer Empire to invade Dai Viet. King Suryavarman II (d. c. 1150) of the Khmer Empire (Cambodia and parts of Laos) then decided to invade Champa. His forces took the Cham capital of Vijaya (Binh Dinh), toppling King Jaya Indravarman III (d. c. 1145) and installing himself as ruler.

In defiance of this conquest, the Chams of Panduranga installed their own king, Rudravarman (d. 1147), and, following his death, his son Jaya Harivarman I (d. 1166–67). Suryavarman dispatched Khmer and Vijayan troops under Senapati Sankara (fl. 12th century), his greatest general, to put an end to defiance in Panduranga. In a stunning military display, Jaya Harivarman met this army at Chaklyang in the Phanrang Valley (in southern Vietnam) and annihilated it. Reeling from the blow, Suryavarman assembled a second army, which was fielded in 1148 and likewise destroyed, at Kayev in the Virapura plain.

Despite these defeats, Suryavarman made his brother-in-law Harideva (d. c. 1149) king of Champa, sending a Khmer army for his protection. In response, Jaya Harivarman pushed north, captured Vijaya and then destroyed this third Khmer force at Mahisa, killing Harideva and all of his chiefs. Jaya Harivarman was crowned king at Vijaya. In 1150, Suryavarman sent a fourth army into Champa. It met the same fate as the others.

See also CHAM CIVIL WAR.

Further reading: Lawrence Palmer Briggs, *The Ancient Khmer Empire* (Philadelphia: American Philosophical Society, 1951); D. G. E. Hall, *A History of South-East Asia*, 4th ed. (New York: St. Martin's Press, 1981).

OUTCOME: In the first phase of the war, the Khmers suffered devastating defeat; the second phase ended, however, in the subjugation of Champa by the Khmer Empire.
APPROXIMATE MAXIMUM NUMBER OF MEN UNDER ARMS: Extremely variable
CASUALTIES: Unknown
TREATIES: None

After he ascended the Cham throne, Jaya Indravarman IV (fl. 1170s) invaded the neighboring Khmer Empire (Cambodia and Laos), partly from motives of traditional enmity and partly to loot its vast stores of treasure. In a battle of 1171, the Chams won victory, in part, by using horses against the Khmers rather than the traditional elephants. The horses were a significant tactical innovation, providing greater speed and mobility and allowing the Chams to outmaneuver their enemy. The Chams emphasized shock tactics, which required speed and surprise. Unfortunately for Jaya Indravarman, he could not obtain horses in China's Kwangtung and Hunan provinces to use in a full-scale invasion of Khmer. In 1177, however, he attacked successfully by sea, sailing a fleet up the Tonle Sap (central Cambodia's "Great Lake") and the Siemreab River to take the undefended Khmer capital of Angkor. Jaya Indravarman burned the wooden city and ravaged its sacred temple (Angkor Wat), stripping it of treasure. He then ordered the death of the Khmer rebel king Tribhuvanadityavarman (fl. 1166–77).

The Khmers were rallied by King Jayavarman VII (c. 1120–c. 1215). In alliance with Thai forces and exiled Chams, the Khmers fought back, winning a significant sea victory in 1181. Jayavarman retook Angkor, rebuilding it as Angkor Thom, north of the old city. By 1190, he mounted an invasion deep into Champa, laying waste to much of its territory and destroying its capital city of Vijaya (Binh Dinh). Champa, defeated and conquered, was divided into two states, which were vassals of the Khmer Empire.

Further reading: Lawrence Palmer Briggs, *The Ancient Khmer Empire* (Philadelphia: American Philosophical Society, 1951); D. G. E. Hall, *A History of South-East Asia*, 4th ed. (New York: St. Martin's Press, 1981).

Khmer-Cham War (1167–1190)

PRINCIPAL COMBATANTS: Khmer Empire vs. Champa
PRINCIPAL THEATER(S): Champa (central Vietnam) and Khmer Empire (Cambodia and Laos)
DECLARATION: None
MAJOR ISSUES AND OBJECTIVES: Champa invaded the Khmer Empire principally to obtain treasure; after suffering defeat, Khmer forces mounted a counteroffensive with the object of conquering Champa.

Khmer-Cham War (1191–1203)

PRINCIPAL COMBATANTS: Khmer Empire vs. Champa
PRINCIPAL THEATER(S): Champa (central Vietnam)
DECLARATION: None
MAJOR ISSUES AND OBJECTIVES: Champa rebelled against conquest by the Khmer Empire.
OUTCOME: Although Champa briefly regained independence, by the end of the war the nation had been reconquered by the Khmers.

APPROXIMATE MAXIMUM NUMBER OF MEN UNDER ARMS:
Unknown
CASUALTIES: Unknown
TREATIES: None

The lengthy KHMER-CHAM WAR (1167–90) resulted in the conquest of Champa by the Khmer Empire. Within a year after the conclusion of this war, however, in 1191, the Chams rebelled. In short order, one of the two Khmer puppets, Prince In (d. after 1203), was overthrown by a Cham prince, who was subsequently crowned King Jaya Indravarman V (d. c. 1192). Jaya Indravarman next marched against and defeated the Khmer puppet ruling the other half of Champa, and Champa was once again reunited under the new king.

The Khmers sent two invasion forces to reconquer Champa, but both were defeated. In 1203, a third expedition, under King Jayavarman VII (c. 1120–c. 1215), recruited the support of Cham rebels opposed to Jaya Indravarman. The use of indigenous troops turned the tide, clearing the way for a successful invasion, which placed a new puppet on Champa's throne, Ong Dhanapatigrama (fl. 1220s). Propped up by the continual presence of a Khmer army, Ong presided over what was effectively a Khmer province for the next two decades. It is not known what reward or benefit the Cham rebels received from their arrangement.

Further reading: Lawrence Palmer Briggs, *The Ancient Khmer Empire* (Philadelphia: American Philosophical Society, 1951); D. G. E. Hall, *A History of South-East Asia,* 4th ed. (New York: St. Martin's Press, 1981).

Khmer Invasion of Champa *See* VIETNAMESE-KHMER WAR.

Khmer-Thai Wars (c. 1352–1444)

PRINCIPAL COMBATANTS: Khmer Empire vs. Ayutthayan Thai invaders
PRINCIPAL THEATER(S): Khmer Empire
DECLARATION: None
MAJOR ISSUES AND OBJECTIVES: The Thais of the Ayutthaya region wanted to conquer the neighboring Khmers.
OUTCOME: Most of the Khmer Empire fell to the Thais.
APPROXIMATE MAXIMUM NUMBER OF MEN UNDER ARMS: Extremely variable
CASUALTIES: Unknown
TREATIES: None

The Thai kingdom of Ayutthaya (south-central Thailand), which had been established by Rama Thibodi I

(1312–69) about 1350, first invaded the Khmer Empire (Cambodia and Laos) about 1352. The initial forces were led by King Rama Thibodi's son Prince Ramesuen (d. 1395), who was governor of Lop Buri Province. Ramesuen was not an able tactician and blundered by splitting his forces, committing to battle only a portion of them, approximately 5,000 troops. This force was crushed by an army of the Khmer crown prince, and it looked as if the invasion would die aborning. At this juncture, however, another Thai prince, Boromoraja I (d. 1388), governor of Sup'an, was dispatched to bolster the faltering invasion. His arrival surprised the Khmers, whose will and capacity to resist suddenly collapsed, and Boromoraja quickly annexed the Khorat and Chanthaburi districts (eastern Thailand).

Ayutthayan Thai invaders were apparently in possession of the Khmer capital of Angkor in 1369 and 1389. It is believed that the occupying forces kept the Khmers weak by threatening to demolish the complex irrigation system and loosing flood waters on the people. Added to this physical threat was continual pressure from the Thais as well as the Chams, which included meddling in Khmer royal politics. All of these factors weakened the Khmer Empire, leading to internal dissension and dynastic squabbling. Thus the position of the Thai occupiers was strengthened.

During 1430–31, Ayutthayan Thai forces led by Boromoraja II (d. 1448) laid siege to Angkor for seven months, at last traducing a pair of Buddhist monks and some Khmer officials, who admitted the invading force into the city. (These turncoats became full-time agents of the Thais following the death of the Khmer king, Dharmasoka in about 1444.) The invaders sacked Angkor and were then driven out in 1432, only to return the following year, when they completely destroyed the Khmer capital. The Khmer court evacuated to Phnom Penh, which became the new capital of a much-reduced kingdom.

Further reading: D. G. E. Hall, *A History of South-East Asia,* 4th ed. (New York: St. Martin's Press, 1981); David K. Wyatt, *Thailand; A Short History* (New Haven, Conn.: Yale University Press, 1984).

Khorasan Rebellion (806–809)

PRINCIPAL COMBATANTS: Khorasan rebels vs. government of Khorasan
PRINCIPAL THEATER(S): Khorasan, Persia
DECLARATION: None
MAJOR ISSUES AND OBJECTIVES: Originally, the rebels agitated for the removal of a despotic governor, but the rebellion escalated to a war for independence.
OUTCOME: The rebels proclaimed an independent kingdom in Transoxiana.
APPROXIMATE MAXIMUM NUMBER OF MEN UNDER ARMS: Unknown

CASUALTIES: Unknown
TREATIES: None

When Harun al-Rashid (766–809), caliph of the Abbasid Empire, received complaints of the despotic rule of the governor of Khorasan, Persia, Ali Ibn Isa ben Mahan (fl. early 800s) the caliph made a journey to investigate personally. Despot or not, the governor was a wise politician, who lavished many gifts on al-Rashid, whose investigation turned up no evidence of malfeasance. Persuaded that all was well, the caliph confirmed the governor in his office and left Khorasan. Having received no satisfaction, Rafi ben Laith (fl. c. 805–810) led a rebellion against the governor, defeating his army in Transoxiana in 806. Alarmed, the governor fled the province, and the caliph promised the rebels that he would install a new governor who would satisfy the rebels' demands. But, at this point, the momentum of the rebellion would not be halted, and Rafi ben Laith proclaimed an independent Muslim province within Transoxiana. The caliph felt he had no choice but to lead an army in person to end the rebellion once and for all. He set off in 809, only to die en route. Leaderless, his troops elected to return to Baghdad without engaging the rebels.

See also MUSLIM CIVIL WAR (809–813).

Further reading: P. M. Holt, Ann K. S. Lambton, and Bernard Lewis, *The Cambridge History of Islam,* 2 vols. (New York: Cambridge University Press, 1970); Hugh Kennedy, *The Prophet and the Age of the Caliphates: The Islamic Near East from the Sixth to the Eleventh Century* (New York: Longman, 1986); A. T. Olmstead, *History of the Persian Empire: Achaemenid Period* (Chicago: University of Chicago Press, 1959).

Khurram's Rebellion   *See* SHAH JAHAN'S REVOLT (1622–1626).

Khurramites' Revolt   (816–838)

PRINCIPAL COMBATANTS: Khurramite rebels (with Byzantine allies) vs. Islamic Persia and Mesopotamia
PRINCIPAL THEATER(S): Mainly Azerbaijan
DECLARATION: Unknown
MAJOR ISSUES AND OBJECTIVES: The Khurramites wanted to destroy Islam.
OUTCOME: After initial successes, the Khurramites were defeated in a war of attrition, and their leader was captured and executed.
APPROXIMATE MAXIMUM NUMBER OF MEN UNDER ARMS: Unknown
CASUALTIES: Unknown
TREATIES: None

The Khurramites were a proto-communist sect, which occupied Azerbaijan on the southwest shore of the Caspian Sea. They advocated the breakup and redistribution of the immense estates. Even more radical was their call for the abolition of Islam. About 816, they began launching attacks on Muslims and Muslim military forces in Persia and in Mesopotamia in fulfillment of a self-proclaimed mission of destroying Islam.

The Khurramites fought with great skill and zeal, and they were aided by the Byzantines, who were at the time engaged in the BYZANTINE-MUSLIM WAR (830–841). Against the forces of Caliph Allah al-Ma'mun (785–833), the Khurramites enjoyed great success. He struck against them four times, and, four times, was defeated, in part because the Khurramites received Byzantine aid. The ascension of a new caliph, Abu Ishak al-Mu'tasim (d. 842), brought a renewed determination to crush the Khurramites as well as their Byzantine allies. Al-Mu'tasim dispatched a large force under the governor of Media, al-Afshin (fl. 830s), to prosecute a vigorous campaign against the rebels. Al-Afshin was unable to force the Khurramites into open battle, but his untiring pursuit of them wore them down. At last, in 838, the remaining Khurramites were defeated in battle, and their leader, Babak al-Khorrami (d. 838), was captured and killed.

Further reading: P. M. Holt, Ann K. S. Lambton, and Bernard Lewis, *The Cambridge History of Islam,* 2 vols. (New York: Cambridge University Press, 1970); Hugh Kennedy, *The Prophet and the Age of the Caliphates: The Islamic Near East from the Sixth to the Eleventh Century* (New York: Longman, 1986); A. T. Olmstead, *History of the Persian Empire: Achaemenid Period* (Chicago: University of Chicago Press, 1959).

Kickapoo Uprising   (1820s–1833)

PRINCIPAL COMBATANTS: Kickapoo Indians vs. the United States
PRINCIPAL THEATER(S): Illinois Territory
DECLARATION: Informal; Illinois settlers petitioned for U.S. troops to stop Indian attacks on settlers (1824)
MAJOR ISSUES AND OBJECTIVES: Kickapoo refusal to vacate lands claimed by white settlers
OUTCOME: Kickapoo ceded lands and moved to present-day Kansas.
APPROXIMATE MAXIMUM NUMBER OF MEN UNDER ARMS: Unknown, most Indian actions were accomplished by small bands of guerrillas.
CASUALTIES: Unknown
TREATIES: Treaty of Castor Hill, 1832

At the start of the 19th century, the Kickapoo Indians lived in central Illinois and in Indiana, principally along the Illinois and Wabash rivers. The easternmost band of this

King George's War 665

tribe established its major settlement on the Vermilion River and were therefore called the Vermilion band. Another tribal group, called the Prairie band, lived farther south in Illinois, along the Sangamon River. Both bands ceded some territory to the United States in 1809, but both sided with the British during the WAR OF 1812.

In 1819, through the Treaty of Edwardsville (Illinois), the majority of the Kickapoos ceded the remainder of their Illinois lands to the federal government and moved west to Missouri. Two factions, one led by Mecina and the other by Kennekuk (d. 1852), refused to move with the majority, and throughout the early 1820s, their warriors conducted guerrilla actions against white settlers, destroying or stealing property. In 1824, settlers petitioned for federal troops, and, after enduring months of military pressure from these soldiers as well as state militiamen, Mecina's faction crossed the Mississippi River into Missouri.

Kennekuk, also known as the Kickapoo Prophet, preached total withdrawal from contact with whites and a return to "pure" Indian ways. Although his followers harassed settlers, Kennekuk's tactics resembled passive resistance more than the kind of guerrilla warfare Mecina had waged. Furthermore, while advocating total avoidance of whites, Kennekuk maintained an ongoing dialogue with federal authorities for more than a decade, repeatedly vowing to move west in peace, but always finding the means to delay that removal.

Beginning in 1831 some of Kennekuk's warriors left his band to join forces with the Sauk and Fox under their charismatic leader, Black Hawk (1767–1838), in BLACK HAWK'S WAR. Still more deserted Kennekuk in 1832, when he signed the Treaty of Castor Hill, formally exchanging his band's land for a tract along the Missouri River in Kansas. Those followers remaining with him moved to their assigned homeland in 1833.

Further reading: Alan Axelrod, *Chronicle of the Indian Wars: From Colonial Times to Wounded Knee* (New York: Prentice Hall General Reference, 1993); Arrell M. Gibson, *Kickapoos: Lords of the Middle Border* (Norman: University of Oklahoma Press, 1990); Joseph B. Herring, *Kenekuk, the Kickapoo Prophet* (Lawrence: University Press of Kansas, 1990).

King George's War (1739–1748)

PRINCIPAL COMBATANTS: British North America and its Indian allies (mostly Iroquois) vs. French North America and its Indian allies (mostly Huron and Abenaki)
PRINCIPAL THEATER(S): Nova Scotia, New England, New York, and the Ohio country, with related violence in the Southeast, the American theater of the War of the Austrian Succession
DECLARATION: October 19, 1739, Great Britain declares war on Spain; France, becoming Spain's ally, declares war on Great Britain, March 15, 1744

MAJOR ISSUES AND OBJECTIVES: Struggle between England and France for control of North America
OUTCOME: Inconclusive; the conflict, which ended in 1748, was largely a rehearsal for the French and Indian War
APPROXIMATE MAXIMUM NUMBER OF MEN UNDER ARMS: Most engagements involved fewer than 100 troops; at Louisbourg, Pepperell commanded militia of 4,200 troops
CASUALTIES: Americans, 500 killed in combat, 1,100 succumbed to disease or exposure; French forces, 350 battle deaths
TREATIES: Treaty of Aix-la-Chapelle, October 18, 1748

King George's War, the American phase of what was fought in Europe as the War of the AUSTRIAN SUCCESSION, had its origin in a conflict known as the War of JENKINS' EAR, essentially a trade dispute between British and Spanish colonial interests.

On October 19, 1739, Great Britain declared war on Spain, and Georgia's founder-governor, James Oglethorpe (1696–1785), launched a series of invasions into Spanish Florida. In the meantime, on the continent of Europe, France, Spain, Bavaria, Saxony, and Prussia faced off against Maria Theresa's (1717–80) Austria and her ally Great Britain. With the signing of the Second Family Compact on October 25, 1743, France joined Spain in its fight against England, declaring war on March 15, 1744.

In America, Virginia and Maryland authorities negotiated the cession of much of the Ohio country from the Iroquois from June 16 to July 7, 1744. Within three months of the treaty, Virginia began granting petitions for western lands totaling 300,000 acres. This was sufficient to provoke the French, whose traders were already working much of the Ohio country, to armed conflict with the English settlers.

Fort Saint-Frédéric in northeastern New York became a staging area for repeated French raids into lower New York and New England. The war heated up after the unsuccessful French assault on Annapolis Royal (Port Royal, Nova Scotia) in 1744, which was followed by the only major "formal" battle in what was otherwise a guerrilla war, the British siege of Louisbourg on Cape Breton Island, Nova Scotia.

On June 16, 1745, after a siege of 49 days, the fort fell to William Pepperell (1696–1759), who commanded 4,200 Massachusetts militiamen. It was an important strategic prize, guarding as it did the approach to the St. Lawrence River. The victory at Louisbourg was in part due to a Cape Cod Indian, probably a Mashpee Wampanoag, who crawled in at one of the fort's embrasures, opened the gate, and simply admitted the English troops.

Throughout King George's War, the French and English vied for alliance with the Indians, whom they employed in guerrilla operations and raids. New York's governor George Clinton (c. 1686–1761) armed Indians for an invasion of Canada, and William Johnson (1715–75), a wealthy landowner very influential among the Mohawks, organized an Indian strike against Montreal in June 1747. Unfortunately for the English, the disparate colonial and Indian forces failed to coalesce into a single effective force. An assault on Fort Saint-Frédéric failed miserably, and the planned attack on Montreal was shelved. Johnson did, however, manage to organize small Mohawk raids against French supply lines.

If anything, the French were more effective at using their Indian allies, who terrorized the outlying settlements of New England with lightning raids, killing many, carrying others into a captivity that sometimes meant hideous torture and slow death.

While western Massachusetts reeled under French-inspired Indian assaults, a combination of French provincials and Abenaki Indians raided remote settlements in Maine beginning in August 1745. The military low point for the English came November 28–29, 1745, when the French, with Indian allies, burned Fort Saratoga, New York.

Throughout 1746, Abenakis and others unrelentingly raided New England's towns. Most of the war's engagements involved small numbers of combatants, usually fewer than a hundred, and engagements were frequently not so much battles as murders.

Only in Nova Scotia was the fighting on a grander, more European scale. Not only had Pepperell taken Louisbourg in 1745, but in 1746 a French fleet attempted a grand assault against Port Royal, but was foiled by the hazardous fogbound coast of Nova Scotia. In 1747, a large French land force did capture the English fort at Grand Pre.

In a significant sense, King George's War was a prelude to the FRENCH AND INDIAN WAR, as the English and French learned the value of Indian allies. In the Northeast, the Mohawks were allied with the English, whereas the other Iroquois tribes struggled to remain neutral—though they leaned toward the English. The English also worked to secure the cooperation of the western tribes of the Ohio country, especially the Shawnee, Wyandots, and Miamis. In the South, the English found support from the Chickasaws and Cherokees, who were themselves at war with the French-allied Creeks and Choctaws. (*See* the CHICKASAW RESISTANCE, the FOX RESISTANCE, and the NATCHEZ REVOLT.)

The French commanded the loyalty of the large Huron tribe as well as other Algonquian Indian groups.

King George's War and the Indian resistances associated with it were costly and resolved virtually nothing, except to create certain European-Indian alliances. The peace brought by the Treaty of Aix-la-Chapelle on October 18, 1748—which ended the War of the Austrian Succession in Europe and, therefore, King George's War in America—was little more than a truce in the violence that preceded the French and Indian War.

Further reading: Alan Axelrod, *Chronicle of the Indian Wars: From Colonial Times to Wounded Knee* (New York: Prentice Hall General Reference, 1993); Allan Gallay, ed., *Colonial Wars of North America, 1512–1763* (New York: Garland, 1996).

King Philip's War (Second Puritan Conquest) (1675–1676)

PRINCIPAL COMBATANTS: Colonists of Massachusetts Bay, Connecticut, Rhode Island, and Plymouth (with various Indian allies) vs. Wampanoag, Narragansett, Nipmuck, and lesser New England Indian tribes

PRINCIPAL THEATER(S): Southern and northern New England

MAJOR ISSUES AND OBJECTIVES: Colonial demands for Indian sale of lands and submission in social, religious, and political matters created the atmosphere in which the killing of an Indian looter by an outraged farmer triggered an almost senselessly destructive war that might be best considered as one of colonial conquest.

OUTCOME: Although suffering crippling losses, the colonists virtually wiped out the Wampanoag tribe, greatly diminished the Narragansetts and Nipmucks, and thoroughly intimidated New England's lesser tribes; in proportion to New England's population, the war was the costliest in American history and of immense significance to future relations with the Indians; the war also gave the New England colonies their first taste of union when they, under what in effect was a mutual defense pact, created the United Colonies of New England.

APPROXIMATE MAXIMUM NUMBER OF MEN UNDER ARMS: Colonists, more than 2,500 (fluctuated greatly and included unorganized militia and varying numbers of Indian allies; largest force officially raised by the United Colonies [Plymouth, Massachusetts Bay, Rhode Island, Connecticut], 1,000); Indian, c. 2,300 (number of warriors based on an estimate of Wampanoag, Narragansett, and Nipmuck combined population of 6,900; in any given engagement, Indians generally fielded a larger force than the colonists)

CASUALTIES: Colonists, at least 600 killed, including many noncombatants; devastation of New England settlements (1,200 houses burned, 8,000 cattle killed); Indians, more than 3,000 killed, including many old men, women, and children; many captives sold into slavery; other survivors dispossessed of land and dispersed into New York and Canada

TREATIES: Taunton Agreement (April 10, 1671); Hutchinson's treaty with the Narragansetts (July 15, 1675); second Narragansett treaty (October 18 or 19, 1675); treaty with the "North Indians" (July 2–3, 1676); no formal treaty ended the war

So far as colonial chroniclers were concerned, the cause of the terrible conflict they called King Philip's War was simple to the point of tautology. King Philip (d. 1676), haughty chief of the Wampanoag Indians, betrayed the traditional friendship between his tribe and the English by waging war against New England's settlers with the object of either annihilating them or driving them out of the country.

In fact, the causes of King Philip's War, as with most white-Indian conflicts, were both more complex and more basic. Colonial land hunger and a rising population, combined with a racism sanctioned by Puritan religious doctrine, met head-on with Philip's growing resentment of English insults to his sovereignty and encroachments on his power. Indians were important to the colonists not only as a kind of spiritual crop waiting to be harvested, but as sources of trade. They were also the means by which the surprisingly heterogeneous New England colonies might each legitimate a stake in America. New England colonial charters, granted as they were to religious and political dissidents, were chronically shaky. With the restoration of Charles II (1630–85) to the English throne, the Massachusetts charter, which had been secure under the Puritan reign of Oliver Cromwell (1599–1658), and that of Rhode Island, which had been granted by Cromwell's government, were most directly threatened. To bolster their sovereignty in the New World, the colonies sought to associate themselves with those whose possession of the soil was acknowledged as a primitive right: the Indians. Colonial governments sought to purchase land from them and, even more important, to establish a protectorate over them. This led to complicated and, ultimately, strained relations between Indians and whites. Two major tribes, the Wampanoags and the Narragansetts, desired the benefits of trade with the English and vied with one another for colonial favor. At the same time, both tribes struggled to maintain some autonomy and retain land. As English pressure to sell more land increased, along with demands for greater and greater submission to colonial authority in matters of politics and religion, the rival tribes began to come together. Culturally, politically, and spiritually, the stage was set for conflict in New England.

Massasoit (d. 1661), chief of the Wampanoags and longtime friend of the English (it was through his aid that the Pilgrims survived their first terrible winter in the New World), died at the age of 81. His son Wamsutta (d. 1664), whom the English called Alexander, succeeded him as the tribe's principal sachem and continued the tradition of friendship with the English. However, under Wamsutta, the Wampanoags were now dividing their loyalty between two English colonies, Rhode Island and Plymouth. Both were perpetually engaged in competition for the purchase of Indian lands, and both sought to establish a protectorate over the Wampanoags. The Plymouth Colony's Major (later governor) Josiah Winslow (c. 1629–80) seized Alexander at gunpoint and took him to Duxbury to answer conspiracy charges and—more particularly—to demonstrate his loyalty to Plymouth by selling land to that colony rather than to Rhode Island. During his captivity, Alexander contracted a fever and died. His 24-year-old brother, Metacom (Metacomet), whom the English called Philip, succeeded him as sachem and, like a number of other Wampanoags, suspected that Winslow had not merely brutalized Wamsutta but had poisoned him.

On August 6, 1664, Philip was summoned to Plymouth Town to answer charges of plotting against the colony. Although he denied the accusations, he did agree to sign a document pledging to seek permission from the colony before concluding any sale or exchange of land, and relations between colonists and Indians remained relatively peaceful until 1665, when a land dispute between Massachusetts and the Narragansetts threatened to erupt into war. A royal commission succeeded in assuaging hostilities only temporarily.

Seeing an opportunity for exploiting the breach between the English and a rival tribe, Philip warned New York colonial authorities that the Narragansetts were plotting war against them. The Narragansett chief, Ninigret, in turn accused Philip of hostile designs, and the next year (1667) Philip was summoned to Plymouth to answer these charges. Proud, even haughty, Philip resented this and other calls to answer to colonial authority. Over the succeeding two years, his animosity toward the English was further aggravated by a dispute over land in the area of Wentham, Massachusetts. And although Ninigret was himself accused in 1669 of combining with the French to stage a rebellion against the English colonies, this failed to vindicate Philip. On the contrary, the accusation served only to make the colonists more wary of Indian "treachery" generally. Early in 1671, Philip, outraged that the new Plymouth settlement of Swansea flagrantly encroached on his land, staged an armed display for the benefit of the town's citizens. On April 10, 1671, he was summoned to Taunton to acknowledge and apologize for such "plotting" and to agree to surrender his people's arms.

After signing the Taunton document, Philip cannily attempted to foment dissension between Plymouth and Massachusetts by suggesting that this retroactive pledge of submission to Plymouth posed a threat to the validity of land titles Massachusetts had earlier secured from the Wampanoags. Despite its political sophistication, Philip's strategy backfired, serving only to bring the two colonies closer together, and by the end of September he was summoned to Plymouth, where he stood trial for failure to abide by the Taunton agreement. Fined £100, the sachem was further humiliated by a requirement that he henceforth obtain colonial permission in all matters involving the purchase or sale of land; he was also forbidden to wage war against other Indians without authority from the colonial government.

For three years, Philip quietly forged anti-English alliances with the Nipmuck Indians and with his tribe's former rivals, the Narragansetts. Then, in January 1675, came another revelation of Wampanoag designs against the English. John Sassamon (d. 1675) (or Saussaman), a Christianized "Praying Indian" who had been Philip's private secretary, alerted the English to the sachem's plotting. On January 29, Sassamon's body was found on the ice of a frozen pond. The death was at first ruled an accident, but later three Wampanoags were convicted of murder. After the noose around the neck of one of the convicted men broke, he—vainly seeking a reprieve—accused Philip himself of complicity in the murder as part of yet another plot against the English.

Haled into court yet again, Philip won release for lack of evidence. On June 11, just three days after the executions, word of Wampanoags arming near Swansea and Plymouth Town reached authorities. They also heard of scattered incidents of cattle killing and looting houses in outlying settlements. Already, settlers were beginning to desert some towns: Swansea, adjacent to Wampanoag country, was the first to be partially abandoned, and Indians began appropriating property left behind. An outraged settler shot a looter—the first blood of the war.

In an uneasy and mistrustful alliance, in which the colonies jockeyed for possible territorial gains that might be tied to defeating the Indians, Massachusetts, Plymouth, and Rhode Island joined forces in a mutual defense pact that would soon develop into a loose-knit league they called the United Colonies of New England. The three colonies mobilized an army, which was mustered during June 21–23 at Miles's Garrison, opposite Philip's base of operations at Mount Hope Neck, Rhode Island—but not before Wampanoags had raided Swansea, on the Sabbath, attacking townsfolk on their way to church. The town was attacked again—and half burned—a few days later, as worshipers returned from church.

Four days later, Rhode Island militia captain Benjamin Church (1639–1718) and his troops fell under attack near beleaguered Swansea at Miles's Bridge, which led into Mount Hope Neck. Church was appalled by the poor showing of the English forces in this first military engagement of the war. During the next year and a half, he would frequently find himself in the minority as he repeatedly counseled—usually in vain—aggressive strategies of attack that called for abandoning formal European battle tactics and fighting the Indians on their own terms. The hastily mustered army proved ineffectual again and again. Wampanoags staged lightning raids in the vicinity of Rehoboth and Taunton on June 29. The next day, troops from Massachusetts, Plymouth, and Rhode Island pursued Philip, but he and his forces handily evaded them by escaping to the swamps of Pocasset country.

Connecticut joined in the New England league's war effort on July 1 when it sent troops to aid Massachusetts, Plymouth, and Rhode Island, but Philip was negotiating an alliance of his own at this time, with the Pocasset squaw-sachem Weetamoo. To forestall the spread of such alliances, a Massachusetts army marched out of Mount Hope Neck and into Narragansett country on the mainland east of present-day Newport around the Great Swamp, to "overawe" that Rhode Island tribe with English might and thereby negotiate a promise of neutrality.

Back in Rhode Island, Benjamin Church, recognizing that feeble diplomacy with Narragansetts and intercolonial strife were siphoning energy from the real menace at hand, pursued Philip in the swamp. In Captain Almy's "pease field," the 20-man party was set upon by 300 Indians for six hours, until they were rescued by an English river sloop.

By mid-July, much of New England was awash in blood, as Wampanoags were joined by Narragansetts and the Nipmucks of eastern and central Massachusetts. Discouraged by their army's performance against the Indians in close combat—and over Church's vigorous objections—colonial authorities soon broke off pursuit of Philip and instead built a fort to besiege him in the swamp, intending to starve the enemy out. This strategic error only prolonged the war. With the English occupied in fort building, Philip was able to escape from the Pocasset swamp on July 29 and make for Nipmuck country to the northeast. Captain Daniel Henchman, with Plymouth troops and Mohegan allies, pursued but was forced to break off the attack due to exhaustion and a shortage of supplies. Philip once again escaped.

Colonial diplomacy was even less successful. Captains Hutchinson and Thomas Wheeler set out for Brookfield (Quabaog) at the beginning of August, attempting once again to treat with the Nipmucks, but were ambushed. Hutchinson was fatally wounded, and Wheeler shot through the arm. Eight other men were also killed, and the Nipmucks pinned down the remainder of the company for 48 hours.

By the end of August, the theater of war had broadened into the upper Connecticut Valley, Merrimac Valley, New Hampshire, and Maine. After refusing an English demand to surrender their arms, a party of Indians attempted to slip away from the English, who pursued them from Hatfield to Hopewell Swamp, south of Deerfield, Massachusetts. The battle of August 24–25 ended in an Indian retreat, but the colonials found it fruitless to pursue their enemy, as fierce rearguard action resulted in nine English deaths, and the Indians were able to escape north.

In the vicinity of Hadley, Massachusetts, colonists demanded that the local Indians surrender their arms as "Proof of their Fidelity." After some stalling, the Indians slipped away from their village on the night of August 25. Realizing that the Hadley Indians had absconded to join

Philip, the colonists marshaled their troops in pursuit of them and skirmished at Sugar Loaf Hill, 10 miles above Hatfield, killing "about 26" Indians and suffering the loss of nine or 10 English.

A week later, Hadley was raided and Deerfield mostly destroyed. This was followed almost immediately by a devastating attack against Northfield (Squakeag). Massachusetts dispatched 36 men to relieve the garrison there, but they were ambushed and about 20 of them were slain.

Having already endured months of bloodshed, the United Colonies officially declared war on September 9, levying an army of 1,000, which, however, was not actually mustered until November and December.

The litany of raid upon raid continued. On September 18, following one of many days of "Public Humiliation" proclaimed in Boston, Lothrop, commanding 80 men, had the grim duty of escorting evacuees, their goods, and provisions out of beleaguered Deerfield. He was ambushed and killed with all but seven or eight of his men.

Repeated attempts at negotiating peace—or even a truce—failed. A hopeful conference at Wickford, Rhode Island, between the English and Narragansetts broke down on September 22. Worse, previously friendly Indians now turned on the colonists. Springfield, Massachusetts, having enjoyed cordial relations with the Indians for some 40 years, maintained no garrisons. On October 4–5, it was raided, and 32 houses—about half the town—were destroyed. On October 18 or 19 700 Indians attacked Hatfield, Massachusetts, but were driven off.

At this time, the Narragansetts at last concluded a new treaty in Boston. Nevertheless, on November 2, Connecticut's colonial council resolved that the best way to prevent war with the Narragansetts was a preemptory strike against them. Plymouth and Massachusetts were in agreement on this, and the army of the United Colonies, called for in September, was at last mustering in November and into December. Assembled at Dedham, Massachusetts; Taunton, Plymouth; and New London, Connecticut, the army united at Wickford, Rhode Island, where, under the command of Plymouth governor Josiah Winslow (1629–80), it awaited provisioning during December 12–18. The army's objective was a Narragansett stronghold near Petenquanscut (Pettiquemscot), Rhode Island. But the sudden fall on December 16 of the garrison house there, which was to have served as a base of operations, foiled this strategy, and Winslow marched his 1,000-man army, including a company under the redoubtable Benjamin Church, into a snowstorm on December 18 to assault another Narragansett fort—stronghold of the sachem Canonchet (d. 1676) (whom the English called Canonicus)—in a frozen swamp at Kingston, Rhode Island.

They reached the Indian fort the following day, having suffered terribly in the intense cold. Worse, the stronghold proved formidable beyond expectation, and the attack was poorly coordinated, as two companies, noting an incomplete palisade at one corner, stormed the fortification prematurely, before the arrival of the main company. Two captains were slain, and the few troops who did make it into the fort were quickly driven out. Benjamin Church led 30 soldiers in another assault and was hit by three bullets. Wounded in the hip and thigh, the frontiersman's only regret was that one shot had pierced and wounded a pair of borrowed mittens. In fierce battle, 80 of Winslow's army perished, including 14 company commanders, and about 600 Narragansetts—half of them women and children—died. Over the protests of the wounded Church, who pointed out that the battered English would need the shelter of the Indians' wigwams for the bitter winter night, the colonials put the encampment to the torch.

Bereft of many of its commanders, its supplies depleted, the army retreated to Wickford, declining to pursue the surviving Narragansetts, who escaped to Nipmuck country. The Great Swamp Fight inflicted heavy losses on the Narragansetts and cut them off from their sources of supply; however, it also served to strengthen desperate anti-English alliances among the Wampanoags, Nipmucks, and Narragansetts.

With the new year, Philip attempted to extend his alliances beyond New England, taking many of his people to Mohawk country near Albany, New York, in search of ammunition and provisions in addition to friends. Unfortunately for Philip, New York governor Edmund Andros (1637–1714) had reached the Mohawks first, persuading them not only to spurn the alliance but to attack Philip, who was compelled to flee back to New England. The alliance Andros established effectively blocked the grand Indian confederacy all colonists feared, but New England forces were not prepared to take immediate advantage of Philip's rebuff; despite the lopsided casualty figures from the Great Swamp Fight, Winslow's army, crippled by their losses (especially at the command level) and a lack of provisions, was immobilized for more than a month, until the end of January, when an Indian raid on Pawtucket, Rhode Island, prompted Winslow to take his newly reinforced but still inadequately provisioned force on a so-called Hungry March into the country of the Nipmucks. The expedition was aborted a week after it had begun, due to wholesale desertion from the ranks.

With the principal English force in disarray, the Indians rallied and renewed their offensive. On February 10, 1676, Lancaster, Massachusetts, was raided a second time, and Mary Rowlandson, wife of the settlement's minister, was captured from Rowlandson Garrison when its defenders were killed or taken prisoner. Mary Rowlandson's account of her ordeal, published in 1682, would become a colonial "best-seller."

On February 21, in another crushing English defeat, 200–300 Indians overcame a 160-man militia force at Medfield, Massachusetts, about 20 miles from Boston, burning half the town and killing 20 persons. Early in March, a colonial cavalry troop pursued Philip near Northampton, but, as usual, he evaded capture as his allies managed a second raid on Pawtucket, which resulted in the burning of a dozen houses.

The colonies reeled under blow after blow. On March 12, Clark's Garrison, Plymouth, was raided and destroyed. The next day, Groton, Massachusetts, was abandoned after a raid. On the day after that, following an attack on Northampton, colonial authorities, reacting to crisis with a siege mentality, began to draw up plans to erect a palisade around Boston, leaving the outlying towns exposed.

In mid-March, Warwick, near Providence, Rhode Island, having been attacked several times, was at last all but deserted. Indians burned it to the ground, killing the sole remaining inhabitant. On March 26, they fell upon worshipers on their way to church at Longmeadow, Massachusetts. On the same day, the town of Marlborough was badly mauled, though colonials gave chase to the retreating Indians and defeated their rear guard. In Connecticut, Simsbury was abandoned and burned. A force of about 50 colonists and 20 friendly Indians near Rehoboth, a Rhode Island settlement bordering Philip's territory, was ambushed as it pursued Philip's warriors. Although the Indians turned their pursuers back, the battle had cost them 140 dead.

The early spring of 1676 marked the low point of the colonists's fortunes. One measure of their desperation was the unorthodox surprise nighttime attack soldiers and citizens of Sudbury, Massachusetts, staged against Indians camped near the town. Despite this minor victory, the Indian raiding continued unabated. On the morning after the colonists' sortie, March 28, 30 barns and 40 houses were burned in Rehoboth, and on the day after that, Providence, Rhode Island, was destroyed. Although Connecticut soldiers operating in western Rhode Island succeeded in capturing the important Narragansett sachem and war leader Canonchet, whom they subsequently executed, by the middle of the month the English area of settlement had greatly contracted. Despite emergency laws forbidding the evacuation of towns without official permission, the outlying settlements around Boston were largely abandoned.

On April 21, Indians repaid Sudbury for its earlier attack on them, hurling as many as 800 or 900 warriors against the town. Militia from Sudbury and surrounding settlements responded and, in a fierce, daylong battle, repelled the attack. Following this engagement, colonial forces at last began to take the offensive, sweeping through eastern Massachusetts by the end of April. On May 1, Indian hostiles at last agreed to negotiate ransom terms for English captives. Yet, as colonial forces prevailed in eastern Massachusetts, Philip's warriors attacked the Plymouth town of Bridgewater on May 6 and launched a desperate general offensive against that colony, raiding Plymouth Town on May 11.

In western Massachusetts, a force of 150 mounted men, attacked an Indian encampment at the Falls of the Connecticut above Deerfield, Massachusetts, on May 19. It was not so much a battle as it was a massacre: The soldiers poked their muskets into the wigwams and shot the Indians—including many women and children—as they slept. While the enemy was routed, the army failed to pursue, and the surviving Indians turned a retreat into a counterattack, killing about 40 men. Yet the loss of many warriors (reportedly more than 100) and supplies made this a Pyrrhic victory for the Indians.

The colonists became more aggressive in attack and pursuit, responding to reports of hostiles fishing in the Pawtucket River near Rehoboth, winning a skirmish there and another on June 2, against Philip in western Massachusetts. Early in the same month, Benjamin Church was authorized to build a new army on behalf of the United Colonies, using white and Indian soldiers. Still, Philip fought on, launching a massive assault against Hadley, Massachusetts. Early on the morning of June 12, 700 Indians descended on the town, which was defended by Connecticut forces, 500 strong (consisting of colonists and friendly Indians: Pequots and Mohegans), in addition to a garrison force. Positioned behind the town's palisades and equipped with some artillery pieces, the colonial army successfully repelled the attackers.

At Nipsachuck, Rhode Island, on July 2, colonists dealt the Narragansetts two crushing blows when they attacked a band of 34 men and 137 women and children, killing all of the men and 92 of the women and children. On the next day, at Warwick, they slew 18 and 22 women and children, taking 27 prisoners as well. At this time, too, war with the so-called North Indians—the Abenakis, Sokokis, and Pennacooks—came to an end when the Pennacook sachem Wannalancet signed a treaty, bringing peace to Maine.

While Benjamin Church prevailed in skirmishes at Middleborough and Monponsett on July 11 and, a week later, skirmished with Philip's men in and around Taunton, Major William Bradford (159–1657) was pursuing Philip himself, narrowly failing to run the Indian leader to ground on July 16.

Church received a second colonial commission on July 24, calling for a larger army of 200 men, of which 140 were to be friendly Indians. The new army set out on July 30 in pursuit of the elusive Philip.

Closing on their quarry, Church's troops killed Philip's uncle on July 31 and the next day captured the sachem's wife and son. Philip himself, however, managed to escape. Nevertheless, the Indians had become demoralized. In August, a deserter from Philip's camp approached Church, offering to lead him and his men to Philip's camp. Church deployed his men around Philip's camp after midnight on August 12 and moved in at first light.

Philip took to his feet, as an English soldier fired and missed. The marksmanship of an English-allied Indian called Alderman was better. Benjamin Church ordered the sachem's body butchered, awarding the head and one hand to Alderman. The remainder of the corpse was quartered and hung on four trees, customary practice in an execution for treason.

With Philip's death, the war had all but come to an end. On September 11, Church captured and executed Annawon, Philip's "chief captain." Sporadic skirmishes occurred through October, but the last sizable band of Indians surrendered on August 28. According to eye-witness accounts, many Indians were left demoralized and abject in their submission to the English. Others, however, had fled to Canada, New York, and the Delaware and Susquehanna valleys, where they would meditate a revenge that exploded in a long series of raids and guerrilla actions culminating in the FRENCH AND INDIAN WAR. As New York's Governor Edmund Andros laconically observed of King Philip's War, "the advantages thereby were none, the disadvantages very great."

King Philip's War was a catastrophe for New England's colonists and Indians alike. In the course of 1675–76, half of the region's towns were badly damaged and 12 destroyed utterly, requiring the work of a generation to rebuild them. The fragile colonial economy suffered devastating blows, both as a result of the direct cost of the war—approximately £100,000—and because of the disruption of the fur trade with the Indians and the virtual cessation of coastal fishing and the seaborne West Indies trade. Not only did the war siphon off the manpower customarily devoted to these industries, many men never returned to their peacetime occupations, for 1 in 16 colonists of military age died. Many others—men, women, children—were also killed, captured, or starved. In proportion to New England's population of 30,000, King Philip's War was the costliest in American history. As for the Indians, at least 3,000 perished, and many of those who did not die were deported and sold into slavery.

Further reading: Alan Axelrod, *Chronicle of the Indian Wars: From Colonial Times to Wounded Knee* (New York: Prentice Hall General Reference, 1993); C. R. Bourne, *The Red King's Rebellion: Racial Politics in New England, 1675–1678* (New York: Atheneum, 1990); James David Drake, *King Philip's War: Civil War in New England, 1675–1676* (Amherst: University of Massachusetts Press, 2000); Francis Jennings, *The Invasion of America* (New York: W. W. Norton, 1975); Jill Lepore, *The Name of War: King Philip's War and the Origins of American Identity* (New York: Random House, 1999); Eric B. Schultz and Michael J. Tougias, *King Philip's War: The History and Legacy of America's Forgotten Conflict* (Woodstock, Vt.: Countryman Press, 2000).

King William's War (1688–1697)

PRINCIPAL COMBATANTS: French and Abenaki Indians vs. English and Iroquois (mostly Mohawk) Indians
PRINCIPAL THEATER(S): New England
DECLARATION: North American theater of the War of the Grand Alliance
MAJOR ISSUES AND OBJECTIVES: Control of North American trade and territory
OUTCOME: Inconclusive
APPROXIMATE MAXIMUM NUMBER OF MEN UNDER ARMS: England raised up to 1,000 troops during the war; French forces organized into small bands of swift-moving, efficient guerrilla warriors
CASUALTIES: English and Iroquois: 1250; French and Abenaki: 400
TREATIES: Treaty of Ryswick, September 1697.

When England's William III (1650–1702) joined the League of Augsburg and the Netherlands on May 12, 1689, to form the Grand Alliance in opposition to Louis XIV's (1638–1717) invasion of the Rhenish Palatinate (September 25, 1688), war broke out not only in Europe, but in North America as well. In Europe, the eight-year-long conflict was fought as the War of the GRAND ALLIANCE; known variously as the War of the League of Augsburg and the Nine Years' War, in America, it was called King William's War and pitted the French and Abenaki Indians (of Maine) against the English and their Iroquois allies.

England and France were bitter trade rivals in North America. After the English took New York from the Dutch in 1664, the Iroquois turned to the colony's new masters, rather than the French, for trade. French settlers and traders were fearful of the English-Iroquois alliance, and northern New Englanders felt menaced by the French-allied Abenakis, who were closely allied with the Malecites, Penobscots, Pennacooks, and Micmacs.

Sir Edmund Andros (1637–1714), governor of Britain's northern colonies from New Jersey to Maine, made a peremptory strike against the trading post of Jean Vincent de l'Abadie (fl. 17th century), baron de Saint Castin, in April 1688, a year before open war broke out. Designed to drive the French out of territory claimed by the English, the raid served only to outrage the Abenakis, who were related to Baron Castin through marriage. The English further provoked the French when settlers at Saco, Maine, took 16 Indians captive in retaliation for their having killed some cattle. This action brought a series of bloody Abenaki raids.

By the late summer of 1688, English settlers began building forts in northern New England, but abandoned the one in North Yarmouth, Maine, when news of the approach of the Indians reached them. At this, the Abenakis unleashed terrifying raids throughout northern

New England. Governor Andros built more forts, at Pemaquid and present-day Brunswick, Maine, and mustered 1,000 troops in the area, but they did not pursue the Indians into their winter hiding places. In the spring, Andros unleashed his army, only to be deposed as royal governor when the Protestant revolt in England dethroned James II (1633–1701)—who had appointed Andros—and replaced him with William III.

In the meantime, Louis XIV dispatched Louis de Buade (1622–98), comte de Frontenac, to America as governor of New France in 1689. Frontenac had been governor earlier, from 1672 to 1682, and was tremendously unpopular, but, despite this and his advanced age (he was nearly 70), he was, in the king's view, the best man for accomplishing not just the defense of Canada, but the invasion of New York.

Frontenac planned to march via Lakes Champlain and George into Albany, forge an alliance with the Iroquois, and take New York City.

It quickly became apparent to the governor, however, that these plans were wildly optimistic. Quebec had been badly shaken by Iroquois raids, particularly one that had taken place on the night of July 25–26, 1689, at Lachine, 10 miles upstream from Montreal, prompting the abandonment of a key Lake Ontario fort.

Unable to carry out a major offensive, Frontenac decided on a strategy of what he called *la petite guerre*—small war, a term that evolved into "guerrilla warfare." He used the Abenaki and allied tribes to terrorize the English throughout Maine and New Hampshire, and the raiding campaign intensified during the summer of 1689. The English withdrew from their outposts east of Falmouth (present-day Portland, Maine). Authorities at Boston raised an army of 600 men, but, as would prove the case in later North American Indian conflicts, conventional military forces were largely ineffective in fighting a wilderness guerrilla war.

As winter approached, Frontenac sent a small force of Indians and Canadians to make a three-pronged assault into New York, New Hampshire, and Maine. On the night of February 8, 1690, Schenectady was ravaged. On March 27, 1690, the attack fell on Salmon Falls, New Hampshire. In May, it was Fort Loyal (Falmouth, Maine), the defenders of which, promised safe conduct out of the fort, fell in massacre.

Reeling under these blows, the English and their Mohawk allies decided to seize the initiative with an invasion of Canada that would coordinate two land forces from New York and New England with a naval force sailing up the Saint Lawrence River. Sir William Phips (1651–95) led 14 ships in a successful assault against Port Royal, Acadia (Annapolis Royal, Nova Scotia) on May 11, 1690, but failed to get the invasion proper under way, and, during the balance of 1690, French forces evicted the English from their Hudson Bay outpost at the mouth of the Severn River. In 1691, they even retook Port Royal.

Although the English suffered many reverses, their Iroquois allies fared worse, suffering the destruction of many villages and the loss of many lives. Yet *la petite guerre* produced no decisive victories for the French, and by the end of 1691, the French-allied Abenakis were exhausted enough to conclude a peace treaty on November 29, 1691.

After a brief interval, the treaty was broken as the Abenakis resumed raiding, attacking York, Maine, on February 5, 1692; Wells, Maine, and Deerfield, Massachusetts, were attacked in June.

In January 1693, Frontenac mounted a large assault against Mohawk villages, capturing 300 Mohawks, most of them women, children, and old men. And so the pattern of raid and counterraid continued, month after month, through the fall of 1697. In September of that year, the Treaty of Ryswick ended the War of the League of Augsburg and also wound down the combat in North America—although the frontier was by no means pacified. During 1698 and 1699, the Iroquois and western tribes (mainly the Ojibwa) did frequent battle. Ojibwa tradition tells of a massive combat on the shores of Lake Erie, fought sometime during this period and resulting in a severe Iroquois defeat.

Further reading: Alan Axelrod, *Chronicle of the Indian Wars: From Colonial Times to Wounded Knee* (New York: Prentice Hall General Reference, 1993); Robert Leckie, *The Wars of America* (New York: Castle Books, 1991); James S. Lemon, "King William's War," in *Colonial Wars of North America 1512–1763,* ed. Alan Gallay (New York: Garland, 1996).

Kiowa War (1874)

PRINCIPAL COMBATANTS: Kiowa, Comanche, and Cheyenne Indians vs. the United States
PRINCIPAL THEATER(S): Texas and Kansas plains
DECLARATION: None
MAJOR ISSUES AND OBJECTIVES: Pursuant to national policy, the army wanted to round up and confine the Indians to reservations.
OUTCOME: During late 1874 and into 1875, a few thousand Indians surrendered and were consigned to reservations.
APPROXIMATE MAXIMUM NUMBER OF MEN UNDER ARMS: United States, 1,500; Indians actively engaged, about 1,000
CASUALTIES: Unknown
TREATIES: None

In the spring of 1874, Kiowa Indians, along with Comanches and Cheyennes, launched extensive raids in Texas and Kansas. On June 27, Comanches and Cheyennes attacked a white hunter village at Adobe Walls in the Texas Panhandle. On July 12, the Kiowa chief Lone

Wolf (c. 1820–79) led an ambush of Texas Rangers in the Lost Valley. Lesser raids preyed upon ranchers and travelers throughout Texas and Kansas. In response to such Indian "depredations," General William Tecumseh Sherman (1820–91), commander in chief of the U.S. Army's western forces, obtained government authority to invade the reservations. Sherman telegraphed his chief field commander, Philip Sheridan (1831–88), on July 20 to begin an offensive. Sheridan and his lieutenants, General John Pope (1822–92) (commanding forces in Kansas, New Mexico, and parts of Colorado and parts of Indian Territory) and General Christopher C. Augur (1821–85) (commanding Texas and part of Indian Territory) planned a campaign in which their forces would converge on the Staked Plains region of the Panhandle. Forces would close in from Fort Sill in Indian Territory (Oklahoma), from Texas, from New Mexico, and from Kansas.

One of Pope's best field commanders, Colonel Nelson A. Miles (1839–1925), led eight troops of the Sixth Cavalry and four companies of the Fifth Infantry south from the Canadian River into Indian Territory. A force of 774 troopers engaged 200 Cheyennes—soon reinforced to a strength of perhaps 600—as they approached the Staked Plains escarpment on August 30. Miles led his attack from one hill to the next, alternating assaults with Gatling guns and howitzers with infantry and cavalry charges. Combat was a five-hour running battle over about 12 miles of rugged territory. At last, the Indians made their stand along the slopes of Tule Canyon. By this time, however, both sides were exhausted—and Miles knew that he lacked provisions to press the attack further. He reluctantly withdrew to resupply his troops, destroying abandoned Indian villages along the way.

In Plains warfare, the climate was typically an enemy more formidable than either Indian or bluecoat. In 1874, the region was plagued by drought, which ended suddenly on September 7 with a rash of torrential rains. Miles, still in search of supplies, joined his men to another 225 soldiers of the Eighth Cavalry commanded by Major William R. Price. Together, they slogged north through all-but-impassable mud, looking to intercept an army supply train. On September 9, however, about 250 Kiowa and Comanche warriors under Lone Wolf, Satanta (c. 1807–78), and Big Tree (c. 1850–1929) intercepted the supply train first. They held it under siege for three days until Price arrived to drive them off. Miles, still hampered by a lack of supplies, was unable to pursue.

In the meantime, approaching from the southeast was Colonel Ranald S. Mackenzie's (1840–89) Fourth Cavalry. His column was attacked during the night of September 26 by 250 Comanches near Tule Canyon. The Indians' purpose was to stampede the cavalry's ponies, but Mackenzie had taken the precaution not only of hobbling the animals, but surrounding them with a special guard. When they found they were unable to stampede the ponies, the Indians began shooting at the troopers.

Mackenzie retaliated in the morning. His 21 officers and 450 men drove the Indians off, then, acting on intelligence provided by Indian scouts, rode on to Palo Duro Canyon. Here he surprised a combined Kiowa-Comanche-Cheyenne village, totally routing the warriors. Three Indians died in the battle, but Mackenzie also destroyed the Indians' store of provisions and appropriated 1,434 horses. He took 400 mounts for his men, then slaughtered the rest.

In October, troops under the command of Colonel George P. Buell destroyed more Indian villages, and Miles and Price pursued Cheyennes under Chief Gray Beard. The Indians evaded their pursuers, but Miles and Price destroyed the village from which they had fled.

The Kiowa War of 1874 ended for the reason that most white-Indian conflicts ended: exhaustion on both sides—and extreme hunger and privation on the side of the Indians. Late in the fall and early in the winter, as the weather on the Plains turned brutal, hungry Kiowas and Cheyennes straggled into Forts Sill and Darlington to surrender and submit to confinement on the reservation. The last group, 407 Kwahadi Comanches, reported to Fort Sill on June 2, 1875. This effectively brought to an end warfare on the southern plains.

See also RED RIVER WAR.

Further reading: Alan Axelrod, *Chronicle of the Indian Wars: From Colonial Times to Wounded Knee* (New York: Prentice Hall General Reference, 1993); Robert Utley, *Frontier Regulars: The United States Army and the Indians, 1866–1890* (Lincoln: University of Nebraska Press, 1984); John R. Wunder, *The Kiowas* (New York: Chelsea House, 1989).

Knights' War (1522–1523)

PRINCIPAL COMBATANTS: German imperial knights vs. Catholic princes
PRINCIPAL THEATER(S): Germany
DECLARATION: None
MAJOR ISSUES AND OBJECTIVES: A bid to secularize ecclesiastical lands and to enhance the Lutheran Reformation
OUTCOME: The revolt against the Catholic princes was crushed.
APPROXIMATE MAXIMUM NUMBER OF MEN UNDER ARMS: Knights, 15,000; princes' numbers unknown
CASUALTIES: Unknown
TREATIES: None

The Knights' War took place in Germany during the period of the Lutheran Reformation, which triggered profound social as well as theological upheaval. The forces of Protestantism tended always to undercut the authority of the nobility.

Two imperial knights, Franz von Sickingen (1481–1523) and Ulrich von Hutten (1488–1523), partisans of the Reformation, embarked on war to secularize noble and ecclesiastical land holdings and to preserve the free status of imperial knights. They formed a league of imperial knights and, with them, laid siege to the Catholic stronghold of Trier on August 13, 1522. Not only did the siege fail to take Trier, it provoked a retaliation in which the Catholic princes of Trier, Hesse, and the Palatinate laid siege to Sickingen in his castle at Landstuhl. He surrendered on May 6, 1523, and succumbed the next day to wounds received during the siege. His colleague, Ulrich van Hutten, fled to Zurich, where he was given refuge by the Swiss Protestant leader Huldreich Zwingli (1484–1531). However, Hutten died soon after securing refuge and did not return to the fight. Although the Protestants raised an impressive force of 15,000, the Knights' War resulted in a victory for the Catholic nobility. The next social rebellion sparked by the Reformation flared up just one year later as the PEASANTS' WAR.

Further reading: Frank Eyck, *Religion and Politics in German History* (New York: St. Martin's Press, 1998); Friedrich Heer, *Holy Roman Empire,* trans. Janet Sondheimer (New York: Sterling, 2002); Lewis W. Spitz, *The Protestant Reformation, 1517–1559: The Rise of Modern Europe* (New York: HarperCollins, 1987).

Korea, Conquest of   *See* SINO-KOREAN WAR (660–668).

Korean-Chinese Wars   *See* SINO-KOREAN WAR (610–614); SINO-KOREAN WAR (645–647); SINO-KOREAN WAR (660–668).

Korean War   (1950–1953)

PRINCIPAL COMBATANTS: United States (nominally allied with 13 other UN member nations) and South Korea (Republic of Korea) vs. North Korea (Democratic People's Republic of Korea) (with assistance from the People's Republic of China)

PRINCIPAL THEATER(S): North and South Korea

DECLARATION: None

MAJOR ISSUES AND OBJECTIVES: Control of Korea

OUTCOME: An armistice left the nation divided along the 38th parallel into a communist North and a democratic South.

APPROXIMATE MAXIMUM NUMBER OF MEN UNDER ARMS: United States, 440,000; North Korea, 100,000; China, 300,000

CASUALTIES: United States, 33,629 killed, 103,284 wounded, 10,218 missing or prisoners; Chinese and North Korean losses not known, but many times greater than U.S. losses

TREATIES: Cease-fire, July 27, 1953

The northern and southern regions of Korea had an ancient heritage of conflict with one another, and all of Korea had often been invaded by China or Japan. In 1910, Japan annexed Korea in violation of international agreements. The United States raised no objection to this until after the December 7, 1941, Japanese attack on Pearl Harbor, Hawaii. The liberation of Korea then became one of the United States's stated war aims in WORLD WAR II. Following the Potsdam Conference during July 27–August 2, 1945, Soviet premier Joseph Stalin (1879–1953) announced his intention to establish, with the Western Allies, a trusteeship for Korea. When the Japanese surrendered on August 14, 1945, the United States proposed that the Soviets receive Japan's surrender in Korea north of the 38th parallel, while the United States accept surrender south of this line. The United States understood that the partition of Korea was a temporary expedient until the nation could be restored to a full peacetime footing, but the Soviets seized on it to divide Korea and bring the northern portion into the communist sphere. The Soviets fortified the dividing line between North and South, the 38th parallel, and the United States requested that the United Nations intervene to bring about Korean unification. With Soviet support, however, North Korean communists barred the United Nations from conducting elections north of the 38th parallel. South of the parallel, the elections proceeded on May 10, 1948, creating the Republic of Korea (ROK) under President Syngman Rhee (1875–1965). The Soviets established a rival government in North Korea on May 25, 1948: the People's Democratic Republic of Korea (DRK), under the leadership of Kim Il-sung (1912–94), a Soviet-trained Korean communist.

UNITED STATES BEGINS MILITARY SUPPORT OF SOUTH KOREA

U.S. policy was to arm South Korea for defense, without giving the appearance of sponsoring South Korean aggression. After training an ROK army of 65,000, a coast guard of 4,000, and a police force of 35,000, and supplying defensive arms, the United States completed its military withdrawal from Korea on June 29, 1949, leaving behind only a 500-man U.S. Korean Military Advisory Group (KMAG).

NORTH KOREA INVADES

The North Korean People's Army (NKPA), numbering about 100,000 troops and supplemented by a small air force of 132 combat aircraft, crossed the 38th parallel at 4 o'clock on the morning of June 25, 1950. Brushing aside the inferior South Korean forces, the principal invading force headed toward Seoul, the South Korean capital, about 35 miles below the parallel, while smaller forces moved down the center of the Korean Peninsula and along the east coast. The NKPA took Seoul, and U.S. president Harry Truman (1884–1972) ordered General Douglas MacArthur (1880–1964), commander of the U.S. Far East Command, to begin supplying the ROK with equipment and ammunition. In addition, Truman ordered the U.S. Seventh Fleet to proceed toward Korea, but then redeployed most of it to Taiwan, to forestall a Communist Chinese attack on this Nationalist Chinese stronghold. On June 30, Truman gave MacArthur permission to use all available U.S. forces to aid the ROK. These included units of the Eighth Army as well as the 29th Regimental Combat Team and modest naval and air forces in the region.

In the midst of the invasion, the Soviets signed a treaty of friendship, alliance, and mutual assistance with the People's Republic of China and boycotted all UN organizations and committees on which Nationalist China participated. The Soviet boycott meant that it was not present to veto the UN Security Council resolution authorizing military action against North Korea. Backed by UN sanctions, President Truman named Douglas MacArthur commander of U.S. and UN forces. On July 24, MacArthur created the United Nations Command (UNC). Although various UN member nations would participate in the Korean War, the United States bore the brunt of the battle.

U.S. ground forces began arriving in Korea just six days after the June 25 invasion. By this time, the NKPA had crossed the Han River *south* of Seoul and was still on the move. By July 3, Kimpo Airfield and the port of Inchon were in communist hands. Concluding that the North Koreans' principal objective was the port of Pusan, MacArthur deployed "Task Force Smith" just above Pusan on July 5, but by July 13, the NKPA had pushed ROK and U.S. forces to Taejon, in south-central South Korea. While fighting delaying actions, MacArthur rushed to build up forces in Japan. Two divisions were moved to South Korea on July 18 to reinforce the defenders of Taejon, but the city was lost to the NKPA on July 20.

MacArthur refused to be disheartened by the defeats the U.S.-UN forces suffered. He understood that the rapid advance of the NKPA had stretched its lines of communication and supply beyond their limit. Moreover, although U.S. ground troops were badly outnumbered at this point, the U.S. Air Force quickly established air superiority and began interdicting the supply lines. A naval blockade was also proving effective in cutting off NKPA supplies.

BATTLE OF PUSAN

Lieutenant General Walton H. Walker (1889–1951), commander of the U.S. Eighth Army, took a make-or-break stand along a line north and west of Pusan, the 140-mile-long "Pusan perimeter," extending in an arc from the Korea Strait to the Sea of Japan. With skill and determina-tion, Walker's troops effectively held the perimeter, buying MacArthur the time he needed to build up forces sufficient for an offensive thrust.

INCHON LANDING

MacArthur wanted to attack the NKPA from its rear, trapping it between the attacking force and the Eighth Army at Pusan. To get a large force north of the NKPA position, MacArthur planned and executed a daring landing at Inchon, a site exposed to hazardous tides and offering difficult terrain. On September 15, 1950, MacArthur committed a large force to the Inchon landing, which proved the most brilliant military operation of MacArthur's career. Within two weeks of the landing, Seoul was once again in ROK hands, and the NKPA lines were severed. During September 16–23, the U.S. Eighth Army fought its way out of the Pusan perimeter, forcing the NKPA to withdraw. The Eighth Army pursued and met up with the landing force on September 26. Although more than 30,000 North Korean troops probably made it back to the 38th parallel, the Inchon landing and the associated breakout from Pusan neutralized the NKPA as a fighting force in South Korea. South Korea had been cleared of invaders.

OFFENSIVE INTO NORTH KOREA

On September 27, President Truman ordered General MacArthur to pursue NKPA across the 38th parallel, warning him to steer clear of the Yalu River (the border with Manchuria) and the Tumen River (the border with the U.S.S.R.). MacArthur was authorized to use South Korean troops exclusively; Truman did not want combat between U.S. and Chinese or Soviet troops.

Two ROK corps crossed the 38th parallel on October 1, and, on October 9, General Walker led Eighth Army's I Corps across as well. By the 19th, I Corps had cleared Pyongyang, the North Korean capital and, by October 24, I Corps was just 50 miles outside of Manchuria. ROK forces were also now positioned close to the Chinese border.

Although China threatened to intervene, Truman authorized the advance to continue. On October 26, MacArthur determined that Communist Chinese troops had entered the fight, but even as the Chinese presence grew, MacArthur continued to believe that Chinese operations were strictly defensive. He ordered the advance to continue, and on November 24, U.S. forces reached the Yalu River, North Korea's border with China.

CHINESE INTERVENTION

On the night of November 25, 1950, Chinese forces attacked the Eighth Army hard on its center and right. Two days later, larger Chinese forces overran units of X Corps on its left flank. By November 28, UN positions were caving in as some 300,000 Chinese troops entered North Korea. General Walker withdrew his troops to

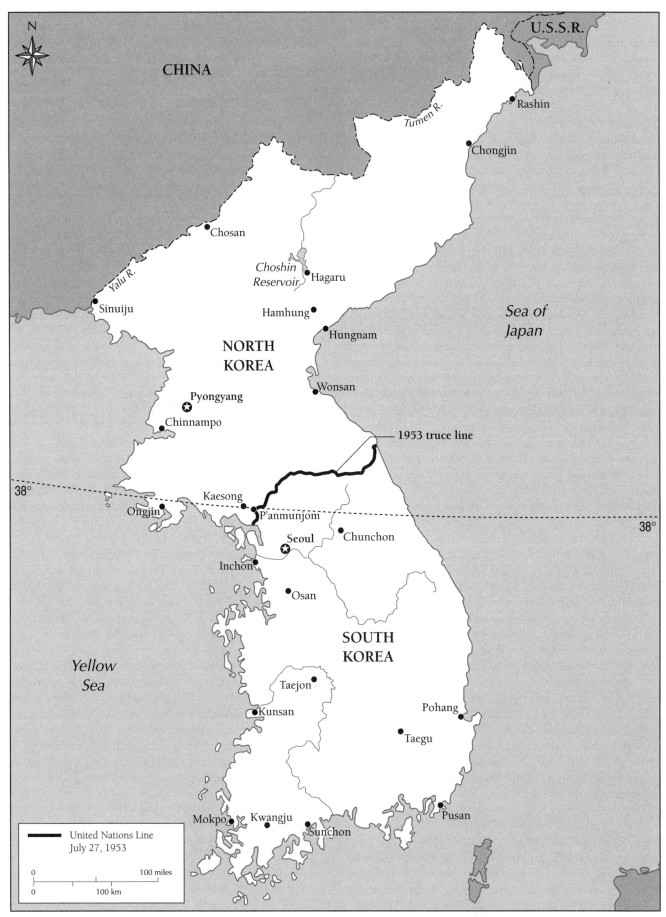

N

CHINA

U.S.S.R.

Tumen R.

Rashin

Chongjin

Chosan

Choshin Reservoir

Hagaru

Yalu R.

Hamhung

Sinuiju

Hungnam

Sea of Japan

NORTH KOREA

Wonsan

Pyongyang

Chinnampo

1953 truce line

Kaesong

38°

Ongjin

P'anmunjom

38°

Seoul

Chunchon

Inchon

Osan

SOUTH KOREA

Yellow Sea

Taejon

Kunsan

Pohang

Taegu

Mokpo

Kwangju

Pusan

Sunchon

United Nations Line
July 27, 1953

0   100 miles

0   100 km

United Nations line established at the 38th parallel, dividing North and South Korea at the time of the armistice prevent envelopment. By December 15, UN forces had withdrawn all the way to the 38th parallel and were now establishing a defensive line across the breadth of the Korean peninsula. A great airlift evacuated X Corps from North Korea. During the evacuation, Walker was killed in an automobile accident, and Lieutenant General Matthew B. Ridgway (1895–1993) replaced him as commander of the Eighth Army.

THE RELIEF OF MACARTHUR

After China's intervention, MacArthur sought permission to attack China directly, especially the airfields in Manchuria. The administration demurred and ordered MacArthur to contain and limit the war, keeping UN forces within Korea. If this became untenable, MacArthur was to evacuate the Korean Peninsula. In response, MacArthur continued to press for a major blockade and attack against China.

While MacArthur and the Truman administration argued, Ridgway prepared an all-out defense north of Seoul. Despite his preparations, a Chinese attack on New Year's Eve drove the Eighth Army into withdrawal toward Seoul. Seoul fell on January 4, 1951, but the Chinese failed to pursue the Eighth Army south of the capital and soon halted the advance. Ridgway recognized that, once again, logistical problems had stalled the Chinese, and he began a slow, methodical offensive (dubbed "Meatgrinder" by troops) on January 25, 1951. Meatgrinder regained Seoul by the middle of March, and, by the 21st, UN troops were back at the 38th parallel.

At the 38th parallel, the UN forces halted. It was decided that holding South Korea below the 38th parallel was an acceptable outcome of the war. When Truman informed MacArthur that negotiations were to open with the Chinese and North Koreans on the basis of currently held positions, the general declared that, if the United Nations would expand the conflict to North Korea's coastal areas and interior strongholds, the Chinese would realize that they were at serious risk of suffering military defeat. Then, on April 5, 1951, Representative Joseph W. Martin (1884–1968) (R-Fla.) read into the *Congressional Record* a letter from MacArthur stating the necessity of opening up a second front against China itself, one using Nationalist Chinese troops. This letter constituted gross—and dangerous—insubordination, and prompted President Truman to relieve MacArthur of command on April 11.

A NEW CHINESE OFFENSIVE

Matthew Ridgway, appointed to replace MacArthur as supreme commander of UN forces, turned over the Eighth Army to Lieutenant General James A. Van Fleet (1892–1992). The Eighth bore the brunt of a massive spring offensive, which inflicted some 7,000 casualties, but cost the communist forces more than 10 times that number. The first phase of the offensive was over by the end of April, but a second phase was launched on May 14,

against the right flank of X Corps. Van Fleet had anticipated just such an attack, however, and so was able to blunt it, inflicting, in the course of a week, some 90,000 casualties.

GUERRILLA PHASE

After the failure of the spring offensive, the communists began to employ hit-and-run attacks by small units instead of deploying massive assaults. The rest of the Korean War became a guerrilla conflict. Van Fleet took the offensive on May 22, 1951, but was soon ordered to halt and hold just north of the 38th parallel.

PEACE NEGOTIATIONS

With the opposing sides arrayed near the 38th parallel, cease-fire negotiations commenced. The talks began at the end of June 1951, but it took until July 26 to even establish an agenda. Breakdowns were frequent, and the talks dragged on for two years, during which combat continued. At length, both sides agreed to an armistice along a demarcation line and demilitarized zone. The truce would be impartially supervised, and arrangements would be made for the return of prisoners of war. UN negotiators wanted prisoners to decide for themselves whether or not they would return home; the communists, fearing mass defection to the South, held out for mandatory repatriation. To break the negotiation stalemate, General Mark Clark (1896–1984), who succeeded Ridgway as UN commander in May 1952, intensified bombing raids on North Korea. It was not until April 1953 that a compromise on the POW issue was reached. At this point, only Syngman Rhee, the president of South Korea, remained dissatisfied with the armistice terms. For him, nothing short of Korean unification (under his leadership) would suffice. He attempted to sabotage the peace process by ordering the immediate release of 25,000 North Korean prisoners who wanted to live in the South. To regain Rhee's cooperation, the United States promised him a mutual security pact and long-term economic aid. However, the armistice signed on July 27, 1953, did not include South Korea. Nevertheless, the shooting war was ended. Korea remained—and remains—divided.

Further reading: Bruce Cumings, *The Origins of the Korean War,* 2 vols. (Princeton, N.J.: Princeton University Press, 1981–1990); T. R. Fehrenbach, *This Kind of War: A Study in Unpreparedness* (New York: Macmillan, 1963); Max Hastings, *The Korean War* (London: M. Joseph, 1987).

Kornilov's Revolt (1917)

PRINCIPAL COMBATANTS: Cossack counterrevolutionary forces vs. the provisional Russian government
PRINCIPAL THEATER(S): Petrograd (St. Petersburg), Russia
DECLARATION: None

MAJOR ISSUES AND OBJECTIVES: Conservative military elements (led by Lavr G. Kornilov) wanted to impose order on Russia through dictatorship following the February Revolution.

OUTCOME: The counterrevolution was quickly suppressed.

APPROXIMATE MAXIMUM NUMBER OF MEN UNDER ARMS: Unknown

CASUALTIES: Unknown

TREATIES: None

Following the FEBRUARY REVOLUTION, which toppled Czar Nicholas II (1868–1918), Russia was adrift in anarchy. Conservative Russian generals, supported by Alexander F. Kerensky (1881–1970), head of the postrevolutionary provisional government, plotted to created a military dictatorship to restore order. However, it soon became apparent that General Lavr G. Kornilov (1870–1918), Kerensky's commander in chief of the army, had ambitions to become sole—and permanent—dictator. Recognizing this, Kerensky denounced Kornilov as a traitor and dismissed him as commander in chief. Kornilov, in turn, sent his loyal Cossack troops to invade Petrograd (subsequently Leningrad and today St. Petersburg). His plan was to reform the soviet (the revolutionary council) to remodel the provisional government along right-wing lines.

Following the incursion of the Cossacks, Kerensky withdrew his support from the military and turned instead to his own left-wing adversaries, the Bolshevik-led workers. In the end, force of persuasion rather than force of arms prevailed. The Cossacks were persuaded to defect, and Kornilov's counterrevolution collapsed, after five days, on September 14, 1917.

General Kornilov was arrested and imprisoned. He escaped from Petrograd following the October Revolution that brought the Bolsheviks to power to participate in the White Russian resistance to government by the soviets (*see* RUSSIAN CIVIL WAR [1917–1922]).

See also BOLSHEVIK REVOLUTION.

Further reading: Sheila Fitzpatrick, *The Russian Revolution* (Oxford, England: Oxford University Press, 1982); Richard Pipes, *The Russian Revolution* (New York: Vintage, 1991); Robert Service, *The Russian Revolution, 1900–1927*, 3rd ed. (New York: St. Martin's Press, 1999).

Kościusko's Uprising   *See* POLISH REBELLION (1794).

Kronstadt Rebellion   (1921)

PRINCIPAL COMBATANTS: Sailors of the Kronstadt Naval Base vs. Bolshevik government troops

PRINCIPAL THEATER(S): Kronstadt Naval Base outside of Petrograd (St. Petersburg), Russia

DECLARATION: None

MAJOR ISSUES AND OBJECTIVES: The sailors demanded an end to Communist Party dictatorship and called for famine relief, as well as other measures.

OUTCOME: The rebellion was quickly and brutally crushed, although it succeeded in spurring reform.

APPROXIMATE MAXIMUM NUMBER OF MEN UNDER ARMS: Kronstadt sailors and allies, 27,000; Bolshevik forces, 45,000

CASUALTIES: Kronstadt forces, 600 killed, 1,000 wounded; Bolshevik forces, 1,912 killed or missing, 1,208 wounded. After the rebellion, 2,103 Kronstadt mutineers were executed, and 6,459 were imprisoned, most of whom died within one year.

TREATIES: None

This brief but bloody uprising came about during the winter of 1921, when the fledgling Soviet Union was stricken by economic disaster and famine brought on in large part by the RUSSIAN CIVIL WAR (1917–1921). One of several major internal uprisings spawned by the Civil War, the Kronstadt Rebellion would have an immense impact on Communist Party policy, influencing it to undertake major economic liberalization.

When the hard-strapped Bolshevik government failed to distribute emergency food supplies to the Russian cities that winter, then imposed repressive laws and strict labor regulations, the sailors at the Kronstadt Naval Base rose up in support of striking workers. The sailors had supported the Bolsheviks in 1917, and their cooperation had been crucial to the success of the October Revolution. During the Civil War, however, they had grown disenchanted with the Bolshevik government, its inability to meet the needs of the population, and its harsh measures against the workers in whose name it ruled. With the striking workers, the sailors formed a Provisional Revolutionary Committee and angrily called for an end to the hegemony of the Communist Party in favor of the full empowerment of the soviets (district councils)—soviets without Bolsheviks. Moreover, they demanded the release of non-Bolshevik political prisoners and a full slate of political freedoms and human rights.

Vladimir I. Lenin (1870–1924), leader of the Bolshevik government, dispatched Leon Trotsky (1879–1940) and Mikhail N. Tukhachevsky (1893–1937) with Red Army soldiers across the ice from Petrograd (Leningrad) to quell the rebellion. Overwhelmed by superior forces, the revolt collapsed. Trotsky ruthlessly shot many of the sailors; others were imprisoned.

The rebellion, so harshly crushed, nevertheless provoked reform. Lenin retreated from strict Marxist communism, allowing a measure of free enterprise and distributing emergency food supplies in an effort to avert the nation's total collapse, in the New Economic Policy of March 1921.

See also BOLSHEVIK REVOLUTION; FEBRUARY (MARCH) REVOLUTION.

Further reading: Sheila Fitzpatrick, *The Russian Revolution* (Oxford, England: Oxford University Press, 1982); Richard Pipes, *The Russian Revolution* (New York: Vintage, 1991); Robert Service, *The Russian Revolution, 1900–1927*, 3rd ed. (New York: St. Martin's Press, 1999).

Kun's Red Terror (1919)

PRINCIPAL COMBATANTS: Hungarian Communists (led by Béla Kun) vs. counterrevolutionaries (led by Admiral Nicholas Horthy) and Romanian invaders
PRINCIPAL THEATER(S): Hungary
DECLARATION: None
MAJOR ISSUES AND OBJECTIVES: Control of the Hungarian government
OUTCOME: The short-lived Hungarian republic was overthrown by Béla Kun's Communists, who were in turn overthrown by a combination of Romanian invaders and Hungarian counterrevolutionaries led by Admiral Nicholas Horthy.
APPROXIMATE MAXIMUM NUMBER OF MEN UNDER ARMS: Unknown
CASUALTIES: Unknown
TREATIES: None

The HUNGARIAN REVOLUTION (1918) gave Hungary independence from the failing Austro-Hungarian Empire and established a republic. However, Soviet Russia, under Vladimir I. Lenin (1870–1924), anxious to spread communism to the newly independent nations of eastern Europe, dispatched Béla Kun (1885–c. 1939) to Hungary to establish a communist party there. The party was created on December 20, 1918, and Kun and his followers did not have long to wait for a moment of instability to exploit. On March 21, 1919, Hungarian president Michael Károlyi (1875–1955) suddenly resigned to protest demands by the Allies of WORLD WAR I for more territorial concessions from Hungary. Károlyi's resignation gave Kun the opportunity he needed, and, immediately, a coalition government was created for Hungary, incorporating communists and social democrats, with Kun as head of state. In short order, Kun terminated the coalition by forcing the social democrats out, and he set up a communist dictatorship.

Kun embarked on an ambitious military program. He created a Hungarian Red Army, with which he invaded Czechoslovakia and reconquered Slovakia from that country. On the domestic front, Kun used his army to force nationalization of Hungary's great estates. When he did not redistribute this land to the peasants, as promised, they turned against Kun. In the meantime,

Kun's increasing use of terror and strong-arm tactics to accelerate the nationalization of land and industry turned the bourgeoisie against him as well. As if this weren't bad enough, the Allies compelled Kun to return Slovakia to the Czechs.

Beleaguered on all sides, Kun fended off a counterrevolutionary attempt at a coup d'etat during mid-1919. No sooner had he succeeded in this, however, than he had to deal with a Romanian invasion. In April, the Romanian army invaded Hungary in a preemptive strike intended to forestall a Hungarian attempt to reconquer Transylvania. Kun defended, but his forces were repulsed. By the summer, Kun's Red Army mutinied, refusing to resist Romanian troops who were now closing in on Budapest, the Hungarian capital. On August 1, 1919, Kun fled to Vienna.

The Romanians occupied Budapest on August 5. The invaders sacked the city, causing significant destruction and loss of life before withdrawing on November 14, 1919. Into the vacuum created by this devastation stepped the counterrevolutionary leader Admiral Nicholas Horthy de Nagybánya (1868–1957). He rode into Budapest and was named head of state and regent in a restored monarchy independent of Austria.

See also HUNGARIAN CIVIL WAR (1921).

Further reading: Jörg K. Hoensch, *A History of Modern Hungary, 1867–1994,* trans. by Kim Traynor, 2nd ed. (New York: Longman, 1996); Paul Ignotus, *Hungary* (New York: Praeger, 1972); Dominic G. Kosáry, *A History of Hungary* (New York: Arno Press, 1971); C. A. Macartney, *Hungary, a Short History* (Edinburgh, Scotland: Edinburgh University Press, 1962); Denis Sinor, *History of Hungary* (Westport, Conn.: Greenwood Press, 1976); John C. Swanson, *The Remnants of the Hapsburg Monarchy: The Shaping of Modern Austria and Hungary, 1918–1922* (Boulder, Colo., and New York: East European Monographs, distributed by Columbia University Press, 2001); Rudolf Tökés, *Béla Kun and the Hungarian Socialist Republic* (Palo Alto, Calif.: Praeger, 1967).

Kurdish Resistance against Iraq (1984–2003)

PRINCIPAL COMBATANTS: The Kurds vs. Turkey; Kurds vs. Iraq; Kurds vs. Iran; Kurdistan Democratic Party (KDP) (sometimes allied with Saddam Hussein's Iraq) vs. Patriotic Union of Kurdistan (PUK); KDP (with Turkish assistance) vs. Kurdistan Workers Party (PKK)
PRINCIPAL THEATER(S): Kurdistan region of Turkey, Iran, and Iraq
DECLARATION: None
MAJOR ISSUES AND OBJECTIVES: Kurdish nationalism and control of the Kurdish nationalist movement
OUTCOME: Unresolved; fighting remains chronic in war marked by genocide and mass displacement of refugees.

APPROXIMATE MAXIMUM NUMBER OF MEN UNDER ARMS:
Unknown
CASUALTIES: Kurdish losses as a result of Turkish counterinsurgency, 20,000 plus displacement of some 2 million refugees; 180,000 Kurds killed by Iraqi forces in 1988 Al-Afan campaign
TREATIES: KDP-PUK cease-fire, October 23, 1996

The Kurds occupy territory encompassed by northern Iraq, eastern Turkey, and Iran, an area denominated Kurdistan, but one that never in modern times existed as an independent state. Since at least the 1920s, the Kurds have attempted, variously, to create an independent nation of Kurdistan or, at least, to gain some measure of autonomy within the nations in which they live. The problems with Kurdish nationalism are twofold: most nations, including those of the West, believe that the creation of a Kurdish state would further destabilize an already volatile region, and, in any case, the Kurds are far from politically homogeneous; it is very difficult to turn a collection of rival clans into a nation. Yet all of this does not alter the fact that the Kurds are chronically mistreated, persecuted, and, especially in the case of Iraqi policy, even subject to a campaign of genocide.

The current chronic state of warfare began in 1984, with the creation in the Turkish-Iraqi border region of the Kurdistan Workers Party (PKK), which was a terrorist organization dedicated to identifying and killing Kurds deemed loyal to the Turkish government. Turkey dispatched troops to Kurdistan in a long campaign of counterinsurgency. The result was a cumulative casualty count in excess of 20,000 among the Kurds. Turkish military action also displaced some 2 million, creating a long-term refugee problem of staggering proportions.

Warfare in Kurdistan is chronic guerrilla action on the part of the Kurds, punctuated by major killing campaigns, most notoriously by Iraq, but also by Turkey and Iran. Under Iraqi dictator Saddam Hussein (b. 1935), mass executions have taken place, as have mass exterminations. The 1988 Al-Afan operation included poison gas attacks and mass executions responsible for the deaths of at least 180,000 Kurds.

Despite the ruthless campaigns mounted against them, the Kurds succeeded in making important territorial gains at the expense of Iraq, in the wake of the PERSIAN GULF WAR, in 1990 and 1991. Guerrillas from the Kurdistan Democratic Party (KDP) and the Patriotic Union of Kurdistan (PUK) ejected Iraqi forces from northern Kurdistan, which became a haven for over 1 million Kurdish refugees. The Persian Gulf War coalition forces guarded an area near the Turkish border to ensure the safety of the refugees, but when the troops left, Saddam Hussein ordered a new attack. It, too, was repulsed.

Under great pressure, Saddam Hussein permitted the Kurds to elect a Kurdish assembly, which was done in April 1992, but within two years fighting between KDP and PUK rivals destroyed the possibility of Kurdish national unity. An attempt to reconcile the rival factions resulted in the establishment of a Kurdish parliament at the Hague in April 1995, but by the early autumn of the next year, the KDP had allied itself with Saddam Hussein in an effort to eliminate the PUK once and for all. KDP forces pushed PUK guerrillas out of Arbīl and Sulaymaniyah, then out of Dokan as well. The KDP conquest was short-lived, however, as, within a month, during October, PUK forces, bolstered by Iran, reconquered most of the lost territory.

Against the backdrop of this internecine fighting, the United States brokered peace talks, which resulted in a cease-fire agreement between the KDP and PUK on October 23, 1996. Within a year, the truce was shattered. Compounding the violence was an invasion of northern Iraq by Turkish and KDP forces to attack Kurdistan Workers Party (PKK) rebels. The PKK was badly beaten, and Turkey rewarded its ally, KDP, by making territorial cessions to it.

Turkish officials sought a definitive end to the PKK rebellion by capturing Abdullah Ocalan (b. c. 1947), a major PKK leader. However, his capture touched off major violent protests on February 16, 1999, and Kurdish-sponsored terrorism in 21 European cities. At the end of 2001, Iraq was in a perpetual stand-off with the Kurds, and Turkey, having claimed victory over Ocalan and the PKK, continues to resist international pressure to grant the Kurds increased political rights. How the downfall of the regime of Saddam Hussein as a result of the UNITED STATES–IRAQ WAR will affect the Kurds had yet to be seen by early 2004.

Further reading: David McDowall, *A Modern History of the Kurds,* 3rd rev. ed. (New York: I. B. Tauris, 2004); Senate Committee on Foreign Relations, *Kurdistan in the Time of Saddam Hussein: A Staff Report to the Committee On Foreign Relations of the United States Senate* (SuDoc Y4.F76/2:S.prt. 102–56) (Washington, D.C.: U.S. Government Printing Office, 1991).

Kurdistan Insurrection (1922–1924)

PRINCIPAL COMBATANTS: The Kurds vs. Great Britain (with Arab allies)
PRINCIPAL THEATER(S): Kurdistan
DECLARATION: None
MAJOR ISSUES AND OBJECTIVES: Independence for the Kurds; protecting the flow of oil for Great Britain
OUTCOME: The Kurds gained considerable autonomy
APPROXIMATE MAXIMUM NUMBER OF MEN UNDER ARMS:
Unknown

CASUALTIES: Unknown
TREATIES: Unknown

In 1909, a British soldier of fortune named William Knox D'Arcy (1849–1917) created the Anglo-Persian Oil Company, which became known as British Petroleum, and launched an economic transformation of the ancient Middle East by the industrialized West, whose political and social effects are still being felt today. When the Middle East collapsed politically, virtually as a whole, during WORLD WAR I, Britain in effect nationalized its Persian oil interests by buying a majority share in the company in 1914 to ensure cheap and ample fuel for its Royal Navy. Thus, in 1922, when the Kurds, a traditional and semi-independent mountain people living in the border region of Iraq, Turkey, and Iran, rebelled against the British and their Arab allies in the region, Great Britain's major concern was to continue the flow of oil from the rich Mosul oil field. The British ultimately suppressed the rebellion, but in the kind of patchwork compromise (sowing the seeds of future conflict) that the Arabs at least were coming to recognize, Britain granted the Kurds considerable autonomy.

Further reading: David McDowall, *A Modern History of the Kurds,* 3rd rev. ed. (New York: I. B. Tauris, 2004); David Fromkin, *A Peace to End All Peace: The Fall of the Ottoman Empire and the Creation of the Modern Middle East* (New York: Henry Holt, 1989); Abdul Rahman Ghassemlou, *Kurdistan and the Kurds* (Prague: Pub. House of the Czechoslovak Academy of Sciences, 1997).

L

Ladislas's ("Last") Crusade *See* HUNGARIAN-TURKISH WAR (1444–1456).

Lamian War (323–322 B.C.E.)

PRINCIPAL COMBATANTS: Athens (and Aetolian League) vs. Macedonia

PRINCIPAL THEATER(S): Macedonia

DECLARATION: None

MAJOR ISSUES AND OBJECTIVES: This was a revolt following the death of Alexander the Great of Macedon; Athenians and other Greek city-states objected to Alexander's recall of the Greek exiles and to the riotous behavior of Alexander's returning troops.

OUTCOME: Athens, overextended and deserted by the other Greek city-states, was defeated on sea and land, and was forced to pay a ruinous indemnity and make other concessions.

APPROXIMATE MAXIMUM NUMBER OF MEN UNDER ARMS: Athens and Aetolian League, 30,000; Macedonian numbers unknown but, when reinforced, greater than 30,000

CASUALTIES: Unknown

TREATIES: No documents survive

Also called the Greek War, the Lamian War was a general revolt in Greece that came in the aftermath of the death of Alexander the Great (356–323 B.C.E.) of Macedon. The revolt was triggered by Alexander's decree recalling the exiles to Athens and was aggravated by the disorderly conduct and criminal actions of troops returning from Alexander's campaigns of conquest. Two focal points of the rebellion were Athens and Taenarum, a place where mercenary troops sold their services; however, the war's name derives from an Athenian siege against Lamia, the Greek city in which the Macedonian regent, Antipater (397–319 B.C.E.), was headquartered.

In October 323, Athens and the Aetolian League fielded 30,000 men and seized Thermopylae, also managing to keep Antipater's army bottled up at Lamia; however, after the Aetolian League deserted the cause, the Athenians lost a major sea battle in 323 B.C.E., then suffered defeat on land, at the Battle of Crannon, Macedonia, in September 322. This left Athens no choice but to surrender unconditionally. The cost to Athens was heavy: some of its most important leaders were executed, and the great orator-philosopher Demosthenes (c. 385–322 B.C.E.) committed suicide. Athens was saddled with a crippling indemnity and lost its democratic status, becoming an oligarchy. Piraeus, its principal port, was relinquished to Macedonian occupation.

See also DIADOCHI, WARS OF THE.

Further reading: M. Cary, *A History of the Greek World from 323 to 146 B.C.* (New York: Barnes and Noble, 1963); Rene Ginones, Gianes N. Akamates, and Iannis Akamates, *Macedonia from Philip II to the Roman Conquest* (Princeton, N.J.: Princeton University Press, 1994); F. W. Walbank, *The Hellenistic World* (Cambridge, Mass.: Harvard University Press, 1993).

Landshut Succession, War of the

See BAVARIAN WAR.

Laodicean War *See* SYRIAN-EGYPTIAN WAR, THIRD.

Laotian-Burmese Wars *See* BURMESE-LAOTIAN WAR (1558); BURMESE-LAOTIAN WAR (1564–1565); BURMESE-LAOTIAN WAR (1571–1575); BURMESE-LAOTIAN WAR (1581–1592).

Laotian Civil War (1954–1973)

PRINCIPAL COMBATANTS: The Laotian neutralist government, right-wing parties, and the communist Pathet Lao vs. each other in various combinations
PRINCIPAL THEATER(S): Laos, especially the Plain of Jars region
DECLARATION: None
MAJOR ISSUES AND OBJECTIVES: Control of the Laotian government
OUTCOME: A coalition was formed among the neutralists, rightists, and Pathet Lao communists; this put the Pathet Lao in a position to take over the government entirely, after neighboring Vietnam was unified as a communist state in 1975.
APPROXIMATE MAXIMUM NUMBER OF MEN UNDER ARMS: Unknown
CASUALTIES: Unknown
TREATIES: Cease-fire of 1961 and of 1973

The Geneva Conference of 1954 recognized Laotian independence from France and acknowledged the new nation's neutrality. The anti-French, leftist Pathet Lao soon gained control of the two northern provinces of Laos and received support from communists in Vietnam. In exchange for this support, the Pathet Lao allowed North Vietnamese communist troops to infiltrate Laos and use it for a supply and staging area in the VIETNAMESE CIVIL WAR (1955–1965) that was escalating into the VIETNAM WAR. In cooperation with the Pathet Lao, the infiltrators attacked Laotian government forces in an effort to overthrow the government and replace it with a communist regime.

Under great pressure from the communists, Prince Souvanna Phouma (1901–84), Laotian premier, attempted to form a coalition government by admitting Pathet Lao leaders into positions of authority. This, however, alienated the right wing of his government, and Souvanna Phouma was ousted. In the wake of his ouster, the pro-Western right wing, drawing economic and military support from the United States, launched a campaign against the Pathet Lao. Most of the fighting, between the Laotian army and the Pathet Lao, was concentrated on the Plain of Jars in north-central Laos.

During the conflict, Souvanna Phouma resurfaced and, in 1960, led a successful coup d'état. He proclaimed himself a middle-of-the-road leader who wanted to restore Laos to the status defined for it by the Geneva Conference. Before the year was out, however, Souvanna found himself locked in a struggle with the Pathet Lao and the right wing. He stepped down and fled to temporary self-imposed exile in Cambodia.

In Souvanna's absence, in 1961, Prince Souphanouvong (1909–95), a Pathet Lao leader, concluded a cease-fire with the remnant of the Laotian government, and, by 1962, a volatile coalition was forged among the left, right, and middle. Not only did each have representation in the government, each also maintained its own private army. Souvanna Phouma returned as the nominal head of state, but in 1964 the political right-wing used the army to oust him from office. When Souvanna agreed to give the right wingers a bigger slice of government representation, he was restored. This, predictably, brought protests and violence from the Pathet Lao, which, supported by the North Vietnamese, broke away from the coalition government and waged an all-out military campaign on the Plain of Jars. From this point forward, the Pathet Lao gradually gained ground—despite U.S. military support for the government of Souvanna Phouma.

By 1973, the Pathet Lao controlled much of the east, north, and south, and the Souvanna government concluded a cease-fire and formed a new coalition in which the Pathet Lao played a prominent role. Souvanna remained premier, with Prince Souphanouvong, the highest-ranking member of the Pathet Lao, as president. The coalition was doomed, however, by the victory of the communist forces in South Vietnam in 1975. Once this neighbor had become a thoroughly communist state, the Pathet Lao felt emboldened to take over Laos.

See also FRENCH-INDOCHINA WAR (1946–1954).

Further reading: MacAlister Brown and Joseph Zasloff, *Apprentice Revolutionaries: The Communist Movement in Laos, 1930–1985* (Palo Alto, Calif.: Stanford University Press, 1986); D. G. E. Hall, *A History of South-East Asia,* 4th ed. (New York: St. Martin's Press, 1981); Joseph Zasloff, *The Pathet Lao* (Lexington, Mass.: Lexington Books, 1973).

Laotian Guerrilla War (1977–1990)

PRINCIPAL COMBATANTS: Pathet Lao (supported by Vietnam) vs. groups favoring royalist restoration (supported by China); Pathet Lao government vs. Thailand in border dispute
PRINCIPAL THEATER(S): Laos
DECLARATION: None
MAJOR ISSUES AND OBJECTIVES: The communist Pathet Lao sought to suppress a movement for the restoration of the monarchy; simultaneously, the Pathet Lao fought a border war with Thailand.

OUTCOME: Once half of the Vietnamese troops occupying Laos withdrew, China ended its military support for the anti-Pathet Lao rebels, and the war quickly wound down. Improved relations with China, Thailand, and other neighbors bolstered the Pathet Lao government and brought a significant degree of stability to the country.
APPROXIMATE MAXIMUM NUMBER OF MEN UNDER ARMS: Unknown
CASUALTIES: Unknown
TREATIES: Formal cease-fire, 1990, but no definitive treaty

Having come to power as a result of the LAOTIAN CIVIL WAR, the Pathet Lao abolished the traditional monarchy of Laos and formally established the People's Democratic Republic, a communist dictatorship. This sent many Laotians fleeing the country, mostly to Thailand. Others, most prominently the Meo tribesmen, loyal supporters of the monarchy, began a guerrilla war against the Pathet Lao government. Because the Pathet Lao supported (and was in turn supported by) communist Vietnam, China, which was locked in enmity against Vietnam, sided with and aided the Meo as well as the Hmong tribespeople—despite their advocacy of the monarchy and opposition to the communist government.

Amid a continual flow of refugees out of Laos and a low-level guerrilla war, the Pathet Lao government weakened, and in 1982, China supported the creation of a Royal Lao Democratic Government, a breakaway government that took control of the southern portion of the country. The Royal Lao forces, already allied with China, planned also to form an alliance with anti-Vietnamese forces in Cambodia. Their immediate objective was to eject some 45,000 Vietnamese troops occupying Laos.

During 1984–88, while guerrilla warfare raged within Laos, Thailand and Laos frequently engaged in combat over a disputed border. The Pathet Lao, barely holding its own against internal rebels, accused Thailand of supporting the Laotian right wing and of giving its members shelter along the border. Then, in 1988, some 20,000 Vietnamese troops were withdrawn from Laos. This was sufficient to allow China to declare a victory and depart the field; it withdrew its military support of the anti–Pathet Lao royalists. The Pathet Lao gained the ascendency now, buoyed in no small measure by vastly improved trade relations with China as well as with Thailand and Vietnam. With economic strength, the Pathet Lao became increasingly popular and, therefore, difficult to oppose. The anti-Pathet Lao rebels gradually withdrew, and a formal cease-fire between Laos and Thailand was also concluded in 1990. By the following year, Thailand withdrew its troops from the border region. Free to focus on the remaining rebels, the Pathet Lao quickly suppressed remaining pockets of rebellion. With stability restored to Laos, some 60,000 refugees returned from camps in Thailand.

Further reading: MacAlister Brown and Joseph Zasloff, *Apprentice Revolutionaries: The Communist Movement in Laos, 1930–1985* (Palo Alto, Calif.: Stanford University Press, 1986); D. G. E. Hall, *A History of South-East Asia,* 4th ed. (New York: St. Martin's Press, 1981); Joseph Zasloff, *The Pathet Lao* (Lexington, Mass.: Lexington Books, 1973); Joseph Zasloff and Leonard Unger, eds., *Laos: Beyond the Revolution* (Houndsmill, Basingstoke, Hampshire: Macmillan, 1991).

Laotian Invasion of Chiengmai   *See* SIAMESE-BURMESE WAR (1593–1600).

"Last" Crusade   *See* HUNGARIAN-TURKISH WAR (1444–1456).

Latin Empire–Byzantine Empire War, First (1204–1222)

PRINCIPAL COMBATANTS: Latin Empire vs. Nicaean Empire
PRINCIPAL THEATER(S): Asia Minor
DECLARATION: None
MAJOR ISSUES AND OBJECTIVES: The belligerents fought over succession to the Byzantine Empire.
OUTCOME: The weak Latin Empire was repeatedly defeated, its territory ultimately reduced to the city of Constantinople itself.
APPROXIMATE MAXIMUM NUMBER OF MEN UNDER ARMS: Unknown
CASUALTIES: Unknown
TREATIES: Armistice of 1206; Armistice of 1214; Armistice of 1222

When the Byzantine Empire collapsed as a result of the disastrous Fourth CRUSADE, the so-called Latin Empire (also known as Romania) was proclaimed under Emperor Baldwin II (1171–1205). The new empire was more an aspiration than an accomplished fact, however, and external threats as well as internal dissension kept it weak. A Bulgarian-Cuman army soundly defeated the forces of the Latin Empire at the Battle of Adrianople in 1205, forcing the withdrawal of the empire's forces and resulting in the capture of Baldwin. The following year, Henry of Flanders (c. 1174–1216) ascended the Latin throne and resolved to reoccupy Asia Minor. He was beaten back by a Nicaean army, and Nicaea forced on him a two-year armistice. In desperation, Henry made a secret pact with the Seljuk Turks, who waged war against Nicaea beginning in 1209. Despite this alliance, the weak army of the Latin Empire was repeatedly bested in battle, so that, by 1214, the Latin

Empire was forced to renounce attempts to conquer Nicaean territory.

When Henry of Flanders died in 1216, the decline of the short-lived Latin Empire accelerated. Three years later, the southern Slavs claimed Nicaea as proper heir to the Byzantine Empire and recognized it as the center of the Greek Orthodox Church. By 1222, the so-called Latin Empire was nothing more than the city of Constantinople, Nicaea having conquered Seleucia from the Latins that year. More enduring was the widening of the gulf between the Christian churches of the East and West. This alienated Greece from the West and killed any hope of Greek reunion with what had been the Byzantine Empire. The Latin Empire had no chance to become a western bulwark against eastern invasion, and thus Europe lay exposed and vulnerable.

See also LATIN EMPIRE–BYZANTINE EMPIRE WAR, SECOND; LATIN EMPIRE–BYZANTINE EMPIRE WAR, THIRD.

Further reading: Michael Angold, *A Byzantine Government in Exile: Government and Society under the Laskanids of Nicaea, 1204–1261* (New York: Oxford University Press, 1975); Cyril A. Mango, ed., *Oxford History of Byzantium* (New York: Oxford University Press, 2002); John Julius Norwich, *Byzantium: The Decline and Fall.* (New York: Alfred A. Knopf, 1996).

Latin Empire–Byzantine Empire War, Second (1224–1237)

PRINCIPAL COMBATANTS: Nicaea vs. Latin Empire and Bulgaria
PRINCIPAL THEATER(S): Asia Minor
DECLARATION: None
MAJOR ISSUES AND OBJECTIVES: As with the First Latin Empire–Byzantine Empire War, the objective was control of the Byzantine Empire.
OUTCOME: After a protracted struggle, Nicaea gained control of Bulgaria and the Latin Empire
APPROXIMATE MAXIMUM NUMBER OF MEN UNDER ARMS: Unknown
CASUALTIES: Unknown
TREATIES: None

The greatly reduced Latin Empire renewed its contest with Nicaea over control of the waning Byzantine Empire in 1224. Nicaea's John III (d. 1254) struck an alliance with Ivan II (d. 1241) of Bulgaria and, together, the allies conquered territory in Asia Minor and among the Aegean islands. John failed, however, to take Constantinople from the Latins. This induced Ivan II to switch allegiance from Nicaea to the Latin Empire. Despite the loss of his ally, however, John III continued to acquire territory in Asia Minor, although he was forced to relinquish Thrace to Epirus.

In the meantime, Ivan II ruled as regent (to Baldwin II [1217–73]) of the Latin Empire until John of Brienne (1170–1237) joined Baldwin as coemperor in 1231. His regency voided, Ivan now declared war on the Latin Empire and attacked Constantinople in 1235 and again in 1236. This proved foolhardy, since the city was such a formidable objective. Both attempts were repulsed. Taking advantage of these defeats, John III attacked Ivan, managing to dominate both Bulgaria and the Latin Empire.

See also LATIN EMPIRE–BYZANTINE EMPIRE WAR, FIRST; LATIN EMPIRE–BYZANTINE EMPIRE WAR, THIRD.

Further reading: Michael Angold, *A Byzantine Government in Exile: Government and Society under the Laskanids of Nicaea, 1204–1261* (New York: Oxford University Press, 1975); Cyril A. Mango, ed., *Oxford History of Byzantium* (New York: Oxford University Press, 2002); John Julius Norwich, *Byzantium: The Decline and Fall.* (New York: Alfred A. Knopf, 1996).

Latin Empire–Byzantine Empire War, Third (1261–1267)

PRINCIPAL COMBATANTS: Restored Byzantine Empire vs. (variously) Latin Empire, Nicaea, Naples and Sicily, Epirus, Genoa, and Bulgaria
PRINCIPAL THEATER(S): Italy and the Peloponnese
DECLARATION: None
MAJOR ISSUES AND OBJECTIVES: Michael VIII Palaeologus sought to restore the Byzantine Empire.
OUTCOME: The empire was largely restored under Michael.
APPROXIMATE MAXIMUM NUMBER OF MEN UNDER ARMS: Unknown
CASUALTIES: Unknown
TREATIES: Treaty with Genoa, 1261; alliance with Venice, 1263

Following the First LATIN EMPIRE–BYZANTINE EMPIRE WAR, and Second LATIN EMPIRE–BYZANTINE EMPIRE WAR, the Latin Empire, never very strong and always wracked by internal dissension, began its final collapse. Michael VIII Palaeologus (1225–82), having usurped the Nicaean throne, now led an army against Constantinople, which had withstood attacks in the First and Second Latin Empire–Byzantine Empire wars, and took the city in 1259. With their last stronghold gone, the Latins yielded to the restoration of the Byzantine Empire. However, the war Michael had started continued now against Charles I (1227–85) of Naples and Sicily, as Michael, in 1261, was proclaimed Byzantine emperor. Michael also faced enemies on the Peloponnese, which he defeated in 1261, and opposition from Genoa, with which he concluded a treaty the same year. A year later, however, Bulgaria rebelled against the renewed Byzantine Empire, and Michael responded with a vigorous campaign that crushed the incipient revolt.

In 1263, its treaty with the empire notwithstanding, Genoa renewed war against the Byzantines, but Michael engaged the enemy on the sea and defeated the Genoese fleet, then struck an alliance with Venice, which effectively checked further aggression from Genoa.

In 1264, Michael moved against Epirus, and scored a victory there, but also lost a major battle against the Latin principality of Achaea at Makry-Plagi. A serious tactical loss, the defeat at Makry-Plagi turned out to be a relatively insignificant strategic setback, for, over the next three years, Michael led a slow but steady campaign against remaining pockets of resistance. Additionally, he conducted a skillful diplomatic offensive. The combination of military momentum and good diplomacy restored the Byzantine Empire and brought it a degree of stability it had not known for many years.

See also BYZANTINE CIVIL WAR (1222–1224); BYZANTINE WAR; CRUSADE, FOURTH; CRUSADE, SIXTH; CRUSADE, EIGHTH.

Further reading: Deno John Geanakoplos, *Emperor Michael Palaeologus and the West, 1258–1282* (Hamden, Conn.: Archon Books, 1973); Donald M. Nicol, *The Last Centuries of Byzantium, 1261–1453,* 2nd ed. (New York: Cambridge University Press, 1993); Cyril A. Mango, ed., *Oxford History of Byzantium* (New York: Oxford University Press, 2002); John Julius Norwich, *Byzantium: The Decline and Fall.* (New York: Alfred A. Knopf, 1996).

Latin War (340–338 B.C.E.)

PRINCIPAL COMBATANTS: Rome vs. Latin rebels
PRINCIPAL THEATER(S): Latium (central Italy)
DECLARATION: None
MAJOR ISSUES AND OBJECTIVES: Rebellious members of the Latin confederation attempted to end Rome's domination of the league.
OUTCOME: After initial victories, the rebellious cities were put down and compelled to acknowledge Rome as the leader of the confederation.
APPROXIMATE MAXIMUM NUMBER OF MEN UNDER ARMS: Unknown
CASUALTIES: Unknown
TREATIES: Revised Latin confederation agreement, 338 B.C.E.

By the fourth century B.C.E., the city-state of Rome came to dominate Latium—central Italy—binding to itself in a loose confederation the other cities in the region. As was common among such confederations, conflict developed over domination of the league. A number of cities, allying

themselves with the Campanians, challenged Roman domination of the confederation beginning in 340 B.C.E.

The first major battle occurred at Vesuvius in 339, when the Roman general Publius Decius Mus (d. 339 B.C.E.) made a suicidal attack against the rebel forces to permit the major Roman army of Titus Manlius Imperiosus Torquatus (fl. mid-fourth century B.C.E.) to withdraw intact. Regrouping, Manlius was able to mount a massive counterattack at the Battle of Trifanum, near the mouth of the Liri River, in 338, achieving a victory so decisive that the Latin rebels were compelled to conclude a revised alliance with Rome, whereby Rome was explicitly acknowledged as the leader of a confederation bound by military alliance and—in a key move toward empire—exchanging citizenship rights among the members of the confederation. Effectively, Rome annexed all of Latium.

Further reading: Joshua Whatmough, *The Foundations of Roman Italy* (New York: Haskell House Publishers, 1971); A. Alföldi, *Early Rome and the Latins* (Ann Arbor: University of Michigan Press, 1965).

Latvian War of Independence (1919–1920)

PRINCIPAL COMBATANTS: Latvian republicans (with German allies) vs. Soviet invaders
PRINCIPAL THEATER(S): Latvia, especially Riga and vicinity
DECLARATION: None
MAJOR ISSUES AND OBJECTIVES: Latvia, having gained independence from Germany, resisted Soviet attempts at domination.
OUTCOME: Latvia obtained Soviet recognition of its independence by the Treaty of Riga (abrogated in 1940).
APPROXIMATE MAXIMUM NUMBER OF MEN UNDER ARMS: Unknown
CASUALTIES: Unknown
TREATIES: Treaty of Riga, August 11, 1920

After the armistice ending WORLD WAR I, Latvia, which had been under German control, declared independence under Prime Minister Karlis Ulmanis (1877–1940). Within weeks, however, during January 1919, Bolshevik forces from Russia invaded Latvia and occupied Riga, its capital city. Ulmanis was ousted, and a Soviet government set up in his place.

Latvian nationalists won the approval of the WORLD WAR I Allies (principally France, Britain, Italy, and the United States) to secure the aid of German troops in combating the invasion. By March, combined Latvian-German forces has expelled the Soviets from Riga but not entirely from Latvia. Now, however, in defiance of the Treaty of Versailles, the Germans refused to evacuate Latvia and remained in control of Riga. Latvian forces were ultimately able to push the Germans out by the end of 1919, but in the process, the Soviets were once again able to advance on Riga. With the aid of the Allied nations, they were at last permanently evicted in January 1920. The Soviets signed an armistice with the Latvians, then concluded the Treaty of Riga on August 11, 1920, recognizing Latvian independence; however, positioned as it was within the jaws of Germany to the west and Soviet Russia to the east, the nation was doomed to reconquest by one great power or the other. In WORLD WAR II, Latvia would become a dismal battlefield.

Further reading: Edgar Anderson, *Latvia, Past and Present: 1918–1968* (Waverly, Iowa: Latva gramata, 1968).

Lava Beds War   *See* MODOC WAR.

League of Augsburg, War of the   *See* GRAND ALLIANCE, WAR OF THE.

League of Cambrai, War of the   (1508–1510)

PRINCIPAL COMBATANTS: League of Cambrai (Holy Roman Empire, France, Aragon) vs. Venice
PRINCIPAL THEATER(S): Northern Italy
DECLARATION: League of Cambrai created December 10, 1508
MAJOR ISSUES AND OBJECTIVES: The pope wanted to regain control of cities of the Romagna seized by Venice.
OUTCOME: Venice relinquished its mainland satellite cities.
APPROXIMATE MAXIMUM NUMBER OF MEN UNDER ARMS: Variable; at the culminating Battle of Agnadello, France fielded 30,000 men against approximately the same number of Venetians.
CASUALTIES: At Agnadello, Venetian casualties were reported "in the thousands."
TREATIES: No treaty ended the war; the creation of the League of Cambrai (December 10, 1508) was the basis of the war.

The Romagna region of northern Italy was titled to the papacy. When Venice seized the region, Pope Julius II (1443–1513), on December 10, 1508, created the League of Cambrai, consisting of the Holy Roman Empire, France, and Aragon—all traditional enemies of Venice—to wage war. The pope authorized the monarchs of the league kingdoms, Holy Roman Emperor Maximilian I (1459–1519), French king Louis XII (1462–1515), and Aragon King Ferdinand II (1452–1516), to divide among themselves the mainland territories of Venice and to bring any papal lands back to the papacy.

The league's first targets were Perugia and the chief city of the Romagna, Bologna. After taking these, Louis's French army of 30,000 attacked a Venetian army (of comparable size) at Agnadello in Cremona on May 14, 1509. The Venetians were soundly defeated, suffering several thousand casualties. The French also captured their artillery. As a result of this decisive battle, the mainland satellite cities of Venice were lost and divided, as the pope had ordered, among the league members and the papacy. However, Venice refused to surrender unconditionally, and when Emperor Maximilian lost control of Padua and the pope had second thoughts about allowing so many foreign monarchs to control Italy, the League of Cambrai dissolved. Venice would eventually regain control of its mainland cities, but it would never recover the extent of power it enjoyed before the League of Cambrai's war.

See also HOLY LEAGUE, WAR OF THE.

Further reading: P. S. Chambers, *The Imperial Venice, 1380–1580* (New York: Harcourt, Brace Jovanovich, 1971); Friedrich Heer, *Holy Roman Empire*, trans. Janet Sondheimer (New York: Sterling, 2002); M. E. Mallett and J. R. Hale, *The Military Organization of a Renaissance State: Venice, c. 1400 to 1617* (New York: Cambridge University Press, 1984); John Jefrees Martin and Dennis Romano eds., *Venice Reconsidered: The History and Civilization of an Italian City State* (Baltimore: Johns Hopkins University Press, 2003); John Julius Norwich, *A History of Venice* (New York: Vintage, 1989).

Lebanese Civil War   (1958)

PRINCIPAL COMBATANTS: Christian (Maronite) Lebanese vs. Lebanese Muslims
PRINCIPAL THEATER(S): Lebanon, especially Beirut
DECLARATION: None
MAJOR ISSUES AND OBJECTIVES: Camille Chamoun, Lebanon's Christian (Maronite) president, developed close ties with the West, a policy that alienated Lebanese Muslims, who favored closer ties with neighboring Arab nations. Muslim groups rebelled against Chamoun.
OUTCOME: U.S. and UN intervention ended the war, with the Christian (Maronite) party still in power.
APPROXIMATE MAXIMUM NUMBER OF MEN UNDER ARMS: U.S. troop strength in Lebanon, 14,000; others variable
CASUALTIES: Mostly civilian
TREATIES: None

Camille Chamoun (1900–87), candidate of the Christian (Maronite) party, was elected to the presidency of Lebanon in 1952 and quickly developed close ties with the West, especially the United States. This policy alienated many Lebanese Muslims, about 50 percent of the population, who favored closer ties with neighboring Arab nations and were hostile to the West. Unrest grew and, during May 9–13, 1958, Muslim groups rebelled against Chamoun. Riots erupted in Tripoli and in the Lebanese capital, Beirut. The riots were apparently orchestrated—or at least supported—by the United Arab Republic (UAR) (the union of Egypt and Syria, formed in January 1958), which also endorsed the activity of Kamal Jumblatt (1918–77), a Druse chieftain who led the most militant aspects of the revolt and who had already defeated Lebanese army forces in several encounters.

Chamoun refused to resign and instead appealed to U.S. president Dwight D. Eisenhower (1890–1969) for military aid. In 1957, Eisenhower had promulgated the so-called Eisenhower Doctrine, which held that the independence of the nations of the Middle East was vital to United States interests and the peace of the world. As the Eisenhower administration saw it, Soviet backing of the United Arab Republic jeopardized the security of Jordan, Turkey, and Iraq, as well as Lebanon—all nations friendly to the West. When Iraqi army officers allied with the UAR overthrew Iraq's King Faisal II (1935–58) in 1957, Egypt and Iraq acted to destabilize Jordan and Lebanon, arming and supporting rebels in these nations. In 1957, the Eisenhower government authorized U.S. Marines and a full army brigade to join a British regiment in Jordan to protect the government of King Hussein (1935–99). At this time, it was also decided to prepare for intervention in Lebanon, and three U.S. Marine battalions were made ready. The army prepared for a massive airlift, if required. Thus the U.S. military was poised to answer Chamoun's appeal for assistance.

On July 15, 1958, marines began to land at Khalde Beach in Lebanon. On July 16, these initial forces were joined by marines airlifted from Europe. On July 19, army troops arrived. The response of the Lebanese was mixed as U.S. soldiers marched into Beirut. Little resistance was encountered, and some even greeted the Americans as friends. Wisely, U.S. commanders established a clear relationship with Lebanese officers. Within a short time, U.S. and Lebanese forces were integrated and working well together to patrol the explosive areas of Beirut.

On July 15, when the first contingent of marines landed, President Eisenhower called on the United Nations to intervene in Lebanon with a multinational peacekeeping force. The Soviet Union vetoed the resolution of intervention, whereupon Eisenhower dispatched Deputy Undersecretary of State Robert D. Murphy (1895–1978) to Lebanon to mediate among the warring factions. In the meantime, the U.S. presence had enabled the establishment of a cease-fire, which, however, was tenuous at best. Sniper incidents were common. Occasionally, skirmishes developed. Despite this, U.S. forces worked with the Lebanese army to create a 20-mile defensive perimeter around Beirut. The principal object of this was to prevent Syrian or Syrian-backed guerrillas from attacking the capital and ousting Chamoun. The U.S. intervention bought time for Murphy to negotiate an agreement to hold new elections. Another Maronite Christian, General Faud Chehab (1902–73), was elected, and, after his inauguration on September 23, 1958, U.S. troops withdrew. At its peak, U.S. troops strength in Lebanon approached 14,000.

Further reading: Helena Cobban, *The Making of Modern Lebanon* (London: Hutchinson, 1985); David Gilmore, *Lebanon, The Fractured Country* (New York: St. Martin's Press, 1983, c. 1984); Kanal S. Salibi, *Crossroads to Civil War* (Delmar, N.Y.: Caravan Books, 1975).

Lebanese Civil War (1975–1992)

PRINCIPAL COMBATANTS: Christian (Maronite) Lebanese (many of the Christian Phalange Party) vs. Lebanese Muslims and Lebanon-based Palestinian refugees, members of the Palestine Liberation Organization (PLO), Palestine Liberation Army (PLA); Syrian military intervention (Arab Deterrent Force, ADF); Israeli military intervention; military intervention by Multinational Force (MNF), consisting of U.S., French, Italian, and British troops

PRINCIPAL THEATER(S): Lebanon, especially Beirut

DECLARATION: None

MAJOR ISSUES AND OBJECTIVES: Long-standing strife between Christian and Muslim factions; war triggered by reprisals for failed attempt to assassinate the Christian president in 1975

OUTCOME: The civil war came to a tentative end after the "Taif Agreement" created Christian-Muslim representation in Lebanese government.

APPROXIMATE MAXIMUM NUMBER OF MEN UNDER ARMS: Arab Deterrent Force (1977), 30,000 men, including 27,000 Syrian troops; Israel Defense Forces (IDF) (1978), 25,000

CASUALTIES: Lebanon (1977), 44,000 dead, 180,000 wounded, mostly civilian, 200,000 refugees; MNF casualties in October 23, 1983, barracks bombing, 298; Lebanese civilian casualties in 1990 Beirut shellings, 900 dead, more than 3,000 wounded

TREATIES: Shtawrah Accord (Syria and Lebanon), July–August 1977; accord for Israeli withdrawal from Lebanon, May 17, 1983; Saudi-brokered cease-fire, September 26, 1983; "Taif Agreement," November 4, 1989 (Christian-Muslim representation in government)

In the second half of the 20th century, Lebanon was divided more or less evenly between Christians and Muslims. The National Pact of 1943 had established the dominant political role of the Christian Phalange Party in the central government. Periodically, this had been a source of violent discontent among the Muslim factions. Further destabilizing the situation in Lebanon was the presence of Palestinian refugees as well as bases from which the Palestine Liberation Organization (PLO) operated against Israel.

On April 13, 1975, gunmen killed four Phalangists during an attempt on the life of Phalange leader Pierre Gemayel (1905–84). Apparently believing that the would-be assassins were Palestinian, Phalangist forces retaliated later that day with an attack against a bus carrying Palestinians through a Christian neighborhood; 26 passengers died. It was these two incidents that triggered a long, extremely destructive civil war.

On April 14, fighting became widespread and intense, with Phalangists engaging Palestinian militiamen, believed by many to have been from the PLO. Much of the violence was disorganized, consisting mainly of random killings in the streets of Beirut. The government quickly proved incapable of responding decisively or effectively. Civil war did not mobilize the government but paralyzed it. Government leaders were unable to agree on whether or not to use the army to stop the killing. Yet when the militant Druse chieftain Kamal Jumblatt (1918–77) tried to cut off the Phalangists politically, other Christian sects rallied to the Phalangist cause. In May, Prime Minister Rashid al-Sulh (served 1992) and his cabinet resigned, and a new government was formed under Rashid Karami (1921–87). Although there were many calls for his resignation, President Sulayman Franjiyah (served 1970–76) refused to step down, and the war intensified and spread throughout Lebanon. In places with mixed sectarian populations, individuals sought the safety of regions where their sect was dominant, thereby further polarizing the country.

The civil war rapidly became chaotic and complex. Opposing militias exchanged fire in a pattern of attack followed by retaliation. Much of the violence was directed against noncombatant civilians. Nor was the civil war a relatively simple matter of Christian versus Muslim. The factions within both groups were many. Generally, however, those in favor of maintaining the status quo came to be known as the Lebanese Front. These groups included primarily the Maronite Christian militias of the Gemayel and other clans. Less well organized was the Lebanese National Movement, largely led by Kamal Jumblatt. This was a loose agglomeration of leftist groups and guerrillas from PLO factions.

By the end of 1975, the first year of the war, no side had made decisive military gains; however, it was clear that the Lebanese Front had performed poorly against the disorganized Lebanese National Movement. This fact alone eroded the national government. Beginning in 1976, Syria attempted diplomatic intervention, organizing a cease-fire and setting up the High Military Committee, through which it negotiated with all sides—albeit with little success at first.

In January 1976, the Lebanese Front began a siege of Tall Zatar, a Palestinian refugee camp in East Beirut. The Lebanese Front also overran and destroyed Karantina, a Muslim quarter in East Beirut. These provocative actions brought the main forces of the PLO, the Palestine Liberation Army (PLA), into the war. Combined PLA and Lebanese National Movement forces took the town of Ad Damur, a Shamun Christian stronghold south of Beirut.

In the midst of these actions, Syria's diplomacy made a breakthrough. On February 14, 1976, Syria was instrumental in hammering out a 17-point reform program called the Constitutional Document. Hopes were high—then soon dashed as, in March, the Lebanese army fell apart. Dissident Muslim troops, led by Lieutenant Ahmad Khatib (fl. 1970s), mutinied, creating the Lebanese Arab Army, which joined the Lebanese National Movement. The Lebanese Arab Army penetrated Christian-controlled Beirut, then attacked the presidential palace, forcing President Franjiyah to flee to Mount Lebanon.

Against this backdrop, in May 1976, the Chamber of Deputies elected Elias Sarkis (1924–85) to take over as president when Franjiyah's term expired in September. Because Sarkis had strong backing from Syria, he was unacceptable to Jumblatt. So the war continued, as the Lebanese National Movement successfully attacked Mount Lebanon and other Christian-controlled areas. Fearing that Jumblatt would prevail and create a state hostile to Syria, Syrian president Hafiz al-Assad (1930–2000) sent troops against Lebanese National Movement forces. Not only did the Syrians encounter far stiffer resistance than they had anticipated, the decision to side with the Christians provoked anti-Syrian outrage from much of the Arab world. Feeling increased pressure, Assad resolved to act even more strongly. In July, he launched a massive drive against Lebanese National Movement strongholds. Well-organized and relentless, the drive very nearly succeeded in neutralizing the opposition within two weeks. However, Syrian leaders chose to stop short of crushing the rebellion. Instead, they participated in an Arab peace conference held in Riyadh, Saudi Arabia, on October 16, 1976. The conference, followed by an Arab League meeting in Cairo also in October 1976, resulted in a formal end to the Lebanese Civil War. Although full-scale warfare did stop, the conference failed to address the causes that underlay the conflict.

By virtue of the Cairo agreement, Syrian troops occupied Lebanon as the main constituents of the Arab Deterrent Force. In January 1977 the ADF consisted of 30,000 men, of whom 27,000 were Syrian. The war, up to this point, had cost the Lebanese about 44,000 dead and approximately 180,000 wounded. Untold thousands became refugees, and Beirut, long celebrated as one of the great cities of the Middle East, was in ruins. By agreement, the city had been divided into Muslim and Christian sectors, separated by the "Green Line."

In December 1976, Prime Minister Salim al Huss (b. 1935) directed the reorganization of the army, most of whose members had deserted during the civil war to join one of the various factions. According to the Cairo Agreement, Lebanese military units were to be stationed in southern Lebanon; instead, the region south of the Litani River was left in the hands of the Palestinians. This meant that relations with Syria would remain a major cause for concern. Worse, by late 1977, as a result of the Egyptian-Israeli peace negotiations and Syria's consequent rapprochement with the PLO, Lebanese-Syrian relations cooled, then began to disintegrate after fighting broke out between the ADF and the Lebanese army in East Beirut in February 1978, followed by a massive ADF bombardment of Christian sectors of Beirut in July. Lebanese president Sarkis resigned in protest but was persuaded to reconsider. Syrian bombardments of East Beirut ended in October 1978 as a result of a UN Security Council cease-fire resolution that indirectly implicated Syria as a party to the Lebanese Civil War. At this point, Syria threatened to withdraw its forces from Lebanon. This forced President Sarkis to come to terms with President Assad in a conference at Damascus in May 1979. The two heads of state agreed that Syrian troops would "remain in Lebanon as long as the Arab interests so require."

Late in 1980 and into the spring of 1981, the ADF moved against the Phalange Party militia, headed by Bashir Gemayel (1947–82), near Zahlah, a short distance from Beirut. For Israel, the Phalange was an ally, and that nation responded with armed intervention, immediately shooting down two Syrian helicopters over Lebanon. Syria responded by bringing surface-to-air missiles into Lebanon, threatening to expand the war. The United States and Lebanon's Arab neighbors mediated the crisis and widespread regional war was averted.

Yet the civil war in Lebanon remained a potentially regional conflict. Especially complex and dangerous were Lebanese relations with the Palestinians. During the early part of the civil war, Lebanese refugees migrated to southern Lebanon, which remained relatively peaceful. After the Palestinians left the area to fight elsewhere, Christian militias, led by Lebanese army officers supported by Israel, took control of a large part of the south. Christian control of southern Lebanon created a buffer zone between the Lebanon-based Palestinians and Israel. The Syrians wanted to eliminate all Israeli influence from the south, while the Israelis wanted direct contact with the population of southern Lebanon and wished to keep both the Syrians and the Palestinians out of the area. Fighting in the south, between the Christian militia under Major Saad Haddad (b. 1936) and the Palestinians, began in 1977 and gradually escalated. Soon war engulfed the south, making refugees of about 200,000 people.

In July and August 1977, Syria and the Lebanese crafted the Shtawrah Accord, calling for the Palestinians to withdraw 15 kilometers from the Israeli border, with this area to be occupied by the Lebanese army. The ADF was assigned to protect the southern coast. However, at this point, Israel Defense Forces (IDF) invaded southern Lebanon in retaliation for a March 11, 1978, Palestinian guerrilla attack on an Israeli bus near Tel Aviv, in which several people were killed. More than 25,000 IDF troops occupied positions as far north as the Litani River and remained in Lebanon for three months. The UN called on Israel to withdraw, and the United Nations Interim Force in Lebanon was sent to replace the Israelis, who withdrew in stages. When Israel withdrew from southern Lebanon in June, Haddad's South Lebanon Army (SLA) took over most of the areas Israel had previously controlled.

Throughout the Sarkis administration, shifts occurred in domestic politics as Prime Minister Huss, a moderate Sunni Muslim, was unable to form a national unity government. In October 1980, Shafiq al Wazzan (1925–99), another moderate Sunni, became prime minister, but he found even greater difficulty, as more than half of the Chamber of Deputies refused to endorse his cabinet. As for the Lebanese army, it remained incapable of maintaining control over the country.

Against the background of a weak central government, the Shia grew in importance, and in 1980 clashes broke out in the south between Amal—the Shia army—and al Fatah, the military arm of the PLO. The Christians were also having internal problems, with serious disputes arising within the leadership of the Lebanese Front.

In July 1980, Bashir Gemayel and his Phalangist militia defeated the Tigers, the militia of the National Liberals under Camille Chamoun (1900–87) and his son Dani (d. 1990). This victory thrust Gemayel into a position of national prominence. In the meantime, in 1981, Israel reduced its support of the Lebanese Front in compliance with conditions set by the Lebanese National Movement and by Syria. The result, however, was a deterioration in Lebanese security during late 1981 and the first half of 1982. In West Beirut, Tripoli, and southern Lebanon, violence was widespread, particularly automobile bombings directed against foreign diplomats. In April 1982, terrorists attacked Muslim and Christian religious leaders, and it had become clear that neither the Lebanese National Movement, the PLO, nor Syria (through the ADF) was able to control the situation. Popular disillusionment paved the way for the ascension to power of more moderate and conservative Sunni and Shia leaders. The Phalange Party also gained support during this period.

At this juncture, Israel again invaded Lebanon on June 6, 1982, in retaliation for the assassination attempt on the Israeli ambassador to London. The object of the Israelis was to remove PLO forces from the country. Israeli forces moved quickly through south Lebanon, encircling west Beirut by mid-June and beginning a three-month siege of Palestinian and Syrian forces in the city. Throughout this period, Israel kept up the pressure with air, naval, and artillery bombardments of west Beirut. At last, in August, an agreement was reached for the evacuation of Syrian troops and PLO fighters from Beirut. The agreement also provided for the deployment of a three-nation Multinational Force (MNF) during the period of the evacuation, and by late August, U.S. Marines, as well as French and Italian units, had arrived in Beirut. When the evacuation ended, these units left, the U.S. Marines departing on September 10.

In a period of relative calm, then, Bashir Gemayel was elected president in August, succeeding Elias Sarkis. On September 14 he was assassinated, and on September 15, Israeli troops entered west Beirut. During the next three days, Lebanese militiamen massacred hundreds of Palestinian civilians in the Sabra and Shatila refugee camps in west Beirut. Bashir Gemayel's brother, Amin (b. 1942), was elected president by a unanimous vote of the parliament. He took office September 23, 1982, and MNF forces returned to Beirut at the end of September to signify their support for the government. In February 1983, a small British contingent joined the U.S., French, and Italian MNF troops in Beirut.

President Gemayel and his government placed primary emphasis on the withdrawal of Israeli, Syrian, and Palestinian forces from Lebanon, and in late 1982, Lebanese-Israeli negotiations commenced with U.S. participation. On May 17, 1983, an agreement was concluded, providing for Israeli withdrawal. But Syria declined to discuss the withdrawal of its troops. While negotiations were thus stalled, a series of terrorist attacks in 1983 and 1984 were aimed at U.S. interests. On April 18, 1983, the U.S. embassy in west Beirut was bombed, with the loss of 63 lives. The U.S. and French MNF headquarters in Beirut were hit on October 23, 1983, with the loss of 298 lives. Eight more U.S. nationals lost their lives in the bombing of the U.S. embassy annex in east Beirut on September 20, 1984.

Druse and Christian forces had clashed during 1982–83, and when Israeli forces withdrew from the Shuf region at the beginning of September 1983, the Druse, backed by Syria, attacked the Christian Lebanese Forces (LF) militia as well as the Lebanese army. The United States and Saudi Arabia brokered a cease-fire on September 26, 1983, which left the Druse in control of most of the Shuf region. By February 1984, the Lebanese army had all but collapsed after many of its Muslim and Druse units defected to opposition militias. With the departure of the U.S. Marines imminent, the Gemayel government was pressured by Syria and its Muslim Lebanese allies to abandon the May 17 accord. At last, on March 5, 1984, the government announced that it was canceling its unimplemented agreement with Israel. The U.S. Marines left shortly afterward. Reconciliation talks at Lausanne under

Syrian auspices failed soon after this. Although a new "government of national unity" under Prime Minister Rashid Karami was declared in April 1984, it made no real progress toward solving Lebanon's internal political and economic crises.

May 1985 saw the beginning of the "camps war," which would flare up twice more in 1986: Palestinians living in refugee camps in Beirut, Tyre, and Sidon fought the Shi'ite Amal militia. Faced with this renewed violence, Syria, late in 1985, negotiated a "tripartite accord" on political reform among the leaders of various Lebanese factions. Gemayel opposed the accord, and the leader of the Lebanese Front was overthrown in January 1986. Syria sought to unseat Gemayel by inducing the Muslim government ministers to cease dealing with him. The government was paralyzed, and the Lebanese economy, once one of the strongest in the Middle East, deteriorated rapidly. On June 1, Prime Minister Karami was assassinated, and Salim al-Huss was appointed acting prime minister. With the end of President Gemayel's term of office approaching, the Lebanese factions could not agree on a successor. Thus, when he left office on September 23, 1988, Gemayel appointed General Michel Aoun (b. 1935) as interim president while Salim al-Huss continued to act as de facto prime minister. Lebanon was thus divided between a Muslim government in west Beirut and a Christian government in east Beirut.

Fresh violence erupted in February 1989, when General Aoun attempted to close illegal ports run by the Lebanese Front. After several days of intense fighting in east Beirut, Aoun's army units concluded a tenuous truce with the Lebanese Front. The following month, however, Aoun's attempt to close illegal militia ports in predominantly Muslim parts of Lebanon triggered six months of shelling of east Beirut by Muslim and Syrian forces and, in return, shelling of west Beirut and the Shuf by the Christian units of the army and the Lebanese Front. At least 1,000 died in the prolonged attack. Many thousands were injured.

With Lebanon in tatters, the Arab League in January 1989 appointed a committee on Lebanon, led by the Kuwaiti foreign minister. At the Casablanca Arab summit in May, the Arab League created a higher committee on Lebanon, composed of Saudi king Fahd (b. 1923), Algerian president Chadli Bendjedid (b. 1929), and Moroccan king Hassan II (1929–99). After much effort, the committee arranged for a seven-point cease-fire in September, followed by a meeting of Lebanese parliamentarians in Taif, Saudi Arabia. After a month of discussions, the deputies agreed on a charter of national reconciliation, the "Taif Agreement." The document was approved on November 4, and René Moawad (d. 1989), a Maronite Christian deputy from Zghorta in north Lebanon, was elected president on November 5. However, General Aoun issued a decree in early November dissolving parliament and rejecting ratification of the Taif Agreement, as well as throwing out the election of Moawad.

On November 22, 1989, President Moawad was assassinated, the victim of a bomb. Parliament quickly elected Elias Hraoui (b. 1926), a Maronite Christian deputy from Zahleh in the Beqaa Valley, to replace him. The new president named Salim al-Huss prime minister. Once again, Aoun refused to recognize Hraoui. When Hraoui replaced Aoun as army commander in early December, Aoun's forces attacked positions of the Lebanese Front in east Beirut during late January 1990. Heavy fighting took place in east Beirut, resulting in the deaths of more than 900 people and the injury of more than 3,000. In August 1990, the National Assembly approved, and President Hraoui signed into law constitutional amendments embodying the political reform aspects of the Taif Agreement, which divided representation equally between Christians and Muslims. This was followed in October 1990 by a joint Lebanese-Syrian military operation against General Aoun, who surrendered and took refuge in the French embassy. On December 24, 1990, Omar Karami (served 1990–92) was appointed Lebanon's prime minister. Aoun remained in the French embassy until August 27, 1991, when a "special pardon" was issued, allowing him to leave Lebanon safely and take up residence in exile in France.

For the most part, the civil war had ended. During 1991 and 1992, the government made progress in reasserting control over Lebanese territory. All militias, except for Hezbollah, were dissolved in May 1991, and the armed forces moved against armed Palestinian elements in Sidon in July 1991. In May 1992 the last of the Western hostages taken during the mid-1980s by Islamic extremists was released.

Further reading: Helena Cobban, *The Making of Modern Lebanon* (London: Hutchinson, 1985); David Gilmore, *Lebanon, The Fractured Country* (New York: St. Martin's Press, 1983, c. 1984); Kanal S. Salibi, *Crossroads to Civil War* (Delmar, N.Y.: Caravan Books, 1975).

Leisler's Rebellion (1689–1691)

PRINCIPAL COMBATANTS: Anti-Catholic rebels led by Jacob Leisler vs. British colonial authorities
PRINCIPAL THEATER(S): New York City
DECLARATION: None
MAJOR ISSUES AND OBJECTIVES: Leisler led merchants and farmers against Catholics in the British colonial administration.
OUTCOME: Leisler remained in power for more than two years before he was arrested as a traitor and executed.
APPROXIMATE MAXIMUM NUMBER OF MEN UNDER ARMS: Unknown
CASUALTIES: Unknown
TREATIES: None

Great Britain's American colonies were beset by a rash of anti-Catholic activity following the ascension of the Protestant monarchs William (1650–1702) and Mary (1662–94) to the British throne in 1688. Throughout the colonies, there was rebellion against Governor Edmund Andros (1637–1714), and royal colonial officials suspected of being Catholics were attacked and sometimes removed from office. In New York City, a band of artisans and merchants, led by Jacob Leisler (c. 1640–91), stormed and seized Fort James in May 1689. Lieutenant Governor Francis Nicholson fled the next month, and in December Leisler proclaimed himself lieutenant governor. Leisler garnered widespread support from nearby farmers, city residents, and, most important, the local militia.

The official colonial government refused to recognize Leisler until 1690, when fear of an impending Indian attack prompted them to acknowledge his authority to secure the services of the militia. The period of official recognition was short-lived, however. In March 1691 a new royal governor, Henry Sloughter (d. 1691), arrived in New York from England, and with him came Major Richard Ingoldesby (fl. early 1690s) with a small force of soldiers. Sloughter demanded the surrender of Fort James. Leisler at first refused, then, on March 30, 1691, did surrender, only to be arrested and tried as a traitor. Convicted, he was hanged in New York City on May 16, 1691. Parliament subsequently—and posthumously—reversed the conviction.

Although the movement Leisler led was essentially anti-Catholic, it was also, in effect, antiaristocratic. Leisler's faction remained powerful in the affairs of New York through the next generation.

See also GLORIOUS REVOLUTION.

Further reading: Jerome R. Reich, *Leisler's Rebellion: A Study in Democracy in New York, 1664–1720* (Chicago: University of Chicago Press, 1953); Charles McCormick, *Leisler's Rebellion* (New York: Garland Publishers, 1989).

Lelantine War (c. 670 B.C.E.)

PRINCIPAL COMBATANTS: The Greek city-state of Khalkís (with allies Corinth, Samos, and the Thessalian League) vs. Eretria (with allies Aegina, Miletus, and perhaps Megara)
PRINCIPAL THEATER(S): Boeotia
DECLARATION: None recorded
MAJOR ISSUES AND OBJECTIVES: Dominance in trade and possession of trading outposts
OUTCOME: Khalkís triumphed, but Eretria eventually became the politically and economically more powerful of the two city-states.
APPROXIMATE MAXIMUM NUMBER OF MEN UNDER ARMS: Unknown
CASUALTIES: Unknown
TREATIES: None recorded

Little is recorded about this major conflict, the most important war among the Greek states following the Trojan War.

It is known that the conflict was sparked by rivalry over trade and the possession of colonial trading posts. The Boeotian city of Khalkís fought Eretria on the Lelantine Plain, the no-man's land that separated them. Khalkís commanded the support of Corinth, Samos, and the Thessalian League, while Eretria had Aegina, Miletus, and possibly Megara on its side.

Combat took place not only on land, but at sea, the decisive battle occurring on the Lelantine Plain. There Thessalian cavalry defeated the Eretrians, yet, despite this triumph, it was Eretria that eventually became the more important and prosperous city. Thus the war, while major in its time, had little enduring effect.

Further reading: John Boardman, *The Greeks Overseas* (Baltimore: Penguin Books, 1964); John Boardman, Jasper Griffin, and Oswyn Murray, eds., *The Oxford History of Greece and the Hellenistic World* (New York: Oxford University Press, 1991); L. H. Jeffery, *Archaic Greece: The City-States, c. 700–500 B.C.* (New York: St. Martin's Press, 1976).

Lepidus, Revolt of (78–77 B.C.E.)

PRINCIPAL COMBATANTS: Marcus Aemilius Lepidus vs. Rome
PRINCIPAL THEATER(S): Northern Italy
DECLARATION: None
MAJOR ISSUES AND OBJECTIVES: Lepidus sought relief for the poor and disenfranchised.
OUTCOME: The rebellion was crushed, and Lepidus fled.
APPROXIMATE MAXIMUM NUMBER OF MEN UNDER ARMS: Unknown
CASUALTIES: Unknown
TREATIES: None

As a Roman senator, Marcus Aemilius Lepidus (d. c. 77 B.C.E.) espoused the cause of the poor and downtrodden, acting politically to improve their situation. Elected consul in 78, he called for renewed distribution of cheap grain, recall of exiles, and restoration of lands confiscated by the former dictator, Sulla (d. 78 B.C.E.). Frustrated because his efforts came to little, he threw his support behind the people of Etruria (in west-central Italy) when they rebelled. He personally raised an army in northern Italy and marched on Rome, only to be repelled by the superior forces of Quintus Lutatius Catulus (d. 60 B.C.E.) and Pompey the Great (106–48 B.C.E.) at the Battle of Milvian Bridge.

Lepidus and a band of his closest followers evaded capture, taking refuge on Sardinia. There Lepidus soon died, perhaps later in 77 B.C.E. In the meantime, those of his followers who remained active in northern Italy were soon routed by Pompey's army.

Further reading: John Boardman, Jasper Griffin, and Oswyn Murray, eds., *The Oxford History of the Roman World* (New York: Oxford University Press, 1991); Colin Wells, *The Roman Empire,* 2nd ed. (Cambridge, Mass.: Harvard University Press, 1995); Richard D. Weigel, *Lepidus: The Tarnished Triumvir* (New York: Routledge, 1992).

Libyan-Egyptian War (1977)

PRINCIPAL COMBATANTS: Libya vs. Egypt
PRINCIPAL THEATER(S): Border region of the two nations
DECLARATION: July 21, 1977, Libya against Egypt
MAJOR ISSUES AND OBJECTIVES: Issues and objectives are unclear; war tension escalated following Libyan assertions that Egypt sought to seize Libyan oil fields.
OUTCOME: Both sides suffered significant loss of materiel in this indecisive war.
APPROXIMATE MAXIMUM NUMBER OF MEN UNDER ARMS: Egypt, 380,000; Libya, 30,000
CASUALTIES: Libya claimed losses of 27 killed and 9 missing, though it is likely that casualties were much higher.
TREATIES: Cease-fire agreement, July 24, 1977

This brief—four-day—but costly border war developed in an atmosphere of escalating friction between Libya and Egypt. During the spring of 1977, mobs in Libya and in Egypt attacked each other's consulates. Following this, Libya's dictator, Colonel Muammar al-Qaddafi (b. 1943), accused Egypt of attempting to provoke a war as a pretext for seizing the Libyan oil fields. Insulted, Egyptian president Anwar Sadat (1918–81) denied the charges. At last, in June 1977, Qaddafi expelled nearly a quarter-million Egyptians residing in Libya, setting July 1 as the deadline for their departure. On July 21, 1977, Libya's seventh armored division crossed the Egyptian border at the town of Salum. Egypt responded vigorously, beating back the incursion and destroying 40 Libyan tanks.

Both sides deployed tanks and aircraft in several desert battles along the border, Egypt making air strikes deep into Libyan territory, concentrating on air bases and destroying many Libyan fighter aircraft before they could get off the ground. Egypt, however, also suffered significant losses of materiel, but admitted losing only two planes.

Immediately after hostilities broke out, Algeria's president, Houari Boumédienne (1927–1978), offered his services as a mediator, and both sides agreed to a cease-fire on July 24, 1977.

Further reading: Derek Hopwood, *Egypt: Politics and Society, 1945–1990,* 3rd ed. (New York: Routledge, 1993);

John L. Wright, *Libya, a Modern History* (Baltimore: Johns Hopkins University Press, 1982).

Lithuanian War of Independence
(1918–1920)

PRINCIPAL COMBATANTS: Lithuania (with German alliance) vs. Soviet Russia; Lithuania (with Polish alliance) vs. Soviet Russia; Lithuania vs. Poland
PRINCIPAL THEATER(S): Lithuania
DECLARATION: Independence declared, February 16, 1918
MAJOR ISSUES AND OBJECTIVES: Lithuania sought independence from Russia, then from partial Polish occupation.
OUTCOME: Independence was achieved by 1922.
APPROXIMATE MAXIMUM NUMBER OF MEN UNDER ARMS: Lithuania fielded as many as 41,000 men, Poland 50,000; strength of other combatants unknown.
CASUALTIES: Unknown
TREATIES: Treaty of Moscow, July 12, 1920

The independence of Lithuania was a product of the BOL-SHEVIK REVOLUTION and WORLD WAR I. The nation declared its independence from Russia on February 16, 1918, after the czar was deposed. The new Soviet government took steps to regain Lithuania, invading almost immediately after the declaration of independence; however, Germany found it advantageous to recognize Lithuanian independence and quickly drove the Soviets out. With Germany's defeat in World War I, on November 11, 1918, its troops were withdrawn from Lithuania, and the Soviets returned, capturing the Lithuanian capital of Vilna (Vilnius) in January 1919. Polish forces intervened on the side of Lithuania and pushed the Soviets out of the capital (*see* RUSSO-POLISH WAR [1919–1920]).

The post–World War I deliberations of the victorious Allies established a border between Lithuania and Poland in December 1919, assigning Vilna to Lithuania; however, the Soviets continued to fight Lithuania for possession of the region until the Treaty of Moscow of July 12, 1920, by which the Soviets recognized Lithuanian independence. Shortly after this, Lithuania's Polish allies turned against Lithuania in a surprise attack on Vilna. A division of 20,000 Belarusian volunteers from the Polish army seized the capital on October 9, 1920. The Poles established a provisional government and conducted a plebiscite on January 8, 1922. When a majority of Vilna's populace voted for union with Poland, Lithuania broke off all relations with its former ally, and Lithuania was recognized as an independent republic in 1922. A 41,000-man Lithuanian army attempted to retake Vilna, but was repulsed by Polish forces now grown to some 50,000. After tortured arbitration, Vilna was awarded to Poland on March 15, 1923. As for Lithuania, it remained an independent republic until it was annexed by the Soviet Union in 1940.

Further reading: Vytas Stanley Vardys and Judith B. Sedaitis, *Lithuania: The Rebel Nation* (Denver: Westview Press, 1966).

Little Turtle's War (1787–1795)

PRINCIPAL COMBATANTS: Shawnee, Miami, Ottawa, and other Indians vs. United States
PRINCIPAL THEATER(S): Ohio country, mainly present-day Ohio and Indiana
DECLARATION: Unknown
MAJOR ISSUES AND OBJECTIVES: Shawnee and Miami refusal to cede lands to the United States
OUTCOME: A "permanent boundary" for white settlement was established in contested territory; the Indians received compensation for their lands; the British vacated the Old Northwest (region bounded by Ohio River, Mississippi River, and the Great Lakes)
APPROXIMATE MAXIMUM NUMBER OF MEN UNDER ARMS: For the United States, under General Josiah Harmar, 1,216 federal troops and 1,100 militia, under Arthur St. Clair, 2,300 federal troops; under General Anthony Wayne, 4,400. For the Indians, small groups of guerrillas armed by British instigators, and 1,200 against General Anthony Wayne's troops
CASUALTIES: Indian losses unknown; U.S. army and militia losses exceeded 1,000 killed.
TREATIES: Treaty of Greenville, January 1795

At the conclusion of the AMERICAN REVOLUTION, the fledgling United States regarded the Indians of the Ohio country—especially the Shawnee—as a conquered people because their allies, the British, had been defeated. The fact was, however, that the Shawnee and other Ohio tribes consistently defeated the Americans during the conflict and were not, therefore, willing to negotiate land treaties as if they had lost the war. Shawnee representatives repeatedly refused to attend treaty conferences until January 1786, when 300 Shawnees came to Fort Finney on the banks of the Ohio and declared to American commissioners that they would relinquish no land. The frontier leader George Rogers Clark (1752–1818) threatened war, and, with his people suffering the effects of a bad winter and wartime destruction of crops and shelter, Chief Kekewepellethe (fl. late 18th century) (known to the Americans as Tame Hawk) backed down and agreed to cede the entire Miami Valley. Other Shawnee bands and the Miami tribe were quick to repudiate the cession, and, led by the war chiefs Blue Jacket (d. c. 1805) (Shawnee) and Little Turtle (1752–1812) (Miami), stepped up a campaign of lightning raids that had never really ceased, even with the end of the Revolution.

The Revolution had also failed to drive British traders out of the Ohio country, and these men now capitalized on the conflict with the Shawnee by supplying them with arms. During the fall of 1786, Clark raised a 2,000-man militia in Kentucky and marched toward the Wabash Valley to engage the Shawnee, Miami, and Ottawa, who were meeting with British agents. But Clark, now aged and ravaged by heavy drinking, proved a far less effective leader than he had been during the Revolution. Within three weeks, his command simply disintegrated without having engaged the enemy. Eight hundred other militiamen, under Colonel Benjamin Logan (1742–1802), attacked Shawnee villages on the Miami River, killing mostly women, children, and old men. In October, Logan's forces destroyed Mackachack, a village actually friendly to the whites. These inept and tragic attacks served only to harden Shawnee hatred of the Americans, and, with other tribes in the region, they vowed all-out war on whites in the Ohio country.

Logan's raid had destroyed large stores of corn, sending the Shawnee, during the summer of 1787, from the Miami River region to Kekionga, near present-day Fort Wayne, Indiana. Here they became closely coordinated with the Miami, Ottawa, Chippewa, Kickapoo, and Potawatomi, launching many devastating raids.

Yet white settlers continued to flood into the region, and in 1790, the federal government assigned 1,216 federal troops, augmented by a 1,100-man militia, to General Josiah Harmar (1753–1813), to police federal lands. Harmar was cautioned to avoid triggering a major Indian conflict, but that is precisely what he did.

Harmar led about 1,500 men, mostly raw militia forces, to Kekionga on October 15, 1790. His army burned the abandoned villages—as Little Turtle and Blue Jacket watched and waited.

On October 19, Little Turtle and his Miami warriors ambushed a small mounted advance party, which panicked, fled, and collided with a detachment of infantry sent to reinforce them. The infantry also fled, so that a mere 30 regulars and nine militiamen were left to fight. Harmar had no choice but to withdraw back to Kekionga, where Blue Jacket and his Shawnee sprang a trap that resulted in a total rout and a stunning defeat for the army. Harmar was saved from complete annihilation by a total lunar eclipse that prompted the Ottawa warriors, who took it as a bad omen, to break off the pursuit—despite Blue Jacket's protests.

After Harmar was defeated, the Shawnee and their allies ravaged the countryside with unorthodox winter raids. At the height of the violence in 1791, the British, who had done much to provoke the warfare to begin with, suddenly turned peacemakers, apparently realizing that the relentless raiding would soon bring a massive American military response that would not only drive out the Indians, but themselves as well.

Yet the negotiations came to nothing, and the federal government assembled a force of 2,300 men—half of them short-term enlistees—under Arthur St. Clair (c. 1736–1818), governor of the federal territory. On October 4, 1791, the punitive expedition got under way, but, with the onset of winter, suffered mass desertions. The desertions prompted St. Clair to advance with 1,400 troops to seek out Little Turtle, Blue Jacket, and their warriors. They marched for a month without a single encounter, making camp on November 3, 1791, on a plateau above the upper Wabash River. At dawn of the next day, the Indians rushed the vulnerable position, killing 623 soldiers and 24 civilian teamsters as well as wounding 271 soldiers. In proportion to the number of men fielded that day, it stands as the worst defeat the U.S. Army has ever suffered.

In 1792, Congress authorized a larger army and hired Iroquois agents to present an American peace proposal—a restriction on white settlement—to the Shawnee and their allies during the summer of 1792. The Shawnee angrily rejected the proposal, and George Washington (1732–99) chose a former Revolutionary Army commander, "Mad Anthony" Wayne (1745–96), to raise an army, which he carefully trained. After another peace commission failed in the summer of 1793, Wayne advanced westward with his forces, but suffered serious delays brought about by inept and corrupt supply agents.

When Wayne failed to attack by May 1794, Little Turtle and Blue Jacket decided to strike the first blow. Twelve hundred warriors under Blue Jacket and Tecumseh (c. 1768–1813) (who within the decade would emerge as a great military and political leader in his own right—see TECUMSEH'S UPRISING; WAR OF 1812) set out from the Maumee River to blockade Fort Recovery near the present Ohio-Indiana state line. On June 30, they ambushed a pack train and its military escorts, completely routing them. When the Indians advanced on the fort itself, however, they were turned back by artillery fire.

Fortunately for the American forces, the Shawnee coalition began to fall into dispute, and the alliance with the British likewise faltered. Wayne advanced his troops and built a new fort, Fort Defiance, in the midst of abandoned Indian villages.

Seeing the renewed strength of the Americans, Little Turtle counseled negotiating for peace, but Blue Jacket and Tecumseh refused to yield. Overall command of the forces now passed to Blue Jacket, with Little Turtle relegated to leading only the 250-man Miami contingent.

Blue Jacket decided to intercept Wayne's army at a place called Fallen Timbers, opposite the rapids of the Maumee River.

Informed of Blue Jacket's position by his scouts, Wayne cached unnecessary equipment at a fortification he called Fort Deposit on August 17. He waited until August

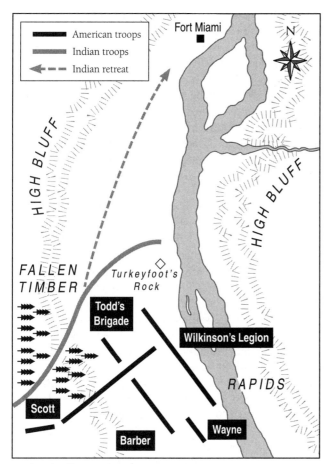

Battle of Fallen Timbers, August 20, 1794

20 before advancing against Blue Jacket. The delay may have been a brilliant stroke of strategy, or perhaps just plain good luck. In either case, it exploited the warriors' custom of fasting before battle. Blue Jacket's men, expecting engagement on the 18th, had advanced without rations on the 17th. By August 20, they had gone without food for three days, and some warriors strayed to forage. Others were weak from hunger. The result was a rout—this time for the Indians.

Fleeing the Battle of Fallen Timbers, Blue Jacket and his surviving warriors were rebuffed by the commandant of a nearby British fort. On August 23, Wayne set about destroying all Indian towns in his path, and, in an act of defiance and contempt, he built Fort Wayne at Kekionga, chief village of the Miamis.

In January 1795, Blue Jacket came to Fort Greenville to negotiate a treaty with Anthony Wayne. The Treaty of Greenville established a "permanent" boundary of white settlement and instituted a program of compensation for Indian territory lost. The British at last agreed to vacate the Old Northwest. And peace reigned in the turbulent Old Northwest until the outbreak of the War of 1812.

Further reading: Alan Axelrod, *Chronicle of the Indian Wars: From Colonial Times to Wounded Knee* (New York:

Prentice Hall General Reference, 1993); Paul David Nelson, *Anthony Wayne: Soldier of the Early Republic* (Bloomington: Indiana University Press, 1985).

Livonian War (1558–1583)

PRINCIPAL COMBATANTS: Russia vs. Livonian Knights; Russia vs. Poland, Lithuania, Sweden, and Denmark
PRINCIPAL THEATER(S): Livonia (modern Estonia and most of modern Latvia)
DECLARATION: None
MAJOR ISSUES AND OBJECTIVES: Russia sought possession of Livonia to acquire a Baltic Sea port.
OUTCOME: After a long war, in which many civilians fell prey to Russian atrocities, Czar Ivan IV renounced all claims to Livonia.
APPROXIMATE MAXIMUM NUMBER OF MEN UNDER ARMS: Russia, 30,000; Poland, 40,000; Sweden, 17,000; other combatant numbers unknown
CASUALTIES: Unknown; civilian losses were very high—perhaps 60,000 at Novgorod
TREATIES: Between Russia and Poland, 1582; Russia and Sweden, 1583

In the 16th century, Livonia encompassed present-day Estonia and most of Latvia and was ruled by the Livonian Knights. In 1558, Russia's aptly named Czar Ivan IV (the Terrible; 1530–84), seeking at all costs an ice-free Baltic Sea port, invaded Livonia with a large force. In a long campaign, Ivan's forces defeated the knights at Narva, Dorpat (Tartu), and elsewhere. By 1561, aware that their situation in Livonia was hopeless, the knights divided Livonia among Poland, Lithuania, Sweden, and Denmark—anything to keep it out of Ivan's hands. Denmark acquired Kurland, and Poland and Lithuania took the rest.

Remarkably, the Russian forces made initial headway against what were now four great adversaries, and the czar's forces committed many atrocities upon the Livonian populace. Most infamous among the atrocities was the slaughter perpetrated not against Livonia, but Russian-held Novgorod. In January 1570, suspicious that the Novgorod citizens had conspired with the Poles, Czar Ivan unleashed 15,000 soldiers against the city. They killed as many as 65,000 people.

Two events began to turn the tide against the Russians. Ivan was faced with an internal rebellion, the BOYARS' REVOLT, and Lithuania, in 1569, formed an effective political union with Poland, thereby allowing the armies of the two kingdoms to work together. For his part, Ivan persuaded Denmark to bow out of the war, but Poland (with Lithuania) commenced a determined offensive under its new king, Stephen Báthory (1533–86), beginning in 1576. The capture of Polotsk in 1579 was a major Polish victory. From here, Stephen marched to

Pskov, sweeping the Russian forces before him. On September 6, 1581, 17,000 Swedes stormed the Russian fortress of Narva and slaughtered the garrison. Although the Poles were unable to capture Pskov during a siege spanning September–November 1581, Czar Ivan yielded to unremitting Polish pressure, concluding a peace in 1582. He renounced all claims to Livonia. This led to peace with the Swedes in 1583 and the loss, to Russia, of towns on the Gulf of Finland.

See also NOVGOROD, SACK OF.

Further reading: Geoffrey A. Hoskin, *Russia and Russians: A History* (Cambridge, Mass.: Harvard University Press, 2001); Arvids Ziedonis, William L. Winter, and Mardi Valgemäe, *Baltic History* (Columbus, Ohio: Association for the Advancement of Baltic Studies, 1974).

Lombard Conquest of Central Danube Valley (c. 500–565)

PRINCIPAL COMBATANTS: The Lombards vs. the Heruli and, separately, vs. the Gepidae
PRINCIPAL THEATER(S): Central Danube valley
DECLARATION: None
MAJOR ISSUES AND OBJECTIVES: Control of territory in and around Pannonia and Noricum
OUTCOME: The Heruli were defeated, but a state of chronic conflict developed between the Lombards and the Gepidae; however, the Lombards came substantially to control the central Danube valley.
APPROXIMATE MAXIMUM NUMBER OF MEN UNDER ARMS: Unknown
CASUALTIES: Unknown
TREATIES: None, save an informal agreement between the Lombards and the Roman emperor Justinian granting approval of Lombard settlement south of the Danube

The Lombards, or Langobardi, related to the Suevi, occupied the area north of Pannonia and Noricum following the Barbarian incursions in these regions. This occupation touched off a conflict with the Heruli, led by Rodulf (d. 508). A Lombard army under Tato defeated Rodulf's Heruli by 508.

With the Heruli neutralized, the Lombards fanned out into the central Danube Valley, pushing north of the river and engaging the Gepidae in a series of sharp wars over territory. The collapse of the Ostrogoth kingdom left Pannonia and Noricum wide open, but the Lombards as well as the Gepidae vied for territory. The Roman emperor Justinian I (483–565) exploited the conflict by skillfully playing one tribe off against the other, ultimately approving Lombard expansion south of the Danube. By 565, this put the Lombards in control of most of the central Danube Valley.

See also LOMBARD INVASION OF ITALY.

Further reading: Neil Christie, *Lombards* (London: Blackwell, 1998).

Lombard Invasion of Italy (568–585)

PRINCIPAL COMBATANTS: The Lombards vs. Rome (and, later, the Franks)
PRINCIPAL THEATER(S): Italy
DECLARATION: None
MAJOR ISSUES AND OBJECTIVES: The Lombards sought conquest of Italy.
OUTCOME: The Lombards defeated imperial forces and gained control of Italy, except for some coastal cities; however, the Lombards failed to install a central government in the region conquered.
APPROXIMATE MAXIMUM NUMBER OF MEN UNDER ARMS: Lombards, about 50,000 warriors, plus 20,000 Saxon allies; Roman imperial strength unknown; Frankish strength unknown
CASUALTIES: Unknown
TREATIES: Alliance between Eastern Empire and Franks against the Lombards, 585

In 568, the Lombards—the entire tribe—advanced into Italy, spearheaded by some 50,000 Lombard warriors and 20,000 Saxon auxiliaries. The Lombard general Alboin (d. 572) led the invasion force over the Julian Alps and, in 569, defeated Roman imperial forces under Longinus in northeast Italy, near Ravenna. This victory achieved, the Lombards quickly overran the Po valley. Milan fell to the invaders in short order, but the capture of Pavia required a three-year siege. The city fell in 572.

In this way, northern Italy became Lombardy, and the Lombards established their capital at Pavia. Thus ensconced, the Lombards were able to drive most of the imperial forces out of Italy, except for large coastal cities, which remained under the control of Constantinople.

In 573, Alboin's wife, Rosamond (fl. c. 570), murdered him, thereby creating a power vacuum among the Lombards. This notwithstanding, the momentum of conquest was hardly diminished. The Lombards continued to expand throughout Italy. Under King Childebert II (r. 570–596), the Franks entered the fray against the Lombards in 585. The Byzantine emperor subsidized Frankish operations, but the imperial forces refused to coordinate their efforts with his, and Childebert soon withdrew, leaving the essentially leaderless Lombards in control of Italy—which was tantamount to creating a state of anarchy there.

See also LOMBARD CONQUEST OF CENTRAL DANUBE VALLEY.

Further reading: Neil Christie, *Lombards* (London: Blackwell, 1998).

Lombard League, Wars of the (1167–1183)

PRINCIPAL COMBATANTS: Holy Roman Empire (under Frederick I Barbarossa) vs. the papacy and the Lombard League
PRINCIPAL THEATER(S): Northern Italy
DECLARATION: None
MAJOR ISSUES AND OBJECTIVES: Frederick sought to dominate both the papacy and the cities of northern Italy; the Lombard League was formed to resist.
OUTCOME: The Lombard League proved extraordinarily successful in resisting five German invasions of Italy led by Frederick I Barbarossa.
APPROXIMATE MAXIMUM NUMBER OF MEN UNDER ARMS: Unknown
CASUALTIES: Unknown
TREATIES: Treaty of Venice, 1177; Peace of Constance, 1183

The Middle Ages witnessed many power struggles between the papacy and the Holy Roman Emperors. The popes jealously guarded their authority to invest abbots and bishops. These offices were highly lucrative, and Holy Roman Emperor Frederick I Barbarossa (c. 1125–90) sought to wrest the power of investiture from the papal grasp. By awarding the offices, a leader purchased loyalty and allegiance, and Frederick was eager to assert his control over as many church officials as possible. Between 1154 and 1186, Frederick led six military campaigns into Italy, hoping to seize control of the papacy. One early campaign forced Pope Alexander III (c. 1105–81) to flee to Avignon, France, in 1162, and between 1159 and 1178, Frederick saw to the elevation of three antipopes.

While Frederick sought to dominate the papacy, he also attempted to subjugate the cities of northern Italy. This prompted Milan, Mantua, Venice, Padua, Lodi, and Brescia to band together as the Lombard League during Frederick's fourth Italian campaign. The league successfully resisted Frederick's invading Germans, who had been weakened by a malaria epidemic. Frederick held Rome for a time, but the sickness, combined with the military prowess of the Lombard League, forced the German army to withdraw from Italy.

Seizing the opportunity, Pope Alexander III formed an alliance with the Lombard League, excommunicated Frederick, and backed the league in the construction of a great fortress at Alessandria, which defended the northern mountain passes against further invasion. Indeed, Frederick's fifth invasion of Italy was disastrously costly to him. His defeat at the Battle of Legnano, northwest of Milan, on May 29, 1176, decimated his knights. The league's infantry, common pikemen, proved far superior to the noble armored warriors. It was the first triumph of infantry over cavalry in the Middle Ages, and it foreshadowed the doom of the knight and the rise of the bourgeoisie. Frederick himself barely escaped with his life, fleeing from Italy in disguise.

Frederick's defeat at Legnano prompted him to sue for peace. The Treaty of Venice of 1177 brought peace between him and the pope. That same year, Frederick made a separate truce with the Lombard League, which was finalized in 1183 as the Peace of Constance. By this treaty, the Lombard League cities were granted a high degree of autonomy, although they acknowledged the limited suzerainty of Frederick I Barbarossa.

The Peace of Constance did not stop Frederick from conducting a sixth Italian campaign during 1184–86. This bypassed the league cities and established imperial control of Milan and much of central Italy.

See also HOLY ROMAN EMPIRE–PAPACY WAR (1228–1241).

Further reading: Friedrich Heer, *Holy Roman Empire*, trans. Janet Sondheimer (New York: Sterling, 2002); Otto of Friesling, *The Deeds of Frederick Barbarossa*, trans. Charles C. Mierow (Toronto: University of Toronto Press, 1991).

Long March *See* CHINESE CIVIL WAR (1927–1937).

"Long War" *See* AUSTRO-TURKISH WAR (1591–1606).

López War *See* PARAGUAYAN WAR.

Lord Dunmore's War (1774)

PRINCIPAL COMBATANTS: Shawnee with Mingo, Wyandot, and Delaware allies vs. colonial Virginia
PRINCIPAL THEATER(S): Ohio River valley
DECLARATION: Lord Dunmore declares war on June 10, 1774
MAJOR ISSUES AND OBJECTIVES: Indian resistance to white treaty violations and usurpation of lands
OUTCOME: Indecisive
APPROXIMATE MAXIMUM NUMBER OF MEN UNDER ARMS: For colonial Virginia, 3,000; Shawnee and allies, 700
CASUALTIES: Colonial troops, about 500; Indians, more than 100
TREATIES: Truce concluded October 26, 1774

John Murray (1732–1809), fourth earl of Dunmore and the royal governor of colonial Virginia, commissioned a survey party under Michael Cresap (1742–75) and John

Louis XIV's Rhenish Invasion 699

Floyd in April 1773 to survey Kentucky land prior to issuing patents to settlers. The next month, Captain Thomas Bullitt (fl. 1770s) informed the Shawnee chief Black Fish (fl. 1770s) that land reserved for the Shawnee by the Fort Stanwix treaty of 1768 would now be opened to settlement by whites. Black Fish warned Bullitt that he would attack anyone who crossed the river into Kentucky. Accordingly, he sent warriors to observe the surveying party, and when some of them did cross the river on May 29, 1773, a Shawnee named Peshewa—Wild Cat—went down to them, unarmed, to warn them back. He was immediately killed. In retaliation, the Shawnee attacked the surveyors, killing several, and sending one back to Wheeling (West Virginia) to warn the other whites not to cross the Ohio River.

Dunmore concluded that the Shawnee were conspiring with fur traders (who wanted to prevent agricultural settlement of the region) and Pennsylvanians (who disputed Virginia's claim to the Ohio country), and he unofficially declared war.

Chief Cornstalk (c. 1720–77), another prominent Shawnee, realized that warfare with the whites was a losing proposition and traveled to Fort Pitt—at the time renamed Fort Dunmore—near present-day Pittsburgh—to negotiate a peaceful resolution to the conflict. Tragically, angry frontiersmen attacked Cornstalk, his brother Silverheels (d. 1773), and another Indian as they returned from the fort. Silverheels was fatally wounded, and all hope of peace was ended.

Cornstalk sought alliance with the Miami, Wyandot, Ottawa, and Delaware, all of whom declined. The Mingo—Iroquois who had migrated to southern Ohio—wanted to remain neutral as well, but were driven to war when the family of one of their principal chiefs, known to the whites as John Logan (and to the Indians as Tah-gah-jute) (c. 1725–89), was slaughtered by some of Cresap's men (see CRESAP'S WAR). Faced with a widespread Indian uprising, Lord Dunmore officially declared war on June 10, 1774. He raised a militia force, which was mobilized by September.

At the head of 1,500 men, Dunmore was supposed to march to Fort Pitt (or Fort Dunmore), travel in boats down the Ohio to its juncture with the Kanawha River, and rendezvous with Colonel Andrew Lewis (1720–81), who was supposed to have recruited an additional 1,500 militiamen. The combined force would cross the Ohio and destroy the Shawnee villages.

A blustering man, Dunmore was in truth a timid commander. Fearing ambush, he abandoned his plan to rendezvous with Lewis on the Ohio and instead proceeded via an arduous overland route to the Scioto River. Lewis, with approximately 1,000 men, had reached Point Pleasant, the appointed rendezvous, on October 6, and, three days later, was told of the change in plan and ordered to cross the Ohio and meet Dunmore near Scioto.

All of the clumsy maneuvering was closely observed by Shawnee scouts. Cornstalk mustered approximately 700 warriors: Shawnees and Mingos (including John Logan), as well as some Wyandots and Delawares. He intended to attack Lewis just as he was about to leave Point Pleasant to unite with Dunmore. However, a foraging party from Lewis's camp discovered the Indians lying in wait and alerted Lewis, who sent troops to attempt an ambush. Although the stratagem failed, Lewis had gained the time to erect a crude defensive cover from fallen trees.

The battle was fiercely fought on October 10. Lewis was able to defend his position, but at the cost of almost one-fourth of his men. Indian casualties numbered more than 100.

No one involved in the bloody engagement claimed victory. Cornstalk berated the poor performance of his Mingo, Delaware, and Wyandot allies, and even his own Shawnee now urged him to seek peace. Cornstalk, who wanted to avoid war in the first place, now judged that, with hostilities commenced, it was foolhardy and disgraceful to seek a truce. But, with his warriors dispirited, he had no choice. Meanwhile, Lord Dunmore's army was near mutiny, his men believing their commander to be incompetent and a coward. For his part, Lewis defied Dunmore's order to halt his advance on the Shawnee towns and was stopped by Dunmore at the point of a sword only a half mile from the villages.

Although parties on both sides clamored for a further fight, a truce was concluded on October 26, 1774.

See also AMERICAN REVOLUTION: FRONTIER THEATER.

Further reading: Alan Axelrod, *Chronicle of the Indian Wars: From Colonial Times to Wounded Knee* (New York: Prentice Hall General Reference, 1993); Warren Skidmore with Donna Kaminsky, *Lord Dunmore's Little War of 1774: His Captains and Their Men Who Opened Up Kentucky & the West to American Settlement* (Bowie, Md.: Heritage Books, 2002).

Louis XIV's Rhenish Invasion (1688–1689)

PRINCIPAL COMBATANTS: France vs. the Holy Roman Empire and German princes
PRINCIPAL THEATER(S): German Rhineland
DECLARATION: France against the Holy Roman Empire, 1688
MAJOR ISSUES AND OBJECTIVES: France's Louis XIV sought more complete control of the Rhineland and Rhine River navigation.
OUTCOME: France retained Alsace and Strasbourg, but relinquished control over the other Rhenish cities, including, most significantly, Cologne
APPROXIMATE MAXIMUM NUMBER OF MEN UNDER ARMS: Unknown

CASUALTIES: Unknown
TREATIES: Treaty of Ryswick, 1697

During the reign of Louis XIV (1638–1715), the great Rhenish city of Cologne (Köln) was a virtual satellite of France. The French king treasured control of the city because it dominated the lower Rhine and thereby gave France a great advantage in trade and military matters. The king's continued control of Cologne depended in large part on maintaining a pliable archbishop in power there. In 1688, Louis's candidate for archbishop of Cologne, Wilhelm Fürstenberg (fl. late 17th century) was summarily rejected by Pope Innocent XI (1611–89). Louis responded by declaring war against the Holy Roman Empire, most of whose troops were engaged in a struggle against the Turks.

Louis believed that a rapid invasion of the Rhine region would force the Holy Roman Empire to withdraw its candidate for archbishop. The French king also sought to resolve certain claims to territory in the Palatinate, and he wanted to neutralize imperial fortifications at Philipsburg.

The invasion went remarkably well—at first. Louis's invading armies met with little resistance and seized the Palatinate, Trier, Mainz, and Cologne. From here, they staged a sweeping and gratuitously violent invasion of Franconia and Swabia. This moved the Holy Roman Emperor and the German princes to conclude hasty truces with the Turks and to rush to the defense of the homeland.

Through a united and coordinated counteroffensive, the Germans liberated Franconia and installed a garrison at Frankfurt. Heidelberg was targeted for attack, but, as the German allies advanced, the French withdrew and relinquished the city—razing Mannheim, Worms, Speyer, and other cities and towns as they retreated.

At this point, the Rhenish invasion dissolved into the far greater conflict that was the War of the GRAND ALLIANCE, from 1688 to 1697. The invasion of the Rhineland was over by 1689, but a definitive settlement of the War of the Grand Alliance did not come until the Treaty of Ryswick of 1697, which gave Louis Alsace and Strasbourg, but forced him to relinquish the other Rhine cities, including Cologne.

Further reading: Philippe Erlanger, *Louis XIV* (London: Phoenix Press, 2003); J. H. Shennan, *Louis XIV* (New York: Routledge, 1993).

Lovewell's War (1725)

PRINCIPAL COMBATANTS: Colonial scalp hunters vs. local Osippee or Pigwacket Indians
PRINCIPAL THEATER(S): New Hampshire and southern Maine
DECLARATION: None

MAJOR ISSUES AND OBJECTIVES: Scalp hunters sought to collect a bounty offered on Indian scalps.
OUTCOME: At least 11 Indians were slain; 17 scalp hunters were killed.
APPROXIMATE MAXIMUM NUMBER OF MEN UNDER ARMS:
At least 87 scalp hunters; in the final "battle" of the "war," 34 scalp hunters were attacked by about 80 Indians.
CASUALTIES: 17 scalp hunters; at least 11 Indians.
TREATIES: None

The venal and ruthless expedition of John Lovewell (1691–1725) entered colonial history and lore as a private "war" against local Indians and earned Lovewell the epithet "King of the Scalp Hunters." During the Third ABENAKI WAR, the colony of Massachusetts offered a bounty of £100 for Indian scalps late in 1724. Seeking his fortune, a farmer named John Lovewell (1691–1725) organized 87 other colonists during February 1725 in an Indian-killing expedition up the Merrimack River near Lake Winnipesaukee. When his party came upon 10 sleeping Osippee or Pigwacket Indians, Lovewell ordered an attack and "harvested" 10 scalps.

In the spring, Lovewell assembled a smaller, 34-man force, which traveled into southern Maine. There they were set upon by approximately 80 Indians near present-day Fryeburg on May 9, 1725, after one of their number (apparently the troop's chaplain) had killed and scalped an Indian earlier in the day. The Indians killed Lovewell and 16 others. The rest of the party escaped death only because the Indians withdrew when their Sachem (medicine man) was shot.

Further reading: Steven C. Eames, "Lovewell, John." In *Colonial Wars of North 1512–1763*, ed. Alan Gallay (New York: Garland, 1996).

Lübeck's War (1531–1535)

PRINCIPAL COMBATANTS: German city-state of Lübeck (and Hanseatic allies, plus Danish rebels) vs. Sweden and Denmark
PRINCIPAL THEATER(S): Malmö, Sweden; Copenhagen, Denmark
DECLARATION: None
MAJOR ISSUES AND OBJECTIVES: Lübeck wanted to assert its absolute monopoly on the Baltic trade.
OUTCOME: Despite initial victories, Lübeck was defeated and lost its monopoly.
APPROXIMATE MAXIMUM NUMBER OF MEN UNDER ARMS:
Unknown
CASUALTIES: Unknown
TREATIES: Treaty of Hamburg, 1536

Lübeck, a north German trading city prominent in the mercantile association known as the Hanseatic League, sought to maintain its trading hegemony in the Baltic region and, therefore, incited a brief war against the Swedes and Danes.

The burgomaster (mayor) of Lübeck, Jürgen Wullenwever (c. 1488–1537), ordered the confiscation of a Swedish ship in Lübeck's port as restitution, he said, for insufficient payment of a war debt incurred by the brother-in-law of Sweden's King Gustavus I (1496–1560). Gustavus responded to this rash act by embargoing all of Lübeck's ships in Swedish ports, whereupon Lübeck and its other Hanseatic allies, aided by anti-government Danish rebels, declared war on both Sweden and Denmark and quickly captured the cities of Malmö and Copenhagen.

Lübeck and its allies were not powerful enough to sustain their victories. Traditional rivals, the Danes and Sweden made common cause and united against Lübeck, readily pushing back the invaders. Lübeck concluded the Treaty of Hamburg with the two nations in 1536 and lost its monopoly on trade in the Baltic. The treaty declared the war debt settled and, in return, allowed favorable toll exemptions for Lübeck's trading vessels. As to Wullenwever, he fled Lübeck, only to suffer imprisonment, torture, and execution in 1537 at the hands of Danish authorities.

See also KALMAR CIVIL WAR (1520–1523).

Further reading: Philippe Dollinger, *The German Hansa,* trans. D. S. Ault and S. H. Steinburg (Palo Alto, Calif.: Stanford University Press, 1970); Franklin D. Scott, *Sweden, the Nation's History* (Carbondale: Southern Illinois University Press, 1988); Byron J. Nordstrom, *The History of Sweden* (Westport, Conn.: Greenwood Press, 2002).

Lübeck's War (1563–1570) *See* DANISH-SWEDISH WAR (1563–1570).

Lubomirski's Rebellion (1665–1667)

PRINCIPAL COMBATANTS: Pro-Russian Polish rebels vs. Royal Polish forces
PRINCIPAL THEATER(S): Poland
DECLARATION: None
MAJOR ISSUES AND OBJECTIVES: Lubomirski wanted to promote Russian domination of Poland.
OUTCOME: Lubomirski's Rebellion weakened Poland, already pressed by war with Russia, forcing it to cede much territory to Russia.
APPROXIMATE MAXIMUM NUMBER OF MEN UNDER ARMS: Rebels, 40,000; Royal forces, 60,000
CASUALTIES: Unknown

TREATIES: The conflict influenced the Treaty of Andrusovo, which ended the Russo-Polish War of 1658–67.

George Lubomirski (1616–67), a Polish nobleman, took part in the ongoing RUSSO-POLISH WAR (1658–1667). Marshaling the support of fellow nobles, he tried to block a royal election in order to place Poland firmly in Russia's political orbit. As a result of this action, the Polish parliament (Sejm) convicted Lubomirski of treason in 1664 and sentenced him to exile. Instead of going off quietly, Lubomirski and his followers harried the Sejm for the next two years, then withdrew to form their own confederation, mustering a military force of some 40,000 men.

When his army was ready, Lubomirski attacked the royal army—some 60,000 men—at Lake Goplo on July 13, 1667, emerging victorious against the numerically superior force. His triumph prompted the abdication of Poland's king John II Casimir (1609–72) in 1668, whereupon Lubomirski withdrew into Austrian Silesia.

Fighting a war within a war, Lubomirski weakened Poland sufficiently to force it to accept the Treaty of Andrusovo, by which the nation ceded most of its eastern lands to Russia.

Further reading: Jerzy Lukowoski, *Concise History of Poland* (New York: Cambridge University Press, 2001); W. F. Reddaway, ed., *The Cambridge History of Poland,* 2 vols. (New York: Cambridge University Press, 1941–50, reprint 1971).

Luccan-Florentine War (1320–1323)

PRINCIPAL COMBATANTS: Ghibellines of Lucca, Italy, vs. Guelfs of Florence, Italy
PRINCIPAL THEATER(S): Florentine territories in Italy
DECLARATION: None
MAJOR ISSUES AND OBJECTIVES: Ghibellines (loyal to the Holy Roman Emperor) wanted to destroy the power and influence of the Guelfs (loyal to the pope).
OUTCOME: Florence lost much territory, which, however, was recovered shortly after the war.
APPROXIMATE MAXIMUM NUMBER OF MEN UNDER ARMS: Unknown
CASUALTIES: Unknown
TREATIES: None

In April 1320, Castruccio Castracani (1281–1328), ruler of Lucca in central Italy and leader of the Ghibelline political party, made war on the rival Guelfs of Florence, a political faction loyal to the pope, as opposed to the Holy Roman Emperor, to whom the Ghibellines owed their allegiance. (*Guelf* comes from German *Welf,* the name of a pro-papal dynasty of Bavarian dukes; *Ghibelline* from *Waiblingen,* the name of the castle of the Welf's opponents.)

Castracani's Luccan army attacked and ravaged Florentine territory until its advance was halted by the arrival of Florentine reinforcements. At this, Castracani allied his own forces with those of Pistoia, another central Italian city. The augmented Luccan forces now laid waste to the countryside within 10 miles of Florence itself during mid-June 1323.

Faced with crisis, Florence scrambled to raise a new army, but Lucca added Milan to its allies, and the combined Luccan-Milanese army dealt the Florentines a decisive blow at the Battle of Altopascio in 1325. Castracani stripped the Florentine lands of treasure to pay war debts and once again menaced the city itself.

Florence looked to other Guelf supporters for aid. However, Castracani was now in control of almost all of Tuscany. A conflict between Castracani and the papacy brought hostilities to a temporary standstill, and before he could resume the war, Castracani died. He had been a brilliant tactician, but an indifferent administrator, who left behind no adequate government for Tuscany. This meant that most of the territory he had taken from Florence was easily reconquered.

Further reading: Gene Adam Brucker, *Florence: The Golden Age, 1138–1737* (Berkeley: University of California Press, 1998); Charles L. Killinger, *The History of Italy* (Westport, Conn.: Greenwood Publishing, 2002); John Larner, *Italy in the Age of Dante and Petrarch, 1216–1380* (New York: Longman, 1980); Giovanni Tabacco, *The Struggle for Power in Medieval Italy: Structures of Political Rule,* trans. Rosalind Brown Jensen (New York: Cambridge University Press, 1989).

Lusitanian War   (147–139 B.C.E.)

PRINCIPAL COMBATANTS: Lusitanian rebels vs. Rome
PRINCIPAL THEATER(S): Iberian Peninsula
DECLARATION: None
MAJOR ISSUES AND OBJECTIVES: The Lusitani wanted independence from Rome.
OUTCOME: Despite victories, the resistance to Rome collapsed after the assassination of the Lusitani's leader.
APPROXIMATE MAXIMUM NUMBER OF MEN UNDER ARMS: Unknown
CASUALTIES: Unknown
TREATIES: None recorded

The Lusitani comprised a group of Celtic tribes who lived in present-day central Portugal and western Spain. After

they were defeated by the Romans during the CELT-IBERIAN WARS in 150 B.C.E., the Roman proconsul on the Iberian Peninsula presided over the massacre of thousands of the unruly Lusitanians—even after he had concluded a treaty of peace with them. A survivor of the massacre, a shepherd named Viriathus (d. 139 B.C.E.), formed a guerrilla army that soon proved extremely effective against the vastly superior Roman forces.

In the end, Viriathus and his cause were in part undone by his own decency. Having trapped an entire Roman army in 139 B.C.E., he refrained from destroying it, but instead concluded a peace and sent it packing. Soon after this, a Lusitanian in the pay of the Romans assassinated Viriathus, and the Roman forces returned, easily crushing the leaderless resistance.

See also NUMANTIAN WAR.

Further reading: John S. Richardson, *Romans in Spain* (London: Blackwell, 1998); Colin Wells, *The Roman Empire,* 2nd ed. (Cambridge, Mass.: Harvard University Press, 1995).

Ly Bon's Rebellion   (541–547)

PRINCIPAL COMBATANTS: Nam Viet people vs. Chinese conquerors of Nam Viet
PRINCIPAL THEATER(S): Nam Viet (northern Vietnam)
DECLARATION: None
MAJOR ISSUES AND OBJECTIVES: The subjugated Nam Viet wanted to retake their nation from the Chinese.
OUTCOME: Briefly successful, the rebellion was ultimately crushed and its principal leader killed.
APPROXIMATE MAXIMUM NUMBER OF MEN UNDER ARMS: Unknown
CASUALTIES: Unknown
TREATIES: None

Oppressed by their Chinese overlord, the people of Nam Viet or Annam (northern Vietnam) rebelled in 541, led by the Chinese-descended Ly Bon (d. 547). Ly Bon succeeded in pushing the Chinese out of Nam Viet. Neighboring Champa, to the south, sought to exploit the turmoil in Nam Viet by invading in 543. Ly Bon managed to defeat Cham forces as well. Ly Bon declared himself king of Nam Viet, but the Chinese renewed their efforts to retake the country, and Ly Bon was defeated and killed by the Chinese victors in 547.

Further reading: D. G. E. Hall, *A History of South-East Asia,* 4th ed. (New York: St. Martin's Press, 1981); Mary Somers Heidhues, *Southeast Asia: A Concise History* (London and New York: Thames and Hudson, 2001).

Macbeth's Wars (1040–1057)

PRINCIPAL COMBATANTS: Macbeth vs. Duncan I (followed by various rebels, followed by Malcolm [Malcolm III], with English assistance)
PRINCIPAL THEATER(S): Scotland
DECLARATION: None
MAJOR ISSUES AND OBJECTIVES: The Scottish throne
OUTCOME: Macbeth attained and held the throne until he was killed in battle by Malcolm (Malcolm III) in 1057.
APPROXIMATE MAXIMUM NUMBER OF MEN UNDER ARMS: Unknown
CASUALTIES: Unknown
TREATIES: No documents survive; may have been formal treaty between Malcolm and the English.

Macbeth (d. 1057), the Scottish warlord and king whose life was the basis for Shakespeare's play, was most likely a grandson of King Kenneth II (r. 971–995). Macbeth married Gruoch (fl. mid-11th century), a descendant of King Kenneth III (r. 997–1005), then, about 1031, succeeded his father, Findlaech (d. 1020), as *mormaer* (chief) of Moray in northern Scotland. In one of the dynastic conflicts common in Scotland, Macbeth killed his cousin, King Duncan I (c. 1010–40), in combat near Elgin on August 14, 1040. This was a killing in battle—not, as Shakespeare portrays it, a murder in Macbeth's castle as an unsuspecting Duncan slept.

Established on the Scottish throne, Macbeth continued to wage war against rebels and other claimants to the Crown. He defeated a rebel army in 1045 near Dunkeld (Tayside), and in 1046 he warded off a coup d'état by Siward (d. 1055), earl of Northumbria, who sought to unseat him in favor of Malcolm (r. 1058–93), eldest son of Duncan I.

In 1050, Macbeth embarked on a pilgrimage to Rome. This may have been unwise, because in 1054 Siward had gained sufficient power to force Macbeth to cede a portion of southern Scotland to Malcolm. Malcolm then mounted a resistance against Macbeth, whom he killed in battle in 1057. Malcolm had allied himself with the English and faced one rival after Macbeth's death. Partisans of Macbeth installed his stepson, Lulach (d. 1058), as king. Lulach was assassinated on March 17, 1058, leaving Malcolm to rule Scotland as Malcolm III Canmore.

Further reading: Peter Somerset Fry and Fiona Somerset Fry, *The History of Scotland* (New York: Barnes and Noble, 1995); Rosalind Mitchison, *A History of Scotland* (New York: Routledge, 2002).

Maccabees, Revolt of the (168–143 B.C.E.)

PRINCIPAL COMBATANTS: Maccabees (powerful Jewish family) vs. Syrian overlords
PRINCIPAL THEATER(S): Judea (southern Palestine)
DECLARATION: None
MAJOR ISSUES AND OBJECTIVES: Jewish independence from Syrian rule.
OUTCOME: After a long period of guerrilla warfare, Judea achieved a short-lived virtual independence.
APPROXIMATE MAXIMUM NUMBER OF MEN UNDER ARMS: Unknown
CASUALTIES: Unknown
TREATIES: None

In 168 B.C.E., the Seleucid king of Syria, Antiochus IV Epiphanes (d. 163 B.C.E.), desecrated the Temple of Jerusalem and decreed that the Jews were to accept his pagan religion. Mattathias (d. 166 B.C.E.), a Jewish priest who was a member of the Maccabee family, resisted, in the process slaying a Syrian soldier. Knowing the fate that awaited him for this act, he and his sons fled to the mountains, where they became the nucleus of a guerrilla movement directed against the Syrians.

Following the death of Mattathias in 166 B.C.E., his son Judas Maccabeus (d. 161 B.C.E.) became the leader of the rebellion and quickly defeated two superior Syrian armies sent against him. In 165, Judas reconquered Jerusalem. He rededicated the desecrated temple (an event Jews commemorate to this day in Hanukkah). Four years after this, in 161, Judas was killed in battle with a third Syrian army sent against him.

His brother Jonathan (d. 143 B.C.E.) assumed command and took a new, diplomatic course, making treaties with Rome and Syria. He was, however, killed in 143 B.C.E. when he accepted a Syrian general's invitation to a peace parley, only to be made captive and slain along with many of his troops.

The last brother of Judas Maccabeus, Simon (d. 135 B.C.E.), constructed a chain of forts throughout Judea (southern Palestine). Recognizing his formidable presence, the king of Syria acknowledged Simon as a high priest and designated him as high governor. This brought an interval of peace and virtual independence to Judea, which, however, lasted only until Simon's death in 135. With the last of the Maccabeus brothers gone, Judea was once again torn by Seleucid invasion and internal conflict.

Further reading: William Reuben Farmer, *Maccabees, Zealots, and Josephus: An Inquiry into Jewish Nationalism in the Greco-Roman War* (Westport, Conn.: Greenwood Publishing Group, 1982).

Macdonald Rebellion (1411)

PRINCIPAL COMBATANTS: Macdonald clan (allied with the Macleans) vs. forces of the regent of Scottish king James I
PRINCIPAL THEATER(S): Region near Aberdeen, Scotland
DECLARATION: None
MAJOR ISSUES AND OBJECTIVES: The Macdonalds and the forces of the regent contested control of the earldom of Ross.
OUTCOME: A draw.
APPROXIMATE MAXIMUM NUMBER OF MEN UNDER ARMS: Unknown
CASUALTIES: Unknown
TREATIES: None; a de facto peace ensued.

This was a war of a single significant battle. After the English captured and imprisoned the Scottish king James I

(1394–1437) in 1406, the Scottish barons amassed a great deal of power during the nearly two decades of his captivity. The Macdonalds of the northwest styled themselves the "kings of the Isles" and ruled as virtual sovereigns. The duke of Rothesay (d. 1406), nephew of James's regent, Robert Stewart, duke of Albany (1341–1420), challenged the clan over control of the earldom of Ross. Donald Macdonald (fl. early 15th century), in alliance with the Maclean clan, attacked the regent's forces at Aberdeen in 1411. The Macdonald-Maclean army was led by a Maclean, Red Hector of the Battles (d. 1411), and fought a brutal engagement known as the Battle of Red Harlaw. The result of the battle was essentially a draw. However, Red Hector was killed, and the Macdonald-Maclean army withdrew. The precipitating dispute was neither resolved nor forgotten, but it was tolerated, and a long period of peace followed.

See also OG's REBELLION.

Further reading: Peter Somerset Fry and Fiona Somerset Fry, *The History of Scotland* (New York: Barnes and Noble, 1995); Rosalind Mitchison, *A History of Scotland* (New York: Routledge, 2002).

Macedonian Insurrection (1902–1903)

PRINCIPAL COMBATANTS: Bulgarian terrorists vs. Ottoman Empire; rival factions within Macedonia itself
PRINCIPAL THEATER(S): Macedonia
DECLARATION: None
MAJOR ISSUES AND OBJECTIVES: The Bulgarian terrorists wanted to position Bulgaria for control of Macedonia.
OUTCOME: Indecisive; violence in Macedonia continued after the end of the insurrection, leading to the First Balkan War.
APPROXIMATE MAXIMUM NUMBER OF MEN UNDER ARMS: Bulgarian forces, 27,000; Ottoman forces, 351,000
CASUALTIES: Bulgar forces, 994 killed; Ottoman forces, 5,328 killed; Bulgarian civilian casualties, 4,700 killed.
TREATIES: None; however, the insurrection yielded an ineffectual agreement (brokered by Austria and Russia) with the Ottoman Empire concerning Macedonia.

The Macedonian Insurrection was an early symptom of the strife that beset the Balkans at the turn of the 20th century and that would eventually trigger WORLD WAR I. Bulgaria, Greece, and Serbia each laid claim to Macedonia—which was controlled by the Ottoman Empire—and in 1899 Bulgaria established what it called a Macedonian Commission, ostensibly to resolve the conflict, but, in fact, to bolster the Bulgarian claim. The aim of the commission was to make Macedonia nominally autonomous, yet controlled—by leave of the Ottoman Empire—by a Bulgarian "inspector." In order to coerce acceptance of the scheme, the Bulgarians conducted a program of covert terrorism through revolutionary bands called *komitadji,* who raided Macedonia.

The activity of the komitadji brought about a civil insurrection within the country, but it was the komitadji's murder of a Romanian professor (who challenged the authority of the commission) and their capture of a female American missionary that prompted intervention from the outside. Together, Austria and Russia proposed political reform of the Macedonian administrative districts of Salonika (Thessaloníki), Monastir (Bitola), and Kosovo in 1903 in an attempt to mollify Bulgaria. The Ottomans approved the reforms, which, however, were never implemented: Escalating internal violence exploded into the First BALKAN WAR, which resulted in the formal division of Macedonia among the three rival claimants to it.

Further reading: Lord Kinross, *The Ottoman Centuries: The Rise and Fall of the Turkish Empire* (New York: Morrow, 1977); Mark Mazower, *Balkans: A Short History* (New York: Random House, 2002); Stanford J. Shaw and E. K. Shaw, *History of the Ottoman Empire and Modern Turkey,* 2 vols. (New York: Cambridge University Press, 1976–1977); Alan Warwick, *The Decline and Fall of the Ottoman Empire* (New York: Barnes and Noble Books, 1995).

Macedonian War, First   (215–205 B.C.E.)

PRINCIPAL COMBATANTS: Macedonians vs. Romans
PRINCIPAL THEATER(S): Northern frontiers of Macedon
DECLARATION: None
MAJOR ISSUES AND OBJECTIVES: Philip V of Macedon wanted to expand his empire.
OUTCOME: Indecisive, except to spawn further warfare.
APPROXIMATE MAXIMUM NUMBER OF MEN UNDER ARMS: Unknown
CASUALTIES: Unknown
TREATIES: Peace of Phoenice, 205 B.C.E.

King Philip V (238–179 B.C.E.) of Macedon was a warlike and restless monarch ambitious to extend his empire at any cost. He exploited the Second PUNIC WAR, in which the forces of Rome were preoccupied with fighting Carthage, to attack the diminished Roman forces in the east, the region known as Illyria. However, the Romans could not decisively defeat the Macedonians, nor could Philip wear down the Romans, and the result was warfare that consumed a decade, producing little result.

Philip took a new tack. Allying himself with Hannibal of Carthage (247–c. 183–181 B.C.E.), he invaded the Greek city-states. Rome, characteristically neutral in the affairs of these states, saw Philip's incursions as an opportunity to expand the Roman sphere of influence. Rome concluded the Peace of Phoenice, which was generous to Philip. However, within five years of the end of the First Macedonian War, the Second MACEDONIAN WAR began.

See also MACEDONIAN WAR, THIRD; MACEDONIAN WAR, FOURTH.

Further reading: M. Cary, *A History of the Greek World from 323 to 146 B.C.* (New York: Barnes and Noble, 1963); N. G. L. Hammond, *The Macedonian State* (New York: Oxford University Press, 1989); Victor Davis Hanson, *The Wars of the Ancient Greeks* (New York: Sterling, 2002); J. F. Lazenby, *Hannibal's War: A Military History of the Second Punic War* (Warminster, England: Aris and Phillips, 1978); Colin Wells, *The Roman Empire,* 2nd ed. (Cambridge, Mass.: Harvard University Press, 1995).

Macedonian War, Second   (200–196 B.C.E.)

PRINCIPAL COMBATANTS: Macedon vs. Rome
PRINCIPAL THEATER(S): Greece
DECLARATION: Rome against Macedon, 200 B.C.E.
MAJOR ISSUES AND OBJECTIVES: Philip V of Macedon wanted to extend his empire into the Greek states.
OUTCOME: Rome defeated Macedon, which agreed to an indemnity.
APPROXIMATE MAXIMUM NUMBER OF MEN UNDER ARMS: Each side fielded about 20,000 men.
CASUALTIES: At Cynoscephalae, the decisive battle of the war, Macedonian losses were 10,000 killed; Roman losses were much lower.
TREATIES: Indemnity agreement

The First MACEDONIAN WAR ended at the northern frontiers of Macedon. Although the Peace of Phoenice offered many favorable terms to Macedon, much was left unsettled, and, in 200 B.C.E., Philip V (238–179 B.C.E.) of Macedon turned southward, intending to make inroads into the Greek city-states. He menaced Rhodes and Pergamum first, then attacked other city-states. Rome demanded Philip's pledge to make no further hostile moves. He refused and, seeing gains to be made in defeating Philip in Greece, Rome engaged him. The climactic battle of the Second Macedonian War came in 197 B.C.E., when Rome's legions soundly beat Philip at Cynoscephalae. Titus Quintius Flaminius (c. 227–174 B.C.E.) led 20,000 Roman legionaries and met the Macedonian force on the heights of Cynoscephalae, in southwestern Thessaly. It was a hard-fought battle, but Philip took by far the worst of it. Half his 20,000 men were killed. Rome's losses, while substantial, did not approach this magnitude. As a result of his defeat, Philip withdrew from Greece and further agreed to render a large indemnity to Rome, which then proclaimed itself the liberator and protector of the Greek states, asserting a benevolent dominance over them.

Philip's son Perseus (c. 212–166 B.C.E.) succeeded him as Macedon's king in 179. Instead of invading Greece, he made alliances among the Greek states. Fearing this

706 Macedonian War, Third

kind of influence as well, Rome initiated the Third MACE-DONIAN WAR.

See also MACEDONIAN WAR, FOURTH.

Further reading: M. Cary, *A History of the Greek World from 323 to 146 B.C.* (New York: Barnes and Noble, 1963); N. G. L. Hammond, *The Macedonian State* (New York: Oxford University Press, 1989); Victor Davis Hanson, *The Wars of the Ancient Greeks* (New York: Sterling, 2002); J. F. Lazenby, *Hannibal's War: A Military History of the Second Punic War* (Warminster, England: Aris and Phillips, 1978); Colin Wells, *The Roman Empire,* 2nd ed. (Cambridge, Mass.: Harvard University Press, 1995).

Macedonian War, Third (172–167 B.C.E.)

PRINCIPAL COMBATANTS: Macedon vs. Rome
PRINCIPAL THEATER(S): Southeastern Macedonia
DECLARATION:
MAJOR ISSUES AND OBJECTIVES: Rome wanted to stop Macedon's meddling in Greek politics.
OUTCOME: Macedon was defeated; Rome divided Macedonia into republics.
APPROXIMATE MAXIMUM NUMBER OF MEN UNDER ARMS: Unknown
CASUALTIES: Macedonian losses at Pydna (168 B.C.E.) were 20,000 killed and 11,000 made prisoner; in contrast, Rome lost about 100 killed.
TREATIES: None

After Perseus (c. 212–166 B.C.E.), who had inherited the Macedonian throne from his father Philip V in 179 B.C.E., began to meddle in Greek affairs by making alliances with various Greek city-states, Rome sent an army to attack his forces at Pydna in southeastern Macedonia. Fought on June 22, 168 B.C.E., this battle proved decisive, the Macedonians lost 20,000 killed and 11,000 taken as prisoners; Roman losses amounted to no more than 100 killed. The following year, Perseus was dethroned and made captive.

To ensure that Macedon would never again threaten the stability of the Roman world, the victors divided it into four republics. However, this only succeeded in causing internal conflict, as the republics soon fell to disputing with one another. In a climate of discontent and confusion, a pretender to the throne attempted to reestablish the Macedonian monarchy in 152 B.C.E., an action that ignited the Fourth MACEDONIAN WAR.

See also MACEDONIAN WAR, FIRST; MACEDONIAN WAR, SECOND.

Further reading: M. Cary, *A History of the Greek World from 323 to 146 B.C.* (New York: Barnes and Noble, 1963); N. G. L. Hammond, *The Macedonian State* (New York: Oxford University Press, 1989); Victor Davis Hanson, *The Wars of the Ancient Greeks* (New York: Sterling, 2002); J. F. Lazenby, *Hannibal's War: A Military History of the Second*

Punic War (Warminster, England: Aris and Phillips, 1978); Colin Wells, *The Roman Empire,* 2nd ed. (Cambridge, Mass.: Harvard University Press, 1995).

Macedonian War, Fourth (151–146 B.C.E.)

PRINCIPAL COMBATANTS: Macedon vs. Rome
PRINCIPAL THEATER(S): Macedonia
DECLARATION: None
MAJOR ISSUES AND OBJECTIVES: When a pretender to the throne vowed to reunify Macedon, the Romans decided to subjugate it fully.
OUTCOME: The Macedonian army was no match for the Romans, who conquered Macedon and annexed it.
APPROXIMATE MAXIMUM NUMBER OF MEN UNDER ARMS: Unknown
CASUALTIES: Unknown
TREATIES: None

Following the Roman partition of Macedon into four republics, a pretender to the throne arose, calling for the reunification of the nation under his leadership. This provoked Rome to dispatch forces to fight the Macedonians for a fourth time, and, once again, Rome easily triumphed over the Macedonian army. The war included no battles of military significance; the Macedonians were simply demoralized by the Roman Legions and melted away before them.

Having tried and failed to render Macedon docile by dividing it into four republics, Rome now annexed the country to itself. This was the first major step in the long expansion of the Roman Empire.

See also MACEDONIAN WAR, FIRST; MACEDONIAN WAR, SECOND; MACEDONIAN WAR, THIRD; PUNIC WAR, THIRD.

Further reading: M. Cary, *A History of the Greek World from 323 to 146 B.C.* (New York: Barnes and Noble, 1963); N. G. L. Hammond, *The Macedonian State* (New York: Oxford University Press, 1989); Victor Davis Hanson, *The Wars of the Ancient Greeks* (New York: Sterling, 2002); J. F. Lazenby, *Hannibal's War: A Military History of the Second Punic War* (Warminster, England: Aris and Phillips, 1978); Colin Wells, *The Roman Empire,* 2nd ed. (Cambridge, Mass.: Harvard University Press, 1995).

Mackenzie's Rebellion (1837)

PRINCIPAL COMBATANTS: William Mackenzie vs. British authorities in Canada
PRINCIPAL THEATER(S): Toronto and Navy Island, Canada
DECLARATION: None
MAJOR ISSUES AND OBJECTIVES: Mackenzie wanted to overthrow the government of Upper Canada (Ontario) to establish a separate republican government.

OUTCOME: Mackenzie failed and fled to the United States.
APPROXIMATE MAXIMUM NUMBER OF MEN UNDER ARMS:
Mackenzie led about 800 followers, who were initially
opposed by 300 government troops; eventually, some
2,000 British troops opposed about 1,000 rebels.
CASUALTIES: Rebels, 132 killed; government troops, 50
killed or wounded
TREATIES: None

This short-lived rebellion was instigated by William Lyon
Mackenzie (1795–1861), a Canadian journalist, who was
a passionate advocate of creating a new, republican government for Upper Canada (that is, Ontario). To this end,
he called for the overthrow of the British-dominated Family Compact, which ruled the country.

Mackenzie was able to muster some 800 followers,
mostly French Canadians, who tried to establish a provisional government at Toronto. When this failed, they fled
to Navy Island, a small piece of land in the Niagara River.
On the island, Mackenzie proclaimed a government and
holed up, supplied from sources in the United States by
the U.S.-registered steamer *Caroline.* A group of Canadians
loyal to the Upper Canada government crossed the river
and burned the *Caroline,* forcing Mackenzie to decamp
from Navy Island and seek refuge in the United States.
There he was arrested, tried, and convicted of violating the
neutrality laws. He served an 11-month prison term.
When, in 1849, the Canadian government declared a general amnesty, Mackenzie returned to his country.

See also PAPINEAU'S REBELLION.

Further reading: William Kilbourn, *Firebrand: Wil-
liam Lyon MacKenzie and the Rebellion in Upper Canada*
(Toronto: Clarke, Erwin, 1964); John Sewell, *Mackenzie: A
Political Biography of William Lyon Mackenzie* (Toronto: J.
Lorimer and Co., 2002).

Madagascar Revolt (1947–1948)

PRINCIPAL COMBATANTS: Madagascar nationalist rebels
(MDRM) vs. French colonial authorities
PRINCIPAL THEATER(S): Eastern Madagascar
DECLARATION: None
MAJOR ISSUES AND OBJECTIVES: The MDRM wanted to
win independence for Madagascar.
OUTCOME: The 1947–48 uprising was quelled at a high
cost in civilian lives; independence came a decade later.
APPROXIMATE MAXIMUM NUMBER OF MEN UNDER ARMS:
Rebels, 4,500; French garrison forces, 6,500; later, 18,000
colonial troops (mostly North African and Senegalese
forces) were deployed; final rebel strength unknown.
CASUALTIES: Rebels, 5,772 killed in action; French and
French colonials, about 1,000 killed. Native civilian
deaths are estimated at 70,000.
TREATIES: None

In the reshuffling of colonies and possessions following
WORLD WAR II, Madagascar became a French "overseas
territory" in 1946. This immediately spurred creation of
the Mouvement Démocratique de la Rénovation Malagache
(MDRM), a political party dedicated to achieving independence. Beginning in 1947, 4,500 Madagascar tribesmen
associated with MDRM staged an armed rebellion on the
eastern end of the island, which threatened to overwhelm
the 6,500 French regulars garrisoning Madagascar. Reinforced by 18,000 colonials, however, the troops put down
the uprising, but at great cost. Rebel combat deaths numbered 5,772, and civilian casualties mounted, reaching
approximately 70,000 by 1948. Total French and French
colonial military losses were about 1,000 killed.

After the 1947 uprising, the MDRM was outlawed,
but the rebellion continued at a lower level of intensity as
a guerrilla war through 1948, when it wound down without any official treaty or armistice. It was not until 1958
that the French government decided to allow the native
population of Madagascar to determine its own direction.
The vote was not for independence, but autonomy within
the French Community. This led to the creation of the
Malagasy Republic in 1958, which became fully independent in two years. Since 1975, the nation has been known
as Madagascar.

See also MADAGASCAR WARS WITH FRANCE.

Further reading: Mervyn Brown, *A History of Mada-
gascar* (Princeton, N.J.: Markus Wiener Publisher, 2001);
Raymond Kent, *From Madagascar to the Malagasy Republic*
(Westport, Conn.: Greenwood Press, 1976).

Madagascar Wars with France (1883–1885, 1894–1899)

PRINCIPAL COMBATANTS: Hovas vs. French forces
PRINCIPAL THEATER(S): Madagascar
DECLARATION: None
MAJOR ISSUES AND OBJECTIVES: The Hova resisted French
attempts first to assert a protectorate over part of
Madagascar and then to colonize the entire country.
OUTCOME: France ultimately made Madagascar a colony.
APPROXIMATE MAXIMUM NUMBER OF MEN UNDER ARMS:
French expeditionary force, 15,431 (plus 7,715 native
porters)
CASUALTIES: Unknown
TREATIES: Treaties at issue include tribal-French
agreements of 1840 and French-Hova treaties of 1868 and
1895

In 1868 France relinquished control of the main island of
Madagascar to the Hova, the chief native Madagascan
group. In 1882, however, France asserted a protectorate
over northwestern Madagascar, citing treaties concluded
in 1840 among individual chieftains. When the Hova

refused to accept the protectorate, French warships were dispatched to bombard the coastal towns of Majunga and Tamatave. In June 1883 French land forces took and occupied Tamatave, which they used as a base from which they recruited a native army to prosecute the war against the Hove more effectively and cheaply. During the next two years there were no set battles, but, rather, continual low-level combat. At last, in 1885, the Hova recognized the French protectorate in the northwest. Diégo-Suarez, a French settlement at the very northern end of Madagascar, was also recognized, and a French "resident," was permitted to serve in Tananarive, the native capital.

Peace did not long endure. The French sought to assert more control, and on June 16, 1894, the Hova mounted an uprising. By 1895, Hova attacks against the French had become so frequent that a force of 15,431 regulars and 7,715 native porters was landed at Majunga, then advanced inland to Tananarive. Using artillery, the troops bombarded Tananarive until it surrendered on September 30, 1895. The Hova were compelled to give up all but a semblance of sovereignty, the Hova queen, Ruha Valona III (r. 1883–96) becoming a figurehead under French government.

The following year, France declared all of Madagascar its colony and dispatched Joseph S. Gallieni (1849–1916)—who would prove the savior of Paris in the opening weeks of WORLD WAR I—as its governor-general. After removing the queen, even as a figurehead, in 1896, Gallieni conducted a long campaign to put down the widespread rebellion that had broken out after colonization was announced, and it was 1899 before the interior was pacified. Gallieni refused to acknowledge Hova supremacy among the tribes and decreed that all residents of Madagascar would be accorded equal treatment under French law.

See also MADAGASCAR REVOLT.

Further reading: Mervyn Brown, *A History of Madagascar* (Princeton, N.J.: Markus Wiener Publisher, 2001); Raymond Kent, *From Madagascar to the Malagasy Republic* (Westport, Conn.: Greenwood Press, 1976).

"Mad Mullah," Holy Wars of the
(1899–1920)

PRINCIPAL COMBATANTS: Muslim dervishes led by Muhammad bin Abd Allah Hasan (the "Mad Mullah") vs. British colonial forces (with Ethiopian and Italian allies)
PRINCIPAL THEATER(S): Somaliland (Somalia)
DECLARATION: None
MAJOR ISSUES AND OBJECTIVES: The Mad Mullah waged a jihad (holy war) to expel all infidels from the region.
OUTCOME: For more than 20 years, the mullah waged a costly war of terror against the interior of Somaliland, but was finally driven out by a combined air and ground attack, with amphibious support.

APPROXIMATE MAXIMUM NUMBER OF MEN UNDER ARMS: The British rarely had more than 8,000 men in the region; the mullah's followers reached as many as 15,000.
CASUALTIES: Military losses include about 500 killed among the dervishes, 300 among the British, and 200 among the Ethiopians; civilian losses were heavy among the mullah's followers and among the tribes of the interior; it is estimated that one-third of the male population in noncoastal Somaliland was killed.
TREATIES: Illig, or Pestalozza Agreement, March 1905

In 1870 Egypt acquired from the Ottoman Empire possession of the Somali coast from Berbera to Seylac. In 1884 problems in the Sudan prompted the Egyptian government to evacuate the Somali colony, and in 1885 Britain concluded treaties with six of the eight Somali tribes living in the region, thereby adding 58,000 square miles to Britain's African empire. In 1899, however, Muhammad bin Abd Allah Hasan (1864–1920), called the "Mad Mullah" because he claimed supernatural powers, declared a jihad, or holy war, to expel the British and other foreigners from what was then known as Somaliland (Somalia). In April 1899, the Mad Mullah, an adherent of a puritanical Islamic sect, attacked Burao, a native settlement 80 miles from Berbera, recruiting or forcibly impressing a number of men into service, mostly dervishes, so that he had raised a force of about 3,000. Next came an attack on the Habr Yunis tribe in August, which enabled him to return to Burao with a total force of 6,000 men. He then lay low for almost a year, but in August 1900, fell upon the Aidegalla tribe and, in September, the Habr Awal tribe.

The British would mount four campaigns, consisting of British regulars and Ethiopian mercenaries, between 1901 and 1904 against the Mad Mullah. The first was launched in April 1901, using some 1,500 locally recruited men. In a campaign that lasted through July, some 1,200 dervishes—the mullah's followers—were killed and wounded and another 800 taken prisoner. This was sufficient to bring about an interval of peace until October 1901, when the mullah renewed his attacks, menacing and pressing into his service most of the Dolbahanta tribe. The British launched a second expeditionary force in June 1902, pitting about 2,000 men against an estimated force of 15,000 dervishes. The culminating Battle of Erigo, in October 1902, resulted in 1,400 dervish casualties, but the mullah was able to retreat with most of his force intact. The British added more troops to their forces and fielded about 3,600 men, to which was added an Abyssinian (Ethiopian) force of 5,000. The advance of these troops sent the mullah into retreat. On April 17, 1903, at Gumburu, however, the mullah, with 1,400 dervishes, attacked a British-led reconnaissance force of 200, slaughtering most of it, including all officers. Of the 46 survivors, 41 were wounded.

To the British and Abyssinian forces arrayed against the mullah were added Italian troops from Italian Somaliland, but even these combined forces—about 8,000 troops—failed to destroy the mullah's power. However, by 1905, the mullah and his followers agreed to settle in Italian Somaliland, concluding in March 1905 the Illig or Pestalozza Agreement with the Italian government, declaring peace with both the British and the Italians. For the next two years, the mullah presided over a small theocracy.

By 1907, the mullah had reestablished himself on the British side and had resumed raiding and looting, killing perhaps a third of the male population in the region. In 1909, the British government decided to withdraw entirely from the interior, effectively abandoning it to the Mad Mullah, who had some 10,000 troops at this time, while concentrating colonial control over three coast towns only. Friendly Somali tribes in the interior were given arms and ammunition to fend for themselves.

Amid increasing mayhem, in 1912, the British formed the Somali Camel Constabulary, 150 strong, to maintain order among friendly tribes near Berbera. At first, the constabulary proved highly effective, but in 1913 the small force was attacked by some 2,000 dervishes at Dulmadoba. The attackers lost between 200 and 600 men, but half the Camel Constabulary were casualties, including the commandant. Following this defeat, the Camel Constabulary was increased to 500 and an Indian contingent of 400 was added to it. Headway was made against the mullah, but the demands of WORLD WAR I drew off troops for service elsewhere, and the Turks and Germans supported the mullah's efforts, to keep the remaining British forces on the defensive throughout the war.

Early in 1920, with World War I concluded, the British launched a new offensive against the Mad Mullah, using Royal Air Force planes, the Somaliland Camel Corps (700 men), a King's African Rifles Contingent (700 men), 400 men of the Indian army, and three warships *Odin*, *Clio*, and *Arc Royal*. On January 21, 1920, the mullah's headquarters at Medishe, near Jidali, was bombed from the air. The bombardment continued over the next three days and was followed by ground assaults. At this, the Mad Mullah fled to Ethiopia, where he succumbed to disease. Only with his death did the long jihad finally end.

Further reading: Douglas J. Jardine, *Mad Mullah of Somaliland* (Westport, Conn.: Greenwood Publishing Group, 1986).

Madura Revolt (1334–1335)

PRINCIPAL COMBATANTS: Delhi sultanate vs. Gulbarga sultanate
PRINCIPAL THEATER(S): Madura, India
DECLARATION: None
MAJOR ISSUES AND OBJECTIVES: The Delhi-appointed governor of Madura declared an independent sultanate.
OUTCOME: Because Delhi's troops had to be recalled to other service, the rebellion continued unchecked.
APPROXIMATE MAXIMUM NUMBER OF MEN UNDER ARMS: Unknown
CASUALTIES: Unknown
TREATIES: None

Muhammad Tughluq (r. 1325–51), sultan of Delhi, whose territories encompassed many Hindu kingdoms, endured many revolts until he established a system of provincial governors. One of these, Jalal-ud-Din Ahsan Shah (fl. mid-14th century) the governor of Madura, proved rebellious himself in 1334 and declared an independent sultanate around the capital city of Gulbarga. The sultan dispatched troops from Delhi, but had to recall them in 1335 to quell rebellions in Lahore and in Delhi itself. This allowed the governor to continue his revolt, which gave rise, in turn, to other rebellions.

See also BAHMANI-DELHI SULTANATE WAR and VIJAYANAGAR CONQUEST OF MADURA.

Further reading: Barbara Daly Metcalf and Thomas R. Metcalf, *Concise History of India* (New York: Cambridge University Press, 2002); Romila Thapar, *A History of India,* vol. 1, in *Comprehensive History of India* of the Indian History Congress (New York: Penguin Books, 1966).

"Mad War" *See* GUERRE FOLLE.

Magnentius and Constantius, War between *See* ROMAN CIVIL WAR (350–351).

Magnentius's Revolt *See* ROMAN CIVIL WAR (350–351).

Magyar Raid, Great (954–955)

PRINCIPAL COMBATANTS: Magyars vs. primarily Germans under Otto I (allied with Conrad of Lorraine)
PRINCIPAL THEATER(S): Bavaria and Franconia
DECLARATION: None
MAJOR ISSUES AND OBJECTIVES: Acquisition of German and Frankish territory.
OUTCOME: The Magyars were ultimately defeated, repulsed, and driven from Germany.
APPROXIMATE MAXIMUM NUMBER OF MEN UNDER ARMS: Magyars, 50,000–100,000; Germans, 10,000 (plus allies)
CASUALTIES: Numbers unknown, but heavy on all sides

TREATIES: Alliance between Magyars and Conrad of Lorraine, then between Otto I and Conrad of Lorraine

In 954, the Magyars mounted their greatest raid ever, sending between 50,000 and 100,000 warriors into Bavaria and Franconia. The devastation was swift, and Conrad of Lorraine, in revolt against the German king Otto I (912–973), made a hasty alliance with the invaders to aid their Rhine crossing at Worms. Conrad also made it easy for the invaders to enter Lorraine. From here, the Magyars crossed the Meuse River to raid northeastern France. They swept through Rheims, then Châlons, and penetrated Burgundy. From Burgundy, they advanced through the Great St. Bernard Pass into Italy, visiting devastation upon parts of Lombardy before crossing the Carnic Alps and into the Drava Valley and the valley of the Danube.

Having terrorized a wide swath of western Europe, the Magyars turned on Bavaria in 955. A force of 50,000 invaded the kingdom and laid siege to Augsburg, where they were met by Otto I leading an army of 10,000. The Magyars lifted their siege and turned instead to battle with Otto. The Battle of Lechfeld, in August, began very badly for the German king. The Magyars wheeled about and surprised the Germans, driving more than 3,000 men from the field. This done, the Magyars took the German camp. Otto, however, secured the aid of his erstwhile foe, Conrad of Lorraine, and was ultimately able to drive out the invaders. Worse for the Magyars, Otto inflicted heavy losses on them and also captured their camp and treasure. He assumed the offensive and harried the fleeing Magyars over a three-day period. Conrad fell in battle. The Great Magyar Raid was at an end, and the Magyars never raided Germany again.

See also MAGYAR RAID INTO EUROPE, FIRST; MAGYAR RAIDS IN FRANCE; and MAGYAR RAIDS IN THE HOLY ROMAN EMPIRE.

Further reading: Paul Ignotus, *Hungary* (New York: Praeger, 1972); Dominic G. Kosáry, *A History of Hungary* (New York: Arno Press, 1971); C. A. Macartney, *The Magyars in the Ninth Century* (reprint, New York: Cambridge University Press, 1968); Miklos Molnar, *A Concise History of Hungary* (New York: Cambridge University Press, 2001); Denis Sinor, *History of Hungary* (Westport, Conn.: Greenwood Press, 1976).

Magyar Raid into Europe, First (862)

PRINCIPAL COMBATANTS: The Magyars vs. the Franks; separately, the Magyars vs. the Pechenegs and Bulgars
PRINCIPAL THEATER(S): Middle Danube Valley region
DECLARATION: None

MAJOR ISSUES AND OBJECTIVES: Menaced by the Pechenegs and Bulgars in their Don Basin homeland, the Magyars sought new territory.
OUTCOME: Ultimately, the Magyars came to occupy the middle Danube Valley region.
APPROXIMATE MAXIMUM NUMBER OF MEN UNDER ARMS: Unknown
CASUALTIES: Unknown
TREATIES: None

During the ninth century, the Magyars (related to the Finns and the Turks) occupied the lower Don Basin as vassals of the Khazar Turks. By the middle of the century, the Magyars had penetrated to the frontiers of the Frankish kingdom in the middle Danube Valley, and they began a series of raids against the frontier Franks. The first Magyar raid west of the Danube took place in 862, when they pushed into Frankish Ostmark.

The raids were attempts to probe for new territory, because the Magyars were menaced in their Don Basin homeland by the Pechenegs and Bulgars. During 862–889, the period of the Magyar western raids, the Magyars were ejected from the Don Basin and resettled in Moldavia. The Magyars would settle permanently in the middle Danube region after 895, when they met defeat at the hands of the Pechenegs.

See also MAGYAR RAID, GREAT; MAGYAR RAIDS IN FRANCE; MAGYAR RAIDS IN THE HOLY ROMAN EMPIRE.

Further reading: Paul Ignotus, *Hungary* (New York: Praeger, 1972); Dominic G. Kosáry, *A History of Hungary* (New York: Arno Press, 1971); C. A. Macartney, *The Magyars in the Ninth Century* (reprint, New York: Cambridge University Press, 1968); Miklos Molnar, *A Concise History of Hungary* (New York: Cambridge University Press, 2001); Denis Sinor, *History of Hungary* (Westport, Conn.: Greenwood Press, 1976).

Magyar Raids in France (907–954)

PRINCIPAL COMBATANTS: Magyars vs. the French
PRINCIPAL THEATER(S): France and northern Italy
DECLARATION: None
MAJOR ISSUES AND OBJECTIVES: The raiders sought wealth.
OUTCOME: Large parts of France were devastated.
APPROXIMATE MAXIMUM NUMBER OF MEN UNDER ARMS: Unknown
CASUALTIES: Unknown
TREATIES: None

The Magyar Raids in France were largely contemporaneous with the MAGYAR RAIDS IN THE HOLY ROMAN EMPIRE from about 894 to 955. Magyar (Hungarian) warriors crossed into

Alsace and Burgundy from Germany, staging raids for many years. Burgundy felt the brunt of this activity during 917 to 919, and King Charles III's (879–929) inability to organize the French barons into an effective resistance allowed the Magyars to advance through the kingdom almost at will. In 926, Rheims was menaced, and Burgundy was again overrun in 936–937. King Raoul of Burgundy (d. 936) mounted a defense, which failed and ended in the king's death.

Raiding was chronic, but some of the worst occurred in Aquitaine in 951. The culminating raid—the so-called Great Magyar Raid—came in 954, when warriors ravaged Cambrai, Laon, and Rheims, then swept through northeastern France, down through Burgundy, and into Italy by way of the Great St. Bernard Pass.

See also MAGYAR RAID INTO EUROPE, FIRST; MAGYAR RAID, GREAT.

Further reading: Paul Ignotus, *Hungary* (New York: Praeger, 1972); Dominic G. Kosáry, *A History of Hungary* (New York: Arno Press, 1971); C. A. Macartney, *The Magyars in the Ninth Century* (reprint, New York: Cambridge University Press, 1968); Miklos Molnar, *A Concise History of Hungary* (New York: Cambridge University Press, 2001); Denis Sinor, *History of Hungary* (Westport, Conn.: Greenwood Press, 1976).

Magyar Raids in the Holy Roman Empire
(c. 894–955)

PRINCIPAL COMBATANTS: The Magyar warriors vs. the Holy Roman Empire
PRINCIPAL THEATER(S): Germany
DECLARATION: None
MAJOR ISSUES AND OBJECTIVES: The Magyars sought riches and conquest.
OUTCOME: After enduring more than five decades of raids, the forces of the Holy Roman Empire, under Otto I, finally evicted the Magyars from Germany.
APPROXIMATE MAXIMUM NUMBER OF MEN UNDER ARMS: At Lechfeld, Magyars: 50,000; Holy Roman Empire, 10,000
CASUALTIES: Unknown
TREATIES: None

The Magyars, seven tribes under a leader named Árpád (c. 840–907), staged a massive western movement from their homes in the northern Caucasus beginning about 889. They swept through Frankish Pannonia—encompassing chiefly eastern Austria and western Hungary—between 894 and 896, raided mercilessly, and seized control of the region by 900. This area became their base of operations for more than five decades of raids into western Europe (*see* MAGYAR RAIDS IN FRANCE).

The Magyars hit Moravia in 906, overwhelming a Bavarian force at the Battle of Ennsburg, which allowed them to occupy the Hungarian Great Plain. The raiders penetrated as far north as Bremen and as far south as Otranto, then pressed west to Orléans and as far east as Constantinople. Within the Holy Roman Empire, Saxony and Thuringia were scourged during 908 and Bavaria in 909–910.

Germany's King Henry I (c. 876–936)—Henry the Fowler—fought effectively against the Magyars during 919–936. In 924, Henry captured a major Magyar chieftain and was able to use him to extort a nine-year truce. During this time, Henry fortified Saxon towns and built up his army, so that in 933, he felt ready to break the truce and take the offensive against the Magyars. He attacked at Riade, seizing their camp and sending them into retreat. A quasi civil war attending the ascension of Otto I (912–973) to the Holy Roman throne weakened the German offensive after 936, but Holy Roman troops were still able to conduct an effective defense in Thuringia, Saxony, and Bavaria during 948–949.

The culminating battle of the Magyar raids was the Battle of Lechfeld, south of Augsburg, Bavaria, in 955. Approximately 50,000 Magyars laid siege to Augsburg in August. Ulric (890–973; canonized St. Ulric in 993), the bishop of Augsburg, led a heroic delaying action against the attackers, which bought sufficient time for the arrival of Otto I at the head of a 10,000-man force. Given the lopsided numbers, the battle predictably began badly for Otto, who suffered a loss of at least a third of his army. However, the timely arrival of Duke Conrad the Red of Lorraine, with reinforcements, turned the tide. The Magyars broke and ran, with Otto in hot pursuit. They retreated far to the east and never menaced the Holy Roman Empire again.

See also MAGYAR RAID INTO EUROPE, FIRST; MAGYAR RAID, GREAT.

Further reading: Paul Ignotus, *Hungary* (New York: Praeger, 1972); Dominic G. Kosáry, *A History of Hungary* (New York: Arno Press, 1971); C. A. Macartney, *The Magyars in the Ninth Century* (reprint, New York: Cambridge University Press, 1968); Miklos Molnar, *A Concise History of Hungary* (New York: Cambridge University Press, 2001); Denis Sinor, *History of Hungary* (Westport, Conn.: Greenwood Press, 1976).

Mahabat Khan's Insurrection (1626–1627)

PRINCIPAL COMBATANTS: Forces of Jahangir, Nur Jahan vs. Mahabat Khan
PRINCIPAL THEATER(S): Punjab, India
DECLARATION: None
MAJOR ISSUES AND OBJECTIVES: Succession to the Mogul throne
OUTCOME: Mahabat Khan succeeded to the throne as Shah Jahan.

APPROXIMATE MAXIMUM NUMBER OF MEN UNDER ARMS:
Unknown
CASUALTIES: Unknown
TREATIES: None

Mahabat Khan (d. 1634) was a general in service to the Mogul emperor Jahangir (1569–1627). Though Mahabat Khan put down the rebellion of the emperor's son Khurram (1592–1666) in 1626 and secured Jahangir on his throne, the general accepted the contrite prince as the emperor's heir (as did Jahangir himself). But Empress Nur Jahan (d. 1645), the favorite among Jahangir's harem, had other ideas about the succession, which she wished to control. She was wary of the general's growing popularity and saw him as a future rival for power behind the throne.

Accordingly, Nur Jahan persuaded Jahangir to appoint Mahabat Khan governor of Bengal, far from the royal court. No sooner did he leave for Bengal than she trumped up charges of treason against him and persuaded Jahangir to order his return to Lahore for trial. Mahabat Khan refused to return and instead sought an audience with the emperor at the royal court in the Punjab. When Jahangir refused to see him, Mahabat Khan took him prisoner. During this exchange, Nur Jahan escaped with her entourage, and Jahangir, too, managed to eventually break free of Mahabat Khan. For his part, the general fled to Khurram's friendly camp in the Deccan. There, however, he was persuaded to return to Jahangir and seek forgiveness or, at least, clemency.

Jahangir died suddenly, before Mahabat Khan returned, and the general thus avoided the wrath of the Mogul emperor. Meanwhile, Nur Jahan's candidate for the throne had been caught pilfering the royal treasury. She was discredited, and he severely punished (he was blinded for his thieving). She was easily shunted aside as the powerful Mahabat Khan threw his support behind Prince Khurram, who became emperor under this throne name: Shah Jahan.

See also MOGUL CIVIL WAR (1657–1659); SHAH JAHAN'S REVOLT.

Further reading: Z. A. Desai, *Shah Jahan Numa of Inayat Khan: An Abridged History of the Mughal Emperor Shah Jahan* (London: Oxford University Press, 1990); Barbara Daly Metcalf and Thomas R. Metcalf, *Concise History of India* (New York: Cambridge University Press, 2002).

Mahdist War *See* SUDANESE WAR (1881–1885).

Mahmud of Ghazna, Conquests of
(c. 1000–1030)

PRINCIPAL COMBATANTS: Ghazna vs. India
PRINCIPAL THEATER(S): Kashmir, the Punjab, and the region of modern Iran

DECLARATION: None
MAJOR ISSUES AND OBJECTIVES: Mahmud desired imperial conquest, in part to acquire treasure, in part to disseminate Islam and suppress Hinduism.
OUTCOME: Over a 30-year period, Mahmud conquered all of the territory he sought.
APPROXIMATE MAXIMUM NUMBER OF MEN UNDER ARMS: In major invasions, Mahmud commanded about 15,000 men. At each of the two major battles of Peshawar, Indian forces numbered about 30,000.
CASUALTIES: Unknown
TREATIES: None

Driven by a combination of Islamic zeal to conquer Hinduism and a desire for treasure, Mahmud (971–1030), ruler of Ghazna (Afghanistan and part of Iran), launched 17 invasions into India between 1000 and 1030. He razed Hindu temples throughout Kashmir and the Punjab, as well as the area encompassed by modern Iran. These vast regions he subjugated and extracted from them great hoards of treasure, which he used to finance a grandiose building program in his capital city.

Three of his Indian raids were major wars. In 1001, he led 10,000 cavalrymen against some 40,000 Indians at the Battle of Peshawar, achieving a signal victory, which resulted in the death of the Indian commander, Rajah Jaipal of Lahore (d. 1001). In 1108, an Indian force of 30,000 attacked him in a second Battle of Peshawar, compelling his retreat. Mahmud was able to regroup, however, and counterattack, defeating the superior Indian forces. This led to the formal Ghaznian annexation of the Punjab. Finally, in 1024, Mahmud invaded Kathiawar, on the southern coast of the subcontinent. He and his army rode into Somnath and there looted and destroyed a magnificent Hindu temple.

By the time of his death in 1030, Mahmud of Ghazna had conducted a total of 17 raids into the Indian Peninsula and came to rule Kashmir, the Punjab, and all of Iran. He was a dictator of unsparing temperament, yet although he looted many Hindu monuments, he never compelled the populace of the conquered territories to renounce their religion and convert to Islam.

Further reading: Barbara Daly Metcalf and Thomas R. Metcalf, *Concise History of India* (New York: Cambridge University Press, 2002); Muhammad Nuzim, *Life and Times of Sultan Mahmad of Ghaza* (Delhi: Vedans eBooks, 2001).

Maillotin Uprising (1382)

PRINCIPAL COMBATANTS: Parisian tax protesters vs. tax collectors, money lenders, and the government of King Charles VI of France
PRINCIPAL THEATER(S): Paris

DECLARATION: None

MAJOR ISSUES AND OBJECTIVES: Oppressed by ruinous taxes levied to finance the ongoing Hundred Years' War, the "Maillots" may have sought a repeal of the taxes but they also sought to express their outrage through violence.

OUTCOME: The uprising was quelled when the ringleaders had been apprehended, tried, and executed; however, the uprising also brought about the repeal of the most outrageous of the taxes.

APPROXIMATE MAXIMUM NUMBER OF MEN UNDER ARMS: Unknown

CASUALTIES: Unknown

TREATIES: None

This uprising of oppressed Parisians, suffering under the privations of the HUNDRED YEARS' WAR, was named for the typical weapon the rioters carried, the *maillot* (a leaden mallet or maul). The "Maillots" turned their wrath against tax collectors and money lenders, whom they hunted down, assaulted, and often killed. During this period in France, Christians were barred from the trade of money lending, which was thus restricted to Jews. Therefore, the uprising took on the character of an anti-Semitic pogrom.

The Maillots refused to negotiate with King Charles VI (1368–1422) and his counselors, and the uprising continued until the ringleaders of the revolt were identified, arrested, tried, and executed. Not content with merely quelling the uprising, Charles VI sought to head off further violence by abolishing the most oppressive of the taxes that had sparked the revolt to begin with.

See also JACQUERIE.

Further reading: Christopher Allmand, *The Hundred Years' War: England and France at War, c. 1300–1450* (New York: Cambridge University Press, 1988); Anne Curry, *The Hundred Years' War*, 2nd ed. (New York: Palgrave Macmillan, 2003); John Bell Henneman, *Oliver de Clisson and Political Society under Charles V and Charles VI* (Philadelphia: University of Pennsylvania Press, 1996); Robin Neillands, *The Hundred Years' War* (New York: Routledge, 2001); Jonathan Sumption, *The Hundred Years' War* (Boston: Faber and Faber, 1999).

Maji Maji Uprising (1905–1907)

PRINCIPAL COMBATANTS: Native people of German East Africa (Tanzania) vs. German colonialists (with African auxiliary troops)

PRINCIPAL THEATER(S): German East Africa

DECLARATION: No formal declaration

MAJOR ISSUES AND OBJECTIVES: Native Africans protested their subjugation at the hands of German colonialists.

OUTCOME: The native uprising was quelled.

APPROXIMATE MAXIMUM NUMBER OF MEN UNDER ARMS: Native forces, 20,000; 500 Germans led thousands of colonial troops.

CASUALTIES: For the Native Africans, 75,000–120,000 killed; Germans, 2,507 killed; African colonials, 4,703 killed

TREATIES: No formal treaty

In July 1905, Abdullah Mapanda (d. 1907) and Kinjikitile Ngwale (d. 1905) led 20,000 native East African rebels in an uprising against the harsh rule of the Germans. They were fortified with maji-maji, a potion they believed rendered them impervious to German bullets. The first major assault fell on a colonial *boma* (fort) at Kilosa on August 16. The garrison of 13 askaris (native troops in the German service) was slaughtered.

The attack on Kilosa triggered a vigorous and unremitting brutal response from colonial governor Adolf Graf von Gotzen (served 1901–06), who led 500 German regulars bolstered by thousands of colonial troops from Africa, as well as New Guinea and Papua (before 1945 a separate territory), and Melanesia. These forces engaged in a rampage of slaughter that killed between 75,000 and 120,000 natives out of a total population of some 2 million. Some were killed outright, others tortured to death, and still others starved after their crops were destroyed. Losses among German and colonial troops were also heavy, many succumbing to disease and exposure.

The rebellion was put down, although fighting continued sporadically through 1918, when, as a result of WORLD WAR I, Germany lost all of its colonies, including East Africa.

Further reading: Erick J. Mann, *Mikono Ya Damu: African Mercenaries and the Politics of Conflict in German East Africa, 1888–1904* (New York: P. Lang, 2002).

Malacca, Siege of (1640–1641)

PRINCIPAL COMBATANTS: The Dutch (with Achinese allies) vs. the Portuguese

PRINCIPAL THEATER(S): The fortress at Malacca

DECLARATION: None

MAJOR ISSUES AND OBJECTIVES: The Dutch and Portuguese vied for control of the important trading center of the western Malay Peninsula.

OUTCOME: The fortress fell to a prolonged siege, resulting in the Dutch usurpation of the spice trade.

APPROXIMATE MAXIMUM NUMBER OF MEN UNDER ARMS: Portuguese-Asian garrison, 3,760; Dutch-Achinese attackers, at least 6,000

CASUALTIES: A total of 7,000 died, more from starvation and disease than from combat

TREATIES: None

Malacca occupied the west coast of the Malay peninsula and was a prize over which Portuguese and Dutch trading interests struggled for years. In 1511, the Portuguese captured Malacca and built a formidable fortress there, A Famosa, with walls 32 feet high and 24 feet thick. The native Achinese resented the presence of the Portuguese and allied themselves with the Dutch in an effort to oust them. In June 1640, a combined Achinese and Dutch fleet blockaded the fortress, and in August ground forces besieged it, cutting off the garrison of 260 Portuguese and some 3,000 locals. Receiving no relief from other Portuguese colonies, the fortress surrendered in January 1641, after some 7,000 had died on both sides, and the Dutch gained mastery of the great spice trade.

Further reading: Diane Lewis, *Jan Compagne in the Straits of Malacca, 1641–1795* (Columbus: Ohio University Press, 1995); George Musselman, *The Cradle of Colonialism* (New Haven, Conn.: Yale University Press, 1963).

Malay Jungle Wars (1948–1960)

PRINCIPAL COMBATANTS: Communist and Red Chinese guerrillas vs. Great Britain and Malay Federation
PRINCIPAL THEATER(S): Malay Federation
DECLARATION: None
MAJOR ISSUES AND OBJECTIVES: The guerrillas wanted an end to British rule and the installation of a communist government.
OUTCOME: Guerrilla activity was effectively suppressed by 1957, except along the Malay-Thai border, where it persisted through 1960.
APPROXIMATE MAXIMUM NUMBER OF MEN UNDER ARMS: Guerrillas, 7,000; Anglo-Malay regulars, 55,000; police, 80,000; Malay Home Guard, 50,000
CASUALTIES: Guerrillas, 6,710 killed, 2,820 wounded, 1,290 captured; Anglo-Malay forces, 2,384 killed, 2,400 wounded; civilian losses, 2,473 killed, 810 abducted and possibly killed
TREATIES: None

The Federation of Malaya was established in 1948 under the mandate supervision of a British high commissioner. Almost immediately after the establishment of the federation, Communist irregulars—many of them Chinese and North Vietnamese—began a widespread guerrilla war against the government, staging raids on government facilities, police stations, and military installations. British and Malay forces swept the country for guerrillas and, by 1949, had succeeded in rounding up or killing hundreds. Within two years, however, the rebels renewed their activities, this time concentrating on rubber plantations, a mainstay of the Malay economy. Plantation workers were killed and rubber trees were destroyed. Sir Herald Briggs

(1891–1989), the British high commissioner, instituted strict controls on food in areas believed to harbor large numbers of guerrillas; this tactic effectively starved out many of the insurgents.

Under the Marxist leader Chin Peng (b. 1922), the guerrillas were organized into the Malayan People's Anti-British Army, reaching a peak strength of 7,000, and later redesignated the Malayan Race Liberation Army (MRLA)—a tiny fraction of Malaya's 5.5 million population. Despite its small size and the absence of popular support, the MRLA fought for a dozen years, against an Anglo-Malayan army of 55,000 (which included troops from the British Commonwealth), a local police force of 84,000, and the Malay Home Guard, a force of 50,000.

In 1957, the Malay Federation become an autonomous state in the British Commonwealth, a step that took the wind out of the insurgents' sails. Activity died down. A substantial number of guerrillas even accepted a government offer of amnesty and gave themselves up. Others moved to Sumatra. Nevertheless, a small number of rebels remained active along the Malay border with Thailand and were the focus of intensive government operations, which defeated the last of them in 1960.

Further reading: Barbara Watson Andaya and Leonard Y. Andaya, *History of Malaysia* (Honolulu: University of Hawaii Press, 2001); D. G. E. Hall, *A History of South-East Asia*, 4th ed. (New York: St. Martin's Press, 1981).

Malvinas War, Islas   *See* FALKLAND ISLANDS WAR.

Mamluk-Ottoman War (1485–1491)

PRINCIPAL COMBATANTS: Mamluks vs. Ottoman Turks
PRINCIPAL THEATER(S): Cappadocia (portion of modern Turkey)
DECLARATION: None
MAJOR ISSUES AND OBJECTIVES: Mamluks sought control of Lesser Armenia.
OUTCOME: Mostly indecisive; peace was reached after minor territorial cessions were made to the Mamluks.
APPROXIMATE MAXIMUM NUMBER OF MEN UNDER ARMS: Unknown
CASUALTIES: Unknown
TREATIES: No documents survive

Sporadic warfare erupted over possession of a Cappadocian Turkoman territory ruled by the Duldakir dynasty, which had the backing of the Egyptian-based military rulers, the Mamluks. In this region, the Mamluks supported Turkoman nomads in rebellion against the Ottoman Turks and declared sovereignty over Lesser Armenia.

Each year, from 1485 to 1491, the Ottomans campaigned against the Mamluks in the region, and each campaign ended indecisively—although the Mamluks scored a minor triumph in 1488. At last, the Mamluks and Ottomans entered into peace negotiations in 1491. The Ottomans bought Mamluk compliance with a relatively modest territorial concession.

See also MAMLUK-PERSIAN-OTTOMAN WAR (1514–1517).

Further reading: Shai Har-el, *Struggle for Domination in the Middle East: The Ottoman-Mamluk War, 1485–1491* (New York: Brill, 1995); Colin Imber, *The Ottoman Empire, 1300–1650: The Structure of Power* (New York: Palgrave, 2002); Lord Kinross, *The Ottoman Centuries: The Rise and Fall of the Turkish Empire* (New York: Morrow, 1977); Donald P. Little, *History and Historiography of the Mamluks* (Burlington, Vt.: Ashgate Publishing, 1986); Stanford J. Shaw and E. K. Shaw, *History of the Ottoman Empire and Modern Turkey,* 2 vols. (New York: Cambridge University Press, 1976–1977).

Mamluk-Persian-Ottoman War (1514–1517)

PRINCIPAL COMBATANTS: Mamluks vs. Ottoman Turks; Ottoman Turks vs. Persians
PRINCIPAL THEATER(S): Syria and Egypt
DECLARATION: None
MAJOR ISSUES AND OBJECTIVES: Ottoman sultan Selim I sought to conquer Mamluk Syria and Egypt, and to put down Shi'ite Persians
OUTCOME: The Mamluk realms fell to Selim; the Persian conflict ended indecisively.
APPROXIMATE MAXIMUM NUMBER OF MEN UNDER ARMS: Unknown
CASUALTIES: Mamluks, 7,000 killed; Persians, 2,000 killed; Ottomans, 9,000 killed
TREATIES: None

The Persian-Ottoman phase of this conflict is treated in the TURKO-PERSIAN WAR (1514–1516). As a result of that conflict, the Ottoman forces of Selim I (1467–1520) encroached into Syria, a Mamluk territory, prompting the Mamluk sultan of Egypt, Kansu al-Gauri (d. 1516), to counterattack by invading the Ottoman Empire from Aleppo. Kansu was met by the forces of Selim at Marj-Dabik, 10 miles north of Aleppo, on August 24, 1516, and was severely defeated. The Ottoman army included 8,000 tunissanes, 3,000 Saphis, 15,000 timariot feudal levies, and some 15,000 irregular auxiliaries; the Mamluks had about 28,000 men. The aged Kansu died of a cerebral hemorrhage during the battle, an event that precipitated the total surrender of the Mamluks, who withdrew from Syria, abandoning it to the Ottomans.

Victorious, Selim now pressed his advantages. His armies captured Damascus, Beirut, Gaza, and Jerusalem. To hold these places, Selim immediately installed Ottoman governors, allowed the princes of Lebanon to continue ruling as his vassals, and offered peace to Tuman Bey (d. 1517), the new sultan of Egypt, in exchange for his acceptance of Ottoman overlordship. Tuman Bey rejected Selim's offer, whereupon Selim advanced against Cairo, defeated the army of the sultan at the Battle of Reydaniyya (Ridanieh) on January 22, 1517, then took Cairo. Six thousand Ottomans died in battle, as did 7,000 Mamluks. Operating from the capital city, Selim soon subdued all of Egypt. Having fled, Tuman Bey tried to mount a guerrilla-style resistance, but was captured and summarily executed.

In the aftermath of the Battle of Reydaniyya and the occupation of Cairo, some 50,000 Mamluks may have been slain; however, after this orgy of violence, Selim I made no further reprisals against those who had been loyal to Tuman Bey and even appointed leading Mamluks to positions of high office in his administration of Egypt.

See also MAMLUK-OTTOMAN WAR (1485–1491).

Further reading: Colin Imber, *The Ottoman Empire, 1300–1650: The Structure of Power* (New York: Palgrave, 2002); Lord Kinross, *The Ottoman Centuries: The Rise and Fall of the Turkish Empire* (New York: Morrow, 1977); Donald P. Little, *History and Historiography of the Mamluks* (Burlington, Vt.: Ashgate Publishing, 1986); Stanford J. Shaw and E. K. Shaw, *History of the Ottoman Empire and Modern Turkey,* 2 vols. (New York: Cambridge University Press, 1976–1977).

Mamluk Revolt *See* CRUSADE, SEVENTH (1248–1254).

Manchu Conquest of China: Manchu-Ming War (1618–1628)

PRINCIPAL COMBATANTS: Manchus vs. Mings (with Korean alliance)
PRINCIPAL THEATER(S): China
DECLARATION: None
MAJOR ISSUES AND OBJECTIVES: The Manchus sought the overthrow of the Ming dynasty.
OUTCOME: Although the Mings suffered many reversals, and the Koreans were badly defeated, the Manchus were unable to overthrow the Mings; however, the Ming dynasty was undermined by the conflict and went into precipitous collapse later in the century.
APPROXIMATE MAXIMUM NUMBER OF MEN UNDER ARMS: Manchu, 170,000; Ming, numbers unknown; Ming-allied Koreans, 20,000
CASUALTIES: Unknown

TREATIES: Presumably, formal agreements were made between the Mings and the Koreans.

The Manchu state emerged in China during 1600–1615, and by 1618, when war broke out between the Manchus and Mings, the Manchu army consisted of Manchus, Mongols, and Chinese: approximately 170,000 men. Led by Nurhachi (1559–1626), also known as Tian Ming (T'ien Ming), part of this force overran and captured a Ming stronghold at Fushun (Fu-shan) in 1618. A counter-attack was launched against the captured position and was repulsed. To help put down what it regarded as a Manchu revolt, the Ming recruited 20,000 Koreans. Despite the augmented force, the Mings suffered a defeat at Shenyang. The city surrendered to the Manchus, who used Ming turncoats to destroy a bridge and thereby trap the Ming army in the city in 1621.

The advance of the Manchus was finally arrested in 1623 when, near the Great Wall, the Ming governor Yuan Chonghuan (Yuan Ch'unghuan; fl. 17th century) used artillery borrowed from Jesuit missionaries to fire on the Manchus. This turned them west, toward Mongolia.

The Manchu leader Nurhachi died in 1626 and was succeeded by his son Abahai (1592–1643, also known as Taizong [T'ai Tsung]). In 1627 he led an invasion into Korea to neutralize this important Ming ally. Abahai invaded during the winter, crossing the frozen Yalu River. His forces succeeded in defeating the Koreans and, this done, he turned back to Ming China. In 1628, however, the renewed Manchu invasion was again repulsed. As before, the victorious Ming general was Yuan Chonghuan, and, also as before, the key weapon was European artillery. The Manchus turned their attention to northern China (see MANCHU CONQUEST OF CHINA: MANCHU RAIDS ON NORTH CHINA).

See also MANCHU CONQUEST OF CHINA: MANCHU INVASION OF KOREA; MANCHU CONQUEST OF CHINA: MANCHU CONQUEST OF INNER MONGOLIA; MANCHU CONQUEST OF CHINA: CHINESE (MING) CIVIL WARS; MANCHU CONQUEST OF CHINA: MANCHU ESTABLISH QING DYNASTY; MANCHU CONQUEST OF CHINA: MANCHU CONQUEST OF KOREA; MANCHU CONQUEST OF CHINA: LI ZICHENG'S REBELLION AND FALL OF THE MING; MANCHU CONQUEST OF CHINA: MANCHU-MING WAR FOR YANGTZE VALLEY; MANCHU CONQUEST OF CHINA: MANCHU CONQUEST OF FUJIAN; MANCHU CONQUEST OF CHINA: GUI WANG'S CAMPAIGNS; MANCHU CONQUEST OF CHINA: MANCHU CONQUEST OF SOUTHWEST CHINA; MANCHU CONQUEST OF CHINA: MANCHU-MING PIRATE WAR; MANCHU CONQUEST OF CHINA: REVOLT OF THE THREE VICEROYS; MANCHU CONQUEST OF CHINA: ANNEXATION OF TAIWAN; MANCHU CONQUEST OF TIBET.

Further reading: Wolfram Eberhart, *A History of China*, 3rd ed. (Berkeley: University of California Press, 1969); Charles O. Hucker, *China's Imperial Past: An Intro-* *duction to Chinese History and Culture* (Stanford, Calif.: Stanford University Press, 1975); J. A. Roberts, *A Concise History of China* (Cambridge, Mass.: Harvard University Press, 1999); Jonathan D. Spence and John E. Wills, Jr., *From Ming to Ch'ing: Conquest, Region and Continuity in Seventeenth-Century China* (New Haven, Conn.: Yale University Press, 1981).

Manchu Conquest of China: Manchu Invasion of Korea (1627)

PRINCIPAL COMBATANTS: Manchus vs. Koreans
PRINCIPAL THEATER(S): Korea
DECLARATION: None
MAJOR ISSUES AND OBJECTIVES: The Manchus wanted dominion over Korea, in part to end the Korean-Ming alliance.
OUTCOME: After a swift invasion, Korea fell to Manchu vassalage.
APPROXIMATE MAXIMUM NUMBER OF MEN UNDER ARMS: Unknown
CASUALTIES: Unknown
TREATIES: Agreement to vassalage and tribute

This invasion resulted more in the conclusion of a vassalage agreement than in an outright conquest. Until forces of the Manchus (Qing [Ch'ing] dynasty) descended upon the Korean Peninsula in 1627, the Koreans had supported the Ming dynasty in China and had supplied military aid to check the advance of the Manchus from the north of Manchuria. Once the Manchus had invaded their country, however, the Koreans found they were no match for the magnificent Manchu army. A stout resistance was offered, but the territory was quickly conquered. In exchange for a change of allegiance from the Ming to the Manchu, the payment of a modest tribute, and an agreement to submit to Manchu vassalage, the Koreans were left essentially to rule themselves—but had been neutralized as Ming allies.

See also MANCHU CONQUEST OF CHINA: MANCHU-MING WAR; MANCHU CONQUEST OF CHINA: MANCHU RAIDS ON NORTH CHINA; MANCHU CONQUEST OF CHINA: MANCHU CONQUEST OF INNER MONGOLIA; MANCHU CONQUEST OF CHINA: CHINESE (MING) CIVIL WARS; MANCHU CONQUEST OF CHINA: MANCHU ESTABLISH Q'ING DYNASTY; MANCHU CONQUEST OF CHINA: MANCHU CONQUEST OF KOREA; MANCHU CONQUEST OF CHINA: LI ZICHENG'S REBELLION AND FALL OF THE MING; MANCHU CONQUEST OF CHINA: MANCHU-MING WAR FOR YANGTZE VALLEY; MANCHU CONQUEST OF CHINA: MANCHU CONQUEST OF FUJIAN; MANCHU CONQUEST OF CHINA: GUI WANG'S CAMPAIGNS; MANCHU CONQUEST OF CHINA: MANCHU CONQUEST OF SOUTHWEST CHINA; MANCHU CONQUEST OF CHINA:

MANCHU-MING PIRATE WAR; MANCHU CONQUEST OF CHINA: REVOLT OF THE THREE VICEROYS; MANCHU CONQUEST OF CHINA: ANNEXATION OF TAIWAN; MANCHU CONQUEST OF TIBET.

Further reading: Wolfram Eberhart, *A History of China,* 3rd ed. (Berkeley: University of California Press, 1969); Charles O. Hucker, *China's Imperial Past: An Introduction to Chinese History and Culture* (Stanford, Calif.: Stanford University Press, 1975); J. A. Roberts, *A Concise History of China* (Cambridge, Mass.: Harvard University Press, 1999); Jonathan D. Spence and John E. Wills, Jr., *From Ming to Ch'ing: Conquest, Region and Continuity in Seventeenth-Century China* (New Haven, Conn.: Yale University Press, 1981).

Manchu Conquest of China: Manchu Raids on North China (1629–1634)

PRINCIPAL COMBATANTS: Manchus vs. Mings
PRINCIPAL THEATER(S): Northern China and Shansi Province
DECLARATION: None
MAJOR ISSUES AND OBJECTIVES: The Manchus wanted to overthrow the Ming dynasty.
OUTCOME: The raids into northern China significantly weakened the already faltering Ming.
APPROXIMATE MAXIMUM NUMBER OF MEN UNDER ARMS: Unknown
CASUALTIES: Unknown
TREATIES: None

Repulsed by the Ming at the conclusion of the MANCHU CONQUEST OF CHINA: MANCHU-MING WAR in 1628, the Manchus turned to the north and launched an invasion into northern China by way of the Chengde Pass. Ming forces repulsed them here; however, the Manchu then descended upon Shanxi (Shansi) province in two sets of raids, during 1632 and 1634, causing considerable destruction.

Recognizing the power and effectiveness of artillery, which had repulsed him twice during the Manchu-Ming War (1618–28), the Manchu leader Abahai (1592–1643) began developing artillery weapons and artillery units of his own. These he began to use against the Ming in open battle, and while the raids into northern China did not culminate in the overthrow of the Ming, they did weaken the dynasty, which went into steep decline before mid-century.

See also MANCHU CONQUEST OF CHINA: MANCHU INVASION OF KOREA; MANCHU CONQUEST OF CHINA: MANCHU CONQUEST OF INNER MONGOLIA; MANCHU CONQUEST OF CHINA: CHINESE (MING) CIVIL WARS; MANCHU CONQUEST OF CHINA: MANCHU ESTABLISH QING DYNASTY; MANCHU

CONQUEST OF CHINA: MANCHU CONQUEST OF KOREA; MANCHU CONQUEST OF CHINA: LI ZICHENG'S REBELLION AND FALL OF THE MING; MANCHU CONQUEST OF CHINA: MANCHU-MING WAR FOR YANGTZE VALLEY; MANCHU CONQUEST OF CHINA: MANCHU CONQUEST OF FUJIAN; MANCHU CONQUEST OF CHINA: GUI WANG'S CAMPAIGNS; MANCHU CONQUEST OF CHINA: MANCHU CONQUEST OF SOUTHWEST CHINA; MANCHU CONQUEST OF CHINA: MANCHU-MING PIRATE WAR; MANCHU CONQUEST OF CHINA: REVOLT OF THE THREE VICEROYS; MANCHU CONQUEST OF CHINA: ANNEXATION OF TAIWAN; MANCHU CONQUEST OF TIBET.

Further reading: Wolfram Eberhart, *A History of China,* 3rd ed. (Berkeley: University of California Press, 1969); Charles O. Hucker, *China's Imperial Past: An Introduction to Chinese History and Culture* (Stanford, Calif.: Stanford University Press, 1975); J. A. Roberts, *A Concise History of China* (Cambridge, Mass.: Harvard University Press, 1999); Jonathan D. Spence and John E. Wills, Jr., *From Ming to Ch'ing: Conquest, Region and Continuity in Seventeenth-Century China* (New Haven, Conn.: Yale University Press, 1981).

Manchu Conquest of China: Manchu Conquest of Inner Mongolia (1633)

PRINCIPAL COMBATANTS: Manchus vs. Mongol army
PRINCIPAL THEATER(S): Inner Mongolia
DECLARATION: None
MAJOR ISSUES AND OBJECTIVES: Conquest of Inner Mongolia, with the object of further weakening the Ming hold on China.
OUTCOME: The Manchus were able to coax massive troop defections from the Mongol ranks and thereby overrun the country.
APPROXIMATE MAXIMUM NUMBER OF MEN UNDER ARMS: Unknown
CASUALTIES: Unknown, but generally light
TREATIES: None

While in the north (*see* MANCHU CONQUEST OF CHINA: MANCHU RAIDS ON NORTH CHINA), a portion of the Manchu invading force was detached and sent into Inner Mongolia. Working with Mongolian defectors (a large group of soldiers who rebelled against harsh conditions in the Mongol army) the Manchu forces systematically overran the country, absorbing more and more Mongol troops into their ranks. By the end of the year, the Mongol army had been thoroughly compromised, and the Manchus were in control of Inner Mongolia.

See also MANCHU CONQUEST OF CHINA: MANCHU INVASION OF KOREA; MANCHU CONQUEST OF CHINA: MANCHU CONQUEST OF CHINA: MANCHU-MING WAR; MANCHU CONQUEST OF CHINA: CHINESE (MING) CIVIL WARS;

MANCHU CONQUEST OF CHINA: MANCHU ESTABLISH QING DYNASTY; MANCHU CONQUEST OF CHINA: MANCHU CONQUEST OF KOREA; MANCHU CONQUEST OF CHINA: LI ZICHENG'S REBELLION AND FALL OF THE MING; MANCHU CONQUEST OF CHINA: MANCHU-MING WAR FOR YANGTZE VALLEY; MANCHU CONQUEST OF CHINA: MANCHU CONQUEST OF FUJIAN; MANCHU CONQUEST OF CHINA: GUI WANG'S CAMPAIGNS; MANCHU CONQUEST OF CHINA: MANCHU CONQUEST OF SOUTHWEST CHINA; MANCHU CONQUEST OF CHINA: MANCHU-MING PIRATE WAR; MANCHU CONQUEST OF CHINA: REVOLT OF THE THREE VICEROYS; MANCHU CONQUEST OF CHINA: ANNEXATION OF TAIWAN; MANCHU CONQUEST OF TIBET.

Further reading: Wolfram Eberhart, *A History of China,* 3rd ed. (Berkeley: University of California Press, 1969); Charles O. Hucker, *China's Imperial Past: An Introduction to Chinese History and Culture* (Stanford, Calif.: Stanford University Press, 1975); J. A. Roberts, *A Concise History of China* (Cambridge, Mass.: Harvard University Press, 1999); Jonathan D. Spence and John E. Wills, Jr., *From Ming to Ch'ing: Conquest, Region and Continuity in Seventeenth-Century China* (New Haven, Conn.: Yale University Press, 1981).

Manchu Conquest of China: Chinese (Ming) Civil Wars (1635–1644)

PRINCIPAL COMBATANTS: Li Zicheng (Li Tzu-ch'eng) (and other warlords, including Manchus and leaders of independent factions) vs. the Ming dynasty
PRINCIPAL THEATER(S): Throughout China
DECLARATION: None
MAJOR ISSUES AND OBJECTIVES: General rebellion against Ming rule
OUTCOME: The Ming dynasty was overthrown.
APPROXIMATE MAXIMUM NUMBER OF MEN UNDER ARMS: Li Zicheng commanded as many as 300,000 men; although Ming forces were of commensurate size, they were led with disastrous ineffectiveness.
CASUALTIES: Unknown, but doubtless extremely heavy among the Ming defenders of Beijing (Peking)
TREATIES: None

The CHINESE CIVIL WAR of 1621–44 may be seen, in part, as a function of Manchu efforts to overthrow the Ming dynasty. As a result of relentless Manchu military campaigning (*see* MANCHU CONQUEST OF CHINA: MANCHU-MING WAR; MANCHU CONQUEST OF CHINA: MANCHU RAIDS ON NORTH CHINA, and MANCHU CONQUEST OF CHINA: MANCHU CONQUEST OF INNER MONGOLIA), the Ming dynasty entered a period of steep decline during 1635–44, coinciding with the culmination of the Chinese Civil War of this period.

Rebellion was widespread throughout China, as the Ming rulers reeled under the Manchu onslaught and fell victim to the devastating effects of famine and flood as well as intense political intrigue. Many throughout China were bereft of their homes, and warlords, some independent, some in the service of the Manchu, recruited legions of the homeless and desperate in a struggle against the Mings.

The warlord Li Zicheng (1606–45) made an unsuccessful attempt to capture the provincial capital of Sichuan (Szechwan) in 1637. Defeated but not beaten, he marched into Shanxi (Shansi), defeated the Ming presence there, then, in 1640, did the same in Henan (Honan). By 1642, both Shanxi and Henan were under his control. Declaring himself emperor, he mustered an army of 300,000 and marched against Beijing, the imperial capital. The capital was defended by forces of ample size; however, two Ming armies were commanded by bitter rivals, who refused to cooperate and coordinate their defense. The result was disastrous defeat. Li Zizcheng's army entered the city in triumph, the last of the Ming emperors committed suicide, and the warlord briefly assumed the throne.

See also MANCHU CONQUEST OF CHINA: MANCHU INVASION OF KOREA; MANCHU CONQUEST OF CHINA: MANCHU ESTABLISH QING DYNASTY; MANCHU CONQUEST OF CHINA: MANCHU CONQUEST OF KOREA; MANCHU CONQUEST OF CHINA: LI ZICHENG'S REBELLION AND FALL OF THE MING; MANCHU CONQUEST OF CHINA: MANCHU-MING WAR FOR YANGTZE VALLEY; MANCHU CONQUEST OF CHINA: MANCHU CONQUEST OF FUJIAN; MANCHU CONQUEST OF CHINA: GUI WANG'S CAMPAIGNS; MANCHU CONQUEST OF CHINA: MANCHU CONQUEST OF SOUTHWEST CHINA; MANCHU CONQUEST OF CHINA: MANCHU-MING PIRATE WAR; MANCHU CONQUEST OF CHINA: REVOLT OF THE THREE VICEROYS; MANCHU CONQUEST OF CHINA: ANNEXATION OF TAIWAN; MANCHU CONQUEST OF TIBET.

Further reading: Wolfram Eberhart, *A History of China,* 3rd ed. (Berkeley: University of California Press, 1969); Charles O. Hucker, *China's Imperial Past: An Introduction to Chinese History and Culture* (Stanford, Calif.: Stanford University Press, 1975); J. A. Roberts, *A Concise History of China* (Cambridge, Mass.: Harvard University Press, 1999); Jonathan D. Spence and John E. Wills, Jr., *From Ming to Ch'ing: Conquest, Region and Continuity in Seventeenth-Century China* (New Haven, Conn.: Yale University Press, 1981).

Manchu Conquest of China: Manchu Establish Qing Dynasty (1636)

PRINCIPAL COMBATANTS: Manchus vs. Mings
PRINCIPAL THEATER(S): China
DECLARATION: None

MAJOR ISSUES AND OBJECTIVES: Consolidation of power, proclamation of a new Qing (Ch'ing) dynasty.
OUTCOME: The culmination of wars on several fronts, the establishment of the Qing dynasty ensured the ultimate success of the Manchus.
APPROXIMATE MAXIMUM NUMBER OF MEN UNDER ARMS: Unknown
CASUALTIES: Unknown
TREATIES: None

Following or concurrently with the MANCHU CONQUEST OF CHINA: MANCHU-MING WAR, from 1618 to 1628, the MANCHU CONQUEST OF CHINA: MANCHU RAIDS ON NORTH CHINA, from 1629 to 1634, the MANCHU CONQUEST OF CHINA: MANCHU CONQUEST OF INNER Mongolia in 1633, MANCHU CONQUEST OF CHINA: CHINESE (MING) CIVIL WARS, from 1635 to 1644, and the MANCHU CONQUEST OF CHINA: MANCHU CONQUEST OF KOREA, from 1636 to 1637, and at the start of Manchu consolidation of positions in the Amur Basin (during 1636–44), Abahai (1592–1643), dynamic leader of the Manchus, proclaimed a new imperial dynasty, the Qing, at Shenyang. Abahai took the title of Chongde (Ch'ung-te).

Further reading: Wolfram Eberhart, *A History of China*, 3rd ed. (Berkeley: University of California Press, 1969); Charles O. Hucker, *China's Imperial Past: An Introduction to Chinese History and Culture* (Stanford, Calif.: Stanford University Press, 1975); J. A. Roberts, *A Concise History of China* (Cambridge, Mass.: Harvard University Press, 1999); Jonathan D. Spence and John E. Wills, Jr., *From Ming to Ch'ing: Conquest, Region and Continuity in Seventeenth-Century China* (New Haven, Conn.: Yale University Press, 1981).

Manchu Conquest of China: Manchu Conquest of Korea (1636–1637)

PRINCIPAL COMBATANTS: Manchus vs. Koreans
PRINCIPAL THEATER(S): Korea
DECLARATION: None
MAJOR ISSUES AND OBJECTIVES: The Manchus sought to compel Korean renunciation of the Mings.
OUTCOME: The renunciation was secured.
APPROXIMATE MAXIMUM NUMBER OF MEN UNDER ARMS: Manchus, 100,000; Koreans, numbers unknown
CASUALTIES: Unknown
TREATIES: None

Allied to the Mings (*see* MANCHU CONQUEST OF CHINA: MANCHU-MING WAR), the Koreans failed to render tribute to the Manchus during the decline of the Ming dynasty. Moreover, the Koreans, for the most part, refused to cooperate with the Manchus in campaigns against the Mings. For these reasons, Abahai, the Manchu leader, invaded Korea with a force of 100,000. This was sufficient to overawe the Koreans, whose rulers agreed to a formal renunciation of the Ming dynasty.

See also MANCHU CONQUEST OF CHINA: MANCHU INVASION OF KOREA; MANCHU CONQUEST OF CHINA: MANCHU RAIDS ON NORTH CHINA: MANCHU CONQUEST OF CHINA: MANCHU CONQUEST OF INNER Mongolia; MANCHU CONQUEST OF CHINA: MANCHU ESTABLISH QING DYNASTY; MANCHU CONQUEST OF CHINA: CHINESE (MING) CIVIL WARS; MANCHU CONQUEST OF CHINA: LI ZICHENG'S REBELLION AND FALL OF THE MING; MANCHU CONQUEST OF CHINA: MANCHU-MING WAR FOR YANGTZE VALLEY; MANCHU CONQUEST OF CHINA: MANCHU CONQUEST OF FUJIAN; MANCHU CONQUEST OF CHINA: GUI WANG'S CAMPAIGNS; MANCHU CONQUEST OF CHINA: MANCHU CONQUEST OF SOUTHWEST China; MANCHU CONQUEST OF CHINA: MANCHU-MING PIRATE WAR; MANCHU CONQUEST OF CHINA: REVOLT OF THE THREE VICEROYS; MANCHU CONQUEST OF CHINA: ANNEXATION OF TAIWAN; MANCHU CONQUEST OF TIBET.

Further reading: Wolfram Eberhart, *A History of China*, 3rd ed. (Berkeley: University of California Press, 1969); Charles O. Hucker, *China's Imperial Past: An Introduction to Chinese History and Culture* (Stanford, Calif.: Stanford University Press, 1975); J. A. Roberts, *A Concise History of China* (Cambridge, Mass.: Harvard University Press, 1999); Jonathan D. Spence and John E. Wills, Jr., *From Ming to Ch'ing: Conquest, Region and Continuity in Seventeenth-Century China* (New Haven, Conn.: Yale University Press, 1981).

Manchu Conquest of China: Li Zicheng's Rebellion and Fall of the Ming (1644)

PRINCIPAL COMBATANTS: Manchus vs. Li Zicheng (Li Tzuch'eng) and, separately, the Ming
PRINCIPAL THEATER(S): Beijing (Peking), China
DECLARATION: None
MAJOR ISSUES AND OBJECTIVES: A desperate Ming general called for Manchu aid to eject rebels from Beijing; this effectively invited Manchu occupation of the capital.
OUTCOME: Victorious over the rebels, the Manchus occupied Beijing, thereby completing the overthrow of the Ming dynasty and its replacement by the Qing (Ch'ing).
APPROXIMATE MAXIMUM NUMBER OF MEN UNDER ARMS: Numbers not known, but the Manchu force was very large and significantly outnumbered the forces under Li Zicheng.
CASUALTIES: Unknown
TREATIES: None

The Manchus had steadily eroded the power of the Ming dynasty through the MANCHU CONQUEST OF CHINA: MANCHU-MING WAR, MANCHU CONQUEST OF CHINA: MANCHU RAIDS ON NORTH CHINA, MANCHU CONQUEST OF CHINA: MANCHU CONQUEST OF INNER Mongolia, MANCHU CONQUEST OF CHINA: CHINESE (MING) CIVIL WARS, and the MANCHU CONQUEST OF CHINA: MANCHU CONQUEST OF KOREA, and in 1636, proclaimed the Qing dynasty (*see* MANCHU CONQUEST OF CHINA: MANCHU ESTABLISH QING DYNASTY). The Ming were ripe to fall, and on May 26, 1644, Li Zicheng (1606–45), a rebel leader and social bandit, overran and occupied Beijing. In desperation, the Ming general Wu Sangui (Wu San-kuei; d. 1678) called on the Manchus for aid in overthrowing Li and his rebel regime. The Manchus rushed in with a large army and, in a momentous battle fought a short distance to the south of the Great Wall, the Manchus defeated Li Zicheng. The Manchus now occupied Beijing, thereby bringing about the final collapse of the Ming dynasty and its replacement by the Qing.

Further reading: Wolfram Eberhart, *A History of China*, 3rd ed. (Berkeley: University of California Press, 1969); Charles O. Hucker, *China's Imperial Past: An Introduction to Chinese History and Culture* (Stanford, Calif.: Stanford University Press, 1975); J. A. Roberts, *A Concise History of China* (Cambridge, Mass.: Harvard University Press, 1999); Jonathan D. Spence and John E. Wills, Jr., *From Ming to Ch'ing: Conquest, Region and Continuity in Seventeenth-Century China* (New Haven, Conn.: Yale University Press, 1981).

Manchu Conquest of China: Manchu-Ming War for Yangtze Valley (1644–1645)

PRINCIPAL COMBATANTS: Manchus vs. Mings (under Prince Fu)
PRINCIPAL THEATER(S): Yangzhou (Yangchow) and Nanjing (Nanking) area
DECLARATION: None
MAJOR ISSUES AND OBJECTIVES: Prince Fu sought to resist the final Manchu takeover.
OUTCOME: After a bloody battle and subsequent massacre, Nanjing fell to the Manchus and Fu fled the field.
APPROXIMATE MAXIMUM NUMBER OF MEN UNDER ARMS: Unknown
CASUALTIES: Virtually all of the Ming army in and around Yangzhou and Nanjing was slaughtered; civilian casualties were extremely high.
TREATIES: None

The Manchu occupation of Beijing (Peking) in Li Zicheng's Li Tzu-ch'eng's (1606–45) 1644 rebellion (*see* MANCHU CONQUEST OF CHINA: LI ZICHENG'S REBELLION AND FALL OF THE MING), for all practical purposes, brought about the final collapse of the Ming dynasty and its displacement by the Qing (Ch'ing) dynasty; however, the Ming prince Fu (r. 1644–45) set up a Ming government in exile at Nanjing, boldly defying Manchu invaders.

The Manchu prince Dorgon (1611–46) led an army against Fu in a week-long battle that centered around Yangzhou. The Ming army was defeated, and the Manchus followed their victory with a general massacre, not only of the defeated army, but of the civilian inhabitants of the Yangzhou area. This rapidly brought about the surrender of Nanjing. Fu fled and became lost to history. The Manchu—as the Qing—now faced sporadic, though stiff, resistance from members of the Ming royal family (cousins of those who had been in the direct line of succession). Although often destructive, this opposition never posed a serious threat of reestablishing the Ming dynasty.

See also MANCHU CONQUEST OF CHINA: MANCHU INVASION OF KOREA; MANCHU CONQUEST OF CHINA: MANCHU-MING WAR; MANCHU CONQUEST OF CHINA: MANCHU RAIDS ON NORTH CHINA; MANCHU CONQUEST OF CHINA: MANCHU CONQUEST OF INNER MONGOLIA; MANCHU CONQUEST OF CHINA: MANCHU ESTABLISH QING DYNASTY; MANCHU CONQUEST OF CHINA: CHINESE (MING) CIVIL WARS; MANCHU CONQUEST OF CHINA: MANCHU CONQUEST OF KOREA; MANCHU CONQUEST OF CHINA: MANCHU CONQUEST OF FUJIAN; MANCHU CONQUEST OF CHINA: GUI WANG'S CAMPAIGNS; MANCHU CONQUEST OF CHINA: MANCHU CONQUEST OF SOUTHWEST CHINA; MANCHU CONQUEST OF CHINA: MANCHU-MING PIRATE WAR; MANCHU CONQUEST OF CHINA: REVOLT OF THE THREE VICEROYS; MANCHU CONQUEST OF CHINA: ANNEXATION OF TAIWAN; MANCHU CONQUEST OF TIBET.

Further reading: Wolfram Eberhart, *A History of China*, 3rd ed. (Berkeley: University of California Press, 1969); Charles O. Hucker, *China's Imperial Past: An Introduction to Chinese History and Culture* (Stanford, Calif.: Stanford University Press, 1975); J. A. Roberts, *A Concise History of China* (Cambridge, Mass.: Harvard University Press, 1999); Jonathan D. Spence and John E. Wills, Jr., *From Ming to Ch'ing: Conquest, Region and Continuity in Seventeenth-Century China* (New Haven, Conn.: Yale University Press, 1981).

Manchu Conquest of China: Manchu Conquest of Fujian (1645–1647)

PRINCIPAL COMBATANTS: Manchus vs. Mings
PRINCIPAL THEATER(S): Fujian (Fukien) Province
DECLARATION: None
MAJOR ISSUES AND OBJECTIVES: The Manchus exploited dissension and disunity among remaining members of the Ming royal family to conquer Fujian.
OUTCOME: Guangzhou (Kwangchow) and Fujian fell to the Manchus.

APPROXIMATE MAXIMUM NUMBER OF MEN UNDER ARMS:
Unknown
CASUALTIES: Unknown
TREATIES: None

As a direct result of the fall of Beijing (Peking) in the 1644 MANCHU CONQUEST OF CHINA: LI ZICHENG'S [LI TZU-CH'ENG'S] REBELLION AND FALL OF THE MING, the Ming dynasty was effectively crushed; however, resistance persisted at Nanjing and Yangzhou (*see* MANCHU CONQUEST OF CHINA: MANCHU-MING WAR FOR YANGTZE VALLEY). This was brutally crushed, but sporadic Ming resistance continued among rival claimants to the Ming throne. Recognizing that the internal disputes among these claimants rendered the remaining Ming useless as a force of resistance, the Manchus exploited the dissension by campaigning through Fujian Province. In 1647, the Manchus were in possession of Guangzhou, and Ming resistance in the province had been completely neutralized, leaving only significant pockets of Ming opposition in Sichuan (Szechwan), Shaanxi (Shensi), and Shanxi (Shansi).

See also MANCHU CONQUEST OF CHINA: MANCHU INVASION OF KOREA; MANCHU CONQUEST OF CHINA: MANCHU-MING WAR; MANCHU CONQUEST OF CHINA: MANCHU RAIDS ON NORTH CHINA; MANCHU CONQUEST OF CHINA: MANCHU CONQUEST OF INNER MONGOLIA; MANCHU CONQUEST OF CHINA: MANCHU ESTABLISH QING DYNASTY; MANCHU CONQUEST OF CHINA: CHINESE (MING) CIVIL WARS; MANCHU CONQUEST OF CHINA: MANCHU CONQUEST OF KOREA; MANCHU CONQUEST OF CHINA: GUI WANG'S CAMPAIGNS; MANCHU CONQUEST OF CHINA: MANCHU CONQUEST OF SOUTHWEST China; MANCHU CONQUEST OF CHINA: MANCHU-MING PIRATE WAR; MANCHU CONQUEST OF CHINA: REVOLT OF THE THREE VICEROYS; MANCHU CONQUEST OF CHINA: ANNEXATION OF TAIWAN; MANCHU CONQUEST OF TIBET.

Further reading: Wolfram Eberhart, *A History of China,* 3rd ed. (Berkeley: University of California Press, 1969); Charles O. Hucker, *China's Imperial Past: An Introduction to Chinese History and Culture* (Stanford, Calif.: Stanford University Press, 1975); J. A. Roberts, *A Concise History of China* (Cambridge, Mass.: Harvard University Press, 1999); Jonathan D. Spence and John E. Wills, Jr., *From Ming to Ch'ing: Conquest, Region and Continuity in Seventeenth-Century China* (New Haven, Conn.: Yale University Press, 1981).

Manchu Conquest of China: Gui Wang's Campaigns (1648–1651)

PRINCIPAL COMBATANTS: Manchus vs. Ming forces under Prince Gui (Kuei Wang)
PRINCIPAL THEATER(S): Southern China

DECLARATION: None
MAJOR ISSUES AND OBJECTIVES: Gui, the last Ming prince, sought to maintain control of southern China.
OUTCOME: Prince Gui was defeated by Manchu forces under Prince Dorgon and forced to retreat to the mountains of the southwest.
APPROXIMATE MAXIMUM NUMBER OF MEN UNDER ARMS:
Unknown
CASUALTIES: More than 100,000 died in Guangzhou.
TREATIES: None

The last prince of the Mings, Gui (d. 1662), attracted a significant following of Ming diehards following the otherwise virtually total collapse of the dynasty. Prince Gui was a fine military leader, who was able to seize control of much of southern China, albeit briefly. Dorgon (1611–46), who had assumed leadership of the Manchus following the death of his brother Abahai (1592–1643), countered Gui by consolidating the Manchu hold on the Yangtze Valley. From this vast base, Dorgon was able to conduct a systematic campaign to retake southern China, mounting a siege of Canton, the most important Ming-held city in the south. In 1651, after eight months, some 100,000 Cantonese had died. Gui was driven out of the region and took refuge in the mountains of the southwest. There he took control, again briefly, over Guizhou (Kweichow) and Yunnan (*see* MANCHU CONQUEST OF CHINA: MANCHU CONQUEST OF SOUTHWEST CHINA).

See also MANCHU CONQUEST OF CHINA: MANCHU INVASION OF KOREA; MANCHU CONQUEST OF CHINA: MANCHU-MING WAR; MANCHU CONQUEST OF CHINA: MANCHU RAIDS ON NORTH CHINA; MANCHU CONQUEST OF CHINA: MANCHU CONQUEST OF INNER MONGOLIA; MANCHU CONQUEST OF CHINA: MANCHU ESTABLISH QING DYNASTY; MANCHU CONQUEST OF CHINA: CHINESE (MING) CIVIL WARS; MANCHU CONQUEST OF CHINA: LI ZICHENG'S REBELLION AND FALL OF THE MING; MANCHU CONQUEST OF CHINA: MANCHU CONQUEST OF KOREA; MANCHU CONQUEST OF CHINA: MANCHU-MING WAR FOR YANGTZE VALLEY; MANCHU CONQUEST OF CHINA: MANCHU CONQUEST OF FUJIAN; MANCHU CONQUEST OF CHINA: MANCHU-MING PIRATE WAR; MANCHU CONQUEST OF CHINA: REVOLT OF THE THREE VICEROYS; MANCHU CONQUEST OF CHINA: ANNEXATION OF TAIWAN; MANCHU CONQUEST OF TIBET.

Further reading: Wolfram Eberhart, *A History of China,* 3rd ed. (Berkeley: University of California Press, 1969); Charles O. Hucker, *China's Imperial Past: An Introduction to Chinese History and Culture* (Stanford, Calif.: Stanford University Press, 1975); J. A. Roberts, *A Concise History of China* (Cambridge, Mass.: Harvard University Press, 1999); Jonathan D. Spence and John E. Wills, Jr., *From Ming to Ch'ing: Conquest, Region and Continuity in Seventeenth-Century China* (New Haven, Conn.: Yale University Press, 1981).

Manchu Conquest of China: **Manchu Conquest of Southwest China** (1651–1659)

PRINCIPAL COMBATANTS: Manchus vs. Mings under Prince Gui (Kuei Wang)
PRINCIPAL THEATER(S): Mountains of southwest China (Guizhou [Kweichow] and Yunnan region)
DECLARATION: None
MAJOR ISSUES AND OBJECTIVES: Kuei Wang sought to retain control of this region.
OUTCOME: Through an arduous campaign, the Manchus wrested the mountainous southwest from Kuei Wang.
APPROXIMATE MAXIMUM NUMBER OF MEN UNDER ARMS: Unknown
CASUALTIES: Unknown
TREATIES: None

Following his defeat in most of southern China, Gui Wang (d. 1662), last of the Ming princes, retreated to the mountains of the southwest, where he continued to control Guizhou and Yunnan (*see* MANCHU CONQUEST OF CHINA: GUI WANG'S CAMPAIGNS). In the southwestern mountains, Gui Wang enjoyed the advantage of rugged terrain that made for effective defensive positions and was extremely difficult on any attacker. Nevertheless, through application of a long, patient, systematic, and persistent campaign, the Manchus gained control of the region. As for Gui Wang, he evaded capture, dying from natural causes in 1662.

See also MANCHU CONQUEST OF CHINA: MANCHU INVASION OF KOREA; MANCHU CONQUEST OF CHINA: MANCHU-MING WAR; MANCHU CONQUEST OF CHINA: MANCHU RAIDS ON NORTH CHINA; MANCHU CONQUEST OF CHINA: MANCHU CONQUEST OF INNER MONGOLIA; MANCHU CONQUEST OF CHINA: MANCHU ESTABLISH QING DYNASTY; MANCHU CONQUEST OF CHINA: CHINESE (MING) CIVIL WARS; MANCHU CONQUEST OF CHINA: LI ZICHENG'S REBELLION AND FALL OF THE MING; MANCHU CONQUEST OF CHINA: MANCHU CONQUEST OF KOREA; MANCHU CONQUEST OF CHINA: MANCHU-MING WAR FOR YANGTZE VALLEY; MANCHU CONQUEST OF CHINA: MANCHU CONQUEST OF FUJIAN; MANCHU CONQUEST OF CHINA: MANCHU-MING PIRATE WAR; MANCHU CONQUEST OF CHINA: REVOLT OF THE THREE VICEROYS; MANCHU CONQUEST OF CHINA: ANNEXATION OF TAIWAN; MANCHU CONQUEST OF TIBET.

Further reading: Wolfram Eberhart, *A History of China*, 3rd ed. (Berkeley: University of California Press, 1969); Charles O. Hucker, *China's Imperial Past: An Introduction to Chinese History and Culture* (Stanford, Calif.: Stanford University Press, 1975); J. A. Roberts, *A Concise History of China* (Cambridge, Mass.: Harvard University Press, 1999); Jonathan D. Spence and John E. Wills, Jr., *From Ming to Ch'ing: Conquest, Region and Continuity in Seventeenth-Century China* (New Haven, Conn.: Yale University Press, 1981).

Manchu Conquest of China: **Manchu-Ming Pirate War** (1652–1662)

PRINCIPAL COMBATANTS: Manchus vs. (separately) Dutch and Ming-allied pirates under Koxinga
PRINCIPAL THEATER(S): Nanjing and nearby coastal provinces
DECLARATION: None
MAJOR ISSUES AND OBJECTIVES: The pirates sought and obtained control of a large coastal region.
OUTCOME: The pirates prevailed wherever they struck, but the death of their leader, Koxinga, in 1662, brought the pirate menace to an end.
APPROXIMATE MAXIMUM NUMBER OF MEN UNDER ARMS: Unknown
CASUALTIES: Unknown
TREATIES: None

Following the collapse of the Mings in 1659, a pirate family in the employ of the Mings continued to wage war against the Manchus. The most famous of the pirate leaders was Zheng Chenggong (Cheg Ch'eng-kung; 1624–62), known to the Europeans (whom the pirates also fought) as Koxinga.

Koxinga's harassment of the Manchus was constant and effective. In 1653, he captured Xiamen and, three years later, Chongming Island. This put him in position to mount a successful assault on Nanjing in 1657.

While he kept the Manchus occupied, Koxinga also attacked the European presence in China, most dramatically at Taiwan, which he attacked with a fleet of 900 ships in 1661. After he held Fort Zelanda (at Anping) under siege from 1661 to 1662, the Dutch surrendered, and the Manchus—or Qing—had to evacuate six coastal provinces. The Qing leaders withdrew settlers 10 miles inland and provided a guarded barrier for their defense.

Ultimately, it was the death of the charismatic Koxinga, not Manchu military might, that ended the pirate scourge in 1662.

See also MANCHU CONQUEST OF CHINA: MANCHU INVASION OF KOREA; MANCHU CONQUEST OF CHINA: MANCHU-MING WAR; MANCHU CONQUEST OF CHINA: MANCHU RAIDS ON NORTH CHINA; MANCHU CONQUEST OF CHINA: MANCHU CONQUEST OF INNER MONGOLIA; MANCHU CONQUEST OF CHINA: MANCHU ESTABLISH QING DYNASTY; MANCHU CONQUEST OF CHINA: CHINESE (MING) CIVIL WARS; MANCHU CONQUEST OF CHINA: LI ZICHENG'S REBELLION AND FALL OF THE MING; MANCHU CONQUEST OF CHINA: MANCHU CONQUEST OF KOREA; MANCHU CONQUEST OF CHINA: MANCHU-MING WAR FOR YANGTZE VAL-

LEY; MANCHU CONQUEST OF CHINA: MANCHU CONQUEST OF FUJIAN; MANCHU CONQUEST OF CHINA: GUI WANG'S CAMPAIGNS; MANCHU CONQUEST OF CHINA: MANCHU CONQUEST OF SOUTHWEST CHINA; MANCHU CONQUEST OF CHINA: REVOLT OF THE THREE VICEROYS; MANCHU CONQUEST OF CHINA: ANNEXATION OF TAIWAN; MANCHU CONQUEST OF TIBET.

Further reading: Wolfram Eberhart, *A History of China*, 3rd ed. (Berkeley: University of California Press, 1969); Charles O. Hucker, *China's Imperial Past: An Introduction to Chinese History and Culture* (Stanford, Calif.: Stanford University Press, 1975); J. A. Roberts, *A Concise History of China* (Cambridge, Mass.: Harvard University Press, 1999); Jonathan D. Spence and John E. Wills, Jr., *From Ming to Ch'ing: Conquest, Region and Continuity in Seventeenth-Century China* (New Haven, Conn.: Yale University Press, 1981).

Manchu Conquest of China: Revolt of the Three Viceroys (1674–1681)

PRINCIPAL COMBATANTS: Manchus (Qing, Ch'ing) vs. rebellious viceroys of Yunnan, Jiangxi (Kiangsi), and Fujian (Fukien) Provinces
PRINCIPAL THEATER(S): Yunnan, Jiangxi, and Fujian Provinces
DECLARATION: None, but the revolt was precipitated by an imperial Qing decree of 1673, ordering the removal of three provincial viceroys
MAJOR ISSUES AND OBJECTIVES: The viceroys resisted an imperial Qing order for their removal.
OUTCOME: The rebel viceroys held a vast territory for several years, but patient and persistent application of military force finally quelled the rebellion.
APPROXIMATE MAXIMUM NUMBER OF MEN UNDER ARMS: Unknown
CASUALTIES: Unknown
TREATIES: None

In 1673, the Qing emperor Kangxi (K'ang-hsi; 1654–1722), concerned over the consolidation of power among three of his provincial viceroys or governors, at Yunnan, Jiangxi, and Fujian, ordered their removal. The viceroy of Yunnan, Wu Sangui (Wu San-kuei; 1612–78), formerly a Ming general, resisted removal and took a stand in Sichuan Guizhou, Hunan, and Guangxi Zhuangzu, tenaciously holding these provinces. He was joined in his resistance by the viceroys of Jiangxi and Fujian. Through continual application of military pressure, however, the rebellion was quelled by 1681, Qing control reestablished, and the removal of the viceroys finally effected.

See also MANCHU CONQUEST OF CHINA: MANCHU INVASION OF KOREA; MANCHU CONQUEST OF CHINA: MANCHU-

MING WAR; MANCHU CONQUEST OF CHINA: MANCHU RAIDS ON NORTH CHINA; MANCHU CONQUEST OF CHINA: MANCHU CONQUEST OF INNER MONGOLIA; MANCHU CONQUEST OF CHINA: MANCHU ESTABLISH QING DYNASTY; MANCHU CONQUEST OF CHINA: CHINESE (MING) CIVIL WARS; MANCHU CONQUEST OF CHINA: LI ZICHENG'S REBELLION AND FALL OF THE MING; MANCHU CONQUEST OF CHINA: MANCHU CONQUEST OF KOREA; MANCHU CONQUEST OF CHINA: MANCHU-MING WAR FOR YANGTZE VALLEY; MANCHU CONQUEST OF CHINA: MANCHU CONQUEST OF FUJIAN; MANCHU CONQUEST OF CHINA: GUI WANG'S CAMPAIGNS; MANCHU CONQUEST OF CHINA: MANCHU CONQUEST OF SOUTHWEST CHINA; MANCHU CONQUEST OF CHINA: MANCHU-MING PIRATE WAR; MANCHU CONQUEST OF CHINA: ANNEXATION OF TAIWAN; and MANCHU CONQUEST OF TIBET.

Further reading: Wolfram Eberhart, *A History of China*, 3rd ed. (Berkeley: University of California Press, 1969); Charles O. Hucker, *China's Imperial Past: An Introduction to Chinese History and Culture* (Stanford, Calif.: Stanford University Press, 1975); J. A. Roberts, *A Concise History of China* (Cambridge, Mass.: Harvard University Press, 1999); Jonathan D. Spence and John E. Wills, Jr., *From Ming to Ch'ing: Conquest, Region and Continuity in Seventeenth-Century China* (New Haven, Conn.: Yale University Press, 1981).

Manchu Conquest of China: Annexation of Taiwan (1683)

PRINCIPAL COMBATANTS: Manchus vs. Taiwanese
PRINCIPAL THEATER(S): Taiwan
DECLARATION: None
MAJOR ISSUES AND OBJECTIVES: Annexation of Taiwan
OUTCOME: Faced with the overwhelming power of the Manchus, the ruler of Taiwan yielded to them and accepted annexation of the island.
APPROXIMATE MAXIMUM NUMBER OF MEN UNDER ARMS: Unknown
CASUALTIES: Unknown
TREATIES: Formal annexation documentation, 1683; this was a political settlement.

Following the Manchu wars of conquest and the successful suppression of rebels between 1674 and 1681 in the Revolt of the Three Viceroys (*see* MANCHU CONQUEST OF CHINA: REVOLT OF THE THREE VICEROYS), Zheng Keshuang (Cheng K'o shuang; 1670–1707 B.C.E.) son and successor to Zheng Jin (Cheng Chin; d. 1681) (fl. mid 17th century), surrendered Taiwan to the Manchus without offering significant resistance.

See also MANCHU CONQUEST OF CHINA: MANCHU INVASION OF KOREA; MANCHU CONQUEST OF CHINA: MANCHU-MING WAR; MANCHU CONQUEST OF CHINA:

MANCHU RAIDS ON NORTH CHINA; MANCHU CONQUEST OF CHINA: MANCHU CONQUEST OF INNER MONGOLIA; MANCHU CONQUEST OF CHINA: MANCHU ESTABLISH QING DYNASTY; MANCHU CONQUEST OF CHINA: CHINESE (MING) CIVIL WARS; MANCHU CONQUEST OF CHINA: LI ZICHENG'S REBELLION AND FALL OF THE MING; MANCHU CONQUEST OF CHINA: MANCHU CONQUEST OF KOREA; MANCHU CONQUEST OF CHINA: MANCHU-MING WAR FOR YANGTZE VALLEY; MANCHU CONQUEST OF CHINA: MANCHU CONQUEST OF FUJIAN; MANCHU CONQUEST OF CHINA: GUI WANG'S CAMPAIGNS; MANCHU CONQUEST OF CHINA: MANCHU CONQUEST OF SOUTHWEST CHINA; MANCHU CONQUEST OF CHINA: MANCHU-MING PIRATE WAR; MANCHU CONQUEST OF CHINA: REVOLT OF THE THREE VICEROYS; MANCHU CONQUEST OF TIBET.

Further reading: Wolfram Eberhart, *A History of China*, 3rd ed. (Berkeley: University of California Press, 1969); Charles O. Hucker, *China's Imperial Past: An Introduction to Chinese History and Culture* (Stanford, Calif.: Stanford University Press, 1975); J. A. Roberts, *A Concise History of China* (Cambridge, Mass.: Harvard University Press, 1999); Jonathan D. Spence and John E. Wills, Jr., *From Ming to Ch'ing: Conquest, Region and Continuity in Seventeenth-Century China* (New Haven, Conn.: Yale University Press, 1981).

Manchu Conquest of Tibet (1720)

PRINCIPAL COMBATANTS: Manchus vs. Dzungar Mongols
PRINCIPAL THEATER(S): Tibet
DECLARATION: None
MAJOR ISSUES AND OBJECTIVES: Control of Tibet
OUTCOME: The Manchus took control of Tibet from the Dzungars, installing a garrison as well as a pliable Dalai Lama.
APPROXIMATE MAXIMUM NUMBER OF MEN UNDER ARMS: Three Chinese armies, presumably a total of about 30,000; Mongol numbers unknown
CASUALTIES: Unknown
TREATIES: None

The Manchu (Qing or Ch'ing) ruler Kanxi (K'ang-hsi; 1645–1722) dispatched two armies to invade Tibet. One advanced from Gansu, and the other from Sichuan. The invasion came swiftly and with much violence. The armies converged against the Dzungars, destroying many, and driving out of the region those who survived.

While this operation was under way, a third Manchu army invaded Junggar and captured Urumqi and Turfan. The Mongol forces resisted in large part with European-supplied muskets—the first time they made use of this weapon. Nevertheless, the weapon was new to them, and they did not use it with tactical effectiveness. The Manchu

forces were larger and better equipped, and they overwhelmed the Mongols here as well.

The Manchus installed a new Dalai Lama, Kelzang Gyatso (1708–57), popular with the Tibetans and yet compliant with Manchu wishes. This puppet ruler was supplemented by a Manchu garrison installed at Lhasa, and thus Manchu control of Tibet was established and consolidated.

See also MANCHU CONQUEST OF CHINA: MANCHU INVASION OF KOREA; MANCHU CONQUEST OF CHINA: MANCHU-MING WAR; MANCHU CONQUEST OF CHINA: MANCHU RAIDS ON NORTH CHINA; MANCHU CONQUEST OF CHINA: MANCHU CONQUEST OF INNER MONGOLIA; MANCHU CONQUEST OF CHINA: MANCHU ESTABLISH QING DYNASTY; MANCHU CONQUEST OF CHINA: CHINESE (MING) CIVIL WARS; MANCHU CONQUEST OF CHINA: LI ZICHENG'S REBELLION AND FALL OF THE MING; MANCHU CONQUEST OF CHINA: MANCHU CONQUEST OF KOREA; MANCHU CONQUEST OF CHINA: MANCHU-MING WAR FOR YANGTZE VALLEY; MANCHU CONQUEST OF CHINA: MANCHU CONQUEST OF FUJIAN; MANCHU CONQUEST OF CHINA: GUI WANG'S CAMPAIGNS; MANCHU CONQUEST OF CHINA: MANCHU CONQUEST OF SOUTHWEST CHINA; MANCHU CONQUEST OF CHINA: MANCHU-MING PIRATE WAR; MANCHU CONQUEST OF CHINA: REVOLT OF THE THREE VICEROYS; MANCHU CONQUEST OF CHINA: ANNEXATION OF TAIWAN.

Further reading: Wolfram Eberhart, *A History of China*, 3rd ed. (Berkeley: University of California Press, 1969); Charles O. Hucker, *China's Imperial Past: An Introduction to Chinese History and Culture* (Stanford, Calif.: Stanford University Press, 1975); J. A. Roberts, *A Concise History of China* (Cambridge, Mass.: Harvard University Press, 1999); Jonathan D. Spence and John E. Wills, Jr., *From Ming to Ch'ing: Conquest, Region and Continuity in Seventeenth-Century China* (New Haven, Conn.: Yale University Press, 1981).

Mandingo-French War, First (1885–1886)

PRINCIPAL COMBATANTS: France vs. the Mandingo tribes
PRINCIPAL THEATER(S): Ivory Coast, Africa
DECLARATION: None
MAJOR ISSUES AND OBJECTIVES: The French sought control of the Ivory Coast; the Mandingo resisted.
OUTCOME: The Mandingo were defeated, and the French asserted control over the country, but the principal Mandingo leader, Almamy Samory Touré, evaded capture and organized a new resistance.
APPROXIMATE MAXIMUM NUMBER OF MEN UNDER ARMS: French and French colonial forces, about 2,000; Mandingo, 40,000
CASUALTIES: Unknown
TREATIES: None

Led by Chief Almamy Samory Touré (d. 1900), the Mandingo tribes of the Ivory Coast, West Africa, resisted French colonial forces, especially in the interior portions of the country. Samory was a natural military leader, who deployed his forces effectively, dividing them into corps, divisions, and companies. A major battle in 1886 resulted in the defeat of the Mandingo, but Almamy Samory Touré escaped, and the Mandingo accepted the Niger River as an absolute frontier. Although the French asserted control of the Ivory Coast, Samory resurfaced in 1894 to continue resistance in the SECOND MANDINGO-FRENCH WAR the following year.

Further reading: J. F. A. Ajayi and Michael Crowder, *History of West Africa,* 2nd ed., 2 vols. (London: Longman, 1976–1987); J. D. Fage and Roland Oliver, eds., *The Cambridge History of West Africa,* 8 vols. (New York: Cambridge University Press, 1975–1980); David L. Lewis, *The Race to Fashoda: Colonialism and African Resistance* (New York: Weidenfeld and Nicolson, 1987); Rodney Steel, *History of West Africa* (New York: Facts On File, 2003).

Mandingo-French War, Second (1894–1895)

PRINCIPAL COMBATANTS: France (with some British aid) vs. the Mandingo tribes
PRINCIPAL THEATER(S): Ivory Coast, Africa
DECLARATION: None
MAJOR ISSUES AND OBJECTIVES: The French sought control of the Ivory Coast; the Mandingo resisted and maintained control of the country's interior.
OUTCOME: Several French campaigns were launched into the interior; all failed.
APPROXIMATE MAXIMUM NUMBER OF MEN UNDER ARMS: Unknown
CASUALTIES: Unknown
TREATIES: None

After their victory in the First MANDINGO-FRENCH WAR, France declared a protectorate over the Ivory Coast; however, renewed resistance led by the Mandingo chief Almamy Samory Touré (d. 1900) kept French colonists out of the country's interior.

The French, sometimes with British assistance, fought 13 major battles and participated in many guerrilla actions, but the war ended inconclusively—although Samory had lost ground. It was not until the Third MANDINGO-FRENCH WAR in 1898 that Samory was captured and the Mandingo resistance definitively ended.

Further reading: J. F. A. Ajayi and Michael Crowder, *History of West Africa,* 2nd ed., 2 vols. (London: Longman, 1976–1987); J. D. Fage and Roland Oliver, eds., *The Cambridge History of West Africa,* 8 vols. (New York: Cambridge University Press, 1975–1980); David L. Lewis, *The Race to Fashoda: Colonialism and African Resistance* (New York: Weidenfeld and Nicolson, 1987); Rodney Steel, *History of West Africa* (New York: Facts On File, 2003).

Mandingo-French War, Third (1898)

PRINCIPAL COMBATANTS: France vs. the Mandingo tribes
PRINCIPAL THEATER(S): Ivory Coast, Africa
DECLARATION: None
MAJOR ISSUES AND OBJECTIVES: This was the third French effort to wrest control of the Ivory Coast interior from the Mandingo under Chief Almamy Samory.
OUTCOME: With the capture of Almamy Samory, the Mandingo resistance collapsed.
APPROXIMATE MAXIMUM NUMBER OF MEN UNDER ARMS: France, unknown; Mandingo, 28,000 combatants, 120,000 noncombatant followers
CASUALTIES: Total Mandingo casualties (all three wars), 50,000 dead; French and French colonial losses unknown
TREATIES: None

Twice before, French colonial forces had attempted to extend into the interior their control over the Ivory Coast. The First MANDINGO-FRENCH WAR resulted in a French victory over the Mandingo, but it did not put a permanent end to their resistance because their leader, Chief Almamy Samory Touré (d. 1900), remained at large and was able to organize an effective guerrilla campaign in the Second MANDINGO-FRENCH WAR. After repeated failures in this second war, a new French military campaign was mounted into the Ivory Coast interior. When the Mandingo fortress town of Sikasso fell to a French siege, Samory lost his chief logistical support. He agreed to negotiate with the French, who violated his flag of truce, and captured him on September 29, 1898. Samory was exiled to Gabon, a decapitating blow to the Mandingo, who relinquished control of the interior to the French. Samory Touré died in exile on June 21, 1900.

Further reading: J. F. A. Ajayi and Michael Crowder, *History of West Africa,* 2nd ed., 2 vols. (London: Longman, 1976–1987); J. D. Fage and Roland Oliver, eds., *The Cambridge History of West Africa,* 8 vols. (New York: Cambridge University Press, 1975–1980); David L. Lewis, *The Race to Fashoda: Colonialism and African Resistance* (New York: Weidenfeld and Nicolson, 1987); Rodney Steel, *History of West Africa* (New York: Facts On File, 2003).

Maniaces, Revolt of (1043)

PRINCIPAL COMBATANTS: Forces of General George Maniaces vs. the Byzantine Empire

PRINCIPAL THEATER(S): Vicinity of Constantinople
DECLARATION: None
MAJOR ISSUES AND OBJECTIVES: Maniaces revolted against the usurping emperor Constantine IX Monomachus
OUTCOME: The revolt ended abruptly when Maniaces fell victim to "friendly fire."
APPROXIMATE MAXIMUM NUMBER OF MEN UNDER ARMS: Unknown
CASUALTIES: Unknown
TREATIES: None

George Maniaces (d. 1043) was an exceedingly capable Byzantine general who was twice unjustly accused of treason. Emperor Michael V Calaphates (d. post 1042) saw to his release from prison after Maniaces was convicted the first time, and, by way of compensation for his wrongful imprisonment, gave him the Italian provinces to rule. In 1043, Maniaces was campaigning against Muslim invaders in his Italian realm when he was again accused of treason, this time by the new emperor, Constantine IX Monomachus (c. 1000–55), who demanded his return to Constantinople. Maniaces, who was loyal to Michael V Calaphates, the emperor whom Constantine IX Monomachus had deposed, refused to return. Instead he raised a rebellion, was proclaimed emperor by his troops, and launched a battle against the forces of the empire. The revolt disintegrated when Maniaces was felled by an arrow accidentally discharged by one of his own men.

Further reading: Cyril A. Mango, ed., *Oxford History of Byzantium* (New York: Oxford University Press, 2002); John Julius Norwich, *Byzantium: The Apogee.* (New York: Alfred A. Knopf, 2001).

Mantuan Succession, War of the
(1628–1631)

PRINCIPAL COMBATANTS: Houses of Savoy and Gonzaga vs. the Holy Roman Empire, and, separately, Duke Charles of Nevers and France
PRINCIPAL THEATER(S): Mantua and Montferrat
DECLARATION: None
MAJOR ISSUES AND OBJECTIVES: The parties each sought possession of Mantua and Montferrat.
OUTCOME: With French military support, the duke of Nevers made good his claim to both Mantua and Montferrat.
APPROXIMATE MAXIMUM NUMBER OF MEN UNDER ARMS: Unknown
CASUALTIES: Unknown
TREATIES: Treaty of Cherasco, April 26, 1631

This war may be seen as a phase of the THIRTY YEARS' WAR. The house of Savoy conferred the duchy of Montferrat on the Mantua-based House of Gonzaga, subject to the further will of the Holy Roman Emperor Ferdinand II (1578–1637). Montferrat fell to a female Gonzaga heir, Maria Gonzaga whereas possession of Mantua went to the French duke of Nevers, Frederico (1573–1637). He married off his son, Charles de Rethel (d. 1665), to the Gonzaga heiress, Maria, in order to secure both Montferrat and Mantua. At this point, the house of Savoy sought to reclaim Montferrat while, simultaneously, a Gonzaga relative laid claim to Mantua. While this conflict developed, Ferdinand II sent an army across the Alps to take Mantua and Milan. His forces sacked Mantua in 1630, forcing Savoy to agree to divide Montferrat with him. At this juncture, King Louis XIII (1601–43) of France sent an army in aid of the duke of Nevers, thereby rescuing Mantua from total destruction by the Holy Roman Emperor's army.

The following year, a French army under Cardinal Richelieu (1585–1642) conquered both Mantua and Montferrat for the duke of Nevers.

Further reading: Ronald G. Ash, *The Thirty Years' War: The Holy Roman Empire and Europe, 1618–1648* (London: Palgrave Macmillan, 1997); Geoffrey Parker, ed. *The Thirty Years' War* (New York: Routledge, 1997).

Manzikert Campaign   See BYZANTINE–SELJUK TURK WAR (1064–1081).

Maori War, First   See BAY OF ISLANDS WAR; WAIRAU AFFRAY IN NEW ZEALAND.

Maori War, Second   See TARANAKI WAR, FIRST; TARANAKI WAR, SECOND; TARANAKI WAR, THIRD.

Maratha-Mogul War   (1647–1665)

PRINCIPAL COMBATANTS: The Marathas vs. the Moguls
PRINCIPAL THEATER(S): India
DECLARATION: None
MAJOR ISSUES AND OBJECTIVES: The Hindu Marathas sought to create an empire at the expense of the Muslim Moguls.
OUTCOME: The Moguls prevailed at the Battle of Purandhar, forcing the surrender of the Maratha prince.
APPROXIMATE MAXIMUM NUMBER OF MEN UNDER ARMS: Marathas, 60,000; Mogul numbers unknown
CASUALTIES: Unknown
TREATIES: Treaty of Purandhar, 1665

The Marathas were a Hindu warrior people with whom the Hindu prince Shivaji Bhonsle (1627–80) identified himself. When, aged 19, he inherited his family's lands in 1647, Shivaji decided to found a Hindu empire free from Mogul oppression and tyranny. Operating from the Western Ghats near Pune, he launched an offensive against Bijapur (a Muslim state) and, after conquering it, constructed a series of hilltop fortifications. He proceeded systematically to acquire territory and by 1653 dominated the region from Goa to the Bhima River and was poised to take much of the Deccan. He called his new empire Maharashtra and, from it, he launched raids against various Mogul holdings. In the meantime, he built a navy to counter any interference from European traders.

In 1664, Shivaji Bhonsle attacked Surat, site of a major English trading facility on the Gulf of Khambhat. This roused the Mogul emperor, Aurangzeb (1618–1707), to action. He sent a force under the able commander Jai Singh (fl. 17th century) to Bijapur. Forming an alliance with Adil Shah (d. 1672), the Muslim sultan there, he mounted an attack in 1665 against Purandhar, a principal Maratha fort. Defeated, Shivaji surrendered most of his forts and consented to send his son, Sambhaji (1657–89) as a political hostage to Agra, the former Mogul capital and still a key city. A short time later, Shivaji decided to go to Agra himself, but, finding that he was to be treated as a prisoner, not a political hostage, he escaped—in 1670—and prepared a new war against the Moguls (see MARATHA-MOGUL WAR [1670–80]).

Further reading: Stewart Gordon, *Marathas 1600–1818* (New York: Cambridge University Press, 1993); Francis Watson, *A Concise History of India* (London: Thames and Hudson, 1981).

Maratha-Mogul War (1670–1680)

PRINCIPAL COMBATANTS: Marathas vs. Moguls
PRINCIPAL THEATER(S): India
DECLARATION: None
MAJOR ISSUES AND OBJECTIVES: Maratha ruler Shivaji Bhonsle resumed his war of conquest against the Moguls.
OUTCOME: Shivaji acquired a vast realm at Mogul expense.
APPROXIMATE MAXIMUM NUMBER OF MEN UNDER ARMS: Unknown
CASUALTIES: Unknown
TREATIES: None

After escaping Mogul captivity, Shivaji Bhonsle (1627–80), founder of the Maratha kingdom of Maharashtra (*see* MARATHA-MOGUL WAR [1647–1665]) resumed war

against the Moguls. He quickly recaptured the 23 forts and associated territories ceded by the Treaty of Purandhar. Surat was sacked, and Khandesh and Berar invaded.

The Muslim leader Jai Singh (fl. 17th century) received Mogul reinforcements and, with these, counterattacked. By 1672, the Mogul army had been increased under a new general, Bahadur Khan (fl. 17th century), and made significant advances against Shivaji. Shivaji outmaneuvered the Moguls, however, and captured large portions of Bijapur after the death of the local sultan, Adil Shah (d. 1672). Within two years, Shivaji acquired enough territory at Mogul expense to prompt him to assume the magnificent title of *chatrapati*, Lord of the Universe.

Bijapur, parts of which Shivaji now controlled, was an independent Muslim state vulnerable to attack by the Moguls. If the Moguls seized Bijapur, they could easily use it as a base from which to mount attacks against Maharashtra. To forestall this, Shivaji invaded the Carnatic region and forged an alliance with the Golconda and conquered the Jinji. Thus greatly strengthened, he was in a position to compel Bijapur to cede territories. In return for these cessions, Shivaji pledged to fight side by side with Bijapur to defeat the Moguls. By 1680, the Maratha territories stretched from the Narmada River to Goa and, eastward, to Nagpur in central India. Shivaji's death in 1680 brought only a year's intermission in the fighting, which resumed in 1681 as the MARATHA-MOGUL WAR (1681–1705).

Further reading: Stewart Gordon, *Marathas 1600–1818* (New York: Cambridge University Press, 1993); Francis Watson, *A Concise History of India* (London: Thames and Hudson, 1981).

Maratha-Mogul War (1681–1705)

PRINCIPAL COMBATANTS: Marathas vs. Moguls
PRINCIPAL THEATER(S): Deccan region of India
DECLARATION: None
MAJOR ISSUES AND OBJECTIVES: The Marathas and Moguls contested for possession of the Deccan.
OUTCOME: War was chronic during this period until, aged and infirm, the Mogul emperor Aurangzeb left the Deccan.
APPROXIMATE MAXIMUM NUMBER OF MEN UNDER ARMS: Maratha numbers unknown; the Mogul camp became a mobile city of 500,000, many of these capable of combat
CASUALTIES: In the hundreds of thousands
TREATIES: None

The MARATHA-MOGUL WAR (1670–80) ended with the death of the founder of Maharashtra, Shivaji Bhonsle (1627–80), but a new war began in 1681 with the ascension to the Maratha throne of Shivaji's son, Sambhaji (1657–89). It was not a straightforward continuation of the earlier conflict, however. As a result of defeat in the

MARATHA-MOGUL WAR (1647–1665), Shivaji had sent Sambhaji to Agra, seat of the Mogul court, as a hostage. Raised among the Moguls, Sambhaji defected for a time to the Mogul side. At the same time, Akbar (d. 1704), son of the Mogul emperor Aurangzeb (1618–1707), defected to the Hindu Rajputs. Akbar prevailed upon Sambhaji to unite with him in an assault upon Agra.

To counter Akbar and Sambhaji, Aurangzeb and his court moved from Agra in 1681 to create a large "temporary" tent city (it actually endured for 24 years) in the Deccan. From this mobile base, housing some 500,000 people, Aurangzeb led successful attacks against Bijapur (in 1686) and Golconda (in 1687) while the Marathas in turn raided him. In 1689, without intending to do so, Aurangzeb captured Sambhaji and other Maratha leaders and put them all to death. Raja Ram (d. 1700), Sambhaji's brother, took up the war, and when he died in 1700, his widow, Tarabai (fl. 17th century), continued to lead the battle in what had become a civil war among the disrupted and divided Marathas and against Aurangzeb, who occupied and left one Maratha fortress town after another, after each was retaken by the Marathas.

Warfare was chronic in the Deccan until 1705, when Aurangzeb, aged and infirm, abandoned the region and settled in Ahmadnagar to the north. His death two years later ensured the absolute end of a war that, in its final years, from about 1700 to 1705, killed perhaps as many as 100,000 annually.

Further reading: Stewart Gordon, *Marathas 1600–1818* (New York: Cambridge University Press, 1993); Francis Watson, *A Concise History of India* (London: Thames and Hudson, 1981).

Maratha War, First (1775–1782)

PRINCIPAL COMBATANTS: British East India Company vs. the Maratha Confederacy
PRINCIPAL THEATER(S): Bombay region
DECLARATION: None
MAJOR ISSUES AND OBJECTIVES: The British East India Company exploited Maratha disunity to make territorial gains.
OUTCOME: The British East India Company acquired an island off Bombay and effectively neutralized the Maratha Confederacy for 20 years, providing an opportunity for the company to gain control of more territory.
APPROXIMATE MAXIMUM NUMBER OF MEN UNDER ARMS: British, 6,000; Maratha, 56,000
CASUALTIES: British, 864 killed; Maratha losses unknown
TREATIES: Treaty of Sabai, May 7, 1782

The Maratha Confederacy was born of the disintegration of Maharashtra, the kingdom founded by Shivaji Bhonsle

(1627–80) about 1647 and that had survived chronic warfare with the Moguls through the beginning of the 18th century (*see* MARATHA-MOGUL WAR [1647–1665], MARATHA-MOGUL WAR [1670–1680], MARATHA-MOGUL WAR [1681–1705]). The confederacy was hardly a kingdom or nation, but merely a loose union of five clans with a capital city at Poona. Leadership authority was ostensibly vested in a *peshwa* (chief) headquartered at Poona, but he never enjoyed uncontested power. The British East India Company exploited the factionalism among the clans of the Maratha Confederacy to acquire control of Indian territories. In 1775, the company backed Narayan Rao (fl. late 18th century), a former peshwa, in his bid for power, promising him troops in exchange for treasure and territory. An early assault on Poona in 1775 failed, as did a campaign in the Deccan in January 1779. On the 12th, 2,600 British troops attacked the Maratha capital at Poona, losing 352 killed or wounded before negotiating a withdrawal from Maratha territory. Despite this negotiated withdrawal, on February 15, 1780, a contingent of 6,000 British soldiers stormed the fortress of Ahmadabad. At the cost of 106 British casualties, the Maratha garrison was dislodged. This victory marked a turning point in the war. On August 3, 1780, the clifftop fortress of Gwalior was breached by 2,000 Anglo-Indian troops and captured without loss. Although this checkmated the Marathas, the war continued, indecisively, for two more years until it was concluded by the Treaty of Sabai on May 7, 1782. The Maratha defeat in 1780 also ended their participation in the First MYSORE WAR.

As a result of the First Maratha War, the British East India Company acquired an island near Bombay and rendered the Maratha Confederacy neutral for the next two decades, during which the British made many more territorial gains, thereby laying the foundation for what would become British domination of the subcontinent.

See also MARATHA WAR, SECOND; MARATHA WAR, THIRD.

Maratha War, Second (1803–1805)

PRINCIPAL COMBATANTS: British East India Company vs. the Sinhai clan of the Maratha Confederacy
PRINCIPAL THEATER(S): Central India
DECLARATION: None
MAJOR ISSUES AND OBJECTIVES: The British East India Company sought to establish its dominance in central India.
OUTCOME: The British East India Company gained control of Poona and much of central India.
APPROXIMATE MAXIMUM NUMBER OF MEN UNDER ARMS: Anglo-British forces, 50,000; Maratha forces, 85,000

CASUALTIES: Anglo-British, 9,209 killed or wounded; Maratha, about 42,000 killed or wounded
TREATIES: Treaty of Bassein, 1802: basis of the war

The victory of the British East India Company against the Maratha Confederacy in the First MARATHA WAR and the conquest of the Mysore in the Fourth MYSORE WAR allowed the British East India Company to focus once again on confederacy in a campaign to acquire control of southern India. Advantageously for the British, the confederacy, after two decades of military inactivity, was no more unified than it had been at the time of the First Maratha War. The *peshwa* (head) of the Maratha Confederacy at this time was Baji Rao II (1775–1851), who was, however, opposed by the Sindhai (one of the confederacy's constituent clans). In 1802, the British had concluded the Treaty of Bassein with Baji Rao, promising defensive aid.

When the Sindhai captured Poona in 1803 and deposed Baji Rao II, the British demanded his restoration. This touched off a war of far greater proportions and cost than the First Maratha War.

The Marathas fielded two armies, approximately 85,000 men. British resources consisted of 50,000 Anglo-British troops.

The British began in earnest in August 1803, when forces under General Arthur Wellesley, the future duke of Wellington (1769–1852), took Ahmadnagar (August 11). On September 23, however, the Marathas counterattacked. Although Wellesley held his position, total Anglo-Indian casualties of 1,584 were among the heaviest sustained in any Indian battle up to that time.

Wellesley was again victorious on November 29, 1803, at Argaum, when his 11,000 Anglo-Indian troops routed 40,000, inflicting some 5,000 casualties. The following month, another Anglo-Indian force laid siege to the fort at Gawilghur from December 12 to December 15, ultimately storming it, then slaughtering 3,000 of the fort's 4,000 defenders—at a cost of only 14 killed and 112 wounded among the attackers.

While these victories were being won in the south, another British force was fighting a brilliant campaign on the north Indian plain. The Maratha fortress of Aligarh fell on September 4, 1803, and, on September 11, near Delhi, the British fielded 4,500 men against a Maratha force of 14,000, inflicting more than 3,000 casualties at a cost of 478 killed or wounded. From here, the Anglo-Indian army marched on Agra, site of the Taj Mahal. Agra was besieged during October 4–18, before finally falling.

At Laswari, on November 1, the British were again victorious, pounding at 9,000 Maratha infantry, who refused to yield until 7,000 of their number had fallen.

The Sindhai Marathas formally surrendered on December 20, but Jaswant Rao Holkar of Indore (d. 1811) remained defiant. British forces pursued him—he had

come to lead some 60,000 cavalry and 15,000 infantry—for months before he suddenly attacked during August 24–29, 1804, at Mokundra Pass. Half of the British regular force of 3,000 was killed, and Holkar laid siege to Delhi for nine days. A British army broke the siege, then pursued Holkar without mercy, running some of his forces to ground at Farrukhabad on November 17, 1804. Three thousand Maratha cavalrymen died in what has been described as a mass execution rather than a battle.

In the meantime, the main armies fought at Dig (Deeg) on November 13, and Holkar was defeated with heavy losses. His stronghold at Dig was besieged from December 10 to December 24, and, with its loss, Holkar ceased to be a threat. Nevertheless, the fortress town of Bhurtpore continued to side with Holkar, and on January 1, 1805, the Anglo-Indian forces laid down siege lines. The defenders held out with fanatical desperation against four major attacks, which cost the Anglo-Indians 3,205 casualties. The city never really fell, but, on April 17, its defenders agreed to withdraw support from Holkar.

Holkar himself was pursued into the Punjab during October 1805. He surrendered in December, thereby ending the war.

See also MARATHA WAR, THIRD.

Further reading: Stewart Gordon, *Marathas 1600–1818* (New York: Cambridge University Press, 1993); Francis Watson, *A Concise History of India* (London: Thames and Hudson, 1981).

Maratha War, Third (1817–1818)

PRINCIPAL COMBATANTS: British East India Company vs. the Pindari bandits and Peshwa Baji Rao
PRINCIPAL THEATER(S): Central India
DECLARATION: Maratha leaders against Britain, November 6, 1817
MAJOR ISSUES AND OBJECTIVES: The British puppet peshwa, Baji Rao, attempted to assert real authority over the Maratha Confederacy.
OUTCOME: The British East India Company put down Baji Rao's bid for power, defeated the Pindari, and established control of all Maratha lands.
APPROXIMATE MAXIMUM NUMBER OF MEN UNDER ARMS: Anglo-Indians, 20,000; Marathas, 200,000
CASUALTIES: Anglo-Indians, 2,000 killed; Marathas, more than 5,000 killed or wounded
TREATIES: None

The Third Maratha War was triggered by the raids of the Pindaris, a piratical outlaw gang, mostly consisting of Marathas. This group was secretly backed by the most important Maratha leaders, Jaswant Rao Holkar of Indore (d. 1811) and Peshwa Baji Rao (1775–1851). On November 6, 1817, Baji Rao declared his backing publicly and thereby began a new war against the British.

In response to what they took as a declaration of war, two British armies were deployed, the Army of the Deccan and the Grand Army, together totaling 20,000 troops. By this time, the Marathas could muster 200,000. As was the case in the first two Maratha wars, however, the British forces were better equipped and much more skillfully led. On November 5, 1817, a force of 2,800 men drove off Baji Rao's force of 26,000 at Kirkee, inflicting 500 Maratha casualties while incurring only 86 killed or wounded. More decisive was the Battle of Mahidpur on December 21, 1817, when 5,500 Anglo-Indian infantrymen used bayonets to charge 30,000 Maratha cavalry and 5,000 infantry under Holkar. The vastly superior Maratha force was driven from its fortifications, and its losses exceeded 3,000 killed or wounded. Anglo-Indian losses were 174 killed, 621 wounded.

British-led sepoys fought smaller actions against Pindaris at Sitabaldi on November 24, 1817, and then at Nagpur on December 16. The key Maratha citadel there fell on December 24. On January 1, 1818, a mere 1,000 Anglo-Indian troops held off 25,000 Maratha attackers at Korygaom long enough for the arrival of reinforcements to drive the attackers off.

On May 10, 1818, an army of 4,000 Anglo-Indians dispersed the remnant of Baji Rao's army, just 7,500 men, at the Battle of Sholapur. The Marathas suffered losses of more than 1,000 killed, whereas British casualties totaled 102 killed or wounded. Baji Rao surrendered on June 2, bringing an end to Maratha political and military power.

See also MARATHA WAR, FIRST; MARATHA WAR, SECOND.

Further reading: Stewart Gordon, *Marathas 1600–1818* (New York: Cambridge University Press, 1993); Francis Watson, *A Concise History of India* (London: Thames and Hudson, 1981).

Marathon Campaign (490 B.C.E.)

PRINCIPAL COMBATANTS: Athens vs. Persia
PRINCIPAL THEATER(S): Plain of Marathon, Greece
DECLARATION: None
MAJOR ISSUES AND OBJECTIVES: Persia sought to punish Athens for its role in the Ionian Revolt, 500–493 B.C.E., and to capture the Plain of Marathon.
OUTCOME: Through a combination of patience and skilled deployment of forces, the Athenian general Miltiades separated the Persian land forces from the Persian fleet and repulsed the invasion.
APPROXIMATE MAXIMUM NUMBER OF MEN UNDER ARMS: Persians, 50,000; Athenians, 20,000
CASUALTIES: Unknown
TREATIES: None

The Marathon Campaign was a Persian expedition to punish Athens for the part it had played in the IONIAN REVOLT, from 500–493 B.C.E. In 492, the Persians dispatched an invasion fleet, which, however, was wrecked in a storm. Two years later, in 490, a second fleet was sent, this one carrying about 50,000 soldiers across the Aegean Sea. The invaders sacked Eretria, reembarked on their vessels, and landed at the Plain of Marathon. This was territory that the pro-Persian Athenian Alcmeonid faction planned to restore to Persia. However, led by Miltiades (d. 489 B.C.E.), an Athenian citizen army staked out the plain, but continually evaded battle. At length, the impatient Persians attacked Athens by sea and with a cavalry force. This was a tactical blunder that exposed the Persians to attack by the waiting Athenians. Miltiades led his forces to a stunning victory.

A soldier, Phidippides (d. 490 B.C.E.), ran from Marathon to Athens to announce the victory—and thus "marathon" has become synonymous with a long-distance run. Phidippides collapsed and died after his effort; it was said that his heart burst. As for the Persian fleet, it withdrew when it heard of the defeat of the land forces.

Further reading: A. R. Burn, *Persia and the Greeks: The Defence of the West, c. 546–478 B.C.* (Palo Alto, Calif.: Stanford University Press, 1984); David Califf, *Marathon* (New York: Chelsea House, 2002); Peter Green, *The Greco-Persian Wars* (Berkeley: University of California Press, 1996); J. F. Lazenby, *The Defence of Greece, 490–479 B.C.* (Warminster, England: Aris and Phillips, 1993).

Marches, Rebellion of the (1322)

PRINCIPAL COMBATANTS: Edward II vs. rebels from the Marches
PRINCIPAL THEATER(S): The Marches (English-Welsh borderlands)
DECLARATION: None
MAJOR ISSUES AND OBJECTIVES: Edward II sought to restore his chamberlain, Hugh le Despenser, to control of Glamorgan after he had been ousted by Marcher rebels.
OUTCOME: The rebellion was crushed and Despenser restored.
APPROXIMATE MAXIMUM NUMBER OF MEN UNDER ARMS: Unknown
CASUALTIES: Unknown
TREATIES: None

The Marches is the borderland between England and Wales, long a region of contention between the two countries. On July 7, 1307, it fell under the suzerainty of King Edward II (1284–1327) who ascended the English throne upon the death of his father, Edward I (1239–1307) ("Longshanks"). There was little love lost between the old king and his son, whose reign proved disastrous. Edward II inherited some of his problems from Longshanks, most significantly a substantial national debt and a war with Scotland (*see* SCOTTISH WAR [1314–1328]), but many of them were of his own making. Surrounded by a ruling nobility related to his family by blood and fealty, Edward had shunned his peers and fallen in love with Piers Gaveston (1284–1312), son of a Gascon knight. Trying to break off their sexual affair, Edward Longshanks had exiled Gaveston, but the newly crowned Edward II immediately recalled him, bestowing on him the highest honors he could manage—the earldom of Cornwall and marriage to the king's niece. This was but one of several acts by which Edward awarded England's highest offices to his father's most prominent opponents. He recalled both Archbishop Winchelsey (d. 1313) and Bishop Bek of Durham, whom Longshanks had also exiled, and he dismissed and put on trial his father's much-trusted treasurer, Walter Langton (d. 1321).

These actions earned Edward the hatred of the English barons, who in 1311 formed a 21-member committee that drafted a document called the Ordinances, which again banished Gaveston and restricted Edward's control over finances and appointments. Though Edward apparently accepted these demands and sent Gaveston abroad, he soon arranged for his lover's return. The barons, led by Edward's enigmatic cousin Thomas, second earl of Lancaster (c. 1278–1322), responded by seizing Gaveston and, in June 1312, executing him. There was little Edward could do. Robert I the Bruce (1274–1329), attempting to rid Scotland of the yoke of English rule, won a major victory at Bannockburn on June 14, 1314 (*see* BRUCE'S REVOLT), which left the king at the mercy of the barons. Thomas's political agenda seemed little more than the enforcement of the Ordinances, but it served to block further action by others. By 1315, Lancaster had made himself the real master of England, and in 1316 a parliament held at Lincoln named him chief councillor.

Thomas soon proved incompetent at government and, by 1318, a group of moderate barons rose to assume the role of arbitrators between Lancaster and Edward, while Edward himself had found two new favourites—Hugh le Despenser (the Elder) (1262–1326), earl of Winchester, and his son and namesake, Sir Hugh le Despenser (the Younger) (d. 1326). The latter married into the Clare family and thereby gained control of Glamorgan on the Welsh border. When the king supported the younger Despenser's territorial ambitions in Wales, Lancaster and the Marcher lords banished both Despensers at Parliament in 1321. Edward then took up arms on their behalf, and the two exiles returned. Edward II attacked the lords of the Marches at the Battle of Boroughbridge in March 1322. In a brilliant tactical innovation, Edward dismounted his cavalry and used them, on foot, together with archers to decimate the rebel cavalry.

In this brief civil war, Edward was totally victorious. He had waited 11 years to annul the Ordinances and avenge Gaveston. Now, he had Lancaster executed for treason after his and the lords of the Marches' ignominious defeat at Boroughbridge. In death, the hardly popular Lancaster began to attract a martyr's sympathy and many rumors spread of miracles at his tomb, but Edward proved adamantine. He executed a large number of Lancaster's followers in a horrific bloodbath. In the same year the Ordinances were repealed in Parliament at York, and in the Statute of York was announced, returning the kingdom to the constitutional practices of the past.

Edward's reliance on the Despensers, however, soon aroused the resentment of his queen, Isabella (1292–1358), who became the mistress of Roger Mortimer (c. 1287–1330), an exiled baron opposed to Edward. In 1326 the couple invaded England, executed the Despensers, and deposed Edward in favor of his son, King Edward III (1312–77). They imprisoned Edward II, who died in September 1327, most likely murdered.

Further reading: Hilda Johnstone, *Edward of Carnarvon* (Manchester, England: Manchester University Press, 1946); Sandra Raban, *Edward II* (London: Blackwell, 2000).

March 1st Movement   *See* SAMIL INDEPENDENCE MOVEMENT (1919–1920).

"March on Rome"   *See* FASCIST MARCH ON ROME (1922).

March Revolution   *See* FEBRUARY (MARCH) REVOLUTION (1917).

Mariposa War   (1850–1851)

PRINCIPAL COMBATANTS: Miwok and Yokut Indians vs. California miners
PRINCIPAL THEATER(S): Sierra Nevada foothills and San Joaquin Valley of California
DECLARATION: None
MAJOR ISSUES AND OBJECTIVES: Miwok and Yokut attempted to drive white miners from the Indians' homeland.
OUTCOME: Indecisive
APPROXIMATE MAXIMUM NUMBER OF MEN UNDER ARMS: Miners, unknown; Indians, Approximately 350
CASUALTIES: Unknown, but certainly minimal
TREATIES: None

This brief conflict began in 1850, when the Miwok and Yokut Indians, living in the foothills of the Sierra Nevada and in the San Joaquin Valley in California, retaliated against the gold miners who had invaded their country. Led by Chief Tenaya (fl. 1850s), warriors attacked isolated prospectors and burned several trading posts belonging to an entrepreneur named James D. Savage (1822–52). Savage responded by raising a local militia—which he dubbed the Mariposa Battalion, after Mariposa County—and by launching a campaign against the Miwoks and Yokuts in 1851.

Tenaya, with approximately 350 warriors, simply evaded Savage's first campaign, but a second foray resulted in the capture of the chief and many of the warriors, which ended the Mariposa War.

Further reading: Alan Axelrod, *Chronicle of the Indian Wars: From Colonial Times to Wounded Knee* (New York: Prentice Hall General Reference, 1993); C. Gregory Crampton, ed., *Mariposa Indian War, 1850–1851* (Provo: University of Utah Press, 1975).

Marjorian's Barbarian Campaigns
(457–461)

PRINCIPAL COMBATANTS: Marjorian's Roman forces vs. the Vandals and Duke Ricimer
PRINCIPAL THEATER(S): Italy, Gaul, and Spain
DECLARATION: None
MAJOR ISSUES AND OBJECTIVES: Marjorian sought to reconstitute the Western Empire of Rome and then to defeat the Vandals in their African homeland.
OUTCOME: Although Marjorian achieved his reunification objective, treachery destroyed his African invasion plans, and a revolt in Italy prompted his abdication.
APPROXIMATE MAXIMUM NUMBER OF MEN UNDER ARMS: Unknown
CASUALTIES: Unknown
TREATIES: None

Ricimer (d. 472), a Swabian-Visigothic duke, drove the Vandals out of Italy and became the major power there. He placed the Roman general Marjorianus—Emperor Marjorian (d. 461)—on the throne, with the intention that he serve as a puppet; however, Marjorian soon took matters of state in his own hands and began a series of vigorous campaigns against the Vandals. When a Vandal force raided near the mouth of the Liris River (the Garigliano), Marjorian easily defeated it. This victory made him ambitious to end the Vandal threat once and for all by taking action against the seat of Vandal power in Africa. However, before he could conduct a successful campaign against the Vandals in their homeland, Marjorian believed that he must reunite the Western Empire. Therefore, in

458, he invaded Gaul. Near Toulouse, he engaged the forces of Visigoth king Theodoric II (d. 466). Marjorian wisely concluded a generous peace with Theodoric, which renewed Roman sway over Gaul as well as Spain during 458–460.

With the Western Empire effectively made whole again, Marjorian set about building an invasion force at Cartagena, Spain, to attack Africa. The Vandal chieftain, Gaiseric (c. 390–477), was a jump ahead of Marjorian, however. Through the judicious application of bribery, he was able to persuade key Romans in Cartagena to turn traitor. Thanks to these "moles," Gaiseric was able to sail a Vandal fleet against the fleet of Marjorian just before it was about to embark in 461. The Roman fleet was virtually destroyed.

Marjorian refused to accept defeat and immediately began rebuilding the fleet. At this point, however, Ricimer, exploiting Marjorian's preoccupation with his African expedition, incited a revolt in Italy. Appalled by what he deemed the ingratitude and disloyalty of the Roman people, Marjorian abdicated. Ricimer, bent on ensuring that Majorian would not return to rise again, had him assassinated. Ricimer emerged as the uncrowned emperor of Italy—and the Western Empire never regained anything approaching its past glory.

Further reading: Arther Ferrill, *The Fall of the Roman Empire: The Military Explanation* (New York: Thames and Hudson, 1986); Peter Heather, ed., *The Visigoths from the Migration Period to the Seventh Century* (Rochester, N.Y.: Boydell Press, 1999); Thomas Hodkins, *Huns, Vandals, and the Fate of the Roman Empire* (Mechanicsburg, Pa.: Stackpole Books, 1996); E. A. Thompson, *Romans and Barbarians: The Decline of the Western Empire* (Madison: University of Wisconsin Press, 2002).

Maroons' Rebellion (1795)

PRINCIPAL COMBATANTS: Maroons (former Jamaican black slaves) vs. Great Britain
PRINCIPAL THEATER(S): Jamaica
DECLARATION: None
MAJOR ISSUES AND OBJECTIVES: The judicial beating of two Maroons triggered a brief, bloody general uprising.
OUTCOME: The uprising was quickly put down.
APPROXIMATE MAXIMUM NUMBER OF MEN UNDER ARMS: Maroons, 300; British troops, 1,500
CASUALTIES: Unknown
TREATIES: Partly at issue was a 1739 treaty between the British and the Maroons, granting the Maroons certain rights.

Freed or escaped black slaves in Jamaica were known as Maroons (from the Spanish *murrano,* meaning wild boar and suggesting an untamed beast) and lived in the woods and mountains. British colonial authorities and British settlers continually harried the Maroons, but in 1739 a treaty was concluded between the British authorities and Maroon leaders granting Maroons territory and autonomy. Under the treaty, the situation was relatively peaceful until 1795, when two Maroons were beaten by British authorities for stealing swine. Other Maroons regarded this as an outrage and rose up in rebellion in July.

The uprising was quick and bloody, and 1,500 British regulars pursued about 300 rebels deep into the woods, using bloodhounds imported from Cuba. Captured, some of the Maroons surrendered. Those who refused to be pacified were packed off to Halifax in the British colony of Nova Scotia. Confined there for a time, they were subsequently, in 1800, transported to Sierra Leone, Africa. As for the rebellion, not only had it been definitively extinguished, but the Maroons remaining in Jamaica agreed to assist British authorities in putting down any future rebellions on the island. In exchange for this pledge, colonial authorities agreed to adopt a hands-off policy with regard to Maroon affairs.

Further reading: Mavis Christine Campbell, *The Maroons of Jamaica: A History of Resistance, Collaboration and Betrayal* (Westport, Conn.: Greenwood Publishing Group, 1988); Edward Long, *History of Jamaica* (Montreal: McGill-Queens University Press 2003).

Marsic War   *See* SOCIAL WAR (91–88 B.C.E.).

Maryland and Virginia's War with the Susquehannocks (1675–1676)

PRINCIPAL COMBATANTS: Maryland and Virginia colonists vs. Susquehannock and allied Indians
PRINCIPAL THEATER(S): Maryland and Virginia
DECLARATION: None
MAJOR ISSUES AND OBJECTIVES: Animosities between settlers and Indians led to violence and calls for revenge, which the colonial governments heeded in part to better control trade relations with various tribes, which in turn sparked a violent dispute between eastern (and mostly aristocratic) and western (and mostly "peasant") colonial factions.
OUTCOME: Inconclusive; many Susquehannock, however, agreed the year after the war ended to move from the Delaware Valley out of reach of the Marylanders
APPROXIMATE MAXIMUM NUMBER OF MEN UNDER ARMS: Colonists, about 1,000; Indian numbers unknown
CASUALTIES: Fewer than 50, total
TREATIES: No official settlement, though the Treaty of Shackamaxon in 1677 set the terms for the move westward of the majority of the Susquehannock

A conflict between the settlers of Maryland and the Iroquois Confederation ignited in 1660, when a party of Oneida—members of the Iroquois Five Nations—killed five Piscataway Indians "for being friends" with Maryland and the Susquehannock. In response, Maryland, either deliberately or through ignorance, failed to distinguish the Oneida from the rest of the Iroquois Confederation and declared war on the entire Five Nations.

The Piscataway were, in effect, a "client" tribe of Maryland, a favored trading partner that was politically dominated by the colony. Since the Five Nations were closely allied with Maryland's chief trading rival, the Dutch, probably war was declared not only to defend the Piscataway, but to gain an advantage over the Dutch and, if possible, to drive them from the Delaware Valley. The Susquehannock were interested in securing all the assistance they could in fighting the ongoing BEAVER WARS against the Iroquois.

Within a very few years, Maryland's perception of which allies were the most valuable shifted, and the colony sought a separate peace with the Iroquois. In 1674, colonists came to terms with the Seneca, an important Iroquois tribe, who were thereby left free to push the Susquehannock south to the Potomac. Tensions now ran high between Maryland and its betrayed ally, the Susquehannock Indians.

In July–August 1675, a group of Maryland Nanticoke (also called Doeg) Indians fell into a dispute with a wealthy Virginia planter named Thomas Mathew (fl. 1670s), who had apparently neglected to pay them for some goods traded. Taking matters into their own hands, the Nanticoke seized some of Mathew's hogs. In retaliation, a gang of Mathew's men killed some of the Indians and recovered the hogs. The Nanticoke now took vengeance by killing three Virginians. At this point, George Brent (fl. 1670s–1680s) and George Mason (fl. 1670s), captains of the local militia, gathered 30 Virginians and crossed into Maryland to confront the Nanticoke. Brent's party surrounded an Indian cabin, called for a talk, and when the Indians emerged, Brent seized one chief, accused him of murder, then shot him when he attempted to escape. A general melee broke out, in which another 10 Nanticoke were killed.

During the confrontation, Mason's detachment had surrounded another cabin nearby. The Indians who had been sleeping inside the cabin were awakened by Brent's gunfire, ran out of the cabin, and were cut down by Mason's men. Fourteen were killed before Mason realized that he was firing not on Nanticoke but on Suquehannock.

The incident was more than enough to ignite fullscale war between the Nanticoke, Susquehannock, and allied tribes on the one hand and Maryland and Virginia on the other.

Governor William Berkeley (1606–77) of Virginia dispatched Colonel John Washington (1632–77) (great-grandfather of the first president of the United States) and Major Isaac Allerton (fl. 1670s) to investigate the causes of the Indian raids. Only if the investigation determined that there was just cause for a war would the militia be deployed. Washington and Allerton, however, overstepped their commission and immediately raised a militia force. Late in September 1675, 1,000 Virginians and Marylanders surrounded the place the Maryland Assembly had designated as the home village of the Susquehannock, at the junction of the Piscataway Creek and the Potomac. A parley was called for, and five chiefs emerged, only to be treacherously slain.

For the next six weeks, the militiamen besieged the Susquehannock town, until the warriors managed to slip out with their women and children. They killed 10 sleeping guards in the process, and they resumed a regime of raiding the white settlements. After 36 settlers had been killed, the Susquehannocks sent a message to Governor Berkeley, declaring that with (approximately) 10 common Englishmen killed for each of their chiefs slain, the score, as it were, was even, and they were willing to make peace.

Berkeley scornfully rejected the offer, yet had little desire to prolong the war. He proposed building a chain of defensive fortifications around the settled parts of the colony and fighting a war of attrition until the Indians gave up. The proposal inflamed the settlers of Virginia's frontier, who would be exposed to the full force of the Indians' wrath. Feeling oppressed and neglected by the central colonial government, the settlers of the outlying areas lined up behind a charismatic braggart named Nathaniel Bacon (1647–76) in what came to be called BACON'S REBELLION. The "rebellion" served to spread and intensify Indian hostilities, and the Indian war became inextricably bound up with Bacon's Rebellion.

In the meantime, while Berkeley was fighting to regain possession of his colony from the likes of Bacon, Governor Edmund Andros (1637–1714) of New York, seeking to forestall the kind of disaster that had beset New England, which was embroiled in the tragic and costly KING PHILIP'S WAR, offered the Susquehannock refuge within his colony. Some accepted, whereas others continued to raid Maryland settlers, and still others—probably the majority of the tribe—now actively sought peace with Maryland authorities. The colony's Indian "clients"—the Piscataway and Mattawoman—demanded that the war continue until the Susquehannock were effectively neutralized. A peace conference convened in early August 1676 was quickly transformed into a strategy meeting for renewing war against the Susquehannock.

At this point Governor Andros, fearing that the entire eastern seaboard would erupt into an Indian war, threatened to take the Susquehannock permanently under his colony's jurisdiction. This temporarily ended hostilities, and Bacon's death in October 1676 (from dysentery) further cooled the situation. The Maryland and Virginia Indian war of 1675–76 ended without any official settlement, though in March 1677, a treaty conference was held at Shackamaxon (today part of Philadelphia) in which many of the Susquehannock consented to removal from the Delaware Valley and beyond the reach of Maryland. However, some 26 Susquehannock families remained in the Delaware Valley by accepting adoption into the Delaware tribe.

Well into the 1680s Maryland as well as Virginia persisted in sporadic conflicts against the Iroquois, who made extensive use of adopted Susquehannocks to conduct raids against the colonies.

Further reading: Alan Axelrod, *Chronicle of the Indian Wars: From Colonial Times to Wounded Knee* (New York: Prentice Hall General Reference, 1993); Francis Jennings, *The Ambiguous Iroquois Empire: The Covenant Chain of Indian Tribes with English Colonies* (New York: W. W. Norton, 1984).

Maryland's Religious War (1644–1646, 1654)

PRINCIPAL COMBATANTS: Royalists vs. pro-Parliament colonists; later, Proprietary forces vs. Puritans
PRINCIPAL THEATER(S): Maryland
DECLARATION: None
MAJOR ISSUES AND OBJECTIVES: Against the background of civil war in England, Royalist factions vied with Parliamentary factions to gain control of Maryland.
OUTCOME: The second Lord Baltimore, proprietor of the colony, regained control of the colony.
APPROXIMATE MAXIMUM NUMBER OF MEN UNDER ARMS: Unknown
CASUALTIES: Unknown
TREATIES: None

By the early 1640s, the English colony of Maryland was beginning to feel the effects of the First ENGLISH CIVIL WAR. Governor Leonard Calvert (1606–47) returned to England and appointed Giles Brent as governor in his stead. Shortly after this, Richard Ingle (fl. 1640s), a pro-Cromwell sea captain from London, arrived in Maryland and led a two-year campaign of sporadic raids throughout the colony known as "the plundering time." Ingle was finally captured, and was tried four times by juries that refused to reach verdicts. He escaped, and continued to ply Maryland waters, both for legal and illegal purposes.

In the meantime, in the fall of 1644, Calvert returned to Maryland, then traveled to Virginia with letters of marque against Parliamentary supporters; he set about recruiting privateers and troops to counter Ingle in Maryland. In 1645, Ingle, however, obtained his own letters of marque against royalists, and, with a growing band of supporters, intensified his Maryland raids, plundering settlements and manors. He took Jesuit missionaries captive, and he also made prisoners of several important political leaders, including the temporary governor, whom he shipped off to England. With Parliamentary forces gaining the upper hand in England, Maryland was thrown into chaos. Calvert was still in Virginia, the temporary governor was now a prisoner in England, and a new government and governor, Giles Brent (served 1643–44), were hurriedly established by the colonial council in an attempt to restore order.

Calvert returned during spring 1647, but died suddenly in June. Just before his death, he appointed Thomas Greene (served 1647–49), a staunch Catholic royalist, as governor. In mid-1648, however, Cecil Calvert (1605–75), the second Lord Baltimore (who had inherited Maryland from his father and who became first lord proprietor of the colony), shifted toward a pro-Parliament stance in an effort to preserve his colonial rights. Although he himself was a Catholic, Baltimore demoted Greene to a position on the council and replaced him with William Stone (served 1649–52), a Protestant friendly to the Cromwellian cause. By this time, the entire council was heavily Protestant, which restored peace to the colony.

New religious strife developed in 1654, however, when Puritan colonists clashed with other Maryland settlers. Lord Baltimore dispatched Governor Stone with a small army to engage an inferior Puritan force near present-day Annapolis on the Severn River. Although outnumbered, Puritan forces won the day at the Battle of the Severn, March 25, 1654, and the second Lord Baltimore was unable to regain complete control of his colony until the Restoration under Charles II (1630–85) in 1660.

Further reading: Morris L. Radoff, ed., *The Old Line State: A History of Maryland* (Annapolis: Maryland State Archives, 1971); Vera Foster Rollo, *The Proprietorship of Maryland: A Documented Account* (Annapolis: Maryland Historical Society, 1988).

Maryland's War with the Susquehannocks (1643–1652)

PRINCIPAL COMBATANTS: Susquehannock Indians vs. colonial Maryland
PRINCIPAL THEATER(S): Maryland
DECLARATION: Maryland declared war on September 23, 1642.
MAJOR ISSUES AND OBJECTIVES: Unknown
OUTCOME: Cessation of hostilities
APPROXIMATE MAXIMUM NUMBER OF MEN UNDER ARMS: Unknown
CASUALTIES: 15 militiamen captured, two tortured
TREATIES: Susquehannock sue for peace, 1652

The reasons for the colony of Maryland's declaration of war on the Susquehannock Indians on September 23, 1642, are unknown. Perhaps it was to halt the intrusion of Susquehannock into territory occupied by Maryland's "client" Indians, the Piscataway (also called Conoy), Patuxent, and Yoamacoe. Whatever the cause, Maryland militiamen mobilized between July 1643 and June 1644, but their first outing seems to have involved nothing that could be called a battle, because the Susquehannock simply fled from the militia's guns. A second expedition resulted in a setback for the Marylanders, because the colony's trading rival New Sweden armed the Indians. About 15 militiamen were captured and two of them were tortured to death. The few records of the Susquehannock victory that exist note the Marylanders fled the field so hastily they abandoned arms, including two artillery weapons—precious commodities in the colonies. But in general, as is frequently true of Indian-colonial conflicts, especially those involving alliances between Indians and one "Christian" colony fighting against another "Christian" colony, no detailed information about this war was ever recorded. It does seem, however, that a relatively inactive state of war existed between the colony and the Susquehannocks from 1643 or 1644 to 1652, when the Susquehannocks, now entangled in the BEAVER WARS against the Iroquois, sued for peace with Maryland and negotiated a treaty. Indeed, within a decade of the treaty, Maryland enlisted the Susquehannocks as allies in combat against the Iroquois.

Further reading: Alan Axelrod, *Chronicle of the Indian Wars: From Colonial Times to Wounded Knee* (New York: Prentice Hall General Reference, 1993); Francis Jennings, *The Invasion of America: Indians, Colonialism, and the Cant of Conquest* (New York: W. W. Norton, 1975) and *The Ambiguous Iroquois Empire: The Covenant Chain of Indian Tribes with English Colonies* (New York: W. W. Norton, 1984).

Masada, Siege of (72–73)

PRINCIPAL COMBATANTS: Roman Legion X Fretensis vs. Jewish zealots defending Masada
PRINCIPAL THEATER(S): Masada, outside of Jerusalem
Declaration: None
MAJOR ISSUES AND OBJECTIVES: The Romans sought to end Jewish resistance in Judea; Masada sheltered the last holdouts.
OUTCOME: After a two-year siege, the Romans finally breached the fortress wall; all but seven defenders (two women and five children) had committed suicide.
APPROXIMATE MAXIMUM NUMBER OF MEN UNDER ARMS: Romans, 15,000; defenders of Masada, 1,000
CASUALTIES: The defenders committed mass suicide—approximately 1,000 died.
TREATIES: None

Following Roman victory at the siege of Jerusalem in 70, Jewish rebels held out in desert fortresses. The Romans made a sweep of these positions, conquering both Herodium and Machaerus by 71. A third fortress, Masada, occupied the entire 18-acre top of an isolated mesa towering some 1,424 feet above the southwest coast of the Dead Sea. There, Herod the Great (r. 37–4 B.C.E.), king of Judea, had constructed a renowned royal citadel of two ornate palaces (one multilevelled), heavily reinforced walls, commanding defensive towers, and cisterns holding almost 200,000 gallons of water fed by a system of aqueducts.

Following Herod's death in 4 B.C.E., Roman legions seized and held the fortress, but, during the JEWISH REVOLT (66–73), the legions lost Masada to Jewish Zealots in 66 C.E. Approximately 1,000 men, women, and children of this Jewish sect, staunchly opposed to domination by Rome, now occupied a fortress whose steep mountain slopes made it virtually unassailable. Against these defenders, the Romans mounted a siege force of some 15,000 (Legion X Fretensis). Despite their overwhelming advantage of numbers, the besieging force hammered away at Masada for two years, without success building elaborate siege engines and employing a massive battering ram. Finally, the besiegers constructed a sloping ramp of earth and stones to bring their soldiers within reach of the stronghold, which fell only after the Romans used the ram to create a breach in the defenders' walls. When the Zealots quickly repaired the breach with wood, the Romans set fire to the repairs and stormed the fortress. The Zealots, however, preferred death to enslavement, and when the Romans entered, they found that the defenders, led by Eleazar ben Jair (d. April 15, 73 C.E.), had taken their own lives. Two women and five children—hidden in a water conduit—survived to tell the story.

In the 20th century, following the creation of a Jewish homeland in Israel, Masada became an icon of Jewish nationalism, and it is now one of Israel's most popular tourist attractions.

Further reading: Flavius Josephus, *The Jewish War,* in *Complete Works,* trans. by William Whitson (Nashville: Nelson Reference and Electronic, 2003); Yigael Yadin *Masada: Herod's Fortress and the Zealots' Last Stand* (New York, Random House, 1966); Mikhah Livneh, *The Last Fortress: The Study of Masada and Its People* (Tel-Aviv: Ministry of Defense, 1989); John W. Welch, *Masada and the World of the New Testament* (Provo, Utah: Brigham Young University Press, 1997).

Masaniello's Insurrection (1647)

PRINCIPAL COMBATANTS: Neapolitan rebels vs. Spain
PRINCIPAL THEATER(S): Naples and vicinity
DECLARATION: None
MAJOR ISSUES AND OBJECTIVES: The rebellion began as a protest against excessive taxation and expanded to a rebellion of the lower classes against the nobles.
OUTCOME: The people of Naples ultimately invited reinstatement of Spanish rule.
APPROXIMATE MAXIMUM NUMBER OF MEN UNDER ARMS: Unknown
CASUALTIES: At least 10,000 were killed in the insurrection.
TREATIES: None

Tommaso Aniello (d. 1647), called Masaniello, was a Neapolitan fisherman who, financed by a lawyer named Giulio Genoino (fl. 17th century) led a rebellion against a tax on fruit levied to finance tribute payments Naples owed Spain. Masaniello's rebels were all of the lower classes, and their insurrection began, on July 7, 1647, with the burning of the customs house and an attack on the Spanish viceroy, who fled the city. The rebels rampaged through Naples, killing members of the nobility at random.

The violence was halted after the viceroy, Antonio Alvarez de Toledo (fl. 17th century), agreed to pardon the rebels, to grant citizens' rights to the Neapolitans, and to rescind the hated tax. However, after these concessions were made Masaniello attempted to provoke his followers into resuming their violence—apparently for the sake of murdering more of the nobility. Although Giulio Genoino put Masaniello into protective custody, the fisherman was assassinated on July 16, 1647, perhaps by agents of the viceroy, the nobles, or even by disillusioned followers.

No sooner was Masaniello dead than the viceroy abrogated his agreement, thereby triggering a new round of rebellion. A Spanish fleet bombarded Naples in an effort to beat it into order, and Spanish troops attempted an invasion of the city, but were beaten back. The Neapolitans proclaimed a republic, but Spain renewed military pressure and, finally, in 1648, the rebels admitted the return of Spanish rule. Spanish authorities rounded up the rebel leaders, whom they subsequently executed.

Further reading: Rosario Villari, *Revolt of Naples* (London: Blackwell, 1999).

Mascates, War of the (1711)

PRINCIPAL COMBATANTS: Pernambuco sugar planters vs. Mascates
PRINCIPAL THEATER(S): Pernambuco, eastern Brazil
DECLARATION: None
MAJOR ISSUES AND OBJECTIVES: The war resulted from conflict between upper-class planters and lower-class Mascates (peddlers)

OUTCOME: The district governor mediated a peace settlement, which included a no-fault general amnesty. Nothing was gained by either side.

APPROXIMATE MAXIMUM NUMBER OF MEN UNDER ARMS: Unknown

CASUALTIES: Planters, 30 killed; Mascates, 25 killed

TREATIES: Mediated settlement, 1711

The sugar planters of the wealthy town of Olina, in Pernambucco, Brazil, scorned the poorer inhabitants—sailors and traders—of neighboring Recife as *Mascates,* peddlers. On June 18, 1711, the Mascates rose against the planters, who responded by laying siege against Recife for three months. The Mascates had control of the town's many cannon and continually bombarded the siege lines. The conflict ended when Portuguese authorities intervened with a promise of amnesty for both sides, neither of which gained anything by the conflict.

Further reading: E. Bradford Burns, *A History of Brazil,* 3rd ed. (New York: Columbia University Press, 1993); Boris Faust, *A Concise History of Brazil* (New York: Cambridge University Press, 1990).

Matanza, La ("The Slaughter") *See* SALVADORAN REVOLT (1931–1932).

Mau Mau Uprising (1952–1956)

PRINCIPAL COMBATANTS: Great Britain vs. Kenya's Mau Mau rebels

PRINCIPAL THEATER(S): British East Africa (Kenya)

DECLARATION: State of emergency declared October 20, 1952

MAJOR ISSUES AND OBJECTIVES: The Mau Mau used terror in an effort to wrest control of the country from the British.

OUTCOME: The uprising was put down, but it served to inspire many other independence movements throughout Africa.

APPROXIMATE MAXIMUM NUMBER OF MEN UNDER ARMS: British, 50,000; Mau Mau and others, unknown

CASUALTIES: Casualties among settlers were high (military losses included 590 killed and 1,500 wounded), but, among the Mau Mau, losses were much higher: 11,503 Mau Mau were killed.

TREATIES: None

By the 1950s, movements were well under way throughout Africa to oust white European colonial governments and settlers. In British East Africa (Kenya), the Mau Mau, concentrated around Nairobi, were a secret terrorist organization made up of Kikuyu tribesmen led by Jomo Kenyatta (1898–1978) and determined to restore the country to native African control. From October 20, 1952, to October 1956, Mau Mau bands marauded throughout the so-called "white highlands," destroying plantations and slaughtering white settlers. The Mau Mau also turned terrorism against other natives, compelling many black Africans to join their ranks or suffer death. The worst incident occurred on March 26, 1953, when 1,000 Mau Mau attacked the "loyal" (friendly to whites) village of Cari, killing 97 and mutilating 37 more.

On October 20, 1952, British authorities declared a state of emergency and sent thousands of regular troops into the field. Ringleaders and assumed ringleaders were targeted for arrest. Despite this action, however, the Mau Mau movement was so well established that, even without key leaders, such as Kenyatta, who was jailed in 1953, the terror continued and even intensified. The British responded by building large concentration camps into which Mau Maus and suspected Mau Maus were thrown. Certain villages were surrounded by contingents of armed guards. Under such pressure, many of the Mau Mau fled into the forests and hills, and waged a guerrilla war from there. However, the British troops proved effective at flushing the terrorists out.

In 1956, the Mau Mau mastermind Dedan Kimathi (d. 1957) was captured, which brought a rapid diminution of Mau Mau activity. He was executed on February 18 of the following year. Although the uprising had been put down, the world was made acutely aware of the injustices of long-established European colonialism in Africa. The great African independence movements of the late 1950s and early 1960s were built on the foundation of the Mau Mau movement.

Further reading: E. S. Atieno Odhiambo and John Lonsdale, eds., *Mau Mau and Nationhood: Arms, Authority, and Narration* (Columbus: Ohio University Press, 2003); Wunyabi O. Maloba, *Mau Mau and Kenya: An Analysis of a Peasant Revolt* (Bloomington: Indiana University Press, 1999).

Mauretania, French Conquest of *See* FRENCH CONQUEST OF MAURETANIA.

Mauryan Empire, Conquests of the (323–180 B.C.E.)

PRINCIPAL COMBATANTS: The Mauryan Empire vs. various kingdoms of India and Hellenic forces

PRINCIPAL THEATER(S): India

DECLARATION: None

MAJOR ISSUES AND OBJECTIVES: The rulers of the Mauryan Empire sought to unify India and repel advances by the Hellenic armies.

OUTCOME: Under the first three rulers of the Mauryan dynasty, the empire expanded its borders and held invaders from the west at bay.

APPROXIMATE MAXIMUM NUMBER OF MEN UNDER ARMS: Unknown

CASUALTIES: Unknown

TREATIES: Unknown

In 323 B.C.E., Chandragupta Maurya (r. 323–298 B.C.E.) seized control of the Magadhan throne in present-day India. This clan had grown from being one of 16 competing political factions in 600 B.C.E. to being the dominant group in the fifth century B.C.E. The Magadha Empire had its capital in Pataliputra (or Patna) and controlled trade along the Ganges River. When Chandragupta Maurya came to the throne, he seized land east of the Indus River and south to the Narmada (or Narbada) River. Ejecting the Macedonians from northwestern India, he was determined to close the avenues of invasion through the mountain passes of present-day Afghanistan. In 305 B.C.E., he defeated the army of Seleucus Nicator (c. 358–280 B.C.E.) of Macedonia. By terms of the treaty between the two powers, Seleucus ceded the provinces east of the Indus River and large areas of Arachosia and Gedrosia west of the river to Chandragupta in exchange for 500 war elephants.

Chandragupta's son, Bindusara (fl. 298–273 B.C.E.), inherited an enormous military force from his father including a secret service and office of naval affairs. During his reign from 297 to 274 B.C.E., he further broadened the reach of the Mauryan Empire through his conquest of the Deccan (central India).

Asoka (fl. 269–232 B.C.E.), the grandson of Chandragupta, conquered the Kalinga kingdom along the eastern coast of India as far as the Godavari River. With these conquests, the Mauryan Empire included all of the subcontinent, except its southern tip, plus Nepal and a large part of Afghanistan. After taking Kalinga, Asoka became a Buddhist, pursued a policy of peace, and ably ruled his vast empire. When he died in 232 B.C.E., the Mauryan Empire became vulnerable to invaders from Bactria, Scythia, and Parthia. Indo-Hellenic forces captured the capital of Pataliputra, and by 180 B.C.E., the empire ceased to exist.

The Magadha Empire managed to survive, however, and reemerged as a considerable force under Chandragupta I (r. c. 320–c. 330 C.E.; no relation to Chandragupta Maurya) in about 320 C.E.

Further reading: R. C. Majumdar, *Ancient India* (Delhi: Motilal Banasidass, 1982); Gurcham Singh Sandhu, *A Military History of Ancient India* (New Delhi: Vision Books, 2000); Francis Watson, *A Concise History of India* (London: Thames and Hudson, 1981).

Maximian's Revolt (310)

PRINCIPAL COMBATANTS: Maximian vs. Constantine
PRINCIPAL THEATER(S): Gaul (Roman Empire)
DECLARATION: None
MAJOR ISSUES AND OBJECTIVES: Maximian wished to overthrow Constantine and reassume his former role as emperor.
OUTCOME: Maximian was defeated and forced to commit suicide.
APPROXIMATE MAXIMUM NUMBER OF MEN UNDER ARMS: Unknown
CASUALTIES: Unknown
TREATIES: None

Diocletian (245–313), emperor of the West, and Maximian (d. 310), emperor of the East, abdicated their thrones in 305 and were succeeded as augusti by, respectively, Constantius (r. 293–306) in the West and Galerius (r. 305–311) in the East. Two new caesars were appointed, Flavius Valerius Severus (r. 305–311) and Galerius Valerius Maximinus Daia (r. 305–313), in preference to Constantius's son Flavius Valerius Aurelius Constantinus (Constantine, r. 306–337) and Marcus Aurelius Valerius Maxentius (r. 306–312), the son of Maximian. This breach of succession triggered the ROMAN CIVIL WAR (306–307).

In the meantime, Rome was continually menaced by barbarians, and Constantine, now junior augustus, set off on a campaign against the Franks in Gaul. Maximian exploited his absence by staging a revolt in Constantine's court at Arelate (modern Arles, France) with the object of becoming sole emperor. To Maximian's consternation, however, Constantine returned swiftly to Arelate and was able to drive Maximian and his partisans out of the city to Marseille. There Constantine captured Maximian. Given a choice between degradation and an honorable suicide, Maximian chose the latter.

See also ROMAN CIVIL WAR (311–312).

Further reading: John Boardman, Jasper Griffin, and Oswyn Murray, eds., *The Oxford History of the Roman World* (New York: Oxford University Press, 1991); Jacob Burkhardt, *The Age of Constantine the Great* (Berkeley: University of California Press, 1982); Arther Ferrill, *The Fall of the Roman Empire: The Military Explanation* (New York: Thames and Hudson, 1986); Colin Wells, *The Roman Empire,* 2nd ed. (Cambridge, Mass.: Harvard University Press, 1995).

Maximilian's Invasion of Switzerland *See* AUSTRO-SWISS WAR (1499).

Mayan Revolt (1546)

PRINCIPAL COMBATANTS: Spanish conquistadores vs.
Mayan Indians
PRINCIPAL THEATER(S): Honduras
DECLARATION: None
MAJOR ISSUES AND OBJECTIVES: Conquest of the Mayans
OUTCOME: After years of effective resistance, the Mayans
were conquered by intense application of utmost brutality
and violence.
APPROXIMATE MAXIMUM NUMBER OF MEN UNDER ARMS:
Unknown
CASUALTIES: Unknown, but nearly genocide among the
Mayans
TREATIES: None

The Spanish conquistador Hernán Cortés (1485–1547)
subjugated the Aztec Empire in 1521, then from 1522 to
1539, he led expeditions south, into southern Mexico and
northern Central America, penetrating as far as El Salvador.
In Central America, especially Honduras, he encountered
extremely fierce resistance from the Mayans (1524–26),
whom he failed to subjugate. It was left to the military successor of Cortés, Francisco de Montejo (c. 1484–c. 1550),
to lead a series of larger expeditions into Honduras during
1539. These suppressed Mayan resistance by the most brutal and violent of means, even to the point of genocide.

See also SPANISH CONQUEST OF MEXICO; SPANISH CON-
QUEST OF NICARAGUA; SPANISH CONQUEST OF YUCATÁN.

Further reading: Inga Clendinnen, *Ambivalent Conquests: Maya and Spaniard in Yucatan, 1517–1570* (New
York: Cambridge University Press, 1990).

Ma Yuan's Southern Campaign (40–43)
See TRUNG SISTERS' REBELLION (39–43).

Mecca, Sack of (930)

PRINCIPAL COMBATANTS: Karmathian raiders vs. the
Muslims of Arabia
PRINCIPAL THEATER(S): Mecca, Saudi Arabia
DECLARATION: None
MAJOR ISSUES AND OBJECTIVES: Bent on plunder, the
Karmathians sacked Mecca and stole the Black Stone, one
of its more sacred objects.
OUTCOME: The Black Stone was held by the Karmathians
for 10 years.
APPROXIMATE MAXIMUM NUMBER OF MEN UNDER ARMS:
Unknown
CASUALTIES: Unknown
TREATIES: None

The Karmathians (*see* KARMATHIAN REVOLT) were Muslim
heretics who lived in northeast Arabia. In the early
decades of the eighth century they frequently invaded
Mesopotamia and raided Baghdad. One such raid occurred
in 930 when they sacked Mecca, Islam's holy city, and
made off with the Black Stone from the Kaaba (the Muslim shrine in Mecca). The Karmathians held onto the
sacred treasure for a decade before the Fatimids, the ruling
dynasty in North Africa, forced them to return it.

Further reading: Karen Armstrong, *A Short History of
Islam* (New York: Random House, 2002); Hugh Kennedy,
*The Prophet and the Age of the Caliphates: The Islamic Near
East from the Sixth to the Eleventh Century* (New York:
Longman, 1986); Michel C. Morony, *Iraq after the Muslim
Conquest* (Princeton, N.J.: Princeton University Press,
1984).

Mecca-Medina War (624–630)

PRINCIPAL COMBATANTS: Followers of Muhammad vs.
Qurayshite pagans
PRINCIPAL THEATER(S): Medina and Mecca
DECLARATION: None
MAJOR ISSUES AND OBJECTIVES: Muhammad fought a jihad
(holy war), to establish Islam throughout the Arab world.
OUTCOME: Mecca fell to Muhammad, who established it
as the holy city of Islam.
APPROXIMATE MAXIMUM NUMBER OF MEN UNDER ARMS:
Muhammad, 3,000; Qurayshites, 10,000
CASUALTIES: Unknown
TREATIES: Treaty of al-Hudaybiyah, 629

An oasis on the old caravan trade route linking the Mediterranean world with the Middle East, Africa, and South
Asia, ancient Mecca had gradually developed by Roman
and Byzantine times into an important trade and religious
center. Ptolemy called it Macoraba, and—according to
Islamic tradition—Abraham and Ishmael, his son by
Hagar, built the Kaaba as the house of God. The Kaaba, a
cube-shaped stone building destroyed and rebuilt many
times, was the goal of pilgrimages to Mecca before the
coming of Islam. The city itself was controlled during bib-
lical times by a series of Yemeni tribes, and under the
pagan Quraysh, the town became something of a city-
state, with commercial ties not only to the rest of Arabia,
but to Ethiopia and to Europe as well. A desert entrepôt
for trade, pilgrimage, and poetry festivals, Mecca grew his-
torically significant with the birth there of Muhammad
(570–632), the founding prophet of Islam.

In the summer of 621, 12 men from Medina—another
desert oasis, this one in the Hejaz region of modern Saudi
Arabia—who were visiting Mecca for the annual pilgrimage to the Kaaba (which, of course, was then still a pagan

shrine), fell under the sway of the new prophet who was denouncing the pagan Arab religion of the native Qurayshites. To Muhammad they secretly professed themselves Muslims before returning home to preach the new faith. Consequently, at the pilgrimage in June 622 a representative party of 75 people from Medina, including two women, not only professed Islam but also took an oath to defend the Prophet as they would their own kin in what became known as the two Pledges of al-'Aqaba. Muhammad urged many among his growing number of followers in Mecca to make their way in small groups to Medina. About 70 did so. Meanwhile, before Muhammad could leave to join them, the Meccans plotted his murder, at which point Muhammad slipped away and traveled to Medina by a devious route, a flight that became known in Latin as the Hegira and marks the beginning of the Muslim calendar—July 16, 622, in the Gregorian system. Muhammad reached Medina safely on September 24, 622.

Medina was a different kind of town from Mecca. Like Mecca, it was an oasis, one where date palms flourished and cereals grew, but here the Jews had become prominent in the centuries following their expulsion from Palestine by the Roman emperor Hadrian about 135 C.E. Several Jewish clans, who had settled among the original Arabs, had developed Medina's agriculture, and they still had the best lands. Here, too, the predominant Yemeni tribe had adopted the Jewish religion around 400 C.E. Later Arab immigrants belonging to the tribes of al-Aws and al-Khazraj, had also become well established in Medina. These eight or so clans, however, had fallen into serious feuds, and these feuds had produced much bloodshed only a few years past. Peace had never been fully restored. Prepared by their close contact with the Jews, many among the Arabs were perhaps looking for a messianic religious leader who would deliver them from oppression and establish a kingdom in which justice prevailed, as well as someone to act as an arbiter among their feuding kin. Little surprise that Muhammad's following continued to grow as he plotted his revenge against Mecca.

Soon he had planned out a military campaign against the Qurayshites. In March 624, he led 300 warriors in an ambush of a 1,000-person Meccan caravan en route from Syria, which traveled under the religious auspices of Mecca's Umayyad leader, Abu Sufyan (563–651), whose extended clan at first rejected Islam. Muhammad's violation of the religious sanctity of the pilgrimage awakened Mecca to the dangers posed by him and his followers.

The next year, the Qurayshites counterattacked Muhammad and his followers at the Hill of Uhud, outside of Mecca. This was followed by an attack on Medina by 10,000 Meccans under Abu Sufyan in 627. With a mere 3,000 men, however, Muhammad successfully defended Medina, and Abu Sufyan agreed to the Treaty of al-Hudaybiyah. This allowed Muhammad and his faithful to make a sacred pilgrimage to Mecca in 629. When a faction of Meccans violated the treaty by attacking the pilgrims in November 629, Muhammad mounted an assault on Mecca in January 630. Meeting no resistance, his army destroyed a large number of pagan idols in the city. Muhammad remained, and his preaching, not the force of his arms, won over to Islam a large portion of the city. He was subsequently invited to establish Mecca as the holy city of Islam.

Further reading: Karen Armstrong, *A Short History of Islam* (New York: Random House, 2002); Ann Holt, K. S. Lambton, and Bernard Lewis, *The Cambridge History of Islam,* 2 vols. (New York: Cambridge University Press, 1970); Hugh Kennedy, *The Prophet and the Age of the Caliphates: The Islamic Near East From the Sixth to the Eleventh Century* (New York: Longman, 1986); Michel C. Morony, *Iraq after the Muslim Conquest* (Princeton, N.J.: Princeton University Press, 1984).

Median-Lydian War (590–585 B.C.E.)

PRINCIPAL COMBATANTS: Media vs. Lydia
PRINCIPAL THEATER(S): Western Anatolia (Asian Turkey)
DECLARATION: None recorded
MAJOR ISSUES AND OBJECTIVES: The kingdoms contested possession of western Anatolia.
OUTCOME: A draw resulting in a boundary agreement
APPROXIMATE MAXIMUM NUMBER OF MEN UNDER ARMS: Unknown
CASUALTIES: Unknown
TREATIES: None recorded; although peace was achieved through a boundary settlement and royal marriage.

Following the collapse of the Assyrian Empire after the fall of Nineveh, the former Assyrian territories were divided between Babylonia and Media. The division precipitated the decline of Lydia, which had been the great power in western Anatolia (the Asian portion of Turkey). The Median-Lydian War was a first major step in the decline.

Media's King Cyaxares (d. 585) attempted to invade and acquire the Anatolian territory of Urartu (Armenia), which Lydia's King Alyattes (c. 619–560) also claimed. By 590, Median forces had advanced to the eastern boundary of Lydia at the Halys (Kizil Irrnak) River. There, the Lydians checked the advance, holding the Medians at the river for the next five years.

Nothing specific is known about these battles, but Babylonia and Cilicia ultimately mediated the dispute, and the two kingdoms, their resources exhausted in futile combat, agreed on the Kizil Irrnak (Halys River) as the boundary between them. The Greek historian Herodotus (c. 484–c. 425) records that the daughter of Alyattes married Cyaxares' son, thereby preserving the peace until the PERSIAN-LYDIAN WAR of 547–46 B.C.E., which brought about the final collapse of Lydia.

Further reading: George C. Cameron, *History of Early Iran* (New York: Greenwood Press, 1968); William Cullican, *The Medes and Persians* (New York: Praeger, 1965); Herodotus, *The Histories,* trans. Aubrey De Selincourt (New York: Penguin, 2003).

Median-Persian Revolt (550–549 B.C.E.)

PRINCIPAL COMBATANTS: Persia (Anshan) vs. the Medes
PRINCIPAL THEATER(S): Anshan
DECLARATION: None recorded
MAJOR ISSUES AND OBJECTIVES: Cyrus II the Great wanted independence from the Median Empire.
OUTCOME: Cyrus achieved his objective and founded the Persian Empire.
APPROXIMATE MAXIMUM NUMBER OF MEN UNDER ARMS: Unknown
CASUALTIES: Unknown
TREATIES: None recorded

Cyrus II the Great (c. 600–529), who ruled the Median (Persian) kingdom of Anshan, rebelled against his grandfather Astyages (fl. 584–549), king of the Medes and, therefore, overlord of the Persians during 584–550.

Cyrus's father was a Persian named Cambyses I (fl. 600–559), and his mother was a Median princess. Cyrus, who founded the Achaemenid dynasty, did not at first seek independence for Persia, but merely the reform of a waning kingdom. However, Cyrus seized upon Persian discontent with Astyages, a cruel and inept ruler, to organize rebellious Medians into an army. During 550, Cyrus led his rebel army in a series of indecisive battles. However, the following year, Astyages' own army mutinied, which gave Cyrus the advantage he needed to defeat the unpopular ruler. Taking Astyages captive, Cyrus made Anshan the core of a revived Persian Empire. He spared the conquered ruler's life, an act of generosity that would lead to the PERSIAN-LYDIAN WAR.

Further reading: William Cullican, *The Medes and Persians* (New York: Praeger, 1965); Josef Wiesehofer, *Ancient Persia* (New York: I. B. Tauris, 2000).

Megiddo, First Battle of (c. 1469 B.C.E.)

PRINCIPAL COMBATANTS: Egypt vs. the Mitanni kingdom and a Syrian-Palestinian coalition
PRINCIPAL THEATER(S): Megiddo, on the frontier of Mesopotamia
DECLARATION: None recorded
MAJOR ISSUES AND OBJECTIVES: Egypt wanted to revive and expand its empire.

OUTCOME: The battle resulted in the collapse of the Syrian-Palestinian coalition and the subjugation of much of southwestern Asia to Egypt.
APPROXIMATE MAXIMUM NUMBER OF MEN UNDER ARMS: Unknown
CASUALTIES: Unknown
TREATIES: None

Megiddo, a fortress city strategically situated at the gateway to Mesopotamia, was the scene of many battles and for that reason was prophesied as the site of the Battle of Armageddon (in Hebrew "Hill of Megiddo"), when the forces of good and evil would contend at the end of the world.

The First Battle of Megiddo followed the decline of Egyptian influence in Syria and Palestine after the expansion of the Mitanni kingdom during the HURRIAN CONQUESTS. Egypt's King Thutmose III (fl. c. 1500–1447 B.C.E.), in an effort to restore Egyptian power, undertook a series of campaigns in the Near East during the 1470s. He managed to regain control of Palestine, and his forces invaded northern Syria. Apparently, however, his advance was checked by a coalition of some 330 Syrian and Palestinian princes under the leadership King Kadesh (fl. 1460s B.C.E.) of the Mitanni.

It was about 1469 B.C.E., near the northern Palestinian fortress city of Megiddo, which effectively guarded entry into Mesopotamia, that the coalition forces engaged the Egyptians. The Egyptians divided their forces into three contingents and surprised the fortress defenders at dawn. The princes' army withdrew into Megiddo, leaving their encampment for the Egyptians to loot. Thutmose then directed a seven-month siege of the city, which ultimately collapsed.

The victory at Megiddo not only revived Egyptian power but established an Egyptian empire in southwestern Asia. Except for the Mitanni king himself, the princes of the coalition subjugated themselves to Egypt, and the mighty kingdoms of Babylonia and Assyria, as well as the Hittites, agreed to pay Egypt tribute. Having gained so much, Thutmose invaded southeastern Mitanni, but failed to conquer the kingdom at this time.

See also MEGIDDO, SECOND BATTLE OF.

Further reading: Hans Goedicke, *The Battle of Megiddo* (Baltimore: Halgo, 2001).

Megiddo, Second Battle of (609 B.C.E.)

PRINCIPAL COMBATANTS: Egypt vs. Judah
PRINCIPAL THEATER(S): Megiddo, at the frontier of Judah
DECLARATION: None
MAJOR ISSUES AND OBJECTIVES: Refused passage across Judah to aid his Syrian allies, King Necho of Egypt engaged Judah's army.

OUTCOME: Outnumbered, the army of Judah was defeated.

APPROXIMATE MAXIMUM NUMBER OF MEN UNDER ARMS: Unknown

CASUALTIES: Unknown

TREATIES: None

Despite Megiddo's conquest by the Egyptians in the First Battle of MEGIDDO, over the centuries, the ancient Palestinian strategic crossroads fell to the Israelites, along with many other sites in the area. Following the Fall of NINEVEH in 612 B.C.E., Assyria's ally Egypt resolved to help the Assyrians retake their lost capital at Harran. Egypt's King Necho II (fl. c. 609–593 B.C.E.) asked leave from the kingdom of Judah to cross its territory in order to come to Syria's aid. Judah refused permission, but sent only a small force against Necho's large army. The two forces clashed at Megiddo, where Judah's troops were vanquished, and the nation's king, Josiah, was killed in the battle by an arrow.

Following his victory, King Necho advanced to his Syrian allies, but his efforts to aid in the retaking of Harran failed. Necho returned to Palestine, where he successfully defended his kingdom against Babylonian incursions.

Further reading: Hans Goedicke, *The Battle of Megiddo* (Baltimore: Halgo, 2001).

Meiji Restoration (1863–1868)

PRINCIPAL COMBATANTS: Tokugawa shogunate vs. forces of the western daimyo (warlords) in support of the Meiji emperor

PRINCIPAL THEATER(S): Edo (Tokyo) and Kyoto, Japan

DECLARATION: None

MAJOR ISSUES AND OBJECTIVES: The daimyo of Japan's western provinces, long opposed to the rule of the shoguns, rebelled against the shogun and threw their support behind the new Meiji emperor to end shogun rule and restore Japanese imperial authority.

OUTCOME: The shogun was maneuvered out of power, and the Meiji emperor restored as full head of the Japanese state.

APPROXIMATE MAXIMUM NUMBER OF MEN UNDER ARMS: Unknown

CASUALTIES: Losses among the Meiji and daimyo forces were light (numbers unknown), but in July 1868, some 3,000 diehard adherents of the Tokugawa shogunate were exterminated.

TREATIES: None

After the early 17th century, the role of the Japanese emperor was reduced to that of a figurehead, with the real governing power lodged in the Tokugawa shogun, a hereditary military ruler. The shogun ruled from Edo (Tokyo), whereas the emperor was ensconced in the ancient city of Kyoto. This dual system of governance was forever altered by the opening of Japan to western trade in the mid-19th century.

At first, the feudal lords of western Japan, the daimyo, were hostile to western traders, but they came to see trade as a positive force and as an opportunity to overthrow the rule of the shoguns. The daimyo advised foreign traders to deal not with the shogun, but with the emperor. This put the shogun at odds with the traders. Nevertheless, when a contingent of Dutch, British, and French trading vessels arrived in November 1865 with armed naval escort, the shogun, fearing naval assault, agreed to persuade the emperor to conclude a trade treaty, which he did.

In 1866, the western province of Choshu rebelled against the shogun, who persuaded the emperor, Komei (d. 1867), to mount a military campaign against the province. The emperor agreed, and the so-called Summer War commenced, but the emperor broke off the campaign as soon as the shogun died in September 1866. Early the next year, the emperor also died and was succeeded by his young son Mutsuhito (1852–1912). Later in the year, the daimyo of the western provinces prevailed upon the new shogun, Yoshinoba (1837–1913), to resign, pointing out to him that the continued existence of the shogunate with imperial rule was tearing the nation apart. Led to believe that he would be given a prominent position in the new imperial government, the shogun resigned in November 1867 and traveled to Kyoto. In fact, the retired shogun was frozen out of power.

At the start of 1868, the daimyo of the western provinces, freed from domination by the shogun, invaded Kyoto and took control of the imperial capital from the Tokugawan troops stationed there. The retired shogun took his troops back to Edo, only to realize that he was greatly outnumbered by the army now prepared to support the emperor. Therefore, he surrendered Edo and retired permanently. Some 3,000 diehard adherents of the shogunate held out on nearby Veno Hill. On July 4, 1868, they were exterminated to a man.

Despite sporadic resistance to the restoration of the full authority of Mutsuhito—now renamed Meiji—in the north, the "revolution" was, for all practical purposes, concluded by the fall of 1868.

Coinciding with the beginning of the Meiji Restoration was the SHIMONOSEKI WAR, which involved the Western powers France, Britain, the United States, and the Netherlands.

Further reading: William G. Beasley, *Meiji Restoration* (Palo Alto, Calif.: Stanford University Press, 1972); John W. Hall, *Japan: From Prehistory to Modern Times* (Tokyo: C. E. Tuttle Co., 1971); Mikiso Hane, *Modern Japan: A Historical Survey,* 3rd ed. (Boulder, Colo.: Westview Press, 2001); James Murdoch, *A History of Japan,* 3 vols. (New

York: Routledge, 1996); George B. Samson, *A History of Japan,* 3 vols. (Palo Alto, Calif.: Stanford University Press, 1958–63).

Memel Insurrection (1923)

PRINCIPAL COMBATANTS: Memel insurrectionists vs. France
PRINCIPAL THEATER(S): Memel (Klaipeda), Lithuania
DECLARATION: None
MAJOR ISSUES AND OBJECTIVES: Governance of the city and district of Memel was disputed between post–World War I Allied authorities and the Lithuanian government.
OUTCOME: The French garrison was driven out of Memel, and the Allies compromised with the Lithuanian government in the creation of Memel as an autonomous district within Lithuania.
APPROXIMATE MAXIMUM NUMBER OF MEN UNDER ARMS: French garrison strength was under 1,000 men; number of insurrectionists much greater.
CASUALTIES: Light
TREATIES: Memel Statute, May 8, 1924

Memel (Klaipeda, Lithuania) was a predominantly German-speaking city in western Lithuania. By the terms of the Treaty of Versailles ending WORLD WAR I, Memel had been governed as a mandate of the Allied powers since 1919. Lithuania asked to be given control of Memel, but the Allies demurred, and established a French garrison to administer the local government. On January 11, 1923, a Lithuanian-backed insurrection took place against the garrison, which withdrew under fire. In the garrison's absence, the Lithuanian government took control of the city and district. Seeking a compromise, Allied authorities declared Memel an autonomous region within Lithuania, a situation the Lithuanian government accepted by the Memel Statute of May 8, 1924.

Further reading: Arvids Ziedonis, William L. Winter, and Mardi Valgemäe, *Baltic History* (Columbus, Ohio: Association for the Advancement of Baltic Studies, 1974); Vytas Stanley Vardys and Judith Sedaitis, *Lithuania: The Rebel Nation* (Denver: Westview Press, 1966).

Menander's Wars of Expansion (c. 150–c. 140 B.C.E.)

PRINCIPAL COMBATANTS: Menander's Greek army vs. the kingdoms in northern India
PRINCIPAL THEATER(S): Northern India
DECLARATION: None
MAJOR ISSUES AND OBJECTIVES: Under pressure from the north and northwest from the Scythians and Parthians, Menander, ruler of Bactria, turned east and conquered the northern portion of present-day India.
OUTCOME: Menander gained control of northern India as far as Pataliputra, but by 100 B.C.E., the Greek kingdom disappeared from India.
APPROXIMATE MAXIMUM NUMBER OF MEN UNDER ARMS: Unknown
CASUALTIES: Unknown
TREATIES: None

During the second century B.C.E., the kingdom of Bactria was in nearly perpetual strife. Euthydemus (fl. early second century B.C.E.) expanded his control to the southwest into Gandhara (northern Afghanistan) and the Punjab. His son Demetrius (fl. mid second century B.C.E.) then conquered the northern half of the Indus Valley. In 175 B.C.E., Eucratides seized control of Bactria itself while Demetrius was away on campaign. During the ensuing civil war, Eucratides captured most of Gandhara and the western Punjab from Demetrius and his successors. After the assassination of Eucratides (c. 162 B.C.E.), one of Demetrius's descendants, Menander (fl. mid second century B.C.E.), was victorious over the descendants of Eucratides, who managed to retain land in the western Punjab and Kabul Valley. Menander then faced invasions by the Scythians and the Parthians, and his control was reduced to southern Bactria, Gandhara, and parts of Arachosia and the Punjab. Pressed from the north and northwest by the Scythians and Parthians, Menander turned his sights east and made conquests in northern India as far as Pataliputra. He had a great influence on India and became known in Indian history as Milinda. The Greek kingdoms declined over the next century as the Hindus and the barbarians pushed the Hellenes out of the region. In about 100 B.C.E., they disappeared from India, and in about 40 B.C.E., they were pushed by the Scythians out of Gandhara.

Further reading: John Boardman, Jasper Griffin, and Oswyn Murray, eds., *The Oxford History of Greece and the Hellenistic World* (New York: Oxford University Press, 1991); M. Cary, *A History of the Greek World from 323 to 146 B.C.* (New York: Barnes and Noble, 1963); William W. Turn, *Greeks in Bactria and India* (Golden, Colo.: Ares Publishers, 1984); F. W. Walbank, *The Hellenistic World* (Cambridge, Mass.: Harvard University Press, 1993).

Mercenaries, Revolt of   See CARTHAGINIAN CIVIL WAR.

Messenian War, First (c. 736–716 B.C.E.)

PRINCIPAL COMBATANTS: Spartans vs. Messenians
PRINCIPAL THEATER(S): Mount Ithome region, Peloponnese

DECLARATION: None recorded
MAJOR ISSUES AND OBJECTIVES: The Spartans wanted to conquer the Messenians to gain access to their fertile lands.
OUTCOME: After two decades of war, the conquest was successful.
APPROXIMATE MAXIMUM NUMBER OF MEN UNDER ARMS: Unknown
CASUALTIES: Unknown
TREATIES: None recorded, but the Messenians were compelled to yield to Sparta half of all crops produced.

The Dorians of northern Greece invaded the Peloponnese between 1100 and 950 B.C.E. They conquered the eastern areas of the peninsula, settling in the valley of Lacedaemon, where they made Sparta their capital. The people they conquered, called helots, were enslaved. Next, the Spartans attacked and subjugated the Laconians, after which, beginning about 736, they commenced their two-decade war against the Messenians, also resident in the Peloponnese.

Messenian resistance was concentrated at Mount Ithome, which guarded passage to the fertile plain of Stenyclarus. Under their king (according to legend), Theopompus (fl. 700s B.C.E.), the Spartans finally prevailed against the Messenians by 716. They extorted from the vanquished people half of all their produce, and they subjected the Messenians to general humiliation.

See also MESSENIAN WAR, SECOND; MESSENIAN WAR, THIRD.

Further reading: John Boardman, Jasper Griffin, and Oswyn Murray, eds., *The Oxford History of Greece and the Hellenistic World* (New York: Oxford University Press, 1991); Victor Davis Hanson, *The Wars of the Ancient Greeks* (New York: Sterling, 2002); W. G. Forrest, *A History of Sparta: 950–192 B.C.* (New York: W. W. Norton, 1978); L. H. Jeffery, *Archaic Greece: The City-States, c. 700–500 B.C.* (New York: St. Martin's Press, 1976).

Messenian War, Second (c. 650–630 B.C.E.)

PRINCIPAL COMBATANTS: Spartans vs. Messenian rebels
PRINCIPAL THEATER(S): Messenia
DECLARATION: None recorded
MAJOR ISSUES AND OBJECTIVES: The Messenians wanted to throw off the Spartan yoke.
OUTCOME: Despite early victories, the Messenians were ultimately defeated and enslaved.
APPROXIMATE MAXIMUM NUMBER OF MEN UNDER ARMS: Unknown
CASUALTIES: Unknown
TREATIES: None

The Messenians were conquered by the Spartans in the First MESSENIAN WAR. About 650 B.C.E., growing increasingly restive under Spartan rule, they rebelled, rallying around the semilegendary leader Aristomenes (fl. seventh century). The war that ensued was both long and costly, driving the Spartans close to bankruptcy. In 630, at the Battle of Mount Eira, a weakened Spartan army was defeated. This catastrophe elevated Lycurgus (fl. seventh century) to leadership among the Spartans. He directed vast social reforms, which included conscription of all males into military service—a move designed to avoid another economic disaster in warfare. Indeed, under Lycurgus, Sparta became the first recorded civilization devoted primarily to war.

The strategy proved effective. The vast citizen-manned Spartan army crushed the Messenians, reducing them to the status of slaves, or helots.

See also MESSENIAN WAR, THIRD.

Further reading: John Boardman, Jasper Griffin, and Oswyn Murray, eds., *The Oxford History of Greece and the Hellenistic World* (New York: Oxford University Press, 1991); Victor Davis Hanson, *The Wars of the Ancient Greeks* (New York: Sterling, 2002); W. G. Forrest, *A History of Sparta: 950–192 B.C.* (New York: W. W. Norton, 1978); L. H. Jeffery, *Archaic Greece: The City-States, c. 700–500 B.C.* (New York: St. Martin's Press, 1976).

Messenian War, Third (c. 464–455 B.C.E.)

PRINCIPAL COMBATANTS: Sparta vs. Messenian helots of Laconia
PRINCIPAL THEATER(S): Peloponnese, especially Mount Ithome
DECLARATION: None
MAJOR ISSUES AND OBJECTIVES: The helots wanted freedom from Spartan domination.
OUTCOME: The helots held out against the Spartans for years; those who survived the war were freed, but exiled.
APPROXIMATE MAXIMUM NUMBER OF MEN UNDER ARMS: Unknown
CASUALTIES: Unknown
TREATIES: None

The third war between the Spartans and Messenians was a slave revolt, the Messenians having been reduced to helots (slaves) by the conquering Spartans. When a major earthquake rocked Sparta in 464, the helots of Laconia took the opportunity to stage a rebellion. However, led by the semilegendary king Archidamus (fl. 476–427 B.C.E.), the Spartans suppressed them.

Still, the Messenians did not give up. They dug in at Mount Ithome in 463 and brilliantly resisted all Spartan attempts at siege. Following this, Sparta turned to Athens for help, securing 40,000 hoplite (Greek infantry) reinforcements. These soldiers immediately proved undependable, however, because many in their ranks were antagonistic toward Sparta. (Perceived as treachery, this situation ignited the FIRST PELOPONNESIAN WAR between Sparta and Athens.) Despite the failure of the Athenian reinforcements, Messenian resistance could not long endure. In 455 B.C.E., the Mount Ithome stronghold collapsed. The Spartans, having no wish to attempt to subjugate the Ithome rebels, freed those who had survived the long siege, albeit exiling them from the Peloponnese. These exiles fled to Athens, where they joined the Peloponnesian wars.

See also MESSENIAN WAR, FIRST; MESSENIAN WAR, SECOND.

Further reading: John Boardman, Jasper Griffin, and Oswyn Murray, eds., *The Oxford History of Greece and the Hellenistic World* (New York: Oxford University Press, 1991); Victor Davis Hanson, *The Wars of the Ancient Greeks* (New York: Sterling, 2002); W. G. Forrest, *A History of Sparta: 950–192 B.C.* (New York: W. W. Norton, 1978).

Messiah War *See* GHOST DANCE UPRISING (1890–1891).

Messinan Rebellion (1674–1679)

PRINCIPAL COMBATANTS: Anti-Spanish rebels (with French support) vs. Spain
PRINCIPAL THEATER(S): Messina, Sicily, and adjacent waters
DECLARATION: None
MAJOR ISSUES AND OBJECTIVES: The rebellion began with a dispute over the authority of the Spanish viceroy and grew into a full-scale rebellion against Spanish control of all Sicily.
OUTCOME: Although French aid allowed the Messinans to achieve victory, the withdrawal of French support brought about the abject subjugation of Messina.
APPROXIMATE MAXIMUM NUMBER OF MEN UNDER ARMS: Unknown
CASUALTIES: Unknown, but heavy as a result of postwar Spanish reprisals.
TREATIES: None

During the 17th century, Messina, Sicily, was controlled by Spain and governed locally by a Spanish viceroy. The contentious citizens of Messina frequently challenged the authority of the Spanish government, and, in 1674, one such challenge erupted into a riot between the viceroy's local supporters, called the Merli (aristocrats), and his opponents, the Malvezzi (democrats). The disturbance led

to the removal of the viceroy, and Sicily offered governance not only of Messina but of the entire island to King Louis XIV (1638–1715) of France in return for his support in their opposition to Spain. Louis agreed, was named king of Sicily, and dispatched a fleet to take and occupy Messina in 1676. This marked the commencement of a three-year naval war between France and Dutch-allied Spain on the sea. Although the French prevailed against the Dutch and the Spanish, the expenses of this war and the ongoing Third DUTCH WAR, created a crisis in France. Louis XIV precipitously withdrew the French fleet from Messina, leaving the city's rebels vulnerable to Spanish reprisals. Many were, in fact, executed. As a result of the rebellion, Messina was reduced from a major city to a backwater. Its population was reduced by half, and Spain enforced upon it a great degree of tyranny.

Further reading: Moses I. Finay Denis, Mack Smith, and Christopher Duggan. *History of Sicily* (New York: Viking Penguin, 1987).

Mexican-American War *See* UNITED STATES–MEXICAN WAR.

Mexican Civil War (1857–1860) *See* REFORM, WAR OF THE.

Mexican Civil War (1871–1877)

PRINCIPAL COMBATANTS: Rebels led by Porfirio Díaz vs. government of Mexico
PRINCIPAL THEATER(S): Tlaxcala and Mexico City
DECLARATION: None
MAJOR ISSUES AND OBJECTIVES: Díaz sought to topple the government and gain election as president.
OUTCOME: After two unsuccessful attempts at rebellion, Díaz defeated government forces in 1876 and was elected president the following year.
APPROXIMATE MAXIMUM NUMBER OF MEN UNDER ARMS: Rebels, 16,000; government strength unknown
CASUALTIES: Rebels, 1,000+ killed; government forces, 1,900 killed, 800 wounded, 3,000 taken prisoner
TREATIES: None

Three candidates competed for election as president of Mexico in 1871, the incumbent Benito Juárez (1806–72), Sebastián Lerdo de Tejada (1825–89), and Porfirio Díaz (1830–1915). Juárez was reelected and appointed Lerdo as chief justice of the supreme court. Excluded from government, Díaz organized a rebellion, which was quickly put down. Díaz took refuge among mountain Indians until the death of Juárez in 1872 and the ascension to the presidency of Lerdo, who proclaimed an amnesty for all those who had participated in the 1871 revolt.

Díaz unsuccessfully opposed Lerdo in the election of 1876, then led a revolt against Lerdo. Government forces defeated Díaz's rebels, who withdrew across the border into the United States, where they regrouped and resupplied. While this army, led by General Manuel Gonzalez (1833–93), recrossed the border, Díaz traveled to Veracruz by way of Cuba, then advanced to Oaxaca, where he assumed command of another army. Gonzalez's army came down from the north while Díaz attacked from Oaxaca, and the two forces converged on government troops in the province of Tlaxcala at the battle of Tecoac, November 16, 1876. The government forces were defeated with disastrous losses, and, Díaz advanced on the capital. Before his advance, Lerdo fled into exile, and Díaz was elected president in 1877. He became a ruthless dictator and was himself overthrown in the MEXICAN CIVIL WAR (1911).

Further reading: Enrique Krause, *Mexico: Biography of Power, A History of Modern Mexico, 1810–1996* (New York: HarperCollins, 1998); Walter V. Scholes, *Mexican Politics during the Juárez Regime, 1855–1872* (Columbia: University of Missouri Press, 1969); Paul Vanderwood, *Disorder and Progress: Bandits, Police, and Mexican Development*, rev. ed. (Wilmington, Del.: SR Books, 1992).

Mexican Civil War (1911)

PRINCIPAL COMBATANTS: Federal forces of Porfirio Díaz vs. forces of Francisco I. Madero, Pascual Orozco, and Francisco Pancho Villa
PRINCIPAL THEATER(S): Mexico
DECLARATION: None
MAJOR ISSUES AND OBJECTIVES: Madero both led and triggered revolutionary opposition to the dictatorship of Porfirio Díaz.
OUTCOME: Díaz was overthrown, but the 1911 war ushered in a long period of violent civil unrest.
APPROXIMATE MAXIMUM NUMBER OF MEN UNDER ARMS: Federals, 70,000; Rebel forces, about 20,000
CASUALTIES: Military deaths were under 1,000 total, but civilians suffered more extensive losses.
TREATIES: Treaty of Ciudad Juárez, 1911

Elected president of Mexico in 1877, Porfirio Díaz (1830–1915) had come to power on the heels of a civil war of his own making (*see* MEXICAN CIVIL WAR [1871–1877]). Thereafter, despite the pretense of national elections, Díaz served as Mexico's absolute ruler (with one brief interruption from 1880 to 1884) until 1911. Then, in the presidential election of 1910 the long-corrupt dictator was faced with a real challenge from the popular liberal candidate. Francisco I. Madero (1873–1913) was a frail but wealthy *hacendado* (rancher) and U.S.-educated lawyer from the northern state of Coahuila, who loudly promoted Díaz's ouster and announced his own Plan of San Luis Potosí, which called for liberal democracy in Mexico. President Díaz, in turn, had Madero arrested during the election and proclaimed himself the victor. On November 20, 1910, an outright rebellion, supported by the exiled Madero, broke out against the Díaz dictatorship.

Among those who rallied to Madero's cause was a band of some 500 peasants and outlaws led by a famous bandito leader named Doroteo Arango but known to his followers—and soon to history—as Francisco "Pancho" Villa (1877–1923). By December, when the rebellion spread to the south, into Morelos, Emiliano Zapata (1880–1919), hero of Mexico's poorest, including its Indians, joined the rebellion. Declaring himself to be fighting for "Land and Liberty," Zapata promised to transform this political uprising into a social revolution. By March Zapata had 3,000 troops in the south, and Madero's forces were growing stronger in the north as the venal, demoralized, and barely competent Federales lost control of extended areas of the country. Madero returned from his exile in Texas, crossing the Rio Grande to lead 500 devoted Mexican revolutionaries in an attack on Casas Grande on March 6, 1911. Although Madero suffered a minor wound and his troops met defeat, the revolution itself continued, especially in Chihuahua, where Pascual Orozco (1882–1915) and Pancho Villa led their troops in fights that grew ever bloodier, and where both sides committed atrocities.

In May 1911, they captured Ciudad Juárez, a victory that immediately revived the revolutionary opposition to Díaz throughout the country. Mexico City was wracked by anti-Díaz demonstrations, and the beleaguered dictator signed the Treaty of Ciudad Juárez, which called for his immediate resignation, after which Madero was elected to the presidency. His election, however, did not stem the tide of revolution. Ultimately Madero's revolution proved too conservative for those like Zapata, who dreamed of land for the landless and bread for the starving, and too moderate for those like Orozco, looking for the kind of spoils Mexico's civil upheavals had afforded its victors in the past. The first to break ranks was Zapata.

Realizing Madero's democracy was good for the bourgeoisie but hardly helped the poor peasantry of Morelos, Zapata resumed his social revolution on August 30, 1911. An unhappy Madero reluctantly sent the Indian general Victoriano Huerta (1854–1916) against his old ally. But Huerta had little luck finding, much less defeating Zapata's guerrillas. In November Zapata proclaimed his revolutionary agenda for Mexico in the Plan of Ayala, which included a vast program for the redistribution of land. Recruits flocked to his cause and before the year was out, Zapata's troops had captured Cuernavaca. Throughout

Madero's presidency and beyond, Zapata continued his agrarian rebellion, while further north the revolution's leaders lusted instead for spoils, plotting Madero's overthrow even as they touted liberal ideals. Madero had easily suppressed an attempted coup by former allies of the Díaz regime on December 13, 1911, and he put down a November rebellion in the north almost as easily, but afterward he felt it prudent to enlarge the Federal army from 30,000 to 70,000.

The most formidable of the northern revolts was led by the greedy Orozco, backed by the large landowners who had been the principal mainstays of Díaz. These aristocrats felt threatened even by Madero's very modest social reforms, and they funded Orozco's rebel army, whose troops marched under a red flag and were soon dubbed Colorados or Red Flaggers. They quickly overran Chihuahua and, by March 1912, had soundly defeated Madero's Federales. In response Madero once more sent out the hard-drinking General Huerta, this time to fight the Colorados. He soon not only checked Orozco's advance, but completely defeated him. Chasing the rebel leader across the border into the United States, Huerta mopped up the rebellion by October.

If Madero hoped for some relief, he was bound for disappointment. Almost immediately, Huerta began to show signs of megalomania (at one point he pretty much insanely threatened to execute Pancho Villa for insubordination). The thoroughly puffed up Huerta was soon scheming with the U.S. ambassador to free former Díaz supporters from prison and stage a coup, which cost Madero the presidency and his life in 1913. For the next 20 years, Mexico would be plagued by revolution and civil war.

See also MEXICAN CIVIL WAR (1920); MEXICAN Insurrections; MEXICAN REVOLT (1914–1915); VILLA'S RAIDS AND PERSHING'S PUNITIVE EXPEDITION.

Further reading: Ronald Atkin, *Revolution! Mexico 1910–1920* (New York: 1969); Enrique Krause, *Mexico: Biography of Power, A History of Modern Mexico, 1810–1996* (New York: HarperCollins, 1998); Stanley R. Ross, *Francisco I. Madero, Apostle of Mexican Democracy* (New York: AMS Press, 1970); Paul Vanderwood, *Disorder and Progress: Bandits, Police, and Mexican Development*, rev. ed. (Wilmington, Del.: SR Books, 1992).

Mexican Civil War (1920)

PRINCIPAL COMBATANTS: Rebels vs. Mexican federal government
PRINCIPAL THEATER(S): Mexico (especially Sonora, Veracruz, Mexico City)
DECLARATION: Creation of Sonora as a separate republic
MAJOR ISSUES AND OBJECTIVES: At issue was the succession to the presidency.

OUTCOME: The incumbent, Carranza, was driven out of office, and succeeded by the rebel leaders, Huerta and Obregón.
APPROXIMATE MAXIMUM NUMBER OF MEN UNDER ARMS: Rebel forces, 25,000; federal forces, 10,000
CASUALTIES: Light; however, Carranza was assassinated.
TREATIES: None

In 1920, Venustiano Carranza (1859–1920), president of Mexico, chose Ignacio Bonillas (fl. 1915–20) as his successor. Álvaro Obregón (1880–1928), minister of war in Carranza's cabinet and a man who had worked faithfully to put Carranza in office, felt betrayed by the anointing of Bonillas. He organized a revolt with Adolfo de la Huerta (1881–1955), former revolutionary and military officer, now governor of Sonora, and General Plutarco Elías Calles (1877–1945), commander of the Sonoran army. Together, they agitated for Carranza's resignation. During this campaign to oust Carranza, a general strike swept Sonora, and Carranza dispatched federal troops to break it. Huerta responded by declaring Sonora a sovereign republic, and Calles and Obregón recruited an army to oppose Carranza. Even Obregón, who had first made Carranza's ascendancy possible by his victories over Francisco "Pancho" Villa (1877–1923), deserted his president. As this popular revolt mounted, Carranza discovered that the government troops would not oppose the rebel army. With his allies and his generals deserting him left and right, he fled Mexico City with 10,000 followers on several trains. They headed toward Veracruz with gold looted from the Mexican treasury. Near Guadalupe, Carranza's lead train was destroyed by a dynamite-filled boxcar and 200 people were killed. As some 20,000 rebels began surrounding the trains, Carranza abandoned the rail lines and fled into the mountains of Puebla with a mere 100 loyalists. On May 14, he was murdered in his sleep by his own bodyguard. Obregón and his army marched into Mexico City unopposed, and Huerta was named provisional president until an election later in the year brought Obregón into office.

See also MEXICAN CIVIL WAR (1871–1877), MEXICAN CIVIL WAR (1911); MEXICAN REVOLT (1914–1915).

Further reading: Ronald Atkin, *Revolution! Mexico 1910–1920* (New York: 1969); Clarence C. Clarendon, *The United States and Pancho Villa; A Study in Unconventional Diplomacy* (Port Washington, N.Y.: Kennikat Press, 1972); John S. D. Eisenhower, *Intervention! The United States and the Mexican Revolution, 1913–1917* (New York: W. W. Norton, 1993); Enrique Krause, *Mexico: Biography of Power, A History of Modern Mexico, 1810–1996* (New York: HarperCollins, 1998); Paul Vanderwood, *Disorder and Progress: Bandits, Police, and Mexican Development*, rev. ed. (Wilmington, Del.: SR Books, 1992).

Mexican-French War (1861–1867)

PRINCIPAL COMBATANTS: France and Mexican conservative forces vs. forces loyal to Mexican president Juárez; U.S. forces were available, but never engaged

PRINCIPAL THEATER(S): Mexico

DECLARATION: None

MAJOR ISSUES AND OBJECTIVES: France deposed President Benito Juárez and installed and supported Austrian archduke Maximilian as emperor.

OUTCOME: After France withdrew its support for Maximilian, he was deposed and executed, and Juárez was reinstated as president.

APPROXIMATE MAXIMUM NUMBER OF MEN UNDER ARMS: French forces, 40,000, augmented by Mexican conservative forces; Liberal forces, 20,000 at any one time; U.S. forces (never engaged) 50,000

CASUALTIES: France, 6,654 killed; Mexican conservatives, 5,671 killed, 2,159 wounded, 4,379 prisoners; Juárez's forces, 31,962 killed (including 11,000 executed), 8,304 wounded, 33,281 prisoners

TREATIES: None

When President Benito Juárez (1806–72) sought to bring economic relief to impoverished Mexico by declaring a moratorium on the payment of foreign debts, he opened the door to European imperialism, providing an excuse for Britain, France, and Spain to send a military force to Mexico, ostensibly to compel the payment of the debt. The joint army landed at Veracruz on December 17, 1861, and advanced to Orizaba. Acting in good faith, however, the British and Spanish contingents withdrew after Juárez persuaded diplomats that the debts would be paid in good time. Emperor Napoleon III (1808–73) of France, however, seized the opportunity to effectively render Mexico a puppet with the intention of creating a new French empire in the New World.

Napoleon III sent an army of 7,500 men under General Charles Ferdinand Latrille de Lorencez (1814–92) against Mexico City, which was defeated at the Battle of Puebla on May 5, 1862, by 12,000 men under General Ignacio Zaragoza (1829–62). (The victory is celebrated today as the Mexican national holiday of Cinco de Mayo.) French casualties were in excess of 400, whereas the Mexicans lost 215 killed and wounded.

After Puebla, Lorencez was relieved and replaced by General Élie Forey (1804–72), who arrived in September 1862 with an additional 30,000 troops. On February 17, 1863, the greatly enlarged French army, augmented by Mexican conservative forces, advanced from Orizaba for a new assault on Puebla, which was defended by a much smaller garrison under General Jesús Gonzales Ortega (1824–81). Under continual guerrilla attack, the French were not able to begin the assault on Puebla until May 4. On May 8, Ignacio Comonfort (1812–63) led a Mexican column to the relief of Puebla, but was ambushed and routed by a French force under General Achille Bazaine (1811–88). Comonfort died in this battle. The situation now hopeless for the Puebla defenders, Ortega surrendered on May 17.

The French army now advanced to Mexico City, marching into the capital on June 7. President Juárez fled the capital and set up a headquarters and government in exile near the Texas border. On June 12, 1863, Archduke Maximilian (1832–67) of Austria was enthroned at the behest of Napoleon III as emperor of Mexico. Although the French emperor intended that Maximilian would govern as his puppet, the new emperor took his office seriously and was determined to govern as his own man and for the benefit of the Mexican people. This notwithstanding, the liberal majority of the Mexican people were opposed to the foreign ruler in their midst, and a guerrilla war commenced.

Throughout the war in Mexico, the ongoing UNITED STATES CIVIL WAR prevented that country's involvement. When the war ended in 1865, however, President Andrew Johnson invoked the Monroe Doctrine, by which the United States had proclaimed its standing position that any act of European aggression against a nation in the Americas would be regarded as an act against the United States itself. General Philip Sheridan (1831–88) was dispatched with 50,000 troops to the Rio Grande, the border with Mexico. A diplomatic standoff developed and, at last, on February 5, 1867, Napoleon III withdrew his troops and support from Maximilian—who, in any case, had proved a disappointment in his failure to bend entirely to the French emperor's will.

With the French forces gone, Maximilian was supported only by conservative Mexicans, but stubbornly refused to abdicate. Juárez dispatched liberal forces under Mariano Escobedo (1827–1902) to attack Maximilian and his forces at Querétaro, which was besieged for 71 days. On May 14, Maximilian was betrayed by one of his own men into surrender. Despite protests and appeals from the international community, he was court-martialed, sentenced to death, and executed on June 19, 1867. With that, the war ended.

Further reading: Michelle Cunningham, *Mexico and the Foreign Policy of Napoleon III* (London: Palgrave, 2001); Enrique Krause, *Mexico: Biography of Power, A History of Modern Mexico, 1810–1996* (New York: Harper-Collins, 1998); Ernst Pittner, *Maximilian's Lieutenant: A Personal History of the Mexican Campaign* (Albuquerque: University of New Mexico Press, 1993); Walter V. Scholes, *Mexican Politics during the Juárez Regime, 1855–1872* (Columbia: University of Missouri Press, 1969).

Mexican Insurrections (1926–1929)

PRINCIPAL COMBATANTS: Mexican government vs. supporters of the Catholic Church (*cristeros*)

PRINCIPAL THEATER(S): Mexico
DECLARATION: None
MAJOR ISSUES AND OBJECTIVES: President Calles (and successive puppets) enforced the harsh anticlerical provisions of Mexico's 1917 constitution, thereby provoking violent uprisings among supporters of the church.
OUTCOME: Sustained government pressure repeatedly suppressed Catholic violence.
APPROXIMATE MAXIMUM NUMBER OF MEN UNDER ARMS: Mexican federal forces, 79,759; Agrarista militia, 25,000; Catholic rebels, 50,000
CASUALTIES: Federal forces and Agraristas, 45,000–60,000 killed; Catholic rebels, 25,000–40,000 killed
TREATIES: None

Mexico's constitution of 1917 included strong anticlerical measures, which went unenforced until the presidency of Plutarco Elías Calles (1877–1945), who entered office in 1924. When, two years later, the Mexican Roman Catholic Church made an official condemnation of the constitutional provisions, Calles responded harshly and provocatively. He closed Catholic schools, convents, and seminaries, and he ordered all priests to register with the government. Adding insult to injury, he condemned the Catholic Church in Mexico as treasonous. These actions incited Catholics all across Mexico to institute an economic boycott intended to bring the country to its knees. Purchases were cut to the barest of bare essentials. For their part, priests protested by ceasing to perform their offices, a move that created great unrest throughout the country. By the end of 1926, militant terrorist bands known as *cristeros* (for their battle cry, *"Viva Cristo Rey!"*—"Long Live Christ the King!") rebelled against the government, raiding and bringing terror throughout all Mexico. Led by a journalist named Rene Capistran Garza, a general named Enrique Gorostieta, and a friar named José Reyes Vegas (whom many called "Pancho Villa in a Cassock"), the *cristeros* came from all over Mexico and every social class, though 60 percent of them were poor or working class, and most lived in the western states of Michoacan and Jalisco. But this, unlike many of Mexico's civil wars, was a religious, not class, conflict. Revolutionary leaders had simply moved the nation too radically away from the Catholic Church for the comfort of Mexico's people. Nevertheless the Catholic Church quickly disavowed the cristeros. That did not, however, stop the Calles government from nationalizing church property and deporting a number of clergymen and even nuns. Certain prominent Catholic leaders were tried for treason and executed. Although this served to exacerbate antigovernment activity, the Calles regime was willing and able to mobilize extensive forces against the cristeros, and the movement was generally suppressed by the end of 1927 and beginning of 1928.

The elections of 1928 brought Calles's ally Álvaro Obregón (1880–1928) into office. He was assassinated less than a month into his term and replaced by Emilio Portes Gil (1891–1978), who governed essentially as a puppet of Calles. The following year, Mexico was swept by a new wave of religiously motivated antigovernment activity, led by a group of conservative generals. Order was restored, and Calles continued to pull the strings, maneuvering into office Pascual Ortiz Rubio (1877–1963). Before the end of 1929, Ortiz Rubio faced a weak insurrection, but continued in office as Calles's anticlerical puppet.

Further reading: Linda B. Hall, *Alvaro Obregón: Power and Revolution in Mexico, 1911–1920* (College Station: Texas A&M University Press, 1981); Enrique Krause, *Mexico: Biography of Power, A History of Modern Mexico, 1810–1996* (New York: HarperCollins, 1998); Jennice Purnell, *Popular Movements and State Formation in Revolutionary Mexico: The Agraristas and Cristeros of Michoacan* (Durham, N.C.: Duke University Press, 1999).

Mexican Revolt (1914–1915)

PRINCIPAL COMBATANTS: Forces of Victoriano Huerta and Álvaro Obregón vs. Emiliano Zapata, Venustiano Carranza, and Francisco "Pancho" Villa. Later, Zapata and Villa vs. Carranza and Obregón.
PRINCIPAL THEATER(S): Mexico
DECLARATION: None
MAJOR ISSUES AND OBJECTIVES: Control of the Mexican government
OUTCOME: Carranza and Obregón defeated Zapata and Villa, and Carranza became president of Mexico.
APPROXIMATE MAXIMUM NUMBER OF MEN UNDER ARMS: Huerta and Obregón, 70,000; Zapata, 25,000; Carranza, 22,000; Villa, 40,000
CASUALTIES: Estimates vary wildly; at least 6,000 troops died on all sides; civilian casualties were much heavier, with estimates reaching 1 million during the height of the conflict and its guerrilla aftermath.
TREATIES: None

The Mexican general Victoriano Huerta (1854–1916) overthrew Mexican president Francisco Madero (1873–1913) in a coup d'état of February 18, 1913. However, Huerta, a right-wing dictator, immediately found himself opposed by four distinct and separate forces: Emiliano Zapata (1880–1919), who controlled much of southern Mexico; Venustiano Carranza (1859–1920), who controlled the northeast; Francisco "Pancho" Villa (1877–1923), the popular leader of the north; and Álvaro Obregón (1880–1928), who held the northwest. These three opponents of Huerta controlled perhaps 75 percent of Mexico—but were in no way united.

By the spring of 1914, Huerta had been fought to a standstill within and outside of Mexico City and in Veracruz on the Gulf coast. For his part, U.S. president Woodrow Wilson (1856–1924) refused to acknowledge the legitimacy of the Huerta regime, which was clearly hostile to the United States. Wilson sent an occupying force to Veracruz on April 21, 1914. This, combined with Villa's taking of Zacatecas and Obregón's seizure of Guadalajara, forced Huerta from office. Both Villa and Obregón raced to fill the resulting power vacuum. Because Obregón reached Mexico City first, he took the opportunity to proclaim his newfound ally, Carranza, "First Chief" of Mexico. Late in the year, Obregón and Carranza hammered out the organization of a government.

They labored against a background of sheer anarchy. Then Villa and Zapata occupied Mexico City, while Obregón and Carranza took Veracruz. Together, Villa and Zapata held about two-thirds of Mexico. The United States, however, recognized the Carranza government, and eight other Western powers followed suit. Because Carranza controlled the Mexican-U.S. border region, he was able to procure arms from the United States. Well supplied, and with Obregón's able military leadership, Carranza retook Mexico City early in 1915. Villa headed for the hills. Although Obregón gave chase and ran Villa and his forces to ground at the town of Celaya, fighting a three-day battle in April 1915, Villa, though essentially defeated, withdrew into the countryside of the north. With Zapata, Villa waged a low-level guerrilla war against the Carranza government, which continued through 1920.

See also MEXICAN CIVIL WAR (1911); MEXICAN CIVIL WAR (1920).

Further reading: Clarence C. Clarendon, *The United States and Pancho Villa; A Study in Unconventional Diplomacy* (Port Washington, N.Y.: Kennikat Press, 1972); John S. D. Eisenhower, *Intervention! The United States and the Mexican Revolution, 1913–1917* (New York: W. W. Norton, 1993); Enrique Krause, *Mexico: Biography of Power, A History of Modern Mexico, 1810–1996* (New York: HarperCollins, 1998); Frank McLynn, *Villa and Zapata: A History of the Mexican Revolution* (New York: Avalon, 2002); John Womack, *Zapata and the Mexican Revolution* (New York: Knopf, 1969).

Mexican Revolt (1994–1998)

PRINCIPAL COMBATANTS: Popular Revolutionary Army (EPR) vs. Mexican government
PRINCIPAL THEATER(S): Southwestern Mexico
DECLARATION: None
MAJOR ISSUES AND OBJECTIVES: The EPR called for a radically new constitution.
OUTCOME: Undecided; a low-level state of guerrilla warfare and general unrest is ongoing as of early 2002.

APPROXIMATE MAXIMUM NUMBER OF MEN UNDER ARMS: Unknown
CASUALTIES: Almost 400 killed, mostly civilians.
TREATIES: None

Beginning in January 1994, Indian guerrillas, proclaiming themselves the political followers of Emiliano Zapata (1880–1919)—see MEXICAN REVOLT (1914–1915)—staged a 12-day uprising in the southern state of Chiapas. Before a truce ended the "Chiapas Rebellion," 145 people were killed.

The peace was tenuous, and sporadic fighting between the Zapatistas and right-wing paramilitary groups in the south continued through 1996, when Mexican president Ernesto Zedillo (b. 1951) was faced with a new and simultaneous revolt, that of the Popular Revolutionary Army (EPR). While attempting to reach a peaceful compromise with the Zapatistas, the Zedillo government was attacked by the EPR in August 1996. The attacks were distributed over six Mexican states, and succeeded only in triggering a major government military counteroffensive, which forced the EPR into the mountains.

Although violence substantially abated by 1998, the EPR has continued to conduct a low-level guerrilla war against government forces and has issued a continual stream of antigovernment propaganda. The object is ultimately to secure a new constitution for Mexico.

Further reading: Tom Hayden, ed. *The Zapatista Reader* (New York: Avalon, 2002).

Mexican Revolts (1810–1815)

PRINCIPAL COMBATANTS: Mexican rebels (led and later inspired by Miguel Hidalgo y Costilla, parish priest of Dolores) vs. Spanish Mexico (Royalists)
PRINCIPAL THEATER(S): Mexico
DECLARATION: The September 16, 1810, *Grito de Dolores*
MAJOR ISSUES AND OBJECTIVES: Popular uprising against Spanish rule
OUTCOME: The initial uprising was crushed and its leader executed; however, the independence movement survived and sparked several other revolts, none of which succeeded before the revolution of 1821.
APPROXIMATE MAXIMUM NUMBER OF MEN UNDER ARMS: Rebels, 80,000; Royalist forces, 35,000–80,000
CASUALTIES: Rebels, 15,450 killed; Royalists, 2,145 killed
TREATIES: None

For 300 years today's Mexico and the Mexican borderlands that would become the American Southwest—California, New Mexico, Arizona, and Texas—had belonged to Spain, the world's oldest western empire. In the late 18th century, Spain had made various efforts to revitalize the northern provinces, setting up a buffer between itself and the United States in hopes of vitiating the "foreign" threat to its North American frontier. Spain's real problems with its empire, however, proved to be internal rather than external. In 1808 Napoleon's (1769–1821) invasion of Iberia had led to a destabilization of the mother country that ultimately cost Spain its holdings in the New World (*see* NAPOLEONIC WARS).

It was the liberals in the Cortes, Spain's traditionally weak parliament, who led the resistance against the French; and it was these same liberals who promulgated reforms during the political chaos created by Napoleon's invasion. They established a representative government under a liberal constitution in 1812 and set up provincial legislatures and town councils in both the mother country and throughout the empire. After Napoleon's defeat and exile to Elba, the Spanish monarchy launched a restoration, dissolving the representative bodies or suspending their privileges, which in turn led to a revolt within Spain by the liberals and their supporters in the military. In the long run, though republican government was restored, the empire fell apart.

The republican movement that began in Spain took firm root in the colonies of the Western Hemisphere. Over the next decade the world witnessed the great Central and South American liberations. In Mexico, the upheavals were fed not only by the liberals' desire for representative government but also by mestizo discontent with social conditions, and the mixture created a cycle of revolt and repression that lasted until Mexico's war for independence became the climax of the New World revolutions. In 1810 a village priest named Miguel Hidalgo y Costillo (1753–1811) joined a group of liberal officers plotting against the Mexican viceroy, rallied 80,000 peasants—mestizos and Indians—into Mexico's first revolutionary army and led them to glory, shouting "Death to the Spaniards!"

Hidalgo y Costilla, parish priest of Dolores, issued his *Grito de Dolores,* the "Cry of Dolores," on September 16, 1810, calling for a revolt against Spanish rule over Mexico. The Grito also called for a policy of racial equality, the breakup of the great haciendas, and the redistribution of the land, which helps explain why Hidalgo y Costillo drew such a substantial following of Indians and mestizos. Led by the priest, they overran a number of towns, then began an advance on the capital, Mexico City. Royalist forces responded by attacking the advancing army at the Battle of Calderón Bridge, near Guadalajara, on January 18, 1811. Hidalgo y Costilla's army was decimated, and the priest himself fled.

A charming but politically naive man, Father Hidalgo imagined peasant dissatisfaction with existing conditions to be aimed mostly at the Spanish-born among the elite (the so-called Gapuchines)—as was his own resentment—rather than at the "white" upper classes in general. Apparently it never occurred to him that the Indians and mestizos might number among their enemies even the Mexican-born, those Creoles who controlled the military and provided most of the officers involved in the coming repressions as well as those leading the revolts. At any rate, after Hidalgo seized Guanajuato, his peasant army slaughtered every ethnic European in the city, Gapuchine and Creole alike. Perhaps deranged by the grisly results of his liberation movement, the priest completely lost control of his followers. Captured by royalist troops in Chihuahua in 1811, Hidalgo was beheaded. His skull remained displayed on a post outside Guanajuato for 10 years.

Nevertheless, his example, together with the *Grito de Dolores,* planted the seed of anti-Spanish revolt. Texas, for example, was embroiled in the Hidalgo revolt from the beginning. More than any other of the empire's borderlands, Texas had continued to suffer under attacks by the Comanche and the Apache, and—late in the 18th century—Spain had consolidated settlement there by ordering its citizens to abandon the missions, presidios, and villages of eastern Texas. In 1779, however, many of those Nacogdoches settlers, unhappy with their new homes around San Antonio de Bexar and the constant Comanche raids to which they were subjected, returned to the area. Enough of them had remained in San Antonio, however, for it to become a Spanish settlement as opposed to a mere cluster of churches, and in 1793, Spain secularized the Alamo mission, distributed its lands, and turned the buildings over to the area's military garrison. By the beginning of the 19th century, only about 3,000 Spaniards, including soldiers and converted Indians, lived in all of Texas, mostly in the scattered eastern settlements, but also around San Antonio and especially along the Rio Grande, where life was dominated by cattle and ranches, run by rancheros to whom the king had granted huge *mercedes* (ranch lands), and manned by mestizo and Indian vaqueros.

It was against the Tejano elite that a militia officer named Juan Bautista de las Casas (d. 1811) in 1811 led a successful uprising fueled by the resentments of poor soldiers and civilians. Answering Hidalgo's call for independence, Bautista unseated the royalist government in San Antonio, only to be captured and executed in a countercoup commanded by local clergy and regular army officers. One of Bautista's supporters—Bernardo Gutierrez de Lara (1774–1841)—escaped the repression to travel to Washington, where he pleaded with Secretary of State James Monroe (1758–1831) for aid in carrying out a revolution in Texas.

Monroe had his own problems: the James Madison (1751–1836) administration was just then staggering under the early defeats of the WAR OF 1812. Monroe did, however, manage to come up with a little money and a few American officers to help Gutierrez raise a motley army of

American mercenaries, Mexican rebels, Indian and mestizo peasants, and even some ethnic French pirates from Louisiana. In effect, Gutierrez had become a figurehead whose function was "to give a Mexican character to the army" of filibusters—soldiers of fortune, who took their name from the Dutch word *vrijbuiter*, who hired their muskets out to the highest bidder, and who were notorious for their dedication to debauchery as well as adventure. Gutierrez provided Madison and Monroe with "deniability" should Spain take umbrage at the coming attack on its sovereignty. Late in 1812, he launched an invasion of the province from the United States.

The Mexican revolutionaries and American soldiers of fortune captured Golidad and took San Antonio; they declared independence; they beheaded the Texas governor, a Spanish general, and 15 others; they began abusing the Mexican and Indian population of the province; and they fell to arguing over the future of Texas. By 1813, Gutierrez's army had swelled to some 1,500 men—850 or so of them American Volunteers, as the freebooters called themselves—and the Spanish viceroy in Mexico City, Francisco Javier de Venegas (r. 1810–13) recognized it for precisely the army of invasion that it was. Not taking kindly to American depredations against Spanish subjects, nor to impudent Mexican revolutionaries, he sent an army under General Joaquin de Arredondo (1768–1837) north to evict the U.S. land pirates and crush the rebellion. Most of the freebooters had deserted Gutierrez's cause by the time royalist forces caught up with them at the Medina River in August of 1814, where the Spanish troops all but annihilated the Americans. Of the 250 freebooters still alive after the battle, 150 of them were slaughtered in flight, "cut . . . in quarters, and suspended on poles and limbs of trees, like beef or pork for the packer. . . ." The republicans of San Antonio, too, suffered a bloody revenge at the hands of Arredondo. He executed 327 people in San Antonio alone.

There were other uprisings similar to Hidalgo's, the most serious led by another priest, Father José Maria Morelos y Pavon (1768–1837). But though Morelos was an altogether more realistic and practical man than Hidalgo, and though he turned his followers against Spain and defined his objectives, his rebellion was put down as brutally by the loyal regular army, and he was captured and executed in 1815. Mexico finally won its independence from Spain not because revolution grew from the class dissatisfactions of the Mexican people, but because its Creole military commanders grew disenchanted with Spanish rule. Thus it was that, six years later, a senior Spanish commander, Agustin de Iturbide (1783–1824), fearing that the more liberal government which had come to power in Spain might deprive him and his fellow officers of their "rights" (and, of course, their privileges), simply switched sides, turned against the viceroy, and launched the MEXICAN REVOLUTION (1821).

See also MEXICAN REVOLUTION (1823).

Further reading: Hugh M. Hamill, Jr., *The Hidalgo Revolt: Prelude to Mexican Independence* (Gainesville: University of Florida Press, 1966); Brian N. Hamnett, *Roots of Insurgency: Mexican Regions, 1750–1824* (New York: Cambridge University Press, 1986); Enrique Krause, *Mexico: Biography of Power, A History of Modern Mexico, 1810–1996* (New York: HarperCollins, 1998); David J. Weber, *The Mexican Frontier, 1821–1846: The American Southwest under Mexico* (Albuquerque: University of New Mexico Press, 1982); Richard White, *"It's Your Misfortune and None of My Own": New History of the American West* (Norman: University of Oklahoma Press, 1991).

Mexican Revolution (1821)

PRINCIPAL COMBATANTS: Mexican coalition for independence vs. Spain
PRINCIPAL THEATER(S): Mexico
DECLARATION: Plan of Iguala, February 24, 1821
MAJOR ISSUES AND OBJECTIVES: Mexican independence from Spain—to escape the effects of the new Spanish liberalism
OUTCOME: A strong coalition of rebels and conservatives easily won independence.
APPROXIMATE MAXIMUM NUMBER OF MEN UNDER ARMS: At least 16,000 pro-independence troops; most of the Spanish royalist forces deserted
CASUALTIES: Few in minor skirmishes during 1821, because Spanish royalists deserted and offered little resistance; however, viewed as the culmination of a struggle that began in 1810, the cost of independence was probably half a million Mexican lives.
TREATIES: Treaty of Córdoba, 1821

This is the war by which Mexico won independence from the Spanish Empire, and it is especially interesting in that, unlike most wars of independence, it was a conservative revolution. In 1820, liberal forces assumed leadership of the Spanish government and compelled King Ferdinand VII (1784–1833) to restore the liberal constitution of 1812 (*see* MEXICAN REVOLTS [1810–1815]). Mexico's conservative element decided that the only way to avoid the great wave of liberalism that was sweeping Spain was to declare independence. This radical step was, in fact, a means of maintaining the status quo.

Thus, Mexico finally won its independence from Spain in 1821, not because the revolution stemmed from the class dissatisfactions of the Mexican people, but because its Creole military commanders grew disenchanted with Spanish rule. Men like Mexico's senior Spanish commander, Agustín de Iturbide (1783–1824), fearing that the more liberal government that had come to power in Spain might deprive him and his fellow officers of their "rights" (and, of course, their privileges), simply switched sides.

To begin the subversion of the Spanish colonial government in Mexico, Iturbide talked the Spanish viceroy, Juan Ruiz de Apodoca (1767–1835), into turning over to him command of the Spanish armies—in order, Iturbide said, to suppress the Mexican rebels led by Vicente Guerrero (1782–1831). With 2,500 Spanish colonial troops under his command, Iturbide did indeed march against Guerrero, not with the purpose of crushing him, however, but of coopting him. Reluctantly, after a few skirmishes, Guerrero was persuaded to join forces with Iturbide.

On February 24, 1821, Iturbide and Guerrero jointly issued the Plan of Iguala, which called for the establishment of an independent Mexican monarchy, the establishment of Roman Catholicism as the state religion, and the proclamation of racial equality for all Mexicans. Rallying to the plan were the rebels Nicolás Bravo (1787?–1854) and Guadalupe Victoria (1789–1843), as well as arch conservatives, such as Anastasio Bustamante (1780–1853). Bustamante had a large contingent under his control, some 6,000 armed men, and he eagerly led them into the cause of independence. As Iturbide and his new allies led their forces in a sweep of Mexico, the remaining Spanish royal forces did not resist, but deserted. This left the new Spanish viceroy, Juan O'Donoju (1755–1821), little choice but to grant Mexico its independence, which was proclaimed in the Treaty of Córdoba of 1821.

Iturbide was proclaimed Emperor Agustín I by his troops, and, like Napoleon (1769–1821), he crowned himself—on May 19, 1822. The United States immediately recognized Mexico as a sovereign state, though Iturbide hardly lasted a year in power (*see* MEXICAN REVOLUTION [1823]).

Further reading: Timothy E. Anna, *The Fall of the Royal Government in Mexico City* (Lincoln: University of Nebraska Press, 1978) and *Mexican Empire of Iturbide* (Lincoln: University of Nebraska Press, 1996); Brian N. Hamnett, *Roots of Insurgency: Mexican Regions, 1750–1824* (New York: Cambridge University Press, 1986); Enrique Krause, *Mexico: Biography of Power, A History of Modern Mexico, 1810–1996* (New York: HarperCollins, 1998); William S. Robertson, *Iturbide of Mexico* (Westport, Conn.: Greenwood Publishing Group, 1986); David J. Weber, *The Mexican Frontier, 1821–1846: The American Southwest under Mexico* (Albuquerque: University of New Mexico Press, 1982); Richard White, *"It's Your Misfortune and None of My Own,"* in *New History of the American West* (Norman: University of Oklahoma Press, 1991).

Mexican Revolution (1823)

PRINCIPAL COMBATANTS: Mexican army vs. government of Agustín I, emperor of Mexico

PRINCIPAL THEATER(S): Mexico
DECLARATION: Plan de Casa Mata, February 1823
MAJOR ISSUES AND OBJECTIVES: Overthrow of the short-lived Mexican monarchy and creation of a Mexican republic
OUTCOME: Under the leadership of Antonio López de Santa Anna and Guadalupe Victoria, the Mexican army forced Agustín I to abdicate, and a republic was declared.
APPROXIMATE MAXIMUM NUMBER OF MEN UNDER ARMS: Essentially, the entire strength of the Mexican army
CASUALTIES: Few
TREATIES: None

As a result of the MEXICAN REVOLUTION of 1821, conservative Mexican leader Agustín de Iturbide (1783–1824) crowned himself Emperor Agustín I of an independent Mexican monarchy. Agustín ruled with the majesty of an Asian potentate, quickly causing a national financial crisis. The Spanish occupied a fortress on the island of San Juan de Ulloa, situated off Veracruz, and from here they blocked Agustín's collection of duties. With this all-important stream of revenue choked off, he began a general program of confiscation to raise funds. His army did not approve, and, even worse, having gone months without pay, rebelled.

The uprising came when General Antonio López de Santa Anna (1794–1876) was ordered by Agustín to capture San Juan de Ulloa. Once he had command of the army, however, Santa Anna called for the overthrow of the monarchy and the establishment of an independent Mexican republic. In this he was joined by General Guadalupe Victoria (1789–1843), and the two of them jointly issued the Plan de Casa Mata in February 1823. This declaration called for the abolition of the empire and the adoption of a new constitution and congress for a new republic. The army immediately fell in behind the Plan de Casa Mata, and, confronted by a general mutiny, Agustín I abdicated in March 1823. He fled into European exile. Guadalupe Victoria became the first president of the independent republic of Mexico.

Further reading: Timothy E. Anna, *The Fall of the Royal Government in Mexico City* (Lincoln: University of Nebraska Press, 1978) and *Mexican Empire of Iturbide* (Lincoln: University of Nebraska Press, 1996); Brian N. Hamnett, *Roots of Insurgency: Mexican Regions, 1750–1824* (New York: Cambridge University Press, 1986); Enrique Krause, *Mexico: Biography of Power, A History of Modern Mexico, 1810–1996* (New York: HarperCollins, 1998); William S. Robertson, *Iturbide of Mexico* (Westport, Conn.: Greenwood Publishing Group, 1986); David J. Weber, *The Mexican Frontier, 1821–1846: The American Southwest under Mexico* (Albuquerque: University of New Mexico Press, 1982); Richard White, *"It's Your Misfortune and None of My Own,"* in *New History of the American West* (Norman: University of Oklahoma Press, 1991).

Mexican War *See* UNITED STATES-MEXICAN WAR (1846–1848).

Mexico, Spanish Conquest of *See* SPANISH CONQUEST OF MEXICO (1519–1521).

Miguelite Wars (War of the Two Brothers) (1828–1834)

PRINCIPAL COMBATANTS: Miguelites vs. Constitutionalists (with British, French, and Spanish allies)
PRINCIPAL THEATER(S): Portugal
DECLARATION: None
MAJOR ISSUES AND OBJECTIVES: Pedro I of Brazil sought to oust his brother Dom Miguel from the Portuguese throne and reinstate a constitutional monarchy under his sister, Maria II.
OUTCOME: Once Pedro gathered international support, his forces were able to defeat the Miguelites and constitutional government was reinstated.
APPROXIMATE MAXIMUM NUMBER OF MEN UNDER ARMS: Miguelites, 80,000; Constitutionalists, under 32,000 (including British, Spanish, and French troops)
CASUALTIES: More than 20,000 killed among all belligerents
TREATIES: Abdication of Dom Miguel, May 26, 1834

Europe was much destabilized by the FRENCH REVOLUTION (1789–1799) and the advent of Napoleon. Portugal struggled, especially in the wake of the PENINSULAR WAR. Its king John VI (1769–1826) had fled to Brazil after the French conquest in 1807, leaving in his wake a French-controlled regency overthrown by Portuguese liberals at Oporto on August 29, 1820 (*see* OPORTO, REVOLUTION AT). They invited John to return to Portugal as a constitutional monarch, and he did so reluctantly on July 4, 1821, leaving behind his eldest son Pedro I (1798–1834) as emperor of the newly independent Brazil. John's return touched off an unsuccessful revolt by his second son, Dom Miguel (1802–66), whose ambitions received the support of absolutist forces in Portugal when his brother ascended in Brazil. In any case, he failed in his attempt to restore the old system (*see* PORTUGUESE CIVIL WAR [1823–1824]) and went into exile in Vienna.

After King John died, the crown fell to Pedro, who—preferring to remain emperor in stable Brazil than to become king in unsteady Portugal—threw his support behind the liberals, issued a constitutional charter based on Britain's parliamentary system, and abdicated in favor of his young daughter, Maria da Gloria (1819–53). The exiled Dom Miguel once again tried to claim the throne and revive the absolute power of the Braganza dynasty,

thus sparking a new PORTUGUESE CIVIL WAR (1826–27). When the British intervened on behalf of the constitutionalists, Dom Miguel came to terms with them and ended his second insurrection on April 18, 1828. He was named regent for the new Queen Maria II, whom he married by proxy, and the British withdrew.

Hardly had the English ships set sail, however, before Dom Miguel violated those terms, removing liberal governors from office and replacing them with conservative aristocrats, dissolving the Cortes and replacing it with a puppet assembly, and having himself declared king of Portugal in May. The ship bearing Maria II from Brazil to Portugal was diverted to England, where the British could protect her against the ambitions of her uncle (and husband). Meanwhile, Maria's backers resisted Dom Miguel's coup, only to be defeated at the battle of Coimbra on June 24, 1828.

Dom Miguel was formally crowned on July 11, 1828. Waging war on the constitutionalists, his supporters rapidly gained control of the Portuguese mainland. Liberals took to the Azores, where they were reinforced by volunteers from Brazil, Britain, and France. On August 12, 1828, Maria's supporters defeated a Miguelite naval attack on the Azores at Praia Bay, and afterward they were able to buy a naval squadron in England. Thus, the Azores remained in constitutionalist hands, and a regency on behalf of Queen Maria II was established there in 1829. Back in Brazil, Pedro abdicated his throne in favor of his son and headed for Europe to join the rebel cause, raise an army, and retake Portugal for his daughter. Thus did the war become popularly known as the "War of the Two Brothers."

The British supported Pedro's landing in the Azores in April 1831, where, again with British aid, he assembled an expedition to take Oporto, which fell to him in February 1832. The Miguelites laid siege to Oporto for a year, but the city was relieved by a naval attack under the command of Sir Charles James Napier (1782–1853) (known as Carlo Ponza) off Cape St. Vincent on July 5, 1833. This opened an opportunity for the constitutionalist forces to take Lisbon on July 24, 1833. At this point, Spain joined the fray on the side of Pedro and the constitutionalists, because Dom Miguel was sheltering Don Carlos (1788–1855), the pretender to the Spanish throne. Spanish troops now invaded Portugal and advanced against the Miguelite headquarters at Coimbra to capture Don Carlos (*see* CARLIST WAR, FIRST).

The international imbroglio over Don Carlos helped prompt Spain and Britain to unite with Portugal and France and form the Quadruple Alliance, dedicated not only to preserving constitutionalism in Portugal, but throughout Europe by opposing the Holy Alliance of Austria, Prussia, and Russia. Backed by the Quadruple Alliance and especially with Spanish aid, the constitutional forces quickly took Viseu, Coimbra, and Tomar, achieving final victory over the Miguelites at the Battle of

Santarém on May 16, 1834. Promised amnesty, Dom Miguel formally surrendered on May 26 at Évora-Monte. He renounced the throne and lived out the rest of his life in Germany. Pedro reinstated the constitution of 1826 and installed Maria II as queen of Portugal.

Further reading: David Birmingham, *Concise History of Portugal* (New York: Cambridge University Press, 1993); H. V. Livermore, *A New History of Portugal*, 2nd ed. (New York: Cambridge University Press, 1976).

Milanese Civil War (1447–1450)

PRINCIPAL COMBATANTS: Francesco Sforza vs. republic of Milan
PRINCIPAL THEATER(S): Milan
DECLARATION: None
MAJOR ISSUES AND OBJECTIVES: Sforza sought to overthrow the newly created republic of Milan and claim what he deemed his right to a dukedom over the city.
OUTCOME: Aided by Venice, Sforza defeated the republic and was proclaimed duke of Milan.
APPROXIMATE MAXIMUM NUMBER OF MEN UNDER ARMS: Unknown
CASUALTIES: Unknown
TREATIES: None

This civil war was associated with the VENETIAN-MILANESE WAR (1448–1454), in which Francesco Sforza (1401–66) seized Milan and Piacenza, then declared war on Venice. Sforza was the son-in-law of Filippo Maria Visconti (1402–47), the duke of Milan, who died without heirs. In this vacuum, a republic was established for Milan, but Sforza decided to seize the city for himself. In the course of his war with Venice, Sforza suddenly switched sides, allied himself with Venice against republican Milan. He laid siege to the city, which fell to him in 1450 and acknowledged him as duke. The short-lived republic came to an end.

Further reading: Thomas Arnold, *The Renaissance at War* (London: Cassell Academic, 2001); P. S. Chambers, *The Imperial Venice, 1380–1580* (New York: Harcourt, Brace Jovanovich, 1971); Lacy Collison-Morely, *The Story of the Sforzas* (New York: Dutton, 1934).

Milanese-Florentine Wars   *See* FLORENTINE-MILANESE WAR (1351); FLORENTINE-MILANESE WAR (1397–1402).

Milanese Revolt   *See* "FIVE DAYS" REVOLT.

Minangkabau War   *See* PADRI WAR.

Minnesota Santee Sioux Uprising
See UNITED STATES–SIOUX WAR (1862–1864).

Mithradatic War, First (88–84 B.C.E.)

PRINCIPAL COMBATANTS: Pontus (with Greek allies) vs. Rome
PRINCIPAL THEATER(S): Asia Minor
DECLARATION: None
MAJOR ISSUES AND OBJECTIVES: Rome responded to the campaign of conquest led by the Pontic king Mithradates VI the Great by launching legions that defeated Greece and Pontus.
OUTCOME: Mithradates was forced back into Pontus and had to relinquish most of his conquests as well as render unto Rome a huge indemnity.
APPROXIMATE MAXIMUM NUMBER OF MEN UNDER ARMS: Unknown
CASUALTIES: Unknown
TREATIES: None

Mithradates VI the Great (c. 132–63 B.C.E.) embarked on a campaign to unite under his leadership as emperor the peoples surrounding his kingdom of Pontus. This led to friction with the Roman Empire, which exploded into war when Mithradates, seizing the major cities of Asia Minor, ordered the mass slaughter of many thousands of Romans.

Rome unleashed legions under Lucius Cornelius Sulla (138–78 B.C.E.)—who marched through Mithradates' ally, Greece, and crushed its army in 85—and Gaius Flavius Fimbria (d. 84 B.C.E.), who attacked Mithradates' forces directly. Although Fimbria fell in battle, by 84 B.C.E. the Romans had succeeded in driving Mithradates back within the confines of Pontus. Most of the territory Mithradates had claimed was forfeit, and Rome also imposed a huge indemnity on him.

See also MITHRADATIC WAR, SECOND; MITHRADATIC WAR, THIRD.

Further reading: John Boardman, Jasper Griffin, and Oswyn Murray, eds., *The Oxford History of the Roman World* (New York: Oxford University Press, 1991); B. C. McGing, *The Foreign Policy of Mithradates VI Eupator, King of Pontus* (Leiden, Netherlands: E. J. Brill, 1986); Colin Wells, *The Roman Empire*, 2nd ed. (Cambridge, Mass.: Harvard University Press, 1995).

Mithradatic War, Second (83–81 B.C.E.)

PRINCIPAL COMBATANTS: Pontus vs. Roman legion under Lucius Licinius Murena
PRINCIPAL THEATER(S): Asia Minor, the region of the Kizil Irmak River
DECLARATION: None

MAJOR ISSUES AND OBJECTIVES: Lucius Licinius Murena wanted to conquer the Kizil Irmak River territory of Mithradates VI the Great, king of Pontus.
OUTCOME: Murena was defeated, and Mithradates formed an important alliance with Quintus Sertorius, another Roman general.
APPROXIMATE MAXIMUM NUMBER OF MEN UNDER ARMS: Unknown
CASUALTIES: Unknown
TREATIES: None

Lucius Licinius Murena (fl. 83–82 B.C.E.), a power-hungry, glory-seeking Roman general, invaded territory held by Mithradates VI the Great (c. 132–63 B.C.E.) in the region of the Kizil Irmak River. Having lost most of his empire in the First MITHRADATIC WAR, from 88 to 84 B.C.E. Mithradates defended what remained with great vigor. He defeated Murena by 81. The war also propelled Mithradates into the arms of a sympathetic Roman general, Quintus Sertorius, with whom he joined forces in 75, thereby precipitating the Third MITHRADATIC WAR, from 75 to 65 B.C.E.

Further reading: John Boardman, Jasper Griffin, and Oswyn Murray, eds., *The Oxford History of the Roman World* (New York: Oxford University Press, 1991); B. C. McGing, *The Foreign Policy of Mithradates VI Eupator, King of Pontus* (Leiden, Netherlands: E. J. Brill, 1986); Colin Wells, *The Roman Empire,* 2nd ed. (Cambridge, Mass.: Harvard University Press, 1995).

Mithradatic War, Third (75–65 B.C.E.)

PRINCIPAL COMBATANTS: Pontus vs. Rome
PRINCIPAL THEATER(S): Asia Minor
DECLARATION: None
MAJOR ISSUES AND OBJECTIVES: Rome sought definitively to crush Mithradates and wrest Pontus from him.
OUTCOME: Mithradates was defeated, and Pontus fell to Rome.
APPROXIMATE MAXIMUM NUMBER OF MEN UNDER ARMS: Unknown
CASUALTIES: Unknown
TREATIES: No documents have been identified.

Together, the Roman general Quintus Sertorius (d. 72 B.C.E.) (*see* MITHRADATIC WAR, SECOND) and Mithradates VI the Great (c. 632–63 B.C.E.), king of Pontus, schemed to attack Rome, Sertorius from the west, and Mithradates from the east. The assassination of Sertorius brought a sudden end to the menace from the west, and General Lucius Licinius Lucullus (c. 110–56 B.C.E.) was dispatched with an army to see to the defeat of Mithradates in the east.

The Romans trounced the Pontic forces in a series of battles, at Cyzicus, Cabira, Tigranocerta, and Artaxata, then attacked Mithradates in Pontus itself. Mithradates left his own country, but, by this time, the legions under Lucullus were worn out. They threatened mutiny, which left the general no choice but to withdraw. Despite having won all the battles, Rome therefore fell short of winning the war.

Pompey the Great (106–48 B.C.E.) replaced Lucullus as commander of the Roman forces and brought about an end to the war by definitively defeating Mithradates at the Battle of Lycus in 66 B.C.E. Mithradates sought refuge in the Crimea, where, in profound disgrace, he commanded a slave to put an end to his life. When his son-in-law and ally, Tigranes (c. 140–55 B.C.E.), king of Armenia, was defeated and captured soon after (*see* ROMAN-ARMENIAN WAR [72–66 B.C.E.]), he was compelled to relinquish to Rome all that he and his father-in-law had once ruled.

See also MITHRADATIC WAR, FIRST.

Further reading: John Boardman, Jasper Griffin, and Oswyn Murray, eds., *The Oxford History of the Roman World* (New York: Oxford University Press, 1991); B. C. McGing, *The Foreign Policy of Mithridates VI Eupator, King of Pontus* (Leiden, Netherlands: E. J. Brill, 1986); Colin Wells, *The Roman Empire,* 2nd ed. (Cambridge, Mass.: Harvard University Press, 1995).

Mitre's Rebellion (1874)

PRINCIPAL COMBATANTS: Liberal forces of presidential candidate Bartolomé Mitre vs. government forces of Domingo Faustino Sarmiento
PRINCIPAL THEATER(S): Argentina, principally Buenos Aires
DECLARATION: None
MAJOR ISSUES AND OBJECTIVES: Claiming election fraud, Mitre rebelled against the government.
OUTCOME: Mitre's liberal uprising was quickly crushed.
APPROXIMATE MAXIMUM NUMBER OF MEN UNDER ARMS: Unknown
CASUALTIES: Unknown, but light
TREATIES: None

Argentine president Bartolomé Mitre (1821–1906) lost his reelection bid to Domingo Faustino Sarmiento (1811–88) in 1868 and again in 1874. Mitre claimed that the second election was fraudulent and led a liberal rebellion against Sarmiento's handpicked successor, Nicolás Avellaneda (1836–85). Sarmiento's candidate had the strong backing of the military, however, and federal troops crushed the rebellion in Buenos Aires on November 6, 1874. Avellaneda's presidency continued Argentina's conservative, military-backed government through the end of the 19th century.

Further reading: Daniel Lewis, *The History of Argentina* (Westport, Conn.: Greenwood Publishing Group, 2001); David Rock, *Argentina, 1516–1982: From Spanish Colonization to the Falklands War* (Berkeley: University of California Press, 1985).

Mixton Rebellion (1541)

PRINCIPAL COMBATANTS: The Zuni, Tewa, and Tiwa Indians vs. colonial forces of Spain
PRINCIPAL THEATER(S): Central New Mexico and Arizona
DECLARATION: None
MAJOR ISSUES AND OBJECTIVES: A pueblo rebelled against Spanish conquest.
OUTCOME: The rebellion was quickly put down, and the Indians were driven out of the pueblos—but they left behind little for the Spanish to enjoy.
APPROXIMATE MAXIMUM NUMBER OF MEN UNDER ARMS: Unknown
CASUALTIES: Unknown
TREATIES: None

As early as the first voyage of Columbus in 1492, Indians told Spaniards tales of villages laden with gold, known as the "Seven Cities of Cibola." In search of these fabled cities, Francisco Vásquez de Coronado (c. 1510–54) set out in February 1540 to explore the unknown region north of the Rio Grande. During July 1540, Coronado and his troops encountered the Zuni pueblo of Hawikuh in central New Mexico. When the conquistador imperiously demanded the surrender of the pueblo, he was attacked, but, after an hour of combat, Hawikuh fell to him. Although he did not find gold in Hawikuh, Coronado occupied it and the surrounding Zuni territory, pillaging, food and anything else of value. After Coronado himself had moved on, the men he left behind to garrison the Tewa pueblos began to molest the women there. In 1541, an Indian named Texamatli (d. 1541) led a rebellion against the garrison conquistadores at a town called Mixton. The governor of New Spain, Niño de Guzmán (d. 1550), responded to this uprising by attacking several pueblos. Those Indians who were not killed in battle were burned at the stake. This demonstration of cruelty was utterly foreign to the traditions of the peaceful people of pueblo country. Tewas and Tiwas abandoned their villages to the Spaniards, but practiced a kind of scorched-earth policy, in which they took with them or destroyed virtually all of their possessions, leaving to the conquerors towns that were empty shells.

See also SPANISH CONQUEST OF NEW MEXICO; SPANISH CONQUEST OF THE PUEBLOS.

Further reading: Hugh Thomas, *Who's Who of the Conquistadors* (New York: Sterling, 2000); David J. Weber, ed., *New Spain's Far Northern Frontier: Essays on Spain in the American West, 1540–1821* (Dallas: Southern Methodist University Press, 1988).

Modena-Parma-Papal States Revolts *See* ITALIAN REVOLTS (1831–1834).

Modoc War (Lava Beds War) (1872–1873)

PRINCIPAL COMBATANTS: Modoc Indians vs. United States
PRINCIPAL THEATER(S): Lava beds of northern California in the vicinity of the Lost River
DECLARATION: None
MAJOR ISSUES AND OBJECTIVES: Modoc resistance to removal to a reservation
OUTCOME: The Modocs capitulated when their leader, Captain Jack, was captured and hanged
APPROXIMATE MAXIMUM NUMBER OF MEN UNDER ARMS: Federal—from 60 to 225 troops and 100 militia for various engagements; Modoc—few, tribe's population about 400
CASUALTIES: Federal—recorded 41 killed, including General Edward R. S. Canby, 52 wounded; Modoc—unknown
TREATIES: None

The Modoc Indians were a small tribe of perhaps 400 individuals living in the rugged Lost River valley of northern California and southern Oregon. During the 1850s, they periodically terrorized travelers along the Applegate Trail, but by the 1860s, under the leadership of Kintpuash (1837–73)—whom the whites called Captain Jack—they sought accommodation and trade with the whites. However, they were unwilling to accept "removal" to a reservation, particularly one they had to share with the Klamath Indians, who were hostile to them. To escape removal, Captain Jack and his followers settled on the Lost River, near Tule Lake, living meagerly by trade with white neighbors.

By the end of the 1860s, increasing numbers of white settlers were moving into the area, and pressure mounted for the Indians' removal. On November 29, 1872, Captain James Jackson (fl. 1870s), heading up a cavalry troop, was sent to Captain Jack's camp to disarm the Indians. A scuffle broke out, shots were exchanged, and one Modoc was killed and another wounded, while two troopers died and six suffered wounds. The army officially dignified the exchange as the Battle of Lost River.

In the meantime, a group of local ranchers took matters into their own hands by attacking a smaller group of Modocs, followers of a man the whites called Hooker Jim (c. 1825–1879). Two ranchers died in the assault and another was wounded, but, as Hooker Jim hurried to join forces with Captain Jack, 14 more settlers, encountered along the way, were killed.

With a combined strength of 60, Captain Jack and Hooker Jim hid in the twisted, remote lava beds south of Tule Lake, which the Indians called the Land of Burnt-Out Fires, and the whites called Captain Jack's Stronghold. Army efforts to dislodge the Indians failed, and a peace commission was appointed by President Ulysses S. Grant (1822–85) to negotiate with the Modocs. On Good Friday, April 11, 1873, despite warnings from the Modoc wife of his interpreter, General E. R. S. Canby (1817–73) and the other three commissioners were attacked by Captain Jack and others. Canby and another commissioner were killed; two others escaped.

General William Tecumseh Sherman (1820–1891), general in chief of the army, dispatched two large infantry units under General John M. Schofield (1831–1906) to hunt down Captain Jack and other Modocs.

On April 26 Modoc warriors surprised a reconnoitering party, killing all five of the party's officers and 20 enlisted men, as well as wounding another 16.

The Modoc victories took a toll on personnel as well as morale, but the Indians could not sustain the effort. By the middle of May, their food and water dwindling, the Modocs dispersed. On May 28, a cavalry detachment located Captain Jack, his family, and a number of followers. They did not surrender until June 3. With three other Modocs, Captain Jack was convicted of murder and hanged.

Further reading: Alan Axelrod, *Chronicle of the Indian Wars: From Colonial Times to Wounded Knee* (New York: Prentice Hall General Reference, 1993); Keith A. Murray, *The Modocs and Their War* (Norman: University of Oklahoma Press, 1985).

Mogul-Afghan War (1565–1581)

PRINCIPAL COMBATANTS: Hindustan vs. Kabul (part of Afghanistan)
PRINCIPAL THEATER(S): Northern India and Afghanistan
DECLARATION: None
MAJOR ISSUES AND OBJECTIVES: Akbar, Mogul emperor of Hindustan, needed to put down rebellious relatives in neighboring Kabul
OUTCOME: All rebellions were quelled; ultimately, Kabul was annexed to the Mogul Empire.
APPROXIMATE MAXIMUM NUMBER OF MEN UNDER ARMS: Mogul forces, 50,000; Kabul numbers unknown
CASUALTIES: Unknown
TREATIES: None

Nations governed by Islamic rulers lacked a system of primogeniture, whereby the oldest son in a family inherits all property and titles. Characteristically, therefore, the question of succession following the death of a ruler was open

to dispute, and it provided fertile ground for many wars. In India, Muslims usually resolved the problem of succession in one of two ways. Either the kingdom in question was divided among the rivals or one contender would do battle with the others.

When Akbar (1542–1605), Mogul emperor of Hindustan (the Ganges plain in north India), chose to divide the kingdom, he gave control of Kabul to his half brother, Mirza Hakim (d. 1585). However, in 1565, the Uzbek nobles attacked Kabul, and Mirza Hakim fled to India to ask Akbar's aid. Akbar agreed and led an army to the defense of his brother-in-law. But a disloyal Mogul faction prevailed upon Mirza Hakim to rebel against Akbar. Fortunately for Akbar, Mirza Hakim had little stomach for a fight when the imperial Mogul army showed up. He quickly backed down, and Akbar made peace with him, only to be required to put down other rebellions among relatives and tributaries in the Second MOGUL WAR AGAINST GUJARAT.

Mirza Hakim led another rebellion in 1581. On February 8, Akbar invaded Afghanistan with 50,000 cavalry and 500 elephants. On August 9, he entered Kabul and defeated Mirza Hakim. Akbar then installed his half sister as governor of Mirza Hakim's lands. Mirza Hakim retained nominal title to Kabul, but he had no real power. When he died in July 1585, Kabul was formally annexed to the Mogul Empire.

Further reading: Barbara Daly Metcalf and Thomas R. Metcalf, *Concise History of India* (New York: Cambridge University Press, 2002); Vincent A. Smith, *The Oxford History India,* 4th ed. (New York: Oxford University Press, 1981); Douglas E. Streusand, *Formation of the Mughal Empire* (New York: Oxford University Press, 1999).

Mogul Conquest of Bihar and Bengal
See MOGUL WARS AGAINST THE SUR DYNASTY, LATER.

Mogul (Akbar's) Conquest of Kashmir, Sind, Orissa, Baluchistan *See* MOGUL CONQUEST OF RAJATHAN.

Mogul (Akbar's) Conquest of Malwa *See* MOGUL CONQUEST OF RAJATHAN.

Mogul Civil War (1600–1605)

PRINCIPAL COMBATANTS: Mogul emperor Akbar vs. his son Salim
PRINCIPAL THEATER(S): Hindustan
DECLARATION: None
MAJOR ISSUES AND OBJECTIVES: The war began as a dispute between father and son, then progressed to a

minor civil war between supporters of Akbar's son and a rival contender for the throne.

OUTCOME: In the first phase of the conflict, father and son reconciled, but the reconciliation was ambivalent, leaving the country ripe for renewed civil conflict in the later phase of the war.

APPROXIMATE MAXIMUM NUMBER OF MEN UNDER ARMS: Akbar: unknown; Salim: 30,000

CASUALTIES: Unknown

TREATIES: None

Late in the reign of Akbar (1542–1605), Mogul emperor of Hindustan (the Ganges plain in north India), his oldest son, Salim (later reigned as Jahangir [1569–1627]), arrogantly governed Allahabad as if he were an independent monarch. This enraged Akbar, who took various opportunities to vent hostility against his son. This seemed only to feed Salim's arrogance. He formed an army and traveled with it throughout India during 1600–02, calling himself emperor and flouting his aging father's authority. At last, in 1602, the situation seemed to come to a crisis when Salim advanced on Agra, his father's capital, at the head of 30,000 troops. Akbar convinced his son not to fight, however.

Upon withdrawing from the abortive Agra confrontation, Salim hatched a scheme to use his troops to assassinate the man he saw as his arch-rival, Akbar's chief adviser. Although the adviser was warned of the scheme, he decided to face down Salim. That proved a grave mistake; for he was taken prisoner and beheaded, the severed head, on Salim's orders, cast into an outhouse.

Still, Akbar restrained himself and did not retaliate. At this point, he judged his son to be a drunk who lacked self-control. For his part, Salim expressed regret and renewed obedience by presenting his father with a gift of 350 elephants, symbolic of disarmament. In return, Akbar proclaimed Salim crown prince, personally placing the royal turban on Salim's head. Then, however, Akbar ordered his son placed under house arrest, in order to break him of his alcohol and opium addictions. The combined actions shocked Akbar's court, who favored the ascension of Khusrau (d. 1622), Salim's son, as crown prince. A riotous fight between followers of Salim and followers of Khusrau broke out during an elephant joust in 1605. With the fight rapidly escalating into a minor war, Akbar directed Salim's 13-year-old son Khurram (1592–1666)—later to rule as Shah Jahan—to stop the combat.

At his death later in the year, Akbar asserted that Salim, unstable and infirm, was his chosen successor. This left the Moguls ripe for renewed conflict in the MOGUL CIVIL WAR (1607).

Further reading: Barbara Daly Metcalf and Thomas R. Metcalf, *Concise History of India* (New York: Cambridge University Press, 2002); Vincent A. Smith, *The Oxford His-*

tory India, 4th ed. (New York: Oxford University Press, 1981); Douglas E. Streusand, *Formation of the Mughal Empire* (New York: Oxford University Press, 1999).

Mogul Civil War (1607)

PRINCIPAL COMBATANTS: Khusrau vs. his father, Jahangir

PRINCIPAL THEATER(S): Lahore (Pakistan)

DECLARATION: None

MAJOR ISSUES AND OBJECTIVES: Khusrau wanted a territory to rule and attempted to seize Lahore.

OUTCOME: Khusrau's rebellion was crushed, but it gave rise to years of civil strife.

APPROXIMATE MAXIMUM NUMBER OF MEN UNDER ARMS: Akbar: Unknown; Salim: 30,000

CASUALTIES: Unknown

TREATIES: None

Jahangir (1569–1627) succeeded his father, Akbar (1542–1605), to the Mogul throne in 1605 after rebelling against his father in the MOGUL CIVIL WAR OF 1600–1605. His own reign was destined to be plagued by civil conflict.

Jahangir was successful in restraining his eldest son Khusrau (d. 1622) briefly, but Khusrau fled the royal court in 1607, quickly assembled a moblike army, and besieged Lahore, to coerce his father into giving him a territory of his own. However, Jahangir's forces quickly defeated Khusrau's rabble, and Khusrau was seized, clapped into irons, and disgraced. His titles and status as crown prince were taken from him and conferred on his brother Khurram (1592–1666), who later ruled as Shah Jahan. Seeking to make an example of the rebels, Jahangir beheaded and impaled them by the hundreds. As to Khusrau, he was bound in golden chains for a year. On his release, he called for the death of his father, who retaliated by putting out one of his eyes and imprisoning him through 1622, when Khurram, who had risen against Jahangir in SHAH JAHAN'S REVOLT, ordered this rival strangled to death.

See also MAHABAT KHAN'S INSURRECTION.

Further reading: Barbara Daly Metcalf and Thomas R. Metcalf, *Concise History of India* (New York: Cambridge University Press, 2002); Vincent A. Smith, *The Oxford History India,* 4th ed. (New York: Oxford University Press, 1981); Douglas E. Streusand, *Formation of the Mughal Empire* (New York: Oxford University Press, 1999).

Mogul Civil War (1657–1659)

PRINCIPAL COMBATANTS: The sons of Shah Jahan, Aurangzeb, Dara Shikoh, Shuja, and Murad, vs. one another; Aurangzeb vs. his father, Shah Jahan

PRINCIPAL THEATER(S): Northern India

DECLARATION: None

MAJOR ISSUES AND OBJECTIVES: The sons contended for succession to their father's throne; Aurangzeb, who triumphed over his brothers, then decided to overthrow his father.

OUTCOME: Aurangzeb emerged as the new Mogul emperor.

APPROXIMATE MAXIMUM NUMBER OF MEN UNDER ARMS: Variable, but, at most Dara commanded 120,000 men; Aurangzeb, 90,000; Shuja, 45,000; Murad, 10,000; numbers for Shah Jahan unknown.

CASUALTIES: Dara Shikoh lost 10,000 killed at the Battle of Samugarh (May 29, 1658).

TREATIES: None

This civil war may properly be called a war of succession. Acting in the service of his father, Shah Jahan (1592–1666), Aurangzeb (1618–1707) proved a brilliant military commander by the age of 16 during the so-called Wars of AURANGZEB. Yet, while he was off fighting, it was his eldest brother, Dara Shikoh (1615–59), whom Shah Jahan was grooming to succeed him on the throne. In part, this was because Dara Shikoh was Shah Jahan's favorite, and in part the treatment was to keep him under control, to forestall a rebellion against the father.

Dara nevertheless grew restive. Seeing in his brother Aurangzeb as a powerful rival, he undercut Aurangzeb's victories against Golconda and Bijapur (1656–57) by substituting indemnities for conquest and annexation. Following this, Dara assumed the reins of government and summarily cut off all contact with Aurangzeb and his other brothers. His act triggered a war of succession.

Shuja (d. c. 1658) and Murad (d. 1661), two of Dara's brothers, each proclaimed himself emperor and assembled armies to march against Agra, the Mogul capital. Shuja was quickly defeated in a battle on February 24, 1658, and was chased to Bengal. Murad, however, allied himself with Aurangzeb. Together, they defeated an imperial force at Dharmat (April 25, 1658) and a force under Dara at Samugarh, near Agra, on May 29, 1658. This proved one of the most decisive battles in Indian history. Dara Shikoh lost 10,000 men, including nine major Rajput lords and 19 high Mogul nobles. Dara fled after this loss, but was captured at Deodari and summarily executed, strangled by Aurangzeb's slaves on August 30, 1659. In the meantime, Aurangzeb engineered the imprisonment and execution of Murad, then directed the ambush and murder of Shuja in Bengal. With his rivals disposed of, Aurangzeb easily overthrew his father, Shah Jahan, whom he imprisoned for the rest of his life in his own Agra fortress. Aurangzeb proclaimed himself emperor on June 26, 1658.

Further reading: Barbara Daly Metcalf and Thomas R. Metcalf, *Concise History of India* (New York: Cambridge University Press, 2002); Vincent A. Smith, *The Oxford His-*tory India, 4th ed. (New York: Oxford University Press, 1981); Douglas E. Streusand, *Formation of the Mughal Empire* (New York: Oxford University Press, 1999).

Mogul Civil War (1707–1708)

PRINCIPAL COMBATANTS: Emperor Bahadur vs. (variously) his brothers, the Rajputs, Maratha, and Sikh rebels

PRINCIPAL THEATER(S): India's Deccan region

DECLARATION: None

MAJOR ISSUES AND OBJECTIVES: Bahadur sought to quell rebellion and rivalry for the throne.

OUTCOME: Bahadur triumphed over his brothers and other rebels, but his campaign against the Sikhs proved inconclusive.

APPROXIMATE MAXIMUM NUMBER OF MEN UNDER ARMS: Unknown

CASUALTIES: Bahadur, 2,000 killed; his brothers probably lost an equal number; other losses unknown

TREATIES: None

At his death, the Mogul emperor Aurangzeb (1618–1707) wanted to divide his kingdom among his sons to avoid the war of succession that customarily followed the death of a Mogul ruler. Despite this, three of his sons violently contended for sole power. Princes Azam (d. 1707) and Kambakhsh (d. 1708), of India's Deccan region, were outraged after their elder brother Muazzam (1643–1712), governor of Kabul (Afghanistan), assumed the Mogul throne in 1707 as Bahadur Shah I. Azam attacked forces under Bahadur and was defeated and slain in 1708. Later that same year, his brother Kambakhsh died in battle.

Bahadur was free of his rivals, but he still needed to solidify his position in an ever-fractious empire. He mollified the Rajputs by releasing Ajit Singh (1678–c. 1720), a crown prisoner since the RAJPUT REBELLION AGAINST AURANGZEB in 1679. He allowed Ajit Singh to rule Marwar (Jodhpur). Bahadur also subverted the Marathas by freeing Shahu (d. 1749), their former ruler, who commenced a civil war against those who had executed his father Sambhagi in 1689 during the MARATHA-MOGUL WAR (1681–1705).

At last, only the Sikhs remained to oppose Bahadur. The emperor launched an assault on Lahore (Pakistan) against the Sikhs in 1710, but the outcome was inconclusive. Although the rebels retreated into the mountains, they remained a threat, and when Bahadur died in 1712, the MOGUL CIVIL WAR (1712–1720) ensued.

See also MOGUL CIVIL WAR (1657–1659).

Further reading: Barbara Daly Metcalf and Thomas R. Metcalf, *Concise History of India* (New York: Cambridge University Press, 2002); Vincent A. Smith, *The Oxford History India,* 4th ed. (New York: Oxford University Press,

1981); Douglas E. Streusand, *Formation of the Mughal Empire* (New York: Oxford University Press, 1999).

Mogul Civil War (1712–1720)

PRINCIPAL COMBATANTS: Jahandar Shah vs. Farrukh-Siyar; Farrukh-Siyar vs. the Sayyid brothers; Sayyid brothers vs. Muhammad Shah
PRINCIPAL THEATER(S): Northern India
DECLARATION: None
MAJOR ISSUES AND OBJECTIVES: Competition for the Mogul throne
OUTCOME: A succession of rulers assumed the throne; the principal result of the civil war was the decline of the Mogul Empire.
APPROXIMATE MAXIMUM NUMBER OF MEN UNDER ARMS: Unknown
CASUALTIES: Unknown
TREATIES: None

After the Mogul emperor Bahadur Shah I (1643–1712) died, India's Mogul Empire was thrown into a bitter struggle over succession, which weakened the empire's resources and helped bring about its decline.

The eldest of Bahadur's four sons assumed the throne as Jahandar Shah (d. 1713). He immediately proved an incompetent ruler and was challenged by a relative, Farrukh-Siyar (d. 1719). Farrukh-Siyar allied himself with the Sayyid brothers—Husayn Ali (d. 1720) and Abdullah (d. c. 1721)—to carry out a coup d'état in 1713. At Farrukh-Siyar's direction, Jahandar Shah was strangled and Farrukh-Siyar installed in his place. With the help of the Sayyids, whose puppet he was, Farrukh-Siyar crushed the rebellious Rajput leader Ajit Singh (1678–c. 1720), as well as a powerful Sikh leader, Sanda Singh Bahadur (1670–1716).

Farrukh-Siyar surprised his Sayyid masters by rebelling against them in 1719. The ruthless brothers engineered his overthrow, took him captive, blinded him, and finally murdered him. However, neither of the Sayyids was in the royal line of succession. They therefore installed two new puppets in succession, a pair of weak and ailing underage boys, who lasted only from February to November 1719. Finally they brought to the throne a grandson of Bahadur Shah I, Muhammad Shah (1702–48).

By 1720 the Moguls were in full decline as the warlike Hindu Marathas extended their influence deeply into Hindustan. Muhammad Shah conspired against Husayn Ali, whom he or his henchmen poisoned. Shortly afterward, Muhammad fought Abdullah at the Battle of Hasanpur, near Delhi. Muhammad was victorious and imprisoned Abdullah, thereby bringing Sayyid control of the Mogul Empire to an end. However, the Mogul Empire itself was tottering. For all practical purposes, it fell in 1764, when the Emperor Shah Alam II (1728–1806) allied himself with the British East India Company, which had established a firm foothold in India (*see* SEVEN YEARS' WAR), displacing French colonial power there. The alliance was one-sided; Shah Alam II effectively became a British vassal.

Further reading: Barbara Daly Metcalf and Thomas R. Metcalf, *Concise History of India* (New York: Cambridge University Press, 2002); Vincent A. Smith, *The Oxford History India,* 4th ed. (New York: Oxford University Press, 1981); Douglas E. Streusand, *Formation of the Mughal Empire* (New York: Oxford University Press, 1999).

Mogul Conquest of Rajasthan (1561–1595)

PRINCIPAL COMBATANTS: Mogul Empire vs. the kingdoms of Rajasthan
PRINCIPAL THEATER(S): Rajasthan, India
DECLARATION: None
MAJOR ISSUES AND OBJECTIVES: The Mogul emperor Akbar wanted to expand the Mogul Empire by dominating the Rajasthan kingdoms.
OUTCOME: All but a few of the Rajasthan kingdoms surrendered.
APPROXIMATE MAXIMUM NUMBER OF MEN UNDER ARMS: Moguls, about 60,000; Rajasthan, about 50,000
CASUALTIES: The siege of Chetor (1567–68) cost the Moguls 30,000 killed; in turn, the Moguls slaughtered 28,000 Rajputs there.
TREATIES: None

The Mogul emperor Humayun (1508–56) had spent so much time away from India during the Early MOGUL WARS AGAINST THE SUR DYNASTY (1535–1536), that the Hindu princes of central and western India, unsupervised, had become virtually autonomous. They formed a loosely structured alliance known as Rajasthan (or Rajputana) and, thus unified, created a threat to the Mogul hegemony.

It fell to Humayun's son and successor, Akbar (1542–1605), to deal with the problem of Rajasthan. In 1561, he launched a military campaign to conquer the central kingdom of Malwa, north of the Deccan. The following year, he established, through marriage, an alliance with the ruler of Amber (Jaipur). In this way, Akbar gained control of Jodhpur, Bhatha (Rewa), and a large portion of the Punjab and western Rajasthan by 1564. Next, between 1567 and 1570, Akbar accumulated control over all of Rajasthan by subduing its system of defensive fortresses, beginning with Chitor. This, the most formidable of the Rajasthan fortresses, took two years to capture (1567–68) and cost Akbar perhaps 30,000 of his men. When, at long last, it became apparent to Chitor's defenders that they were doomed, they performed the ritual of *jauhar*—burning their woman to death in preparation for a suicidal battle. This completed, the garrison of 8,000 sortied out against Akbar and was cut down to a man. After the fall of the fortress, Chitor was sacked with the loss of some 20,000 inhabitants. Ranthambhor, another fortress, also required a long siege, conducted from 1568 to 1569.

Following these brutal victories, Akbar, in 1570, called the Rajput rulers to a conference. Four Rajasthan kingdoms readily acknowledged his sovereignty. Another four soon followed. The only holdout was the western Mewar kingdom, which set up a kind of government in exile on an island in an artificial lake at Udaipur. Remarkably, Mewar managed to remain independent for the balance of Akbar's rule, even as he continued to enlarge the Mogul Empire by annexing Kashmir (1586), taking Sind (1590), annexing Orissa to Bengal (1592–94), and subduing Baluchistan (1595).

See also MOGUL WAR AGAINST GUJARAT, FIRST; MOGUL WAR AGAINST GUJARAT, SECOND.

Further reading: Barbara Daly Metcalf and Thomas R. Metcalf, *Concise History of India* (New York: Cambridge University Press, 2002); Vincent A. Smith, *The Oxford History India,* 4th ed. (New York: Oxford University Press, 1981); Douglas E. Streusand, *Formation of the Mughal Empire* (New York: Oxford University Press, 1999).

Mogul-Maratha Wars   *See* MARATHA-MOGUL WAR (1647–1665); MARATHA-MOGUL WAR (1670–1680); MARATHA-MOGUL WAR (1681–1705).

Mogul-Persian War   (1622–1623)

PRINCIPAL COMBATANTS: Mogul Empire vs. Persia
PRINCIPAL THEATER(S): Region around the fortress-city of Kandahar, Afghanistan
DECLARATION: None
MAJOR ISSUES AND OBJECTIVES: The Persians wanted to take Kandahar from the Moguls; the Moguls wanted to recover it.
OUTCOME: The city was taken, and the Moguls failed to retake it.
APPROXIMATE MAXIMUM NUMBER OF MEN UNDER ARMS: Unknown
CASUALTIES: Unknown
TREATIES: None

Abbas I the Great (1557–c. 1628), shah of Persia, wanted to capture the strategically situated fortress-city of Kandahar, which was held by the Moguls. He made an assault against it in 1605–06, but was pushed back by forces under the Mogul emperor Jahangir (1569–1627). In 1622, Abbas led another army against Kandahar, taking it after a

siege of 45 days. Immediately, Jahangir planned a campaign to recover the fortress-city, ordering his son Khurram (1592–1666)—who subsequently ruled as Shah Jahan—to take an army from the Deccan into Kabul (Afghanistan) and make the assault. However, Khurram delayed his departure, and his father accused him of being in revolt. This prompted him to lead an army against his father in the so-called SHAH JAHAN'S REVOLT. Weakened by this action, the Mogul imperial forces were unable to retake Kandahar when they finally reached it in 1623, but the city would become a constant bone of contention between Persia and the Mogul Empire.

See also MAHABAT KHAN'S INSURRECTION; MOGUL-PERSIAN WAR (1638); MOGUL-PERSIAN WAR (1648–1653).

Further reading: David Morgan, *Medieval Persia, 1040–1797* (New York: Longman, 1988); Douglas E. Streusand, *Formation of the Mughal Empire* (New York: Oxford University Press, 1999).

Mogul-Persian War   (1638)

PRINCIPAL COMBATANTS: Mogul Empire vs. Persians
PRINCIPAL THEATER(S): Kandahar in Kabul (Afghanistan)
DECLARATION: None
MAJOR ISSUES AND OBJECTIVES: Mogul emperor Shah Jahan wanted to retake Kandahar, lost earlier.
OUTCOME: The fortress-city was retaken, not through force of arms, but by bribery. Shah Jahan's grander plan, to recapture Samarkand, was aborted.
APPROXIMATE MAXIMUM NUMBER OF MEN UNDER ARMS: Unknown
CASUALTIES: Unknown
TREATIES: None

The strategic fortress-city of Kandahar had been lost by the Moguls during the MOGUL-PERSIAN WAR (1622–1623). In 1638, the Mogul emperor Shah Jahan (1592–1666) wanted to retake it as a step in a campaign to recover his ancestral Timurid homeland of Samarkand. Shah Jahan bribed the Persian governor of Kandahar, thereby obtaining the city's surrender without laying siege to it. Next, Shah Jahan refortified Kandahar and the surrounding area.

Shah Jahan did not succeed in his grand plan of taking Samarkand. Moreover, in the next war with Persia, the MOGUL-PERSIAN WAR (1649–53), Shah Jahan once again lost Kandahar to the Persians—this time permanently, although the Persian occupation continued to raise the ire of the Moguls.

Further reading: David Morgan, *Medieval Persia, 1040–1797* (New York: Longman, 1988); Douglas E. Streusand, *Formation of the Mughal Empire* (New York: Oxford University Press, 1999).

Mogul-Persian War (1648–1653)

PRINCIPAL COMBATANTS: Mogul Empire vs. Persia
PRINCIPAL THEATER(S): Kandahar, Afghanistan
DECLARATION: None
MAJOR ISSUES AND OBJECTIVES: The Moguls wanted to retake the strategically critical fortress-city of Kandahar.
OUTCOME: The Moguls repeatedly failed to retake the city.
APPROXIMATE MAXIMUM NUMBER OF MEN UNDER ARMS: Moguls, 60,000 (under Aurangzeb) and 70,000 (under Dara Shikoh); Persian numbers were greater.
CASUALTIES: Dara's assault on August 21, 1653, resulted in 1,000 Moguls killed and 1,000 wounded; Persian losses unknown.
TREATIES: None

In 1639 Persia invaded the Mogul Empire, capturing the Afghan city of Bamian and threatening the previously contested fortress-city of Kandahar to the south. Shah Jahan (1592–1666), the Mogul emperor, redoubled the fortifications at the strategically critical Kandahar, but for years no further Persian attack came.

In the meantime, Shah Jahan sent his son Murad (d. 1661) to invade Uzbek-controlled Badakhshan in 1646. He was soundly defeated, an event that prompted the Persians finally to mobilize against Kandahar. Preoccupied on other fronts, Shah Jahan delayed dispatching troops to the fortress-city until 1649, by which time Kandahar had fallen to the combined armies of the Persians and Uzbek Turks. The following year, Shah Jahan's son Aurangzeb (1618–1707) led an attack on Kandahar, but failed to retake it. Aurangzeb withdrew from the area, and, in 1652, returned with a larger army of 60,000 men. After two months of fighting, the still-superior Persian forces drove the Moguls into a second retreat. In disgrace, Aurangzeb turned over command of the armies to his oldest brother, Dara Shikoh (1615–59). Augmented to 70,000 men, that army conducted a five-month siege, but also failed to retake the fortress-city. Dara withdrew, having suffered 1,000 killed and an equal number wounded. Kandahar remained in Persian hands.

See also MOGUL-PERSIAN WAR (1622–1623); MOGUL-PERSIAN WAR (1638).

Further reading: David Morgan, *Medieval Persia, 1040–1797* (New York: Longman, 1988); Douglas E. Streusand, *Formation of the Mughal Empire* (New York: Oxford University Press, 1999).

Mogul-Sikh War (1675–1708)

PRINCIPAL COMBATANTS: Mogul Empire vs. Sikh rebels
PRINCIPAL THEATER(S): Northern India
DECLARATION: None
MAJOR ISSUES AND OBJECTIVES: The Sikhs wanted freedom from religious persecution.
OUTCOME: The Sikhs fought a long defensive war, but were finally subdued.
APPROXIMATE MAXIMUM NUMBER OF MEN UNDER ARMS: Unknown
CASUALTIES: Unknown
TREATIES: None

The Sikhs of northern India, who combined elements of the Muslim as well as Hindu religions, were favored by the Muslim Mogul emperor Akbar (1542–1605), but were disliked by orthodox Muslims as well as Hindus. In 1606, a Sikh guru named Arjun (1563–1606) was tortured to death by order of the orthodox Muslim Mogul emperor Jahangir (1569–1627) on charges that Arjun had supported the rebellion of the emperor's son Khusrau (d. 1622) in the MOGUL CIVIL WAR (1607). The seventh guru, Har Rai (1630–61)—Arjun had been the fifth—threw Sikh support behind the liberal Muslim prince Dara Shikoh (1615–59) against his brother, the new Mogul emperor Aurangzeb (1618–1707). In retaliation, Aurangzeb forced Dara to send his son as a hostage to the Mogul court.

Such incidents steadily heightened the enmity between the Sikhs and the Moguls. At last, the ninth guru, Tegh Bahadur (c. 1621–75) staged a revolt in the Punjab. It proved short-lived, and the guru was taken captive to Delhi, the Mogul capital, where he was beheaded. The execution prompted Tegh Bahadur's son and the 10th guru, Gobind Rai Singh (1666–1708), to assemble a large Sikh army of the Khalsa ("pure"), with which they conducted a defensive war in the Punjab against far superior Mogul forces. Although this army held out for more than three decades, no major battles were fought, and Sikh resistance finally ended when the guru was assassinated in 1708.

See also MOGUL-SIKH WAR (1709–1716).

Further reading: K. S. Duggal, *Sikh Gurus: Their Lives and Teachings* (New Delhi: UBS Publishers, 1998); Barbara Daly Metcalf and Thomas R. Metcalf, *Concise History of India* (New York: Cambridge University Press, 2002); Vincent A. Smith, *The Oxford History India*, 4th ed. (New York: Oxford University Press, 1981); Douglas E. Streusand, *Formation of the Mughal Empire* (New York: Oxford University Press, 1999).

Mogul-Sikh War (1709–1716)

PRINCIPAL COMBATANTS: Mogul Empire vs. Sikh rebels
PRINCIPAL THEATER(S): Punjab region of India
DECLARATION: None
MAJOR ISSUES AND OBJECTIVES: Sikhs wanted independence from the Moguls.

OUTCOME: In the course of the war, the Sikhs made many gains, but the resistance collapsed when the Sikh's principal leader was captured and killed.
APPROXIMATE MAXIMUM NUMBER OF MEN UNDER ARMS: Extremely variable
CASUALTIES: Unknown
TREATIES: None

Bahadur Shah I (1643–1712), Mogul emperor of India, secured an alliance with the Sikh followers of Guru Gobind Rai Singh (1666–1708) against the rival Marathas. Following Gobind's death in 1708, the Sikhs under Banda Singh Bahadur (1670–1716) turned on the Mogul garrisons that had been established in their country— the Punjab—and seized the fort at Sirhind in 1710. After this, the Sikhs were virtual rulers of the region, as only the city of Lahore (Pakistan) remained under Mogul control.

Banda conducted a guerrilla war against the Moguls, raiding from hillside strongholds. When Bahadur Shah died in 1712, Banda was able to retake Sadhaura and Longarh, and when the Mogul Empire was weakened by the MOGUL CIVIL WAR (1712–1720), which followed Bahadur's death, Banda and the Sikhs made further inroads. However, Bahadur Shah's successor, Farrukh-Siyar (d. 1719), defeated the wily Banda in battle. Taken captive, he was transported to Delhi, where he was publicly humiliated and tortured to death in June 1716.

See also MOGUL-SIKH WAR (1675–1708).

Further reading: K. S. Duggal, *Sikh Gurus: Their Lives and Teachings* (New Delhi: UBS Publishers, 1998); Barbara Daly Metcalf and Thomas R. Metcalf, *Concise History of India* (New York: Cambridge University Press, 2002); Vincent A. Smith, *The Oxford History India,* 4th ed. (New York: Oxford University Press, 1981); Douglas E. Streusand, *Formation of the Mughal Empire* (New York: Oxford University Press, 1999).

Mogul War against Gujarat, First
(1535–1536)

PRINCIPAL COMBATANTS: Mogul India vs. Gujarat
PRINCIPAL THEATER(S): Region near Delhi, west coast of India, and Kabul (Afghanistan)
DECLARATION: None
MAJOR ISSUES AND OBJECTIVES: Moguls attempted to consolidate their territorial gains in India.
OUTCOME: Bahadur, the Gujarat sultan, was temporarily defeated, only to resume his opposition to the Moguls.
APPROXIMATE MAXIMUM NUMBER OF MEN UNDER ARMS: Unknown
CASUALTIES: Unknown
TREATIES: None

After the death of Babur (1483–1530), first Mogul emperor of India, his son Humayun (1518–56) assumed the throne. He proved a grossly incompetent ruler at a time when great vigor was called for. Although Babur had acquired a vast realm, stretching across north India from the Amu Dar'ya (oxus) to the Brahmaputra River, the Moguls at this stage were little more than military occupiers. (*See* BABUR'S CONQUEST OF BIHAR AND BENGAL; BABUR'S INVASION OF NORTHERN INDIA; BABUR'S LAHORE CAMPAIGN; BABUR'S RAIDS ON PUNJAB.) Babur's gains had yet to be forged into a genuine empire. Humayun began his reign in 1530 by failing to subdue the Hindu principality of Kalinjar in Bundelkhand, south of Delhi. Next, he provoked war with the Sur (Afghan) dynasty's Sher Khan (1486–1545), governor of Bihar. In this conflict, Humayun failed to take Sher Khan's key fortress at Chunar. Then Humayun moved south and west to invade Malwa and Gujarat (1535).

This time, Humayun seemed to be on the way to victory. He captured the forts of Mandu and Champaner and pushed Sultan Bahadur (d. c. 1536) of Gujarat all the way down India's west coast, where he secured refuge among the Portuguese. In the meantime, however, Sher Khan proclaimed independence and invaded Bengal in 1536. Worse, Humayun returned to Delhi without leaving behind occupation forces. Bahadur simply reentered his lands, resumed control of them, and continued to oppose Mogul authority.

See also MOGUL WAR AGAINST GUJARAT, SECOND (1572–1573).

Further reading: Barbara Daly Metcalf and Thomas R. Metcalf, *Concise History of India* (New York: Cambridge University Press, 2002); Vincent A. Smith, *The Oxford History India,* 4th ed. (New York: Oxford University Press, 1981); Douglas E. Streusand, *Formation of the Mughal Empire* (New York: Oxford University Press, 1999).

Mogul War against Gujarat, Second
(1572–1573)

PRINCIPAL COMBATANTS: Mogul Hindustan vs. Gujarat (with Portuguese aid)
PRINCIPAL THEATER(S): Gujarat
DECLARATION: None
MAJOR ISSUES AND OBJECTIVES: Moguls wanted to crush Gujarat resistance to their authority in India.
OUTCOME: The Mogul emperor Akbar succeeded in subduing Gujarat opposition.
APPROXIMATE MAXIMUM NUMBER OF MEN UNDER ARMS: Moguls, 20,000; Gujarat rebels, 20,000
CASUALTIES: Unknown
TREATIES: Treaty between Akbar and Portuguese colonists of Diu, 1573

Akbar (1542–1605), Mogul emperor of Hindustan, successfully completed the MOGUL CONQUEST OF RAJASTHAN, then advanced west, toward the kingdom of Gujarat, which had long opposed Muslim authority. Gujarat was defended by a complex of fortresses and fortress-cities, each of which required the mounting of a siege to capture it.

First to fall was Ahmadabad in November 1572. In December, Akbar subdued the fortress at Cambay and scored a victory against usurpers at Sarnal. Following these triumphs, Akbar retired to the court city of Fatehpur Sikri, which he had commissioned to be built to replace the traditional capitals, Agra and Delhi. Insurgents returned to plague Akbar by laying siege to Ahmadabad in 1573. They had counted on the monsoon to prevent Akbar from defending Ahmadabad, but Akbar led his troops through monsoon conditions across more than 500 miles in 11 days. Akbar retook Ahmadabad on September 2, 1573, captured the insurgent leaders and took many other prisoners from among the 20,000 rebels there. The Portuguese, who had supported Gujarat (they occupied the Gujarat island of Diu), concluded a hasty peace with Akbar.

See also MOGUL WAR AGAINST GUJARAT, FIRST.

Further reading: Barbara Daly Metcalf and Thomas R. Metcalf, *Concise History of India* (New York: Cambridge University Press, 2002); Vincent A. Smith, *The Oxford History India,* 4th ed. (New York: Oxford University Press, 1981); Douglas E. Streusand, *Formation of the Mughal Empire* (New York: Oxford University Press, 1999).

Mogul Wars against the Sur Dynasty, Early (1535–1536)

PRINCIPAL COMBATANTS: Moguls (with Persian allies) under Humayun vs. Surs under Sher Khan
PRINCIPAL THEATER(S): Punjab and Bengal, India
DECLARATION: None
MAJOR ISSUES AND OBJECTIVES: Sher Khan and Humayun were locked in a struggle over the Indian throne.
OUTCOME: Sher Khan overthrew Humayun, who later was able to win back his throne.
APPROXIMATE MAXIMUM NUMBER OF MEN UNDER ARMS: Unknown
CASUALTIES: Unknown
TREATIES: None

Sher Khan (1486–1545) became Sur (Afghan) governor of Bihar after he participated in Babur's (1483–1530) Mogul conquest of India. (*See* BABUR'S CONQUEST OF BIHAR AND BENGAL; BABUR'S INVASION OF NORTHERN INDIA; BABUR'S LAHORE CAMPAIGN; BABUR'S RAIDS ON PUNJAB.) When Babur's successor, the Emperor Humayun (1508–56), failed to seize the Bihari fortress of Chunar in 1532, Sher Khan became his rival for power. Humayun left Delhi in 1535 to fight the Fisrt MOGUL WAR AGAINST GUJARAT, and Sher

Khan took the opportunity to invade Bengal. At this, Humayun broke off his campaign in Gujarat and marched his army east through the monsoon, reaching Bengal in 1537.

Humayun engaged Sher Khan, only to be called away yet again, this time to combat a revolt in Delhi by younger brothers. In a ruthless masterstroke of strategy, Sher Khan positioned his forces between Humayun and Delhi. The emperor's troops, weakened by the hardships of the monsoon, were slaughtered at the Battle of Chausa in 1539. Humayun himself managed narrowly to escape by floating across the Ganges on inflated animal skins used to carry water. He fled to Agra, where he pardoned his brothers, naming one of them, Kamran (d. 1557), ruler of Kabul and Kandahar. After this, Humayun fled west, where he lost another battle, at Kanauj in 1540, this time nearly drowning in the sacred river before escaping with his defeated troops to Lahore (Pakistan).

In the meantime, Sher Khan established himself as emperor. Wanting to leave no loose ends, Sher Khan pressed the pursuit of Humayun, first into Sind, then east to Rajasthan, then back to Sind and Kandahar. There Humayun's own brother refused to give him refuge, and he fled to Persia. There he unsuccessfully offered to bribe the shah with the 240-carat Koh-i-noor ("mountain of light") diamond in exchange for an army.

It was 1547 before Humayun was able to raise an army and begin the return to Delhi. That journey consumed seven years of fighting in Kamran before he crossed into India in 1554. By this time, however, the mighty Sur armies were embroiled in a three-way war of succession, so that Humayun's combined Mogul-Persian forces were able to defeat the fragmented Sur armies, first in the Punjab and then at Rohtas (Rohtak) in 1555.

The long-suffering Humayun went to Delhi and Agra and reclaimed his throne, only to fall to his death down a flight of stone steps the following year while in a drunken stupor.

See also MOGUL WARS AGAINST THE SUR DYNASTY, LATER (1556–1557; 1575–1576).

Further reading: Barbara Daly Metcalf and Thomas R. Metcalf, *Concise History of India* (New York: Cambridge University Press, 2002); Vincent A. Smith, *The Oxford History India,* 4th ed. (New York: Oxford University Press, 1981); Douglas E. Streusand, *Formation of the Mughal Empire* (New York: Oxford University Press, 1999).

Mogul Wars against the Sur Dynasty, Later (1556–1557; 1575–1576)

PRINCIPAL COMBATANTS: Moguls vs. Surs
PRINCIPAL THEATER(S): India, principally Punjab and Bengal
DECLARATION: None
MAJOR ISSUES AND OBJECTIVES: The Moguls and Surs contended for control of India.
OUTCOME: The Surs were defeated.

APPROXIMATE MAXIMUM NUMBER OF MEN UNDER ARMS:
Moguls, 20,000; Surs, 180,000
CASUALTIES: Precise numbers unknown, but, following the
Battle of Tukra (Tukuroi), March 3, 1575, the Moguls be-
headed their prisoners, creating 80 towers of severed skulls.
TREATIES: None

Akbar (1542–1605), son of the Mogul emperor Humayun
(1508–56), inherited the troubled Mogul Indian throne at
age 13. The young ruler was faced with the ongoing threat
from the Sur dynasty, as well as opposition from the Hindu
Rajput rulers (see the MOGUL CONQUEST OF RAJASTHAN),
the rivalry of his brother, opposition from Gujarat (see Second MOGUL WAR AGAINST GUJARAT), and a rebellious son.

Humayun's 1555 victory at Rohtas (Rohtak) in the
Early MOGUL WARS AGAINST THE SUR DYNASTY (1535–1536)
had not entirely eliminated the Sur rivals for the throne.
Sikander Sur (d. 1558) was vying for control of the Punjab,
and Hemu (d. 1556), Hindu prime minister of Sur-domi-
nated Bihar and Bengal, seized Delhi and Agra, establishing
himself as the Rajah Vikramaditya. Akbar attended to this
threat first, but soon found himself losing the second Battle
of Panipat. Some 1,500 Hindu elephants were charging for
the coup de grâce when, suddenly, Hemu was felled by an
arrow that penetrated his eye. His army broke and ran, and
the wounded Hemu was taken captive and executed.

With Delhi and Agra retaken, Akbar returned to the
west, where he met Sikander Sur at the Battle of Sirhind
(1557) and defeated him. At the defeat, a final Sur pretender, Daud Khan (d. 1576), fled to Orissa. Akbar determined that he could leave the weakly supported man
alone for the time being. Years later, in 1574, during the
course of Akbar's conquest of Bihar, Daud invaded Bengal
with an army of 40,000 cavalry, 140,000 infantry, and
3,600 elephants. By vastly superior tactics, this massive
force was defeated by 20,000 Mogul horsemen at the Battle of Tukra on March 3, 1575. While relatively few Sur
warriors were killed in the battle, many were made prisoner. These unfortunate men were beheaded, the victors
creating 80 towers of their severed skulls.

Daud attacked again at Rajmahal on July 12, 1576,
but was defeated, captured, and executed. His death
brought an end to Sur opposition to the Moguls in India.

Further reading: Barbara Daly Metcalf and Thomas R.
Metcalf, *Concise History of India* (New York: Cambridge
University Press, 2002); Vincent A. Smith, *The Oxford His-
tory India,* 4th ed. (New York: Oxford University Press,
1981); Douglas E. Streusand, *Formation of the Mughal
Empire* (New York: Oxford University Press, 1999).

Mohawk-Mahican War (1626–1628)

PRINCIPAL COMBATANTS: Iroquoian Mohawks vs.
Algonquian Mahicans

PRINCIPAL THEATER(S): Vicinity of Albany, New York
DECLARATION: None recorded
MAJOR ISSUES AND OBJECTIVES: The Mohawks sought first
to break the Mahican monopoly on the Dutch beaver
trade, then to take control of it themselves
OUTCOME: The Dutch reached trading arrangements with
both tribes
APPROXIMATE MAXIMUM NUMBER OF MEN UNDER ARMS:
Unknown
CASUALTIES: Unknown
TREATIES: None

The Indian policy of Dutch colonists in America vacillated
between aggression and cruelty on the one hand and timid
defensiveness on the other. The Dutch initially enjoyed
friendlier relations with the Indians than did the Spanish
or English because, unlike the Spanish, they did not come
to conquer, and, unlike the English, they were less interested in settling than in trading.

Henry Hudson (d. 1611), an Englishman sailing for
the Dutch, discovered the river that bears his name in
1609. Five years after this, Fort Nassau, a trading post,
was built on Castle Island near Albany, the country of the
Mahican Indians, with whom they struck a trade agreement in 1618. Fort Nassau was flooded out and abandoned in 1617, but the Dutch West Indies Company,
formed in 1621, built Fort Orange on the site of Albany in
1624. The first Indian conflict came two years later, when
the Mohawks launched a war against the Mahicans. The
Dutch sent a small force under Daniel van Krieckebeeck
(d. 1624) to help their trading partners, but were defeated,
with the loss of three men in addition to van Krieckebeeck. The Dutch withdrew and concluded a treaty with
the Mohawks.

Four years later, in 1628, Mohawk warriors once
again hit the Mahicans, but they did not press their advantage. The Mohawks seemed less intent on annihilating the
Mahicans than on taking control of the lucrative Dutch
trade, much desired by all the beaver-hunting Indians (see
BEAVER WARS). After 1628, the two tribes apparently
reached an accord, because both conducted a profitable
trade with the Fort Orangers.

Further reading: Alan Axelrod, *Chronicle of the Indian
Wars: From Colonial Times to Wounded Knee* (New York:
Prentice Hall General Reference, 1993); Wilcomb E.
Washburn, *The Cambridge History of the Native Peoples of
the Americas,* 3 vols. (New York: Cambridge University
Press, 1996–2000).

Moldavian Revolt   See AUSTRO-TURKISH WAR (1591–1606).

Monfort's Rebellion   See BARONS' WAR.

Mongol-Burmese War (1277–1287)

PRINCIPAL COMBATANTS: Mongols vs. Burmese Pagans
PRINCIPAL THEATER(S): Borderlands of Burma (Myanmar) and Mongolia
DECLARATION: None
MAJOR ISSUES AND OBJECTIVES: The king of Pagan in Burma resisted Mongol demands for vassalage and tribute.
OUTCOME: The Pagan king ultimately accepted Mongol suzerainty over his kingdom.
APPROXIMATE MAXIMUM NUMBER OF MEN UNDER ARMS: Numbers unknown; but, at their greatest extent, Burmese forces outnumbered Mongol forces 3 to 1.
CASUALTIES: Unknown
TREATIES: No documents survive

The Mongol dynastic founder Kublai Khan (1216–94) attempted to force vassalage on the king of Pagan, Narathihapate (d. 1287). The king not only refused, but, as an insult to Kublai Khan, executed the emissary who bore the demand. Taking the initiative, Narathihapate then led an offensive against Kublai Khan in the Yunnan region of China. Narathihapate's elephant-mounted troops terrified the Mongol cavalry at the Battle of Ngasaunggyan in 1277, but commanders were able to avoid a panicked rout by ordering archers to dismount. On foot, the archers were able to disperse the Burmese elephants. That accomplished, they remounted and quickly counterattacked against the vastly superior Burmese forces, which outnumbered them 3 to 1. The counterattack was so vigorous that the Burmese withdrew. (The battle was described in detail by the European traveler Marco Polo [1254–1324], who witnessed it.)

In 1283, the Mongols staged a counteroffensive against the Burmese after turning away another border raid. After defeating the raiders at Bhamo, Yesin Timur (1267–1307), grandson of Kublai Khan, continued to advance through the Irrawaddy Valley and took Narathihapate's capital of Pagan. Narathihapate himself had escaped south to Bassein. Yesin Timur set up a Mongol puppet government—a circumstance that ultimately persuaded Narathihapate to accept Mongol suzerainty over his kingdom; however, his son, objecting to this capitulation, murdered Narathihapate in 1287. War would erupt anew in 1299 (MONGOL-BURMESE WAR OF 1299–1300).

Further reading: G. E. Harvey, *History of Burma* (London: Cass, 1967); David Morgan, *The Mongols* (New York: Oxford University Press, 1986); Sir Arthur P. Phayre, *History of Burma* (London: Susil Gupta, 1967); J. J. Saunders, *History of the Mongol Conquests* (Philadelphia: University of Pennsylvania Press, 2001).

Mongol-Burmese War (1299–1300)

PRINCIPAL COMBATANTS: Shan (Mongolian Thai people of northeast Burma) vs. Mongols
PRINCIPAL THEATER(S): Pagan, kingdom in Burma (Myanmar)
DECLARATION: None
MAJOR ISSUES AND OBJECTIVES: Mongols sought to reassert control of Pagan after the Shan overthrew the Mongol puppet government established in 1287.
OUTCOME: The Mongol force withdrew from Pagan, control of which remained with the Shan.
APPROXIMATE MAXIMUM NUMBER OF MEN UNDER ARMS: Unknown
CASUALTIES: 500 Mongols were killed at the Battle of Myinsaing, 1300
TREATIES: None

Mongol triumph in the MONGOL-BURMESE WAR (1277–1287) resulted in the establishment of a puppet government in the Burmese kingdom of Pagan. In 1299, the Shans of northeast Burma overthrew this government, prompting the Mongols to dispatch a small army to reestablish control. Shan forces resisted from within their fortified city of Myinsaing, killing 500 of the Mongol invaders, checking their advance, but failing to drive them out. The leader of the Shan believed that the Mongols would now send a much larger force and sought to forestall this by bribing the Mongol commander to withdraw. The Mongol commander accepted the bribe and withdrew to the Yunnan province of China. His deed did not go unpunished, however, as Mongol leaders later executed the corrupt commander; the Shan nevertheless remained in control of Pagan, because the Mongols never sent another army to mount a new attack.

Further reading: G. E. Harvey, *History of Burma* (London: Cass, 1967); David Morgan, *The Mongols* (New York: Oxford University Press, 1986); Sir Arthur P. Phayre, *History of Burma* (London: Susil Gupta, 1967); J. J. Saunders, *History of the Mongol Conquests* (Philadelphia: University of Pennsylvania Press, 2001).

Mongol-Chinese War (1356–1368)

PRINCIPAL COMBATANTS: Chinese (primarily under Zhu Yuanchang [Chu Yüan-chang]) vs. the Mongol overlords
PRINCIPAL THEATER(S): China, especially Yangtzi (Yangtse or Chang) River valley
DECLARATION: None
MAJOR ISSUES AND OBJECTIVES: The Chinese sought to overthrow their Mongol overlords.
OUTCOME: Amid a weakening Mongol administration, Zhu Yuanchang evicted the Mongols and established the Ming dynasty.

APPROXIMATE MAXIMUM NUMBER OF MEN UNDER ARMS:
Unknown
CASUALTIES: Unknown
TREATIES: None; the Mongols, though defeated, refused to surrender

---

The Yuan dynasty, established in China by Kublai Khan (1216–94), was inherently flawed. Kublai Khan failed to respect Chinese culture and highhandedly appointed Muslim officials to high office, thereby offending the indigenous Chinese officials, the mandarins. He generally relegated the Chinese to a status inferior to the Mongols. Far from subjugating the Chinese, this approach provoked a number of revolts, which Kublai Khan quickly crushed. Over the years, however, the quality of the Yüan emperors declined, and the Mongols became less involved in administering China. By the 1350s, the rebellions became more numerous and intense, especially in the Yangtzi River valley. Local warlords usurped authority, and one of them, Zhu Yuanchang (1328–98), proclaimed himself emperor, establishing a capital at Nanjing (Nanking). From this base, Zhu Yuanchang invaded Beijing (Peking) in 1368, which easily fell to him. He drove the Mongols out of Beijing and the surrounding territory, pushing them to Shangdu (Shang-tu) and, ultimately, to Outer Mongolia. Zhu Yüanchang founded the Ming dynasty, although the dispossessed Mongols persisted in calling themselves the rulers of China.

Further reading: Wolfram Eberhart, *A History of China,* 3rd ed. (Berkeley, University of California Press, 1969); Charles O. Hucker, *China's Imperial Past: An Introduction to Chinese History and Culture* (Stanford: Stanford University Press, 1975); David Morgan, *The Mongols* (New York: Oxford University Press, 1986); J. A. Roberts, *A Concise History of China* (Cambridge, Mass.: Harvard University Press, 1999); J. J. Saunders, *History of the Mongol Conquests* (Philadelphia: University of Pennsylvania Press, 2001).

Mongol Civil War (1260–1264)

PRINCIPAL COMBATANTS: Forces of Kublai Khan vs. forces of Arik-Böke, his brother and rival
PRINCIPAL THEATER(S): Mongolia, especially vicinity of Karakorum
DECLARATION: None
MAJOR ISSUES AND OBJECTIVES: This was a civil war fought between rival factions.
OUTCOME: The faction led by Kublai Khan prevailed.
APPROXIMATE MAXIMUM NUMBER OF MEN UNDER ARMS:
Unknown
CASUALTIES: Unknown
TREATIES: No document survives

Mangu Khan (c. 1207–59) ruled the Mongols in harmony with his brother Kublai Khan (1216–94). When Mangu died in 1259, however, a younger brother, Arik-Böke (d. 1255), assumed leadership of the "Old Mongol" faction, to oppose Kublai Khan's Chinese-influenced, modern faction. Their respective factions elected both Kublai Khan and Arik-Böke to supreme leadership of the Mongols, and this ignited civil war.

One aspect of the war was the GOLDEN HORDE–IL-KHAN CIVIL WAR, which pitted another of Kublai Khan's brothers, Hülegü (d. 1265), against Berke (d. 1266), the leader of the Golden Horde. Another aspect of the war directly involved Kublai Khan against Arik-Böke. In 1260, Kublai Khan marched an army toward Arik-Böke's capital at Karakorum, sending Arik-Böke into retreat. The following year, the two armies engaged, but fought to a draw. Nevertheless, Arik-Böke attempted to retake Karakorum. Failing in this, he lost a succession of lesser engagements before he finally surrendered to Kublai Khan in 1264. Kublai Khan did not exact personal vengeance on his brother, but released him. It was enough that his forces had been defeated, and, indeed, Arik-Böke was finished as a political power.

Further reading: Wolfram Eberhart, *A History of China,* 3rd ed. (Berkeley: University of California Press, 1969); Charles O. Hucker, *China's Imperial Past: An Introduction to Chinese History and Culture* (Stanford: Stanford University Press, 1975); David Morgan, *The Mongols* (New York: Oxford University Press, 1986); J. A. Roberts, *A Concise History of China* (Cambridge, Mass.: Harvard University Press, 1999); Morris Rossabi, *Kublai Khan: His Life and Times* (Berkeley: University of California Press, 1989); J. J. Saunders, *History of the Mongol Conquests* (Philadelphia: University of Pennsylvania Press, 2001).

Mongol Conquest of the Abbasid Caliphate (1255–1260)

PRINCIPAL COMBATANTS: Mongols vs. the Abbasid Caliphate and Egypt
PRINCIPAL THEATER(S): Mesopotamia (Iraq) and Syria
DECLARATION: None
MAJOR ISSUES AND OBJECTIVES: The Mongols sought the conquest of Mesopotamia, Syria, and, ultimately, Egypt
OUTCOME: The Abbasid Caliphate fell, and the Mongols conquered Mesopotamia and Syria, but failed to hold Syria and also failed to conquer Egypt.
APPROXIMATE MAXIMUM NUMBER OF MEN UNDER ARMS:
Maximum Mongol strength, 400,000
CASUALTIES: Mongol casualties approached 10,000; other casualties unknown. Many civilian losses in the sack of Baghdad
TREATIES: None

Preparatory to an assault on Egypt, the Mongol khakhan (supreme ruler) Mangu Khan (c. 1207–59) assigned the conquest of the Abbasid caliphate to his brother Hülegü (d. 1265), who had founded the Il-Khan dynasty, which bordered the caliphate. Hülegü advanced from the Oxus (Amu Dar'ya) River to within a few miles of the Nile. Simultaneously, Hülegü's general, Ked-Buka (d. 1260), led a massive Mongol force out of Samarqand in 1256 and attacked the Assassins, a secret Muslim terrorist sect, destroying their power and putting Ked-Buka's army in position to take Baghdad, capital of the caliphate. With brilliant execution of a careful plan, Ked-Buka was able to surround Baghdad and assault it from three sides. The capital fell in 1258, after a yearlong siege, and Hülegü entered it, sacked it, seized the caliph, Al Mustasim (d. 1258), and ordered him trampled to death by horses.

Having captured the Abbasid capital and having killed its caliph, Hülegü invaded the rest of Mesopotamia (Iraq) with a vast army of 400,000. In 1259, he expanded the attack to Syria, and in 1260 the cities of Aleppo, Damascus, Gaza, and Sidon fell to him. These major conquests put Hülegü in position to take Egypt, but Hülegü had to abandon these plans when Mangu Khan died. With a power vacuum back home, Hülegü had no choice but to return. He left Ked-Buka and a garrison of 10,000 soldiers in charge of the conquered territory. This, of course, left him vulnerable to Egyptian attack, which came in 1260. Ked-Buka was killed and his 10,000-man force defeated. An Egyptian army went on to retake Syria.

Further reading: Guy LeStrange, *Baghdad during the Abbasid Caliphate: From Contemporary Arabic and Persian Sources* (Westport, Conn.: Greenwood Publishing Group, 1983); J. J. Saunders, *History of the Mongol Conquests* (Philadelphia: University of Pennsylvania Press, 2001).

Mongol Conquest of the Jin Empire
(1231–1234)

PRINCIPAL COMBATANTS: Mongols vs. Jin dynasty
PRINCIPAL THEATER(S): Northern China
DECLARATION: None
MAJOR ISSUES AND OBJECTIVES: Mongol conquest
OUTCOME: The Jin (Chin) dynasty fell to the conquest.
APPROXIMATE MAXIMUM NUMBER OF MEN UNDER ARMS: About 80,000 Mongols; numbers of other combatants unknown
CASUALTIES: Unknown
TREATIES: None

The Mongol conquest of the Jin in northern China was the prelude to the MONGOL CONQUEST OF THE SONG [Sung] EMPIRE and the MONGOL INVASION OF EUROPE. It was led by the son of Genghis Khan (c. 1167–1227), Ögedei (d.

1241), who became khakhan (supreme ruler) of the Mongols after the death of his father.

With his brother Tolui (d. 1232) and his leading commander, Sübedei (d. c. 1258), Ögedei advanced into Henan (Honan) Province, Jin territory. Like his father, Ögedei was a master of military strategy and had developed a plan whereby he and Sübedei advanced from the north and Tolui from the south. Tolui fended off Jin opposition and forced the Jin to withdraw into their capital, Kaifeng. Although Tolui died in battle, he had driven the Jin warriors precisely where Ögedei and Sübedei wanted them. Sübedei now led a siege against Kaifeng, constructing a great wall around the capital, by which the Jin were starved into submission. Seeing the collapse of the Jin to be imminent, Song warriors joined the Mongols in their siege. The Jin emperor Ai Zong (Ai Tsung; r. 1224–34), managed to slip through the siege lines, but, believing his situation hopeless, hanged himself. Ögedei's intervention forestalled wholesale destruction of the fallen Jin capital, much of which was preserved.

Further reading: Wolfram Eberhart, *A History of China*, 3rd ed. (Berkeley: University of California Press, 1969); Charles O. Hucker, *China's Imperial Past: An Introduction to Chinese History and Culture* (Stanford: Stanford University Press, 1975); David Morgan, *The Mongols* (New York: Oxford University Press, 1986); J. A. Roberts, *A Concise History of China* (Cambridge, Mass.: Harvard University Press, 1999); J. J. Saunders, *History of the Mongol Conquests* (Philadelphia: University of Pennsylvania Press, 2001).

Mongol Conquest of the Song Empire
(1234–1279)

PRINCIPAL COMBATANTS: Mongols vs. Song (Sung) dynasty
PRINCIPAL THEATER(S): China and Southeast Asia
DECLARATION: None
MAJOR ISSUES AND OBJECTIVES: Mongol conquest
OUTCOME: After sporadic and protracted warfare against stubborn resistance, the Mongols conquered the Song and founded the Yuan dynasty.
APPROXIMATE MAXIMUM NUMBER OF MEN UNDER ARMS: Kublai Khan fielded an army of 100,000; other numbers unknown
CASUALTIES: Often heavy. Kublai Khan lost 60,000 of his army of 100,000; Song losses were heavy, as Song warriors typically fought to the death.
TREATIES: None

Immediately after the MONGOL CONQUEST OF THE JIN [Chin] EMPIRE in 1231, 1233, and 1234, Ögedei (d. 1241), khakhan (supreme ruler) of the Mongols, commenced a war against the Song dynasty. In contrast to the conquest of the Jin, war against the Song proved long and arduous —in no small part because the Mongol program of conquest at this point was so ambitious, encompassing the Middle East and Europe, as well as China, that Mongol resources were spread thin.

Warfare against the Song was chronic and indecisive for the first 20 years of campaigning, but was stepped up in intensity under Kublai Khan (1216–94) in the 1250s. Sübedei (d. c. 1258), serving as his chief commander, led a series of sieges, and, in 1252, Kublai Khan himself led an army of 100,000 through Tibet into Yunnan, defeating a Song army there before advancing through modern Laos, where he attacked the Song army from the south. He advanced northward and engaged a large Song army in 1254. Losses to the Song in men and territory were great, but so were losses to Kublai Khan's army, which, by 1254, had dwindled to 20,000.

After Kublai Khan had fought his running war of attrition, his brother, Mangu Khan (c. 1207–59), defeated the Song in a series of speedy victories between 1257 and 1259, when he succumbed to disease. Mangu Khan's death brought a long intermission in the war, which allowed the Song to regroup and, to a large extent, revive. It was not until 1268 that Sübedei's grandson Bayan (1237–95) resumed in earnest the conquest of the Song in a series of devastating victories culminating in the fall of Hangzhou (Hangchow), the Song capital. So determined was Song resistance, however, that the fighting continued even after Hangzhou had been taken. In 1279, a small Song force evacuated the boy emperor in a fleet that rode in the bay of Canton. Mongol vessels attacked, sinking the emperor's ship and drowning him. This at long last ended Song resistance.

The fall of the Song dynasty was the culmination of Mongol efforts to unite all China under its rule. Kublai Khan established the Yüan dynasty in place of the Jin and Song.

Further reading: Wolfram Eberhart, *A History of China*, 3rd ed. (Berkeley: University of California Press, 1969); Charles O. Hucker, *China's Imperial Past: An Introduction to Chinese History and Culture* (Stanford: Stanford University Press, 1975); David Morgan, *The Mongols* (New York: Oxford University Press, 1986); J. A. Roberts, *A Concise History of China* (Cambridge, Mass.: Harvard University Press, 1999); J. J. Saunders, *History of the Mongol Conquests* (Philadelphia: University of Pennsylvania Press, 2001).

Mongol Dynastic Wars   *See* GOLDEN HORDE DYNASTIC WAR.

Mongol Invasion of Annam and Champa
See VIETNAMESE-MONGOL WAR (1257–1288).

Mongol Invasion of Europe (1237–1242)

PRINCIPAL COMBATANTS: Mongols vs. Poles and Hungarians
PRINCIPAL THEATER(S): Poland, Hungary, Austria
DECLARATION: None
MAJOR ISSUES AND OBJECTIVES: Mongol conquest
OUTCOME: The Mongols swept through Poland and Hungary, bringing great destruction, but they withdrew on the death of the khakhan Ögedei.
APPROXIMATE MAXIMUM NUMBER OF MEN UNDER ARMS: Mongols, 150,000; at the Battle of Wahlstadt, Poland fielded 40,000; at the Battle of Mohi, Hungary fielded 70,000
CASUALTIES: Totals unknown; at the Battle of Mohi, Hungary suffered 40,000 casualties out of an army of 70,000
TREATIES: None

The Mongol invasion of Europe was part of a vast program of conquest including the MONGOL CONQUEST OF THE ABBASID CALIPHATE, the MONGOL CONQUEST OF THE JIN [CHIN] EMPIRE, and the MONGOL CONQUEST OF THE SONG [SONG] EMPIRE. The movement west of some 150,000 Mongol troops commenced in 1237 and began with the conquest of Russian principalities (Second MONGOL INVASION OF RUSSIA). By 1240, the Mongol army, under the remarkable commander Sübedei (d. c. 1258), was in Poland. Lublin, Sandomierz, Boleshlav, Chmielnik, and Kraków were either captured or destroyed. The culminating battle came on April 9, 1241, at Wahlstadt, where Henry I of Silesia (1168–1241) led 40,000 troops, including a contingent of Teutonic Knights, in a defensive counterattack against the Mongols. The European troops were heterogeneous, poorly disciplined, and indifferently led. The Mongols, in contrast, were highly trained, highly motivated, and brilliantly led by commanders bred on strategy and tactics. When Sübedei noted that Henry had divided his forces into four units, he employed a so-called suicide tactic (*mangudai*), using a small advance force as a lure to draw the enemy out to attack. The small force would hold the enemy in place, absorbing its blows, until the hidden wings of the Mongol army would close upon the attacker like the jaws of a giant trap. This is precisely what happened at Wahlstadt. Not only was an army of 40,000 routed and decimated, Europe's finest warriors, the Teutonic Knights, were all but wiped out. As for Henry of Silesia, although he fled, Mongol patrols tracked him down, and he was beheaded. This act was intended to intimidate the citizens of nearby Liegnitz into instant capitulation; however, shown Henry's severed head, they resolved instead to resist. The Mongols destroyed the city, albeit incurring heavy losses themselves.

From the bloody triumph of Wahlstadt, the Mongols advanced into Hungary via the Carpathian Mountains, Galicia, Moldavia, Transylvania, and Saxony. Thus the Hungarians were surrounded by hostiles on four sides. Hungary's King Béla IV (1206–70) foolishly sent the bulk of his army (the most formidable in Europe) to the north, near Pest (Budapest), where he thought the main attack would come. At Mohi on the Sajo River, on April 11, 1241, Béla divided his 70,000 men, making a probing attack with an advance unit against a small Mongol detachment. Sübedei, always the master of tactics, hid his main force and, at night, struck the main part of Béla's force, which was sleeping in camp. Surprise was total and resulted in the loss of 40,000 Hungarians, more than half of Béla's army. Thoroughly demoralized after the Battle of Mohi, the rest of the army fled, as did Béla, leaving Pest open to the Mongols. On December 25, 1241, they invaded the city and burned it. From here they raided into Austria (1242) and, doubtless, would have continued their westward advance had word of the death of the khakhan (supreme ruler) Ögedei (d. 1241) not prompted them to return to Asia. Thus the Mongol army returned home undefeated.

Further reading: Jesse Chambers, *The Devil's Horsemen: The Mongol Invasion of Europe* (New York: Sterling, 2001); David Morgan, *The Mongols* (New York: Oxford University Press, 1986); J. J. Saunders, *History of the Mongol Conquests* (Philadelphia: University of Pennsylvania Press, 2001).

Mongol Invasion of Japan, First (1274)

PRINCIPAL COMBATANTS: Mongol (with Korean allies) vs. Japan
PRINCIPAL THEATER(S): Kyushu, Japan
DECLARATION: None
MAJOR ISSUES AND OBJECTIVES: Mongol conquest
OUTCOME: A storm forced an end to the Mongol and Korean amphibious invasion, and the forces withdrew to Korea.
APPROXIMATE MAXIMUM NUMBER OF MEN UNDER ARMS: Unknown
CASUALTIES: Unknown
TREATIES: None

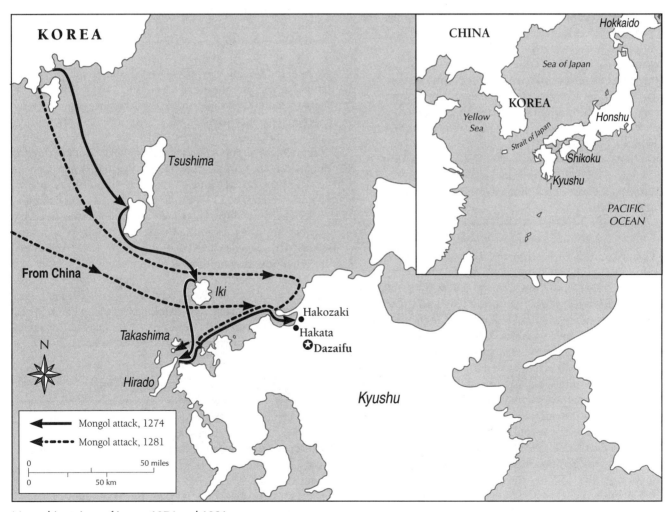

Mongol invasions of Japan, 1274 and 1281

Having conquered Korea in 1241 (MONGOL INVASION OF KOREA), the Mongols decided to use the country as a platform from which to launch an invasion of Japan. When the Japanese refused a surrender demand, a combined Mongol-Korean fleet landed at Kakata in Kyushu. Although the Mongols possessed military superiority over the Japanese, a storm wrecked some of the landing fleet, delaying the operation and buying the Japanese time to mass more defenders. Under this pressure, the Mongols and Koreans aborted the invasion and withdrew to Korea.

See also MONGOL INVASION OF JAPAN, SECOND (1281).

Further reading: John W. Hall, *Japan; From Prehistory to Modern Times* (Tokyo: C. E. Tuttle Co., 1971); David Morgan, *The Mongols* (New York: Oxford University Press, 1986); James Murdoch, *A History of Japan,* 3 vols. (New York: Routledge, 1996); George B. Samson, *A History of Japan,* 3 vols. (Palo Alto, Calif.: Stanford University Press, 1958–63); J. J. Saunders, *History of the Mongol Conquests* (Philadelphia: University of Pennsylvania Press, 2001).

Mongol Invasion of Japan, Second (1281)

PRINCIPAL COMBATANTS: Mongols (with Korean allies) vs. Japan
PRINCIPAL THEATER(S): Kyushu, Japan
DECLARATION: None
MAJOR ISSUES AND OBJECTIVES: Mongol conquest
OUTCOME: The Mongols were unable to breach strong Japanese fortifications and, at sea, were defeated by a combination of a Japanese fleet and a terrible storm or kamikaze ("divine wind").
APPROXIMATE MAXIMUM NUMBER OF MEN UNDER ARMS: Mongols, 150,000; Japanese forces were lesser
CASUALTIES: Most of the Mongol army was destroyed.
TREATIES: None

Kublai Khan (1216–94) delayed a second invasion attempt against Japan long after the failure of the first attempt (*see* MONGOL INVASION OF JAPAN, FIRST) and was provoked to the second foray only after Japan not only rejected Mongol demands for submission but also killed Mongol envoys. In 1281, Kublai Khan assembled a Mongol-Korean fleet of 4,500 vessels carrying 150,000 invasion troops. As in the earlier attempt, the invaders seized outlying islands and, from these, mounted an invasion at Kyushu. This time, however, they met intense resistance. Taking a lesson from the first invasion attempt, the Japanese built strong fortifications on Kyushu. These held the Mongol army at bay while a Japanese fleet battled the Mongol armada at sea.

About two months into the operation, disaster struck the Mongol fleet, which was mostly wrecked in a storm (the Japanese believed this to have been a "divine wind, [or *kamikaze*]"), leaving the beleaguered attackers on land without supplies. The Japanese counterattacked, wiping out most of the Mongol-Korean army. Japan was never menaced by the Mongols again.

Further reading: John W. Hall, *Japan; From Prehistory to Modern Times* (Tokyo: C. E. Tuttle Co., 1971); David Morgan, *The Mongols* (New York: Oxford University Press, 1986); James Murdoch, *A History of Japan,* 3 vols. (New York: Routledge, 1996); George B. Samson, *A History of Japan,* 3 vols. (Palo Alto, Calif.: Stanford University Press, 1958–63); J. J. Saunders, *History of the Mongol Conquests* (Philadelphia: University of Pennsylvania Press, 2001).

Mongol Invasion of Korea (1231–1241)

PRINCIPAL COMBATANTS: Mongols vs. Korea
PRINCIPAL THEATER(S): Korea
DECLARATION: None
MAJOR ISSUES AND OBJECTIVES: Mongol conquest
OUTCOME: The initial conquest was swift, but subsequent rebellions brought a long period of raiding and suppression of rebel forces.
APPROXIMATE MAXIMUM NUMBER OF MEN UNDER ARMS: Unknown
CASUALTIES: Unknown
TREATIES: None

When a Mongol envoy conveyed the demand of the khakhan (supreme ruler), Ögedei (d. 1241), that Korea must submit to Mongol suzerainty, the messenger was, by way of response, murdered. Ögedei ordered his leading general, Sübedei (d. c. 1258), to invade. Within less than a year, a Mongol puppet was installed on the Korean throne, but a rebellion in 1232 sent him fleeing. When Ögedei ordered the puppet king to report to him at Karakorum, he refused and, in 1235, Ögedei dispatched a force to punish him by subjugating Korea anew. Over the next six years, the Mongols methodically raided Korea and suppressed all opposition. At last, the king submitted entirely to the Mongols, who reinstated him.

Further reading: John W. Hall, *Japan; From Prehistory to Modern Times* (Tokyo: C. E. Tuttle Co., 1971); David Morgan, *The Mongols* (New York: Oxford University Press, 1986); J. J. Saunders, *History of the Mongol Conquests* (Philadelphia: University of Pennsylvania Press, 2001).

Mongol Invasion of Russia, First (1221–1223)

PRINCIPAL COMBATANTS: Mongols vs. Khivans, Alans, Cherkess, Kipchak Turks, and Russian princes
PRINCIPAL THEATER(S): Uzbekistan, Georgia, Caucasus, and Crimea
DECLARATION: None
MAJOR ISSUES AND OBJECTIVES: Mongol conquest
OUTCOME: The theater of the war was conquered by the Mongols and became the Kipchak Khanate.

APPROXIMATE MAXIMUM NUMBER OF MEN UNDER ARMS: At the Battle of the Kalka River, the Kipchaks and Russian princes fielded 80,000 men against an inferior number of Mongols.

CASUALTIES: The Battle of Kalka River resulted in the loss of most of the Kipchak-Russian army of 80,000.

TREATIES: None

The Mongols' first invasion of Russia was incidental to a punitive pursuit of the shah of Khwarazm (Khiva), who had fled after the Mongols destroyed Bukhara in central Uzbekistan. The shah was run to ground near the Caspian Sea and found dead there in 1221. With two Mongol armies now in the area, however, the Mongol commanders set about raiding through Azerbaijan and Georgia. In Georgia, Tiflis (Tbilisi) fell to the Mongols before the end of the year. The raiders then destroyed Margaha and Hamadan, and in 1222 raided the steppes north of the Caucasus. Here they were confronted by allied Alan, Cherkess, and Kipchak tribes. The Kipchaks were rapidly defeated, but the others united with the Russian princes at the Kalka River. Here, in 1223, the Kipchak-Russian force, approximately 80,000 men, attacked the smaller Mongol army under Sübedei (d. c. 1258). Despite their inferiority of numbers, the Mongols were far better trained,

equipped, and led. Sübedei used a fast-moving circling tactic, pouring fire from his archers into the Kipchak-Russian ranks, almost entirely destroying the enemy.

From the Battle of the Kalka River, the Mongols captured the Genoese port of Sudak on the Crimean Peninsula, then marched up the Volga River, where they harassed Bulgars and Kangli Turks. After this, the Mongols returned to Persia. The Mongol emperor Genghis Khan (c. 1167–1227) gave the conquered Russian territory to his eldest son, Jöchi (d. 1227), and, after the Second MONGOL INVASION OF RUSSIA in 1236, it became known as the Kipchak Khanate.

Further reading: Charles J. Halperin, *Russia and the Golden Horde: The Mongol Impact on Medieval Russian History* (Bloomington: Indiana University Press, 1987); Geoffrey A. Hoskin, *Russia and Russians: A History* (Cambridge, Mass.: Harvard University Press, 2001); David Morgan, *The Mongols* (New York: Oxford University Press, 1986); J. J. Saunders, *History of the Mongol Conquests* (Philadelphia: University of Pennsylvania Press, 2001).

Mongol Invasion of Russia, Second
(1236–1240)

PRINCIPAL COMBATANTS: Mongols vs. Russians
PRINCIPAL THEATER(S): Western and central Russia

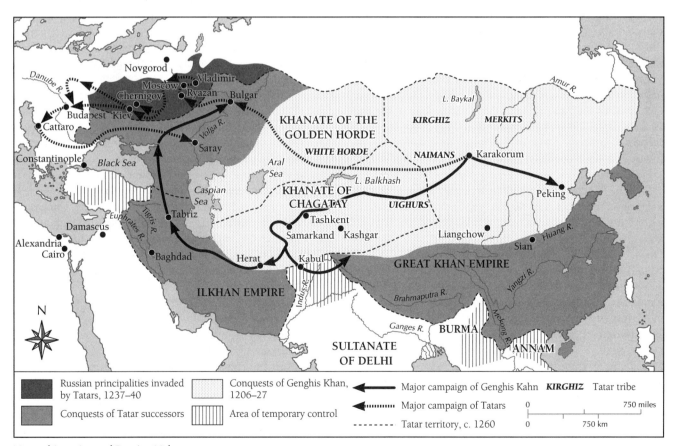

Mongol invasions of Russia, 13th century

DECLARATION: None

MAJOR ISSUES AND OBJECTIVES: Mongol conquest

OUTCOME: By 1240, the Kipchak Khanate (central Russia) was firmly in the hands of the Golden Horde, as was Kievan Russia (Ukraine).

APPROXIMATE MAXIMUM NUMBER OF MEN UNDER ARMS: Unknown

CASUALTIES: Unknown, but heavy among the conquerors and conquered alike

TREATIES: None

The First MONGOL INVASION OF RUSSIA made great inroads into Russian territory and staked out the Kipchak Khanate, but it did not deliver the territory wholly into the hands of what became known as the Golden Horde of Batu Khan. Therefore, in 1236, Mongol forces assembled in Great Bulgaria, near the Volga River, and, after ravaging Great Bulgaria, advanced into European Russia.

Mangu Khan (c. 1207–59) subdued Great Hungary in 1236, defeating the Bashkirs and Kipchaks, then advanced into Hungary proper by 1241. In the meantime, Batu Khan (d. 1256) destroyed the Russian cities of Riazan and Kilomna in 1237, conquered most of central Russia in 1238—the realm of Prince Vladimir falling to him—then went on toward Novgorod. Like many other conquerors after him, Batu Khan was defeated not by an opposing army, but by the elements. His troops survived the bitter winter, only to become bogged down in a vast muddy thaw. Unable to make further headway, Batu Khan withdrew and was idle throughout 1239. In 1240, he renewed the invasion, ravaging Kievan Russia (Ukraine) along the Dnieper River. He destroyed Kiev itself, then established complete control of the area.

Further reading: Charles J. Halperin, *Russia and the Golden Horde: The Mongol Impact on Medieval Russian History* (Bloomington: Indiana University Press, 1987); Geoffrey A. Hoskin, *Russia and Russians: A History* (Cambridge, Mass.: Harvard University Press, 2001); David Morgan, *The Mongols* (New York: Oxford University Press, 1986); J. J. Saunders, *History of the Mongol Conquests* (Philadelphia: University of Pennsylvania Press, 2001).

Mongol Invasion of Syria (1299–1300)

PRINCIPAL COMBATANTS: Mongols vs. Syrians

PRINCIPAL THEATER(S): Syria

DECLARATION: None

MAJOR ISSUES AND OBJECTIVES: Essentially a massive hit-and-run raid rather than an occupation

OUTCOME: The invasion was successful, but the Mongols either failed or chose not to occupy the region on a permanent basis.

APPROXIMATE MAXIMUM NUMBER OF MEN UNDER ARMS: Unknown

CASUALTIES: Unknown

TREATIES: None

During the great age of Mongol expansion, the two centuries spanning 1200 to 1400, Mongol forces under Il-Khan Mahmud Ghazan (r. 1294–1303) attacked and captured Damascus and used this Syrian capital as a base from which they overran all Syria. However, Mahmud Ghazan failed to establish a permanent presence in the region and, no sooner had he completed his conquest, than he withdrew from Syria—which, however, would be subject to periodic Mongol raids.

Further reading: David Morgan, *The Mongols* (New York: Oxford University Press, 1986); J. J. Saunders, *History of the Mongol Conquests* (Philadelphia: University of Pennsylvania Press, 2001).

Mongol Invasions of India (1221–1398)

PRINCIPAL COMBATANTS: Mongols vs. India

PRINCIPAL THEATER(S): India, chiefly the Punjab

DECLARATION: None

MAJOR ISSUES AND OBJECTIVES: Mongol conquest

OUTCOME: The Mongol raids during this period were disorganized and random.

APPROXIMATE MAXIMUM NUMBER OF MEN UNDER ARMS: At the Battle of the Indus, Mongol forces numbered 40,000 against Indian forces of 30,000.

CASUALTIES: At the Battle of the Indus, Indian losses were much more than half of the 30,000-man force.

TREATIES: None

Generally, Mongol invasions were major campaigns guided by detailed plans and carefully formulated strategies. In contrast to this, however, the first invasion of India was almost accidental. It came about when the son of the Khwarazm shah, Jalal-ad-Din (or Jalal al-Din; d. 1231), escaped Mongol captivity and fled to Khorasan, where he mobilized resistance, then fled to Afghanistan and organized resistance there as well. From there he took refuge in the Hindu Kush Mountains.

Genghis Khan (c. 1167–1227) led a Mongol army in the Battle of Bamian, laying waste that city, then pressed his pursuit of Jalal-ad-Din into India. He ran his quarry to ground at the Indus River. Genghis Khan commanded about 40,000 troops against Jalal-ad-Din's 30,000. The Muslim forces had the river at their backs, but were protected on the right flank by a bend in the river and, on the left, by a mountain ridge. Genghis Khan perceived that the weaker position was the enemy's left, and he dispatched specially trained mountain cavalry to attack it. Rolling up Jalal-ad-Din's flank, Genghis Khan was able to envelop him completely. Most of the 30,000-man force was wiped out, although Jalal-ad-Din himself escaped.

After the Indus River battle, Genghis Khan decided to focus his attention on gaining control of Khorasan, so he withdrew from India. The next invasion came in 1241 and was not followed by another until 1292. Another hiatus came until 1299. From this time until 1308, Mongols frequently raided in and about Lahore and throughout the Punjab. After 1308, the Mongols refrained from invasion except for a brief raid on Delhi in 1329. It was not until TAMERLANE'S INVASION OF INDIA in 1398 that the Mongols made a concerted effort to gain control of the region.

Further reading: Barbara Daly Metcalf and Thomas R. Metcalf, *Concise History of India* (New York: Cambridge University Press, 2002); David Morgan, *The Mongols* (New York: Oxford University Press, 1986); J. J. Saunders, *History of the Mongol Conquests* (Philadelphia: University of Pennsylvania Press, 2001); Vincent A. Smith, *The Oxford History India*, 4th ed. (New York: Oxford University Press, 1981).

Mongol-Persian War, First (1218–1221)

PRINCIPAL COMBATANTS: Mongols vs. Persia, especially Khwarazm (Khiva)
PRINCIPAL THEATER(S): Persia
DECLARATION: Genghis Khan against Khwarazm
MAJOR ISSUES AND OBJECTIVES: The invasion began as retribution for the killing of Mongol trade emissaries.
OUTCOME: Much of Persia was subjugated.
APPROXIMATE MAXIMUM NUMBER OF MEN UNDER ARMS: Mongol, 200,000; other numbers unknown, but much smaller in any single engagement
CASUALTIES: Unknown
TREATIES: None

The war began after Genghis Khan (1167–1227) sent military aid to Muslim Turks suppressing an uprising in Kara-Khitai. The Mongol mission liberated Kara-Khitai, from which Genghis Khan decided to send a peaceful trading mission into neighboring Khwarazm, one of the three realms that at the time made up Persia (the other two were Transoxiana and Khorasan). Muhammad (r. 1200–20), the shah of Khwarazm, seized the caravan and executed the Mongol emissaries, whereupon Genghis Khan demanded reparation. When no reparation was forthcoming, the Mongol leader declared war.

Genghis Khan sent a 200,000-man army into Persia, destroying all cities that failed to surrender. The population of each resisting city was killed, except for artisans and engineers, who were recruited into the Mongol number. Those cities Genghis Khan destroyed were permitted to rebuild, once they acknowledged Genghis Khan's suzerainty.

In the face of this destruction, the Khwarazmian shah fled. The Mongols gave chase, sacking along the way Bukhara and the capital city of Samarkand in 1220. By timely surrender, Herat and Merv, major centers of trade, wisely avoided destruction. The war continued through 1221 as one of many MONGOL INVASIONS OF INDIA, but Muhammad Khwarazm Shah had been permanently deposed.

See also MONGOL-PERSIAN WAR, SECOND (1230–1243).

Further reading: David Morgan, *Medieval Persia, 1040–1797* (New York: Longman, 1988) and *The Mongols* (New York: Oxford University Press, 1986); J. J. Saunders, *History of the Mongol Conquests* (Philadelphia: University of Pennsylvania Press, 2001).

Mongol-Persian War, Second (1230–1243)

PRINCIPAL COMBATANTS: Mongols vs. Persia
PRINCIPAL THEATER(S): Persia
DECLARATION: None
MAJOR ISSUES AND OBJECTIVES: Mongol conquest
OUTCOME: Persia and the surrounding region fell to the Mongols.
APPROXIMATE MAXIMUM NUMBER OF MEN UNDER ARMS: Unknown
CASUALTIES: Unknown
TREATIES: None

Having escaped the general slaughter of the 1221 Battle of the Indus River during the first of the MONGOL INVASIONS OF INDIA, Jalal-ad-Din (or Jalal al-Din; d. 1231), son of the shah of Khwarazm, fled to Delhi, where he married the daughter of the local sultan. With his father-in-law's aid, he advanced across the Indus in 1224, raided Lahore and the Punjab, both controlled by the Mongols, and captured Tabriz and Tiflis (Tbilisi) in 1225 and Armenia in 1227, where he defeated a small Mongol army. In 1230, the Mongol khakhan (supreme ruler) Ögedei (d. 1241) assembled a major Mongol army to destroy the forces of Jalal-ad-Din. He was surrounded at Diyarbakir in 1231, but eluded capture; however, Syria, Syrian Mesopotamia, and Anatolia (Turkey) fell to the Mongols, along with Persia.

See also MONGOL-PERSIAN WAR, FIRST.

Further reading: David Morgan, *Medieval Persia, 1040–1797* (New York: Longman, 1988) and *The Mongols* (New York: Oxford University Press, 1986); J. J. Saunders, *History of the Mongol Conquests* (Philadelphia: University of Pennsylvania Press, 2001).

Mongol Revolts (1755–1760)

PRINCIPAL COMBATANTS: China vs. Mongol tribes
PRINCIPAL THEATER(S): Eastern Turkistan and western Mongolia

DECLARATION: None
MAJOR ISSUES AND OBJECTIVES: The Chinese acted to suppress rebellion among the Mongols.
OUTCOME: The Mongols were suppressed, and their territory became an autonomous region under Chinese suzerainty.
APPROXIMATE MAXIMUM NUMBER OF MEN UNDER ARMS: Unknown
CASUALTIES: Unknown
TREATIES: None

The Mongol tribes, especially the Dzungars, in eastern Turkistan and western Mongolia frequently rebelled against the government of the Chinese emperor Qianlong (Ch'ien-lung; 1711–99). The Chinese general Zhaohui (Chao-hui; 1708–64) led an expedition to crush the rebellions and, in 1757, defeated the Dzungars and other Mongol tribes. Eastern Turkistan and western Mongolia became the Xinjiang Uighur (Sinkiang Uygur) Autonomous Region under the suzerainty of China.

Further reading: Wolfram Eberhart, *A History of China,* 3rd ed. (Berkeley: University of California Press, 1969); Charles O. Hucker, *China's Imperial Past: An Introduction to Chinese History and Culture* (Stanford: Stanford University Press, 1975); David Morgan, *The Mongols* (New York: Oxford University Press, 1986); J. A. Roberts, *A Concise History of China* (Cambridge, Mass.: Harvard University Press, 1999); J. J. Saunders, *History of the Mongol Conquests* (Philadelphia: University of Pennsylvania Press, 2001).

Monks, War of the (1465)

PRINCIPAL COMBATANTS: Tendai warrior monks vs. Shin warrior monks
PRINCIPAL THEATER(S): In and about Kyoto, Japan
DECLARATION: None
MAJOR ISSUES AND OBJECTIVES: Religious rivalry
OUTCOME: Inconclusive
APPROXIMATE MAXIMUM NUMBER OF MEN UNDER ARMS: Unknown
CASUALTIES: Unknown
TREATIES: None

This was a conflict between rival warrior monks: the Tendai, based on a hill in northeast Kyoto called the Hieisan, and the Shin, within Kyoto proper. The Tendai invaded the city and burned down the Shins' Hongwanji Temple. The violence sparked an uprising outside the city as well; other sects began to fight with one another. Despite quick expansion, the war soon petered out, albeit without resolution.

The War of the Monks was a manifestation of the anarchy that prevailed during this period, in which neither emperor nor shoguns (military overlords) had effective power and authority.

Further reading: John W. Hall, *Japan; From Prehistory to Modern Times* (Tokyo: C. E. Tuttle Co., 1971); James Murdoch, *A History of Japan,* 3 vols. (New York: Routledge, 1996); George B. Samson, *A History of Japan,* 3 vols. (Palo Alto, Calif.: Stanford University Press, 1958–63).

Monmouth's Rebellion (1685)

PRINCIPAL COMBATANTS: England vs. the duke of Monmouth
PRINCIPAL THEATER(S): Somersetshire, England
DECLARATION: None
MAJOR ISSUES AND OBJECTIVES: Monmouth sought to succeed Charles II to the throne.
OUTCOME: The rebellion was crushed, Monmouth beheaded, and the other rebels punished.
APPROXIMATE MAXIMUM NUMBER OF MEN UNDER ARMS: Monmouth's army, 9,000; royalist forces, 2,700
CASUALTIES: Monmouth's army, 1,384 killed in action, 1,000 made prisoner, of whom 200 were executed and 800 transported to Barbados exile; royalists, 400 killed or wounded
TREATIES: None

James Scot (1649–85), duke of Monmouth, was proposed by the first earl of Shaftesbury as the heir to the throne of Charles II (1630–85) in preference to the Catholic duke of York, James (subsequently King James II [1633–1701]). When Monmouth attracted many supporters, he was threatened and had to flee for his life to Holland. He returned to England after the death of Charles II, where he proclaimed himself king and raised an army of 9,000 supporters. The duke of York, having ascended the throne as James II, sent an army under Louis de Durfort, the second earl of Feversham (1641–1709) to intercept Monmouth's force. Colonel John Churchill (1650–1722), commanding the Household Cavalry, defeated Monmouth, largely with artillery fire, at the Battle of Sedgemoor, in Somersetshire, on July 6, 1685. Monmouth's force was decimated, and although Monmouth himself escaped death in battle, he was soon captured and beheaded. Of 1,000 of Monmouth's men taken prisoner, 200 were hanged and the rest shipped off to Barbados by judgment of Chief Justice George Jeffreys (c. 1645–89) in what came to be called the Bloody Assizes.

Further reading: David Johnson, *Monmouth's Rebellion* (New York: Viking Penguin, 1968).

Mon Revolt *See* BURMESE CIVIL WAR (1740–1752).

Montenegran-Turkish Wars   *See* TURKO-
MONTENEGRIN WAR, FIRST; TURKO-MONTENEGRIN WAR, SECOND.

Montenegro Revolt   *See* VENETIAN-TURKISH WAR (1714–1718).

Moorish-Christian Wars in Spain   *See*
SPANISH CHRISTIAN-MUSLIM WAR (912–928); SPANISH CHRISTIAN-MUSLIM WAR (977–997); SPANISH CHRISTIAN-MUSLIM WAR (1001–1031); SPANISH CHRISTIAN-MUSLIM WAR (1172–1212); SPANISH CHRISTIAN-MUSLIM WAR (1230–1248); SPANISH CHRISTIAN-MUSLIM WAR (1481–1492).

Moorish-Frankish Wars   *See* FRANKISH-
MOORISH WAR, FIRST; FRANKISH-MOORISH WAR, SECOND.

Moors' Conquest of Spain   *See* MUSLIM
CONQUEST OF SPAIN.

Morant Bay Rebellion   (1865)

PRINCIPAL COMBATANTS: Great Britain vs. native Jamaican rebels
PRINCIPAL THEATER(S): Morant Bay
DECLARATION: None
MAJOR ISSUES AND OBJECTIVES: The protestors wanted access to government lands.
OUTCOME: The rebellion was put down harshly, and the British government, to avoid full-scale rebellion, acted to mitigate the effect of the action.
APPROXIMATE MAXIMUM NUMBER OF MEN UNDER ARMS: Rebels, 2,000; government numbers unknown
CASUALTIES: Fifteen were killed and 31 wounded in the initial ation, the Morant Bay courthouse arson; three more whites were slain in subsequent action; 439 rebels were executed and 600 more flogged.
TREATIES: None

After hard-pressed Jamaicans were refused permission to use government lands for planting, mobs in St. Ann and St. Thomas parishes set fire to the courthouse at Morant Bay on October 10, 1865, while the parish council was in session. The chief magistrate and 14 other whites were killed (it is not known how many black Jamaicans died). In response, Jamaica's British governor Edward John Eyre (1815–1901) imposed martial law and dispatched troops to suppress the "rebellion." George William Gordon (d. 1865), a prominent black merchant, was executed as a

ringleader, producing outrage throughout the island. In a successful effort to forestall a greater rebellion, the Jamaican assembly voted itself out of existence, the Crown recalled Governor Eyre, and Parliament created Jamaica as a crown colony under a royal governor. However, government troops burned some 1,000 native huts, executed 439 rebels, and sentenced another 600 to flogging. Eyre, brought up on government charges for his brutality in suppressing the uprising, was acquitted.

Further reading: Gad J. Heuman, *The Killing Time: The Morant Bay Rebellion in Jamaica* (Knoxville: University of Tennessee Press, 1994); Edward Long, *History of Jamaica* (Montreal: McGill-Queens University Press 2003).

Morgan's Raids on Panama   (1668–1671)

PRINCIPAL COMBATANTS: Morgan's buccaneers vs. Spanish colonial forces
PRINCIPAL THEATER(S): Panama
DECLARATION: None
MAJOR ISSUES AND OBJECTIVES: Morgan was hired by the British Crown to harass the Spanish along the Spanish Main.
OUTCOME: Morgan's raids in Panama disrupted Spanish interests there and netted Morgan a personal fortune.
APPROXIMATE MAXIMUM NUMBER OF MEN UNDER ARMS: Morgan's raiders numbered about 2,000. Panama was defended by fewer than 3,000 Spanish troops.
CASUALTIES: 406 buccaneers killed or wounded; 782 Spanish troops killed or wounded
TREATIES: None

Henry Morgan (c. 1635–88), a Welsh mariner, was hired by the English Crown to harass vessels on the so-called Spanish Main—the South American coastal region between Panama and the Orinoco River. On July 10, 1668, Morgan led a fleet of a dozen ships manned by 460 pirates, who captured the port town of Porto Bello on the Caribbean side of the Panamanian isthmus. One hundred thirty men of the Spanish garrison were killed before the survivors surrendered.

The following year, Morgan sailed again, but his 200-gun flagship, *Oxford,* exploded, with the loss of 200 men. It was December 16, 1670, before he made a new assault, with 37 ships manned by about 2,000 "buccaneers." They raided the rich Spanish fortress-city of Panama in January 1671. In February the city's defenses were breached and the city sacked.

Morgan withdrew on February 24 with a vast hoard of treasure and 600 prisoners, ripe for lucrative ransom. Although Morgan deserted some of his men and sailed off, he was knighted in 1673 and returned to Jamaica the following year as its deputy royal governor.

Further reading: Peter Earle, *Sack of Panama* (New York: Viking Penguin, 1982); Albert Marrin, *Terror of the Spanish Main: Sir Henry Morgan and His Buccaneers* (New York: Penguin, 1999).

Moriscos, Revolt of the (1568–1571)

PRINCIPAL COMBATANTS: Spanish vs. Moriscos rebels
PRINCIPAL THEATER(S): Andalusia, Spain
DECLARATION: None
MAJOR ISSUES AND OBJECTIVES: The Crown wanted to suppress all Muslim practice within Spain.
OUTCOME: The rebellion was crushed in Andalusia and the surviving Moriscos dispersed throughout Spain.
APPROXIMATE MAXIMUM NUMBER OF MEN UNDER ARMS: Spain, 5,000; Moriscos, 30,000
CASUALTIES: Spain, 1,550 killed or wounded; Moriscos, 21,000 killed
TREATIES: None

The Moriscos were Spanish Muslims who had been forcibly baptized by order of the Spanish Crown. In Andalusia, the Moriscos defiantly continued to speak and write in Arabic and to wear Muslim dress. To enforce religious conformity, King Philip II (1527–98) decreed harsh measures of subjugation, thereby provoking an armed rebellion at Alpujarras beginning on December 25, 1568. The initial attack was repulsed, but the violence spread to Granada, which was badly damaged by the Moriscos, and the rebels soon controlled the Alpujarras region.

In January 1569, 5,000 Spanish troops slaughtered large numbers of Moriscos at the Battle of Alfajarali Pass, but by August, the Moriscos had recruited some 30,000 troops and the revolt continued. At last, in 1571, Don Juan (John of Austria, 1547–78) led a substantial force against the Moriscos. His first assault failed, but a second attack on the Moriscos stronghold of Galera, on February 10, resulted in the deaths of 2,500 rebels. Further action prompted some Moriscos to surrender and others to disperse throughout Spain, where they persisted in clinging to Muslim practices and dress until they were deported from Spain by royal order in 1609. They were resettled mainly in North Africa.

Further reading: Henry Charles Lea, *The Moriscos of Spain: Their Conversion and Expulsion* (Westport, Conn.: Greenwood Publishing Group, 1968); J. B. Trend, *Origins of Modern Spain* (London: Russell and Russell, 1965).

Mormon War   *See* UTAH WAR (MORMON WAR) (1857–1858).

Moroccan Civil War   (1645–1668)

PRINCIPAL COMBATANTS: Hassani Berbers vs. Sa'ad dynasty
PRINCIPAL THEATER(S): Morocco
DECLARATION: None
MAJOR ISSUES AND OBJECTIVES: The Hassani sought to overthrow the Sa'ad dynasty and establish their own.
OUTCOME: The Hassani dynasty was proclaimed in 1649, but the civil war continued until the fall of Marrakesh in 1668.
APPROXIMATE MAXIMUM NUMBER OF MEN UNDER ARMS: Unknown
CASUALTIES: Unknown
TREATIES: None

During the reign of Sultan Zidan (1608–28) the Sa'ad dynasty, rulers of Morocco, entered a sharp decline. This led to a long period of civil war, from about 1645 to 1668, waged chiefly by the Hassani Berbers, who lived on the desert's edge. In 1649, the civil war reached a climax when Muhammad XIV (fl. 17th century) captured Fez and established the Hassani dynasty. However, this did not bring an end to rebellion and civil war throughout Morocco. Hassani forces continually fought resistance and did not complete the conquest of the country until 1668, when Marrakesh at last fell to them. It was then under Mulay al-Rashid, as Rashid II (r. 1668–72), that final consolidation of Morocco was achieved, from 1668 to 1672.

Further reading: Howard H. Hourami and Malise Ruthven, *A History of Arab Peoples* (Cambridge, Mass.: Harvard University Press, 2002).

Moroccan Insurrection   *See* RIF WAR (1919–1926).

Moroccan War   (1907–1912)

PRINCIPAL COMBATANTS: Morocco vs. France and Spain; Germany vs. France
PRINCIPAL THEATER(S): Morocco
DECLARATION: None—although the war may be traced to the Algeciras Convention of April 7, 1906
MAJOR ISSUES AND OBJECTIVES: Control of Morocco
OUTCOME: France was granted a protectorate over Morocco
APPROXIMATE MAXIMUM NUMBER OF MEN UNDER ARMS: Morocco, 15,000; France, 32,000; numbers for other belligerents unknown
CASUALTIES: Morocco, more than 3,000 killed; France, 1,424 killed or wounded; casualties for other belligerents unknown

TREATIES: Algeciras Convention, April 7, 1906; Treaty of Fez, March 30, 1912

In Algeciras, Spain, on April 7, 1906, Germany, Austria-Hungary, Belgium, Spain, France, Great Britain, Italy, Morocco, Netherlands, Portugal, Russia, Sweden, and the United States concluded the Algeciras Convention, which affirmed the territorial integrity of Morocco even as it authorized France and Spain to police the country. The convention had come about after Germany challenged the impending partition of Morocco by France and Spain.

North Africa, in the early 20th century, became an arena for European power politics. In 1898 the French had unsuccessfully attempted to gain control of the Egyptian Sudan, and now, through agreements with Spain, Italy, and Britain, France sought to strengthen its hold on Saharan Africa by converting the Sultanate of Morocco to a French protectorate. Kaiser Wilhelm II (1859–1941) of Germany moved to preempt this by intervening personally with the sultan of Morocco, Abd al-Aziz IV (1878–1943) in 1905. Wilhelm believed his call on the sultan would persuade Britain to back down from its recently concluded Entente Cordiale with France. The diplomatically inept kaiser had miscalculated, and his overtures to the sultan succeeded only in drawing Britain and France closer together.

Finding himself caught in a European squeeze, the sultan of Morocco requested an international conference at Algeciras, Spain, during January 16–April 7, 1906, to resolve peacefully what was developing into an explosive crisis. The convention concluded the following: Affirmation of the independence of Morocco (which pleased Germany) and the award to France of control over much of "independent" Morocco, including regulation of the Moroccan police and finances (which was contrary to the German interest). France and Spain were permitted to establish within Morocco a paramilitary police force, and France was authorized to create a substantially French-controlled state bank.

In 1907, Moroccans rose up against foreigners in Casablanca. This brought a violent and overwhelming response from French troops, who killed thousands of Moroccans and occupied Casablanca. Yet native Moroccan dissent and resistance only increased. Abd al-Hafiz (1875–1937), brother of Sultan Abd al-Aziz IV, deposed the sultan on grounds that he had sold out Morocco and failed in his stewardship of Islam. In 1909, the brother was proclaimed sultan, but he found himself engulfed in the momentum of the ongoing uprising—and called on the French and Spanish for military aid in restoring order.

On the Moroccan coast, Rif tribespeople attacked the Spanish troops, who were defeated at the Battle of Melilla in 1909. When the Rif attacked Fez, the French responded with a major force and occupied the city.

Wilhelm II, never pleased with the Algeciras Convention and now alarmed by French military actions in Morocco, sent in 1911 the German gunboat *Panther* to Agadir. Emergency negotiations between France and Germany averted war when the kaiser backed down and formally recognized French rights in Morocco. The kaiser was allowed to save face by obtaining from France the cession of a small area of the Congo.

On March 30, 1912, the sultan of Morocco concluded with France the Treaty of Fez, by which France was granted a full protectorate over Morocco.

Further reading: Edmund Burke III, *Prelude to a Protectorate: Precolonial Protest and Resistance, 1860–1912* (Chicago: University of Chicago Press, 1976); C. R. R. Pennell, *Morocco since 1830: A History* (New York: New York University Press, 2001).

Moroccan Wars in West Africa (1591–1618)

PRINCIPAL COMBATANTS: Morocco (with a largely mercenary army of Spanish and Portuguese troops) vs. Songhai Empire and other West African peoples
PRINCIPAL THEATER(S): West Africa
DECLARATION: None
MAJOR ISSUES AND OBJECTIVES: Colonial conquest
OUTCOME: Morocco overran, devastated, and colonized West Africa, only to withdraw when colonization proved costly and insufficiently profitable.
APPROXIMATE MAXIMUM NUMBER OF MEN UNDER ARMS: Moroccan forces, 4,000 against Songhai; Songhai opposition numbers unknown
CASUALTIES: Numbers unknown, but heavy among the Songhai
TREATIES: None

In 1591, a Moroccan army, consisting mainly of Spanish and Portuguese mercenary troops, about 4,000 strong and equipped with European firearms, invaded the Songhai Empire in West Africa. The Songhai warriors had never experienced European weapons before and were quickly overwhelmed. The mercenaries overran and sacked Timbuktu (Tombouctou) and they destroyed Gao, the Songhai capital. This devastation ended the Songhai Empire.

From Songhai, the Moroccans fanned out over the central Niger Valley, and when the university at Timbuktu threatened to become a center of religious and political opposition, the Moroccans destroyed it. In the end, the Moroccan military triumph was total, but the cost of maintaining colonial dominion in West Africa grew prohibitive, and Sultan Zidan (d. 1606) of Morocco withdrew all of his forces in 1618. Many Moroccan colonists remained, and some prospered whereas others perished in the power vacuum that was left by the precipitous withdrawal of the conquerors.

Further reading: J. F. A. Ajayi and Michael Crowder, *History of West Africa,* 2nd ed., 2 vols. (London: Longman, 1976–1987); J. D. Fage and Roland Oliver, eds., *The Cambridge History of West Africa,* 8 vols. (New York: Cambridge University Press, 1975–1980); Rodney Steel, *History of West Africa* (New York: Facts On File, 2003).

Moro Wars (1901–1913)

PRINCIPAL COMBATANTS: Moros of southern Philippines vs. the United States
PRINCIPAL THEATER(S): Luzon and other southern Philippine islands
DECLARATION: None
MAJOR ISSUES AND OBJECTIVES: Moros resisted U.S. occupation and administration, largely on religious and cultural grounds.
OUTCOME: Moro resistance was eventually suppressed.
APPROXIMATE MAXIMUM NUMBER OF MEN UNDER ARMS: 1,200 U.S. troops; 5,000 Moros
CASUALTIES: U.S. casualties light, fewer than 100 battle deaths total; 600 Moros died in the fall of Bud Dajo, 1906
TREATIES: None

The principal United States effort in the suppression of the PHILIPPINE INSURRECTION (1899–1902) was in the northern Philippines, especially on Luzon. The southern islands were largely neglected, and it was here that resistance to the U.S. presence grew early in the 20th century. In 1899, Brigadier General John C. Bates (1842–1919) had negotiated an agreement with the sultan of Sulu, nominal leader of the Moros, an Islamic people living on Mindanao and the Sulu Archipelago, by which the sultan recognized U.S. sovereignty. In return, the United States agreed to provide protection for the sultan's subjects, grant him sovereignty in criminal cases, respect Islamic religious customs, and even permit slavery in the area. But the sultan's control of the Moros, a people with a strong warrior tradition, was tenuous at best, and their resistance to the Americans took on the intensity of a religious war.

In November 1901, Captain John J. Pershing (1860–1948) led two troops of the 15th Cavalry and three infantry companies to Mindanao with the purpose of persuading the Moros to cooperate with the U.S. government. With great diplomatic skill, Pershing won over those Moros living on the north shore of Lake Lanao. Those on the southern shore, however, frequently skirmished with U.S. troops as well as with a U.S.-sanctioned native Moros constabulary. Brigadier General George Davis (fl. late 19th and early 20th centuries) sent 1,200 U.S. troops to take the Moro stronghold at Pandapatan, which was neutral-ized at the cost of 60 Americans killed and many more wounded. At this site, the army established Camp Vicars, with Pershing in command. From this base, between June 1902 and May 1903, Pershing launched a new diplomatic campaign, but failed to cajole cooperation from the Moros. Pershing then conducted a series of restrained but highly effective military expeditions, which also included diplomatic elements.

By the summer of 1903, when Pershing returned to the United States, the most acute Moros violence had been quelled—but flare-ups were chronic, and the new military governor of the Moro province, Major General Leonard Wood (1860–1927), entirely lacked Pershing's understanding, skill, and tolerance in dealing with the Moro people. He was determined to beat them into absolute submission to U.S. authority, and he was especially zealous in his effort to eliminate slavery in the province. Wood's approach provoked a guerrilla war, fought from Moro strongholds called *cottas.* In October 1905, a major guerrilla leader, Dato Ali (d. 1905), was targeted by Wood, who sent Captain Frank R. McCoy (fl. early 20th century) with 115 men against his cotta. McCoy's command ambushed and killed Dato Ali on October 22. Even this victory, however, did not end the Moro resistance. At the end of 1905, a large contingent of Moros took up positions at Bud Dajo, a crater atop a 2,100-foot-high extinct volcano, which proved to be a formidable natural fortress. The existence of this stronghold became a great embarrassment to U.S. authority in the province, and, on March 5, 1906, Colonel Joseph W. Duncan (fl. early 20th century) attacked the position in force. Bud Dajo fell on March 8, 18 of Duncan's troops having died, along with some 600 Moros.

The reduction of Bud Dajo brought relative peace to the Moro province for the next three years, but it did nothing to salve Moro resentment against American dominion. Pershing, now a general, returned to the Philippines in 1909 and was assigned to the Mindanao region. He was distressed by attitudes there, which he considered dangerous, and, as he had done years earlier, he embarked on a campaign of building trust and relationships. He resolved to bring enduring peace to the Moro province by disarming the tribe. He issued a disarmament order on September 8, 1911, setting a deadline of December 1. In October, however, the Moros reacted violently and, on December 3 and 5, Pershing dispatched troops to put down an incipient rebellion. The Moros sent word that they wished to negotiate peace, but they used the ensuing armistice to begin the reoccupation of Bud Dajo on December 14. Pershing responded by surrounding the stronghold on December 22. Bud Dajo was evacuated within two days, and, once again, Moro resistance died down, but did not completely end. In January 1913, following two more major skirmishes, more than 5,000 Moros, including women and children, holed up on Bud

Bagsak, another extinct volcano. Pershing had no desire to precipitate the slaughter of families and so attempted to persuade the Moros to evacuate. When they would not, on June 11, 1913, Pershing launched a coordinated land and amphibious assault on Bud Bagsak. Moro guerrillas had established well-defended cottas at Langusan, Pujagan, Matunkup, Puyacabao, Bunga, and at Bagsak, but, one by one, these fell to the assault. On June 15, Bud Bagsak was captured, and the Moro Wars quickly ended.

See also PHILIPPINE INSURRECTION (1896–1898); PHILIPPINE INSURRECTION (1899–1902); SPANISH-AMERICAN WAR (1898).

Further reading: Brian McAllister Linn, *The U.S. Army and Counterinsurgency in the Philippine War, 1899–1902* (Chapel Hill: University of North Carolina Press, 1989); John E. Walsh, *Philippine Insurrection, 1899–1902* (New York: Scholastic, 1973).

Mountain Meadows Massacre (1857)

PRINCIPAL COMBATANTS: Utah Indians, Mormons vs. California-bound emigrants of the Francher Company
PRINCIPAL THEATER(S): Southern Utah
DECLARATION: None
MAJOR ISSUES AND OBJECTIVES: The Utah Indians and a group of Mormons attacked anti-Mormon emigrants who had threatened to annihilate the Mormons.
OUTCOME: Following a federal investigation, Brigham Young punished those involved, but failed to stem the tide of anti-Mormon sentiment in the West.
APPROXIMATE MAXIMUM NUMBER OF MEN UNDER ARMS: 50 Mormon militiamen; 200 Utah; 100 Francher Company emigrants
CASUALTIES: 82 emigrants
TREATIES: None

In September 1857, Utah Indians and local Mormon settlers ambushed and killed 100 California-bound emigrants, known as the Francher Company, in a remote area of southern Utah. There were several interrelated factors that precipitated the incident, called the Mountain Meadows Massacre. First, the doomed emigrant company, composed entirely of non-Mormons, arrived in Utah at an extremely tense time. In 1857, during what became known as the UTAH WAR (or Mormon War), the Mormons anticipated armed conflict with the federal government and U.S. Army troops then traveling into the region. Second, the Francher Company's members were from Missouri and Arkansas and made no secret of their intense dislike for Mormons. Some emigrants actually bragged of direct involvement in earlier anti-Mormon violence in Missouri and Illinois. In response, the Mormons refused to trade with the emigrants or sell them badly needed food and supplies.

Further aggravating the situation was a third factor stemming from ongoing difficulties with the Indians of southern Utah. The Indians, after years of tense relations and some armed conflict with Mormon settlers, had finally established a reasonably good relationship with their new neighbors. In this relationship, the Indians believed (or wanted to believe) that the Mormons had given them tacit approval to raid and steal from non-Mormon emigrant companies passing through the region. To make matters worse, the Indians accused the Francher Company itself of killing their livestock and poisoning their wells.

Thus, when the Francher Company reached southern Utah, the situation had become critical, particularly after local Mormons refused to sell the emigrants food. The angry emigrants retaliated by destroying Mormon property and vowing to return to Utah with an armed force to wipe "every damn Mormon off the earth." The alarmed Mormons, in conjunction with their Indian allies, decided to take a drastic course of action. On September 11, 1857, at Mountain Meadows, 50 Mormon militiamen and 200 local Indians surrounded and killed all the Francher Company members, except for 18 small children.

When news of the massacre first reached church leader Brigham Young (1801–77) in Salt Lake City, he did not believe that local Mormons were involved and initially viewed the incident as an Indian affair. Young sought to cover up details of direct Mormon involvement, in particular that of John D. Lee (1812–77), the primary local Mormon leader involved; however, under national public pressure, Young finally excommunicated him.

Mormon involvement in the Mountain Meadows Massacre contributed to a negative image of the entire Latter-day Saints movement. That image persisted among many non-Mormon Americans for years to come.

Further reading: Juanita Brooks, *The Mountain Meadows Massacre* (Norman: University of Oklahoma Press, 1987); Morris Shirts, *The Mountain Meadows Massacre: Another Look* (Cedar City: Southern Utah University Press 1992).

Mozambican Civil and Guerrilla Wars
(1976–1996)

PRINCIPAL COMBATANTS: The Front for the Liberation of Mozambique (FRELIMO) ruling party vs. the Mozambican National Resistance Organization (RENAMO) and other anti-Marxist factions (with support from South Africa); FRELIMO guerrillas also raided neighboring Rhodesia (Zimbabwe)
PRINCIPAL THEATER(S): Mozambique
DECLARATION: None
MAJOR ISSUES AND OBJECTIVES: Control of the Mozambican government

OUTCOME: The brutal civil war brought general ruin to Mozambique and was resolved mainly through exhaustion on all sides; the Marxist regime was ended, and a democratic government installed.

APPROXIMATE MAXIMUM NUMBER OF MEN UNDER ARMS: FRELIMO, 40,000 (supported by 30,000 troops from neighboring countries); RENAMO, 15,000

CASUALTIES: At least 500,000 died on all sides, and at least 2 million refugees were created by the conflict, combined with drought, disease, and starvation.

TREATIES: Cease-fire, October 4, 1992

As a result of the MOZAMBICAN WAR OF INDEPENDENCE, which ended in 1974, the African country of Mozambique had won its independence from Portugal. The success of that revolution was due largely to the leadership of the Front for the Liberation of Mozambique (FRELIMO). FRELIMO not only led the revolution, but, afterward, installed a Marxist government and outlawed all competing political parties.

Within two years of FRELIMO's ascendency, Mozambique was in political and economic chaos. Skilled workers, especially whites, had fled the country. Food and all manner of imported goods were at critical shortages due to an inept and ruinous nationalization of commerce and industry and the collectivization of agriculture. The result was universal discontent and outrage. Rebellion was frequent and corruption rampant. The government dealt summarily and brutally with any offenders it caught. Many were packed into "reeducation camps," which quickly became overcrowded, squalid concentration camps.

During this period of intense internal conflict, guerrilla forces from Mozambique began a war of incursion and raids into neighboring Rhodesia, which, at the time, was still ruled by a white colonial government. The border between the two nations was closed from 1976 until 1980, when Rhodesia became independent as Zimbabwe. During this period, border clashes were routine.

In the meantime, FRELIMO found itself under siege by an array of anti-Marxist factions, the most important of which was the Mozambican National Resistance (MNR), which sought to undermine the regime by concentrating its attacks on what was left of the nation's infrastructure. Roads, railroads, and, most important of all, oil pipelines were sabotaged.

From South Africa (at the time ruled by a white government), troops invaded southern Mozambique, from which the African National Congress (ANC), a South African nationalist organization, mounted raids into South Africa.

Under pressure from all quarters, Samora Moisés Machel (b. 1933), president of Mozambique, assumed direct command of his country's military in 1983. He intensified campaigns against the various rebel factions within Mozambique, and in 1984 made what was to him a distasteful agreement with South Africa. In exchange for Mozambique's pledge to expel the ANC, the South African government promised to withdraw its support for the MNR. In fact, support was officially withdrawn, but the government continued to funnel covert aid to the right-wing movement.

In 1986, Joaquim Chissanó (b. 1929) replaced Machel as president of Mozambique and presided over a wholly defensive war against multiplying numbers of anti-Marxist rebel factions. Always companions of war in poor nations, starvation and disease swept Mozambique by the late 1980s, killing thousands. Nearly 2 million refugees fled the more ravaged areas, creating a hopeless situation.

In 1989, Afonso Dhlakama (b. 1954), leader of the MNR, opened talks with representatives of the Roman Catholic clergy to formulate a peace plan that might begin to heal the desperate nation. The clergy brokered talks between the MNR and other rebel factions and President Chissanó; Zimbabwe's president, Robert Mugabe (b. 1924), served as moderator of the rancorous talks. At last, in 1990, FRELIMO turned its back on Marxism, deeming it a failure. The party acceded to most of the MNR demands, and a new democratic constitution was adopted.

On paper, at least, Mozambique became a free-market democracy, in which all political parties were welcome and civil rights assured. In fact, dissident MNR rebels continued their program of sabotage of the infrastructure, but when a formal cease-fire was hammered out on October 4, 1992, the fighting stopped. By this time, disease, starvation, and a killing drought had sapped even the guerrillas' will and ability to fight. The nation was in extremis, having lost at least 500,000 in battles and massacres as well as to disease and famine created or exacerbated by the war. UN peacekeeping forces arrived, oversaw the disarmament of all parties, and arranged multiparty, free elections. Chissanó won reelection in October 1994, and, amid international aid and reconstruction work, most of Mozambique's 2 million refugees had returned by 1995.

Further reading: Hilary Andersson, *Mozambique: A War against the People* (New York: St. Martin's Press, 1992); William Finnegan, *A Complicated War: The Harrowing of Mozambique* (Berkeley: University of California Press, 1993).

Mozambican War of Independence
(1962–1974)

PRINCIPAL COMBATANTS: Portugal vs. Mozambican rebels

PRINCIPAL THEATER(S): Mozambique (Portuguese East Africa)

DECLARATION: None

MAJOR ISSUES AND OBJECTIVES: Mozambican independence from Portugal

OUTCOME: After unremitting pressure, Portugal, its own government transformed by a coup d'état, granted Mozambique its independence.
APPROXIMATE MAXIMUM NUMBER OF MEN UNDER ARMS: Portuguese forces, about 40,000 troops; FRELIMO, 10,000
CASUALTIES: Unknown
TREATIES: Cease-fire, 1974; independence granted, 1974

Mozambique was a longtime colony of Portugal, known as Portuguese East Africa, and was caught up in the general movement, during the 1960s, for the independence of all European African colonies. In 1962, the leaders of many nationalist factions met in Dar es Salaam the capital of Tankanyika (Tanzania in 1964) in an effort to create a united front. The result was the Front for the Liberation of Mozambique (FRELIMO).

FRELIMO's leader, Eduardo Mondlane (d. 1969), took a core group of several hundred guerrillas into Algeria for training in guerrilla warfare tactics. In the meantime, other rebels began a war of resistance against the Portuguese military in Mozambique. This conflict remained at a relatively low level until 1964, when Mondlane's specially trained guerrillas were committed to battle. The FRELIMO squads soon overwhelmed the Portuguese patrols in Mozambique's two northern provinces, and Portuguese authorities rushed reinforcements to the south in an effort to hold the line there. The guerrillas kept up the pressure, however, and Portugal found that its defensive war was a costly drain on its national resources. Portuguese agents were dispatched to Dar es Salaam to assassinate Mondlane. He was murdered in 1969, but command of FRELIMO was quickly taken up by another guerrilla leader, Samora Moisés Machel (b. 1933). Unlike Mondlane, Machel was a committed Marxist, and from this point forward, FRELIMO became a Marxist rebel movement.

Machel attacked the Portuguese with renewed resolve. Although he was outnumbered 4 to 1, he more than held his own against the Portuguese. Then, in 1974, a military coup d'état toppled the Lisbon government, and the new Portuguese regime was prepared to negotiate. In 1974, during a cease-fire, Mozambique was offered limited independence. Machel held out for full independence, and the new Portuguese regime, seeking to avoid further drain on its resources, agreed.

The war ended, but white colonial rebels attempted to undermine the settlement by seizing the government in a coup in 1975. FRELIMO—now aided by Portuguese troops—suppressed the white rebels, and Machel became the first president of independent Mozambique. Within a year, the new nation, which Machel immediately transformed into a Marxist dictatorship, was torn by the MOZAMBICAN CIVIL AND GUERRILLA WARS (1976–1992).

Further reading: William Finnegan, *A Complicated War: The Harrowing of Mozambique* (Berkeley: University of California Press, 1993); Thomas H. Henriksen, *Revolution and Counterrevolution: Mozambique's War of Independence, 1964–1974* (Westport, Conn.: Greenwood Publishing Group, 1983).

Muhammad of Ghur, Conquests of
(1175–1206)

PRINCIPAL COMBATANTS: Forces of Ghur (led by Muhammad) vs. Ghaznivid India and other Indian kingdoms
PRINCIPAL THEATER(S): India and Pakistan
DECLARATION: None
MAJOR ISSUES AND OBJECTIVES: Conquest
OUTCOME: Muhammad built a vast Ghurid empire in India, established Islam in India, and created the basis of what would become the Mogul Empire.
APPROXIMATE MAXIMUM NUMBER OF MEN UNDER ARMS: Unknown
CASUALTIES: Unknown
TREATIES: No documents identified; existence of formal treaties unlikely

Muhammad of Ghur (Mu'izz-ud-Din Muhammad ibn Sam, d. 1206) was the greatest of the Ghurid leaders and one of the principal founders of Islamic rule in India. He operated in conjunction with his brother, Ghiyas-ud-Din Muhammad (fl. late 12th century) and began his military career by participating in the Ghurid conquest of Khorosan in 1173. In that same year, he led his army in the successful conquest of Ghazni.

From 1175 until he died in 1206, Muhammad of Ghur conducted a dozen campaigns of conquest in India.

In 1179, he attacked and defeated the Ghaznivid garrison of Peshawar. Sind fell to his armies in 1182, and three years later the Ghaznivid principality of Sialkor (Kashmir) also fell under his domination. The key city of Lahore was captured in 1186, and the entire Punjab region came under the control of Ghur the following year. This completed his conquest of what had been the Ghaznivid Empire in India. (Driven from India, the Ghaznivids fled east to Bihar and Bengal, where Muhammad's forces conquered them by 1200.)

In 1191, Muhammad of Ghur suffered his only reversal in India. The Rajput rulers, among them the western Chalukyas, attacked his forces at the Battle of Taraori near Thanesar along the Sarsuti River. The next year, however, he redressed this defeat by returning to the same battlefield and destroying the Rajput army.

In 1193, Muhammad of Ghur overran and conquered Delhi, took Kannauj, and, in 1194, sacked Benares (Varanasi). The great fortress at Gwalior fell to him in 1195, and Bihar succumbed in 1197. In 1198, Muhammad led an invasion of Bengal; a by-product of the campaign was the disruption of Indian Buddhism.

In each region he conquered, Muhammad of Ghur set up a brutally oppressive government. He was well aware that Muslims were a minority in India, and he was determined to suppress the Hindu majority by whatever means were necessary. Perhaps inevitably, Muhammad of Ghur was assassinated, in 1206. His chief lieutenant, a former slave named Qutb-ud-Din Aybak (d. 1210), assumed control of the Ghurid empire, establishing what would come to be called the "slave dynasty" and the Delhi sultanate, which, together, endured for almost 90 years—from 1206 to 1290. This was the forerunner of the great Mogul Empire.

Further reading: Barbara Daly Metcalf and Thomas R. Metcalf, *Concise History of India* (New York: Cambridge University Press, 2002); David Morgan, *The Mongols* (New York: Oxford University Press, 1986); J. J. Saunders, *History of the Mongol Conquests* (Philadelphia: University of Pennsylvania Press, 2001); Vincent A. Smith, *The Oxford History India*, 4th ed. (New York: Oxford University Press, 1981); Douglas E. Streusand, *Formation of the Mughal Empire* (New York: Oxford University Press, 1999).

Muqanna, Revolt of (775–778)

PRINCIPAL COMBATANTS: Shi'ite followers of Muqanna vs. the Abbasid caliph
PRINCIPAL THEATER(S): Khorasan, Persia
DECLARATION: None
MAJOR ISSUES AND OBJECTIVES: Religious dispute over the basis of power of the caliphate
OUTCOME: The rebellion was put down, but the underlying controversy remained unresolved.
APPROXIMATE MAXIMUM NUMBER OF MEN UNDER ARMS: Unknown
CASUALTIES: Unknown
TREATIES: None

Muqanna, the so-called Veiled Prophet, was Hashim ibn Hakim (d. 779), a Shi'ite who was also animated by Zoroastrian and Manichaean beliefs, who led a revolt of Shi'ites who challenged the basis on which the Abbasid caliph claimed authority: descent from Abbas (d. 653), the prophet Muhammad's (570–632) uncle. The Shi'ites claimed the power to govern derived from Ali (c. 600–661), husband of Fatima (606–632), Muhammad's daughter.

Muqanna led his followers in a three-year revolt, which ended in his defeat at the hands of Abbasid caliph, Muhammad al-Mahdi (742–786) in 778. Muqanna retired to his stronghold at Sanam and, the following year, committed suicide. With this, the revolt was suppressed, but the religious controversy remained unresolved and persists today.

Further reading: Karen Armstrong, *A Short History of Islam* (New York: Random House, 2002); P. M. Holt, Ann K. S. Lambton, and Bernard Lewis, *The Cambridge History of Islam*, 2 vols. (New York: Cambridge University Press, 1970); Hugh Kennedy, *The Prophet and the Age of the Caliphates: The Islamic Near East from the Sixth to the Eleventh Century* (New York: Longman, 1986); Muhammad-Husagh al-Tuba-Tabai, *Shiite Islam* (Albany: State University of New York Press, 1975).

Murrel's Uprising (1835)

PRINCIPAL COMBATANTS: Rebel slaves vs. U.S. authorities
PRINCIPAL THEATER(S): Mississippi and Tennessee
DECLARATION: None
MAJOR ISSUES AND OBJECTIVES: Abortive slave uprising designed to create a criminal empire.
OUTCOME: With the arrest of the leader of the uprising, the revolt failed.
APPROXIMATE MAXIMUM NUMBER OF MEN UNDER ARMS: Unknown
CASUALTIES: 45 participants in the uprising were hanged.
TREATIES: None

This abortive rebellion was planned by a Tennessee plantation owner, John A. Murrel (1794–1844). The leader of a horse-stealing and slave-stealing gang working in Tennessee and elsewhere in the South, Murrel conceived a scheme to organize a large-scale slave revolt with the object of creating a crime empire in the southern states. He planned a coordinated uprising among slaves in Nashville, Memphis, Natchez, New Orleans, and other southern cities to commence on July 4, 1835. When authorities discovered his scheme, however, Murrel was arrested. The rebellion fell apart, but uprisings did occur in some places. Thirty blacks and 15 whites were apprehended in Mississippi and Tennessee. Tried and convicted of conspiracy, all were hanged. Murrel, the instigator of it all, had been arrested, so did not participate in any of the action; therefore, he was sentenced to a prison term of 10 years. Released after having served a portion of his sentence, he was broken in health and died very shortly after he left prison.

Further reading: Thomas Wentworth Higgenson, *Black Rebellion: Five Slave Revolts* (New York: Da Capo Press, 1998).

Muscovite Conquest of Novgorod
(1471–1479)

PRINCIPAL COMBATANTS: Muscovy under Ivan III (with aid from Tver and Pskov) vs. Novgorod (with Polish aid)
PRINCIPAL THEATER(S): Novgorod
DECLARATION: None

MAJOR ISSUES AND OBJECTIVES: Conquest of Novgorod
OUTCOME: Novgorod fell to Ivan III.
APPROXIMATE MAXIMUM NUMBER OF MEN UNDER ARMS:
Unknown
CASUALTIES: Unknown
TREATIES: Alliances between Novgorod and Lithuania and between Novgorod and Poland; alliances between Muscovy and Tver and Pskov

In the Middle Ages, Muscovy was the core of what would become the Russian Empire. Ivan III (the Great; 1440–1505), grand prince of Muscovy, took up the mantle of his father, Basil II (1415–62), and was committed to the aggrandizement of Muscovy. He set his sights on Novgorod, a key trading city, which controlled vast territories in the Russian north. Not only was Novgorod an attractive prize, it had for years competed with Moscow for trade and power in the region. In addition, there was a profound religious conflict between the two principalities. Novgorod championed Roman Catholicism, whereas Moscow was the seat of Orthodox Christianity.

In 1471, Novgorod struck an alliance with Poland. Realizing that this portended an invasion, Ivan III seized the initiative and preemptively declared war on Novgorod. He put his troops on the march immediately, but his first two major victories did not come until 1475, at the Battle of the Shelon River and the Battle of the Shilenga River. Novgorod was betrayed by Poland, which reneged on its promises of military aid. Fearing annihilation, Novgorod surrendered to Ivan III, paying him a massive indemnity of 15,000 rubles and conceding to him the right to nominate an archbishop for the city. Moreover, Novgorod agreed to forswear any alliance with Lithuania, which would have posed both a military and an economic threat to Muscovy.

As much as Ivan III had gained in his war against Novgorod, he demanded more, namely, the title of "lord" of Novgorod. This was too much for some of the citizens of Novgorod, who staged a rebellion in 1477 and attempted to take over the city. Ivan III secured military aid from the cities of Pskov and Tver, which furnished large armies to march against Novgorod. The Novgorodians sued for peace and asked for negotiation. Ivan III refused and forced the city into unconditional surrender after the resignation of its leader in January 1478. Ivan confiscated all monastery estates under Novgorod control and imprisoned many Novgorod boyars (aristocrats). Although Novgorod secured Polish aid in 1479 for another uprising, it was quickly crushed—and Ivan acted against the city with a brutality so decisive that no further rebellion was possible.

Further reading: Ian Grey, *Ivan III and the Unification of Russia* (London: English Universities Press, 1964); Geoffrey A. Hoskin, *Russia and Russians: A History* (Cambridge, Mass.: Harvard University Press, 2001).

Muslim-Byzantine Wars   *See* BYZANTINE-MUSLIM WAR (633–642); BYZANTINE-MUSLIM WAR (645–656); BYZANTINE-MUSLIM WAR (668–679); BYZANTINE-MUSLIM WAR (698–718); BYZANTINE-MUSLIM WAR (739); BYZANTINE-MUSLIM WAR (741–752); BYZANTINE-MUSLIM WAR (778–783); BYZANTINE-MUSLIM WAR (797–798); BYZANTINE-MUSLIM WAR (803–809); BYZANTINE-MUSLIM WAR (830–841); BYZANTINE-MUSLIM WAR (851–863); BYZANTINE-MUSLIM WAR (871–885); BYZANTINE-MUSLIM WAR (960–976); BYZANTINE-MUSLIM WAR (995–999); BYZANTINE-MUSLIM WARS (1030–1035).

Muslim Civil War (657–661)

PRINCIPAL COMBATANTS: Mu'awiyah (and supporters) vs. the caliphate line of Ali
PRINCIPAL THEATER(S): Syria
DECLARATION: None
MAJOR ISSUES AND OBJECTIVES: Mu'awiyah sought the caliphate of the Muslim Empire.
OUTCOME: Mu'awiyah prevailed over the line of Ali ibn Abi Talib, thereby creating the Umayyad caliphate and bringing about the division of the Muslim world into two major sects, the Shi'ites and the Sunnis.
APPROXIMATE MAXIMUM NUMBER OF MEN UNDER ARMS:
Unknown
CASUALTIES: Unknown
TREATIES: None

The war was fought over a dispute as to the identity of the true Muslim caliph. Mu'awiyah (c. 602–680), Syrian governor, had reason to believe that the fourth caliph, Ali ibn Abi Talib (c. 600–661) had participated in the murder of his predecessor, Uthman ibn Affan (d. 656), who was Mu'awiyah's cousin. Mu'awiyah led an uprising against Ali ibn Abi Talib, to which Ali responded by invading Syria. Ali's forces clashed with Mu'awiyah's in a protracted battle at Siffin in 657. After three months of combat, the two sides called a truce and opened negotiations to determine the true caliph. During this period, Mu'awiyah unilaterally proclaimed himself caliph in Jerusalem in 660, and, in 661, Ali was assassinated by a member of the Kharijite sect. This sect, which developed during the negotiations between Mu'awiyah and Ali ibn Abi Talib, believed that piety and worth, not right of inheritance, should determine who would become caliph. Under pressure from the Kharijites and Mu'awiyah, al-Hassan (628–673), Ali's eldest son, renounced the caliphate in 661. Thus Mu'awiyah became the first Umayyad caliph. He established Damascus as the capital of the Muslim world. However, Mu'awiyah's ascension had a profound effect on Muslim life, dividing the faith between two major sects: the Shi'ites, who support the divine right of the line of Ali, and the Sunnis, who support the Umayyad line.

See also MUSLIM CIVIL WAR (680–692); MUSLIM CIVIL WAR (743–747); MUSLIM CIVIL WAR (809–813); MUSLIM CIVIL WAR (861–870); MUSLIM CIVIL WAR (936–944); MUSLIM CIVIL WAR (945–948); MUSLIM CIVIL WAR (976–977); MUSLIM CIVIL WAR (1102–1108).

Further reading: Karen Armstrong, *A Short History of Islam* (New York: Random House, 2002); P. M. Holt, Ann K. S. Lambton, and Bernard Lewis, *The Cambridge History of Islam*, 2 vols. (New York: Cambridge University Press, 1970); Hugh Kennedy, *The Prophet and the Age of the Caliphates: The Islamic Near East from the Sixth to the Eleventh Century* (New York: Longman, 1986).

Muslim Civil War (680–692)

PRINCIPAL COMBATANTS: Umayyad clan vs. Ali clan
PRINCIPAL THEATER(S): Syria and Mesopotamia
DECLARATION: None
MAJOR ISSUES AND OBJECTIVES: The clans disputed the right to rule as caliph.
OUTCOME: Abd al-Malik ascended the throne and eliminated his chief rival.
APPROXIMATE MAXIMUM NUMBER OF MEN UNDER ARMS: Unknown
CASUALTIES: Unknown
TREATIES: None

Mu'awiyah (c. 602–680), who came to power as a result of the MUSLIM CIVIL WAR (657–661), died in 680, leaving the succession to the caliphate unsettled. His son Yazid I (c. 645–683) ascended the throne, but was opposed by factions in Mesopotamia (Iraq) and Syria. The Kufan clan supported Husayn ibn Ali (629–680), who was a son of Ali ibn Abi Talib (c. 600–661), the caliph Mu'awiyah had opposed. Thus the war was a conflict between the Umayyad clan (partisans of Yazid I) and the Ali clan (partisans of Husayn).

Husayn set out from Mecca to meet the forces of Yazid, but Husayn was killed after the Kufans deserted him at the Battle of Kerbela in 680. Abdallah ibn Zubayr (d. 692) successfully led an army of Meccans and Medinans in opposing the invasion of Yazid's army in 682. Yazid died the following year, leaving Zubayr to be recognized as caliph of most of the Muslim Empire, Arabia, Mesopotamia, and Egypt.

Zubayr's caliphate proved short-lived. Marwan ibn al-Hakam (623–685) fought Zubayr's forces to defeat at the Battle of Marj Rahit, just outside Damascus, in 684. Al-Hakam became caliph, but presided over a deeply divided realm. His son, Abd al-Malik (646–705), who succeeded him after his death in 692, attempted to bring unity by leading a siege against Mecca, the capital from which Zubayr ruled as a rival caliph. Al-Malik's Syrian forces killed Zubayr, leaving Al-Malik the sole caliph.

See also MUSLIM CIVIL WAR (657–661); MUSLIM CIVIL WAR (743–747); MUSLIM CIVIL WAR (809–813); MUSLIM CIVIL WAR (861–870); MUSLIM CIVIL WAR (936–944); MUSLIM CIVIL WAR (945–948); MUSLIM CIVIL WAR (976–977); MUSLIM CIVIL WAR (1102–1108).

Further reading: Karen Armstrong, *A Short History of Islam* (New York: Random House, 2002); P. M. Holt, Ann K. S. Lambton, and Bernard Lewis, *The Cambridge History of Islam*, 2 vols. (New York: Cambridge University Press, 1970); Hugh Kennedy, *The Prophet and the Age of the Caliphates: The Islamic Near East from the Sixth to the Eleventh Century* (New York: Longman, 1986).

Muslim Civil War (743–747)

PRINCIPAL COMBATANTS: Marwan II vs. various rebel groups
PRINCIPAL THEATER(S): Arab empire
DECLARATION: None
MAJOR ISSUES AND OBJECTIVES: Marwan II sought to eliminate rebellion from his caliphate.
OUTCOME: All of the major rebel groups were put down, except for the Abbasids.
APPROXIMATE MAXIMUM NUMBER OF MEN UNDER ARMS: Unknown
CASUALTIES: Unknown
TREATIES: None

After the death of Abd al-Malik (646–705) in 705, the Arab empire was ruled by successively less effective caliphs, and during 743–744, three weak rulers rose and fell in succession, unable to command the support of the people. The typically stormy empire was rocked by rebellion during this period until the ascension in 744 of Marwan II (d. 750), last of the Umayyad caliphs. Marwan II made liberal use of military force to put down rebellions in Arabia, Syria, Persia (Iran), and Mesopotamia (Iraq), but one group, the Abbasids, centered in Khorasan, Persia, remained undefeated and went on to oppose the Umayyad clan in the ABBASID REBELLION of 747–750.

See also KHARIJITE REVOLT; MUSLIM CIVIL WAR (657–661); MUSLIM CIVIL WAR (680–692); MUSLIM CIVIL WAR (809–813); MUSLIM CIVIL WAR (861–870); MUSLIM CIVIL WAR (936–944); MUSLIM CIVIL WAR (945–948); MUSLIM CIVIL WAR (976–977); MUSLIM CIVIL WAR (1102–1108).

Further reading: Karen Armstrong, *A Short History of Islam* (New York: Random House, 2002); Holt, Ann K. S. Lambton, and Bernard Lewis, *The Cambridge History of Islam*, 2 vols. (New York: Cambridge University Press, 1970); Hugh Kennedy, *The Prophet and the Age of the Caliphates: The Islamic Near East from the Sixth to the Eleventh Century* (New York: Longman, 1986).

Muslim Civil War (809–813)

PRINCIPAL COMBATANTS: Allah al-Ma'mun vs. his brother, Muhammad al-Amin
PRINCIPAL THEATER(S): Khorosan, Persia
DECLARATION: None
MAJOR ISSUES AND OBJECTIVES: Allah al-Ma'mun sought to assume sole rule over the Arab Empire.
OUTCOME: Allah al-Ma'mun defeated his brother's forces, then imprisoned his brother, who was subsequently killed; al-Ma'mun thus became sole caliph.
APPROXIMATE MAXIMUM NUMBER OF MEN UNDER ARMS: Unknown
CASUALTIES: Unknown
TREATIES: None

The ABBASID REBELLION of 747–750 ushered in the Abbasid caliphate over the Arab Empire, and in 802 Caliph Harun al-Rashid (766–809) declared that his two sons would jointly inherit the throne, Muhammad al-Amin (785–813) succeeding him as caliph and Allah al-Ma'mun (785–833) as ruler of Khorosan and the eastern portion of the empire. After al-Rashid died, however, al-Ma'mun rebelled, seeking to seize the entire empire from his brother. He was backed by Persian forces under Tahir ibn Husain (d. 822), who defeated al-Amin's army in Khorosan, advanced into Mesopotamia, acquired most of al-Amin's holdings, then laid siege to Baghdad in 809. After two years under siege, the capital fell. In 812, al-Amin surrendered and was made a prisoner. He attempted to escape in 813, but was killed.

The death of al-Amin left al-Ma'mun sole caliph, but the bitter warfare between the brothers had brought permanent unrest to Mesopotamia, Syria, and Egypt.

See also MUSLIM CIVIL WAR (657–661); MUSLIM CIVIL WAR (680–692); MUSLIM CIVIL WAR (743–747); MUSLIM CIVIL WAR (861–870); MUSLIM CIVIL WAR (936–944); MUSLIM CIVIL WAR (945–948); MUSLIM CIVIL WAR (976–977); MUSLIM CIVIL WAR (1102–1108).

Further reading: Karen Armstrong, *A Short History of Islam* (New York: Random House, 2002); P. M. Holt, Ann K. S. Lambton, and Bernard Lewis, *The Cambridge History of Islam,* 2 vols. (New York: Cambridge University Press, 1970); Hugh Kennedy, *The Prophet and the Age of the Caliphates: The Islamic Near East from the Sixth to the Eleventh Century* (New York: Longman, 1986).

Muslim Civil War (861–870)

PRINCIPAL COMBATANTS: Turkish interests in the caliphate vs. various rebel groups
PRINCIPAL THEATER(S): Arab Empire, especially Uzbekistan, Persia, Arabia, Egypt, and Mesopotamia
DECLARATION: None

MAJOR ISSUES AND OBJECTIVES: The Turks sought to dominate the caliphate, creating disorder and rebellion in the process.
OUTCOME: After years of misrule, the Turks withdrew their interest in the caliphate.
APPROXIMATE MAXIMUM NUMBER OF MEN UNDER ARMS: Unknown
CASUALTIES: Unknown
TREATIES: None

During the mid-ninth century, Turks were included in the government of the Arab caliphate, an action that led to disorder. During the period of the civil war of 861–870, Turks installed their own puppet caliphs, who were disposed of—either deposed or assassinated—when they ceased to do Turkish bidding. Without a strong central government, the far-flung empire was swept by revolt and rebellion. Transoxiana (Uzbekistan), Persia (Iran), Arabia, and Egypt all saw rebellion, and in 869, the ZANJ REBELLION, a revolt among black slaves in Mesopotamia (Iraq), lasted 15 years.

At last, in 870, unwilling to continue financing chronic warfare, the Turks suddenly broke off their involvement in the caliphate. They left al-Mo'tamid (d. 892) on the throne, and the Arab Empire in economic and political shambles.

See also MUSLIM CIVIL WAR (657–661); MUSLIM CIVIL WAR (680–692); MUSLIM CIVIL WAR (743–747); MUSLIM CIVIL WAR (809–813); MUSLIM CIVIL WAR (936–944); MUSLIM CIVIL WAR (945–948); MUSLIM CIVIL WAR (976–977); MUSLIM CIVIL WAR (1102–1108).

Further reading: Karen Armstrong, *A Short History of Islam* (New York: Random House, 2002); P. M. Holt, Ann K. S. Lambton, and Bernard Lewis, *The Cambridge History of Islam,* 2 vols. (New York: Cambridge University Press, 1970); Hugh Kennedy, *The Prophet and the Age of the Caliphates: The Islamic Near East from the Sixth to the Eleventh Century* (New York: Longman, 1986).

Muslim Civil War (936–944)

PRINCIPAL COMBATANTS: Abbasid forces under Muhammad ibn-Ra'iq vs. Hamdanids and Ikshidids
PRINCIPAL THEATER(S): Syria
DECLARATION: None
MAJOR ISSUES AND OBJECTIVES: The Abbasid caliph employed ibn-Ra'iq to restore the Arab Empire.
OUTCOME: Syria was restored, except for two cities; the war ended in an uneasy truce.
APPROXIMATE MAXIMUM NUMBER OF MEN UNDER ARMS: Unknown
CASUALTIES: Unknown
TREATIES: Treaty of 944

Turkish misrule during the MUSLIM CIVIL WAR (861–870) left the Arabian caliphate greatly weakened and reduced. What had once been a vast empire had been cut down to the province of Baghdad. In an effort to restore the empire, Abbasid caliph Ahmad ar-Radi (d. 940) appointed Muhammad ibn-Ra'iq (d. 942) to command an army and serve essentially as dictator over the realm. The idea was to give ibn-Ra'iq sufficient power to restore order and control.

Ibn-Ra'iq first confronted the Hamdanids in Syria, then repulsed an invasion by the Egyptian Ikshidids. In this way, Syria was returned to the caliph's fold. However, the Hamdanids returned to capture Aleppo and Hims in northern Syria after the death of ibn-Ra'iq. At this point, in 944, the caliph concluded a truce with the Hamdanids.

See also MUSLIM CIVIL WAR (657–661); MUSLIM CIVIL WAR (680–692); MUSLIM CIVIL WAR (743–747); MUSLIM CIVIL WAR (809–813); MUSLIM CIVIL WAR (945–948); MUSLIM CIVIL WAR (976–977); MUSLIM CIVIL WAR (1102–1108).

Further reading: Karen Armstrong, A Short History of Islam (New York: Random House, 2002); P. M. Holt, Ann K. S. Lambton, and Bernard Lewis, The Cambridge History of Islam, 2 vols. (New York: Cambridge University Press, 1970); Hugh Kennedy, The Prophet and the Age of the Caliphates: The Islamic Near East from the Sixth to the Eleventh Century (New York: Longman, 1986).

Muslim Civil War (945–948)

PRINCIPAL COMBATANTS: Hamdanids vs. Ikshidids vs., separately, Byzantines
PRINCIPAL THEATER(S): Syria
DECLARATION: None
MAJOR ISSUES AND OBJECTIVES: The Hamdanids had to resist invasion both from the Ikshidids and the Byzantines.
OUTCOME: Although the Hamdanids successfully resisted the Byzantine invasion to retain northern Syria, the drain on military resources caused the Hamdanids to relinquish the southern and central regions to the Ikshidids.
APPROXIMATE MAXIMUM NUMBER OF MEN UNDER ARMS: Unknown
CASUALTIES: Unknown
TREATIES: None

After a truce ended the MUSLIM CIVIL WAR (936–944), a new war erupted the next year when Sayf al-Dawla (d. 967), in Syria, led the Hamdanids against invading Ikshidids from Egypt. The Hamdanids held Aleppo, in northwestern Syria, and, from this base, were at first highly successful in repelling Ikshidid incursions; however, when the Byzantines invaded the north, Hamdanid forces became too widely dispersed, and the Hamdanids were com-

pelled to relinquish central and southern Syria to the Ikshidids by 948. Al-Dawla was able to retain northern Syria against the Byzantines.

See also MUSLIM CIVIL WAR (657–661); MUSLIM CIVIL WAR (680–692); MUSLIM CIVIL WAR (743–747); MUSLIM CIVIL WAR (809–813); MUSLIM CIVIL WAR (861–870); MUSLIM CIVIL WAR (976–977); MUSLIM CIVIL WAR (1102–1108).

Further reading: Karen Armstrong, A Short History of Islam (New York: Random House, 2002); P. M. Holt, Ann K. S. Lambton, and Bernard Lewis, The Cambridge History of Islam, 2 vols. (New York: Cambridge University Press, 1970); Hugh Kennedy, The Prophet and the Age of the Caliphates: The Islamic Near East from the Sixth to the Eleventh Century (New York: Longman, 1986).

Muslim Civil War (976–977)

PRINCIPAL COMBATANTS: Hamdanids, and Karmathians vs. Fatimids
PRINCIPAL THEATER(S): Syria
DECLARATION: None
MAJOR ISSUES AND OBJECTIVES: The Hamdanids and Karmathians sought to seize control of central and southern Syria from the Fatimids.
OUTCOME: Despite initial Hamdanid-Karmathian success, the Fatimids ultimately retained control of central and southern Syria.
APPROXIMATE MAXIMUM NUMBER OF MEN UNDER ARMS: Unknown
CASUALTIES: Unknown
TREATIES: None

The Muslim Fatimids, who claimed direct descent from Fatima (c. 606–632), daughter of the prophet Muhammad (570–632), invaded southern and central Syria in 969 and seized control of the region from the Ikshidids. In an effort to eject the Fatimids from the region, the Hamdanids, based in northern Syria, allied with the Karmathians, who had already been victorious against the Fatimids in Egypt, and mounted an offensive in 976. The Fatimids fled, but returned in 977 and scored a decisive victory against the allied Hamdanids and Karmathians at the Battle of Ramleh. Once again, southern and central Syria were in Fatimid hands.

See also KARMATHIAN REVOLT; MUSLIM CIVIL WAR (657–661); MUSLIM CIVIL WAR (680–692); MUSLIM CIVIL WAR (743–747); MUSLIM CIVIL WAR (809–813); MUSLIM CIVIL WAR (861–870); MUSLIM CIVIL WAR (936–944); MUSLIM CIVIL WAR (945–948); MUSLIM CIVIL WAR (1102–1108).

Further reading: Karen Armstrong, A Short History of Islam (New York: Random House, 2002); P. M. Holt, Ann

K. S. Lambton, and Bernard Lewis, *The Cambridge History of Islam,* 2 vols. (New York: Cambridge University Press, 1970); Hugh Kennedy, *The Prophet and the Age of the Caliphates: The Islamic Near East from the Sixth to the Eleventh Century* (New York: Longman, 1986).

Muslim Civil War (1102–1108)

PRINCIPAL COMBATANTS: Rival Muslim groups, principally Seljuks led by Kilij Arslan I, vs. Seljuks led by Ridwan.
PRINCIPAL THEATER(S): Central and southern Syria
DECLARATION: None
MAJOR ISSUES AND OBJECTIVES: In an era of instability brought about by the First Crusade, rivals sought dominance of large portions of Syria.
OUTCOME: Ridwan took the principal city of northern Mesopotamia (Iraq), Mosul, but failed in his bids to subdue other rivals throughout the region, especially in rural areas.
APPROXIMATE MAXIMUM NUMBER OF MEN UNDER ARMS: Unknown
CASUALTIES: Unknown
TREATIES: None

The incursions of the Crusaders not only posed an external threat to the Arab world, but brought about internal warfare as well. The Seljuk Turks, who held most of urban central and southern Syria, were pitted against other Muslim groups, which controlled the rural districts in the region. Dissent among the Seljuks was bitter.

Mosul, the major city of northern Mesopotamia, fell to the Seljuk warrior leader Kilij Arslan I (d. 1108) in 1102. Attacked by another Seljuk leader, Ridwan (d. 1117), Kilij fought the Battle of the Khabur River against him in 1108 and was killed. Ridwan took over Mosul and, from this city, attempted to conquer more territory and defeat other Muslim groups as well as rival Turks. He made little progress, and the region remained fragmented under repeated European onslaught.

See also MUSLIM CIVIL WAR (657–661); MUSLIM CIVIL WAR (680–692); MUSLIM CIVIL WAR (743–747); MUSLIM CIVIL WAR (809–813); MUSLIM CIVIL WAR (861–870); MUSLIM CIVIL WAR (936–944); MUSLIM CIVIL WAR (945–948); MUSLIM CIVIL WAR (976–977).

Further reading: Karen Armstrong, *A Short History of Islam* (New York: Random House, 2002); P. M. Holt, Ann K. S. Lambton, and Bernard Lewis, *The Cambridge History of Islam,* 2 vols. (New York: Cambridge University Press, 1970); Steven Runciman, *A History of the Crusades,* vol. 2, *The Kingdom of Jerusalem and the Frankish East* (Cambridge: Cambridge University Press, 1951).

Muslim Conquest of the Deccan   *See* DELHI SULTANATE RAIDS IN SOUTH INDIA (1307–1313).

Muslim Conquest of Persia (634–651)

PRINCIPAL COMBATANTS: Muslim Arabs vs. Sassanid Persians
PRINCIPAL THEATER(S): Persia (Iran and Iraq)
DECLARATION: None
MAJOR ISSUES AND OBJECTIVES: The Muslims sought to conquer Persia.
OUTCOME: After a long struggle, the Sassanids were defeated.
APPROXIMATE MAXIMUM NUMBER OF MEN UNDER ARMS: At al-Qadisiyah, the Persians fielded 50,000 men, the Arabs 30,000.
CASUALTIES: Persian casualties at the Battle of Nhavand (641) were reported in excess of 100,000; Arab casualties were far less.
TREATIES: None

After the death of the Muslim prophet Muhammad (570–632), Islam began an era of expansion outside Arabia. Muslim armies swept into Mesopotamia, then through Palestine and Syria into Byzantine Damascus, where they stalled for a six-month siege. They were also stymied at first by the Sassanids when they attempted to invade the Persian Empire. At the Battle of the Bridge, in 634, the Sassanid army dealt the Muslims a severe defeat, sending Muhammad's army in retreat to Hira. However, Muhammad counterattacked at Buwayb in 635, near Kufah (Iraq). This checked the Persian advance, while a new Muslim army of 30,000 men under Caliph Omar (c. 581–644) defeated the superior Persian army (50,000 troops) at al-Qadisiyah in 637. This was followed later the same year by the capture of Ctesiphon, the Persians' winter headquarters. In December 637, the Arabs enjoyed another triumph, at the Battle of Jalula, north of Ctesiphon. These victories brought central Persia under Muslim control.

The Islamic forces continued to consolidate their gains over the rest of the decade. In 641, a major victory at Nahavand devastated Persian forces. A small Muslim force lured a much larger Persian army into pursuit, then fell upon this army when it was trapped between two narrow mountain passes. Persian casualties were catastrophic, reportedly in excess of 100,000 men. Despite continued resistance through 651, Sassanid control of Persia disintegrated. Yazdegerd III (d. 651), last Sassanid king of Persia, took refuge in Merv and was assassinated there in 651. This brought the Muslim conquest of Persia to an end.

Further reading: Karen Armstrong, *A Short History of Islam* (New York: Random House, 2002); P. M. Holt, Ann

K. S. Lambton, and Bernard Lewis, *The Cambridge History of Islam,* 2 vols. (New York: Cambridge University Press, 1970); Hugh Kennedy, *The Prophet and the Age of the Caliphates: The Islamic Near East from the Sixth to the Eleventh Century* (New York: Longman, 1986); Bernard Lewis, *The Middle East: A Brief History of the Last 2000 Years* (New York: Simon and Schuster, 1997).

Muslim Conquest of Sind (708–712)

PRINCIPAL COMBATANTS: Muslim Arabs vs. Baluchistan and Sind
PRINCIPAL THEATER(S): Northern India
DECLARATION: None
MAJOR ISSUES AND OBJECTIVES: Conquest
OUTCOME: Sind was subdued and used as a base from which further conquests were launched.
APPROXIMATE MAXIMUM NUMBER OF MEN UNDER ARMS: Unknown
CASUALTIES: Unknown
TREATIES: None

Following the death of Muhammad the Prophet (570–632) his heirs expanded Islam far beyond Arabia, sweeping through Byzantine-held territories and the Sassanids' Persian Empire. Muslim invaders arrive in northern India about 650 and, between this time and 707, overran and conquered Baluchistan, a desert region in modern western Pakistan. This was followed by the Arab invasion of Sind, led by Muhammed ibn Kasim, who subdued the region by 712. From the bases they established in Sind, the Muslims mounted raids into Rajputana and Gujarat. Although Rajputana largely yielded, Gujarat resisted and prevailed, repulsing the Arab invaders.

Further reading: Karen Armstrong, *A Short History of Islam* (New York: Random House, 2002); P. M. Holt, Ann K. S. Lambton, and Bernard Lewis, *The Cambridge History of Islam,* 2 vols. (New York: Cambridge University Press, 1970); Barbara Daly Metcalf and Thomas R. Metcalf, *Concise History of India* (New York: Cambridge University Press, 2002); Vincent A. Smith, *The Oxford History of India,* 4th ed. (New York: Oxford University Press, 1981).

Muslim Conquest of Spain (711–718)

PRINCIPAL COMBATANTS: Arabs (Moors) vs. Visigoths and Spanish Christians
PRINCIPAL THEATER(S): Spain
DECLARATION: None
MAJOR ISSUES AND OBJECTIVES: The Arabs sought conquest of Spain.
OUTCOME: Most of Spain fell into Arab (Moorish) hands.
APPROXIMATE MAXIMUM NUMBER OF MEN UNDER ARMS: Arabs commanded at least 50,000 men.
CASUALTIES: Unknown, but consistently heavy among the Visigoths
TREATIES: Treaty with the Visigoths at Murcia, 713

When the Umayyad clan took over the Islamic Empire at the end of the seventh century, Muslims began a new wave of conquests that would extend Islam to its utmost. During this period, Spain was controlled by the Visigoths, who had earlier conquered certain Arab territories. Musa ibn-Nusayr (c. 660–c. 714), Arab viceroy in North Africa, decided to invade Spain in an effort to regain some of what had been lost. Tarik ibn-Ziyad (d. c. 720) was sent at the head of an Arab-Berber army to attack across the Gibraltar strait in 711. On July 19, 711, at the Battle of Laguna de Janda, ibn-Ziyad defeated King Roderick (d. 711) and his forces. Roderick, last of the Visigoth kings, fell in battle.

The force of ibn-Ziyad's personality was such that many in Roderick's defeated army joined him in completing the conquest of Spain. Córdoba and Toledo, the Visigoth capital, fell by early 712. At this point, Musa ibn-Nusayr joined the campaign at the head of 18,000 Arabs, who landed at Algeciras in June 712. The army advanced to Medina-Sidonia, which fell to it, then to Seville and Mérida, the latter falling to the Arabs on June 30, 713. At this point, ibn-Nusayr and ibn-Ziyad linked up, ibn-Ziyad having by this time acquired the support of Spain's Jews.

After campaigning together for a time, ibn-Ziyad launched a separate campaign against northwest Spain, conquering León and Astorga. Musa ibn-Nusayr returned to Damascus, Syria, in 713 after installing his son, Abd al-Aziz (d. 716) as emir in the south of Spain. Negotiating from a position of great strength, al-Aziz made peace with the Visigoths at Murcia, making the remaining Visigoths in southern Spain Arab vassals. In the meantime, elsewhere in Spain, the Arab conquests continued: Saragossa fell in 714 and Barcelona in 717. The culmination of the Arab conquest came in 718, after the Spanish Christians had been pushed to the mountainous regions of northern and western Spain and the Muslims—now known as the Moors—controlled territory touching the Pyrenees.

Further reading: Karen Armstrong, *A Short History of Islam* (New York: Random House, 2002); P. M. Holt, Ann K. S. Lambton, and Bernard Lewis, *The Cambridge History of Islam,* 2 vols. (New York: Cambridge University Press, 1970); Charles C. Torrey, ed. *History of the Conquest of Egypt, North Africa, and Spain* (New Haven: Yale University Press, 1922).

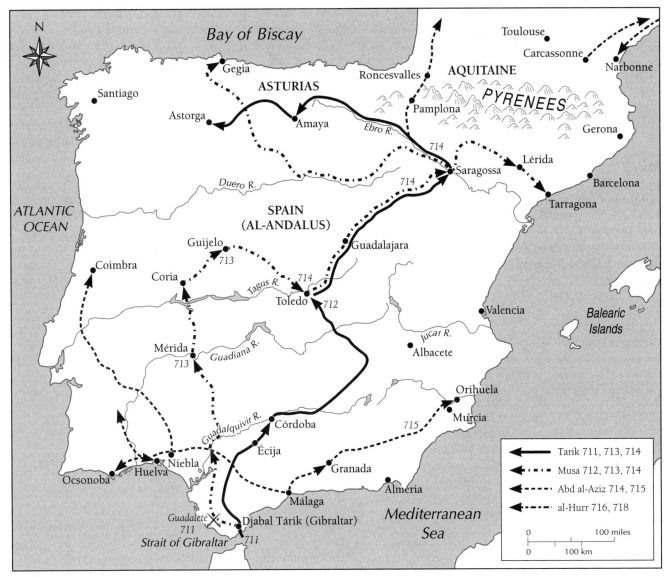

Muslim conquest of Spain, 711–718

Muslim Dynastic War   (1196–1200)

PRINCIPAL COMBATANTS: Al-Malik al-Adil vs. the sons of Saladin

PRINCIPAL THEATER(S): Egypt

DECLARATION: None

MAJOR ISSUES AND OBJECTIVES: The original dispute involved control of the sultanate of Cairo, but grew to encompass the entire Ayyubid Empire.

OUTCOME: Al-Malik al-Adil achieved control of the empire Saladin had divided between his sons.

APPROXIMATE MAXIMUM NUMBER OF MEN UNDER ARMS: Unknown

CASUALTIES: Unknown

TREATIES: None

Hoping to avoid a ruinous dynastic struggle, the Muslim leader Saladin (c. 1137–93) wisely apportioned his great Ayyubid Empire in Egypt and Syria among designated heirs before his death. Unfortunately, he overlooked the sultanate of Cairo, and in 1196, three years after Saladin's death, two of his sons, al-Afdal (r. 1186–96) and al-Aziz (r. 1193–98), the sultan of Syria and the sultan of Egypt, fell to disputing over control of Cairo. Al-Malik al-Adil (d. 1218), Saladin's brother, also participated in the dispute, fighting on both sides until he himself gained the upper hand over his nephews. In January 1200, al-Adil fought the critical Battle of Bilbeis, Egypt, and was able to seize control not only of Cairo but of the entire empire Saladin had left to his sons. Thus, for a time, Egypt and Syria were united under his rule. Nevertheless, the defeat of Saladin's heirs did not bring peace to the Ayyubid dynasty. Disputes, quarrels, and armed conflict persisted, the Ayyubids were progressively weakened, and Ayyubid control of the empire finally collapsed in 1250 in a rebellion by the Mamluks.

Further reading: Karen Armstrong, *A Short History of Islam* (New York: Random House, 2002); P. M. Holt, Ann K. S. Lambton, and Bernard Lewis, *The Cambridge History of Islam,* 2 vols. (New York: Cambridge University Press, 1970).

Muslim Invasion of Egypt (639–642)

PRINCIPAL COMBATANTS: Muslim Arabs vs. Egypt
PRINCIPAL THEATER(S): Egypt
DECLARATION: None
MAJOR ISSUES AND OBJECTIVES: Conquest
OUTCOME: The Muslims overran Egypt and occupied its major cities.
APPROXIMATE MAXIMUM NUMBER OF MEN UNDER ARMS: Unknown
CASUALTIES: Unknown
TREATIES: None

During the first epoch of Islamic expansion, an army under Amr ibn al-'As (d. 633) defeated Byzantine forces at the Battle of Babylon, which took place near Heliopolis in July 640. This victory served as al-Aslon's springboard to an assault on the fortress city of Babylon itself in April of the following year. From here, al-Aslon led a Muslim assault on the Egyptian capital, taking Alexandria in September 642 after a prolonged siege.

Further reading: Karen Armstrong, *A Short History of Islam* (New York: Random House, 2002); Sir John Bagot Glubb, *The Great Arab Conquests* (London: Hodder and Stoughton, 1963); P. M. Holt, Ann K. S. Lambton, and Bernard Lewis, *The Cambridge History of Islam,* 2 vols. (New York: Cambridge University Press, 1970); Charles C. Torrey, ed. *History of the Conquest of Egypt, North Africa, and Spain* (New Haven, Conn.: Yale University Press, 1922).

Muslim Invasion of India (661–663)

PRINCIPAL COMBATANTS: Muslim Arabs vs. India
PRINCIPAL THEATER(S): Sind and lower Indus Valley, India
DECLARATION: None
MAJOR ISSUES AND OBJECTIVES: Raids, preparatory to invasion and eventual conquest
OUTCOME: The raids were successful, but the invasion was not immediately succeeded by occupation.
APPROXIMATE MAXIMUM NUMBER OF MEN UNDER ARMS: Unknown
CASUALTIES: Unknown
TREATIES: None

The Muslim Arabs, having expanded through India and having made a truce with the Byzantine Empire (in 659), turned their attention to an advance into India. Under the command of Ziyad ibn Abihi (d. 672), Arab forces reached the borderlands of India by 661, then conducted raids into Sind and the lower Indus Valley. At this point, the invasion did not result in occupation.

Further reading: Karen Armstrong, *A Short History of Islam* (New York: Random House, 2002); Sir John Bagot Glubb, *The Great Arab Conquests* (London: Hodder and Stoughton, 1963); P. M. Holt, Ann K. S. Lambton, and Bernard Lewis, *The Cambridge History of Islam,* 2 vols. (New York: Cambridge University Press, 1970); Charles C. Torrey, ed. *History of the Conquest of Egypt, North Africa, and Spain* (New Haven, Conn.: Yale University Press, 1922).

Muslim Invasion of Morocco (681–683)

PRINCIPAL COMBATANTS: Arab Muslims vs. the Berbers of Morocco (with Byzantine allies)
PRINCIPAL THEATER(S): Morocco
DECLARATION: None
MAJOR ISSUES AND OBJECTIVES: Conquest
OUTCOME: The Arabs penetrated deeply into Morocco before they were driven out by a Berber counterattack conducted in concert with Byzantine action.
APPROXIMATE MAXIMUM NUMBER OF MEN UNDER ARMS: Unknown
CASUALTIES: Unknown
TREATIES: None

Egypt having been invaded and occupied during the MUSLIM INVASION OF EGYPT from 639 to 642, the Arabs used it as a staging area for an invasion of Morocco, which started in 681 under the command of Okba ibn Nafi (fl. late seventh century). The invaders advanced all the way to the Atlantic before they were beaten back to Cyrene by Berbers who had allied themselves with the Byzantine garrison at Carthage. Ibn Nafi was killed in the retreat.

Further reading: Karen Armstrong, *A Short History of Islam* (New York: Random House, 2002); Sir John Bagot Glubb, *The Great Arab Conquests* (London: Hodder and Stoughton, 1963); P. M. Holt, Ann K. S. Lambton, and Bernard Lewis, *The Cambridge History of Islam,* 2 vols. (New York: Cambridge University Press, 1970); Charles C. Torrey, ed. *History of the Conquest of Egypt, North Africa, and Spain* (New Haven, Conn.: Yale University Press, 1922).

Muslim Invasion of Southern France *See*

FRANKISH-MOORISH WAR, FIRST.

Muslim Invasion of Transcaspia (716)

PRINCIPAL COMBATANTS: Muslim Arabs vs. the peoples of the Transcaspian region
PRINCIPAL THEATER(S): Territory between the Oxus River and the Caspian Sea
DECLARATION: None
MAJOR ISSUES AND OBJECTIVES: Conquest
OUTCOME: The Arabs dominated the region.
APPROXIMATE MAXIMUM NUMBER OF MEN UNDER ARMS: Unknown
CASUALTIES: Unknown
TREATIES: None

One of the landmarks in the great movement of Muslim expansion out from the Middle East (*see* MUSLIM INVASION OF EGYPT) was the overrunning of the Transcaspian region. The Yemenite commander Yazid ibn Mohallib (fl. early eighth century) led an invasion that swept through and dominated the territory bounded by the Oxus (Amu Dar'ya) River and the Caspian Sea.

Further reading: Karen Armstrong, *A Short History of Islam* (New York: Random House, 2002); Sir John Bagot Glubb, *The Great Arab Conquests* (London: Hodder and Stoughton, 1963); P. M. Holt, Ann K. S. Lambton, and Bernard Lewis, *The Cambridge History of Islam,* 2 vols. (New York: Cambridge University Press, 1970).

Muslim Invasion of Transoxiana (674–676)

PRINCIPAL COMBATANTS: Arab Muslims vs. the Byzantines
PRINCIPAL THEATER(S): Transoxiana Uzbekistan and Anatolia (Turkey)
DECLARATION: None
MAJOR ISSUES AND OBJECTIVES: Conquest
OUTCOME: Initially victorious in Transoxiana, the Arabs lost heavily in Anatolia and were forced to withdraw from Anatolia as well as the entire Transoxiana region.
APPROXIMATE MAXIMUM NUMBER OF MEN UNDER ARMS: Unknown
CASUALTIES: Unknown
TREATIES: A treaty was concluded between the Arabs and Byzantines in 679, pledging 30 years of peace and an Arab tribute to the Byzantines.

After raiding India (*see* MUSLIM INVASION OF INDIA) and while engaged in general warfare against the Byzantines, the Muslims invaded Transoxiana. In 674, Muslim forces took Bukhara and, two years later, the leading trading city of Samarqand. However, these conquests were temporary, as the Byzantines defeated the Arabs in a major land battle at Armorium (in Anatolia, 669) and also in two major sea battles, at Cyzicus (Kapidagi) in the Sea of Marmara (672) and at Syllaeum (679).

Further reading: Karen Armstrong, *A Short History of Islam* (New York: Random House, 2002); Sir John Bagot Glubb, *The Great Arab Conquests* (London: Hodder and Stoughton, 1963); P. M. Holt, Ann K. S. Lambton, and Bernard Lewis, *The Cambridge History of Islam,* 2 vols. (New York: Cambridge University Press, 1970).

Muslim Raids on Aquitaine and South France *See* FRANKISH-MOORISH WAR, FIRST.

Muslim Rebellion in China (1863–1877)

PRINCIPAL COMBATANTS: Manchu Chinese forces vs. Muslim rebels in Turkistan; Russian peripheral involvement
PRINCIPAL THEATER(S): Turkistan
DECLARATION: Yakub Beg proclaims an independent Turkistan, 1863
MAJOR ISSUES AND OBJECTIVES: China sought to reclaim rebellious Turkistan.
OUTCOME: The rebellion was put down, but a separate treaty had to be made with a Russian occupation force.
APPROXIMATE MAXIMUM NUMBER OF MEN UNDER ARMS: Manchu forces, 100,000; rebel strength unknown
CASUALTIES: Known to be very high among Muslim civilians
TREATIES: Treaty between China and Russia, 1881

In 1863, Muslim tribes in Chinese Turkistan—west of Tibet—rebelled against the Manchu (Qing or Ch'ing) rulers. Under Yakub Beg (1820–77), the rebels established a breakaway government at Kashi, near territory controlled by Russia. Always fearful of rebellion, the Russians sent troops into Turkistan in 1871, but in 1872 signed a trade treaty with Yakub Beg, thereby legitimating his claim to sovereignty.

Although the Russians were satisfied that they had controlled the Muslim rebellion as far as their interests were concerned, the Chinese sent an army of 100,000 under General Zuo Zongtang (Tso Tsung-t'ang; 1812–1885) to put down the rebels in Turkistan. In 1876, Tso engaged Beg at Kashi and defeated him. Later that year, Tso captured the Muslim capital at Urümqi, and on May 16, 1877, took the principal Muslim stronghold of Turfan. This forced Beg to acknowledge Chinese authority over Turkistan. Now, however, it was the Russians who presented a problem. They declined to leave Turkistan until 1881, when they concluded a treaty with China in which Turkistan reverted back to the Chinese—in exchange for 9 million rubles. The money was compensation to Russia for the cost of the occupation—even though China had not authorized that occupation.

Further reading: Aitchen Wu, *Turkistan Tumult* (New York: Oxford University Press, 1985); P. M. Holt, Ann K. S. Lambton, and Bernard Lewis, *The Cambridge History of Islam,* 2 vols. (New York: Cambridge University Press, 1970).

Muslim Revolt (656)

PRINCIPAL COMBATANTS: Caliph Ali ibn Abi Talib vs. the rebels Talha and Al-Zubair
PRINCIPAL THEATER(S): Mesopotamia (Iraq)
DECLARATION: None
MAJOR ISSUES AND OBJECTIVES: The rebels sought to topple Ali ibn Abi Talib.
OUTCOME: The rebels were defeated.
APPROXIMATE MAXIMUM NUMBER OF MEN UNDER ARMS: Rebel forces numbered 30,000; Ali ibn Abi Talib's strength was similar.
CASUALTIES: Unknown
TREATIES: None

The Arab world was rocked by turbulence after the passing of the prophet Muhammad (570–632). In 656, the third caliph, Uthman ibn Affan (d. 656), was assassinated and succeeded by the cousin and son-in-law of Muhammad, Ali ibn Abi Talib (c. 600–661). Two followers of Muhammad, Talha (d. 656) and Al-Zubair (d. 656) rebelled against him with the support of Muhammad's widow, A'ishah (614–678). The rebels recruited a 30,000-man army and fought the so-called Battle of the Camel near Basra, Mesopotamia (Iraq) on December 4, 656. (A'ishah observed the battle at close quarters while seated on a camel.) The battle ended when Talha and Al-Zubair were killed. A'ishah was captured and sent into exile. However, Ali's ascension to the caliphate did not bring stability, but ignited the MUSLIM CIVIL WAR (657–661).

See also AFGHAN REVOLT.

Further reading: Karen Armstrong, *A Short History of Islam* (New York: Random House, 2002); P. M. Holt, Ann K. S. Lambton, and Bernard Lewis, *The Cambridge History of Islam,* 2 vols. (New York: Cambridge University Press, 1970); Hugh Kennedy, *The Prophet and the Age of the Caliphates: The Islamic Near East from the Sixth to the Eleventh Century* (New York: Longman, 1986).

Mysore War, First (1767–1769)

PRINCIPAL COMBATANTS: British East India Company vs. Mysore

PRINCIPAL THEATER(S): Mysore (modern location's name), India
DECLARATION: None
MAJOR ISSUES AND OBJECTIVES: The East India Company sought dominance in the region.
OUTCOME: After the company's chief allies withdrew, Mysore defeated the army of the company and concluded a peace favorable to Mysore.
APPROXIMATE MAXIMUM NUMBER OF MEN UNDER ARMS: British East India Company, 1,400 British infantry, 800 British cavalry, 9,000 Sepoy troops; Mysore forces, 42,000 infantry, 28,000 cavalry
CASUALTIES: East India Company forces, fewer than 1,000 killed or wounded; Mysore forces, 7,000 killed or wounded
TREATIES: Treaty of 1769

The British East India Company competed for supremacy in Indian trade with the Mysore kingdom and the Marathas. Striking an uneasy alliance with the Marathas and Hyderabad, the East India Company attacked Mysore in 1767 and defeated Mysore forces led by the Muslim Hyder Ali (1722–82). On September 24, 1767, an Anglo-sepoy force of more than 11,000 fought a Mysore force of 42,000 infantrymen and 28,000 cavalry troops at Trinco-malee. Despite being massively outnumbered, the Anglo-sepoy army scored a major victory, inflicting some 4,000 casualties on the enemy while suffering 48 British and 67 sepoy casualties. Just a few days later, 65,000 Mysori attacked the Anglo-sepoy camp at Changama and were repelled, losing 2,000 killed or wounded. The defenders suffered 170 casualties.

While this action was taking place, another Anglo-sepoy force stormed the Mysore fortress at Mulwagal, inflicting 1,000 casualties at a cost of 230 killed or wounded.

In 1768, both the Marathas and the forces from Hyderabad withdrew from the alliance, and Haidar, who had always evaded the British, menaced the East India Company headquarters at Madras in 1769. In April of that year, Britons concluded a peace, primarily on Mysore terms, and the stage was set for a Second MYSORE WAR.

Further reading: Barbara Daly Metcalf and Thomas R. Metcalf, *Concise History of India* (New York: Cambridge University Press, 2002); Vincent A. Smith, *The Oxford History of India,* 4th ed. (New York: Oxford University Press, 1981); Jac Weller, *Wellington in India* (London: Greenhill Books, 2001).

Mysore War, Second (1780–1784)

PRINCIPAL COMBATANTS: Mysore (with French aid) vs. the British East India Company (Anglo-Indian forces)

PRINCIPAL THEATER(S): Mysore (Karnataka) and Madras (Tamil Nadu), India
DECLARATION: None
MAJOR ISSUES AND OBJECTIVES: Dominance of Mysore
OUTCOME: After initial successes, Mysore was defeated.
APPROXIMATE MAXIMUM NUMBER OF MEN UNDER ARMS: Mysore, 90,000; France, 1,000; Anglo-Indian forces, 12,000
CASUALTIES: Mysore, 16,500 killed or wounded; Anglo-Indian, 4,573 killed, wounded, or taken prisoner; French losses unknown
TREATIES: Treaty of Mangalore, 1784

As with the AMERICAN REVOLUTION, Britain fought the Second Mysore War against both indigenous people and the French, who had established a presence in India, allied with Hyder Ali (1722–82), at Pondicherry on the Karnataka coast. Before the war got under way in earnest, the British had seized Pondicherry as well as Mahe (on the Malabar coast) from the French.

In July 1780, Hyder led an army of 55,000 infantry, 28,000 cavalry, 7,000 rocketeers and artillerymen, and 400 French gunners against the British in the Karnataka. This massive force readily overwhelmed the Anglo-Indian garrison of 3,853 at Perambakam (Pollilur) on September 10. More than 300 British soldiers were killed in battle, as were some 1,700 sepoys. At least 1,000 prisoners were taken, most of whom died in captivity, making this one of Britain's costliest defeats in India.

After triumphing at Perambakam, Hyder overran the Karnataka and menaced the British stronghold of Madras. An Anglo-Indian force of about 10,500 met Hyder's army of 40,000 at Porto Novo on June 1, 1781, defeating it soundly. Three thousand Mysoris died, and twice that number were wounded. This Anglo-Indian victory was followed by two more, at the Second Battle of Pollilur (August 27), in which 12,000 Anglo-Indian troops defeated more than 80,000 Mysoris, and at Sholingarh, where fewer than 9,000 Anglo-Indians defeated 70,000 of Hyder's troops. Sholingarh brought the Mysoris close to defeat; however, French naval forces intervened with the capture of Trincomalee on the coast of Ceylon (Sri Lanka) on August 30, 1782. From here, the French were able to send aid and arms to Haidar, and, on June 13, 1783, the French garrison at Cuddalore, consisting of 3,000 French regulars, 3,000 sepoys, and 5,000 Mysori troops, coordinated with the French fleet to defeat an Anglo-Indian force of nearly 10,000. Despite this victory, however, the 1783 Treaty of Paris, which ended the American Revolution, mandated the withdrawal of French support from Mysore, and, the following year, the Mysoris had little choice but to make peace.

See also MYSORE WAR, FIRST; MYSORE WAR, THIRD; MYSORE WAR, FOURTH.

Further reading: Barbara Daly Metcalf and Thomas R. Metcalf, *Concise History of India* (New York: Cambridge University Press, 2002); Vincent A. Smith, *The Oxford History of India,* 4th ed. (New York: Oxford University Press, 1981); Jac Weller, *Wellington in India* (London: Greenhill Books, 2001).

Mysore War, Third (1790–1792)

PRINCIPAL COMBATANTS: Mysore vs. the Anglo-Indian forces of the British East India Company
PRINCIPAL THEATER(S): Mysore (Karnataka), India
DECLARATION: None
MAJOR ISSUES AND OBJECTIVES: Domination of Mysore
OUTCOME: Mysore relinquished about half of its territory to the British East India Company.
APPROXIMATE MAXIMUM NUMBER OF MEN UNDER ARMS: Mysore, 45,000; Anglo-Indian forces, 61,000
CASUALTIES: Mysore, 23,000 killed, wounded, or died from illness; Anglo-Indian forces, 1,500 killed or wounded
TREATIES: None

The successor of Hyder Ali (1722–82) as leader of the Mysori opposition to the hegemony of the British East India Company was Tippu Sultan (1749–99). On December 28, 1789, he attacked British defenses at Travancore and was repulsed at terrible cost: 2,000 killed or wounded out of the 15,000 he committed to the battle.

Seeking to forestall any further attacks, Charles, Lord Cornwallis (1738–1805), recently named governor-general of British India, invaded the territory controlled by Tippu, laying siege to the Mysore stronghold of Bangalore during March 5–21, 1791. Of the 8,000 Mysoris holding this position, 3,000 were killed or wounded before resistance collapsed. Moreover, Tippu's attempt, on March 7, to relieve the siege was likewise repulsed at great loss to the Mysori—2,000 killed or wounded.

Maintaining the momentum of these victories, Cornwallis led 23,000 men against Mysore fortifications of Carigat; the resulting battle, sometimes called the Battle of Arikera, resulted in 2,000 casualties among the 20,000 Mysori defenders and the loss of the fortifications.

In 1792, Cornwallis led a massive army, consisting of 9,000 British regulars, 22,000 sepoys, 18,000 Hyderabad cavalrymen, 12,000 Maratha mercenary troops, complete with artillery, in a wide-ranging campaign. Of this number, 8,700 were deployed against Seringapatam, Tippu's stronghold, a fortification celebrated as perhaps the most formidable on the subcontinent and garrisoned by 45,000 Mysoris. Despite being overwhelmingly outnumbered, Cornwallis stormed the bastion on February 6 and, at the cost of 535 killed and wounded, inflicting3,000 casualties among the Mysori. When an additional 9,000 Anglo-Indian troops arrived a few days later, Tippu surrendered, but no definitive treaty was concluded. Indeed, Tippu used the truce that commenced in March 1792 to regroup for a new war, which came seven years later.

See also MYSORE WAR, FIRST; MYSORE WAR, SECOND; and MYSORE WAR, FOURTH.

Further reading: Barbara Daly Metcalf and Thomas R. Metcalf, *Concise History of India* (New York: Cambridge University Press, 2002); Vincent A. Smith, *The Oxford History of India*, 4th ed. (New York: Oxford University Press, 1981); Franklin B. Wickwire and Mary B. Wickwire, *Cornwallis: The Imperial Years* (Durham: University of North Carolina Press, 1980).

Mysore War, Fourth (1799)

PRINCIPAL COMBATANTS: Mysore (with a limited French aid) vs. the British East India Company and Hyderabad
PRINCIPAL THEATER(S): Mysore (Karnataka), India
DECLARATION: None
MAJOR ISSUES AND OBJECTIVES: Domination of Mysore
OUTCOME: Tippoo, son of Haydar Ali, died in battle; that portion of Mysore not lost in the Third Mysore War was now divided between the British and their Hyderabad allies.
APPROXIMATE MAXIMUM NUMBER OF MEN UNDER ARMS: Mysori forces, 25,000; Anglo-Indian forces, 57,000
CASUALTIES: Mysori losses, 11,000 killed; Anglo-Indian losses, 1,464 killed or wounded
TREATIES: None

The final bout between Britain and Tippu Sultan (1749–99) was staged in 1799.

Anglo-Indian commanders used about half of the available force of 57,000 men against the Mysori when war resumed in 1799, as British authorities responded to an attempt by Tippu, leader of the Mysori, to make an anti-British alliance with France. Two Anglo-Indian forces converged on Tippu's stronghold at Seringapatam. Tippu unsuccessfully attempted to stop the convergence at Sedaseer Hill on March 6, 1799, but was defeated with the loss of 2,000 troops. On March 27, Tippu offered battle at Malavelley and was again defeated, losing half of his attacking force of 2,000.

The two defeats left Seringapatam ripe for attack, although, as in the Third MYSORE WAR, it remained a formidable objective, excellently situated and garrisoned by 13,737 Mysori and 120 French troops. In addition, 8,100 Mysori soldiers were positioned on a fortified island southeast of the fortress city. The Anglo-Indian force began its siege on April 17, and the fortress fell on May 4, with great loss of life. The attackers lost 389 killed or wounded, whereas the garrison suffered at least 6,000 deaths, including that of Tippu Sultan. Added to the number of defenders killed during the siege itself, Mysori losses at Seringapatam reached 9,000 killed.

See also MYSORE WAR, FIRST; MYSORE WAR, SECOND; and MYSORE WAR, THIRD.

Further reading: Barbara Daly Metcalf and Thomas R. Metcalf, *Concise History of India* (New York: Cambridge University Press, 2002); Vincent A. Smith, *The Oxford History of India*, 4th ed. (New York: Oxford University Press, 1981); Franklin B. Wickwire and Mary B. Wickwire, *Cornwallis: The Imperial Years* (Durham: University of North Carolina Press, 1980).

Nadir Shah's Abdalis Campaign *See* PERSIAN-AFGHAN WAR (1726–1738).

Nadir Shah's Conquest of Bokhara and Khiva (1740)

PRINCIPAL COMBATANTS: Persia vs. Uzbeks
PRINCIPAL THEATER(S): Region of Bukhara and Khiva (Uzbekistan)
DECLARATION: None
MAJOR ISSUES AND OBJECTIVES: Conquest and territorial expansion
OUTCOME: Nadir Shah achieved quick victory and annexed territory south of the Aral Sea.
APPROXIMATE MAXIMUM NUMBER OF MEN UNDER ARMS: Unknown
CASUALTIES: Unknown
TREATIES: None

Nadir Shah (1688–1747), perhaps the greatest military mind in later Persian history and the last of the great Asian conquerors, decided to annex the region south of the Aral Sea. He invaded the land of the Uzbeks and defeated that tribe in two battles, one at Charjui and one at Khiva. After Charjui, the great trading city of Bukhara fell to him. The Battle of Khiva yielded Khiva and put Nadir Shah in position to annex the region he desired.

Further reading: Peter Avery, Gavin Hamblin, and Charles Melville, eds., *From Nadir Shah to the Islamic Republic: The Cambridge History of Iran,* 7 vols. (New York: Cambridge University Press, 1993); Percy Sykes, *A History of Persia,* 2 vols. (New York: RoutledgeCurzon, 2003).

Nadir Shah's Conquest of Meshed
See PERSIAN-AFGHAN WAR (1726–1738).

Nadir Shah's Coup d'Etat *See* PERSIAN-AFGHAN WAR (1726–1738); PERSIAN-CIVIL WAR (1725–1730).

Nadir Shah's Invasion of Afghanistan *See* PERSIAN-AFGHAN WAR (1726–1738).

Nadir Shah's Invasion of India *See* PERSIAN INVASION OF MOGUL INDIA (1738–1739).

Nadir Shah's Invasion of Mesopotamia
See TURKO-PERSIAN WAR (1730–1736).

Namibian War of Independence (1966–1990)

PRINCIPAL COMBATANTS: SWAPO (Namibian nationalist guerrillas) vs. Union of South Africa
PRINCIPAL THEATER(S): Namibia and Angola
DECLARATION: UN Resolution 435, calling for Namibian independence, passed in 1966, was the closest thing to a declaration of war.

MAJOR ISSUES AND OBJECTIVES: SWAPO sought to drive out the South African mandate government from Namibia and achieve full independence.

OUTCOME: After years of guerrilla fighting, independence was achieved in 1990.

APPROXIMATE MAXIMUM NUMBER OF MEN UNDER ARMS: SWAPO, 18,000; South African forces, 30,000

CASUALTIES: Total deaths, about 25,000, including civilians

TREATIES: U.S.-brokered peace, 1988

During the 1960s, African countries were swept by a tide of independence, as former colonies, protectorates, and mandate territories stirred with nationalism and, in most cases, achieved independence. Namibia, formerly a German colony—and, since the end of WORLD WAR I, a mandate territory of South Africa—was nominally given its independence by a UN resolution in 1966. The white government of South Africa refused to abide by the resolution, however, and did not relinquish control of Namibia. This led Namibian nationalists to organize the South West Africa People's Organization (SWAPO), a guerrilla liberation movement.

At first, SWAPO was ineffective; however, when the Portuguese were driven out of neighboring Angola in the ANGOLAN WAR OF INDEPENDENCE, that newly independent nation offered Namibian guerrillas aid and bases of operations in Angolan territory. Cuban troops in Angola offered to train the SWAPO guerrillas. After these developments, the guerrilla war in Namibia intensified, and South African troops made incursions into Angola to raid guerrilla bases. SWAPO, however, continued to retaliate in Namibia.

The war ground on for a decade before the United Nations condemned South Africa in 1976 for its illegal occupation of Namibia. In 1977, the United Nations declared SWAPO the exclusive legal representative of Namibia, and in 1978 called for an international conference to resolve the long Namibian crisis. As a result of the conference, South Africa agreed to allow free elections in Namibia; however, the South African government soon reneged on the offer. In 1979, South Africa rejected a new UN initiative to settle the dispute, and a 1981 peace conference in Geneva also broke down. By this time, however, the stumbling block had been defined: control of Namibia's only deep-water port, Walvis Bay. The United States, fearing Cuban influence in Namibia, sided with South Africa to the extent that it favored refusing to pull out until the Cubans left Angola. Although the dispute remained unresolved, a cease-fire was agreed on in 1984, to be supervised by a UN commission. The following year, South Africa agreed to the installation of a multiracial government.

Despite these concessions, SWAPO pressed on with the war, demanding both the implementation of the UN resolution for Namibian independence and the withdrawal of Cuban troops from Angola—for these now loomed as a menace to an independent Namibia. The United States mediated an agreement in December 1988, whereby Cuba, South Africa, and Angola agreed on a timetable for Namibian independence. For its part, Cuba agreed to make a phased withdrawal of its troops from Angola.

On April 1, 1989, SWAPO guerrillas invaded Namibia from their bases in Angola. They were met by Namibian security police forces, which killed several hundred of the invaders and effectively put an end to SWAPO raids across the border. The peace process then continued, as thousands of Namibian refugees peacefully left Angola to return to Namibia. One of these refugees, the nationalist leader Samuel S. Nujoma (b. 1929), won election as Namibian president when South Africa finally pulled out of the country. Namibia achieved full independence on March 21, 1990. SWAPO became a powerful force in the nation's Constituent Assembly.

Further reading: Ronald F. Dreyer, *Namibia and Southern Africa: Regional Dynamics of Decolonization, 1945–1990* (New York: Routledge, 1994); Stanley Shoeman and Elna Shoeman, *Namibia* (Santa Barbara, Calif.: ABC-Clio, 1997).

Naning War (1831–1832)

PRINCIPAL COMBATANTS: Great Britain vs. Naning

PRINCIPAL THEATER(S): Naning, Malay Peninsula

DECLARATION: 1831, Britain against Naning

MAJOR ISSUES AND OBJECTIVES: Britain sought to compel Naning to pay to them the annual tribute formerly paid to the Dutch.

OUTCOME: After a brief but inordinately costly war, Naning agreed to pay the tribute.

APPROXIMATE MAXIMUM NUMBER OF MEN UNDER ARMS: Unknown

CASUALTIES: Unknown

TREATIES: None

During the 17th and 18th centuries, Minangkabau immigrants from Sumatra settled in Naning, a Malay state, paying a regular tribute for this privilege to the Dutch East India Company. In 1799, the Dutch government assumed control of the financially ailing Dutch East India Company. By a treaty of 1824, the Dutch ceded Malacca—including nearby Naning—Singapore, and Pinang to the British. In 1829 the British attempted to collect the annual tribute (amounting to 10 percent of the agricultural output of the country) that had been paid by Naning to the Dutch. The ruler of Naning, Datuk Abdul Saiyid (r. 1801–32), refused. Two years later, British authorities dispatched a small expeditionary army to enforce payment, but it was defeated. A larger expedition was mounted in 1832 and was resisted for three months. Although the British eventually extracted the tribute payment, the costly effort discouraged other countries on the Malay Peninsula from negotiating trade treaties with the British. The net effect was to retard the progress of British trade in the East Indies through the mid-19th century, making this a very costly conflict.

See also ANGLO-DUTCH WAR IN JAVA; PADRI WAR.

Further reading: Barbara Watson Andaya and Leonard Y. Andaya, *History of Malaysia* (Honolulu: University of Hawaii Press, 2001); D. G. E. Hall, *A History of South-East Asia*, 4th ed. (New York: St. Martin's Press, 1981).

Napoleonic Wars (1795–1815)

PRINCIPAL COMBATANTS: France vs. the major European powers, Great Britain, and the Ottoman Empire
PRINCIPAL THEATER(S): Europe, Russia, Egypt, Syria
DECLARATION: Various
MAJOR ISSUES AND OBJECTIVES: The rise of Napoleon Bonaparte from an obscure artillery officer to emperor of France during the French Revolution inspired his attempt at world conquest, after the Revolution itself had sparked a series of conflicts across Europe.
OUTCOME: Napoleon was ultimately defeated and expelled from France to die in exile, while a Europe transformed by the Napoleonic Wars tried to put together a lasting peace.
APPROXIMATE MAXIMUM NUMBER OF MEN UNDER ARMS: Some 12 million men were mobilized among all belligerents during the era of the Napoleonic Wars.
CASUALTIES: Estimates of casualties during the Napoleonic Wars vary widely but most historians agree that nearly 6 million troops were killed on all sides.
TREATIES: Major treaties of 1795–1805 include Treaty of Campo Formio (October 17, 1797); Treaty of Amiens (March 27, 1802); Treaty of Pressburg (December 26, 1805); Treaty of Tilsit (July 7–9, 1807); Treaty of Schönbrunn (October 14, 1809); First Peace of Paris (May 30, 1814); Second Peace of Paris (November 20, 1815).

This entry covers the rise of Napoleon Bonaparte (1769–1821) to supreme power in France and an overview of his wars of conquest. For a full account of Napoleon's role in the Revolution, *see* FRENCH REVOLUTION. For Napoleon's role in the French Revolutionary wars, *see* the COALITION, WAR OF THE FIRST, and the COALITION, WAR OF THE SECOND. For more on the post-Revolutionary conquests themselves, *see* COALITION, WAR OF THE THIRD; NAPOLEON'S WAR WITH AUSTRIA; PENINSU-LAR WAR; and NAPOLEON'S INVASION OF RUSSIA. For the conclusion of the wars, the peace settlement, and their historic impact, *see* HUNDRED DAYS' WAR.

For some 20 years the history of Europe at the end of the 18th and beginning of the 19th centuries was intertwined and inseparable from the fortunes of a single man, Napoleon Bonaparte. From his relatively obscure origins in Corsica, Bonaparte's military prowess and political acumen swept him to personal dominance over most of the Continent. At its height, Napoleon's empire stretched from Spain to the Russian border. Napoleon ruled France, Catalonia, the Netherlands, the Dalmatian coast, and northern Italy, and members of his family reigned over Spain, modern-day Germany and Poland, and the rest of Italy. For some of these countries, French occupation brought a centralized rule and liberal institutions that provided them for the first time with a true sense of national identity. Even after Napoleon's downfall in 1815, the empire's legal codes and administrative systems continued to operate for decades or longer in the once-occupied territories. Certainly the history of warfare during the first decades of the new century centered on the doings of the man who made himself Emperor Napoleon I.

During two decades of revolution and war, Napoleon changed the history of France and of the world. When that ended, a Europe much rattled by revolution and its global impact met in victory at Vienna to try to put the Old World back together, only to discover that Europe as conceived by the conservative representatives of the traditional regimes had vanished. Ultimately, in the wake of the French Revolution and the rise to power of one of the preeminent personalities of the 19th century, Napoleon Bonaparte, the old regimes of continental Europe eventually, if quietly, modernized their governments and internationalized their relations.

Destined to become perhaps the most brilliant figure in military history, the emperor-to-be was born Napoleone Buonaparte on August 5, 1769, in Ajaccio, Corsica, a politically turbulent island recently acquired by the French Crown from the Republic of Genoa. He was the second surviving son of Carlo Buonaparte (1746–85), a lawyer who claimed descent from the 12th-century military aristocracy of Tuscany, and his wife, Maria Letizia Ramolino (1750–1835). Carlo Buonaparte had married the comely and strong-willed Letizia when she was 14, and they eventually had eight children, whom they raised through difficult times. A number of Corsicans, led by Pasquale Paoli (1725–1807), resisted France's occupation of the island, and Carlo Buonaparte counted himself among them. But when Paoli fled the island, Carlo came to terms with the French ancien régime, winning the protection of a new governor and appointment to the judicial district of Ajaccio as an assessor.

Using his political connections, Carlo obtained Napoleone's admission to the preparatory military academy at Autun, where the nine-year-old Buonaparte learned to speak French and temporarily dropped the "e" from his Christian name. A few months later, Carlo saw years of struggle culminate in success when the French court recognized the Buonapartes' Corsican patents of nobility, a vital step in securing the military future of his son, because the French officer corps recruited only from the aristocracy. Napoleon received a king's scholarship for the offspring of poor nobles and moved on to a more distinguished school in the Champagne region of eastern France, the Royal Military College at Brienne-le-Château, which he attended from April 1779 to October 1784. Spurned as a provincial and a foreigner, Corsican by birth, blood, and the bonds of childhood, Napoleon continued for some time after his arrival on the Continent to feel he was an outsider, and he kept aloof and threw himself into his studies.

If he was never the reincarnation of a typical 14th-century condottiere that some biographers later made him out to be, from the beginning Napoleon shared few, if any, of the traditions and adopted almost none of the prejudices of his new country, however French his education. Remaining Corsican by temperament, he became, through both that education and his own reading, a man of the 18th century, of both its belief in enlightenment and its absolutism. Though in Champagne, he managed to graduate only near the bottom of his class, 42nd of 58 members, a final report praised his conduct and mathematical skills (his accomplishments were weak, said the school, in music, dancing, and other social skills) and concluded, "This boy will make an excellent sailor." But Napoleon abandoned the navy for the artillery, which enjoyed little prestige among the country's officer nobility but was the most forward-looking arm of the French military and on the cutting edge of 18th-century technology. At 15, Napoleon pursued his studies at the École Militaire in Paris, and a year later—about half the time it took most cadets to graduate—he was assigned as a second lieutenant in the artillery regiment of Le Fere, a kind of training school for young artillery officers.

Back in February 1785, Napoleon's father had died of stomach cancer, leaving his family in straitened circumstances. Although not yet 16 and not the eldest son, the young lieutenant had assumed the position of head of the family. In these twilight years of the ancien régime, garrison duty was leisurely, with light workloads and long leaves, which Napoleon not only took but abused. Garrisoned at Valence, Napoleon read more widely than the average young officer. Plunging especially into works on strategy and tactics, he fell under the influence of the military theorist J. P. du Teil (fl. 18th century). He wrote *Lettres sur la Corse*, a history of Corsica that revealed his romantic feelings for his native island. At the same time, having read Voltaire and Rousseau and steeped himself in the liberal ideas sweeping France, he believed political change was imperative, although as a career officer he seemed leery of radical social reform. He went back to Corsica in September 1786 and did not rejoin his regiment until June 1788. He soon garnered a post at the Auxonne artillery depot, and—as an aide to senior officers engaged in technical experiments—he acquired practical experience as well as influential friends. It was here, in 1789, that Buonaparte first saw active service when he and his troops were sent to quell food riots.

Later that year, the National Assembly, meeting to write a national constitution, granted Pasquale Paoli permission to return to Corsica. Napoleon asked for leave to follow him and joined Paoli's group in September 1789. But Paoli did not much care for the Buonapartes. In Paoli's eyes not only had Napoleon's father deserted the Corsican cause back in the days of the ancien régime, but these days, his son was nothing better than a foreigner. The disenchanted young soldier returned to France, where he was transferred to the Grenoble artillery regiment in February 1791, securing promotion to first lieutenant. He immediately joined the Jacobin Club of Grenoble, at a time when that debating society still favored a constitutional monarchy. Soon the local club's president, Napoleon made speeches declaiming against nobles, monks, and bishops. In September 1791, Napoleon took three months' leave to return to Corsica. There he contrived to have himself elected lieutenant colonel of the newly formed Ajaccio National Guard, whose commander in chief was none other than Pasquale Paoli, with whom he soon had yet another falling out. When he failed to return to France, he was listed as a deserter in January 1792, but after France declared war on Austria in April, he was both forgiven his offense and—apparently through patronage—promoted to the rank of captain. However, instead of rejoining his regiment, in October 1782 Napoleon returned to Corsica, which was well on the way toward civil war, and joined the Corsican Jacobins. Many of the island's natives, including Paoli, had always seen in France's revolutionary turmoil a chance to seize their own independence. Rising to power on the back of the National Guard, Paoli was by this time acting as a virtual dictator and preparing to separate Corsica from France. Only the Jacobins stood in his way, and when civil war broke out in April 1793, Napoleon—at the head of the pro-French Ajaccio Volunteers—acted vigorously, if unsuccessfully, to suppress what was now considered a rebellion. As a result, in June, Paoli had the Buonaparte family sentenced to "perpetual execration and infamy." With his family, Napoleon fled to Marseille on June 10, 1793.

Back in France, Maximilien Robespierre (1758–94) and his radical Jacobins, despite pockets of resistance, were running the country. Now a republic, France was beleaguered on all fronts, at war with most of Europe and fighting rebellion in the countryside. She needed all the soldiers she could get, especially young Jacobins like

Napoleon who, upon rejoining his regiment in Nice in late June, wrote a pamphlet entitled *Souper de Beaucaire*, which argued fervently for united action by all republicans rallied around the Jacobins and the National Convention who had, the past autumn, abolished the monarchy. The exhortation caught the attention of Augustin Robespierre (1764–94), brother of Maximilien and the Jacobin government's representative in the south, and Napoleon would soon use this new contact in the government to good advantage.

At the end of August 1793, government troops had retaken control of Marseille, but they were brought up short at the port of Toulon, where defecting royalists had allowed the British to occupy the town. The scratch revolutionary army was trying to dislodge them, so far unsuccessfully, making Toulon Augustin's biggest headache. When the French artillery commander was wounded, Buonaparte obtained the post through the commissioner to the army, Antoine Saliceti (fl. late 18th century), who was a Corsican deputy to the National Assembly and a friend of Napoleon's family. It was the first real opportunity in Napoleon's career, and the greatest opportunist of the age played it for all it was worth, rising to major in September and adjutant general in October. With backing from Augustin Robespierre, he persuaded his reluctant superiors to adopt his plan of employing artillery to force the port's British supporting fleet to withdraw, and in December he carried out the plan. Receiving a bayonet wound on December 16, he nevertheless watched the next day as British troops, harassed by his artillery, evacuated the port and the British ships sailed away. Toulon, an embarrassment to the republic for months, had fallen within 48 hours of Napoleon's taking direct charge. On December 22, Buonaparte, aged 24, still hobbling from his leg wound, was promoted again, to brigadier general. Augustin Robespierre wrote to his brother Maximilien, by then head of the government in all but name and the leading figure behind the Reign of Terror, praising what Augustin called the "transcendent merit" of the young republican officer.

As a reward for his able command of the artillery, Napoleon was designated artillery commander of the French army in Italy in February 1794. Following the overthrow of Maximilien Robespierre in July of that year, however, Buonaparte was thrown into prison from August 6 to September 14, but he was already too well connected politically to long remain there. Following his release, he declined artillery command of the Army of the West and was assigned instead to the war office's Topographical Bureau. Soon appointed second in command of the Army of the Interior, he ended the Parisian uprising of 13 Vendémiaire (October 5, 1795), which was mounted in protest against the new constitution introduced by the National Convention. Napoleon dispersed the insurrectionists with his beloved artillery, thereby saving the Con-

vention. The Directory, as the new government was called, rewarded him with full command of the Army of the Interior, at which point he married Josephine de Beauharnais (1763–1814), the rather notorious widow of a titled republican general, and changed his name to Bonaparte.

Once in command of the Army of the Interior, Napoleon moved vigorously against Piedmontese (Sardinian) and Austrian forces, bringing about an armistice with the Piedmontese by the end of April after defeating them at Ceva and Mondovi in April, thereby securing the cession of Savoy and Nice to France. He next moved swiftly and brilliantly against the Austrians, defeating them at Lodi on May 10, then entering Milan on May 15. He drove the Austrian forces out of Lombardy during May and June. Mantua, the last Austrian stronghold in the region, fell to Napoleon in February 1797 following a lengthy siege. Next Napoleon advanced toward Vienna itself, a move that sent the Austrians to the peace table. The commander himself negotiated the Treaty of Campo Formio on October 17, 1797, by which the War of the First Coalition—the first of the French Revolutionary Wars—was ended.

Napoleon reshaped Italian politics, creating the Cisapline Republic, establishing what were in effect various puppet governments in Italy, and pillaging Italian art collections to help finance French military operations. He was hailed as a hero by the Directory, which proposed to send the conqueror of Italy to invade England. But Napoleon successfully promoted another grand strategy: the invasion of Egypt in order to secure a staging area for an invasion of British India, in what is known as the War of the Second Coalition.

Taking Malta on the way, while deftly avoiding the British navy under Horatio Nelson, Napoleon managed to occupy Alexandria and Cairo in late 1798, where he wisely guaranteed the preservation of Islamic law but set about modernizing the secular government. But then the British fleet destroyed the French fleet at Aboukir Bay, cutting off Napoleon from France, and the Ottoman Turks declared war on France in February 1799. Napoleon preemptively invaded Syria, only to be stopped at Acre by British-led Ottoman troops, and the French army fell prey to the plague. By the time Bonaparte returned to Cairo in June, the French government had reached a crisis under the onslaught of the Second Coalition victories in Europe.

Napoleon embarked for France on August 24, 1799, arriving in Paris on October 14 to discover that he had been recalled by the members of the Directory to help again to "save" the Revolution. He participated in the coup d'état of 18 Brumaire (November 19) against the Directory, which was reconstituted with Napoleon as one of its three consuls. Appointed commander of the Paris garrison, Napoleon was elected first consul under the new constitution of the Year VIII, with power to appoint members of the Consulate itself, government officials, and judges. Installed in February 1800, Napoleon consolidated what soon amounted to dictatorial power and radically centralized the government, bringing it under his personal control. The French Revolution was over.

The nation favored the first consul, and there was remarkably little opposition. Wracked by years of revolutionary terror and lawlessness, still faced with a formidable royalist faction, the people—whose yearning for stability was almost tangible—were willing to hand over authority to one strong man. Buttressed by the new and highly authoritarian constitution that a plebiscite of his weary fellow citizens backed almost unanimously, Napoleon radically restructured the French national debt, setting the French economy on a sound footing. He encouraged the development of industry and the improvement of the educational system, and he initiated an ambitious program of construction inspired by the classical examples of imperial Rome. He created the Code Napoleon, which codified civil law by amalgamating the old customs of northern France with the Roman law of the south. Also included was a new criminal code to be enforced by judges. These changes were sweeping, and over the years the code would be extended to regulate and transform every aspect of French life, and then, as it came to cover Napoleon's conquests, the life of much of Europe. One provision in particular, requiring the equal division of property between sons, did more than the Revolution to destroy the power of France's—then the Empire's—landed gentry. Equally as significant, the first consul concluded the 1801 Concordat with Pope Pius VII (1742–1823), reestablishing Roman Catholicism as the state religion, or—as the Concordat would have it—at least "the religion of the great majority of the French people," whose practice was authorized "in conformity with any police regulations that may be necessary for public order."

In April 1802, church bells rang out for the first time since the onset of the Revolution, as if in celebration of a new civic harmony within France and a new peace in Europe. For Napoleon, needing peace at home and abroad to give time for his reforms to take effect, had moved decisively in May 1800 to bring an end to the War of the Second Coalition. Crushing the Austrians at the Battle of Marengo on June 14, 1800, he did indeed initiate a brief interval of peace with all Europe, including Britain, the next year. The failure of William Pitt's (1759–1806) coalition on the Continent forced him to resign as British prime minister, and the incoming government—its members emotionally fatigued by almost a decade of fruitless fighting—signed the Treaty of Amiens on March 27, 1802. Although the peace—with Great Britain still deeply suspicious and France full of expansionist ambition—was destined to be not much more than a brief truce, it did nevertheless provide Napoleon nearly 15 months to complete his civic and clerical reforms and to reshape his

army. A grateful France made Napoleon first consul for life on August 2, 1802.

To the chagrin of the British, much of France's newfound energy seemed devoted to ship building, and not just to constructing ships of the line, but also flat-bottomed barges that could only, they decided, be intended for an invasion of their island. Worse still, in 1803 Napoleon set about once again to reshape the face of Europe. In Holland he occupied the Batavian Republic and in Switzerland the Helvetian Republic. He annexed Savoy-Piedmont, then took the first step toward abolishing the Holy Roman Empire by means of the Imperial Recess of 1803, which consolidated free cities and minor states dominated by the Holy Roman Empire. He also attempted to recover the Caribbean island of Haiti, which had rebelled against French colonial domination. To help fund these adventures and to ensure, at the very least, America's neutrality in what was surely the coming war with Britain, Napoleon sold Louisiana—ceded to France by its ally, Spain, in 1800 under the secret Treaty of San Ildefonso—to the United States at a cut-rate price, extracting in exchange vague promises of friendship that fell far short of Bonaparte's hopeful prediction to the U.S. diplomats that the Americans would fight Britain again.

Britain was even more irritated by Napoleon's determination to turn Europe into a huge market reserved exclusively for French goods. Not only did France control the continental coastline from Genoa to Antwerp, it was also charging extortionate customs duties that much affronted the commercially minded island sea power. Thus Napoleon's renewed aggression in Europe, coupled with his refusal to grant trade concessions to Britain, led the English to reignite war—on the slim pretext that he was not living up to the Treaty of Amiens—in May 1803. As Napoleon prepared to invade England with an army of 170,000 troops, an assassination scheme, financed by the British, was discovered. Alarmed by the plot, the French Senate—nudged along by Napoleon—petitioned the first consul to establish a hereditary dynasty. Once more, Bonaparte eagerly seized opportunity and, on December 2, 1804, as Pope Pius VII looked on, he crowned himself emperor.

Eliminating the republic for which he had supposedly fought for so long and so ostentatiously, Napoleon created a royal court populated by former republicans and royalists alike. Not content merely to create a dynasty for France, he would eventually install members of his family on the thrones of the newly created kingdoms of Naples, Holland, Westphalia, and Spain. Meanwhile, he went to war with the world.

From the moment he became emperor, Napoleon was almost constantly at war. Great Britain proved his most dogged opponent, but Prussia, Russia, and Austria also joined in the series of coalitions stitched together to stop Napoleon's march across Europe. Backed by an entirely new kind of army—ideologically conscripted rather than professionally recruited—he was a master strategist, particularly skilled at the rapid deployment of masses of troops and mobile field artillery. Until 1812—with some important exceptions—the French military was usually successful. One of those exceptions came in October 1805, when British admiral Horatio Nelson (1758–1805) annihilated the French navy at the Battle of Trafalgar off the coast of Spain. Preoccupied with Austria and Russia, Napoleon was probably not aware that the battle—which cost Nelson his life—was one of the turning points in history. In the short term, it meant Napoleon had to call off his elaborate plans to invade England; in the long run, Nelson's victory ensured the British navy would rule the seas for more than a century.

Forcing the Russians to capitulate and sign the Treaty of Pressburg after the Battle of Austerlitz in December (his single greatest military victory), Napoleon abolished the Holy Roman Empire and organized in its stead the Confederation of the Rhine, a French protectorate of German states. In an attempt to ease hostilities with Britain, Napoleon offered to return Hanover to British control, which provoked a war with Prussia in September, though Napoleon easily defeated this Fourth Coalition. Once again, he forced major concessions from Prussia and its ally, Czar Alexander I, creating the French-controlled Grand Duchy of Warsaw, gaining Russian recognition of other European entities spawned by Napoleon, and removing from Prussia all lands between the Rhine and Elbe rivers.

The emperor now enjoyed unparalleled sway over Europe, but he was not satisfied. Unable to defeat Britain by military means, he instituted in 1806 the Continental System, a blockade of British trade intended to destroy England's economy. Britain responded with the Orders in Council, which called for its own naval blockade of Napoleonic Europe. The Continental System, and the British response, created tremendous unrest throughout Europe, and Portugal immediately announced that it would not participate. Napoleon launched the Peninsular War to compel Portugal's obedience, which provoked unrest in Spain and led to the abdication of King Charles IV (1748–1819) and his son Ferdinand VII (1784–1833). When Napoleon replaced them with his brother, Joseph Bonaparte (1768–1844), a popular revolt broke out in Spain and in Spanish holdings around the world. With Napoleon embroiled on the Iberian Peninsula, Austria formed the Fifth Coalition, won a few early victories, then lost decisively. Napoleon's marriage to Marie-Louise of Austria followed the 1809 armistice.

By 1809 Napoleonic France had annexed the Low Countries and western Germany and set up satellite kingdoms in eastern Germany and Italy, Spain, and Poland. Despite the enmity his empire provoked, Napoleon hoped that his union with one of Europe's oldest royal families, in addition to providing an heir, would guarantee him Austrian friendship and bring peace to Europe. Instead, English-backed guerrillas continued to threaten his grasp on Spain and Portugal, and Russia—nervous about the substantial French forces in Poland—also refused to participate in the Continental System. These irritations provoked Napoleon to overreach himself beginning in 1810.

Following an enormous effort requiring every country in Europe, including a reluctant Prussia, to contribute a contingent, the emperor assembled 650,000 troops along the Russian frontier, where he planned one of his lightning campaigns that would destroy the Russian forces in six weeks and allow him to impose a humiliating peace. But the invasion failed miserably in the cold Russian winter, and by December of 1812, the Prussians had deserted the Grand Army and turned against the French, the Austrians had likewise withdrawn and were growing increasingly hostile, and even stalwart Italy was turning its back on Napoleon. They would all hail the formation of yet another anti-French Coalition—the sixth—consisting of Prussia, Russia, Britain, and Sweden. In Austria, Napoleon's own father-in-law was mobilizing against him.

This time, the forces arrayed against France would no longer be armies of mercenaries but those of nations fighting for their freedom. And even though, in Paris, the emperor built a new army, with which he defeated coalition forces in 1813 and brought about a brief armistice, the French themselves had lost their enthusiasm for a European empire. Napoleon's goal of conquest was no longer that of the French nation. In August, Austria joined the Sixth Coalition. Napoleon promptly defeated Austrian troops at Dresden but, badly outnumbered, the French were in turn trounced at the Battle of the Nations at Leipzig on October 16–19, 1813. Napoleon retreated across the Rhine, but refused to surrender any conquered territory. The next year, when coalition armies invaded France itself, the emperor prevailed against each attempt to penetrate to Paris until repeated mauling of his dwindling forces prompted a mutiny of his marshals and the fall of the capital on March 31, 1814. A few days later, on April 4, Napoleon abdicated in favor of his son.

The allies rejected this "solution," and Napoleon abdicated unconditionally on April 6. He was exiled to the British-controlled island of Elba. In a matter of days, the empire had vanished, and in Napoleon's place the victors had enthroned the Bourbon Louis XVIII (1755–1824), whose brother had lost his head to the Revolution 21 years before. On May 30, the new king signed the First Peace of Paris, which Charles Maurice de Talleyrand-Périgord (1754–1838) negotiated to retain those "natural" frontiers of France in place since 1792. A great congress was summoned at Vienna to set in order a post-Napoleonic Europe, but within weeks, thanks to Talleyrand's diplomacy, the allies' wartime unity had begun to evaporate and the diplomats were engaged in bitter squabbles. They had at least managed to agree to the creation of a

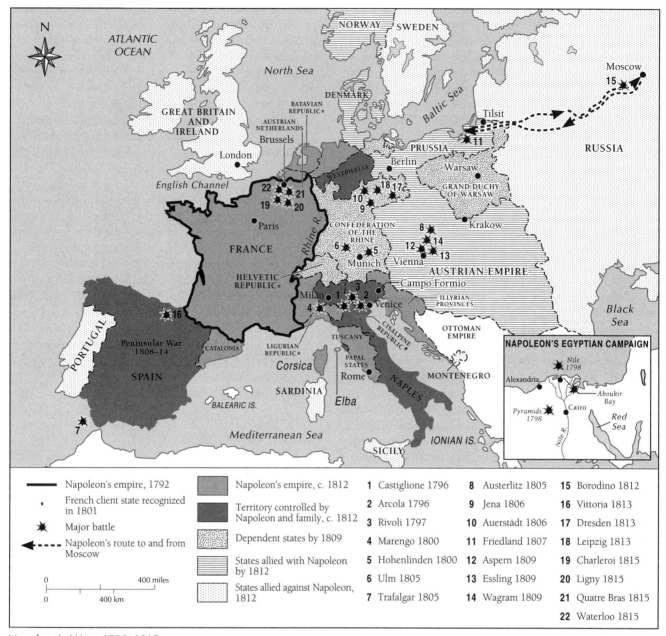

Napoleonic Wars, 1792–1815

moderately powerful state in the Netherlands as a buffer against a resurgent France when the congress was interrupted by news that Napoleon had escaped from exile and was on his way to Paris.

He landed, with a few hundred followers, at Cannes on March 1, 1815, aware that Louis XVIII was unpopular, that the peasants feared a restoration of the aristocracy would cost them all they had gained in the Revolution, and that the middle class hated a reactionary regime threatening to its own class hegemony. Troops sent by the king to arrest Napoleon instead joined him, and yet again a Bourbon monarch fled Paris. Napoleon occupied the

city, which joyfully acclaimed the return of its emperor on March 20. The Congress of Vienna spurned Napoleon's claim that his intentions were peaceful and labeled him an outlaw. Seeking to forestall combined attack by Russian and Austrian armies, Napoleon decided to strike first in order to divide and destroy Prussian and Anglo-Dutch armies in Belgium. Indeed, Napoleon prevailed against the Austrians at Ligny on June 16 and against the British at Quatre-Bras on the same day, but he was defeated at Waterloo by Arthur Wellesley (1769–1852), duke of Wellington, reinforced by troops under Gebhard von Blücher (1742–1819) on June 18, 1815.

The duke of Wellington claimed Waterloo had been nearly a draw and a very close call, but even had Napoleon won, the world was determinedly arrayed against him and would have quickly crushed his restoration. Now he was on the run, a mere fugitive, who reached the port of Rochefort in early July hoping to find a ship to take him to the United States. But the British, always his nemesis, were still strictly enforcing their blockade, and Napoleon had no way out. Napoleon returned to Paris, abdicated for the second time on June 22, and surrendered to the captain of the *Bellerophon*, a British warship, cheekily seeking asylum in England. The British demurred, and he was exiled again, this time to the desolate South Atlantic island of Saint Helena. There he composed his memoirs and grew increasingly ill. Some authorities believe that he succumbed, like his father, to cancer of the stomach on May 5, 1821; others have theorized that he died of gradual arsenic poisoning, which may have been the result of a deliberate assassination effort or due to overmedication with the arsenic-based drugs popular at the time.

HISTORICAL IMPACT OF THE WARS

The Congress of Vienna, which had been so shocked by Napoleon's escape that it interrupted its bickering, picked up where it had left off in March. Both a diplomatic conference and a glittering social occasion, the delegates discussed the fate of their world amid a gala of balls and receptions where old Europe celebrated its survival. Austria's foreign minister, Prince Klemens von Metternich (1773–1859), whose shadow stretched long over the future of Europe, dominated the proceedings as diplomats from Britain, Russia, and Prussia worked to restore a balance of power that would ensure their old order continued to thrive indefinitely. Much of their attention focused on the undoing of Napoleon's reforms in Europe, but—terrified by both the Revolution and the attendant nationalism that gave rise to France's empire—they hoped to do more than merely restore the balance of power.

They hoped to come up with a settlement designed to prevent any such events from recurring. Thus all the powers, including the constitutionally governed Britain, placed great emphasis on principles of legitimacy for monarchies. Some of Napoleon's innovations, long envied and often imitated, the congress was not willing to forego. Having striven to copy his efficient and centralized administration, they retained the improved bureaucratic and fiscal systems he had imposed on his conquests, and where these conflicted with the old feudal aristocracy, they often set aside old and once-cherished privileges. Napoleon's Civil Code, too, they left intact, underpinning the legal systems not just of France, but also of Holland, Belgium, Italy—wherever had trodden the troops of the Grand Army.

Napoleon's rise had transformed many institutions beyond the ability of the European peacemakers to change—indeed, beyond remedy by the art of diplomacy altogether. Not only did his conquests spread revolutionary ideology to much of western Europe and destroy the old order inherited from the 18th century in major sections of the Continent, but in such areas as Belgium, western Germany, and northern Italy, Napoleon's armies consolidated what before had been scattered territories. This welter of states was never truly restored. Such developments, added to an intense resentment toward Napoleonic hegemony, did indeed spark a growing nationalism in these areas, as well as in Spain and Poland. And even Prussia and Russia, more resistant to the siren call of revolution, had introduced political reforms to strengthen their states and resist Napoleon's war machine.

Napoleon's impact was felt outside Europe as well, most spectacularly in Latin America. When Bonaparte placed his inept brother on the Spanish throne, he unintentionally united all Creole society in opposition to Joseph, and mobs drove French emissaries out of capitals across the lower half of the Western Hemisphere. Then Spanish officialdom itself, increasingly viewed as the puppet of a French usurper, came under attack. For a year, Spanish viceroys clung to power, but in 1810, Latin America's Creole population arose, almost as one, to depose their already powerless rulers. The rebellions struck every Latin country in the New World but Peru. Years later, Spain and Portugal would make a feeble stab at reclaiming some of their lost colonial empires, but by then the United States, backed by Great Britain, was determined to stop them, setting the stage for U.S. president James Monroe to issue the seminal Monroe Doctrine, by which the United States proclaimed itself the defender of republican government in the Americas.

Perhaps just as significantly, Great Britain, protected by the English Channel from Napoleon's army, was also transformed by the long series of conflicts. Fifteen years of continuous war against the French emperor (and 10 years of war against the French Revolution before that), although arduous for those at the front on land or sea, was nevertheless a godsend for British industrialists and empire builders. Honed by Napoleon's constant pressure, the Royal Navy came to rule the waves, not only protecting the island kingdom from invasion but also keeping the ocean lanes open for British export. The navy enforced the Orders in Council, which not only blockaded France and her allies but also permitted neutrals to trade with the enemy only if they paid duty on their cargoes. Although this ultimately provoked the WAR OF 1812 with the United States, it also gave Britain's fledgling industries the security they needed to expand.

Britain's military victories in the Napoleonic Wars also expanded its empire. French possessions in the Caribbean and Mediterranean soon joined its growing—and captive—imperial market. When Holland fell to France, the British seized Dutch territories in Africa and Asia. The expanded colonial demands for British goods helped offset the decline in trade with a continental Europe squeezed by economic sanctions, but more important, it stoked the fires of Britain's industrial revolution and gave rise to one of the greatest colonial empires the world had ever seen. But even the protection afforded by the British navy, and the expanding industrial economy that ultimately helped to wear Napoleon down, could not prevent the French revolutionary example from spurring a new wave of democratic agitation in British society.

Thus Britain was as anxious to preserve some of the old order as the Europeans coming under Metternich's sway. The Treaty of Vienna they produced disappointed the growing number of nationalists, who had hoped for an officially unified Germany and Italy, and it certainly daunted democrats and liberals, but—thanks in no small measure to Talleyrand—it was not truly reactionary, nor as punitive toward France as it might have been. After Vienna, conservatism dominated the diplomatic and political agenda of Europe through the mid-1820s, with major governments, even in Britain, employing police agents to ferret out revolutionary agitators. The balance of power worked out at the congress would preserve the peace in Europe for more than half a century, but in the long run the conservative political order it worked to reestablish was doomed by the boost given to national movements in the Napoleonic Wars.

Further reading: Louise Bergeron, *France under Napoleon* (Princeton, N.J.: Princeton University Press, 1990); David G. Chandler, *The Campaigns of Napoleon* (New York: Scribner, 1966); John R. Elting, *A Military History and Atlas of the Napoleonic Wars* (Philadelphia: Stackpole, 1999); Pieter Geyl, *Napoleon For and Against* (London: Jonathan Cape, 1957); Alan Schom, *Napoleon Bonaparte* (New York: HarperCollins, 1997).

Napoleon's Egyptian Campaign

See COALITION, WAR OF THE SECOND.

Napoleon's German Campaign

See COALITION, WAR OF THE SECOND.

Napoleon's Invasion of Russia (1812)

PRINCIPAL COMBATANTS: France vs. Russia
PRINCIPAL THEATER(S): Russia
DECLARATION: France against Russia, April 8, 1812
MAJOR ISSUES AND OBJECTIVES: When Russia renounced Napoleon's Continental System, because the trade boycott against Britain was ruining the Russian economy, and made peace with the British, Napoleon invaded his erstwhile ally.
OUTCOME: Napoleon's Grand Army nearly perished in the harsh Russian winter, leaving Napoleon vulnerable to a new coalition of forces in Europe.

APPROXIMATE MAXIMUM NUMBER OF MEN UNDER ARMS: France, 500,000 in Russia; Russia, 409,000
CASUALTIES: France, 334,000 killed, 180,000 wounded, 100,000 captured; Russia, 150,000–200,000 killed, 150,000 wounded, 50,000 deserted
TREATIES: First Peace of Paris, May 30, 1814

Since the Congress of Erfurt in the fall of 1808, Russia's Czar Alexander I (1777–1825) had shown himself increasingly less willing to deal with Napoleon (1769–1821) as a trusted ally or to enforce his Continental System of trade restrictions against the British. By the summer of 1812, Napoleon had massed his troops in Poland to intimidate Alexander into staying the course, but in June 1812—after attempts to heal the rift had failed—the czar made peace with Great Britain, and Napoleon's Grand Army of 500,000 invaded Russia.

The Russians retreated, adopting a "scorched earth" defense that kept the French army from the approaches to Moscow until the beginning of September. At Borodino, the Russian commander, Mikhail Kutuzov (1745–1813), engaged Napoleon in a savage, bloody, indecisive battle that did not prevent the French from entering Moscow a week later, after the Russians had abandoned the city. A huge fire broke out that same day, although no one knows whether it was deliberately set by the Russians or occurred accidentally at the hands of French looters. In any case, it destroyed the greater part of the town, and afterward, Alexander refused to treat with Napoleon. Stranded in the heart of Russia with winter coming on, Napoleon withdrew. But early snows made the retreat disastrous. By December, although he managed to preserve himself and the core of his Grand Army, much of his forces were destroyed or had deserted him, and although 40,000 made it out alive, fewer than 10,000 men fit for combat remained in Napoleon's main force.

THE AFTERMATH

The French catastrophe cheered all Europe. Though Arthur Wellesley (1769–1852), duke of Wellington, had earlier failed to take Burgos in Spain, in 1813 he routed the French at Vitoria and pursued them back into their home country. Napoleon's Prussian allies, smelling weakness in the Russian and Spanish setbacks, formed a new coalition with Russia, Sweden, and Austria to wage a "War of Liberation." Having pursued Napoleon's army into France itself, Wellington laid siege to Bayonne and Bordeaux, where his efforts merged with the general allied effort. This brought the PENINSULAR WAR—which had brutalized Spain and detonated Latin American revolutions—to a close.

Meanwhile, at the Battle of Nations in Leipzig on October 16–19, 1813, coalition powers defeated the Grand Army. Napoleon rejected the allies' offer of a peace that stipulated France's pre-1792 frontiers on the Rhine and

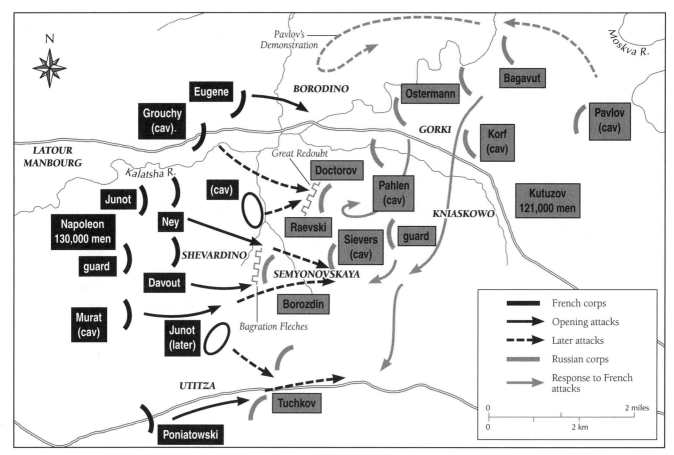

Battle of Borodino, September 7, 1812

along the Alps as its "natural" borders and stubbornly held his ground. But in March 1814, Paris was captured by the allies, and Napoleon relinquished the battle, abdicating as emperor and accepting—under the Peace of Paris—exile from Europe to the island of Elba (*see* NAPOLEONIC WARS).

Further reading: Alan Palmer, *Napoleon in Russia* (New York: Carroll and Graf Publishers, 2003); Richard K. Riehn, *1812: Napoleon's Russian Campaign* (New York: Wiley, 1991).

Napoleon's North Italy Campaign
See COALITION, WAR OF THE FIRST.

Napoleon's Peninsular Campaign
See PENINSULAR WAR.

Napoleon's Reconquest of Egypt
See COALITION, WAR OF THE SECOND.

Napoleon's Second Italian Campaign
See COALITION, WAR OF THE SECOND.

Napoleon's War with Austria   (1809)

PRINCIPAL COMBATANTS: France (including Bavarian forces) vs. Austria (nominally heading a Fifth Coalition)
PRINCIPAL THEATER(S): Austria
DECLARATION: Austria on France, February 9, 1809
MAJOR ISSUES AND OBJECTIVES: The Austrian Hapsburgs, always jealous of Napoleon's domination of Europe, attacked France while Napoleon was preoccupied with fighting in Spain and Portugal.
OUTCOME: Napoleon soundly defeated the Hapsburgs and allied himself to them by marriage.
APPROXIMATE MAXIMUM NUMBER OF MEN UNDER ARMS: France, 169,400; Austria, 136,200
CASUALTIES: France, about 30,000 killed or wounded; Austria, 80,855 killed or wounded
TREATIES: Treaty of Schönbrunn (or Treaty of Vienna), October 14, 1809

In 1809 while Napoleon (1769–1821) was caught up in the PENINSULAR WAR, the Hapsburgs invaded Bavaria on April 9, 1809, in hopes of rousing all Germany against a common foe, but they only succeeded in catching Napoleon's undivided attention. Napoleon marshaled a large army to confront the Austrians, but the first action of the war was against the Tyrolean peasantry, which rose in rebellion against Bavarian garrisons on the southern flank of Napoleon's main army. Although a French force of 36,000 attacked 40,000 Austrians at Sacile on April 16, the combination of the uprising and Austrian resistance overwhelmed the attack: 3,500 French soldiers were killed or wounded, and another 6,000 taken prisoner.

Three days later, on the war's main front in Bavaria proper, a French army was more successful, penetrating Austrian lines, albeit at great cost. Of 22,000 French troops engaged, 4,000 were killed or wounded, whereas Austrian casualties were about 3,000. Nevertheless, Napoleon personally led a force to exploit the breach in the Austrian lines and scored a stunning victory at Abensberg on April 19–20. Of about 14,000 men, the Austrians lost 2,700 killed or wounded and 4,000 taken prisoner. French losses were negligible. This action exposed the left wing of the Austrian army of 27,000 men, which

Napoleon attacked on April 21 and drove back across the Iser River at Landshut. Austrian losses were about 2,000 killed or wounded, 3,312 captured, and another 2,653 missing. Of some 70,000 French soldiers in the region, 1,500 were killed or wounded.

From the triumph at Landshut, Napoleon turned north to reinforce the 36,000 French troops menaced by an army of 75,000 on the Danube. Napoleon arrived just in time on April 22 to repulse an Austrian attack at Eggmühl. The repulse cost the French 3,000 killed or wounded, about the same as the casualties inflicted on the Austrians.

Although it had suffered a series of stinging defeats, the Austrian army withdrew in good order, whereupon Napoleon turned down the Danube in an advance on Vienna. This brought an Austrian counterattack on April 24 at Neumarkt-St. Vieth, which took a sharp toll on the Bavarian division there, but failed to stop Napoleon, who entered Vienna without resistance on May 13.

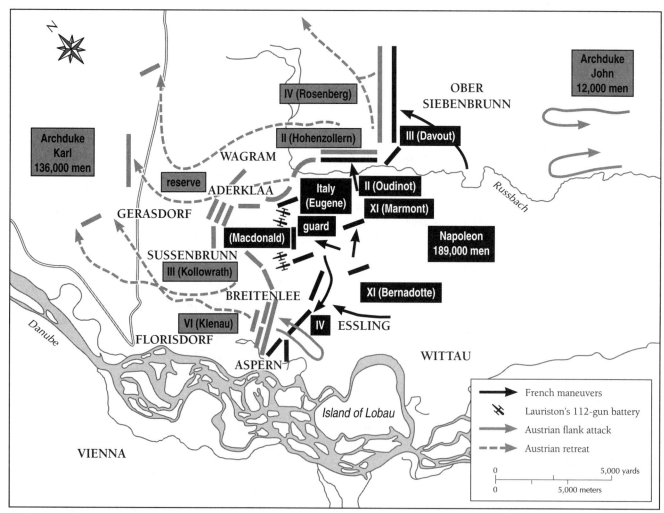

Battle of Wagram, July 4–6, 1809

In the meantime, the French Army of Italy engaged in an offensive on the Piave River beginning May 7–8. A large force of 44,800 Frenchmen defeated 20,750 Austrians and broke through to the Isonzo River by May 18. Here the French cleared the Austrian border defenses—which, badly outnumbered, nevertheless fought valiantly—and invaded Austrian territory from the south.

During the action in Bavaria and Italy, an Austrian army defeated combined French and Polish forces in Poland and, on April 19, took Warsaw. Thus Poland fell under Austrian control.

In the meantime, the main Austrian army, though so far defeated, remained intact and, on May 21, repulsed a major thrust by Napoleon at Aspern-Essling. Thirty percent of the French forces engaged, 21,000 men, were killed or wounded, at a cost, however of 23,340 Austrians killed, wounded, captured, or missing.

The costly repulse at Aspern-Essling inspired the people of the Tyrol, who once again rose up in rebellion. However, the Austrians were having their own trouble in Poland, and when the nation erupted into widespread rebellion, the Austrian army had to relinquish Warsaw and begin a general withdrawal southward.

As for Napoleon, after the terrible defeat at Aspern-Essling, he regrouped with 188,900 men for an all-out push against 146,000 Austrians on the Danube. Crossing this river on July 4–5, Napoleon engaged the Austrian forces in the culminating Battle of Wagram beginning on July 5. The battle continued the next day and would stand with Leipzig and Borodino as the bloodiest clash of the NAPOLEONIC WARS. Napoleon lost 24 percent of his army during these two days, 6,901 killed and 26,757 wounded (some authorities put the losses even higher). Austria lost 5,631 killed, 18,119 wounded, and 18,000 captured (again, some historians believe the losses were significantly greater). Despite his staggering losses, Napoleon forced the retreat of the Austrians, who, fighting a desperate rearguard action, sued for an armistice on July 10. While this ended fighting on the main Bavarian front, combat in the Tyrol continued until the conclusion of the Treaty of Schönbrunn on October 14, whereupon the Austrians summarily abandoned the Tyrolean rebels. These warriors were finally pacified the following year.

By terms of the October treaty, Austria ceded some 32,000 square miles of territory and 3 million of its 16 million subjects.

Further reading: James R. Arnold, *Napoleon Conquers Austria: The 1809 Campaign for Vienna* (Westport, Conn.: Greenwood Publishing Group, 1995); Robert M. Epstein, *Napoleon's Last Victory and the Emergence of Modern War* (Lawrence: University Press of Kansas, 1994).

Napoleon's Waterloo Campaign
See HUNDRED DAY'S WAR.

Naresuen's First Invasion of Burma
See SIAMESE-BURMESE WAR.

Naresuen's Second Invasion of Burma
See BURMESE CIVIL WAR (1599); SIAMESE-BURMESE WAR.

Natchez Revolt (1729)

PRINCIPAL COMBATANTS: Natchez Indians vs. French settlers
PRINCIPAL THEATER(S): Lower Mississippi Valley
DECLARATION: None
MAJOR ISSUES AND OBJECTIVES: Natchez resistance to French invasion
OUTCOME: The Natchez were defeated.
APPROXIMATE MAXIMUM NUMBER OF MEN UNDER ARMS: Unknown
CASUALTIES: At least 200 colonists in initial raids
TREATIES: None

In the 18th century, the Natchez Indians lived just east of the present-day Mississippi city that bears their name. On November 28, 1729, the tribe attacked Fort Rosalie, a French settlement and military outpost, killing about 200 French colonists. The initial assault was followed by scattered raids throughout the lower Mississippi Valley. The "revolt" was the culmination of long-deteriorating relations between the French and the Natchez. There had been outbursts of violence in the past, but open warfare had been avoided largely through the diplomacy of Tattooed Serpent, brother of the Natchez principal chief, known as the Great Sun. After the death of Tattooed Serpent, however, the French governor of Louisiana, Sieur Chepart (d. 1729), summarily ordered the removal of the Natchez from their sacred Great Village, opposite Fort Rosalie on the bluffs of the Mississippi. Even at this outrage, the tribal "queen mother," Tattooed Arm, counseled peace, but to no avail. The Natchez Revolt was under way.

Among those taken captive in the attack on Fort Rosalie was the governor, whom the Natchez warriors regarded with such contempt that none of them would defile a weapon by taking his life. Sieur Chepart's execution was assigned to a Stinkard, a member of the lowest caste in the hierarchy of Natchez society. Death by the blade was deemed too noble, and the Stinkard was ordered to club the governor to death.

French colonial officials retaliated against the Natchez with vigor, dispatching several invasion forces out of New Orleans. The Natchez and the Yazoo Indians, who had joined in the uprising, were soon defeated in battle. Those captured (about 400) were sold into West Indian slavery. Survivors who evaded capture sought refuge among the Chickasaws.

The defeat of the Natchez brought peace to the lower Mississippi Valley only until 1732, when the French renewed prior demands that the Chickasaws expel English traders from their villages and, with them, refugees from the Natchez Revolt (see CHICKASAW RESISTANCE).

Further reading: Alan Axelrod, *Chronicle of the Indian Wars: From Colonial Times to Wounded Knee* (New York: Prentice Hall General Reference, 1993); Wilcomb E. Washburn, *The Cambridge History of the Native Peoples of the Americas*, 3 vols. (New York: Cambridge University Press, 1996–2000).

Nat Turner's Rebellion   *See* TURNER'S REBELLION.

Navajo War (1861–1863)

PRINCIPAL COMBATANTS: Navajo Indians vs. United States
PRINCIPAL THEATER(S): New Mexico
DECLARATION: None
MAJOR ISSUES AND OBJECTIVES: The Navajos were responding to the provocations of New Mexican settlers and an unprovoked attack by the U.S. Army with raids; the United States intended to subdue the Navajos and imprison them at Bosque Redondo to keep them from hampering its war against the Confederacy, or worse, from joining forces with the South's Rebels.
OUTCOME: The Navajos were defeated under a harsh, take-no-prisoners campaign by the U.S. Army and forced en masse onto Bosque Redondo.
APPROXIMATE MAXIMUM NUMBER OF MEN UNDER ARMS: Kit Carson's regiment, 736; Navajo, unknown
CASUALTIES: Navajo, around 500 killed or died, wounded unknown, 8,000 taken captive and forced onto Bosque Redondo; U.S. and CSA—Unknown
TREATIES: None, but a later Peace Commission, formed to investigate the charges of inhumane conditions at Bosque Redondo, negotiated a treaty in 1868 that returned the Navajo to their traditional homelands in New Mexico.

At the beginning of the American Civil War, the United States found itself faced not only with half a country in rebellion (see UNITED STATES CIVIL WAR: WESTERN THEATER), but also two major Indian uprisings—one with the Apaches (see APACHE UPRISING), the other with the Navajos. The outbreak of civil war drained the army of the West, especially its officers. One-third of the army's officer corps—313 officers—left primarily western commands to take up arms on the side of the Confederacy. At this time, Confederate Lieutenant Colonel John Robert Baylor (1822–94) took advantage of the Union army's weakness to sweep through the southern New Mexico Territory,

from the Rio Grande to California, and proclaim the Confederate Territory of Arizona, which encompassed all of present-day Arizona as well as New Mexico south of the 34th parallel. Baylor appointed himself governor. There was not much the Union could do about it. Colonel Edward R. S. Canby (1817–73), commander of the Department of New Mexico, had his hands full with Navajo raids in New Mexico and unauthorized, provocative New Mexican counterraids.

Indeed, the very people Canby was trying to protect, the citizens of New Mexico, repeatedly provoked the Navajo by raiding them and taking captives whom they subsequently sold as slaves. In retaliation, the Navajo, joined by Mescalero Apaches, Utes, Comanches, and Kiowas, ravaged the countryside in the spring of 1860. Learning that the majority of New Mexicans were loyal to the Union, Canby hastily sought to organize them as the First and Second Regiments of New Mexican Volunteers. This gesture, however, failed to bring the volunteers under Canby's control.

In September and October 1860, New Mexico volunteers invaded Canyon de Chelly and destroyed Navajo crops, seized Navajo livestock, and took Navajo captives, killing one of the major peace-minded chiefs—Zarcillos Largos (d. 1860). The attack marked a period in Navajo history that the Indians came to call "the Fearing Time," a period of war and, ultimately, of defeat and exile.

Meanwhile, Navajos, Utes, and Apaches continued to raid freely as the distracted U.S. Army geared up to meet the Confederate invasion of New Mexico. Then, at Fort Faunteroy on September 13, 1861, the New Mexico volunteers engaged in a massacre of Navajos gathered there peacefully, enraging tribesmen and swelling the ranks of the war-minded faction, whose members—led by Manuelito (c. 1818–93)—struck out with renewed fury.

It had become clear to Canby that the army proper was going to have to take the matter in hand, and he proposed a firm policy for dealing with the Navajos. Those, he announced, who agreed to settle on a reservation would be spared and protected by the United States government; those who refused would be branded enemies and hunted down. It fell to Canby's successor—General James H. Carleton (1814–73)—to carry out the plan.

A veteran Indian fighter, Carleton was also considered a humanitarian, which in the second half of the 19th century meant he wished to see a transformation of Native American culture and the ultimate assimilation of the Indians into Anglo-American society. To further that end, he set up a reservation at Bosque Redondo, a barren flat on eastern New Mexico's Pecos River. He then turned his attention to the Mescaleros, whom he quickly defeated and resettled on the reservation. Then, he unleashed on the Navajos his best colonel—Christopher Houston "Kit" Carson (1809–69). Ordered to prosecute his campaign until headquarters concluded that the Navajo had been effectively punished, Carson succeeded in killing 13 warriors before the end of the month, taking 11 women and children captive. Far more significant was the widespread destruction of Navajo fields and orchards. Carleton offered a $20 bounty for each horse or mule captured and a dollar for each sheep. Although Navajo raiding continued—10,000 sheep were stolen in August alone—the Indians did begin to surrender to confinement at the Bosque Redondo: 51 at the end of September, 188 in November, more than 500 in January. By March, a total of 2,138 Navajos were sent from Fort Canby, New Mexico, to the Bosque.

Not to be satisfied, however, until every last Navajo had been consigned to the reservation, Carleton pressed his campaign relentlessly. He repeatedly admonished Carson and his officers that they were to negotiate nothing with the Navajo, for the Indians' choice was as simple as it was absolute: either go to the Bosque or be destroyed. On December 31, 1863, Carleton issued an order for the kind of hard winter campaign soldiers dreaded almost as much as the Indians did.

On January 6, 1864, Carson and 389 officers and men set out from Fort Canby to strike from the west the Navajo's ancient stronghold, Canyon de Chelly. Two more companies approached from the east. On January 12, a patrol in advance of Carson's main body engaged a party of Navajo, killing 11 of them. Otherwise, Carson's command fought no Navajos. Instead, on January 15, 60 Navajos surrendered to Carson, complaining that the ceaseless warfare was starving them. After destroying dwellings and orchards, Carson declared the Canyon de Chelly Expedition ended, and even more Navajos dejectedly marched off to the Bosque. By late 1864, three-quarters of the Navajo tribe had accepted concentration on the reservation.

The Bosque Redondo was a place to be dreaded. Although government wagons were furnished to transport the very young, the old, and the infirm, the remainder took an infamous "Long Walk." Conditions at Fort Canby, the jumping-off point for the Bosque, were deplorable, and 126 Navajos died of dysentery there. More died en route to the Bosque itself; reportedly, some, no longer able to march, were shot by their soldier escorts. The entire affair was reminiscent of the Cherokees' Trail of Tears. Eventually, 8,000 Navajos crowded the reservation, but, with an inefficiency and inhumanity that had become routine, the government failed to supply sufficient rations to feed this population. To his credit, General Carleton was unremitting in his pleas for 2 million pounds of food, 13,000 yards of cloth for clothing, 7,000 blankets, 20 spinning wheels, 50 mills for grinding corn, farm implements, and seeds. Finally—perhaps it was his special nod toward the amenities of white civilization—Carleton asked for 600 cotton handkerchiefs.

Congress did appropriate funds, but the amount fell short of what was needed. Attempts to teach the traditionally peripatetic Navajo and Apache Indians sedentary farming techniques likewise failed. By 1864, conditions at "Fair Carletonia"—as the soldiers sardonically christened the Bosque—were desperate. After enduring through 1868, Manuelito, Barboncito, and other chiefs were permitted to journey to Washington, D.C., to inform President Andrew Johnson of conditions at the reservation. A month later, peace commissioners visited the Bosque Redondo and concluded that the Navajos "had sunk into a condition of absolute poverty and despair." A treaty was concluded on June 1, 1868, returning the Indians to their homeland and declaring it their new reservation.

Further reading: Alan Axelrod, *Chronicle of the Indian Wars: From Colonial Times to Wounded Knee* (New York: Prentice Hall General Reference, 1993); Alvin M. Josephy, *The Civil War in the American West* (New York: Alfred A. Knopf, 1991); F. Stanley, *The Apaches of New Mexico, 1549–1590* (Pampa, Tex.: Pampa Print Shops, 1962); Ruth Roessel, ed., *Navajo Stories of the Long Walk Period* (Tsaile, Ariz.: Navajo Community College Press, 1973); Robert M. Utley, *The Indian Frontier of the American West, 1845–1890* (Albuquerque: University of New Mexico Press, 1984).

Neapolitan Revolt (1485–1486)

PRINCIPAL COMBATANTS: Angevin barons vs. Ferdinand I of Naples
PRINCIPAL THEATER(S): Naples
DECLARATION: None
MAJOR ISSUES AND OBJECTIVES: The Angevin barons, oppressed by high taxes, sought to overthrow Ferdinand I.
OUTCOME: With the aid of Lorenzo de' Medici of Florence, Ferdinand I defeated the barons and maintained his throne.
APPROXIMATE MAXIMUM NUMBER OF MEN UNDER ARMS: Unknown
CASUALTIES: Unknown
TREATIES: None

Ferdinand I (1423–94) ruled Naples with an iron fist, imposing a heavy tax burden on the Angevin barons of that city-state. At length, the barons rebelled against Ferdinand in 1485, seeking to replace him with René II (1451–1508) of Lorraine or Frederick of Aragon, Ferdinand's own second son. At first, Ferdinand acted against the rebellion through police actions, including arrests of subversives, followed by trials and executions, but as the movement against him gained ground, especially after Pope Innocent VIII (1432–92) threw his support behind the barons, he appealed to Lorenzo de' Medici (1449–92) of Florence for military assistance (*see* FLORENTINE WAR WITH THE PAPAL STATES). Lorenzo's intervention in 1486 defeated the papal supporters of the Angevin barons and preserved Ferdinand on the throne. This, in turn, led Milan's Lodovico Sforza (1451–1508), who feared Ferdinand's growing power, to invite Charles VIII (1470–98) of France to intervene in the wars among the Italian city-states. (*See* ITALIAN WAR OF CHARLES VIII.)

Further reading: Benedetto Croce, *History of the Kingdom of Naples* (Chicago: University of Chicago Press, 1970); Christopher Duggan, *A Concise History of Italy* (New York: Cambridge University Press, 1994); Charles L. Killinger, *The History of Italy* (Westport, Conn.: Greenwood Publishing, 2002).

Neapolitan Revolt (1820–1821)

PRINCIPAL COMBATANTS: Neapolitan nationalists (Muratists) vs. Ferdinand I, king of the Two Sicilies (backed by the Holy Alliance)
PRINCIPAL THEATER(S): Naples
DECLARATION: None
MAJOR ISSUES AND OBJECTIVES: The Muratists rebelled against the despotism of Ferdinand I.
OUTCOME: Ferdinand I secured Austrian aid in crushing the rebellion and reestablishing despotic rule over Naples.
APPROXIMATE MAXIMUM NUMBER OF MEN UNDER ARMS: Neapolitans: 50,000; Holy Alliance: 60,000
CASUALTIES: Unknown
TREATIES: None

The fall of Napoleon (1769–1821) in 1815 brought an end to the Decennio, the decade of French rule in Italy. Resented by Italian nationalists, Napoleon's puppets were often admired by liberals for the political reforms they brought in their wake. Thus, when the old despot, Ferdinand I (1751–1825) was restored as king of the Two Sicilies (that is, Naples and Sicily), the Muratists, followers of Joachim Murat (1767–1815), the late Napoleonic king of Naples, attempted to carry out democratic reforms to government under Ferdinand's reactionary rule. When the reforms failed, a Muratist cavalry regiment mutinied in the town of Nola on July 11, 1820. Ferdinand I called on the army to put down the mutiny, but the officers, sympathetic to the Muratist soldiers, refused. Their cause attracted support from the Carbonari, a nationalist fraternity that had been formed under the French dominance and had since become chief among those groups calling for a liberal revolution against Ferdinand. Led by veteran general Guglielmo Pepe (1783–1855), the insurgency burgeoned and the violence magnified into a week of riot and revolt. The king felt that he had no choice but to grant Naples the con-

stitution the revolutionaries sought. However, a Sicilian junta opposed the Neapolitan constitution, and the new Neapolitan parliament sent an army under Pietro Colletta (1775–1831) to suppress the Sicilian government. This touched off a revolt in Palermo, the chief city of Sicily, which prompted the Holy Alliance, a reactionary league of European nations, to send troops to "restore order" in Sicily and Naples. The Neapolitans called on Ferdinand I to travel to Ljubljana, Austria (today the capital of Slovenia), to block intervention from the Holy Alliance. He agreed to go but betrayed Naples by formally requesting military aid from Austria. Sixty thousand Austrian troops marched on Naples in March 1821. The Neapolitan army, consisting of some 50,000 citizen-soldiers mobilized by the constitutionalists, could hardly stand up to the Hapsburg regulars. They crumpled even before the Austrians reached the border. Ferdinand resumed his despotic reign over Naples and denounced the constitution. He enforced his rule by means of an Austrian army of occupation, which remained in Naples through 1827.

Further reading: Benedetto Croce, *History of the Kingdom of Naples* (Chicago: University of Chicago Press, 1970); Christopher Duggan, *A Concise History of Italy* (New York: Cambridge University Press, 1994); Charles L. Killinger, *The History of Italy* (Westport, Conn.: Greenwood Publishing, 2002).

Netherlands' War of Independence
See EIGHTY YEARS' WAR.

Nebuchadnezzar's Campaigns
(605–561 B.C.E.)

PRINCIPAL COMBATANTS: Babylon vs. (variously) Judah, Arab tribes, and Egypt
PRINCIPAL THEATER(S): Judah, Syria, Palestine, and Egypt
DECLARATION: None
MAJOR ISSUES AND OBJECTIVES: Conquest; expansion of the Babylonian Empire
OUTCOME: Despite some reversals, Nebuchadnezzar was an active and successful conqueror, who greatly enlarged Babylon in extent and influence.
APPROXIMATE MAXIMUM NUMBER OF MEN UNDER ARMS: Unknown
CASUALTIES: Unknown
TREATIES: Unknown

Nebuchadnezzar II (c. 630–562 B.C.E.) was the second king of the Chaldean dynasty of Babylonia. His entire reign, from about 605 to about 561 B.C.E., was marked by military campaigns. His first significant campaign came in 607–606, when, as crown prince under his father, Nabopolassar (fl. 625–605 B.C.E.), he commanded an army in the mountains north of Assyria. When Nabopolassar returned to Babylon, Nebuchadnezzar led military operations entirely in his own right.

When Babylonian forces were defeated in battle by the Egyptians during 606–605, Nebuchadnezzar was appointed to command Babylonian forces. He proved a brilliant general—far superior to his father—and defeated the Egyptian army at the battles of Carchemish and Hamath. These victories gave Babylon control of all Syria.

Following the death of Nabopolassar on August 16, 605, Nebuchadnezzar returned to Babylon and assumed the throne. Then, between June and December of 604, after receiving the submission of local states, including Judah, he captured the important city of Ashqelon. He set about expanding his armies by hiring Greek mercenaries, whom he sent campaigning into Palestine. Within three years, Babylon controlled the region. However, during 601–600, his armies tangled with Egyptian forces and suffered severe losses. This defeat precipitated the desertion of some vassal states, including Judah.

During 600–599 B.C.E., Nebuchadnezzar regrouped his forces and, in particular, repaired and refitted his war chariots. By the end of 599–598 (December to March), Nebuchadnezzar resumed campaigning to regain control of Palestine. He attacked the Arab tribes of northwestern Arabia to clear the way for an assault on and occupation of Judah. That attack came in 597, and on March 16 of that year, Nebuchadnezzar took Jerusalem, ousting the king, Jehoiachin, and deporting him to Babylon.

After the conquest of Judah, Nebuchadnezzar led a campaign into Syria during 596–595. However, he had to return to Babylonia to repel a threatened invasion of the eastern portion of his realm, apparently from Elam (southwestern Iran). Nebuchadnezzar also faced internal dissension during this period. Late in 595–594, a rebellion broke out among some elements of the army. Evidently, the rebellion was extinguished, because Nebuchadnezzar launched two new campaigns in Syria during 594.

Nebuchadnezzar's military activities after 594 are not recorded in any surviving chronicles, but are mentioned in the Old Testament. Here we learn of another attack on Jerusalem and a 13-year siege against Tyre. Nebuchadnezzar may also have invaded Egypt. According to the Bible, the second siege of Jerusalem was successful. The city fell to Nebuchadnezzar in 587–586. Nebuchadnezzar purged the city of certain prominent citizens, who were deported to Babylon. A second wave of deportations occurred in 582.

Fragmentary cuneiform references suggest that Nebuchadnezzar's culminating operation was an invasion of Egypt, in 568–567 B.C.E.

See also ASSYRIA, FALL OF; MEGIDDO, SECOND BATTLE OF; NINEVEH, FALL OF.

Further reading: Sabatino Moscati, *Ancient Semitic Civilizations* (New York: G. P. Putnam's Sons, Capricorn Books, 1960); Donald John Wiseman, *Nebuchadnezzar and Babylon* (London: Oxford University Press, 1985).

Neuchâtel, Insurrection at (1856–1857)

PRINCIPAL COMBATANTS: Neuchâtel republicans vs. Neuchâtel royalists (backed by Prussia)
PRINCIPAL THEATER(S): Neuchâtel, Switzerland
DECLARATION: None
MAJOR ISSUES AND OBJECTIVES: The royalists sought to overthrow the republican government of Neuchâtel and establish Prussia's Frederick William IV as prince of Neuchâtel.
OUTCOME: A stand-off developed between Prussia and Neuchâtel, but war was averted by diplomatic compromise.
APPROXIMATE MAXIMUM NUMBER OF MEN UNDER ARMS: Unknown
CASUALTIES: None
TREATIES: Compromise of 1857

The Congress of Vienna that followed the conclusion of the NAPOLEONIC WARS temporized in the case of Neuchâtel, establishing it simultaneously as a new Swiss canton and as the property of the king of Prussia. This prompted the Swiss to rebel in 1848, a year in which revolution swept Europe, and to declare Neuchâtel a republic. In 1852, the major European powers responded with the London Protocol, which confirmed the rights of Prussia's Frederick William IV (1795–1861) to the canton, but also advised him to forestall action unless the powers concurred. Frederick William agreed to the London Protocol but nevertheless endorsed a coup by Neuchâtel's royalists in 1856. The coup d'état fizzled, resulting in the mass arrest of 530 aristocrats. When the republic of Neuchâtel refused to release the plotters, Prussia vowed to go to war. The Swiss then mobilized for combat as well, but war was staved off by the diplomatic intervention of France's Napoleon III (1808–73). He decided to back the claims of Neuchâtel, and the British supported this decision. Frederick William was thus put in an embarrassing position, which French diplomats resolved by suggesting that he retain his title of prince of Neuchâtel but simultaneously renounce sovereignty over it, thereby allowing the canton to remain an independent republic. In return, Neuchâtel officials agreed to release the aristocrats without taking further action against them. Prussia and Neuchâtel demobilized their armies, and war was averted.

Further reading: Edgar Bonjour, H. S. Offler, and G. R. Potter, *A Short History of Switzerland* (Westport, Conn.:

Greenwood Press, 1985); William Martin, *Switzerland: From Roman Times to the Present* (London: Elek, 1971).

Nez Percé War (Chief Joseph's Uprising) (1877)

PRINCIPAL COMBATANTS: Nez Percé Indians vs. United States

PRINCIPAL THEATER(S): Portions of Idaho, Washington, Oregon, and Montana

DECLARATION: No formal declaration

MAJOR ISSUES AND OBJECTIVES: A Nez Percé faction refused to relinquish their lands and move to a reservation; when pressured by the United States, they fled for Canada; the U.S. Army sought to prevent their escape and their joining Sioux leader Sitting Bull in Canada

OUTCOME: Nez Percé surrender and removal to reservations

APPROXIMATE MAXIMUM NUMBER OF MEN UNDER ARMS: United States—5,000; Nez Percé—300 warriors

CASUALTIES: United States, civilian and military—92 killed, about 57 wounded; Nez Percé—(according to Nelson Miles) 120 killed in action, 205 died en route, 150 captured and turned over to Cheyenne, wounded unknown, though many who survived the journey, wounded, sick, or exhausted, died soon thereafter

TREATIES: None

The Nez Percé of central Idaho, southeastern Washington, northeastern Oregon, and parts of Montana fell into sharply divided "treaty" (pro-white) and "non-treaty" (anti-white) factions after an 1863 gold rush had prompted a revision of an earlier treaty that had defined the boundaries of the Nez Percé homelands. The revised covenant carved the mineral-rich lands out of the original allocation. Those Indians whose homes remained within the revised boundaries signed the treaty; those who were dispossessed refused to sign. Prominent among the latter was the revered Chief Joseph (d. 1871), who repudiated the treaty and lived with his people in land now claimed by the government.

For many years, few whites were actually interested in the particular area, however, and Joseph was left in peace. Indeed, in 1873, two years after Joseph's death, President Ulysses S. Grant (1822–85) set aside part of the Wallowa Valley as a reservation. At this very time, however, Oregon settlers began to covet the land for grazing and lobbied for its reopening to white settlement. General Oliver O. Howard (1830–1909) headed a negotiating committee charged with persuading the nontreaty Nez Percés to leave the disputed lands. The conference, which took place between November 12 and November 15, 1876, broke down, but Young Joseph (c. 1840–1904), who had become

chief upon the death of his father, nevertheless marched off with the nontreaty faction to the reservation, realizing that war with the whites would be useless.

As was frequently the case, the younger men in the tribe could not reconcile themselves to the situation. On June 13 and 14, 1877, while traveling to the reservation, some young warriors, drunk, killed four whites. Although Young Joseph tried to convince his followers to seek reconciliation with white authorities, the nontreaty Indians now decided to turn south, toward the Salmon River, instead of continuing to the reservation, and in the course of their run, 15 more settlers were slain.

General Howard dispatched 100 cavalrymen under Captain David Perry out of Fort Lapwai. Persuaded by panic-stricken civilians to strike, Perry confronted the Indians on June 17 at White Bird Canyon. Joseph sent a delegation under a flag of truce, intending to talk peace, but a party of trigger-happy civilian volunteers opened fire, inciting an attack on Perry's troops, one-third of whom—more than 30 men—were killed.

On June 22, Howard moved about 400 men to White Bird Canyon. Once again, a Nez Percé leader, Chief Looking Glass (c. 1823–77), offered reconciliation, and, once again, civilian volunteers attached to the army force provoked a fight. Under attack on July 1, the regulars trained their Gatling guns against the village, killing several people, including women and children, and sending Looking Glass over to the side of the hostiles.

Ten days of pursuit and attack followed, with the Indians usually maintaining the advantage. On July 9 and 10, the Indians besieged a force of volunteers at a place the whites dubbed Mount Misery. Howard was able to bring his main force to the Nez Percés' rear, and on July 11, the two-day Battle of Clearwater began, which ended in the Indians' withdrawal. However, exhausted by the battle, Howard could not give chase and thereby failed to bring the war with the Nez Percé to an immediate conclusion.

The army pursued the fugitive Indians until August 9, when Colonel John O. Gibbon (1827–96), leading 15 officers, 146 enlisted regulars, and 45 volunteers, surprised a camp on the Big Hole River, Montana. Looking Glass led a quick and successful counterattack, killing two of Gibbon's officers, 22 regulars, and six civilians, and wounding five more officers, 30 enlisted men, and four civilians. The Nez Percés then traveled 100 miles, killing nine whites, seizing 250 horses, and raiding a wagon train before they entered the newly established Yellowstone National Park, where they terrorized visitors.

Howard gave chase while the seventh Cavalry, under Colonel Samuel D. Sturgis (1822–76), attempted unsuccessfully to block the escape route. On August 19, 200 warriors skirmished with troopers on Camas Meadows and made off with 150 army mules, having killed one trooper and wounded seven. On September 13, the seventh Cavalry engaged Nez Percé at the site of present-day

Billings, Montana, and, once again, the army took serious casualties. Sturgis lost three men killed and 11 wounded.

The Nez Percés fled northward, toward Canada, where they hoped Sitting Bull (c. 1831–90), in exile there, would welcome them. But, only 40 miles south of the border, they paused to rest. On September 30, on the northern edge of the Bear Paw Mountains, they were attacked by about 400 regulars under Colonel Nelson A. Miles (1839–1925). The Indians dug in, and the Battle of Bear Paw Mountain lasted six snowy, miserable days, from September 30 to October 5.

During the battle, the Indians held council. Chief Joseph argued for surrender. Looking Glass wanted to fight, but they agreed to talk terms. On October 1, under a flag of truce, Joseph went to meet Miles to negotiate surrender terms. Talks broke down, and Miles decided to hold the chief hostage but exchanged him for one of his own men held captive. On October 5, Looking Glass was struck in the forehead by a stray bullet and killed, whereupon Chief Joseph surrendered to Miles, making a speech of heart-wrenching, desperate eloquence:

> I am tired of fighting. Our chiefs are killed. Looking Glass is dead. Toohoolhoolzote is dead. The old men are all dead. It is the young men who say yes or no. He who led on the young men [Joseph's brother, Ollokot] is dead. It is cold and we have no blankets. The little children are freezing to death. My people, some of them, have run away to the hills, and have no blankets, no food; no one knows where they are—perhaps freezing to death. I want to have time to look for my children and see how many of them I can find. Maybe I shall find them among the dead. Hear me, my chiefs! I am tired; my heart is sick and sad. From where the sun now stands I will fight no more forever.

For three months, 800 Nez Percés traveled more than 1,700 miles, consistently eluding or defeating the army. Chief Joseph, aided by Miles and Howard, who had come to respect him deeply, spent the rest of his life unsuccessfully petitioning for the land originally promised by President Grant. Joseph died on a reservation in 1904.

Further reading: Alan Axelrod, *Chronicle of the Indian Wars: From Colonial Times to Wounded Knee* (New York: Prentice Hall General Reference, 1993); Merrill D. Beal, *"I Will Fight No More Forever": Chief Joseph and the Nez Percé War* (Seattle: University of Washington Press, 1963); Mark H. Brown, *The Flight of the Nez Percé* (Lincoln: University of Nebraska Press, 1967); Alvin M. Josephy, *The Nez Percé Indians and the Opening of the Northwest* (New Haven, Conn.: Yale University Press, 1965).

Nian Rebellion (1853–1868)

PRINCIPAL COMBATANTS: Nian (Nien) rebels vs. Manchu China

PRINCIPAL THEATER(S): Yellow (Huang) River Valley of China

DECLARATION: None

MAJOR ISSUES AND OBJECTIVES: The Nian rebelled against the ineffectual Manchu government.

OUTCOME: For many years, the Nian controlled much of northern China, but, following the death of their leader, the movement began to collapse, and the rebellion was crushed by 1868.

APPROXIMATE MAXIMUM NUMBER OF MEN UNDER ARMS: Nian rebels, 50,000

CASUALTIES: Civilian and military casualties, more than 4 million

TREATIES: None

An offshoot of the Buddhist-inspired White Lotus secret societies, the Nian were outlaw bands of Chinese peasants army deserters, and smugglers living along the Yellow River, who had raided the Manchu (Qing or Ch'ing) Empire sporadically since the early 1800s. Victims of long-term famine, they took to plundering Anhui (Anwei), Henan (Honan), and Shandong (Shantung) during the early 1850s when the Manchus were preoccupied with the TAIPING REBELLION. Soon, the Nian assumed paramilitary status, fortifying villages and using these as bases from which to conduct their raids. The Manchu government acted ineffectually against the Nian, who now numbered between 30,000 and 50,000, organized into five armies, and who came to control much of northern China, establishing in this region a kind of shadow government.

The death of the Nian leader Zhang Luoxing (Chang Lo-hsing) in 1863 at the government's siege at Zhi-ho (Chih-ho), the Nian citadel, brought disorder to the Nian. Had they been able to coordinate their actions with the Taiping rebels of southern China, the Manchu dynasty might well have been overthrown. But, disorganized now, the Nian fell prey to an imperial assault under a series of generals, Senggelinqin (Seng-ko lin-ch'in; d. 1865), Zeng Guofan (Tseng Kuo-fan; 1811–72), and Li Hongzhang (Li Huang-chang; 1823–1901). The imperial troops laid siege to all of the Nian fortress villages, starving the inhabitants into surrender. Through systematic sieges, the rebellion was put down by 1868.

Further reading: Jean Chesneaux, comp., *Secret Societies in China in the Nineteenth and Twentieth Centuries* (Ann Arbor: University of Michigan Press, 1971); Albert Feuerwerker, *Rebellion in Nineteenth Century China* (Ann Arbor: University of Michigan Press, 1975); Elizabeth J. Perry, *Rebels and Rebellion in North China, 1845–1945* (Palo Alto, Calif.: Stanford University Press, 1980).

Nicaragua, Spanish Conquest of See SPANISH CONQUEST OF NICARAGUA.

Nicaraguan Civil War (1909–1912)

PRINCIPAL COMBATANTS: Conservative Party opposition (backed by U.S. intervention) vs. the nationalist forces of President José Santos Zelaya.

PRINCIPAL THEATER(S): Nicaragua

DECLARATION: Demonstrations against Zelaya's government began at Bluefields on October 10, 1909.

MAJOR ISSUES AND OBJECTIVES: Conservatives, supported by the United States, rebelled against nationalist and dictatorial government.

OUTCOME: Installation of a Conservative Party regime, friendly to the United States

APPROXIMATE MAXIMUM NUMBER OF MEN UNDER ARMS: Fewer than 1,000 U.S. Marines; rebel and government forces at variable strength

CASUALTIES: Unknown

TREATIES: None

A backwater of the old Spanish Empire, Nicaragua had been inspired by the revolutions in Mexico and El Salvador to depose its imperial intendant in 1811. When Guatemala declared its independence from Spain in 1821, both countries united briefly with Mexico but often fought against one another for supremacy until 1826, when Nicaragua joined the United Provinces of Central America. By the time it seceded from that federation in 1838, liberal and conservative factions were already battling with each other and would continue to do so throughout Nicaraguan history. The discovery of gold in California in 1848 made Nicaragua a strategic location for interocean travel, which caught the attention of U.S. railroad and shipping magnate Cornelius Vanderbilt (1794–1877). Backing the Conservative Party, Vanderbilt just about owned the country when famed soldier of fortune William Walker (1824–60) attempted his ill-starred invasion at the behest of the Liberals, then made himself president in 1856 (see WALKER'S INVASION OF NICARAGUA.)

After Vanderbilt's transit-company army and the forces of five republics from the former United Provinces routed Walker the following year, Nicaragua was ruled until 1893 by Conservatives, supported by the United States and routinely in the pay of North America's profit-minded big business interests. The Conservatives brought relative peace but little in the way of freedom or democracy to the people of Nicaragua, and they were ousted by the Liberal presidency of José Santos Zelaya (1853–1919).

Zelaya, a committed nationalist but a brutal dictator, promoted schemes for Central American reunification and refused to grant U.S. businesses the kind of concessions they demanded to build a canal across his country, which encouraged Theodore Roosevelt (1858–1919) and his friends to turn to Panama. As if that weren't dangerous enough, rumors spread that Zelaya planned to invite Japan to construct a canal that would compete with the projected U.S. waterway. Not content to alienate U.S. business interests and foil North American "progress," Zelaya displayed open hostility toward U.S. diplomats in the capital, Managua. The United States promptly turned its support to Zelaya's Conservative opposition and urged its members to stage a revolt.

Juan J. Estrada, Adolfo Díaz (1874–1964), and Emiliano Chamorro Vargas (1871–1966) led a group of powerful and influential Nicaraguans in the rebellion beginning on October 10, 1909. At first localized near Bluefields, on Nicaragua's eastern coast, the conflict slowly spread west. Two American citizens, Leonard Croce and Leroy Canon, volunteered for service as officers in Chamorro's revolutionary army and were captured by Zelaya's troops. Despite the warnings of his own advisers, Zelaya ordered the execution of the two Americans, an act that prompted U.S. secretary of state Philander Knox (1853–1921) to sever diplomatic relations with the Zelaya government on December 1, 1909.

Simultaneously, the navy was ordered to organize the Nicaraguan Expeditionary Brigade of marines, which arrived at Cristobal, Canal Zone, on December 12. The marines then boarded the USS *Buffalo* bound for Corinto, Nicaragua. Their arrival in Nicaragua persuaded Zelaya to resign office, on December 16, in favor of José Madriz (fl. 1909–10) and to flee to political asylum in Mexico. Immediately, relations with the United States improved, and the marines sailed back to Panama on March 22, 1910.

The departure of Zelaya by no means left Nicaragua peaceful, however. In the vicinity of Bluefields, where the revolt had started, fighting broke out between rebels loyal to Juan J. Estrada and forces loyal to President Madriz. Seeking to restore order, U.S. naval commander William W. Gilmer, skipper of the USS *Paducah*, riding off Bluefields, issued a proclamation to both sides forbidding fighting within the city. Gilmer requested a contingent of marines to enforce his proclamation. Two hundred marines under Major Smedley D. Butler (1881–1940) arrived from the Canal Zone on May 30.

The principal dispute at Bluefields was the disposition of the customs house there. Estrada's rebels had seized it and used it as a source of finance. On May 27, Madriz's army retook it, even though Estrada's forces still occupied the city. Estrada demanded that customs duties be paid to his men in the city, whereas Madriz insisted that they be paid at the customs house he now controlled. U.S. authorities, feeling that Madriz was becoming dictatorial and dangerous, ordered that customs duties be paid to Estrada. This provided the financial support he needed to continue his revolt against Madriz. While the U.S. Marines maintained civil order in Bluefields—and oversaw the rebuilding of the local hospital, market, and sanitary facilities there—Estrada took Managua on August 23. He was inaugurated as president on August 30, and, on September 4, the Marines pulled out of Bluefields and sailed back to Panama.

However, Nicaragua was still rocked by unrest. Zelaya's followers were still active, and many in Estrada's own party became dissatisfied over the paltry shares of power and spoils they received. Nicaraguans more generally objected to U.S. imperialism and the various trade considerations and monopolies the United States received. When fighting broke out in Managua, Elliott Northcott (1869–1946), U.S. minister to Nicaragua, persuaded Estrada to resign in favor of his vice president, Adolfo Díaz. This relieved tensions for a short time, but in 1912, General Luis Mena, who had been war minister under Estrada, took a portion of the army to Masaya and then instigated the seizure of American-owned steamships on Lake Managua.

U.S. officials appealed to Díaz for assistance. He replied, in turn, with a request for U.S. military aid, and 100 sailors from the USS *Annapolis* arrived in Managua on August 4, 1912, while 353 marines, under Smedley Butler, set off from Panama for Corinto. On August 14, the Marines and 80 more seamen left Corinto by train for Managua, arriving on August 15. Thus backed, George F. Weitzel (b. 1873), who had replaced Northcott as minister in Managua, demanded that Mena immediately return the vessels that had been appropriated. When Mena refused, more marines were called up.

On September 6, the First and Second Marine Battalions of the First Provisional Regiment, Colonel Joseph H. Pendleton (1860–1942) commanding, arrived in Managua to join the small force already there. Assuming command of the combined forces, Pendleton loaded three marine companies onto a train bound for Granada, to confront Mena. At La Barranca, a hill near the town of Masaya, the forces of General Benjamin Zeledon (1879–1912), a supporter of Mena, blocked the train. Butler set up a conference between Pendleton (along with Admiral William H. H. Southerland [1852–1933]) and Zeledon, who eventually agreed to allow the marines to pass. On September 19, however, within the city limits of Masaya, revolutionary troops ambushed the train, which, putting on full speed, managed to get through the city without serious harm. At San Blas, on the outskirts of Granada, Butler informed General Mena's representatives that he would attack Granada if Mena did not surrender. Ailing, Mena gave up in return for safe conduct to political asylum in Panama.

The marines had achieved control of the rail line but still had to take Zeledon's stronghold in the Barranca-Coyatepe hills and his rebel positions in Masaya and León. On October 2, marine and Nicaraguan government troops commenced artillery bombardment of the hills, then, on October 3, stormed Zeledon's positions, readily taking them. Now the Nicaraguan troops descended on Masaya, which they ravaged and looted. Seeking to avoid Masaya's fate, León quickly surrendered to the U.S. Marines. This ended the revolt against the Díaz regime. In November 1913, most of the marines returned to Panama, leaving behind a contingent of 100 to guard the U.S. legation— and to supply the muscle needed to bolster the U.S.-friendly, Conservative Díaz government.

See also HONDURAN CIVIL WAR; NICARAGUAN CIVIL WAR (1925–1933).

Further reading: Thomas P. Anderson, *Politics in Central America: Guatemala, El Salvador, Honduras, and Nicaragua* (New York: Praeger, 1988); Jonathan R. Barton, *Political Geography of Latin America* (New York: Routledge, 1997); Eduardo Crawley, *Nicaragua in Perspective* (New York: St. Martin's Press, 1984); Thomas W. Walker, *Nicaragua,* 4th ed. (Boulder, Colo.: Westview Press, 2003).

Nicaraguan Civil War (1925–1933)

PRINCIPAL COMBATANTS: Nicaraguan Liberals vs. Nicaraguan Conservatives (aided by U.S. troops)
PRINCIPAL THEATER(S): Nicaragua
DECLARATION: None
MAJOR ISSUES AND OBJECTIVES: After the failure of a U.S.-sponsored Liberal-Conservative coalition government and the withdrawal of long-standing U.S. occupation forces, liberal and conservative factions vied for control of the country.
OUTCOME: Conservatives retained power; Augusto César Sandino, the leading Liberal guerrilla commander, was assassinated.
APPROXIMATE MAXIMUM NUMBER OF MEN UNDER ARMS: U.S. military contingent, 2,000 marines; Nicaraguan government and rebel forces at variable strength
CASUALTIES: Unknown
TREATIES: None

Though the citizens of the United States liked to think of their country as a champion of democracy and human rights, those living in Central and South America often had a different historical notion about the behemoth to their north. Beginning in the late 19th and early 20th centuries, when U.S. foreign policy more openly served the economic imperialism of American big business interests, the United States helped to create a series of Latin American client republics. The conservative governments of such countries were supported by the U.S. military and often controlled behind the scenes by U.S. corporations interested only in the profits they could exploit. Because these corrupt governments tended to be brutal and repressive, popular national liberation movements in Latin America usually took on a decidedly anti-North American, anticapitalist tone.

In Nicaragua, from the time the country became independent in 1838, Liberals struggled for power with Conservatives, who were in the thrall of Cornelius Vanderbilt (1794–1877) and his transportation companies from the start and who grew especially friendly toward U.S.-owned fruit producers. In 1893, Liberals regained power but, under threat by the United States, were forced to yield to the Conservatives in the NICARAGUAN CIVIL WAR (1909–1912). To shore up the new government and protect American business interests, the United States dispatched a detachment of marines to the scene. This small force of about 100 men continuously occupied Nicaragua until 1925, when the United States helped engineer a coalition government between Conservative president Carlos Solórzano (fl. 1920s) and Liberal vice president Bautista Sacasa (1874–1946). Believing it had "solved" the long-standing animosities, the U.S. government withdrew its marines, which sparked another civil war.

On October 25, 1925, shortly after the marines left, General Emiliano Chamorro Vargas (1871–1966) and Adolfo Díaz (1874–1964) staged a coup, which drove the Liberals, including Sacasa, out of office. Soon after, Solórzano also resigned, and, in January 1926, Chamorro became president. The United States refused to recognize his elevation to office, and, in the meantime, the charismatic General Augusto César Sandino (1893–1934) led Liberals in a revolt against Chamorro. In the course of the revolt, Sandino's followers ("Sandinistas") seized U.S. businesses and property in Nicaragua, which prompted the United States to dispatch gunboats and marines to the country. Their presence brought about a truce, during which Chamorro stepped down as president and left Nicaragua. In October 1926, the Nicaraguan congress elected the Conservative Díaz president.

At this point, Sacasa returned from his exile in Mexico and, with Mexican support, set up a rival Liberal government on the east coast of Nicaragua. This triggered a civil war between Sacasa's followers—a rebel army under General José María Moncada (1868–1945)—and the government forces of Díaz. At the urging of U.S. business and the request of the Conservative president, U.S. president Calvin Coolidge (1872–1933) authorized military aid in 1927, including several warships and a contingent of 2,000 marines. The United States also supplied Díaz with weapons and other materiel.

U.S. intervention in the Nicaraguan Civil War incited Augusto Sandino to join the fight, leading a brilliant guerrilla campaign against the marines and other gringo interlopers. In the face of this new development, Coolidge dispatched former secretary of war Henry L. Stimson (1867–1950) to Nicaragua to mediate between the rival leaders Díaz and Moncada. He persuaded them to disarm and to allow the United States to supervise the upcoming election. On November 4, 1928, Moncada, the Liberal candidate, was elected. But Sandino refused to accept the U.S.-mediated result placing a rival general, even if he was Liberal, in power, and his guerrillas continued to clash

with the marines. The United States responded by sending light bombers over the mountain regions known to harbor Sandinista guerrillas. After the bombings, Sandino fled to Mexico but continued to direct guerrilla activities from there.

In 1932, Sacasa himself was elected to the presidency in another U.S.-supervised election and began negotiating with Sandino. The rebel leader agreed to end the war as soon as U.S. Marines withdrew, which they did in 1933 after training the Nicaraguan National Guard to maintain order for the new civilian president and leaving a hand-picked man, Anastasio Somoza García (1896–1956), in charge of the guard. Granted amnesty by Sacasa, Sandino returned to Nicaragua and, in 1934, was assassinated by soldiers of the Somoza-controlled force in Managua. This created a Liberal political martyr and an enduring symbol of resistance to oppression and to U.S. imperialism in Nicaragua. Four decades later, liberal socialist elements, calling themselves Sandinistas, would clash with the ruling Somoza presidential regime, which was supported by the United States, in yet another civil conflict, the NICARAGUAN CIVIL WAR (1978–1979).

Further reading: Thomas P. Anderson, *Politics in Central America: Guatemala, El Salvador, Honduras, and Nicaragua* (New York: Praeger, 1988); Jonathan R. Barton, *Political Geography of Latin America* (New York: Routledge, 1997); Eduardo Crawley, *Nicaragua in Perspective* (New York: St. Martin's Press, 1984); Donald Clark Hodges, *Intellectual Foundations of the Nicaraguan Revolution* (Austin: University of Texas Press, 1986); Thomas W. Walker, *Nicaragua*, 4th ed. (Boulder, Colo.: Westview Press, 2003).

Nicaraguan Civil War (Sandinista Revolution) (1978–1979)

PRINCIPAL COMBATANTS: Sandinista rebels vs. Nicaragua's government forces under dictator Anastasio Somoza

PRINCIPAL THEATER(S): Nicaragua

DECLARATION: None

MAJOR ISSUES AND OBJECTIVES: The growing brutality and greed of the Somoza dynasty had long fed unrest in Nicaragua, which exploded in a Marxist revolution in 1979.

OUTCOME: Somoza fell from power, fled the country, and was later assassinated, whereas the Sandinistas assumed control of the country and installed a military junta.

APPROXIMATE MAXIMUM NUMBER OF MEN UNDER ARMS: Sandinistas, 5,000; National Guard, 13,000

CASUALTIES: 10,000 Nicaraguans killed including 7,000 civilians

TREATIES: None

On July 17, 1979, the longtime president and brutal dictator of Nicaragua, Anastasio Somoza Debayle (1925–80), resigned his office and fled before the advancing revolutionary army of the Marxist Sandinistas. Nicaragua had undergone a revolution, and the United States was deeply implicated in the struggle.

For about a century after Nicaragua became independent in 1838, the nation was torn by power struggles between Liberals and Conservatives. The Conservatives were especially friendly to outside business interests, and that included U.S. fruit producers. In 1893, the Liberals regained power but were persuaded under threat of force by the United States to yield to the Conservatives in 1909. To back up the new government and to protect American business interests in Nicaragua, a U.S. Marine detachment was dispatched to the scene (see NICARAGUAN CIVIL WAR [1909–1912]). It remained until 1925, when its withdrawal sparked an outright civil war between Liberals and Conservatives (see NICARAGUAN CIVIL WAR [1925–1933[).

Before the U.S. Marines left, a coalition government had been formed with the election of a Conservative as president and a Liberal as vice president, but hardly had the marines reached home before the Nicaraguan Army staged a coup d'état, which led to a Liberal revolt. In 1927, the United States again sent thousands of marines to put down the Liberal insurrection. However, two elections held under U.S. supervision resulted in the election of Liberal presidents in 1928 and 1932. After training the Nicaraguan National Guard to maintain order, the marines withdrew in 1933, leaving a handpicked man, Anastasio Somoza Garcia (1896–1956), in charge of the guard. The Liberal government of the early 1930s was far more moderate than earlier Liberal regimes; however, one important "radical" leader remained, Cesar Augusto Sandino (1893–1934), who led a resistance movement not only against the Conservatives, but opposed to the U.S. presence as well. Somoza, knowing the United States would support him if he made a bid for power, took his chance and invited Sandino to a peace conference but arranged to have him abducted and murdered by the National Guard. With Sandino out of the way, Somoza rallied support for the ouster of President Juan Bautista Sacasa (1874–1946) in 1936, after which Somoza was elected president. Somoza ran the country with an iron hand until 1956, when he was assassinated by a nationalist poet. But during his long tenure, Somoza laid the foundation of a modern dynasty, appointing his family members to the highest government posts and manipulating government policy to facilitate his amassing a fortune in money and land. Following Somoza's assassination, first his oldest son Luis (1922–1967) and then his third son, Anastasio Somoza Debayle (1922–1967), succeeded him as president.

The new leader transformed the National Guard into a private palace army under his personal control. He struck a deal with the Conservative Party to succeed himself as president in 1971 in return for giving the Conservatives 40 percent of the legislature. Then the devastating 1972 earthquake, which destroyed a large part of the capital city of Managua and brought in millions of dollars in foreign aid, mostly from the United States, swelled the Somoza fortune in real estate, construction, finance and insurance companies, and a range of businesses. By then, the Somoza family already held half of the nation's land deeds and owned outright a quarter of the best arable land. Given its wealth and American business contacts, the regime, distastefully arrogant and distressingly repressive though it was, came to be regarded by the United States as a bastion against incursions of communism into a chronically unstable Central America.

After Somoza's "election" to a third term in 1974, the Sandinistas, a leftist guerrilla force named in honor of Augusto César Sandino, stepped up their hitherto sporadic attacks and abducted high-ranking members of the Somoza government. The president waged a two-and-a-half-year counterinsurgency campaign, killing thousands. In 1977 the U.S. State Department signaled a change in attitude toward Somoza (and developing country dictators in general) under President Jimmy Carter (b. 1924) by citing the regime for human rights violations. That same year Nicaragua's Roman Catholic hierarchy accused the government of torturing and summarily executing civilians in its brutal anti-Sandinista campaign. The murder of opposition publisher Pedro Joaquin Chamarro (d. 1978), owner of the newspaper La Prensa, in 1978 led to rioting by thousands of Nicaraguans, who not without reason blamed Somoza for his death.

Antigovernment activity grew apace, and calls came for Somoza's resignation both at home and in the United States. In August 1978, Sandinista guerrillas invaded the national palace and held some 1,500 people hostage, including members of the Nicaraguan Congress, until Somoza—in a telling show of weakness—released 59 political prisoners and gave them safe passage out of the country. Invading Sandinistas from Costa Rica sparked a successful revolution on May 29, 1979, which after seven weeks of fighting reached the capital in Managua. The summary execution of a U.S. news reporter by Somoza's troops, caught on camera and broadcast nationwide in the United States, not only enlisted popular support for the Sandinistas in North America, but also ensured there would be no U.S. Marines rushing in to save wealthy conservatives this time around. On July 17, 1979, Anastasio Somoza Debayle resigned as president, fleeing two days later, first to Miami and then to Paraguay, where he was assassinated in a September 1980 bazooka attack.

The Sandinistas broadcast over government radio that a cease-fire was in place. A five-man military junta was installed and immediately set about reforming the country's institutions and economy, nationalizing all of the

Somozas' vast holdings, banks, insurance companies, mineral reserves and forests. Turning to the United States with requests for foreign loans and expanding ties with many noncommunist nations, Nicaragua also established particularly close relations with Cuba, a country that had much resembled Nicaragua during the early days after the CUBAN REVOLUTION. The new U.S. president, Ronald Reagan (1911–2004), took the growing ties between the only Marxist-Leninist governments in the Western Hemisphere as evidence of an expanding communist presence in Central America and not only cut off economic aid to Nicaragua, but authorized some $20 million to create and arm Nicaraguan counterrevolutionaries to fight the Sandinistas. Reagan justified his actions by pointing to the fact that the Sandinistas were building a huge army themselves and, so he claimed, were acting in concert with Cuba to destabilize the government of neighboring El Salvador. Whether or not Reagan's claims were justified—and there were soon Congressional white papers to say they were not—his funding of a counterrevolutionary force operating out of neighboring nations was both a venerable dollar-diplomacy tradition and insurance that another civil war would follow (see NICARAGUAN CIVIL WAR [1982–1989]).

Further reading: Thomas P. Anderson, *Politics in Central America: Guatemala, El Salvador, Honduras, and Nicaragua* (New York: Praeger, 1988); Jonathan R. Barton, *Political Geography of Latin America* (New York: Routledge, 1997); Eduardo Crawley, *Nicaragua in Perspective* (New York: St. Martin's Press, 1984); Donald Clark Hodges, *Intellectual Foundations of the Nicaraguan Revolution* (Austin: University of Texas Press, 1986); Thomas W. Walker, *Nicaragua,* 4th ed. (Boulder, Colo.: Westview Press, 2003).

Nicaraguan Civil War (1982–1990)

PRINCIPAL COMBATANTS: The contras (adherents of the former Nicaraguan dictator Anastasio Somoza) vs. Nicaragua's Sandinista government
PRINCIPAL THEATER(S): Nicaragua's border regions
DECLARATION: None
MAJOR ISSUES AND OBJECTIVES: Right-wing remnants of Somoza's National Guard sought, with massive U.S. aid, to overthrow the new revolutionary government of the Marxist Sandinistas.
OUTCOME: The Sandinistas were able to contain the rebels, but at the cost of U.S. hostility and economic ruin, which led to their defeat by a U.S.-backed opposition candidate in the first general election under the new constitution
APPROXIMATE MAXIMUM NUMBER OF MEN UNDER ARMS: Contras—15,000; Sandinistas—60,000
CASUALTIES: More than 30,000 Nicaraguans killed

TREATIES: 1990 cease-fire between contras and UNO (National Opposition Union), followed by 1991 treaty in Managua

Some of the former Nicaraguan National Guard called *Somocistas* because of their loyalty to the late dictator, Anastasio Somoza Debayle (1925–80), went into exile in Miami with Somoza when he first fled the country after the Marxist Sandinistas had staged their successful national revolution in 1979 (*see* NICARAGUAN CIVIL WAR [1978–1979]). Others fled to neighboring Honduras, El Salvador, and Costa Rica. All of them were soon plotting to overthrow the National Liberation Front's five-man military junta that the Sandinistas had installed. The country the Sandinistas inherited was devastated economically and socially, so Sandinistas turned to the United States, and received from the administration of President Jimmy Carter (b. 1924) recognition and economic aid, but they also established particularly close relations with Cuba.

When U.S. president Ronald Reagan (1911–2004) took office in 1980 he made much of these growing ties with Cuba, claiming they were evidence of an expanding communist presence in Central America. In 1981, he suspended U.S. economic aid and authorized some $20 million to create and arm Nicaraguan counterrevolutionaries to fight the Sandinistas. The Sandinistas, he claimed, were curtailing civil liberties and setting up a socialist economy, which was clearly true. Also, he pointed to the fact that the Sandinistas were building a huge army themselves. Finally, he claimed that not only were the Sandinistas in league with Communist Cuba, together they aimed to destabilize all of Central America, beginning with neighboring El Salvador. Congress openly questioned that claim. On the other hand, it was certainly clear that the Reagan administration wanted to destabilize Nicaragua.

By the mid-1980s, the Somocistas were joined by Nicaragua's Miskito Indians, who were resisting the Sandinistas' attempts to resettle them away from the Coco River on the Nicaraguan-Honduran border. In January 1982, Nicaraguan troops crossed the border into Honduras, raided several Miskito villages, and killed more than 100 Indians, alienating in the process many Sandinista sympathizers at home and abroad. Some Miskitos headed for rebel camps across the border while others joined a guerrilla outfit in southern Nicaragua called the Alianza Revolucionaria Democratia, which accused the Sandinistas of being Stalinists. In Honduras and El Salvador, the contras—as the counterrevolutionaries there had come to be called—now numbered about 15,000 soldiers. In 1983 and 1984, the contras, financed by the United States and trained covertly by the Central Intelligence Agency, made incursions into Nicaragua, inflicting costly damage by blowing up bridges and oil tanks, and earning a brutal reputation for the zeal with which they avenged themselves on the mostly Sandinista-sympathizing population.

The Sandinista government responded with a further military buildup and by speeding up their domestic political reforms. In November 1984, the Sandinista National Liberation Front (FSLN) and its presidential candidate, Daniel Ortega Saavedra (b. 1945), won 63 percent of the vote in an election that international observers, including former U.S. president Jimmy Carter, deemed fair and competitive, and Ortega was inaugurated in January 1985. Two years later the Constituent Assembly produced a constitution that called for regular elections, the first for national office to be held in 1990. Growing ever more legitimate in the eyes of other nations, the Nicaraguan government was eventually able to acquire critical equipment for its military, such as assault helicopters, and to mount an effective counterinsurgency campaign that by the late 1980s contained and demoralized the contras.

President Reagan wanted to provide additional backing for the contras, but he encountered domestic resistance to more massive aid. In El Salvador, the United States found itself supporting a client regime that openly violated human rights, including the widely documented murder of U.S. missionary nuns. Congress wanted no part in protecting the brutal government of El Salvador from the perhaps chimerical threat of the Sandinistas, nor in supporting a counterrevolutionary campaign linked to the Somoza family's interests and its savage former national guard. In 1987, it voted against supplying further military aid to the contras.

That led to one of the century's more bizarre presidential scandals, which cast a telling light on the tangled web of world diplomacy and shadow government in the late 20th century and moved the Nicaraguan civil war from the battlefield to the plane of international politics. In 1979, Iranian followers of the Ayatollah Ruhollah Khomeini (1901–89) seized 90 American diplomats at the U.S. embassy in Tehran. The resulting "Iran Hostage Crisis" blighted Jimmy Carter's last year in office but ended on the day Ronald Reagan became president, when Khomeini—much to Reagan's political benefit—released the hostages. However, another round of kidnappings, inspired by those in Iran, soon followed in Lebanon. Most of the new hostages were to remain in captivity, their whereabouts unknown and their kidnappers unidentified throughout the Reagan presidency. The Reagan administration was especially worried about hostage William Buckley (1928–85), because his captors knew that Buckley was the CIA's head of station in Beirut. Fearing the political cost of appearing weak, President Reagan declared he would not under any circumstances negotiate with terrorists for hostages. Then, in 1985, a group of Israelis told Reagan's National Security Advisor, Robert MacFarlane (b. 1937), that an Iranian arms dealer could gain the release of the hostages if the United States were willing to trade antitank missiles, which Iran desperately needed for its war with Iraq (see the IRAN-IRAQ WAR), in exchange for Tehran's promise to use its influence over the kidnappers. MacFarlane outlined the arms-for-hostages plan for President Reagan, but Secretary of State George Schultz (b. 1920) and Secretary of Defense Caspar Weinberger (b. 1917) both strongly opposed it. They left the meeting with Reagan and MacFarlane, believing the plan was dead and buried.

Instead, according to MacFarlane, the president told him to go ahead. MacFarlane got one arms shipment off and one hostage returned. MacFarlane then turned a second shipment over to one of his Security Council deputies, Colonel Oliver North (b. 1943). North, a Vietnam veteran and right-wing zealot, had—so he claimed—become the protégé of CIA director William Casey (1913–87) when he (North) came up with a plan to transfer money received from arms sales to Iran to the contras. This would need to be done secretly because Congress had banned such funding. Casey gave North the go-ahead, North recruited former CIA and U.S. military men to help him. Soon he was talking about expanding the mission into a permanent, off-the-shelf covert enterprise, always ready for use in circumventing congressional oversight of secret CIA operations.

Unfortunately for North, the second shipment of arms-for-hostages went sour, and, while he was preparing to arrange a third, an obscure Middle Eastern magazine broke the story that would lead to the unraveling of the Iran-contra plans. Within days of finding out that North and MacFarlane had been to Iran, U.S. newspapers ran stories about the affair. As in the Watergate scandal that had torpedoed Richard Nixon's presidency, the White House issued baldly conflicting statements. President Reagan rushed to appoint a commission headed by Senator John Tower (1925–91), which produced a scathing indictment of the administration. Congress also followed the Watergate pattern by creating a special committee to investigate, and a special prosecutor was appointed. President Reagan invoked "national security" as an excuse for withholding evidence, a strategy that famously had failed Nixon in the case of Watergate. Meanwhile, Oliver North, under a congressional grant of immunity, freely admitted at least those of his lies, deceptions, and illegal activities covered by the immunity, in all of which he implicated his superiors, including the president.

CIA director Casey, whom North had identified as the prime mover of the entire operation, had died of a stroke, and others in the administration either remained adamant in their denials or claimed loss of memory. Oliver North was given a suspended sentence on a number of the counts on which he was found guilty, and even these convictions were overturned on appeal. (He would later run for the U.S. Senate, then became a radio talk-show host).

MacFarlane unsuccessfully attempted suicide early in the scandal. Ronald Reagan emerged legally unscathed, though the scandal, coupled with the precipitous crash of the stock market, cast a pall over the final days of his administration.

In some ways, the Iran-Contra scandal, born of the war in Central America and hostilities in the Middle East, was the greatest nonevent of the 20th century. Although its implications were staggering (an out-of-touch president, a fanatical junior officer running major illegal foreign-policy initiatives unsanctioned by any elected authority, a Central Intelligence Agency making plans to institutionalize the illegal circumvention of Congress) U.S. citizens seemed not much to care. For the Nicaraguans, however, the Reagan administration's meddling approach to their internal affairs was very much a matter of concern.

Reagan had denounced the 1984 Nicaraguan election as a sham. Since 1982, the United States had used its leverage within the World Bank and the Inter-American Development Bank to block Nicaraguan loan requests. In 1985, the Reagan administration declared an outright embargo against the country. Such measures, combined with the social and economic dislocations of the civil war with the Sandinistas' own economic errors, caused an already weak economy to plummet after 1985. In response to an annual inflation rate in 1988 of 30,000 percent, the Sandinistas introduced harsh and unpopular austerity measures in 1989, slashing government programs in health, education, housing, and nutrition, which formed the background for the 1990 elections. Held under intense international scrutiny, the elections were marred by increased contra violence, but they were held nevertheless, and ended with a surprise. The U.S.-backed and -financed National Opposition Union and its presidential candidate, Violeta Barros de Chamorro (b. 1929), widow of a newspaper publisher martyred by former dictator Anastasio Somoza, won in an upset, and a peaceful transition ensued between the Sandinista administration and hers. The contras agreed to an immediate cease-fire, and eventually Barros persuaded them—despite the resistance of some very strong factions—to lay down their arms altogether. The civil war was over.

Further reading: Thomas P. Anderson, *Politics in Central America: Guatemala, El Salvador, Honduras, and Nicaragua* (New York: Praeger, 1988); Jonathan R. Barton, *Political Geography of Latin America* (New York: Routledge, 1997); Robert Busby, *Reagan and the Iran-Contra Affair* (New York: St. Martin's Press, 1987); Eduardo Crawley, *Nicaragua in Perspective* (New York: St. Martin's Press, 1984); Jiri Valenta and Esperanza Durán, eds., *Conflict in Nicaragua: A Multidimensional Perspective* (Boston: Allen Unwin, 1987); Thomas W. Walker, *Nicaragua*, 4th ed. (Boulder, Colo.: Westview Press, 2003).

Nicopolis, Crusade of (1396)

PRINCIPAL COMBATANTS: Crusaders (under Sigismund of Hungary) vs. Ottoman Turks (under Bayazid I)
PRINCIPAL THEATER(S): Bulgaria
DECLARATION: Papal call to arms, 1396
MAJOR ISSUES AND OBJECTIVES: The crusaders wanted to check ongoing Ottoman conquests.
OUTCOME: The crusaders suffered disastrous defeat at the Battle of Nicopolis.
APPROXIMATE MAXIMUM NUMBER OF MEN UNDER ARMS: 100,000 crusaders (of whom many subsequently deserted)
CASUALTIES: Thousands of crusaders fell, and some 10,000 were taken prisoner.
TREATIES: None

In 1396, Pope Boniface IX (c. 1355–1404) proclaimed a crusade against the Ottoman Turks, who spread panic throughout Europe because of their conquests in the Balkans and their assault upon Constantinople. An army of some 100,000 assembled in Buda, from which Hungary's King Sigismund (1368–1437) led them down the Danube to seize two Ottoman forts. The crusaders were charged with liberating from the Ottomans those towns and villages through which they advanced; however, the crusaders behaved poorly and pillaged most of the communities that lay in their path.

At Nicopolis (Nikopol, Bulgaria), the ill-disciplined crusader army began to fall apart in earnest. The crusaders laid siege against the Ottoman fortress but soon grew restless in this thankless work. Without a firm battle plan or an agreed-upon chain of command, individual leaders took action on their own. John the Fearless (1371–1419) of France led his knights in an ill-advised attack against Sultan Bayazid I's (1347–1403) army. He and his forces fell victim to the Ottoman tactic of luring the enemy with an apparently vulnerable front line, only to envelop and destroy the attackers from the flanks. John's knights were slaughtered, and the 16,000 men Sigismund sent to his relief fared little better. In addition to thousands slain in battle, 10,000 were made prisoner. Some of these were subsequently ransomed at great cost, while others were executed.

Sigismund fled the battle, escaping back to Hungary by ship. For his part, Sultan Bayazid I continued unchecked his conquest of the Balkans.

Further reading: Aziz Suryal Atiya, *Crusade of Nicopolis* (New York: AMS Press, 1918); Colin Imber, *The Ottoman Empire, 1300–1650: The Structure of Power* (New York: Palgrave, 2002); Kemal H. Karpat, ed., *The Ottoman State and Its Place in World History* (Leiden: Brill, 1974); Lord Kinross, *The Ottoman Centuries: The Rise and Fall of the Turkish Empire* (New York: Morrow, 1977); Mark

Mazower, *Balkans: A Short History* (New York: Random House, 2002); Peter F. Sugar, *Southeastern Europe under Ottoman Rule*, 2354–1804 (Seattle: University of Washington Press, 1977).

Nigerian-Biafran War (1967–1970)

PRINCIPAL COMBATANTS: Nigeria vs. Biafra
PRINCIPAL THEATER(S): Biafra
DECLARATION: Biafra declared independence on May 30, 1967.
MAJOR ISSUES AND OBJECTIVES: Biafra sought independence; Nigeria sought to reclaim Biafra.
OUTCOME: Biafra was defeated, mainly as a result of a long and intensive blockade that held the nation under a state of siege.
APPROXIMATE MAXIMUM NUMBER OF MEN UNDER ARMS: Nigerian army, 200,000; Biafran army, 50,000
CASUALTIES: Battle deaths, 45,000 on both sides; 500,000 civilians died, mainly as a result of starvation
TREATIES: None

Biafra broke away from Nigeria in 1967, seven years after Nigeria achieved independence from Britain. In 1960, when independence came, the Ibo people of eastern Nigeria, who—under British colonial rule—had become an educated elite and were now essentially a privileged class, assumed economic and political dominance in the new nation. This alienated the less privileged Islamic Hausa people of the north, who rioted against the Christian Ibo. In an effort to establish some semblance of home rule, the Nigerian government divided the nation into three states, corresponding to the territorial concentrations of the Ibo, the Hausa, and the Yoruba peoples. Far from bringing peace, this prompted the Ibo to secede from Nigeria. After the military governor of the eastern region, Lieutenant Colonel Chukwuemeka Odumegwo Ojukwu (b. 1933), declared an independent state of Biafra on May 30, 1967, the new country's Ibo army went on the offensive and made a major push toward the Nigerian capital of Lagos. The Nigerian army stopped the advance and counterattacked, invading Biafra and overcoming stout resistance to capture the Biafran capital, Enugu, on October 4, 1967. This was followed by peace negotiations early in 1968, which, however, came to nothing.

As the Civil War continued, the Nigerian government—determined to bring the oil-rich area back into its territory waged total war against Biafra, mainly in the form of a blockade, which created a famine throughout the region. European powers intervened in the struggle, the British, the Soviets, and Italy giving aid to Nigeria, whereas France supplied arms to beleaguered Biafra. For the new nation, however, it was a losing battle. Port Har-

court, Aba, and Owerri, all key cities, fell in 1968. Although Owerri was retaken in 1969, the Biafran army was overwhelmed by a counteroffensive from a now well-equipped Nigerian army of 200,000 men. Biafra's military defeat took place against a background of great civilian suffering, as the nation's name became an international byword for want and starvation. Biafra surrendered to Nigeria on January 12, 1970. Ojukwu fled to exile in the Ivory Coast. Civilian losses in Biafra topped 500,000, almost all from starvation and diseases related to malnutrition.

See also CONGOLESE CIVIL WAR.

Further reading: J. F. A. Ajayi and Michael Crowder, *History of West Africa*, 2nd ed., 2 vols. (London: Longman, 1976–1987); J. D. Fage and Roland Oliver, eds., *The Cambridge History of West Africa*, 8 vols. (New York: Cambridge University Press, 1975–1980); Rodney Steel, *History of West Africa* (New York: Facts On File, 2003); John De St. Jorre, *The Nigerian Civil War* (London: Hodder and Stoughton, 1972).

Nigerois Civil War (1990–1995)

PRINCIPAL COMBATANTS: Nigerois government vs. Tuareg rebels
PRINCIPAL THEATER(S): Northern Niger
DECLARATION: None
MAJOR ISSUES AND OBJECTIVES: The Tuaregs sought autonomy.
OUTCOME: Limited autonomy was granted.
APPROXIMATE MAXIMUM NUMBER OF MEN UNDER ARMS: Unknown
CASUALTIES: Thousands of civilian deaths, mainly due to general privation created by the war
TREATIES: Treaty of Ouagadougou (Burkina Faso), October 9, 1994; additional treaty, April 24, 1995

In Niger, Africa, the Tuareg tribe of the northern desert was frequently at odds with the mainstream government. Tuareg separatists often fought with government troops in the capital city of Niamey. At last, in May 1990, the government retaliated with a major raid in Tchin Tabaraden, in which hundred of Tuaregs were killed or arrested. In response, the Tuaregs stepped up attacks in the north, hitting government security forces as well as foreign tourists. The government mounted a new sweep against rebel activity in August 1992, rounding up members of the Tuareg Liberation Front of Air and Azawad (FLAA) and declaring a state of emergency in the northern region.

The civil war created great hardship for the people, and the FLAA agreed to a truce while the government sent aid to the starving. Although fighting between the government and the Tuaregs was largely suspended during 1993, violent unrest was common elsewhere in Niger, triggered mainly by the depressed economy. Under general pressure, the government negotiated in 1994 terms of limited autonomy for some 750,000 Tuaregs affiliated with the Coordination of Armed Resistance (CRA) organization. On October 9, 1994, CRA signed the formal Treaty of Ouagadougou, and other Tuareg groups fell into line with a treaty of April 24, 1995. With the war formally concluded, the Nigerois government granted amnesty to all Tuaregs and released its political prisoners. At this point, only a single rebel group, the Democratic Renewal Front, held out, but even the DRF agreed to the treaty terms in 1997.

Further reading: Samuel Decalo, *Historical Dictionary of Niger* (Lanham, Md.: Scarecrow Press, 1996); Rodney Steel, *History of West Africa* (New York: Facts On File, 2003).

Nika Revolt (532)

PRINCIPAL COMBATANTS: Nika rebels (supporters of Hypatius) vs. Byzantine emperor Justinian I
PRINCIPAL THEATER(S): Constantinople
DECLARATION: None
MAJOR ISSUES AND OBJECTIVES: The Nika rebels protested general corruption and extortionate taxation.
OUTCOME: The rebellion was crushed, but it did prompt Justinian I to step up reform of Byzantine government.
APPROXIMATE MAXIMUM NUMBER OF MEN UNDER ARMS: Unknown
CASUALTIES: 30,000 rebels were killed
TREATIES: None

The Byzantine Empire was plagued by despotism and corruption at regional levels of government, a situation the emperor Justinian I (483–565) attempted to alleviate by acting against many imperial officials and administrators. This produced some improvement, but not enough to prevent a popular uprising in Constantinople in protest against exorbitant taxes and government-sanctioned extortion. The battle cry of the rebellion was *Nika!*, meaning victory.

When a mob surrounded Justinian's palace, the emperor contemplated fleeing the city, but his wife, Theodora (c. 508–548), stood firm and persuaded her husband to do likewise. Justinian ordered his two top generals, Belisarius (c. 505–565) and Narses (c. 478–573), to lead the imperial bodyguard and other troops against the rebels. In a fierce action, some 30,000 Nika rebels, having proclaimed Hypatius (d. 532) emperor, were killed. Hypatius was captured and executed as a traitor. Although the rebellion thus collapsed, it did move Justinian to act more aggressively against corrupt

and abusive officials. More administrators were removed from office.

See also GOTHIC (ITALIAN) WAR; JUSTINIAN'S FIRST PERSIAN WAR; JUSTINIAN'S SECOND PERSIAN WAR; ROMAN-PERSIAN WAR (572–591); VANDAL-ROMAN WARS IN NORTH AFRICA.

Further reading: Cyril A. Mango, ed., *Oxford History of Byzantium* (New York: Oxford University Press, 2002); John Julius Norwich, *Byzantium: The Early Centuries* (New York: Alfred A. Knopf, 2003).

Nineveh, Fall of (612 B.C.E.)

PRINCIPAL COMBATANTS: Medes, Babylonians, Scythians, and Persians vs. Assyrians
PRINCIPAL THEATER(S): Nineveh, Assyria
DECLARATION: None
MAJOR ISSUES AND OBJECTIVES: Presumably conquest
OUTCOME: Nineveh fell.
APPROXIMATE MAXIMUM NUMBER OF MEN UNDER ARMS: Unknown
CASUALTIES: Unknown
TREATIES: No documents exist

The capital city of the great Assyrian Empire, Nineveh, on the Tigris, was so strongly fortified that it was deemed impregnable. It was surrounded by seven miles of walls, which, in some places, were almost 150 feet thick. Despite this, a combination of Medes, Babylonians, Scythians, and Persians overran Nineveh and destroyed the city in 612 B.C.E. Beyond this fact nothing is known, and no details of the military operation exist. It is possible that the main assault was amphibious, using rafts with battering rams and other siege devices on the Tigris, which was at high flood stage during this time.

See also ASSYRIAN WARS (c. 746–609 B.C.E.).

Further reading: William Cullican, *The Medes and Persians* (New York: Praeger, 1965); Josef Wiesehofer, *Ancient Persia* (New York: I. B. Tauris, 2000).

Nine Years' War *See* GRAND ALLIANCE, WAR OF THE.

Norman-Byzantine War, First (1081–1085)

PRINCIPAL COMBATANTS: Normans vs. Byzantine Empire
PRINCIPAL THEATER(S): Southern Italy and the Balkans
DECLARATION: None
MAJOR ISSUES AND OBJECTIVES: Ultimately, the Normans' leader, Robert Guiscard, intended to seize the Byzantine throne.

OUTCOME: Guiscard died before he could carry out his plan in earnest.
APPROXIMATE MAXIMUM NUMBER OF MEN UNDER ARMS: Unknown
CASUALTIES: Unknown
TREATIES: None

The dashing Norman soldier Robert Guiscard (c. 1015–85) campaigned with his brother Roger I (c. 1031–1101) to gain control of Apulia, Calabria, and Sicily, lands granted him by the pope. In the process of fighting Muslim forces in southern Italy, Guiscard ran afoul of the Byzantine Empire. This prompted the avaricious Guiscard, with his son Bohemund I (c. 1056–1111), to mount an invasion of the Balkans. He captured Corfu and Dyrrachium, then decided to attack the emperor, Alexius I Comnenus (1048–1118), with the objective of taking the imperial crown for himself. His scheme was delayed by the ongoing wars in Italy, however, and by the time he was ready to commence his attack against Cephalonia in 1085, he succumbed to the plague.

See also NORMAN-BYZANTINE WAR, SECOND.

Further reading: David C. Douglas, *The Norman Achievement, 1050–1100* (Berkeley: University of California Press, 1969)); Cyril A. Mango, ed., *Oxford History of Byzantium* (New York: Oxford University Press, 2002); John Julius Norwich, *Byzantium: The Decline and Fall* (New York: Alfred A. Knopf, 1996).

Norman-Byzantine War, Second
(1098–1108)

PRINCIPAL COMBATANTS: Normans vs. Byzantine Empire
PRINCIPAL THEATER(S): Byzantine Empire and Jerusalem
DECLARATION: None
MAJOR ISSUES AND OBJECTIVES: Norman leader Bohemond sought to complete his late father's plan to topple Alexius I Comnenus from the Byzantine throne.
OUTCOME: Bohemond was ultimately defeated.
APPROXIMATE MAXIMUM NUMBER OF MEN UNDER ARMS: Unknown
CASUALTIES: Unknown
TREATIES: None

In the First NORMAN-BYZANTINE WAR, from 1081 to 1085, Robert Guiscard (c. 1015–85) had planned to topple Alexius I Comnenus (1048–1118) from the Byzantine throne and seize it for himself. Guiscard's death from plague in 1085 ended this scheme until 1098, when Guiscard's son Bohemond I (c. 1056–1111) attacked the empire. During this war, he also participated in the First CRUSADE and became vassal to Geoffrey of Bouillon (c. 1053–1100), the

Latin ruler of Jerusalem. His campaign against the empire was interrupted during 1100–03, when he was held prisoner by the Muslims in the Holy Land. On his return to Europe in 1103, he pressed his campaign against Alexius I Comnenus, whom his father had been unable to defeat, but was himself defeated by 1108. His bid for the Byzantine throne came to an end.

Further reading: David C. Douglas, *The Norman Fate, 1100–1150* (London: Eyre Methuen, 1976); Cyril A. Mango, ed., *Oxford History of Byzantium* (New York: Oxford University Press, 2002); John Julius Norwich, *Byzantium: The Decline and Fall* (New York: Alfred A. Knopf, 1996).

Norman Conquest (1066)

PRINCIPAL COMBATANTS: William I (Normans) vs. Harold Godwinson (Saxons)
PRINCIPAL THEATER(S): England
DECLARATION: None
MAJOR ISSUES AND OBJECTIVES: William fought Harold for the English throne.
OUTCOME: William won the decisive Battle of Hastings and thereby claimed the throne.
APPROXIMATE MAXIMUM NUMBER OF MEN UNDER ARMS: 4,000–7,000 on each side
CASUALTIES: Both side lost about one-quarter of their troops.
TREATIES: None

The Normans, named for the Vikings ("Norsemen") from whom they were descended, made their homeland in northwestern France. Over the course of about three generations of intermarriage with the area's Frankish tribes, they had transformed themselves from pagan raiders into devout, if fierce, Christian crusaders. From Normandy, they launched sporadic conquests by which, during the course of the 11th century, they created a patchwork empire from the North Sea to the Mediterranean. Leading the way were freelancing Norman knights fighting for feuding Lombards and Greeks, and picking up what fiefs they could along the way. By mid-century they had taken most of southern Italy, and in 1061 they defeated the Muslim occupiers of Sicily. Soon the knights would seize Greek Corfu and invade the Byzantine Balkans. In 1098, as a result of their service in the First CRUSADE, they established the principality of Antioch. Long before that, however, their much-hailed leader William I (the Conqueror; c. 1027–87) had added Anglo-Saxon England to the piecemeal dominions of Normandy.

England's King Edward (c. 1003–1066), known as the Confessor for his piety, was related to the Norman

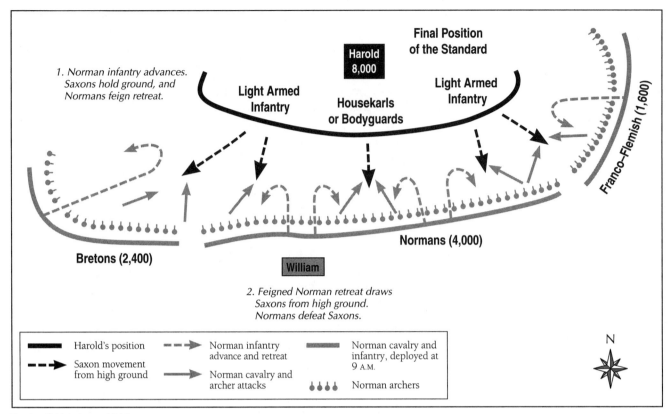

1. Norman infantry advances. Saxons hold ground, and Normans feign retreat.

Final Position of the Standard

Harold 8,000

Light Armed Infantry

Housekarls or Bodyguards

Light Armed Infantry

Franco-Flemish (1,600)

Bretons (2,400)

Normans (4,000)

William

2. Feigned Norman retreat draws Saxons from high ground. Normans defeat Saxons.

▬▬▬ Harold's position	---▶ Norman infantry advance and retreat	▬▬▬ Norman cavalry and infantry, deployed at 9 A.M.	
---▶ Saxon movement from high ground	──▶ Norman cavalry and archer attacks	♠♠♠♠ Norman archers	

N

Battle of Hastings, 1066

nobility through his mother. During the years of Canute's reign in England (c. 995–1035), Edward had spent much of his youth and young manhood 100 miles across the English Channel in exile at the Norman court. Nine years after he ascended to the throne in 1051, he named William, duke of Normandy, as his heir. It was this claim that William sought to assert after Edward died on January 5, 1066.

However, William was not the only contender.

Harold Hadrada (d. 1066), king of Norway and the most renowned Viking warrior of his day, hoped to reassert the Scandinavian claim to the Crown established early in the century by King Canute (d. 1035). Edward had further complicated matters by changing his mind on his deathbed and naming Harold Godwinson (c. 1022–66) as his successor, or so Godwinson, the earl of Wessex, claimed. Not only an English baron, he was the most powerful magnate on the island, and he moved decisively to have himself crowned Harold II of England at Westminster Abbey only hours after Edward had been buried in the famous church.

Harold had trouble justifying his actions. Only two years before he had appeared at the Norman court and sworn fealty upon holy relics to William as the rightful heir to the English throne. Now, however, he claimed he had been forced to take the oath when his ship acciden-

tally ran aground on the Normandy coast, but neither the knights in France nor the pope in Rome accepted his version of events. Set to march with Pope Alexander II's (d. 1075) blessing under the three-tailed papal banner, William's forces swelled mightily as knights from every principality in northern France rushed to join the now holy cause.

Meanwhile, Harold was suffering problems enough at home. His own brother, Tostig (d. 1066), rose up to challenge him, and upon being quickly defeated, united with Hadrada in the Norwegian invasion of England. Harold not only repulsed the Norwegian invasion at the Battle of Stamford Bridge on September 25, 1066, but killed both Tostig and Hadrada. This left only William as his rival for the throne.

Now time and distance worked against Harold Godwinson and became the key factors in the Norman conquest of England. When the Norman fleet landed at Pevensey on the southwest coast of England in late September, King Harold's Anglo-Saxon army was in York, about 200 miles away, celebrating its victory over the Norwegians.

At least 7,000 Normans disembarked from the 700 or so vessels of William's armada in an operation that was a nightmare of logistics. Some 3,000 cavalry mounts had to be offloaded from makeshift wattle stalls down shaky wooden ramps. The invaders brought ashore cartloads of arms and the heavy armor the Normans were becoming famous for wearing, and they dragged onto the beach the tools and planks they needed for building fortifications, the pots and supplies for setting up camp and cooking, and barrels of French wine to shore up their courage. Blessed by favorable winds for the passage over, they now managed to land virtually unopposed, securing a beach-head without a single loss of life.

Godwinson rushed south to do battle with William. The army Harold Godwinson had force-marched to Sussex was of approximately the same size as William's—somewhere between 4,000 and 7,000 troops—but it consisted mainly of untrained and poorly armed peasants, whereas William commanded a professional force. Moreover, Harold lacked both archers and cavalry. He compensated for this by deploying his troops on a ridge about 10 miles northwest of Hastings, but he made the serious tactical error of packing his soldiers closely together. This transformed them into ready targets for William's fine archers. Yet Harold's men did fight back, exacting a terrible toll on Williams's bowmen and prompting him to pull them back. William then sent in his cavalry. From their well-defended positions, Harold's troops decimated the horsemen in their first assault.

Not one to panic, William persisted. He wore away at the Saxons by alternating cavalry charges and bow attacks all day. When he saw that Harold's army was wearing down, William feigned two retreats late in the day. These lured the Saxon troops out of their protected position. Once they were in the clear, William suddenly wheeled about and counterattacked, routing the tired Saxon army.

Harold fell in battle, killed by a stray arrow, and the leaderless army began to fall apart. Those who did not surrender scattered in defeat. William advanced against London to cut off the city. He met with no resistance from the nobles in the surrounding area, and, at Westminster, on Christmas, 1066, William was crowned King William I of England.

Although the Norman victory at the battle of Hastings had been decisive, it was yet another five years before the Anglo-Saxons were fully subjugated. Meanwhile, William's army of occupation frequently faced rebel forces, most notably in Yorkshire and on the isle of Ely in the east. At length, the conquest was completed in 1072, when the Normans secured England's northern border with an attack through Scotland.

See also NORMAN-FRENCH WAR; WILLIAM I'S INVASION OF SCOTLAND.

Further reading: Timothy Baker, *The Normans* (London: Cassell, 1966); R. Allen Brown, *The Norman Conquest* (London and Baltimore, Md.: E. Arnold, 1984); N. J. Higham, *The Norman Conquest* (Stroud, Gloucestershire: Sutton Pub., 1998).

Norman-French War (1077–1082)

PRINCIPAL COMBATANTS: Normans under William I the Conqueror vs. the French under his son, Robert Curthose
PRINCIPAL THEATER(S): Normandy
DECLARATION: None
MAJOR ISSUES AND OBJECTIVES: Robert Curthose sought to topple his father.
OUTCOME: The rebels were defeated.
APPROXIMATE MAXIMUM NUMBER OF MEN UNDER ARMS: Unknown
CASUALTIES: Unknown
TREATIES: None

Once William the Conqueror (c. 1027–87) had completed the NORMAN CONQUEST of England, he chose to reign, for the most part, from his native Normandy, and leave the administration of his island kingdoms to regents. Back in the north of France, except for an attempted coup by a few English earls and yet one more—the final—Danish invasion in 1085, his time was taken up with defending Normandy's frontiers against hostile neighbors. Not the least of these was King Philip I (1052–1108) of France, who very much desired to prevent the union of Normandy and England under a single ruler. Toward that end he backed William's first son, young Robert Curthose (c. 1054–1134), in a series of rebellions. Not that Curthose needed much encouragement—he bitterly resented his father's refusal to let him play a vital role in the governing of the French province, which William had nominally handed over to him in 1066 when he went off to invade Anglo-Saxon England. Easily defeated in his initial outing, Robert for a while reconciled with his father, until further disagreements led to renewed fighting. At one point, the son's challenge was serious enough, that William was forced to launch an operation from England (*see* WILLIAM I'S INVASION OF NORMANDY) and ultimately he was forced to send his son into exile. Thus thwarted, Philip I would prevail briefly when Robert returned to Normandy in 1087, on the death of William, and inherited the title of duke of Normandy, reigning as Robert II. He did not lay claim to the throne of England, which fell to his brother William II. Shortly, however, this William, too, reunited the kingdoms.

Further reading: Timothy Baker, *The Normans* (London: Cassell, 1966); Richard F. Cassidy, *The Norman Achievement* (London: Sedquick and Jackson, 1986); David C. Douglas, *The Norman Achievement, 1050–1100* (Berkeley: University of California Press, 1969) and *William the Conqueror* (London: Eyre and Spottiswoode, 1964).

North Africa, French Conquest of
See FRENCH CONQUEST OF NORTH AFRICA.

North America, Spanish Conquests in

See SPANISH CONQUEST OF NORTH MEXICO (NORTH AMERICA).

Northern Ireland Civil War (1969–2001)

PRINCIPAL COMBATANTS: Northern Irish Protestants vs. Northern Irish Catholics; also involved: British peacekeeping and policing troops
PRINCIPAL THEATER(S): Northern Ireland, with some terrorist activity in England (mainly London)
DECLARATION: None
MAJOR ISSUES AND OBJECTIVES: In general, Northern Irish Catholics wanted independence from England and union with the Republic of Ireland; Northern Irish Protestants, the nation's majority, have wanted to remain politically connected with England, which provided defense.
OUTCOME: After a new National Assembly was created and the Irish Republican Army (IRA) disarmed, hopes ran high for a sustained end to the civil war.
APPROXIMATE MAXIMUM NUMBER OF MEN UNDER ARMS: Unknown
CASUALTIES: Approximately 3,000
TREATIES: Agreement of May 22, 1998, establishing a Northern Ireland National Assembly

For centuries, Britain had oppressed the Irish. The British put down the 1916 EASTER UPRISING, but it produced a great wave of support for Irish independence—both in Ireland and among many in Britain. In 1921, the Irish Free State was created, divided from Northern Ireland, which was still a part of Britain (*see* ANGLO-IRISH CIVIL WAR). Subsequently, the Free State became a sovereign nation. The chief difference between independent Ireland and Northern Ireland was religion. Ireland was and is about 95 percent Roman Catholic. Northern Ireland is 60 percent Protestant. The Catholic minority in Northern Ireland, feeling politically and economically oppressed by the Protestant majority, demanded union with independent Ireland. The Protestant majority, fearing absorption into Catholic Ireland, sought to remain attached to the United Kingdom.

Catholics and Protestants in Northern Ireland fought frequently after the break with the Irish Free State. However, in 1968, when the Catholic minority staged massive civil rights protests, violence became acute, and British troops were called in to maintain order. The British military presence has remained a part of Northern Irish life —much resented by the Catholics, who saw themselves as oppressed not only by their Protestant fellow citizens but by an army of occupation from a Protestant nation, England, and in the service of Protestantism in Northern Ireland.

Both the Catholics and the Protestants developed paramilitary organizations to wage civil war. The Irish Republican Army (IRA) and its even more radical and violent wing, the Provisional Wing (Provos) of the IRA, carried out the Catholic military agenda, whereas the Protestant Ulster Defence Association was the militant arm of Northern Ireland Protestants. Caught in the middle were noncombatant citizens and the British military. From 1969 into the 1970s, these paramilitary organizations staged violent demonstrations, engaged in street fighting, planted bombs, and carried out political assassinations.

To cope with the crisis, the British government suspended the Stormont, the Northern Ireland parliament, in 1972 and took over administration of the government. The following year, a plebiscite was held on the question of union with Ireland. By an overwhelming majority, union was rejected, and a coalition government—Catholic and Protestant—was formed. However, radical Protestants, led by the Reverend Ian Paisley (b. 1926), set out to destroy the coalition. They did so primarily through political means, sending a hard-line slate of members to the British parliament and calling a general strike that brought about the collapse of the reconstituted Stormont.

In the meantime, violence continued—a daily affair of action and reaction, offense and reprisal. Catholic terrorism was carried out against British troops in Ulster and against British civilians in England, especially London. At last, in 1983, a new bill was introduced in the British parliament, attempting to form a third home rule government for Northern Ireland, but a Roman Catholic boycott killed the bill. The following year a new plan for union with Ireland was also developed, and, this time, a majority approved it—but the union did not come to pass, and the violence continued through the early 1990s.

In 1993, the Downing Street Declaration pledged the commencement of peace talks between Britain and Ireland. In response, in September 1994, the IRA declared a cease-fire, which the Protestant paramilitary organizations agreed to the following month. In 1995, a "Framework Document" outlined and addressed key political issues. The atmosphere was generally hopeful until a bomb was exploded in London in an IRA terrorist attack in February 1996. This was followed by renewed street fighting in Portadown, Northern Ireland, in July. The IRA, however, was determined to play a role in the joint British-Irish peace talks, which were restricted to peaceful groups only. Therefore, the IRA unilaterally reinstated the cease-fire in July 1997. In September, the IRA's political wing, known as Sinn Fein, headed by the fiery Gerry Adams (b. 1948), was admitted to the talks—and Adams presented himself in a statesmanlike manner. The talks produced, on April 10, 1998, an agreement that created a National Assembly for Northern Ireland, which would work cooperatively with the Republic of Ireland and which included a balance of Protestant and Catholic representation.

Hard-liners and diehards continued to perpetrate acts of violence—the most notorious group calling itself the "Real IRA." However, public disgust at the renewed killings—most notably a car bomb detonation at Omagh on August 15, 1998, which killed 28 and wounded some 330—undercut support for the militants. At the end of October 2001, the IRA announced, unilaterally, that it had begun to destroy its arsenal. This act of good faith seemed to mark an end to 32 years of Irish civil war. Since then fitful initiatives attempting to establish real peace have made uneasy headway, and while Northern Ireland remains volatile both socially and politically, the once almost universal violence has abated.

Further reading: Jack Holland, *Hope against History: The Course of Conflict in Northern Ireland* (New York: Henry Holt, 1999); George J. Mitchell, *Making Peace* (Berkeley: University of California Press, 2000).

Northern War, First (1655–1660)

PRINCIPAL COMBATANTS: Sweden vs. Poland and Denmark
PRINCIPAL THEATER(S): Poland, Holstein, Schleswig, and Denmark
DECLARATION: Sweden against Poland, 1655
MAJOR ISSUES AND OBJECTIVES: Sweden's Charles X sought glory and conquest.
OUTCOME: The Swedes made remarkable initial advances but ultimately failed to hold the territories gained, except in Poland.
APPROXIMATE MAXIMUM NUMBER OF MEN UNDER ARMS: Sweden, 50,000; Poland and Denmark, unknown
CASUALTIES: Unknown
TREATIES: Treaty of Roskilde, 1658, and Treaty of Oliva, 1660

The great Swedish warrior king Charles X (1622–60) sought to push his kingdom's dominion into the Baltic and, by the Second POLISH-SWEDISH WAR FOR LIVONIA from 1600 to 1611, asserted a claim as "Protector of Poland." King John II Casimir (1609–72) of Poland refused to recognize the protectorate, whereupon Charles declared war.

Charles personally led a large army of invasion, which seized Warsaw after a three-day battle. With this, Poland was conquered, and Charles now pressed on into Lithuania, which the Swedes quickly occupied. Charles's Prussian ally, Frederick William (1620–88), secured peace with Poland, which allowed Charles to advance westward to fight Denmark (Poland's ally) for possession of Holstein, Schleswig, and most of Jutland. Having secured these territories, Charles led an extraordinary assault across the ice from Jutland with the object of taking Copenhagen, the Danish capital. For the moment, the

Swedish king contented himself with holding the island of Fünen, pending the terms of a Danish-Swedish peace. Displeased with the Treaty of Roskilde, Charles advanced on Copenhagen and laid siege to the city. Ships of the Dutch fleet—Holland was a Danish ally—forced the lifting of the Swedish blockade of Copenhagen.

In the meantime, in Schleswig and Holstein, Polish forces drove out the invading Swedes. Next, the Danes and Norwegians defeated the Swedes at Bornholm and Trondheim, prompting Charles to sue for peace.

Negotiations dragged on, then faltered, but the Danish victory at the Battle of Nyborg in November 1659, which resulted in the defeat and capture of Sweden's best soldiers, prompted the Swedish government—now under the control of a regency, Charles having succumbed to a fever—to conclude the Treaty of Oliva in 1660. By this treaty, Sweden was confirmed in its rights to Livonia, while the Danes claimed Bornholm and Trondheim, and Brandenburg retained East Prussia.

Further reading: Robert I. Frost, *The Northern Wars: State and Society in Northeastern Europe, 1558–1721* (New York: Longman, 2000); W. Glyn Jones, *Denmark: A Modern History* (Dover, N.H.: Croom Helm, 1986); Jerzy Lukowoski, *Concise History of Poland* (New York: Cambridge University Press, 2001); Byron J. Nordstrom, *The History of Sweden* (Westport, Conn.: Greenwood Press, 2002); Stewart Oakley, *War and Peace in the Baltic, 1560–1790* (New York: Routledge, 1992); W. F. Reddaway, ed., *The Cambridge History of Poland*, 2 vols. (New York: Cambridge University Press, 1941–50, reprinted 1971); Michael Roberts, ed., *Sweden's Age of Greatness, 1632–1718* (London: Macmillan, 1973); Franklin D. Scott, *Sweden, the Nation's History* (Carbondale: Southern Illinois University Press, 1988); Vytas Stanley Vardys and Judith Sedaitis, *Lithuania: The Rebel Nation* (Denver: Westview Press, 1966); Arvids Ziedonis, William L. Winter, and Mardi Valgemäe, *Baltic History* (Columbus, Ohio: Association for the Advancement of Baltic Studies, 1974).

Northern War, Second (Great Northern War) (1700–1721)

PRINCIPAL COMBATANTS: Sweden vs. Poland, Russia, Prussia, Saxony, Hanover, and Denmark
PRINCIPAL THEATER(S): The Baltic, Poland, Denmark, Russia
DECLARATION: None
MAJOR ISSUES AND OBJECTIVES: Charles XII wanted to achieve dominance in the Baltic and beyond.
OUTCOME: Sweden was ultimately defeated by a large coalition.
APPROXIMATE MAXIMUM NUMBER OF MEN UNDER ARMS: The largest army fielded was a Swedish force of 80,000.

CASUALTIES: At the disastrous Battle of Poltava, Charles XII lost virtually all of his 80,000-man army, by death, capture, and desertion.

TREATIES: The Treaties of Stockholm, 1719–1720 and the Treaty of Nystad, 1721

During the 16th and 17th centuries, Sweden had expanded its hold over the coasts of the Baltic Sea, much to the irritation of its neighbors. Russia resented having its access to a northern port blocked by such Swedish-controlled lands as Estonia, Ingria, Karelia, and Livonia. Denmark-Norway, already glum over the loss of its Scandinavian provinces to the Swedes, was especially unhappy about Sweden's alliance with Holstein-Gottrop. For it was this alliance that held Denmark in check from the south and prevented the Danes from again taking control of Schleswig and Holstein. The Germans, the house of Brandenburg in particular, which lusted after Swedish Pomerania, deplored the role Sweden played in

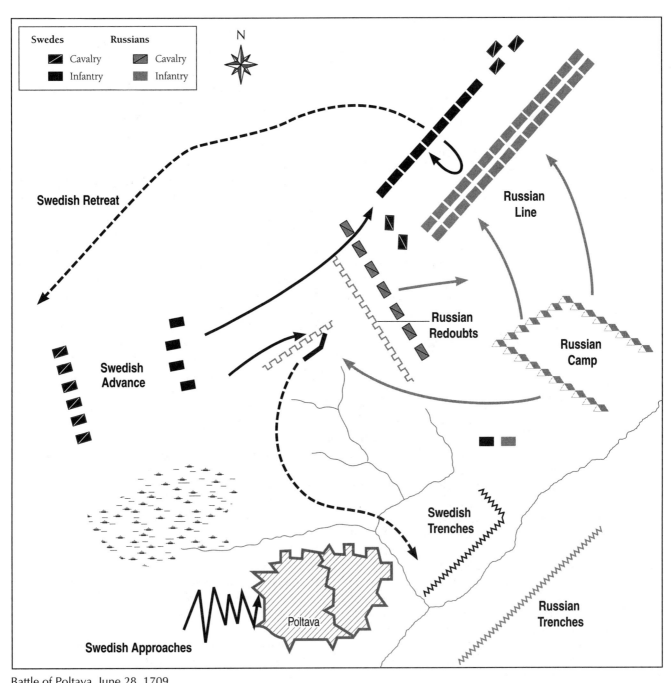

Battle of Poltava, June 28, 1709

the Holy Roman Empire. Finally, the Poles continued to stew over the loss of Livonia, holding it still Polish by any honest reckoning.

The atmosphere was already charged with danger, then, when Sweden's Charles XI (1655–97) died, making a 14-year-old the heir to the throne. Denmark-Norway took Charles XII's (1682–1718) ascension as the signal to organize an anti-Swedish coalition, and the young king was immediately confronted by three threats: the Danes invading Holstein-Gottrop, King Augustus II (1670–1733) of Poland attacking Livonia at Riga, and Russian czar Peter I (the Great; 1672–1725) laying siege to Narva in a bid for Ingermanland.

The new king showed some strategic brilliance when he concentrated his forces first on Denmark, forcing King Frederick IV (1670–1730) to withdraw Denmark and Norway from the anti-Swedish alliance and to sign, in August 1700, the Treaty of Traventhal, which returned the status quo ante bellum. Then, quickly, Charles turned his attention to Peter's army at Narva, forcing the Russians to lift the siege there, before he marched to the relief of Riga, driving the Poles and the Saxons into retreat as he pushed on through Livonia to invade first Lithuania, then Poland itself, where he seized both Cracow and Warsaw.

Augustus II of Poland, commanding some 10,000 men, met Charles at the Battle of Pultusk, about 32 miles north of Warsaw, on April 13, 1703. The two armies were fairly evenly matched, but Charles XII trounced Augustus, sending his army into full retreat. On the heels of this victory, the Polish diet installed Charles's candidate, Stanislaus I Leszczynski (1677–1766), on the Polish throne in 1704. Two years after taking Poland, Charles moved against Lithuania and chased Augustus II into Saxony. It was this invasion of Saxony, finally, that led Augustus, after six years of fighting, to relinquish his Polish throne. For, though he fought Charles to a standstill, he nevertheless agreed, under the Treaty of Altranstadt in September 1706, to renounce his royal claim in favor of Stanislaus and to break with his Russian allies. For his part, Charles clearly intended to continue on into Peter the Great's vast kingdom.

Meanwhile, the czar had used the period when Charles had focused on defeating Augustus to reorganize the Russian army and to entrench Russia on the east coast of the Baltic, where in 1703 Peter founded both the city of Saint Petersburg and the naval port of Kronstadt.

Thus was Russia the better prepared when Charles marched from Saxony in September 1707 at the head of an 80,000-man army through Poland and Lithuania and into Russia. Like other invaders who would come after him, including Napoleon I (1769–1821) and Adolf Hitler (1889–1945), Charles fell victim to the Russian winter and to the dogged resistance of the Russian soldier. He failed to reach Moscow and turned instead toward the Ukraine, where he joined forces with the Cossack insurrectionist leader Ivan Mazeppa (c. 1640–1709). His army greatly reduced by the hardships of Russia, Charles was badly defeated at the Battle of Poltava on June 28, 1709. He had only 1,800 men with him when he fled to Turkish Moldavia.

While Charles was in ignominious retreat, Augustus returned to Poland and overthrew Stanislaus, and Peter I invaded Ingermanland, as well as Livonia and Finland. Prussia conquered Pomerania. Poland, Russia, Prussia, Saxony, Hanover, and Denmark now leagued against Sweden. The Swedes managed to defeat a Danish army in Skåne, Sweden, and a combined Danish-Saxon army in Pomerania, but a Russian, Danish, and Saxon coalition defeated the Swedish army in Holstein. At this time, too, the Swedish fleet fell to Russia.

Sweden began negotiating a peace, but the process was interrupted by Charles XII, who goaded the Turks into war with Russia. From a headquarters at the Baltic town of Stralsund, Charles ordered the war to resume, but the anti-Swedish coalition quickly besieged Stralsund, which fell in December 1715. Charles made for Sweden, where he raised a new army to invade Norway (at the time a Danish possession), but the king fell victim to an enemy bullet while he was commanding the siegeworks outside of Frederikshald in December 1718.

Without their commander in chief, the Swedish army withdrew and marched home, and Sweden now entered into negotiations that resulted in the Treaties of Stockholm. Hanover collected from Sweden the duchies of Bremen and Verden in exchange for an indemnity. To Prussia went Stettin and parts of Pomerania. Denmark relinquished most of its war gains, except for Schleswig, taking an indemnity payment in exchange. By the Treaty of Nystad, Sweden ceded Livonia, Ingermanland, a portion of Karelia, and various Baltic islands to Russia, which relinquished Finland in return. Russia became the dominant power in eastern Europe.

Further reading: Robert I. Frost, *The Northern Wars: State and Society in Northeastern Europe, 1558–1721* (New York: Longman, 2000); R. M. Hattan, *Charles XII of Sweden: Union, Disunion, and Scandinavian Integration* (New York: Weybright and Talley, 1969); W. Glyn Jones, *Denmark: A Modern History* (Dover, N.H.: Croom Helm, 1986); Jerzy Lukowoski, *Concise History of Poland* (New York: Cambridge University Press, 2001); Byron J. Nordstrom, *The History of Sweden* (Westport, Conn.: Greenwood Press, 2002); Stewart Oakley, *War and Peace in the Baltic, 1560–1790* (New York: Routledge, 1992); W. F. Reddaway, ed., *The Cambridge History of Poland*, 2 vols. (New York: Cambridge University Press, 1941–50, reprinted 1971); Michael Roberts, ed., *Sweden's Age of Greatness, 1632–1718* (London: Macmillan, 1973); Franklin D. Scott, *Sweden, the Nation's History* (Carbondale: Southern Illinois University Press, 1988); Vytas

Stanley Vardys and Judith Sedaitis, *Lithuania: The Rebel Nation* (Denver: Westview Press, 1966); Arvids Ziedonis, William L. Winter, and Mardi Valgemäe, *Baltic History* (Columbus, Ohio: Association for the Advancement of Baltic Studies, 1974).

Northumberland's Rebellion (1408)

PRINCIPAL COMBATANTS: Scottish rebels (under the earl of Northumberland) vs. England
PRINCIPAL THEATER(S): Northern England
DECLARATION: None
MAJOR ISSUES AND OBJECTIVES: Northumberland was rebelling against Henry IV.
OUTCOME: The rebel army was crushed and Northumberland killed in battle.
APPROXIMATE MAXIMUM NUMBER OF MEN UNDER ARMS: Unknown
CASUALTIES: Unknown
TREATIES: None

Henry IV (1357–1413) could hardly have gained his throne without the support of Henry Percy (1342–1408), first earl of Northumberland, and early in Henry's reign Northumberland remained an important member of the English privy council. But the earl and his son (Shakespeare's "Hotspur," Sir Henry Percy [1366–1403]) both grew disenchanted with the Crown when Henry failed to reward them sufficiently for their service in Scotland. They ultimately rose up against the king in PERCY'S REBELLION, which led to Hotspur's death and Northumberland's complete alienation. He joined the conspiracy to oust King Henry and replace him with Edmund Mortimer (1376–1409) that lay at the heart of GLENDOWER'S REVOLT. Informed of the plot, Henry caused the arrest of Northumberland's coconspirators, who were subsequently executed. As for Northumberland, he escaped to Scotland, then to Holland. In the summer of 1406 he returned to Scotland, where he raised a small army to raid the north of England just across the Scottish border. The raids had little effect, and on February 19, 1408, he was trapped at Bramham Moor by a force under the local sheriff, Thomas Rokeby. The rebels were soundly defeated, and Northumberland was among the slain.

Further reading: Bryan Beran, *Henry IV* (London: Palgrave Macmillan, 1994); E. F. Jacob, *The Fifteenth Century, 1399–1485* (Oxford: Clarendon Press, 1961).

Northwest Rebellion   *See* RIEL'S SECOND REBELLION.

Norwegian Invasion of Scotland (1263)

PRINCIPAL COMBATANTS: Norway vs. Scotland
PRINCIPAL THEATER(S): Largs, Scotland—on the Clyde River
DECLARATION: None
MAJOR ISSUES AND OBJECTIVES: King Haakon IV of Norway sought conquest.
OUTCOME: A storm wrecked Haakon's fleet, and his land forces were readily defeated; ultimately, Norway sold the Hebrides to Scotland.
APPROXIMATE MAXIMUM NUMBER OF MEN UNDER ARMS: Unknown; Haakon's fleet numbered 100 ships.
CASUALTIES: Unknown, although well over half of Haakon's fleet was lost.
TREATIES: No treaty ended the war; the 1266 Treaty of Perth transferred sovereignty of the Hebrides to Scotland.

Haakon IV (1204–63), king of Norway, invaded Scotland in the summer of 1263 by sending a fleet of 100 ships to the port of Largs. King Alexander III (1241–86) of Scotland entered into deliberately protracted negotiations with Haakon, extending talks into the fall, which, he knew, was the stormy season. Haakon's fleet was decimated by storms, leaving his land troops without supply. Alexander defeated Haakon at the Battle of Largs, which sent the Norwegian king fleeing back to his homeland. He died en route, however, at Kirkwall in the Orkneys, and his successor, King Magnus IV (1238–80), sold Alexander control of the Hebrides Islands in 1266. To cement relations between Scotland and Norway, Magnus married his sons to the daughters of the Scottish king.

Further reading: T. K. Derry, *A Short History of Norway*, 2nd ed. (Westport, Conn.: Greenwood Press, 1968).

November Insurrection   *See* POLISH REBELLION (1830–1831).

November (October) Revolution
See BOLSHEVIK REVOLUTION; FEBRUARY (MARCH) REVOLUTION; KORNILOV'S REVOLT.

Novgorod, Sack of (1569–1570)

PRINCIPAL COMBATANTS: Czar Ivan IV "the Terrible" vs. Novgorod
PRINCIPAL THEATER(S): Novgorod
DECLARATION: None

MAJOR ISSUES AND OBJECTIVES: The czar sought retribution for what he falsely asserted was the disloyalty of the metropolitan of Novgorod.
OUTCOME: The city was all but completely destroyed.
APPROXIMATE MAXIMUM NUMBER OF MEN UNDER ARMS:
Unknown
CASUALTIES: 60,000 citizens of Novgorod were killed outright; others subsequently died of plague brought on by their inability to dispose of corpses. The death toll in Tver (Kalnin) and other towns along the czar's route to Novgorod is unknown.
TREATIES: None

In the 14th and 15th centuries, Novgorod—one of the oldest of Russia's cities whose history stretches back at least to 859—engaged in a long, bitter, and often destructive battle for supremacy with Moscow. During the course of this struggle, Novgorod not uncommonly turned to Lithuania for help. Soundly defeated by Moscow in 1386, the city stubbornly continued its opposition to and maintained its alliance with Lithuania, however sporadic. Then in 1471, Grand prince of Moscow Ivan III (the Great; 1440–1505) defeated Novgorod and annexed much of its northern territories (see MUSCOVITE CONQUEST OF NOVGOROD).

Though forced in 1478 finally to recognize Moscow's sovereignty, opposition by the city's leading citizens remained a Novgorod tradition until Ivan IV (the Terrible; 1530–84) became czar and decided to put an end to Novgorod's history of disloyalty. In December 1569, Ivan relied on trumped-up evidence that the Novgorod metropolitan had secretly concocted an alliance with Lithuania to justify launching a military expedition against the city. On the way to Novgorod, his troops destroyed various villages and towns, including, most notably, Tver (Kalinin), whose citizens were massacred.

On January 2, 1570, Ivan and his troops arrived at Novgorod. They swept through the city, looting and destroying churches and monasteries and putting to death, by cold-blooded, methodical execution, some 60,000 residents of the city at the rate of 500 to 1,000 daily. At length exhausted, the czar pardoned the survivors of the massacre—but the town was piled so high with rotting corpses that plague broke out and killed many of those who had escaped execution.

To impress the people back in Moscow, Ivan returned bearing the corpses of the Novgorod metropolitan and other church and city leaders suspected of plotting against Russia.

See also LIVONIAN WAR.

Further reading: Robert Auty and Dimitri Obolensky, *An Introduction to Russian History* (Cambridge, U.K.: Cambridge University Press, 1976); Robert O. Crummey, *The Formation of Muscovy* (London: Longman, 1987); Henri Troyat, *Ivan the Terrible* (London: New English Library, 1985).

Numantian War   (137–133 B.C.E.)

PRINCIPAL COMBATANTS: Rome vs. Numantia
PRINCIPAL THEATER(S): Numantia, Spain
DECLARATION: None
MAJOR ISSUES AND OBJECTIVES: Rome sought to conquer the stubbornly defended Spanish town of Numantia.
OUTCOME: After an eight-month siege, the town fell.
APPROXIMATE MAXIMUM NUMBER OF MEN UNDER ARMS:
Rome, 60,000; Numantia, numbers unknown, but certainly far inferior to Rome
CASUALTIES: Only 4,000 Numantians survived the eight-month Roman siege.
TREATIES: None

This may be seen as a phase of the CELTIBERIAN WARS, from 154 to 133 B.C.E. Numantia was a Celtiberian town located near modern-day Soria, Spain, along the Duero River. In the past, the town had repulsed a number of Roman attempts at conquest. In 137, Gaius Hostilius Mancinus (fl. mid-second century) B.C.E.) led 20,000 Roman legionnaires against Numantia and was forced to surrender, leading to the general demoralization of Roman troops in Spain.

In 134, Scipio Aemilianus (c. 185–129 B.C.E.) was sent to take charge of the legions and revive their spirit. With 60,000 men, he renewed the siege of Numantia, which endured for eight months before a mere 4,000 starving survivors surrendered. Scipio Aemilianus gave no quarter. After destroying Numantia, he ordered the execution of some of his prisoners and the enslavement of the rest.

See also LUSITANIAN WAR.

Further reading: John S. Richardson, *Romans in Spain* (London: Blackwell, 1998); Colin Wells, *The Roman Empire*, 2nd ed. (Cambridge, Mass.: Harvard University Press, 1995).

Numidian War   *See* JUGURTHINE WAR (NUMIDIAN WAR) (112–106 B.C.E.).

Octavian's War against Antony

(33–30 B.C.E.)

PRINCIPAL COMBATANTS: Mark Antony and Cleopatra vs. Octavian

PRINCIPAL THEATER(S): Egypt

DECLARATION: None

MAJOR ISSUES AND OBJECTIVES: Possession and control of Egypt

OUTCOME: Antony and Cleopatra were defeated; Octavian conquered Egypt and subsequently, as Caesar Augustus, was the first emperor of the Roman Empire.

APPROXIMATE MAXIMUM NUMBER OF MEN UNDER ARMS: Antony and Cleopatra's forces, 40,000; Octavian's forces, 40,000

CASUALTIES: At Actium, 5,000 of Antony's men died.

TREATIES: Egyptian capitulation and tribute, 30 B.C.E.

After the assassination of Julius Caesar (100–44 B.C.E.) in 44 B.C.E., two of his cohorts, his second-in-command Marcus Aemilius Lepidus (d. c. 13 B.C.E.) and his right-hand man Marcus Antonius (c. 83–30 B.C.E. ["Mark Antony" to the English-speaking, Shakespeare-reading world]) formed the Second Triumvirate with Caesar's nephew and adopted heir, 18-year-old Gaius Octavius (63 B.C.E.–14 C.E.; called Octavian by English scholars and soon to be known throughout the world and for eternity as Rome's first and greatest emperor, Augustus Caesar. Though the three, with good reason, hardly trusted one another, they managed to coexist until 36 B.C.E., when Lepidus—resentful of the growing domination of the triumvirate by Octavian and Antony—attacked Octavius in Sicily, only to lose his army to the younger man and find himself placed under lifelong armed guard.

Meanwhile, Antony—having taken Rome's Eastern Empire as his share of the Triumvirate's division of power—was refused aid by Octavian in the further execution of the ongoing ROMAN-PARTHIAN WAR (55–38 B.C.E.) So, instead, Antony turned to Julius Caesar's former lover, Cleopatra (69–30 B.C.E.), queen of Egypt. Thus began one of the great sexual-political-military liaisons of history, a heated affair hardly affected by the fact that in 40 B.C.E., when Antony returned to Rome to patch up matters with Octavian, he entered into a politically necessary marriage with Octavian's sister, Octavia (69–11 B.C.E.). The speed with which Antony returned to Egypt and the openness of his infidelity with Cleopatra affronted not only his official wife but enraged her powerful brother. Octavian was soon joined in his anger by the whole of Rome itself when news spread that Antony was turning over liberal patches of the Eastern Empire to Cleopatra and her children, three of them in fact sired by Mark Antony.

Pushed by Octavian, the Roman Senate declared war on Antony and Egypt. Antony was portrayed throughout Rome as a traitor, and Octavian was thereby able to persuade all of Italy and the western Roman provinces to withdraw allegiance from Antony and swear loyalty to himself. Officially, Antony was stripped of all Roman titles and honors, and the Senate declared war on Cleopatra, which was also war against Antony.

Together, Antony and Cleopatra assembled an army and a fleet, which sailed to Greece during 32–31 B.C.E. to wait out the winter. In the spring, Octavian and his lieutenant, Marcus Vipsanius Agrippa (63–12 B.C.E.), crossed the Adriatic with a force of comparable size to that of

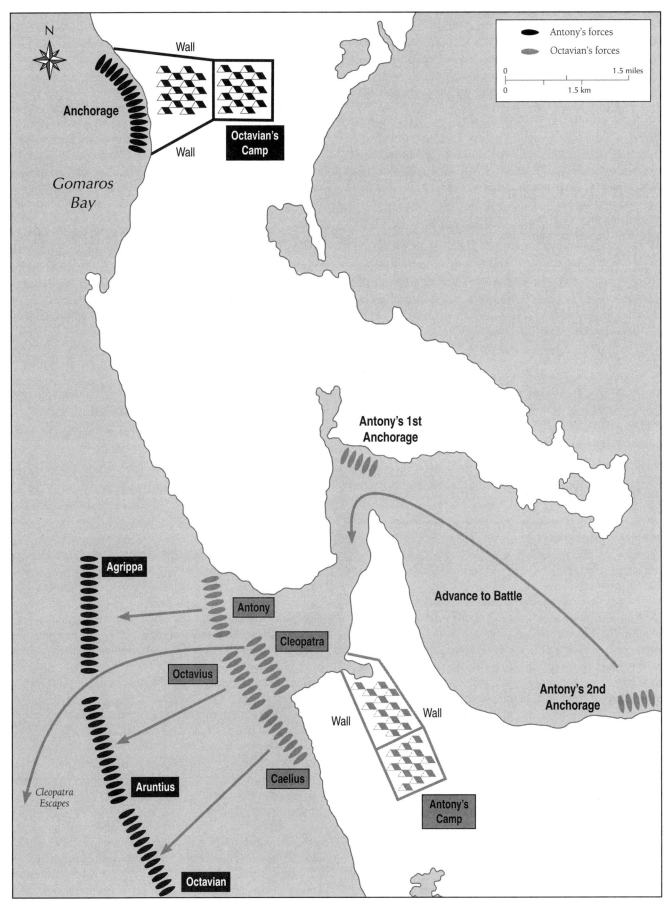

N

Wall

Anchorage

Octavian's Camp

Gomaros Bay

Wall

Antony's forces
Octavian's forces

0   1.5 miles
0   1.5 km

Antony's 1st Anchorage

Advance to Battle

Agrippa

Antony

Cleopatra

Octavius

Antony's 2nd Anchorage

Wall   Wall

Cleopatra Escapes

Aruntius

Caelius

Antony's Camp

Octavian

Battle of Actium, 31 B.C.E.

Antony. On September 2, 31, the Battle of Actium was fought on the Ionian coast of Greece. While Agrippa blockaded Antony's fleet, Octavian cut off the overland supply routes of his army. Antony then ordered a retreat and took his chances running the naval blockade. Most of the ships, together with the troops they held, were sunk or surrendered. Antony and Cleopatra made it successfully through the blockade, however, and managed to regroup. In 30, when Octavian invaded Egypt, Antony was at first able to mount a creditable defense, pushing the Romans back before they reached Alexandria. However, Antony's army soon deserted to the enemy, leading both Antony and Cleopatra to commit suicide.

Octavian looted the treasures of Ptolemaic Egypt and forced the Egyptians to pay a heavy tribute. With the conquest of Egypt, Octavian was the preeminent leader of the known world. As Caesar Augustus, he became the first emperor of the Roman Empire.

See also OCTAVIAN'S WAR AGAINST POMPEY; ROMAN CIVIL WAR (49–44 B.C.E.); ROMAN CIVIL WAR (43–31 B.C.E.).

Further reading: Anthony Everitt, *Cicero: The Life and Times of Rome's Greatest Politician* (New York: Random House, 2002); A. H. Jones, *Augustus* (New York: W. W. Norton, 1970); E. S. Schuckburgh, *Augustus Caesar* (New York: Barnes and Noble, 1995).

Octavian's War against Pompey
(40–36 B.C.E.)

PRINCIPAL COMBATANTS: Octavian vs. Pompey the Younger
PRINCIPAL THEATER(S): Sicily and Sardinia
DECLARATION: None
MAJOR ISSUES AND OBJECTIVES: At issue was control of Sardinia and Sicily in an effort to secure a reliable supply of grain for Rome.
OUTCOME: Octavian ultimately prevailed, capturing both Sardinia and Sicily and ensuring the free passage of grain to Rome.
APPROXIMATE MAXIMUM NUMBER OF MEN UNDER ARMS: Unknown; Octavian dispatched a fleet of 120 vessels against Pompey's smaller fleet.
CASUALTIES: Unknown
TREATIES: Treaty of Misenium, 39 B.C.E.

Following the death of Pompey the Great (106–48 B.C.E.) in the Great ROMAN CIVIL WAR (50–49 B.C.E.), his son Pompey the Younger (Sextus Pompeius Magnus) (75–35 B.C.E.) fled to Egypt and then to Spain, where he continued to oppose the forces of Julius Caesar (100–44 B.C.E.) and his successors. Pompey the Younger captured Sicily and, operating from there, blockaded shipments of grain

to Rome. From there, too, he launched an attack on Sardinia, which he seized from Octavian (63 B.C.E.–14 C.E.) in 40 B.C.E. This prompted Octavian and Mark Antony (c. 83–30 B.C.E.) to conclude the Treaty of Misenium with Pompey the Younger, by which Pompey was made governor of Sicily and Sardinia and was compensated for property seized from Pompey the Great. In return, Pompey the Younger agreed to transport grain to Rome.

The treaty did not long endure. In 38, Octavian regained Sardinia, but when he attempted to capture Sicily as well, his fleet fell victim to a combination of Pompey's sailors and a severe storm.

In 36, Octavian launched a new naval attack against Pompey's Sicily, sending against him 120 ships under Marcus Vipsanius Agrippa (63–12 B.C.E.). At the naval Battle of Naulochus, Pompey's fleet was defeated. Pompey himself escaped to Asia Minor, but was captured in 35 by Mark Antony and was subsequently killed. Rome never again suffered a threat to its supply of grain.

See also OCTAVIAN'S WAR AGAINST ANTONY; ROMAN CIVIL WAR (43–31 B.C.E.).

October (November) Revolution
See BOLSHEVIK REVOLUTION; FEBRUARY (MARCH) REVOLUTION; KORNILOV'S REVOLT.

"October War"   *See* ARAB-ISRAELI WAR (YOM KIPPUR WAR) (1973).

Odaenathus's Gothic Campaign   (266)

PRINCIPAL COMBATANTS: Odaenathus vs. Goth raiders
PRINCIPAL THEATER(S): Asia Minor
DECLARATION: Unknown
MAJOR ISSUES AND OBJECTIVES: Backed by his patron, Rome's emperor Gallienus, Odaenathus launched a punitive expedition against the Goths.
OUTCOME: Odaenathus subdued the barbarian raids but was soon afterward murdered.
APPROXIMATE MAXIMUM NUMBER OF MEN UNDER ARMS: Unknown
CASUALTIES: Unknown
TREATIES: None

In the middle of the third century, the Goths took advantage of Rome's wars with Persia to ravage Asia Minor. Teutonic "barbarians" of mixed Scythian and German stock, though less Asian than the Sarmatians, they consisted of two main groups: the Ostrogoths, or East Goths, from the Dnieper-Don steppes, who were primarily horsemen, and Visigoths, or West Goths, from the Carpathians, who relied primarily on infantry. But the Goths also became a seafaring people, and their most destructive raids into the Roman Empire came by water, across the Black and Aegean Seas.

During the ROMAN-PERSIAN WAR (257–261), a Romanized Arab, Septimus Odainath (or Odaenathus) (d. c. 267), prince of Palmyra, rose to prominence by effectively defending the empire's eastern provinces against Shapur I (d. 272), who had captured the Roman emperor Valerian (d. c. 261) in battle, and by defeating and executing one of the "Thirty Tyrants" named Quietus (d. c. 261). After Valerian died in captivity, the new emperor Gallienus (d. 268) graced Odaenathus with the title "Dux Orientus" and made him a virtual coruler of the Eastern Empire. Accompanied and aided by his wife, Zenobia (d. after 274), Odaenathus led the ARAB INVASION OF PERSIA in 262 and had recaptured Rome's lost provinces east of the Euphrates by 264.

Because he was already in the area, it was only natural that Odaenathus take on the Goths then raiding throughout Asia Minor. Backed by Gallienus and reinforced with Roman troops, Odaenathus launched his army of light foot soldiers and Arabian cavalry on a successful punitive expedition against the Goths in 266. The expedition, however, is mostly significant for its conclusion. Soon after completing his last "mission" for Rome, the Dux Orientus was murdered, at which point his title passed to his son, Vaballathus (d. c. 273), but his power—over Palmyra and the Eastern Empire—effectively passed to his widow, celebrated for her beauty and her military acumen, but not necessarily for her loyalty to Rome (see ZENOBIA'S CONQUEST OF EGYPT and AURELIAN'S WAR AGAINST ZENOBIA).

Further reading: Peter Brown, *The World of Late Antiquity, A.D. 150–750* (New York: W. W. Norton, 1989); Richard Stoneman, *Palmyra and Its Empire: Zenobia's Revolt against Rome* (reprint, Ann Arbor: University of Michigan Press, 1995).

Offa's Wars (771–796)

PRINCIPAL COMBATANTS: Mercia's Offa vs. various rebellious lords and subkings and the Welsh
PRINCIPAL THEATER(S): England below Yorkshire
DECLARATION: None
MAJOR ISSUES AND OBJECTIVES: The forging of Anglo-Saxon England
OUTCOME: Offa obtained and maintained control over most of England south of Yorkshire; Wales remained wildly independent.
APPROXIMATE MAXIMUM NUMBER OF MEN UNDER ARMS: Unknown
CASUALTIES: Unknown
TREATIES: No documents survive

From ancient Mercian lineage, Offa (d. July 796) became one of the more powerful Anglo-Saxon kings in England after he seized the throne during a civil war following the murder of his cousin, King Aethelbald (r. 716–57). Ruthlessly suppressing the small states in and around Mercia, he forged a united kingdom south of Yorkshire. By 774, lesser kings in the region were paying him homage as "king of the English," and he married his daughters to the rulers of Wessex and Northumbria. Offa's England was, however, an unstable place, and in addition to the wars he had waged to unite the kingdom before 774, he was forced afterward to engage in a number of disciplinary conflicts from 775 through 796 against upstart rebels, most often in Kent, but also in Wessex and East Anglia.

Offa's goal throughout was to establish himself on a par with the monarchs of continental Europe, and though he quarreled frequently with the king of the Franks, Charlemagne (c. 742–814) nevertheless concluded a commercial treaty with Offa in 796. Offa was also on good terms with Rome and allowed Pope Adrian I (pope from 772–95) to increase his control over the sometimes maverick English church. None of his European prestige, however, helped Offa much with the Welsh, who stoutly resisted conquest, and Offa ultimately gave up on these stubborn people, erecting an earthen boundary, Offa's Dyke, to separate England from Wales—and to provide something of a fortified position to defend against raids and other incursions.

See also AETHELBALD'S WARS.

Further reading: Frank Stenton, *Anglo-Saxon England*, 3rd ed. (Oxford, UK: Clarendon Press, 1971).

Og's Rebellion (1480)

PRINCIPAL COMBATANTS: Angus Og vs. the Macdonald and Maclean clans
PRINCIPAL THEATER(S): Northwestern Scottish Highlands
DECLARATION: None
MAJOR ISSUES AND OBJECTIVES: Domination of the Highlands
OUTCOME: Og defeated his father, the Lord of the Isles, and caused great and violent feuding throughout the Highlands.
APPROXIMATE MAXIMUM NUMBER OF MEN UNDER ARMS: Unknown
CASUALTIES: Unknown, but the Battle of Bloody Bay is believed to have been extraordinarily savage.
TREATIES: None

In the northwest of Scotland, the Macdonald clan dubbed themselves the "Lords of the Isles" and rebelled against the Scottish Crown in the MACDONALD REBELLION in 1411. After years of chronic unrest and uprising, the

Crown reached an agreement with the Macdonalds, which, however, turned Angus Og (d. 1490), bastard son of the current lord of the Isles, against his father as well as the Crown. His break with his father divided the northwestern Highlands into two warring factions. In 1480, at the Battle of Bloody Bay, Og, allied now with the Macleod and MacKenzie clans, fought his father and his allies, the Macleans. Og not only enjoyed victory, he captured and imprisoned his father (as well as two of his principal Maclean officers) and persisted in stirring up violent feuding in the Highlands. The assassination of Og in 1490 ended this.

Further reading: W. Croft Dickinson, *Scotland from the Earliest Times to 1603,* 3rd rev. ed. (Oxford: Clarendon Press, 1977).

Old Zurich War (1436–1450)

PRINCIPAL COMBATANTS: Zurich and Austria (with French aid) vs. Schwyz, Glarus, and the Swiss Confederacy
PRINCIPAL THEATER(S): Zurich and the Toggenburg
DECLARATION: None
MAJOR ISSUES AND OBJECTIVES: Control of the Toggenburg
OUTCOME: Zurich relinquished the Toggenburg to Schwyz, and the house of Savoy was installed in the Aargau (Switzerland).
APPROXIMATE MAXIMUM NUMBER OF MEN UNDER ARMS: Schwyz and Swiss Confederacy, 20,000; Zurich and allies, 40,000
CASUALTIES: Unknown
TREATIES: Peace of Ensisheim, 1444; Peace of Constance, 1446

The Old Zurich War grew from a territorial dispute created by the death of the last count of Toggenburg in 1436. The Toggenburgs, always vassals of either German kings or Holy Roman Emperors, boasted extensive possessions in what is now northeastern Switzerland. The dying off of the dynasty not only raised questions about who would rule some of the large Toggenburg holdings but fed the greed of nearby towns. The Toggenburg lands were bounded to the west and to the southwest by the free cities of Zurich, Schwyz, and Glarus—all members of the Swiss Confederation. To the southeast, Toggenburg possessions bordered lands held by two of the three leagues later known collectively as the Grisons.

While the southeasternmost part of the territory was quickly claimed (and occupied) by the newly formed Zehngerichtenbund (League of Ten Jurisdictions), the rest of the Toggenburg inheritance fell open to dispute. The House of Raron (in distant Valais) managed successfully to claim most of the countship, but the dependencies nearest to Lake Zurich and a tract to the east of them was promptly invaded by the men of Schwyz, who blocked the road to Zurich. These moves were, of course, fiercely resented by Zurich, whose leaders desired to control at least the shore of the lake if nothing else. When a meeting of the Swiss confederates in 1437 authorized Schwyz and Glarus to retain nearly all the occupied zone, Zurich rejected the settlement out of hand and appealed to the Imperial Diet in 1440. The Austrian duke and German king Frederick III (1415–43) allied his forces with Zurich, which prompted Schwyz and its ally Glarus to declare war on Zurich and Austria.

During the opening clash, Zurich's burgomaster, at the head of its army, was killed, sending the forces of Zurich into headlong retreat. The Imperial Diet now called for conciliation, whereupon Zurich broke with Austria, which rejected the directive of the Diet. Joining the side of Schwyz, the Swiss Confederacy aided the city with some 20,000 troops in its siege against Zurich. Frederick obtained aid from France—40,000 men—who were nevertheless defeated by the much smaller Schwyz-Swiss Confederacy force in 1444.

The Peace of Ensisheim was concluded in 1444, but Zurich refused to be a party to it. Two years later, however, the Peace of Constance ended the Austrian-Zurich alliance and gave some territory back to Zurich, but yielded to Schwyz most of Toggenburg. Austria remained involved in sporadic fighting in the region until a special court of arbitration ordered Austria out of the Aargau (Switzerland) altogether and installed there the house of Savoy. Ultimately, the major portion of the Toggenburg countship was sold by the house of Raron to the prince-abbot of Sankt Gallen in 1468, only to become a ground for discord during the Swiss Reformation (*see* the VILLMERGEN WAR, SECOND).

Further reading: William Martin, *Switzerland: From Roman Times to the Present* (New York: Praeger, 1971).

Onin War (1467–1477)

PRINCIPAL COMBATANTS: Rival shogun clans
PRINCIPAL THEATER(S): Kyoto and environs
DECLARATION: None
MAJOR ISSUES AND OBJECTIVES: Succession to the shogunate
OUTCOME: The issues of succession remained unresolved throughout the long and ruinous war.
APPROXIMATE MAXIMUM NUMBER OF MEN UNDER ARMS: Unknown
CASUALTIES: Unknown
TREATIES: None

A feudal dispute erupted into chaotic warfare in western Japan. Yoshimasa (1435–90), the Ashikaga shogun (military overlord), retired in 1467, triggering a dispute over succession to his shogunate. Rival families started a full-scale war in and about Kyoto, which was largely destroyed in the conflict. Even though the leaders of the warring factions, Yamana Mochitoyo (1404–73) and Hosokawa Katsumoto (c. 1430–73), both died in 1473, their partisans continued to fight, ultimately bringing some dozen major military families into the fray and laying waste to the entire region around Kyoto. The Onin War produced nothing but general ruin and failed to resolve the succession to the shogunate.

See also JAPANESE CIVIL WARS (1450–1550).

Further reading: Thomas Keirstead, *The Geography of Power in Medieval Japan* (Princeton, N.J.: Princeton University Press, 1992); H. Paul Valery, *The Onin War* (New York: Columbia University Press, 1966).

"Operation Iraqi Freedom"   *See* UNITED STATES–IRAQ WAR.

"Operation Just Cause"   *See* UNITED STATES INVASION OF PANAMA.

Opium War, First   (1839–1842)

PRINCIPAL COMBATANTS: Great Britain vs. China
PRINCIPAL THEATER(S): The China coast
DECLARATION: China attacked the British ships sent to protect the opium trade on September 4, 1839.
MAJOR ISSUES AND OBJECTIVES: The British used Chinese trade policies against the importation of opium and China's treatment of opium merchants as a cause for going to war and forcing "open" trade policies on the traditionally insular Qing (Ch'ing) dynasty.
OUTCOME: China was forced to open its ports to British and other foreign trade and to grant a number of humiliating concessions
APPROXIMATE MAXIMUM NUMBER OF MEN UNDER ARMS: British forces, 12,000; Chinese forces, 45,000
CASUALTIES: Britain, about 100 killed or wounded; China, about 6,800 killed, wounded, or captured
TREATIES: Treaty of Nanking, August 29, 1842

Basically trade wars in which Western nations gained commercial privileges in China, the Opium Wars (fought from 1839 to 1842 and 1856 to 1860) were the first major military confrontations between China and the European West. Since the beginning of the 19th century British traders had been illegally importing the drug into China, leading to widespread social and economic disruption and degradation. They not only ended Chinese isolation from other civilizations, but began for China a century of mistreatment and humiliation at the hands of foreign powers, leading to the decay of the Qing dynasty and, ultimately, revolution, civil war, and the ascendancy of communist rule.

The First Opium War began when British merchants ignored a Chinese prohibition against the importation of opium. On March 30, 1839, the Chinese imperial commissioner, Lin Zexu (Lin Tse-hsü)—frustrated by the insouciance of British merchants toward official China—confiscated and destroyed all the smuggled opium in British warehouses and ships in Canton (Guangzhou [Kwangchow]), British tempers, from merchant to skivvy, flared, and the antagonism between the British and Chinese officialdom only increased a few days later when drunken British sailors killed a Chinese villager. The British government, which did not recognize the Chinese legal system, refused to turn the accused men over to the local courts.

Hostilities broke out, and Britain responded by dispatching warships and troops to attack the China coast. In rapid succession, the cities of Hangzhou (Hangchow), Hong Kong, and Canton fell under attack and were blockaded by the British. A small amphibious force sailed up the Pearl River and assaulted the fortifications surrounding Canton. The city fell in May 1841, followed soon by Amoy and Ningbo (Ning-po). After a lull in the fighting when disease struck the British forces, renewed efforts resulted in the taking of Shanghai and Xinjiang (Chinkiang). Outmatched by British troops and equipment, the Chinese capitulated when British navy ships appeared in August 1842.

The subsequent Treaty of Nanjing (Nanking) was harsh. In addition to agreeing to pay a $20 million indemnity, the Chinese opened the ports of Canton, Xiamen (Amoy), Fuzhou (Foochow), Ningbo, and Shanghai to British trade and residence. China also granted Britain the right of "extraterritoriality," whereby British residents in China were subject not to Chinese legal jurisdiction but to that of special consular courts. The greatest prize ceded to the Crown was Hong Kong, which was transferred to Britain in perpetuity.

The trade and legal concessions made to the British under the treaty were soon extended to other Western powers, and China's long isolation came to an end. The Second OPIUM WAR erupted in 1856.

Further reading: Jack Beeching, *The Chinese Opium Wars* (New York: Harcourt, 1977); Hsin-pao Chang, *Commissioner Lin and the Opium War* (Cambridge, Mass.: Harvard University Press, 1964); Peter Ward Fay, *The Opium War, 1840–1842* (Chapel Hill: University of North Carolina Press, 1975); W. Travis Hanes and Frank Sanello, *The Opium Wars: The Addiction of One Empire and the Corruption of Another* (Naperville, Ill.: Sourcebooks Inc., 2002).

Opium War, Second (1856–1860)

PRINCIPAL COMBATANTS: Great Britain and France vs. China

PRINCIPAL THEATER(S): The China coast

DECLARATION: England and France attacked China after the *Arrow*, a Chinese-owned ship flying the British flag, was seized by the Chinese.

MAJOR ISSUES AND OBJECTIVES: After the First Opium War, the British and the French (and other Western powers, including the United States) sought further trade concessions and, once again, used China's enforcement of its ban on the opium trade as an excuse to go to war and get them.

OUTCOME: China was forced to open more of its ports to British and other foreign trade and to grant Great Britain further land around Hong Kong in a "lease" to last 99 years

APPROXIMATE MAXIMUM NUMBER OF MEN UNDER ARMS: Anglo-French forces, 17,700; Chinese forces, 30,000

CASUALTIES: Anglo-French, nearly 900 killed or wounded; Chinese, more than 7,000 killed, wounded, or captured

TREATIES: Treaty of Tientsin (Tianjin or Tianjian [Tientsin]), June 28, 1858 (reaffirmed and expanded in 1860) plus copycat treaties with France, Russia, and the United States

The First OPIUM WAR resulted in the opening of several Chinese ports as well as the cession of Hong Kong to Great Britain. By 1856, the British (and the French) were restless for further trade concessions. In that year, Chinese officials seized the *Arrow*, a Chinese-owned ship flying the British flag and engaged in smuggling opium. The British, seeking to extend their trading rights in China, used the seizure as an excuse to renew hostilities. They were joined in the hostilities by the French, who used as *their* excuse the murder of a French missionary in the interior of China. In late 1857 a combined English and French force attacked, occupying Canton (Guangzhou [Kwangchow]). Next, the force took forts near Tianjin, and treaties were concluded between China and Britain as well as similar treaties between China and France, Russia, and the United States.

The new treaties with the Western powers caused widespread outrage in China and failed to receive ratification. Foreign diplomats were refused entrance to Beijing (Peking), and a British force was slaughtered outside of Tianjin in 1859. A renewed Anglo-French assault captured Tianjin and defeated a Chinese army outside of Beijing. The Chinese emperor, Xianfeng (Hsien-feng; 1831–61), fled, and his commissioners concluded new treaties embodying the provisions of the Tianjin agreement and adding four more ports to the list of those now open to foreign trade.

Of special importance, the Kowloon Peninsula on the Chinese mainland was added to the Hong Kong colony,

and in 1898 a large area beyond Kowloon, together with the surrounding islands (the "New Territories"), was leased to Great Britain for 99 years.

See also BOXER REBELLION.

Further reading: Jack Beeching, *The Chinese Opium Wars* (New York: Harcourt, 1977); D. Bonner-Smith, *The Second China War, 1856–1860* (New York: Hyperion, 1994); W. Travis Hanes and Frank Sanello, *The Opium Wars: The Addiction of One Empire and the Corruption of Another* (Naperville, Ill.: Sourcebooks Inc., 2002); Douglas Hurd, *The Arrow War: an Anglo-Chinese Confusion, 1856–1860* (New York: Macmillan, 1967).

Oporto, Revolution at (1820)

PRINCIPAL COMBATANTS: Oporto Jacobins vs. Great Britain

PRINCIPAL THEATER(S): Oporto and Lisbon, Portugal

DECLARATION: Coup of August 24, 1820

MAJOR ISSUES AND OBJECTIVES: The Jacobins sought the ouster of the British regency in Portugal.

OUTCOME: In a bloodless revolution, the British regency was evicted and the Portuguese king returned to his throne as a constitutional monarch.

APPROXIMATE MAXIMUM NUMBER OF MEN UNDER ARMS: Unknown

CASUALTIES: None

TREATIES: None

As a result of the British victory over Napoleon Bonaparte (1769–1821) in the PENINSULAR WAR from 1808 to 1814, Portugal came under the rule of a British regency, its king, John VI (1769–1826), having fled to Brazil to establish a government in exile. During the regency, Portuguese radical nationalists—popularly called Jacobins—fomented rebellion, calling for the removal of the British marshal in charge of the Portuguese army, William Carr Beresford (1768–1854). To counter the Jacobin movement, Beresford went to Brazil in an effort to persuade the king to return. In Beresford's absence, on August 24, 1820, the Jacobin Club of Oporto conspired with high-ranking military officers to stage a coup d'état. A junta was summarily established, and the revolution was accomplished with nothing more than a volley of musket fire.

The revolution spread to the Portuguese capital, Lisbon, within a matter of days. A quick revolt took place on September 15, 1820, and the junta ousted the regency and convened a session of the Cortes (parliament). The small contingent of British military was ejected from the country, Beresford was recalled to Britain, and John VI did return to Portugal, without the intermediation of a foreign regency and as a constitutional monarch. The king had left his first son behind as Emperor Pedro I (1798–1834) of Brazil, but his second son, Don Miguel

(1842–66) could not reconcile his father's return with his own ideas of absolute monarchy and his own ambitions for such a crown. Backed by his Braganza family in Portugal, he tried to extend their dynasty in a stop-and-go rebellion that ultimately led to the MIGUELITE WARS (1828–34).

See also BRAZILIAN WAR OF INDEPENDENCE; PORTUGUESE CIVIL WAR (1823–1824); SPANISH CIVIL WAR (1820–1823).

Further reading: James M. Anderson, *History of Portugal* (Westport, Conn.: Greenwood Publishing Group, 2000); Antonio Henrique R. De Oliveira Marques, *History of Portugal* (New York: Columbia University Press, 1972); H. V. Livermore, *A New History of Portugal* (New York: Cambridge University Press, 1976).

Orange River War (1846–1850)

PRINCIPAL COMBATANTS: The Boers vs. Great Britain
PRINCIPAL THEATER(S): South Africa, between the Vaal and Orange rivers
DECLARATION: None
MAJOR ISSUES AND OBJECTIVES: Frontier conflict between colonial rivals
OUTCOME: Inconclusive, although the British beat back a Boer incursion across the Vaal River
APPROXIMATE MAXIMUM NUMBER OF MEN UNDER ARMS: Boers, 1,000; British, 1,000
CASUALTIES: 100 killed or wounded on both sides
TREATIES: None

Throughout much of the 19th century, the Boers (Dutch colonial farmers of South Africa) came into increasing conflict with the British who had control of the region. During 1835–37, some 12,000 Boers migrated northward and established their own independent states. Along the frontier between these new Boer states and the British colonial holdings warfare developed during 1846–50. There was only a single set battle, and no war was formally declared. However, the chronic conflict near the Great Kei River and in the area between the Orange River and the Vaal River was dubbed the Orange River War.

The single major battle of the war, at Boomplaats, on August 29, 1848, resulted in the defeat of the Orange Colony Boers under General Andreas Pretorius (1798–1853) by a British force commanded by Sir Harry Smith (1787–1860). As a result, the Boers retreated across the Vaal, but violence continued sporadically.

See also BOER UPRISING; BOER WAR, FIRST; BOER WAR, SECOND; BOER-ZULU WAR; JAMESON RAID.

Further reading: Leonard Thompson, *A History of South Africa* (New Haven, Conn.: Yale University Press, 2001).

Oranges, War of the (1801)

PRINCIPAL COMBATANTS: France and Spain vs. Portugal
PRINCIPAL THEATER(S): Portugal
DECLARATION: None
MAJOR ISSUES AND OBJECTIVES: France wanted Portuguese cessions of territory and concessions of trade; under pressure from Napoleon, Spain cooperated in war against Portugal.
OUTCOME: Portugal ceded territory in Brazil and Portugal and made other concessions; Napoleon was unsatisfied.
APPROXIMATE MAXIMUM NUMBER OF MEN UNDER ARMS: Unknown
CASUALTIES: Unknown
TREATIES: Treaty of Badajoz, June 6, 1801

Threatened by Napoleon I (Napoleon Bonaparte; 1769–1821), Spain joined France in a brief war to compel Portugal to cede much of its territory to France and to close its ports to British trade. French forces, joined by Spanish troops under General Manuel Godoy (1767–1851), invaded in April 1801. The Portuguese were defeated along the Spanish border at the Battle of Olivenza, whereupon Godoy sent to the queen of Spain a basket of oranges picked at nearby Elvas, with a message announcing his intention to march to Lisbon. However, Portugal quickly agreed to the Treaty of Badajoz on June 6, 1801, shutting its ports to British trade, granting special trading status to France, ceding Olivenza to Spain, ceding part of Brazil to France, and paying monetary reparations. Napoleon, wanting more of Portugal itself, denounced the treaty, prompting Spain to take a stand against France. Napoleon threatened to devastate both Spain and Portugal, but he was unable to make good on his threat because of war pressures elsewhere.

See also NAPOLEONIC WARS.

Further reading: David Chandler, *Campaigns of Napoleon* (London: Cassell, 1997); Charles J. Esdaile, *The Wars of Napoleon* (London: Pearson, 1996); Gunther Eric Rothenberg, *The Napoleonic Wars* (London: Cassell, 1999).

Orléans, Siege of (1429)

PRINCIPAL COMBATANTS: English forces for Henry VI and Burgundian allies vs. Joan of Arc and forces for the French heir Charles
PRINCIPAL THEATER(S): City of Orléans in southern France
DECLARATION: No formal declaration
MAJOR ISSUES AND OBJECTIVES: A contest for the French throne following the death of King Charles VI.
OUTCOME: The dauphin ascended to the throne.

APPROXIMATE MAXIMUM NUMBER OF MEN UNDER ARMS:
English, 5,000; Joan was accompanied to Orléans by
several hundred troops.
CASUALTIES: English, 500 killed or captured; French,
unknown
TREATIES: None

In 1420, during the HUNDRED YEARS' WAR, England's King
Henry V (1387–1422) became heir to the French throne,
by courtesy of the Treaty of Troyes, upon the death of
French king Charles VI (1368–1422). The deal was
denounced by Charles's son, the dauphin, and his followers, and when Charles died, the dauphin claimed the crown
as Charles VII (1403–61). Unfortunately, the English, too,
decided to press their claim, and they allied with Philip III
(the Good; 1396–1467), duke of Burgundy—whose forces
controlled much of northern France—to keep Charles from
taking the throne. As it happened, Henry V died the same
year as Charles VI, so it was not he but his infant son,
Henry VI (1421–71), in whose name the English regent,
John Plantagenet (1389–1435), duke of Bedford, took control of English holdings in northern France. Five years after
the death of this father, Charles VII had not yet been
crowned, since Reims, traditional site of French corona-
tions, lay under the control of his enemies.

Even worse, Bedford soon attacked the south, sending
5,000 troops to conquer Maine, a border region between
those French lands recognizing Henry of England as king
and those recognizing Charles as king. After taking Maine,
Thomas de Montacute (d. 1428), earl of Salisbury,
launched the siege of Orléans, a city which had become
key to maintaining the dauphin's ambition. Not only the
French were unhappy with Salisbury. His action had been
taken against the advice of the duke of Bedford himself,
who argued for an advance into Anjou instead. Salisbury
managed to capture some important places upstream and
downstream from Orléans, along with the bridgehead fort
on the south bank of the Loire River opposite the city
itself, before he died from a battle wound on November 3.

His successor in command, William de la Pole (1396–
1450), earl of Suffolk, did little to advance the siege before
December of 1428, when John Talbot (1384–1453 [later earl
of Shrewsbury]) and Thomas Scales arrived to push him forward. Under their influence the English began to build
impressive siegeworks, including forts, and to press harder
on the city, and a French attempt to cut the besiegers' line of
supply was defeated in the Battle of the Herrings on February 12, 1429. Still, as the weeks went by, Orléans held out.

Part of the reason lay with a young French peasant
girl, the deeply religious Joan of Arc (1412–31), who
would lead the defense against the siege after forcing an
audience with the dauphin and persuading him to accept
what she saw as her divine mission to save the city. In fact,
the defenders, under Jean d'Orléans (1403–68), comte de
Dunois (bastard son of Charles VII's late uncle Louis, duc

d'Orléans [1372–1407]), were considering capitulation
when Joan had her audience. At length, she persuaded
Charles to send an army to relieve the besieged town.

With several hundred of the dauphin's troops, Joan set
out for Orléans. From Chézy five miles upstream, Joan
distracted the English with a diversionary feint against
one of the English forts, and entered Orléans with supplies on April 30. On May 4 she attacked the principal
English forts, and within three days they had all been
stormed. Suffolk abandoned the siege. What was more,
the English were forced out of Troyes, Châlons, and
Reims. There, at last, Charles was crowned. Although ultimately the English would execute Joan as a witch and a
heretic, the "Maid of Orléans" had loosened England's grip
on French lands for good.

See also ROSES, WARS OF THE.

Further reading: Anne Curry, *The Hundred Years War*
(New York: Palgrave Macmillan, 2003); Desmond Stewart,
The Hundred Years' War: England in France, 1337–1453
(New York: Penguin USA, 1999); Jonathan Sumption, *The
Hundred Years' War: Trial by Fire* (Philadelphia: University
of Pennsylvania Press, 2000).

Oruro Revolt (1736–1737)

PRINCIPAL COMBATANTS: Spain vs. the Oruro Indians
PRINCIPAL THEATER(S): Central Peru
DECLARATION: None
MAJOR ISSUES AND OBJECTIVES: Rebellion against
intolerable working and living conditions in the mines of
central Peru
OUTCOME: The rebels sacked the city of Oruro, but the
rebellion was extinguished by Spanish colonial troops.
APPROXIMATE MAXIMUM NUMBER OF MEN UNDER ARMS:
Unknown
CASUALTIES: Unknown
TREATIES: None

The Oruro Indians of Peru were treated essentially as
slaves by the mine owners in the central portion of that
colony. The horrific conditions drove the Oruros to desperation, and they rallied behind Juan Santos, who led
them in revolt. In 1737, they overran the city of Oruro
before colonial troops put down the rebellion.

Further reading: J.R. Fisher, *Silver Mines and Silver
Miners in Colonial Peru, 1776–1824* (Liverpool: Centre for
Latin-American Studies, University of Liverpool, 1977).

Oswald's Wars (1633–641)

PRINCIPAL COMBATANTS: Oswald, king of Bernicia, and
Penda, king of Mercia vs. Cadwallon, king of Gwynedd,
Wales; later, Oswald vs. Penda

PRINCIPAL THEATER(S): England, primarily Northumbria and Wales
DECLARATION: None
MAJOR ISSUES AND OBJECTIVES: Domination over Anglo-Saxon England
OUTCOME: Oswald amassed a large Anglo-Saxon kingdom, but was killed in battle by his former ally, Penda, who elevated Mercia to a long period of dominance over Anglo-Saxon England.
APPROXIMATE MAXIMUM NUMBER OF MEN UNDER ARMS: Unknown
CASUALTIES: Unknown
TREATIES: No documents survive

During the Middle Ages, England was a region of fragmented kingdoms. The death of Edwin (585–632), king of Deira, enabled Oswald (c. 605–641), son of the Bernician king Aethelfrith (fl. 593–616), to regain dominance of both Bernicia and Deira after he had been exiled from Northumbria (the region encompassing Bernicia and Deira) in 616. With King Penda (c. 577–655) of Mercia, Oswald now attacked King Cadwallon (d. 634) of Gwynedd, in northern Wales. After a year of combat, the forces of Cadwallon were defeated, and Cadwallon himself killed at the Battle of Heavenfield in 634.

Oswald now fought to secure his Northumbrian borders and extend his realms south. Along with battle, he used a dynastic marriage to secure control of Wessex. This, however, turned his ally Penda against him, and the two led armies into combat at the Battle of Maserfeld in 641. There Oswald fell, propelling Penda and the kingdom of Mercia to dominance over Anglo-Saxon England. Mercia would come to dominate England for a century and a half. Oswald, who had tried to bring peace to his realm and who founded a famous monastery at Lindisfarne to bring Christianity into pagan Northumbria, was later canonized.

See also AETHEBALD'S WARS (733–750); AETHELFRITH'S WARS (593–616).

Further reading: Frank Stenton, *Anglo-Saxon England,* 3rd ed. (Oxford, UK: Clarendon Press, 1971).

Ottoman-Byzantine Wars *See* BYZANTINE-OTTOMAN TURK WAR (1302–1326); BYZANTINE-OTTOMAN TURK WAR (1329–1338); BYZANTINE-OTTOMAN TURK WAR (1359–1399); BYZANTINE-OTTOMAN TURK WAR (1422); BYZANTINE-OTTOMAN TURK WAR (1453–1461).

Ottoman Civil War (1403–1413)

PRINCIPAL COMBATANTS: Four sons of Sultan Bayazid I of the Ottoman Empire
PRINCIPAL THEATER(S): Ottoman Empire
DECLARATION: None
MAJOR ISSUES AND OBJECTIVES: Succession to the Ottoman sultanate
OUTCOME: After a long civil war, one son emerged victorious and ruled as Muhammad I.
APPROXIMATE MAXIMUM NUMBER OF MEN UNDER ARMS: Unknown
CASUALTIES: Unknown
TREATIES: None

When Sultan Bayazid I (1347–1403) was killed at the Battle of Angora in 1403, his death began a period known as the Interregnum, during which four of his six sons tore the fledgling Ottoman Empire apart in their quest for domination of the sultanate. Muhammad, or Mehmed I (1389–1421), captured Karaman and made this city his stronghold. Süleyman (d. 1411) had control of the empire's European territories. Both Isa Bey (d. 1405) and Mustafa, or Musa Bey (d. 1413), took territories in Anatolia Turkey.

Süleyman struck an alliance with the Byzantine Empire in 1405 and met Isa in battle. Defeating Isa's army, he strangled his brother. Mustafa attacked Süleyman in 1406, fighting him and the Byzantine co-emperor John VIII Palaeologue (1390–1448) in Thrace. When Mustafa's Serbian and Bulgarian allies fled the field, however, Süleyman was able to take Adrianople (Edirne), the Ottoman European capital. Mustafa regrouped, assembling an army of Turks and Wallachians, against Adrianople. In the course of the battle, Mustafa persuaded Süleyman's contingent of Janissaries to defect to his side, and Süleyman was captured. Mustafa had him strangled as well.

After the death of Süleyman, Mustafa laid siege to Constantinople but suffered defeat at sea. Despite this loss, Mustafa was still more powerful than Muhammad and was dominant in the region. He attacked Serbia in 1406 and conquered Salonika, blinding its ruler, a son of Süleyman. Muhammad, however, with a large Turkish force and allied with the Byzantines, lifted Mustafa's siege of Constantinople and regained the loyalty of the Janissaries. He waged unremitting war on Mustafa, fighting him in three separate battles before he definitively defeated his brother in 1413. Like Isa and Süleyman, Mustafa was executed by strangulation. Muhammad I assumed the Ottoman throne and set about rebuilding the empire.

Further reading: Ducas, *Decline and Fall of Byzantium to the Ottoman Turks,* trans. Harry J. Magonlias. (Detroit: Wayne State University Press, 1975); Jason Goodwin, *Lords of the Horizon: A History of the Ottoman Empire* (New York: Picador, 2003); Colin Imber, *Ottoman Empire: 1300–1650* (London: Palgrave Macmillan, 2003); Halil Inalcik, *The Ottoman Empire: The Classical Age, 1300–1600* (London: Phoenix Press, 2001).

Ottoman Civil War (1481–1482)

PRINCIPAL COMBATANTS: Bayazid II vs. Djem
PRINCIPAL THEATER(S): Ottoman Empire
DECLARATION: None
MAJOR ISSUES AND OBJECTIVES: Succession to the Ottoman sultanate following the death of Muhammad II the Conqueror
OUTCOME: Djem was defeated several times and ultimately fled to Rhodes, where he was imprisoned for the rest of his life.
APPROXIMATE MAXIMUM NUMBER OF MEN UNDER ARMS: Unknown
CASUALTIES: Unknown
TREATIES: None

Although Sultan Muhammad, or Mehmed II (the Conqueror; 1429–1481) had greatly expanded the Ottoman Empire, leaving a firm foundation for the great future conquests of the 16th-century sultans, his death left unresolved many of the problems caused by his internal policies. The taxes he had imposed to finance his conquests, for example, had led during the last year of his reign to a virtual civil war in Constantinople between major factions of the janissaries and the Turkish aristocracy. Muhammad's son, Bayazid (1447–1513), left Amaysa to assume the throne at the behest of the Janissaries, who dominated the capital militarily and whom Bayazid had courted with promises of a full amnesty for their rebellion and an increase in pay for their services, the latter always a key attraction for mercenary troops. Bayazid II's first act was to kill the grand vizier, who had backed the other candidate for Muhammad's throne, Djem (1459–95), governor of Karaman and Bayazid's younger brother, who had already been proclaimed sultan in the old Ottoman capital of Bursa. Djem proposed to his brother that Bayazid rule Ottoman Europe and let Djem assume control of Anatolia. Bayazid rejected this proposal. He then managed to conciliate the nobility with his essentially pacific plans for consolidating his father's empire, which downgraded the Janissaries. Bereft of his major support, Djem nevertheless came to fight. The two met in battle at Yenishehr in 1481. Defeated, Djem fled into exile in Mamluk Syria in the summer of 1481. In Cairo, he regrouped, and, in 1482, renewed his attack on Bayazid II, this time with Mamluk aid. Djem failed, however, to recruit support in Karaman, where the Turkoman nomads he had hoped to rally were instead attracted to Bayazid's heterodoxy. Consequently, Djem was again defeated by his brother. This time, he fled to Rhodes, where the Knights Hospitalers kept him a captive—apparently at the request of Bayazid II, who paid them an annual fee for the service. However, another condition of Djem's captivity—either explicit or understood—was that the Ottomans refrain from attacking Europe. For 13 years, Bayazid II left Europe unmolested, fearing that the Knights Hospitalers would

release Djem. Upon Djem's death (by poisoning, probably on Bayazid's orders), Bayazid launched the VENETIAN-TURKISH WAR (1499–1503).

Further reading: Jason Goodwin, *Lords of the Horizon: A History of the Ottoman Empire* (New York: Picador, 2003); Colin Imber, *Ottoman Empire: 1300–1650* (London: Palgrave Macmillan, 2003); Halil Inalcik, *The Ottoman Empire: The Classical Age, 1300–1600* (London: Phoenix Press, 2001).

Ottoman Civil War (1509–1513)

PRINCIPAL COMBATANTS: Bayazid II vs. his sons
PRINCIPAL THEATER(S): Ottoman Empire
DECLARATION: None
MAJOR ISSUES AND OBJECTIVES: Succession to the Ottoman sultanate
OUTCOME: Selim prevailed over his father and brothers and assumed the throne as Selim I.
APPROXIMATE MAXIMUM NUMBER OF MEN UNDER ARMS: Unknown
CASUALTIES: Casualties included 40,000 Anatolian Shi'ites slain.
TREATIES: None

Although Bayazid II (1447–1513) had inherited a considerable empire from his father, Muhammad, or Mehmet, II (1429–81), he was never able to undertake the new conquests in Europe that the expansion-minded old sultan might have imagined to be the Ottoman legacy. For one thing, Bayazid had to turn much of his attention in the later years of his life to internal rebellion, especially in eastern Anatolia, where Turkoman nomads resisted not just the extension of the Ottoman administrative bureaucracy but also the empire's Sunni orthodoxy. They developed a fanatical attachment to the Sufi and Shi'ite mystic orders, the most successful of which, the Safavids, used a combined religious and military appeal to conquer most of Persia. They then spread a message of religious heresy and political revolt, not only among the tribesmen but also to farmers and some city dwellers, Ottoman citizens who were beginning to imagine in this movement the answers to their own problems.

At the same time, Bayazid was having trouble with the Janissaries who had been so instrumental in his own rise to power (*see* OTTOMAN CIVIL WAR [1481–1482]). Whereas Bayazid wished to name his son Ahmed (d. 1513) as his successor, the Janissaries much preferred his brother, Selim (1467–1520), governor of Trebizond. Bayazid, who had been put on the throne by the Janissaries despite his peace-loving nature, had throughout his reign only carried out military activities with reluctance, and Ahmed seemed to share his father's personality. Selim, on the other hand, like the mercenary Janissaries, longed to return to Muhammad

II's aggressive style of conquest. When Bayazid seemed to be prepared to abdicate in Ahmed's favor, Selim, governor of Trebizond, led an army to Adrianople, demanding that he be given a European province to govern. He wanted to ensure that he had sufficient power to topple Ahmed. Bayazid refused to accede to Selim's demand, and Selim was defeated in battle. He returned to Trebizond in 1509.

Then, in 1511, all the grievances disturbing the empire coalesced into a fundamentally religious uprising against the central government. The Shi'ite Turkoman nomads rebelled and took Bursa, the old Ottoman capital, about 150 miles from Adrianople. Bayazid dispatched his grand vizier Ali Posa (fl. 1512) with a force to put down the Turkoman rebellion, an action that left him vulnerable to Ahmed's pressure for abdication. The Janissaries threatened to revolt if Ahmed ascended the throne, so Bayazid decided not to abdicate. This prompted Ahmed to join with another brother, Kortud (d. 1513), in a rebellion in Anatolia. However, in 1512, Selim, backed by Persian allies, defeated Ahmed, then advanced to Adrianople. With the aid of the Janissaries, he at last compelled Bayazid's abdication. Both Bayazid and Kortud were soon dead—poisoned. Selim pursued Ahmed, who was defeated in battle in 1513. Captured, he was put to death by strangulation. To ensure that he would now rule unopposed, Selim—now Selim I—ordered the deaths of all seven of his nephews, and four of his five sons. He then massacred 40,000 Anatolian Shi'ites to prevent another Turkoman rebellion. With his sultanate secure, Selim could then turn to new conquests.

See also PERSIAN CIVIL WAR (1500–1503); TURKO-PERSIAN WAR (1514–1516).

Further reading: Jason Goodwin, *Lords of the Horizon: A History of the Ottoman Empire* (New York: Picador, 2003); Colin Imber, *Ottoman Empire: 1300–1650* (London: Palgrave Macmillan, 2003); Halil Inalcik, *The Ottoman Empire: The Classical Age, 1300–1600* (London: Phoenix Press, 2001).

Ottoman Civil War (1559)

PRINCIPAL COMBATANTS: Son of Süleyman I the Magnificent, Selim vs. his brother, Bayazid
PRINCIPAL THEATER(S): Ottoman Empire
DECLARATION: None
MAJOR ISSUES AND OBJECTIVES: Succession to the Ottoman sultanate
OUTCOME: Selim prevailed against Bayazid, who was executed.
APPROXIMATE MAXIMUM NUMBER OF MEN UNDER ARMS: Unknown
CASUALTIES: Unknown
TREATIES: None

Süleyman I (the Magnificent; 1496–1566), was warned by his favorite wife, Roxelana (d. 1559), that his eldest son,

Mustafa (d. 1553), was plotting against him. This was untrue, but the sultan did not pause to investigate; instead, he had Mustafa arrested and beheaded in 1553. This left the sons Süleyman had had by Roxelana in position to inherit the throne; however, upon Roxelana's death, the two young men, Selim (c. 1524–74), and Bayazid (d. 1561), fell to disputing their inheritance. Bayazid raised an army to oppose Selim, Süleyman's favorite. Selim defeated Bayazid at the Battle of Konya in 1559, whereupon Bayazid fled to Persia. Süleyman subsequently authorized Selim to dispatch executioners to Persia and paid Shahtahmasp I (r. 1524–76) to deliver Bayazid into their hands. Bayazid was killed in 1561.

Further reading: Andre Clot: *Suleiman the Magnificent: The Man, His Life, His Epoch* (London: Saqi Books, 1992); Jason Goodwin, *Lords of the Horizon: A History of the Ottoman Empire* (New York: Picador, 2003); Colin Imber, *Ottoman Empire: 1300–1650* (London: Palgrave Macmillan, 2003); Halil Inalcik, *The Ottoman Empire: the Classical Age, 1300–1600* (London: Phoenix Press, 2001).

Ottoman Conquest of Bulgaria (1369–1372)

PRINCIPAL COMBATANTS: Ottoman Turks (principally the Janissary corps) vs. the Bulgarians and Serbs
PRINCIPAL THEATER(S): Bulgaria and Macedonia
DECLARATION: None
MAJOR ISSUES AND OBJECTIVES: Conquest of eastern Europe
OUTCOME: The Ottomans seized control of Bulgaria and much of Macedonia.
APPROXIMATE MAXIMUM NUMBER OF MEN UNDER ARMS: Unknown
CASUALTIES: Unknown
TREATIES: None

Under Murad I (1319–89), the Ottoman Empire pressed a program of invasion and expansion into eastern Europe. The conquest of Bulgaria was accomplished chiefly by the elite corps of troops Murad created. The Janissaries were former Christians who had been captured in childhood and raised as violently fanatic Muslims. Murad harnessed their fanaticism by shaping them into a disciplined body of infantry archers. The Janissary victory at the Battle of Cernomen in 1371 neutralized Serb resistance in the region of the Maritza River and led to the conquest not only of Bulgaria, but Macedonia as well.

Over the next half millennium, the Janissaries would figure as an extremely powerful—and ultimately self-serving—force in Ottoman history.

Further reading: Godfrey Goodwin, *The Janissaries* (London: Saqi Books, 1997); Colin Imber, *Ottoman Empire: 1300–1650* (London: Palgrave Macmillan, 2003); Halil Inalcik, *The Ottoman Empire: The Classical Age, 1300–1600* (London: Phoenix Press, 2001).

Ottoman-Druse War (1585)

PRINCIPAL COMBATANTS: Ottoman Turks vs. Lebanese Druse
PRINCIPAL THEATER(S): Lebanon
DECLARATION: None
MAJOR ISSUES AND OBJECTIVES: The Ottomans sought to suppress rebellion among the Druse.
OUTCOME: The Druse rebellion was suppressed, but, in Lebanon, the Druse remained an important political force.
APPROXIMATE MAXIMUM NUMBER OF MEN UNDER ARMS: Unknown
CASUALTIES: Unknown
TREATIES: None

The Islamic sect known as the Druse was small but important during the 16th century. The Ottoman sultan Selim I (1467–1520) sought to placate Druse interests by naming Lebanon's Fakhr ad-Din (d. 1544) emir of the Ottoman Empire's Druse. However, in 1585, the Shi'ite ruler of Tripoli, Yusuf Sayfa (fl. 1580s), led an insurrection against the Ottoman sultan. The rebel forces encompassed a number of religious groups, including Druse led by Korkmaz (1544–85), the son of Fakhr ad-Din. The Ottomans put down the rebellion and executed Korkmaz. He was succeeded first by his uncle and then by Fakhr ad-Din II (1572–1635), grandson of Fakhr ad-Din. Although nominally under Ottoman control, the Druse came to dominate Lebanese politics.

See also MAMLUK-PERSIAN-OTTOMAN WAR (1516–1517).

Further reading: Jason Goodwin, *Lords of the Horizon: A History of the Ottoman Empire* (New York: Picador, 2003); Colin Imber, *Ottoman Empire: 1300–1650* (London: Palgrave Macmillan, 2003); Halil Inalcik, *The Ottoman Empire: The Classical Age, 1300–1600* (London: Phoenix Press, 2001).

Ottoman-Druse War (1611–1613)

PRINCIPAL COMBATANTS: Ottoman Empire (through the pasha of Damascus) vs. Fakhr ad-Din II and the Druse of Lebanon
PRINCIPAL THEATER(S): Lebanon
DECLARATION: None
MAJOR ISSUES AND OBJECTIVES: The Ottoman sultan wanted to punish the Druse for an unauthorized alliance with Tuscany (Holy Roman Empire).
OUTCOME: Fakhr ad-Din was driven into exile.
APPROXIMATE MAXIMUM NUMBER OF MEN UNDER ARMS: Druse army, 40,000; pasha's forces were larger
CASUALTIES: Unknown
TREATIES: None

Fakhr ad-Din II (1572–1635), emir of the Druse in Lebanon, made the Druse dominant in the region. In 1608, when he struck an alliance with Tuscany—effectively an alliance with the Holy Roman Empire—Ottoman sultan Ahmed (1589–1617) ordered the pasha of Damascus to conduct a punitive expedition against the Druse. Fakhr commanded an army of 40,000, a formidable force that readily countered the Ottoman action. The pasha mounted a larger assault in 1613, which defeated the Druse and sent Fakhr fleeing into Tuscan exile. (He returned in 1618 at the invitation of a new sultan, Osman II [1604–22].)

See also AUSTRO-TURKISH WAR (1591–1606); TURKO-PERSIAN WAR (1603–1612).

Further reading: M. A. Cook, ed., *A History of the Ottoman Empire to 1730* (Cambridge, England: Cambridge University Press, 1976); Jason Goodwin, *Lords of the Horizon: A History of the Ottoman Empire* (New York: Picador, 2003); Colin Imber, *Ottoman Empire: 1300–1650* (London: Palgrave Macmillan, 2003).

Ottoman-Druse War (1631–1635)

PRINCIPAL COMBATANTS: Ottoman Empire vs. the Druse
PRINCIPAL THEATER(S): Lebanon
DECLARATION: None
MAJOR ISSUES AND OBJECTIVES: Suppression of the Druse
OUTCOME: The Druse were defeated, and their leader, Fakhr ad-Din, executed.
APPROXIMATE MAXIMUM NUMBER OF MEN UNDER ARMS: Ottoman forces, 80,000; Druse, 25,000
CASUALTIES: Unknown
TREATIES: None

Exiled to Tuscany after the OTTOMAN-DRUSE WAR (1611–1613), Fakhr ad-Din II (1572–1635) returned to Lebanon in 1618, then continued a program of territorial expansion and opposition to the Sublime Porte (the government of the Ottoman Empire). Armed exchanges were taking place by 1631, and, in 1633, Sultan Murad IV (1609–40) sent a major amphibious expedition against the Druse. While Murad's fleet blockaded the coast of Lebanon, an 80,000-man army (made up of Syrians and Egyptians) defeated a Druse army numbering 25,000 men (and consisting of Maronites and mercenary troops in addition to the Druse). Fakhr fled the field and took refuge in the mountains. One of his sons was immediately captured and executed, and Fakhr was captured in 1634 and executed the following year, as were two more of his sons. This brought an end to the war, but not to the Druse presence and influence in the region. As a ruling dynasty (called the Ma'n), the line of Fakhr ad-Din ended in 1697.

See also TURKO-PERSIAN WAR (1623–1638).

Further reading: M. A. Cook, ed., *A History of the Ottoman Empire to 1730* (Cambridge, England: Cambridge University Press, 1976); Jason Goodwin, *Lords of the Hori-*

zon: *A History of the Ottoman Empire* (New York: Picador, 2003); Colin Imber, *Ottoman Empire: 1300–1650* (London: Palgrave Macmillan, 2003).

Ottoman-Hapsburg Wars *See* AUSTRO-TURKISH WAR (1537–1547); AUSTRO-TURKISH WAR (1551–1553); AUSTRO-TURKISH WAR (1566).

Ottoman (Turkish) War with Serbia and Montenegro *See* SERBO-TURKISH WAR (1876–1878).

Ottoman-Venetian War over Crete

See CANDIAN WAR (1645–1669).

Otto the Great, Conquests of (942–972)

PRINCIPAL COMBATANTS: Otto I vs. various rebels within Germany; Otto vs. the Slavs of middle Europe; Otto vs. the Magyars; Germany vs. France; Germany vs. Italy
PRINCIPAL THEATER(S): Central Europe and northern Italy
DECLARATION: None
MAJOR ISSUES AND OBJECTIVES: Otto I sought to centralize German-speaking Europe and expand his kingdom.
OUTCOME: Otto consolidated the German Reich and gained hegemony over much of Europe.
APPROXIMATE MAXIMUM NUMBER OF MEN UNDER ARMS: At Lechfeld, Otto led an army of 10,000.
CASUALTIES: Unknown
TREATIES: None

The son of Germany's Henry I (c. 876–936), Otto I (the Great; 912–73) consolidated the German Reich by suppressing rebellious vassals (led by Thanknar, his half brother, and Henry, his younger brother) in the GERMAN CIVIL WARS (938–941) and ultimately by winning a decisive victory against the Hungarians at the battle of Lechfeld in 955 (*see* MAGYAR RAID, GREAT). But Otto's ambition stretched beyond Germany, and even as he was quelling the early rebellions against his reign, he took the time to strengthen and expand his kingdom's frontiers.

In the East, he attacked and defeated the Slavs, consolidating his gains by founding a monastery in Magdeburg in 941 and establishing two bishoprics in 948. In the North, he extended Christendom into Denmark, establishing four bishoprics there by 968. However, an early campaign in Bohemia failed, and it took Otto till 950 to force its prince, Boleslav I (d. 967), to submit and pay tribute.

Otto was then in a position to deny any French claims to Lorraine, which he had taken when be put down the French-backed rebellion of 939 to 941. He also assumed

the role of mediator in France's internal struggles. He held a similar sway over Burgundy. In fact, when Burgundian princess Adelaide, the widowed queen of Italy, appealed to him after being taken prisoner by the Lombard prince Berengar (c. 900–966), Otto marched into Italy in 951, declared himself king of the Lombards, and married Adelaide (his first wife having died). Berengar became his vassal for the kingdom of Italy.

Otto was forced to cut his first Italian campaign short when a revolt broke out in Germany in 953. Led by his son Liudolf (930–957), and backed by Conrad (d. 955), duke of Lorraine, and Frederick, bishop of Mainz, the rebellion at first succeeded, forcing Otto to withdraw to Saxony. But the rebellion began to fail when the Magyar invasion allowed Otto to paint the rebels as traitors and enemies of the Reich in league with the invaders. In 955, not only did Otto defeat the Magyars so decisively at Lechfeld that they never invaded again, he also captured the rebel stronghold at Regensburg, ending the rebellion. That year, too, Otto also won another major victory over the Slavs, which he followed with a series of campaigns that, by 960, had forced the utter subjugation of all the Slavs between the middle Elbe and the middle Oder rivers. By 968, even Mieszko (Mieczyslaw I) (c. 930–992), prince of Poland, was paying tribute to the German king.

Meanwhile, Otto's old enemy and former vassal Berengar, free of German interference, was now threatening Rome. Pope John XII (d. 964) appealed to the German king for help. Otto's price was the Holy Roman Empire. When Otto arrived in Rome on February 2, 962, he was crowned emperor, and 11 days later, he and the pope reached an agreement called the *Privilegium Ottoianum*, which regulated relations between emperor and pope and gave the emperor the right to ratify papal elections. Some say this provision was added later by Otto after he deposed John XII in December for treating with Berengar. In any case, Otto replaced John with Leo VIII (d. 965) as pope, then captured Berengar and dragged him back to Germany. In 966, Otto was back in Italy for a third campaign, this time to suppress a revolt by the Romans against his puppet pontiff, Leo VIII. Since Leo had been deposed by Benedict V (d. 966), and had since died, in 972 Otto appointed a new pope, John XIII (d. 972).

Otto consolidated the German Reich and gave it peace and security from foreign attack. Enjoying something approaching hegemony over Europe, Germany under his rule experienced a cultural flowering that some scholars call the "Ottonian renaissance."

See also MAGYAR RAIDS IN FRANCE; MAGYAR RAIDS IN THE HOLY ROMAN EMPIRE; MAGYAR RAID INTO EUROPE, FIRST.

Further reading: G. Barraclough, *The Origins of Modern Germany* (Oxford: B. Blackwell, 1947); K. J. Leyser, *Rule and Conflict in Early Medieval Society: Ottonian Saxony* (Göttingen: Vandenhoeck and Ruprecht, 1984).

DENMARK

FRISIA

SAXONY

NORTH MARK

Elbe R.

POLAND

Vistula R.

EAST MARK

THURINGIA

MEISSEN MARK

Oder R.

Rhine R.

LORRAINE

FRANCONIA

BOHEMIA

MORAVIA

FRANCE

Seine R.

Danube R.

SWABIA

BAVARIA

EAST MARK
(AUSTRIA)

Danube R.

HUNGARY

Loire R.

BURGUNDY

CARINTHIA

Drave R.

Rhone R.

Po R.

Save R.

CROATIA

SERBIA

KINGDOM OF ITALY

Corsica

Sardinia

EASTERN EMPIRE

EASTERN
EMPIRE

0   125 miles

0   125 km

Empire of Otto the Great at the time of his death

P

Pacific War of the (1879–1884)

PRINCIPAL COMBATANTS: Chile vs. Bolivia and Peru
PRINCIPAL THEATER(S): Atacama Desert region and adjacent sea
DECLARATION: Chile against Bolivia and Peru, April 5, 1879
MAJOR ISSUES AND OBJECTIVES: Control of this nitrate-rich region
OUTCOME: Chile triumphed, winning important portions of the Atacama region from the Peruvian-Bolivian alliance.
APPROXIMATE MAXIMUM NUMBER OF MEN UNDER ARMS: Chile fielded as many as 25,000 troops and had a reserve of 50,000; Peru, 9,680 plus 30,000 reserves; Bolivia, 7,959
CASUALTIES: Chile, 3,276 killed, 5,610 wounded; Peru, 9,672 killed, 14,431 wounded; Bolivia, 920 killed, 1,210 wounded
TREATIES: Treaty of Ancón (Chile and Peru), October 20, 1883; Treaty of Valparaiso (Chile and Bolivia), April 4, 1884

The War of the Pacific ranks with the PARAGUAYAN WAR as one of the two greatest international conflicts in 19th-century South American history. Here Chile waged war against Peru and Bolivia for control of the guano and nitrate deposits (vital in the manufacture of fertilizer, explosives, and economically important chemicals) found in the Atacama Desert. Although Chile claimed Tacna, Arica, and Tarapacá, and Bolivia Antofagasta, the boundary between the two was uncertain, despite the fact that they had settled on the 24th parallel as the dividing line in 1866. Chilean-financed mining concerns took advantage of the instability. They swarmed into the region, threatening both Peruvian and Bolivian holdings. In response, these two nations signed a secret accord in 1873, pledging to assist one another in defense of their Atacama territory. In 1875, Peru seized the property of Chilean mining companies. Three years later, Bolivia made seizures of its own in 1878. Chile responded in turn. Its president, Aníbal Pinto (1825–84), dispatched 200 troops to take and occupy the port of Antofagasta in February 1879, and on April 5, 1879, Chile declared war on Bolivia and Peru.

The war began at sea, when Chilean warships blockaded Peruvian and Bolivian ports. Peru dispatched its ironclad *Huáscar* to attack the blockading vessels, which it did with considerable success until it was sunk in the Battle of Antofagasta on October 8, 1879. Not only did Peru lose one of its two ironclads, but one of its important naval officers, Admiral Miguel Grau (1838–79), perished along with most of his crew.

After the sinking of the *Huáscar,* the action shifted to land. The Peruvian and Bolivian armies were ill-trained and poorly armed, possessing none of the modern weapons to match those boasted by Chile's well-drilled infantry armed with Gras rifles, its veteran Winchester-toting cavalry, or its formidable artillery, equipped with Krupp and Armstrong field guns and a smattering of Gatlings and Nordenfelts. Thus it was a confident Chilean army that staged a counteroffensive against the combined forces of Peru and Bolivia in the Tarapacá region during the closing months of 1879. Chilean forces took and occupied both Antofagasta and Tarapacá, then invaded Arica and Tacna. These towns would fall to Chile by June 1880.

Bolivia reeled in defeat, but Peru stayed in the fight, determined to regain Tarapacá. However, while this fighting continued, peace negotiations were opened. Chilean leaders took advantage of the ongoing negotiations to increase the pressure on Peru by invading that country, at Pisco, with some 25,000 troops. Outnumbered, the Peruvian defenders fell back, and the Chilean army marched north. At the village of Concepción on June 9–10, 1883, a company of 77 Chileans went down bravely fighting some 1,800 Peruvians in a battle that came to represent for Chile what the Alamo represented for Texans or Thermopylae for the Greeks. More determined than ever, the Chilean soldiers redoubled their efforts, the Peruvian resistance collapsed, and the government itself tottered. On December 17, 1879, Peru's capital, Lima, fell. It proved a decapitating blow. A cease-fire was declared, and, on October 20, 1883, Peru and Chile concluded the Treaty of Ancón, by which Peru ceded Tarapacá to Chile. Peru was to retain Tacna and Arica for a period of 10 years, after which possession would be decided by plebiscite. On April 4, 1884, Chile and Bolivia concluded the Treaty of Valparaiso, by which Bolivia ceded to Chile the city and the province of Antofagasta. Diplomatic wrangling delayed formal implementation of these terms for many years, until 1904.

See also CHACO WAR.

Further reading: Robert N. Burr, *By Reason or Force: Chile and the Balancing of Power in South America, 1830–1905* (Berkeley: University of California Press, 1965); Bruce W. Farcau, *The Ten Cents War: Chile, Peru, and Bolivia in the War of the Pacific, 1879–1884* (New York: Praeger, 2000).

Padri War (1821–1837)

PRINCIPAL COMBATANTS: Padri Muslim reformers vs. various leaders in Minangkabau, Sumatra, and Dutch colonial forces
PRINCIPAL THEATER(S): Minangkabau, Sumatra
DECLARATION: None
MAJOR ISSUES AND OBJECTIVES: Suppression of the Padri
OUTCOME: After a long (15-year) siege, the major Padri stronghold fell, and the Padri surrendered; guerrilla warfare continued sporadically.
APPROXIMATE MAXIMUM NUMBER OF MEN UNDER ARMS: Unknown
CASUALTIES: Unknown
TREATIES: None

The Padri were fundamentalist Islamic reformers who essentially forced their beliefs on the Muslims of Minangkabau, Sumatra, during the early 19th century. Local chiefs rebelled against the Padris but failed to suppress them. The local leaders appealed to Dutch trade and colonial interests in Java for aid. Seeing the fanatical Padris as a threat to Dutch interests in the region, the Dutch intervened in the conflict and mounted a 15-year siege against the Padri fortress-city of Bondjol. Although the city finally fell in 1837, bringing the main phase of the war to an end, many Padri dispersed into the mountains, from which they continued to wage sporadic guerrilla warfare against the Dutch as well as non-Padri natives.

The conflict was also known as the Minangkabau War.

See also JAVA WAR, GREAT; NANING WAR.

Further reading: Barbara Watson Andaya, *To Live as Brothers: Southeastern Sumatra in the Seventeenth and Eighteenth Centuries* (Honolulu: University of Hawaii Press, 1993); Edwin M. Loeb, *Sumatra* (New York: University of Oxford Press, 1990).

Pahang Civil War (1857–1863)

PRINCIPAL COMBATANTS: Rival claimants to the throne of Pahang, each with foreign allies (mainly Britain and Siam)
PRINCIPAL THEATER(S): Pahang, Malaya
DECLARATION: None
MAJOR ISSUES AND OBJECTIVES: Succession to the Pahang sultanate
OUTCOME: The war ended with the death (from natural causes) of one of the two claimants to the throne.
APPROXIMATE MAXIMUM NUMBER OF MEN UNDER ARMS: Unknown
CASUALTIES: Unknown
TREATIES: None

Two rival brothers claimed the throne of the Malay state of Pahang after the death of their father, Sultan Bendahara Tun Ali in 1857. The rival claims erupted into war, in which the older brother, Tun Mutahir (d. 1863), found support from Johore, a neighboring sultanate, and from the British, who were attempting to achieve colonial domination of Malaya. The younger claimant, Wan Ahmad (fl. 1860s), was aided by the Trengganu sultanate and by the Siamese, who were opposed to the British. In effect, Britain and Siam used the war as a pretext for fighting one another for dominance in Malaya.

The war consisted mainly of hit-and-run raids, ambushes, and skirmishes, with occasional assaults on fortified positions. British naval vessels destroyed a Siamese fleet in 1862, which drew the war close to a conclusion. When Tun Mutahir died in 1863, the cause of war died with him, and Wan Ahmad was recognized as the new sultan.

Further reading: Barbara Watson Andaya, *A History of Malaysia* (Honolulu: University of Hawaii Press, 2001);

William R. Roff, *The Origins of Malay Nationalism* (New Haven, Conn.: Yale University Press, 1967).

Paiute War (Pyramid Lake War) (1860)

PRINCIPAL COMBATANTS: Local miners and the United States vs. the Paiute Indians
PRINCIPAL THEATER(S): Comstock mining region of Nevada
DECLARATION: None
MAJOR ISSUES AND OBJECTIVES: When local miners raped two Paiute women, the Indians sought revenge by attacking a trading post; the miners sent a force to exact their revenge for the raid but fell victim to an ambush; the U.S. Army was sent in to punish the Paiutes.
OUTCOME: The army skirmished with a small Paiute force, killing 25 Indians and bringing the war to a close, afterward establishing Fort Churchill to protect overland trails through Nevada to California.
APPROXIMATE MAXIMUM NUMBER OF MEN UNDER ARMS: 105 miners; 800 U.S. Army regulars and volunteers; Paiutes, unknown
CASUALTIES: 100 soldiers and civilians; 25 Indians
TREATIES: None

The last significant Indian-white conflict before the U.S. Civil War was between Nevada miners and the Southern Paiutes. Williams Station was one of two trading posts in the Carson Valley along the California Trail. The station served the Central Overland Mail and the Pony Express and was a vital link to the outside world for the miners of Carson City, Virginia City, Gold Hill, and Genoa. Early in May 1860, traders at Williams Station abducted and raped two young Indian women. The Southern Paiutes, already resentful of white intrusions into their lands, were moved to revenge. A party of Indian soldiers rode to the station, rescued the two girls, then burned the station and killed five whites.

Word of the "massacre" reached Virginia City's Wells Fargo office on May 8. Anticipating a major Indian attack, a large and rowdy "army" of miners—perhaps as many as 2,000 men—immediately assembled. The miners telegraphed the governor of California asking for arms. As quickly as they banded together, the miners, totally undisciplined and thoroughly disorganized, dispersed. A miner named Henry Meredith organized and armed a new force drawn from the mining towns. At Dayton, Nevada, Meredith's men were joined by Major William M. Ormsby (d. 1860) and a group from Carson City. Ormsby now assumed command of the combined force of 105 men, which made its way to Pyramid Lake in Paiute country—not merely to defend the mining towns but also to exact revenge.

The Paiute chief Numaga (d. 1871) had hoped to avoid further violence, but he realized that the miners would be satisfied with nothing less than blood. He set up an ambush at the Big Bend of the Truckee River valley. In the narrow pass, about four in the afternoon of May 12, the trap was sprung. It was deadly and effective. The Paiutes' poison-tipped arrows accounted for 46 fatalities—almost half the force that had been organized against them.

The Comstock country was thrown into a panic, but the governor of California responded with troops under the command of Colonel Jack Hayes (d. 1883), a former Texas Ranger. A small body of U.S. infantry regulars out of the Presidio in San Francisco, together with some local volunteer groups, brought the force to about 800 men, who headed toward the Truckee at the end of May. The force encountered a few Paiutes near the site of the original ambush and, after a skirmish, pursued the Indians to Pinnacle Mountain, killing about 25 Paiute soldiers. The short-lived Paiute War was over, but to ensure the peace and keep the California Trail open, the U.S. Army established Fort Churchill near Buckland Station.

Further reading: Alan Axelrod, *Chronicle of the Indian Wars: From Colonial Times to Wounded Knee* (New York: Prentice Hall General Reference, 1993); Ferol Egan and Richard Dillon, *Sand in a Whirlwind: The Paiute Indian War of 1860* (Reno: University of Nevada Press, 2002); Sessions S. Wheeler, *Paiute* (Reno: University of Nevada Press, 1996).

Pakistani Civil War (1971)

PRINCIPAL COMBATANTS: West Pakistan vs. East Pakistan (Bangladesh), with aid from India
PRINCIPAL THEATER(S): East Pakistan (Bangladesh)
DECLARATION: Bangladesh declared independence on March 26, 1971.
MAJOR ISSUES AND OBJECTIVES: East Pakistan wanted independence as Bangladesh.
OUTCOME: Bangladesh achieved independence.
APPROXIMATE MAXIMUM NUMBER OF MEN UNDER ARMS: Pakistan, 60,000; Bangladesh and India, the numbers are unknown, but they are much larger.
CASUALTIES: Pakistan, heavy casualties and many prisoners; Bangladesh, hundreds of thousands of civilians killed, 10 million refugees created
TREATIES: Treaty of Friendship and Peace between India and Bangladesh, March 19, 1972; no formal peace treaty between Pakistan and Bangladesh

By the mid-1960s, a strong independence movement gathered momentum in East Pakistan. Although this region accounted for some 75 percent of Pakistan's foreign trade, West Pakistan remained politically dominant, and the East received disproportionately less representation in government and far fewer economic benefits. Riots broke out in

East Pakistan during 1968 and 1969, prompting the new Pakistani president, General Agha Muhammad Yahya Khan (1907–74), to call for a vote for a national assembly. Held in December 1970, these were Pakistan's first general elections held by Pakistan since independence in 1947. The Awami League—an organization calling for the independence of eastern Pakistan and headed by the popular Bengali leader Sheikh Mujib Rahman (1920–75)—won a majority in the new assembly. Yahya Khan promptly refused to honor the outcome, first by postponing the assembly, then by cancelling the result of the elections.

This, predictably, triggered civil war, beginning with a general strike throughout East Pakistan and the withholding of all taxes. The Pakistani president then declared martial law and sent 60,000 troops into East Pakistan. Negotiations between the East and West quickly broke down at the end of March 1971, after Mujib demanded virtual independence for East Pakistan. Instead, Yahya Khan ordered a military massacre in Dacca. When Yahya Khan had Mujib arrested and flown to prison in West Pakistan, the Bengali firebrand called upon his followers in the East to rise up and proclaim their independence as "Bangladesh," which translates into English as "Land of the Bengalis." Demonstrations and riots followed, and Pakistani troops, on March 25, 1971, fired on civilians —students in dormitories and people in crowded marketplaces—prompting Bangladesh to declare its independence on March 26.

The declaration unleashed the full force of the Pakistani army in the region. Troops rounded up and killed hundreds of thousands of Bangladeshi "rebels" and sent some 10 million terrified refugees fleeing Bangladesh for the neighboring Indian state of West Bengal. This refugee crisis, in turn, became the basis for the INDO-PAKISTANI WAR (1971), as Pakistan attacked the Indian-held portion of Kashmir on December 3.

The attack on India was ill-advised. When the monsoon season had passed, India's army moved quickly up to the Bangladesh border. By early December the Indians had advanced virtually unopposed to Dacca. Pakistan surrendered the city in mid-December 1971. Yahya Khan resigned in disgrace and was replaced by Zulfikar Ali Bhutto (b. 1921), who ordered the release of Sheik Mujib, who flew home to a hero's welcome. In January 1972, he became the first prime minister of the People's Republic of Bangladesh, but it was not until 1973 that a prisoner of war exchange was concluded between Pakistan and Bangladesh. A year later, Pakistan formally recognized the independence of the nation.

Meanwhile, India's stunning victory over Pakistan in the Bangladesh war was achieved in part due to Soviet support, and—with the birth of Bangladesh—India came to dominate South Asia and its foreign policy. Officially nonaligned, it tilted toward the Soviet Union, which led the United States to veer toward supporting Pakistan. Belatedly the United States sent a nuclear-armed carrier from its Pacific Fleet to the Bay of Bengal, ostensibly to evacuate civilians from Dacca. Instead it only stirred up the dangerous cold war stew by provoking a nuclear arms race between India and Pakistan.

Further reading: Craig Baxter, *Bangladesh: From a Nation to a State* (Boulder, Colo.: Westview Press, 1997); D. K. Palit, *The Lightning Campaign: The Indo-Pakistan War of 1971* (New Delhi: Thomson Press [India], 1972); Richard Sisson, *War and Secession: Pakistan, India, and the Creation of Bangladesh* (reprint, Berkeley: University of California Press, 1991).

Palan Wars (800–1025)

PRINCIPAL COMBATANTS: Pala dynasty vs. various Indian states (especially the Rashtrakutas, the Rajput alliance, and the Cholas)
PRINCIPAL THEATER(S): India
DECLARATION: None
MAJOR ISSUES AND OBJECTIVES: Pala expansion
OUTCOME: The Pala were unable to establish permanent expansion of their empire.
APPROXIMATE MAXIMUM NUMBER OF MEN UNDER ARMS: Unknown
CASUALTIES: Unknown
TREATIES: No documents survive

The Palan Wars encompass a long period of violent chaos in northern India following the failure of Harsha Vardhana (c. 590–c. 647) to revive the Gupta Empire, which disintegrated during the CHALUKYAN WAR AGAINST HARSHA in 620. Over the years, many of the small Indian states that broke away from the Gupta Empire expanded, leading to many conflicts.

One of the most aggressive of the breakaway kingdoms was Bengal under the Pala dynasty. Between 800 and 1025, the Palas made three major attempts to expand west, meeting with ultimate defeat each time. Under Dharmapala (fl. 770–810), the Palas reached Harsha's former capital, Kannauj, but were met there by the Rashtrakutas, who checked the advance. In the ninth century, Devapala (fl. 810–850), who succeeded Dharmapala, attempted to assert rights to the Deccan and mounted a campaign along the Narmada River. Once again, the Rashtrakutas checked the Pala advance.

In the Rajput, a number of states leagued against the Palas to counter their activity along the Ganges. The army of this alliance marched into Bengal in 916, which neutralized Palan expansionism until the early 11th-century reign of Mahipala (fl. 988–1038). Under his leadership, the Pala dynasty pushed its influence as far west as Benares and south along the east coast of the subcontinent. The latter advance brought the Palas into conflict with the Cholas, who, beginning in 1021, mounted a strong military campaign against the invaders. By 1025, the Cholas had entered Bengal, dealt Mahipala a strong defeat, and sent the Pala dynasty into a sharp decline.

See also MUHAMMAD OF GHUR, CONQUESTS OF.

Further reading: Jhunu Bagchi, *The History and Culture of the Palas of Bengal and Bihar* (c. 750 A.D.–c. 1200 A.D.) (New Delhi: Abhinav Publications, 1993); R. C. Majumdar, *The History of Bengal* (Ramna, Dacca: University of Dacca, 1963).

Palestinian Guerrilla War (c. 1960s–ongoing)

PRINCIPAL COMBATANTS: Palestinian guerrillas (especially Palestine Liberation Organization, or PLO) vs. Israel
PRINCIPAL THEATER(S): Israeli territory, West Bank, Gaza, and various international locations of terrorist attacks
DECLARATION: None
MAJOR ISSUES AND OBJECTIVES: Palestinian self-rule; Palestinian possession of territory; Palestinian challenge to the right of Israel to exist
OUTCOME: Violence continues as of January 2004 despite two important peace accords.
APPROXIMATE MAXIMUM NUMBER OF MEN UNDER ARMS: Unknown
CASUALTIES: In the tens of thousands, mostly among Palestinians
TREATIES: PLO-Israel Accord, September 13, 1993; Wye River Memorandum, October 28, 1998

Until 1988, Palestine did not exist as an independent state, but was a loosely constituted political entity consisting of Muslims who had been, in effect, internally displaced by the creation of the State of Israel. Beginning in the 1960s, various Palestinian organizations, primarily the Popular Front for the Liberation of Palestine (PFLP, a Marxist organization) and, even more centrally, Al Fatah, led by Yasser Arafat (b. 1929), launched a low-level but persistent guerrilla war and program of terrorism against Israel. In military terms, the actions of the Palestinians might best be characterized as guerrilla raids.

In 1964, Arafat emerged as the most highly visible of the Palestinian leaders—although he by no means had full control of the people—and formed the Palestine Liberation Organization (PLO). Five years later, Arafat became chairman of the organization.

The PLO seemed to gear its program of attacks to the lulls between the more formal wars between Arabs and Israelis during the 1960s and early 1970s. PLO terror tactics included rocket attacks on markets and other civilian public places, assassinations, raids on Israeli schools, and attacks on transport buses. The PLO guerrillas based their operations variously in Syria, then Jordan, and, for much of the 1970s and early 1980s, war-torn Lebanon.

PLO and PLO-backed actions were not directed solely against the territory of Israel. The organization engaged in international terrorism, as when the so-called Black September group hijacked commercial airliners during September 6–9, 1970, taking 435 hostages to Amman. Most infamous were the PLO attacks at the 1972 Olympics in Munich, in which 11 Israeli athletes were taken captive and killed.

As a result of the LEBANESE CIVIL WAR (1975–92), the PLO was forced out of Lebanon in 1983, and the group became less effective and less capable of applying a steady program of raids. After a period of relative quiescence, however, Palestinians living in Israeli-controlled Gaza staged massive riots against Israeli troops and paramilitary police in 1987. The violence spread to other Israeli-occupied territories, and, emboldened, the PLO proclaimed an independent state of Palestine in 1988. At this point, Israel granted Palestine a nominal—and quite limited—diplomatic recognition, and the United States followed suit.

This did not bring an end to the violence, which shifted to the West Bank and Gaza. In a campaign of popular Palestinian uprisings known as the Intifada, the PLO orchestrated battles with Israeli troops during 1989 and 1990. These were one-sided affairs, which resulted in the wounding and death of many Palestinians—all of whom were regarded as martyrs to the cause. Moreover, against this backdrop of continual violence, both the Israeli government and the Palestinian leadership showed an unprecedented willingness to come to a modus vivendi. In 1993 agreements brokered by the U.S. government and, personally, by President Bill Clinton (b. 1946), Israel and Palestine concluded peace accords. Whereas Israel agreed to accept the PLO as the representative government of Palestine, the PLO retracted its adamantly held objective of destroying Israel and now conceded the right of Israel to exist. In 1994 and 1995, the Palestinians were given a significant measure of self-rule on the West Bank and in Gaza.

There was an aura of hope during this period, but among many Palestinians as well as Israelis, there was also a backlash and resistance to the peace process. In 1996, Israelis elected right-wing candidate Benjamin Netanyahu (b. 1949) as prime minister. His hard line provoked new clashes between Israeli troops and Palestinians in the fall of 1996. In 1998, President Clinton brought the Israelis and Palestinians to Wye River, Maryland, to negotiate further peace terms. Israel agreed to cede additional territory in return for various U.S.-backed security guarantees. Feeling some political heat from home and abroad, Netanyahu signed the Wye River Memorandum, but when the peace process nevertheless faltered, he lost the next election on May 19, 1999, to Labor Party leader Ehud Barak (b. 1942). Barak had campaigned on a platform of bringing an end to Israel's conflicts with all its neighbors—Syria and Lebanon, for example—in addition to the Palestinians. On September 5, 1999, Israel and the

Palestinian Authority agreed to a new, revised deal on the stalled Wye River accord, hoping to revive the Middle East peace process. On November 8, 1999, they resumed "final status" talks.

In February 2000, a summit between Barak and Arafat fell apart over the promised Israeli withdrawal from the West Bank under the revised Wye accord, new deadlines were missed, and the "final status" negotiations deadlocked. Regardless of disagreements on the final stages of peace, however, in March Israel did indeed hand over part of the West Bank to Palestinians as part of a land transfer agreed to at Wye River back in 1998. Then, in May 2000, Israel unilaterally withdrew from the area of Lebanon it had been occupying since 1982. The seesaw swung the other way in July, when a peace summit at Camp David foundered on competing claims to Jerusalem and the issue of Palestinian refugees. By October, President Clinton had helped patch up matters some, presiding over yet another summit at the Egyptian resort of Sharm el-Sheikh, where the attendees announced a cease-fire and plans to bring an end to the Palestinian-Israeli violence. No sooner was the cease-fire created than it came undone, and Barak—feeling the need to seek a mandate to see the process through—stepped down and called for new elections on December 10.

Instead of a mandate, he lost the election to Likud Party candidate Ariel Sharon (b. 1928) by 20 percentage points. Sharon campaigned on a platform calling for "Peace with Security," and promised that he would take a different approach to the Palestinian conflict, which most read as a conservative attempt to turn back the clock. The Palestinians, who disliked Sharon for his harsh policies in Israel's 1982 invasion of Lebanon and distrusted him because of his outspoken support of Israel's settlement activity, soon raised the stakes with a wave of "suicide" attacks.

Then on February 14, 2001, following the deaths of eight soldiers and civilians killed when a Palestinian bus driver ploughed his vehicle into a waiting line of passengers, Israel reimposed a total blockade on the occupied territories. By the time Ariel Sharon formally took office on March 7, his fragile seven-party coalition included veteran Labor leader Shimon Peres (b. 1923) as foreign minister. Peres had persuaded his party to join Sharon's right-wing government in the name of national unity. A month later, a more united Israel was ready to respond to the newest wave of Palestinian "terrorism." In April, Israeli troops seized territory controlled by the Palestinians for the first time since the start of the Oslo peace process, taking the Gaza Strip and dividing its territory into three parts. The United States responded by setting up a commission under former U.S. senator George Mitchell (b. 1933) to explore the new deadlock and look for ways around it. In May, the Mitchell Commission called for an immediate cease-fire, to be followed by confidence-building measures and ultimately by renewed peace negotiations.

Tellingly, Mitchell also called for a freeze on expansion of Jewish settlements in the occupied territories about the same time that the European Union accused Israel of employing "disproportionate" force in the occupied territories and called for the dismantling of Jewish settlements in the West Bank and Gaza Strip. But the world pressure on Israel was immediately undermined when a suicide bomber killed 19 young Israelis at a nightclub in Tel Aviv. With the pressure now reversed, Arafat ordered his forces in the occupied territories to enforce a cease-fire.

But Israel was having none of it. On July 4, 2001, the Israeli security cabinet voted to give the Israeli Defense Forces (IDF) a broader license to target Palestinian terrorists, permitting their assassination anywhere and anytime they could be found, rather than, as formerly, only when they were on the verge of committing an attack. "Targeted assassination" was the Israeli policy response to suicide bombing, although it was attacked by the Palestinians as extrajudicial execution, a war crime under Geneva conventions.

On August 10, in retaliation for a Hamas-sponsored suicide bombing in Jerusalem the day before, Israeli war planes destroyed the headquarters of the Palestinian police in the West Bank city of Ramallah. Israeli Special Forces also seized the offices of the Palestine Liberation Organization at Orient House in East Jerusalem. Several days later, Israeli tanks moved into the West Bank city of Jenin and opened fire on the Palestinian police station, utterly destroying it. This, the biggest incursion into Palestinian-controlled territory since 1994, was roundly criticized by Washington, which was increasingly coming under international pressure to step up its intermediary role in the region.

Regardless of U.S. desires, on August 28, 2001, Israeli troops moved into the West Bank town of Beit Jala, near the southern outskirts of Jerusalem, and both the United States and Britain strongly condemned the Israeli action. Throughout the late summer and fall, Israel occupied major Palestinian cities for various lengths of time, including Jericho, Ramallah and Tulkarm.

Then came the terrorist attacks on New York and Washington, D.C., on September 11, and the Bush administration began to manifest a much greater interest in bringing Israel and the Palestinians to negotiations, partly in response to requests from Arab and Muslim governments that were, many quite reluctantly, supporting the UNITED STATES WAR ON TERRORISM. Also, it was clear that that war could be more effectively fought if the Palestinian cause were removed as a justification for terror by Muslim extremists. On October 2, George W. Bush (b. 1946) announced a dramatic break with his administration's previous Middle East policy by stating that he was prepared to back the creation of a Palestinian state, and U.S. secretary of state Colin Powell (b. 1937) spearheaded a new American initiative, which—as it turned out—involved the removal of Yasser Arafat as the only spokesman for the Palestinian cause. Thus, even though the Israeli-Palestinian conflict escalated once more after the October 17, 2001, assassination of the Israeli hard-line minister of tourism Rehavam Zeevi (1926–2001) by Palestinian militants, there was ample evidence of a renewed Israeli interest in peace talks in the two years following.

As of 2004, the seesaw violence between terrorist attack and brutal reprisal continued, as did the peace initiatives. However much the United States may have been determined to solve the long intractable problems of the Arab-Israeli conflict in the wake of 9/11, it had yet to find the key.

See also ARAB-ISRAELI WAR (1948–1949); ARAB-ISRAELI WAR (1956); ARAB-ISRAELI WAR (1967); ARAB-ISRAELI WAR (1973).

Further reading: Reuters, *The Israeli-Palestinian Conflict: Crisis in the Middle East* (New York: Reuters Prentice Hall, 2002); Charles D. Smith, *Palestine and the Arab-Israeli Conflict,* 3rd ed. (New York: St. Martin's Press, 1996); Mark A. Tessler, *A History of the Israel: Palestinian Conflict* (South Bend: Indiana University Press, 1994).

Panama Invasion *See* UNITED STATES INVASION OF PANAMA ("OPERATION JUST CAUSE") (1989).

Panamanian Revolution (1903)

PRINCIPAL COMBATANTS: Panama (with U.S. backing) vs. Colombia
PRINCIPAL THEATER(S): Panama
DECLARATION: Panamanian Declaration of Independence, November 3, 1903
MAJOR ISSUES AND OBJECTIVES: U.S.-backed parties with an interest in building a canal across the Isthmus of Panama fomented a revolt in Colombia that led to the declaration of an independent Republic of Panama, ready to comply with American plans for the canal.
OUTCOME: Panama achieved independence and U.S. recognition; the United States gained the rights to build and administer the Panama Canal.
APPROXIMATE MAXIMUM NUMBER OF MEN UNDER ARMS: Unknown
CASUALTIES: Unknown
TREATIES: Hay-Bunau-Varilla Treaty (also called the Panama Canal Treaty) of November 18, 1903

For centuries Europeans had dreamed of joining the Atlantic and Pacific oceans by cutting a canal through the Isthmus of Panama, which separates the Caribbean Sea from the Pacific. The United States did not begin to take the idea seriously until after the UNITED STATES–MEXICAN WAR. In 1848, the United States negotiated an agreement with New Granada (a nation consisting of present-day Panama and Colombia) for rights of transit in exchange for a guarantee of New Granada's sovereignty over the isthmus province. The 1849 California gold rush, which sent tens of thousands of easterners west, prompted the United States to fund the Panama Railroad across the isthmus, but the ultimate dream remained a canal.

Meanwhile, U.S. diplomats—influenced by speculators such as railroad magnate Cornelius Vanderbilt (1794–1877) and adventurers such as famed filibuster William Walker (1824–60)—had become mired in the affairs of the tiny and politically volatile Republic of Nicaragua, which a number of them saw as being every bit as promising a site as Panama for an interocean canal. Here, however, the Americans were in competition with Britain, whose world trade, transoceanic navy, and numerous colonies ensured that she also was keenly interested in such a canal. London had kept close watch on U.S. ambitions in Central America, and attempted to establish a political beachhead at the mouth of the San Juan River, the most likely terminus for a Nicaraguan canal, by claiming a protectorate of the Miskito Indians on Nicaragua's east coast. This set off alarms within the U.S. foreign policy community, and the two countries exchanged diplomatic notes warning they would not permit the other exclusive control over a canal through the isthmus. In 1850 the British minister to the United States, Sir Henry Lytton Bulwer (1801–72), and Zachary Taylor's (1784–1850) secretary of state, John Clayton (1796–1856), got together and agreed to terms in a treaty settling the dispute. The Clayton-Bulwer Treaty provided that any canal built through either Panama or Nicaragua would be unfortified, neutral during war, and open to shipping from any country on equal terms, and that neither the United States nor Great Britain was to colonize or try to establish dominion over any part of Central America.

The treaty was ratified by the U.S. Senate and remained in force for half a century, but it was never very popular. Britain only made matters worse when it maintained that the treaty was not retroactive—meaning it still got to keep its protectorate over the Mosquito Coast. The Americans responded in typical fashion—Tennessee filibuster William Walker led an expedition to Nicaragua in 1855 and took over the country (*see* WALKER'S INVASION OF NICARAGUA). He was soon driven out, but not by the British. Cornelius Vanderbilt had at first given Walker clandestine support to take control of the isthmus across which he planned to build his own railroad. When Walker instead assumed power, Vanderbilt became the driving force behind his removal. Despite the brouhaha, what the treaty said was ultimately not of much importance. Until someone actually tried to build a canal—and negotiated the rights to do so—the impact of the Clayton-Bulwer Treaty was academic.

Decades later, a French firm under the direction of the brilliant Ferdinand de Lesseps (1805–94) did indeed negotiate the necessary rights with New Granada to build a canal across the Isthmus of Panama. The firm began construction in 1881 but went bankrupt in short order. The project was taken over by the reorganized New Panama Canal Company (officially, the Compagnie Universelle du Canal Interocéanique) which hired another French engineer, Philippe Bunau-Varilla (1860–1940) in 1884 to oversee completion. Bunau-Varilla fared no better than his predecessor, and by 1880 the French Panama canal project had clearly failed. Bunau-Varilla approached the United States with an offer to sell the rights to build the canal, but got no takers. Then, in the flush of victory after the 1898 SPANISH-AMERICAN WAR (and encouraged, after 1901, by the expansionist president Theodore Roosevelt [1858–1919]), who had played a prominent role in that war), the United States persuaded Great Britain to relinquish its claims to share control of a Central American canal. The treaty, which had been negotiated in 1899 and 1901 by the U.S. secretary of state John Hay (1838–1905) and Baron Julian Pauncefote (1828–1902) of Preston, British ambassador to the United States, had been amended by the Senate in 1900, and was rejected by the British. The second version of the Hay-Pauncefote treaty, which the British government accepted and which the Senate ratified in December 1901, superseded the Clayton-Bulwer treaty and gave the United States the right to construct and fully control an isthmian canal in Central America. It retained, at least nominally, the principle of neutrality under the sole guarantee of the United States and provided that the canal would be open to ships of all nations on equal terms, but it omitted a clause contained in the first draft that, following Clayton-Bulwer, had forbidden fortifications.

Before the treaty was passed, however, an American commission of experts authorized by Congress in 1901 and advised by Bunau-Varilla had come to prefer a lock canal through Panama. This, argued the commission, would provide the cheapest and shortest route between the two U.S. coasts, over the original plan to build the canal in Nicaragua, whose Mosquito Coast—and British protection of that coast—had been behind the controversy that led to Clayton-Bulwer in the first place. Accordingly, in June 1902, Congress directed the president to negotiate with Colombia the acquisition of a strip of land in Panama after the New Panama Canal Company, successors to de Lesseps's defunct firm, agreed to a reasonable timetable and reasonable terms for selling the United States its titles and equities in the area. Rather than the original asking price of $109 million for this right-of-way, the French company took the $40 million at which the American commission had valued their holdings.

Roosevelt then pressed Colombia, which had jurisdiction over New Granada, to surrender control over the 10-mile-strip of land in return for a $10 million cash payment and annual rent of $250,000. These were the terms negotiated by the U.S. secretary of state John Hay and Colombian foreign minister Tomas Herrán (1843–1904) and presented to both the U.S. and the Colombian senates. Early in 1902, the Congress authorized construction and the next year ratified the Hay-Herrán Treaty. The Colombian Senate, however, delayed ratification in the hope of increasing the price offered by the United States and, in the end, on August 12, 1903, refused to ratify the treaty—not only because of dissatisfaction with the financial terms but also in response to a popular movement to resist "Yankee imperialism" and popular objections to relinquishing a significant measure of national sovereignty. Faced with Colombian intransigence, an outraged Roosevelt called the new financial demands—reasonable enough from the Colombians' point of view—"blackmail" and let it be known privately to those interests backing the canal that he would smile upon an insurrection in Panama.

To the surprise of few, an insurrection did indeed occur in 1903; and if one had not, President Roosevelt would have been fully prepared to ask Congress for the authority to seize the zone from Colombia. The ubiquitous Bunau-Varilla helped organize the revolt. He cooperated with a group of railway workers, firemen, and soldiers at Colón, Panama, in an uprising during November 3–4. The rebels proclaimed Panamanian independence, and, just offshore, the U.S. Navy cruiser *Nashville* prevented an attempt by Colombian general Rafael Reyes (c. 1850–1918) to land troops intended to quell the rebellion. Immediately after this action, on November 6, President Roosevelt recognized the newly independent Republic of Panama and then received Bunau-Varilla as its first foreign minister. He and Secretary of State Hay concluded the Hay-Bunau-Varilla Treaty on November 18, which provided for the acquisition of a canal zone and the right to build and control a canal in exchange for the same monetary terms that had been offered Colombia. Called officially the "Convention for the Construction of a Ship Canal," the treaty was ratified in 1904.

Afterward Teddy Roosevelt often boasted that he "took Panama," and most Americans, certainly the American elite, at the time not only condoned but applauded his behavior. Nevertheless—in the eyes of much of Europe, some Americans, all Colombians, many in Latin America, and any number of historians since—the episode was a national disgrace. Some hinted at scandal, and the agents of the French Panama Canal Company, anxious to dump their worthless stock, had surely influenced the State Department and a number of members of Congress to adopt their favorable view of the Panama route. When the time came, those agents just as surely had helped stir up the Panamanian revolution.

Roosevelt personally had no stake in their game, and he probably could not have cared less about the ethics of their actions in pursuit of profit, but he was no less ruthless than they in pushing what he perceived as America's national interest, and he was certainly much better than they at persuading primarily himself but also many others of the righteousness of his cause in stamping out lawlessness in Colombia and disorder in Panama. Thus did "stability" become a watchword for American imperialism in Latin America.

Further reading: Ovido Diaz Espino, *How Wall Street Created a Nation: J. P. Morgan, Teddy Roosevelt, and the Panama Canal* (New York: Four Walls Eight Windows Press, 2001); Walter LaFeber, *Panama Canal* (New York: Oxford University Press, 1993); David McCullough, *The Path between the Seas: The Creation of the Panama Canal, 1870–1914* (New York: Simon and Schuster, 1999, c. 1977).

Pan Chao's Central Asia Campaigns (73–102)

PRINCIPAL COMBATANTS: Chinese forces of Pan Chao (Pinyin: Ban Zhao) vs. the tribes of Turkistan and the Kushan kingdom
PRINCIPAL THEATER(S): Turkistan and the region of the Hindu Kush
DECLARATION: None
MAJOR ISSUES AND OBJECTIVES: Conquest
OUTCOME: Pan Chao's brilliant campaign extended Chinese control into Turkistan and the region between the Hindu Kush and the Aral Sea; it is possible that control was pushed as far as the eastern shore of the Caspian.
APPROXIMATE MAXIMUM NUMBER OF MEN UNDER ARMS: Unknown, but the proportions of Pan Chao's army were certainly modest.
CASUALTIES: Unknown
TREATIES: Tribute pledge from the Kushans, about 90 C.E.

One of the most celebrated generals in Chinese military history, Pan Chao (32–102) first proved himself as a subordinate in campaigns against the Xiongnu (Hsiung-nu). After this, he was given command of a modest army and sent into the southwest, where he conquered the Tarim Basin, encompassing eastern Turkistan. This accomplished, he marched over the Tian (Tien) Shan Mountains into the western reaches of Turkistan. Here he fought and suppressed a host of nomadic tribes, sweeping through the vast region lying between the Hindu Kush and the Aral Sea. The nomads yielded to Chinese suzerainty.

Having built a power base among the nomadic tribes of Turkistan, Pan Chao carried battle to the formidable Kushans, who around 90 C.E., agreed to send annual tribute to China.

It is a certainty that advance elements of Pan Chao's army reached as far as the eastern shore of the Caspian; whether the general actually imposed Chinese control this far is not known.

Further reading: Myra Immell, *The Han Dynasty* (San Diego: Lucent Books, 2003).

Pannonian Revolts (6–9 C.E.)

PRINCIPAL COMBATANTS: Roman legions vs. Pannonian rebels
PRINCIPAL THEATER(S): Pannonia (Hungary)
DECLARATION: None
MAJOR ISSUES AND OBJECTIVES: The Romans sought to put down a Pannonian uprising and assert firm control of Pannonia as a frontier province of the Roman Empire.
OUTCOME: By means of a patient, systematic campaign of attrition, the Romans established suzerainty over the Pannonian rebels.
APPROXIMATE MAXIMUM NUMBER OF MEN UNDER ARMS: Unknown
CASUALTIES: Unknown
TREATIES: None

The era of the great Pax Romana was not altogether peaceful. Rome faced revolts among the conquered people of northern and eastern Europe, notably in Pannonia (Hungary). Here, for three years, violent uprisings prompted Tiberius (42 B.C.E.–37 C.E.) to break off his campaigning in Germania (Germany)—he left some legions there under the command of his legate, P. Quintilius Varus (d. 9 C.E.)—and rush to the Danube.

Tiberius understood that his legions possessed a weapon superior to any that the Pannonian tribes, no matter how fierce, commanded. His army was highly disciplined, patient, and as willing to expend time and effort as blood. Accordingly, he led his legions in gradual, methodical operations against the Pannonian rebels. By 9 C.E., the Romans had worn down the rebellion. There were no spectacular battles, no great victories, just journeyman military work leading to the attrition of the enemy. Both upper Pannonia and Moesia became firm provinces on the vast Roman frontier.

See also ROMAN NORTHERN FRONTIER WARS.

Further reading: András Mócsy, *Pannonia and Upper Moesia: A History of the Middle Danube Provinces of the Roman Empire* (London, Boston: Routledge and Kegan Paul, 1974); Pavel Oliva, *Pannonia and the Onset of Crisis in the Roman Empire* (Prague: Ceskoslovenské akademie ved, 1962).

Papacy—Holy Roman Empire Wars *See* HOLY ROMAN EMPIRE–PAPACY WAR (1081–1084); HOLY ROMAN EMPIRE–PAPACY WAR (1228–1241); HOLY ROMAN EMPIRE–PAPACY WAR (1243–1250).

Papineau's Rebellion (1837)

PRINCIPAL COMBATANTS: French-Canadian rebels vs. Canada
PRINCIPAL THEATER(S): Montreal vicinity
DECLARATION: None
MAJOR ISSUES AND OBJECTIVES: The French-Canadians sought an end to British domination of Quebec.
OUTCOME: The rebellion was quickly extinguished.
APPROXIMATE MAXIMUM NUMBER OF MEN UNDER ARMS: Unknown
CASUALTIES: Numbers not known, but casualties were light.
TREATIES: None

After the WAR OF 1812, political unrest spread through Canada, some of it as a result of Canada's 1791 constitution, but much of it a result of resentment toward the country's ruling elites—the so-called Family Compact in Upper Canada (southern Ontario) and the Château Clique in Lower Canada (southern and eastern Quebec). The wealthy members of the Family Compact modeled themselves on England's landed gentry, while the Château Clique consisted in the main of merchants, bankers, and shipping magnates. Colonial oligarchies formed the inner circle of government, shared religious and cultural ties, and married among themselves as a matter of course. Coming from the same circles, they not surprisingly chased similar social, economic, and political aims, and so they quite naturally supported each other politically. In Upper Canada the Family Compact used its political power to attempt to create a class-ordered society on the British model, and the tensions caused by its land hunger led to MACKENZIE'S REBELLION. In Lower Canada, the situation was more nuanced.

The Château Clique sought to spend liberally the tax monies raised by the French-Canadian–dominated legislature to improve the colony's infrastructure, thereby improving commerce and further enriching members of the Clique, which threatened the standing of the more traditional French-speaking and Roman Catholic majority. Indeed, these French *habitants* soon became convinced that the English-speaking, Protestant Château Clique aimed to destroy their way of life. In many ways, they were right: since the turn of the century, the French Canadian standard of living, especially in rural areas, had fallen dramatically as grain prices steadily dropped with, it seemed, no hope of recovery. At the same time, the British colonial regime had heavily increased the habitants' seigniorial dues. Their strong resentment of the ever-growing number of non-French immigrants exploded into riots when Montreal was hit by cholera and typhoid epidemics, and soon the resentment spread to open rebellion.

The habitants were represented in the colonial assembly by the Parti Canadien (later called the Parti Patriote), and this was headed by Louis-Joseph Papineau (1786–1871). Farmers made up the majority of the rebels, farmers from the parishes to the west and south of Montreal, and they first took up arms when the government moved to arrest leading members of the Parti Patriote, including Papineau. When Papineau and others fled to the countryside, the governor sent troops to arrest them. The first battle was fought in November at St. Denis, near Montreal; the government forces were repelled. But the rebels were defeated in subsequent battles at St. Charles and St. Eustache, and Papineau was forced to flee to the United States to escape arrest and a charge of treason. The rebels tried unsuccessfully to renew the fighting in the months that followed, but in 1839 Papineau took flight aboard a ship for France. Papineau eventually returned to Canada after he was pardoned in 1845, but a number of his followers were jailed, executed, or deported to Australia.

Further reading: J. M. S. Careless, ed., *Colonists & Canadiens, 1760–1867* (Toronto: Macmillan of Canada, 1971).

Paraguayan Civil War (1947)

PRINCIPAL COMBATANTS: Liberal Febrerista party vs. government of Higinio Morínigo
PRINCIPAL THEATER(S): Paraguay
DECLARATION: None
MAJOR ISSUES AND OBJECTIVES: The liberals sought to overthrow the nation's military dictatorship.
OUTCOME: The civil war was quickly over and the Febreristas crushed.
APPROXIMATE MAXIMUM NUMBER OF MEN UNDER ARMS: Unknown
CASUALTIES: Unknown
TREATIES: None

General José Felix Estigarribia, architect of Paraguay's military strategy in the CHACO WAR with Bolivia, was elected president in 1939 on the heels of the failed military coup conducted by radical officers called Febreristas (for the February Revolutionary Party or Partido Revolucionario Febrerista, PRF), but before he could implement the new constitution, which gave him immense authoritarian powers, he died in a plane crash. Replacing him in 1940 was General Higinio Morínigo (1897–1983), a harsh opportunist who moved immediately to shore up the fascistic Colorados, and to persecute the Liberales. He suspended the nation's constitution and ruled as a military dictator. Because he maintained the military in so privileged a position, the army remained intensely loyal to Morínigo, despite frequent civil unrest. Nevertheless, in July 1946, yielding to unremitting popular pressure, Morínigo allowed political activity to resume legally, and he formed a coalition two-party cabinet. The coalition did not long endure. Morínigo's opposition, the Febreristas, all resigned from the cabinet, and their leader, Rafael Franco (1896–1973), attempted a liberal coup. The result was a brief civil war from March to August 1947, which was crushed by the military. The revolt, which devastated the countryside and left thousands dead, greatly destabilized the Morínigo government, which was toppled the following year, on June 6, 1948, not by liberals, but by a military unhappy with Morínigo's handling of the crisis.

In the next six years, Paraguay had six weak presidents before General Alfredo Stroessner (b. 1912), backed by both the Colorados and the military, seized power in 1954.

See also PARAGUAYAN REVOLT (1954).

Further reading: Carlos R. Miranda, *The Stroessner Era: Authoritarian Rule in Paraguay* (Boulder, Colo.: Westview Press, 1990); Charles Washburn, *History of Paraguay*, 2 vols. (New York: AMS Press, 1975).

Paraguayan Revolt (1954)

PRINCIPAL COMBATANTS: Forces of General Alfredo Stroessner vs. President Federico Chavéz
PRINCIPAL THEATER(S): Paraguay
DECLARATION: Coup proclaimed on May 5, 1954
MAJOR ISSUES AND OBJECTIVES: Stroessner wanted to seize power from the current government.
OUTCOME: The military coup quickly succeeded, putting Stroessner in position to run for president without opposition.
APPROXIMATE MAXIMUM NUMBER OF MEN UNDER ARMS: Unknown
CASUALTIES: Unknown
TREATIES: None

Following the toppling of General Higinio Morínigo (1897–1983) in 1948, Paraguay became severely destabilized, and Federico Chavéz (d. 1978) was the sixth president in as many years when General Alfredo Stroessner (b. 1912), commander in chief of the Paraguayan armed forces, led a revolt against Chavéz's weak government on May 5, 1954. With Chavéz deposed, Stroessner put himself up for election, unopposed, to the office of president. He quickly purged the government of all current and potential adversaries, maintaining power through the military suppression of attempted coups and revolts. He placated capitalists by stabilizing the Paraguayan economy, while pleasing the people at large with a program of major public works.

So successful was Stroessner, with much help from the United States, at breaking down Paraguay's traditional isolation, both internal and external, that, after about 1960, he began to relax some of the harshness of his rule and permitted elections at all levels of government. However, the ultra-right-wing Colorado Party never lost such elections, and Stroessner was returned to office like clockwork every five years. For its part, the Catholic Church continued to decry Stroessner's brutal treatment of his country's Indian minority and to protest the government's strict censorship. During the 1970s, when the U.S. administration under Jimmy Carter stressed human rights in its foreign relations policy, Paraguay's relationship with the United States began to deteriorate and Carter much reduced U.S. aid. As a result, Paraguay drew ever closer to the right-wing regime in Brazil, which helped replace some of the lost U.S. funding for Stroessner's public works programs. Not until the 1980s, when Paraguay's economy took a serious nosedive, did the regime find itself threatened by rebellion (*see* the PARAGUAYAN REVOLT [1989]).

See also PARAGUAYAN CIVIL WAR (1947).

Further reading: Carlos R. Miranda, *The Stroessner Era: Authoritarian Rule in Paraguay* (Boulder, Colo.: Westview Press, 1990); Charles Washburn, *History of Paraguay*, 2 vols. (New York: AMS Press, 1975).

Paraguayan Revolt (1989)

PRINCIPAL COMBATANTS: Military forces under General Andrés Rodríguez vs. government of General Alfredo Stroessner
PRINCIPAL THEATER(S): Paraguay
DECLARATION: February 3, 1989, coup d'état
MAJOR ISSUES AND OBJECTIVES: Seizure of power from the prevailing dictator
OUTCOME: The government of Alfredo Stroessner was toppled.
APPROXIMATE MAXIMUM NUMBER OF MEN UNDER ARMS: Unknown
CASUALTIES: Approximately 300
TREATIES: None

General Alfredo Stroessner (b. 1912) came to power in the PARAGUAYAN REVOLT (1954) and maintained his dictatorship for far longer than any previous Paraguayan ruler. Although this brought an unprecedented degree of stability to Paraguay, the people paid a high price in human rights and liberty. When he assumed his seventh five-year terms in office in 1988, Stroessner was not only aging, he was seen to be aging. Now, worry began to grow within his own Colorado Party, where the traditionalists and the militant factions were squaring off for a fight over the succession to the presidency. In the end, they could not simply wait for the old man to pass away. On February 3, 1989, General Andrés Rodríguez (1923–98), Stroessner's chief lieutenant, staged a short, violent coup against the government in its Asunción capital. Three hundred people were killed, including troops and civilians in the government, and Stroessner was placed under close house arrest. He was subsequently permitted to seek refuge abroad.

Although Rodríguez carried out the revolt in the name of restoring democracy to Paraguay, his enemies alleged he was a criminal and known cocaine trafficker. In 1993, he did allow an election, which replaced him with Juan Carlos Wasmosy (b. 1939), a civilian and a democrat. He presided uneasily over a government that was still strongly influenced by the military, which remained the most powerful force in the government of Paraguay.

Further reading: Carlos R. Miranda, *The Stroessner Era: Authoritarian Rule in Paraguay* (Boulder, Colo.: Westview Press, 1990); Charles Washburn, *History of Paraguay*, 2 vols. (New York: AMS Press, 1975).

Paraguayan Uprisings (1959–1960)

PRINCIPAL COMBATANTS: Paraguayan rebels vs. government of Alfredo Stroessner
PRINCIPAL THEATER(S): Paraguay-Argentine border region
DECLARATION: None
MAJOR ISSUES AND OBJECTIVES: The rebels wanted to topple the Stroessner government.
OUTCOME: The rebels (operating from Argentina) and the guerrillas (operating from within Paraguay) were largely suppressed.
APPROXIMATE MAXIMUM NUMBER OF MEN UNDER ARMS: Initial incursion, 1,000 rebels
CASUALTIES: Unknown
TREATIES: None

General Alfredo Stroessner (b. 1912) brought unprecedented stability to Paraguayan government—at the cost of human rights and liberty. During the years that followed the establishment of the Stroessner regime (after the PARAGUAYAN REVOLT [1954]), thousands of Paraguayans fled across the border into Argentina, where they established a guerrilla base from which they mounted attacks against their homeland, seeking to overthrown Stroessner. To combat these incursions, Stroessner ordered the southern border of Paraguay closed in September 1959. On December 12, 1959, a force of about 1,000 rebels crossed the border and advanced several miles into Paraguay until government forces checked their advance. After this incident, Stroessner declared a state of siege, and Paraguay and Argentina teetered on the brink of war.

The uprisings consisted of periodic rebel incursions from Argentina, culminating in six major attempts in 1960. When the rebels failed to penetrate far into Para-

guayan territory, they fomented rebellion by guerrillas living in Paraguay. Stroessner's forces cracked down, and by the end of 1960, most of the rebel and guerrilla activity had been suppressed.

Further reading: Carlos R. Miranda, *The Stroessner Era: Authoritarian Rule in Paraguay* (Boulder, Colo.: Westview Press, 1990); Charles Washburn, *A History of Paraguay*, 2 vols. (New York, AMS Press, 1975).

Paraguayan War (1864–1870)

PRINCIPAL COMBATANTS: Paraguay vs. the Triple Alliance (Brazil, Argentina, Uruguay)
PRINCIPAL THEATER(S): Brazil and Paraguay
DECLARATION: Paraguay against Brazil, 1864; against Argentina, 1865
MAJOR ISSUES AND OBJECTIVES: Seeking expansion, Paraguay waged war against its larger neighbors.
OUTCOME: Paraguay was devastated by the costliest war ever fought on the South American continent.
APPROXIMATE MAXIMUM NUMBER OF MEN UNDER ARMS: Unknown
CASUALTIES: 220,000 Paraguayans killed; Alliance casualties, 190,000
TREATIES: Concluded on June 20, 1870

The Paraguayan War, also called the López War and the War of the Triple Alliance, was the bloodiest conflict in Latin American history. It began when Francisco Solano López (1827–70)—the callow pampered son of an iron-willed dictator—conceived a longing to establish Paraguay as the center of a vast South American state. Overestimating Paraguay's military strength, he imagined a showdown with Brazil as a first step toward realizing his dream. That showdown came in August 1864 when Brazil ignored López's increasingly strident warnings and intervened in Uruguay's civil war in support of the pro-Brazilian right-wing Colorados faction, who were opposed to the López-backed liberal Blancos. When the Brazilians ignored López's demands that they immediately withdraw, he declared war on Brazil. In November, he ordered the capture of a Brazilian war steamer and dispatched both his army and navy north to invade the Mato Grosso.

When Argentina foiled López's plan to send troops into southern Brazil by refusing him permission to march through Argentine territory, Paraguay declared war on Argentina as well in March 1865.

In response to tiny Paraguay's belligerence, Brazil, Argentina, and Uruguay formed the Triple Alliance on May 1, 1865, and mounted major counterattacks against Paraguayan forces. Argentine general Bartolomé Mitre (1821–1906) led the ground forces of the Alliance, and the Brazilian navy conducted a successful campaign on the Paraná River south of Corrientes in mid-1865. The Paraguayan invaders shortly retreated to their own territory and were obliged to fight a desperate defensive war.

López suffered defeat after defeat, although he scored a significant victory at the Battle of Curupayti on September 22, 1866. Despite this, the Alliance steadily advanced up the Paraguay River, pushing the Paraguayan defenders before them. In May 1866 López lost the cream of his army—almost 20,000 of his best men—in a series of suicidal attacks against allied forces at Tuyutí. In addition to heavy battlefield losses, after 1866 widespread epidemics of Asiatic cholera depleted the population at large.

In 1867, the key Paraguayan river fortress of Humaitá fell to the Alliance, forcing López to withdraw north to Angostura and Ypacaraí. These two towns were lost to the Alliance by the end of 1867, leaving Asunción, capital of Paraguay, vulnerable. A Brazilian army, led now by Luís Alves de Lima e Silva (1803–80), duke of Caxias, who had assumed command from Mitre, sacked the capital.

López was now reduced to fighting a guerrilla war in the remote regions of northern and eastern Paraguay. In 1869 and 1870 López fled before the huge allied forces, dragging his shattered army and thousands of civilian refugees behind him into the interior, trailing famine, disease, and death in his wake. Some historians think that by now he had become unhinged, and he certainly grew Lear-like, grimly ordering the executions of hundreds, including his own two brothers, two brothers-in-law, and many of his officers.

Ultimately, he was killed on March 1, 1870, in a battle in the province of Concepción. This cleared the way for the provisional Paraguayan government that replaced López to sue for peace. The treaty concluded on June 20, 1870, ceded to Argentina and Brazil 55,000 square miles of Paraguayan country. But the loss in land was as nothing compared to the human toll: of a population of 525,000, 220,000 Paraguayans were killed. Only 29,000 adult males survived the war. Not only did López's country by then lay in ruins, it was under the control of a Brazilian army of occupation, which continued to further drain the country until 1876.

Further reading: Charles J. Kolinski, *Independence Death: The Story of the Paraguayan War* (Gainesville: University of Florida Press, 1965); Harris Gaylord Warren, *Paraguay and the Triple Alliance: The Postwar Decade, 1869–1878* (Austin: Institute of Latin American Studies, University of Texas at Austin, 1978).

Paraguayan War of Independence
(1810–1811)

PRINCIPAL COMBATANTS: Paraguay vs. the United Provinces of the Río de la Plata and, separately, Spain
PRINCIPAL THEATER(S): Paraguay; mainly Asunción
DECLARATION: None

MAJOR ISSUES AND OBJECTIVES: Paraguay wanted independence from both Spain and the United Provinces
OUTCOME: Independence was achieved, although governing power was soon vested in an absolute dictator.
APPROXIMATE MAXIMUM NUMBER OF MEN UNDER ARMS: Unknown
CASUALTIES: Unknown
TREATIES: None

In 1776, the Spanish combined the present countries of Paraguay, Argentina Bolivia, and Uruguay (then called Banda Oriental) into the Río de la Plata, under the rule of a viceroy. But when Napoleon (1769–1821) deposed Spain's Ferdinand VII (1784–1833), Argentines in Buenos Aires formed a junta to govern what they called the United Provinces of the Río de la Plata. In 1810, Paraguay, asserting its autonomy, refused to join. A year later, a United Provinces army under Manuel Belgrano (1770–1820) marched out of Buenos Aires to attack the Paraguayan capital, Asunción, to compel Paraguayan compliance. Belgrano met stiff resistance and was forced to withdraw from the capital. Having defeated the United Provinces, the Paraguayans turned on the Spanish royal governor, whom they ousted. After declaring independence from Spain, a junta established a government at Asunción, and, in 1814, José Gaspar Rodríguez de Francia (1766–1840) was named first consul. In 1816, he was vested with dictatorial powers for life.

See also ARGENTINE WAR OF INDEPENDENCE; NAPOLEONIC WARS.

Further reading: John Hoyt Williams, *The Rise and Fall of the Paraguayan Republic, 1800–1870* (Austin: Institute of Latin American Studies, University of Texas at Austin, 1979).

Paraguay's Jesuit-Indian War against Portuguese Slave Traders (1609–1642)

PRINCIPAL COMBATANTS: Paraguayan missionaries and Indians vs. Portuguese invaders
PRINCIPAL THEATER(S): Paraguay
DECLARATION: None
MAJOR ISSUES AND OBJECTIVES: The Jesuits sought to resist an invasion by Paraguayan slave traders.
OUTCOME: By rallying and organizing the Indians, the Jesuits fashioned an effective defensive force, which ultimately succeeded in ejecting all Portuguese slave traders from Paraguay.
APPROXIMATE MAXIMUM NUMBER OF MEN UNDER ARMS: Unknown
CASUALTIES: Unknown
TREATIES: None

Little is known about this long conflict, which included no recorded set battles. Spain and Portugal competed for territory and trade in South America. Paraguay became subject to dispute. Spain had dispatched Jesuit missionaries to convert the Indians. For many years, these Jesuit priests were the only representatives of Spanish authority in the region. During the early 17th century, Portuguese slave traders invaded Paraguay. They were repeatedly repulsed by small forces of Indians organized by the Jesuit fathers. This makeshift "army" succeeded in driving all of the Portuguese out of the region by 1642.

Further reading: Sélim Abou, *The Jesuit "Republic" of Guaranis (1609–1768) and Its Heritage* (New York: Crossroad Publishing Company, 1997); Charles Washburn, *History of Paraguay*, 2 vols. (New York: AMS Press, 1975).

Parthian Conquest of Media (150 B.C.E.)

PRINCIPAL COMBATANTS: Parthia vs. Seleucid Syria
PRINCIPAL THEATER(S): Media
DECLARATION: None
MAJOR ISSUES AND OBJECTIVES: Conquest
OUTCOME: By exploiting chaos within the Seleucid dynasty, Parthia's King Mithradates I made a lightning conquest in Media.
APPROXIMATE MAXIMUM NUMBER OF MEN UNDER ARMS: Unknown
CASUALTIES: Unknown
TREATIES: Unknown

From 162 to 143 B.C.E., the Seleucid dynasty in Syria was torn by internecine strife and internal rebellion. Mithradates I (fl. 171–138 B.C.E.), king of Parthia, exploited the Seleucid disarray by advancing against Media and, in a single, sweeping campaign, conquering the region. The Seleucids were powerless to respond until 141 B.C.E., when, following Mithradates I's invasion of Babylonia, a full-scale war was waged between the Seleucids and Parthia.

Parthian-Roman Wars   *See* ROMAN-PARTHIAN WAR (55–38 B.C.E.); ROMAN-PARTHIAN WAR (56–63 B.C.E.); ROMAN-PARTHIAN WAR (195–202).

Parthian-Syrian War   *See* SYRIAN-PARTHIAN WAR (141–139 B.C.E.); SYRIAN-PARTHIAN WAR (130–127 B.C.E.).

Pastry War   (1838)

PRINCIPAL COMBATANTS: France vs. Mexico
PRINCIPAL THEATER(S): Veracruz, Mexico
DECLARATION: Mexico declared war on France in 1838.
MAJOR ISSUES AND OBJECTIVES: The pretext was reparations for foreign losses during Mexican civil unrest, but there was something of a bully's need to push around a weaker power in the newly installed French king's provocative dispatch of the French fleet to collect a debt owed to a French pastry chef for abuses he suffered at the hands of rowdy Mexican army officers.
OUTCOME: Mexico agreed to pay France's demands for reparations, and France withdrew, but not before making just enough of a martyr of the retired general Santa Anna to launch him once again on the road to becoming Mexico's president.
APPROXIMATE MAXIMUM NUMBER OF MEN UNDER ARMS: France, 4,000; Mexico, 1,600
CASUALTIES: France, 12 killed, 99 wounded; Mexico, 65 known dead, about 347 either killed or wounded
TREATIES: None

In 1836, Texan general Sam Houston (1793–1863) defeated the Mexican army under Mexico's president, General Antonio López de Santa Anna (1794–1876), the self-styled Napoleon of the West, at the Battle of San Jacinto (*see* TEXAN WAR OF INDEPENDENCE). Afterward Houston had treated the ingloriously captured Santa Anna decently enough as the defeated former head of an enemy country, but Houston's Texas troops threw the generalissimo in jail the minute Houston left on a politically motivated trip to the United States. Santa Anna remained in chains for two months while Houston was out of the country. Finally the Texans, not knowing exactly what to do with him, sent His Excellency to Washington. There Andrew Jackson (1767–1845), too, treated Santa Anna courteously, receiving him as a head of state on January 19, 1837. As Jackson's guest, Santa Anna discussed with the president the state of affairs in Texas, the two men agreeing to disagree on Mexican recognition of Texas as an independent republic, before Jackson sent him on his way to Veracruz under naval escort.

The United States, Texas, and most of Mexico fully expected the deposed Santa Anna to live out his retirement there. But Santa Anna remained in Veracruz for only a year or so before he heard himself recalled to the defense of his country by public acclaim. His mission was to expel the French who had occupied his hometown on a silly pretext. In the early years of the Mexican republic, foreigners sometimes found their property destroyed during Mexico's frequent civil disorders, and unable to get satisfactory compensation from Mexico, they had taken to petitioning their own governments for help.

Just before leaving with Santa Anna for Texas and the Alamo three years before, some of Santa Anna's officers had visited a French restaurant in Veracruz. They had wrecked the place and carried off all the French pastry they could find. The proprietor, knowing that a suit against the Mexican government was an exercise in futility, sought out the French minister, who had been collecting similar claims, all totaling about $600,000. By 1838, Mexico did not have $600,000. In fact, it had a 17-million-peso national debt. So when the French minister pressed Mexico for payment, the government ignored him. France, once again a monarchy, decided to use the incident as a pretext for chastising the arrogant little republic: thus the so-called Pastry War.

The French king, Louis Philippe (1773–1850) sent a fleet to collect the pastry chef's debt, along with all the others, and the French navy sailed into the port at Veracruz and began bombarding the nearby fortress of San Juan de Ulúa, which the French then seized, briefly occupying Veracruz itself. Mexico declared war in 1838, and Santa Anna immediately put himself at the head of a Mexican force and marched against the French at Veracruz. He acted without authority; no one in the current administration, and certainly not President Anastasio Bustamante (1780–1853) (an old rival), wanted to see Santa Anna come out of retirement, but Santa Anna had never been one for legal niceties. He chased the French out of Veracruz with little problem, especially because the Mexican government, upon hearing he was involved, quickly promised to pay the $600,000, and the French just as quickly agreed to withdraw. Santa Anna, who lost a leg from a stray volley from the departing French ship, parlayed his wound and his success in the Pastry War into an 1841 coup that made him, once again, president of Mexico.

Further reading: John S. D. Eisenhower, *So Far from God: The U.S. War with Mexico, 1846–1848* (New York: Anchor, 1990); Oakah L. Jones, Jr., *Santa Anna* (New York: Twayne Publishers, 1968).

Paulician War (867–872)

PRINCIPAL COMBATANTS: Byzantine Empire vs. the Paulician sect
PRINCIPAL THEATER(S): Tephrike, Byzantine Empire (Divrigu, Turkey)
DECLARATION: None
MAJOR ISSUES AND OBJECTIVES: The Byzantine objective was to wipe out a "heretical" sect.
OUTCOME: The Paulicians were totally defeated, many were killed, and others were forced to flee the empire.
APPROXIMATE MAXIMUM NUMBER OF MEN UNDER ARMS: Unknown
CASUALTIES: Unknown, but a high percentage of the Paulicians were killed.
TREATIES: None

The Paulicians, a Christian sect, created a Paulician state in the Byzantine city of Tephrike (Divrigu, Turkey). Although they were mercilessly persecuted by Byzantine religious authorities as heretics, the Paulicians continued to spread their teachings and, to counter their Byzantine persecutors, they allied themselves with the Muslims in the BYZANTINE-MUSLIM WAR (851–863). At last, in 867, Basil I (c. 813–886), Byzantine emperor, mounted a concerted military campaign against the Paulicians, seeking to wipe out the sect once and for all. The campaign was more protracted than anticipated, but by 872, Byzantine troops had invaded and occupied Tephrike and killed the sect's spiritual and political leader, Chrysocheir (d. 872), as well as many other Paulicians. The survivors fled their fallen capital and sought refuge in Armenia and Syria.

Further reading: Romilly James Heald Jenkins, *Byzantium; the Imperial Centuries, A.D. 610–1071* (New York: Random House, 1967).

Paxton Riots (1763)

PRINCIPAL COMBATANTS: A mob of Scotch-Irish Presbyterians from the Pennsylvania frontier vs. Conestoga and Delaware Indians
PRINCIPAL THEATER(S): Vicinity of Philadelphia and the Pennsylvania frontier
DECLARATION: None
MAJOR ISSUES AND OBJECTIVES: Settlers indiscriminately sought vengeance against Indians.
OUTCOME: Nothing conclusive
APPROXIMATE MAXIMUM NUMBER OF MEN UNDER ARMS: British colonies, 57 from Paxton and Donegal settlements, others from the Delaware Valley Irish settlement; Indians, unknown
CASUALTIES: 20 Conestoga Indians, 56 Delaware Indians died in protective custody; colonial casualties not recorded
TREATIES: None

During the period of the FRENCH AND INDIAN WAR, settlers made little or no effort to distinguish between combatant and noncombatant Indians. On December 14, 1763, a mob of 57 Scotch-Irish Presbyterians from Paxton and Donegal, Pennsylvania frontier settlements subject to violent Indian raids, slaughtered six innocent Conestoga Indians in Lancaster County. Provincial lieutenant governor John Penn (1729–95) issued an arrest warrant for the mob, but no official dared execute it. Most frontier Pennsylvanians heartily approved of the actions of the mob they called the "Paxton Boys."

In order to protect the Conestogas who had survived the attack from further harm, the magistrates of Lancaster County placed them in protective custody in a public workhouse. But the Paxton Boys struck again on December 27, killing 14 Conestogas while they knelt in prayer.

In the meantime, the residents of the so-called Irish Settlement in the Delaware Valley were harassing and even killing their Delaware Indian neighbors, who had been converted to Christianity by Moravian missionaries. Colonial authorities removed these Indians to Province Island, Philadelphia, whereupon the Paxton Boys descended on the City of Brotherly Love and were confronted by a band of young citizens who had rallied to the Indians' defense. The timely intervention of no less a figure than Benjamin Franklin (1706–90) averted violence; he persuaded the Paxton Boys to go home.

Tragically, 56 of the Indians given refuge on the island sickened and died in the harsh winter. When the survivors returned to the Delaware Valley, they found their villages had been destroyed. Some moved farther west. Others were killed by frontiersmen.

Further reading: Alan Axelrod, *Chronicle of the Indian Wars: From Colonial Times to Wounded Knee* (New York: Prentice Hall General Reference, 1993); Francis Jennings, *Empire of Fortune: Crowns, Colonies and Tribes in the Seven Year War in America* (reprint, New York: Norton, 1990).

Peach War (1655–1657)

PRINCIPAL COMBATANTS: The Delaware (and allied Indian tribes) vs. Dutch settlers
PRINCIPAL THEATER(S): Southern New Netherland (New York)
DECLARATION: None
MAJOR ISSUES AND OBJECTIVES: Indian retaliation for a Dutch farmer's murder of an Indian woman who picked peaches in the farmer's orchard
OUTCOME: Inconclusive; no definitive ending to the conflict
APPROXIMATE MAXIMUM NUMBER OF MEN UNDER ARMS: Unknown
CASUALTIES: In early raids, 28 Dutch farms were burned, 50 colonists killed, at least 100 taken captive; number of Indian casualties unknown
TREATIES: None

The Peach War began when a Dutch farmer (in present-day New York City) killed a Delaware Indian woman for picking peaches in his orchard. Her family retaliated by waylaying and killing the farmer. Word of the incident spread rapidly, inciting other Delaware bands to strike out against Dutch settlers. Several settlers were killed at New Amsterdam, and 150 were taken captive there. Governor Peter Stuyvesant (c. 1592–1672) called out the militia, which liberated most of the captives, then destroyed a number of Indian villages. Following this exchange,

Dutch-Indian violence continued sporadically, to the detriment of the Indians as well as the settlers.

Many wars between settlers and Indians began, like this one, with an isolated incident; however, the killing in the orchard was hardly the sole motive for Indian action. While Stuyvesant and his troops were campaigning against the Swedes for dominance in the Delaware Valley, a band of several hundred Delawares entered New Amsterdam one September morning in 1655. Although they did not attack anyone, they did break into a house, claiming that they were in search of "Northern Indians," their enemies. Then the invaders refused to vacate Manhattan until they received news that the farmer who had killed the Delaware woman in his orchard had been slain. This confirmed, the Indians prepared to leave, only to be attacked by the local militia. A battle ensued, which drove the Indians to retreat across the Hudson River to Staten Island and Pavonia (Jersey City, New Jersey).

The Dutch attack in Manhattan was doubtless intended to intimidate the Delawares; it failed. Instead, it moved the tribe to exact vengeance on local Dutch settlements near Manhattan in a series of raids conducted over a three-day period. Twenty-eight Dutch farms were burned, 50 colonists were killed, and at least 100 colonists taken captive.

Returning from the Delaware Valley campaign against the Swedes, Stuyvesant turned his attention to the Indians, negotiating the release of at least 70 prisoners in exchange for a ransom of trade goods, including gunpowder and lead. The Delaware band known as the Hackensacks quickly concluded negotiations, but other bands stubbornly held onto their captives. After much debate, Stuyvesant prepared to attack at least one of the recalcitrant bands, with the object not only of recovering the captives but also to discourage Indians from taking hostages as a tool of extortion. But Stuyvesant was unable to mount the new offensive. History does not record the reason for this failure, but it is likely that at least some of the remaining captives were retained by the Indians precisely to discourage a Dutch assault. Stuyvesant could not risk an attack that would result in the immediate murder of the prisoners. With this anticlimax, the Peach War faded by early 1656, concluded without any treaty or other formal ending.

Further reading: Alan Axelrod, *Chronicle of the Indian Wars: From Colonial Times to Wounded Knee* (New York: Prentice Hall General Reference, 1993); Michael Kammen, *Colonial New York: A History* (New York: Oxford University Press, 1996).

Peasants' War (1524–1525)

PRINCIPAL COMBATANTS: German peasants vs. German nobles

PRINCIPAL THEATER(S): Germany and Austria
DECLARATION: None
MAJOR ISSUES AND OBJECTIVES: Inspired by Protestant paeans to individual freedoms, German peasants revolted against the country's upper classes.
OUTCOME: The rebels were crushed.
APPROXIMATE MAXIMUM NUMBER OF MEN UNDER ARMS: Peasants, 30,000 at any given time; nobles, 10,000 at any given time.
CASUALTIES: 130,000 peasants killed; casualties among nobles, unknown.
TREATIES: None

Beginning on August 24, 1524, German peasants, inspired by the Protestant fervor of Martin Luther (1483–1546), Huldrych Zwingli (1484–1531), and John Calvin (1509–64), rose up against the papacy and the Holy Roman Empire in Swabia and Franconia and pillaged churches and nobles' lands across much of southern Germany. Some landholders sympathized with the rebels and their desires for new rights and freedoms, and they even won the support of several towns as the rebellion escalated into Hesse, Thuringia, Saxony, and the Tyrol. The German nobility, now awakened to the danger, organized quickly to quell this uprising of the poor.

In April 1525, Jaecklein Rohrbach (d. 1525?) led rebels against the town of Weinsberg, overcame the men-at-arms defending the town, and forced Count Ludwig von Helfenstein (d. 1525) and 16 of his knights to walk to their deaths along a gauntlet of men carrying pikes and daggers.

The response was swift. Martin Luther himself denounced the uprising, and the Catholic Swabian League engaged mercenary troops under Georg von Truchsess (fl. 1525) to recapture the towns that had fallen to the peasants and to put down the uprising with utmost brutality. Truchsess did both. With about 10,000 men, he swept through Alsace and slaughtered perhaps 20,000 rebels.

While Truchsess operated in the west, armies were formed in Hesse and Saxony and attacked the headquarters of rebel leader Thomas Munzer (d. 1525) at Mühlhausen (Mulhouse). Munzer mustered some 8,000 troops, but was defeated at the Battle of Frankenhausen on May 15, 1525. Five thousand of his men were slaughtered, and he was led off to torture and execution. About 1,200 rebel diehards continued to defend Mühlhausen, but were soon overwhelmed.

Although sporadic rebellion continued in Austria until 1526, the German Peasants' War had been effectively crushed by the spring of 1525. The death toll among the peasants reached 130,000.

Further reading: Douglas Miller, *German Peasants' War* (London: Osprey, 2003).

Pecheneg Invasion of Russia (967–968)

PRINCIPAL COMBATANTS: Pechenegs vs. Russians
PRINCIPAL THEATER(S): Russia
DECLARATION: None
MAJOR ISSUES AND OBJECTIVES: Conquest of Russian territory in a general Pecheneg expansion
OUTCOME: The Pechenegs were driven out of Russia.
APPROXIMATE MAXIMUM NUMBER OF MEN UNDER ARMS: Unknown
CASUALTIES: Unknown
TREATIES: None

The Pechenegs were a nomadic Turkic people who lived in the steppes north of the Black Sea from the sixth through the 12th centuries. By the 10th century, having driven out the Hungarians, they reached the height of their power and extent, controlling the territory between the Don and lower Danube rivers. From here, they menaced Byzantium and Russia.

In 967, the Pechenegs were poised to take Kiev, which prompted Sviatoslav (d. 972), the son of the Russian prince Igor (877–945), to return from campaigning in Bulgaria. Sviatoslav engaged the Pechenegs and drove them out of Russia by 968. Encouraged by this triumph, he returned to Bulgaria, scoring success against the enemy there. Sviatoslav was defeated by the Byzantines shortly after his victories against the Pechenegs and the Bulgarians. On his return to Russia from a renewed campaign against Bulgaria in 972, he was intercepted by a Pecheneg army, which defeated his forces and killed him.

See also BYZANTINE-RUSSIAN WAR; RUSSIAN-BULGARIAN WAR.

Further reading: George Vernadsky, *A History of Russia* (New Haven, Conn.: Yale University Press, 1961).

Peddlars' War   *See* MASCATES, WAR OF THE.

Peloponnese War, First (460–445 B.C.E.)

PRINCIPAL COMBATANTS: Athens vs. Sparta (and her allies, especially Corinth)
PRINCIPAL THEATER(S): The Peloponnese, Greece
DECLARATION: None
MAJOR ISSUES AND OBJECTIVES: Ultimately, resentment against Athens's growing influence in Greece, mainly from Sparta and Corinth
OUTCOME: After initial triumphs, Athens fell victim to multiple revolts, and the war ended with the situation essentially restored to its prewar status.
APPROXIMATE MAXIMUM NUMBER OF MEN UNDER ARMS: Unknown

CASUALTIES: Unknown
TREATIES: Truce in 451; "30 years' peace" in 445

By 462 B.C.E., Sparta and Corinth, trade and political rivals to Athens and the Athens-dominated Delian League, had developed an intense enmity toward Athens. That year Sparta insulted Athens by spurning Athenian aid in putting down a revolt of Spartan helots, which sent Athens into a series of alliances with the enemies of Sparta.

But it was the Corinthians, even more than the Spartans, who grew to hate the Athenians. Corinth saw the series of alliances—first with Argos and Thessaly, and more recently with Megara (which had turned to Athens after Corinth put pressure on its borders) as a direct challenge. The First Peloponnese war is best viewed, then, as a conflict between Athens and Corinth, in which Sparta—as Athens's principal rival—sometimes intervened.

Athens took the initiative in 460, attacking the Corinthian fleet at Hailes, in the Gulf of Argolis, a Corinthian victory. The next battle, however, went the other way, when in 459 Athens defeated a Corinthian force that attacked Megara. Two years later, Athens launched a successful invasion of Aegina, Corinth's ally. At this point, Sparta sent an expedition into Boeotia in support of its ally Thebes, which had the effect of taking pressure off Aegina. Near Thebes, it was the Spartans who triumphed over the Athenians at the Battle of Tanagra in 457. But, Sparta unwisely relinquished the initiative by recalling its forces, leaving an opening for an Athenian counteroffensive at Oenophyta, which fell in 457. The defeat left Boeotia exposed, and Athens took control of it.

The great Athenian dictator Pericles (c. 495–429 B.C.E.) led his country's forces to a series of victories along the coast of Achaea in 455, thereby securing the Spartan helots as vassals of Athens. They were dispatched to colonize the Gulf of Corinth. Athens under Pericles had rapidly established a Greek empire, and the city's ambition did not end with the Peloponnese. It would continue to try to expand throughout the Aegean.

Following this whirlwind of Athenian triumphs, a five-year truce was concluded in 451. But Boeotia rose up in revolt against Athens, and, with this, Sparta and its allies resumed the war. With Megara, Phocis, and Euboea all in rebellion against Athens, Pericles barely managed to block a Spartan advance against Athens. He also recovered Euboea, but, in 445, when a peace was concluded, most of the quickly won Athenian empire had vanished.

The belligerents pledged 30 years of peace. The Second (Great) PELOPONNESE WAR would break out within half that time.

Further reading: Donald Kagan, *The Peloponnesian War* (New York: Viking Press, 2003); David M. Lewis, "The Origins of the First Peloponnesian War," in Gordon Spencer Shrimpton and David Joseph McCargar, eds., *Classical Contributions* (Locust Valley, N.Y.: J.J. Augustin, 1981), pp. 71–78.

Peloponnese War, Second (Great)
(431–404 B.C.E.)

PRINCIPAL COMBATANTS: Athens (and allies) vs. Sparta (and allies)
PRINCIPAL THEATER(S): The Peloponnese, Greece; Sicily
DECLARATION: None
MAJOR ISSUES AND OBJECTIVES: Sparta and Athens vied for dominance in the Mediterranean world.
OUTCOME: Although Athens frequently held the upper hand, Sparta prevailed, ultimately reducing Athens to complete subordination.
APPROXIMATE MAXIMUM NUMBER OF MEN UNDER ARMS:
CASUALTIES: At the siege of Syracuse, Athens lost 40,000 men killed; survivors were enslaved.
TREATIES: Truce of 424; Peace of 421; Peace of 404

In the spring of 431, just about halfway through the promised 30-year peace that ended the First PELOPONNESE WAR, Thebes—Sparta's ally—attacked Plataea, which was allied with Athens. Eighty days later, Sparta itself struck at Athens, launching the Great Peloponnese War.

According to the Greek historian Thucydides (c. 460–390), the cause of the war was Sparta's fear of Athens and its imperial ambitions, though it was more immediately Sparta's allies who precipitated the war. Corinth had recently and unofficially sent a force to its former colony at Potidaea to help those now in rebellion there against Athens. Corinth convened a congress of Spartan allies to discuss their many grievances against Athens, and—with Thebes's enthusiastic support—pushed through a decision to go to war with Athens. Even Sparta later admitted that the Theban attack on peaceful Plataea, which followed the congress, was unprovoked and a just cause for Athenian anger. Sparta nevertheless ignored Athens's call for arbitration and invaded Attica just as the Spartans' provocative allies had hoped.

During the early phases of the war, Pericles (c. 495–429 B.C.E.) followed a canny strategy of avoiding out-and-out battle, and he did manage to drive off a Spartan siege of Athens. However, a plague epidemic killed not only Pericles but also approximately a quarter of the population of Athens. When Cleon (d. 422 B.C.E.) replaced Pericles as the new Athenian leader, he discarded the policy of battle avoidance. Whereas Pericles had exhausted the Spartans with hit-and-run raids and a blockade, which closed the Gulf of Corinth in 429, Cleon impatiently took the offensive. In 428, he put down a revolt in Lesbos, then

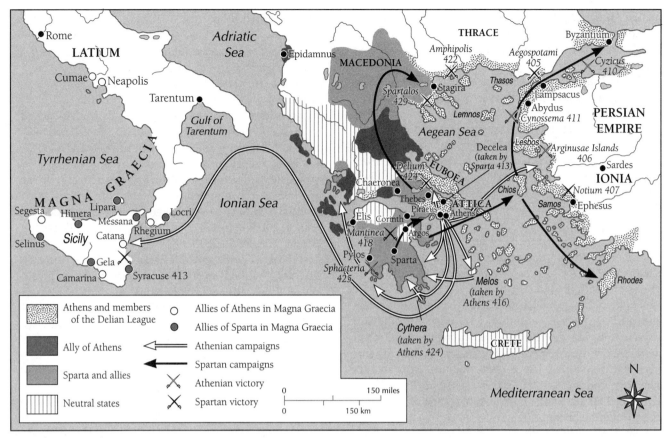

Second (Great) Peloponnese War, 431–404 B.C.E.

advanced into Boeotia the following year. He failed to take Boeotia, but he did manage to capture every military base along the Gulf of Corinth save one.

Under Cleon, in 425, the Athenians boldly established a military base at Sphacteria, in the heart of Spartan territory. This enabled victories at Megara and the port city of Nisaea the following year.

Despite Cleon's aggressive triumphs, his failure to take Boeotia and the collapse of the Boeotian campaign at the Battle of Delium disheartened Athens. A peace faction rose up. Its leader, Nicias (d. 413 B.C.E.), opposed Cleon, and the momentum of his monolithically aggressive strategy was frittered away. As a result, the Spartan commander Brasidas (d. 422 B.C.E.) crushed the Athenians at the Battle of Amphipolis in 424, precipitating a yearlong truce. After regrouping, Athens made a new attempt against Amphipolis, but failed.

The deaths of both Brasidas and Cleon in 422 left Nicias the undisputed leader of Athens, and his peace policy was unopposed. He hastily concluded a peace in 421, whereby Athens retained the important Messenian harbor of Pylos, and Sparta retained its great port, Amphipolis. At this time, however, the charismatic military leader Alcibiades (c. 450–404 B.C.E.) stirred Athens to break the peace. Under Alcibiades' direction, Athens stole Argos, Mantinea,

and Tegea from the camp of Spartan allies. Alcibiades promoted a grandiose plan to conquer Syracuse, Sicily, and an Athenian fleet was launched in 415. Incredibly, however, even though he was the leader of the invasion, Alcibiades, was recalled to Athens to face charges of religious sacrilege involving the defilement of sacred objects. This prompted the mercurial Alcibiades to defect to the Spartan cause. He successfully prevailed upon Sparta to send troops to the defense of Syracuse, where they could trap the Athenian invasion force.

As a result of Alicibiades' defection, the Athenian siege of Syracuse was a disaster. In 414, the Athenian land forces were themselves laid under siege, and in 413, the Athenian fleet was destroyed. Approximately 40,000 Athenian troops died, and 240 ships were lost. Athenian survivors were enslaved. Nicias and Demosthenes (d. 413 B.C.E.), leaders of the Athenian forces, were taken prisoner and put to death.

Following the defeat of Athens, Alcibiades established a Spartan garrison at Declea, on Attic territory, directly threatening Athens itself. Worse, Declea straddled Athenian access to its silver mines at Laurium, thereby cutting off the Athenian treasury from replenishment. In the meantime, Sparta reached out to Sardis, a Persian province, concluded an alliance with it, and together they incited Athenian colonies to revolt—Sparta having agreed to allow Persia to hold sway over any colonies acquired in exchange for financial support of a naval expedition against Athens.

By 412, despite all hardships, Athens rebuilt its fleet and reorganized its army. The ever-treacherous Alcibiades entered into secret negotiations with Athens and was given command of the new Athenian fleet in 411. This he led the following year to victory at the Battle of Cynossema and the Battle of Abydos, defeating the Spartan fleet in both battles. In 410, at Cyzicus, a combined Spartan-Persian fleet was defeated, as were the alliance's land forces.

Reeling from the unexpected disasters of 411 and 410, Sparta sued for peace to restore the status quo antebellum. The plea fell upon the deaf ears of the dictatorial Cleophon (d. 405 B.C.E.), new leader of Athens. He pressed on with the war.

At first, this seemed a good idea. Thanks to the generalship of Alcibiades, Byzantium fell under the Athenian yoke in 408. The general had little enough time to relish his victory, however. In 406, while he was back in Athens, his sea forces were defeated by a combined Spartan-Persian fleet under Lysander (d. 395 B.C.E.) at the Battle of Notium. This led to the complete blockade of the Athenian fleet at Mytelene.

With nearly miraculous resilience, the Athenians built a *third* new fleet—despite the paucity of silver in the treasury—and advanced against the Spartan fleet at the Battle of Arginusae in 406. Dealt a defeat here, the Spartans once again sued for peace, and, once again, Cleophon spurned the plea.

Thus circumstances stood in 405 when Lysander led a Spartan fleet in a surprise attack against the 200-ship Athenian fleet riding at anchor off the Hellespont at Aegospotami. The Athenian fleet was destroyed, and all hands were either killed or captured. Capitalizing on his victory, Lysander sailed to Piraeus and Athens, laying siege to both. After six months, the starving Athenians surrendered, and Cleophon was executed. Sparta forced extremely punitive peace conditions on Athens. All of its military fortifications were razed, and its mighty fleet was limited to no more than a dozen vessels. The government of Athens was decreed as an oligarchy (the so-called Thirty Tyrants), a virtual puppet of Sparta, to which it was subject as an involuntary ally. The conclusion of the Great Peloponnese War brought the end of Athenian hegemony in ancient Greece.

Further reading: Donald Kagan, *The Peloponnesian War* (New York: Viking Press, 2003) and *The Fall of the Athenian Empire* (Ithaca, N.Y.: Cornell University Press, 1987); G.E.M. de Ste. Croix, *The Origins of the Peloponnesian War* (Ithaca, N.Y.: Cornell University Press, 1972); Thucydides, *History of the Peloponnesian War*, trans. Rex Warner (New York: Viking Press, 2003).

Peninsular War (1808–1814)

PRINCIPAL COMBATANTS: France and Napoleonic Spain vs. Spanish rebels, Portugal, and Great Britain
PRINCIPAL THEATER(S): Spain and Portugal
DECLARATION: July 14, 1807, summons to war
MAJOR ISSUES AND OBJECTIVES: Portugal's British-backed resistance to French trade policies and Spanish patriots' hatred of Napoleon and his puppet rulers led to a long and bloody rebellion against French rule.
OUTCOME: Ultimately Napoleon was defeated and driven first from the Iberian Peninsula, then from power.
APPROXIMATE MAXIMUM NUMBER OF MEN UNDER ARMS: France, 230,000 in 1812; Spain, Portugal, and Great Britain, 172,000 in 1813
CASUALTIES: France and allies, 91,000 killed in battle, 237,000 wounded; Spain, 25,000 guerrillas killed plus tens of thousands of regular Spanish and Portuguese troops; Great Britain, 35,630 killed; 32,429 wounded. Including noncombatants, total deaths from all causes may have exceeded 1 million.
TREATIES: First Peace of Paris, May 30, 1814

After the humiliating concessions made by Prussia and the less humiliating accord with Russia that followed the WAR OF THE THIRD COALITION, Napoleon Bonaparte (1769–1821) moved in November and December 1807 against Portugal when that country refused to answer his July 19, 1807, summons to declare war on Great Britain. His Continental System—aimed at killing the world's trade with archenemy Britain—was failing, and he realized for the blockade to work, he needed to enforce it throughout Europe; that meant seizing Portugal, a country that, from the beginning, had made clear its opposition to Napoleon's trade restrictions. Spain's Charles IV (1748–1819) allowed French troops passage across the Iberian Peninsula, and they soon occupied Lisbon. The presence of Napoleon's legions in northern Spain, however, did not sit well with Charles's subjects, and they rebelled, forcing him to abdicate in favor of his son, Ferdinand VII (1784–1833). Napoleon saw in the abdication a chance to rid Europe and himself of the last Bourbon rulers, and he peremptorily summoned the Spanish royal family to Bayonne in April 1808. There, he removed both Charles and Ferdinand from the throne and interned them in the chateau of French foreign minister Charles Maurice de Talleyrand-Périgord (1754–1838). In their stead Napoleon named his brother, Joseph Bonaparte (1768–1844), king of Naples, as the new ruler of Spain.

Spaniards were no happier with a Bonaparte on the throne than they were with a Bonaparte army roaming the countryside. When Napoleon brutally suppressed an uprising in Madrid, the insurrection spread across the whole of the peninsula. Encouraged at the sight of Iberia up in arms, the British decided to use the area as a bridgehead on the Continent and sent a small force under the energetic Arthur Wellesley (1769–1852) (subsequently the duke of Wellington) to support the rebellion. The French, after setbacks at Bailén and Vimeiro, surrendered Lisbon. Napoleon met with his reluctant ally, Czar Alexander I (1777–1825) of Russia, at the Congress of Erfurt in September and October of 1808, to extract promises of help in a situation that might well become desperate. Despite the august company of princes assembled by Napoleon, the czar made no clear commitments. So damaged was Napoleon's prestige by the sensational blows he had received during what could only be considered a national uprising in Spain and Portugal that even Talleyrand—always a harbinger of informed French opinion—had grown dismayed by his emperor's policies and was already negotiating with Alexander behind Napoleon's back.

With little choice, Napoleon personally led an expedition onto the peninsula during November 1808 through January 1809. Taking most of his Grand Army with him, he nearly defeated the British, who narrowly escaped at Coruña in early 1809. Thus, Napoleon was on the brink of putting down the entire revolt when Austria—seeing him preoccupied in Spain—attempted to regain her autonomy (*see* NAPOLEON'S WAR WITH AUSTRIA).

From 1809 onward, Spanish guerrillas, sometimes backed by British ships and British troops, harassed the French while Napoleon was preoccupied in Austria. In fact, the British under Wellington returned to drive the French from Portugal and invade Spain, winning an important victory at Talavera on July 28, 1809. But Napoleon sent reinforcements to lance what he described as his "Spanish ulcer" and enforce the Continental System in the only way he could after losing his fleet at Trafalgar. Freshly spilled blood did for the moment restore French ascendancy, but in 1811 Wellington's forces began their inexorable recovery of Portugal's frontier fortress. Although the Spanish field armies had been smashed and scattered by Napoleon's marshals the year before, guerrillas continued the struggle and, with British aid, proved effective. Without the British, the guerrillas would hardly have survived; without the guerrillas, the outnumbered British would have been swept away by the more experienced French; together—supplied by the Royal Navy—Wellington's regulars and the Spanish irregulars were devastating, although at an appalling cost to Spain's civil population.

In 1812, the national Cortes, convened at Cadiz by the rebels, promulgated a constitution inspired by both the FRENCH REVOLUTION and by British institutions, which in turn would spark revolutions throughout the old Spanish Empire's holdings in the New World. For now, it cheered the allies on to Salamanca and Madrid, where they evicted the French from southern Spain by 1812. Wellington failed to take Burgos in 1812, but he did better in 1813, routing the French at Vitoria and chasing them back into France. There, he joined the general effort of the European allies to bring down Napoleon (*see* NAPOLEONIC WARS; NAPOLEON'S INVASION OF RUSSIA) by besieging Bayonne and Bordeaux.

See also COALITION, WAR OF THE FIRST; COALITION, WAR OF THE SECOND; FRENCH REVOLUTIONARY WARS; HUNDRED DAYS' WAR; NAPOLEONIC WARS.

Further reading: David Chandler, *The Campaigns of Napoleon* (New York: Scribner, 1973); Charles J. Esdaile, *The Wars of Napoleon* (London: Pearson Education UK, 1996); David Gates, *The Napoleonic Wars* (London: Edward Arnold, 1997).

Penruddock's Revolt (1655)

PRINCIPAL COMBATANTS: Penruddock's "army" vs. Cromwellian Britain
PRINCIPAL THEATER(S): Salisbury and vicinity
DECLARATION: None
MAJOR ISSUES AND OBJECTIVES: Penruddock sought the restoration of the British Crown.
OUTCOME: Penruddock was captured, tried for treason, and executed.
APPROXIMATE MAXIMUM NUMBER OF MEN UNDER ARMS: Penruddock had about 200 followers.
CASUALTIES: None, except for Penruddock himself
TREATIES: None

After the Lord Protector, Oliver Cromwell (1599–1658), dissolved Parliament in 1655, a number of royalists responded to this dictatorial and tyrannical measure by raising revolts with the objective of bringing about the return of the monarchy. In Wiltshire, John Penruddock (1619–55), a royalist who had been persecuted by Cromwell's regime, raised an "army" of 200 followers and occupied Salisbury. There he abducted judges who were in the process of trying a number of royalists for treason. His point made by the abductions, Penruddock declined to harm the judges and marched into Devon. There he was taken prisoner by a regiment of Cromwell's troops. Remanded to the judges he had abducted and released, he was tried for treason, found guilty, and beheaded. Acknowledging that Penruddock had not harmed the judges, however, Oliver Cromwell personally saw to it that a portion of Penruddock's estate, subject to forfeiture because of his treason, was given to his children.

See also ENGLISH CIVIL WAR, FIRST; ENGLISH CIVIL WAR, SECOND.

Further reading: J. P. Kenyan, *Stuart England* (New York: St. Martin's Press, 1978).

Pepin's Campaigns in Aquitaine (760–768)

PRINCIPAL COMBATANTS: Pepin III vs. Waifer, duke of Aquitaine
PRINCIPAL THEATER(S): Aquitaine
DECLARATION: None
MAJOR ISSUES AND OBJECTIVES: Pepin sought to put down the rebellion of Waifer, who wanted to maintain Aquitaine's independence from France.
OUTCOME: After a protracted war, Waifer was defeated, and Aquitaine became a province of Pepin's Frankish Empire.
APPROXIMATE MAXIMUM NUMBER OF MEN UNDER ARMS: Unknown
CASUALTIES: Unknown
TREATIES: None

Pepin III (c. 714–814, also known as Pepin the Short), son and successor of Charles Martel (c. 688–741), succeeded in driving the Muslims over the Pyrenees and out of France. Pepin held the nominal title of Mayor of the Palace but ruled as the true power behind the Merovingian throne for 10 years until he deposed Childeric III (d. 755) and brought about his own coronation as king of the Franks in 751. This accomplished, he campaigned against the Lombards and in Germany (*see* PEPIN'S CAMPAIGNS IN GERMANY). Then he launched a campaign against the forces of Waifer, the duke of Aquitaine. Waifer sought to keep Aquitaine independent of France. Over the course of a bitter eight-year campaign, Pepin defeated Waifer and brought Aquitaine firmly into the fold of his growing empire.

Further reading: Margaret Deanesly, *A History of Early Medieval Europe, from 476 to 911*, 2nd ed. (London: Methuen, 1969).

Pepin's Campaigns in Germany (757–758)

PRINCIPAL COMBATANTS: Franks vs. Saxons
PRINCIPAL THEATER(S): Bavaria
DECLARATION: None
MAJOR ISSUES AND OBJECTIVES: Tassilo III, duke of Bavaria, sought independence from the Frankish empire.
OUTCOME: Under the leadership of Pepin III, the Franks crushed the rebellion and forced a heavy tribute on the Saxons.
APPROXIMATE MAXIMUM NUMBER OF MEN UNDER ARMS: Unknown
CASUALTIES: Unknown
TREATIES: Tribute agreement, 758

After driving the Muslims from France and subduing the Lombards in Italy and before commencing a protracted campaign against Waifer, duke of Aquitaine (*see* PEPIN'S CAMPAIGNS IN AQUITAINE), Pepin III (c. 714–814, also known as Pepin the Short), king of the Franks and effectively king of France, invaded Germany, primarily to put down a rebellion led by Tassilo III (fl. 788), duke of Bavaria. Tassilo sought to break with the Frankish empire and proclaim Bavarian independence. Pepin quickly defeated Tassilo and extracted from the Saxons a heavy tribute.

Further reading: Bernard S. Bachrach, *Merovingian Military Organization* (Minneapolis: University of Minnesota Press, 1972); Rosamond McKitterick, *The Frankish Kingdoms under the Carolingians, 751–987* (London, New York: Longman, 1983).

Pepin's War with Muslims   *See* FRANKISH-MOORISH WAR, SECOND.

Pequot War (First Puritan Conquest) (1634–1638)

PRINCIPAL COMBATANTS: Pequot Indians vs. colonists of New England
PRINCIPAL THEATER(S): Western Massachusetts and Connecticut
DECLARATION: None
MAJOR ISSUES AND OBJECTIVES: After years of tension caused by white encroachment upon Pequot-held lands, the murder of a colonial captain ignited hostilities.
OUTCOME: Essentially, the annihilation of the Pequot tribe
APPROXIMATE MAXIMUM NUMBER OF MEN UNDER ARMS: Colonists, at Block Island, 90; at Pequot Harbor, 90 whites and 60 Mohegan and some 500 Narragansett and Niantic allies. Pequots, unknown.
CASUALTIES: Colonists, unknown; Pequots, 600–700 at Mystic fort, others
TREATIES: Treaty of Hartford, September 21, 1638

By the 1630s, growing numbers of settlers in the Connecticut River valley were encroaching upon the territory of the Pequots, an Algonquian tribe related to the Mohegans and, like them, originally settled along the Hudson. In 1634, Captain John Stone fell victim to an Indian raid. The only thing certain about the incident is that the raiders were not Pequots, but western Niantics, a tribe dominated by the Pequots; however, on November 7, Pequot representatives agreed to hand over those guilty of Captain Stone's murder, to pay an exorbitant indemnity, to relinquish rights to Connecticut land the English might wish to settle, and to trade with the English "as friends."

When the Pequot council failed to ratify what the tribe's ambassadors had agreed to, the English grumbled for two years over a breach of treaty but took no action.

On June 16, 1636, however, colonial officials received a message from Uncas (fl. 17th century), chief of the friendly Mohegan tribe, warning that the Pequots were about to strike. A conference was called, and the colonists reasserted the demands of the 1634 treaty, again calling for the killers of Captain Stone and full payment of the tribute. It is not clear what the Pequot response was to these demands, but a few days following it, another trading captain, John Oldham (c. 1600–36), and his crew were killed on Block Island by Narragansetts or members of a tribe subject to them.

Although the Narragansett sachems Canonchet (c. 1630–76) (whom the English called Canonicus) and Miantonomo (c. 1600–43) condemned the murder and offered reparations and a pledge of loyalty, colonial authorities dispatched Captain John Endecott (c. 1588–1665), with Captain John Underhill (c. 1597–1672) and Captain William Turner (1623–76) and a force of 90 men to Block Island on August 25. By the time Endecott reached Block Island, however, most of the Indians had fled, so he and his troops sailed to the English fort at Saybrook, Connecticut, on the Connecticut River to punish the Pequots—even though they had had nothing to do with the death of John Oldham.

Endecott proceeded to Pequot Harbor at the mouth of the Pequot (Thames) River. The Pequots there greeted him, Endecott proclaimed his mission of revenge, and the Pequots asked for a parley. Endecott refused and called the Indians to battle. The Indians refused to fight, whereupon Endecott set about burning dwellings and crops, thereby provoking a full-scale war.

A band of Pequots besieged the Saybrook fort for months, and other groups raided nearby settlements. In the meantime, the English and the Pequots vied for an alliance with the powerful Narragansett tribe. Largely due to the skillful negotiations of religious dissident Roger Williams (c. 1603–83), the sachem Miantonomo pledged the Narragansetts to an alliance with the English.

Despite the alliance, the war became increasingly brutal. By the spring of 1637, Wethersfield, Connecticut, had been ravaged, and other settlements fell under attack. On May 1, the Plymouth, Massachusetts, and Connecticut colonies resolved to unite in fighting the Pequots. Yet political and religious wrangling delayed organization of an effective fighting force.

While Massachusetts and Plymouth floundered, Captain John Mason (c. 1600–74) set out from Hartford, Connecticut, on May 10 with 90 colonists and 60 Mohegans under Chief Uncas to attack the principal Pequot stronghold, the fort of Sassacus (d. 1637), on Pequot Harbor. As he neared his objective, Mason decided to recruit more Indian allies before attacking.

On May 25, Mason, with 500 Narragansett and Niantic allies, drew near Sassacus's Pequot Harbor fort. Instead of attacking it, however, Mason turned to Mystic to attack another fort, which harbored not warriors but mostly women, children, and old men. The May 26 assault on the fort at Mystic was less a battle than a slaughter of innocents. Within an hour 600–700 Pequots were slain.

In late May or early June, Mason joined his troops to a Massachusetts unit and attacked a large number of Pequots near the Connecticut River, causing a general rout, with many of the surviving Indians fleeing south to Manhattan. A pursuit detachment of about 160 troops was organized in July, and on the 13th they ran the Mystic survivors to ground in a swamp near New Haven. After surrounding the Indians, the English announced that they would guarantee old men, women, and children safe conduct out of the swamp. Almost 200 emerged, whereupon they were made prisoners, the male children to be sold into West Indian slavery, and the females to be distributed as slaves to various colonial towns as well as to the Indian allies of the English.

The 80 Pequot warriors who remained holed up in the swamp fought valiantly as the colonial troops cut through the swamp with their swords, all the while shooting at them.

Despite the unrelenting assault, a sizable number of Pequots, perhaps including the sachem Sassacus, slipped through the English lines on July 14. The remainder were (as one eyewitness put it) "killed in the Swamp like sullen Dogs."

Sassacus and other Pequot fugitives sought sanctuary among neighboring tribes, but the terror tactics of the English had so intimidated the Indians of the region that no tribe took Sassacus in. Finally, the Mohawks sent colonial officials the severed head of Sassacus, who had—unsuccessfully—sought refuge among them.

The Treaty of Hartford, concluded on September 21, 1638, divided the survivors of the swamp siege as slaves among the Indian allies. The treaty also directed that no Pequot might inhabit his former country and ordered that the very name *Pequot* be expunged; those enslaved had to take the name of their "host" tribe. Those Pequots who escaped death or enslavement fell easy prey to surrounding tribes, who had long endured their raids and depredations.

Shortly after the treaty was signed, a number of Pequots settled at Pawcatuck, in former Pequot country and, therefore, in violation of the treaty. Mason was dispatched with 40 colonists and 120 Mohegans, led by Uncas, to clear them out, which he did, allowing his men and the Indian allies to plunder freely, and, with this, the Pequot War ended.

Further reading: Alan Axelrod, *Chronicle of the Indian Wars: From Colonial Times to Wounded Knee* (New York: Prentice Hall General Reference, 1993); Francis Jenning, *The Invasion of America: Indians, Colonialism, and the Cant of Conquest* (New York: Norton, 1975).

Perak War (1874–1876)

PRINCIPAL COMBATANTS: Perak vs. Great Britain
PRINCIPAL THEATER(S): Perak, Malaysia

DECLARATION: None

MAJOR ISSUES AND OBJECTIVES: A rebellion against British occupation by a group of dissident Malay chiefs led to the assassination of the first British resident at Perak, then to reprisals that crushed the resistance.

OUTCOME: The dissident native leaders were arrested and removed from power, failing to curb British economic and political influence.

APPROXIMATE MAXIMUM NUMBER OF MEN UNDER ARMS: Unknown

CASUALTIES: Unknown

TREATIES: Violation of the Pangkor Treaty of 1874 triggered the war.

The Pangkor Treaty of 1874 between the British government and the local Malay chiefs permitted Britain to install a resident in Perak, a country in northwestern Malaysia, to administer trade and other commercial and governmental functions. When the first resident, James W. W. Birch (d.1875), arrived in Perak in November 1874 to take up his post as official British adviser to the sultan, he embarked on a program of reform that ended both corrupt revenue collection policies and slavery in Perak. Birch hoped through his influence not only to modernize the traditional administrative system, under which government had been based on personal relationships between the sultan and the chiefs, but also to have Raja Abdullah accepted as sultan in Upper Perak, in other words, as its supreme ruler, the one man who dealt directly with the British. But Birch's rapid and revolutionary changes quickly alienated both Abdullah and most local chiefs. At a meeting in July 1875, the sultan organized a movement to end foreign influence in Perak by assassinating Birch.

Later that month, when Birch was in Upper Perak posting his new tax proclamations, one of the chiefs, Maharaja Lela, and his men assassinated the resident. The conspirators failed, however, to follow up with the planned attack on the residency itself. His murder prompted immediate reprisal from the British government, which dispatched troops to put down all resistance to British administration in the region.

By the middle of 1876, the rebellious chiefs and leaders had been rounded up. They were later tried and punished. The sultan Abdullah was deposed, and the British assumed an increasing degree of influence over Malay affairs. However, the lesson of the Birch affair was not lost on subsequent British residents. Instead of acting unilaterally to impose changes and reforms, they worked cooperatively with indigenous rulers, and made few drastic changes in traditional institutions.

Further reading: William R. Roff, *The Origins of Malay Nationalism* (New Haven, Conn.: Yale University Press, 1967).

Percy's Rebellion (1403)

PRINCIPAL COMBATANTS: Henry "Hotspur" Percy vs. Henry IV

PRINCIPAL THEATER(S): Shrewsbury, England

DECLARATION: None

MAJOR ISSUES AND OBJECTIVES: Hotspur wanted to topple Henry from the throne and replace him with Edmund Mortimer.

OUTCOME: Hotspur's forces were defeated—and Hotspur killed—at the Battle of Shrewsbury, bringing about the collapse of the rebellion.

APPROXIMATE MAXIMUM NUMBER OF MEN UNDER ARMS: Unknown

CASUALTIES: Unknown

TREATIES: None

Prominent among those who helped Henry Bolingbroke depose Richard II (1367–1400) to become England's king Henry IV (1367–1413) were Henry Percy (1342–1408), first earl of Northumberland, and his son Sir Henry Percy (1366–1403), nicknamed "Hotspur" by his Scottish enemies for the alacrity with which he patrolled their borders. A grateful Henry IV rewarded the Percys liberally with lands and offices in northern England and Wales, making them the largest landowners in Northumberland. But their ambitions were deeper than Henry's purse could ever accommodate—ultimately they sought to control the throne itself. As it happened, they parted ways with the new king over a trifle—falling into a dispute over the ransom of a Scottish rebel. When Hotspur captured the earl of Douglas at the battle of Homildon Hill, Henry demanded the prisoner and claimed the ransom for himself. The break had been building, and now it came—the Percys withdrew their support from Henry and backed Edmund Mortimer.

Mortimer (1376–1413) was the uncle of Richard II's legitimate heir, the earl of March (d. 1428). He had been captured by the French-backed Welsh rebel Owen Glendower (c. 1359–1416) and persuaded to make common cause against Henry. The Percys dispatched an army to join Glendower, but it was intercepted en route by royalist forces under Henry IV and his son, Prince Hal (1387–1422, later Henry V). On July 21, 1403, the armies clashed in the Battle of Shrewsbury. The Percys were defeated before Glendower could reinforce them. Hotspur fell in battle, and his leaderless troops surrendered.

See also GLENDOWER'S REVOLT; NORTHUMBERLAND'S REBELLION.

Further reading: Bryan Bevan, *Henry IV* (London: Palgrave Macmillan, 1994).

Pergamum, Conquest of (133–129 B.C.E.)

PRINCIPAL COMBATANTS: Rome (with Cappadocian aid) vs. Aristonicus of Pergamum

PRINCIPAL THEATER(S): Pergamum, Italy
DECLARATION: None
MAJOR ISSUES AND OBJECTIVES: Aristonicus resisted
Roman annexation of Pergamum.
OUTCOME: Aristonicus was ultimately defeated, and
Pergamum became the Roman province known as Asia.
APPROXIMATE MAXIMUM NUMBER OF MEN UNDER ARMS:
Unknown
CASUALTIES: Unknown
TREATIES: None, save underlying bequest of Attalus III,
king of Pergamum

On his death, Attalus III (c. 170–133 B.C.E.), ruler of the
Italian kingdom of Pergamum, bequeathed his realm to
Rome. However, a pretender to the throne, Aristonicus,
intervened and blocked Roman efforts to assume control
of Pergamum. It took forces under the command of proconsul P. Licinius Crassus (c. 180–130 B.C.E.), in alliance
with a Cappadocian army, to defeat Aristonicus. With the
pretender driven from the throne, Pergamum became the
Roman province of Asia.

Peronist Revolts (1956–1957)

PRINCIPAL COMBATANTS: Peronists vs. Argentine
government
PRINCIPAL THEATER(S): Argentina
DECLARATION: None
MAJOR ISSUES AND OBJECTIVES: The Peronists wanted to
restore Juan Perón as dictator of Argentina.
OUTCOME: The Peronists were partially suppressed, but a
low-level civil war ensued, to the great detriment of the
Argentine economy.
APPROXIMATE MAXIMUM NUMBER OF MEN UNDER ARMS:
Unknown
CASUALTIES: Casualty numbers unknown; 2,000
Peronistas were arrested; 38 executed.
TREATIES: None

Juan Perón (1895–1974), dictator of Argentina, was
deposed in the ARGENTINE REVOLT (1955), but his supporters were still very much present in Argentine politics.
In the power vacuum left by Perón's ouster, General
Eduardo Lonardi (1896–1956) assumed control of a provisional government. On November 13, 1955, Lonardi
was deposed by General Pedro Pablo Eugenio Aramburu
(1903–70) in a bloodless coup. A hard-line anti-Peronist,
Aramburu took steps to ensure that the Peronist party
would never again assume power. The party was outlawed
—a step that served only to intensify the Peronists' sub-
versive activities.

Juan Perón, living in exile in Paraguay, directed the
Peronists in a campaign of antigovernment activity, rang-
ing from harassment to terrorism, including sabotage and
rioting. On June 14, 1956, Peronist rebels staged major
uprisings in Santa Fe, La Pampa, and Buenos Aires. The
government responded by declaring martial law, and Peronists and government troops clashed in bloody battles.
The first wave of revolts was put down, with the arrest of
some 2,000 Peronists, of whom 38 were subsequently executed.

In the meantime, although the Peronist party had
been declared illegal, a neo-Peronist "Popular Union
Party" was established. It urged voters to signal protest in
the upcoming general elections by casting blank ballots.
In an atmosphere of increasing hostility, more violence
erupted between Peronists and the government as the
elections of 1957 approached. The Peronists exercised
their considerable influence and swung their support
behind Arturo Frondizi (1908–95), a radical leader who
promised to reopen political life in Argentina for them.
Frondizi won majorities in both houses of Congress,
but when his reformist majority proved more interested in
foreign investment than in the adverse effect his currency
devaluation was having on the middle and lower classes,
he had to use the military to shore up his unpopular policies against these traditional strongholds of Peronists. An
ongoing, low-level civil war resulted, which greatly disrupted the already beleaguered Argentine economy.

Further reading: Frederick C. Turner and José
Enrique Miguens, eds., *Juan Perón and the Reshaping of
Argentina* (Pittsburgh: University of Pittsburgh Press,
1983).

Pershing's Punitive Expedition See VILLA'S
RAIDS.

Persian-Afghan War (1726–1738)

PRINCIPAL COMBATANTS: Safavid Persians (with Abdali
Afghan allies) vs. Ghilzai Afghans
PRINCIPAL THEATER(S): Persia (Iran)
DECLARATION: None
MAJOR ISSUES AND OBJECTIVES: Nadir Khan (later Nadir
Shah) sought to reconquer Persia from the Ghilzai
Afghans.
OUTCOME: The Ghilzai were largely driven out of Persia,
which was restored to Safavid rule—under Nadir Shah.
APPROXIMATE MAXIMUM NUMBER OF MEN UNDER ARMS:
Hundreds of thousands (100,000 Abdalis at Meshed;
80,000 troops to lay siege against Kandahar)
CASUALTIES: Unknown
TREATIES: None

Over the course of the first three decades of the 18th century, Afghan tribes seized control of nearly half of Persia

(Iran). In 1722, Ghilzai Afghan rebels had driven the Safavid shah, Hussein (c. 1675–1726), from his throne (see AFGHAN REBELLIONS [1709–1727]). Meanwhile the Safavid dynasty's weakness had attracted other invaders—first the Russians from the East (see RUSSO-PERSIAN WAR of 1722–1723), then the Ottoman Turks from the West. As Persia collapsed, not so surprisingly, into civil war (see PERSIAN CIVIL WAR [1725–1730]), the Afghans continued to make the most of the chaos, taking Tehran in 1725 and soundly defeating both the Russians and the Ottomans. Only the rise of Nadir Kahn (1688–1747, later, Nadir Shah) put a stumbling block between the rebels and their dream of Afghan liberation.

From an obscure beginning in the Afshar tribe of Turks loyal to the Safavids—where he served under a local chieftain—Nadir Kahn first evidenced his remarkable leadership qualities when he formed and led a band of robbers. By 1726, as head of the gang, he persuaded 5,000 of his followers to support the putative Safavid shah Tahmasp II (d. 1739), now seeking to regain the throne his father had lost four years earlier to the Afghan usurpers. Under Tahmasp's banner Nadir reformed Persia's military forces, slowly assembling and carefully training the army he would need to retake the lost reaches of the empire.

Nadir initially fought a limited, stealthy war, retaking areas near Afghan-held Herat but always avoiding large-scale engagements while he continued to build up and prepare his forces.

By 1728, Nadir had captured Mazandrin, which controlled the routes to Tehran. With these routes closed, Nadir advanced on Herat itself in 1729, defeating the Abdali Afghans. Having defeated them, he engaged them as allies to fight their rivals, the Ghilzai Afghans. In 1729, Nadir and his Abdali allies defeated the forces of Ashraf (d. 1730), the Ghilza Afghan to whom Hussein had abdicated, at the Battle of Mihmandust. The allies collaborated again on a victory at Murchalkur later in the year. After this series of brilliant victories, by which Nadir utterly defeated the Ghilzai, he restored Isfahan (near Murchalkur) Tahmasp II to the Persian throne.

Nadir then attacked and routed the Ottoman Turks, who had occupied adjacent areas of Azerbaijan and Iraq. Despite these early successes in the TURKO-PERSIAN WAR (1730–1736), Nadir was soon frustrated by the inept aggression of the new shah. Even as Nadir fought the Turks, the Afghans continued to rebel at Herat. Then, while Nadir was absent quelling the revolt, Tahmasp rashly attacked the Turks only to be heavily defeated. The Turks forced an ignominious peace on the shah, all of which enraged Nadir when he heard about it. He rushed back, deposed Tahmasp, placed the shah's infant son, Abbas III, on the throne, and declared himself regent. When he suffered a defeat at the hands of the Turks in Iraq, Nadir redoubled his effort and relentlessly drove them completely out of Persia. Fresh from that victory, he

turned to Russia, threatening war. To avoid fighting Nadir, an uneasy Russia gave up its Caspian provinces in favor to Persia. Then, in 1736, Nadir deposed the child king Abbas III and took the Persian throne himself, assuming now the title of Nadir Shah.

And still, the war with the Afghans went on. In 1736, Nadir transferred 100,000 of his Abdali allies to Meshed, where they were to safeguard Khorasan. This generally stabilized Persia, enabling Nadir to conclude the war with the Turks. Once the Ottoman Turks were defeated, Nadir turned in 1737 to the task of taking the great fortified Ghizali city of Kandahar, considered impregnable. With 80,000 troops, most of them Abdalis, Nadir laid siege to the fortress city, which fell in 1738. Nadir attempted to raze Kandahar, but its 30-foot-thick walls were so stout that he was unable to destroy it. He evacuated it of Ghizalis, redeeming prisoners of war for captured Abdalis. With Persia largely won back from Afghan control, Nadir's ambitions expanded as he prepared to invade Mogul India (see PERSIAN INVASION OF MOGUL INDIAN).

Further reading: Willem M. Floor, *The Afghan Occupation of Safavid Persia, 1721–1729* (Paris: Association pour l'avancement des études iraniennes); Laurence Lockhart, *Nadir Shah* (New York: AMS Press, 1973).

Persian-Afghan War (1798)

PRINCIPAL COMBATANTS: Muhammad Barakzai (with Persian allies) vs. his brother, Zaman Barakzai
PRINCIPAL THEATER(S): Afghanistan
DECLARATION: None
MAJOR ISSUES AND OBJECTIVES: Muhammad Barakzai wanted to depose his brother and assume leadership of the Afghans.
OUTCOME: With Persian help, Muhammad Barakzai prevailed; his brother was deposed, blinded, and imprisoned.
APPROXIMATE MAXIMUM NUMBER OF MEN UNDER ARMS: Unknown
CASUALTIES: Unknown
TREATIES: None

When Zaman Shah (r. 1793–1800) seized the Afghan throne with the intention of following in the footsteps of his grandfather, Ahmad Shah (d. 1772)—the founder of the Durrani dynasty, who had extended Afghan control from Meshed to Kashmir and Delhi—British imperialists grew nervous. Seeking above all to defend their growing hold on India, they persuaded the shah of Persia, Fath Ali (1766–1834), to pressure Zaman to call off his planned attack on India. Zaman, refusing to comply with the shah's wishes, invaded India, whereupon Fath Ali goaded Zaman's older brother, Muhammad (fl. 1798–1816), to take advantage of Zaman's absence by usurping the Afghan throne. With Persian assistance, Muhammad took the fortress city of Kandahar and then the Afghan capital of Kabul. When Zaman returned from India, he found that he had been deposed. Falling captive to his brother, he was blinded and imprisoned.

Further reading: Sir Percy Sykes, *History of Afghanistan*, 2 vols. (New York: AMS Press, 1975); Stephen Tanner, *Afghanistan: A Military History from Alexander the Great to the Fall of the Taliban* (New York: Da Capo Press, 2002).

Persian-Afghan War (1816)

PRINCIPAL COMBATANTS: Persia vs. Afghanistan
PRINCIPAL THEATER(S): Persian-Afghan frontier
DECLARATION: None
MAJOR ISSUES AND OBJECTIVES: Fath Ali, shah of Persia, wanted to seize Herat, a city held by the Afghans.
OUTCOME: Muhammad, the Afghan king, was able to appease the Persian shah, who broke off his advance on Herat.
APPROXIMATE MAXIMUM NUMBER OF MEN UNDER ARMS: Unknown
CASUALTIES: Unknown
TREATIES: None

Fath Ali (1766–1834), shah of Persia, mounted an invasion of Afghanistan in 1816, marching a large army to Ghorian, a Persian fortress on the frontier. His objective was the capture of Herat, an Afghan city claimed by the Persians. However, the Afghan governor of Herat proposed to pay the Persian army to abort the invasion. The Afghan vizier disapproved of this bribery scheme and ordered the Herat governor to be deported. This done, Fath Ali's troops continued their advance on Herat. To appease Fath Ali, Muhammad (fl. 1798–1816), king of the Afghans, ordered that the vizier be blinded. Although Fath Ali did break off his campaign against Herat, the blinding of the vizier induced his relatives to seize the Afghan throne from Muhammad by way of vengeance.

Further reading: Sir Percy Sykes, *History of Afghanistan*, 2 vols. (New York: AMS Press, 1975): Stephan Tanner, *Afghanistan: A Military History from Alexander the Great to the Fall of the Taliban* (New York: Da Capo Press, 2002).

Persian-Afghan War (1836–1838)

PRINCIPAL COMBATANTS: Persia vs. Afghanistan (allied with Great Britain)
PRINCIPAL THEATER(S): Herat, Afghanistan

DECLARATION: None
MAJOR ISSUES AND OBJECTIVES: The Persians wanted to take Herat.
OUTCOME: With British aid, the Afghans resisted a 10-month Persian siege, forcing the Persians to withdraw.
APPROXIMATE MAXIMUM NUMBER OF MEN UNDER ARMS: Unknown
CASUALTIES: Unknown
TREATIES: None

The Russian czar Nicholas I (1796–1855) induced Muhammad Shah (1810–1848), ruler of Persia, to invade Afghanistan. Muhammad assembled his invasion force at Khorasan, preparatory to an assault on the often-disputed city of Herat. The siege was begun on November 23, 1837. Meanwhile, the British, grown fearful that Persia was falling completely under Russia's spell, decided to aid the Afghans in defending Herat, which the British tended to see as the key to India. Entering into an alliance with the rulers not only of Herat but also of Kabul and Kandahar, they sent a formal mission to meet with Dost Muhammad (1793–1863), founder of the Afghan ruling dynasty—the Barakzai (or Mohammadzai). When Captain (later Sir) Alexander Burnes (1805–41) arrived in Kabul in 1837, he was thinking of protecting India from Russia, while Dost Muhammad was thinking of his failure the year before to take Peshawar, India, from the Sikhs.

The British helped the Afghans resist the Persian siege of Herat for 10 months, but after the Persians withdrew on September 28, 1838, Burnes refused to give Dost Muhammad the assurances of support he felt he needed and deserved to invade Peshawar again. If the British would not be enticed, however, the Russians might, and the Afghan ruler turned to the czar's government. A Russian agent appeared in Kabul ready to intrigue with the Afghans against the interests of their erstwhile allies, and the British promptly withdrew back to India, where they began their own plottings. Indeed, the failure of Burnes's mission made the First AFGHAN WAR (1839–42) almost inevitable.

Further reading: Sir Percy Sykes, *History of Afghanistan*, 2 vols. (New York: AMS Press, 1975); Stephan Tanner, *Afghanistan: A Military History from Alexander the Great to the Fall of the Taliban* (New York: Da Capo Press, 2002).

Persian-Afghan War (1855–1857)

PRINCIPAL COMBATANTS: Persia vs. Afghanistan (allied with Great Britain)
PRINCIPAL THEATER(S): Herat, Afghanistan
DECLARATION: None

MAJOR ISSUES AND OBJECTIVES: Persia wanted to seize Herat.

OUTCOME: Under combined Afghan and British pressure, the Persians withdrew.

APPROXIMATE MAXIMUM NUMBER OF MEN UNDER ARMS: Unknown

CASUALTIES: Unknown

TREATIES: Afghan-British alliance was created by the Treaty of Peshawar of 1855.

Although the Afghan ruler Dost Muhammad (1793–1863) and most of his family had been deported to India after he surrendered to the British in Kabul at the close of the First AFGHAN WAR (1839–42), the British were never able to control postwar Afghanistan. When they tried to discuss terms for their withdrawal with Akbar Kahn, Dost Muhammad's son, they only managed to get their agent, Sir William Hay Macnaghten (1793–1841), assassinated during the parley. By the summer of 1842, the new governor general, Edward Law, Lord Ellenborough (1790–1871), decided to withdraw his country entirely from Afghanistan. The following year Dost Muhammad returned to Kabul ready to begin some 20 years of consolidating his rule.

By 1855, he had occupied Kandahar. That same year Britain and Afghanistan concluded the Treaty of Peshawar, which established, for the moment, friendship between the two nations. The treaty was timely; for also in 1855, a Persian army invaded Afghanistan, with the object of taking Herat, and the British answered the Afghans' call for aid. Under British pressure, the Persians withdrew. This freed Dost Muhammad to further consolidate his kingdom, uniting what had previously been many independent local rulers under his dynasty. In 1859 he occupied Balkh and then Herat in 1863 less than a month before his death in June.

See also ANGLO-PERSIAN WAR; PERSIAN-AFGHAN WAR (1836–1838).

Further reading: Sir Percy Sykes, *History of Afghanistan,* 2 vols. (New York: AMS Press, 1975); Stephan Tanner, *Afghanistan: A Military History from Alexander the Great to the Fall of the Taliban* (New York: Da Capo Press, 2002).

Persian Civil War (522–521 B.C.E.)

PRINCIPAL COMBATANTS: Gautama (the "false Smerdis") vs. Darius I

PRINCIPAL THEATER(S): Persia

DECLARATION: None

MAJOR ISSUES AND OBJECTIVES: An internecine struggle within the Achaemenid dynasty for control of the Persian Empire

OUTCOME: Darius I ascended the Persian throne.

APPROXIMATE MAXIMUM NUMBER OF MEN UNDER ARMS: Unknown

CASUALTIES: Unknown

TREATIES: None

Like that of many of the Achaemenid kings of Persia, the reign of Cambyses II from 529 to 522 B.C.E. was marred by a struggle for power within the dynasty. Cambyses was the eldest son of King Cyrus II (the Great; c. 600–529 B.C.E.), and his mother, Cassandane, was the daughter of a fellow Achaemenid. Cyrus put Cambyses in charge of Babylonian affairs in 538, and in 530, before Cyrus set out on his last campaign, he appointed Cambyses regent in Babylon, but it was the Persian conquest of Egypt, planned by Cyrus, that proved the major achievement of Cambyses reign.

Aided by Polycrates (c. 535–522 B.C.E.), tyrant of Samos, well-informed by Phanes, a Greek general in the Egyptian army, and supplied by Arabs with the water essential for crossing the Sinai, Cambyses defeated the army of Psamtik III (d. c. 523) at the battle of Pelusium in 525 in the Nile Delta. When he subsequently captured Heliopolis and Memphis, Egyptian resistance collapsed. According to the Greek historian Herodotus (c. 484–between 430–420 B.C.E.), Cambyses was a madman and guilty of many atrocities in Egypt, though later historians have questioned his judgments based on contemporary Egyptian sources, which suggest—at least in the beginning—Cambyses pursued a conciliatory policy toward Egypt while he planned new expeditions against Ethiopia and Carthage.

Herodotus based his judgments on the propaganda spread by Cambyses' distant cousin and successor Darius I (the Great; c. 558–486 B.C.E.). According to Darius, Cambyses, before going to Egypt, had secretly killed his brother, Bardiya (whom Herodotus called Smerdis [d. c. 525 B.C.E.), so he could claim sole rule over Persia. The murdered prince was, however, impersonated by Gaumata (d. 521 B.C.E.), the Magian, a Median priest who seized the Achaemenid throne in March 522. Cambyses abruptly broke off his plans for other expeditions and headed back to Persia from Egypt, dying along the way in the summer of 522, either by accident or, possibly, suicide.

Gautama-Smerdis continued to rule for seven months but was overthrown and killed by Darius (c. 558–486 B.C.E.). Darius now ascended the throne as Darius I and, after hard-fought campaigns to thwart rebellions all across Persia, would reign as Darius the Great.

See also PERSIAN REVOLTS.

Further reading: Herodotus, *Wars of Greece and Persia,* W. D. Lowe, ed. (Wauconda, Ill.: Bolchazy Carducci, 1990); Sir Percy Sykes, *A History of Persia* (New York: RoutledgeCurzon, 2003).

Persian Civil War (1500–1503)

PRINCIPAL COMBATANTS: The Koyunlu sect vs. the Shi'ite sect
PRINCIPAL THEATER(S): Persian Empire (Iran and Iraq)
DECLARATION: None
MAJOR ISSUES AND OBJECTIVES: Ismail, Shi'ite leader, sought to unify the Persian Empire under Shi'ism.
OUTCOME: To a great extent, Ismail succeeded in suppressing the Sunnis and establishing the dominance of Shi'ism in the Persian Empire and beyond.
APPROXIMATE MAXIMUM NUMBER OF MEN UNDER ARMS: Unknown
CASUALTIES: Unknown
TREATIES: None

Religion was at the root of this conflict between the Turkoman Al Koyunlu dynasty and the Shi'ites (and other sects) of Persia. The Koyunlus reformed Timurid and Mongol laws to comply with Sunni religious canons, seeking to reapply rigorous orthodox rules for collecting taxes. This enraged the Sufi Shi'ite sheikh Heydar (d. 1488) of Ardebil, who was killed by Sunnis in 1488. Meanwhile, the reforms had damaged the popularity of the regime and discredited Sunni fanaticism, leaving the path clear for Heydar's son, Ismail (1486–1524), who swore revenge and used his father's Kizilbash warrior society to fight the Koyunlus and ultimately establish the Safavid dynasty. Through a combination of his own military skill and charisma and by exploiting the fractious nature of the Koyunlu dynasty, Ismail established himself as shah in Tabriz in 1501. At the Battle of Shurur later in the year, he defeated the last of the Koyunlu rulers, then went on to conquer the territory encompassing most of modern Iran and Iraq. When he captured Hamadan in 1503, Ismail had such power and influence that he was able to convert most of the region's Sunnis into Shi'ites, and he firmly established Shi'ism as the state religion of the Persian Empire. Ismail's spiritual influence extended even further than his political power, encompassing Turkoman sects in Anatolia (Turkey) and into eastern Europe (southern Romania). Ismail's family, riding the swelling Shi'ite tide, would occupy the throne until 1722.

Further reading: David Morgan, *Medieval Persia, 1040–1797* (London, New York: Longman, 1988); Sir Percy Sykes, *A History of Persia* (New York: RoutledgeCurzon, 2003).

Persian Civil War (1725–1730)

PRINCIPAL COMBATANTS: Forces of Tahmasp II (under Nadir Khan) vs. various Persian factions and the Ottoman Turks

PRINCIPAL THEATER(S): Persia
DECLARATION: None
MAJOR ISSUES AND OBJECTIVES: Establishment of Tahmasp II as shah of Persia
OUTCOME: Thanks to the military skill of Nadir Khan, Tahmasp was established on the Persian throne, and the occupying Ottoman Turks were pushed out of Persia.
APPROXIMATE MAXIMUM NUMBER OF MEN UNDER ARMS: Unknown
CASUALTIES: Unknown
TREATIES: None

Amid the early disintegration of the Safavid dynasty in Persia, Shah Hussein (c. 1675–1726) was murdered by an Afghan in 1726, thereby precipitating Persia into full-scale civil war. The Ottoman Turks exploited Persia's chaos by invading and occupying vast territories, from Georgia to Hamadan. In the meantime, Nadir Khan (1688–1747) served Tahmasp II (d. 1739), the uncrowned shah of Persia, as his leading general. He patiently assembled, enlarged, and continually trained a formidable army, which made Tahmasp dominant in Persia. By 1730, Nadir Khan had forced the Ottomans out of Hamadan, Kirmanshah, and Tabriz. With that, the Persian Civil War of 1725–30 came to a close.

See also AFGHAN REBELLIONS; PERSIAN-AFGHAN WAR (1726–1738); TURKO-PERSIAN WAR (1730–1736).

Further reading: Willem M. Floor, *The Afghan Occupation of Safavid Persia, 1721–1729* (Amsterdam: Cleeters, 1998); David Morgan, *Medieval Persia, 1040–1797* (London, New York: Longman, 1988).

Persian Civil War (1747–1760)

PRINCIPAL COMBATANTS: The late Nadir Shah's military commanders
PRINCIPAL THEATER(S): Persia
DECLARATION: None
MAJOR ISSUES AND OBJECTIVES: The military commanders fought one another for control of the Persian Empire.
OUTCOME: Karim Khan founded the Zand dynasty and emerged as the dominant ruler of Persia.
APPROXIMATE MAXIMUM NUMBER OF MEN UNDER ARMS: Unknown
CASUALTIES: Unknown
TREATIES: None

In 1736, Nadir Khan (1688–1747) established the Afshar dynasty in Persia, reigned as Nadir Shah, and reestablished the greatness of the Persian Empire. However, Nadir Shah was assassinated in 1747, and the Persian Empire fell prey to the ambition of Nadir Shah's various military commanders, who—bent on establishing their own states—scrambled for territorial spoils. Ahmid Shah Durran (1725–75) founded a kingdom in Afghanistan, based at Kandahar; Shah Rokh, Nadir's blind grandson, remained at the helm of the Afsharid ship of state in Khorasan; the Qajar chief, Muhammad Hasan, took the region of Mazanderan south of the Caspian Sea, then expelled Azad Kahn from Azerbaijan. From 1747 to 1760, a half dozen men struggled to dominate the Persian Empire.

In 1760, central and southern Persia had been consolidated under the nominal rule of an infant, Shah Ismail III (fl. c. 1755–80), who was controlled by his regent, Karim Khan (c. 1705–79), founder of the Zand dynasty. Karim Khan was content never to assume the title of shah for himself, but he worked behind the scenes in an effort to return Persia to the greatness it had enjoyed under Nadir Shah. He succeeded to some extent, rebuilding the country, reforming taxation, and expanding trade; however, on his death in 1779, the empire was once again torn by civil war (see PERSIAN CIVIL WAR [1779–1794]).

Further reading: Laurence Lockhart, *Nadir Shah* (New York: AMS Press, 1973); David Morgan, *Medieval Persian, 1040–1797* (London, New York: Longman, 1988).

Persian Civil War (1779–1794)

PRINCIPAL COMBATANTS: Kajars vs. Zands and, subsequently, various rebel factions
PRINCIPAL THEATER(S): Persia
DECLARATION: None
MAJOR ISSUES AND OBJECTIVES: Rule over Persia
OUTCOME: By 1794, Agha Muhammad Khan had founded and firmly established the Kajars as the ruling dynasty of Persia.
APPROXIMATE MAXIMUM NUMBER OF MEN UNDER ARMS: Unknown
CASUALTIES: Unknown
TREATIES: None

The assassination of Karim Khan (c. 1705–79), founder of the Zand dynasty, touched off a struggle for power among members of the dynasty. Lotf Ali Khan Zand (1769–94) rose to dominance after a struggle that lasted until 1789. However, once placed on the Persian throne, Lotf Ali became the target of Agha Muhammad Khan (1742–97), head of the rival Kajar (or Qajar) family. He met Lotf Ali in battle at Kerman in 1794, defeated him, captured him, and had him killed. This having been done, Agha turned his wrath on the people of Kerman, whom he massacred. Those who escaped death were mutilated or blinded—all in retribution for their having supported Lotf Ali.

Within two years after killing Lotf Ali, Agha had subdued all of Persia, save the always rebellious Khorasan.

Crowning himself "king of kings," Agha led an attack on Khorasan in 1796, taking its ruler Shah Rokh (d. 1796) captive and torturing him to death to make him reveal the location of all the Afsharid treasure. Although Agha's rapacity and sheer cruelty dismantled the Persian economy, he ruled with such a degree of terror that all rebellions—and there were many—quickly withered. His Kajar dynasty held Persia in thrall until the ascension of the Pahlavi dynasty with the PERSIAN REVOLUTION (1921). Agha himself was assassinated in 1797.

See also PERSIAN CIVIL WAR (1747–1760).

Further reading: David Morgan, *Medieval Persia, 1040–1797* (London, New York: Longman, 1988); Sir Percy Sykes, *A History of Persia* (New York: RoutledgeCurzon, 2003).

Persian Conquests (559–509 B.C.E.)

PRINCIPAL COMBATANTS: Persia vs. Scythia, the Getae, Thrace, the Greek cities of Asia Minor, and Macedonia
PRINCIPAL THEATER(S): Scythia, the Getae, Thrace, the Greek cities of Asia Minor, and Macedonia
DECLARATION: None
MAJOR ISSUES AND OBJECTIVES: Territorial conquest
OUTCOME: Persia greatly expanded under Darius I the Great.
APPROXIMATE MAXIMUM NUMBER OF MEN UNDER ARMS: Unknown
CASUALTIES: Unknown
TREATIES: No documents survive

After securing his authority over Persia, Darius I (the Great; c. 558–486 B.C.E.) embarked on an ambitious campaign of imperial expansion, beginning by fighting against the Scythians on Persia's borders, pushing them east of the Caspian Sea and thereby expanding the Persian domain as far east as the valley of the Indus. This accomplished, in 513 B.C.E. he attacked the Scythians of eastern Thrace and the eastern territories of the Getae. This campaign took the forces of Darius into Europe, as the emperor pushed the Scythians and Getae into the territory now encompassed by Romania.

Unfortunately, Darius had ventured so far that supply became a major problem, especially as the conquered people began destroying crops and other resources to foil foraging. Darius withdrew his troops and left the rest of the task of conquering Thrace and Asia Minor to a network of satraps (royal governors). As for Macedonia, Darius never conquered it, but he did compel its submission to Persian authority. In 509, the first great phase of Persian conquest was completed with the acquisition of the Aegean islands of Lemnos and Imbros.

See also GRECO-PERSIAN WARS.

Further reading: J. M. Cook, *The Persian Empire* (New York: Schocken Books, 1983); Herodotus, *Wars of Greece and Persia*, W. D. Lowe, ed. (Wauconda, Ill.: Bolchazy Carducci, 1990); A. T. Olmstead, *History of the Persian Empire* (Chicago: University of Chicago Press, 1959); Sir Percy Sykes, *A History of Persia* (New York: Routledge-Curzon, 2003).

Persian-Greek Wars *See* GRECO-PERSIAN WARS.

Persian Gulf War (1990–1991)

PRINCIPAL COMBATANTS: Iraq vs. Kuwait and a U.S.-led coalition of 48 nations
PRINCIPAL THEATER(S): Saudi Arabia, Iraq, and Kuwait
DECLARATION: UN-set deadline for Iraqi withdrawal from Kuwait, January 15, 1991
MAJOR ISSUES AND OBJECTIVES: A UN-sanctioned, U.S.-led coalition—with the objective of protecting key oil supplies in the Middle East—sought to liberate Kuwait from occupation by Iraq.
OUTCOME: Kuwait was liberated, but Iraq's dictator, Saddam Hussein, remained in power.
APPROXIMATE MAXIMUM NUMBER OF MEN UNDER ARMS: Coalition, 450,000, in addition to vast air and naval assets; Iraq, 530,000
CASUALTIES: Coalition casualties: 95 killed, 368 wounded, 20 missing in action; Iraqi casualties: 50,000 killed, 50,000 wounded, 60,000 taken prisoner
TREATIES: Iraqi capitulation, February 28, 1991

After prevailing in an eight-year war against Iran so costly that it nearly led to a military coup in Iraq (*see* IRAN-IRAQ WAR), dictator Saddam Hussein (b. 1935) on August 2, 1990, invaded and attempted to annex the small, oil-rich neighboring nation of Kuwait. The invasion was swift; in less than a week, the Iraqi army, fourth-largest ground force in the world, was in complete control of Kuwait. The United States, its allies, and much of the world now feared that Iraq would go on to mount an attack southward into Saudi Arabia. This could give Hussein a stranglehold on much of the world's oil supply; even if he chose to press the attack no farther, his seizure of Kuwait put him in a position to threaten Saudi Arabia and thus control the flow of oil.

The United States responded to the invasion by freezing Iraqi assets in the United States and by cutting off trade with the country. The administration of President George H. W. Bush (b. 1924) then worked to secure UN resolutions condemning the invasion and supporting military action against it. Bush and Secretary of State James Baker (b. 1930) worked quickly to forge an unprecedented coalition among 48 nations. Of these, 30 provided military forces, with the United States making the largest contribution; 18 other nations provided economic, humanitarian, and other noncombat assistance. Saudi Arabia and other Arab states near Iraq provided port facilities, airfields, and staging areas for the buildup of ground forces. Because the participation of Israel would drive a wedge between the Arab members of the coalition and the United States and other Western members, Israel agreed not to take part in any military action, except in direct self-defense.

The U.S. buildup in the Middle East began on August 7, 1990, in response to a Saudi request for U.S. military aid to defend against possible Iraqi invasion. Operation Desert Shield was initiated to deploy sufficient forces to deter further Iraqi aggression and to defend Saudi Arabia. The first step was a naval blockade of Iraq. On August 8, U.S. Air Force fighters began to arrive at Saudi air bases. Lead elements of the army arrived on August 9. By September, the coalition had sufficient resources deployed to deter any further invasion. U.S. forces in the region included, by the fall, four aircraft carrier battle groups, each of which consisted of 74 aircraft, one guided missile cruiser, three to five destroyers or frigates, and one or two support vessels in addition to one aircraft carrier. Six to eight nuclear submarines were also in the Persian Gulf area. The U.S. Air Force had 400 combat aircraft in the theater of operations by September 2. By the end of October, 210,000 U.S. Army and Marine troops had been deployed, in addition to 65,000 troops from other coalition nations. These forces put the United States and the coalition countries in a position to attempt the diplomatic negotiation of an Iraqi withdrawal from Kuwait. But Saddam Hussein proved unresponsive, despite a series of UN resolutions condemning him. President Bush prepared the American people to accept the necessity of military action against Hussein. Bush and the State Department also successfully lobbied for a UN resolution authorizing military force to expel Iraq from Kuwait. This was secured on November 29. The resolution set a withdrawal deadline of January 15, 1991.

Mid-January was also when the United States anticipated completing a second phase of the military buildup in the Middle East. As the deadline approached, 450,000 coalition troops were on the ground, to oppose a larger Iraqi force, some 530,000, in Kuwait. Except in troop numbers, the coalition enjoyed an overwhelming advantage: more than 170 ships were now in the area, including six aircraft carriers and two battleships. Air power consisted of 2,200 combat craft.

When the deadline passed, Operation Desert Shield became Operation Desert Storm, and on the morning of January 16 a massive air campaign was unleashed against Iraq and Iraqi positions in Kuwait. This air war continued for five weeks, during which coalition forces flew more than 88,000 missions with losses of only 22 U.S. aircraft and nine craft from other coalition countries. The Iraqi air force offered almost no resistance, and antiaircraft fire and surface-to-air missiles had little effect against the coalition sorties. The Iraqis attempted to hide some of their planes in hardened revetments; others were flown into Iran.

The Iraqis did make use of Scud surface-to-surface missiles, which were directed against Israel and Saudi Arabia. Israel was targeted specifically in the hope that the attacks would goad it into entering the war, thereby alienating the Arab members of the coalition. Through deft diplomacy, the United States kept Israel out of the war. The United States deployed mobile Patriot missile launchers to intercept Scud attacks. Although most of the incoming Scuds were successfully deflected, the coalition was far less successful in destroying Scud launchers on the ground. Iraqi missile crews were skilled at camouflaging the mobile Scud launchers, then quickly moving the launchers to a new site.

Impressively destructive as the coalition air campaign was, its main purpose was to prepare the way for the ground campaign, which was led primarily by U.S. general H. Norman Schwarzkopf (b. 1934). The overwhelming air supremacy of the coalition kept Iraqi reconnaissance aircraft from discovering anything about the deployment of coalition ground troops; however, it was the Iraqis who made the first move on the ground, launching an attack on the Saudi town of Khafji on January 29, with three tank brigades. Although the Iraqis occupied the lightly defended town, they were pushed out the next day by a Saudi counterattack. The Battle of Khafji suggested to coalition military planners that the Iraqis were no match for U.S.-style mobile warfare.

The coalition ground offensive stepped off at 4 A.M., February 24, 1991. The plan was for the army's 18th Airborne Corps to be positioned on the coalition's left flank. This unit would move into Iraq on the far west and, striking deep within the country, cut off the Iraqi army in Kuwait, isolating it from any support or reinforcement from the north. The French Sixth Light Armored Division covered the 18th Airborne Corps's own left flank. The center of the ground force consisted of the U.S. Seventh Corps, the U.S. Second Armored Cavalry, and the British First Armored Division—celebrated as the "Desert Rats" who defeated Erwin Rommel's Afrika Korps in WORLD WAR II. The center units would move north into Iraq after the left and right flanks had been secured, then make a sharp right turn to advance into Kuwait from the west to attack Iraqi units there, including the elite Republican Guard. The right flank was also charged with breaching Iraqi lines in Kuwait. The units composing this flank were mainly U.S. Marines.

The attacks on the first day were intended, in part, to screen the main attack and to deceive the Iraqis into thinking that the principal assault would come on the coast of Kuwait. Although Iraqi defenses were well developed, relatively light resistance was offered, and many Iraqi prisoners were taken. By the second day of the ground war, French troops had secured the left flank of the coalition advance, and the U.S. forces had cut off all avenues of Iraqi retreat and reinforcement. The U.S. 24th Division ended its advance in Basra, Iraq, which sealed the remaining avenue of escape from Kuwait.

With the Iraqis in Kuwait occupied on the right, the Eighth Airborne Corps made a surprise attack on the left, in the west. By nightfall of February 25, well ahead of schedule, the Eighth Airborne Corps was already turning east into Kuwait. When the corps encountered units of the Republican Guard, the vaunted Iraqi elite fled before their advance. By February 27, however, with the 24th Infantry having taken Basra, the Republican Guard was bottled up. The Hammurabi Division, the elite of the elite Republican Guard, attempted to engage the Eighth Airborne Corps in a delaying action to allow the remainder of the Republican Guard to escape. The attempt failed, and the Hammurabi Division was wiped out.

Among the American public, haunted by memories of Vietnam, the war against Iraq had been fraught with much trepidation. In fact, the air and ground campaigns were probably the most successful military operations in modern history. This was due in large measure to overwhelming force and technology, as well as planning that was both careful and bold; but it was also due to the universal ineptitude of the Iraqi response to the coalition and to the poor generalship of Saddam Hussein, who took personal command of much of the war. In the end, the Scud missiles were the only significant element of Iraqi resistance to the coalition attack. The Iraqi air force was essentially a no-show in the war, as were the 43 ships of the Iraqi navy.

A cease-fire was declared at 8 A.M. on February 28, shortly after Iraq capitulated on U.S. terms. The ground war had lasted 100 hours. Operation Desert Storm had achieved its mission of liberating Kuwait, and it had done so with minimal coalition casualties: 95 killed, 368 wounded, 20 missing in action. Iraqi casualties were perhaps as many as 50,000 killed and another 50,000 wounded; 60,000 Iraqi troops were taken prisoner. Iraqi military hardware was destroyed, as were communication equipment and military bases, barracks, and other facilities.

During the war, Iraqi forces in Kuwait terrorized citizens and laid waste 300 oil fields, setting numerous blazes. The oil-field fires were one of the worst legacies of the war, burning for years to come. In addition, Saddam committed unprecedented acts of ecological terrorism by creating massive and deliberate oil spills into the Persian Gulf, hoping to foul Saudi desalinization plants, which produce drinking water for the nation. In Iraq itself varying degrees of civil unrest followed in the wake of the ruinous war, especially in outlying provinces and particularly in the chronically rebellious Kurdish provinces. But

Saddam managed to hold on to power and continuously to indulge in bouts of defiance against sanctions leveled and conditions imposed by the United Nations.

In its immediate aftermath, the Persian Gulf War appeared to many Americans to be the first "good" war the United States had fought since World War II. In an era marked by ambiguity of motives and murky options that often amounted to attempting to determine the least of any number of manifest evils, here was a conflict that seemed a simple matter of choosing to defend the hapless against the hateful. There had been a number of voices raised in the United States—both among the public and in Congress—at the outset protesting the exchange of "blood for oil." But to most, Hussein soon appeared the devil incarnate and a stark contrast to the head of the coalition forces, General Schwarzkopf, who was frank and professional in his many wartime press conferences, and to the head of the American joint chiefs, the clear-thinking, politically astute African-American general, Colin Powell (b. 1937). The pleasure most Americans took in the victory over Saddam Hussein was evident in the public adulation accorded Schwarzkopf and Powell and in the unprecedented 90-percent-plus popular approval rating President Bush garnered during and immediately following the war.

To be sure, Saddam Hussein was a tyrant. But the century had seen many tyrants, and many far worse—in terms of body count—than he: Stalin, Hitler, Mao Zedong (Mao Tse-t'ung), Pol Pot, and others. The difference was —and it was a difference that made the Gulf War unique at the time—never had so many people seen the work of a tyrant so close and immediate. CNN, the cable television 24-hour news network, covered the war in such thorough and intimate detail that Powell, Schwarzkopf, and others admitted to using the broadcasts as valuable supplements to official intelligence. Vietnam had, of course, been reported on television—and the effect was powerful—but here television audiences nationwide not only got reports on the Persian Gulf War, they also saw it unfold at the same time as the commanders did.

It was a late 20th-century war, creating around it an electronic community and, in the process, translating complex moral and political issues into real-time television melodrama. Certainly George Bush treated the war as a miniseries depicting the triumph of good guys over bad as he began to talk boldly about a "new world order" based on this first post–cold war conflict, which would see a confluence of world powers policing "outlaw" nations and protecting the globe from the threat they represented. But even as the smoke continued to billow into the atmosphere from sabotaged Kuwaiti oil wells, ethnic conflicts in Africa and the Balkans raised issues that appeared to befuddle the same world that had united against Hussein. When the United States and the United Nations seemed to ignore the genocide of "ethnic cleansing" in these new trouble spots, their irresolution called into question just how much the Gulf War had to do with humanitarian rescue and how much with fossil fuels.

However hard President Bush tried to make Desert Storm into the antidote for America's so-called Vietnam syndrome, he could not maintain his popularity when the war degenerated into something of a personal squabble with Saddam after the fighting was over. Bush found himself attacked for sending Saddam the confused diplomatic signals that encouraged the Iraqi dictator to invade Kuwait in the first place, for saving that country only to return it to a few incredibly wealthy and arrogant oil autocrats, for failing to finish the job he had started by deposing Saddam, and for floundering in his responses to Saddam's flouting of UN-imposed sanctions and peace conditions.

Bush's telegenic military commanders, however, fared much better. Schwarzkopf had become a media darling by the time he retired, conducting a well-received and enriching speaking tour and producing a best-selling autobiography centered on his Gulf War experiences. Colin Powell, his authority swelled by the success of the war, proved a thorn in the side of the new U.S. president, Bill Clinton (b. 1946), blocking Clinton's attempts to integrate openly gay men into the military and frustrating Clinton's efforts to make drastic cuts in the defense budget shortly after he assumed office.

As an African American who enjoyed tremendous prestige and great popularity, Powell seemed poised to run for political office himself as he resigned early in the Clinton administration. Instead, he wrote his own best-selling autobiography and conducted an extended publicity tour to sell it. In the book, Powell admitted that it was he—and not George Bush—who refused to continue the war in order to bring down Saddam Hussein and, in fact, that he had been opposed to going to war with Iraq from the start. Ironically enough, President George W. Bush (b. 1946)—George H. W. Bush's son—would make Powell his secretary of state primarily because of the reputation he gained from a war he did not want to fight and, most felt, had called off too early.

See also UNITED STATES–IRAQ WAR.

Further reading: Deborah Amos, *Lines in the Sand: Desert Storm and the Remaking of the Arab World* (New York: Simon and Schuster, 1992); Rick Atkinson, *Crusade: The Untold Story of the Persian Gulf War* (New York: Houghton Mifflin Co., 1993); Lawrence Freedman and Efrain Karsh, *The Gulf Conflict, 1990–1991: Diplomacy and War in the New World Order* (Princeton, N.J.: Princeton University Press, 1993); A. Sue Goodman, *Persian Gulf War, 1990–1991: Desert Shield/Desert Storm* (Maxwell Air Force Base, Ala.: Air University Library, 1991); Michael R. Gordon and General Bernard E. Trainor, *The Generals' War: The Inside Story of the Conflict in the Gulf* (Boston: Little Brown and Co., 1996); Richard P. Hallion, *Storm over Iraq: Air Power and the Gulf War* (Washington, D.C.: Smithsonian Institution Press, 1992).

Persian Invasion of Greece (480–479 B.C.E.)

PRINCIPAL COMBATANTS: Persia and Greece
PRINCIPAL THEATER(S): The Aegean coast of southern Greece
DECLARATION: None
MAJOR ISSUES AND OBJECTIVES: Persia sought to invade, conquer, and subjugate the Greek city-states; Greece sought to stave off the invasion.
OUTCOME: At Thermopylae, Xerxes defeated the Spartans only to see the invasion ultimately fail because of Athenian prowess at sea.
APPROXIMATE MAXIMUM NUMBER OF MEN UNDER ARMS: Unknown
CASUALTIES: Unknown
TREATIES: None

After the Persian defeat during the MARATHON CAMPAIGN in 490 B.C.E., Darius I (the Great; c. 558–486 B.C.E.) made plans to invade and conquer Greece but died before he could execute them. In 480, his son Xerxes (c. 519–465 B.C.E.) fell heir to the throne and to his father's ambitions and led the invasion, attacking from Macedonia and moving south through Thessaly. Led by Sparta's king, Leonidas (d. 480 B.C.E.), the small Greek army met the vastly superior Persian force at Thermopylae. For two days Leonidas withstood the Persian onslaught and held in check Xerxes' advance. At length, the Persians, attacking from the rear, trapped the Greeks in a narrow pass. By then the Spartan king had ordered most of his troops to retreat, while he and his 300-member royal guard remained behind to fight the invaders down to the last man. The episode clearly made a deep impression on the Greek imagination, and—thanks in no small measure to Herodotus—Thermopylae gave rise to the legend that Spartans never surrendered.

Meanwhile, the Greek navy, mostly Athenian, fought the Persians in the Aegean. Indeed the Greek navy saved the day, destroying Xerxes' fleet, causing the Persians to flee back to Asia Minor, and greatly enhancing the power and prestige of Athens. Left in charge of the Persian force in Greece, Mardonius (d. 479 B.C.E.) attacked Boeotia in 479 but was thwarted by Pausanius (d. 471 B.C.E.), who led the bedraggled Greeks through some ingenious manueverings into the heart of the Persian camp, which they sacked, killing Mardonius in the process. The Greek fleet finished the Persian navy at Cape Mycale near Samos, cutting off all possibility of a Persian attack through Europe.

See also GRECO-PERSIAN WARS.

Further reading: A. R. Burn, *Persia and the Greeks: The Defence of the West, c. 546–478 B.C.E.* (Stanford, Calif.: Stanford University Press, 1984); Herodotus, *Wars of Greece and Persia,* W. D. Lowe, ed. (Wauconda, Ill.: Bolc- hazy Carducci, 1990); Sir Percy Sykes, *A History of Persia* (New York: RoutledgeCurzon, 2003).

Persian Invasion of Mogul India (1738–1739)

PRINCIPAL COMBATANTS: Mogul Empire vs. Persia
PRINCIPAL THEATER(S): India
DECLARATION: Nadir Shah invaded India on May 10, 1738.
MAJOR ISSUES AND OBJECTIVES: To punish the Indians for coming to the aid of the Afghans under Persian attack, Nadir Shah invaded India.
OUTCOME: The Persians defeated and sacked the Mogul Empire, but left the current emperor in power.
APPROXIMATE MAXIMUM NUMBER OF MEN UNDER ARMS: Persians, 50,000; Moguls, 300,000
CASUALTIES: Persians, 3,400 killed; 5,000 wounded; Moguls, 17,000 killed; 20,000 citizens of Delhi massacred by Nadir Shah
TREATIES: None

When Muhammad Shah (1702–48), the Mogul emperor, allied himself with the Afghans and against the Persians during the PERSIAN-AFGHAN WAR (1726–1738), he unfortunately brought India to the attention of the Persian ruler, Nadir Shah (1688–1747). After forcing Kabul to surrender in September of 1738, Nadir drove on into the Mogul Empire looking for loot to shore up his war-depleted resources. Brushing the Mogul force aside at the Khyber Pass, Nadir and his 50,000 men marched toward the Punjab, seizing Peshawar and Lahore as they went. At Karnal the Moguls mustered some 300,000 Indians and 2,000 elephants to halt the Persian advance, but the clever Nadir sneaked past their encampment to set up an ambush at a nearby village. Nadir lured part of the Indian force from its camp and routed it after a four-hour battle, which led to an abject Indian surrender. After the triumphant Nadir entered Delhi, rumors of his murder led his soldiers to riot, which almost cost him his life at the hand of Indians resisting the rioting troops. A vengeful shah ordered the massacre of some 20,000 Indians as the Persians sacked and burned Delhi. Though he left Muhammad Shah in power, Nadir took the Peacock Throne on which the Indian ruler sat back with him to Persia, along with the crown jewels, the Koh-i-noor diamond, and a huge indemnity of 700 million rupees collected from the Indian citizens. So great was the Indian booty, Nadir was able to exempt the whole of Persia from taxes for three years, at least temporarily solving the vexing problem of how to make his empire financially sound.

Further reading: Laurence Lockhart, *Nadir Shah* (New York: AMS Press, 1973); David Morgan, *Medieval*

Persia, 1040–1797 (London, New York: Longman, 1988); Sir Percy Sykes, *A History of Persia* (New York: Routledge-Curzon, 2003).

Persian-Kushan War (c. 250)

PRINCIPAL COMBATANTS: Persia vs. the Kushans
PRINCIPAL THEATER(S): Bactria or Gandhara
DECLARATION: None
MAJOR ISSUES AND OBJECTIVES: Presumably, Shapur I of Persia wanted to make conquests in central and western Asia.
OUTCOME: Shapur I defeated the Kushans under Vasuveda but failed to follow up on his triumph; thus, while the Kushans were driven out of central and western Asia, the Persians did not step in to fill the vacuum.
APPROXIMATE MAXIMUM NUMBER OF MEN UNDER ARMS: Unknown
CASUALTIES: Unknown
TREATIES: None

Shapur I (d. 272), the Sassanid emperor of Persia, mounted an expedition against the Kushans, who were led by Vasuveda. The exact date of the expedition is unknown, as is the precise location of the brief war, which, however, is believed to have taken place in Bactria or Gandhara.

Unfortunately for Persia, internal strife and Shapur's own preoccupation with the ongoing struggle against Rome prevented exploitation of the triumph over the Kushans, who were, in fact, driven from central as well as western Asia.

Further reading: Richard Frye, *Golden Age of Persia* (London: Phoenix Press, 2000); Sir Percy Sykes, *A History of Persia* (New York: RoutledgeCurzon, 2003).

Persian-Lydian War (547–546 B.C.E.)

PRINCIPAL COMBATANTS: Persia vs. Lydia (with Chaldea, Egypt, and Sparta)
PRINCIPAL THEATER(S): Lydia and Ionia
DECLARATION: None
MAJOR ISSUES AND OBJECTIVES: Lydia's King Croesus sought either conquest or to forestall Persian invasion; Persia's Emperor Cyrus sought conquest.
OUTCOME: Lydia fell to Persia, as did the former Lydian satellite cities along the Ionian coast.
APPROXIMATE MAXIMUM NUMBER OF MEN UNDER ARMS: Persians, 50,000; Lydian forces were larger
CASUALTIES: Unknown, but certainly heavy among the Lydians
TREATIES: None

By about 550 B.C.E., Croesus (d. 547 B.C.E.), king of Lydia, had successfully annexed a number of the Greek cities along the coast of Asia Minor. From these conquests, Croesus moved on, in 547, to invade Cappadocia, a province of Persia-Media. Just why Croesus crossed the Halys into this territory is unclear. He may have wanted to restore his brother-in-law Astyages (fl. 584–549 B.C.E.) to the Median throne, or he may have been moving preemptively against what he believed would be a Persian invasion of Lydia. Allied with Croesus were the forces of Chaldea, Egypt, and Sparta.

The Persian army was led by Cyrus II (c. 600–529 B.C.E.), who engaged Croesus's forces at the Battle of Pteria in 547 or 546. The battle, under harsh winter conditions, was fierce, but ultimately indecisive—although it did result in the retreat of Croesus back across the Halys.

Returned to Sardis, Croesus communicated with his allies in an attempt to organize a new invasion during a more favorable season; however, Cyrus stole a march on him by invading Lydia with at least 50,000 men. As Cyrus closed in on Sardis, Croesus hastily assembled a superior force to meet him. The greatly outnumbered Cyrus deployed his forces with consummate and innovative skill, using a great square formation rather than the conventional parallel order of battle. This formation tempted the superior Lydian army to attempt an easy envelopment. Anticipating this movement, however, Cyrus was able to exploit the gaps that were created by it. His forces drove the Lydians to great disorder and ultimately routed the army of Croesus. Cyrus took Sardis but treated the conquered people with great magnanimity.

A short time later, during 546, the Persian general Harpagus (fl. sixth century B.C.E.) conquered the Ionian cities, which had been under the control of Croesus. After that king's defeat, these cities made bold to assert their independence. Harpagus quickly crushed the incipient rebellions and seized control of the cities for Persia.

Further reading: A. R. Burn, *Persia and the Greeks: The Defence of the West, c. 546–478 B.C.E.* (Stanford, Calif.: Stanford University Press, 1984); Herodotus, *Wars of Greece and Persia*, W. D. Lowe, ed. (Wauconda, Ill.: Bolchazy Carducci, 1990); Sir Percy Sykes, *A History of Persia* (New York: RoutledgeCurzon, 2003).

Persian-Mesopotamian Wars   *See* ROMAN-PERSIAN WAR (337–363).

Persian-Mogul Wars   *See* MOGUL-PERSIAN WAR (1622–1623); MOGUL-PERSIAN WAR (1638); MOGUL-PERSIAN WAR (1648–1653); PERSIAN INVASION OF MOGUL INDIA.

Persian Revolts (521–519 B.C.E.)

PRINCIPAL COMBATANTS: Forces of Darius I vs. various pretenders and rebel forces
PRINCIPAL THEATER(S): Persia, Media, Susiana, Babylonia, Sagartia, Margiana, and Armenia
DECLARATION: None
MAJOR ISSUES AND OBJECTIVES: Consolidation of control over the Persian Empire
OUTCOME: Darius I firmly established himself as ruler of the empire and put himself in position for further conquests.
APPROXIMATE MAXIMUM NUMBER OF MEN UNDER ARMS: Unknown
CASUALTIES: Unknown
TREATIES: None

After he became ruler of Persia in the course of the PERSIAN CIVIL WAR of 522–521 B.C.E., Darius I (the Great; c. 588–486 B.C.E.) embarked on a ruthless campaign to enforce and secure his rule. He led an expedition to Media to assassinate the putative son of Cyrus II (the Great; c. 600–529 B.C.E.)—Gaumata (d. 521 B.C.E.), a Magian, who claimed to be Bardiya (d. c. 521 B.C.E.) (called by Herodotus "Smerdis"). Darius claimed the real heir had been secretly murdered by his brother, Cambyses II (d. 522 B.C.E.), who had recently died, perhaps a suicide, while in Egypt. The priest Gaumata, then, was a fraud, who had usurped the Median throne in 522.

The assassination of Gaumata accomplished, Darius led or dispatched forces to Susiana, Babylonia, Sagartia, and Margiana to crush uprisings in these places. Each had taken advantage of the internal chaos of Persia during the civil war and had established independent governments. Darius brought these to an end.

In the meantime, back at home in Persia and in Babylonia, impostors claiming descent from Cyrus or Cyaxares (d. 585 B.C.E.) attempted to usurp the throne. Darius crushed their forces quickly.

In 519 B.C.E., Armenia and Parthia rose against his rule. Troops nipped budding revolts there, then had to return to Susiana, where a third revolt was under way. Archaeological evidence exists that, in Susiana, Darius fought 19 battles in which he crushed nine rebel leaders.

After 519 B.C.E., Darius had so thoroughly secured his empire that he launched invasion offensives to acquire more (see PERSIAN CONQUESTS).

Further reading: Herodotus, *Wars of Greece and Persia,* W. D. Lowe, ed. (Wauconda, Ill.: Bolchazy Carducci, 1990); Sir Percy Sykes, *A History of Persia* (New York: RoutledgeCurzon, 2003).

Persian Revolution (1906–1909)

PRINCIPAL COMBATANTS: Kajar Shah of Persia (with Russian aid) vs. liberal revolutionaries
PRINCIPAL THEATER(S): Persia (Iran)
DECLARATION: None
MAJOR ISSUES AND OBJECTIVES: The shah sought to preserve an absolute monarchy; liberals sought to introduce constitutional government.
OUTCOME: Despite Russian aid, the shah was ultimately forced to abdicate.
APPROXIMATE MAXIMUM NUMBER OF MEN UNDER ARMS: Unknown
CASUALTIES: Unknown
TREATIES: None

Persia entered the 20th century as a faltering absolute monarchy, its shah, Mozaffar od-Din Shah (1852–1907), weak, and its economy weaker. In 1906, the shah bowed to popular pressure for a constitution and signed the Fundamental Law, by which Persia became a constitutional monarchy. Shortly after signing the document, the shah died, leaving the nation to his son, Muhammad Ali (1872–1925). Immediately, the new shah sought to abrogate the constitution by overthrowing the Majles, the new parliament. He was aided by the Russian czar Nicholas II (1868–1918), who had recently put down the RUSSIAN REVOLUTION (1905). Muhammad Ali formed a brigade of Persian Cossacks, which terrorized the parliament into suspending itself. This did not prevent revolutionaries from assassinating the shah's reactionary prime minister, Mirza Mahmoud Khan (d. 1906). The newly formed parliament yielded to the shah in enacting an absolutist constitution, yet it simultaneously declined to abrogate the original liberal document. The new prime minister, Aynu'd-Dawlih a liberal, united with others in the parliament in supporting the original constitution and was arrested for this in December 1907. A few months later, in June 1908, the shah used his Persian Cossacks to break up the second parliament. A third was formed and, in obedience to the shah's will, repudiated the original 1906 constitution, claiming that it ran contrary to Muslim law.

Yet the seeds of revolution had been sown. In 1908, Tabriz rebelled against Muhammad Ali, and Rasht and Isfahan followed the next year. In March 1909, Persian and Russian forces combined to crush the rebels, but Bakhtiaro tribespeople overran the capital, Tehran, in July 1909, forcing Muhammad Ali to abdicate in favor of his 12-year-old son, Ahmed Mirza (1898–1930). He was subject to a regent who initially accepted some reform, but when Ahmed Mirza came into his majority, he proved a corrupt, inept, and ineffective leader. A new revolution erupted in 1921 (see PERSIAN REVOLUTION [1921]).

Further reading: Peter Avery, *Modern Iran* (New York: Praeger, 1965); Edward G. Browne, *The Persian Revolution of 1905–1909* (Washington, D.C.: Mage Publishers, 1995); Sir Percy Sykes, *A History of Persia* (RoutledgeCurzon, 2003).

Persian Revolution (1921)

PRINCIPAL COMBATANTS: Forces loyal to Reza Khan Pahlavi vs. the government of Ahmed Shah
PRINCIPAL THEATER(S): Persia (Iran)
DECLARATION: Coup of February 21, 1921
MAJOR ISSUES AND OBJECTIVES: Overthrow of the Kajar dynasty
OUTCOME: Pahlavi overthrew Ahmed Shah and established the Pahlavi dynasty.
APPROXIMATE MAXIMUM NUMBER OF MEN UNDER ARMS: The coup was accomplished with 3,000 troops.
CASUALTIES: Few
TREATIES: None

Ahmed Shah (1898–1930), who came to power as a result of the PERSIAN REVOLUTION (1906–1909), proved a corrupt and incompetent ruler, who brought Persia to the edge of total political and economic collapse, subject to the whim of Great Britain and Russia, which, between them, had commercial control of the country. Then, during WORLD WAR I, Iran was the scene of much intrigue from the pro-British and pro-German groups among the Persian nobility, which had pretty much gained control of the Iranian parliament (called in Iran the Majles). When the war-spawned economic and political disruptions were greatly exacerbated by growing famine and the looming national bankruptcy, Great Britain offered both financial and military assistance. But the Nazi faction won out in the Majles, Iran refused the British offer (with all the strings it implied) and Great Britain withdrew its financial and military experts from Persia.

It was into this chaos that an Iranian officer, Reza Khan (1877–1944), of the Persian Cossack Brigade, stepped in to take charge. In collaboration with a political writer, Sayyid Zia od-Din Tabataba'i, he staged a coup d'état on February 21, 1921. Immediately seizing control of all the military forces, Pahlavi named himself minister of war in the new provisional government and quickly seized dictatorial control. He cleared Russian troops out of the country, then, in 1923, as prime minister, negotiated the withdrawal of British forces as well. In 1925, he pushed the Majles (parliament) to make Ahmed Shah's removal official and he himself was named shah. Thus fell the last of the Kajar shahs, and thus was the Pahlavi dynasty established under the man now known as Reza shah.

Further reading: Edward Abrahamian, *Iran between the Two Revolutions* (Princeton, N.J.: Princeton University Press, 1982); Peter Avery, *Modern Iran* (New York: Praeger, 1965); George Lenczowski (ed.), *Iran under the Pahlavis* (Washington, D.C.: Hoover Institution Press, 1978).

Persian-Roman Wars   *See* ROMAN-PERSIAN WAR (230–233); ROMAN-PERSIAN WAR (241–244); ROMAN-PERSIAN WAR (257–261); ROMAN-PERSIAN WAR (282–283); ROMAN-PERSIAN WAR (295–297); ROMAN-PERSIAN WAR (337–364); ROMAN-PERSIAN WAR (421–422); ROMAN-PERSIAN WAR (441); ROMAN-PERSIAN WAR (502–506); ROMAN-PERSIAN WAR (572–591).

Persian-Russian Wars   *See* RUSSO-PERSIAN WAR (1722–1723); RUSSO-PERSIAN WAR (1804–1813); RUSSO-PERSIAN WAR (1825–1828); RUSSO-PERSIAN WAR (1911).

Persian-Turkish Wars   *See* TURKO-PERSIAN WAR (1514–1516); TURKO-PERSIAN WAR (1526–1555); TURKO-PERSIAN WAR (1578–1590); TURKO-PERSIAN WAR (1603–1612); TURKO-PERSIAN WAR (1616–1618); TURKO-PERSIAN WAR (1623–1638); TURKO-PERSIAN WAR (1730–1736); TURKO-PERSIAN WAR (1743–1747); TURKO-PERSIAN WAR (1821–1823).

Persian Wars   *See* GRECO-PERSIAN WARS.

Persia's Georgian Expedition (1613–1615)

PRINCIPAL COMBATANTS: Persia vs. Georgia
PRINCIPAL THEATER(S): Georgia
DECLARATION: None
MAJOR ISSUES AND OBJECTIVES: Persia sought control of Georgia.
OUTCOME: Georgia submitted after invasion, but thereby created a crisis between Persia and Turkey.
APPROXIMATE MAXIMUM NUMBER OF MEN UNDER ARMS: Unknown
CASUALTIES: Unknown
TREATIES: None

Georgia agreed to suzerainty of the Persian shah Abbas (the Great; 1557–c. 1628) after he sent an army to invade the country. This, however, provoked a conflict with Turkey, which also claimed control, if not outright suzerainty, over Georgia.

Further reading: David Morgan, *Medieval Persia* (New York: Praeger, 1965).

Peru, Spanish Civil Wars in (1537–1548)

See SPANISH CIVIL WARS IN PERU (1537–1548).

Peru, Spanish Conquest of (1531–1533)

See SPANISH CONQUEST OF PERU (1531–1533).

Perusian War (Perusine War) *See* ROMAN CIVIL WAR (43–31 B.C.E.).

Peruvian-Bolivian Confederation, War of the (1836–1839)

PRINCIPAL COMBATANTS: Chile vs. Peruvian-Bolivian Confederation
PRINCIPAL THEATER(S): Chile
DECLARATION: Chile on Peru (and, therefore, Peruvian-Bolivian Confederation), November 11, 1836
MAJOR ISSUES AND OBJECTIVES: Chile (with Argentine support) sought to break up the Peruvian-Bolivian Confederation.
OUTCOME: The confederation was dissolved.
APPROXIMATE MAXIMUM NUMBER OF MEN UNDER ARMS: Unknown
CASUALTIES: Unknown
TREATIES: Treaty of Paucarpata, 1837; rejected

In 1835 Bolivian dictator Andrés Santa Cruz (1792–1865) invaded Peru, ostensibly to help quell an army rebellion against Peruvian president Luís José de Orbegoso. Having conquered the country instead, Santa Cruz created what proved to be a short-lived union of Peru and Bolivia that he called the Peruvian-Bolivian Confederation. Bolivia itself he split into two parts, allowing Orbegoso to remain as president in the north and placing General Ramón Herrera in charge in the south. With both these states then joined to Bolivia, Santa Cruz made General José Miguel de Velasco president of the latter. For himself Santa Cruz created the office of "protector" of the confederation, a lifetime and hereditary office in which the true power lay.

Perhaps because of his reputation as the able leader of Bolivia, not only did many influential Peruvians welcome his rule, but also Great Britain, France, and the United States quickly recognized the confederation. But the sudden appearance of a new and powerful state in South America worried some of Santa Cruz's neighbors, especially Argentina and Chile who feared and opposed the powerful new state. Moreover, Chile was locked in a financial dispute with Peru. Callao (a major port near Lima) was a major economic rival of Chile's port at Valparaíso, and relations had been rapidly deteriorating

between Chile and Peru even when Peru was still an independent country. Now, backed by Peruvians opposed to Santa Cruz, Chile declared war on Peru on November 11, 1836. But an invasion early the following year resulted in a standoff. Andrés Santa Cruz, who now presided over the Peruvian-Bolivian Confederation, sued for peace, but Chile rejected the proposed Treaty of Paucarpata. Invasion efforts were renewed, and in 1838 General Manuel Bulnes (1799–1866), leading a Chilean army, captured Lima. Santa Cruz's army recaptured it before the end of the year, but the Peruvian-Bolivian forces were badly defeated in the next major battle—January 20, 1839, at Yungay. Santa Cruz sought refuge in Ecuador, and the Peruvian-Bolivian Confederation was dissolved.

See also PERUVIAN-BOLIVIAN WAR; PERUVIAN WAR OF INDEPENDENCE.

Further reading: David Scott Palmer, *Peru: The Authoritarian Tradition* (New York: Praeger, 1980); Frederick B. Pike, *The Modern History of Peru* (New York: Praeger, 1967).

Peruvian-Bolivian War (1841)

PRINCIPAL COMBATANTS: Peru vs. Bolivia
PRINCIPAL THEATER(S): Bolivia
DECLARATION: Peru on Bolivia, 1841
MAJOR ISSUES AND OBJECTIVES: Peru attempted to annex Bolivia.
OUTCOME: The invasion was quickly defeated.
APPROXIMATE MAXIMUM NUMBER OF MEN UNDER ARMS: Unknown
CASUALTIES: Unknown
TREATIES: Treaty of peace, June 1842

When former Bolivian dictator Andrés Santa Cruz (1792–1865) fled into exile before an advancing Chilean army during the War of the PERUVIAN-BOLIVIAN CONFEDERATION, Agustín Gamarra (1758–1841) assumed the presidency of Peru. Gamarra had been one of those Peruvian generals whose revolt led Santa Cruz to invade Peru and set up the confederation in the first place. He and the few other Peruvians of note who were disgruntled with the new union headed by the effective and charismatic Santa Cruz, had supported Chile in the war, despite the fact that Chile was fighting as much to keep Peru from becoming its economic rival as it was to remove Santa Cruz from power.

As president of Peru, Gamarra longed to turn the tables completely on Bolivia. In 1841 he launched an invasion in an effort this time to annex Bolivia to Peru. Bolivian forces crushed the invaders at the Battle of Ingavi on November 18, 1841. Gamarra, who led Peruvian forces, was killed on the battlefield. A treaty was concluded the following year. Meanwhile, both Peru and Bolivia entered into a period of great internal conflict and massive disorder.

See also PERUVIAN-BOLIVIAN CONFEDERATION; WAR OF THE; PERUVIAN CIVIL WAR.

Further reading: David Scott Palmer, *Peru: The Authoritarian Tradition* (New York: Praeger, 1980); Frederick B. Pike, *The Modern History of Peru* (New York: Praeger, 1967).

Peruvian Civil War (1842–1845)

PRINCIPAL COMBATANTS: Constitutionalist forces vs. dictatorship of Manuel Ignacio Vivanco
PRINCIPAL THEATER(S): Peru
DECLARATION: None
MAJOR ISSUES AND OBJECTIVES: The Constitutionalists wanted to end the Vivanco dictatorship.
OUTCOME: After a single decisive battle, Vivanco's forces were defeated, and he fled the country.
APPROXIMATE MAXIMUM NUMBER OF MEN UNDER ARMS: Unknown
CASUALTIES: Unknown
TREATIES: None

After Peru's ignominious defeat in its over-hasty invasion of Bolivia in 1841, the country fell into a period of civic unrest during which there emerged two parties—the liberals and the conservatives—with ill-defined political agendas and programs that only enhanced the instability. Following a year of political chaos and fighting, conservative champion Manuel Ignacio Vivanco (the Regenerator; fl. 1840s) used the army to seize power. Vivanco set up a dictatorship, and he abrogated the 1839 constitution, refused to convene congress, and shot anyone who crossed him. In southern Peru, Constitutionalist opponents of Vivanco formed under the leadership of liberal Ramón Castilla (c. 1797–1867). He led troops into Lima and, in Vivanco's absence, seized the capital. Vivanco fought Castilla's forces at the Battle of Carmen Alto on July 22, 1844, and suffered a decisive defeat. Vivanco fled the country, but civil strife persisted until the following year, when Castilla was elected to the presidency. A degree of order was then restored to Peru, as Castilla—despite his mestizo background—managed to dominate the political scene for the better part of the next two decades.

See also PERUVIAN-BOLIVIAN WAR (1841).

Further reading: David Scott Palmer, *Peru: The Authoritarian Tradition* (New York: Praeger, 1980); Frederick B. Pike, *The Modern History of Peru* (New York: Praeger, 1967).

Peruvian Guerrilla War (1980–ongoing)

PRINCIPAL COMBATANTS: Shining Path vs. MRTA guerrillas and Peruvian government forces
PRINCIPAL THEATER(S): Peru, especially Ayacucho and Lima
DECLARATION: None
MAJOR ISSUES AND OBJECTIVES: The guerrillas apparently seek to establish a radical Maoist/Incan government.
OUTCOME: As of mid-2002, a low-level guerrilla war continues.
APPROXIMATE MAXIMUM NUMBER OF MEN UNDER ARMS: Unknown
CASUALTIES: Between 1980 and 2001, more than 25,000 people, mostly civilians, have been killed; in the worst single incident, 66 civilians were massacred in an Ayacucho village.
TREATIES: None

The Sendero Luminoso ("Shining Path") guerrilla group, who combined radical Maoism with ancient Incan tribal traditions, began raiding parts of Peru in 1980. Initially, the attacks centered on Ayacucho but then targeted the capital city of Lima as well.

Raids included an attack on an Ayacucho prison, which liberated about 250 prisoners, sabotage of utilities, bombing of rail lines and public buildings, and a horrific raid on an Ayacucho village, which resulted in the deaths of 66 villagers. Lima and the port city of Callao were repeatedly attacked. In conjunction with military action, the Shining Path incited civil disturbances and strikes. In 1990, they targeted the new president, Alberto Fujimori (b. 1938), joining forces with another terrorist group, Movimiento Revolucionario Tupac Amarú (MRTA). In 1992, the two groups attempted to assassinate Fujimori.

Fujimori responded to the escalation in guerrilla violence by declaring war on "all guerrillas." Government forces enjoyed some success, but, on December 17, 1996, a band of MRTA guerrillas attacked the residence of the Japanese ambassador during a state reception and took 600 hostages. The guerrillas demanded the release of their captured comrades, showing their good faith in the standoff by releasing most of the hostages. On April 22, 1997, Peruvian government forces stormed the ambassador's residence, killed the guerrillas, and successfully freed the remaining 72 hostages.

This did not bring an end to the guerrilla war, which continues fitfully as of mid-2004.

Further reading: Gustavo Gorriti Ellenbojen, *The Shining Path: A History of the Millenarian War in Peru* (Chapel Hill: University of North Carolina Press, 1999); David Scott Palmer, ed., *The Shining Path of Peru* (New York: Palgrave Macmillan, 1994); Steve J. Stern, ed.,

Shining and Other Paths: War and Society in Peru, 1980–1995 (Durham, N.C.: Duke University Press, 1998).

Peruvian Revolt (1780–1782)

PRINCIPAL COMBATANTS: Indian rebels under Tupac Amarú vs. Spain
PRINCIPAL THEATER(S): Peru
DECLARATION: None
MAJOR ISSUES AND OBJECTIVES: Tupac Amarú sought to overthrow Spanish rule in Peru.
OUTCOME: Spain regained control of the country.
APPROXIMATE MAXIMUM NUMBER OF MEN UNDER ARMS: 75,000 Indian rebels; 60,000 Spanish colonial troops
CASUALTIES: Unknown
TREATIES: None

The Spanish conquistadores never succeeded in entirely suppressing Indian rebellion in Peru, and as late as 1780, José Gabriel Condorcanqui (c. 1742–81), assuming the name of Tupac Amarú II, after his ancestor and the last of the great Inca chieftains, led a rebellion. A hereditary chief—the Indians called them *caciques*—in the Tinta region of southern Peru, Tupac Amarú II had been schooled by the Jesuits but lived the traditional life among the Indians. He sparked the revolt in 1780, when he arrested and executed the provincial administrator—or *corregidor,* Antonio Arriaga, on charges of cruelty.

It was to be the last general Indian rebellion against Spain, and at first it enjoyed the support of some among the Creoles (Spaniards born in the Americas), who disliked Spanish cruelty toward the Indians and were in theory opposed to their enforced labor. His army consisted of Incas of the highlands, who, although poorly equipped, were large in number. Late in 1780, some 75,000 rebels, aided by the Creoles, stormed across southern Peru and into present-day Bolivia and part of Argentina. Resistance crumbled before the onslaught, and Tupac Amarú declared himself Peru's liberator.

But, as the revolt spread, it had become a violent battle between Indians and Europeans, and Tupac Amarú II lost the support of the Creoles, turning the tide against him. When he led two assaults against the Spanish colonial stronghold of Cuzco, he and his family were taken prisoner during the second assault. In March 1781, they were taken to Cuzco and, after Tupac was forced to witness the execution of his wife and sons, he was mutilated, drawn and quartered, and beheaded. This, however, did not put an end to the revolt, which was continued by Tupac Amarú's half brother, Tupac Amarú III (d. 1787). The rebels laid siege against La Paz twice. By this time, however, the Spanish had amassed a well-armed force of 60,000, which crushed the rebellion. In an effort to appease the rebels, Spanish officials granted a general amnesty.

See also PERUVIAN WAR OF INDEPENDENCE.

Further reading: Timothy E. Anna, *The Fall of the Royal Government in Peru* (Lincoln: University of Nebraska Press, 1979).

Peruvian Revolt (1948)

PRINCIPAL COMBATANTS: Conservative forces led by Manuel Odría vs. leftist forces of the Alianza Popular Revolucionaria Americana (APRA)
PRINCIPAL THEATER(S): Peru
DECLARATION: None
MAJOR ISSUES AND OBJECTIVES: Struggle between left-wing and right-wing forces; the right wing sought to topple a government sympathetic to and rife with APRA members.
OUTCOME: The forces of Odría prevailed, propelling Odría to the Peruvian presidency.
APPROXIMATE MAXIMUM NUMBER OF MEN UNDER ARMS: Unknown
CASUALTIES: Unknown
TREATIES: None

Peru's American Popular Revolutionary Alliance (Alianza Popular Revolucionaria Americana [APTA]), known as the "Aprista movement," had been formed in 1924 by a Peruvian intellectual named Victor Raul Haya de la Torre (1895–1979) then living in exile in Mexico City. Calling for the unity of the American Indians and an end to American imperialism, and supporting a planned economy and the nationalization of foreign-owned business inside Peru, the Partido Aprista suffered its up and downs, falling permanently afoul of the powerful Peruvian military when some party members assassinated the head of a ruling military junta in 1933. Declared illegal after the assassination, the party's fortunes rebounded when it backed the winner of the 1939 presidential elections, Manuel Prado (1889–1967). WORLD WAR II brought not only economic prosperity to Peru, but something like the promise of real democracy, as crypto-fascist militarism fell out of favor. Pressured by public opinion, the retiring President Prado in 1945 approved the candidacy of José Luis Bustamante y Rivero (1894–1979). And Bustamante, a left-leaning lawyer from Arequipa, won the election with the not inconsiderable help of Victor Raul Haya de la Torre and the Partido Aprista.

The Apristas may have been riding Bustamante's more respectable coattails, but they did nevertheless take numerous seats in both houses of the Peruvian legislature and accepted three posts in the cabinet. In power at last, they were determined to make changes and embarked on a program of liberal reform. This provoked a conservative reaction, and when a conservative newspaper editor was slain in 1947, the Apristas were blamed. The accusations moved Aprista government officials essentially to boycott the government, which, in turn, ground to a halt.

Under deteriorating political and economic conditions, dissident Apristas stormed and took the port town of Callao in October 1948. This prompted the seizure of warships in port by discontented sailors and civilians. Civil war seemed unavoidable, and as the country tottered on the brink, General Manuel Odría (1897–1974), chief of staff of the Peruvian army, suddenly led military loyalists against the Apristas during October 27–29. The action quickly assumed the form of a full-scale rebellion against the Bustamante government, which collapsed. Odría assumed power and immediately outlawed the APRA and other leftist parties. Military and paramilitary troops were sent to arrest leftists, many of whom were imprisoned or sent into exile. Haya de la Torre fled to the asylum of the Colombian embassy in Lima. As for Odría, he was formally elected president on July 2, 1950.

Further reading: Peter F. Klaren, *Modernization, Dislocation, and Aprismo: Origins of the Peruvian Aprista Party, 1870–1932* (Austin: University of Texas Press, 1973); Frederick B. Pike, *The Politics of the Miraculous Peru: Haya de Torre and the Spiritualist Tradition* (Lincoln: University of Nebraska Press, 1986).

Peruvian War of Independence (1820–1825)

PRINCIPAL COMBATANTS: Peruvian and other independence fighters vs. Spanish royalists
PRINCIPAL THEATER(S): Peru and Upper Peru (Bolivia)
DECLARATION: Peruvian independence declared, July 1821
MAJOR ISSUES AND OBJECTIVES: Independence from Spain
OUTCOME: Independence was achieved, both for Peru and the newly created state of Bolivia.
APPROXIMATE MAXIMUM NUMBER OF MEN UNDER ARMS: 9,000 independence fighters (Peruvian and others) vs. 9,300 royalists
CASUALTIES: At Juní, the rebels lost 55 killed and 99 wounded; the royalists lost 374 killed and 80 captured. At Ayacucho, the rebels lost 310 killed, 609 wounded; the royalists lost 1,400 killed, 700 wounded, 2,600 captured.
TREATIES: None

Napoleon's invasion of Spain in 1808 sparked revolutions throughout Central and South America. For more than a decade, the Creoles (those of Spanish descent born in the Americas) launched successful wars of independence in all the Spanish colonies but Peru, where an entrenched and conservative aristocracy, including a relatively high number of native Spaniards, led to the concentration of royal military power in Lima and to the grimly effective suppression of the kind of Indian uprisings that often lent support to Creole revolts elsewhere.

As a result, liberating Peru fell to outsiders, among them the great South American revolutionary leader José de San Martín (1778–1850), who saw Peru as the key to the liberation of all South America from the Spanish yoke. Not only did he wish to disable this bastion of Spanish imperial power on the continent, he also wanted for Argentina the silver mines of Upper Peru, now in the hands of the Spanish. Having already lost earlier to the imperial forces in the mountains, San Martín decided in 1818 to surround them by liberating Chile (*see* CHILEAN WAR OF INDEPENDENCE) and using that country as a base for a seaborne assault on Peru. San Martín led 4,000 troops from that struggle, along with the new Chilean navy (under the command of the British Lord Thomas Cochrane [1775–1860]) to Pisco, Peru. The troops landed and established a camp at Huacho. San Martín used this as his recruiting headquarters, and, soon, his small Chilean army became the nucleus of a Peruvian army of independence.

With San Martín's forces threatening, the Spanish colonial government evacuated Lima, and took refuge in the interior. The citizens of the capital then invited San Martín to enter the city in July 1821. Upon entering Lima, San Martín proclaimed the independence of Peru and "Upper Peru" (Bolivia).

San Martín well understood that it was one thing to proclaim independence and quite another to make it a fact. To attack the strong, entrenched Spanish forces in the interior, he called upon the "Great Liberator," Simón Bolívar (1783–1830), and the two leaders pooled their forces at Guayaquil in July 1822. This completed, San Martín decided to relinquish control of the army entirely to Bolívar. With Antonio José de Sucre (1785–1830), Bolívar led a 9,000-man army to victory against Spanish royalist forces at the Battle of Junín on August 6, 1824. On December 9, 1824, Sucre led 6,000 men against a significantly superior royalist force (9,300 men) at the Battle of Ayacucho. Sucre was not only victorious, but he captured the entire Spanish force led by José de La Serna (1770–1832). This compelled the Spanish to withdraw from Peru.

Upper Peru remained in royalist hands. The revolution had not been going well there. But the victory in Peru freed Bolívar and Sucre's troops to aid the freedom fighters in Upper Peru, and in 1824 a 4,000-man Spanish royalist force capitulated to the reinforced independence army. Upper Peru gained its independence as Bolivia.

See also ARGENTINE WAR OF INDEPENDENCE; COLOMBIAN WAR OF INDEPENDENCE; VENEZUELAN WAR OF INDEPENDENCE.

Further reading: Timothy E. Anna, *The Fall of the Royal Government in Peru* (Lincoln: University of Nebraska Press, 1979); Frederick B. Pike, *The Modern History of Peru* (New York: Praeger, 1967).

Philip of Macedon's Northern Conquests
(345–339 B.C.E.)

PRINCIPAL COMBATANTS: Macedon vs. Epirus, Thessaly, Illyria, and Danubian tribes, as well as Perinthus and Byzantium
PRINCIPAL THEATER(S): Middle East and middle Europe
DECLARATION: None
MAJOR ISSUES AND OBJECTIVES: Conquest
OUTCOME: Philip greatly extended the Macedonian empire.
APPROXIMATE MAXIMUM NUMBER OF MEN UNDER ARMS: Unknown
CASUALTIES: Unknown
TREATIES: None

Philip II of Macedon (382–336 B.C.E.) conducted a campaign of conquest through Epirus, Thessaly, and the southern portion of Illyria during 344–342 B.C.E. With these regions subdued, he moved north into the wild Danube region, where he intimidated the northern tribal peoples. This accomplished, Philip pushed his conquests eastward within Thrace, acquiring territory as far as the Black Sea.

In 339, Philip met united opposition from the peoples of Perinthus and Byzantium, who were backed by Athenian finance. Repulsed in battles for these territories, Philip withdrew and from 339 to 338 B.C.E. turned his attention to the Fourth SACRED WAR.

See also SACRED WAR, FIRST; SACRED WAR, SECOND; SACRED WAR, THIRD.

Further reading: D. G. Hogarth, *Philip and Alexander of Macedon* (Freeport, N.Y.: Books for Libraries Press, 1971).

Philippine Guerrilla Wars (1969–1986)

PRINCIPAL COMBATANTS: Philippine government vs. Huk and Moro guerrillas
PRINCIPAL THEATER(S): The Philippines, especially Luzon and Sulu
DECLARATION: None
MAJOR ISSUES AND OBJECTIVES: For the rebels, the overthrow of Ferdinand Marcos; for Marcos, the continuation of his personal rule
OUTCOME: Marcos fell from power, and rebel activity markedly dissipated.
APPROXIMATE MAXIMUM NUMBER OF MEN UNDER ARMS: Unknown
CASUALTIES: Unknown
TREATIES: None

After the United States liberated its former protectorate, the Philippines, from their Japanese conquerors in WORLD WAR II, the Americans came under international pressure to act as it was urging European powers with former colonies in the Pacific and Southeast Asia to act. In 1946, the United States finally granted the islands the independence it had been more or less promising Filipinos for half a century. But, during the war, intense fighting, especially around Manila, during the Japanese retreat had virtually destroyed the Filipino capital and the country's economy. It also had left the islands subject to special conditions set by the U.S. government through the Bell Act and other heavy-handed postwar policies. Some of these were more onerous than others, but they all fueled Filipino resentment. For example, free trade with the islands was extended for eight years, with gradually increasing tariffs, and the United States leased a number of military bases for 99 years. The latter ensured an extensive military presence over which the Filipinos had no control because U.S. authority on the bases amounted to all but territorial rights. Finally, in return for the release of U.S. payments to cover damages done by the war, the Philippine government was forced under the so-called Parity Amendment to change its constitution to grant U.S. citizens (read American big business) equal rights with Filipinos in exploiting the islands' ample natural resources.

Soon resentment flared into open dissent and then outright rebellion from the Communist-led Huk militants. The U.S.-backed government responded with heavy-handed repression and clearly fraudulent national elections, which placed Elpidio Quirino (1890–1956) in the presidency. By 1954, the HUKBALAHAP REBELLION had been quelled, partly with U.S. military aid but also as a result of the opening of the political process to greater participation by the Filipino masses. Still, under the charismatic Ramon Magsaysay (1907–1957) and his successors, true reform remained elusive—for such reform faced adamantine resistance from a corrupt legislature and an entrenched bureaucracy. Unrest was nevertheless usually handled through the electoral process and legal protest.

In November 1965, Ferdinand E. Marcos (1917–89) was elected president. Grave economic problems were exacerbated by Marcos's own venality and arrogance, though these did not prevent him from being the first elected president of the Philippines to win reelection in 1969. By then the Huks had renewed hostilities in central Luzon, where the sense of social injustice among tenant farmers had always been strong. Now their voices were joined by those of the intensely nationalistic Moro (Muslim) rebels in Mindanao. No longer did Filipinos take pride as a matter of course in being an outpost of Christianity in an Asian world; instead, many began to look to precolonial times for an Asian cultural identity and a language, Pilipino, other than English or Spanish. Responding to these cultural pressures and fears of Communist influence among the growing number of rebels, the Filipino authorities, pushed by a troubled U.S. administration, held one of the more honest—and certainly more peaceful—elections in Philippine history. The voting produced a widely representative Constitutional Convention intended to undertake a fundamental restructuring of power in the waning years of Marcos's legally limited term in office.

Instead, backed by big business interests, mostly American, Marcos used the 1972 typhoon floods in rebel-infested Luzon as an excuse to declare martial law, intending to set up a parliamentary-style government that would allow him to hold onto power. He immediately began suppressing the ongoing violent student demonstrations and arresting opposition politicians in both the Congress and the Convention. To the rebels he offered amnesty if they surrendered their weapons, and many members of the New People's Army, the military wing of the officially banned Communist Party of the Philippines (PKP), did so. On the other hand, the Moros mostly held out, and—with help from Muslim radicals in Malaysia and Libya—even spread their rebellion to the Sulu Archipelago. As Marcos collected unregistered firearms in the streets and countryside, he introduced a prohibition on strikes by organized labor, launched a land reform program, and granted important new concessions to foreign investors. They helped celebrate in turn the new parliamentary system under which Marcos became both president and prime minister, though he failed to convene the legislature called for by his new constitution.

The Moro resistance continued, reaching a peak in 1974, when the Sulu city of Jolo was all but destroyed in the fighting, causing Marcos to increase security there with 35,000 government troops. Afterward, guerrilla activity became sporadic. But now it was also as endemic as the rioting in Manila since Marcos's assumption of dictatorial power.

In 1978, when elections were finally held for an interim National Assembly, rigged results gave the opposition (led by formerly jailed senator Benigno S. Aquino [1932–83]) no seats, which sparked further unrest. In 1980, Aquino went into exile in the United States. In 1981, Marcos, under renewed pressure from the United States, suspended martial law and recalled the legislature. Though the National Assembly had token power, Marcos won a new six-year term in a virtually uncontested election. When Aquino attempted to return in 1983, he was assassinated by Marcos's military, which resulted in more rioting and another rigged election. Increasing internal and international pressure led to Marcos's resignation and a new election, which brought Aquino's widow, Corazon C. Aquino (b. 1933), to power in 1986. Marcos sought exile in the United States, where he died, in Hawaii, in 1989.

Thereafter, as the United States reduced its presence and its influence in the islands, rebel activity in the hills and the jungles decreased. The Moro groups degenerated into outlaw organizations, terrorizing rich tourists for ransom and justifying their greed as part of the late 20th-century radical Muslim attack on the international hegemony of the United States. The administration of Aquino was threatened by six attempted coups, and in 1992, Aquino decided against running for reelection.

Further reading: John Bresnan, ed., *Crises in the Philippines: The Marcos Era and Beyond* (Princeton, N.J.: Princeton University Press, 1986); Gary Hawes, *The Philippine State and the Marcos Regime: The Politics of Export* (Ithaca, N.Y.: Cornell University Press, 1987); Monina Allarey Mercado, ed., *People Power: The Philippine Revolution of 1986* (Manila: James B. Reuter, S.J., Foundation, 1986); Primitivo Mijares, *The Conjugal Dictatorship of Ferdinand and Imelda Marcos* (San Francisco: Union Square Publications, 1976).

Philippine Insurrection (1896–1898)

PRINCIPAL COMBATANTS: Filipino rebels vs. Spain
PRINCIPAL THEATER(S): The Philippines, especially Luzon in the north
DECLARATION: A rebel call to arms on August 26, 1896
MAJOR ISSUES AND OBJECTIVES: Independence and social justice
OUTCOME: The rebellion was defeated, but Spain's hold on the Philippines was weakened.
APPROXIMATE MAXIMUM NUMBER OF MEN UNDER ARMS: Rebels, 30,000; Spanish 25,000
CASUALTIES: 2,000 combat deaths on both sides
TREATIES: Pact of Biak-na-bato, December 15, 1897

By the late 18th century, Spain's long colonial decline had resulted in the loss of its trade monopoly in the Philippines, which by the 1830s were open virtually without restrictions to foreign merchants. European demand for commercial agricultural products, such as sugar and hemp, gave birth to a class of Chinese-Filipino mestizos who, in time, provided the seeds of a revolutionary independence movement. A passion for nationalism and for reform also blossomed in the late 1800s among the sons of the Filipino elite, who eschewed the parochial schools of the islands for liberal educations in Europe. Among this group of talented overseas students was José Rizal (1861–96), whose political novels and leadership of the so-called Propaganda Movement had a huge impact on the islands.

In 1892, Rizal returned home to form a modestly reformist society called the "Liga Filipino," whose members were careful never to utter the word "independence."

Nevertheless, the always excitable Spanish colonial authorities arrested Rizal in 1892, exiled him to one of the more remote southern islands, and eventually executed him in 1896. Shocked by the arrest, Rizal's followers formed a secret revolutionary society called the "Katipunan," headquartered in Manila and dedicated to expelling the Spaniards from the islands. Under the leadership of a self-educated warehouse worker named Andres Bonifacio (1863–1897), the Katipunan made preparations for armed revolt.

Thus, even before the SPANISH-AMERICAN WAR, many Filipino freedom-fighters—inspired by José Rizal—had already taken up arms in opposition to Spain's corrupt colonial government. When the Katipunan's purpose was unmasked by government agents in the summer of 1898, Bonifacio called for an armed and immediate insurrection on August 26. But rebel attempts to secure independence for the islands failed. Outfought by the Spanish, Filipino revolutionaries were forced to retreat to northern Luzon, but their resistance became entrenched when the Spanish executed Rizal, now considered the father of the independence movement.

Challenging Bonifacio for leadership of the movement in Luzon was a new revolutionary firebrand named Emilio Aguinaldo (1869–1964). Mayor of the Luzon city of Cavite, Aguinaldo had also been arrested for treason by the Spanish, who intentionally crippled the Filipino leader by shooting him in the foot. Under Aguinaldo's leadership, Luzon became the center of the fighting. The province fell again under Spanish control by the end of 1897, when rebel leaders agreed to the Pact of Biak-na-bato. In return for Spanish promises to introduce reforms, Aguinaldo accepted some 400,000 pesos and exile in Hong Kong, where he and other rebel leaders continued to plot a Filipino revolution. With U.S. backing, Aguinaldo returned to the islands on May 19, 1898, after Spain went to war with the United States. When the victorious Americans proved themselves intent on colonizing the Philippines, Aguinaldo launched another rebellion—the PHILIPPINE INSURRECTION (1899–1902).

See also CAVITE MUTINY.

Further reading: Fronio M. Alip, *A Philippine History,* new rev. ed., 2 vols. (Manila: Manlapaz Pub. Co., 1974); Renato Constantino, *The Philippines: From the Spanish Colonization to the Second World War* (New York: Monthly Review Press, 1975).

Philippine Insurrection (1899–1902)

PRINCIPAL COMBATANTS: United States vs. Filipino independence fighters
PRINCIPAL THEATER(S): Philippines
DECLARATION: Philippine Republic proclaimed, January 20, 1899; shots first fired on February 4, 1899.

MAJOR ISSUES AND OBJECTIVES: Filipinos, led by Emilio Aguinaldo, proclaimed the Philippine Republic, refused to recognize U.S. annexation of Cuba following the Spanish-American War, and launched an insurrection against American occupation.
OUTCOME: The independence movement was defeated but not permanently suppressed.
APPROXIMATE MAXIMUM NUMBER OF MEN UNDER ARMS: U.S., 70,000; Filipino insurgents, 40,000.
CASUALTIES: United States, 1,073 killed in battle; 3,161 died of disease and other causes; 2,911 wounded. Filipino forces, 16,000 killed in battle. About 200,000 civilians died of disease, starvation, and other causes.
TREATIES: Treaty, May 6, 1902; U.S. proclamation ending the war and granting a general amnesty, July 4, 1902.

After the fall of Manila in the SPANISH-AMERICAN WAR, Philippine nationalist insurgents under Emilio Aguinaldo (1869–1964) reached an informal truce with the occupying forces of the United States. In January 1899, following the conclusion of the Peace of Paris with Spain, the United States announced annexation of the Philippines, having purchased the islands from Spain for $20 million. Explaining his decision to annex the Philippines to a group of ministers visiting the White House, President William McKinley (1843–1901) said he had looked at all the options and decided he could not give the islands back to Spain, which would be cowardly and dishonorable; nor could he turn them over to Germany or France, America's rivals in the Orient, because that would be bad business and discreditable; nor could he leave them to themselves, since they were "unfit" for self-government and would soon have anarchy and misrule, worse than Spain's domination. There was nothing left for us to do, McKinley continued, but take "them all" and to educate the Filipinos, to "uplift" and "civilize" and Christianize them, and by God's grace do the very best we could by them, as our fellow men for whom Christ also died. And then, he concluded, he went to bed and went to sleep and slept soundly.

But Aguinaldo's rebels had proclaimed Philippine independence on June 12, 1898, and they now refused to accept annexation. On January 20, 1899, the Philippine Republic was proclaimed under the Malolos Constitution, with Emilio Aguinaldo as president. In February 1899, the Filipinos rose in revolt against U.S. colonial rule. A year earlier U.S. warships had brought Aguinaldo back from exile in China to lead his countrymen against Spain. Now that he and his *insurrectos* were demanding Filipino independence within a U.S. protectorate, what U.S. correspondents described as his "ingratitude" sparked outrage "back home" in the states.

McKinley claimed the fighting began when the insurgents attacked U.S. forces, though U.S. troops later testified that the occupying army fired the first shot. At any rate, the rebellion was under way, and the same *Harper's Weekly* that in early January had hailed Aguinaldo as a hero excoriated him as a savage in March. This "beast" had ordered his men, according to the magazine, to exterminate without compassion or distinction of age or sex all "the civilized race" in the islands. *Harper's* had merely sounded the clarion call for a propaganda war that would treat the Philippine insurrection as a replay of Theodore Roosevelt's (1858–1919) celebrated history *The Winning of the West*. Ironically, before it was over McKinley would be dead and the chief Rough Rider would be in the saddle of the presidency.

THE PHILIPPINES QUESTION AND AMERICA'S IMPERIAL IMPULSE

When Theodore Roosevelt returned from Cuba as the hero of San Juan Hill, he ran for governor of New York and made the Philippine "question" the centerpiece of his campaign. Not only did Roosevelt win the gubernatorial contest, but in 1900 he was nominated as McKinley's running mate in the president's bid for a second term. As in 1896, Populist sentiment ran strong through the Democratic Party, and its candidate—yet again William Jennings Bryan (1860–1925)—was in a strong position going into the election because of the party's critique of big business. But the key to the election became Bryan's anti-imperialism. With unremitting, even gleeful, demagoguery, vice-presidential candidate Roosevelt lashed out at Bryan by focusing on his unpopular foreign policy positions. Aided by the Republican press, Roosevelt identified Bryan as a backer of Emilio Aguinaldo, leader of the Filipino opposition to annexation, and in cartoon after cartoon, editorial after editorial, speech after speech, Bryan was denounced as a coward and a sissy.

After the election, when anarchist Leon Czolgosz (c. 1873–1901) assassinated McKinley at the Pan-American Exposition in Buffalo "TR" had what he called a "bully pulpit" from which to urge his imperial agenda. Many in Congress shared that agenda and, like the new president, compared the troubles in the Philippines to those recently settled with the American Indians on the western Plains. If Americans had not subjugated and dispossessed the Indian, argued Senator Albert Beveridge (1862–1927), there would be no America. If an American argued for Filipino independence, he was arguing that savages had a right to self-government. In taking the Philippines and crushing the natives, Americans weren't violating their most basic principles, they were instead only doing what their fathers had done, pitching the tents of liberty farther westward and continuing the march of the flag. Dissenters were "infidels" to America's manifest destiny.

The army high command was itself controlled by old Indian fighters who had learned their trade fighting in the Plains and Apache wars, and they adapted what they had learned to defeat Moro tribesmen (*see* MORO WARS). As the U.S. Army in the American West used Indian scouts, now it also hired Filipino scouts. And when it came to setting up refugee camps or "pacifying" districts, they had picked up the tricks of doing so on Indian reservations, or perhaps during the Civil War in the antiguerrilla campaigns of Missouri, where the rules of civilized warfare had been suspended by decree. As with the Indian wars, then, so with the Filipino revolt. Once this foreign adventure became a war against savages, massacre became not only possible, but likely.

THE INSURRECTION

The fighting began on the night of February 4, 1899, when an insurgent patrol challenged a U.S. guard post near Manila. On the eve of ratification of the Peace of Paris, the challenge was most likely calculated to embarrass and intimidate American forces, which had yet to be reinforced. The troops of VIII Corps were not overawed, however. Major General Elwell S. Otis commanding 12,000 U.S. soldiers against 40,000 insurgents (1838–1909), nevertheless responded vigorously with several attacks that drove back the insurgents and inflicted at least 3,000 casualties on the Filipinos. During February 22–24, insurgents under General Antonio Luna (1866–99) retaliated with a concerted attack on Manila, but U.S. forces led by General Arthur MacArthur (1845–1912) forced them into retreat and by March 31 had pushed the insurgents back to their capital and stronghold in Malolos. After this setback, Aguinaldo took flight, disbanded the formally constituted army, and instituted a guerrilla campaign. Reinforced U.S. forces took the offensive, carrying the war into southern Luzon, the Visayan Islands, Mindanao, and Sulu.

In general, U.S. firepower overwhelmed all the Filipinos could throw together. Before it was all over, the United States would send 70,000 troops, four times as many as it sent to Cuba, and they inflicted many more times the casualties. In the opening battle, Admiral George Dewey (1837–1917) steamed up the Pasig River and fired 500-pound shells into Filipino trenches, creating so many dead natives that the Americans used their bodies for breastworks. A British witness mourned: "This is not war; it is simply massacre and murderous butchery." And that was only the beginning. The *insurrectos* held out for three long years, and to do so against such odds, they had to have had the support of the population. General Arthur MacArthur, commander of the war, was reluctant to accept that fact. At first believing that Aguinaldo's troops represented only a faction and refusing to even think that all of Luzon was opposed to the Americans, he later admitted that he was "reluctantly compelled" to understand that Filipino guerrilla tactics depended upon almost the complete unity of action of the entire native population. This meant, of course, that every Filipino was the enemy.

In response, the army targeted Aguinaldo, who was captured by General Frederick Funston's (1865–1917) Filipino scouts on March 23, 1901. Aguinaldo was pressured into swearing allegiance to the United States and into issuing a proclamation calling for peace. By this time, however, the guerrilla war had taken on a life independent from its original leader. For the next year, U.S. forces were subject to sporadic attack until virtually all of the Filipino military leaders had been located, rounded up, and placed under arrest. The last of these leaders concluded a treaty with U.S. authorities on May 6, 1902, and the U.S. military administration of the islands was replaced by a U.S.-controlled civil government. Its first appointed governor was William Howard Taft (1857–1930), who would later become the 27th president of the United States.

THE OPPOSITION AND THE AFTERMATH

Despite what U.S. newspapers and magazines had reported openly during the fighting, federal officials responded to charges of brutality with what became typical dissimulation. Said Secretary of War Elihu Root (1845–1937): "The war in the Philippines has been conducted by the American army with the scrupulous regard for the rules of civilized warfare . . . with self restraint and with humanity never surpassed." Some were sickened by the slaughter and hated the war. In the four black regiments serving in the Philippines, many of the black soldiers established a rapport with the natives, and an unusually large number of them deserted. The Philippines "situation" aroused many prominent blacks and black congregations in the United States to militant opposition to the war. And they weren't the only ones. Invocations to savage war were one thing, actual atrocities another. As Howard Zinn notes, William James (1842–1910) cursed: "God damn the U.S. for its vile conduct in the Philippine Isles!" And Mark Twain (1835–1910) wrote in the *New York Herald*: "I bring you the stately matron named Christendom, returning bedraggled, besmirched, and dishonored from pirate raids in Kiao-Chou, Manchuria, South Africa, and the Philippines, with her soul full of meanness, her pocket full of boodle, and her mouth full of pious hypocrisies."

Eventually, even Secretary Root was forced to admit that there had been "marked severities," severities that became notorious when several officers involved in the activities at Samar were court-martialed. But Roosevelt and his allies were able to turn the Samar massacres from an embarrassment into renewed public support for the war by insisting even more vehemently than they had before on the "savage" nature of the Filipino rebels. Congress held investigations following the unsuccessful trials, and testimony that should have been damaging about freely employed water torture and similar "inhuman conduct" not within "the ordinary rules of civilized warfare" was vitiated by General J. Franklin Bell's (1856–1919) observation that he had never been dressed down for taking the same or similar measures against the Indians and by General MacArthur's contention that he had simply been fulfilling the destiny of America's "Aryan ancestors." They used the myth of the American Indian wars to justify the Philippine slaughter, and in doing so fully resuscitated old frontier metaphysics to rally the imperial impulse of a new domestic policy. Teddy Roosevelt was launched on a campaign to build up the navy into a two-ocean force and make America policeman of the world. By 1904, he could employ the Philippines "question" yet again to defeat William Jennings Bryan in the presidential elections and get on with his plans.

Further reading: Robert Beisner, *Twelve against Empire: The Anti-Imperialists, 1892–1902* (New York: McGraw-Hill, 1968); Thomas Dyer, *Theodore Roosevelt and the Idea of Race* (Baton Rouge: Louisiana State University Press, 1980); Philip Foner, *The Spanish-Cuban-American War and the Birth of American Imperialism*, 2 vols. (New York: Monthly Review Press, 1972); Willard B. Gatewood, comp., *"Smoked Yankees" and the Struggle for Empire: Letters from Negro Soldiers, 1898–1902* (Urbana: University of Illinois Press, 1971); David Healy, *U.S. Expansionism: The Imperialist Urge in the 1890s* (Madison: University of Wisconsin Press, 1970); Eric Hobsbawm, *The Age of Empire, 1875–1914* (New York: Pantheon Books, 1987); Gerald F. Linderman, *The Mirror of War: American Society and the Spanish American War* (Ann Arbor: University of Michigan Press, 1974); Brian McAllister Linn, *The Philippine War, 1899–1902* (Lawrence: University Press of Kansas, 2000); Stuart Creighton Miller, *"Benevolent Assimilation": The American Conquest of the Philippines, 1899–1903* (New Haven, Conn.: Yale University Press, 1982); Richard Slotkin, *Gunfighter Nation: The Myth of the Frontier in Twentieth-Century America* (New York: Atheneum, 1992); William Appleman Williams, *The Roots of the Modern American Empire* (New York: Random House, 1969) and *The Tragedy of American Diplomacy* (New York: Dell Publishing, 1972); Howard Zinn, *A People's History of the United States* (New York: Harper and Row, 1980).

Phocas's Mutiny (602)

PRINCIPAL COMBATANTS: Phocas vs. Emperor Maurice of the Byzantine Empire
PRINCIPAL THEATER(S): Constantinople
DECLARATION: None
MAJOR ISSUES AND OBJECTIVES: Mutinous troops protested pay cuts and harsh living conditions; Phocas led them in an assault upon the emperor.
OUTCOME: The emperor and his sons were assassinated, and Phocas was acclaimed emperor by the army.
APPROXIMATE MAXIMUM NUMBER OF MEN UNDER ARMS: Unknown

CASUALTIES: Unknown
TREATIES: None

The Byzantine centurion Phocas (d. 610) led a mutiny by Byzantine soldiers who were protesting severe winter conditions and a cut in pay they had suffered at the end of the BYZANTINE-AVAR WAR (595–602) against the Mongolian Avars from the Volga River area. The enraged troops overthrew their designated commander, Priscus, and replaced him with Phocas, who then led them in a march on Constantinople, where they overran the royal palace and assassinated Emperor Maurice (c. 539–602) as well as his five sons. Phocas was then elevated to the throne.

Further reading: John F. Haldon, *Byzantium in the Seventh Century: The Transformation of a Culture* (Cambridge, UK; New York: Cambridge University Press, 1997).

P(h)ra Naret's Revolt *See* SIAMESE-BURMESE WAR (1584–1592); SIAMESE-CAMBODIAN WAR (1587).

Piedmontese Revolt (1821)

PRINCIPAL COMBATANTS: Piedmont constitutionalists vs. the House of Savoy
PRINCIPAL THEATER(S): Piedmont, Italy
DECLARATION: None
MAJOR ISSUES AND OBJECTIVES: Piedmont liberals wanted independence from Sardinia and the rule of King Victor Emmanuel I.
OUTCOME: Victor Emmanuel I was forced to abdicate, but the even more reactionary new king, Charles Felix, brutally crushed the rebellion.
APPROXIMATE MAXIMUM NUMBER OF MEN UNDER ARMS: Unknown
CASUALTIES: Unknown
TREATIES: None

The 1814 Congress of Vienna, ending the Napoleonic Wars, made possible, in theory, the restoration of the old order throughout Europe, although this proved impossible in practice, and in Italy gave rise to decades of struggle by freedom fighters such as those who formed the secret political society known as the Carbonari (or Charcoal Burners). Already founded during the period of French control, this cabal of the bourgeoisie, with its vaguely nationalist and decidedly republican agenda, spread from its lodges in the south throughout Italy to the Marches and the Romagna, to Milan and the Piedmont.

In the Piedmont, a considerable wing of the nobility, liberal and cultivated, was quite hostile to the reactionary policies of the restored king of Sardinia, Victor Emmanuel I (1795–1824), whose hegemony included the Piedmont. The Carbonari rebels, with their constitutional hopes, allied themselves with these nobles. When the king declined to accept a constitutional monarchy, the groups entered into a conspiracy, which had the covert support of the successor-designate to the throne, Charles Albert (1798–1849), of the house of Savoy. Between March 9 and March 13, 1821, the conspiracy spawned a revolt, planned by the military and the bourgeoisie, which spread from Alessandria to Turin and ultimately forced Victor Emmanuel I to abdicate in favor of his brother, Charles Felix (1765–1831). No sooner was Charles Felix enthroned, however, than he turned against the rebels and opposed the constitution. On April 8, 1821, Charles Felix allied Sardinia with Austria, and a combined Austro-Sardinian force invaded Piedmont and easily defeated the rebel forces at the Battle of Novara. Charles Felix turned his wrath on the army, purging it of disloyal officers and executing three liberal ringleaders.

Further reading: George Martin, *The Red Shirt and the Cross of Savoy: The Story of Italy's Risorgimento, 1748–1871* (New York: Dodd, Mead, 1969).

"Pig" War (1906–1909)

PRINCIPAL COMBATANTS: Serbia (with Russian aid) vs. Austria-Hungary
PRINCIPAL THEATER(S): Serbia and Austria-Hungary
DECLARATION: None
MAJOR ISSUES AND OBJECTIVES: Serbia wanted to achieve economic independence from Austria-Hungary.
OUTCOME: A more favorable trade treaty was negotiated between Serbia and Austria-Hungary.
APPROXIMATE MAXIMUM NUMBER OF MEN UNDER ARMS: No combat ensued; but the nations prepared to mobilize their armies.
CASUALTIES: None
TREATIES: Commercial treaty of 1909

Serbia sought to free itself from economic dependency on Austria-Hungary by importing French munitions and establishing a customs union with Bulgaria, which would mean that high-tariff Austro-Hungarian goods would not be able to compete in the Serbian market. Austria-Hungary responded in 1906 by barring the importation of Serbian pork. For its part, Serbia secured international investment to open more international export markets for its pork. Serbia also pressed Bosnia-Herzegovina, provinces of the Austro-Hungarian Empire, to provide an outlet to the Adriatic Sea.

When Russia, pursuing a pan-Slavic policy, backed Serbia's actions, war between Russia and Austria-Hungary loomed. Russia backed down, however, in response to a 1909 German ultimatum. Once Russian aid to Serbia was cut off, Serbia and Austria-Hungary concluded a new trade treaty; however, Serbia's own pan-Slavic nationalism continued unabated. Its activity, both public and secret, stirred up an independence movement in Bosnia-Herzegovina, creating the conditions that sparked WORLD WAR I.

See also BALKAN WAR, FIRST; BALKAN WAR, SECOND.

Further reading: Samuel R. Williamson, Jr., *Austria-Hungary and the Origins of the First World War* (New York: St. Martin's Press, 1991).

Pima Revolt, First (1695)

PRINCIPAL COMBATANTS: Pima Indians vs. Spanish settlers in Mexico and southern Arizona

PRINCIPAL THEATER(S): Territory of present-day Sonora, Mexico, and southern Arizona

DECLARATION: Unknown

MAJOR ISSUES AND OBJECTIVES: Pima bid for independence of Spanish rule

OUTCOME: After a short-lived revolt, Spanish rule was reinstated.

APPROXIMATE MAXIMUM NUMBER OF MEN UNDER ARMS: Unknown

CASUALTIES: Unknown

TREATIES: None

In 1695, the Pima Indians of lower Pimeria Alta—Sonora, Mexico, and southern Arizona—staged a short-lived revolt against their colonial Spanish overlord, destroying property and terrorizing missionaries. The uprising, about which very little is known, was quickly put down.

Further reading: Frank Russell, *Pima Indians* (Tempe: University of Arizona Press, 1975).

Pima Revolt, Second (1751)

PRINCIPAL COMBATANTS: Pima Indians vs. colonial Spanish overlords

PRINCIPAL THEATER(S): Northern Arizona

DECLARATION: Unknown

MAJOR ISSUES AND OBJECTIVES: Pima attempt to overthrow colonial Spanish domination

OUTCOME: Indecisive; Pimas remained under Spanish rule

APPROXIMATE MAXIMUM NUMBER OF MEN UNDER ARMS: Unknown

CASUALTIES: Spanish, 17 by Oacpicagigua's hand, others unrecorded; Pima, unknown

TREATIES: None

In 1751, 50 years after the First PIMA REVOLT, the Pima Indians of upper Pimeria Alta, many of them descendants of earlier rebels who had fled north, followed Luis Oacpicagigua in a rebellion against the colonial Spanish overlords.

Oacpicagigua had once served the Spanish as captain-general of the western Pimas but had come to believe that the influx of Spanish settlers would eventually force his people into slavery. Accordingly, Oacpicagigua secretly worked to unite many Pimas, Papagos, Sobaipuris, and Apaches in an organized resistance.

On the night of November 20, 1751, Oacpicagigua and some of his men attacked 18 Spaniards whom he had been entertaining at his home in Saric. All were killed except for Padre Nentvig, who escaped to spread the alarm. But it was too late. During the succeeding weeks, rebels attacked missions and ranches in Caborca, Sonoita, Bac, and Guevavi.

The raids were destructive, but they did not coalesce into the general revolution Oacpicagigua had hoped for. The Sobiapuris and the Apaches backed out of the action at the decisive moment, and many Papagos and Pimas also failed to participate.

Spanish officials dispatched an army under the colonial governor, who, after several months of combat, finally quelled the insurrection. Luis Oacpicagigua managed to evade execution by a pledge to rebuild the churches destroyed during the uprising. In fact, he failed to keep this promise, and the people he had led never fully submitted to Spanish rule. For the next century and a half, they waged sporadic guerrilla warfare against the Spanish, then the Mexicans, and finally, in their turn, the Americans.

Further reading: Frank Russell, *Pima Indians* (Tempe: University of Arizona Press, 1975).

Polish-Bohemian War (1305–1312)

PRINCIPAL COMBATANTS: Poland vs. Bohemia

PRINCIPAL THEATER(S): Poland

DECLARATION: Effective Polish declaration of independence, 1305

MAJOR ISSUES AND OBJECTIVES: Polish independence from Bohemia.

OUTCOME: Under Ladislas of Kujavia, Poland secured its independence and the principalities of Little Poland and Great Poland were united into a sovereign kingdom.

APPROXIMATE MAXIMUM NUMBER OF MEN UNDER ARMS: Unknown

CASUALTIES: Unknown

TREATIES: None

As a result of the HAPSBURG-BOHEMIAN WAR, King Wenceslaus II (1271–1305) achieved full control over Bohemia. He embarked on a reign that greatly augmented the power and prestige of the kingdom. In 1300, he won victories in Little Poland, which gained him the Polish crown, so that he now ruled both Poland and Bohemia. However, the authority of Wenceslaus II did not survive his passing. Upon his death in 1305, his son, Wenceslaus III (1289–1306), was beset by challenges to his right to rule Poland, and en route to his coronation as Poland's king in 1306, he was assassinated in Olomuoc, a town in Moravia.

Into the vacuum created by Wenceslaus III's death stepped Duke Ladislas "Lokietek" (1260–1333), a renowned Polish champion from Kujavia. His ambition was to unify the disparate principalities of Poland and thereby gain independence from Bohemia. In the year before the murder of Wenceslaus III, he secured the backing of the Polish church and retook Little Poland from the Bohemians. Following the death of the Bohemian monarch, he campaigned in Great Poland, winning several decisive victories. By 1312, he was in a position to unite Little and Great Poland, and, having accomplished this, he was finally crowned King Ladislas I in 1320.

See also HUNGARIAN CIVIL WAR (1301–1308).

Further reading: Norman Davies, *God's Playground: A History of Poland,* 2 vols. (New York: Columbia University Press, 1982); O. Halecki (with additional material by A. Polonsky and Thaddeus V. Grommada), *A History of Poland,* new ed. (New York: Dorset Press, 1992); W. F. Reddaway, et al., eds., *The Cambridge History of Poland,* 2 vols. (reprint, Cambridge, UK: Cambridge University Press, 1971).

Polish-Bohemian War (1438–1439)

PRINCIPAL COMBATANTS: Partisans of King Albert II vs. partisans of Ladislas III; Ladislas III vs. Slovakian Hussites
PRINCIPAL THEATER(S): Bohemia
DECLARATION: None
MAJOR ISSUES AND OBJECTIVES: Control of Bohemia and Slovakia
OUTCOME: The Hussites achieved control of much of Slovakia.
APPROXIMATE MAXIMUM NUMBER OF MEN UNDER ARMS: Unknown
CASUALTIES: Unknown
TREATIES: Truce of 1439

Albert II (1397–1439), Hapsburg (Austrian) king of Germany, succeeded to the throne of the Holy Roman Empire that had been occupied by his late father-in-law, Sigismund (1368–1437). Because Sigismund had ruled both Hungary and Bohemia, Albert II assumed rule over these kingdoms as well. This did not sit well with a faction that supported the bay-king of Poland, Ladislas III (1424–1444), as candidate for Holy Roman Emperor and ruler of Hungary and Bohemia.

In 1438, the partisans of Albert II and Ladislas III clashed. The war seemed about to end, however, almost before it had begun when Albert II fell in battle while campaigning against the Turks in 1439. However, after he assumed the Hungarian throne in 1440, the 16-year-old Ladislas found himself facing new opposition, from Slovakian Hussites (religious radicals, followers of the nationalist and religious dissident Jan Hus [1369–1415]) led by John Jiskra z Brandysa (d. 1470). The Hussites had control of Slovakia before the end of 1440. As for Ladislas, he never had the opportunity to resolve the power struggle between his throne and the Hussites. In 1444, at only 20 years of age, Ladislas III was killed in battle against the Turks at Varna on the coast of the Black Sea.

Following the death of Ladislas III, one of his commanders, General John Hunyadi (1387–1456), proclaimed himself "overseer" of Slovakia. He was challenged by Jiskra z Brandysa, but Hunyadi, a skilled tactician and strategist, repeatedly defeated him in battle, culminating in the Battle of Lucenec in 1451. A truce was concluded, by which Jiskra z Brandysa retained some control over Slovakia.

See also BOHEMIAN CIVIL WAR (1448–1451); HUNGARIAN-TURKISH WAR (1441–1444); HUSSITE WARS.

Further reading: Norman Davies, *God's Playground: A History of Poland,* 2 vols. (New York: Columbia University Press, 1982); O. Halecki (with additional material by A. Polonsky and Thaddeus V. Grommada), *A History of Poland,* new ed. (New York: Dorset Press, 1992); W. F. Reddaway, et al., eds., *The Cambridge History of Poland,* 2 vols. (reprint, Cambridge, UK: Cambridge University Press, 1971).

Polish Civil War (1573–1574)

PRINCIPAL COMBATANTS: A variety of Polish factions
PRINCIPAL THEATER(S): Poland
DECLARATION: None
MAJOR ISSUES AND OBJECTIVES: Following the death of King Sigismund II Augustus and amid liberal reforms, Poland was thrown into chaos.
OUTCOME: General civil war ended with the election of the duc d'Anjou to the Polish throne, but the violence resumed when he stepped down after a 13-month reign.
APPROXIMATE MAXIMUM NUMBER OF MEN UNDER ARMS: Unknown
CASUALTIES: Unknown
TREATIES: None

When Poland's King Sigismund II Augustus (1520–72) died in 1572 without issue, the choice of successor to the throne was left to the Polish people. This matter added to the political chaos that prevailed as a result of opposition to the Union of Lublin, by which Poland had been formally united with Lithuania. A congress was convened in Warsaw in April 1573 to select a new king from among foreign contenders; the hope was that installation of a foreign-born monarch would avoid many conflicts among supporters of domestic candidates.

However, the liberal reforms that followed upon the Compact of Warsaw (January 28, 1573) so constrained the power of the Polish monarch that, 13 months after he was elected Polish king, Henry of Valois (1551–89), duc d'Anjou, returned to France to assume the throne there as Henry III following the death of his brother, Charles IX (1550–74) of France. Henry's departure reawakened the dormant civil war, and this time it was the Polish nobles who brought in a new king, Prince Stephen Bathory (1533–86) of Transylvania. The nobles enforced his coronation by military means.

See also RELIGION, FIFTH WAR OF.

Further reading: Norman Davies, *God's Playground: A History of Poland,* 2 vols. (New York: Columbia University Press, 1982); O. Halecki (with additional material by A. Polonsky and Thaddeus V. Grommada), *A History of Poland,* new ed. (New York: Dorset Press, 1992); W. F. Reddaway, et al., eds., *The Cambridge History of Poland,* 2 vols. (reprint, Cambridge, UK: Cambridge University Press, 1971).

Polish Civil War (1768–1773)

PRINCIPAL COMBATANTS: Confederation of Bar (with French, Ottoman, and Austrian support, but not direct military involvement) vs. the government of Stanislaus II Augustus (with Russian military aid and Prussian political support)

PRINCIPAL THEATER(S): Poland

DECLARATION: None

MAJOR ISSUES AND OBJECTIVES: Control of Poland; subsequently, the partition of parts of Poland among Russia, Prussia, and Austria

OUTCOME: Stanislaus II Augustus, effectively a Russian puppet, remained on the throne; about one-third of Poland was partitioned among Russia, Prussia, and Austria.

APPROXIMATE MAXIMUM NUMBER OF MEN UNDER ARMS: Unknown

CASUALTIES: Unknown

TREATIES: First Partition of Poland, five treaties, July 25, 1772, September 18, 1773, March 15–18, 1775, February 9, 1776, and August 22, 1776

The conclusion of the SEVEN YEARS' WAR in Europe in 1763 left both Austria and Prussia dissatisfied—Austria had failed in its bid to regain Silesia from Prussia; Prussia had failed to acquire Saxony. Meanwhile, Russia was making advances against its traditional rival, Ottoman Turkey,

and Catherine II (the Great; 1726–96) was anxious to forestall any aggression from a frustrated Austria. In 1764, she engineered the election of a puppet monarch, Stanislaus Poniatowski (1732–98) to the Polish throne, thereby making that hapless nation a virtual Russian satellite. Her plan was to use Poland as a means of placating both Prussia and Austria in order to maintain a balance of power in Europe that would protect her flank as she carried out her campaign against Turkey.

Some Poles resisted, especially when the new king, Stanislaus II Augustus, under pressure from Catherine, granted full rights to non-Catholic Poles. The Confederation of Bar was a league of Polish Catholic noblemen formed to counter Russian influence in Poland and to fight against equality for Protestants and Russian Orthodox Poles. The Bar sought to compel Stanislaus to abdicate. In this, the Bar enjoyed support from France and from the Ottomans, both wanting to halt Russian expansionism.

In June 1770, Catherine sent troops into Poland to intervene in the civil war that had developed between the Confederation of the Bar and the government of Stanislaus—whom the Bar had declared deposed. The Russian forces easily defeated the smaller, ad hoc army of the Confederation of the Bar, but Austria now threatened to intervene. Like France and the Ottomans, Austria feared Russian expansion. In response to the Austrian threat, Catherine turned to Prussia's Frederick II (1712–86, Frederick the Great). Although Frederick had no desire to trigger a general European war, he did want to expand into Polish territory, and so Catherine was able to play her Polish card. In a series of five treaties in 1772, Poland was partitioned: Russia gained part of northeast Poland, Austria annexed Galicia, and Prussia acquired Polish Pomerania and Ermeland. Overall, Poland was forced to cede about one-third of its territory.

See also CATHERINE THE GREAT'S FIRST WAR WITH THE TURKS.

Further reading: Norman Davies, *God's Playground: A History of Poland,* 2 vols. (New York: Columbia University Press, 1982); O. Halecki (with additional material by A. Polonsky and Thaddeus V. Grommada), *A History of Poland,* new ed. (New York: Dorset Press, 1992); W. F. Reddaway, et al., eds., *The Cambridge History of Poland,* 2 vols. (reprint, Cambridge, UK: Cambridge University Press, 1971); Piotr Sefan Wandyez, *The Lands of Partitioned Poland* (Seattle: University of Washington Press, 1974).

Polish Rebellion (1606–1607)

PRINCIPAL COMBATANTS: Zebrzydowski's Polish Catholic nobles vs. King Sigismund III

PRINCIPAL THEATER(S): Poland

DECLARATION: None
MAJOR ISSUES AND OBJECTIVES: Zebrzydowski sought reform of Sigismund's policies.
OUTCOME: The rebellion was defeated militarily, but it succeeded in pushing through the desired reforms.
APPROXIMATE MAXIMUM NUMBER OF MEN UNDER ARMS: Unknown
CASUALTIES: Unknown
TREATIES: None

Many Poles were alienated by the policies of King Sigismund III (1566–1632), who was anti-Catholic, who sent Polish armies to secure the Swedish throne, who compromised Polish nationalism by courting Austria, and who sought to curtail the Polish constitution to increase his power over parliament. Cracow's governor, Mikolaj Zebrzydowski (fl. 1605–07), led other Polish nobles in a militant protest of the king's order for a standing army to be constituted under royal authority. Zebrzydowski presented a list of demands to the king. When these were rejected, he led a violent rebellion, which prompted Sigismund to recall his armies from Sweden to put down the rebels. Zebrzydowski was defeated in a July 1607 battle, but his point had been made. In 1609, the Polish parliament proclaimed an amnesty for all the rebels, and the supremacy of the constitution was affirmed. Thus the rebellion, though militarily defeated, secured the preeminence of the Polish Catholic nobility in politics and the subjection of the Crown to parliamentary rule.

The conflict is often called Zebrzydowski's Insurrection.

Further reading: Norman Davies, *God's Playground: A History of Poland*, 2 vols. (New York: Columbia University Press, 1982); O. Halecki (with additional material by A. Polonsky and Thaddeus V. Grommada), *A History of Poland*, new ed. (New York: Dorset Press, 1992); W. F. Reddaway, et al., eds., *The Cambridge History of Poland*, 2 vols. (reprint, Cambridge, UK: Cambridge University Press, 1971).

Polish Rebellion (1715–1717)

PRINCIPAL COMBATANTS: Polish people and nobles vs. Augustus II
PRINCIPAL THEATER(S): Poland
DECLARATION: None
MAJOR ISSUES AND OBJECTIVES: The people rebelled against the presence, thievery, and general destructiveness of Saxon troops quartered throughout Poland.
OUTCOME: The king's threat to summon Russian troops prompted the negotiation of peace.
APPROXIMATE MAXIMUM NUMBER OF MEN UNDER ARMS: Unknown

CASUALTIES: In the hundreds among civilians and military alike.
TREATIES: 1717 agreement on Saxon troop withdrawal and limitation on the size of the Polish standing army.

Saxon troops quartered in Poland by King Augustus II (1670–1733) during the Second (or Great) NORTHERN WAR wreaked havoc on the populace with acts of theft and vandalism. With the support of the Polish nobility, a popular uprising erupted, and armed clashes between the people and the king's troops became frequent. Soon, the army ran amok—far beyond the king's ability to control it. Polish citizens were slain by the hundreds, and the people, in return, waged intensive guerrilla warfare against the army, bringing about substantial losses. At length, Augustus appealed to the Russian czar for aid. Fearing that Poland would now be overrun by Russians, the Polish nobles intervened and entered into negotiations with the king's government. By agreement in 1717, the Saxon army would withdraw from Poland, and Polish standing forces would be reduced to 18,000 troops.

Further reading: Norman Davies, *God's Playground: A History of Poland*, 2 vols. (New York: Columbia University Press, 1982); O. Halecki (with additional material by A. Polonsky and Thaddeus V. Grommada), *A History of Poland*, new ed. (New York: Dorset Press, 1992); W. F. Reddaway, et al., eds., *The Cambridge History of Poland*, 2 vols. (reprint, Cambridge, UK: Cambridge University Press, 1971).

Polish Rebellion (1794)

PRINCIPAL COMBATANTS: Nationalist forces under Thaddeus Kościusko vs. Russia and Prussia
PRINCIPAL THEATER(S): Poland
DECLARATION: March 1794, uprising declared
MAJOR ISSUES AND OBJECTIVES: Kościusko wanted to recover territory lost in the First and Second Partitions of Poland.
OUTCOME: The rebellion was crushed and Poland was totally dismembered by the Third Partition; Poland effectively ceased to exist as a nation.
APPROXIMATE MAXIMUM NUMBER OF MEN UNDER ARMS: Nationalists, 90,000 plus 50,000 peasants; Russians, 65,000; Prussians, 25,000
CASUALTIES: Nationalists, 29,000 killed or wounded; Russians, 9,100 killed or wounded; Prussians, 573 killed or wounded
TREATIES: Second Partition of Poland, January 23, 1793; Third Partition of Poland, October 24, 1795

Humiliated by the high-handed encroachments on their sovereignty by the major European powers during the first partitioning of Poland 20 years earlier (*see* the POLISH

CIVIL WAR (1768–1773), the Poles had reformed and strengthened their government, abolishing the trappings of what had been a hopelessly outmoded feudal state and replacing their weak elective monarchy with hereditary kingship. Now, afraid that Poland might indeed revive as a nation and fight to recover its land, Russia launched a pre-emptive invasion and concluded the second partition of Poland in 1793, which gave Russia most of eastern Poland and Prussia Gdansk and the region known as Great Poland.

Poland, not even invited to sign this set of agreements, broke out in a national revolt in 1794. Thaddeus Kościusko (1746–1817), a veteran of the American Revolution, led other exiled Polish nationalists in planning the rebellion from his headquarters in Leipzig, Germany.

Kościusko went to Cracow in March 1794, where he recruited the support of disaffected Polish army officers. This secured, he proclaimed a national uprising and assumed dictatorial powers. His first military objective was Russian-held Warsaw. During the advance on the Polish capital, he encountered Russian forces and defeated them. This victory inspired a general popular uprising.

Under Kościusko's leadership, three-quarters of the territory lost as a result of the First and Second Partitions was recovered. Although both Warsaw and Vilna were taken from foreign hands, a combined Prussian-Russian army defeated Kościusko at Kulm (Chelmno). When Cracow fell to the Russians on June 15, a panic spread among Poles in Warsaw, who feared the work of spies and traitors. The city was gripped by a rash of executions, until Kościusko personally restored order.

Warsaw girded for a siege, which lasted a month before Prussian and Russian forces suddenly lifted it in September 1794 (their presence was required to put down uprisings in Prussian-occupied areas of Poland).

By the fall of 1794, Kościusko had seized control of Great Poland, but he had lost Lithuania to Russia. At last, at the Battle of Maciejowice on October 10, 1794, Kościusko was defeated and taken prisoner. The rebellion collapsed both suddenly and violently when the Russian invaded the Warsaw suburb of Praga on November 3, 1794. The 22,000 Russian troops defeated the 25,000 Polish defenders, killing as many as 13,000 combatants and 7,000 noncombatants and taking 11,000 prisoners.

Poland was now subject to a Third Partition, concluded on October 24, 1795, which divided among Russia, Prussia, and Austria what remained after the Second Partition. In effect, Poland ceased to exist as a nation.

See also POLISH REBELLION (1715–1717); POLISH REBELLION (1830–1831).

Further reading: Norman Davies, *God's Playground: A History of Poland,* 2 vols. (New York: Columbia University Press, 1982); O. Halecki (with additional material by A. Polonsky and Thaddeus V. Grommada), *A History of Poland,* new ed. (New York: Dorset Press, 1992); W. F. Reddaway, et al., eds., *The Cambridge History of Poland,* 2 vols.

(reprint, Cambridge, UK: Cambridge University Press, 1971); Piotr Sefan Wandyez, *The Lands of Partitioned Poland* (Seattle: University of Washington Press, 1974).

Polish Rebellion (1830–1831)

PRINCIPAL COMBATANTS: Polish nationalists vs. Russia
PRINCIPAL THEATER(S): Poland
DECLARATION: Rebellion commenced on November 29, 1830.
MAJOR ISSUES AND OBJECTIVES: The rebels sought to free Poland from Russian control.
OUTCOME: The rebellion, disorganized, was ultimately crushed, and Poland was incorporated into Russia as a Russian state.
APPROXIMATE MAXIMUM NUMBER OF MEN UNDER ARMS: Nationalists, 81,000; Russians, 127,000
CASUALTIES: Nationalists, 15,000–20,000 killed; Russians, 15,000 killed
TREATIES: None

Called the November Insurrection to distinguish it from the Polish Rebellion (1863–1864), which became known as the January Insurrection, this conflict began when Russia's czar Nicholas I (1796–1855), hoping to take advantage of the French Revolution of 1830, made plans to invade France and Belgium using the Polish army, which he supposed to be under his autocratic control. But among the many conspiratorial revolutionary groups Poland was producing at the time, there was a secret society—the National Association—formed by Polish troops with the object of coordinating an uprising against Poland's Russian overlords. As a result of the FRENCH REVOLUTION (1830), the Polish rebels believed their efforts would receive strong support from France.

The rebellion broke out in Warsaw on November 20, 1830, when Polish officers and troops at the military academy acted on their fear of an imminent Russian takeover of the academy and, ultimately, the army itself in keeping with Nicholas's plan. Russian cavalry companies were attacked, and an assault on the Warsaw residence of Russian grand duke Constantine (1779–1831) was mounted. Soon, almost the entire Polish army, liberated convicts, and the general Polish citizenry joined in a chaotic uprising. The result was not a revolution, but mob violence on a massive scale. After Russian authorities fled for their lives, Polish general Josef Chlopicki (1771–1854) proclaimed a revolutionary dictatorship and declared that the Russian succession to the Polish throne was at an end.

Czar Nicholas I (1796–1855) responded to the Polish rebellion by sending large numbers of troops into the country. Despite some Polish successes, the Russians advanced deep into Poland but were fought to stand at the Battle of Grochow on February 25, 1831. The Russians went into winter quarters, and during the resulting lull in combat, the Poles, never well organized, began to fight among themselves, so that when the fighting resumed in the spring the rebels were considerably weakened. The Russians triumphed at the Battle of Ostroleka on May 26, 1831, then advanced on Warsaw, which fell to them on September 8, 1831. This rebellion collapsed, and rebel leaders fled the country.

The czar now cracked down on Poland harder than ever before. Poland was not merely annexed but incorporated into Russia as a Russian state. Nicholas I was determined to stamp out any vestiges of Polish nationality. His tyranny, however, only served to intensify already powerful Polish patriotism.

See also CRACOW INSURRECTION.

Further reading: Norman Davies, *God's Playground: A History of Poland,* 2 vols. (New York: Columbia University Press, 1982); O. Halecki (with additional material by A. Polonsky and Thaddeus V. Grommada), *A History of Poland,* new ed. (New York: Dorset Press, 1992); W. F. Reddaway, et al., eds., *The Cambridge History of Poland,* 2 vols. (reprint, Cambridge, UK: Cambridge University Press, 1971).

Polish Rebellion (1863–1864)

PRINCIPAL COMBATANTS: Polish nationalists vs. Russia
PRINCIPAL THEATER(S): Poland
DECLARATION: Rebellion proclaimed, January 22, 1863
MAJOR ISSUES AND OBJECTIVES: The nationalists wanted to liberate Poland from Russian control.
OUTCOME: Russia crushed the rebellion and made Poland a Russian province.
APPROXIMATE MAXIMUM NUMBER OF MEN UNDER ARMS: Unknown
CASUALTIES: Nationalists, 5,000–8,000 killed; Russians, 5,000 killed
TREATIES: None

The CRIMEAN WAR (1853–56) and turmoil caused by the Eastern Question (the threat to Europe's balance of power posed by the crumbling of the Ottoman Empire) led Russia's Czar Alexander II (1818–81) to take a more conciliatory stance toward Poland. Hoping to pacify the Poles, Alexander introduced a series of comparatively liberal reforms, but the salutary effect of these was mitigated by the autocratic policies and manner of the Russian authorities in Poland itself. By the beginning of the 1860s, even moderate Poles had been radicalized, and the country was gripped by mass demonstrations calling for independence. Once again seeking to placate the Poles, Alexander II installed his brother Constantine (1827–92) as viceroy in Warsaw, instructing him to give the Poles local voting rights. The Poles responded with an assassination attempt,

provoking Constantine to crack down by issuing an order to conscript Polish rebels into the czar's army. This provoked the rebels to form a revolutionary assembly, and on January 22, 1863, an armed rebellion erupted, quickly spreading across Poland and into Lithuania.

The rebellion took the form of a guerrilla war, poorly conducted by young men inexperienced in military matters, but nevertheless persistent. When the Western powers—Britain, France, and Austria—attempted to mediate, Russia reacted with greater determination to subdue Poland once and for all. French emperor Napoleon III (1808–73) promised the rebels military aid (he wished to counter Prussia's support of Russia in Poland) but failed to deliver adequately. By May 1864, superior Russian forces had suppressed the guerrillas and had put an end to the secret rebel governments set up in Warsaw and Lithuania. Russian authorities executed or exiled everyone suspected of having participated in the rebellion. All of Alexander's mildly liberal reforms were reversed. Poland was made a Russian province, and laws were enacted to stamp out Polish culture and language.

The net result of the January Insurrection, as it was called to distinguish it from the POLISH REBELLION (1830–1831), known as the November Insurrection, was to extinguish all hopes that the Poles might create an autonomous national state for the next 50 years.

Further reading: Norman Davies, *God's Playground: A History of Poland,* 2 vols. (New York: Columbia University Press, 1982); O. Halecki (with additional material by A. Polonsky and Thaddeus V. Grommada), *A History of Poland,* new ed. (New York: Dorset Press, 1992); W. F. Reddaway, et al., eds., *The Cambridge History of Poland,* 2 vols. (reprint, Cambridge, UK: Cambridge University Press, 1971).

Polish Succession, War of the (1733–1738)

PRINCIPAL COMBATANTS: Stanislaus I Leszczynski (backed by France, Spain, and Sardinia) vs. Augustus III (backed by Russia and Austria)
PRINCIPAL THEATER(S): Poland, Rhineland, Italy, and Austria
DECLARATION: October 10, 1733
MAJOR ISSUES AND OBJECTIVES: Succession to the Polish throne following the death of Augustus II
OUTCOME: After an Austrian victory in the decisive Battle of Bitonio, the supporters of Stanislaus yielded to the supporters of Augustus III, who became king of Poland. In addition, the war led to a redistribution of Italian territories and inflated Russia's influence over Poland.
APPROXIMATE MAXIMUM NUMBER OF MEN UNDER ARMS: In Poland—pro-Hapsburg forces: 30,000 Russians, 10,000 Saxons; pro-Stanislaus forces: large but unknown number of Poles and a small French reinforcement of 1,950. In the Rhineland—no estimates for the large French

invasion force or the overall Hapsburg resistance. In Italy—40,000 Spanish and 30,000 French-Sardinian troops; 50,000–60,000 Hapsburg forces.

CASUALTIES: At least 50,000 Frenchmen killed or wounded overall and more than 30,000 Austrians. Overall figures for other belligerents were not tabulated, although the Spanish lost 3,000 men at Bitonto alone.

TREATIES: Treaty of Vienna, November 18, 1738

When Poland's King Augustus II (1670–1733) died on February 1, 1733, Austria and Russia supported the succession of his son Frederick Augustus (1696–1763), elector of Saxony, to the throne. Most Poles, and certainly the major Polish nobles, preferred Stanislaus I Leszczynski (1677–1766), who, as the father-in-law of Louis XV (1710–74), had the backing of both France and Spain. In fact, Stanislaus had been the Poles' king once already for a brief five years after the Swedes, back in 1704, helped to depose Augustus in the Second (or Great) NORTHERN WAR—temporarily as it turned out. In any case, the Polish sejm (Diet, or parliament), consisting of some 12,000 delegates, on September 12 elected Stanislaus king.

This the Hapsburgs' ally, Russia, could not abide, and quickly dispatched an army 30,000 strong toward Warsaw. With the approach of the Russians, both Stanislaus and most of the Diet's delegates fled, the king, pursued by Russian and Saxon troops, to Danzig. Meanwhile, the Russians occupied the city and forced a rump parliament of some 3,000 to declare Frederick Augustus as Poland's new king, Augustus III, on October 5, 1733.

In response to the mobilization of the Russian army, France had formed anti-Hapsburg alliances with Sardinia on September 26 and Spain on November 7. They declared war on Austria on October 10. With some dispatch, Don Carlos (1716–88), the Spanish *infante* (heir apparent), led a Spanish army of 40,000 across Tuscany and the Papal States to Naples, defeated the Austrians at Bitonto on May 25, 1734, conquered Sicily, and was crowned king of Naples and Sicily (25 years later, he would become Spain's Charles III). The French war, however, did not proceed so smoothly. After overrunning Lorraine when they invaded the Rhineland, the French were effectively checked in southern Germany by the Hapsburg forces; the French-Sardinian forces invading Lombardy could not manage to take Mantua, and the small French contingent sent by sea to relieve the Russian siege of Danzig failed miserably.

Danzig fell in June 1734, but by then Stanislaus had escaped to Prussia. Although the Poles organized the Confederation of Dzików in November 1734 to support his cause, they were no match for the Russians and Augustus. Worse for the Poles, the Spaniards and the Sardinians fell to bickering, fracturing the Italian campaign of 1735. Worried that the British and the Dutch might join the fighting as Hapsburg allies, the French made a hasty, half-baked peace with Austria on October 3, 1735, which was followed by the definitive Treaty of Vienna on November 18, 1738. Don Carlos was allowed to retain Naples and Sicily but he had to give the Hapsburgs both Parma and Piacenza, which he had inherited in 1731, and to renounce his claims to Tuscany. Stanislaus renounced the Polish throne and was compensated for this with the dukedom of Lorraine. Augustus III was recognized as the rightful Polish king.

See also SPANISH-PORTUGUESE WAR (1735–1737).

Further reading: Norman Davies, *God's Playground: A History of Poland*, 2 vols. (New York: Columbia University Press, 1982); O. Halecki (with additional material by A. Polonsky and Thaddeus V. Grommada), *A History of Poland*, new ed. (New York: Dorset Press, 1992); W. F. Reddaway, et al., eds., *The Cambridge History of Poland*, 2 vols. (reprint, Cambridge, UK: Cambridge University Press, 1971).

Polish-Swedish War for Livonia, First
(1600–1611)

PRINCIPAL COMBATANTS: Sweden vs. Poland

PRINCIPAL THEATER(S): Livonia (Estonia and portions of Latvia)

DECLARATION: None

MAJOR ISSUES AND OBJECTIVES: Possession of Livonia

OUTCOME: Undecided; Sweden occupied parts of Livonia but failed to gain control of the region.

APPROXIMATE MAXIMUM NUMBER OF MEN UNDER ARMS: At the major Battle of Kirchholm, Sweden fielded 14,000 men, Poland 3,500

CASUALTIES: Unknown (but the Poles claimed 9,000 Swedish dead)

TREATIES: Armistice of 1611

Long an area of contention among Sweden, Poland, and Russia, the Baltic became the locus of fighting yet again when Sweden invaded and occupied most of Estonia and Livonia in 1600. They were halted by the Poles at the fortress city of Riga, where Herman Jan Karol Chodkiewicz (1560–1621) launched a counterattack, driving the Swedes out of most of Livonia with victories at Dorpat (Tartu) and Revel (Tallinn), but failing to secure complete control over the disputed region.

Then, in 1604, Charles IX (1550–1611), the newly declared and ambitious Swedish king, landed a fresh army of 14,000 in Estonia and marched on Riga to try his fortunes against Chodkiewicz. The two armies met at the battle of Kirchholm, where the Poles mustered only some 3,500 men—although 2,500 of them were horsemen in Poland's heavy cavalry, hailed as the best in Europe. They mounted a savage, reckless charge that swept the Swedes from the field and themselves forever into Polish history. They not only won the battle, they came very close to capturing Sweden's warrior king himself, and Polish chroniclers would soon be claiming that the bodies of some 9,000 Swedish soldiers littered the abandoned battlefield. Afterward, the war fizzled, and continued only in sporadic fighting until ended by truce in 1611.

See also POLISH-SWEDISH WAR FOR LIVONIA, SECOND.

Further reading: Norman Davies, *God's Playground: A History of Poland,* 2 vols. (New York: Columbia University Press, 1982); O. Halecki (with additional material by A. Polonsky and Thaddeus V. Grommada), *A History of Poland,* new ed. (New York: Dorset Press, 1992); W. F. Reddaway, et al., eds., *The Cambridge History of Poland,* 2 vols. (reprint, Cambridge, UK: Cambridge University Press, 1971).

Polish-Swedish War for Livonia, Second
(1617–1629)

PRINCIPAL COMBATANTS: Sweden vs. Poland
PRINCIPAL THEATER(S): Livonia (Estonia and portions of Latvia), Courland (southwestern Latvia), and northern Prussia
DECLARATION: None
MAJOR ISSUES AND OBJECTIVES: Possession of Livonia and Baltic ports
OUTCOME: Sweden triumphed, acquiring Livonia and the use of major Prussian ports.
APPROXIMATE MAXIMUM NUMBER OF MEN UNDER ARMS: Sweden: more than 32,000; Poland: 9,000; 7,000 Austrians.
CASUALTIES: Unknown, but deaths from disease far outnumbered combat casualties.
TREATIES: Truce of Altmark (1629)

The long Baltic Sea contest between the Poles and the Swedes flared up once again in 1617, six years after the death of Sweden's Charles IX (1550–1611) and the armistice that ended the First POLISH-SWEDISH WAR FOR LIVONIA. Charles's son, Gustavus II (1594–1632), having already faced Denmark from 1611 to 1613 in the War of KALMAR and fought the Russians in the inconclusive RUSSO-SWEDISH WAR (1613–1617), now turned to Poland, hoping to take advantage of the Poles' distractions with both the Russians and the Turks (see RUSSO-POLISH WAR [1609–1618] and POLISH-TURKISH WAR [1614–1621]). He quickly reconquered much of the Baltic coast of Livonia in 1617, then just as quickly arranged a two-year armistice. Come 1620, however, he was back, with an army of 16,000, which he led against Riga. The city fell in September of the following year, and Swedish forces overran all of Livonia and southwestern Latvia, then known as Cour-

land. From here, they invaded northern Prussia, taking much of that territory and posing a threat to Poland's Baltic outlet by 1626.

A Polish counterattack, led by Herman Stanislaws Koniecpolski (1591–1646), threatened these Swedish conquests, but in May 1627 Gustavus broke the Polish offensive at Tczew, where 9,000 Poles, including the famed Polish heavy cavalry that had destroyed his father's army a generation before, were routed. Gustavus then returned to Sweden to bring back to the Polish borderlands some 32,000 reinforcements, which in 1628 he used to drive south and extend his conquests. At this point, the Holy Roman Empire intervened, dispatching a corps of 7,000 men to the aid of Polish king Sigismund III (1566–1632) and halting the Swedish advance. The Baltic coast, however, remained in Gustavus's hands.

By 1628, the war became one of attrition and deadlock. Anxious to enter the THIRTY YEARS' WAR—Gustavus agreed to the Truce of Altmark in 1629, securing most of the conquests he had made during the war.

Further reading: Norman Davies, *God's Playground: A History of Poland,* 2 vols. (New York: Columbia University Press, 1982); O. Halecki (with additional material by A. Polonsky and Thaddeus V. Grommada), *A History of Poland,* new ed. (New York: Dorset Press, 1992); W. F. Reddaway, et al., eds., *The Cambridge History of Poland,* 2 vols. (reprint, Cambridge, UK: Cambridge University Press, 1971).

Polish-Turkish War (1484–1504)

PRINCIPAL COMBATANTS: Poland vs. Ottoman Empire and Moldavia
PRINCIPAL THEATER(S): Moldavia
DECLARATION: None
MAJOR ISSUES AND OBJECTIVES: Moldavia sought autonomy from both Poland and the Ottoman Empire.
OUTCOME: Combat between Poland and the Ottoman Empire ended indecisively with a truce. Moldavia achieved victory over the Poles but was forced to maintain its autonomy from the Ottoman Empire by paying an annual tribute to the sultan.
APPROXIMATE MAXIMUM NUMBER OF MEN UNDER ARMS: The largest single force was the Polish invasion army of 1485, 20,000 men.
CASUALTIES: Unknown
TREATIES: Truce of 1492 (Poland–Ottoman Empire), Truce of 1500 (Poland–Ottoman Empire); Treaty of 1504 (Moldavia–Ottoman Empire)

Moldavia, which Poland had annexed in the late 15th century during the reign of King Casimir IV (1427–92), became the subject of conflict between Poland and the

Ottoman Empire. In 1484, the Turkish navy took Kiliya at the mouth of the Danube River and Akkerman (Belgorod-Dnestovsky) at the mouth of the Dniester in an effort to sever Poland from outlets to the Black Sea. Casimir responded by forming an anti-Ottoman league and marched 20,000 troops into Moldavia to eject the Turks. From here, in 1485, he advanced against Kolomyya on the Pruth River. Cornered, Bayazid II (1447–1513), the Ottoman sultan, sued for peace. Although the disposition of the captured fortresses of both sides was never settled, Casimir and Bayazid concluded a truce.

The Polish-Ottoman truce ended with the death of Casimir in 1492. Sporadic fighting broke out, and in 1496 Poland's new king, John I Albert (1459–1501), Casimir's son, launched a major campaign that allied Poland with King Stephen (c. 1433–1504, Stephen the Great) of Moldavia. The objective was to keep the Turks out of Moldavia; however, Stephen came to believe that John I Albert wanted to depose him. Therefore, Moldavian forces resisted Polish intervention and defeated the Poles at the Battle of Suceava in 1497. Taking advantage of Stephen's preoccupation with his erstwhile allies, Ottoman forces invaded Moldavia, but finding the winter unusually severe, they withdrew in 1498 after fighting only a few minor engagements. Hostilities between the Poles and the Turks were definitively ended by a truce in 1500, but the Moldavians refused to sign on, and combat between them and the Ottomans continued at a low level until Stephen died in 1504. At that time, Moldavia agreed to pay the Ottoman sultan an annual tribute in exchange for autonomy.

Further reading: Norman Davies, *God's Playground: A History of Poland,* 2 vols. (New York: Columbia University Press, 1982); O. Halecki (with additional material by A. Polonsky and Thaddeus V. Grommada), *A History of Poland,* new ed. (New York: Dorset Press, 1992); W. F. Reddaway, et al., eds., *The Cambridge History of Poland,* 2 vols. (reprint, Cambridge, UK: Cambridge University Press, 1971).

Polish-Turkish War (1614–1621)

PRINCIPAL COMBATANTS: Poland vs. the Ottoman Empire
PRINCIPAL THEATER(S): Moldavia and Wallachia
DECLARATION: None
MAJOR ISSUES AND OBJECTIVES: Poland attempted to gain control of Moldavia and Wallachia from the Ottomans.
OUTCOME: The Ottoman Empire retained control of the area.
APPROXIMATE MAXIMUM NUMBER OF MEN UNDER ARMS: Maximum Polish forces 75,000; Ottoman forces were somewhat smaller.
CASUALTIES: Polish casualties in Moldavia approached 10,000 killed.
TREATIES: Truce of 1621

By the 17th century, the Ottomans were once again in control of Moldavia as well as Wallachia. Poland encouraged and aided anti-Ottoman rebellions in these areas. The Ottomans responded with fierce raids against the Polish Ukraine. To put an end to these, a 10,000-man Polish army under General Stanislas Zolkiewski (d. 1620) invaded Moldavia where, joined by Cossacks and Moldavians, it defeated a substantially more numerous Ottoman-Tatar force at the Battle of Jassy on September 20, 1620.

Osman II (1604–22), the Ottoman sultan, responded by marching an even larger force from Constantinople into Moldavia, which forced the Poles into retreat. Despite the Poles' attempt to withdraw, the Ottoman forces engaged them in Moldavia and destroyed the army, killing Zolkiewski. A new Polish army of 75,000 troops under Stanislas Lubomirski (1583–1641) fought to a bloody draw at the Battle of Chocim on the Dniester in 1621, prompting the sultan to agree to a truce. Although no further major battles were fought, sporadic raiding continued on both sides.

See also RUSSO-POLISH WAR (1609–1618); THIRTY YEARS' WAR.

Further reading: Norman Davies, *God's Playground: A History of Poland,* 2 vols. (New York: Columbia University Press, 1982); O. Halecki (with additional material by A. Polonsky and Thaddeus V. Grommada), *A History of Poland,* new ed. (New York: Dorset Press, 1992); W. F. Reddaway, et al., eds., *The Cambridge History of Poland,* 2 vols. (reprint, Cambridge, UK: Cambridge University Press, 1971).

Polish-Turkish War (1671–1677)

PRINCIPAL COMBATANTS: Poland vs. the Ottoman Empire
PRINCIPAL THEATER(S): Polish Ukraine
DECLARATION: None
MAJOR ISSUES AND OBJECTIVES: Poland sought to regain from the Ottoman Empire control of the Polish Ukraine.
OUTCOME: The Poles regained western Ukraine, but the Ottoman Empire retained the province of Podolia.
APPROXIMATE MAXIMUM NUMBER OF MEN UNDER ARMS: Ottoman Empire, as many as 250,000 men in a single campaign; the Poles commanded far fewer numbers—at Zorawno, the Ottoman Empire fielded 200,000 men to the Poles' 20,000.
CASUALTIES: Unknown
TREATIES: Treaty of Buczacz, 1672; Treaty of Zorawno, October 16, 1676

Polish forces were in the process of suppressing a Cossack rebellion in the Polish Ukraine when a massive force of a quarter-million Turks under Sultan Muhammad IV (1641–91) bore down on the much smaller force of John Sobieski (1624–96). As Sobieski retreated, the Turks took

Podolia province and, in 1672, occupied the fortress of Kamieniec. Unable to muster forces sufficiently large to counter the invasion, Polish king Michael (1638–73) signed the 1672 Treaty of Buczacz, ceding to the Ottoman Empire all of Podolia and relinquishing to an Ottoman protectorate the Polish Ukraine. However, the Polish parliament refused to ratify the treaty, and proud Poles rallied behind John Sobieski to resume the war.

Sobieski's troops scored a major triumph at the Battle of Chocim on November 11, 1673, and the Turks withdrew from Polish territory. King Michael had died the preceding day, so that when Sobieski returned to Warsaw, he was elected king, to reign as John III.

The Ottoman Turks were not finished, however. In 1675, 150,000 Turks and Tatars invaded and once again seized Podolia but were ejected by a much smaller Polish force at the Battle of Lvov. Nevertheless, the Turks pressed on with an augmented general invasion in 1676. John found himself unable to raise an army larger than 20,000 men to go up against the new 200,000-man invasion force. Incredibly, outnumbered 10 to 1, John defeated the invaders at the Battle of Zorawno in October 1676. The Ottoman defeat was not militarily definitive, but the sultan was so impressed by what John III had done that he agreed to the Treaty of Zorawno on October 16, 1676, by which the Ottoman Empire returned to Poland much of western Ukraine, retaining only Podolia.

See also RUSSO-POLISH WAR (1658–1667); RUSSO-TURKISH WAR (1678–1681).

Further reading: Norman Davies, *God's Playground: A History of Poland,* 2 vols. (New York: Columbia University Press, 1982); O. Halecki (with additional material by A. Polonsky and Thaddeus V. Grommada), *A History of Poland,* new ed. (New York: Dorset Press, 1992); W. F. Reddaway, et al., eds., *The Cambridge History of Poland,* 2 vols. (reprint, Cambridge, UK: Cambridge University Press, 1971).

Polish-Turkish War (1683–1688) *See* AUSTRO-TURKISH WAR (1683–1699).

Pompey-Pirate War (67 B.C.E.)

PRINCIPAL COMBATANTS: Roman forces under Pompey the Great vs. Mediterranean pirates
PRINCIPAL THEATER(S): Mediterranean coastal regions
DECLARATION: None
MAJOR ISSUES AND OBJECTIVES: Elimination of piracy in the region
OUTCOME: Pompey scored a rapid victory.
APPROXIMATE MAXIMUM NUMBER OF MEN UNDER ARMS: Unknown
CASUALTIES: Unknown
TREATIES: None

The Roman general and statesman Pompey the Great (106–48 B.C.E.) was commissioned by the Senate to campaign throughout the Mediterranean and its littorals (up to 50 miles inland) for the purpose of defeating the widespread piracy endemic to the region. Conducting a sweep of 90 days, Pompey routed the pirates who plagued the eastern and western Mediterranean. His brilliant victory earned him praise from the Senate—and a grant of dictatorial powers.

See also GALLIC WARS; LEPIDUS, REVOLT OF; MITHRADATIC WAR, THIRD; OCTAVIAN'S WAR AGAINST POMPEY; ROMAN CIVIL WAR, GREAT (50–45 B.C.E.); SECTORIAN WAR.

Further reading: Peter A. L. Greenhalgh, *Pompey: The Roman Alexander* (Columbia: University of Missouri Press, 1981).

Pontiac's Rebellion (Pontiac's Conspiracy; Pontiac's War) (1763–1764)

PRINCIPAL COMBATANTS: Ottawa, Delaware, Iroquois Indians vs. colonial British forces and settlers
PRINCIPAL THEATER(S): The Ohio country
DECLARATION: No formal declaration; on April 27, 1763, Pontiac urged Potawatomi and Huron to join his raid on British Detroit
MAJOR ISSUES AND OBJECTIVES: An attempt by an Indian confederation to reclaim lands lost in the French and Indian War
OUTCOME: Inconclusive; Pontiac gained no lands and was forced to pledge obedience to the king of England.
APPROXIMATE MAXIMUM NUMBER OF MEN UNDER ARMS: At Fort Detroit, May 1763: British, 120; Pontiac, 300
CASUALTIES: British forces entire garrisons wiped out at Fort Venango (June 16, 1763) and Fort Presque Isle (June 20, 1763); Delaware Indians, in addition to battle-induced casualties, suffered a smallpox epidemic when Simon Ecuyer presented their chiefs with smallpox-infected gifts.
TREATIES: September 7, 1764

The Ottawa chief Pontiac (1720–69), for whom the rebellion is named, was actually only one among several Indian leaders who collaborated in resistance to English encroachment on their land. The "rebellion"—a term born of the white perspective on the events—included Delaware, Iroquois (principally the Seneca), and Shawnee in addition to the Ottawa.

The conflict began with the fall of French-held Detroit to the British during the FRENCH AND INDIAN WAR on November 29, 1760, and General Jeffrey Amherst's (1717–97) decision (in February of the next year) to abolish the French custom of giving gifts to the Indians, in particular their supply of ammunition. Following the edict, a religious leader known as the Delaware Prophet began preaching that the Indians should reject all the ways of the white man. British military authorities interpreted the Delaware Prophet's preachings as part of a widespread conspiracy against forts and settlements. General Amherst dispatched Major Henry Gladwin (1729–91) with reinforcements to Detroit.

Perhaps this action forestalled the raids, for nothing happened until 1763, when France capitulated in the French and Indian War, ceding virtually all of its territory to Britain. This prompted Pontiac to call a grand council on April 27, 1763, urging the Potawatomi and Huron to join his Ottawa in an attack upon Detroit.

Pontiac planned to enter Fort Detroit, with some warriors, on pretext of making a social call, then, having gained entrance, commence battle. The operation was scheduled for May 7, but Gladwin learned of the plan and twice foiled it.

Frustrated, Pontiac began raiding the settlers in the vicinity of the fort, then, joined by Wyandot, Potawatomi, and Ojibwa, began firing into the fort itself. After six hours, the attackers withdrew.

Following this battle, on May 10, Pontiac called for a parley, and Captain Donald Campbell (c. 1735–63) left the fort to negotiate. No sooner was Campbell outside of the fort than he was seized by the Indians and held hostage. Pontiac massed a large number of warriors and demanded the surrender of the fort. When Gladwin refused, Pontiac laid siege while also ambushing and raiding settlers in the vicinity of the fort.

Pontiac also managed to win the support of French settlers and farmers and was able to unleash widespread attacks against many forts. On May 16, 1763, Fort Sandusky fell. On May 25, Fort Saint Joseph was taken. Two days later, Fort Miami (near present-day Fort Wayne, Indiana) was breached. On the 28th, a relief column bound for Detroit was ambushed, resulting in heavy casualties. On June 1, Fort Ouiatenon (Lafayette, Indiana) was taken. And Fort Michilimackinac, in Michigan, was overrun soon after.

Following the fall of Michilimackinac, attacks began farther east. Forts Pitt, Ligonier, and Bedford in Pennsylvania were all besieged but managed to hold out. About June 16, 1763, Senecas killed the entire 15- or 16-man garrison at Fort Venango (Franklin, Pennsylvania). On June 18, the Senecas moved on to Fort Le Boeuf (Waterford, Pennsylvania) and burned it. Joined by Ottawas, Hurons, and Chippewas, the Senecas attacked Fort Presque Isle (Erie, Pennsylvania) on June 20, torching it and killing the garrison after promising it safe conduct.

When a group of Delawares demanded the surrender of Fort Pitt on June 24, Simon Ecuyer, acting commander, refused. He summoned the Delaware chiefs to the fort for a parley and presented them with a handkerchief and two blankets—from the fort's smallpox-ridden hospital. This early instance of biological warfare not only caused the attackers to retreat but apparently created a smallpox epidemic within the tribe.

Forts Niagara and Detroit both survived long sieges, and Fort Detroit was periodically able to launch offensives, one of which, on July 4, 1763, resulted in the death of two Indians, including the nephew of Wasson, an important Chippewa chief.

On August 5, Colonel Henry Bouquet (1719–65) was leading a relief column to Fort Pitt, when he was attacked at Edge Hill, Pennsylvania, by a party of Delawares, Shawnees, Mingos, and Hurons. Despite being outnumbered, Bouquet prevailed on August 6, 1763. Called the Battle of Bushy Run, after the stream beside which Bouquet was camped, the battle turned the tide of Pontiac's Rebellion against the Indians.

The siege at Detroit was lifted in September, and, on October 3, 1763, Pontiac at last agreed to a peace, but a treaty was not concluded until September 7, 1764, following two more major English offensives. By virtue of the treaty, Pontiac and the other chiefs involved in the "rebellion" pledged obedience to the king of England.

The conflict had been costly, more on civilians, white and Indian alike, than on the military. At least 2,000 white settlers died. The Indian death toll, especially when the effects of smallpox are taken into consideration, was doubtless even greater.

As to Pontiac, he kept the peace until 1769, when he was assassinated as he was leaving a trading post in Cahokia, Illinois. The Indian who killed him may have been in the employ of local British traders.

Further reading: Francis Jennings, *Empire of Fortune: Crowns, Colonies, and Tribes in the Seven Years' War* (New York: Norton, 1988).

Pope's Rebellion   *See* Pueblo Uprising (1680).

Portuguese Conquest of Malacca
See Portuguese Conquests in India and the East Indies.

Portuguese Campaigns against Diu (1509–1547)

PRINCIPAL COMBATANTS: Portugal vs. Egypt and Gujarat
PRINCIPAL THEATER(S): Diu, an island in the Arabian Sea
DECLARATION: None
MAJOR ISSUES AND OBJECTIVES: Portugal wanted to seize Giu in order to control commerce on the Arabian Sea.

OUTCOME: Portugal conquered the island and other key ports.
APPROXIMATE MAXIMUM NUMBER OF MEN UNDER ARMS: Unknown
CASUALTIES: Unknown
TREATIES: None

The contest for preeminence in the East Indian spice trade pitted Portugal against Egyptian Muslim trading interests. In 1509, Portugal sank an Egyptian fleet off Diu, an island in the Arabian Sea that was a possession of the Indian Muslim state of Gujarat. But it wasn't until 1531 that the Portuguese mounted a major campaign against Diu itself, a land mass from which the possessor could control commerce on the Arabian Sea by dominating key ports. The island was defended by a combination of Egyptian and Gujarat troops, who resisted siege and attack for two years, before finally surrendering in 1533.

In 1538, the Gujaratis attempted to retake Diu, but failed, losing the ports of Goa and Daman in the process. During 1546–47, the Gujaratis mounted a new siege against Diu, which would have succeeded had not a Portuguese relief expedition made a timely arrival from Goa.

Further reading: James M. Anderson, *History of Portugal* (Westport, Conn.: Greenwood Publishing Group, 2000); Christopher Bell, *Portugal and the Quest for the Indies* (New York: Barnes and Noble, 1974); H. V. Livermore, *A New History of Portugal* (Cambridge, UK: Cambridge University Press, 1976); Antonio Henrique R. De Oliveria Marques, *History of Portugal* (New York: Columbia University Press, 1972).

Portuguese-Castilian War (1140)

PRINCIPAL COMBATANTS: Portugal vs. Castile and Léon
PRINCIPAL THEATER(S): Portugal
DECLARATION: None
MAJOR ISSUES AND OBJECTIVES: Independence of Portugal and the disposition of Galicia
OUTCOME: The matter was settled by a tournament in Portugal's favor.
APPROXIMATE MAXIMUM NUMBER OF MEN UNDER ARMS: Unknown
CASUALTIES: Unknown
TREATIES: Peace of Zamora, 1143

In 1139, Count Alfonso Henriques (1112–85) triumphed over the Moors at the Battle of Ourique and then declared Portuguese independence from Castile and Léon, which were ruled by his cousin, Alfonso VII (d. 1157). Thus Alfonso Henriques became the first king of Portugal. This achieved, he pursued the claim of his mother, Teresa (an illegitimate daughter of Alfonso VI of Castile), to western Galicia (northwest Spain). The following year, 1140, Alfonso VII responded by invading Portugal. With Spanish troops occupying his kingdom, Alfonso Henriques met with his cousin, and it was decided to settle the matter of the Galician claims not with a full-scale war but with a tournament between Portuguese and Castilian knights at Val-de-Vez. When the Portuguese champions proved triumphant, the Castilian king was as good as his word. The Galician matter was settled, and, by the Peace of Zamora in 1143, Alfonso VII formally recognized Alfonso Henriques as king of Portugal.

Further reading: James M. Anderson, *History of Portugal* (Westport, Conn.: Greenwood Publishing Group, 2000); H. V. Livermore, *A New History of Portugal* (Cambridge, UK: Cambridge University Press, 1976); Antonio Henrique R. De Oliveria Marques, *History of Portugal* (New York: Columbia University Press, 1972).

Portuguese-Castilian Wars (1369–1388)

PRINCIPAL COMBATANTS: Portugal (with English alliance) vs. Castile (with French alliance)
PRINCIPAL THEATER(S): Portugal and Castile
DECLARATION: None
MAJOR ISSUES AND OBJECTIVES: Independence of Portugal from Castile; succession to the Castilian throne
OUTCOME: Portugal become independent; the English claim to the Castilian throne was abandoned.
APPROXIMATE MAXIMUM NUMBER OF MEN UNDER ARMS: Unknown
CASUALTIES: Unknown
TREATIES: Peace of Alcoutin, 1371; Treaty of Windsor, 1386; Peace of Bayonne; Portuguese-Castilian peace treaty, 1411

The war between Portugal and Castile may be regarded as a phase of the HUNDRED YEARS' WAR. Pedro I (the Cruel; 1320–67), king of Portugal, disputed possession of the throne of Castile with Count Henry of Trastamara (1333–79). In 1367, however, Pedro fell to an assassin. Pedro's son Ferdinand I (the Handsome; 1345–83) succeeded to the Portuguese throne, whereupon a number of Castilian towns pledged allegiance to him. Despite this, in 1369, Henry of Trastamara assumed the Castilian throne as Henry II and decided on a preemptive strike against Portugal to prevent his rule from being progressively undermined.

Henry invaded, and by 1371 Ferdinand I, having suffered defeat, acceded to the Peace of Alcoutin, by which he ceded claim to Castile and made an arrangement to marry Henry's daughter. When, however, Ferdinand immediately demonstrated his bad faith by engaging in an affair with Leonor Teles (d. 1386), a married Portuguese noblewoman, Henry II invaded again.

Henry successfully besieged Lisbon, the Portuguese capital, and compelled Ferdinand not only to give up a number of castles but also to sever his alliance with England's John of Gaunt (1340–99), who had a claim to the Castilian throne through marriage to the elder daughter of Pedro I.

Thus circumstances stood in 1372. Seven years later, when Henry II died, Ferdinand merely picked up the English alliance where he had left it. In 1380, John of Gaunt allied with Ferdinand for an invasion of Castile. Gaunt's expeditionary force arrived the following year, led by his brother, Edmund of Langely (then earl of Cambridge, later duke of York) (1362–85), who betrothed his son Edward to Ferdinand's only legitimate child, Beatrice. But in August 1382, halfway through the campaign, Ferdinand come to terms with the Castilians, agreeing now to marry Beatrice to a Castilian prince, and John of Gaunt's forces withdrew.

Beatrice became the wife of the prematurely decrepit King John I (1358–90) of Castile; at least when Ferdinand died, Leonor Teles became regent in her name, and Castile claimed the Portuguese Crown when, in 1383, Ferdinand I—a failed sovereign detested by his people—died.

The people of Portugal effectively repudiated Ferdinand's capitulation to Castile and, defiantly opposing Castile's claim on Portugal, elevated the bastard son of Pedro I, John (grand master of Aviz; 1357–1433) to the position of defender of the realm. The popular forces drove Leonor Teles out of Lisbon. She fled to Santarem, where she was met by Castilian invaders in 1384. They sent her packing to a convent for her protection.

The Castilian invaders laid siege to Lisbon, but the onset of plague and almost universal opposition from the people of Portugal caused the siege to collapse. King John I and his forces returned to Castile.

With the Castilians out of the country, the Portuguese Cortes (parliament) elevated John of Aviz to the Portuguese throne on April 6, 1385. He led forces in a series of sieges against pockets of resistance to his rule. This action moved John I of Castile to form an alliance with France and, once again, invade Portugal.

The invasion culminated in the Battle of Aljubarrota, outside of Lisbon, fought on August 14, 1385. Although the Portuguese were outnumbered by the combined Castilian and French forces, their English archers were instrumental in defeating the invaders, who, once again, withdrew from the country. This battle may be said to have secured the independence of Portugal.

The Treaty of Windsor, concluded in 1386, established a long-term alliance between England and Portugal, giving John of Gaunt the backing he needed to assert his claim to the throne of Castile. With Portuguese aid, he invaded Castile in 1387 but was repulsed. He settled for a compromise in 1388 by concluding the Peace of Bayonne, by which he renounced his claim to Castile in return for a cash settlement. Although Portugal had concluded a truce with Castile in 1387, a full and formal treaty was not signed until much later, 1411.

Further reading: James M. Anderson, *History of Portugal* (Westport, Conn.: Greenwood Publishing Group, 2000); Christopher Bell, *Portugal and the Quest for the Indies* (New York: Barnes and Noble, 1974); H. V. Livermore, *A New History of Portugal* (Cambridge, UK: Cambridge University Press, 1976); Antonio Henrique R. De Oliveria Marques, *History of Portugal* (New York: Columbia University Press, 1972).

Portuguese Civil War (1449)

PRINCIPAL COMBATANTS: Alfonso V vs. the duke of Braganza and Pedro, duke of Coimbra
PRINCIPAL THEATER(S): Coimbra, Portugal
DECLARATION: None
MAJOR ISSUES AND OBJECTIVES: The king's brother persuaded him that Pedro was disloyal.
OUTCOME: Pedro and his supporters were defeated in battle and slain.
APPROXIMATE MAXIMUM NUMBER OF MEN UNDER ARMS: Alfonso fielded as many as 30,000 men against a far inferior force.
CASUALTIES: Numbers unknown, but Pedro and almost all of his army were killed.
TREATIES: None

When Alfonso V (1432–81) became king of Portugal in 1438, he was still a child, and his uncle, Pedro (d. 1449), duke of Coimbra, became regent, despite the opposition of the powerful Braganza family, related to the king through the duke of Braganza, also named Alfonso (d. 1461), who was an illegitimate son of John I of Aviz (1357–1433). Although Pedro managed to arrange for the young king to marry his daughter Isabella in 1446, the Braganzas continued to poison Alfonso V's mind against his uncle, who was forced to resign his regency. Seeking to avoid confrontation, Pedro withdrew to his lands in Coimbra. The Braganzas, however, did not cease their calumnies, and an increasingly manipulated Alfonso V demanded the surrender of Pedro's arms. When Pedro refused, the duke of Braganza urged the king to go to war. Braganza's troops were soundly defeated by Pedro's partisans at the Battle of Panella. Alfonso then raised an army of 30,000 and advanced to the Alfarrobeira River where, on May 21, 1449, Alfonso defeated the much smaller forces of Pedro, who, together with most of his army, fell in battle.

Further reading: James M. Anderson, *History of Portugal* (Westport, Conn.: Greenwood Publishing Group,

2000); H. V. Livermore, *A New History of Portugal* (Cambridge, UK: Cambridge University Press, 1976); Antonio Henrique R. De Oliveria Marques, *History of Portugal* (New York: Columbia University Press, 1972).

Portuguese Civil War (1481–1483)

PRINCIPAL COMBATANTS: King John II vs. various nobles
PRINCIPAL THEATER(S): Portugal
DECLARATION: None
MAJOR ISSUES AND OBJECTIVES: The king sought to curtail the power of a corrupt nobility.
OUTCOME: With popular support, King John II suppressed the abuses practiced by the nobles.
APPROXIMATE MAXIMUM NUMBER OF MEN UNDER ARMS: Unknown
CASUALTIES: Unknown
TREATIES: None

When John II (1455–95) ascended the Portuguese throne in 1481, he reacted perhaps to the open-handed and negligent rule of his father, Alfonso V (1432–81), who had been something of a puppet to the powerful Braganza family. He immediately set about curtailing the power of a nobility grown not only powerful but also quite corrupt by convening the Cortes (parliament) at Évora in 1481. The king forced restrictions on the great families and demanded a detailed oath of homage from them. When they responded by joining conspiracies against the king, John countered through a merciless purge, meting out death on the field as well as judicial executions. Indeed, the suspicion of treason served the king's purposes very well, allowing him to arrest Fernando II, duke of Braganza, and many of his followers. Although it was rumored the king had killed two of his conspiratorial cousins on the spot, that is, in his own castle, the duke at least was sentenced to death and executed in 1484 at Évora. The ruthless suppression of the aristocracy had lasted three years, and enjoyed strong support from the Portuguese middle class and peasantry, who were tired of inefficient, exploitative, and generally abusive government.

Further reading: James M. Anderson, *History of Portugal* (Westport, Conn.: Greenwood Publishing Group, 2000); Christopher Bell, *Portugal and the Quest for the Indies* (New York: Barnes and Noble, 1974); H. V. Livermore, *A New History of Portugal* (Cambridge, UK: Cambridge University Press, 1976); Antonio Henrique R. De Oliveria Marques, *History of Portugal* (New York: Columbia University Press, 1972); A. J. R. Russell-Wood, *The Portuguese Empire, 1415–1808* (reprint, Baltimore: Johns Hopkins University Press, 1998).

Portuguese Civil War (1823–1824)

PRINCIPAL COMBATANTS: King John VI vs. his rebellious son, Dom Miguel
PRINCIPAL THEATER(S): Portugal
DECLARATION: None
MAJOR ISSUES AND OBJECTIVES: Restoration of an absolutist monarchy—under Dom Miguel
OUTCOME: Failing to obtain popular support, Dom Miguel ultimately stepped down and was exiled.
APPROXIMATE MAXIMUM NUMBER OF MEN UNDER ARMS: Unknown
CASUALTIES: Unknown
TREATIES: None

Despite two major royalist attempts to overthrow the constitutional monarchy and reinstall an absolutist government, Portugal drafted a democratic constitution in 1823.

The first rebellion began in Vila Real; the second, bigger, insurrection originated in Vila Franca de Xira and was sponsored by Dom Miguel (1802–66), third son of King John VI (1769–1826). On April 30, 1824, Dom Miguel and his forces attacked Lisbon, receiving support from the troops of the Lisbon garrison, who acclaimed him king. Dom Miguel brought in his mother, Queen Carlota Joaquina, and all the advisers of John VI fled the capital. In the meantime, Dom Miguel arrested Lisbon's chief of police and others loyal to John VI, then installed into high military office his followers.

What Dom Miguel had failed to calculate, however, was the loyalty of the people toward John VI. Without popular support, Dom Miguel's coup collapsed, and the young man was compelled to beseech forgiveness from his father. John VI responded by exiling Dom Miguel to Vienna. John VI now authorized the constitution.

See also BRAZILIAN WAR OF INDEPENDENCE; MIGUELITE WARS; OPORTO, REVOLUTION AT.

Further reading: James M. Anderson, *History of Portugal* (Westport, Conn.: Greenwood Publishing Group, 2000); H. V. Livermore, *A New History of Portugal* (Cambridge, UK: Cambridge University Press, 1976); Antonio Henrique R. De Oliveria Marques, *History of Portugal* (New York: Columbia University Press, 1972).

Portuguese Civil War (1826–1827)

PRINCIPAL COMBATANTS: Miguelites vs. constitutionalists (backed by Great Britain)
PRINCIPAL THEATER(S): Portugal
DECLARATION: None
MAJOR ISSUES AND OBJECTIVES: The Miguelites supported an absolute monarchy for Portugal, while the constitutionalists supported a constitutional monarchy.

OUTCOME: With British aid, the constitutionalists triumphed, forcing Dom Miguel to accept constitutional government.
APPROXIMATE MAXIMUM NUMBER OF MEN UNDER ARMS: Unknown; the British interventionist force, highly effective, consisted of only 5,000 men.
CASUALTIES: Unknown
TREATIES: None

With the death of John VI (1769–1826), his son, Pedro I (1798–1834) of Brazil, was recognized as King Pedro IV of Portugal. After promulgating a constitutional charter for Portugal, emulating Britain's parliamentary democracy, Pedro remained emperor of Brazil but abdicated the Portuguese throne in favor of his infant daughter Maria da Gloria (1819–53), with the proviso that she become betrothed to Dom Miguel (1802–66), his younger brother. Dom Miguel was pledged to accept constitutional government; however, his absolutist supporters, dubbed Miguelites, clashed with the constitutionalists under General John Carlos de Oliveira e Daun Saldanha (1791–1876). The Miguelites overran and occupied Lisbon, while the constitutionalists operated out of Oporto. In 1827, a 5,000-man British expeditionary force landed at Lisbon and engaged the Miguelites. Only after Miguel agreed to honor Pedro's constitutional charter did the British leave. Miguel was duly appointed regent.

See also MIGUELITE WARS; OPORTO, REVOLUTION AT; PORTUGUESE CIVIL WAR (1823–1824).

Further reading: James M. Anderson, *History of Portugal* (Westport, Conn.: Greenwood Publishing Group, 2000); H. V. Livermore, *A New History of Portugal* (Cambridge, UK: Cambridge University Press, 1976); Antonio Henrique R. De Oliveria Marques, *History of Portugal* (New York: Columbia University Press, 1972).

Portuguese Conquest of Ceuta (1415)

PRINCIPAL COMBATANTS: Portugal vs. the Moors
PRINCIPAL THEATER(S): Ceuta, Gibraltar Strait
DECLARATION: None
MAJOR ISSUES AND OBJECTIVES: Portugal wanted a toehold in Africa.
OUTCOME: Ceuta, poorly defended at the time, fell.
APPROXIMATE MAXIMUM NUMBER OF MEN UNDER ARMS: Unknown
CASUALTIES: Unknown
TREATIES: None

When John of Aviz (1357–1433) came to the throne of Portugal during the PORTUGUESE-CASTILIAN WARS (1369–1388), he founded a new dynasty that, despite the misgivings of many among the nobility and clergy, was immensely popular with the common folk. As he consolidated his hold on Portugal, his conquests came to represent what historians describe as the victory of the country's national yearnings over the feudal attachments of the traditional order. Because so many of the older nobles held tenaciously to Castile, John I rewarded his followers at their (and the crown's) expense, fostering a commerce that continued to flourish with the marriage of his daughter, Isabella, to Philip the Good (1396–1467) of Burgundy and the consequent closer trade relations between Portugal and Flanders. Almost naturally, then, with the onset of peace in 1388, John and his soldiers of fortune turned to Moorish Africa as an outlet for their frontiering ways and launched the great age of Portuguese expansion. Standing smack in their path was Ceuta, the fortress guarding the Strait of Gibraltar.

When the Moorish sultan left Ceuta all but undefended to put down a revolt in the Maghreb (part of Morocco, Algeria, and Tunisia), King John I of Portugal acted. Seeking in part to gain a little favor, as a crusader, with a standoffish pope and the still seething Spanish, John set sail with his sons from Lisbon on July 25, 1415. Among the boys was young Prince Henry (1394–1460), the king's third son, who John hoped would gain some valuable experience with the expedition and who would become known to history as Henry the Navigator. The fleet anchored at Tarifa, then launched the assault. Despite the skeleton crew, the fortress withstood the first attack. Townspeople as well as Moors from the mountains came to the defense of the fortress, but it yielded to a second Portuguese assault on August 24, 1415. From this foothold, Portuguese conquest would expand onto the mainland of Africa, and Ceuta became a redoubtable Portuguese outpost, which withstood repeated assaults by the Moors and others.

Further reading: James M. Anderson, *History of Portugal* (Westport, Conn.: Greenwood Publishing Group, 2000); C. R. Boxer, *The Portuguese Seaborne Empire, 1415–1825* (New York: Knopf, 1969); James Duffy, *Portuguese Africa* (Cambridge, Mass.: Harvard University Press, 1968); H. V. Livermore, *A New History of Portugal* (Cambridge, UK: Cambridge University Press, 1976); Antonio Henrique R. De Oliveria Marques, *History of Portugal* (New York: Columbia University Press, 1972); A. J. R. Russell-Wood, *The Portuguese Empire, 1415–1808* (reprint, Baltimore: Johns Hopkins University Press, 1998).

Portuguese Conquests in India and the East Indies (1500–1545)

PRINCIPAL COMBATANTS: Portugal vs. Indian, Egyptian, and Ottoman Empire
PRINCIPAL THEATER(S): India and the East Indies
DECLARATION: None

MAJOR ISSUES AND OBJECTIVES: Conquest and commercial domination
OUTCOME: The Portuguese gained control of large parts of coastal India and Ceylon (Sri Lanka)
APPROXIMATE MAXIMUM NUMBER OF MEN UNDER ARMS: Unknown
CASUALTIES: Unknown
TREATIES: Alliances among the Muslim powers

On June 7, 1494, the Treaty of Tordesillas asserted Portugal's right—as opposed to Spain's—to the exploration of Africa and the seaway to India, and three years later Vasco da Gama (c. 1469–1524) set sail with four ships on the first expedition to India. They reached Calicut on the Malabar coastline in the spring of 1498 and set up a trading post. In the autumn of 1499, the survivors sailed into Lisbon, laden with all the rich spices and trade goods of the Orient, and Portuguese exploration became an opiate of national ambitions in the East. Converting the pagans and crushing the infidels became the clarion call of a Portugal intent on muscling its way into the Muslim trade monopoly along the Mediterranean and growing rich beyond imagining off the traffic in exotic merchandise.

Portugal's plan called for no immediate colonies. Instead, Portuguese sailors would establish commercial trading posts from the East Indies to the Arabian Sea and protect them with garrisons patrolled by the well-armed Portuguese fleet. But when the first Portuguese viceroy, Francisco de Almeida (c. 1450–1510), arrived in 1505, he made immediately clear the impact of the region's new traders by backing the Cochin rajah against the Calicut sultan. The Portuguese may not yet have been colonizers officially, but they fired off the cannon of every departing export-laden ship as a kind of fireworks display to impress the local Hindus and deflate the local Muslims with Portugal's imperial majesty.

Little wonder that Mahmud Begarha, sultan of Gujarat, formed an alliance with Kansu al-Gauri of Egypt in 1508 to counter the Portuguese assault. This led to the naval Battle of Dabul later in the year. Although the battle ended inconclusively, Almeida's son Lorenzo (d. 1508) was killed. While Almeida made plans to avenge Lorenzo's death, Afonso de Albuquerque (1453–1515) arrived in India to replace Almeida as viceroy. Almeida responded by imprisoning Albuquerque, then, during January–February 1509, he raided Muslim ports, razing Goa and Dabul. In February, Almeida attacked the Muslim fleet at Diu. Achieving total surprise, he destroyed the fleet, then returned to Cochin. The battle reestablished Portuguese supremacy at sea, the chief ingredient of Portugal's newfound wealth and power in the East. As for Almeida, his vengeance secured, he at last heeded the Portuguese king's order to acknowledge Albuquerque as the new viceroy.

Now installed, Albuquerque led a military expedition to Malaya and captured Goa in 1510. The following year, he took Malacca, establishing a military base from which he sent expeditions to the Moluccas during 1512–14. In the meantime, Goa rebelled against the Portuguese invaders, but Albuquerque managed to put down the revolt.

In 1513, the viceroy led an expedition to Aden, to which he unsuccessfully laid siege, then, two years later, took Ormuz, which would serve as a Portuguese stronghold for a century and a half. Despite his triumphs on behalf of Portugal, Albuquerque was recalled in 1515. He died on the voyage back to Europe.

Albuquerque had established a powerful Portuguese presence in India and the Indies. A great fort was built at Columbo, Ceylon (Sri Lanka), in 1518, which Portuguese traders used to establish an important presence in Burma. The new Portuguese viceroy, Numbo da Cunha (fl. 16th century), led an expedition of conquest to Diu, which fell to him in 1528.

During 1536–37, Sultan Bahadur of Gujarat (fl. 16th century) formed an alliance with the Ottoman Turks. In response, the Portuguese viceroy invited Bahadur to negotiations—only to have him captured and assassinated. Despite the death of Bahadur, the Ottoman fleet coordinated with a Gujarat land force to attack and lay siege to Diu. The Portuguese defenders managed to repulse the attackers. It was 1546 before a new Indian-Ottoman alliance was concluded, but Muslim forces repeatedly failed to evict the Portuguese.

Further reading: James M. Anderson, *History of Portugal* (Westport, Conn.: Greenwood Publishing Group, 2000); Christopher Bell, *Portugal and the Quest for the Indies* (New York: Barnes and Noble, 1974); C. R. Boxer, *The Portuguese Seaborne Empire, 1415–1825* (New York: Knopf, 1969); James Duffy, *Portuguese Africa* (Cambridge, Mass.: Harvard University Press, 1968); H. V. Livermore, *A New History of Portugal* (Cambridge, UK: Cambridge University Press, 1976); Antonio Henrique R. De Oliveria Marques, *History of Portugal* (New York: Columbia University Press, 1972); A. J. R. Russell-Wood, *The Portuguese Empire, 1415–1808* (reprint, Baltimore: Johns Hopkins University Press, 1998).

Portuguese-Dutch Wars in the East Indies
(1601–1641)

PRINCIPAL COMBATANTS: Netherlands vs. Portugal
PRINCIPAL THEATER(S): East Indies and coastal India
DECLARATION: None
MAJOR ISSUES AND OBJECTIVES: Domination of trade (chiefly spices)
OUTCOME: Over the course of four decades, the Dutch displaced the Portuguese as masters of the East India trade.

APPROXIMATE MAXIMUM NUMBER OF MEN UNDER ARMS:
Extremely variable
CASUALTIES: Unknown
TREATIES: Armistice of 1608

At the beginning of the 16th century the Portuguese had broken the Muslim monopoly on trade with the Orient (*see* PORTUGUESE CONQUESTS IN INDIA AND THE EAST INDIES). They controlled Goa as the chief port of western India; Hormuz, the key to the Persian Gulf; and Malacca, the gateway from the Indian Ocean to the South China Sea. Portugal maintained a string of fortified trading posts along the coast of East Africa and on the Indian gulf, as well as on the shores of Ceylon. The Portuguese had established trading settlements from Bengal to China, and they were the major foreign trade influence in the Spice Islands. If never in total control of the Oriental trade, they certainly dominated it until the joining of the Portuguese and the Spanish Crowns deprived the Dutch of their traditional trade with Lisbon and sent them seeking spices at their source. In 1601, the Dutch made the diplomatically critical move of concluding an alliance with the ruler of Ceylon (Sri Lanka). Dutch and Ceylonese forces defeated the Portuguese on the island, driving them off.

In 1602, Dutch naval forces defeated the Portuguese fleet near the Banda Islands in east Indonesia. Three years after this, in 1605, the Portuguese were forced off the island of Amboina (Ambon), and the Dutch compelled the Portuguese to agree to a 12-year armistice. In 1619, the Dutch returned to the offensive, taking and destroying the Javanese town of Jakarta and building Batavia adjacent to it, a walled fortress town that became headquarters of the powerful Dutch East India Company.

Batavia was more than a trading center. It became military headquarters for a sustained war against the remaining Portuguese interests in the East Indies. Also subject to attack were the British and any native powers that resisted Dutch domination. Through a combination of naval and land offensives, the Dutch acquired full control over Amboina, Banda, Ceylon, Java, and Ternate, as well as lesser areas. In this way, they came to dominate the East Indian spice trade.

With Dutch power consolidated in the East Indies, the Dutch launched attacks on Portuguese India and on Point de Galle, the Portuguese port-stronghold in Ceylon. This bastion fell to the Dutch in 1640. Emboldened by this victory, Dutch forces laid siege to Malacca, the most important Portuguese port on the southern Malay Peninsula. After enduring a long siege, the city fell to the Dutch in 1641. This marked the end of Portuguese hegemony in the East Indies and the culmination of Dutch supremacy there.

Further reading: James M. Anderson, *History of Portugal* (Westport, Conn.: Greenwood Publishing Group,

2000); Christopher Bell, *Portugal and the Quest for the Indies* (New York: Barnes and Noble, 1974); C. R. Boxer, *The Portuguese Seaborne Empire, 1415–1825* (New York: Knopf, 1969); James Duffy, *Portuguese Africa* (Cambridge, Mass.: Harvard University Press, 1968); H. V. Livermore, *A New History of Portugal* (Cambridge, UK: Cambridge University Press, 1976); Antonio Henrique R. De Oliveria Marques, *History of Portugal* (New York: Columbia University Press, 1972); A. J. R. Russell-Wood, *The Portuguese Empire, 1415–1808* (reprint, Baltimore: Johns Hopkins University Press, 1998).

Portuguese-Mogul War (1631–1632)

PRINCIPAL COMBATANTS: Moguls vs. Portuguese
PRINCIPAL THEATER(S): Hugli, Bengal
DECLARATION: None
MAJOR ISSUES AND OBJECTIVES: The Moguls sought to crush the Portuguese traders, who had monopolized Bengal trade and oppressed the natives.
OUTCOME: The major Portuguese trading base of Hugli was taken.
APPROXIMATE MAXIMUM NUMBER OF MEN UNDER ARMS:
Moguls, 150,000; Portuguese, 1,100 defenders of Hugli
CASUALTIES: Moguls, 1,000 killed; Portuguese, all of the defenders were either killed in battle or subsequently executed; most of the civilian inhabitants of Hugli were killed as well.
TREATIES: None

From Hugli, in the Ganges-Brahmaputra delta, the Portuguese had been conducting an immensely profitable Indian trade since 1537. Portuguese interests enjoyed a monopoly on salt production and the tobacco trade and, in fact, managed most of Bengal's trade, cutting the Moguls out of the profits. Even worse, Portuguese traders routinely kidnaped Muslim as well as Hindu children and sold them into slavery.

At last, on June 24, 1631, Shah Jahan (1592–1666), the Mogul emperor, sent 150,000 troops under Qasim Kahn, the governor of Bengal, against Hugli, which was defended by a mere 300 Portuguese and a native Christian force of 700. Shah Jahan's army held Hugli under siege for three months before it finally collapsed. Many of the townspeople drowned in an effort to escape by boat. Only 400 people survived to surrender, and these were subsequently put to death (in 1635) for refusing to convert to Islam. About 1,000 of Shah Jahan's troops were killed in the assault on Hugli, which was greatly reduced in importance as a trading port.

Further reading: James M. Anderson, *History of Portugal* (Westport, Conn.: Greenwood Publishing Group, 2000); Christopher Bell, *Portugal and the Quest for the*

Indies (New York: Barnes and Noble, 1974); C. R. Boxer, *The Portuguese Seaborne Empire, 1415–1825* (New York: Knopf, 1969); Antonio Henrique R. De Oliveria Marques, *History of Portugal* (New York: Columbia University Press, 1972); H. V. Livermore, *A New History of Portugal* (Cambridge: Cambridge University Press, 1976); A. J. R. Russell-Wood, *The Portuguese Empire, 1415–1808* (reprint, Baltimore: Johns Hopkins University Press, 1998).

Portuguese-Moroccan War (1458–1471)

PRINCIPAL COMBATANTS: Portugal vs. Muslims in Morocco
PRINCIPAL THEATER(S): Morocco
DECLARATION: None
MAJOR ISSUES AND OBJECTIVES: Alfonso V the African of Portugal wanted to defeat the Muslims in the name of Christianity.
OUTCOME: The Portuguese acquired Tangier in 1471.
APPROXIMATE MAXIMUM NUMBER OF MEN UNDER ARMS: The Portuguese fielded a maximum of 30,000 troops; Muslim numbers, unknown.
CASUALTIES: Portuguese casualties were heavy in the first assault on Tangier, with battle deaths in excess of 10,000.
TREATIES: None

After the fall of Constantinople to the Ottomans in 1453, Portugal's King Alfonso V (the African; 1432–81) and Castile's King Henry IV (1425–74) united in a crusade against the Muslims. Henry's task was to attack the Moors in Granada, Spain, and Alfonso was to conquer the Muslims in Morocco, Africa. In the first of three military expeditions against Morocco, Alfonso led 25,000 men across the Strait of Gibraltar, with the objective of attacking Tangier. Advisers, however, persuaded him to lay siege to Alcázarquivir (Ksar el-Kebir) instead. He did so, and the city quickly fell to him.

Alfonso was slow to capitalize on his triumph. He did not launch his second expedition, the attack on Tangier, until 1464, and when he did, he met with catastrophe. His army was badly defeated, and he himself barely escaped. Meanwhile, that same year Henry reconquered Gibraltar from the Muslims. Alfonso's defeat discouraged him from continuing his crusade, but when the Portuguese sailors in 1468 captured and burned Anfa, a Muslim part on the Atlantic at the site of modern Casablanca, a reinvigorated Alfonso led about 30,000 men on his third and final expedition, a new assault on Tangier. Massacring Muslim civilians along the way, Alfonso's troops assembled before a city that had been deserted by its terrified inhabitants. Alfonso seized it. Castile, meanwhile, despite Henry's conquest, collapsed into political chaos, as factions among the nobility fell to feuding in the absence of a strong monarch.

See also SPANISH CHRISTIAN–MUSLIM WAR (1481–1492).

Further reading: James M. Anderson, *History of Portugal* (Westport, Conn.: Greenwood Publishing Group, 2000); C. R. Boxer, *The Portuguese Seaborne Empire, 1415–1825* (New York: Knopf, 1969); Antonio Henrique R. De Oliveria Marques, *History of Portugal* (New York: Columbia University Press, 1972); James Duffy, *Portuguese Africa* (Cambridge, Mass.: Harvard University Press, 1968); H. V. Livermore, *A New History of Portugal* (Cambridge, UK: Cambridge University Press, 1976); A. J. R. Russell-Wood, *The Portuguese Empire, 1415–1808* (reprint, Baltimore: Johns Hopkins University Press, 1998).

Portuguese-Moroccan War (1578)

PRINCIPAL COMBATANTS: Portugal vs. Muslim Morocco
PRINCIPAL THEATER(S): Morocco
DECLARATION: None
MAJOR ISSUES AND OBJECTIVES: King Sebastian of Portugal wanted to overthrow the Muslim sultan and install a pro-Christian pretender.
OUTCOME: Total defeat for Portugal
APPROXIMATE MAXIMUM NUMBER OF MEN UNDER ARMS: Portugal, 25,000; Morocco, 70,000
CASUALTIES: Portugal suffered losses of 8,000 dead, including Sebastian and the pretender to the throne of Fez; 15,000 were taken prisoner.
TREATIES: None

In 1578, contrary to the wishes of Pope Gregory XIII (1502–85) and King Philip II (1527–98) of Spain, Portugal's king Sebastian (1554–78)—a religious zealot, who wished to subject Muslim Morocco to Christian rule—led 25,000 mostly mercenary troops in a crusade to replace Morocco's current sultan, 'Abd al-Malik (d. 1578), with a more pliable pretender, the former, now deposed sultan, al-Mutawakkil (d. 1578). Landing at Tangier, weighed down by artillery and an army unfamiliar with desert warfare, Sebastian encountered the far superior, 50,000- to 70,000-strong, forces of Sharif 'Abd al-Malik at Ksar el-Kebir (Alcázarquivir). On August 4, 1578, at the so-called Battle of the Three Kings (the sultan, the pretender, and Sebastian), the Portuguese advance withered under the fire of Morocco's mounted harquebusiers, and as the Christians retreated to Larache on the coast, many drowned or surrendered in crossing the Wadi al-Makhazin, which was at high tide. Among the casualties were Sebastian and the pretender, both of whom drowned.

Many in a stunned Portugal refused to believe that Sebastian had been slain, and in later years, he was looked on as a savior who would someday return to rescue Portugal from Spanish domination. In reality, the death of the head-strong young Sebastian, without heir, brought the Portuguese empire under Spanish control for the next 60 years.

On the other hand, although the already seriously ill 'Abd al-Malik, died the morning after the battle (thus the European name of the battle), the victory provided the Muslim soldiery with a rich booty and Morocco a new prestige in Europe, enhancing both its diplomacy and its commerce.

See also SPANISH-PORTUGUESE WAR (1580–1589).

Further reading: James M. Anderson, *History of Portugal* (Westport, Conn.: Greenwood, 2000); Christopher Bell, *Portugal and the Quest for the Indies* (New York: Barnes and Noble, 1974); C. R. Boxer, *The Portuguese Seaborne Empire, 1415–1825* (New York: Knopf, 1969); Antonio Henrique R. De Oliveria Marques, *History of Portugal* (New York: Columbia University Press, 1972); James Duffy, *Portuguese Africa* (Cambridge, Mass.: Harvard University Press, 1968); H. V. Livermore, *A New History of Portugal* (Cambridge: Cambridge University Press, 1976); A. J. R. Russell-Wood, *The Portuguese Empire, 1415–1808* (reprint, Baltimore: Johns Hopkins University Press, 1998).

Portuguese North Java Wars (1535–1600)

PRINCIPAL COMBATANTS: Portugal vs. the Muslim states in northern Java
PRINCIPAL THEATER(S): Northern Java
DECLARATION: None
MAJOR ISSUES AND OBJECTIVES: Conquest and commercial domination
OUTCOME: Through a long series of very small wars, the Portuguese gained control of northern Java.
APPROXIMATE MAXIMUM NUMBER OF MEN UNDER ARMS: Unknown
CASUALTIES: Unknown
TREATIES: None

During the 16th century, Portugal established itself as the chief power in Malaysia by capturing Malacca, using it as a base from which to create a well-defended trading empire throughout the region. For the last two-thirds of the century, Portuguese trading interests chronically warred with the small Muslim states that constituted northern Java. These wars consisted of largely inconclusive battles, in which, nevertheless, the Portuguese almost always prevailed. Over a long period, the power of the Muslim rulers in this region diminished, so that Portugal could claim victory in the region.

See also PORTUGUESE CONQUESTS IN INDIA AND THE EAST INDIES.

Further reading: C. R. Boxer, *The Portuguese Seaborne Empire* (New York: Knopf, 1969); A. J. R. Russell-Wood, *The Portuguese Empire, 1415–1808* (reprint, Baltimore: Johns Hopkins University Press, 1998).

Portuguese-Omani Wars in East Africa (1652–1730)

PRINCIPAL COMBATANTS: Portugal vs. Oman (and native African forces)
PRINCIPAL THEATER(S): East Africa and coastal islands
DECLARATION: None
MAJOR ISSUES AND OBJECTIVES: For the natives, political liberation; for Portugal and Omani, commercial domination of the East African trade in slaves and gold
OUTCOME: Both the Portuguese and Omani presence in the region was diminished, then removed.
APPROXIMATE MAXIMUM NUMBER OF MEN UNDER ARMS: Extremely variable
CASUALTIES: Unknown
TREATIES: Various agreements between native rulers and Portuguese and Omani interests

Although commonly practiced in Africa itself, especially by the Arabs, and once widespread in the ancient Mediterranean world, slavery had nearly died out in medieval Europe before it was revived by the Portuguese during the time of Henry the Navigator (1394–1460). Beginning with his enslavement of Berbers in 1442, Portugal's intrepid explorers populated Cape Verde, Fernando Po (now Bioko), and São Tomé mostly with black slaves, many of whom they eventually took home. As Europe expanded into the New World, the traffic in slaves expanded, too, along with the new discoveries of gold that helped fund it. By the mid-17th century, based on the island of Mombasa, off the coast of Kenya, the Portuguese controlled the East African slave trade and the trade in gold. Suffering under the Portuguese yoke for many years, the Mombasan natives appealed in 1652 to the sultan of Oman (on the Arabian Peninsula) for military aid in driving off the Portuguese. The sultan dispatched a fleet to attack Zanzibar, a Portuguese-controlled island south of Mombasa. This began a long state of warfare between the Omanis and the Portuguese, which was both a war for trade domination—the prize being the commercial exploitation of the African east coast—and a religious conflict between the forces of Islam and the forces of Catholic Christianity.

The next major phase of combat came in 1687, when a former ruling house of Pate, an island nation off Kenya, asked the Portuguese to help it regain its realm from Omani control. The Portuguese suffered from poor intelligence information. Approaching Pate, they were confronted by a substantially superior Omani fleet, which forced them to retreat to Mombasa.

In 1696, the Omani fleet attacked Mombasa, laying siege against Fort Jesus. The spectacular siege spanned three years before the beleaguered Portuguese finally capitulated, having lost all trading outlets north of Cape Delgado. The Omani ruler installed a garrison at Fort Jesus, which mutinied in 1727. Seeing that the Omani presence was weakening, the king of Pate again appealed to Portugal for help in finally driving the Omanis from his island. Oman itself was beset by internal disorder and could not reinforce Pate or Mombasa. The Portuguese easily prevailed against them and quickly reestablished a slave trading post at Zanzibar.

Inevitably, conflict developed between the natives and the returned Portuguese. A massive native uprising laid siege to the Portuguese installations in Zanzibar, Mombasa, and Pate, and by 1730 all of the Portuguese had again fled. They retreated to Portuguese colonies in western India (Goa) and in Mozambique (Portuguese East Africa).

Further reading: James Duffy, *Portuguese Africa* (Cambridge, Mass.: Harvard University Press, 1968).

Portuguese Revolution (1640)

PRINCIPAL COMBATANTS: Portugal vs. Spain
PRINCIPAL THEATER(S): Lisbon, Braga, and Évora, Portugal
DECLARATION: None
MAJOR ISSUES AND OBJECTIVES: The people of Portugal wanted an end to Spanish overlordship.
OUTCOME: A popular uprising ejected the Spanish colonial government and replaced it with a Portuguese king.
APPROXIMATE MAXIMUM NUMBER OF MEN UNDER ARMS: Unknown
CASUALTIES: Unknown
TREATIES: None

Restive under the Spanish yoke, the people of Lisbon, Braga, and Évora rioted in 1640 and rallied behind the leadership of John (1605–56), duke of Braganza, the highest noble in Portugal. The Spanish overlords summoned the nobles and army of Portugal to Madrid, but, by that time, under John's leadership, the popular uprising had expelled the Spanish governor from Portugal (on December 1, 1640). Instead of obediently traveling to Madrid, the nobles in Portugal's Cortes (parliament) offered John the Portuguese crown, and he accepted, becoming King John IV two weeks after the fall of the Spanish colonial government.

Further reading: H. V. Livermore, *A New History of Portugal,* 2nd ed. (New York: Cambridge University Press, 1976).

Portuguese-Spanish Wars *See* SPANISH-PORTUGUESE PHILIPPINE WARS; SPANISH-PORTUGUESE WAR (1580–1589); SPANISH-PORTUGUESE WAR (1641–1644); SPANISH-PORTUGUESE WAR (1657–1668); SPANISH-PORTUGUESE WAR (1735–1737); SPANISH-PORTUGUESE WAR (1762).

Portuguese War against Ternate (1550–1588)

PRINCIPAL COMBATANTS: Portugal vs. Ternate
PRINCIPAL THEATER(S): Ternate, Indonesia
DECLARATION: None
MAJOR ISSUES AND OBJECTIVES: The sultan of Ternate sought to drive out the Portuguese and to exact vengeance for the murder of Sultan Hairun.
OUTCOME: The Portuguese were defeated on Ternate.
APPROXIMATE MAXIMUM NUMBER OF MEN UNDER ARMS: Unknown
CASUALTIES: More than 500 Portuguese died on a siege of their garrison.
TREATIES: None

In the 16th century, Portugal expanded its commercial empire into the Arabian Sea and the East Indies, seeking trade in pepper and other spices, and defending that trade with ample amounts of gunpowder. By mid-century, Portugal had set its sites on the island of Ternate, in the Malaccas. There, Portuguese forces did battle with the army of Sultan Hairun (d. 1570) off and on for years, beginning in 1550. In 1570, Portuguese agents assassinated Hairun, an act that escalated warfare under the sultan's successor Baabullah (fl. 1570s), who pledged undying enmity for the Portuguese. The vengeful new ruler attacked and laid siege to the Portuguese fort on Ternate. The installation held out for four years, from 1570 to 1574, before Baabullah finally breached its defenses and massacred the entire garrison. Beleaguered in Malacca, which was held under siege by the Achanese, and under attack elsewhere, the Portuguese had been unable to relieve the siege of Ternate. In April 1606 a combined Spanish-Portuguese fleet recaptured the island, which the Portuguese held until the Dutch began to dominate the South Pacific in 1595.

Further reading: C. R. Boxer, *The Portuguese Seaborne Empire* (New York: Knopf, 1969).

Potato War *See* BAVARIAN SUCCESSION, WAR OF THE.

Pottawatomie Massacre *See* KANSAS-MISSOURI BORDER WARS.

Powhatan War (1622–1644)

PRINCIPAL COMBATANTS: Indians of the Powhatan Confederacy vs. England's Virginia colony
PRINCIPAL THEATER(S): Virginia
DECLARATION: No formal declaration
MAJOR ISSUES AND OBJECTIVES: The Indians were resisting colonial incursions onto Powhatan lands.
OUTCOME: Powhatan agreed to formal boundaries to pledge loyalty to the king of England, and to submit their choice of future tribal chiefs for the Virginia governor's approval.
APPROXIMATE MAXIMUM NUMBER OF MEN UNDER ARMS: Unknown
CASUALTIES: Virginians, 347 in 1622, 400 in 1644; Powhatan, 200 after being served poisoned food
TREATIES: Signed in October 1646

The English colonists who settled Jamestown, Virginia, encountered Indians who were members of a remarkable confederacy of at least 32 Algonquian-speaking tribes (a total of perhaps 10,000 people) distributed among 200 villages and held together by a revered chief named Wahun-sen-a-cawh (or Wahunsonacock) (c. 1550–1618), whom the English named Powhatan after the town in which he lived. Generations of schoolchildren have learned the story of Captain John Smith (1580–1631), who accompanied the first 105 Jamestown settlers. Captured by some of Powhatan's men in December 1607, he was taken before Powhatan and saved from execution by the chief's 13-year-old daughter Pocahontas (c. 1595–1617), who also facilitated Smith's adoption by the tribe. Once Smith had won Powhatan's favor, he was able to obtain corn from the Indians, which saved the colonists from starvation.

The settlers were remarkably ungrateful to the Indians and, although an active trade grew up between them, the Virginians and the Powhatans (as the member tribes were known) distrusted and resented one another. Friction between the two groups increased in proportion to the colonists' hunger for land as the Virginians began cultivating tobacco for export. Planters wanted to usurp the Indians' already cleared and cultivated fields and even proposed taking Powhatan prisoner in order to gain control of his people.

Although that scheme was not carried out, Sir Thomas Gates (fl. 1585–1621) (who later became the colony's governor) murdered some Indian priests, and, in 1613, Samuel Argall (1572–1626), mariner and colonist, kidnapped Pocahontas, who was held hostage for a time. Her subsequent marriage to colonist John Rolfe (1585–c. 1622) may well have forestalled the war that these and other outrages might have otherwise provoked. In any event, whatever Powhatan may have felt about the English, he valued trade with them and managed to preserve peace until his death in 1618.

Powhatan's half brother Opechancanough (d. 1644) succeeded him as sachem of the confederation, and, although he promised friendship with the colonists, war was not long in coming.

In 1622 a planter named Morgan disappeared. His servants claimed that an Indian named Nemattanow (or Nematanou), prominent among the Powhatans, had ordered his death, and Nemattanow was killed. For this, Opechancanough vowed revenge, and the colonists likewise hurled threats. Opechancanough apparently backed down, renewing his pledge of friendship only to launch an all-out raid on every English settlement along the James River on Good Friday, March 22, 1622. By the end of that day, 347 settlers had been killed—about one-third of the colony.

In response to the assault, colonist patrols attacked Indians indiscriminately up and down the coast. There were no formal battles or campaigns, just 14 years of murder and raiding, punctuated by occasional peace conferences. It was not until 1632 that an uneasy truce, born of mutual exhaustion, was concluded. It lasted 12 years, until April 18, 1644, when Opechancanough, now old and blind, launched a coordinated offensive against the James River settlements. More than 400 colonists were killed in a series of lightning raids, but, as quickly as they had come, the attackers withdrew.

Virginia's Governor William Berkeley (1606–77) retaliated with a campaign of burning and destruction, but by March 1646, the Virginia assembly had had enough of war, and it negotiated with the Indians. Berkeley, who differed sharply with the assembly's decision, personally led a party of soldiers to Opechancanough's village, took the aged sachem prisoner, and brought him back to Jamestown. Although Berkeley commanded that the chief be treated with courtesy and respect, a mob taunted him, and one of the men who was guarding him shot him dead.

With the death of Opechancanough, Berkeley agreed with the assembly to conclude a peace, which they did in October 1646. Under that peace, the Powhatans pledged loyalty to the king of England, agreed that the appointment of future chiefs would be approved by the governor, and agreed to formal boundaries.

Further reading: Alan Axelrod, *Chronicle of the Indian Wars: From Colonial Times to Wounded Knee* (New York: Prentice Hall General Reference, 1993); James Axtell, *The Rise and Fall of the Powhatan Empire: Indians in Seventeenth-Century Virginia* (Williamsburg, Va.: Colonial Williamsburg Foundation, 1995); Philip L. Barbour, *The Three Worlds of Captain John Smith* (Boston: Houghton Mifflin, 1964).

Praguerie (1440)

PRINCIPAL COMBATANTS: French nobility vs. King Charles VII of France
PRINCIPAL THEATER(S): Poitou and Bourbon
DECLARATION: None
MAJOR ISSUES AND OBJECTIVES: The nobles challenged the authority of the king.
OUTCOME: The rebellious nobles were defeated and agreed to an uneasy peace.
APPROXIMATE MAXIMUM NUMBER OF MEN UNDER ARMS: Unknown
CASUALTIES: Unknown
TREATIES: Peace of Cusset, 1440

French nobles rebelled against their king, Charles VII (1403–61), in emulation of a similar revolt in Prague, Bohemia—hence the name. The spirit of rebellion—in France as well as Bohemia—was fostered by the general political instability created by the HUNDRED YEARS' WAR, which diminished the authority of the king and enhanced the power of the nobles. As early as the spring of 1437, some of those princes excluded from the royal council had begun plotting a seizure of power. They did not manage to pull it off, but their schemes provoked King Charles into attempting to curb further mischief by forbidding the aristocracy to raise and maintain private armies. This, the first of his great military reforms, threatened the captains of the realm's mercenary military. Many nobles, including the dauphin (Charles's own son, later Louis XI, 1423–83), united with these mercenary leaders in a revolt at Poitou in February 1440. Royalist forces put down the rebels there, sending them into Bourbon country, where, under Charles, duke of Bourbon (1401–56), they were again defeated.

The rebels negotiated the Peace of Cusset, which ended the uprising and secured generous treatment of the rebels. However, conflict between the king and the nobles continued for decades.

See also ANGLO-FRENCH WAR (1475); BURGUNDIAN-SWISS WAR (1447–1477); HUSSITE WARS; ROSES, WARS OF THE.

Further reading: David Potter, *A History of France, 1460–1560: The Emergence of a Nation-State* (London: Macmillan, 1995); Jonathan Sumption, *The Hundred Years' War* (Philadelphia: University of Pennsylvania Press, 1995).

Procopius's Eastern Revolt (366)

PRINCIPAL COMBATANTS: Procopius's rebels vs. Eastern Roman Empire
PRINCIPAL THEATER(S): Constantinople
DECLARATION: None
MAJOR ISSUES AND OBJECTIVES: Procopius usurped the throne of the Eastern Empire.
OUTCOME: The revolt was short-lived; Procopius was defeated and executed.
APPROXIMATE MAXIMUM NUMBER OF MEN UNDER ARMS: Unknown
CASUALTIES: Unknown
TREATIES: None

The Roman general Procopius (d. 366), in service to Julian (331–363, known to history as "The Apostate"), seized control of Constantinople and its environs in 366. He then declared himself emperor but was attacked and defeated by generals Arbetio (fl. fourth century) and Lupicinus (fl. fourth century) in service of Valens (c. 328–378), brother of Valentinian I (321–375) and coemperor of the Roman Empire. Procopius was captured and summarily executed.

Further reading: Noel Emmanuel Lenski, *Failure of Empire: Valens and the Roman State in the Fourth Century A.D.* (Berkeley: University of California Press, 2002).

Pueblos, Conquest of the *See* SPANISH CONQUEST OF THE PUEBLOS.

Pueblo Uprising (Popé's Rebellion) (1680)

PRINCIPAL COMBATANTS: Pueblo Indians vs. Spanish colonizers
PRINCIPAL THEATER(S): Pueblo country of present-day Arizona and New Mexico
DECLARATION: No formal declaration
MAJOR ISSUES AND OBJECTIVES: The Pueblo Indians attempted to overthrow Spanish rule.
OUTCOME: Inconclusive; after chasing the Spanish to present-day El Paso, Popé's oppressive rule lasted eight years; once the Spanish regained control of Santa Fe, all pueblos submitted to Spanish rule within four years.
APPROXIMATE MAXIMUM NUMBER OF MEN UNDER ARMS: For the Pueblo assault on Santa Fe, 500; for the Spanish, about 50
CASUALTIES: Spanish, 400 settlers, 21 missionaries; Pueblos, unknown
TREATIES: None

The Spanish conquerors of the American Southwest combined a zealous concern for the souls of the native population—dispatching an army of missionaries and erecting scores of missions—with a heartless policy of exploitation of labor through the *encomienda* system, by which each colonist was granted designated Indian families—sometimes the inhabitants of several towns—from whom he could exact labor as well as commodity tribute. By the middle of the 17th century, after 50 years of life under this system, the Pueblo Indians concluded a desperate alliance with their hereditary enemies, the Apaches (the name itself is derived from the Zuni word for "enemy"), and made several attempts at rebellion, but were defeated each time.

During the 1670s, the Apaches and Pueblos launched an all-out campaign of guerrilla terrorism throughout the Spanish Southwest. Two years of this activity virtually strangled Spanish colonial trade, and Governor Antonio de Otermin (fl. 1677–83) acted against those he deemed most responsible for the rebelliousness, arresting 47 Pueblo "medicine men," three of whom he hanged and the remainder imprisoned. Among the latter was Popé (d. c. 1688), from the important Tewa Pueblo.

Popé was released after several years and went into hiding in Taos, where he secretly organized a large-scale, highly coordinated rebellion.

It was an ambitious project, not only because absolute secrecy was vital, but also because none of the pueblo towns would act without the unanimous consent of its council, and that meant Popé had to persuade a wide variety of individuals to participate. Once this was accomplished, he had to coordinate the strike among the widely dispersed pueblos, for he realized that the only hope for success lay in coordinated action.

Popé dispatched runners to the various towns, each bearing a knotted cord designed so that the last knot would be untied in each pueblo on the day set for the revolt: August 13, 1680. When, despite his precautions (including the murder of a loose-tongued brother-in-law), word of the plot leaked out, Popé launched the assault on the 10th.

Despite the change in plan, the rebellion proved devastating. The Taos, Pecos, and Acoma missions were burned to the ground and the priests killed. Lesser missions also fell, and scores of haciendas were destroyed. On August 15, Popé and his army of 200 advanced on Santa Fe, the colonial capital, killing 400 settlers and 21 of 33 missionaries. Although the Santa Fe garrison was outnumbered 10 to 1, the 50 defenders did have a brass cannon, with which they held Popé at bay for four days. But then the city fell.

Popé entered Santa Fe and installed himself in the palace Governor Otermin had hurriedly evacuated on August 21. Before his onslaught, some 2,500 settlers fled far downriver as far as present-day El Paso, Texas, abandoning all their property.

Like so many "liberators" before and after him, Popé became a dictator, if anything, more corrupt and oppressive than any Spaniard had been. For eight years he plundered and taxed his people, ruling them with terror. When Popé died c. 1688, the pueblos were in a chronic state of civil war and were easy pickings for the Spanish.

In 1689, the Zia Pueblo fell to colonial forces, and in 1692, Governor Don Diego da Vargas (fl. 1691–97) retook Santa Fe. Within another four years the pueblos had again submitted to Spanish rule—with the single exception of the Hopis, whom the Spanish seem simply to have overlooked.

Further reading: Jack D. Forbes, *Apache, Navajo, and Spaniard* (Norman: University of Oklahoma Press, 1960); Charles Wilson Hackett, *Revolt of the Pueblo Indians and Oterman's Attempted Reconquest, 1680–1682*, 2 vols. (Albuquerque: University of New Mexico Press, 1942); Robert Silverberg, *The Pueblo Revolt* (New York: Weybright and Talley, 1970).

Puerto Rico, Spanish Conquest of

See SPANISH CONQUEST OF PUERTO RICO.

Pugachev's Revolt (1773–1774)

PRINCIPAL COMBATANTS: Peasant rebels led by Pugachev vs. the armies of Catherine II of Russia
PRINCIPAL THEATER(S): Steppe region of Russia
DECLARATION: None
MAJOR ISSUES AND OBJECTIVES: Pugachev claimed to be the rightful czar and promised to abolish serfdom and end oppression.
OUTCOME: The rebellion was crushed and Pugachev executed.
APPROXIMATE MAXIMUM NUMBER OF MEN UNDER ARMS: Pugachev's forces, 15,000; government forces, unknown
CASUALTIES: About 20,000 of the 200,000 rebels who took part in the revolt were killed. At Ufa, 75 government troops were killed or wounded; at Fort Tatischev, 2,000 killed; at Kazan, 291 killed or wounded.
TREATIES: None

After Czar Peter III (1728–62) was secretly murdered by the courtiers of Catherine II (the Great; 1729–96) during the RUSSIAN REVOLUTION (1762), a number of pretenders had appeared, hoping to lead the Russian peasants against a German-born empress they despised. One of these, a Volga Cossack named Fedot Bogomolov (d. 1772) appeared, claiming to be the missing Peter and displaying the "czar's signs," scars in the shape of a cross. His revolt, however, was quickly crushed, and he was captured, brutally tortured and mutilated, and sent into exile in Siberia, dying en route.

The same year saw by far the most successful of these Cossack revolts raised against Catherine. In November 1772, a man named Emelyan Ivanovich Pugachev (1726–75) appeared among the Yaik Cossacks, claiming to be the "deposed" czar. In September 1773, Pugachev emerged from the steppes east of the Volga, backed by an army of 4,000, seized Fort Tatischev, with its 1,400 defenders, and executed all the officers. Immediately, Bashkir tribesmen and factory peasants flooded into his camp, and by the end of the year Pugachev commanded some 15,000 rebels.

It was a ragtag bunch—1,500 Cossacks, 5,000 tribesmen, 1,000 workers, and the rest made up of serfs, Tatars, and Kalmyks—but they had 100 cannon, and by 1774, they were ready to attack and laid siege to the Ural River towns of Ufa and Orenberg. These failed, but Catherine's imperial forces were at first unable to halt the growing rebellion, and Pugachev attacked and ravaged Kazan and then Saratov.

As news of these actions spread through the countryside, the oppressed lower orders of Russia began to see Pugachev as their savior. But he could not long sustain his rabble in the field. An imperial army under Count Aleksandr Suvorov (1729–1800) crushed Pugachev's forces at Tzadtsyn (Volgograd) in September 1774. Pugachev himself was captured but managed to escape, only to suffer betrayal at the hands of one of his own lieutenants. Recaptured, he was brought to Moscow and executed in 1775. His rebellion prompted a reactionary backlash, which actually bolstered the practice of serfdom in Russia.

Further reading: Simon Dixon, *Catherine the Great* (New York: Longman, 2001); Aleksandr Sergeevich Pushkin, *The History of Pugachev*, trans. Earl Sampson (London: Phoenix Press, 2001).

Punic War, First (264–241 B.C.E.)

PRINCIPAL COMBATANTS: Rome vs. Carthage
PRINCIPAL THEATER(S): Sicily and the Mediterranean Sea
DECLARATION: None
MAJOR ISSUES AND OBJECTIVES: Rome and Carthage fought for control of the island of Sicily.
OUTCOME: Rome won control of western Sicily and forced Carthage to pay a large indemnity.
APPROXIMATE MAXIMUM NUMBER OF MEN UNDER ARMS: Unknown
CASUALTIES: Unknown
TREATIES: None

The Battle of Messina in Sicily in 264 B.C.E. precipitated full-scale war between Rome and Carthage. This battle began after an attack by the Syracusans, under Hieron II (d. 216 B.C.E.), and the Carthaginians on the Mamertimes, the Campanian mercenaries hired by Syracuse to hold the seaport of Messina. The Mamertimes called on Rome for help, and the Carthaginians took control of the city. The Roman army then repelled the Carthaginians, and the Syracusans allied themselves with Rome. The Romans invaded western Sicily and besieged Agrigentum, a Carthaginian stronghold.

Carthage sent Hanno (fl. third century B.C.E.) with an army to relieve Agrigentum in 262, but he was defeated. At that point, Rome controlled most of the island of Sicily.

At Mylae in 260, the Roman fleet won a battle against the Carthaginians by using new methods of naval warfare—the corvus, a narrow plank employed to form a bridge to the enemy ship, and fore and aft turrets from which missiles were hurled. After invading the islands of Corsica and Sardinia, Rome turned her attention to northern Africa. Setting sail with about 150,000 soldiers and sailors, a Roman fleet of 330 ships clashed with the Carthaginians at Cape Ecnomus off the coast of Sicily. After a decisive victory, the Romans continued toward Carthage and landed 20,000 troops under M. Atilius Regulus (fl. third century B.C.E.), who won a victory at the Battle of Adys in 256 and offered terms to the Carthaginians. These terms, however, were so severe that the Carthaginians rejected them and continued fighting. To bolster their strength, the Carthaginians engaged the aid of Xanthippus and a band of Greek mercenaries.

The hiring of Xanthippus proved to be beneficial to the Carthaginians. At the Battle of Tunis in 255, he defeated Regulus by using his cavalry, elephants, and phalanx of Greek mercenaries to good advantage. Approximately 2,500 Romans managed to escape back to their ships.

The following year, Carthage reinforced her strongholds on Sicily and recaptured Agrigentum. Suffering from the loss of nearly 100,000 soldiers when the Roman fleet went down in a storm, Rome nevertheless mounted an amphibious assault at Panormus in northwestern Sicily. In 251, at the Battle of Panormus, the Roman consul L. Caecilius Metellus (d. 221 B.C.E.) defeated the Carthaginian general Hasdrubal (d. 221 B.C.E.), who lost his entire force of elephants in Sicily. The Carthaginians sued for peace and sent the Roman general Regulus, who had been held hostage since the Battle of Tunis, to Rome to negotiate terms. Legend holds that Regulus advised his fellow Romans to reject Carthage's proposals and then returned voluntarily to Carthage to honor his parole. He was then tortured to death.

The next major engagement took place at Drepanum. The Roman and Carthaginian fleets, each of about 100 warships, fought a battle that resulted in the loss of 93 Roman ships and 8,000 men, and a victory for Carthage. The Carthaginian commander Hamilcar Barcas (c. 270–228 B.C.E.) then repulsed the Romans at Eryx. Barcas fought off Roman assaults in western Sicily for the next five years, between 247 and 242. Rome continued to rebuild her military force and in 242 captured the Carthaginian strongholds of Lilybaeum and Drepanum.

The final battle of the First Punic War occurred on the Aegates Islands in 241. The Roman commander, L. Lutatius Catulus (fl. third century B.C.E.), won a decisive victory, sinking 50 Carthaginian ships and capturing 70 others. The Carthaginians sued for peace, evacuated Sicily, and agreed to pay an indemnity of 3,200 talents over the next 10 years. Rome continued to hold western Sicily as her first overseas province, whereas Syracuse remained in control of the eastern portion of the island.

See also PUNIC WAR, SECOND; PUNIC WAR, THIRD.

Further reading: Nigel Bagnall, *Punic Wars* (London: Trafalgar Square, 1991); Brian Caven, *Punic Wars* (London: Palgrave Macmillan, 1980); Adrian Goldsworthy, *The Punic Wars* (London: Cassell, 2001); J. F. Lazenby, *The First Punic War: A Military History* (Stanford, Calif.: Stanford University Press, 1996).

Punic War, Second (219–202 B.C.E.)

PRINCIPAL COMBATANTS: Rome vs. Carthage
PRINCIPAL THEATER(S): Spain, Africa, and Italy
DECLARATION: None
MAJOR ISSUES AND OBJECTIVES: Carthage, under the leadership of Hannibal, sought revenge for her loss in the First Punic War with Rome.
OUTCOME: Rome defeated Carthage and extracted from her a large indemnity and a promise to keep the peace.

APPROXIMATE MAXIMUM NUMBER OF MEN UNDER ARMS: Carthaginians, forces, 59,000; Romans, 87,000
CASUALTIES: At Trebia River, Carthaginians, 5,000; Romans, 30,000. At Lake Trasimene, 30,000 Romans. At Cannae, Carthaginians, 6,000; Romans, 54,000. At Zama, Carthaginians, 35,000
TREATIES: None

After being defeated in the First PUNIC WAR, Carthage relinquished her claims to Sicily and established a colony in eastern Spain. Known as New Carthage, the colony was ruled first by the Carthaginian general Hamilcar Barca (c. 270–228 B.C.E.), who had been victorious in the first war at Eryx and in western Sicily. When the general's son, Hannibal (247–183 B.C.E.), became ruler of the colony in 221, he set out to punish Italy for the crippling defeat Carthage suffered at her hands in the earlier conflict. In 221, he besieged Saguntum, the only city in Spain south of the Ebro River not under Carthage's control. Saguntum, a Greek stronghold, was an ally of Rome, and when Hannibal refused to call off the siege, Rome declared war on Carthage. After an eight-month siege, Hannibal stormed Saguntum, thereby capturing the city from which he would launch his invasion of Rome.

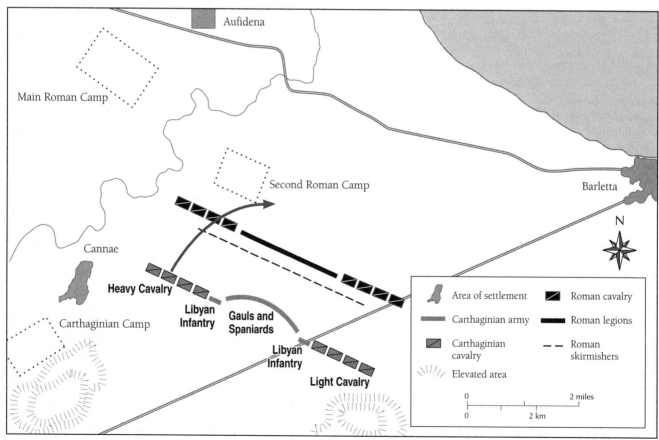

Battle of Cannae, 216 B.C.E.

Realizing that Rome controlled the sea, Hannibal decided to carry out his invasion by land. Setting out in March 218, Hannibal crossed the Ebro River with 90,000 men. After gaining control of the region between the Ebro and the Pyrenees, he left a garrison there to maintain his line of communication back to Spain and entered Gaul with about 50,000 infantry, 9,000 cavalry, and 80 elephants.

From July to October 218, Hannibal marched through Gaul. Having heard of Hannibal's approach, Rome sent Publius Cornelius Scipio (237–183 B.C.E.) to Massilia (Marseilles) to cut off the Carthaginians' route. Hannibal evaded this block by turning north up the Rhone Valley. Scipio sent the bulk of his force to Spain and returned with a small army to the coast of northern Italy.

Hannibal then faced a formidable challenge: the snow-covered Alps. He managed to cross the mountains in 15 days but sustained heavy losses due to the climate and attacks by mountain tribes. Twenty thousand infantry, 6,000 cavalry, and a few surviving elephants reached the Po Valley.

Hannibal first engaged his enemy at the Battle of the Ticinus River, where he defeated the Roman army under Scipio in November 218. The following month, at the Battle of the Trebia River, Hannibal's army, reinforced by recruits from Gaul, enticed the Romans to attack across the river while Mago (d. 203 B.C.E.), Hannibal's brother, struck the Roman flank and rear. Roman losses totaled about 30,000; Hannibal lost about 5,000. The Cisalpine Gauls were pleased with Hannibal's victory over Rome, their longtime enemy, and about 10,000 Gallic soldiers attached themselves to the Carthaginian military.

Hannibal then took up winter quarters in the Po Valley near modern-day Bologna. In March, he was ready to press on. His army of 40,000 crossed the Apennine passes north of Genoa, marched along the seacoast, and pushed through the Arnus marshes to the Rome-Arretium road. The Roman commander, Gaius Flaminius (d. 217 B.C.E.), rushed to meet Hannibal in battle, but the Carthaginian strategist had set an ambush for his enemy at Lake Trasimene. When the entire Roman force had marched into a narrow defile, Hannibal ordered his cavalry to close the northern end and his infantry to attack the Romans' east flank. In the ensuing battle, one of the bloodiest ambushes in history, 30,000 Romans were killed or captured.

Over the next several months, from May to October 217, the Romans engaged in delaying tactics and sought only to harass Hannibal's approaching army. At Geronium, the Roman commander, M. Minucius Rufus (fl. early 200s B.C.E.), engaged Hannibal and was nearly defeated but was saved by the arrival of Quintus Fabius (d. 203 B.C.E.), dictator of Rome. Hannibal quickly withdrew.

While Hannibal continued his push for Rome, his armies in Spain were forced to withdraw from the Ebro line. In Africa, the Romans persuaded the king of Numidia to rebel against Carthage in 213, but this outbreak was put down by Hasdrubal (d. 221 B.C.E.) and a Numidian prince named Masinissa (c. 240–148 B.C.E.). Hasdrubal returned to Spain, but there the Romans had regained control of Saguntum.

Meanwhile, the Romans organized 16 legions (80,000 infantry and 7,000 cavalry) to battle Hannibal's army of 40,000 infantry and 10,000 cavalry. On August 2, 216, at the Battle of Cannae, Roman consul Terentius Varro (fl. early 200s B.C.E.) sent 11,000 men to attack Hannibal's camp. As the rest of the Roman army—72,000 infantry and cavalry—pushed Hannibal's central line back toward the Aufidus River, the Carthaginian infantry wings wheeled inward and the cavalry struck from the rear. The Romans were surrounded, and a slaughter ensued. Compared to Hannibal's losses of 6,000, the Romans suffered staggering casualties: 50,000 killed and 4,500 captured.

Despite three crippling defeats—at Trebia, Lake Tresimene, and Cannae—Rome persevered. The new commander, Marcus Claudius Marcellus (c. 268–208 B.C.E.), raised an army by pressing all able-bodied men into service. His two legions marched south from Rome to shore up the support from Rome's allies. At the First and Second Battles of Nola, Marcellus gained a victory against Hannibal, further encouraging Rome's allies to remain loyal. After the indecisive Third Battle of Nola, Hannibal marched toward the seaport of Tarentum, while his brother Hanno was defeated at Beneventum.

Beginning in 213 B.C.E., Marcellus besieged Syracuse, and in 211 he overwhelmed the garrison. Hannibal was successful at Tarentum in 212, but the Romans then besieged Capua, and Hannibal was forced to send Hanno (fl. third century B.C.E.) to the city's aid. The Romans foiled Hanno's attempts and resumed their siege. Hannibal attacked the Romans at the First Battle of Capua, brought supplies to Capua, and moved on to the south coast.

Over the next winter, the Romans increased their efforts to capture Capua, keeping the city cut off from any aid from the Carthaginians. Hannibal's army of 30,000 men made another attempt to relieve the city but was repelled. Instead of withdrawing in defeat, Hannibal pushed on toward Rome to try to draw the enemy force at Capua back to the capital city. The ploy failed, however, and Capua surrendered to the Romans in 211.

At the Second Battle of Herdonia, Hannibal defeated Roman proconsul Fulvius Centumalus (fl. early 200s B.C.E.) and went on to Numistro, where he defeated Marcellus. Suffering a crisis of leadership, the Roman Senate called on 25-year-old Publius Cornelius Scipio (also known as Scipio Africanus) to take charge of the Roman army in Spain. This new commander soon gained control of territory north of the Ebro and then marched to New Carthage, while his fleet blockaded the city. The town fell in 209.

Battles followed at Tarentum, Asculum, Baecula, and Grumentum. The next major engagement, the Battle of the Metarus in 207 B.C.E., began when Hasdrubal withdrew his Carthaginian army, as reinforcements for M. Livius Salinator's (fl. early 200s B.C.E.) Roman army arrived on the

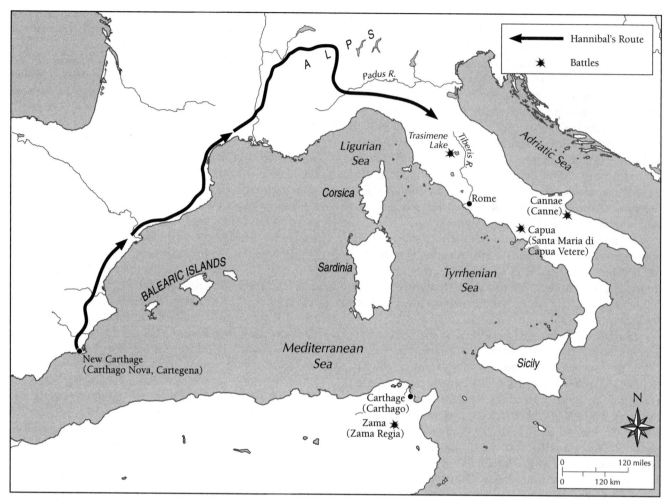

Hannibal's transalpine invasion of Rome, 218–201 B.C.E.

scene. Hasdrubal's forces got lost during the withdrawal and were forced to prepare for battle quickly at dawn. During the battle, Gaius Claudius Nero (fl. early 200s B.C.E.) attacked Hasdrubal from the rear. This surprise attack demoralized the Carthaginians, who lost more than 10,000 men, including Hasdrubal, in the battle. Hannibal learned of his brother's death when the Roman army catapulted the severed head of Hasdrubal into Hannibal's camp.

The Roman army continued to press the advantage, and at the Battle of Ilipa in 206, Scipio's army of 48,000 defeated 70,000 Carthaginians, thereby ending Carthaginian rule in Spain. In 204, Scipio invaded North Africa with an army of 30,000. During the winter of 203, Scipio attacked the Carthaginian and Numidian camps at night, wiping out the entire army, and then renewed his siege of Utica. The Carthaginian Senate soon sent for Hannibal, and the general set sail from Italy. Upon his arrival, the Senate helped him raise a new army. He then marched to Zama with 45,000 infantry and 3,000 cavalry in an attempt to draw Scipio's army away from Carthage. The

ploy worked, and Scipio soon followed Hannibal toward Zama with 34,000 infantry and 9,000 cavalry. At the Battle of Zama in 202, the Romans quickly smashed the first two lines of Carthaginian infantry as the Roman and Numidian cavalry drove Hannibal's cavalry off the field. At first, the third line of Carthaginians, the hardened veterans of many battles, held their own, but when the Roman and Numidian cavalry attacked the line from the rear, the battle was over. More than 20,000 Carthaginians were killed in the battle, and 15,000 were taken prisoner. Carthage sued for peace, surrendered all warships and elephants, and gave up control of Spain and her Mediterranean islands. Carthage also agreed to seek the permission of Rome before engaging in war and to pay Rome 10,000 talents over the next 50 years.

See also PUNIC WAR, FIRST; PUNIC WAR, THIRD.

Further reading: Nigel Bagnall, *Punic Wars* (London: Trafalgar Square, 1991); Brian Caven, *Punic Wars* (London: Palgrave Macmillan, 1980); Adrian Goldsworthy, *The Punic Wars* (London: Cassell, 2001); J. F. Lazenby, *Hanni-*

bal's War: A Military History of the Second Punic War (Norman: University of Oklahoma Press, 1998); John Prevas, *Hannibal Crosses the Alps: The Invasion of Italy and the Second Punic War* (New York: Da Capo, 2001).

Punic War, Third   (149–146 B.C.E.)

PRINCIPAL COMBATANTS: Rome and Carthage
PRINCIPAL THEATER(S): Northern Africa
DECLARATION: 149 B.C.E.
MAJOR ISSUES AND OBJECTIVES: Rome wanted to keep Carthage under its control and prevent her from waging war on Numidia.
OUTCOME: Rome utterly destroyed Carthage, sold the surviving Carthaginians into slavery, and took control of North Africa.
APPROXIMATE MAXIMUM NUMBER OF MEN UNDER ARMS: Unknown
CASUALTIES: Only 50,000 of 225,000 Carthaginians survived the destruction of their city.
TREATIES: None

Fifty years after the end of the Second PUNIC WAR, hostilities broke out between Carthage and Rome's ally Numidia, despite promises made at the close of the Second Punic War by Carthage to gain permission from Rome before waging war. The Roman Senate demanded that Carthage cease operations against Numidia, send 300 hostages to Rome, surrender her weapons, and dismantle her battlements. Carthage complied with these demands but refused to accede to Rome's final demand: to abandon the city of Carthage and move the population inland. In 149, Rome sent a large force to Carthage, but the Carthaginians mounted a strong defense and managed to thwart Roman's attack. In 147, Scipio Aemilianus (c. 185–129 B.C.E.) arrived in Africa with the Roman army and blockaded the city of Carthage by land and sea. After holding out for three years, the city fell in 146 B.C.E., following a house-to-house conflict. At the end of the battle, 78 percent of the Carthaginian population had perished from starvation, disease, or in battle. The Roman Senate ordered the city completely destroyed and sold all survivors into slavery.

See also CELTIBERIAN WARS; PUNIC WAR, FIRST.

Further reading: Nigel Bagnall, *Punic Wars* (London: Trafalgar Square, 1991); Brian Caven, *Punic Wars* (London: Palgrave Macmillan, 1980); Adrian Goldsworthy, *The Punic Wars* (London: Cassell, 2001).

Punjab Revolt   *See* MOGUL CIVIL WAR (1607).

Puritan Conquest, First   *See* PEQUOT WAR (1634–1638).

Puritan Conquest, Second   *See* KING PHILIP'S WAR (1675–1676).

Pursuit of the Northern Cheyenne
See CHEYENNE, PURSUIT OF THE NORTHERN (1878–1879).

Pyramid Lake War   *See* PAIUTE WAR.

al-Qaeda, United States' War against *See* United States's "War on Terrorism."

Quadruple Alliance, War of the (1718–1720)

PRINCIPAL COMBATANTS: Spain (with Scottish Jacobites) vs. Britain, France, Netherlands, and Austria (the Quadruple Alliance)
PRINCIPAL THEATER(S): Spain, Sicily, and Scotland
DECLARATION: None
MAJOR ISSUES AND OBJECTIVES: Philip V of Spain sought the French Crown and an extension of Spain's territory.
OUTCOME: Philip V of Spain renounced his Italian holdings in return for a pledge from Austria that his son would inherit the duchies of Parma, Piacenza, and Tuscany.
APPROXIMATE MAXIMUM NUMBER OF MEN UNDER ARMS: Spain, about 48,000; Jacobites, 1,000; Quadruple Alliance, 51,000
CASUALTIES: Spain, 30,000 killed or wounded; Jacobites, 200 killed or wounded; Quadruple Alliance, 15,000-plus killed or wounded (mostly Austrian)
TREATIES: Treaty of The Hague (February 17, 1720)

At the death of Louis XIV (1638–1715) of France, his grandson Philip V (1683–1746) of Spain sought the French Crown for himself. At the same time, Philip's second wife, Elizabeth Farnese (1692–1766) of Parma, wanted to secure the family's holdings in Italy for her children. Opposing Philip in his quest for France were Britain, Holland, and Austria. These three countries, along with France, formed the Quadruple Alliance on August 2, 1718,

to stop Philip from occupying Sardinia and Sicily. Later that month, a British fleet transported Austrian troops to Sicily, and 21 British warships under Admiral George Byng (1663–1733) defeated a Spanish naval force of 29 ships off Cape Passaro on the southeast coast of Sicily. Byng captured or destroyed 7 ships of the line, 9 frigates, and 4 smaller Spanish crafts, and the Spanish commander Don Antonio Castañeda (d. 1718) was mortally wounded. The way was then clear for the Austrian troops to seize Messina, Sicily, from Spanish control. The first attempt by a force of 21,000 Hapsburg troops was repulsed by the Spanish at Francavilla, and 3,100 Hapsburgs fell. However, a new attack in October 1719 took Messina, albeit at a cost of 5,200 killed or wounded out of a force of 18,000.

While the war raged in Sicily, Spain sent an expedition to Scotland to aid the Jacobites in a planned revolt against England. Although the initial force of 29 ships and 6,000 troops, sent in April 1719, wrecked in a storm, never reached its destination, a smaller Spanish force of 300 troops under George Keith (1693?–1778), earl of Marischal, did reach Scotland. There they were joined by 1,000 Highlanders under Rob Roy MacGregor (1671–1734) and other Scottish chiefs. This combined force faced British troops at Glenshiel on June 10, 1719, but fled or surrendered after a brief British bombardment.

In April 1719, 30,000 French troops invaded Spain and ranged over the northern part of the country with little resistance until November, when bad weather and disease prompted a withdrawal.

By December 1719, Philip had regained his senses. The French Crown was not to be his, and his efforts in Scotland to aid the Jacobites against the king of England had come to nothing. On February 17, 1720, he signed the Treaty of The Hague, by which he renounced his claims in Italy in return for a promise by Austria that the duchies of Parma, Piacenza, and Tuscany would be inherited by Charles (1716–88), his eldest son. Also included in the treaty was a provision that Sicily would be ceded to Austria and Sardinia to Savoy.

See also ANGLO-SPANISH WAR (1727–1729); AUSTRIAN SUCCESSION, WAR OF THE (1745–1748).

Further reading: Henry Arthur Kamen, *Philip V of Spain: The King Who Reigned Twice* (New Haven, Conn.: Yale University Press, 2001).

Quantrill's Raids See UNITED STATES CIVIL WAR: TRANS-MISSISSIPPI THEATER.

Queen Anne's War (1702–1713)

PRINCIPAL COMBATANTS: Colonial England and its Indian allies vs. colonial France and its Indian allies
PRINCIPAL THEATER(S): Eastern seaboard of North America, from Nova Scotia to Florida
DECLARATION: War in Europe declared, May 2, 1702; no formal declaration in North America
MAJOR ISSUES AND OBJECTIVES: American theater of the War of the Spanish Succession was a struggle for dominance in North America.
OUTCOME: The French retained New France, including Cape Breton and Prince Edward Island, but lost Newfoundland, Hudson Bay, and Acadia; Abenakis and other French-allied Indians pledged loyalty to Britain's queen Anne.
APPROXIMATE MAXIMUM NUMBER OF MEN UNDER ARMS: English: 5,200 in the Caribbean; 6,500 in North America; French: unknown.
CASUALTIES: English, 270 people killed at Deerfield, Massachusetts, and 1,600 shipwrecked in an attempted assault on Quebec; otherwise casualties were light; 200 dead in New England, 150 in the Carolinas. French and Indians: 60 French and Spanish soldiers in the North and 50 Indians (but many more were killed among the southern tribal allies of the French)
TREATIES: Treaty of Utrecht, July 13, 1713

Queen Anne's War was the American phase of a larger European conflict, the War of the SPANISH SUCCESSION. Britain, Holland, and Austria, fearing an alliance between France and Spain, formed the Grand Alliance after Charles II (1661–1700) of Spain, a Hapsburg, chose a Bourbon as his successor. When Charles II died in 1700, the French naturally supported the king's chosen successor, a grandson of Louis XIV (1638–1715). Britain, Holland, and Austria supported an obscure Bavarian prince,

and the issue sparked war, which was declared on May 4, 1702.

In the American colonies, Queen Anne's War began on September 10, 1702, when the South Carolina legislature sent troops to seize the Spanish fort and town of St. Augustine, Florida. After a British naval expedition sacked the town, a force of 500 South Carolina colonists and Chickasaw Indian attacked the fort. Failing to penetrate it, they pillaged what little was left in the town and then burned it.

A cycle of raids and retribution began until former South Carolina governor James Moore (c. 1640–1729) led militiamen and Chickasaws through the territory of the Appalachee Indians of western Florida during July 1704. This expedition ravaged seven Appalachee villages—virtually annihilating the tribe—and destroyed 13 of the 14 Spanish missions in the country.

The way was now open to invade French Louisiana territory and the settlements on the Gulf. The French bribed Choctaw, Cherokee, Creek, and Chickasaw in an attempt to gain alliances. The Chickasaws remained pro-English, and the Cherokee maintained neutrality. Although some elements of the Creek Indians did side with the French, it was the Choctaws who proved France's most powerful ally, stopping Moore's advance.

In the North, the French had developed more extensive alliances with the Indians, especially the Abenakis of Maine. On August 10, 1703, English settlers plundered the Maine house belonging to the son of Jean Vincent de l'Abadie, baron de St. Castin, whose trading post had been similarly attacked in April 1688, during KING WILLIAM'S WAR. Through marriage, the younger St. Castin was deemed an Abenaki chief, and the attack touched off Indian raids all along the northern New England frontier.

Among the towns hardest hit was Deerfield, Massachusetts, a prosperous village of 41 houses and 270 people, which had borne the brunt of numerous raids during KING PHILIP'S WAR and King William's War.

Farther north, in Nova Scotia, a superannuated Benjamin Church, hero of King Philip's War, led 550 men into Acadian French territory, terrorizing the villages of Minas and Beaubassin on July 1 and 28, 1704. During August 18–29, a mixed force of French and Abenakis retaliated by destroying the English at Bonavista, Nova Scotia.

For the most part, Queen Anne's War dragged on in the North as well as the South as a litany of raids and individual murders. Some larger actions were attempted, as when the English unsuccessfully attempted to take Port Royal, Nova Scotia, in 1706, and the French and Spanish assaulted Charleston, South Carolina, from the sea but likewise failed to take the city. The French were successful in capturing St. Johns, Newfoundland, on December 21, 1708.

In an effort to garner more support from the mother country, the colonies sent a delegation of English-allied Mohawk chiefs to the court of Queen Anne (1665–1714) in 1710. The monarch was so impressed that she sent land reinforcement to the colonies under Colonel Francis Nicholson (1655–1728) and a fleet under Sir Francis Hobby (fl. early 18th century). Together, they reduced Port Royal on October 16, 1710, and, the following summer, all Acadia fell to the English.

Even more ambitious was a naval expedition against Quebec, which, however was shipwrecked at the mouth of the St. Lawrence River with the loss of 1,600 men. The next year, in 1712, another assault against Quebec likewise failed. However, by this time, Louis XIV of France could no longer foot the bill of this far-flung war, the original cause of which had been rendered moot in any case when the Bavarian candidate supported by the Grand Alliance died. Louis's grandson ascended the Spanish throne by default.

By the Treaty of Utrecht, concluded on July 13, 1713, France ceded Hudson Bay and Acadia to the English but retained Cape Breton Island and other small islands in the St. Lawrence. The Abenakis and other French-allied Indians promised to become loyal subjects to Queen Anne.

Further reading: Robert Leckie, *A Few Acres of Snow: The Saga of the French and Indian Wars* (New York: Wiley, 2000); John Williams, *The Redeemed Captive Returning to Zion* (reprinted, Westport, Conn.: Hopkins, Bridgeman, 1987).

R

Rajput Rebellion against Aurangzeb
(1675–1707)

PRINCIPAL COMBATANTS: Rajputs and Sikhs vs. the Mogul Empire
PRINCIPAL THEATER(S): Northern India
DECLARATION: None
MAJOR ISSUES AND OBJECTIVES: The Rajputs and allied Sikhs sought to overthrow Mogul rule after Aurangzeb instituted a campaign of oppression against non-Muslims.
OUTCOME: Aurangzeb prevailed in straight combat but became bogged down in a long, ruinous guerrilla conflict.
APPROXIMATE MAXIMUM NUMBER OF MEN UNDER ARMS:
Unknown
CASUALTIES: Unknown
TREATIES: None

In 1658, Aurangzeb (1618–1707) crowned himself emperor of India at Delhi and commenced a program of persecution of non-Muslims. In 1675, he turned in particular against the Sikhs and Rajputs, who responded by fanatically devoting themselves to wiping out Aurangzeb and all Muslims.

Led by the Mewar Durgadas, the Rajputs staged a massive rebellion during 1675–81, managing to drive out the Mogul garrisons of Aurangzeb. In 1681, Aurangzeb's own son, Akbar (d. 1704), joined the Rajputs in rebellion. Aurangzeb defeated the young man, who fled for his life to Persia.

The rebellion of the Rajputs deprived Aurangzeb's army of one of its most valuable assets, the Rajput cavalry, which rendered Aurangzeb vulnerable to the rising power of the Marathas. Aurangzeb decided to move preemptively against the Marathas and prevailed against them during 1686–89 but was then plagued by a long guerrilla conflict with their supposedly defeated forces. This marked the beginning of a long decline, during which Aurangzeb's empire became bankrupt, its soldiers mutinous, and its far-flung empire impossible to hold together. Aurangzeb's death in 1707 marked the end of Mogul hegemony.

See also MOGUL CIVIL WAR (1707–1708).

Further reading: Robert C. Hallissey, *The Rajput Rebellion against Aurangzeb: A Study of the Moghul Empire in Seventeenth-Century India* (Columbia: University of Missouri Press, 1977).

Rashtrakutan-Cholan War (c. 940–972)

PRINCIPAL COMBATANTS: The Rashtrakuta vs. Chola dynasties of India
PRINCIPAL THEATER(S): India
DECLARATION: None
MAJOR ISSUES AND OBJECTIVES: The Rashtrakuta dynasty sought to expand its territory into southern India.
OUTCOME: The Chola dynasty was overwhelmed in battle by the Rashtrakuta dynasty and lost much territory.
APPROXIMATE MAXIMUM NUMBER OF MEN UNDER ARMS:
Unknown
CASUALTIES: Unknown
TREATIES: None

As former vassals of the Chalukyas, the Rashtrakutas grew more powerful from the eighth century onward and began to annex territory including Malwa to the north. The Rashtrakutan king, Krishna III (fl. 939–968), also began preparing to annex land that formerly belonged to the Pallavas. This region, however, was being claimed by the Cholas under Parantaka I (fl. 907–953). The Cholas took Nellore from the Rashtrakutas, but Krishna and Indra IV (r. ended 973), his successor, battled the Cholas and gained territory in the Vengi and Tamil plains and the Chola capital at Kanchipuram. With these territorial gains, the Rashtrakutas controlled southern India. The CHALUKYAN-RASHTRAKUTAN WARS, ending in 975, brought a decline to the Rashtrakuta dynasty and prominence to a western Chalukya dynasty.

Further reading: Brajadulal D. Chattopadhaya, *The Making of Early Medieval India* (New York: Oxford University Press, 1994).

Ravenna, Revolt in (726–731)

PRINCIPAL COMBATANTS: The army of the Byzantine Empire vs. military force raised by Pope Gregory II in Italy
PRINCIPAL THEATER(S): Northeast Italy
DECLARATION: None
MAJOR ISSUES AND OBJECTIVES: Leo III, Byzantine emperor, sought to strengthen the Christian Church by banning the worship of images; the Italian clergy vehemently opposed the edict.
OUTCOME: The army raised by Pope Gregory II repelled the advance of the Byzantine army.
APPROXIMATE MAXIMUM NUMBER OF MEN UNDER ARMS: Unknown
CASUALTIES: Unknown
TREATIES: None

In 726, Byzantine emperor Leo III (c. 675–680 to 741) forbade the worship of images in the Roman Catholic Church. This edict by the emperor, who became known as the Iconoclast, was an attempt to remove "frills" from the church and make it better able to compete with the fast-growing, simpler Muslim faith. When most of the Italian clergy disagreed with Leo's edict, the emperor decided to enforce compliance by sending a military force to Ravenna, the Byzantine capital in Italy. There the Byzantine army clashed with the army of Pope Gregory (669–731), who drove back Leo's army and forced it to retreat to Constantinople. This battle further pointed to the growing schism between the Orthodox Church of the Byzantine Empire and the Roman Catholic Church.

Further reading: John Julius Norwich, *Byzantium: The Early Centuries* (New York: Knopf, 1989); Cyril A. Mango, ed., *Oxford History of Byzantium* (New York: Oxford University Press, 2002).

Razin's Revolt (1665–1671)

PRINCIPAL COMBATANTS: Cossack and peasant army led by Stenka Razin vs. imperial Russian forces
PRINCIPAL THEATER(S): Lower Volga and Caspian Sea region
DECLARATION: None
MAJOR ISSUES AND OBJECTIVES: Razin sought relief from czarist oppression.
OUTCOME: Although Razin acquired a substantial number of followers, his rebellion was crushed.
APPROXIMATE MAXIMUM NUMBER OF MEN UNDER ARMS: Razin's army, 20,000; Czarist forces, 30,000
CASUALTIES: Total deaths, including civilians, 100,000+
TREATIES: None

Although often serving as military assets of the czars, the Cossacks also staged numerous revolts against them, the most celebrated being that of Stenka Razin (d. 1671), a Cossack *hetman,* or leader.

In the summer of 1670, at the head of 7,000 Cossack warriors, Razin took Tsaritsyn, then advanced down the Volga River, picking up more followers. In June, some 10,000 Cossacks attacked and captured Astrakhan, killing 441 of the 6,000 czarist troops defending the city. This triggered a larger rebellion among the Cossacks; by mid-September some 20,000 were under arms, advancing in two columns, up the Volga and up the Don.

At Simbirsk, 4,000 Cossacks repeatedly assaulted the garrison of *streltsy* (czarist musketeers) who held the city. After repelling the onslaught three times, the defenders were finally reinforced by a relief column of 6,000 men. Razin attempted to intercept the column but was defeated at the Battle of Sviyaga River on October 1. Thus Simbirsk was saved, and the rebel cause was dealt a severe blow.

In the meantime, on the Don, a Cossack force was defeated at the Battle of Korotoyak. Combined with the defeat outside of Simbirsk, this setback brought the Cossack advance to a standstill and presented czarist forces with an opening for a smashing counteroffensive. Many Cossacks at this point deserted Razin and collaborated with the czarist army. At Kagolnik, on April 14, 1671, Razin was defeated. Taken prisoner, he was tortured for two months until, on June 6, 1671, he was publicly drawn and quartered in Moscow's Red Square.

The death of Razin all but extinguished the rebellion. Some 30,000 *streltsy* and militiamen were dispatched to Astrakhan in August 1671 to mop up the last rebel holdouts. The city fell to the czarist army on November 26.

Further reading: Paul Avrich, *Russian Rebels, 1600–1800: Four Great Rebellions Which Shook the Russian State in the Seventeenth Century* (New York: Norton, 1990); George Vernadsky, *A History of Russia* (New Haven, Conn.: Yale University Press, 1961).

Red Cloud's War   *See* Bozeman Trail, War for the.

Red Eyebrow Revolt (c. 17 c.e.)

PRINCIPAL COMBATANTS: Xin (Hsin) emperor Wang Mang vs. peasant rebels in Shandong (Shantung)
PRINCIPAL THEATER(S): Yellow River region of Shandong
DECLARATION: None
MAJOR ISSUES AND OBJECTIVES: When the Yellow River flooded in 17, desperate peasants rebelled against the unpopular usurper of the Han dynasty.
OUTCOME: The rebellion, while suppressed, sapped Wang's strength and caused his rule to spiral out of control.
APPROXIMATE MAXIMUM NUMBER OF MEN UNDER ARMS: Unknown
CASUALTIES: Unknown
TREATIES: None

First and only emperor of the Xin ("New") dynasty, Wang Mang (33 B.C.E.–C.E. 23) was the nephew of the dowager empress of the decadent Han dynasty in China. He had served as her chief minister for a decade or so before he disposed of the infant emperor, Ru-zi (4 C.E.–?), to whom he was acting as regent and seized the Chinese throne for himself. The sweeping reforms he introduced, such as abolishing slavery and imposing an income tax, alienated the powerful Chinese landlords. He tried to justify these changes as a revival of the Zhou (Chou) dynasty's "Golden Age," but his argument failed to win over the landlords. As for the peasants, they were oppressed by his massive levies to fund the invasion and annexation of the tribal lands of the nomadic Xiongnu (Hsiung-nu).

Around the year 17 C.E., heavy rains caused the Yellow River to flood, bursting through dikes neglected by Wang Mang's government and driving tens of thousands of peasants from their homes. As a result, a peasant revolt, led by an aggressive Chinese woman named Mother Lu (fl. early first century), broke out in Shandong (Shantung) Province. Inspired by a religious fanaticism, the rebels painted their eyebrows red to make themselves resemble demons. The revolt reached such proportions as to sap Wang's military strength and cause the invasion of Xiongnu territory to fail. Thereafter, Wang—unable to withstand the combined opposition of aristocratic warlords and desperate peasants—faced a succession of revolts at home, causing him to lose much of Turkestan, which had long been under Han control. As anarchy swept China, Wang Mang was killed in another revolt, and the Han dynasty was soon restored to power.

Further reading: Rudi Thomsen, *Ambition and Confucianism: A Biography of Wang Mang* (Aarhus, Den.: Aarhus University Press, 1988).

Red River Rebellion (1869–1870)   *See* Riel's First Rebellion.

Red River War (1874–1875)

PRINCIPAL COMBATANTS: Comanche and Kiowa Indians vs. United States
PRINCIPAL THEATER(S): Indian Territory (Oklahoma), Texas, and Kansas
DECLARATION: None
MAJOR ISSUES AND OBJECTIVES: Kiowa-Comanche raids on white settlers and resistance to confinement on reservations
OUTCOME: Kwahadi Comanche, for the first time ever, consent to live on the reservation; 74 militant chiefs are exiled to Castillo de San Marcos, Florida.
APPROXIMATE MAXIMUM NUMBER OF MEN UNDER ARMS: Indians, about 1,200 warriors; U.S. Army, fewer than 1,000
CASUALTIES: Indians, 84 killed; army, 2 killed, 7 wounded
TREATIES: None

After President Ulysses S. Grant (1822–85) proclaimed a policy of conciliation and peace in dealing with the Indians of the West, the Kiowa, mainly led by Chief Satanta (1830–78) raided throughout neighboring Texas, withdrawing to the reservation for refuge. In response to complaints from outraged Texans, General William Tecumseh Sherman (1820–91) made a personal tour of inspection of the reservation and nearby Fort Sill.

As Sherman's wagon train approached the area, on May 18, 1871, Satanta, Satank (c. 1810–70), Big Tree (c. 1847–1929), and about 100 Kiowa braves ambushed a 10-wagon train, killing eight teamsters and stealing property. Ironically, they had let pass a smaller train—which (unknown to them) carried General Sherman, who ordered the arrest of Satanta, Big Tree, and Satank. They were transported to Texas to stand trial for murder. Satank was shot en route during an escape attempt; Satanta and Big Tree were convicted in a Texas court and sentenced to hang. However, the sentences were commuted to prison terms, and in 1873 Satanta and Big Tree were paroled.

Once released, Satanta and Big Tree led new raids in the Texas Panhandle, prompting General Sherman to launch the major offensive that came to be known as the Red River War. By this time, the Kiowa had been joined by Comanche and Cheyenne and conducted ever more destructive raids. On June 27, Comanches and Cheyenne hit a white hunter village at Adobe Walls in the Texas Panhandle; on July 12, the Kiowa chief Lone Wolf (c. 1820–79) ambushed Texas Rangers at Lost Valley; throughout this period, warriors struck at ranchers and wayfarers in Kansas and Texas.

Sherman launched a campaign in the Staked Plains region of the Texas Panhandle, a campaign made especially arduous by a severe drought, which, on September 7, suddenly yielded to torrential rains that rendered travel all but impossible. Cut off from support, Colonel Nelson A. Miles (1839–1925) held off an Indian siege for three days, from September 9 to September 11, before the attackers finally withdrew.

Colonel Ranald Mackenzie (1840–89) commanding the 4th Cavalry, was attacked on the night of September 26 near Tule Canyon. Mackenzie struck back in the morning, chasing the attackers to the Palo Duro Canyon, where he destroyed a combined Kiowa-Comanche-Cheyenne village. During the fall, other troops burned more villages, leaving the Indians poorly supplied for the winter.

During the late fall and winter, parties of Kiowa and Cheyenne straggled in to Forts Sill and Darlington to submit to life on the reservation. On June 2, 1875, more than 400 Kwahadi Comanches consented to live on a reservation—the first time they had done so in their history.

Satanta, together with other Kiowa war chiefs, surrendered on October 7, 1874. Satanta was sent to the Texas state penitentiary, from which he had been previously paroled. On March 11, 1878, he leaped to his death from a window. Seventy-four other militant chiefs were exiled to Castillo de San Marcos, a former Spanish fortress in St. Augustine, Florida.

See also UNITED STATES–SIOUX WAR (1876–1877).

Further reading: Alan Axelrod, Chronicle of the Indian Wars: From Colonial Times to Wounded Knee (New York: Prentice Hall General Reference, 1993); Stan Haig, Tribal Wars of the Southern Plains (Norman: University of Oklahoma Press, 1993); Robert M. Utley, Frontier Regulars: The United States Army and the Indian 1866–1890 (New York: Macmillan, 1973).

Reform, War of the (1857–1860)

PRINCIPAL COMBATANTS: Mexican Conservatives vs. Liberals (Constitutionalists)
PRINCIPAL THEATER(S): Mexico
DECLARATION: None
MAJOR ISSUES AND OBJECTIVES: The conservatives fought against the implementation of the reforms of the constitution of 1857.
OUTCOME: After losing many battles, Liberal forces finally turned the tide, defeated the Conservatives, and installed Benito Juárez as president; he instituted the reforms of the 1857 constitution.
APPROXIMATE MAXIMUM NUMBER OF MEN UNDER ARMS: Conservatives, about 25,000; Liberals, 35,000
CASUALTIES: 70,000 combatants and civilians killed
TREATIES: None

The Mexican constitution of 1857 introduced reforms supported by the Liberals and opposed by the Conservatives, prompting them to revolt. In January 1858, General Félix Zuloaga (1814–76), a Conservative leader, led forces that overran Mexico City and forced the constitutional president, Benito Juárez (1806–72), to flee to Veracruz. Zuloaga assumed presidential powers, then was replaced by another Conservative, Miguel Miramón (1832–67). In the meantime, Juárez rallied the weak militia of the Liberals, which repelled Conservative attempts to take Veracruz, in March 1859 and March 1860. Despite these victories, the Conservatives, whose forces were both better equipped and better led than those of the Liberals, seemed likely to prevail. The Conservatives were also willing to fight on the most ruthless terms, throwing the nation into a bitter and bloody civil war. Indeed, during the first two years of the conflict, most of the triumphs went to the Conservatives. Their greatest victory was at the Battle of Ahuaalulco de los Pinos on October 29, 1858, in which the Liberal army was ignominiously routed. Although the Liberal commander, General Santos Degollado (d. 1861) lost every engagement he fought, he managed to keep the army intact, and this accomplishment bought time for Juárez to plead successfully for support from the United States, which sent arms and funding to the Liberals.

Not through military victory but by staying in the war did the Liberals ultimately prevail. In March 1859, General Miramón renewed his offensive against the Liberals, attempting again to push Juárez out of Veracruz. Miramón found himself defeated not by Liberal arms so much as by tropical diseases endemic to the Mexican lowlands. Taking advantage of the debilitated state of the Conservative army, Degollado led his forces in an assault against Mexico City, only to be defeated, yet again, at Chapultepec in April 1859.

Juárez ordered the confiscation of church property to raise funds to continue the battle against the well-financed Conservatives. With his forces now better armed, he put them in the charge of Jesus Gonzalez Ortega (1824–81), who won a striking victory against the Conservatives near Guadalajara and then at Calderón, both in 1860. On December 20, 1860, Ortega led Liberal forces to a mighty victory against Miramón at the Battle of Calpulalpam. This victory laid bare Mexico City, into which Juárez rode in triumph on January 1, 1861. With the war suddenly reversed in the Liberals' favor, Juárez assumed the presidency and implemented the reforms of the 1857 constitution.

See also MEXICAN-FRENCH WAR.

Further reading: Brian R. Hamnetet, Juárez (London: Longman, 1995); Enrique Krause, Mexico: Biography of Power, A History of Modern Mexico, 1810–1996 (New York: HarperCollins, 1998); Walter V. Scholes, Mexican Politics during the Juárez Regime, 1855–1872 (Columbia: University of Missouri Press, 1969).

Regulators' Revolt (1771)

PRINCIPAL COMBATANTS: Regulators (militant frontiersmen) vs. colonial militia
PRINCIPAL THEATER(S): Carolina backcountry
DECLARATION: None
MAJOR ISSUES AND OBJECTIVES: Disaffected Carolina frontiersmen rebelled against corrupt, unresponsive, tax-hungry, and repressive royal colonial government.
OUTCOME: The Regulators were suppressed.
APPROXIMATE MAXIMUM NUMBER OF MEN UNDER ARMS: Regulators, 2,000; militia forces, 1,200
CASUALTIES: Six Regulators executed; other minor casualties
TREATIES: None

After the English victory in the FRENCH AND INDIAN WAR, many Americans were proud to be part of the triumphant British Empire, but many others felt oppressed and outraged by the series of taxes and duties the Crown imposed on the colonies in an attempt to recoup some of the expense of the long wilderness war. The towns of New England, especially Boston, harbored the strongest streak of radicalism and ultimately agitated for and organized the Revolution. In the frontier regions, much of the population was Tory in sympathy (i.e., loyal to Britain), but many on the frontier were disaffected, feeling that the East Coast centers of government, as well as the mother country across the Atlantic, cared little about the inland settlements. The alienation of the frontier was intensified by George III's (1738–1820) Proclamation of 1763, which fixed the Appalachians as the absolute western limit of white settlement. Although most of the organized demonstrations against British authority in the pre-Revolutionary years took place in the cities and towns of the East Coast, the first armed preludes to outright revolution occurred on the frontier.

The poor farmers of the western counties of North Carolina were among those with grievances against the Tidewater aristocrats who held the reins of colonial government. In 1768, they formed an association to protest what they saw as unjust taxation and thoroughly corrupt justices of the peace, who had been sent from the East to administer law for the frontier. In 1769, the association turned militant, as a group of farmers and settlers formed the Regulators, a political and paramilitary vigilante band. The Regulators won control of the provincial assembly, which sufficiently alarmed the British colonial governor, William Tryon (1729–88), to prompt him to dissolve the assembly before it could take any action.

Cut off even from quasi-legal action, the Regulators increasingly turned to vigilante violence. For example, when a lawyer convicted of extortion was freed by the provincial magistrate, the Regulators pillaged the court-house and assaulted the lawyer. In response to this and similar acts, the colonial government passed the Bloody Act (1771), which proclaimed the rioters guilty of treason. Amid escalating tension later in 1771, Governor Tryon dispatched 1,200 militiamen into the area. They confronted some 2,000 Regulators on May 16, 1771, at the Battle of Alamance Creek. Although outnumbered, the militiamen were much better armed and disciplined. After soundly defeating the Regulators, they arrested a number identified as ringleaders. Six Regulator leaders were subsequently hanged, and the others were compelled to swear allegiance to the eastern Tidewater government. With this single battle and subsequent punishment, the Regulators' Revolt ended.

Further reading: Marjoleine Kars, *Breaking Loose Together: The Regulator Rebellion in Pre-Revolutionary North Carolina* (Chapel Hill: University of North Carolina Press, 2002).

Religion, First War of (1562–1563)

PRINCIPAL COMBATANTS: Catholics vs. Huguenots (with English aid) in France
PRINCIPAL THEATER(S): France
DECLARATION: None
MAJOR ISSUES AND OBJECTIVES: The Huguenots sought religious freedom.
OUTCOME: A degree of tolerance was granted to the Huguenots.
APPROXIMATE MAXIMUM NUMBER OF MEN UNDER ARMS: Catholics, 23,000; Huguenots, 15,000 (including 3,000 English troops)
CASUALTIES: Military losses were about 4,000 killed on each side; Huguenot civilian losses were about 3,000 killed.
TREATIES: Peace of Amboise (March 1563)

On March 1, 1562, supporters of the Catholic duke François de Guise (1519–63) killed a congregation of Protestants at Vassy. This massacre was instigated by the granting of limited toleration to the Protestants by Catherine de' Medici (1519–85), the queen mother who took control of the throne at the death of King Francis II (1544–60). The Catholics, under François de Guise, the Constable de Montmorency (Anne, duc de Montmorency; 1493–1567), and Prince Antoine de Bourbon (1518–62), king of Navarre, and the Protestants, under Louis I de Bourbon, prince of Condé (1530–69), and Comte Gaspard de Coligny (1519–72), admiral of France, were soon pitted against each other in a battle known as the First War of Religion. Louis de Condé and Gaspard de Coligny ordered the Huguenots to seize Orléans to retaliate for the Vassy massacre and called on all Protestants in France to rebel. In September 1562, the English sent John Dudley (fl. 16th century) of Warwick to help the Huguenots, and his force captured Le Havre. About one month later, the Catholics defeated Rouen, a Protestant stronghold. One of the leaders of the Catholic movement, Antoine de Bourbon, was killed during the attack. The Huguenots continued to rise in rebellion, and in December 15,000 Protestants under Condé and Coligny marched north to join the English troops at Le Havre. En route, they encountered about 19,000 Catholics at Dreux. The Catholics under Guise were victorious, but one of their leaders, Montmorency, was captured, as was the Protestant leader Condé. On February 18, 1563, Guise was killed while besieging Orléans. Peace was finally secured in March when Montmorency and Condé, both prisoners since the Battle of Dreux, negotiated a settlement at the request of Queen Catherine. The Peace of Amboise stipulated a degree of tolerance. The opposing sides then combined forces to push the English from Le Havre, which fell on July 28, 1563.

See also RELIGION, SECOND WAR OF; RELIGION, THIRD WAR OF; RELIGION, FOURTH WAR OF; RELIGION, FIFTH WAR OF; RELIGION, SIX AND SEVENTH WARS OF; RELIGION, EIGHTH WAR OF; and RELIGION, NINTH WAR OF.

Further reading: R. J. Knecht, *The French Civil Wars, 1562–1598* (New York: Pearson Education, 2000); R. J. Knecht and Mabel Segun, *French Wars of Religion* (New York: Addison-Wesley Longman, 1996).

Religion, Second War of (1567–1568)

PRINCIPAL COMBATANTS: Catholics vs. Huguenots in France
PRINCIPAL THEATER(S): France
DECLARATION: None
MAJOR ISSUES AND OBJECTIVES: The Huguenots sought religious freedom.
OUTCOME: A degree of tolerance was granted to the Huguenots.
APPROXIMATE MAXIMUM NUMBER OF MEN UNDER ARMS: 16,000 French (Catholics); 3,500 Huguenots
CASUALTIES: Numbers unknown, but heavy on both sides
TREATIES: Peace of Longjumeau (March 1568)

The Peace of Amboise (July 28, 1563), which stipulated a greater degree of tolerance between the Catholics and the Huguenots in France, ended the FIRST WAR OF RELIGION. However, peace lasted only four years. On September 29, 1567, the Huguenots under Louis de Bourbon, prince de Condé (1530–69), and Comte Gaspard de Coligny (1519–72) tried to capture the royal family at Meaux. Although they were unsuccessful, other Protestant bands threatened Paris and captured Orléans, Auxerre, Vienne, Valence, Nîmes, Montpellier, and Montaubon. At the Battle of St. Denis, a force of 16,000 men under Constable de Montmorency (Anne, duc de Montmorency; 1493–1567),

attacked Condé's small army of 3,500. Despite the long odds, the Huguenots managed to remain on the field for several hours. Montmorency, aged 74, was killed during the fray. This war ended on March 23, 1568, with the Peace of Longjumeau by which the Huguenots gained substantial concessions from Queen Catherine de' Medici (1519–85).

See also RELIGION, THIRD WAR OF (1568–1570); RELIGION, FOURTH WAR OF; RELIGION, FIFTH WAR OF; RELIGION, SIX AND SEVENTH WARS OF; RELIGION, EIGHTH WAR OF; and RELIGION, NINTH WAR OF.

Further reading: R. J. Knecht, *The French Civil Wars, 1562–1598* (New York: Pearson Education, 2000); R. J. Knecht and Mabel Segun, *French Wars of Religion* (New York: Addison-Wesley Longman, 1996).

Religion, Third War of (1568–1570)

PRINCIPAL COMBATANTS: Catholics vs. Huguenots in France
PRINCIPAL THEATER(S): France
DECLARATION: None
MAJOR ISSUES AND OBJECTIVES: The Huguenots sought religious freedom.
OUTCOME: A degree of tolerance was granted to the Huguenots.
APPROXIMATE MAXIMUM NUMBER OF MEN UNDER ARMS: Catholics, 18,000; Huguenots, 16,500
CASUALTIES: Catholics, 1,000 killed or wounded; Huguenots, 8,400 killed or wounded
TREATIES: Peace of St. Germain, August 8, 1570

The Third War of Religion broke out on August 18, 1568, when Catholics attempted to capture Louis de Bourbon, prince de Condé (1530–69), and Comte Gaspard de Coligny (1519–72), the primary Protestant leaders. The Royalist Catholics continued to suppress Protestantism. Sporadic fighting occurred throughout the Loire Valley for the remainder of 1568. In March 1569, the Royalists under Marshal Gaspard de Tavannes (1509–73) engaged in battle with Condé's forces in the region between Angoulême and Cognac. Later in March, Tavanne crossed the Charente River near Châteauneuf and soundly defeated the Huguenots at the Battle of Jarmac. Although Condé was captured and murdered, Coligny managed to withdraw a portion of the Protestant army in good order. About three months later, help for the Huguenots arrived in the form of 13,000 German Protestant reinforcements. This enlarged force laid siege to Poitiers. Then on August 24, 1569, Coligny sent Comte Gabriel de Montgomery (c. 1530–74) to Orthez, where he repulsed a Royalist invasion of French-held Navarre and defeated Catholic forces arranged against him. Royalist marshal Tavanne then relieved Poitiers and forced Coligny to raise the siege. The major battle of the Third War of Religion occurred on October

3, 1569, at Moncontour. The Royalists, aided by a force of Swiss sympathizers, forced the Huguenot cavalry off the field and then crushed the Huguenot infantry. The Huguenots lost about 8,000, whereas Royalist losses numbered about 1,000. The following year, however, Coligny marched his Huguenot forces through central France from April through June and began threatening Paris. These actions forced the Peace of St. Germain, which granted many religious freedoms to the Protestants.

See also RELIGION, FIRST WAR OF; RELIGION, SECOND WAR OF; RELIGION, FOURTH WAR OF; RELIGION, FIFTH WAR OF; RELIGION, SIX AND SEVENTH WARS OF; RELIGION, EIGHTH WAR OF; RELIGION, NINTH WAR OF.

Further reading: R. J. Knecht, *The French Civil Wars, 1562–1598* (New York: Pearson Education, 2000); R. J. Knecht and Mabel Segun, *French Wars of Religion* (New York: Addison-Wesley Longman, 1996).

Religion, Fourth War of (1572–1573)

PRINCIPAL COMBATANTS: Catholics vs. Huguenots in France
PRINCIPAL THEATER(S): France
DECLARATION: None
MAJOR ISSUES AND OBJECTIVES: The Huguenots sought religious freedom.
OUTCOME: A degree of tolerance was granted to the Huguenots, and a group of moderate Catholics formed a new political party known as the Politiques.
APPROXIMATE MAXIMUM NUMBER OF MEN UNDER ARMS: Unknown
CASUALTIES: Unknown
TREATIES: None

A massacre of 3,000 Protestants and their leader Louis de Bourbon, prince of Condé (1530–69), precipitated the outbreak of the Fourth War of Religion between Catholics and Protestants in France. After the massacre of St. Bartholomew's Eve in Paris, August 24, 1572, Prince Henry IV of Navarre (1553–1610) took charge of the Protestant forces. Marked primarily by a long siege of La Rochelle by Royalist forces under another Prince Henry, the younger brother of Charles IX (1550–74), this Fourth War of Religion resulted in the Protestants' gaining military control over most of southwest France. However, at least 3,000 more Huguenots were massacred in the provinces before the war ended.

The St. Bartholomew's Day Massacre outraged even Catholic moderates, who, seeking to counter the extremes of the Catholic Royalists, formed a new political party, the Politiques, to negotiate with the Protestants and establish peace and national unity.

See also RELIGION, FIRST WAR OF (1562–1563); RELIGION, SECOND WAR OF (1567–1568); RELIGION, THIRD

WAR OF (1568–1570); RELIGION, FIFTH WAR OF (1575–1576); RELIGION, SIXTH AND SEVENTH WARS OF (1576–1577; 1580); RELIGION, EIGHTH WAR OF (1585–1589); RELIGION, NINTH WAR OF (1589–1598).

Further reading: R. J. Knecht, *The French Civil Wars, 1562–1598* (New York: Pearson Education, 2000); R. J. Knecht and Mabel Segun, *French Wars of Religion* (New York: Addison-Wesley Longman, 1996).

Religion, Fifth War of (1575–1576)

PRINCIPAL COMBATANTS: Catholics vs. Huguenots in France
PRINCIPAL THEATER(S): France
DECLARATION: None
MAJOR ISSUES AND OBJECTIVES: Henry, duc de Guise; and his Royalist faction wanted to take the French throne away from Henry III, who was more tolerant of religious differences than they.
OUTCOME: The Royalist Catholics under Henry, duke de Guise, formed a Holy League with King Philip of Spain to secure the French throne for the Catholics.
APPROXIMATE MAXIMUM NUMBER OF MEN UNDER ARMS: Unknown
CASUALTIES: Unknown
TREATIES: Peace of Mousieur, May 5, 1576

Protestants and Catholics in France had been fighting sporadically since 1562 in the First War of RELIGION, the Second War of RELIGION, the Third War of RELIGION, and the Fourth War of RELIGION when violence again erupted in 1575. In the most important action of this war, Henry, duc de Guise (1555–88), led the Catholic Royalists to victory at the Battle of Dormans. Aligned against Guise, however, were not only the Protestants under Henry IV of Navarre (1553–1610) but also the Politiques, moderate Catholics who wanted the king to make peace with the Protestants and restore national unity. Henry III (1551–89) was not wholeheartedly in support of Guise, and he offered pledges of more religious freedom to the Protestants at the Peace of Mousieur, signed on May 5, 1576. Guise refused to accept the terms of the peace and began negotiating with Philip II (1527–98) of Spain to organize a Holy League and secure Spain's help in capturing the French throne.

See also RELIGION, SECOND WAR OF; RELIGION, THIRD WAR OF; RELIGION, FOURTH WAR OF; RELIGION, SIXTH AND SEVENTH WARS OF; RELIGION, EIGHTH WAR OF; and RELIGION, NINTH WAR OF.

Further reading: R. J. Knecht, *The French Civil Wars, 1562–1598* (New York: Pearson Education, 2000); R. J. Knecht and Mabel Segun, *French Wars of Religion* (New York: Addison-Wesley Longman, 1996).

Religion, Sixth and Seventh Wars of
(1576–1577, 1580)

PRINCIPAL COMBATANTS: Catholics vs. Huguenots in France
PRINCIPAL THEATER(S): France
DECLARATION: None
MAJOR ISSUES AND OBJECTIVES: The Huguenots sought religious freedom.
OUTCOME: After subduing the Protestants, Henry III wavered in his determination to carry out the terms of the Peace of Bergerac.
APPROXIMATE MAXIMUM NUMBER OF MEN UNDER ARMS: Unknown
CASUALTIES: Unknown
TREATIES: Peace of Bergerac (1577)

The Sixth War of Religion between the Catholics and Protestants in France included only one campaign and was settled by the Peace of Bergerac of 1577. During this period, Henry III (1551–89) tried to persuade the Holy League, formed in 1576 by Catholic leader Henry, duke de Guise (1555–88), and Philip II (1527–98) of Spain, to support an attack on the Protestants. Henry succeeded in subduing the Protestants but wavered in his determination to carry out the terms of the Peace of Bergerac.

The Seventh War of Religion in 1580, also known as the "Lovers' War," had little to do with hostilities between the Catholics and Protestants. Instead fighting was instigated by the actions of Margaret, the promiscuous wife of Henry IV of Navarre (1553–1610). Over the next five years, Catholics, Protestants, and the moderate Politiques (*see* RELIGION, FOURTH WAR OF; RELIGION, FIFTH WAR OF) all engaged in intrigue in their attempts to name a successor to the childless Henry III. Although Henry of Navarre was next in line by direct heredity, the Holy League maneuvered to ensure that Henry, duc de Guise, would gain the throne after the reign of Charles de Bourbon (1566–1612), proposed as the successor to Henry III.

See also RELIGION, FIRST WAR OF; RELIGION, SECOND WAR OF; RELIGION, THIRD WAR OF; RELIGION, FOURTH WAR OF; RELIGION, FIFTH WAR OF; RELIGION, EIGHTH WAR OF; RELIGION, NINTH WAR OF (1589–1598).

Further reading: R. J. Knecht, *The French Civil Wars, 1562–1598* (New York: Pearson Education, 2000); R. J. Knecht and Mabel Segun, *French Wars of Religion* (New York: Addison-Wesley Longman, 1996).

Religion, Eighth War of (1585–1589)

PRINCIPAL COMBATANTS: Catholics vs. Huguenots in France
PRINCIPAL THEATER(S): France
DECLARATION: None
MAJOR ISSUES AND OBJECTIVES: The Catholic Royalists in France wanted to ensure that one of their numbers would be named successor to the childless Henry III.
OUTCOME: King Henry named the Protestant leader Henry of Navarre as his successor.
APPROXIMATE MAXIMUM NUMBER OF MEN UNDER ARMS: Catholics, 8,700+; Huguenots, 6,500
CASUALTIES: Catholics, 3,400 killed; Huguenots, 200 killed
TREATIES: None

The Eighth War of Religion, also known as the "War of the Three Henrys," pitted the Royalist Henry III (1551–89), Henry of Navarre (1553–1610), and Henry de Guise (1555–88) against each other in a struggle over succession to the French throne. The war began when Henry III withdrew many of the concessions he had granted to the Protestants during his reign. At the Battle of Coutras on October 20, 1587, the army of Henry of Navarre, 1,500 cavalry and 5,000 infantry, smashed the Royalist cavalry—1,700 lancers—and 7,000 infantry. More than 3,000 Royalists were killed; Protestant deaths totaled 200. Especially effective against the Royalist was the massed fire of the Protestant arquebuses, primitive muskets.

Despite the Protestant victory at Coutras, the Catholics under Henry of Guise prevailed at Vimoy and Auneau and checked the advance of a German army marching into the Loire Valley to aid to Protestants. Henry's next victory was in Paris, where he forced the king to capitulate in May 1588. In subsequent intrigues, Henry de Guise and his brother Cardinal Louis I de Guise (1527–78) were assassinated. Fleeing the Catholics' rage over the murders, Henry III sought refuge with Protestant leader Henry of Navarre. The king failed to find permanent safety and was assassinated, stabbed to death, by a Catholic monk on August 2, 1589. On his deathbed, the king named Henry of Navarre his successor. The Catholics refused to acknowledge him king, insisting instead that Cardinal Charles de Bourbon (1566–1612) was the rightful ruler of France. This conflict sparked the NINTH WAR OF RELIGION.

See also RELIGION, FIRST WAR OF; RELIGION, SECOND WAR OF; RELIGION, THIRD WAR OF (1568–1570); RELIGION, FOURTH WAR OF; RELIGION, FIFTH WAR OF; RELIGION, SIXTH AND SEVENTH WARS OF; and RELIGION, NINTH WAR OF.

Further reading: R. J. Knecht, *The French Civil Wars, 1562–1598* (New York: Pearson Education, 2000); R. J. Knecht and Mabel Segun, *French Wars of Religion* (New York: Addison-Wesley Longman, 1996).

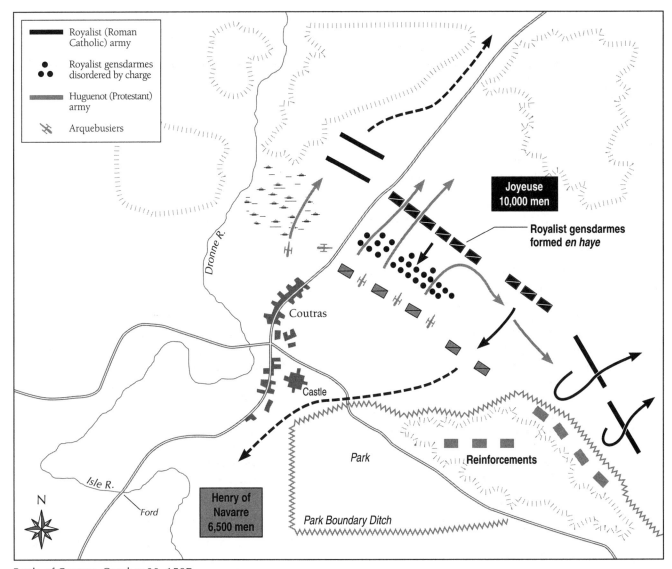

Battle of Coutras, October 20, 1587

Religion, Ninth War of (1589–1598)

PRINCIPAL COMBATANTS: Catholics vs. Huguenots in France

PRINCIPAL THEATER(S): France

DECLARATION: None

MAJOR ISSUES AND OBJECTIVES: The Protestants in France sought religious freedom.

OUTCOME: Henry III, although he had returned to the Catholic faith, issued the Edict of Nantes, which proclaimed religious freedom for French Protestants.

APPROXIMATE MAXIMUM NUMBER OF MEN UNDER ARMS: Catholics, 26,000; Huguenots, 20,000

CASUALTIES: Catholics, 13,550 killed or wounded; Huguenots, 12,040 killed or wounded

TREATIES: Edict of Nantes (1598)

The naming of Henry of Navarre (1553–1610) as successor to the French throne sparked the final War of Religion between Protestant Huguenots and Catholics in France. Insisting that Charles, duke de Bourbon (1566–1612), was the rightful successor to Henry III (1551–89), the Catholics enlisted the aid of the Spanish. Charles, duke of Mayenne (1554–1611), the younger brother of Henry of Guise (1555–88), led the Catholic efforts.

At the Battle of Arques on September 21, 1589, Henry of Navarre (1553–1660) ambushed Mayenne's army of 24,000 French Catholic and Spanish soldiers. Having lost 600 men, Mayenne withdrew to Amiens, while the victorious Navarre, whose casualties numbered 200 killed or wounded, rushed toward Paris.

A Catholic garrison near Paris repulsed Navarre's advance on November 1, 1589. Not to be daunted in his quest for the throne, Henry withdrew but promptly proclaimed himself Henry IV and established a temporary capital at Tours.

Henry of Navarre won another important battle at Ivry on March 14, matching 11,000 troops against Mayenne's 19,000. Mayenne lost 3,800 killed, whereas Navarre suffered only 500 casualties.

Civil war continued unabated. Between May and August 1590, Paris was reduced to near starvation during Navarre's siege of the city. Maneuvers continued, especially in northern France until May 1592; however, in July 1593 Henry of Navarre reunited most of the French populace by declaring his return to the Catholic faith. His army then turned to counter a threat of invasion by Spain and the French Catholics allied with Mayenne.

On March 21, 1594, Henry of Navarre entered Paris in triumph and over the next few years battled the invading Spanish: at Fontaine-Française on June 9, 1596, at Calais on April 9, 1596, and at Amiens on September 17, 1596. No further major campaigns ensued.

On April 13, 1598, Henry of Navarre ended the decades of violence between the Catholics and the Protestants by issuing the Edict of Nantes, whereby he granted religious freedom to the Protestants. Then on May 2, 1598, the war with Spain ended with the Treaty of Vervins, whereby Spain recognized Henry as king of France. The next major conflict between the Catholics and Protestants in France occurred 27 years later when the Protestants rose in revolt in 1625 and the English joined their cause in the ANGLO-FRENCH WAR (1627–1628).

See also RELIGION, FIRST WAR OF; RELIGION, SECOND WAR OF; RELIGION, THIRD WAR OF; RELIGION, FOURTH WAR OF; RELIGION, FIFTH WAR OF; RELIGION, SIXTH AND SEVENTH WARS OF; and RELIGION, EIGHTH WAR OF.

Further reading: R. J. Knecht, *The French Civil Wars, 1562–1598* (New York: Pearson Education, 2000); R. J. Knecht and Mabel Segun, *French Wars of Religion* (New York: Addison-Wesley Longman, 1996).

Revolutionary War, United States

See AMERICAN REVOLUTION.

Revolution of 1688   *See* GLORIOUS REVOLUTION.

Revolutions of 1848   *See* AUSTRIAN REVOLUTION 1848–1849); FRENCH REVOLUTION (1848); GERMAN REVOLUTION (1848); HUNGARIAN REVOLUTION (1848–1849); ITALIAN REVOLUTION (1848–1849).

Rhodesian Civil War   (1971–1980)

PRINCIPAL COMBATANTS: White supremacist Rhodesian government vs. black rebels

PRINCIPAL THEATER(S): Rhodesia (Zimbabwe) and neighboring Zambia and Mozambique
DECLARATION: None
MAJOR ISSUES AND OBJECTIVES: The black majority sought control of the government.
OUTCOME: Rhodesia gained independence as Zimbabwe.
APPROXIMATE MAXIMUM NUMBER OF MEN UNDER ARMS: Rhodesian government forces, 58,700; rebels, 20,000+
CASUALTIES: Total lives lost, 21,000 within Rhodesia/Zimbabwe; 6,000 in neighboring Zambia and Mozambique; the overwhelming majority of casualties were among black civilians and the rebel forces.
TREATIES: A 1979 London-based peace conference produced no formal treaty, but the war was resolved by the election of 1980.

Prime Minister Ian Smith (b. 1919), head of the white supremacist government of Rhodesia (Zimbabwe), broke away from the British Commonwealth in 1965 and, despite the fact that he represented only 250,000 whites in an overwhelmingly black nation of six million people, declared independence for the nation under his leadership. This provoked sporadic guerrilla warfare, which developed into a full-scale civil war in December 1972.

From December 1972 to December 1975, the black rebels proved unsuccessful against the white Rhodesian security forces. During this period, 720 rebel guerrillas were killed, whereas only 75 government troops died. The situation began to improve for the rebels at the end of 1975 when they acquired bases in newly independent Mozambique (*see* MOZAMBICAN WAR OF INDEPENDENCE). The rebels began to attack on two fronts—Mozambique and Zambia. Nevertheless, they were outnumbered, mustering by 1976 about 20,000 men against a total of 58,700 government army, air force, reserve, and police personnel. Moreover, the insurgents were divided between forces loyal to the Zambian-based Zimbabwe African People's Union (ZAPU) and the Mozambique-based Zimbabwe African National Union (ZANU).

Despite the strain of fighting a two-front war, Rhodesian government forces continued to enjoy success against the divided rebels, whom they called "terrs"—terrorists. However, each year took a greater toll on both sides, and a pattern of raid and reprisal developed, culminating (on September 2, 1978) in the downing of a Rhodesian airliner by a rebel-fired SAM-7 missile. This moved Prime Minister Smith to arrange a compromise by turning over leadership to a majority black government under a moderate black leader, Bishop Abel Muzorewa (b. 1925). Guerrilla leaders who were not included in the government, however, continued the war, claiming that Muzorewa was a white puppet.

Elections early in 1980 brought the two most important "outlaw" rebel leaders to power. Robert Mugabe (b.

1924) was elected president, and Joshua Nkomo (1917–1999) became vice president. With this Rhodesia became Zimbabwe, and the war ended.

Further reading: Martin Meredith, *Our Votes, Our Guns: Robert Mugabe and the Tragedy of Zimbabwe* (New York: Public Affairs, 2002).

Riel's First Rebellion (Red River Rebellion) (1869–1870)

PRINCIPAL COMBATANTS: Métis rebels vs. Canadian government

PRINCIPAL THEATER(S): Red River area of Manitoba

DECLARATION: None

MAJOR ISSUES AND OBJECTIVES: When the Hudson's Bay Company transferred ownership of Rupert's Land to the Canadian government, the Métis people, living in the Red River settlement included in the transfer, feared they would lose their traditional rights and rebelled.

OUTCOME: Setting up a provincial government at present-day Winnipeg, the rebels petitioned to be included in the new province of Manitoba, which Canada was forming out of the vast Rupert's holdings. When fighting broke out between the Métis and local English settlers, Canada repressed the rebellion.

APPROXIMATE MAXIMUM NUMBER OF MEN UNDER ARMS: Métis: 10,000 (4,000 of whom were "mixed blood" Scottish and English settlers); Canadian numbers unknown

CASUALTIES: Numbers unknown, but losses light on both sides.

TREATIES: None

Sometimes called the "Métis Messiah," Louis David Riel (1844–85) was a leader of the Métis peoples of western Canada. Riel's father, also named Louis (fl. early 19th century), had organized a brief rebellion against Hudson's Bay Company rule over the Red River Settlement (present-day Manitoba) in 1849, when the boy was not yet five years old, and he grew up surrounded by anti-English and anti-Canadian feeling. Sent to study for the priesthood in Montreal, the youthful Riel there gave the first evidence of the moodiness, distraction, and quarrelsome personality that would seem to the Métis messianic but would lead the Canadian government to confine him for a while in mental asylums in Quebec. Possibly distraught by the death of his father, Riel gave up the priesthood; scorned by the white parents of his lover when he proposed marriage, Riel returned to the West.

In 1869 the Hudson's Bay Company turned Rupert's Land, the company's vast holdings in the Canadian West, over to the British Crown. When the government launched a survey as the first step in transferring those lands to Canadian jurisdiction, the Métis at Red River reacted with fear and anger. Generally of mixed French and Indian ancestry, the Métis believed, with good cause, that neither their land rights nor the separate culture they had developed over centuries would be respected by the English-speaking Canadians. Given his father's status, Riel quickly became their spokesman after standing firm against a party of surveyors who were trying to enter the settlement. Under his leadership, the Red River people established the Comité National des Métis, which blocked the region's new Canadian governor William McDougal (1822–1905) from entering the territory and seized nearby Fort Garry (Winnipeg).

The 6,000 Métis turned for help to local English-speaking settlers, 4,000 or so of them also "mixed bloods" with Scottish or English fathers and grandfathers and often lumped together with the Métis by white Canadians as *bois brulé,* or "scorched wood." Because they too were leery of the Canadians, they joined with the Métis in a provisional government headed by Riel. In 1870, the Red River Settlement negotiated with the Canadians to become part the province of Manitoba. Though both parties came to terms, the agreement was shattered when rebellious Métis court-martialed and executed some local sympathizers with the Canadian cause for bearing arms against the state. One of them—an obscure Irishman named Thomas Scott (d. 1870), who had threatened to kill Riel—became a martyr for white Canadians.

Canada's government in Ottawa responded by denying the rebel Métis amnesty, and the rebels fled to Métis settlements on the Saskatchewan River. Riel ensconced himself in Fort Garry when Ottawa sent Colonel Garnet Wolseley (1833–1913) in August to "maintain order" in Manitoba. When Wolseley and his British regulars arrived, Riel gave up the fort without a fight on August 24, 1870. He too fled the area. That year, the Red River area was incorporated into the new Manitoba Province, which granted many of the rights—such as separate French schools for the Métis—demanded by Riel and his rebels.

Further reading: Marcel Giraud, *The Métis in the Canadian West,* trans. George Woodcock (Edmonton: University of Alberta Press, 1986); Joseph Kinsey Howard, *Strange Empire: Louis Riel and the Métis People* (1952; reprint ed., Toronto: Lewis and Samuel, 1974); Charles Phillips, "Louis David Riel" and "The Metis," in *Encyclopedia of the American West,* ed. Charles Phillips and Alan Axelrod, vols. 3 and 4 (New York: Macmillan Reference USA, 1996).

Riel's Second Rebellion (Northwest Rebellion) (1885)

PRINCIPAL COMBATANTS: Métis rebels vs. the Northwest Mounted Police and the Canadian army

PRINCIPAL THEATER(S): Saskatchewan, Canada
DECLARATION: None
MAJOR ISSUES AND OBJECTIVES: When the Métis, who had removed to Saskatchewan after Riel's First Rebellion, and other Indians in the area began to feel the impact of the westward settlement of English-speaking whites, they called on their exiled leader, Louis David Riel, who returned from the United States to head up a second revolt.
OUTCOME: The resistance was crushed, and Riel was tried for treason and executed, helping to create a bitter legacy the impact of which is still felt today between French-speaking and English-speaking Canadians.
APPROXIMATE MAXIMUM NUMBER OF MEN UNDER ARMS: Rebels, 400+; Canadian government forces, 8,000+
CASUALTIES: Rebels, 35 killed; Canadian government forces, 40 killed, 115 wounded
TREATIES: None

In the Canadian parliamentary elections of 1873 following RIEL'S FIRST REBELLION, the leader of that rebellion, Louis David Riel (1844–85) was elected as the new province of Manitoba's representative. Denied his seat, he was reelected in 1874, and again the government declined to let him hold office. The following year Riel was banished from all of Canada. Caught on Canadian soil, he was thrown into a Quebec mental institution for two years—between 1876 and 1878. After he was released, he headed south to Montana, took out papers for American citizenship, and began calling himself David—rather than Louis—Riel. Back in Canada, four members of the Thomas Scott jury, who had ruled on the case of the white Canadian court-martialed and executed by the rebel Métis during the first rebellion, were murdered. Another was beaten within an inch of his life and left for dead just across the border in the United States. White-Métis racial tension escalated; Métis land was appropriated, and the Métis people were harassed and scorned by white Canadians arriving in the new Canadian West.

Riel had been teaching at a Jesuit mission school near Sun River for several years when the Métis in Saskatchewan appealed to him in 1884 to return to Canada to help them fight off the growing number of English settlers and the Canada Pacific Railway, which ominously had begun to survey their lands. Hailed as a messiah, the perhaps mentally unstable Riel refused all compromise with the Canadians. Turning his back on Canada's legal channels of redress and protest, Riel deliberately provoked Canadian authorities. Once again, he set up a provisional government, this time in Saskatchewan. Growing increasingly suspicious of those around him, including some of his oldest friends, Riel broke with the Catholic Church in the spring of 1885, declared a new Métis provincial government, and enlisted local Indians in his fight against the whites. In March, he defeated a force of the Northwest

Mounted Police and attacked settlers along Frog Creek. Canada sent its army out after Riel, which defeated the Métis guerrillas at Bartoche on May 12, 1885.

Tried for treason at Regina, Riel refused to plead insanity, as his lawyers recommended, before an English-speaking jury. The jury found him guilty and sentenced him to hang. After a number of postponements, the government carried out the execution on November 6, 1885. Riel's death became a national scandal, provoking outbursts of protest among French Canadians in Quebec and a bitter controversy over Catholic (and French-speaking) schools in Manitoba and Quebec. For the Métis, and for French-speaking Canadians in general, Riel remained a martyr though English-speaking Canadians continued mostly to consider him a madman. Both attitudes remained common even in the early 21st century, when cultural tensions spawned more than a century before continued to mar the relations between Canada's ethnic groups.

Further reading: Marcel Giraud, *The Métis in the Canadian West,* trans. George Woodcock (Edmonton: University of Alberta Press, 1986); Joseph Kinsey Howard, *Strange Empire: Louis Riel and the Métis People* (1952; reprint ed., Toronto: Lewis and Samuel, 1974); Charles Phillips, "Louis David Riel" and "The Métis," in *Encyclopedia of the American West,* ed. Charles Phillips and Alan Axelrod, vols. 3 and 4 (New York: Macmillan Reference USA, 1996).

Rif War (1893)

PRINCIPAL COMBATANTS: Rif tribesmen vs. Spanish colonists at Melilla
PRINCIPAL THEATER(S): Morocco
DECLARATION: None
MAJOR ISSUES AND OBJECTIVES: Spain wanted to subdue the Rif, who raided the Spanish enclave of Melilla.
OUTCOME: The Rif were suppressed, and the sultan of Morocco agreed to pay an indemnity.
APPROXIMATE MAXIMUM NUMBER OF MEN UNDER ARMS: Rif numbers unknown; Spanish troops, 25,000
CASUALTIES: Unknown
TREATIES: Treaty of Fez (1894)

Spanish possessions along the northern Mediterranean coast of Morocco were threatened by Muslim Berbers known as the Rif, because they lived in the Rif region of Morocco. The sultan of Morocco proved unable to suppress the Rif, whereupon Spain fortified its Melilla enclave there. Nevertheless, Melilla was besieged by the Rif, provoking a public outcry in Spain. Accordingly, in November 1893 the Spanish government to Melilla dispatched 25,000 troops, who pushed the Rif back. The following year, the Treaty of Fez (1894) was concluded between Spain and the sultan of Morocco, who agreed to pay Spain a war indemnity of 20 million pesetas and to conduct a punitive campaign against the Rif. For its part, Spain was given explicit leave to complete its fortification of Melilla, creating a buffer zone between it and Morocco.

See also RIF WAR (1919–1926).

Further reading: C. R. Pennell, *Morocco since 1830: A History* (New York: New York University Press, 2001).

Rif War (Abd el-Krim's Revolt) (1919–1926)

PRINCIPAL COMBATANTS: Spain and France vs. Rifs
PRINCIPAL THEATER(S): Morocco
DECLARATION: None
MAJOR ISSUES AND OBJECTIVES: The Rifs under Abd el-Krim wanted to establish Morocco as an independent republic.
OUTCOME: Initial victories against Spain alone were decisive; later, the Rifs lost to an alliance of France and Spain.
APPROXIMATE MAXIMUM NUMBER OF MEN UNDER ARMS: Spain, 150,000; France, 160,000; Rifs, 80,000–120,000
CASUALTIES: Spain, 50,000 killed; France, 10,000 killed; Rifs, 30,000 killed or wounded
TREATIES: Paris Conference of June 16–July 10, 1926

In the largest anticolonial rebellion of the early 20th century, Spanish possessions in northern Morocco came under attack in the east by the Rif—66 Berber tribes living in the Rif Mountain region—led by Abd el-Krim (1882–1963), and in the west by Moroccans under Ahmed ibn-Muhammad Raisuli (1875–1925).

The first uprisings occurred in 1919. While troops under the Spanish high commissioner of Morocco, Damaso Berenguer (1873–1953), succeeded against those led by Raisuli, General Fernandez Silvestre was dealt a devastating defeat by Abd el-Krim's Rifs. The general, together with 13,000 out of 20,000 Spanish troops engaged, fell at the Battle of Anual on July 21, 1921, utterly defeated by a mere 6,000 Rif warriors.

In the wake of this disaster, panic gripped the colony, and Spain withdrew from eastern Morocco. Abd el-Krim immediately set up the Republic of the Rif, with himself as president. His triumph against Silvestre drew to his side a huge army of between 80,000 and 120,000 rebel warriors. With the Spanish out of the way, Abd el-Krim moved next against the French, his object being to gain control of all Morocco. Leading 20,000 men out of his large army, he took many French outposts as he marched to Fez in 1925. Forty-three of 66 French outposts and blockhouses fell to Krim's advance.

Krim's triumph prompted the French to reinforce their army, to 60,000 by July and to 160,000 by the end of the year. Moreover, traditional rivals for the Moroccan prize, France and Spain now joined forces. Spain's dictator General Miguel Primo de Rivera (1870–1930) led a combined Spanish-French expeditionary force that landed at Alhucemas Bay on Morocco's Mediterranean coast in September 1925. He advanced against Abd el-Krim's headquarters at Targuist, while from the south a 160,000-man French army led by WORLD WAR I hero Marshal Philippe Pétain (1856–1951) moved northward, boxing the Rif troops into an area north of Taza. This combined attack rapidly turned the tide of the war. In the face of vastly superior forces—some 360,000 men in all, the largest army mobilized for colonial warfare to that time—Abd el-Krim surrendered on May 26, 1926, and suffered exile to the island of Réunion. At a Paris conference held during June 16–July 10, 1926, France and Spain restored the borders of their Moroccan zones as established by a 1912 treaty.

See also RIF WAR (1893).

Further reading: Rupert Furneaux, *Abdel Krim: Emir of the Rif* (London: Secker and Warburg, 1967); C. R. Pennell, *Morocco since 1830: A History* (New York: New York University Press, 2001).

Río de la Plata, Wars of the   See ARGENTINE WAR OF INDEPENDENCE; PARAGUAYAN WAR OF INDEPENDENCE (1810–1811); URUGUAYAN REVOLT.

Robert's Revolt (921–923)

PRINCIPAL COMBATANTS: Robert, count of Paris, vs. Charles III, king of France
PRINCIPAL THEATER(S): France
DECLARATION: None
MAJOR ISSUES AND OBJECTIVES: Robert sought to depose the king.
OUTCOME: Charles III was toppled, but Robert died in battle; the throne was occupied by the Carolingian duke Rudolph of Burgundy.
APPROXIMATE MAXIMUM NUMBER OF MEN UNDER ARMS: Unknown
CASUALTIES: Unknown
TREATIES: None

Robert I, count of Paris (c. 865–923), rebelled against Charles III (the Simple; 879–929) of France after his many military successes increased both his prestige and his ambition. Initially, Robert enjoyed great success against Charles, forcing him to retreat to Lorraine. In June 922, the nobles elected Robert king at Reims, and he was crowned on the 29th. Charles, however, recruited an army in Lorraine and marched to Laon. The following year, on June 15, 923, Charles engaged Robert at the Battle of Soissons. Although the forces of the count emerged victorious, Robert himself fell, apparently killed in a duel with Charles.

Rudolph (d. 936), the Carolingian duke of Burgundy, assumed the throne and went on to triumph against the Normans and the men of Aquitaine.

Further reading: Heinrich Fichtenau. *The Carolingian Empire* (Toronto: University of Toronto Press, 1978).

Rogue River War (1855–1856)

PRINCIPAL COMBATANTS: "Rogue" Indians vs. United States

PRINCIPAL THEATER(S): Oregon-California border region

DECLARATION: None

MAJOR ISSUES AND OBJECTIVES: Deteriorating relations between white settlers and marauding Indians, exacerbated by the memory of an Indian "massacre" of Oregon missionaries and by the local territorial officials' policy of removing Indians to reservations, broke out into a minor war that involved reluctant federal troops.

OUTCOME: The Indians were defeated and removed to a reservation.

APPROXIMATE MAXIMUM NUMBER OF MEN UNDER ARMS: "Rogue" Indians, 200; United States, est. 180

CASUALTIES: Indians 48+ killed; U.S. 38 killed, 25 killed or wounded

TREATIES: None

Following the WHITMAN MASSACRE of 1847 and the reprisal led by Cornelius Gilliam (d. 1848), Indian-white relations in the Northwest steadily deteriorated until, by 1854, Indians and whites fell into the habit of shooting each other on sight. Fearful and outraged settlers called for aid from the regular army. General John E. Wool (1784–1869), who commanded the U.S. Army's Department of the Pacific, was charged with policing the Indian situation in the Northwest. One of a distinct white minority who favored reason and moderation in dealing with the Indians, Wool soon found himself facing not only an Indian "situation" but a white "situation" as well. The general not only refused to annihilate the Indians, as the settlers loudly demanded, but repeatedly and publicly excoriated the citizenry of Oregon for their lust after Indian extermination. By the autumn of 1855, the army found itself caught between Indians and settlers.

Settlers called the Takelma and Tututni, who lived near the Oregon-California border, "Rogue" Indians because they repeatedly attacked travelers along the Siskiyou Trail near the Rogue River. In August, drunken Indians killed 10 or 11 miners along the Klamath River. In retaliation, whites killed some 25 Indians—though not those who had killed the miners; they had fled. The Rogue River War was now under way, and, in September 1855, the local violence was intensified by rumors of a developing war between Yakamas and whites east of the Cascades. As whites began to menace all Indians, hostile or not, Captain Andrew Jackson Smith (fl. mid-19th century), commanding Fort Lane, found it necessary to offer Indian men, women, and children the protection of the fort. Before Lane could admit all of the endangered Indians into the fort, however, a band of settlers raided a nearby camp, killing 23 "Rogue Indians," including old men, women, and children. The next day, October 17, Indian war parties took revenge, killing 27 settlers in the Rogue Valley and burning the hamlet of Gallice Creek.

With the bulk of General Wool's regulars engaged in fighting the Yakamas, Walla Wallas, Umatillas, and Cayuses in what was now being called the Yakama War, Captain Smith could do little with his small garrison except keep it from being overrun itself. By the time relief was scheduled to arrive at Fort Lane, the Rogue River War actually seemed to be winding down of its own volition. The Takelma and Tututni chiefs known to the whites as Limpy, Old John, and George (all fl. mid-19th century), weary of warfare, agreed to surrender to Captain Smith at a place called Big Meadows. Apparently at the very last minute, the chiefs thought better of it and instead mustered some 200 warriors for an attack on Smith's 50 dragoons and 30 infantrymen. The element of surprise was lost when two Indian women informed Smith of the planned attack. Outnumbered, the captain did the best he could, deploying his men on a hilltop that offered a good defensive position.

When it came, the attack was fierce and unremitting. The soldiers dug in the night after the first day of fighting. Morning revealed that 25 men had been killed or wounded. By the afternoon of May 28, 1856, the Indians were massing for a final assault.

At that moment, with the good timing of a bad Hollywood western, the promised reinforcements arrived, commanded by Captain Christopher C. Augur (served 1843–85). Overjoyed, Smith rallied his men for a downhill charge as Augur's infantry charged up from the rear. It was one of the few times that a classic military charge was effective against Indians, as Smith and Augur played out the cliché situation in which victory is snatched from the jaws of defeat. Indeed, the "Rogues" were so utterly routed that within the month all had surrendered and meekly submitted to life on a reservation.

Further reading: Alan Axelrod, *Chronicle of the Indian Wars: From Colonial Times to Wounded Knee* (New York: Prentice Hall General Reference, 1993); E. A. Schwartz, *The Royal River Indian War and Its Aftermath, 1850–1980* (Norman: University of Oklahoma Press, 1997); Robert M. Utley, *Frontiersman in Blue: The United States Army and the Indian, 1848–1865* (Lincoln: University of Nebraska Press, 1981).

Rohan's Revolts *See* BEARNESE REVOLT, FIRST; BEARNESE REVOLT, SECOND; BEARNESE REVOLT, THIRD.

Rohilla War (1774)

PRINCIPAL COMBATANTS: The Rohillas vs. the Marathas (and, subsequently, Oudh), aided by British East India Company mercenaries
PRINCIPAL THEATER(S): Rohilkhand, India
DECLARATION: None
MAJOR ISSUES AND OBJECTIVES: The British wanted to maintain Oudh as a buffer against the Marathas and to this end aided the nawab of Oudh in defeating the Marathas and in annexing Rohilkhand.
OUTCOME: The Marathas were pushed out of Oudh and Rohilkhand, the Rohillas were subjugated, and Rohilkhand was annexed to Oudh.
APPROXIMATE MAXIMUM NUMBER OF MEN UNDER ARMS: Unknown
CASUALTIES: Unknown
TREATIES: None

The Rohillas were Afghans who had been displaced by the forces of Nadir Shah (1688–1747) of Persia and settled in Rohilkhand, north-central India by 1740. When the Marathas menaced them in 1771, they asked for aid from the nawab of Oudh, Asaf-ud-Daula (1749–97), who sent mercenary troops. The Rohillas, however, failed to pay the troops, who attacked Oudh, already beleaguered by Maratha forces.

At this point, Warren Hastings (1772–1818), Britain's governor-general of Bengal, intervened. He believed Oudh was vital to British interests as a buffer between Maratha and the British settlements in eastern India. Therefore, Hastings dispatched to the nawab a brigade of soldiers in the employ of the British East India Company. Together, the nawab's troops and the British mercenary brigade pushed back the Marathas. This left the British mercenaries free to move against the Rohillas, whose territory the nawab had decided to annex. The Rohillas were defeated at the Battle of Miranput Katra in February 1774, whereupon Oudh annexed Rohilkhand. Oudh was enlarged, and Hastings had thus gained an augmented buffer against the Marathas. Parliament belatedly impeached Hastings for having exceeded his authority, but he was acquitted upon trial, and Britain had made a further step in what would be its ultimate conquest of India.

See also MARATHA WARS.

Further reading: Lawrence Jones, *The Raj: the Making and Unmaking of British India* (New York: St. Martin's, 2000); Barbara Daly Metcalf and Thomas P. Metcalf, *Concise History of India* (New York: Cambridge University Press, 2002).

Roman-Alemannic War (271)

PRINCIPAL COMBATANTS: Alemanni invaders vs. Rome
PRINCIPAL THEATER(S): Northern and central Italy
DECLARATION: None
MAJOR ISSUES AND OBJECTIVES: The Alemanni invaded Italy and sought to take Rome itself.
OUTCOME: After suffering defeat, Emperor Aurelian rallied and drove the Alemanni out of Italy; although triumphant, he took steps to reduce the Roman Empire and to protect Rome future invasions.
APPROXIMATE MAXIMUM NUMBER OF MEN UNDER ARMS: Unknown
CASUALTIES: Unknown
TREATIES: None

By 270 C.E. the Alemanni, Germanic tribespeople, who were highly successful in their attacks against the Romans, had overrun the Agri Deumates (Baden-Württemberg) on Rome's German frontier. From here, joined by the Jutungi and the Vandals, they invaded northern Italy and were met at Placentia (Piacenza) on the Po River by a Roman army under Emperor Aurelian (c. 212–275). The Alemanni dealt Aurelian a severe defeat and advanced down the Italian Peninsula toward Rome. Undaunted, Aurelian regrouped and rallied his troops, then gave chase, overtaking the Alemanni at Faro, in central Italy. Here Aurelian triumphed, driving the Alemanni north. Unwilling to relinquish the initiative, Aurelian pursued the retreating barbarians to Pavia, where he forced them to a stand in a battle that nearly destroyed the invading forces. Surviving Alemanni dispersed into the Alps.

Although he was ultimately victorious, Aurelian was greatly abashed by the invasion. He ordered a withdrawal from Agri Decumates and erected a chain of forts on the south bank of the Danube. By the end of the 270s, the city of Rome itself had been walled.

Further reading: E. A. Thompson, *Romans and Barbarians: The Decline of the Western Empire* (Madison: University of Wisconsin Press, 2002); Alaric Watson, *Aurelian and the Third Century* (London: Routledge, 1999).

Roman-Armenian War (93–92 B.C.E.)

PRINCIPAL COMBATANTS: Rome (with Parthia) vs. Armenia
PRINCIPAL THEATER(S): Cappadocia, Asia Minor
DECLARATION: None
MAJOR ISSUES AND OBJECTIVES: Rome sought to drive the Armenians out of Cappadocia, a client state.
OUTCOME: Roman legions triumphed over the Armenian invaders.
APPROXIMATE MAXIMUM NUMBER OF MEN UNDER ARMS: Unknown

CASUALTIES: Unknown
TREATIES: Alliance between Rome and Parthia, 92 B.C.E.

Seeking to expand his power and his kingdom, Tigranes I (the Great; c. 140–55 B.C.E.), king of Armenia, annexed parts of eastern Asia Minor, then allied himself with the Pontine emperor Mithradates VI (the Great) (r. 120–64 B.C.E.) and, in 93 B.C.E., to invade the Roman protectorate of Cappadocia, in east-central Asia Minor. With Parthian king Mithradates II (the Great; r. 123–86 B.C.E.), the Roman praetor and military commander Cornelius Sulla (138–78 B.C.E) formed an alliance against Tigranes and the Pontine Mithradates. Yet even before Parthian reinforcements arrived, the Roman legions drove the Armenians out of Cappadocia. Tigranes was thus defeated by Roman arms alone.

See also ROMAN-ARMENIAN WAR (72–66 B.C.E.).

Further reading: Neilson C. Debevoise, *Political History of Parthia* (Chicago: University of Chicago Press, 1969); Mark Dunster, *Parthia* (Fresno, Calif.: Linden Publishers, 1979).

Roman-Armenian War (72–66 B.C.E.)

PRINCIPAL COMBATANTS: Rome vs. Armenia and Pontus
PRINCIPAL THEATER(S): Armenia
DECLARATION: None
MAJOR ISSUES AND OBJECTIVES: Rome sought to punish Mithradates VI (the Great), king of Pontus, who had taken refuge with his son-in-law, Tigranes I (the Great) of Armenia; when Tigranes refused to surrender Mithradates, Rome sought the conquest of Armenia.
OUTCOME: Mithradates returned to Pontus, and Armenia fell to Rome.
APPROXIMATE MAXIMUM NUMBER OF MEN UNDER ARMS: Unknown
CASUALTIES: Unknown
TREATIES: None

After Mithradates VI (the Great; r. 120–64 B.C.E.) king of Pontus, was defeated by Rome in the Third MITHRADATIC WAR, he took refuge with Tigranes II (the Great) (c. 140–55 B.C.E.) of Armenia. Tigranes II had brought a unity to Armenia that would last 500 years, and this "King of Kings" (as he was called) gladly gave sanctuary to his father-in-law, Mithradates VI. Lucius Licinius Lucullus (c. 110–56 B.C.E.), commanding the Roman legions against Mithradates, demanded that Tigranes surrender the fugitive. When Tigranes refused, Lucullus attacked and overran Armenia, looting its capital city, Tigranocerta, on October 6, 69. From the base he established in the fallen capital, Lucullus set out to subjugate all of Armenia. However, the difficult mountainous terrain and inhospitable

climate of Armenia proved more formidable. While Lucullus's legions were struggling with weather and topography, Tigranes and Mithradates raised and trained a new army, only to be defeated by the Romans at the Battle of Artaxata in 68. Following this victory, Lucullus, determined to capture the new Armenian capital, drove his reluctant and exhausted troops northward until they mutinied, refusing to march farther. Lucullus had no choice but to retreat to the valley of the Euphrates. Mithradates responded to this retreat by returning to Pontus, where he was determined to take a stand once again against the Romans. Lucullus followed, but was recalled to Rome in 66 before he could give battle.

In 66, Pompey the Great (106–48 B.C.E.) led Roman forces against Armenia, defeating Tigranes with the aid of his disloyal son. The Armenian king agreed to Roman vassalage.

See also ROMAN-ARMENIAN WAR (93–92 B.C.E.).

Further reading: Mack Chahin, *The Kingdom of Armenia* (London: Taylor and Francis, 2001).

Roman-Armenian War (113–117) *See* ROMAN EASTERN WAR (113–117).

Roman-Armenian War (162–165) *See* ROMAN EASTERN WAR (162–165).

Roman Civil War (88–82 B.C.E.)

PRINCIPAL COMBATANTS: Lucius Cornelius Sulla vs. his Roman rivals
PRINCIPAL THEATER(S): Italy and the environs of Rome
DECLARATION: None
MAJOR ISSUES AND OBJECTIVES: Control of the Roman Empire
OUTCOME: Sulla converted or defeated all rivals and was named dictator for life.
APPROXIMATE MAXIMUM NUMBER OF MEN UNDER ARMS: Sulla, 40,000; opposition substantially smaller
CASUALTIES: Unknown
TREATIES: None

In 88 B.C.E., the tribune Publius Sulpicius Rufus (124–88 B.C.E.) led a democratic revolt against the dictatorship of Lucius Cornelius Sulla (138–78 B.C.E.) while Sulla was on his way to fight the First MITHRADATIC WAR. Sulla quickly returned and crushed the incipient revolt, then set out for Greece again. The very next year, a new uprising of democrats, this one led by Lucius Cornelius Cinna (d. 84 B.C.E.), began. This time, the democrats seized power, and Caius Marius (157–86 B.C.E.), who had conspired with

Rufus and then fled with other rebels to Africa in 88 B.C.E., returned. Marius set up a tyrannical and despotic regime in 86, and although he died later that year, Cinna continued his despotic rule.

Seeking to neutralize the power of Sulla, Cinna dispatched Gaius Flavius Fimbria (d. 84) to replace him as commander in the East during the ongoing First Mithradatic War. Sulla, however, managed to persuade Fimbria to join his side, and in 83, reinforced with Fimbria's troops, Sulla marched back to Italy. Resistance from Italian tribes and from Romans he neutralized either by defeating the opposing forces in battle or winning them over to his cause. Desperate, those who opposed Sulla attempted to capture the city of Rome itself. Sulla and his allies met the rival forces at the Colline Gate and there destroyed them in November 82. The Senate immediately named Sulla dictator for life.

See also ROMAN CIVIL WAR, GREAT.

Further reading: P. A. Kildahl, *Caius Marius* (New York: Twayne, 1968); Rex Warner, tr., *The Fall of the Roman Republic: Six Lives—Marius, Sulla, Crussus, Pompey, Caesar, Cicero* (New York: Penguin, 1972).

Roman Civil War, Great (50–45 B.C.E.)

PRINCIPAL COMBATANTS: Caesar's legions vs. the Roman army of Pompey
PRINCIPAL THEATER(S): Spain, Egypt, Africa, Asia Minor
DECLARATION: None
MAJOR ISSUES AND OBJECTIVES: Julius Caesar sought to cement his control over the Roman Empire.
OUTCOME: Caesar succeeded in subduing all opponents and was appointed dictator of Rome.
APPROXIMATE MAXIMUM NUMBER OF MEN UNDER ARMS: Caesar, 60,000; Pompey, 180,000
CASUALTIES: At the great Battle of Pharsalus (August 9, 48 B.C.E.), Caesar lost 230 killed, and 2,000 wounded, whereas Pompey lost 15,000 killed and wounded, and 24,000 prisoners.
TREATIES: None

Having conquered Gaul, Julius Caesar (100–44 B.C.E.) was a military hero. The Roman Senate, fearful of his power, ordered Caesar to relinquish his province of Gaul, disband his army, and return to Rome. Caesar refused. Instead he crossed the Rubicon River with his army into Italy, despite the fact that the Roman law forbade generals from entering Italy proper with their armies without permission from the Senate. Pompey (the Great; 106–48 B.C.E.), having been appointed sole consul by the Senate, took his army and most of the Senate into Greece, where he hoped to increase his forces to battle Caesar. Caesar entered Rome and took control of the city.

ILERDA CAMPAIGN

Rather than pursue Pompey in Greece, Caesar turned toward Spain. First, however, he was forced to take the city of Massilia (Marseille). Lucius Domitius Ahenobarbus (d. 48 B.C.E.), a supporter of Pompey, had arrived in Massilia with a small force and persuaded the city to declare its allegiance to Pompey. Caesar used three legions under Gaius Trebonius (d. 43 B.C.E.) to besiege the city, while the others proceeded to the passes of the Pyrenees. There they were able to block the advance of Pompey's armies under Lucius Afranius (d. 46 B.C.E.) and Marcus Petreius (fl. 50–44 B.C.E.). These two Pompeian generals then waited for Caesar at Ilerda while the rest of Spain was held by Vibellius Rufus (fl. 50–44 B.C.E.) and Marcus Varro (116–27 B.C.E.). At Ilerda, Caesar's 37,000-strong army confronted the Pompeian force in July 49 B.C.E. Caesar had decided not to destroy the Pompeian army but to try to capture it, thereby adding to his force by recruiting captives. As Afranius and Petreius began their withdrawal from Ilerda, Caesar outmaneuvered them and cut off their retreat. They returned to Ilerda, where Caesar surrounded them and captured their water supply. On August 2, 49, the two Pompeian leaders surrendered, their legions were disbanded. Caesar then gained control over Gades (Cadiz) and marched to Massilia. Upon his arrival, Massilia surrendered on September 6, 49 B.C.E. Caesar returned to Rome, and in October 49, the senators who had remained in Rome appointed him dictator.

Meanwhile, Gaius Curio (d. 49 B.C.E.), Caesar's legate, had gained control of Sicily and had moved on to Africa. There he faced a Pompeian force under Attius Varus (fl. 50–48 B.C.E.) and his ally Juba (c. 85–46 B.C.E.), king of Numidia. Curio defeated the allies near Utica but was himself defeated at the Bagradas River on August 24, 49.

SIEGE OF DYRRHACHIUM

Caesar, deciding to pursue Pompey, set sail on January 4, 48, with seven legions and a few cavalry. Landing to the south of Pompey's base at Dyrrhachium, Caesar then sent his ships back to Brundisium to pick up Mark Antony (82/81–30 B.C.E.). Pompey's troops got word of Caesar's attempt to join Mark Antony's forces with his own and blockaded Antony in Brundisium. Pompey, with nearly 100,000 men, moved from eastern Epirus (southern Albania) to Dyrrhachium. By March 48 Antony was able to break out of Brundisium, and he joined Caesar in a siege of Pompey's numerically superior forces in Dyrrhachium. On July 10, Pompey's army broke through the lines of investment, while Caesar withdrew his forces to Thessaly. In July and August, the two armies camped on either side of the Pharsalus plain. On August 9, 48, Caesar's outnumbered army soundly defeated Pompey, who fled in disguise to the coast, where he set sail for Egypt. The battle had inflicted 2,200 casualties on Caesar and 15,000 on Pompey. About 24,000 Pompeian troops were taken prisoner.

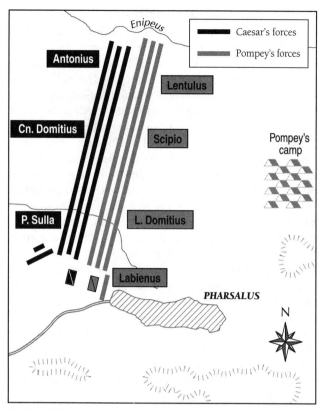

Battle of Pharsalus, 48 B.C.E.

EGYPTIAN CAMPAIGN

Caesar and 4,000 of his men pursued Pompey to Egypt, but upon their arrival in Alexandria they were told that Pompey had been assassinated by his associates. The former Pompeians had also encouraged Ptolemy XII (c. 112–51 B.C.E.) and his sister Cleopatra (69–30 B.C.E.) to defy Caesar, who had taken up positions in a portion of Alexandria. From August 48 until January 47, the former Pompeians laid siege to Alexandria. Learning that his ally Mithradates of Pergamum (fl. 50–44 B.C.E.) had arrived at the Nile River, Caesar slipped out of Alexandria with part of his force. In February at the Battle of the Nile, Caesar and Mithradates completely defeated Ptolemy and the Roman-Egyptian army. Over the following months, Caesar established control over Egypt and placed Cleopatra, who had become his ally and his lover, on the throne with her younger brother Ptolemy XIII (63–47 B.C.E.).

PONTIC CAMPAIGN

In April 47, Caesar set sail for Syria with a portion of his army. There he had plans to defeat Pharnaces (fl. 50–44 B.C.E.), king of the Bosporus Cimmerius, who had taken advantage of the Roman civil war to reestablish the kingdom of Pontus. At the Battle of Zela in May 47, Caesar defeated Pharnaces and sent to Rome his message, *"Veni, vidi, vici"* ("I came, I saw, I conquered"). He gave control of the kingdom of Pharnaces to his ally Mithradates of Pergamum.

AFRICAN CAMPAIGN

After returning to Rome, where he subdued a mutiny by many of his veteran legionnaires who wanted to be discharged from the army and rewarded for their victories, Caesar sent 25,000 men first to Sicily and then to Africa, where he confronted the remnants of the Pompeian force defeated earlier in Spain and Greece. Under the leadership of Metellus Scipio (d. 46 B.C.E.) and Caesar's former lieutenant Labienus, the army also included a Numidian force under King Juba. Caesar arrived at Ruspina and, maneuvering away from this base, was encircled by the army of Labenius. Caesar broke free of the encircling army and returned to Ruspina, where he was blockaded by the army of Scipio and Juba. In December 47 and January 46, Caesar marched inland and laid siege to Thapsus. At the Battle of Thapsus in February 46 the Pompeian-Numidian army, earlier decimated by illness and desertions, attacked Caesar's troops and was completely defeated. Having subdued Africa, Caesar returned to Rome in May 46.

SPANISH THEATER

Caesar did not remain long in Rome, however. In December 46, he sailed to Spain and took control of the force he had left there after the Ilerda campaign. In Spain, Roman-Pompeian troops who had fled Africa after the Battle of Thapsus had rallied under Pompey's sons. At the Battle of Munda on March 17, 45, Caesar attacked the army of Gnaeus Pompey (d. 45 B.C.E.) and Labienus (d. 45 B.C.E.) in their hilltop positions but was nearly defeated. Rushing to the center of the battle line, Caesar was able to forestall panic, and his reinvigorated army surged forward. The battle was a massacre; 30,000 Pompeians were killed. Labienus was killed, and Gnaeus Pompey was captured and executed. Sextus (fl. 48–34 B.C.E.), the younger brother of Gnaeus Pompey, escaped along with a remnant of the Pompeian fleet. Caesar marched through Spain and then returned to Rome, in July 45. His reign there as monarch of the Roman empire was now undisputed, but it lasted only a short time. On March 15, 44 B.C.E., Caesar was assassinated by a group of Roman senators alarmed at the despotism of his rule. Following his death, Rome was ruled by Caesar's grandnephew Octavian (63–14 B.C.E.) (later known as Augustus), Mark Antony, and Marcus Lepidus (d. c. 77). This Second Triumvirate faced another round of civil war, which lasted from 43 to 31 B.C.E.

See also ROMAN CIVIL WAR (43–31 B.C.E.).

Further reading: Julius Caesar, *Civil War* (after 49 B.C.E.; trans. and reprint ed., New York: Penguin, 1976); Philip Matyszak, *Chronicle of the Roman Republic: The Rulers of Ancient Rome from Romulus to Augustus* (New York and London: Thames and Hudson, 2003).

Roman Civil War (43–31 B.C.E.)

PRINCIPAL COMBATANTS: Marc Antony, Octavian and Lepidus ("Second Triumvirate") vs. Pompey and other Roman generals leaders of the Roman Senate; subsequently, the Triumvirs fought among themselves.

PRINCIPAL THEATER(S): Roman Empire

DECLARATION: None

MAJOR ISSUES AND OBJECTIVES: Following the murder of Julius Caesar, his friend, Marc Antony, his heir, Octavian, and Roman general Lepidus formed the Second Triumvirate to punish those responsible, then fell to fighting among themselves.

OUTCOME: Over the course of little more than a decade, Octavian destroyed Caesar's enemies, defeated his rivals, and consolidated the Roman state under his rule as Augustus Caesar.

APPROXIMATE MAXIMUM NUMBER OF MEN UNDER ARMS: Triumvirate, 120,000; Pompey, perhaps 80,000 maximum

CASUALTIES: Unknown

TREATIES: Treaty of Brundisium (40 B.C.E.) and Treaty of Tarentum (37 B.C.E.)

Following the Punic Wars (see PUNIC WAR, FIRST; PUNIC WAR, SECOND; PUNIC WAR, THIRD), the Roman Republic began to lose its authority as Rome itself expanded toward a worldwide empire. By the time Julius Caesar (100–44 B.C.E.), began his rise to power, the old peasant militia of the Republic had become a professional army, the soldiers of which owed their allegiance not to the Roman state, much less to the Senate, but to the individual generals upon whom their fortunes literally depended. Inevitably, Rome's legions became a political tool. For a generation, Rome's fate was decided by powerful generals, as its politics became volatile and expensive. From this combination three men emerged within a few years to claim leadership of the state—a renowned and revered general named Gnaeus Pompey (106–48 B.C.E.); a wealthy landowner, speculator, and moneylender named Marcus Crassus (115–53 B.C.E.); and Julius Caesar himself, the scion of an obscure patrician family but also a skilled writer, spellbinding orator, astute politician, and accomplished general. The three men formed a coalition, an informal compact called later the "First Triumvirate."

After Crassus was killed in a foreign war in Parthia (see ROMAN-PARTHIAN WAR [55–36 B.C.E.]), Pompey colluded with a powerful oligarchy in the Senate to trump up charges of treason against Caesar, who had been appointed governor of Gaul (see GALLIC WARS). Ordered to return alone to Rome to face the charges, Caesar came instead with his extensive and loyal army, and Pompey fled to Egypt, where he was put to death by the nominally independent country's teen-aged king, Ptolemy XIII (63–47 B.C.E.). Caesar, arriving in Egypt in pursuit of Pompey,

quickly replaced Ptolemy with Ptolemy's sister, Cleopatra (69–30 B.C.E.). Cleopatra and Caesar became lovers; she was pregnant with Caesar's child when he returned to Rome to a hero's welcome and a humbled but secretly seething Senate (see GREAT ROMAN CIVIL WAR). Declared dictator, he announced his intentions to assume the position for life, which lead the Senate oligarchy to plot his assassination. On March 15—the Ides of March—in 44 B.C.E. some 60 senators surrounded Caesar in the forum as he presided over the assembly and stabbed him 23 times.

News of Caesar death reached Caesar's 18-year-old grandnephew and protégé, Gaius Octavian (63–19 B.C.E.), in Appollinia, a Greek city on the Adriatic coast, where he was completing his education. Octavius rushed back to Italy to find he had been named in the dictator's will as his adopted son and heir. Urged on by his stepfather and others, Octavian decided to take up what was bound to be a perilous inheritance, and he proceeded on to Rome, where he would discover there were others vying for the position his dead "father" had created—Caesar's chief lieutenant, the swaggering and handsome Mark Antony (82/81–30 B.C.E.); Caesar's second in command, Marcus Aemilius Lepidus (d. 13/12 B.C.E.), who succeeded the great Roman as chief priest in the state religion; and two powerful senators, Marcus Junius Brutus (85–42 B.C.E.) and Gaius Cassius Longinus (d. 42 B.C.E.), who had led the assassination conspiracy.

Antony, who had assumed he would be Caesar's heir, had taken possession of his papers and assets, and refused to hand over any of Caesar's funds. Upon his arrival in Rome, Octavian paid from his own pockets the late dictator's bequests that Antony had refused to pay and underwrote the public games instituted by Caesar to ingratiate himself with the Roman populace. In the process, Octavian managed to win considerable numbers of Caesar's former troops to his cause. Brutus and Cassius left Rome, more or less ignoring the new pretender to power, and took command of the eastern half of the empire. The Senate, encouraged by Cicero (106–43 B.C.E.), broke with Antony and swung its support to the young man who was now calling himself Gaius Julius Caesar. Cicero had assumed that Octavian (as historians by tradition continue to refer to him before he assumes the title "Augustus") would be easier for the Senate to manipulate than either Antony or Lepidus, and eventually he would pay for that mistake with his life.

After several months of battling for supremacy, the three men agreed to a division of power in a coalition called the "Second Triumvirate." Formed in part to seek retribution against Caesar's assassins, this triumvirate, unlike the first, became official when the Senate in 43 B.C.E. granted to the triumvirs five years of autocratic power in order to reconstitute the fractured state. Antony and Octavian hunted down the two leading tyrannicides in Macedonia, where both Brutus and Cassius chose suicide on the battlefield rather than capture at Philippi. The triumvirs then turned on Rome itself, drawing up a list of proscribed enemies and executing 200 senators and 2,000 nobles. Among the condemned senators, at Antony's insistence, was Cicero, whose head and hands were nailed to the Rostra in the forum, one nail—in mockery of the great orator's eloquence—driven through his tongue. Finally, the triumvirs had Julius Caesar officially recognized as a god of the Roman state, which enhanced Octavian's prestige. To Antony, the coalition's senior partner, went the Eastern Empire and Gaul.

Upon his return to Italy, Octavian found himself embroiled in the Perusine War against Antony's brother, Lucius Antonius (fl. 43–31 B.C.E.) over the settlement of Octavian's veterans. Pompey's son, Sextus Pompeius (67–35 B.C.E.), was causing trouble as well, having seized Sicily and Rome's sea routes. To appease Sextus and win time to finish the Perusine conflict, Octavian married one of his relatives, Scribonia (divorced 40 B.C.E.) but this did not stop Sextus from making overtures to Antony once the war was concluded. Meanwhile, Antony had formed a strong political bond with Egypt's wealthy queen and Caesar's former lover, Cleopatra. Soon that bond became a romantic one as well. Octavian was no doubt relieved when Antony rejected Sextus's blandishments. In 40 B.C.E., Octavian and Antony reached a fresh understanding in the Treaty of Brundisium.

Under the new agreement, Octavian was to have the whole of the Western Roman Empire, including Gaul and excepting Africa, which went to Lepidus. Italy itself was declared neutral ground, although in fact it was controlled by Octavian. Antony kept the eastern half of the empire, but having spent—much to the dismay of Rome—the previous winter with Cleopatra, he now agreed under the treaty to a marriage with Octavian's sister, Octavia (69–11 B.C.E.). The treaty delighted the peoples of the empire, east and west, because it seemed to promise an end to generations of social strife and occasional civil war. Just as Antony was closely linking his future to Octavian by marrying into his family, Octavian sought to strengthen his ties to the Senate aristocracy, many members of which supported either Antony or Sextus, by a new marriage of his own to Livia Drusilla (58–29 B.C.E.).

The goodwill established by the treaty did not last, and in the long run provisions of the treaty themselves became sources of discord. Reconciliation with Sextus proved abortive, and Lepidus, unhappy with his portion of power, rebelled. Antony's true love lay in Egypt, not in Italy, but when he returned to Cleopatra the insult was not only to his new wife but to her brother as well. In 37 B.C.E., with Antony's reluctant help, Octavian destroyed Sextus (see OCTAVIAN'S WAR AGAINST POMPEY). In 36 B.C.E., when Lepidus attacked, Octavian defeated him and placed him under guard for the rest of his life. In 32 B.C.E. Octavian renounced the triumvirate outright, and Antony responded by divorcing Octavia. Urged on by Octavian, the next year the Senate declared war on Antony. Octavian

himself accompanied the Roman ships that defeated Antony and Cleopatra at the Battle of Actium in 31 B.C.E. (see OCTAVIAN'S WAR AGAINST ANTONY). Like Brutus and Cassius before them, the pair chose suicide over capture by the ruthless Octavian.

Octavian went on to reign as Caesar Augustus, the first Roman emperor. The Republic had died, replaced by the rule of a single strong man. Under such rule would grow a Roman Empire whose glory became the touchstone of civilization thereafter. But such rule also created the problem of succession, which the empire never solved. Instead, the habit of political assassination, having brought Augustus to power, would plague his empire throughout its history.

Further reading: Robin Seager, *Pompey the Great* (London: Blackwell, 2002); Pat Southern, *Mark Antony* (London: Tempus, 1999); Richard D. Weigel, *Lepidus: The Tarnished Triumvir* (London: Routledge, 1992).

Roman Civil War (68–69 C.E.)

PRINCIPAL COMBATANTS: Vindex and Galba vs. Nero; Rufus and Galba vs. Vindex; Otho vs. Galba and, separately, Vitellius; Vespasian vs. Vitellius
PRINCIPAL THEATER(S): Mostly Italy
DECLARATION: None
MAJOR ISSUES AND OBJECTIVES: Ascension to the imperial throne of Rome
OUTCOME: After a succession of rebellions and ascensions, Vespasian was proclaimed emperor of Rome.
APPROXIMATE MAXIMUM NUMBER OF MEN UNDER ARMS: Unknown
CASUALTIES: Unknown
TREATIES: None

This Roman civil war began as a revolt against Nero (37–68), the ruler among whom none of the legion of "bad" Roman emperors is more infamous for sadistic, corrupt, and incompetent rule. Gaius Julius Vindex (d. 68), legate (governor) of Gaul, led a revolt against Nero in 68 B.C.E. and was joined by Servius Sulpicius Galba (3–69), legate of Spain. At the urging of Vindex, Galba's troops proclaimed him emperor. In the meantime, however, the legate of Upper Germany, Lucius Verginius Rufus (15–69), led an army against Vindex and crushed his revolt, Vindex committed suicide. Although Rufus's troops wanted to proclaim him emperor, Rufus refused and threw his support behind Galba. When the Praetorian Guard—the emperor's own bodyguard—joined Rufus in this acclamation, the Senate proclaimed Galba emperor and condemned Nero, who promptly killed himself.

Yet the matter of Roman rule was hardly resolved. 69 C.E. would become known as the "Year of the Four Emperors," as, in turn, four contenders occupied the imperial throne. Galba was only the first. Aulus Vitellius (15–69), legate of Lower Germany, accepted acclamation as emperor by his legions, which he led toward Italy. Galba, in the meantime, was slain by the very Praetorians who had acclaimed him but now supported Marcus Salvius Otho (32–69), legate of Lusitania (modern Portugal) and a longtime opponent of Nero. Otho won recognition from the Senate as emperor, then marched against the advancing Vitellius. At the First Battle of Bedriacum (near Cremona, Italy), on April 16, 69, Vitellius was victorious. Defeat prompted Otho to commit suicide, leaving the way clear for Vitellius to complete his march on Rome, where he was acclaimed emperor by the Senate.

During this time, however, in Judea, Vespasian (9–79) was proclaimed emperor by his troops and with the additional support of the legates of Syria and Egypt, who sent a large combined army under Antonius Primus (fl. first century) into Italy. Antonius triumphed over Vitellius at the Second Battle of Bedriacum (fought probably in November of 69). Vitellius himself was assassinated in Rome on December 20, 69, as Antonius's army arrived in the capital. On December 21, the Roman Senate ratified Vespasian as the new emperor of Rome.

Further reading: Barbara Levick, *Vespasian* (London: Routledge, 199); Kenneth Wellesley, *Year of the Four Emperors* (London: Routledge, 2000).

Roman Civil War (193–197)

PRINCIPAL COMBATANTS: Severus vs. (variously) Pescennius Niger and Slodius Septimus Albinus
PRINCIPAL THEATER(S): Chiefly Byzantium and Gaul
DECLARATION: None
MAJOR ISSUES AND OBJECTIVES: Succession to the imperial Roman throne
OUTCOME: Severus defeated his two rivals and assumed the throne, effectively initiating a military dictatorship of the empire.
APPROXIMATE MAXIMUM NUMBER OF MEN UNDER ARMS: Unknown
CASUALTIES: Unknown
TREATIES: None

Commodus (161–192)—yet another of Rome's "bad emperors"—reigned from 180 to 192, when he was assassinated. He was succeeded by the elderly Publius Helvius Pertinax (126–193), who sought to restore Rome to moral and financial soundness by introducing a program of severe austerity, beginning with the imperial court. The Praetorians bridled at this and, in 193, assassinated Pertinax. The throne was offered for sale to the highest bidder. The claimant was Marcus Didius Julianus (133–193), who, however, was immediately confronted by three rivals, each of whom was a general and enjoyed the backing of the legions they respectively commanded. In Britain, Clodius Septimus Albinus (d. 197) pressed his claim. In Pannonia (Hungary), it was Luscius Septimus Severus. In Syria, the claimant was Pescennius Niger (d. 194).

On his way to Rome, Severus quickly usurped power, the Senate having just ordered the execution of Didius Julianus because it resented the manner in which he had assumed power. Severus set to work purging and reforming the treacherous Praetorian Guard, then neutralized opposition from Albinus by (quite deceitfully) promising him succession to the throne. During his march toward Rome, Severus also dealt with Pescennius Niger, defeating him at the Battle of Cyzicus in 193, again at Nicaea later in the year, and finally at Issus in 194. Severus's pursuing legions caught up with Niger as he fled from the last battle and promptly executed him.

Despite the death of Niger, Byzantium, a stronghold of forces loyal to him, held off a siege by Severus. He persisted and in 196 at last overran the city, which his troops mercilessly sacked. By this time, however, conflict between Severus and Albinus had reached a boil, and Albinus preemptively declared himself emperor. He led his British legions into Gaul, where he clashed with the Pannonian legions under the command of Severus. At the Battle of Lugdunum (Lyon, France) in 197, Albinus met his end, and Severus turned the wrath of his legions against the city of Lugdunum, leveling it.

Following his victory over Albinus, Severus marched his legions back to Macedonia to resume the ROMAN-PARTHIAN WAR (195–202). Over the empire of Rome, Severus created a military dictatorship, supplanting with the army the power formerly enjoyed by the Senate.

Further reading: Edward Gibbon, *The Decline and Fall of the Roman Empire*, 3 vols., edited by J. B. Bury (New York: Modern Library, 1993); Michael Grant, *Sick Caesars: Madness and Malady in Imperial Rome* (New York: Barnes and Noble, 2003).

Roman Civil War (235–268)

PRINCIPAL COMBATANTS: Publius Licinius Egnatius Gallienus vs. many rivals and pretenders, in addition to Germanic invaders
PRINCIPAL THEATER(S): Italy and the northern and eastern borders of the Roman Empire
DECLARATION: None
MAJOR ISSUES AND OBJECTIVES: Control of the imperial throne and survival of the empire
OUTCOME: Gallienus successfully retained his throne, albeit of an increasingly imperiled and reduced empire, until he was assassinated by his own troops.
APPROXIMATE MAXIMUM NUMBER OF MEN UNDER ARMS: Unknown
CASUALTIES: Unknown
TREATIES: None

Like the ROMAN CIVIL WAR (43–31 B.C.E.), this period was less a discrete war than an epoch of internal conflict often verging on outright anarchy. During this period, the empire was assailed not only by intense political and economic instability but by continual menace and incursions from Germanic peoples, and, between 251 and 265, an epidemic of plague. Only the long tradition of military discipline among the legions kept Rome from immediate collapse during this time. Nevertheless, even the legions suffered from pervasive corruption and debility.

The reign of Publius Licinius Egnatius Gallienus (253–268) was dubbed the "Reign of Thirty Tyrants" because of the number of petty rulers (according to the historian Edward Gibbon, 19 rather than 30) and others who vied for the imperial throne. Armed conflict was endemic throughout three decades, although Gallienus enjoyed remarkable success in retaining power over his increasingly attenuated empire. His life and reign came to an end in 268, when he was assassinated by members of his own legions during a campaign to crush a rebellion in Milan.

See also ROMAN CIVIL WAR (238).

Further reading: Edward Gibbon, *The Decline and Fall of the Roman Empire*, 3 vols., edited by J. B. Bury (New York: Modern Library, 1995); Ramsay MacMullen, *Corruption and the Decline of Rome* (New Haven, Conn.: Yale University Press, 1990); E. A. Thompson, *Romans and Barbarians: The Decline of the Western Empire* (Madison: University of Wisconsin Press, 2002).

Roman Civil War (238)

PRINCIPAL COMBATANTS: Thrax (Gaius Julius Verus Maximinus) vs. (variously) Clodus Pupienus Maximus, Decimus Caelius Balbinus, Gordianus I, Gordianus II, Gordianus III, and his own troops
PRINCIPAL THEATER(S): Carthage and Italy
DECLARATION: None
MAJOR ISSUES AND OBJECTIVES: Control of the imperial throne
OUTCOME: Thrax defeated most of his external enemies but was killed by his own troops; Gordianus III became emperor.
APPROXIMATE MAXIMUM NUMBER OF MEN UNDER ARMS: Unknown
CASUALTIES: Unknown
TREATIES: None

The reign of Gaius Julius Verus Maximinus (173–238)—known as Thrax, in honor of his Thracian birth—was consumed in battles against invading Germans. Thrax's continual absence from Rome cost him recognition by the Senate, which in 238 proclaimed Clodius Pupienus Maximus (d. 238) and Decimus Caelius Balbinus (d. 238) co-emperors of Rome. In the meantime, disaffected Roman

legionnaires in northern Africa proclaimed Gordianus I (158–238) emperor. Superannuated, Gordianus I conferred co-emperor status on his son Gordianus II (192–238). The young man, however, was soon killed in battle in Carthage by supporters of Thrax. After this, his father committed suicide, and Gordianus III (c. 224–244), grandson of Gordianus I, was proclaimed emperor by the Senate, which now formally deposed Thrax. In response, he advanced into northeaster Italy, where he laid siege against Aquileia. The siege settled into a frustrating stalemate, during which Thrax's own restive troops assassinated him.

With Thrax disposed of, the Praetorian Guard now made its preference known by killing Pupienus Maximus and Balbinus, thereby affirming the Senate's choice of Gordianus III as emperor.

See also ROMAN CIVIL WAR (235–268).

Further reading: Edward Gibbon, *The Decline and Fall of the Roman Empire*, 3 vols., edited by J. B. Bury (New York: Modern Library, 1995); Ramsay MacMullen, *Corruption and the Decline of Rome* (New Haven, Conn.: Yale University Press, 1990); E. A. Thompson, *Romans and Barbarians: The Decline of the Western Empire* (Madison: University of Wisconsin Press, 2002).

Roman Civil War (284–285)

PRINCIPAL COMBATANTS: Carinus vs. Diocletian
PRINCIPAL THEATER(S): Moesia (modern Bulgaria)
DECLARATION: None
MAJOR ISSUES AND OBJECTIVES: Emperor of the West, Carinus wanted to become emperor of the East as well.
OUTCOME: Although militarily victorious, Carinus was killed by one of his own troops, and Diocletian became sole emperor of a united Rome.
APPROXIMATE MAXIMUM NUMBER OF MEN UNDER ARMS: Unknown
CASUALTIES: Unknown
TREATIES: None

Marcus Aurelius Carinus (d. 285), who long served as administrator and *virtual* emperor of the West, was proclaimed emperor of the West in fact upon the death of his father, Marcus Aurelius Carus (c. 223–283). In the East, however, the Roman legions proclaimed Diocletian (245–313) emperor. Carinus was not content with rule only in the West and therefore led an army against Diocletian.

Initially, Carinus enjoyed a heartening success in small engagements in Moesia (Bulgaria) and seemed destined to win a major victory against Diocletian at the Battle of Margus (Morava). However, at the height of the combat he was suddenly killed, apparently by one of his own troops. This catapulted Diocletian to victory and to imperial rule over both the Western and Eastern Empires. In a single stroke, the civil war was over.

Further reading: Edward Gibbon, *The Decline and Fall of the Roman Empire*, 3 vols., edited by J. B. Bury (New York: Modern Library, 1995); Ramsay MacMullen, *Corruption and the Decline of Rome* (New Haven, Conn.: Yale University Press, 1990); E. A. Thompson, *Romans and Barbarians: The Decline of the Western Empire* (Madison: University of Wisconsin Press, 2002); Stephen Williams, *Diocletian and the Roman Recovery* (London: Routledge, 1996).

Roman Civil War (306–307)

PRINCIPAL COMBATANTS: Maxentius vs. Severus (with help from Galerius)
PRINCIPAL THEATER(S): Environs of Rome
DECLARATION: None
MAJOR ISSUES AND OBJECTIVES: Succession to the imperial throne.
OUTCOME: Severus was killed, and Maxentius proclaimed himself emperor; however, four other contenders made the same claim, and the empire was essentially divided among them.
APPROXIMATE MAXIMUM NUMBER OF MEN UNDER ARMS: Unknown
CASUALTIES: Unknown
TREATIES: None

Diocletian (245–313) introduced a host of military and administrative reforms that helped stave off the disintegration of the Roman Empire. However, aged and ailing, he abdicated in 305 C.E., thrusting the beleaguered empire into yet another civil war. Years earlier, the emperor had taken pains to appoint successors—giving the Eastern Empire to Galerius (d. 311) and the Western to Constantius I (250–306)—but conflict developed. Constantius died in 306, and the army chose his son, Constantine I (c. 280–337), to succeed him. Galerius, however, supported Severus (d. 307) as emperor of the West. The situation was further clouded by the claim of Maxentius (d. 312), who, aided by his father, Maximian (d. 310), met the armies of Galerius and Severus in battle just outside of Rome. Severus was suddenly deserted by his forces and threw himself on the mercy of Maximian, who responded by having him executed. This ended a year of great turmoil, and, in 307, Maxentius proclaimed himself emperor. Within three years, however, he was joined by four other self-proclaimed emperors. An uneasy peace—riddled with schemes and conspiracies—was maintained, none of the five contenders wishing to risk their hold on the piece of the now-fragmented Roman Empire he respectively ruled.

Further reading: Edward Gibbon, *The Decline and Fall of the Roman Empire*, 3 vols., edited by J. B. Bury (New York: Modern Library, 1995); Ramsay MacMullen, *Corruption and the Decline of Rome* (New Haven, Conn.: Yale Uni-

versity Press, 1990); Stephen Williams, *Diocletian and the Roman Recovery* (London: Routledge, 1996).

Roman Civil War (311–312)

PRINCIPAL COMBATANTS: Constantine I the Great vs. Maxentius
PRINCIPAL THEATER(S): Environs of Rome
DECLARATION: None
MAJOR ISSUES AND OBJECTIVES: Control of the imperial throne of the West
OUTCOME: Constantine, victorious, became emperor of the Western Empire.
APPROXIMATE MAXIMUM NUMBER OF MEN UNDER ARMS: At Milvian Bridge, Constantine fielded 50,000 men against Maxentius's 75,000; total strength, 311–312: Constantine, 100,000; Maxentius, 170,000
CASUALTIES: Unknown
TREATIES: None

Constantine I (the Great; c. 280–337) opposed Maxentius (d. 312), his rival emperor, by invading northern Italy with 40,000 men. In rapid succession he triumphed at Susa, Turin, and Milan, each time winning brilliant victories against numerically superior forces. After victories at Brescia and Verona, Constantine marched on Rome. With reinforcements, Constantine had about 50,000 men when late in 312 he was met at the Tiber, just outside of Rome, at Milvian Bridge by a 75,000-man army under Maxentius. Constantine won an outstanding victory that gave him the throne of the Western Empire. The early church historian Pamphili Eusebius of Caesarea (c. 260–before 341) created an enduring legend about the battle, writing that Constantine had a vision of a flaming cross, bearing the legend *In hoc signo vinces*—"By this sign conquer"—and there and then converted to Christianity in exchange for victory. In fact, Constantine did not convert until he was on his deathbed in 337, but in 313, with Licinius (270?–325), emperor of the East, he issued an edict proclaiming toleration of Christianity in the Roman Empire.

Further reading: G. P. Baker, *Constantine the Great and the Christian Revolution* (New York: Rowman and Littlefield, 2001); Edward Gibbon, *The Decline and Fall of the Roman Empire*, 3 vols., edited by J. B. Bury (New York: Modern Library, 1995); Ramsay MacMullen, *Corruption and the Decline of Rome* (New Haven, Conn.: Yale University Press, 1990).

Roman Civil War (313)

PRINCIPAL COMBATANTS: Licinius vs. Maximinus (Daia)
PRINCIPAL THEATER(S): Thrace and western Asia Minor
DECLARATION: None

MAJOR ISSUES AND OBJECTIVES: Maximinus wanted to seize the Eastern Empire from Licinius.

OUTCOME: Maximinus was defeated and yielded territory to Licinius, who lived out the rest of his life as the unchallenged emperor of the Eastern Empire.

APPROXIMATE MAXIMUM NUMBER OF MEN UNDER ARMS: Licinius, 30,000; Maximinus, 70,000

CASUALTIES: Unknown

TREATIES: None

Maximinus (Daia) (d. 313) opposed Licinius (c. 270–325), Roman emperor of the East, in 313. He led an army of 70,000 across the Bosporus and attacked the emperor's much smaller force of 30,000 at Thrace. Despite his superiority of numbers, Maximinus was beaten back into Asia Minor. Licinius then led his veterans of the Danubian campaigns in a counterattack against Maximinus in western Asia Minor, defeating him at the Battle of Tzirallum and sending his rival into full retreat. Soon after this battle, Maximinus died, and Licinius annexed the territory he had controlled. From this point on, Licinius reigned, without further contest, as the emperor of the East.

Further reading: G. P. Baker, *Constantine the Great and the Christian Revolution* (New York: Rowman and Littlefield, 2001); Edward Gibbon, *The Decline and Fall of the Roman Empire*, 3 vols., edited by J. B. Bury (New York: Modern Library, 1995); Ramsay MacMullen, *Corruption and the Decline of Rome* (New Haven, Conn.: Yale University Press, 1990).

Roman Civil War (314–324)

PRINCIPAL COMBATANTS: Constantine I (the Great) vs. Licinius

PRINCIPAL THEATER(S): Pannonia (Hungary), Thrace, Asia Minor, Hellespont

DECLARATION: None

MAJOR ISSUES AND OBJECTIVES: Licinius, emperor of the East, wanted to seize control of the West from Constantine I.

OUTCOME: Constantine I defeated Licinius and had him executed.

APPROXIMATE MAXIMUM NUMBER OF MEN UNDER ARMS: In Pannonia, Constantine commanded 20,000, Licinius, 35,000; by the First Battle of Adrianople, each army consisted of 120,000–150,000 men

CASUALTIES: Totals unknown, but Licinius lost 35,000–50,000 men at Adrianople (July 3, 323)

TREATIES: None

Licinius (c. 270–325), emperor of the Eastern Empire, attempted to ignite a revolt against his western counterpart, Constantine I (the Great; c. 280–337) in 314. In

response, Constantine led 20,000 soldiers in an invasion of the East, narrowly defeating Licinius's forces in eastern Pannonia (Hungary) later in the year. He pursued Licinius's retreating army, which took a stand at Mardia and lost decisively there. Licinius then agreed to acknowledge Constantine as emperor of all Roman European holdings, save Thrace. In turn, Constantine renounced his perquisites as "senior" emperor. Left unresolved, however, was the disposition of the Christians, Constantine advocating toleration, Licinius objecting. Still, an uneasy peace endured until 323 C.E., when Constantine, in pursuit of marauding Goths, made an incursion into Thrace, thereby reigniting war with the Eastern Empire.

In the new conflict, Constantine seized the initiative, attacking Licinius's army at Adrianople (Edirne) on July 3, 323. Shortly after this land victory, Flavius Hulius Crispus (305–26), Constantine's son, led a 200-ship fleet against Licinius's superior 350-ship fleet and defeated it at the Hellespont (Dardanelles). Totally defeated, Licinius fled deep into Asia Minor. He recruited a new army and returned to confront Constantine's forces at the Battle of Chrysopolis (Scutari) in September 323. After an exceptionally hard-fought battle, Licinius was defeated and once again fled the field only to surrender later. He was executed as a traitor.

Further reading: G. P. Baker, *Constantine the Great and the Christian Revolution* (New York: Rowman and Littlefield, 2001); Edward Gibbon, *The Decline and Fall of the Roman Empire*, 3 vols., edited by J. B. Bury (New York: Modern Library, 1995); Ramsay MacMullen, *Corruption and the Decline of Rome* (New Haven, Conn.: Yale University Press, 1990).

Roman Civil War (350–351)

PRINCIPAL COMBATANTS: Constantius vs. Magnentius

PRINCIPAL THEATER(S): Italy and Yugoslavia

DECLARATION: None

MAJOR ISSUES AND OBJECTIVES: Constantius sought to punish the murderer of his brother Constans and to reunite the Roman Empire under his rule.

OUTCOME: Constantius defeated Flavius Popilius Magnentius and become the sole emperor in 351.

APPROXIMATE MAXIMUM NUMBER OF MEN UNDER ARMS: At the Battle of Mursa (351), each army numbered about 100,000 men.

CASUALTIES: At Mursa and in the retreat following the battle, Magnentius lost 12,000 men killed, Constantius lost 15,000.

TREATIES: None

In 337 C.E., when Constantine I (c. 280–337) died, the Roman Empire was divided among his three sons. Constantine II (c. 317–40) inherited Gaul, Spain, and Britain;

Constantius II (317–361) received Greece, Thrace and the East; Constans (c. 323–350) became ruler of Italy, Africa, and Illyricum (the Balkan Peninsula). Constantine II invaded Italy almost immediately. After he was killed in an ambush near Aquileia, a large city used as a port of entry for Italy and a key defense zone, in 340, Constans seized his holdings. But Constans himself fell victim to an intrigue when his general, Flavius Popilius Magnentius (d. 353), led a revolt against him and killed the Roman ruler. Magnentius then declared himself emperor. Constantius was occupied in a war with Shapur II (309–79) of Persia at this time. Once peace was secured, Constantius marched west to have a showdown with the murderer of his brother. Reaching Illyricum, modern Dalmatia and an important but troublesome Roman province, he found that his sister, Constantina (d. 354), had crowned Magnentius Augustus. The armies of Constantius and Magnentius (about 100,000 men each) marched toward lower Pannonia—modern Hungary, a major frontier province. At the Battle of Mursa (Osijek, Yugoslavia), Constantius's army proved more maneuverable and superior. His troops enveloped the left flank of Magnentius's army, on September 28, 351, and his cavalry charged through the Gallic legions. Magnentius lost about 12,000 soldiers and withdrew to Italy. Constantius's army—which suffered as many as 15,000 casualties—pursued Magnentius, but at the Battle of Pavia, Magnentius was victorious. Despite that victory, the Roman populace rose against him, and he retreated to Gaul, where not only the local populace but his own army turned against him. Magnentius committed suicide in 353, and Constantius became the sole Roman emperor.

Further reading: G. P. Baker, *Constantine the Great and the Christian Revolution* (New York: Rowman and Littlefield, 2001); Edward Gibbon, *The Decline and Fall of the Roman Empire*, 3 vols., edited by J. B. Bury (New York: Modern Library, 1995); Ramsay MacMullen, *Corruption and the Decline of Rome* (New Haven, Conn.: Yale University Press, 1990).

Roman Civil War (360–361)

PRINCIPAL COMBATANTS: Constantius II vs. Julian
PRINCIPAL THEATER(S): Constantinople
DECLARATION: None
MAJOR ISSUES AND OBJECTIVES: A jealous Constantius II sought to punish his cousin Julian for accepting the title of emperor from soldiers in Gaul.
OUTCOME: Constantius died before confronting Julian, who became the legitimate emperor and continued the war against Persia.
APPROXIMATE MAXIMUM NUMBER OF MEN UNDER ARMS: Julian was able to raise an army of 95,000 in the wake of this conflict.
CASUALTIES: Unknown
TREATIES: None

After Muslim Persians invaded the Christian kingdom of Armenia, Roman emperor Constantius II (317–61) took an army to the East to wage war against the Persians. Constantius was defeated in the war and sent word to his cousin Flavius Claudius Julianus (Julian) (331–63) to come to his aid. Not only was Constantius anxious for victory against the Persians, but he also wanted to remove from Gaul Julian and the cream of the Roman Legions faithful to him. Julian represented a grave threat to Constantius's power. Famed for his conversion to Christianity, Julian was extremely popular among his men, who had waged successful wars in Gaul against the Franks and Alemanni. Julian's soldiers refused to leave Gaul and defiantly proclaimed Julian emperor. Constantius, hearing of this rebellion, rushed toward Constantinople from the East; Julian hurried across southern Germany and parts of Austria, Hungary, and Yugoslavia to meet his cousin in battle. During the march, he learned that Constantius had fallen ill in Asia Minor and had died. At that moment, Julian repudiated Christianity—becoming known to history as Julian the Apostate—in order to claim the throne as emperor of the Roman Empire. This done, he turned his attention to Persia and raised an army of 95,000 men, the largest expeditionary force Rome had ever assembled in the East.

See also ROMAN-PERSIAN WAR (337–363).

Further reading: G. P. Baker, *Constantine the Great and the Christian Revolution* (New York: Rowman and Littlefield, 2001); G. W. Bowersock, *Julian the Apostate* (Cambridge, Mass.: Harvard University Press, 1997); Robert Louis Wilken, *The Christians as the Romans Saw Them* (New Haven, Conn.: Yale University Press, 2003).

Roman Civil War (394)   *See* ARBOGAST AND EUGENIUS, REVOLT OF.

Roman Conquest of Britain (43–61 C.E.)

PRINCIPAL COMBATANTS: Rome vs. British tribesmen
PRINCIPAL THEATER(S): Britain
DECLARATION: None
MAJOR ISSUES AND OBJECTIVES: Rome sought to subjugate the British tribes and securely attach the region to the Roman Empire.
OUTCOME: Rome won complete control of Britain by 61 C.E.
APPROXIMATE MAXIMUM NUMBER OF MEN UNDER ARMS: Roman legions, 50,000; tribal numbers unknown
CASUALTIES: Unknown
TREATIES: None

Although Julius Caesar (43–61) had first invaded Britain during the GALLIC WARS of 58–51 B.C.E., the British tribes remained unsubdued. Emperor Claudius I (10 B.C.E.–54) sent Aulus Plautius (fl. 43–61), commander of four Roman legions and auxiliaries, to the region in 43 C.E. He landed at Rutupiae (Richborough, Kent), and was soon reinforced (in 44) by troops under the personal leadership of Claudius, who brought elephants intended to overawe the tribesmen.

Aulus Plautius and Claudius defeated the Catuvellauni and Trinovantes, and drove the Catavellauni chieftain, Caratacus (fl. 43–61), into Wales. Along the route of his retreat, Caratacus recruited support from the Silures and Orgovices of Wales and appealed to Queen Cartimandua (fl. 30–70) of Brigante. Cartimandua treacherously betrayed him to Roman authorities. Nevertheless, Caratacus made numerous raids into Roman-held territory before he was defeated at the Battle of Caer Craddock (in modern Shropshire) in 50. He was sent, a prisoner, to Rome.

By 61, not only were Londinium (London), Camulodunum (Colchester), and Verulamium (St. Albans), the three main population centers, firmly a part of the Roman Empire, but the British frontier of Wales was as well. The last major resistance was BOUDECCA'S REVOLT (from 60 to 61).

Further reading: T. W. Potter and Catherine Johns, *Roman Britain* (Berkeley: University of California Press, 1993); Malcolm Todd, *Roman Britain* (London: Blackwell, 1999).

Roman Eastern War (113–117)

PRINCIPAL COMBATANTS: Rome and Armenia, Assyria, and Parthia
PRINCIPAL THEATER(S): Armenia and Mesopotamia
DECLARATION: None
MAJOR ISSUES AND OBJECTIVES: Rome sought to secure extend her reach into Armenia and Mesopotamia.
OUTCOME: Rome annexed Armenia and Assyria as provinces and gained control of Parthia.
APPROXIMATE MAXIMUM NUMBER OF MEN UNDER ARMS: Unknown
CASUALTIES: Unknown
TREATIES: None

After Osroes (c. 109–129) of Parthia violated an ancient treaty concluded in 20 B.C.E. by placing a puppet ruler on the Armenian throne, Emperor Trajan (53–117) of Rome set out with an army to evict the puppet. In 144 he invaded Armenia, overthrew the king, and annexed the region as an imperial province. From here, Trajan moved into Mesopotamia and established the province of Assyria. Continuing his advance, he targeted Babylon but turned his forces around when Assyria and Armenia suddenly rose in rebellion and, in disarray, were invaded by Parthia. Osroes now exploited the fragmented state of Roman forces in Mesopotamia and Assyrian by attacking. By 115,

Trajan found himself cut off, but after suffering a defeat at Hatra, he managed to consolidate and reunite his forces, so that by 116 he regained control of the region.

Trajan placed on the throne of Parthia a nobleman loyal to the Romans, Publius Aelius Hadrianus (known as Hadrian) (76–138). Nevertheless, the succession of battles had exhausted the aged Trajan, who died on the return journey to Rome. Hadrian thus became emperor of Rome and made peace with Parthia in the process, forsaking the projected Roman program of conquest east of the Euphrates River.

Further reading: Julian Bennett, *Trajan: Optimus Princeps* (Bloomington: Indiana University Press, 2002); Neilson C. Debevoise, *Political History of Parthia* (Chicago: University of Chicago Press, 1969); Stewart Perowne, *Hadrian* (New York: Barnes and Noble, 1990).

Roman Eastern War (162–165)

PRINCIPAL COMBATANTS: Rome vs. Parthia
PRINCIPAL THEATER(S): Armenia and Mesopotamia
DECLARATION: None
MAJOR ISSUES AND OBJECTIVES: Parthia sought to oust the Romans from Armenia and Mesopotamia.
OUTCOME: Rome subdued Parthia and regained control of Armenia.
APPROXIMATE MAXIMUM NUMBER OF MEN UNDER ARMS: Unknown
CASUALTIES: Unknown
TREATIES: None

In 162, Vologasus III (fl. 147–191), king of Parthia, invaded Armenia and defeated the Roman army stationed in the province. Vologasus continued into Mesopotamia and crushed Roman garrisons stationed there. Newly installed, Emperor Marcus Aurelius (121–180) sent his righthand man and virtual assistant emperor Lucius Aurelius Verus (130–169) with a Roman army to the East. Operating from Antioch, Verus regained Armenia by 163, while, over the next two years, Avidius Cassius (d. 175) led a Roman counteroffensive at Seleucia and Ctesiphon, the capital of Parthia. This prompted Parthia to sue for peace, after which many of the Roman soldiers returned home. En route to Italy, the troops were infected by plague, which spread throughout the Roman Empire. The resulting depopulation made it impossible for Rome to hold Parthia.

Further reading: Anthony R. Birley, *Marcus Aurelius* (London: Routledge, 2000); Neilson C. Debevoise, *Political History of Parthia* (Chicago: University of Chicago Press, 1969).

Roman-Etruscan Wars   *See* ETRUSCAN-ROMAN WARS, EARLY; ETRUSCAN-ROMAN WARS, LATER.

Roman Gothic War, First (249–252)

PRINCIPAL COMBATANTS: Rome vs. Goths
PRINCIPAL THEATER(S): Danube River region to northern Greece
DECLARATION: None
MAJOR ISSUES AND OBJECTIVES: Goths sought to exploit internal dissension in Rome to invade the Roman frontier.
OUTCOME: Rome bought transitory peace with tribute money.
APPROXIMATE MAXIMUM NUMBER OF MEN UNDER ARMS: Unknown, but Gothic numbers reported as "great"
CASUALTIES: Unknown
TREATIES: A tribute agreement, probably more or less formalized

Cuiva (fl. 240s–250s), king of the Goths, led a very large army across the Danube and confronted the Roman legions at Philippopolis (in modern Bulgaria). The legions were soundly defeated, and Cuiva rolled over them, penetrating into northern Greece. Here, Emperor Decius (201–251) mounted a major defensive campaign against the Goths, blocked them, then forced them to fall back into the marshes south of the Danubian mouth.

Cuiva now found himself in a corner, and in 251 the Battle of Forum Terebronii was fought at a distinct Roman advantage. However, desperation made the Goths that much more determined. Cuiva's forces held out, and when Romans under C. V. Tribonianus Gallus (d. 253) faltered, then failed to maintain the initiative and press home the attack, Cuiva made his move. The Goths launched a counterattack that devastated the Roman legions. Decius fell in battle, leaving Gallus to make a craven truce. He not only allowed the Goths to retain the spoils of war and to withdraw—intact—across the Danube but also accepted a tribute agreement, bribing Cuiva to refrain from further invasions or raids.

See also ROMAN GOTHIC WAR, SECOND; ROMAN GOTHIC WAR, THIRD; ROMAN GOTHIC WAR, FOURTH; ROMAN GOTHIC WAR, FIFTH.

Further reading: Edward Gibbon, *The Decline and Fall of the Roman Empire*, 3 vols., edited by J. B. Bury (New York: Modern Library, 1995); Peter Heather, *The Goths* (London: Blackwell, 1996). Ramsay MacMullen, *Corruption and the Decline of Rome* (New Haven, Conn.: Yale University Press, 1990).

Roman Gothic War, Second (252–268)

PRINCIPAL COMBATANTS: Rome vs. Goths
PRINCIPAL THEATER(S): Danube River and Aegean region
DECLARATION: None
MAJOR ISSUES AND OBJECTIVES: The Goths violated the peace concluded after the First Gothic War.
OUTCOME: The Goths gained control of most of the Aegean region, except for Greece.
APPROXIMATE MAXIMUM NUMBER OF MEN UNDER ARMS: Unknown
CASUALTIES: Unknown
TREATIES: None

No sooner had the Goths agreed, in exchange for tribute, to refrain from incursions into Roman territory (*see* ROMAN GOTHIC WAR, FIRST) than they once again crossed the Danube. Aemilianus (d. 253), legate of Moesia, rushed to repel the invasion and soundly defeated this Gothic incursion. Flushed with victory, Aemilianus rushed back to Rome in a bid to seize the throne. He succeeded, only to be assassinated by his own troops, whereupon Marcus Aurelius Claudius (d. 268) assumed command on the Danube under emperors Valerian (r. 253–259) and Gallienus (r. 259–268) and stoutly resisted further Goth incursions.

Battles were sporadic during the period of Marcus Aurelius Claudius's command, but the Goths did not recross the Danube; however, Goth "sea rovers" plied the Black Sea and raided the coasts of Moesia, Thrace, and northern Asia Minor from 252 to 268. Valerian dispatched a series of expeditions to end these depredations but fared miserably, especially in shore actions during 257–258. Worse for Rome, the Goths were joined by a related tribe, the Heruli, with whom they expanded inland from their Black Sea beachheads. Combined Goth-Heruli raiders devastated parts of the Caucasus, Georgia, and Asia Minor, notoriously sacking Ephesus, where in 262 they destroyed the Temple of Diana, famed as one of the Seven Wonders of the World. From Asia Minor, the raiders invaded Greece and captured or sacked Athens, Corinth, Sparta, Argos, and other towns during 265–267.

For the most part, the raiders enjoyed unalloyed triumph, except for sharp defeats at the hands of Odaenathus (d. 267/268) and Publius Herennius Dexippus (c. 210–after 270). The latter managed to drive the invaders out of central Greece by 267. Thus, except for Greece, the Goths and Heruli controlled most of the Aegean region when the Second Roman Gothic War wound down in 268.

See also ROMAN GOTHIC WAR, THIRD; ROMAN GOTHIC WAR, FOURTH; ROMAN GOTHIC WAR, FIFTH.

Further reading: Edward Gibbon, *The Decline and Fall of the Roman Empire*, 3 vols., edited by J. B. Bury (New York: Modern Library, 1995); Peter Heather, *The Goths* (London: Blackwell, 1996); Ramsay MacMullen, *Corruption and the Decline of Rome* (New Haven, Conn.: Yale University Press, 1990).

Roman Gothic War, Third (270)

PRINCIPAL COMBATANTS: Rome vs. Goths
PRINCIPAL THEATER(S): Danube River region, Moesia (lower Danube area), and Dacia (encompassing most of Romania)
DECLARATION: None
MAJOR ISSUES AND OBJECTIVES: After the death of Emperor Claudius, the Goths decided to exploit Roman internal disorder.
OUTCOME: The Goths were driven out of Moesia, but Dacia was lost to Rome.
APPROXIMATE MAXIMUM NUMBER OF MEN UNDER ARMS: Unknown
CASUALTIES: Unknown
TREATIES: None

Gallienus (r. 259–268) was succeeded as emperor by Claudius II (214–270), known as Gothicus. His death in 270 prompted the Goths to recross the Danube and invade Moesia and Dacia. Aurelian (c. 212–75), who had succeeded to the throne, confronted the incursion with considerable vigor and managed to drive the Goths out of Moesia. However, he decided on a course of discretion rather than valor when it came to Dacia, which he decided to sacrifice as a lost cause. He evacuated as many Roman colonists as he could, resettled them in Moesia, and left Dacia to the Goths.

Further reading: Edward Gibbon, *The Decline and Fall of the Roman Empire*, 3 vols., edited by J. B. Bury (New York: Modern Library, 1995); Peter Heather, *The Goths* (London: Blackwell, 1996); Ramsay MacMullen, *Corruption and the Decline of Rome* (New Haven, Conn.: Yale University Press, 1990).

Roman Gothic War, Fourth (367–369)

PRINCIPAL COMBATANTS: Rome vs. Visigoths and Ostrogoths
PRINCIPAL THEATER(S): Thrace
DECLARATION: None
MAJOR ISSUES AND OBJECTIVES: In response to pressure from invading Huns, the Visigoths and Ostrogoths invaded Roman-held Thrace.
OUTCOME: The Ostrogoths and Visigoths were granted permission to settle certain frontier regions of the empire.
APPROXIMATE MAXIMUM NUMBER OF MEN UNDER ARMS: Unknown
CASUALTIES: Unknown
TREATIES: Formal agreement that Visigothic settlement would remain north of the Danube

During the continued unrest that followed the ROMAN CIVIL WAR (360–361), the rebel Procopius (fl. 360s) had been aided by various Gothic mercenaries. In response, Valens (c. 328–78), emperor of the East, captured and imprisoned some of the mercenaries. This was met with protests from the Visigothic king, Athanaric (d. 381), who sent an army into Roman-held Thrace. In the meantime, pressure from invading Huns was driving both Visigoths and Ostrogoths westward, into Thrace and other Danubian regions. The fighting that resulted was largely confused and indecisive—until 369, when a concerted Roman offensive resulted in a substantial victory. Athanaric agreed that his Visigoths would remain north of the Danube. However, the continued advances of the Huns soon wrecked the peace, as more Gothic tribes settled in Thrace and then, after the fact, sought Valens's permission to resettle there. Valens agreed and also released his Gothic prisoners; however, he simultaneously invaded Visigothic territory north of the Danube. Moreover, Roman officials within the region Valens had allotted for Gothic settlement preyed upon the settlers, robbing them and extorting tribute from them.

Further reading: Thomas S. Burns, *A History of the Ostrogoths* (Bloomington: Indiana University Press, 1991); Edward Gibbon, *The Decline and Fall of the Roman Empire*, 3 vols., edited by J. B. Bury (New York: Modern Library, 1995); Peter Heather, *The Goths* (London: Blackwell, 1996); Ramsay MacMullen, *Corruption and the Decline of Rome* (New Haven, Conn.: Yale University Press, 1990).

Roman Gothic War, Fifth (377–383)

PRINCIPAL COMBATANTS: Rome vs. Visigoths and allied Germanic tribes
PRINCIPAL THEATER(S): Thrace and Moesia
DECLARATION: None
MAJOR ISSUES AND OBJECTIVES: Goth depredations within Roman territory combined with Roman abuse of Goth settlers to create a new war.
OUTCOME: The Romans negotiated a peace permitting the Goths to remain on Roman lands in exchange for military service.
APPROXIMATE MAXIMUM NUMBER OF MEN UNDER ARMS: Goths and allies, 100,000–200,000; Roman strength at the Second Battle of Adrianople (August 9, 378), 60,000
CASUALTIES: 40,000 Romans fell at the Second Battle of Adrianople (August 9, 378)
TREATIES: Agreement to exchange Goth settlement rights for Roman military service.

Following the Fourth ROMAN GOTHIC WAR, Goth settlers poured into Roman-controlled Thrace in large numbers. For their part, the new settlers were often wild and unruly; Roman officials were abusive. The inevitable result was friction that rapidly escalated into a new Roman Gothic war.

This time, the Goths decided to find strength in numbers by making alliances with other Germanic tribes, including the Ostrogoths. Roman negotiators sought to act preemptively by attacking the Visigoth leaders Fritigern (d. 380) and Alavius (d. 377) at a parley in 377. Alavius was killed, but Fritigern escaped and led a vengeance counterattack against Romans under Lupicinius (fl. 370s–380s) at Marianopolis (modern Shumla, in eastern Bulgaria). After victory in this exchange, Fritigern united with other Goth leaders between the lower Danube and the Black Sea (the area of modern Dobruja).

The Roman emperor Valens (c. 328–378) dispatched legions to Thrace, forcing the Goths to fall back and confining them to the marshes south of the Danube's mouth. The Goths and their allies took a stand here at the Battle of the Salices or Willows. The Romans failed to make a decisive move, and Fritigern was able to withdraw with his forces intact.

His retreat was neither furtive nor abject. He led his troops through Thrace and Moesia, raiding, pillaging, and destroying, often in concert with Alans, Sarmatians, and even Huns. In response, Valens called on his nephew and co-emperor, Gratian (359–383). However, by 378 the Gothic tribes had formed a powerful alliance. Gratian was delayed in his arrival in Thrace by Frankish and Alemanni incursions in Gaul. After disposing of this menace, he made his way toward Thrace during the summer of 378. Even without Gratian's assistance, Valens's forces had made substantial gains against the barbarians during July and August 378. Perhaps as many as 200,000 Visigoths, Ostrogoths, Sarmatians, Alans, and Huns were held at bay in a wagon camp near Adrianople by August. It would have been prudent for Valens to await the arrival of Gratian before pushing the attack; however, craving glory, Valens led his 60,000 troops against the Goth camp on August 9, 378. This Second Battle of Adrianople resulted in disaster for the legions, which were overwhelmed by horsemen. Forty thousand Romans died, including Valens. Nevertheless, the Goths proved unable to take Adrianople and, instead, once again fell to destructive raiding throughout Thrace.

Gratian assumed to full function of emperor of the West and recruited Theodosius I (c. 346–395) as the new emperor of the East, charging him with defending against the barbarians. Theodosius was as wise as Valens had been rash. He did not attempt to sweep the Visigoths (and others) from Thrace but instead continually harassed them with small, sharp actions. Exhausted, the barbarians agreed to negotiate, and in 383 an unprecedented agreement was made whereby the Visigoths were permitted to live unmolested in designated areas of Thrace in exchange for military service to Rome.

Further reading: Edward Gibbon, *The Decline and Fall of the Roman Empire*, 3 vols., edited by J. B. Bury (New York: Modern Library, 1995); Peter Heather, *The Goths* (London: Blackwell, 1996); Ramsay MacMullen, *Corruption and the Decline of Rome* (New Haven, Conn.: Yale University Press, 1990); Stephen Williams and Gerard Friell,

Theodosius: The Empire at Bay (New Haven, Conn.: Yale University Press, 1995).

Roman Northern Frontier Wars
(24 B.C.E.–16 C.E.)

PRINCIPAL COMBATANTS: Rome vs. Germanic tribes
PRINCIPAL THEATER(S): Bavaria, Austria, Hungary, and France
DECLARATION: None
MAJOR ISSUES AND OBJECTIVES: The Republic of Rome struggled to hold back the invasion of Germanic tribes from the north.
OUTCOME: Rome was forced to abandon the colonization of Germany.
APPROXIMATE MAXIMUM NUMBER OF MEN UNDER ARMS: Unknown
CASUALTIES: Unknown
TREATIES: None

This period saw the beginning of the great Pax Romana, a time of relative peace punctuated by some military operations in the north. To secure the border protecting Gaul and Italy, Emperor Augustus (63–14 B.C.E.) sent his legions to the north to capture more territory and provide a buffer between Rome and the Germanic tribes. In 51 B.C.E. he founded Aosta in northern Italy and took control of Illyria (Yugoslavia) and Moesia (northern Bulgaria). In 16 B.C.E., Augustus went to Gaul to take personal command. His stepsons Tiberius (42 B.C.E.–37 C.E.) and Drusus (13 B.C.E.–23 C.E.) led punitive expeditions in Rhaetia (Bavaria), Noricum (Austria) and Pannonia (western Hungary) and annexed these regions to the Roman Empire. Drusus was victorious against the Germanic tribes in Gaul, marched to Germany, and won a battle at the Lippe River, traditional battlefield between the forces of Rome and the German tribes. At the death of Drusus, who had injured himself in a fall from his horse, Tiberius continued the campaigns in Germany. He put down tribal revolts in 4 C.E. and uprisings in Pannonia and Illyria between 6 and 9 C.E., leaving Publius Quintilius Varus (d. 9 C.E.) in Germany with five legions and several auxiliary forces. Varus angered the commander of one of the auxiliaries, Arminius (c. 18 B.C.E.–19 C.E.), a young German chief of the Cherusci tribe, which although not the most powerful of the German tribes, was the most famous. Planning his revenge on Varus, Arminius staged a rebellion in the region between the Visurgis and Aliso. Varus and 20,000 soldiers, accompanied by some 10,000 noncombatants, crossed the Visurgis and entered the Teutoberg Forest. When the legions became mired in the forest's muddy trails, Arminius and his followers deserted from the Roman ranks and attacked a Roman detachment. Varus continued to press northward, but his progress was slowed by his lengthy baggage train and by the number of noncombatants among his columns. After several days, the Germans—mostly Cherusci—broke through the legions. Twenty thousand Roman troops were killed, and Varus and his surviving officers committed suicide. Although Tiberius continued punitive expeditions against the Germans between 11 and 16, Rome, whose people were stunned by the annihilation of Varus's legions at Teutoberg, was forced to establish the Rhine and Danube rivers rather than the Elbe as the boundaries of her holdings in Germany, and tribal warfare and internal violence were rampant in Germany for the next several centuries.

Further reading: Edward Gibbon, *The Decline and Fall of the Roman Empire*, 3 vols., edited by J. B. Bury (New York: Modern Library, 1995); Ramsay MacMullen, *Corruption and the Decline of Rome* (New Haven, Conn.: Yale University Press, 1990).

Roman-Parthian War (55–38 B.C.E.)

PRINCIPAL COMBATANTS: Rome vs. Parthia
PRINCIPAL THEATER(S): Parthia and Rome-Parthian borderlands
DECLARATION: None
MAJOR ISSUES AND OBJECTIVES: Pompey (of the First Triumvirate) craved the glory of conquest.
OUTCOME: The Roman legions were defeated in two major attempts at invasion.
APPROXIMATE MAXIMUM NUMBER OF MEN UNDER ARMS: Rome, 39,000; Parthian forces larger
CASUALTIES: Rome lost 4,000 killed and 10,000 prisoners at Carrhae (53 B.C.E.)
TREATIES: None

In 55, the Roman governor of Syria, Aulus Gabinius (d. 47), aided Mithradates III (d. 54 B.C.E.), who had been forced into exile by his brother Orodes II (d. 37/36 B.C.E.), in his bid to regain the Parthian throne. Orodes, however, defeated Mithradates III at the Battle of Seelucia in 55 and captured and killed him the following year.

Gabinius's action opened the door to a Roman invasion of Parthia. An army of 39,000 under Marcus Licinius Crassus (c. 115–53 B.C.E.) commenced a campaign in Carrhae during 54–53. Shortly after crossing the Euphrates, the Romans were set upon by Parthian cavalry and archers. The legions assumed defensive positions, whereupon the Parthians besieged them, continually attacking at long distance with arrows. At last, Crassus dispatched 6,000 men under his son, Publius Crassus (55–15 B.C.E.), to attack the Parthian cavalry so that the main Roman force could break out. The Parthians fell back, only to counterattack with great ferocity. Four thousand Romans fell, and another 10,000 were taken prisoner.

The Carrhae campaign left Mesopotamia in Parthian hands and cemented an enmity between Rome and Parthia, leading to sporadic, bloody, and inconclusive combat from 53 to 38 B.C.E., mostly provoked by Parthian invasions of Roman-held Syria.

Further reading: Neilson C. Debevoise, *Political History of Parthia* (Chicago: University of Chicago Press, 1969); Mark Dunster, *Parthia* (London: Linden, 1979); Plutarch, "Life of Crassus," in *The Fall of the Roman Republic: Six Lives: Marius, Sulla, Crassus, Pompey, Caesar, Cicero*, trans. Rex Warner (New York: Penguin, 1972).

Roman-Parthian War (56–63)

PRINCIPAL COMBATANTS: Rome vs. Parthia
PRINCIPAL THEATER(S): Armenia
DECLARATION: None
MAJOR ISSUES AND OBJECTIVES: Both empires wanted to control Armenia.
OUTCOME: A Parthian king was placed on the Armenian throne with the proviso that he acknowledge the Roman emperor Nero as his overlord.
APPROXIMATE MAXIMUM NUMBER OF MEN UNDER ARMS: Unknown
CASUALTIES: Unknown
TREATIES: No documents survive

The first century C.E. was a time of great turmoil in Southwest Asia. Parthia, the greatest kingdom in the region, was often at odds with Rome, even though both Parthia and Rome had a common enemy in the barbarians to the north. It was over control of one of the northern regions, Armenia, that the war of 56–63 was fought. In 56, Rome controlled Armenia through a puppet ruler, Radamistus (d. 56) who was killed in 56. Upon his death, Vologesus I (fl. 51–77), king of Parthia (northern Iran), attempted to put his brother Tiridates (d. c. 73) on the Armenian throne. The Roman emperor Nero (37–68) responded by ordering Corbulo (d. 67), his military commander in Asia Minor, to install another Roman puppet. Accordingly, in 57, Corbulo led an army into Armenia, ousted Tiridates, and replaced him with a pliant ruler, Tigranes VI of Cappadocia (d. 62). Because Vologesus was using his army to quell internal disorders at the time, he did not oppose the invasion; however, in 61, he mounted an invasion of Armenia and defeated Corbulo's legions. With the Romans out of the country, Tiridates was reinstated, and Corbulo wisely allowed Nero to save face by negotiating his agreement to permit Tiridates to rule, provided Tiridates acknowledge Nero as his overlord.

Further reading: Neilson C. Debevoise, *Political History of Parthia* (Chicago: University of Chicago Press, 1969); Mark Dunster, *Parthia* (London: Linden, 1979).

Roman-Parthian War (195–202)

PRINCIPAL COMBATANTS: Rome vs. Parthia
PRINCIPAL THEATER(S): Mesopotamia (modern Iran)
DECLARATION: None
MAJOR ISSUES AND OBJECTIVES: Rome sought to curtail Parthian incursions into Armenia and then to annex some part of Parthia itself.
OUTCOME: Parthia was almost totally defeated.
APPROXIMATE MAXIMUM NUMBER OF MEN UNDER ARMS: Unknown
CASUALTIES: Unknown
TREATIES: None

Mesopotamia had been under nominal Roman rule since the reign of Marcus Aurelius (121–180), but during the ROMAN CIVIL WAR (193–197), which pitted rivals for the imperial throne against one another and thereby fragmented Roman power, the Parthian king Vologesus IV (fl. 191–209) invaded Armenia and laid siege against the Mesopotamian city of Nisibis. It was not until Lucius Septimus Severus (146–211) won out against his rivals to become sole emperor of Rome that the Roman legions were able to mount a credible response, even though Severus had to deal with other potential rivals. In 196, the emperor led his forces across the Euphrates to capture the great Parthian city of Seleucia. From the conquest, the legions attacked Ctesiphon, which also fell to them. Severus then marched north, forcing Vologesus to lift his siege of Nisibis and retreat into the mountains.

Only Hatra, defended by a formidable Parthian force, remained firm. The legions hammered this objective fruitlessly in 197 and again in 199; however, Nisibis was returned firmly into Roman hands, and Severus made it his capital to govern the Roman province he carved out of the defeated Vologesus's realm. Hatra remained unbreached, a lonely Parthian outpost and a constant thorn in the emperor's side.

Further reading: Neilson C. Debevoise, *Political History of Parthia* (Chicago: University of Chicago Press, 1969); Mark Dunster, *Parthia* (London: Linden, 1979).

Roman-Persian War (230–233)

PRINCIPAL COMBATANTS: Rome vs. Persian Empire
PRINCIPAL THEATER(S): Roman-Persian borderlands
DECLARATION: None
MAJOR ISSUES AND OBJECTIVES: Rome sought to counter the aggression of the newly expanded Persian Empire.
OUTCOME: Rome regained its Mesopotamian possessions and reestablished the Roman-Persian frontier.
APPROXIMATE MAXIMUM NUMBER OF MEN UNDER ARMS: Unknown

CASUALTIES: Unknown
TREATIES: None; no formal peace was established

Ardashir I (d. 241)—also known as Ataxerxes I—king of Persia, rebelled against his Parthian masters in 226 and, by the following year, had not only shed the Parthian yoke but conquered Parthia itself, to found the Sassanid dynasty. From this vast conquest, he moved on to lay claim to all of Asia Minor; in 230–231 he led an invasion into Roman Mesopotamia and boldly asserted Persian sovereignty by minting coins in the invaded region.

At first, the Roman emperor, Marcus Aurelius Alexander Severus (c. 208–235), attempted political negotiation with Ardashir. One of the abler emperors and generals of the late Roman period, Alexander led a three-pronged invasion of Persia after negotiations collapsed. But Alexander was more courageous than experienced, and his "prong" of the invasion was defeated. The other two Roman forces fared better, however, yet also failed to achieve decisive victories. Ardashir held his ground, but suffered severe losses and was unable to turn his defensive action into a counterattack. Thus the war ended in a draw, although both sides declared victory—Rome with more justification, since, strategically, the war reestablished the empire's frontier.

Further reading: A. T. Olmstead, *History of the Persian Empire* (Chicago: University of Chicago Press, 1972); Josef Wiesehofer, *Ancient Persia, 550 B.C.–A.D. 650* (New York: St. Martin's Press, 1998).

Roman-Persian War (241–244)

PRINCIPAL COMBATANTS: Rome vs. Persia
PRINCIPAL THEATER(S): Syria
DECLARATION: None
MAJOR ISSUES AND OBJECTIVES: Persia, under Shapur I, continued its Sassanid program of expansion by invading Syria; Rome countered.
OUTCOME: Persia gave up Syria, and the prewar Persian-Roman frontier was reestablished.
APPROXIMATE MAXIMUM NUMBER OF MEN UNDER ARMS: Unknown
CASUALTIES: Unknown
TREATIES: Presumably a formal agreement reestablishing status quo ante bellum

The second of the Sassanid kings of Persia, Shapur I (d. 272), son of the dynasty's founder, Ardashir I (d. 241), and, for a time, coruler with his father, continued Ardashir's practice of nibbling at the Roman borderlands to expand the Persian Empire. Even before Ardashir's death, he mounted a major invasion of Syria, conquered much of it, and besieged the great city of Antioch. Shapur counted on Rome's internal strife to weaken the empire's ability and will to respond; however, Marcus Antonius Gordianus III (c. 224–244), emperor of Rome, in company with his best general (and father-in-law), Gaius Furius Sabinus Aquila Timesithesus (d. 243), marched into Syria in 242 and met Shapur's forces at the Battle of Resaena on the upper Araxes River the following year. The battle proved decisive, and Shapur withdrew from Syria.

Timesithesus and Gordianus were anxious to capitalize on their victory by driving into Persia itself. But Timesithesus died late in 243 and the next year Gordianus was assassinated, possibly at the instigation of his successor, Philip (c. 204–249) (called Philip the Arabian). Having no desire to press the campaign against Shapur any further, Philip negotiated a peace that reestablished the prewar Persian-Roman frontier.

Further reading: A. T. Olmstead, *History of the Persian Empire* (Chicago: University of Chicago Press, 1972); Josef Wiesehofer, *Ancient Persia, 550 B.C.–A.D. 650* (New York: St. Martin's Press, 1998).

Roman-Persian War (257–261)

PRINCIPAL COMBATANTS: Rome vs. Persia; Persia vs. Palmyra
PRINCIPAL THEATER(S): Syria
DECLARATION: None
MAJOR ISSUES AND OBJECTIVES: Persian king Shapur I sought conquest of Syria.
OUTCOME: Rome was defeated and Emperor Valerian taken captive—although Shapur himself suffered a serious defeat at the hands of a Palmyran prince.
APPROXIMATE MAXIMUM NUMBER OF MEN UNDER ARMS: Unknown
CASUALTIES: Unknown
TREATIES: None

As with the ROMAN-PERSIAN WAR (241–244), internal disorder in Rome encouraged Shapur I (d. 272) to seize the opportunity to attack. He moved into Armenia, which his forces conquered by 258. Shapur had installed a Persian puppet on the Armenian throne, he then stabbed with raiding forces into Mesopotamia and Syria, plundering the important city of Antioch later in 258. Roman emperor Valerian (d. c. 261) was able to make an effective response to this. He expelled the Persians from Antioch but was unable to follow up this victory with a triumph over Shapur's main forces, which remained very much intact. Valerian lost the Battle of Edessa in 260, and Shapur blocked, then surrounded, the Roman armies. In a desperate situation and seeking to avoid the destruction of his legions, Valerian sued for peace and was taken captive. Leaderless, the Roman army panicked and instantly surrendered. Valerian was hauled off to Persia, where he died a prisoner.

Unopposed, Shapur overran Syria, retook Antioch, then redoubled raids into all the Roman regions of the East, including Cilicia and Cappadocia, both of which he devastated, although he met stout resistance in Cappadocia. In the end, Shapur was defeated not by Rome but by Palmyran forces, which attacked Shapur's booty-laden army as it returned to Persia. The defeat was so severe that Shapur ended his aggression against Syria and Asia Minor.

Further reading: A. T. Olmstead, *History of the Persian Empire* (Chicago: University of Chicago Press, 1972); Josef Wiesehofer, *Ancient Persia, 550 B.C.–A.D. 650* (New York: St. Martin's Press, 1998).

Roman-Persian War (282–283)

PRINCIPAL COMBATANTS: Rome vs. Persia
PRINCIPAL THEATER(S): Upper Mesopotamia
DECLARATION: None
MAJOR ISSUES AND OBJECTIVES: Rome wanted to retake Mesopotamia from Persia.
OUTCOME: Upper Mesopotamia was retaken, and Rome negotiated peace with the Persians; however, internal intrigue resulted in the deaths of Emperor Carus and his son Numerianus, and ultimately resulted in the elevation of Diocletian as emperor of Rome.
APPROXIMATE MAXIMUM NUMBER OF MEN UNDER ARMS: Unknown
CASUALTIES: Unknown
TREATIES: Treaty of 283; no document survives

Marcus Aurelius Carus (c. 223–283), a Praetorian who became emperor of Rome, together with his son Marcus Aurelius Numerianus (d. 284), invaded Persian-occupied Mesopotamia in 282, retaking upper Mesopotamia, along with the Persian provincial capital of Ctesiphon. From here, Carus advanced east of the Tigris, presumably with the intention of invading the Sassanid Empire. Before Carus proceeded much farther, however, Persia's king Bahram I (d. 276) sued for peace and negotiated a settlement with the Romans.

The legions did not vacate Persian territory after the peace, however, but resumed their march eastward, deep into Sassanid territory. The invasion was halted by the sudden death of Carus in 283. The cause of death was officially recorded as a lightning bolt, but most scholars believe he had been the victim of assassination, killed by the prefect of the Praetorian Guard, Arius Aper (d. 285).

The death of Carus turned the Roman legions back toward Rome, and Numerianus was now jointly emperor with his brother Carinus (d. 285). Before the Roman army reached the Bosporus, however, Numerianus was killed. Arius Aper was accused of having assassinated him, and Diocletian (245–313), a commander who had served under Carus, personally executed the Praetorian prefect. After this action, the army proclaimed Diocletian emperor.

See also ROMAN CIVIL WAR (284–285 C.E.).

Further reading: A. T. Olmstead, *History of the Persian Empire* (Chicago: University of Chicago Press, 1972); Josef Wiesehofer, *Ancient Persia, 550 B.C.–A.D. 650* (New York: St. Martin's Press, 1998); Peter Wilcox, *Rome's Enemies: Parthians and Sassanids,* vol. 175 (London: Osprey, 1988).

Roman-Persian War (295–297)

PRINCIPAL COMBATANTS: Rome vs. Persia
PRINCIPAL THEATER(S): Upper Mesopotamia
DECLARATION: None
MAJOR ISSUES AND OBJECTIVES: Rome wanted to retake upper Mesopotamia from the Persians.
OUTCOME: After suffering a decisive defeat in a surprise attack along the Tigris, Narses made vast concessions to Rome.
APPROXIMATE MAXIMUM NUMBER OF MEN UNDER ARMS:
Rome, 25,000; Persia, 100,000
CASUALTIES: Unknown
TREATIES: Peace of Nisibis, 297

Throughout the third century, Persia had taken advantage of the internal disintegration of the Roman Empire to move against often weakly held Roman provinces. Narses (d. c. 302), king of Persia, invaded Armenia in 295 and removed the Roman puppet Tirdates III (c. 238–314) from the throne. This provoked the Roman caesar of the East, Galerius (d. 311), to assemble a small force, which included Tirdates and a cadre of Armenian exiles, and attack Narses. After defeating small Persian forces in Mesopotamia, Galerius and his army were routed near Carrhae in 296. This was the very scene of the defeat of Crassus (c. 115–53 B.C.E.) in the ROMAN-PARTHIAN WAR (55–38 B.C.E.).

Emperor Diocletian (c. 245–313?) publicly chastised Galerius but allowed him to retain his command. The following year, Galerius regrouped and reinforced his army, then advanced against the Persians once again. Commanding 25,000, he encountered a vastly superior Persian force of 100,000 near the upper Tigris but nevertheless managed to surprise it. The element of surprise served him well, and the Persian force, though larger, was nearly destroyed. Galerius and his men ran riot, looting the treasures carried by the army and capturing Narses's harem as well as his family. The Persian emperor desperately sued for peace and concluded the Peace of Nisibis in 297, whereby Persia restored all of upper Mesopotamia to Rome and, in addition, ceded five provinces northeast of the Tigris. Narses also acknowledged Tiridates III as king of Armenia. In return, the Persian emperor's harem and family were restored to him.

Further reading: A. T. Olmstead, *History of the Persian Empire* (Chicago: University of Chicago Press, 1972); Josef Wiesehofer, *Ancient Persia, 550 B.C.–A.D. 650* (New York: St. Martin's Press, 1998); Peter Wilcox, *Rome's Enemies: Parthians and Sassanids,* vol. 175 (London: Osprey, 1988).

Roman-Persian War (337–364)

PRINCIPAL COMBATANTS: Rome vs. Persia
PRINCIPAL THEATER(S): Armenia and Mesopotamia
DECLARATION: None
MAJOR ISSUES AND OBJECTIVES: Persia sought to regain upper Mesopotamia and Armenia from the Romans.
OUTCOME: War was, for the most part, chronic and indecisive—until the death of Emperor Julian disordered the Roman legions and left Persian emperor Shapur II essentially free to possess the disputed territories.
APPROXIMATE MAXIMUM NUMBER OF MEN UNDER ARMS:
Rome, 95,000; Persian strength unknown
CASUALTIES: Unknown
TREATIES: None

Constantius II (317–361), son and heir of Constantine I (the Great; c. 228–337), inherited the throne of the Eastern Empire upon the death of his father in 337. Immediately, he was assailed by the forces of Persia's Shapur II (309–79), who was determined to regain Armenia and northern Mesopotamia from Rome. Presumably, Shapur was motivated to a large degree by religious zeal. Initial Persian raids into these regions inaugurated a long, sporadic state of war between Rome and Persia, which, however, resulted in only the sketchiest of historical records.

It is believed that the war encompassed nine great battles, of which the best known is Singara (Sinjar, Iraq), which may have taken place in 344 or as late as 348. While it is known that Constantius at first prevailed, historians are divided on the ultimate issue of the battle. Some believe the Romans succeeded in capturing Shapur's camp, only to be driven out of it in a nighttime counterattack. Others hold that the battle ended in a draw.

Singara was the scene of a Roman offensive. Repeatedly, however, Shapur seized the initiative and put the legions on the defensive. Three times he attacked the Mesopotamian fortress of Nisibis (337, possibly in 344, and again in 349), and three times he was repulsed by the Roman defenders.

The first major phase of the war ended in 350 with a truce, as both Constantius and Shapur became preoccupied with other threats to their empires. However, in 358, war recommenced with a new Persian invasion of Armenia. The Romans valiantly held the fortress of Amida (in Diyarbekir, Turkey) against a 73-day siege. The siege not only proved costly to Shapur but forced him to delay his campaign until the end of winter. But in 359 he pressed on, capturing Singara and Bezabde, two Roman fortress towns. Constantius rushed to the region with reinforcements but was unable to retake Bezabde. He summoned aid from his cousin Julian (331–363), who assembled a force of 95,000 legionnaires during 363–363, then invaded early in 363. At Ctesiphon on the Tigris River, Julian coordinated a brilliant amphibious assault on Shapur's position. The Persian army was badly cut up and retreated into the city of Ctesiphon. Unfortunately for Julian, promised aid from the Armenians did not materialize, and he decided not to lay siege to Ctesiphon but to penetrate farther into Persian territory. The invaders, however, were greeted by a Persian scorched-earth policy and soon found themselves short of supplies. Julian therefore began a withdrawal to the north, traveling up the Tigris with the intention of establishing a new base of operations in Armenia. It was during this retreat that Shapur again showed himself, repeatedly attacking the Roman columns with light cavalry. In one attack, at night against a Roman camp, Julian was mortally wounded.

Julian was replaced by Flavius Claudius Jovian (d. 365) as commander of the legions. That general quickly buckled. Fearing a fatal shortage of supplies, he sued for peace. Shapur shrewdly kept the hungry army waiting with deliberately drawn-out negotiations. On the verge of starvation, Jovian agreed to cede to Persia all provinces east of the Tigris as well as the major Roman fortresses, including Nisibis. On behalf of Rome, Jovian further renounced suzerainty over both Armenia and the Caucasian region. He led his emaciated army abjectly back to Antioch. On his way back to Constantinople in 365 Jovian died suddenly and mysteriously, quite likely the victim of assassination.

Further reading: A. T. Olmstead, *History of the Persian Empire* (Chicago: University of Chicago Press, 1972); Josef Wiesehofer, *Ancient Persia, 550 B.C.–A.D. 650* (New York: St. Martin's Press, 1998); Peter Wilcox, *Rome's Enemies: Parthians and Sassanids,* vol. 175 (London: Osprey, 1988).

Roman-Persian War (421–422)

PRINCIPAL COMBATANTS: Rome vs. Persia
PRINCIPAL THEATER(S): Mesopotamian provinces of Persia
DECLARATION: None
MAJOR ISSUES AND OBJECTIVES: Rome sought to compel Persia's king Bahram V to reinstate a policy of toleration of Christianity.
OUTCOME: After suffering a number of minor defeats, Bahram agreed to tolerate Christianity throughout the Persian Empire in exchange for a Roman pledge to tolerate Zoroastrianism throughout Rome.
APPROXIMATE MAXIMUM NUMBER OF MEN UNDER ARMS: Unknown
CASUALTIES: Unknown
TREATIES: Treaty of 422

When King Bahram V (d. 439)—known as Gor ("the Wild Ass")—ascended the Sassanid throne, he overturned the policy of religious toleration maintained by his father, Yazdegerd I, assassinated in 420, and instituted a program of violent persecution against Christians—or, at least, allowed his powerful chief minister, Mihr-Naresh (fl. fifth century) to persecute them. Rome responded by attacking Bahram's forces in Mesopotamia, inflicting a series of defeats against him in minor battles. Thoroughly intimidated, Bahram V sued for peace and agreed by treaty to tolerate Christianity throughout his empire. Rome, in turn, agreed to tolerate the dominant religion of Persia, Zoroastrianism, and the balance of Bahram V's reign became known not for religious persecution but for a combination of romantic chivalry and noble huntsmanship.

Further reading: A. T. Olmstead, *History of the Persian Empire* (Chicago: University of Chicago Press, 1972); Josef Wiesehofer, *Ancient Persia, 550 B.C.–A.D. 650* (New York: St. Martin's Press, 1998); Peter Wilcox, *Rome's Enemies: Parthians and Sassanids,* vol. 175 (London: Osprey, 1988).

Roman-Persian War (441)

PRINCIPAL COMBATANTS: Rome vs. Persia
PRINCIPAL THEATER(S): Persia's Mesopotamian provinces
DECLARATION: None
MAJOR ISSUES AND OBJECTIVES: Rome sought to compel Persia to reinstate its former policy of toleration of Christianity.
OUTCOME: Persian king Yazdegerd II agreed to reinstate the toleration policy.
APPROXIMATE MAXIMUM NUMBER OF MEN UNDER ARMS: Unknown
CASUALTIES: Unknown
TREATIES: No documents survive

Although Bahram V (d. 439) had agreed not to persecute Christians in Persia (*see* ROMAN-PERSIAN WAR [421–422]), his son and successor, Yazdegerd II (d. 457), reinstated violent persecution, thereby provoking intervention from Rome. At first Rome sought to achieve a diplomatic solution, but when this failed, a small number of troops were sent to harass Persian forces in Mesopotamia. Like his father, Yazdegerd was easily intimidated, and nothing more than a brief foray into the Persian provinces was sufficient to persuade him to reaffirm his father's agreement to pursue a policy of toleration.

Further reading: A. T. Olmstead, *History of the Persian Empire* (Chicago: University of Chicago Press, 1972); Josef Wiesehofer, *Ancient Persia, 550 B.C.–A.D. 650* (New York: St. Martin's Press, 1998); Peter Wilcox, *Rome's Enemies: Parthians and Sassanids,* vol. 175 (London: Osprey, 1988).

Roman-Persian War (502–506)

PRINCIPAL COMBATANTS: Rome (Eastern Empire/Byzantine Empire) vs. Persia
PRINCIPAL THEATER(S): Roman Armenia and Roman Mesopotamia
DECLARATION: None
MAJOR ISSUES AND OBJECTIVES: The Persian king was provoked by Rome's refusal to help Persia pay tribute to the White Huns.
OUTCOME: After many initial reverses, Roman forces defeated the Persians and the prewar frontier was reestablished.
APPROXIMATE MAXIMUM NUMBER OF MEN UNDER ARMS: Unknown
CASUALTIES: Unknown
TREATIES: Frontier agreement of 506

Anastasius I (430?–518), emperor of the Eastern Empire, refused the appeal of Persian king Kavadh I (d. 531) for financial aid to help him pay tribute owed to the White Huns (Ephthalites), who had been instrumental in regaining the throne for Kavadh after he was deposed by his brother. His refusal was motivated by a desire to halt Persian expansion along the Black Sea; however, the effects of the refusal were compounded by unwelcome Roman incursions into Armenia. Provoked, Kavadh invaded Roman Armenia in 502 and captured the principal city, Theodosiopolis (Erzurum, Turkey) and, in 503, followed this triumph with a victory in Roman Mesopotamia when Amida (Diyarbakir, Turkey) fell to Persian forces after a 90-day siege.

Anastasius was able gradually to mount an effective counterattack and, during 504–506, repeatedly defeated Persian forces after initially repulsing an attempt to take Edessa (in modern Greece). After Amida was retaken by Anastasius's forces in 506, Kavadh sued for peace and agreed to the restoration of the Roman-Persian border on its prewar terms.

Further reading: Mack Chahin, *The Kingdom of Armenia* (New York: Taylor and Francis, 2001); Robert H. Hewsen and Christopher C. Salvatico, *Armenia: A Historical Atlas* (Chicago: University of Chicago Press, 1999); A. T. Olmstead, *History of the Persian Empire* (Chicago: University of Chicago Press, 1972); Josef Wiesehofer, *Ancient Persia, 550 B.C.–A.D. 650* (New York: St. Martin's Press, 1998); Peter Wilcox, *Rome's Enemies: Parthians and Sassanids*, vol. 175 (London: Osprey, 1988).

Roman-Persian War (524–532) *See* JUSTINIAN'S FIRST PERSIAN WAR.

Roman-Persian War (539–562) *See* JUSTINIAN'S SECOND PERSIAN WAR.

Roman-Persian War (572–591)

PRINCIPAL COMBATANTS: Persia vs. Rome and the Turks
PRINCIPAL THEATER(S): Persia, Macedonia, Media, and Armenia
DECLARATION: None
MAJOR ISSUES AND OBJECTIVES: Persia sought territorial expansion at the expense of the East Roman Empire
OUTCOME: Persia was defeated, suffered civil war, and made peace with Rome.
APPROXIMATE MAXIMUM NUMBER OF MEN UNDER ARMS: Roman army at the time of the intervention (590), 60,000; Persian forces at this time numbered about 40,000
CASUALTIES: Unknown
TREATIES: Truce, 573–575; peace treaty between Maurice of Rome and Chosroes II of Persia, 591

Chosroes I (d. 579), emperor of Persia, sent an expeditionary force into Roman Mesopotamia after Justin II (d. 578), emperor of Rome, struck a threatening alliance with the Turks in support of an uprising among Christian Armenians. Simultaneously, Chosroes fought a defensive action against the Turks in the East.

Chosroes's grandson, also named Chosroes (591–628), laid siege to Dara and dispatched forces to raid Syria. The Persians penetrated as far as Antioch. Rome, recognizing that the war it had provoked was going badly, sued for peace and secured a three-year truce spanning 573–575. During this period, the Romans—and the Persians—prepared for an expanded war.

In 575, Chosroes dispatched his grandson into Roman territory again but was driven out of Cappadocia; in 577, the Roman general Justinian (527–565) defeated young Chosroes at the Battle of Melitene, just west of the upper Euphrates River. This drove the Persian forces to the west. Justinian exploited the advantage he had gained by invading Persian Armenia, advancing to the Caspian Sea, where he established a base and constructed a fleet of warships late in 577.

In 578, Justinian invaded Assyria, which prompted the elder Chosroes to sue for peace. This was negotiated when the old man died in 579, and the new Persian king, Hormizd IV (r. 579–590), repudiated his father's negotiations, refusing to yield any territory. The war, therefore, continued—and continued to go badly for the Persians. They lost most of Armenia and were forced to withdraw from the Caucasus. For their part, the Turks overran Khorasan, penetrating as far as Hyrcania on the Caspian Sea. Within Persia, the reign of Hormizd IV proved disastrous. His tyranny provoked internal dissent and rebellion.

By 588, the Sassanid Empire of Persia was on the verge of collapse. At that point General Bahram Chobin (d. 591) performed a miracle: ambushing a larger Turkish force, he achieved a complete victory at the Battle of the Hyrcanian

Rock. By pressing his advantage, he pushed the Turks out of most of the area south of the Oxus River (near Mus), but was defeated at the hands of the Roman emperor Maurice (539–602) at the Battle of Nisibis later in the year. This loss resulted in a Persian withdrawal to Armenia. Still later, in 589, Bahram sought to regain lost ground by going on the offensive at the Battle of the Araxes. After this defeat, Hormizd ordered Bahram's relief, but the general refused to relinquish command. He now turned against the unpopular Persian emperor, whom he overthrew. The younger Chosroes now assumed the throne, but Bahram again refused to yield and seized the throne for himself. Chosroes found refuge with Persia's Roman enemies.

Emperor Maurice took advantage of the Persian disarray by supporting Chosroes against Bahram. He dispatched a Roman army under Narses via Assyria to restore Chosroes. Simultaneously, Roman legions advanced into Media. Bahram met Narses in battle at the Zab River. Outnumbered (60,000 to 40,000), Bahram was defeated, fled, and was killed. Restored to the throne as Chosroes II, the new Persian ruler made peace with Rome.

Further reading: Geoffrey Greatrex and Samuel N. C. Lieu, eds., *Roman Eastern Frontier and the Persian Wars: Part II, 363–628 A.D., a Narrative Sourcebook* (New York: Routledge, 2002); A. T. Olmstead, *History of the Persian Empire* (Chicago: University of Chicago Press, 1972); Peter Wilcox, *Rome's Enemies: Parthians and Sassanids*, vol. 175 (London: Osprey, 1988).

Roman-Syrian War   See SYRIAN-ROMAN WARS.

Romanus's Early Campaigns (1068–1069)

PRINCIPAL COMBATANTS: Byzantine Empire vs. the Seljuk Turks
PRINCIPAL THEATER(S): Syria, Media, Anatolia (Turkey)
DECLARATION: None
MAJOR ISSUES AND OBJECTIVES: Romanus rebuilt his army and mounted campaigns to protect his Byzantine Empire from attacks by the Seljuk Turks.
OUTCOME: Romanus drove the Turks out of the Byzantine Empire.
APPROXIMATE MAXIMUM NUMBER OF MEN UNDER ARMS: Unknown
CASUALTIES: Unknown
TREATIES: None

Romanus IV Diogenes (d. 1072) married Eudocia Macreom Dolitissa (fl. 11th century), the widow of Constantine X (d. 1067) in 1067. The new ruler of the Byzantine Empire spent his first year on the throne rebuilding the empire's armies, which had been allowed to deteriorate over the previous 25 years. His first action was against the

Seljuk Turks, who had set up winter quarters in Phrygia and Pontus. At the Battle of Sebastia, Romanus defeated Alp Arslan (d. c. 1030), the Seljuks' leader, and forced him to withdraw to Armenia and Mesopotamia. Romanus then struck in Syria against Arabs who had risen against the Byzantine rule there. He next marched to Cappadocia, where he drove off the Turks. He pressed onward to Akhlat, the Turkish stronghold on Lake Van. Part of his army moved to Media, where it was defeated by Alp Arslan. The Seljuk Turk leader then raided into Anatolia, but Romanus devised a clever attack and defeated the Turks at the Battle of Heraclea. By the end of the campaigns of 1069, Romanus had driven the Seljuk Turks out of the Byzantine Empire.

Further reading: John F. Haldon, *The Byzantine Wars* (Mount Pleasant, S.C.: Arcadia, 2000); Cyril A. Manso, ed. *History of Byzantium* (New York: Oxford University Press, 2002).

Roman War against Pyrrhus of Epirus (281–272 B.C.E.)

PRINCIPAL COMBATANTS: Rome vs. Tarentum (forces led by Pyrrhus of Epirus)
PRINCIPAL THEATER(S): Southern Italy
DECLARATION: Tarentum against Rome
MAJOR ISSUES AND OBJECTIVES: Tarentum sought to stem Roman expansion in the region.
OUTCOME: Tarentum succeeded in its objective, but at great cost.
APPROXIMATE MAXIMUM NUMBER OF MEN UNDER ARMS: Rome, 70,000; Pyrrhus, 70,000
CASUALTIES: Rome lost 7,000–15,000 killed at Heraclea (280), and Pyrrhus lost 4,000–11,000; each side lost about 11,000 men at Asculum (279 B.C.E.)
TREATIES: None

When Tarentum (in southern Italy) feared that Roman expansion would soon engulf it, that city-state declared war on Rome and sought aid from Pyrrhus (319–272 B.C.E.), king of Epirus. He arrived with 20,000 infantrymen and some 3,000 Thessalian and Epirote cavalry troopers and set up as ruler of the Greek city-states of southern Italy.

In 280, Publius Valerius Laevinus (fl. 280s–270s B.C.E.) led about 35,000 Romans against what was now 30,000 troops deployed by Pyrrhus at Heraclea on the Siris River. Pyrrhus brilliantly deployed his elephants, surprising and overwhelming the Romans, who had never seen such creatures. He effected a rout, driving the legions across the Siris and inflicting 7,000 to 15,000 deaths. Pyrrhus's losses were also heavy, between 4,000 and 11,000 killed. Later congratulated on this victory, Pyrrhus reportedly replied, "One more such victory and I am lost."

Thereafter a "Pyrrhic victory" described a triumph not worth its cost.

Pyrrhus advanced toward Rome and, learning that a new Roman-allied army was marching to intercept him, recruited a force that may have numbered 70,000 and included Samnites and Greeks. In 279, Pyrrhus's forces clashed with the Roman-allied army (also numbering perhaps 70,000) near Asculum (modern Ascoli, Italy). The first day of battle proved indecisive, but the second day was carried by Pyrrhus, again largely because of judicious use of elephants. However, this time there was no rout, and the Roman forces withdrew intact. Both sides sustained heavy losses of about 11,000 each, and Pyrrhus himself was seriously wounded. Like Heraclea, Asculum was a "Pyrrhic victory."

Following Asculum, Pyrrhus answered a call for aid from Syracuse on the island of Sicily, this time against the Carthaginians, who had laid siege to Syracuse. During 278–76 B.C.E., Pyrrhus repeatedly prevailed against the Carthaginians but never drove them off the island. Worse, his struggle against the Carthaginians prompted them to conclude an alliance with Rome. Despite this, Pyrrhus might well have come to control all of Sicily had he stayed; however, in 275 he returned to the southern Italian mainland and fought the Battle of Beneventum against Roman forces. At first, it looked as if Pyrrhus's elephants would yet again carry the day, for they drove the Romans against the walls of their own camp. At a critical moment, however, the Romans managed to turn the elephants back against the attackers, creating great confusion and panic. The Romans exploited this success with a sharp counterattack that defeated Pyrrhus, who suffered heavy losses. Later in 275, Tarentum fell to the Romans, and Pyrrhus departed the field.

Further reading: Petros Garoufalias, *Pyrrhus, King of Epirus* (London: Stacey International, 1978); C. A. Kinkaid, *Successors of Alexander the Great: Ptolemy I-Pyrrhus of Epirus-Antiochus III* (Golden, Colo.: Ares, 1980).

Roman War with the Quadi and Sarmatians (374–375)

PRINCIPAL COMBATANTS: The Quadi and Sarmatians vs. the Roman Empire
PRINCIPAL THEATER(S): Romania, Bulgaria, Austria, Hungary, and Yugoslavia
DECLARATION: None
MAJOR ISSUES AND OBJECTIVES: The Quadi wanted the Roman Empire to remove the fortification it had erected from Quadi territory.
OUTCOME: Romans battled the Quadi and their allies the Sarmations until the death of Valentinian.
APPROXIMATE MAXIMUM NUMBER OF MEN UNDER ARMS: Unknown

CASUALTIES: Unknown
TREATIES: None

The invading Huns pushed the Germanic people known as the Quadi westward into Dacia (Romania), where they settled in about 359. They remained there with little to do with the Roman Empire to the south until Emperor Valentinian I (321–375) ordered fortifications constructed on the south bank of the Danube River in Quadi territory. Gabinus (d. 374), the Quadi king, at first tried to appeal to the fort commander but was killed for his efforts by the Roman general Marcellinus (330–395). The Quadi then rose in protest with the Sarmatians. They swept across Moesia (Bulgaria) and Pannonia (Austria, Hungary, and Yugoslavia). In 374, the Roman army under Theodosius (c. 346–395) forced the Sarmatians to make a separate peace in Moesia, while Valentinian marched into Quadi territory in 375 and wreaked havoc in the region. The Quadi then sent envoys to Valentinian to ask for peace. Valentinian became so angry at their attempts to blame the war on Roman incursions into Quadi territory that he suffered a stroke and died. Flavius Gratianus (Gratian) (359–383), his son, then became emperor in the West, and the Quadi lived in peace until they invaded Italy with the Visigoths in 405.

Further reading: Stephen Williams and Gerard Friell, *Theodosius: The Empire at Bay* (New Haven, Conn.: Yale University Press, 1995).

Roman War with the Cimbri and Teutones (104–101 B.C.E.)

PRINCIPAL COMBATANTS: Rome vs. the Germanic tribes of Cimbri and Teutones
PRINCIPAL THEATER(S): Gaul and northern Italy
DECLARATION: None
MAJOR ISSUES AND OBJECTIVES: The barbarian tribes of Cimbri and Teutones sought to invade the territory of the Roman Republic.
OUTCOME: Rome defeated the barbarian tribes of Cimbri and Teutones.
APPROXIMATE MAXIMUM NUMBER OF MEN UNDER ARMS: Unknown
CASUALTIES: At the Battle of Vercellae (101 B.C.E.), 140,000 Cimbri were killed and 50,000 captured.
TREATIES: None

In about 109 B.C.E. the Germanic tribes of the Cimbri and the Teutones migrated through Switzerland to Gaul. At the Rhone River, they were met by and they defeated the Roman army of M. Junius Silanus (fl. second century B.C.E.). Disaster struck the Romans again in 105 at the Battle of Arausio (Orange), where the Roman army was nearly annihilated and some 40,000 Roman noncombatants were also killed.

In 104, Caius Marius (155?–86 B.C.E.), who had been fighting in Numidia, took command in Gaul. As the Cimbri and Teutones prepared to invade Italy, Marius made sweeping military reforms and recruited new troops. He fortified his camp at the Rhone and Isere rivers in preparation for new assaults. In 102, the barbarian tribes divided their forces. The Teutones moved toward Italy, but Marius's army ambushed the horde at the Battle of Aquae Sextae (Aix-en-Provence), killing 90,000 and capturing 20,000. The Cimbri, however, managed to move through Switzerland and the Brenner Pass and to defeat a Roman force in the Adige River valley in northern Italy. They continued toward the south into the Po River valley. Marius hurried his forces back to Italy, where they thoroughly defeated the Cimbri horde at the Battle of Vercellae in 101. About 140,000 barbarians were killed, and more than 50,000 were captured. No further attacks from Gaul threatened Italy.

Further reading: John B. Bury, *The Invasion of Europe by the Barbarians* (New York: W. W. Norton, 2000); Peter Wilcox, *Barbarians against Rome: Rome's Celtic, Germanic, Spanish and Gallic Enemies* (London: Osprey, 2000).

Roman War with the Vandals (468)

PRINCIPAL COMBATANTS: Rome vs. the Vandals
PRINCIPAL THEATER(S): The Mediterranean
DECLARATION: None
MAJOR ISSUES AND OBJECTIVES: Emperor Leo I of the Eastern Roman Empire wanted to push the Germanic Vandals out of the Mediterranean region.
OUTCOME: The Roman general Basiliscus was defeated near Cape Bon (Tunisia), and the Vandals retained control of the Mediterranean.
APPROXIMATE MAXIMUM NUMBER OF MEN UNDER ARMS: Rome, more than 100,000 men; Vandal numbers unknown
CASUALTIES: Unknown
TREATIES: None

Having been pushed from the Danube River basin, Gaul, and Spain, the Germanic Vandals, an ancient tribe originally from Denmark, relocated to North Africa in 429. Under the leadership of King Gaiseric (390–477), the Vandals began increasing their territory in the Mediterranean region, making Carthage their capital in 439. In 455, the Vandals marched on Rome and sacked the city. Withdrawing to Carthage with Licinia Eudoxia (c. 422–480), widow of Emperor Valentinian III (419–455), as their hostage, by 468 the Vandals had gained control over Roman Africa, Sicily, and other eastern Mediterranean islands. Leo I (c. 400–74), emperor of the Eastern Roman Empire, sent his brother-in-law Basiliscus (d. 478) to attack the Vandals at their North Africa base. Basiliscus postponed the attack for so long that the Vandals were able to decimate the Roman fleet at Cape Bon (Tunisia). As for Basiliscus, he fled back to Constantinople with his large but unused army. The Vandals continued to hold power in the Mediterranean region, and the Eastern Empire made peace with the Vandals in 476.

Further reading: Frank M. Clover, *Late Roman West and the Vandals* (London: Ashgate, 1993); Thomas Hodgkin, *Huns, Vandals, and the Fall of the Roman Empire* (London: Lionel Leventhal, 1996).

Roman Wars with Veii (438–426 B.C.E., 405–396 B.C.E.)

PRINCIPAL COMBATANTS: Rome vs. Veii
PRINCIPAL THEATER(S): Central Italy
DECLARATION: None
MAJOR ISSUES AND OBJECTIVES: Rome sought to end the Etruscan dominance in central Italy.
OUTCOME: Rome won a prolonged siege of Veii and became the leading state in central Italy.
APPROXIMATE MAXIMUM NUMBER OF MEN UNDER ARMS: Unknown
CASUALTIES: Unknown
TREATIES: None

Located about 10 miles to the northwest of Rome on the banks of the Tiber River, the Etruscan state of Veii was first engaged in war with Rome between 438 and 425 B.C.E. At the siege of the Veii outpost Fidenae, King Tolumnius (d. c. 430) of Veii was killed. Although asked to come to Veii's aid, few other Etruscan states entered the fray. Rome won the siege of Fidenae in 426 and went on to besiege the state of Veii for nine years. Realizing that the Romans would soon reach Veii after the defeat of Fidenae, the citizens of Veii fortified their city. Veii at last fell to the Romans in 396 after the troops of Marcus Furius Camillus (d. c. 365) crawled through tunnels into the city, which they sacked. The people and territory of Veii were absorbed by Rome. As a result of the siege of Veii, Rome had established a new career path for its citizens by offering regular payments to troops in the field. The Roman Republic by this time was the leading state in central Italy.

Further reading: A. Alfödi, *Early Rome and the Latins* (Ann Arbor: University of Michigan Press, 965); Graeme Barker, *Etruscans* (London: Blackwell, 2000); Howard H. Soullard, *Etruscan Cities and Rome* (Baltimore: Johns Hopkins University Press, 1998).

Rome, Celtic Sack of (390 B.C.E.)

PRINCIPAL COMBATANTS: Celts vs. Etruscan Rome
PRINCIPAL THEATER(S): Rome and environs

DECLARATION: None
MAJOR ISSUES AND OBJECTIVES: Celtic expansion
OUTCOME: The Etruscan city-state of Rome was sacked, except for the Capitol.
APPROXIMATE MAXIMUM NUMBER OF MEN UNDER ARMS: Unknown
CASUALTIES: Unknown
TREATIES: None

The Celts (Senones) of Britain first invaded Italy about 450 B.C.E., and they made a full-scale assault against Rome in 390 (some authorities say 387), achieving victory against Roman (Etruscan) forces at the Battle of Clusium (or Clisium). Rome, during this period an Etruscan city-state, appealed to its neighbors for military aid, and, in violation of accepted behavior for diplomats, Roman ambassadors rushed to the defense of the Clusium. In response, the Celts, led by Brennus (fl. latter fourth century B.C.E.) (the Welsh word *brenin* is the equivalent of "king") marched on Rome itself. Celtic forces routed the Roman army at Allia, then went on to overrun and sack Rome, destroying everything except the Capitol.

The Celtic sack of Rome had a profound long-term effect on the Roman collective psychology. Even centuries later, after the rise of Roman power and after Rome had subjugated most of the Celtic kingdoms, fear of the Celtic threat persisted and influenced Rome's aggressive foreign policy.

See also ETRUSCAN-ROMAN WARS, EARLY.

Further reading: Peter Berresford Ellis, *Celt and Roman: The Celts of Italy* (New York: St. Martin's Press, 1998).

Rome, March on *See* FASCIST MARCH ON ROME.

Rome, Republican Revolt in *See* ETRUSCAN-ROMAN WARS, EARLY.

Rome, Vandal Sack of *See* VANDAL SACK OF ROME.

Rome, Visigothic Sack of *See* VISIGOTHIC SACK OF ROME.

Roses, Wars of the (1455–1487)

PRINCIPAL COMBATANTS: Two houses of the English nobility—the Yorks vs. the Lancasters.
PRINCIPAL THEATER(S): England
DECLARATION: The intrigue and fighting was continuous.

MAJOR ISSUES AND OBJECTIVES: These were dynastic conflicts, fought between two factions both to seize immediate control of the kingdom and to achieve an uncontested claim to the throne.
OUTCOME: In effect, the wars led to the founding of a new ruling house, the Tudor family, whose monarchs were to bring strong and relatively stable government to England.
APPROXIMATE MAXIMUM NUMBER OF MEN UNDER ARMS: Unknown
CASUALTIES: Unknown, but concentrated in the partisan nobility
TREATIES: None

Less a series of wars in the traditional sense, the Wars of the Roses were a sequence of intrigues, rebellions, and attacks that took place over the dozen years from 1455 and 1487, in three distinct stages. Between 1455 to 1464, what began as a battle between rival factions under the weak Lancaster king Henry VI (1421–71) became in the end a war for possession of the crown, which settled briefly on the head of House of York candidate Edward IV (1442–83). In the second phase, from 1469 to 1471, renewed factional wrangling led to dynastic war between Edward IV and supporters of Henry VI, who was (also briefly) restored to the throne. The final stage, from 1483 to 1487, consisted of outright dynastic war and led to the accession of Henry VII (1457–1509), the first Tudor king. The wars are familiar to the English reading public as the backdrop and sometimes subject of a number of Shakespeare's historical plays, best known among them, perhaps, *Richard III*. They were first called the "Wars of the Roses" many years later by Tudor propagandists—the idea being that the warring houses of Lancaster (represented by a red rose) and York (represented by a white rose) had been reconciled in the Tudor ascendancy, thus replacing an insecure age of upheaval and unrest by orderly times of peace and prosperity.

Although both the Lancasters and the Yorks had some claim to the monarchy through descent from the sons of Edward III (1312–77), a Lancaster had actually sat on the throne since 1399. If it had not been for the near anarchy rampant in England during the middle of the 15th century, the Yorkists might never have made a bid for power. But after the death of Henry V (1387–1422), the Lancasters did not acquit themselves well in France, where the HUNDRED YEARS' WAR ground to a halt, having done little for the English but bankrupt the government and discredit Lancastrian rule. Great lords with private armies commanded the English countryside, where lawlessness ran rife and taxation hung heavy. The catalysts of struggle between York and Lancaster lay in the long minority of Henry VI. Henry proved to be a simpleton, slouching toward madness, and was from the start under the thumb of his ambitious queen, Margaret of Anjou (c. 1430–82). Her party, the Beauforts, had allowed the English position in France to deteriorate and caused the English themselves to turn to the Yorkists with the fall of Bordeaux in 1453.

That year Henry lapsed into insanity, causing a powerful baronial cabal, backed by Richard Neville (the "Kingmaker"; 1428–71), earl of Warwick, to make its move. The barons invested Richard (1411–60), duke of York, as protector of the realm. When Henry recovered his sanity in 1455, he brought the Beauforts back to court, reestablishing Margaret's authority. York took up arms, in self-protection as well as ambition. At the battle of St. Albans on May 22, 1455, York proved victorious, and an uneasy truce followed. Civil war broke out again four years later, when York rose once more in rebellion. The Yorkists had some initial success before they scattered following defeat at Ludford Bridge on October 12, 1459. Many fled to France, where Warwick was regrouping the Yorkist forces. In June 1460, they returned to England, where Warwick and Richard's son and heir Edward (1470–83) decisively defeated the Lancastrian forces at Northampton on July 10. Thereafter, York tried to lay claim to the throne but settled instead for the right to succeed upon the death of Henry. Because this effectively disinherited King Henry's son, also named Edward, Queen Margaret continued her strident opposition.

Gathering forces in northern England, Margaret led the Lancastrians on a surprise attack and killed York at Wakefield in December. She then marched south toward London, defeating Warwick on the way at the Second Battle of St. Albans on February 17, 1461, which left the Yorkist cause in the hands of the 18-year-old Edward of York. On February 2, he had defeated a Lancastrian force at Mortimer's Cross, and now he too was marching on London. Arriving before Margaret on February 26, within the week the young duke of York was proclaimed King Edward IV at Westminster, on March 4. Then, with what was left of Warwick's army, Edward chased Margaret north to Towton, where they would fight the bloodiest battle of the war. At Towton, Edward won a complete victory for the Yorkist cause. Henry, Margaret, and their son Prince Edward fled to Scotland. The first stage of the Wars of the Roses drew to a close as the fighting waned, except for seesaw struggles for the castles of Northumbria between 1461 and 1464 and the reduction of a few pockets of Lancastrian resistance, such as the battles of Hedgeley Moor and Hexham in April–May 1464.

The next round grew from disputes within the Yorkist ranks. Warwick and Edward fell out over foreign policy, and Warwick and his cronies found themselves increasingly passed over at court. Soon Warwick was fomenting rebellion with the king's ambitious brother George (1449–78), duke of Clarence. By 1469 civil war had broken out once more as Warwick and Clarence backed risings in the north. By July, they had defeated Edward's supporters at Edgecote (near Banbury), and soon they took the king himself prisoner. However, Edward was rescued by March 1470. He regained control of his govern-ment and forced the conspirators to flee to France. There they allied themselves with the French king Louis XI (1423–83) and their former enemy, Margaret of Anjou.

Warwick and Clarence returned to England in September 1470, defeated and deposed Edward, and restored the crown to Henry VI. Edward himself now fled with his supporters to the Netherlands. Securing aid from Burgundia, he returned to England in March 1471. Edward outmaneuvered Warwick long enough to regain the loyalty of his brother, the duke of Clarence. The two joined forces to defeat Warwick at Barnet on April 14. That same day, Margaret landed at Weymouth. When she learned of Warwick's disastrous defeat, she turned west and rushed toward the safety of Wales. But Edward's army beat hers to the River Severn; at the battle of Tewkesbury on May 4 Edward captured Margaret, destroyed her forces, and put her son to death. Shortly afterward, he had Henry VI murdered in the Tower of London.

Edward's throne was safe for the rest of his life, but when he died in 1483 his brother, Richard (1461–83), the duke of Gloucester, disregarded the claims of his nephew, the young Edward V, and had himself crowned Richard III. In doing so, he alienated many Yorkists, his only natural constituency. These men now turned to the House they had so long opposed and to the last hope of the Lancastrians, Henry Tudor (later Henry VII). Backed by the Yorkist defectors, allied with the French, Henry rebelled. As all readers of William Shakespeare know, Henry defeated and killed Richard at Bosworth Field (on August 22, 1485). The next year Henry married Edward IV's daughter Elizabeth of York (1466–1503) thus uniting the Yorkist and Lancastrian claims. There was still some persuading to do, some malcontents to put down. It was only when Henry defeated a Yorkist rising supporting the pretender Lambert Simnel (see SIMNEL'S REBELLION) on June 16, 1487, that what Henry's descendants would call the Wars of the Roses came to a close.

More recent historians have downplayed the significance of these wars, claiming that the Tudor writers and later historians following their lead exaggerated the level of casualties and the extent of the disorder they caused. Most of the fighting was limited not merely to the nobility but to the two factions and those most closely associated with them, so that even at the height of the fighting, most common people continued about their everyday business. The conflicts did not much disrupt the growing prosperity and the rising standard of living of ordinary men and women in England in the second half of the 15th century, though the political crisis they created no doubt had a larger effect. Their most lasting impact was probably to produce the new dynasty of the Tudors—a lusty, expansive, and confident lot who would take England to glories no previous rulers, Lancaster or York, would have imagined possible.

See also BUCKINGHAM'S REVOLT; CADE'S REBELLION; WARWICK'S REBELLION.

Further reading: Anthony Goodman, *The Wars of the Roses* (London: Routledge, 1981); A. J. Pollard, *The Wars of the Roses* (New York: St. Martin's Press, 1988); John Gillingham, *The Wars of the Roses: Peace and Conflict in Fifteenth Century England* (Baton Rouge: Louisiana State University Press, 1981); B. Alison Weir, *The Wars of the Roses* (New York: Random House, 1996).

Ruandan (Rwandan) Civil War (1959–1961)

PRINCIPAL COMBATANTS: Tutsi (and Twa) tribe vs. Hutu tribe
PRINCIPAL THEATER(S): Ruanda (Rwanda), Africa
DECLARATION: None
MAJOR ISSUES AND OBJECTIVES: The oppressed Hutu rebelled against the dominant minority Tutsi.
OUTCOME: The Hutu prevailed, but the stage was set for further civil war.
APPROXIMATE MAXIMUM NUMBER OF MEN UNDER ARMS: Unknown
CASUALTIES: Unknown, but some 150,000 Tutsis became exiles.
TREATIES: None, except for a UN-sponsored referendum effectively ending Tutsi rule

The German defeat in WORLD WAR II resulted in the transfer of the former East African colony to a Belgian protectorate, Ruanda-Urundi, under the aegis of the United Nations. In 1959, after UN-supervised elections, the Belgian administrators granted self-government to Ruanda-Urundi. This sparked a revolt of the long-suppressed and long-oppressed Hutu against the Tutsi (Watusi). The Tutsi traditionally dominated the region, culturally and economically as well as in government, even though they constituted only 15 percent of the population. The Hutu, the majority tribe, were long held in servitude by the Tutsi. As the Tutsi moved to seize the power granted by Belgium, the Hutu commenced a war not only against the Tutsi but their allies the Twa (pygmies).

The war was bloody and bitter, but the Hutu prevailed. In a 1961 UN-sanctioned referendum, the vast majority of Ruandans voted to depose the Tutsi king and replace him with a republic. On July 1, 1962, Ruanda officially became independent. Following the elections and independence some 150,000 Tutsis went into exile. Many of them would invade their former country in 1963. This and other Tutsi-Hutu conflicts became the basis of the disastrous RWANDAN CIVIL WAR of 1990–94.

Further reading: Alain Destexhe, *Rwanda and Genocide in the Twentieth Century* (New York: New York University Press, 1996); Mahmood Mamdani, *When Victims Become Killers: Colonialism, Nativism, and the Genocide in Rwanda* (Princeton, N.J.: Princeton University Press, 2002); Gerard Prunier, *The Rwanda Crisis: History of a Genocide* (New York: Columbia University Press, 1995).

Ruandan Civil War   *See* RWANDAN CIVIL WAR.

Russian-Bulgarian War (969–972)

PRINCIPAL COMBATANTS: Kievan Russia vs. Bulgaria
PRINCIPAL THEATER(S): Bulgaria
DECLARATION: None
MAJOR ISSUES AND OBJECTIVES: The Kievan prince Sviatoslav sought territorial conquest.
OUTCOME: Some of Bulgaria fell to Sviatoslav, who, however, provoked war with the Byzantine Empire.
APPROXIMATE MAXIMUM NUMBER OF MEN UNDER ARMS: Unknown
CASUALTIES: Unknown
TREATIES: None

This war is important because it relates to the BYZANTINE-RUSSIAN WAR of 970–972, which erupted over a dispute as to how Bulgaria should be divided between Russia and the Byzantine Empire. During 967–969, combined Russian and Byzantine forces invaded Bulgaria. In 969, Kievan Russians led by Prince Sviatoslav (d. 972) sought to exploit the disarray in Bulgaria created by the death, in 927, of the Bulgarian czar Symeon (d. 927). Sviatoslav led an army into Bulgaria, took Philippopolis, then captured the new Bulgarian ruler, Boris II (d. 984). After this, the Russians overran the country. The Bulgarians resisted, but it was ultimately Russia's erstwhile Byzantine ally that transformed the war into one between Byzantium and Russia. The Byzantine emperor, John Tzimisces (925–976), moved in 970 to check the Russian advance. This resulted in exhausting and inconclusive combat for the next two years.

Further reading: R. J. Crampton, *A Concise History of Bulgaria* (New York: Cambridge University Press, 1997).

Russian Civil War (1425–1453)

PRINCIPAL COMBATANTS: Internecine dispute within Muscovy (ancient Russia) and between Muscovy and the Tartars
PRINCIPAL THEATER(S): Muscovy (Russia)
DECLARATION: None
MAJOR ISSUES AND OBJECTIVES: Control of the throne of Muscovy
OUTCOME: Ultimately, the reign of Ivan III the Great was assured.
APPROXIMATE MAXIMUM NUMBER OF MEN UNDER ARMS: Unknown
CASUALTIES: Unknown
TREATIES: None

The reign of Basil II (1415–62) was marked by universal anarchy in Russia. He came to the throne at age 10 as grand prince of Moscow following the death of his father, Basil I (1371–1425), in 1425. Immediately, the boy's uncle, Yuri (d. c. 1434), attempted to seize control of Russia with the support of the Tartars. This put him in opposition to the *boyars* (nobility), who supported Basil II. However, in 1432, the boyars suddenly transferred their allegiance to Yuri because of a dispute over an arranged marriage between Basil and a boyar girl. Assisted by the boyars, Yuri managed to seize control of Moscow, but his death in 1434 abruptly ended his royal ambitions. His ineffectual son, also named Yuri (d. after 1432), half-heartedly attempted to capitalize on his father's gains but was quickly defeated, taken captive, and blinded.

In 1446, Dimitri Shemiaka (d. 1453), another of Yuri's sons, prince of Galicia (part of Poland), allied himself with other princes and effectively conquered Muscovy in 1446. Basil, captured, was blinded—but, inexplicably, Dimitri Shemiaka restored Basil to the throne in 1447.

In 1447 and, again in 1451, the Tartars invaded, the second invasion reaching the walls of Moscow itself. The defeat of Yuri and his son left the Tartars as Basil II's only significant threat. The Muscovites managed to repel the Tartar invasions, successfully defending the walled city of Moscow, even though the Tartars sporadically gained the advantage and even once captured Basil, holding him for an exorbitant ransom.

During the 1450s, Basil II's son Ivan (1440–1505) invaded Galicia, defeating Dimitri Shemiaka and forcing him into exile at Novgorod. Despite his blindness, Basil began to unify Muscovy, laying the foundation for the empire that would grow under the rule of Ivan—as Czar Ivan III (the Great).

Further reading: Robert O. Crummey, *The Formation of Muscovy, 1304–1613* (London: Longman, 1991); Geoffrey A. Hasking, *Russia and the Russians: A History* (Cambridge, Mass.: Harvard University Press, 2001).

Russian Civil War (1604–1613) *See* TIME OF TROUBLES, RUSSIA'S.

Russian Civil War (1917–1922)

PRINCIPAL COMBATANTS: "Red" Soviet (communist, Bolshevik) revolutionary government vs. "White" czarist counterrevolutionaries (with varied foreign interventions)
PRINCIPAL THEATER(S): Russia, Siberia, and the Baltic states (Latvia, Lithuania, Estonia)
DECLARATION: None
MAJOR ISSUES AND OBJECTIVES: Following the communist victory in the Bolshevik Revolution of 1917, this civil war was essentially a counterrevolution to overthrow the new Soviet (communist) regime.

OUTCOME: The counterrevolution was defeated.
APPROXIMATE MAXIMUM NUMBER OF MEN UNDER ARMS: Soviet Red Army, 5,427,273 (but only 498,891 effective peak strength); White, 317,800 effective peak strength
CASUALTIES: Soviet Red Army, 418,768 battle deaths, 283,079 deaths from disease and other causes, 536,725 wounded; Whites, 175,000 battle deaths, 150,000 deaths from disease and other causes
TREATIES: None

Almost immediately following the triumph of the communist regime in the BOLSHEVIK REVOLUTION (1917), the Don Cossacks revolted on December 9, 1917, in the first organized counterrevolutionary opposition. These men joined czarist loyalists known as the Whites by the end of 1917 and created an army of 3,500, which soon grew to about 5,000 and repeatedly engaged Bolshevik militia forces over an 80-day period called the First Kuban Campaign, or the Ice March. The most experienced of the White commanders, General Lavr Kornilov (1870–1918), fell in battle on April 13, 1918, but the White forces continued to grow. Under General Anton Denikin (1872–1947), some 9,000 counterrevolutionary troops rallied by the summer of 1918, including 3,500 fierce Cossacks. With these troops, Denikin launched the Second Kuban Campaign and by October had seized the Kuban region from Bolshevik control. Following this triumph, the White ranks swelled to 40,000, and a full-scale civil war was at hand.

Encouraged by the success of the counterrevolutionary movement, a number of foreign powers, hostile to the Bolsheviks, intervened on behalf of the Whites. Japan occupied Vladivostok in December 1917 and committed 74,000 soldiers to action in Siberia. Small numbers of French and Greek troops fought in the Ukraine and occupied Odessa until April 8, 1919. A combined U.S., British, and French expeditionary force seized the ports of Murmansk (June 23, 1918) and Archangel (August 1, 1918), retrieving materiel they had sent to the now-fallen czar. This materiel they now turned over to the Whites. Yet the commitment by the major powers to the civil war was never compelling, and the Americans (some 5,800 men) were withdrawn in August 1919 from northern Russia after losses of 144 killed in action, 100 dead from other causes, and 305 wounded. French and British forces withdrew in September and October—the Royal Navy having done considerable damage to Bolshevik naval forces on the Baltic. Two Russian battleships were sunk, as were five destroyers, two submarines, a cruiser, and a submarine depot ship. The British lost one submarine, two destroyers, and 10 smaller craft.

In August 1918, the United States deployed 8,358 men—two regiments—to Siberia, less to aid the Whites directly than to prevent the Japanese from seizing the Russian Maritime Provinces should the Bolsheviks prove victorious. The Americans reinforced 4,000 Canadian, 3,000

French, and 2,000 British troops already in place. These forces engaged in skirmishes with the Bolsheviks for two years before withdrawing in April 1920. By that time, the Japanese had mostly withdrawn, though they did not completely evacuate Siberia until October 25, 1922. While few casualties were suffered among the foreign and Bolshevik forces in these engagements, Bolshevik partisans attacked the pro-czarist stronghold of Nikolaevsk on May 25, 1920, killing 700 Japanese troops and slaughtering as many as 6,000 civilians.

Although the major foreign powers did not throw major troop support behind the White cause, they did contribute significant quantities of munitions. The Whites also received aid from the so-called Czech Legion, 50,000 poorly equipped but experienced troops formerly belonging to the Austro-Hungarian army who had recently been released from WORLD WAR I prisoner-of-war camps. The legion seized control of the Trans-Siberian Railroad in June 1918 and advanced along the line into eastern Russia. As they approached Yekaterinburg, the village in which Bolshevik partisans were holding the deposed czar, Nicholas II (1868–1918), his wife, and children, the partisans apparently panicked and summarily executed the royal family. In this sense, the last of the Romanov dynasty fell victim not to the Bolshevik Revolution but to the civil war that followed.

As the Czechs and Whites pressed their offensive, a provisional anti-Soviet government was established at Omsk. Former Imperial Russian navy admiral Alexander Kolchak (1874–1920) seized control of the Omsk government and thereby effectively proclaimed himself head of the White government. Rallying to him, the Whites advanced deeply into eastern Russia with an army of about 120,000 men. In December 1918, this force captured Perm and took some 30,000 Bolshevik prisoners.

The White momentum of late 1918 continued into the next year. Ufa fell in the spring of 1919 and was followed by the wanton massacre of 670 Bolshevik prisoners of war. Thinly deployed across a 700-mile front, the Whites continued to advance until Leon Trotsky (1879–1940), one of the primary architects of the Bolshevik Revolution, at last organized a truly effective Red Army force of 119,214 men. Beginning in late April, General Mikhail Tukhachevsky (1893–1937) led this army in a counteroffensive against the Whites, compelling Kolchak to make a long fighting retreat through the summer and fall of 1919.

On June 6, 1919, the Red Army's most distinguished commander, Mikhail Frunze (1885–1925), retook Ufa, killing about 3,000 White soldiers. Throughout the fall, Kolchak's forces suffered one defeat after another, losing nearly 20,000 killed or wounded during September–October. Kolchak himself was captured and executed on February 7, 1920, and about 40,000 Whites became POWs. In the meantime, the Czech Legion fought an eastward retreat along the Trans-Siberian Railroad, reaching

Vladivostok, from which 57,459 men (the entire legion and associated units) were evacuated and thereby removed from the fighting. This left only the so-called White Guards, mostly Cossacks, in Siberia. The White Guards became a much-feared guerrilla force that murdered untold thousands of civilians.

While fighting, often irregular and disorganized, raged in Siberia, Red forces took the offensive in the Baltic, invading Latvia, Lithuania, and Estonia during 1918–19. German and Allied troops, bitter enemies in the just-concluded World War I, were sent to the Baltic States, forcing the Bolsheviks to withdraw back into Russia by spring 1919. Estonia then became a staging area for a White counteroffensive. A White army of 18,500 marched across the Estonian frontier into Russia on October 6, 1919, and made a daring assault on Leningrad (St. Petersburg). Trotsky rallied 24,000 civilian defenders from the city. Soon reinforced to a strength of 73,000, these fighters repulsed the White army, forcing it back into Estonia.

A third front of great importance, in addition to Siberia and the Baltic, was the Don River region in the Ukraine and southern Caucasus. Here Trotsky built up his largest Red Army force, 380,000 combat-capable troops, by January 1919. Fighting on this huge front was exceptionally fierce and at first greatly favored the Whites. The northern Caucasus fell to the Whites by early 1919, Tsaritsyn (later Stalingrad) was conquered on June 17, 1919, and 40,000 Reds became POWs. Kiev, capital city of the Ukraine, was taken by White forces on September 2. By this time the Whites had found a powerful ally in Ukrainian nationalists, who turned their wrath not only against the Reds but also against Ukrainian Jews. Estimates of Jews slaughtered by the nationalists vary from 31,071 (the actual burial count) to 100,000, and some estimates reach 200,000.

By October 1919, the White offensive had largely swept the Reds out of southern Russia, and White forces were now on the march to Moscow. At Tula, however, a large city on the road to Moscow, a massive 175,000-man Red Army force counterattacked the White advance of some 100,000 men. The White army collapsed, unit by unit, and began a retreat back into the Ukraine. The Reds pursued, and, on December 17, 1919, retook Kiev. The White army retreated all the way to the Black Sea, where its survivors were evacuated by Allied ships in March 1920. A small White force under General Peter Wrangel (1878–1928) remained in Crimea, but otherwise the counterrevolution seemed to have been defeated.

The sudden demands of the RUSSO-POLISH WAR (1919–1920) briefly revived White hopes. Wrangel rebuilt an army of 40,000 and went on a new offensive north of the Sea of Azov. Unfortunately for Wrangel, however, the war with Poland soon ended, allowing Trotsky to release more Red Army troops against the offensive. General Frunze led about 130,000 Reds in a vast sweep of the

Crimea, driving Wrangel and the entire remainder of the White military as well as many sympathizing civilians, a total of 145,693 men, women, and children, to seek evacuation to Constantinople aboard a fleet of 126 British ships. With the end of the evacuation on November 15, 1920, the major phase of the Russian Civil War ended—although sporadic and disorganized violence, mostly from anarchists, continued into 1922.

Further reading: Orlando Figes, *A People's Tragedy: The Russian Revolution, 1891–1924* (New York: Penguin, 1998); W. Bruce Lincoln, *Red Victory: A History of the Russian Civil War* (New York: Da Capo, 1999); Evan Mawdsley, *The Russian Civil War* (Edinburgh, U.K.: Berlinn, 2001); Rex A. Wade, *The Bolshevik Revolution and the Russian Civil War* (Westport, Conn.: Greenwood, 2000).

Russian Conquest of Buryat Mongols

See RUSSIAN CONQUEST OF CENTRAL ASIA.

Russian Conquest of Central Asia
(1604–1689)

PRINCIPAL COMBATANTS: Russia vs. peoples of the region and the Manchu Chinese
PRINCIPAL THEATER(S): Central Asia and the Chinese frontier
DECLARATION: None
MAJOR ISSUES AND OBJECTIVES: Territorial expansion and conquest
OUTCOME: The Russians were remarkably successful in expanding their holdings until the Manchu retaliated in the border country; here, the Russians backed down after a long war of raiding and attrition.
APPROXIMATE MAXIMUM NUMBER OF MEN UNDER ARMS: Extremely variable
CASUALTIES: Unknown
TREATIES: Treaty of Nerchinsk, 1689

Russian expansion into Central Asia began with the founding of the settlement of Tomsk on the middle Yenisei River. From here, Russian settlement progressed, sometimes violently, to the upper Yenisei, where Yaniseisk, a fort, was built in 1618. In 1628, Russian expansion had reached the middle Lena River. Kirensk was founded in 1630, followed two years later by Yakutsk. In 1639, Russian settlement reached the Sea of Okhotsk, the first Russian outpost on the Pacific.

Throughout the 1640s, culminating in 1652, Russian armies fought the Buryat Mongols, ultimately defeating them and thereby gaining control of Lake Baikal and the surrounding territory. Simultaneously, during 1643–46, Russian forces set out from Yakutsk and reached the Chinese frontier. In 1644, they were at the mouth of the

Kolyma River, which put Russia into contact with the Arctic Ocean. Two new settlements were established, Okotsk in 1648 and Irkutsk and Khabarovsk in 1651. With this, commander Verofey Khabarov (fl. 17th century) erected forts throughout the Amur Valley and, to the north, the land of the Daur.

Russian penetration to the doorstep of China touched off skirmishes and pitched battles from 1653 to 1685. Although the Manchus had little enough interest in the Amur Valley, they were outraged by the persecution of Chinese settlers at the hands of Russian conquerors in the region. This prompted frequent Manchu raids against Russian positions in the valley. The ceaseless raiding wore the Russians down, and in 1660 a Manchu army forced the Russians out of the Amur Valley. This triggered a three-year war between Russia and Manchu China (1683–85). The result was the permanent ouster of the Russians from the Amur region. Russian czar Peter I (the Great; 1672–1725), ruling jointly with his half brother Ivan V (1682–96), concluded the Treaty of Nerchinsk with the Manchus in 1689, which brought peace and prosperous trade between China and Russia for some 175 years.

See also RUSSIAN-MANCHU WAR (1660) and RUSSIAN-MANCHU WAR (1683–1685).

Further reading: Fred W. Bergholz, *Partition of the Steppe: The Struggle of the Russians, Manchus, and the Zunghar Mongols to Empire in Central Asia, 1619–1758* (New York: Peter Lang, 1993); Robert K. Massie, *Peter the Great: His Life and World* (New York: Ballantine, 1981).

Russian Conquest of Finland *See* RUSSO-SWEDISH WAR.

Russian Conquest of Merv (1884–1885)

PRINCIPAL COMBATANTS: Russia vs. Merv
PRINCIPAL THEATER(S): Merv, Turkmenistan
DECLARATION: None
MAJOR ISSUES AND OBJECTIVES: Russian colonial expansion
OUTCOME: Merv fell in a sustained campaign.
APPROXIMATE MAXIMUM NUMBER OF MEN UNDER ARMS: Unknown
CASUALTIES: Unknown
TREATIES: None

By 1881, Russia had annexed virtually the entire Transcaspian Region (*see* RUSSIAN CONQUESTS IN CENTRAL ASIA [1864–1881]). The only Moslem principality of Central Asia that retained its independence was Merv. Once the Russians established control elsewhere in the region, the surrender of Merv became inevitable. A sustained campaign during 1884–85 resulted in the annexation of the principality and pushed the Russian border to the doorstep of Afghanistan. This heightened tension between the Russians and the British, since their colonial interests now threatened to encroach on one another.

Further reading: Geoffrey A. Hosking, *Russia and the Russians: A History* (Cambridge, Mass.: Harvard University Press, 2001); Dominic Lieven, *Empire: The Russian Empire and Its Rivals* (New Haven, Conn.: Yale University Press, 2002).

Russian Dynastic War (972–980)

PRINCIPAL COMBATANTS: Struggle among heirs to the medieval Russian throne, Oleg, Yaropolk, and Vladimir
PRINCIPAL THEATER(S): Russia and Kiev
DECLARATION: None
MAJOR ISSUES AND OBJECTIVES: Sole possession of the Russian throne
OUTCOME: After defeating and killing Oleg, Yaropolk was in turn defeated, then executed, by Vladimir, who become sole ruler of Russia.
APPROXIMATE MAXIMUM NUMBER OF MEN UNDER ARMS: Unknown
CASUALTIES: Unknown
TREATIES: None

Russia in the Middle Ages was a fragmented, feudal realm, and when the powerful Prince Sviatoslav (d. 972) died in 972, he left Russia in the hands of his three sons, Oleg (d. 977?), Yaropolk (d. c. 979), and Vladimir (956–1015). Almost immediately, they began to fight each other for sole possession of the throne. Combat was indecisive until 977, when Yaropolk's Kievan forces defeated Oleg's Drevlian army, and Oleg apparently fell in battle; his death was not confirmed, but he disappeared forever. Alarmed by Yaropolk's success, Vladimir sought an alliance with Scandinavia but managed only to recruit the costly services of Norse mercenaries. It proved a sound investment. Vladimir used them to obtain control of Polotsk in 978 and the following year Novgorod as well. In 980, Vladimir's forces marched on Kiev and took Yaropolk prisoner. He then surrendered Kiev without giving battle—and was soon executed, leaving Vladimir sole ruler of feudal Russia.

Further reading: Paul Dukes, *A History of Russia: Medieval, Modern, Contemporary, 882–1996* (Durham, N.C.: Duke University Press, 1998); Lawrence N. Langer, *Historical Dictionary of Medieval Russia* (Lanham, Md.: Scarecrow Press, 2002); David Nicolle, *Medieval Russian Armies 838–1252* (London: Osprey, 1999).

Russian Dynastic War (1015–1025)

PRINCIPAL COMBATANTS: Struggle among the heirs of Grand Prince Vladimir (with Polish intervention)

PRINCIPAL THEATER(S): Kiev and Novgorod
DECLARATION: None
MAJOR ISSUES AND OBJECTIVES: Succession to the thrones of Kiev and Novgorod
OUTCOME: Yaroslav emerged triumphant over his brothers.
APPROXIMATE MAXIMUM NUMBER OF MEN UNDER ARMS: Unknown
CASUALTIES: Unknown
TREATIES: None

Like his father Sviatoslav (d. 972), before him (*see* RUSSIAN DYNASTIC WAR [972–980]), Grand Prince Vladimir (956–1015) left on his death in 1015 a Russia divided among contending heirs—a situation that created inevitable conflict.

Vladimir's nephew Sviatopolk (d. 1021) sought sole rule and did not hesitate to murder his younger brothers Boris and Gleb (both died 1015) immediately following his uncle's death. This made him sole ruler of Kievan Russia and earned him the sobriquet of "the Damned"). In the meantime, however, another of Sviatopolk's brothers, Yaroslav (d. 1054), heir to the Novgorod throne, marched on Kiev, attacked Sviatopolk, and sent him fleeing to Poland to the protection of his father-in-law, Boleslav I (d. 1054). With Boleslav, Sviatopolk recruited a large army—precise numbers unknown—and invaded Russia, driving Yaroslav's forces back into Kiev, then all the way back to Novgorod.

In this way, Sviatopolk regained Kiev, but, always treacherous, suddenly betrayed his father-in-law and turned against his Polish allies. This gave Yaroslav an opening to counterattack Sviatopolk. He deftly allied his forces to those of the spurned Poles and attacked Kiev, defeating Sviatopolk, who was killed in battle. Yaroslav was now grand prince of Kiev and Novgorod. Subsequently, yet another heir, Mstislav (d. 1036), successfully fought Yaroslav for a portion of the realm. Yaroslav drove him east of the Dnieper, where Mstislav ruled independently until his death. However, Yaroslav remained sole ruler of Kiev and Novgorod.

Further reading: Paul Dukes, *A History of Russia: Medieval, Modern, Contemporary, 882–1996* (Durham, N.C.: Duke University Press, 1998); Lawrence N. Langer, *Historical Dictionary of Medieval Russia* (Lanham, Md.: Scarecrow Press, 2002); Robert Mitchell and Nevill Forbes, trans., *Chronicle of Novgorod, 1016–1471* (New York: Best Books, 1914).

Russian-Krim Tartar War   *See* RUSSIAN-TARTAR WAR.

Russian-Manchu War (1660)

PRINCIPAL COMBATANTS: Russia vs. Manchu China
PRINCIPAL THEATER(S): Manchu borderlands

DECLARATION: None
MAJOR ISSUES AND OBJECTIVES: The Manchu sought to prevent a Russian invasion.
OUTCOME: The Russians were ejected from the region.
APPROXIMATE MAXIMUM NUMBER OF MEN UNDER ARMS: Unknown
CASUALTIES: Unknown
TREATIES: None

In the course of the RUSSIAN CONQUEST OF CENTRAL ASIA (1604–89) Russian attacks along the Manchu borderlands resulted in a strong retaliation by Manchu forces. Little is known about military operations in this region at the time, but, within a brief span, Russian troops were pushed out of the Amur River area and also from positions occupied near the Sungari River.

Further reading: Geoffrey A. Hosking, *Russia: People and Empire, 1552–1917* (Cambridge, Mass.: Harvard University Press, 1996).

Russian-Manchu War (1683–1685)

PRINCIPAL COMBATANTS: Russia vs. Manchu China
PRINCIPAL THEATER(S): Amur Valley, near the Manchu border
DECLARATION: None
MAJOR ISSUES AND OBJECTIVES: The Manchus reacted to Russian persecution of Manchu and Chinese settlers in the Amur Valley.
OUTCOME: The Russians were ejected from the valley for a second time.
APPROXIMATE MAXIMUM NUMBER OF MEN UNDER ARMS: Unknown
CASUALTIES: Unknown
TREATIES: Treaty of Nerchinsk, 1689

During the late phase of the RUSSIAN CONQUEST OF CENTRAL ASIA (1604–89), Russians reoccupied the Amur Valley, from which they had been ousted in the RUSSIAN-MANCHU WAR (1660). They conducted a program of persecution of Chinese and Manchu settlers in the region. This provoked a response from Manchu China in the form of frequent raids against Russian settlers in the valley. The Manchus intensified the raiding, ultimately conducting well-developed military campaigns against the Russians, whom, for a second time, they had succeeded in driving out of the Amur Valley. Four years later, the Treaty of Nerchinsk established a prosperous peace between Russia and China, based on trade and enduring for some 175 years.

Further reading: Geoffrey Hosking, *Russia: People and Empire, 1552–1917* (Cambridge, Mass.: Harvard University Press, 1996).

Russian Rebellion against the Mongols (1381–1382)

PRINCIPAL COMBATANTS: Mongols (White Horde) vs. Russians
PRINCIPAL THEATER(S): Northern and central Russia, especially Moscow and environs
DECLARATION: None
MAJOR ISSUES AND OBJECTIVES: Conquest
OUTCOME: The White Horde conquered much territory, including Russia, but failed to hold onto it.
APPROXIMATE MAXIMUM NUMBER OF MEN UNDER ARMS: Unknown
CASUALTIES: Unknown
TREATIES: None

Across a broad front, the Russians mounted a rebellion against their Mongol occupiers beginning in 1381. However, within a year, Toktamish (r. c. 1376–c. 1395), who had become khan of the White Horde—thanks to the support of the great Tamerlane—suppressed the rebellion in northern and central Russia. On August 23, 1382, Toktamish overran and captured Moscow, unleashing wholesale slaughter within the city.

Fortunately for the Russians, Toktamish soon turned against Tamerlane, and the forces of the two fell to fighting during 1385–95. Under Dmitri Donskoi (1350–89), Russia was able to regain not only Moscow but many other holdings lost to the Mongols.

Further reading: David Christian, *A History of Russia, Central Asia and Mongolia:* vol. 1, *Inner Eurasia from Prehistory to the Mongol Empire* (London: Blackwell, 1999); Charles J. Halperin, *Russia and the Golden Horde: The Mongol Impact on Medieval Russian History* (Bloomington: Indiana University Press, 1987); Geoffrey A. Hosking, *Russia and the Russians: A History* (Cambridge, Mass.: Harvard University Press, 2001).

Russian Revolution (The Revolution of 1762) (1762)

PRINCIPAL COMBATANTS: Catherine I the Great vs. Czar Peter III
PRINCIPAL THEATER(S): Russia
DECLARATION: None
MAJOR ISSUES AND OBJECTIVES: Catherine wanted to depose her husband and become czarina of Russia.
OUTCOME: Catherine succeeded in accomplishing a bloodless coup d'état—although, afterward, Peter III was killed.
APPROXIMATE MAXIMUM NUMBER OF MEN UNDER ARMS: Unknown

CASUALTIES: None except for Peter III, killed in a "brawl" several days after the coup.
TREATIES: None

Although often called the Revolution of 1762, this brief struggle was a coup d'état by Catherine I (the Great; 1729–96) to overthrow her dim-witted husband, Czar Peter III (1728–62). He had undermined Russian national solidarity by attempting to impose on the Russian Orthodox Church his own Lutheran beliefs and practices. Seeing an opportunity to both save Russia and acquire absolute power, Catherine, a woman of extraordinary intellect and vision, ambitious, ruthless, and pragmatic, conspired with her lover Grigori Orlov (1734–83), a highly placed courtier whose brother Aleksei (1737–1809) was an influential army officer, to win over the army to her cause. When Peter attempted to mount a campaign to assist his native Holstein in its effort to annex Schleswig, his troops, who had no respect for him, refused to join the effort, and the time was therefore ripe for the coup.

While Peter was absent from the royal court, Catherine, Grigori Orlov, and the imperial guard traveled to St. Petersburg, where on July 9, 1762, the Russian senate and the Orthodox Church acclaimed her ascension to the throne. She was crowned czarina almost immediately. From the throne, she quickly proclaimed Peter's removal and led her troops to nearby Oranienbaum, where Peter was staying, to compel his abdication. He did so, without the necessity of bloodshed, on July 10. It is unlikely that the dissolute and feckless Peter would have posed a continuing threat to Catherine's power; however, Aleksei Orlov arranged an altercation a few days later, which resulted in Peter's death. Thus Catherine managed the permanent removal of her husband and rival.

Further reading: Simon Dixon, *Catherine the Great: Profiles in Power Series* (New York: Pearson, 2001); Carolly Erickson, *Great Catherine* (New York: St. Martin's Press, 1995); Isabel de Madariaga, *Catherine the Great: A Short History* (New Haven, Conn.: Yale University Press, 2002); Henri Troyat, *Catherine the Great* (New York: New American Library, 1994).

Russian Revolution (1905)

PRINCIPAL COMBATANTS: Russian peasants, workers and others vs. the czarist government
PRINCIPAL THEATER(S): Russia, especially St. Petersburg and Moscow
DECLARATION: No formal declaration
MAJOR ISSUES AND OBJECTIVES: Various groups had different objectives; the major objective was to liberalize the Russian government.
OUTCOME: The czar promised reform but delivered repression.

APPROXIMATE MAXIMUM NUMBER OF MEN UNDER ARMS: Unknown
CASUALTIES: By 1906, 3,611 government officials had been killed, along with about 1,500 soldiers; 15,000 rebels died, and 20,000 were wounded.
TREATIES: None

By the late 19th century, Russia seethed with discontent among many classes, including the rising industrial proletariat and the rural peasantry but also among the nobility and ethnic peoples in the border regions. This discontent intensified during the RUSSO-JAPANESE WAR (1904–05), in which Russia suffered a costly and humiliating defeat that dramatically illustrated the ineptitude and corruption of the old czarist regime.

On January 22, 1905, an Orthodox priest, Father Georgi Gapon (c. 1870–1906), led workers in a march on the czar's Winter Palace in St. Petersburg to present Nicholas II (1868–1918) with a petition of grievances. Unknown to the marchers, the czar was absent at the time, but government troops fired on the unarmed petitioners, killing 70 and wounding perhaps 300 in what became the infamous "Bloody Sunday."

Rage swept Russia, touching off a rash of workers' strikes. When Nicholas's minister of the interior, Vyacheslav Plehve (1846–1904) proposed placating the people with a new moderate constitution, leftists were emboldened to take more extreme action. Plehve, a much-hated reactionary and architect of turn-of-the-century pogroms, was assassinated by a bomb blast on July 28, 1904. Next, during October 20–30, 1905, a general strike gripped all of Russia. During this period of intense ferment, a radical Soviet (council) of Workers' Deputies formed under the leadership of Leon Trotsky (1879–1940), and a more moderate Constitutional Democratic Party was also created. In the meantime, in rural districts, peasants occupied or vandalized the property of their landlords, while the urban proletariat demanded civil rights reforms and general pardons.

Yielding to the advice of his prime minister, Count Sergei Witte (1849–1915), Czar Nicholas II allowed the promulgation of the October Manifesto (on October 30, 1905), which granted broad civil liberties, promised a new constitution, and created an elected Duma, or national parliament.

On the surface, the relatively bloodless revolution seemed to have succeeded. However, the czar had bargained in bad faith and openly supported the "Black Hundreds," right-wing terrorists who assaulted radicals, workers, and other suspected revolutionaries. On December 16, 1905, the czar approved the roundup of some 200 members of the St. Petersburg Soviet. Their arrest and imprisonment effectively crushed the organization but incited the Moscow Soviet to organize a violent insurrection that government troops brutally suppressed after five days of street combat. As for the Duma, it was dissolved in 1906 after elections produced an anti-czarist majority, even though the government had engineered a narrow franchise to eliminate radical elements.

Further reading: Andrei Bely, *Petersburg* (Bloomington: Indiana University Press, 1990); Richard E. Pipes, *The Russian Revolution* (New York: Knopf, 1991); Walter Sablinsky, *The Road to Bloody Sunday: Father Gapon and the Petersburg Massacre of 1905* (Princeton, N.J.: Princeton University Press, 1976); Andrew M. Verner, *The Crisis of Russian Autocracy: Nicholas II and the 1905 Revolution* (Princeton, N.J.: Princeton University Press, 1990).

Russian Revolution (1917) *See* BOLSHEVIK REVOLUTION; FEBRUARY (MARCH) REVOLUTION; KORNILOV'S REVOLT.

Russian-Tartar War (1571–1572)

PRINCIPAL COMBATANTS: Russia vs. Krim Tartars
PRINCIPAL THEATER(S): Russia, especially Moscow
DECLARATION: None
MAJOR ISSUES AND OBJECTIVES: The Krim raided Russia for loot and prisoners to ransom.
OUTCOME: Initial raids were devastating; the Krim were eventually driven out of the country.
APPROXIMATE MAXIMUM NUMBER OF MEN UNDER ARMS: Tartars, 40,000; Russian numbers unknown
CASUALTIES: Reportedly, 60,000 Muscovites died and 100,000 captives were taken from the city.
TREATIES: None

While Russian czar Ivan IV (The Terrible; 1530–84) was engaged in one of his numerous wars with the Turks (*see* RUSSO-TURKISH WAR [1568–1569]), repulsing an Ottoman invasion of Astrakhan, the khan of the Krim Tartars (a Crimean Tartar group) staged cavalry raids along the Crimean frontier with Russia, then penetrated as far as Moscow itself on May 24, 1571. Mounting a full-scale assault, the Krim breached the walls of the then lightly defended city and burned most of it, save the Kremlin. It is reported that 60,000 Muscovites died in the rampage and 100,000 prisoners were taken before the attackers were finally repulsed in 1572 by Russian forces returned from the Turkish front. Later in the year, the Krim Tartars closed within 30 miles of Moscow but were checked at the Battle of Molodi, during July 29–August 2. The Krim were soundly defeated at a cost of some 3,000 Russian musketeers. Although the Tartars withdrew from Muscovy (the ancient Russian territory), they remained a menace for many more years.

Further reading: Donald Ostrowski, *Muscovy and the Mongols: Cross-Cultural Influences on the Steppe Frontier, 1304–1589* (New York: Cambridge University Press, 1998); E. H. Parker, *A Thousand Years of the Tartars* (London: Kegan Paul, 2001).

Russo-Afghan War (1885)

PRINCIPAL COMBATANTS: Russia vs. Afghanistan
PRINCIPAL THEATER(S): Russian-Afghan border region
DECLARATION: None
MAJOR ISSUES AND OBJECTIVES: Russia and Afghanistan disputed their frontier; Britain contemplated intervention to prevent Russian possession of Afghan routes into India.
OUTCOME: Combat between Russian and Afghan forces was short, sharp, and one-sided (favoring the Russians); threatened British military intervention never materialized; the border dispute was resolved primarily through negotiation.
APPROXIMATE MAXIMUM NUMBER OF MEN UNDER ARMS: Unknown
CASUALTIES: Unknown
TREATIES: Agreement of September 10, 1885

Disputes over the Russian-Afghan border were frequent in the 19th century, and in 1884, Russian troops occupied the border city of Merv; the following year, they crossed the border and ejected Afghan forces from the Penjdeh region. At this point, the British, who were part of an Anglo-Russian boundary commission established to resolve the Russian-Afghan border dispute, prepared to intervene militarily to protect the city of Herat. This was felt to be essential to the defense of British India. The prospect of British intervention prompted the Russians to back down and agree to an interim settlement, whereby Russian forces would hold their present positions pending ultimate resolution of the border.

On March 30, 1885, Russian troops, violating orders to stay in place, attacked the Afghans at Ak-Teppe, dealing them a severe defeat. The British government decided to withhold a military response and instead negotiated an agreement of September 10, 1885, which gave Russia the Penjdeh district in exchange for Afghan possession of the Zulfkar Pass—the vulnerable gateway to India. Within two years, the Anglo-Russian commission settled the entire Russian-Afghan border dispute.

Further reading: Ludwig W. Adamec, *Historical Dictionary of Afghanistan* (Lanham, Md.: Scarecrow Press, 1997); Martin Ewans, *Afghanistan: A Short History of Its People and Politics* (New York: HarperCollins, 2002); Svatopluk Soucek, *History of Inner Asia* (New York: Cambridge University Press, 2000).

Russo-Finnish War ("Winter War") (1939–1940)

PRINCIPAL COMBATANTS: Soviet Union vs. Finland
PRINCIPAL THEATER(S): Finland

DECLARATION: Russia invaded on November 30, 1939, without a declaration.

MAJOR ISSUES AND OBJECTIVES: The Soviets wanted Finland as a buffer zone against anticipated German aggression.

OUTCOME: After a hard-fought 104-day war, costly to the Soviets, Finland surrendered.

APPROXIMATE MAXIMUM NUMBER OF MEN UNDER ARMS: Soviet Union, 710,578; Finland, 350,000

CASUALTIES: Soviet Union, 126,875 killed, 264,908 wounded; Finland, 23,157 killed, 43,557 wounded

TREATIES: March 12, 1940

Despite having concluded with Germany a nonaggression pact on August 23, 1939, the Soviet government feared an eventual Nazi invasion and was anxious to secure its borders for defense and to obtain buffer zones to absorb anticipated German attacks. One such buffer zone was secured by invading and annexing the eastern third of Poland, and also by annexing small Baltic and Balkan states. This left only one area of critical vulnerability: The Russo-Finnish border, from which Leningrad (St. Petersburg) lay only 20 miles distant, well within reach of Finnish artillery. All things being equal, the Russian government was willing to respect Finland's independence, but Moscow planners believed that Germany planned to effect a landing in Finland and use it as a base from which to attack into Russia.

At first, the Soviets sought a military alliance with the Finns. This was rejected by the Finnish government as a violation of its policy of neutrality. Although Finland assured Russia that it would oppose any German landings—or, for that matter, any Russian incursion—Russia demanded what it called certain "concrete guarantees," which, as the Finns saw it, violated their neutrality. Negotiations between Finland and the USSR became increasingly heated. Then, on November 26, 1939, four Soviet soldiers were killed, and nine were wounded when seven artillery shells were fired near the Russian village of Manila. According to the Russians, the shells had been fired by the Finns; however, the Finnish artillery was actually stationed so far behind the border that it was impossible for Finland to have fired these shots. Clearly, the incident had been Russian in origin—an excuse to go to war with Finland. The so-called "Manila shots" were the justification for Russia's invasion of Finland on November 30, 1939.

The Russians launched an aerial bombardment of Helsinki on the first day of the war, accompanied by an attack along the Mannerheim Line with seven Soviet divisions. Although outgunned and outnumbered, the Finns had the advantage of superior tactics, which used the snow and rugged terrain to advantage. All along the border, the Soviets were repulsed. Then, under Colonel Paavo Tavela (1897–1973), a Finnish counterattack hit the Soviets hard at Tolvajarvi. By December 23, however, the

counterattack had petered out. Still, Soviet losses were heavy: 4,000 killed, 5,000 wounded, compared to only 630 Finns killed and 1,320 wounded.

If Soviet ground forces performed poorly, the Red Air Force produced even more disappointing results. Aircraft flew more than 44,000 sorties and dropped 7,500 tons of ordnance on Finland yet produced no decisive effect.

The Finns refused to remain on the defensive. On the eastern border, the 9th Finnish Division scored a great victory at Suomussalmi during December 11–January 8, destroying two entire Soviet divisions; some 27,500 Red Army soldiers were killed. North of Lake Ladoga, separating Russia and Finland, the Finns attacked at Great Mottis, destroying an entire Soviet division in January 1940.

Yet the Soviets refused to cut their losses. If the Finns had superior commanders and better tactics, the Soviets had almost limitless numbers and Stalin's equally limitless will to commit these numbers to battle, even to slaughter.

Of 2,500 aircraft deployed, the Soviets lost 725; of 3,200 tanks, they lost 1,600. Soviet casualties were staggering—126,875 killed out of 710,578 deployed. Nevertheless, Soviet strength remained far superior, and the Finns knew they could not long hold out. The Finns sued for peace and on March 12, 1940, accepted a Soviet puppet government—although, ostensibly, Finland remained independent. Finland also ceded the strategically valuable Karelian Isthmus and Viipuri. Never happy with the March 12, 1940, treaty, Finland joined the German invasion of the Soviet Union in June 1941.

Further reading: Eloise Engle, *The Winter War: The Soviet Attack on Finland, 1939–1940* (Mechanicsburg, Penn.: Stackpole Books, 1992); William R. Trotter, *A Frozen Hell: The Russo-Finnish Winter War of 1939–1940* (Chapel Hill, N.C.: Algonquin Books of Chapel Hill, 2000); Olli Venvilainen, *Finland in the Second World War: Between Germany and Russia* (London: Palgrave Macmillan, 2002).

Russo-Japanese War (1904–1905)

PRINCIPAL COMBATANTS: Russia vs. Japan

PRINCIPAL THEATER(S): Korea, Manchuria, and the North Pacific

DECLARATION: Began with a surprise Japanese attack on February 8, 1904, after which Russia declared war.

MAJOR ISSUES AND OBJECTIVES: When imperial Russia refused to accept the demands of a Japan grown equally imperial in the previous half-century, the Japanese launched a surprise attack on the Russian fleet, intending to take Manchuria and Korea with a war of expansion.

OUTCOME: Russia was defeated, Japan became a world power, and a naval arms race began that ultimately contributed to World War I.

APPROXIMATE MAXIMUM NUMBER OF MEN UNDER ARMS: Russia, 1,365,000; Japan, 1,200,000

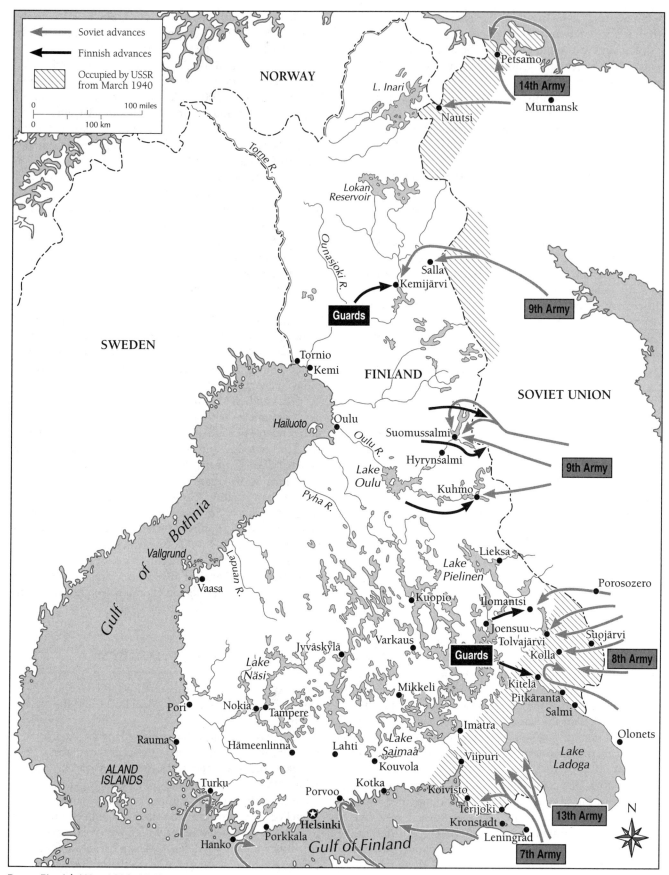

Legend:
- Soviet advances
- Finnish advances
- Occupied by USSR from March 1940

0   100 miles
0   100 km

NORWAY

L. Inari

Petsamo

14th Army

Murmansk

Nautsi

Torne R.

Lokan Reservoir

Ounasjoki R.

Salla

Kemijärvi

9th Army

Guards

SWEDEN

Tornio

Kemi

FINLAND

SOVIET UNION

Hailuoto

Oulu

Oulu R.

Suomussalmi

Hyrynsalmi

9th Army

Lake Oulu

Kuhmo

Pyha R.

Gulf of Bothnia

Lapuan R.

Vallgrund

Vaasa

Lieksa

Lake Pielinen

Porosozero

Kuopio

Ilomantsi

Joensuu

Tolvajärvi

Suojärvi

Jyväskylä

Varkaus

Guards

Kolla

8th Army

Lake Näsi

Mikkeli

Kitelä

Pitkäranta

Salmi

Pori

Nokia

Tampere

Imatra

Olonets

Rauma

Hämeenlinna

Lahti

Lake Saimaa

Kouvola

Viipuri

Lake Ladoga

ALAND ISLANDS

Turku

Kotka

Koivisto

Porvoo

Terijoki

13th Army

Helsinki

Porkkala

Kronstadt

N

Hanko

Gulf of Finland

Leningrad

7th Army

Russo-Finnish War, 1939–1940

CASUALTIES: Russia, 71,453 killed, 141,800 wounded; Japan, 80,378 killed, 153,673 wounded

TREATIES: Treaty of Portsmouth, September 5, 1905.

On February 8, 1904, the Japanese fleet laid siege to a Russian naval squadron anchored at Russian-controlled Port Arthur on the coast of the Liaodong (Liaotung) Peninsula in southern Manchuria. Japan's surprise attack on Russia launched one of the largest armed conflicts the world had ever witnessed, a war that saw the first large-scale use of automatic weapons and in which for the first time in modern history an Asian country defeated a European power.

For half a century Japan had watched with apprehension the Russian Empire expand into eastern Asia, threatening Japan's own imperial designs. Since Russia had begun the construction of the Trans-Siberian Railroad in 1891, it had looked longingly toward China's huge Manchurian province. After the decadent Manchu dynasty lost a war with Japan in 1894, China had entered into an anti-Japanese alliance with Russia, granting the czar rights to extend the railroad across Manchuria to Vladivostok and giving Russia in the process control over an important strip of Chinese territory. In 1898, Russia pressured the Chinese into leasing the strategically important Port Arthur (today called Lu-shun), and in 1903 Czar Nicholas II (1868–1918) reneged on his agreement to withdraw his troops from Manchuria, making the military occupation of the Liao-tung Peninsula permanent. With Russia's navy stationed at Port Arthur and its army occupying the peninsula, it seemed to the Japanese only a matter of time before the czar would stake a claim to Korea, which lay just to the east of Manchuria like a dagger pointed at the heart of Japan.

Since defeating China, Japan had been building up its army, and by the turn of the century it enjoyed a marked superiority over Russia in the number of ground troops in the Far East. All that held the Japanese in check was Great Britain, which ruled the sea with its all-powerful navy. However, Britain abandoned its policy of "splendid isolation"—namely, its refusal to enter into official alliances with any national power—in 1902 and signed a treaty with Japan in order to stop the headlong expansionism of Nicholas II. Confident of Britain's neutrality, Japanese military leaders began planning for the war that world leaders, certainly not unaware of the constantly escalating hostility between Russia and Japan, had long expected.

Late in 1903, Russia and Japan undertook talks, with the Japanese proposing that each side should recognize the other's special interests and economic rights in both Manchuria and Korea. But the Russians responded in a desultory fashion, and the Japanese ambassador broke of the negotiations in a fit of pique on February 6, 1904. Three days later Japan sank two Russian warships at Chemulpo (Inchon, Korea) and torpedoed the main Russian fleet at Port Arthur. When the attack came, Japan was a small country little known in the West, and Russia was one of Europe's five Great Powers. Most of the world expected Russia to make short work of the island kingdom. No country, certainly not Japan's new-found ally Britain, much less Russia itself, imagined the Japanese could so easily debilitate the czar's Pacific fleet. However, there was little the czar could do, since the rest of the Russian navy in the area remained icebound at Vladivostok.

More shocking was the speed with which Japan's army overran Korea and crossed the Yalu River into Manchuria. Having achieved superiority at sea, Japan was able to send thousands of troops into both Korea and Manchuria. By May 1 vast areas in those countries belonged to the Japanese, and by September the Russians had been driven north and west to Mukden (Shenyang), and Port Arthur itself was surrounded. Russian ground forces fought back in two bloody but indecisive battles before retreating farther north. After a long, grueling siege, Port Arthur fell on January 5, 1905.

Nicholas, his czarina, and imperial court—all under the influence of the half-crazed monk Grigory Yefimovich Rasputin (c. 1872–1916)—was slow to react to Japanese advances. Yet overmatched and outgunned, Nicholas refused to back down, vaguely trusting in God rather than sound military action to defend the honor and glory of Russia. Before the fall of Port Arthur, Nicholas dispatched his large Baltic Fleet to the Pacific. On its way to Vladivostok, it suffered the same fate as the Pacific fleet the year before. Caught in the straits off the Japanese islands of Tsushima, the Russian navy fought the Battle of Tsushima, which lasted two days and resulted in the complete destruction of the Russian fleet at the cost of three Japanese torpedo boats. Meanwhile, during the same month in Manchuria, the Japanese took the offensive again, winning the Battle of Mukden.

Although many Japanese troops died, within little more than a year, Japan brought the mighty Russian Empire to its knees. The consequences of Japan's great victory were swift and far-reaching. Theodore Roosevelt (1858–1919), a U.S. president who scarcely concealed his own imperial ambitions, offered to mediate a peace. A conference was held at Portsmouth, New Hampshire, between August 9 and September 5, 1905, where a peace treaty was signed on September 5, 1905. Japan's conquest of Korea was recognized. It gained control of the Liao-tung Peninsula and Port Arthur—and the South Manchurian Railroad that led to Port Arthur. A humiliated Russia meekly agreed to evacuate southern Manchuria.

Within two months of signing the treaty, Nicholas II was faced with a revolution. Ragged Russian workers, starving peasants, and dispirited soldiers rose up en masse to plead for succor from their "Little Father," only to have their pleas and bodies crushed under the hooves of

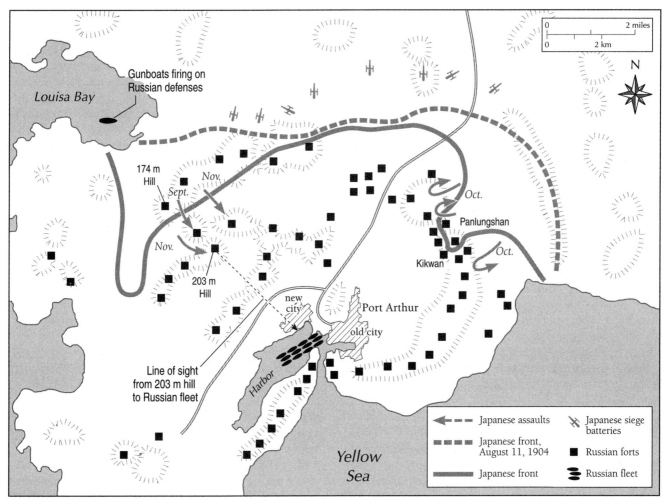

Siege of Port Arthur, June 1, 1904–January 2, 1905

Cossack horses. Though Nicholas suppressed the RUS-SIAN REVOLUTION (1905), he did so only after buying off middle- and upper-class reformers by issuing the October Manifesto, a kind of constitutional charter.

Russia never recovered from the war and the revolution. As for Japan, its victory, costly though it was, proved a turning point for Asia, which awoke to the fact that Europe was not invincible.

Further reading: Geoffrey Jukes, *Russo-Japanese War 1904–1905* (London: Osprey, 2002); Bruce W. Menning, *Bayonets before Bullets: The Imperial Russian Army, 1861–1914* (Bloomington: Indiana University Press, 1999); David Schimmelpenninck Van Der Oye, *Toward the Rising Sun: Russian Ideologies of Empire and the Path to War with Japan* (De Kalb: Northern Illinois University Press, 2001); Denis Ashton Warner and Peggy Warner, *Tide at Sunrise: A History of the Russo-Japanese War, 1904–05* (London: Frank Cass, 2001).

Russo-Lithuanian War *See* RUSSO-POLISH WAR (1499–1503).

Russo-Persian War (1722–1723)

PRINCIPAL COMBATANTS: Russia vs. Persia (with the peripheral involvement of the Ottoman Empire)
PRINCIPAL THEATER(S): Caspian coastal region
DECLARATION: None
MAJOR ISSUES AND OBJECTIVES: Russia sought to counter Ottoman expansion by occupying as much of Persia as possible.
OUTCOME: Russia acquired significant control of the Caspian Sea, but nearly provoked a war with Turkey.
APPROXIMATE MAXIMUM NUMBER OF MEN UNDER ARMS: Unknown
CASUALTIES: Unknown
TREATIES: Treaty of St. Petersburg, September 12, 1723

The first quarter of the 18th century saw the almost fatal collapse of Persia, which was invaded by Afghan armies (PERSIAN-AFGHAN WAR [1726–38]) and by the Ottomans (TURKO-PERSIAN WAR [1730–36]), as well as the Russians. To counter Ottoman expansion toward the Caspian Sea,

Czar Peter I (the Great; 1672–1725) decided to move against weak, Ottoman-dominated Persia, and he overran and took Derbent in 1722. In 1723, he captured Baku and Resht. The Ottomans responded by invading Georgia (then part of Persia) and taking its capital, Tiflis. This counterthrust moved Peter to conclude the Treaty of St. Petersburg with Persia on September 12, 1723. By this treaty, Russia annexed the Caspian coast between Derbent and Resht, whereas the shah received in return the services of Russian troops to keep order in his unstable kingdom.

The treaty provoked protest from the Ottoman Empire, which, backed by Britain, challenged Russia's acquisition of control of the Caspian Sea. War now threatened to break out directly between Russia and the Ottomans but was averted by the Treaty of Constantinople in 1724, which ceded western Persia to Turkey and northern Persia to Russia, including the Caspian territory gained in the 1722–23 war.

Further reading: Lindsey Hughes, *Russia in the Age of Peter the Great* (New Haven, Conn.: Yale University Press, 2000); Robert K. Massie, *Peter the Great: His Life and World* (New York: Ballantine Books, 1986); David Morgan, *Medieval Persia 1040–1797* (New York: Pearson Education, 1989).

Russo-Persian War (1804–1813)

PRINCIPAL COMBATANTS: Russia vs. Persia (and rebel forces in Georgia and Karabakh)
PRINCIPAL THEATER(S): Georgia and Karabakh in the Caucasus
DECLARATION: None
MAJOR ISSUES AND OBJECTIVES: Persia sought to aid rebels in these regions to prevent Russian annexation.
OUTCOME: After much inconclusive combat, the decisive Battle of Aslanduz resulted in an overwhelming Persian defeat and the capitulation of Persian and rebel forces.
APPROXIMATE MAXIMUM NUMBER OF MEN UNDER ARMS: Unknown
CASUALTIES: At the Battle of Aslanduz (October 13, 1812), 10,000 Persians were killed or wounded; two months later, 4,000 Persians died in the fall of Lenkoran.
TREATIES: Treaty of Gulistan, 1813

In 1800, Russia annexed Georgia and Karabakh, regions in the Caucasus that had been controlled by Persia. Resistance was immediate, and rebels within these regions secured Persian aid. Thus, when Russian forces laid siege against rebel-held Erivan in 1804, they were forced into retreat by the arrival of Persian troops commanded by Shah Fath Ali (c. 1762–1835) and Crown Prince Abbas Mirza (1789–1833). The pair had defeated the Russians in a three-day battle at Echmiddzin and thus, unexpectedly, broke through to relieve Evrian.

Following the end of the Erivan siege was a long period of desultory and ultimately inconclusive war, which the Russian czar, Alexander I (1777–1825), sought to end by ordering a massive surprise attack against a Persian army led by Abbas Mirza. The Battle of Aslanduz was a defeat so stunning that the shah of Persia formally ceded Georgia, Karabakh, and additional Caucasian territories to Russia in the 1813 Treaty of Gulistan. The peace did not prove permanent, as war erupted again 12 years later as the RUSSO-PERSIAN WAR of 1825–1828.

Further reading: Nicholas Griffin, *Caucasus: Mountain Men and Holy Wars* (New York: St. Martin's Press, 2003); Leonid Ivan Strakhovsky, *Alexander I of Russia, the Man Who Defeated Napoleon* (Westport, Conn.: Greenwood, 1970); Henri Troyat, *Alexander of Russia: Napoleon's Conqueror* (New York: Grove/Atlantic, 2002).

Russo-Persian War (1825–1828)

PRINCIPAL COMBATANTS: Persia vs. Russia
PRINCIPAL THEATER(S): Georgia and Persia
DECLARATION: Persia against Russia, 1825
MAJOR ISSUES AND OBJECTIVES: Persia denounced the Treaty of Gulistan and attempted to retake Georgia, which it had ceded to Russia.
OUTCOME: Persia suffered total defeat and was forced to make crippling and humiliating concessions to Russia.
APPROXIMATE MAXIMUM NUMBER OF MEN UNDER ARMS: Persia, 30,000; Russia, 15,000
CASUALTIES: Persian losses are unknown; Russian battle deaths reached 5,000.
TREATIES: Treaty of Turkomanchi, 1828

The death of Nadir Shah (1688–1747) brought a long decline in the Persian Empire, which became most acute early in the 19th century. Dispute over certain aspects of the Treaty of Gulistan, which ended the RUSSO-PERSIAN WAR (1804–1813) and by which Persia ceded Georgia to Russia, Karabakh, and other Caucasian regions, prompted the shah, Fath Ali (1771–1834), to denounce the treaty, especially in the face of Russia's formal annexation of the territory. The treaty abrogated, Persia launched an attack in Georgia with the aim of retaking it, but defeat at the Battle of Ganja (September 26, 1826) ended the offensive ignominiously. Modern Russian artillery created panic throughout the Persian cavalry, the Persian line broke, and the Persians fled.

Taking advantage of the rout at Ganja, Russian forces pursued the retreating Persians into Persia. General Ivan Paskevich (1782–1856) led his troops against Erivan and Tabriz, both of which fell to him in October 1827. To make matters worse for the Persians, the onset of winter caused the army to break up, leaving the Persian capital city of Tehran vulnerable. Paskevich's army took Tehran and captured the principal Persian artillery arsenal.

With its capital and a major means of its defense in Russian hands, the Persian government capitulated. The shah concluded the Treaty of Turkomanchi, which moved the Persian-Russian border back to the Aras River, conceded to Russia the exclusive right to station warships on the Caspian Sea, levied an indemnity against Persia, and gave to Russia generous commercial and territorial privileges. The defeat put Persia in a much worse situation than it had found itself at the conclusion of the 1804–13 war, and its days as a formidable military power were over. However, the cost to Russia was also great: 5,000 of the 15,000-man army in the region were lost. And there was worse. Although the shah's government had been defeated, Shamil tribesmen waged a chronic guerrilla war in the Caucasus, which proved a severe drain on czarist forces in the region for years to come.

Further reading: Thomas M. Barrett, *At the Edge of Empire: The Terek Cossacks and the North Caucasus Frontier, 1700–1860* (Boulder, Colo.: Westview, 1999); Ariel Cohen, *Russian Imperialism: Development and Crisis* (Westport, Conn.: Greenwood, 1996); Michael Khodarkovsky, *Russia's Steppe Frontier: The Making of a Colonial Empire, 1500–1800* (Bloomington: Indiana University Press, 2001).

Russo-Persian War (1911)

PRINCIPAL COMBATANTS: Russia vs. Persia
PRINCIPAL THEATER(S): Northern Persia (Iran)
DECLARATION: None
MAJOR ISSUES AND OBJECTIVES: Claiming that they were looking out for Russian interests following the Persian Revolution of 1906–09, Russian forces occupied a portion of Persia and backed an abortive counterrevolution. After clashing with revolutionary Persia's American treasurer, the Russians threatened full-scale invasion, unless the American was removed.
OUTCOME: The revolutionary government was overthrown by coup d'état, and the new Persian government acceded to Russian demands for the removal of the American official. The war ended.
APPROXIMATE MAXIMUM NUMBER OF MEN UNDER ARMS: Unknown
CASUALTIES: Unknown
TREATIES: None

This brief conflict was touched off by William M. Schuster (1877–1960), an American hired as the treasurer-general of Persia. His mission was to sort out the nation's finances, which had been left in chaos by the PERSIAN REVOLUTION (1906–1909). In the aftermath of the revolution, Russia sent troops to occupy Kazvin, a city in northern Persia, claiming that the military presence was necessary to protect Russian interests in the city. Schuster protested and clashed with the Russians, pointing out that the Russian occupation violated an Anglo-Russian accord of 1907. Furthermore, it was clear to Schuster that the Russians decided to back an attempt by the former shah of Persia, Muhammad Ali (1872–1925), to carry out a counterrevolution and reclaim control of the country. Although the czarist government had previously opposed Ali, he was preferable to an upstart republic. The counterrevolution failed, but the Russians refused to withdraw their troops and twice presented the new Persian national assembly with demands for Schuster's removal. The assembly rejected the demands in November 1911, and Russian troops committed various atrocities in Tabriz, northern Persia. They next invaded and conquered Azerbaijan, then marched toward the Persian capital, Tehran.

At this point, exploiting the pressure exerted by the Russians, the regency government (which ruled during the minority of Ahmed Shah [1898–1930]) conspired with the cabinet to carry out a coup d'état on December 24, 1911. Once the regents had seized power, they promptly dissolved the revolutionary assembly and established a governing directory. Among the first acts of this body was to accede to the Russian demand for Schuster's withdrawal. With that, the Russians withdrew to Kazvin, and the war ended, but Russia continued to dominate Persian government until the fall of the Romanov dynasty in the BOLSHEVIK REVOLUTION of 1917.

Further reading: Ariel Cohen, *Russian Imperialism: Development and Crisis* (Westport, Conn.: Greenwood, 1996); Taras Hunczak, *Russian Imperialism from Ivan the Great to the Revolution* (Washington, D.C.: University Press of America, 2000).

Russo-Polish War (1019–1025)

PRINCIPAL COMBATANTS: Boleslav I, duke of Poland, vs. Sviatopolk, deposed Russian ruler of Kiev
PRINCIPAL THEATER(S): Region near Kiev
DECLARATION: None
MAJOR ISSUES AND OBJECTIVES: Boleslav enlisted Polish aid in defeating his brother and rival, Yaroslav, grand prince of Novgorod; once this was accomplished, however, Sviatopolk planned to attack his Polish allies.
OUTCOME: The Poles preempted Sviatopolk's attack on them, and Boleslav I defeated Sviatopolk and his army, making large territorial gains in the process.
APPROXIMATE MAXIMUM NUMBER OF MEN UNDER ARMS: Unknown
CASUALTIES: Unknown
TREATIES: None

After Yaroslav (d. 1054), grand prince of Novgorod, defeated his brother, Prince Sviatopolk (d. 1021) of Kiev, Sviatopolk sought refuge in the court of Boleslav I (d. 1025), his father-in-law and the ruling duke of Poland. While in Boleslav's court, Sviatopolk roused Boleslav and other Poles to war against Yaroslav with the object of regaining territories earlier lost to Novgorod—and, of course, with the additional object of restoring him to the throne in Kiev.

Boleslav led a Polish army into Russia, engaging Yaroslav in 1020 at the Battle of Bug. After a protracted fight, Boleslav prevailed, advanced into Kiev, restored Sviatopolk to the throne, and occupied the city. No sooner was this accomplished, however, than Sviatopolk bristled under Polish domination. He decided to betray his father-in-law and laid plans to massacre the Polish army of occupation in Kiev. Unfortunately for Sviatopolk, his plan was discovered, which incited the Poles to riot. The Poles looted Kiev, then left the city, with Sviatopolk and his forces in pursuit.

At the Bug River, Boleslav's army suddenly wheeled about and attacked its pursuer. Sviatopolk's army was defeated and retreated to Kiev. Realizing that the Russian army was weak, the Poles laid siege to Kiev, which soon surrendered. Thus Boleslav amassed all territory bounded by the Elbe and the Bug rivers, and from the Baltic Sea to the Danube. Unwilling to rely on military conquest alone, Boleslav solidified his authority by securing papal sanction for his coronation by the archbishop of Ghiezno on December 25, 1024.

Further reading: Janet Martin, *Medieval Russia, 980–1584* (Cambridge, U.K.: Cambridge University Press, 1995); David Nicolle, *Medieval Russian Armies 838–1252* (London: Osprey, 1999).

Russo-Polish War (1499–1503)

PRINCIPAL COMBATANTS: Russia vs. Poland-Lithuania
PRINCIPAL THEATER(S): Poland and Lithuania
DECLARATION: Ivan III (the Great) declared war on Alexander I.
MAJOR ISSUES AND OBJECTIVES: Ivan III of Russia acted punitively against his son-in-law, Alexander I, king of Poland-Lithuania, for having violated his marriage contract.
OUTCOME: A treaty gave Ivan III all territory he had already conquered and acknowledged him as czar of all Russia.
APPROXIMATE MAXIMUM NUMBER OF MEN UNDER ARMS: Unknown
CASUALTIES: Unknown
TREATIES: Treaty of 1503, conceding territory and authority to Ivan III

Ivan III (the Great; 1440–1505), grand duke of Moscow, declared war on his son-in-law, Alexander I (d. 1506), king of Poland-Lithuania, over a dispute in Alexander's marriage contract with Ivan. The Russians invaded Poland, causing significant destruction and engaging Lithuanian troops in battle on July 14, 1500. Although the Russians emerged victorious in this battle, they were not able to wrest Smolensk from Lithuanian control. While the struggle for Smolensk was under way, the Livonian Knights—elite independent Polish troops—intervened on behalf of the Lithuanian forces. The Knights defeated the Russians at the Battle of Siritza, then laid siege against Pskov in 1502. However, they failed to take the city, and the resulting inconclusive combat soon exhausted all sides, prompting a treaty in 1503. In the end, Ivan III emerged the winner, retaining all territory he had conquered and earning acknowledgment as czar of all the Russias.

Further reading: Janet Martin, *Medieval Russia, 980–1584* (Cambridge, U.K.: Cambridge University Press, 1995); Saulius Suziedelis, *Historical Dictionary of Lithuania* (Lanham, Md.: Scarecrow Press, 1997).

Russo-Polish War (1506–1508)

PRINCIPAL COMBATANTS: Russia vs. Poland and Lithuania
PRINCIPAL THEATER(S): Border region between Russia and Lithuania
DECLARATION: None
MAJOR ISSUES AND OBJECTIVES: Russia sought to dominate Poland-Lithuania.
OUTCOME: The opponents never engaged in full-scale war; by the time both sides were ready to do so, a truce had been concluded, one mainly beneficial to Russia.
APPROXIMATE MAXIMUM NUMBER OF MEN UNDER ARMS: Unknown
CASUALTIES: Light
TREATIES: Truce of 1508

This was an escalation of a dispute between Sigismund I (1467–1548), duke of Lithuania and king of Poland, and Basil III (1479–1533), grand duke of Moscow. Basil III controlled the services of a number of lesser foreign princes. He ordered them to conduct a major campaign against Lithuania, sparing nothing. As these commanders were on the verge of embarking and as Sigismund I prepared to mount a large-scale defense, some desultory combat took place; however, preparations consumed so much time that by 1508, when the armies were ready to clash, a truce was concluded. By the terms of this agreement, Russia retained all conquered territories. The truce did not resolve the tension between Russia, the Poles, and the Lithuanians, and warfare would resume in the RUSSO-POLISH WAR (1512–1521).

Further reading: Samuel Fiszman, ed., *Polish Renaissance in Its European Context* (Bloomington: Indiana University Press, 1989); Janet Martin, *Medieval Russia, 980–1584* (Cambridge, U.K.: Cambridge University Press, 1995); Saulius Suziedelis, *Historical Dictionary of Lithuania* (Lanham, Md.: Scarecrow Press, 1997).

Russo-Polish War (1512–1521)

PRINCIPAL COMBATANTS: Russia vs. Poland-Lithuania (and Crimean Tatar allies)
PRINCIPAL THEATER(S): Smolensk, Moscow, Russian-Tartar frontier areas
DECLARATION: Grand Duke Basil III of Moscow against Sigismund I of Poland-Lithuania, 1512
MAJOR ISSUES AND OBJECTIVES: Basil renewed war against Poland-Lithuania when he discovered a secret agreement between that kingdom and the Tartars.
OUTCOME: Russia gained control of contested Smolensk.
APPROXIMATE MAXIMUM NUMBER OF MEN UNDER ARMS: Unknown
CASUALTIES: 30,000 Russians lost at the Battle of Orsha
TREATIES: Treaty in 1517 and definitive armistice in 1521

About 1512, Poland concluded a treaty with the Tartars (Crimean Tatars), who agreed to attack their frontier with Muscovy-Byelorussia. The grand duke of Moscow, Basil III (1479–1533), discovered the agreement and decided to reopen the war between his country and Poland-Lithuania that had been fought periodically over more than a decade (*see* RUSSO-POLISH WAR [1499–1503] and RUSSO-POLISH WAR [1506–1508]).

Basil began with sieges against Smolensk, which was in Lithuanian hands. Two sieges were mounted in December 1512, both failed to breach the city walls. Basil backed away and conducted raids elsewhere, accumulating other Lithuanian-held territory. Two years after the first sieges, he returned to the gates of Smolensk, mounted a new assault, and took the city in June 1514.

Elsewhere, the Russians did not fare so well. At the Battle of Orsha, some 30,000 Russians fell, and it became apparent to Sigismund I (1467–1548) of Poland-Lithuania that the Russian forces were thinly spread and were vulnerable. In 1517, he persuaded his Tartar allies to attack the Russians at Tula, south of Moscow. To Sigismund's surprise and consternation, the hard-pressed Russians managed to repulse the attack, and the Tartars soon withdrew.

With both sides weary of war, negotiations were commenced. But by this time, border warfare had become virtually reflexive, and even as representatives of Basil III and Sigismund I negotiated, the Tartars continued to clash with the Russians at the Crimean frontier. This warfare at last ceased in 1521, when Basil III obtained a firm armistice that brought Smolensk under his control.

Further reading: Samuel Fiszman, ed., *Polish Renaissance in Its European Context* (Bloomington: Indiana University Press, 1989); Janet Martin, *Medieval Russia, 980–1584* (Cambridge, U.K.: Cambridge University Press, 1995); E. H. Parker, *A Thousand Years of the Tartars* (London: Kegan Paul, 2001); Saulius Suziedelis, *Historical Dictionary of Lithuania* (Lanham, Md.: Scarecrow Press, 1997).

Russo-Polish War (1534–1537)

PRINCIPAL COMBATANTS: Russia vs. Poland-Lithuania
PRINCIPAL THEATER(S): Russian-Polish frontier regions
DECLARATION: None
MAJOR ISSUES AND OBJECTIVES: King Sigismund I of Poland-Lithuania hoped to make territorial gains by exploiting the Russian chaos following the death of Grand Duke Basil III
OUTCOME: The Polish-Lithuanian offensive failed, and the war ended, by a truce, with Russia still in control of contested Smolensk.
APPROXIMATE MAXIMUM NUMBER OF MEN UNDER ARMS: Unknown
CASUALTIES: Unknown
TREATIES: Truce concluded in 1537; no larger treaty

The death of Basil III (1479–1533), grand duke of Moscow, put Muscovy in the hands of his widow as regent to his son, Ivan IV (1530–84), who would later rule as "Ivan the Terrible." During his minority (1533–47), Ivan was well schooled in the brutality of Russian politics, living through the intrigue and murder that followed on the death of his father. Rightly fearing danger and treachery from all quarters, especially from her own family, Ivan's mother, Yelena Glinskaya (d. 1538), ordered mass imprisonments. When Basil's brother was intercepted on the way to Sigismund I (1467–1548) of Poland-Lithuania, traditional foe of Muscovy (*see* RUSSO-POLISH WAR [1506–1508] and RUSSO-POLISH WAR [1512–1521]), she had him charged with treason. The seizure of Basil's brother prompted Sigismund to invade Russia and to incite rebellion in frontier regions. Although Sigismund mustered a sizable army, and even in the face of chaos in Muscovy, Polish and Lithuanian forces were forced into retreat. As was often the case, Russian forces prevailed by dint of their size. Smolensk, held by Russia only since the Russo-Polish War of 1512–1521, was retained by Russia, and the inconclusive war was ended with a truce.

Further reading: Samuel Fiszman, ed., *Polish Renaissance in Its European Context* (Bloomington: Indiana University Press, 1989); Janet Martin, *Medieval Russia,*

980–1584 (Cambridge, U.K.: Cambridge University Press, 1995); E. H. Parker, *A Thousand Years of the Tartars* (London: Kegan Paul, 2001); Saulius Suziedelis, *Historical Dictionary of Lithuania* (Lanham, Md.: Scarecrow Press, 1997).

Russo-Polish War (1609–1618)

PRINCIPAL COMBATANTS: Russia vs. Poland
PRINCIPAL THEATER(S): Russian-Polish frontier and Moscow and environs
DECLARATION: None
MAJOR ISSUES AND OBJECTIVES: Exploiting Russian weakness during the "time of troubles," Sigismund III of Poland attempted to seize the Russian throne.
OUTCOME: The Poles failed to achieve their principal objective, seizure of the Russian throne, but they did obtain control of Smolensk.
APPROXIMATE MAXIMUM NUMBER OF MEN UNDER ARMS: The largest single invasion force was 30,000 Poles; at Smolensk, 70,000 Russian civilians joined 12,000 soldiers in the defense.
CASUALTIES: Russia lost 15,000 killed in the attempt to relieve Smolensk.
TREATIES: 15-year armistice signed on December 1, 1618

The beginning of the 17th century brought a long spasm of violent instability to Russia known as the "time of troubles" (*see* TIME OF TROUBLES, RUSSIA's), Sigismund III (1566–1632) decided to exploit the time of troubles to usurp the throne of Muscovy for himself, like his grandfather, Sigismund I (1467–1548), king of Poland-Lithuania, had attempted to do during the RUSSO-POLISH WAR (1512–1521), when the death of Grand Duke Basil III left Russia similarly destabilized.

In 1609, Sigismund III led a large army in an invasion of Russia and laid siege to Smolensk. While he did this, he called upon all Poles living in Russia to rise up. Basil IV Shuiski (d. 1612), a Russian warlord, led an army of 30,000 to the relief of Smolensk but was ambushed by a much smaller Polish force under Stanislas Zolkiewski (d. 1620). The Russians were defeated at the Battle of Klushino in September 1610. Basil IV Shuiski fled the field and made for Moscow, where, word of his defeat having preceded him, he was immediately deposed. With the city leaderless, it readily fell to Polish forces on October 8, 1610. (Smolensk would hold out longer, but yielded early the following year.)

Muscovites offered the Russian throne to Ladislas (1595–1648), son of Sigismund III, pursuant to an earlier treaty (Treaty of Smolensk). Surprisingly, Sigismund balked at this; he wanted himself and not his son on the Russian throne. Instead of accepting the Russian offer, he used German troops, in addition to his own Polish forces, to storm the Kremlin and establish his government. This incited a popular uprising among Muscovites and the peasantry of the surrounding area. The Kremlin was attacked; Sigismund responded by burning much of Moscow. This did not lift the siege of the Kremlin. When Sigismund III (who, fortunately for himself, had not yet traveled to the Kremlin in person) sent a force to relieve the Kremlin, Russian citizens intercepted and defeated it. The Kremlin fell to the Russians.

In 1613, a measure of stability was brought to Russia by the election of Michael Romanov (1596–1645) as czar. Defeated and demoralized Polish troops retreated to the frontier, from where they continued to wage sporadic and desultory war. In 1617, Ladislas rallied his forces for a new assault on Moscow. When the attack was defeated, Ladislas agreed to a 15-year armistice on December 1, 1618. At great cost, the Poles had failed to seize the Russian throne but had gained control of long-contested Smolensk. As for Russia, it saw the commencement of the Romanov dynasty, which would endure until the FEBRUARY (MARCH) REVOLUTION and the BOLSHEVIK REVOLUTION, both of 1917.

Further reading: Samuel Fiszman, ed., *Polish Renaissance in Its European Context* (Bloomington: Indiana University Press, 1989); Janet Martin, *Medieval Russia, 980–1584* (Cambridge, U.K.: Cambridge University Press, 1995); E. H. Parker, *A Thousand Years of the Tartars* (London: Kegan Paul, 2001); S. F. Platanov, *The Time of Troubles: A Historical Study of the Internal Crisis and Social Struggle in Sixteenth- and Seventeenth-Century Muscovy* (Lawrence: University Press of Kansas, 1970); Saulius Suziedelis, *Historical Dictionary of Lithuania* (Lanham, Md.: Scarecrow Press, 1997).

Russo-Polish War (1632–1634)

PRINCIPAL COMBATANTS: Russia vs. Poland
PRINCIPAL THEATER(S): Smolensk and environs
DECLARATION: Russia against Poland, 1632
MAJOR ISSUES AND OBJECTIVES: Russian czar Michael Romanov wanted to reclaim sovereignty over Smolensk.
OUTCOME: The Russians were defeated, renounced Smolensk and associated territories but received in return a pledge from Polish king Ladislas IV to make no future claim on the Russian throne.
APPROXIMATE MAXIMUM NUMBER OF MEN UNDER ARMS: Russia, 35,000; Poland, 40,000
CASUALTIES: Russia lost 27,000 men, a casualty rate of 77 percent.
TREATIES: Treaty of Polianovka, 1634

The RUSSO-POLISH WAR (1609–1618) ended with a 15-year armistice and the delivery of Smolensk into Polish hands. With the approaching expiration of the 15-year period, Russian czar Michael Romanov (1596–1645) laid plans for a campaign to recover Smolensk. Although the armistice was not scheduled to expire until 1633, the death of Poland's king, Sigismund III (1566–1632), in 1632 prompted Michael to take action sooner. Arguing that the armistice was valid only during the reigns of both signatories, in September 1632 he ordered Russian troops to lay siege to the walled city of Smolensk. The Poles, who had relied on the armistice, garrisoned Smolensk lightly with only 3,000 men and were therefore overwhelmingly outnumbered. Nevertheless, they defended the city in the expectation of the arrival of a relief force under Poland's Ladislas IV (1595–1648). However, when food and water ran out, the defenders gave up the city after a three-month siege.

In the meantime Ladislas's army engaged and defeated a Russian force under Boris Shein (fl. 17th century), which they pursued to Smolensk. When the Russian took refuge inside the captured city, it was now the Poles who laid siege. After six months, the Russian army surrendered, in February 1634. By that time, only 8,000 of Shein's 35,000 men were still alive.

By the Treaty of Polianovka, Czar Michael Romanov formally ceded Smolensk to Poland, along with the surrounding province and a large swath of the northeastern Baltic coast. On his part, Ladislas willingly renounced all future claims to the Russian throne and acknowledged Michael Romanov as rightful czar. As for Boris Shein, his heroism was poorly rewarded. Back in Moscow, he was seized by the czar, who saw in him the perfect scapegoat. Boris was tried and executed for treason.

Further reading: Samuel Fiszman, ed., *Polish Renaissance in Its European Context* (Bloomington: Indiana University Press, 1989); W. Bruce Lincoln, *The Romanovs: Autocrats of All the Russias* (New York: Dell, 1983).

Russo-Polish War (1654–1656)

PRINCIPAL COMBATANTS: Russia vs. Poland (with Tartar aid at the end of 1655)
PRINCIPAL THEATER(S): Ukraine, Lithuania, Poland
DECLARATION: Russia on Poland, 1654
MAJOR ISSUES AND OBJECTIVES: The war began as Cossack retaliation for losses suffered in Chmielnicki's Revolt, 1648–54, but expanded into a Russian attempt to regain Ukraine and make territorial gains in Lithuania.
OUTCOME: Russia made gains in Lithuania before Russia and Poland made an alliance against their common enemy, Sweden.
APPROXIMATE MAXIMUM NUMBER OF MEN UNDER ARMS: Russia, more than 100,000; Tartars, 150,000, Poland, numbers far inferior to Russian forces

CASUALTIES: At Vilna (July 28, 1655), 20,000 Lithuanians and Poles died.
TREATIES: Treaty of Nimieza, 1656

After suffering defeat in the Ukraine at the hands of Poland during CHMIELNICKI'S REVOLT, the Cossack leader Bogdan Chmielnicki (c. 1593–1657) allied his Cossack forces with regular Russian troops to attack Polish occupiers of Kiev and Smolensk. This initiated the Russo-Polish War of 1654–1656.

With the Poles under attack in Kiev and Smolensk, Czar Alexis (1629–76) personally led an army of 100,000 against Polish forces in Lithuania. Overwhelming the Poles with superior numbers, Alexis quickly occupied much of Lithuania. In the meantime, Poland was also attacked by Sweden in 1655 (see NORTHERN WAR, FIRST), and its forces thus spread even more thinly. Alexis took advantage of this to proclaim himself grand duke of Lithuania, while combined Russian-Cossack armies ranged across the Ukraine, retaking most of the territory that had been yielded to Poland. From the Ukrainian frontier region, these forces also launched a succession of raids into Poland itself; however, in November 1655, a force of 150,000 Tartars under Mahmet Girei (fl. 1650) switched allegiance from Russia to the Poles and attacked Chimielnicki, driving his forces back. Thus the Russians failed to complete the conquest of Ukraine.

Fearing a full-scale Russian invasion, Poland's John II Casimir (1609–72) fled to Silesia, then negotiated an alliance with Holy Roman Emperor Leopold I (1640–1705). In the meantime, however, Poland was in the hands of invading Russians and Swedes. The presence of the Swedes made the czar eager to conclude a treaty with John II Casimir. The Russians withdrew from the territories of John II Casimir, and were free to mount a concentrated attack on Swedish forces in Swedish Livonia, part of modern Poland, at the time occupied by Sweden.

The war between Russia and Poland was ended by the Treaty of Nimieza, of 1656, which constituted an alliance against the common Russian-Polish enemy, Sweden.

See also RUSSO-SWEDISH WAR (1656–1658).

Further reading: Samuel Fiszman, ed., *Polish Renaissance in Its European Context* (Bloomington: Indiana University Press, 1989); Michael F. Hamm, *Kiev* (Princeton, N.J.: Princeton University Press, 1993).

Russo-Polish War (1658–1667)

PRINCIPAL COMBATANTS: Russia vs. Poland (with Ukrainian and Tartar aid)
PRINCIPAL THEATER(S): Ukraine and Lithuania
DECLARATION: Poland on Russia, 1658

MAJOR ISSUES AND OBJECTIVES: Poland aimed to end Russia's occupation of Lithuania.

OUTCOME: Despite a series of strong Polish victories, internal strife within Poland put Russia in an advantageous negotiating position; Smolensk and Kiev reverted to Russia for a specified period of two years, the Ukraine was divided between Russia and Poland, and the Cossacks were put under the joint control of Russia and Poland.

APPROXIMATE MAXIMUM NUMBER OF MEN UNDER ARMS: Russia, 150,000; Polish-Ukrainian forces, 40,000

CASUALTIES: At Konotop (1659), Russia lost 30,000 men.

TREATIES: Treaty of Andrusovo, 1667

The RUSSO-POLISH WAR (1654–1656) ended with a Russian-Polish alliance against Sweden. As soon as that three-year pact expired, however, John II Casimir (1609–72) of Poland resumed warfare against the Russians, who had invaded and occupied Lithuania in the earlier war. Initially, the Polish forces were beaten at the Battle of Vilna and the Battle of Kaunas. In Ukraine, however, a Russian army of 150,000 was driven off with the loss of 30,000 killed. The Poles also regrouped and rallied, mounting a fierce counterattack that drove the Russian army out of Lithuania. Some 60,000 Russians were defeated at Lvov in 1660 by 40,000 Poles and Tartars. Sustaining momentum, the Polish forces went on to invade the regions surrounding Vitebsk and Polotsk later that year.

The Russian loss of Lithuania was bad enough, but the defeat and rout of a better-equipped and larger Russian army by an inferior force of Poles—allied with Tartars—under George Lubomirski (1616–67) was devastating. The Russian forces limped away from the Battle of Lubar in 1660, and an associated Cossack army was similarly defeated a short time afterward.

After the crushing defeat at the Battle of Lubar, the Russians were unable or unwilling to mount any major counteroffensive. Warfare degenerated into sporadic border clashes until the Poles organized an aggressive drive to victory at the Battle of Lublin in 1664. This set the stage for what promised to be peace negotiations favorable to the Poles; however, internal strife during LUBOMIRSKI'S REBELLION (1665–67) caused chaos throughout the Polish leadership. Despite its heavy losses, Russia now found itself in an advantageous negotiating position, and the Treaty of Andrusovo of 1667 obligated Poland to cede Smolensk and Kiev to Russia for a period of two years. The Ukraine was divided between Poland and Russia along the Dnieper River, and the Cossacks were put under the combined control of the Russians and Poles. (Although control of Kiev was to revert to Poland after two years, the Poles in fact never regained control of the Ukrainian city.)

Further reading: Samuel Fiszman, ed., *Polish Renaissance in Its European Context* (Bloomington: Indiana Uni-

versity Press, 1989); Michael F. Hamm, *Kiev* (Princeton, N.J.: Princeton University Press, 1993).

Russo-Polish War (1919–1920)

PRINCIPAL COMBATANTS: Bolshevik Russia vs. Poland

PRINCIPAL THEATER(S): Poland and Ukraine

DECLARATION: None

MAJOR ISSUES AND OBJECTIVES: The Bolshevik government sought control over Polish territory.

OUTCOME: The seesaw course of the war ended with a major Polish triumph and the imposition of an eastern border for Poland within the Ukraine.

APPROXIMATE MAXIMUM NUMBER OF MEN UNDER ARMS: Russia, 757,000; Poland, 737,767

CASUALTIES: At the turning-point Battle of Warsaw (August 25, 1920), Russia lost 100,000 killed, wounded, or captured; Poland lost 4,362 killed, 21,751 wounded.

TREATIES: Treaty of Riga, March 18, 1921

Bolshevik Russian forces took advantage of the withdrawal of German forces from Poland following the armistice that ended WORLD WAR I to invade Poland. By February 1919, elements of the Red Army had crossed the Bug River and were engaged by Polish forces led by Jozef Pilsudski (1867–1935), which drove the Bolsheviks back across the Polish frontier and into the Ukraine as far as the Berezina River.

In the aftermath of World War I, the Supreme Council of the Allies assigned an eastern Polish border that was within Russia, but the Bolsheviks sought to establish the border farther west, along the actual war front. As for Pilsudski, he sought an even more eastern border, that of 1772, which encompassed the entire Ukraine. Pilsudski allied Polish forces with anti-Bolshevik Ukrainians led by Simon Petlyura (1879–1926) and advanced against Kiev. The city was besieged on April 25, 1920, and fell to Pilsudski on May 7. This incited a determined Bolshevik counterthrust, which pushed the Polish forces out of Kiev and also out of Vilna, Lithuania. Under the command of Mikhail Tukhachevskiy (1893–1937), the Red Army pursued the retreating Poles all the way to the outskirts of the Polish capital, Warsaw. Aided by a French force under Maxime Weygand (1867–1965), the Poles took a stand outside of their capital and defeated the Red Army after a costly 10-day battle. One hundred thousand Russians were killed, wounded, or captured.

The repulse from Warsaw severely depleted the Bolshevik invading forces, and the Poles took advantage of this to pursue the retreating Russians. On August 31, 1920, Poland unleashed Europe's last full-scale cavalry offensive, defeating Russian forces at Zamosa. On September 12, the Poles advanced along the Pripet Marshes, and on September 26 defeated the Russians at the Niemen River. A battle on the Shchara River followed, the next day, in which 50,000 Russians where taken prisoner. The Bolsheviks sued for peace, and an armistice was imposed on October 12. This was followed by the Treaty of Riga, concluded on March 18, 1921, by which the Soviet government was compelled to accept Poland's territorial claims along the lines that had been specified by Pilsudski.

Further reading: Jan T. Gross, *Revolution from Abroad: The Soviet Conquest of Poland's Western Ukraine and Western Belorussia* (Princeton, N.J.: Princeton University Press, 2002); Janusz Cisek Kosciuszko, *We Are Here! American Pilots of the Kosciuszko Squadron in Defense of Poland, 1919–1921* (Jefferson, N.C.: McFarland, 2002).

Russo-Swedish War (1240–1242)

PRINCIPAL COMBATANTS: Swedish, Danish, and Lithuanian forces vs. Novgorod
PRINCIPAL THEATER(S): Neva River region
DECLARATION: None
MAJOR ISSUES AND OBJECTIVES: The Swedish coalition wanted territory claimed by Novgorod.
OUTCOME: Russian troops under Alexander Nevski defeated the coalition.
APPROXIMATE MAXIMUM NUMBER OF MEN UNDER ARMS: Unknown
CASUALTIES: Unknown
TREATIES: Peace agreement concluded at Novgorod, 1242.

Sweden, Denmark, and Lithuania were eager to exploit the disarray created by the Second MONGOL INVASION OF RUSSIA to gain territory for themselves and, not incidentally, to extend the reach of Christianity. The latter motive gained them the support of Pope Gregory IX (1147[?]–1241). Under a Swedish soldier-statesman named Birger (d. 1266), a combined army of Swedes, Danes, and Livonian knights invaded Russia, where they challenged Novgorod's claims on the Neva River and Gulf of Finland. Prince Alexander (c. 1220–1263) of Novgorod, champion of Orthodox Christianity, engaged Birger's forces near present-day St. Petersburg and won a great victory. He took the precaution of building a series of forts on the Neva, then returned home to Novgorod, where he was honored with the surname Nevski ("of the Neva") and is still celebrated as one of Russia's seminal heroes.

Still, the Swedish coalition was not finished. No sooner had Nevski left the region than they seized Pskov. The Livonian knights built a fort at Koporie on the Neva, extorted tributes from the people, and pillaged the region corresponding to modern Estonia. In response, Alexander Nevski returned with an army that drove the knights out of Koporie and Pskov, an action culminating in the celebrated April 5, 1242, "Battle on the Ice," fought on a frozen channel leading to Lake Peipus. This ended the war, and Alexander returned to Novgorod, where a definitive peace was concluded. In later years, Russians would invoke the memory of Nevski and the Battle on the Ice to inspire resistance to invaders from Napoleon to Hitler.

Further reading: Henrik Birnbaum, *Novgorod in Focus: Selected Essays* (Bloomington, Ind.: Slavica, 1996); Janet Martin, *Medieval Russia, 980–1584* (Cambridge, U.K.: Cambridge University Press, 1995); Robert Mitchell and Nevill Forbes. trans., *Chronicle of Novgorod, 1016–1471* (London: Best Books, 1914).

Russo-Swedish War (1590–1595)

PRINCIPAL COMBATANTS: Russia vs. Sweden
PRINCIPAL THEATER(S): Estonia and Livonia
DECLARATION: None recorded
MAJOR ISSUES AND OBJECTIVES: Russia wanted to wrest control of Estonia from Sweden.
OUTCOME: The two sides fought to a truce favorable to Russia; after reinforcing its army, Sweden resumed fighting and not only retained Estonia but acquired much of Livonia.
APPROXIMATE MAXIMUM NUMBER OF MEN UNDER ARMS: Swedish strength at Narva, 20,000
CASUALTIES: Unknown
TREATIES: Armistice in 1591; treaty in 1593

Russian czar Feodor I (1557–98) hungered after Swedish-controlled northern Estonia and in particular wanted to acquire Reval (Tallinn), its principal city. At the urging of his chief adviser and power-behind-the-throne, Boris Godunov (c. 1551–1605), Feodor authorized an invasion. Godunov led a Russian army toward Narva, where it engaged and defeated a Swedish force of 20,000 men early in 1590. While laying siege to Narva, the Russians also menaced Estonia, which convinced Sweden to come to a one-year truce, granting Russia sovereignty over a number of towns, most notably the Baltic ports of Kaporye, Ivangorod, and Yani, while delaying Russian occupation of Estonia. Sweden's John III (1537–92), however, soon grew impatient with these terms and decided to retake the ceded towns. Negotiations over Narva and northern Estonia were reopened, but John died during them, the talks collapsed, and the war resumed.

Sweden sought to exploit a Tartar threat against Russia by augmenting its forces in Estonia, but initially met with no success and, in 1593, concluded a treaty that allowed Russia to retain most of what it had gained. However, the peace was soon broken once again, as Swedish forces regained control of Estonia's Baltic coast and much of Livonia (including parts of modern Estonia and Latvia) by 1695.

Further reading: Samuel Fiszman, ed., *Polish Renaissance in Its European Context* (Bloomington: Indiana University Press, 1989); S. F. Platanov, *The Time of Troubles: A Historical Study of the Internal Crisis and Social Struggle in Sixteenth- and Seventeenth-Century Muscovy* (Lawrence: University Press of Kansas, 1970); Toivo U. Raun, *Estonia and the Estonians* (Washington, D.C.: Hoover Institution Press, 2001).

Russo-Swedish War (1613–1617)

PRINCIPAL COMBATANTS: Sweden vs. Muscovite Russians
PRINCIPAL THEATER(S): Novgorod and Pskov
DECLARATION: None
MAJOR ISSUES AND OBJECTIVES: Muscovites wanted to seize Swedish-held Novgorod; Swedes wanted to gain control of the Russian throne.
OUTCOME: Swedes ceded Novgorod to Moscow; they gained in return all territories on the Gulf of Finland; Russia relinquished claims on Estonia and Livonia.
APPROXIMATE MAXIMUM NUMBER OF MEN UNDER ARMS: Unknown
CASUALTIES: Unknown
TREATIES: Treaty of Stolbovo, January 26, 1617

During the internal Russian conflict known as the TIME OF TROUBLES, Muscovite forces attacked Novgorod, which was held by the Swedes, who had made a bid to gain control of the Russian throne, which, in the time of troubles, was very much in play. With the election of Czar Michael Romanov (1596–1645), however, the Swedes' hopes were dashed, and Sweden's Gustavus II (1594–1632) cast aside conquest by intrigue. He now opted for military action, launching an invasion of Moscow after first defeating the Russian expedition against Novgorod.

Despite his success at Novgorod, Gustavus was stopped in 1614 by the defenders of the formidable fortress of Pskov, which withstood a six-month siege. Short of supplies, his forces depleted, Gustavus withdrew his army and opened peace negotiations culminating in the Treaty of Stolbovo on January 26, 1617. By this agreement, the Swedes ceded Novgorod to Moscow, but gained all territories on the Gulf of Finland in return. Moreover, Russia relinquished claims on Estonia and Livonia.

Further reading: S. F. Platanov, *The Time of Troubles: A Historical Study of the Internal Crisis and Social Struggle in Sixteenth- and Seventeenth-Century Muscovy* (Lawrence: University Press of Kansas, 1970); B. F. Porshnev, *Muscovy and Sweden in the Thirty Years' War, 1630–1635* (New York: Cambridge University Press, 1995).

Russo-Swedish War (1656–1658)

PRINCIPAL COMBATANTS: Russia vs. Sweden
PRINCIPAL THEATER(S): Estonia and Livonia
DECLARATION: None
MAJOR ISSUES AND OBJECTIVES: Russia wanted to reclaim lands lost to Sweden.
OUTCOME: Despite a driving offensive, the Russians lost to Sweden and withdrew from the contested lands.
APPROXIMATE MAXIMUM NUMBER OF MEN UNDER ARMS: Unknown
CASUALTIES: Several thousand Russians fell at Riga (1656).
TREATIES: Truce concluded in 1658

This conflict may be regarded as a phase of the First NORTHERN WAR, during which Russian czar Alexis (1629–1676) decided to seize an opportunity to recover lands earlier lost to Sweden in the RUSSO-SWEDISH WAR (1613–1617). He concluded a hasty peace with Poland to end the RUSSO-POLISH WAR (1654–1656), so that he could concentrate his forces for an invasion of Swedish-held Livonia and Estonia.

The czar captured numerous towns and fortresses before massing his army outside of Riga, to which he laid siege during July and August 1656. The Swedes countered with a devastating sortie out of Riga, which overran the Russian lines, broke the siege, and resulted in the slaughter of thousands. Stunned, Czar Alexis fled the field. With the Russians gone, the Swedes generally reinforced their defenses throughout the Baltic area. This enabled them to withstand another Russian offensive in 1658, after which an abashed Alexis agreed to a truce, which endured well into the next century.

Further reading: Robert I. Frost, *The Northern Wars: War, State, and Society in Northeastern Europe, 1558–1721* (New York: Longman, 2000); S. F. Platanov, *The Time of Troubles: A Historical Study of the Internal Crisis and Social Struggle in Sixteenth- and Seventeenth-Century Muscovy* (Lawrence: University Press of Kansas, 1970).

Russo-Swedish War (1741–1743)

PRINCIPAL COMBATANTS: Russia vs. Sweden
PRINCIPAL THEATER(S): Finland
DECLARATION: None
MAJOR ISSUES AND OBJECTIVES: Sweden wanted to regain Finnish territories lost to Russia.
OUTCOME: Greatly outnumbered, the Swedish army was soundly defeated, and Russia was confirmed in its possession of southern Finland.
APPROXIMATE MAXIMUM NUMBER OF MEN UNDER ARMS: Sweden, 17,000; Russia, 26,000
CASUALTIES: At Wilmanstrand, Russia lost 2,400 killed or wounded; Sweden lost 3,300 killed or wounded and 1,300 captured.
TREATIES: Treaty of Åbo, August 7, 1743

When the hawkish Hattar Party (literally, the "Hats") gained control of Swedish politics, it yielded to French entreaties to start a war with Russia to regain lost territory. Although Sweden's standing army consisted of only 20,000 men, the nation began hostilities in 1741. Russia's superior army had been on a war footing since the freshly concluded RUSSO-TURKISH WAR (1736–1739). Accordingly, Russian troops took the offensive, winning the Battle of Wilmanstrand in Finland on September 3, 1741, inflicting 4,600 casualties (including 1,300 captured) on 6,000 Swedes engaged.

In the meantime, a bloodless coup put Elizabeth Petrovna (1709–62) on the Russian throne. Despite Russia's triumph, she had no wish to press the war further and invited peace. Unwisely, the Swedes responded with unreasonable terms, and Elizabeth sent Russian troops to invade Finland again. They easily overran the main contingent of the Swedish army. Seventeen thousand Swedes laid down their arms at Helsingfors (Helsinki) on August 20, 1742, and fighting ceased.

Despite Russia's overwhelming victory, peace negotiations dragged on for nearly a year before culminating in the Treaty of Åbo on August 7, 1743. The treaty provided that Russia would retain the southern part of its Finnish territory to the Kymmene River, which became the new border. Sweden's childless Frederick I (1676–1751) further agreed to Elizabeth's election of Holstein's duke Adolphus Frederick (1710–71), a Russian ally, to inherit the Swedish Crown.

Further reading: Max Engman and David Kirby, eds., *Finland: People, Nation, State* (Bloomington: Indiana University Press, 1989); Eino Jutikkala, *A History of Finland* (New York: Praeger, 1974); Anatole Gregory Mazour, *Finland between East and West* (Princeton, N.J.: Van Nostrand, 1956).

Russo-Swedish War (1788–1790)

PRINCIPAL COMBATANTS: Russia vs. Sweden
PRINCIPAL THEATER(S): Finland
DECLARATION: Made unilaterally by Gustavus III
MAJOR ISSUES AND OBJECTIVES: Acting without legislative authority, Gustavus III wanted to retake Finnish territories lost to Russia.
OUTCOME: A return to the status quo ante bellum
APPROXIMATE MAXIMUM NUMBER OF MEN UNDER ARMS: Russia, 31 ships of the line, and 24 frigates; Sweden, 21 ships of the line and 13 frigates.
CASUALTIES: Russia lost four ships of the line; Sweden lost 12 ships of the line
TREATIES: Treaty of Wereloe, August 15, 1790

In 1788, Sweden's Gustavus III (1746–92) saw that Russia was preoccupied with CATHERINE THE GREAT'S SECOND WAR WITH THE TURKS. In June, acting without the approval of the Swedish diet, Gustavus invaded the Russian-held portion of Finland. Unfortunately for the Swedish king, many of his officers rightly deemed the war illegal and refused to fight. As a result, operations during 1788 and 1789 were failures, culminating in a disastrous defeat at the Finnish town of Fredrikshamm (Hamina).

Following Fredrikshamm, the dissident officers formed the Anjala League to negotiate peace with Russia's Catherine II (the Great; 1729–1796). During this period, while the dissidents negotiated, Gustavus conducted a sea war, which became one of the greatest conflicts fought on the Baltic. By 1799, Sweden mustered 21 ships of the line and 13 frigates against 17 Russian ships of the line and eight frigates. On July 17, 1788, the Battle of Hogland pitted 20 Swedish ships against all of the Russian fleet's ships of the line. Although the battle ended indecisively, the Swedes managed to capture a 74-gun Russian ship at the cost of a lesser 70-gun vessel. At Svensksund (August 24, 1789) and at Vyborg (July 3, 1790), the Russian fleet emerged victorious, although casualties were heavy on both sides. Svensksund was a duel between small coastal craft, 81 Russian boats versus 49 Swedish vessels. The Swedes lost 11 craft, the Russians two. At Vyborg, 31 Russian ships of the line and 24 frigates overwhelmed seven Swedish ships of the line, three frigates, and about 30 smaller warships and 30 transports. The engagement was a disaster for the Swedes, who lost some 5,000 men (many taken prisoner), although the bulk of the fleet was able to withdraw intact. Russia lost more than 2,000 killed or wounded.

Six days after Vyborg, the Swedes retaliated by mustering a very large mixed fleet of 196 ships against 141 Russian vessels in the Second Battle of Svenskund. At a cost of four ships and 181 killed, the Swedes sunk 64 Russian ships and inflicted 7,369 casualties, including 900 killed. This Swedish triumph staved off ignominious defeat at the hands of the Russians, who concluded the Treaty of Wereloe in 1790, restoring the status quo ante bellum.

Further reading: Simon Dixon, *Catherine the Great: Profiles in Power Series* (New York: Pearson, 2001); Carolly Erickson, *Great Catherine* (New York: St. Martin's Press, 1995); Isabel de Madariaga, *Catherine the Great: A Short History* (New Haven, Conn.: Yale University Press, 2002); Byron J. Nordstrom, *The History of Sweden* (Westport, Conn.: Greenwood, 2000); Henri Troyat, *Catherine the Great* (New York: New American Library, 1994).

Russo-Swedish War (1808–1809)

PRINCIPAL COMBATANTS: Russia vs. Sweden
PRINCIPAL THEATER(S): Finland

DECLARATION: Russia against Sweden, February 1808

MAJOR ISSUES AND OBJECTIVES: Seizing on Sweden's refusal to end its alliance with Britain, Russia invaded Finland in order to acquire that country.

OUTCOME: Russia prevailed; Finland became a Russian duchy.

APPROXIMATE MAXIMUM NUMBER OF MEN UNDER ARMS: Russia, 9,000; Sweden, 11,000

CASUALTIES: At Revolax (April 27, 1808), 3,000 out of 4,000 Russians were killed.

TREATIES: Treaty of Fredrikshamm, September 17, 1809

The NAPOLEONIC WARS occasioned a great deal of diplomatic maneuvering among belligerents. After France and Russia made peace by the Treaty of Tilsit in 1807, they called on Sweden to end its anti-French alliance with Britain. Sweden refused, and Czar Alexander I (1777–1825) responded by invading Swedish-held Finland in February 1808 with an army under Mikhail Bogdonovich (1761–1818), prince Barclay de Tolly.

On April 16, 1808, 3,000 Russian troops laid siege to the fortress of Sveaborg, forcing the surrender of its 7,000-man garrison after scarcely a fight. Following this, the Russians marched unimpeded through Finland, which, by the end of 1808, the Swedes had evacuated.

The Swedes did score a major triumph at Revolax on April 27, 1808, when their 8,000-man force overwhelmed 4,000 Russians, killing all but 1,000 of them. The Battle of Orawis, on September 15, 1808, proved inconclusive. Meanwhile, at sea, Sweden held out well against the Russians. Nevertheless, the losses in Finland were too much for Sweden's King Gustavus IV (1778–1837), whose repressive autocracy was overthrown by a coup d'état on March 13, 1809, forcing him into exile. For its part, however, Russia refused to negotiate peace terms with the unstable provisional government that followed. The czar did not want to recognize a revolutionary regime; besides, he was not finished with his campaign of expansion. The Russians pressed the fight to the Åland Islands, which fell to the invaders, and then fought two battles in northern Sweden. After an 11,000-man Swedish army was trapped and held on the Ratun Peninsula in August 1809, Swedish forces totally evacuated Finland, and the new Swedish king, Charles XIII (1748–1818), negotiated the Treaty of Fredrikshamm with the Russians on September 17, 1809. Sweden formally ceded Finland and the Åland Islands to Russia. Finland thus became a Russian duchy.

Further reading: George C. Schoolfield, *Helsinki of the Czars: A Cultural History 1808–1918* (London: Boydell and Brewer, 1996); Fred Singleton, *Short History of Finland* (New York: Cambridge University Press, 1998).

Russo-Turkish War (1568–1569)

PRINCIPAL COMBATANTS: Russia vs. Ottoman Turks

PRINCIPAL THEATER(S): Astrakhan, on the Volga River

DECLARATION: None

MAJOR ISSUES AND OBJECTIVES: Turkish grand vizier Muhammad Sokollu wanted to build a canal linking the Don and Volga; he needed to seize Russian-held Astrakhan to do this.

OUTCOME: Canal construction bogged down; the grand vizier failed to take Astrakhan; his troops withdrew, only to be lost at sea.

APPROXIMATE MAXIMUM NUMBER OF MEN UNDER ARMS: Unknown

CASUALTIES: Unknown

TREATIES: None

Muhammad Sokollu (1505–79), Ottoman grand vizier under Sultan Selim II (1524–74), devised a scheme to curb Russian expansion by digging a canal linking the Don and Volga rivers. This would allow Turkish vessels to pass between the Black and Caspian seas, giving Turkey direct access to Persia and Central Asia. To accomplish this objective, the grand vizier sent troops to Azov in 1568 in order to take Astrakhan from Russia. Soldiers marched up the Don River and began construction of the canal, but when they had progressed about a third of the way, engineering difficulties forced a halt.

Undaunted, the grand vizier ordered his ships portaged to the Volga. From this position, he invested Astrakhan on the Volga delta in 1569. The city, which had been in Russian hands for only 13 years, withstood the siege long enough for a relief column to arrive. At the approach of the column, the weary Turks withdrew. Although a major battle was avoided, all of the siege troops perished in a storm on the Black Sea as they returned home. The sultan responded by ordering Sokollu to attempt no more canals.

Further reading: Daniel Goffman, *The Ottoman Empire and Early Modern Europe* (New York: Cambridge University Press, 2002); Alan Warwick Palmer, *The Decline and Fall of the Ottoman Empire* (New York: Barnes and Noble Books, 1995).

Russo-Turkish War (1678–1681)

PRINCIPAL COMBATANTS: Russia vs. Turkey

PRINCIPAL THEATER(S): Ukraine

DECLARATION: None

MAJOR ISSUES AND OBJECTIVES: The Turks wanted to acquire the Ukraine.

OUTCOME: After suffering severe casualties, the Turks withdrew and agreed to renounce their claims to the Ukraine.

APPROXIMATE MAXIMUM NUMBER OF MEN UNDER ARMS:
Unknown
CASUALTIES: Unknown
TREATIES: Treaty of Radzin, January 8, 1681

The origin of this war lay in Sultan Muhammad IV's (1641–91) refusal to honor what he deemed the overly generous terms of the Treaty of Zorawno, which ended the POLISH-TURKISH WAR (1671–77). He dispatched an army under Grand Vizier Kara Mustafa (d. 1683), determined to push the Russians and Poles out of the Ukraine.

Though the next two years the Turks ravaged the Ukraine, destroying many towns, they suffered heavy casualties and lost much of their artillery. When the Ukraine refused to yield, the Turks at last withdrew, and on January 8, 1681, the sultan concluded the Treaty of Radzin, renouncing all claims to Ukraine. By resisting the Turks, Ukraine prevailed, but at a terrible lost to the civilian population.

Further reading: Daniel Goffman, *The Ottoman Empire and Early Modern Europe* (New York: Cambridge University Press, 2002); Alan Warwick Palmer, *The Decline and Fall of the Ottoman Empire* (New York: Barnes and Noble Books, 1995); Anna Reid, *Borderland: A Journey through the History of the Ukraine* (Denver: Westview, 2000).

Russo-Turkish War (1695–1700)

PRINCIPAL COMBATANTS: Russia vs. Ottoman Turks
PRINCIPAL THEATER(S): Delta of the Don River
DECLARATION: None
MAJOR ISSUES AND OBJECTIVES: Peter I the Great wanted to take the Turkish-held fortress-city of Azov.
OUTCOME: Despite heavy losses, the Russians took Azov.
APPROXIMATE MAXIMUM NUMBER OF MEN UNDER ARMS:
Russia, 75,000; Turkey, 31,000
CASUALTIES: Some 32,000 Russians died; Turkish losses unknown
TREATIES: Truce, 1700

Acting on the advice of his Swiss-Scotch adviser François Lefort (1656–99), Czar Peter I (the Great; 1672–1725) made an assault on the Turkish-held city-fortress of Azov at the Don River delta. The czar personally led 31,000 men in this first siege in 1695. The assault failed, forcing the Russians to withdraw with heavy losses, including 2,000 killed in action.

Peter determined that the failure had occurred because, without a navy, he had been unable to blockade Azov. Within a year, Peter built a fleet and dispatched it to blockade the city. The fleet overcame Ottoman naval opposition, and Peter's land forces took Azov in July 1696. The cost, however, was great: more than 30,000 Russians

fell. Mindful of the cost, Peter resolved to ensure that the sacrifice would not be in vain. He decided to undertake a great expedition against the Ottomans in order to end permanently the threat they posed. In preparation, Peter toured Europe, seeking allies as well as knowledge of Western technical, scientific, and military advances. During the period of Peter's travels, the Hapsburgs concluded a peace in the AUSTRO-TURKISH WAR (1683–1699), which prompted Peter to abandon his Turkish plans to join Poland against Sweden in the Great Northern War. In 1700, Peter concluded a truce with the Ottoman Empire, trading the Russian Black Sea fleet for permanent possession of Azov.

See also NORTHERN WAR, SECOND.

Further reading: Daniel Goffman, *The Ottoman Empire and Early Modern Europe* (New York: Cambridge University Press, 2002); Robert K. Massie, *Peter the Great: His Life and World* (New York: Ballantine Books, 1987); Alan Warwick Palmer, *The Decline and Fall of the Ottoman Empire* (New York: Barnes and Noble Books, 1995).

Russo-Turkish War (1710–1711)

PRINCIPAL COMBATANTS: Russia vs. Ottoman Turks
PRINCIPAL THEATER(S): Moldavia (part of Romania)
DECLARATION: Turkey against Russia, 1710
MAJOR ISSUES AND OBJECTIVES: The Turks refused to surrender Sweden's king Charles XII to the Russians.
OUTCOME: Superior Turkish numbers defeated the army of Czar Peter I the Great, who had to relinquish the fortress-city of Azov, so hard won in the Russo-Turkish War of 1695–1700.
APPROXIMATE MAXIMUM NUMBER OF MEN UNDER ARMS:
Russia, 54,000; Ottomans, 200,000
CASUALTIES: Unknown
TREATIES: Treaty of the Pruth, July 21, 1711

The warrior-king Charles XII (1682–1718) of Sweden suffered a disastrous defeat at the hands of the Russians during the GREAT NORTHERN WAR. With his army all but destroyed, Charles took refuge in Turkish Moldavia, whereupon, in October 1710, Czar Peter I (the Great; 1672–1725) demanded that the Ottoman sultan surrender his guest. In response to this imperious demand, the sultan made war against Peter.

With the Turks arrayed along the Russian border, the recklessly overconfident czar led 54,000 soldiers in an invasion of Moldavia in March 1711. He was met by 120,000 Ottoman infantry men and 80,000 cavalry, which pushed the Russians back to the Pruth River, trapping him against this natural barrier as he anxiously awaited reinforcements from Slavs, Moldavians, and Wallachians, with whom he had secret alliances. When these troops failed to materialize, Peter had no choice but to negotiate a peace, and he was indeed fortunate that he had the opportunity for such negotiations. Had the Ottomans chosen to attack Peter his badly outnumbered forces would almost surely have been destroyed. As it was, the Treaty of the Pruth, signed on July 21, 1711, compelled Russia to return Azov (acquired at great cost in the RUSSO-TURKISH WAR [1695–1700]) to the Turks and to dismantle its border fortresses. The czar also had to grant Sweden's Charles free passage back to Sweden—but the bellicose monarch remained among the Turks for three more years, trying unsuccessfully to persuade the Ottomans to launch an all-out war against Russia.

Further reading: Daniel Goffman, *The Ottoman Empire and Early Modern Europe* (New York: Cambridge University Press, 2002); Robert K. Massie, *Peter the Great: His Life and World* (New York: Ballantine Books, 1987); Alan Warwick Palmer, *The Decline and Fall of the Ottoman Empire* (New York: Barnes and Noble Books, 1995); François Marie Arouet de Voltaire, *Lion of the North: Charles XII of Sweden* (Madison, N.J.: Fairleigh Dickinson University Press, 1981).

Russo-Turkish War (1722–1724) *See* RUSSO-PERSIAN WAR (1722–1723).

Russo-Turkish War (Austro-Turkish War) (1736–1739)

PRINCIPAL COMBATANTS: Russia (with Austria) vs. Ottoman Turks (with Tartar allies)
PRINCIPAL THEATER(S): Ukraine
DECLARATION: Russia on the Ottoman Empire, 1736
MAJOR ISSUES AND OBJECTIVES: Russia wanted to secure possession of the Turkish Ukraine.
OUTCOME: Despite initial gains, Russia agreed to an unfavorable peace after its Austrian allies abandoned the war.
APPROXIMATE MAXIMUM NUMBER OF MEN UNDER ARMS: At the Battle of Khotin (August 17, 1739), Russia deployed 68,000 men, Turkey 90,000.
CASUALTIES: Total Russian casualties have been estimated at 100,000 dead, as a result of battle, disease, and general privation. Austria lost about 20,000 men. Turkish losses are unknown.
TREATIES: Treaty of Nissa, October 3, 1739

The War of the POLISH SUCCESSION was among the European conflicts that brought into play a complex network of alliances and enmities. When Russia discovered that France had solicited military aid from the Ottoman Empire during that war, Russia declared war on the Ottomans in 1736. Russian forces were dispatched to Turkish areas north of the Black Sea. However, having struck an alliance with the Tartars, the Ottomans severely punished the invaders, who withdrew into the Russian Ukraine, having lost 30,000 men out of a force of 58,000. The withdrawal brought Tartar raids into the Ukraine, so costly that Russia's ally, Austria, declared war on the Turks in January 1737.

Austrian armies invaded Bosnia, Wallachia, and southern Serbia. The fortress city of Nish fell, but a Turkish counter offensive forced Austria to withdraw. In the meantime, in the Turkish Ukraine, Russian and Turkish armies contended for Azov and Ochakov, frequently taking, losing, and retaking these cities. The French mediated a peace agreement, which was honored more in the breach than in the observance, and the Turks fought their way along the Danube toward Belgrade during 1738. The Austrians fared poorly against the Turks in the Balkans, but the Russian army, under Count Burkhard C. von Münnich (1683–1767), defeated 90,000 Turks with his 68,000 Russians at Chocim (Khotin) on August 17, 1739. After this, he took Jassy (Iaşi), Moldavia's capital.

Münnich was preparing to invade Constantinople (Istanbul), the Ottoman capital, when Austria, Russia's ally, signed a separate peace at Belgrade on September 18, 1739, following the fall of that city to the Turks. The Austrians ceded Belgrade, northern Serbia, parts of Bosnia, and Wallachia to the Turks, who were now free to turn all of their attention to Münnich's army. The prospect of a concentrated attack by the Turks was enough to prompt the Russians to negotiate peace. By the Treaty of Nissa, signed on October 3, 1739, Russia relinquished all that it had conquered, save the often-contested Azov. Russia agreed to dismantle the town's fortifications and further agreed that Russian naval vessels would stay out of the Sea of Azov and the Black Sea.

Further reading: Daniel Goffman, *The Ottoman Empire and Early Modern Europe* (New York: Cambridge University Press, 2002); Robert K. Massie, *Peter the Great: His Life and World* (New York: Ballantine Books, 1987); Alan Warwick Palmer, *The Decline and Fall of the Ottoman Empire* (New York: Barnes and Noble Books, 1995); E. H. Parker, *A Thousand Years of the Tartars* (London: Kegan Paul, 2001).

Russo-Turkish War (1768–1774) *See* CATHERINE THE GREAT'S FIRST WAR WITH THE TURKS.

Russo-Turkish War (1787–1792) *See* CATHERINE THE GREAT'S SECOND WAR WITH THE TURKS.

Russo-Turkish War (1806–1812)

PRINCIPAL COMBATANTS: Russia (with British alliance) vs. Ottoman Empire (with French alliance)

PRINCIPAL THEATER(S): Moldavia, Wallachia (Romania) and waters off Constantinople
DECLARATION: Ottoman Empire on Russia, November 6, 1806
MAJOR ISSUES AND OBJECTIVES: Russia and the Ottomans contended for control of Moldavia and Wallachia.
OUTCOME: The war ended indecisively, by means of a British-mediated peace; Moldavia and Wallachia remained under Ottoman control, but Russia gained Bessarabia.
APPROXIMATE MAXIMUM NUMBER OF MEN UNDER ARMS: At Batin (September 7, 1810) Russia fielded 22,000 against 35,000 Turks.
CASUALTIES: At Batin, Russia lost 2,000 killed or wounded, Turkey 5,000 killed or wounded and 5,000 captured.
TREATIES: Armistice of 1807; Treaty of Bucharest, May 28, 1812

France, locked in combat with Russia during the NAPOLEONIC WARS, took every opportunity to weaken its opponent. The French ambassador to the Ottoman Empire encouraged Sultan Selim III (1761–1808) to declare war on Russia because of its interference with Ottoman affairs in Moldavia and Wallachia. The declaration came on November 6, 1806, prompting Russia to invade Moldavia and Wallachia. However, the first major battle—indeed, the most important engagement of the war—came not on land but at sea. The Battle of Lemnos (or Athos) took place on June 30, 1807, when 10 Russian battleships tangled with 10 Ottoman ships of the line, five frigates, and five smaller vessels. Although outgunned, the Russians defeated the Ottoman squadron, sinking three ships of the line and three frigates. This was sufficient to prompt an armistice in August 1807, which endured until October 21, 1809, when a force of 30,000 Turks defeated 15,000 Russians at the Battle of Tataritza in Bulgaria. Despite the victory, the Turks lost 2,000 men versus 1,000 casualties among the Russians. At Bazardjik on June 3, 1810, Russian forces, 23,000 strong, overwhelmed a 5,000-man Turkish garrison, killing or wounding 3,000 and taking the rest captive.

The Ottomans regained the initiative at Schumla on June 23–24, 1810, using 30,000 men to defeat a Russian force of 20,000. On August 2, the Russians replied with a victory at Tachlimechle, inflicting 3,000 casualties on an Ottoman force of 30,000. This was followed by a series of Russian victories in Bulgaria, including a large battle at the Danubian city of Batin on September 7, 1810, when 22,000 Russians decisively defeated 35,000 Turks, inflicting 5,000 Turkish casualties, killed or wounded, and capturing another 5,000 Turks. In the meantime, the Russians laid siege to Turkish-held Rustchuk from July 20 to September 26, 1810, killing or wounding 6,000 of 15,000 Ottoman defenders, but in the process losing 3,000 killed and 5,000

wounded. The Russians fared better at Lovca, Bulgaria, on February 11, 1811, driving out a Turkish garrison of 10,000. A Second Battle of Rustchuk, on July 4, 1811, was a magnificent Russian victory—20,000 Russians decisively defeated 60,000 Turks. The Turks gained a measure of revenge at Giurgevo, Romania, on September 9, 1811, but their victory was short-lived. On September 10, a Russian counterthrust forced the Turks to surrender Giurgevo and compelled the Ottoman government to sue for peace. By the Treaty of Bucharest (May 28, 1812), Bessarabia was ceded to Russia, but Moldavia and Wallachia were returned to Ottoman control.

Further reading: Emory C. Bogle, *Modern Middle East: From Imperialism to Freedom, 1800–1958* (Englewood Cliffs, N.J.: Prentice Hall Professional Technical Reference, 1995); Alexander Mikhailovsky-Danilevsky, *Russo-Turkish War of 1806–1812* (West Chester, Ohio: Nafziger Collection, 2002); Gunther E. Rothenberg, *The Napoleonic Wars* (London: Cassell, 1998).

Russo-Turkish War (1828–1829)

PRINCIPAL COMBATANTS: Russia vs. Ottoman Empire
PRINCIPAL THEATER(S): Wallachia (part of Romania), Caucasus, and Crimea
DECLARATION: Russian on the Ottoman Empire, April, 26, 1828
MAJOR ISSUES AND OBJECTIVES: Ostensibly, Russia had come to aid the cause of Greek independence; other objectives included territorial gain.
OUTCOME: The Turks were repeatedly defeated, Russia made territorial gains, the Ottomans agree to pay an indemnity, and Greece was granted independence.
APPROXIMATE MAXIMUM NUMBER OF MEN UNDER ARMS: Russia 113,920; Ottoman Empire, 80,000
CASUALTIES: Russia, 42,515 dead; Ottomans, 80,000 dead; most succumbed to disease.
TREATIES: Treaty of Adrianople, September 16, 1829

Russia declared war on the Ottoman Turks on April 26, 1828, ostensibly in aid of Greece during the GREEK WAR OF INDEPENDENCE; however, the Russian czar was moved less by nationalist or republican zeal than by hunger for territory. Besides, the Turks were at an especially low ebb during this time. Militarily weak, they were highly vulnerable.

Russian armies successfully besieged Braila in Wallachia, then crossed the Danube to assault the Turkish fortresses at Ruschuk (Ruse) and Widdin (Vidin). Another Russian force captured the city of Varna after a three-month siege in 1828. Simultaneously, in the Caucasus, the Russians took Kars and penetrated as far as Akhaltsikhe, where, after scoring a victory, they were stopped by Kurds.

The next year, 1829, began badly for the Turks as well. They lost Silistra and suffered defeat at the hands of Russian general Hans Diebitsch-Zabalkansky (1785–1831) at Tcherkovna (June 11) and at Sliven (August 12). Eight days after the second victory, Diebitsch-Zabalkansky marched into Adrianople (Edirne)—although his army was exhausted and suffering from the effects of plague. Disease was a far more formidable enemy than any opposing army. Of the 42,515 Russians who died in this war, 29,658 succumbed to disease. Likewise, most of the 80,000 Turks who perished were victims of plague and other scourges.

Elsewhere, Russia was also victorious. Erivan (Yerevan) fell to the Russians, though Diebitsch-Zabalkansky had already agreed to the Treaty of Adrianople on September 16, 1829, by which the Danubian Principalities (Moldavia and Wallachia) were made semiautonomous, and by which Russia gained control of the mouth of the Danube. The treaty also granted all peaceful states access to the Turkish straits—and granted Greece its independence. Additionally, the Ottoman Empire agreed to pay heavy war reparations and confirmed (Russian) Orthodox freedom of religion in its territories.

Further reading: Elizabeth Wormeley Latimer, *Russia and Turkey in the Nineteenth Century* (Honolulu: University Press of the Pacific, 2002); Alan Warwick Palmer, *The Decline and Fall of the Ottoman Empire* (New York: Barnes and Noble Books, 1995).

Russo-Turkish War (1877–1878)

PRINCIPAL COMBATANTS: Russia (with Romanian allies) vs. Ottoman Empire
PRINCIPAL THEATER(S): The Balkans
DECLARATION: Russia on the Ottoman Empire, April 24, 1877
MAJOR ISSUES AND OBJECTIVES: Russia wanted to secure religious freedom for Orthodox Serbs oppressed by the Ottomans; Russia also wanted to expand its territory.
OUTCOME: Romania and Serbia became independent; Bulgaria, enlarged at the expense of the Turks, became semi-autonomous under Russian authority.
APPROXIMATE MAXIMUM NUMBER OF MEN UNDER ARMS: Russia, 933,726; Ottoman numbers unknown
CASUALTIES: Russia, 117,621 killed; Ottoman Empire, 90,000; most deaths were from disease.
TREATIES: Treaty of San Stefano, March 3, 1878

In the name of pan-Slavism, 19th-century Russian czars supported the Balkan states in their bid to gain independence from the Ottoman Empire. This motivated the war that Russia declared on April 24, 1877. It began with mostly desultory naval action as Russian land forces assembled and prepared to cross the Danube. It was not until June 23, 1878, that the first Russian units made the crossing, only to find themselves bogged down in a five-month siege against the fortress of Plevna in Bulgaria. Fanatical defenders hurled back two Russian assaults, inflicting terrible casualties. On July 20, 1878, 3,000 of 6,500 Russian attackers fell. Ten days later, 7,305 Russians were killed or wounded (out of a force of 30,000) in another unsuccessful assault. The third attack, or "Great Assault," came on September 11 and pitted 95,000 Russians against a garrison of 30,000 plus other defenders. Over the next two days, the Russians lost 18,600 killed or wounded, and still Plevna remained in Turkish hands—although the siege remained in place.

The Turks could not hold out forever. On the night of December 9–10, they attempted a breakout but were driven back with the loss of 5,000 killed or wounded and some 43,340 captured. At this, the Turks surrendered, and the 143-day siege ended. Russian losses in this operation topped 50,000 men.

Following the fall of Plevna, Russia concentrated on Ottoman forces south of the Shipka River. At the Battle of Senova on January 8–9, 1878, a 36,000-man Ottoman army collapsed. This was followed on January 17 by the fall of the Ottoman-held fortress town of Plovdiv, a success that allowed Russian forces to advance to the doorstep of Constantinople. This action prompted an armistice on January 31, 1878.

In the meantime, war raged on another front, the Caucasus. Here, the opposing armies were evenly matched at about 70,000 each. At the Battle of Aladja Dagh (October 15–18, 1877), Russian forces killed or wounded 6,000 Turks and captured another 12,000; Russian losses were light,—1,600 killed or wounded. The victory put the Russians in position to invest the great fortress at Kars, which they stormed on November 17, 1877. The attackers inflicted 7,000 casualties on the Turkish garrison of 24,000 before the fort surrendered.

Turkish losses in the Balkans and on the Caucasus front prompted the Ottoman government to agree to the Treaty of San Stefano on March 3, 1878, by which it recognized the independence of Serbia, Montenegro, Romania, and Bulgaria. Even more important, the war had rendered the Ottoman Empire effectively obsolete. It no longer figured as a major power in Eurasian politics; became known as the "sick man of Europe." To achieve this, Russia had mobilized 933,726 troops, of which 117,621 died. As in other wars with the Ottoman Empire, the greatest enemy was disease. More than 80,000 Russian deaths were the result of plague and other maladies. Two-thirds of Turkish losses, which amounted to about 90,000 men, were also due to disease.

Further reading: Emory C. Bogle, *Modern Middle East: From Imperialism to Freedom, 1800–1958* (Englewood Cliffs, N.J.: Prentice Hall Professional Technical Reference, 1995); Alexander Mikhailovsky-Danilevsky, *Russo-Turkish War of 1806–1812* (West Chester, Ohio: Nafziger Collection, 2002); Alan Warwick Palmer, *The Decline and Fall of the Ottoman Empire* (New York: Barnes and Noble Books, 1995); Gunther E. Rothenberg, *The Napoleonic Wars* (London: Cassell, 1998).

Rwandan Civil War (1959–1961)   *See* RUANDAN (RWANDAN) CIVIL WAR.

Rwandan Civil War (1990–1994)

PRINCIPAL COMBATANTS: Hutus vs. Tutsis in Rwanda
PRINCIPAL THEATER(S): Rwanda
DECLARATION: None
MAJOR ISSUES AND OBJECTIVES: Control of the Rwandan government
OUTCOME: Genocide against the Tutsis, panic among the Hutus; control of the government was ultimately divided between the tribes.
APPROXIMATE MAXIMUM NUMBER OF MEN UNDER ARMS: Extremely variable, with much civilian involvement
CASUALTIES: 10,000 combatants on both sides in guerrilla warfare; 500,000–1,000,000 civilians slain by Hutu troops and death squads
TREATIES: Arusha Accords, August 1993 and July 1994

The African nation of Rwanda (formerly Ruanda) achieved independence from Belgium, then engaged in the bloody RUANDAN (RWANDAN) CIVIL WAR of 1959–61, emerging from it as Rwanda. The 1959–61 conflict pitted the majority Hutu tribe against the Tutsi, who, although a minority, were socially, economically, and politically dominant. Following the first civil war, many Tutsi fled to neighboring Uganda. For more than 30 years, resentment simmered among the exiles, who created the Rwandan Patriotic Front (RPF) and, beginning in 1990, infiltrated Rwanda. Their goal was to reclaim the nation under Tutsi control.

The Tutsi invasion came at a bad time for the Hutu government of Rwanda. The nation was chronically poor—the departure of the Tutsi having contributed to this poverty—and was beset by drought and famine. Unable to feed its people, let alone resist an invasion, the Hutu government concluded the Arusha Accords in August 1993, ceding considerable power to the Tutsi. Before the accords could be implemented, however, Hutu president Juvénal Habyarimana (c. 1937–94) intervened and sabotaged the peace process. He backed down to some extent, however, as the Tutsi became increasingly menacing. By this time about 10,000 lives had been lost in guerrilla fighting. Habyarimana granted some cabinet posts to Tutsis, and he agreed to fly to Tanzania to participate in a 1994 conference on the Tutsi-Hutu problem. On April 6, 1994, during the flight back to Rwanda, Habyarimana's plane exploded—apparently as a result of Hutu sabotage, a hard-line Hutu element objecting to any rapprochement with the Tutsis.

After the assassination of Habyarimana, chaos reigned in Rwanda. During a period of 14 weeks, the Hutu army and special Hutu death squads rampaged throughout the country, killing hundreds of thousands of civilians (estimates vary from 500,000 to 850,000). Targeted victims of this genocide were mostly Tutsis, but many Hutu moderates were also slain.

The Hutu genocide against the Tutsis prompted some three million Hutus to flee Rwanda for fear of Tutsi reprisals. The reprisals were not forthcoming, but the refugee problem created by the mass exodus was deadly for the region. The Tutsis did capture the Rwandan capital on April 6, 1994—the day of Habyarimana's death—but fighting continued. Government officials were assassinated, and between April 6 and the beginning of July, a genocide of perhaps as many as one million Tutsis and moderate Hutus was perpetrated by organized bands of militia known as the Interahamwe.

The RPF continued to pour into Rwanda, and civil war raged concurrently with the genocide for two months. French forces intervened in June, an action that helped to quell the genocide. However, the RPF quickly defeated the Rwandan army, the surviving members of which fled across the border to Zaire, with some two million civilian refugees in their wake. The civilians sought refuge in Zaire, Tanzania, and Burundi.

On July 4, 1994, the RPF took Kigali. The war officially ended on July 16, 1994, with full implementation of the so-called Arusha Accords. A UN peacekeeping mission remained in Rwanda until March 8, 1996. Genocide and war crimes trials began in 1996 and as of late 2003 were still under way. Low-level fighting continued throughout Rwanda.

Further reading: Alain Destexhe, *Rwanda and Genocide in the Twentieth Century* (New York: New York University Press, 1996); Gerard Prunier, *The Rwanda Crisis: History of a Genocide* (New York: Columbia University Press, 1995).